Collins Gem

School
DICTIONARY

Collins Gem

An Imprint of HarperCollinsPublishers

first edition 2003

© HarperCollins Publishers 2003

latest reprint 2003

HarperCollins Publishers
Westerhill Road, Bishopbriggs, Glasgow G64 2QT
Great Britain

www.collinsdictionaries.com

Collins Gem® and Bank of English® are registered
trademarks of HarperCollins Publishers Limited

ISBN 0-00-716004-6 (blue cover)
ISBN 0-00-714849-6 (pink cover)

Acknowledgements
We would like to thank those authors and publishers who
kindly gave permission for copyright material to be used
in the Bank of English. We would also like to thank
Times Newspapers Ltd for providing valuable data.

Note
Entered words that we have reason to believe constitute
trademarks have been designated as such. However, neither
the presence nor absence of such designation should be
regarded as affecting the legal status of any trademark.

A catalogue record for this book is
available from the British Library

Dictionary text typeset by John Podbielski
Supplement typeset by Wordcraft

Printed and bound in Great Britain
by The Bath Press, Bath

EDITORIAL STAFF

Managing Editor
Marianne Davidson

Editors
Andrew Holmes   Elspeth Summers   Kay Cullen
Alice Grandison   Jenny Kumar

Computing Support
John Podbielski

Publishing Director
Lorna Sinclair Knight

Publishing Manager
Elaine Higgleton

CONTENTS

FOREWORD

The **Collins Gem School Dictionary**, a special edition for students, is easy to use and easy to understand. An open modern layout makes it a pleasure to read. Every definition is presented in straightforward English. Where a word has more than one sense, the one given first is the most common meaning in today's language. Other senses of a word – for example, historical and technical senses – are explained after the main present-day meaning.

The entries show the spelling and meaning of each word. Another feature which makes this dictionary particularly helpful is the simple pronunciations for words that may be unfamiliar.

New words and new senses have been gathered through the Collins language monitoring programme. There is also specialist vocabulary from subjects such as science, technology, and computing.

In compiling this dictionary the lexicographers have been able to consult the Bank of English, a unique electronic database of over 450 million words of written and spoken English from a huge variety of sources. By analysing this data, lexicographers have ensured that the dictionary user is given the most up-to-date information about how English is spoken and written today. Many examples have been taken from real English to help illustrate meaning within the definitions.

An added bonus is the reference supplement. The *Word Power* section provides help with using English, while the *Fact Finder* section contains a wealth of information relating to geography, maths, science, politics and more.

These features mean that the **Collins Gem School Dictionary** is not only the most up-to-date and user-friendly small dictionary available, but is also the ideal homework reference.

USING THE DICTIONARY

Main Entry Words   printed in large bold type, e.g.

> **abbey**

All main entry words, including
abbreviations and
combining forms, in one alphabetical
sequence, e.g.

> **abbot**
>
> **abbreviate**
>
> **ABC**
>
> **abdicate**

Variant Spellings   shown in full, e.g.

> **adrenalin, adrenaline**

Note: where the spellings **-ize** and **-ization**
are used at the end of a word, the
alternative forms **-ise** and **-isation** are
equally acceptable.

Pronunciations   given in square brackets for words that
are difficult or confusing; the word is
respelt as it is pronounced,
with the stressed syllable in bold type,
e.g.

> **antipodes** [an-**tip**-pod-deez]

Parts of Speech   shown in italics as an abbreviation, e.g.

> **ablaze** *adj*

When a word can be used as more than
one part of speech, the change of part of
speech is shown after an arrow, e.g.

> **mock** *v* make fun of; mimic. ▸ *adj* sham
> or imitation.

Parts of speech may be combined for
some words, e.g.

> **alone** *adj, adv* without anyone or
> anything else.

vi

USING THE DICTIONARY

Cross References shown in small capital letters, e.g.
doner kebab *n* see KEBAB.

Irregular Parts or confusing forms of verbs, nouns, adjectives, and adverbs shown in bold type, e.g.
begin *v* **-ginning, -gan, -gun.**
regret *v* **-gretting, -gretted.**
anniversary *n*, *pl* **-ries.**
angry *adj* **-grier, -griest.**
well *adv* **better, best.**

Meanings separated by semicolons, e.g.
casual *adj* careless, nonchalant; (of work or workers) occasional; for informal wear; happening by chance.

Phrases and Idioms included immediately after the meanings of the main entry word, e.g.
hand *n* ... *v* ... **have a hand in** be involved **lend a hand** help ...

Related Words shown in the same paragraph as the main entry word, e.g.
absurd *adj* incongruous or ridiculous.
absurdly *adv* **absurdity** *n*
Note: where the meaning of a related word is not given, it may be understood from the main entry word, or from another related word.

Compounds shown in alphabetical order at the end of the paragraph, e.g.
ash *n* ... **ashtray** *n* receptacle for tobacco ash and cigarette butts.
Ash Wednesday first day of Lent.

ABBREVIATIONS USED IN THE DICTIONARY

AD	anno Domini	pron	pronoun
Meteorol	Meteorology	E	East
adj	adjective	Psychol	Psychology
Mil	Military	e.g.	for example
adv	adverb	®	Trademark
n	noun	esp.	especially
Anat	Anatomy	RC	Roman Catholic
N	North	etc.	et cetera
Archit	Architecture	S	South
Naut	Nautical	fem	feminine
Astrol	Astrology	S Afr	South Africa(n)
NZ	New Zealand	foll.	followed
Aust	Australia(n)	Scot	Scottish
Obs	Obsolete	Geom	Geometry
BC	before Christ	sing	singular
Offens	Offensive	Hist	History
Biol	Biology	US	United States
orig.	originally	interj	interjection
Brit	British	usu.	usually
Photog	Photography	Lit	Literary
Chem	Chemistry	v	verb
pl	plural	masc	masculine
C of E	Church of England	W	West
prep	preposition	Med	Medicine
conj	conjunction	Zool	Zoology

A a

a *adj* indefinite article, used before a noun being mentioned for the first time.

AA Alcoholics Anonymous; Automobile Association.

aardvark *n* S African anteater with long ears and snout.

AB able-bodied seaman.

aback *adv* **taken aback** startled or disconcerted.

abacus *n* beads on a wire frame, used for doing calculations.

abalone [ab-a-**lone**-ee] *n* edible sea creature with a shell lined with mother of pearl.

abandon *v* desert or leave (one's wife, children, etc.); give up (hope etc.) altogether. ▶ *n* lack of inhibition. **abandoned** *adj* deserted; uninhibited. **abandonment** *n*

abase *v* humiliate or degrade (oneself). **abasement** *n*

abashed *adj* embarrassed and ashamed.

abate *v* make or become less strong. **abatement** *n*

abattoir [ab-a-**twahr**] *n* place where animals are killed for food.

abbess *n* nun in charge of a convent.

abbey *n* dwelling place of, or a church belonging to, a community of monks or nuns.

abbot *n* head of an abbey of monks.

abbreviate *v* shorten (a word) by leaving out some letters. **abbreviation** *n* shortened form of a word or words.

ABC¹ *n* alphabet; basics of a subject.

ABC² Australian Broadcasting Corporation.

abdicate *v* give up (the throne or a responsibility). **abdication** *n*

abdomen *n* part of the body containing the stomach and intestines. **abdominal** *adj*

abduct *v* carry off, kidnap. **abduction** *n* **abductor** *n*

aberration *n* sudden change from what is normal, accurate, or correct; brief lapse in control of one's thoughts or feelings. **aberrant** *adj* showing aberration.

abet *v* **abetting**, **abetted**. help or encourage in wrongdoing. **abettor** *n*

abeyance *n* **in abeyance** not in use.

abhor *v* **-horring**, **-horred**. detest utterly. **abhorrent** *adj* hateful, loathsome. **abhorrence** *n*

abide *v* endure, put up with; *Obs* stay or dwell, e.g. *abide with me*. **abide by** *v* obey (the law, rules, etc.). **abiding** *adj* lasting.

ability *n*, *pl* **-ties**. competence, power; talent.

abject *adj* utterly miserable; lacking all self-respect. **abjectly** *adv*

abjure *v* deny or renounce on oath.

ablative *n* case of nouns in Latin and other languages, indicating source, agent, or instrument of action.

ablaze *adj* burning fiercely.

able *adj* capable, competent. **ably** *adv* **able-bodied** *adj* strong and healthy.

ablutions *pl n* act of washing.

abnormal *adj* not normal or usual. **abnormally** *adv* **abnormality** *n*

aboard *adv*, *prep* on, in, onto, or into (a ship, train, or plane).

abode *n* home, dwelling.

abolish *v* do away with. **abolition**

n **abolitionist** *n* person who wishes to do away with something, esp. slavery.

abominable *adj* detestable, very bad. **abominable snowman** large apelike creature said to live in the Himalayas. **abominably** *adv*

abomination *n* someone or something that is detestable.

aborigine [ab-or-**rij**-in-ee], **aboriginal** *n* original inhabitant of a country or region, esp. **(A-)** Australia. **aboriginal** *adj*

abort *v* have an abortion or perform an abortion on; have a miscarriage; end a plan or process before completion. **abortive** *adj* unsuccessful.

abortion *n* operation to end a pregnancy; *Informal* something grotesque. **abortionist** *n* person who performs abortions, esp. illegally.

abound *v* be plentiful. **abounding** *adj*

about *prep* concerning, on the subject of; in or near (a place). ▶ *adv* nearly, approximately; nearby. **about to** shortly going to. **not about to** determined not to. **about-turn** *n* complete change of attitude.

above *adv, prep* over or higher (than); greater (than); superior (to). **above board** in the open, without dishonesty.

abracadabra *n* supposedly magic word.

abrasion *n* scraped area on the skin.

abrasive *adj* harsh and unpleasant in manner; tending to rub or scrape. ▶ *n* substance for cleaning or polishing by rubbing.

abreast *adv, adj* side by side. **abreast of** up to date with.

abridge *v* shorten by using fewer words. **abridgment,**

abridgement *n*

abroad *adv* to or in a foreign country; at large.

abrogate *v* cancel (a law or agreement) formally. **abrogation** *n*

abrupt *adj* sudden, unexpected; blunt and rude. **abruptly** *adv* **abruptness** *n*

abscess *n* inflamed swelling containing pus.

abscond *v* leave secretly.

abseil [ab-**sale**] *v* go down a steep drop by a rope fastened at the top and tied around one's body.

absent *adj* not present; lacking; inattentive. ▶ *v* stay away. **absently** *adv* **absence** *n* being away; lack. **absentee** *n* person who should be present but is not. **absenteeism** *n* persistent absence from work or school. **absent-minded** *adj* inattentive or forgetful. **absent-mindedly** *adv*

absinthe *n* strong green aniseed-flavoured liqueur.

absolute *adj* complete, perfect; not limited, unconditional; pure, e.g. *absolute alcohol.* **absolutely** *adv* completely. ▶ *interj* certainly, yes. **absolutism** *n* government by a ruler with unrestricted power.

absolve *v* declare to be free from blame or sin. **absolution** *n*

absorb *v* soak up (a liquid); take in; engage the interest of (someone). **absorption** *n* **absorbent** *adj* able to absorb liquid. **absorbency** *n*

abstain *v* choose not to do something; choose not to vote. **abstainer** *n* **abstention** *n* abstaining, esp. from voting. **abstinence** *n* abstaining, esp. from drinking alcohol. **abstinent** *adj*

abstemious *adj* taking very little alcohol or food. **abstemiousness** *n*

abstract *adj* existing as a quality or

idea rather than a material object;
theoretical; (of art) using patterns
of shapes and colours rather than
realistic likenesses. ▶ n summary;
abstract work of art; abstract word
or idea. ▶ v summarize; remove.
abstracted adj lost in thought.
abstraction n

abstruse adj not easy to
understand.

absurd adj incongruous or
ridiculous. **absurdly** adv
absurdity n

abundant adj plentiful.
abundantly adv **abundance** n

abuse v use wrongly; ill-treat
violently; speak harshly and rudely
to. ▶ n prolonged ill-treatment;
harsh and vulgar comments;
wrong use. **abuser** n **abusive** adj
abusively adv **abusiveness** n

abut v **abutting, abutted.** be next
to or touching.

abysmal adj Informal extremely
bad, awful. **abysmally** adv

abyss n very deep hole or chasm.

AC alternating current.

a/c account.

acacia [a-kay-sha] n tree or shrub
with yellow or white flowers.

academy n, pl -mies. society to
advance arts or sciences;
institution for training in a
particular skill; Scot secondary
school. **academic** adj of an
academy or university; of
theoretical interest. ▶ n
lecturer or researcher at a
university. **academically** adv
academician n member of an
academy.

acanthus n prickly plant.

ACAS (in Britain) Advisory
Conciliation and Arbitration
Service.

ACC (in New Zealand) Accident
Compensation Corporation.

accede v consent or agree (to);

take up (an office or position).

accelerate v (cause to) move
faster. **acceleration** n
accelerator n pedal in a motor
vehicle to increase speed.

accent n distinctive style of
pronunciation of a local, national,
or social group; mark over a letter
to show how it is pronounced;
stress on a syllable or musical
note. ▶ v place emphasis on.

accentuate v stress, emphasize.
accentuation n

accept v receive willingly; agree to;
consider to be true. **acceptance** n
acceptable adj tolerable;
satisfactory. **acceptably** adv
acceptability n

access n means of or right to
approach or enter. ▶ v obtain
(data) from a computer.
accessible adj easy to reach.
accessibility n

accession n taking up of an office
or position.

accessory n, pl -ries.
supplementary part or object;
person involved in a crime
although not present when it is
committed.

accident n mishap, often causing
injury; event happening by
chance. **accidental** adj happening
by chance or unintentionally. ▶ n
Music symbol indicating that a
sharp, flat, or natural note is not a
part of the key signature.
accidentally adv

acclaim v applaud, praise. ▶ n
enthusiastic approval.
acclamation n

acclimatize v adapt to a new
climate or environment.
acclimatization n

accolade n award, honour, or
praise; award of knighthood.

accommodate v provide with
lodgings; have room for; oblige,

do a favour for; adapt or adjust (to something). **accommodation** n house or room for living in. **accommodating** adj obliging.

accompany v **-nying, -nied.** go along with; occur with; provide a musical accompaniment for. **accompaniment** n something that accompanies; *Music* supporting part that goes with a solo. **accompanist** n

accomplice n person who helps another to commit a crime.

accomplish v manage to do; finish. **accomplishment** n completion; personal ability or skill. **accomplished** adj expert, proficient.

accord n agreement, harmony. ▶ v fit in with.

accordance n **in accordance with** conforming to or according to.

according adv **according to** as stated by; in conformity with. **accordingly** adv in an appropriate manner; consequently.

accordion n portable musical instrument played by moving the two sides apart and together, and pressing a keyboard or buttons to produce the notes. **accordionist** n

accost v approach and speak to, often aggressively.

account n report, description; business arrangement making credit available; record of money received and paid out with the resulting balance; person's money held in a bank; importance, value. ▶ v judge to be. **on account of** because of. **accountable** adj responsible to someone or for something. **accountability** n

accounting n skill or practice of maintaining and auditing business accounts. **accountant** n person who maintains and audits business accounts. **accountancy** n

accoutrements pl n clothing and equipment for a particular activity.

accredited adj authorized, officially recognized.

accretion [ak-**kree**-shun] n gradual growth; something added.

accrue v **-cruing, -crued.** increase gradually. **accrual** n

accumulate v gather together in increasing quantity. **accumulation** n **accumulative** adj **accumulator** n *Brit & Aust* rechargeable electric battery.

accurate adj exact, correct. **accurately** adv **accuracy** n

accursed adj under a curse; detestable.

accusative n grammatical case indicating the direct object.

accuse v charge with wrongdoing. **accused** n **accuser** n **accusing** adj **accusation** n **accusatory** adj

accustom v make used to. **accustomed** adj usual; used (to); in the habit (of).

ace n playing card with one symbol on it; *Informal* expert; *Tennis* unreturnable serve. ▶ adj *Informal* excellent.

acerbic [ass-**sir**-bik] adj harsh or bitter. **acerbity** n

acetate [ass-it-tate] n *Chem* salt or ester of acetic acid; (also **acetate rayon**) synthetic textile fibre.

acetic [ass-**see**-tik] adj of or involving vinegar. **acetic acid** colourless liquid used to make vinegar.

acetone [ass-it-tone] n colourless liquid used as a solvent.

acetylene [ass-**set**-ill-een] n colourless flammable gas used in welding metals.

ache n dull continuous pain. ▶ v be in or cause continuous dull pain.

achieve v gain by hard work or ability. **achievement** n something accomplished.

Achilles heel [ak-kill-eez] n small but fatal weakness.

Achilles tendon n cord connecting the calf muscle to the heel bone.

achromatic adj colourless; Music with no sharps or flats.

acid n Chem one of a class of compounds, corrosive and sour when dissolved in water, that combine with a base to form a salt; Slang LSD. ▶ adj containing acid; sour-tasting; sharp or sour in manner. **acidic** adj **acidify** v **acidity** n **Acid (House)** n type of funk-based electronically edited disco music with hypnotic sound effects. **acid rain** rain containing acid from atmospheric pollution. **acid test** conclusive test of value.

acknowledge v admit, recognize; indicate recognition of (a person); say one has received. **acknowledgment, acknowledgement** n

acme [ak-mee] n highest point of achievement or excellence.

acne [ak-nee] n pimply skin disease.

acolyte n follower or attendant; Christianity person who assists a priest.

aconite n poisonous plant with hoodlike flowers; poison obtained from this plant.

acorn n nut of the oak tree.

acoustic adj of sound and hearing; (of a musical instrument) not electronically amplified. **acoustics** n science of sounds. ▶ pl features of a room or building determining how sound is heard within it. **acoustically** adv

acquaint v make familiar, inform. **acquainted** adj **acquaintance** n person known; personal knowledge.

acquiesce [ak-wee-ess] v agree to what someone wants.

acquiescence n **acquiescent** adj

acquire v gain, get. **acquisition** n thing acquired; act of getting. **acquisitive** adj eager to gain material possessions. **acquisitiveness**, n

acquit v -quitting, -quitted. pronounce (someone) innocent; behave in a particular way. **acquittal** n

acre n measure of land, 4840 square yards (4046.86 square metres). **acreage** [ake-er-rij] n land area in acres.

acrid [ak-rid] adj pungent, bitter.

acrimonious adj bitter in speech or manner. **acrimony** n

acrobat n person skilled in gymnastic feats requiring agility and balance. **acrobatic** adj **acrobatics** pl n acrobatic feats.

acronym n word formed from the initial letters of other words, such as NASA.

across adv, prep from side to side (of); on or to the other side (of). **across the board** applying equally to all.

acrostic n lines of writing in which the first or last letters of each line spell a word or saying.

acrylic n, adj (synthetic fibre, paint, etc.) made from acrylic acid. **acrylic acid** strong-smelling corrosive liquid.

act n thing done; law or decree; section of a play or opera; one of several short performances in a show; pretended attitude. ▶ v do something; behave in a particular way; perform in a play, film, etc. **act of God** unpredictable natural event. **acting** n art of an actor. ▶ adj temporarily performing the duties of someone. **actor, actress** n person who acts in a play, film, etc.

ACT Australian Capital Territory.

actinium n Chem radioactive

chemical element.

action n process of doing something; thing done; lawsuit; operating mechanism; minor battle. **actionable** adj giving grounds for a lawsuit. **action replay** rerun of an event on a television tape.

active adj moving, working; busy, energetic; Grammar (of a verb) in a form indicating that the subject is performing the action, e.g. threw in Kim threw the ball. **actively** adv **activity** n state of being active; (pl **-ties**) leisure pursuit. **activate** v make active. **activation** n **activator** n **activist** n person who works energetically to achieve political or social goals. **activism** n

actual adj existing in reality. **actually** adv really, indeed. **actuality** n

actuary n, pl **-aries**. statistician who calculates insurance risks. **actuarial** adj

actuate v start up (a device).

acuity [ak-kew-it-ee] n keenness of vision or thought.

acumen [ak-yew-men] n ability to make good judgments.

acupuncture n medical treatment involving the insertion of needles at various points on the body. **acupuncturist** n

acute adj severe; keen, shrewd; sharp, sensitive; (of an angle) less than 90°. ▶ n accent (´) over a letter to indicate the quality or length of its sound, as in café. **acutely** adv **acuteness** n

ad n Informal advertisement.

AD anno Domini.

adage n wise saying, proverb.

adagio n, pl **-gios**, adv Music (piece to be played) slowly and gracefully.

adamant adj unshakable in determination or purpose.

adamantly adv

Adam's apple n projecting lump of thyroid cartilage at the front of the throat.

adapt v alter for new use or new conditions. **adaptable** adj **adaptability** n **adaptation** n thing produced by adapting something; adapting. **adaptor**, **adapter** n device for connecting several electrical appliances to a single socket.

add v combine (numbers or quantities); join (to something); say or write further.

addendum n, pl **-da**. addition; appendix to a book etc.

adder n small poisonous snake.

addict n person who is unable to stop taking drugs; Informal person devoted to something. **addicted** adj **addiction** n **addictive** adj causing addiction.

addition n adding; thing added. **in addition** besides, as well. **additional** adj **additionally** adv **additive** n something added, esp. to a foodstuff, to improve it or prevent deterioration.

addled adj confused or unable to think clearly.

address n place where a person lives; direction on a letter; location; formal public speech. ▶ v mark the destination, as on an envelope; make a speech; give attention to (a problem, task, etc.). **addressee** n person addressed.

adduce v mention something as evidence or proof.

adenoids [ad-in-oidz] pl n mass of tissue at the back of the throat. **adenoidal** adj having a nasal voice caused by swollen adenoids.

adept adj, n very skilful (person).

adequate adj sufficient, enough; not outstanding. **adequately** adv

adequacy n

adhere v stick (to); be devoted (to). **adherence** n **adherent** n devotee, follower. **adhesion** n sticking (to); joining together of parts of the body that are normally separate, as after surgery. **adhesive** n substance used to stick things together. ▶ adj able to stick to things.

ad hoc adj, adv Latin for a particular purpose only.

adieu [a-dew] interj Lit farewell, goodbye.

ad infinitum [ad in-fin-eye-tum] adv Latin endlessly.

adipose adj of or containing fat.

adj. adjective.

adjacent adj near or next (to); having a common boundary; Geom (of a side in a right-angled triangle) lying between a specified angle and the right angle.

adjective n word that adds information about a noun or pronoun. **adjectival** adj

adjoin v be next to. **adjoining** adj

adjourn v close (a court) at the end of a session; postpone temporarily; Informal go elsewhere. **adjournment** n

adjudge v declare (to be).

adjudicate v give a formal decision on (a dispute); judge (a competition). **adjudication** n **adjudicator** n

adjunct n subordinate or additional person or thing.

adjure v command (to do); appeal earnestly.

adjust v adapt to new conditions; alter slightly so as to be suitable. **adjustable** adj **adjuster** n **adjustment** n

adjutant [aj-oo-tant] n army officer in charge of routine administration.

ad-lib v -**libbing**, -**libbed**. improvise a speech etc. without preparation.

▶ n improvised remark.

admin n Informal administration.

administer v manage (business affairs); organize and put into practice; give (medicine or treatment).

administrate v manage (an organization). **administrator** n

administration n management of an organization; people who manage an organization; government, e.g. the Bush administration.

administrative adj of the management of an organization.

admiral n highest naval rank. **Admiralty** n (in Britain) former government department in charge of the Royal Navy.

admire v regard with esteem and approval. **admirable** adj **admirably** adv **admiration** n **admirer** n **admiring** adj **admiringly** adv

admissible adj allowed to be brought in as evidence in court. **admissibility** n

admission n permission to enter; entrance fee; confession.

admit v -**mitting**, -**mitted**. confess, acknowledge; concede the truth of; allow in. **admittance** n permission to enter. **admittedly** adv it must be agreed.

admixture n mixture; ingredient.

admonish v reprove sternly. **admonition** n

ad nauseam [ad naw-zee-am] adv Latin to a boring or sickening extent.

ado n Lit fuss, trouble.

adobe [ad-oh-bee] n sun-dried brick.

adolescence n period between puberty and adulthood. **adolescent** n, adj (person) between puberty and adulthood.

adopt v take (someone else's child)

as one's own; take up (a plan or principle). **adoption** n **adoptive** adj related by adoption.

adore v love intensely; worship. **adorable** adj **adoration** n **adoring** adj **adoringly** adv

adorn v decorate, embellish. **adornment** n

adrenal [ad-**reen**-al] adj near the kidneys. **adrenal glands** glands covering the top of the kidneys.

adrenalin, adrenaline n hormone secreted by the adrenal glands in response to stress.

adrift adj, adv drifting; without a clear purpose.

adroit adj quick and skilful. **adroitly** adv **adroitness** n

adsorb v (of a gas or vapour) condense and form a thin film on a surface. **adsorption** n

adulation n uncritical admiration.

adult adj fully grown, mature. ▶ n adult person or animal. **adulthood** n

adulterate v spoil something by adding inferior material. **adulteration** n

adultery n, pl **-teries.** sexual unfaithfulness of a husband or wife. **adulterer, adulteress** n **adulterous** adj

adv. adverb.

advance v go or bring forward; further (a cause); propose (an idea); lend (a sum of money). ▶ n forward movement; improvement; loan. ▶ pl approaches to a person with the hope of starting a romantic or sexual relationship. ▶ adj done or happening before an event. **in advance** ahead. **advanced** adj at a late stage in development; not elementary. **advancement** n promotion.

advantage n more favourable position or state; benefit or profit; Tennis point scored after deuce.

take advantage of use (a person) unfairly; use (an opportunity). **advantageous** adj **advantageously** adv

advent n arrival; (**A-**) season of four weeks before Christmas.

Adventist n member of a Christian sect that believes in the imminent return of Christ (also **Seventh Day Adventist**).

adventitious adj added or appearing accidentally.

adventure n exciting and risky undertaking or exploit. **adventurer, adventuress** n person who unscrupulously seeks money or power; person who seeks adventures. **adventurous** adj

adverb n word that adds information about a verb, adjective, or other adverb. **adverbial** adj

adversary [**ad**-verse-er-ree] n, pl **-saries.** opponent or enemy.

adverse adj unfavourable; antagonistic or hostile. **adversely** adv **adversity** n very difficult or hard circumstances.

advert n Informal advertisement.

advertise v present or praise (goods or services) to the public in order to encourage sales; make (a vacancy, event, etc.) known publicly. **advertisement** n public announcement to sell goods or publicize an event. **advertiser** n **advertising** adj, n

advice n recommendation as to what to do. **advise** v offer advice to; notify (someone). **advisable** adj prudent, sensible. **advisability** n **advisory** adj giving advice. **advised** adj considered, thought-out, e.g. ill-advised. **advisedly** adv deliberately.

adviser, advisor n person who offers advice, e.g. on careers to students or school pupils.

advocaat n liqueur with a raw egg base.

advocate v propose or recommend. ▸ n person who publicly supports a cause; *Scot & S Afr* barrister. **advocacy** n

adze n tool with an arched blade at right angles to the handle.

aegis [ee-jiss] n sponsorship, protection.

aeolian harp [ee-oh-lee-an] n musical instrument that produces sounds when the wind passes over its strings.

aeon [ee-on] n immeasurably long period of time.

aerate v put gas into (a liquid), as when making a fizzy drink. **aeration** n

aerial adj in, from, or operating in the air; relating to aircraft. ▸ n metal pole, wire, etc., for receiving or transmitting radio or TV signals. **aerial top dressing** spreading of fertilizer from an aeroplane onto remote areas.

aerobatics pl n stunt flying. **aerobatic** adj

aerobics n exercises designed to increase the amount of oxygen in the blood. **aerobic** adj

aerodrome n small airport.

aerodynamics n study of how air flows around moving solid objects. **aerodynamic** adj

aerofoil n part of an aircraft, such as the wing, designed to give lift.

aerogram n airmail letter on a single sheet of paper that seals to form an envelope.

aeronautics n study or practice of aircraft flight. **aeronautical** adj

aeroplane n powered flying vehicle with fixed wings.

aerosol n pressurized can from which a substance can be dispensed as a fine spray.

aerospace n earth's atmosphere and space beyond.

aesthetic [iss-thet-ik] adj relating to the appreciation of art and beauty. **aesthetics** n study of art, beauty, and good taste. **aesthetically** adv **aesthete** [eess-theet] n person who has or affects an extravagant love of art. **aestheticism** n

aether n same as ETHER.

aetiology [ee-tee-ol-a-jee] n same as ETIOLOGY.

afar adv **from afar** from or at a great distance.

affable adj friendly and easy to talk to. **affably** adv **affability** n

affair n event or happening; sexual relationship outside marriage; thing to be done or attended to. ▸ pl personal or business interests; matters of public interest.

affect[1] v act on, influence; move (someone) emotionally.

affect[2] v put on a show of; wear or use by preference. **affectation** n attitude or manner put on to impress. **affected** adj displaying affectation; pretended.

affection n fondness or love. **affectionate** adj loving. **affectionately** adv

affianced [af-fie-anst] adj *Old-fashioned* engaged to be married.

affidavit [af-fid-dave-it] n written statement made on oath.

affiliate v (of a group) link up with a larger group. **affiliation** n

affinity n, pl -ties. close connection or liking; close resemblance; chemical attraction.

affirm v declare to be true; uphold or confirm (an idea or belief). **affirmation** n **affirmative** n, adj (word or phrase) indicating agreement.

affix v attach or fasten. ▸ n word or syllable added to a word to change its meaning.

afflict v give pain or grief to. **affliction** n

affluent adj having plenty of money. **affluence** n wealth.

afford v have enough money to buy; be able to spare (the time etc.); give or supply. **affordable** adj

afforest v plant trees on. **afforestation** n

affray n Brit, Aust & NZ law noisy fight, brawl.

affront v, n insult.

Afghan adj of Afghanistan or its language. **Afghan hound** large slim dog with long silky hair.

aficionado [af-fish-yo-nah-do] n, pl -dos. enthusiastic fan of something or someone.

afield adv **far afield** far away.

aflame adj burning.

afloat adv, adj floating; at sea.

afoot adv, adj happening, in operation.

aforesaid, aforementioned adj referred to previously.

aforethought adj premeditated, e.g. with malice aforethought.

Afr. Africa(n).

afraid adj frightened; regretful.

afresh adv again, anew.

African adj or Africa. ▶ n person from Africa. **African violet** house plant with pink or purple flowers and hairy leaves.

Afrikaans n language used in S Africa, descended from Dutch.

Afrikaner n White S African whose mother tongue is Afrikaans.

Afro- combining form African, e.g. Afro-Caribbean.

aft adv at or towards the rear of a ship or aircraft.

after prep following in time or place; in pursuit of; in imitation of. ▶ conj at a later time than. ▶ adv at a later time. **afters** pl n

Brit informal dessert.

afterbirth n material expelled from the womb after childbirth.

aftercare n support given to a person discharged from a hospital or prison; regular care required to keep something in good condition.

aftereffect n result occurring some time after its cause.

afterglow n glow left after a source of light has gone; pleasant feeling left after an enjoyable experience.

afterlife n life after death.

aftermath n results of an event considered together.

afternoon n time between noon and evening.

aftershave n lotion applied to the face after shaving.

afterthought n idea occurring later; something added later.

afterwards, afterward adv later.

Ag Chem silver.

again adv once more; in addition.

against prep in opposition or contrast to; in contact with; as a protection from.

agape adj (of the mouth) wide open; (of a person) very surprised.

agaric n fungus with gills on the underside of the cap, such as a mushroom.

agate [ag-git] n semiprecious form of quartz with striped colouring.

age n length of time a person or thing has existed; time of life; latter part of human life; period of history; long time. ▶ v ageing or aging, aged. make or grow old. **aged** adj [ay-jid] old; [rhymes with raged] being at the age of. **ageing, aging** n, adj **ageless** adj apparently never growing old; seeming to have existed for ever. **age-old** adj very old.

agency n, pl -cies. organization providing a service; business or function of an agent; *Old-fashioned* power or action by which something happens.

agenda *n* list of things to be dealt with, esp. at a meeting.

agent *n* person acting on behalf of another; person or thing producing an effect.

agent provocateur [azh-on prov-vok-at-**tur**] *n, pl* **agents provocateurs** [azh-on prov-vok-at-**tur**] person employed by the authorities to tempt people to commit illegal acts and so be discredited or punished.

agglomeration *n* confused mass or cluster.

aggrandize *v* make greater in size, power, or rank. **aggrandizement** *n*

aggravate *v* make worse; *Chiefly informal* annoy. **aggravating** *adj* **aggravation** *n*

aggregate *n* total; rock consisting of a mixture of minerals; sand or gravel used to make concrete. ▶ *adj* gathered into a mass; total or final. ▶ *v* combine into a whole. **aggregation** *n*

aggression *n* hostile behaviour; unprovoked attack. **aggressive** *adj* showing aggression; forceful. **aggressively** *adv* **aggressiveness** *n* **aggressor** *n*

aggrieved *adj* upset and angry.

aggro *n Brit, Aust & NZ slang* aggressive behaviour.

aghast *adj* overcome with amazement or horror.

agile *adj* nimble, quick-moving; mentally quick. **agility** *n*

agitate *v* disturb or excite; stir or shake (a liquid); stir up public opinion for or against something. **agitation** *n* **agitator** *n*

aglow *adj* glowing.

AGM annual general meeting.

agnostic *n* person who believes

that it is impossible to know whether God exists. ▶ *adj* of agnostics. **agnosticism** *n*

ago *adv* in the past.

agog *adj* eager or curious.

agony *n, pl* **-nies.** extreme physical or mental pain. **agonize** *v* worry greatly; (cause to) suffer agony. **agonizing** *adj* **agony aunt** journalist who gives advice in an agony column. **agony column** newspaper or magazine feature offering advice on personal problems.

agoraphobia *n* fear of open spaces. **agoraphobic** *n, adj*

agrarian *adj* of land or agriculture.

agree *v* **agreeing, agreed.** be of the same opinion; consent; reach a joint decision; be consistent; (foll. by *with*) be suitable to (one's health or digestion). **agreeable** *adj* pleasant and enjoyable; prepared to consent. **agreeably** *adv* **agreement** *n* agreeing; contract.

agriculture *n* raising of crops and livestock. **agricultural** *adj* **agriculturalist** *n*

agronomy [ag-**ron**-om-mee] *n* science of soil management and crop production. **agronomist** *n*

aground *adv* onto the bottom of shallow water.

ague [aig-yew] *n Old-fashioned* periodic fever with shivering.

ahead *adv* in front; forwards.

ahoy *interj* shout used at sea to attract attention.

AI artificial insemination; artificial intelligence.

aid *v, n* (give) assistance or support.

aide *n* assistant.

aide-de-camp [aid-de-kom] *n, pl* **aides-de-camp** [aid-de-kom] military officer serving as personal assistant to a senior.

AIDS acquired immunodeficiency

syndrome, a viral disease that destroys the body's ability to fight infection.

AIH artificial insemination by husband.

ail v trouble, afflict; be ill. **ailing** adj sickly. **ailment** n illness.

aileron n movable flap on an aircraft wing which controls rolling.

aim v point (a weapon or missile) or direct (a blow or remark) at a target; propose or intend. ▶ n aiming; intention, purpose. **aimless** adj having no purpose. **aimlessly** adv

ain't Not standard am not; is not; are not; has not; have not.

air n mixture of gases forming the earth's atmosphere; space above the ground, sky; breeze; quality or manner; tune. ▶ pl affected manners. ▶ v make known publicly; expose to air to dry or ventilate. **on the air** in the act of broadcasting on radio or television. **airless** adj stuffy. **air bag** vehicle safety device which inflates automatically in a crash to protect the driver or passenger when they are thrown forward. **airborne** adj carried by air; (of aircraft) flying. **airbrush** n atomizer spraying paint by compressed air. **airfield** n place where aircraft can land and take off. **air force** branch of the armed forces responsible for air warfare. **air gun** gun fired by compressed air. **air hostess** female flight attendant. **airlift** n transport of troops or cargo by aircraft when other routes are blocked. ▶ v transport by airlift. **airlock** n air bubble blocking the flow of liquid in a pipe; airtight chamber. **airmail** n system of sending mail by aircraft; mail sent in this way. **airman** n member of

the air force. **air miles** miles of free air travel that can be earned by buying airline tickets and various other products. **airplay** n broadcast performances of a record on radio. **airport** n airfield for civilian aircraft, with facilities for aircraft maintenance and passengers. **air raid** attack by aircraft. **airship** n lighter-than-air self-propelled aircraft. **airspace** n atmosphere above a country, regarded as its territory. **airstrip** n cleared area where aircraft can take off and land. **airtight** adj sealed so that air cannot enter.

air conditioning n system that controls the temperature and humidity of the air in a building. **air conditioner**

aircraft n any machine that flies, such as an aeroplane. **aircraft carrier** warship for the launching and landing of aircraft.

airing n exposure to air for drying or ventilation; exposure to public debate.

airline n company providing scheduled flights for aircraft and cargo. **airliner** n large passenger aircraft.

airworthy adj (of aircraft) fit to fly. **airworthiness** n

airy adj airier, airiest. well-ventilated; light-hearted and casual. **airily** adv

aisle [rhymes with **mile**] n passageway separating seating areas in a church, theatre, etc., or row of shelves in a supermarket.

ajar adj, adv (of a door) partly open.

akimbo adv with arms akimbo with hands on hips and elbows outwards.

akin adj akin to similar, related.

alabaster n soft white translucent stone.

à la carte *adj, adv* (of a menu) having dishes individually priced.

alacrity *n* speed, eagerness.

à la mode *adj* fashionable.

alarm *n* sudden fear caused by awareness of danger; warning sound; device that gives this; alarm clock. ▶ *v* fill with fear.

alarming *adj* **alarmist** *n* person who alarms others needlessly.

alarm clock clock which sounds at a set time to wake someone up.

alas *adv* unfortunately, regrettably.

albatross *n* large sea bird with very long wings.

albeit *conj* even though.

albino *n, pl* -**nos**. person or animal with white skin and hair and pink eyes.

album *n* book with blank pages for keeping photographs or stamps in; long-playing record.

albumen *n* egg white.

albumin, albumen *n* protein found in blood plasma, egg white, milk, and muscle.

alchemy *n* medieval form of chemistry concerned with trying to turn base metals into gold and to find the elixir of life. **alchemist** *n*

alcohol *n* colourless flammable liquid present in intoxicating drinks; intoxicating drinks generally. **alcoholic** *adj* of alcohol. ▶ *n* person addicted to alcohol. **alcoholism** *n* addiction to alcohol.

alcopop *n Brit, Aust & S Afr informal* alcoholic drink that tastes like a soft drink.

alcove *n* recess in the wall of a room.

aldehyde *n* one of a group of chemical compounds derived from alcohol by oxidation.

alder *n* tree related to the birch.

alderman *n* formerly, senior member of a local council.

ale *n* kind of beer.

alert *adj* watchful, attentive. ▶ *n* warning of danger. ▶ *v* warn of danger; make (someone) aware of (a fact). **on the alert** watchful. **alertness** *n*

alfalfa *n* kind of plant used to feed livestock.

alfresco *adv, adj* in the open air.

algae [al-jee] *pl n* plants which live in or near water and have no true stems, leaves, or roots.

algebra *n* branch of mathematics using symbols to represent numbers. **algebraic** *adj*

ALGOL *n Computers* programming language for mathematical and scientific purposes.

algorithm *n* logical arithmetical or computational procedure for solving a problem.

alias *adv* also known as. ▶ *n* false name.

alibi *n* plea of being somewhere else when a crime was committed; *Informal* excuse.

alien *adj* foreign; repugnant (to); from another world. ▶ *n* foreigner; being from another world.

alienate *v* cause to become hostile. **alienation** *n*

alight¹ *v* step out of (a vehicle); land.

alight² *adj* on fire; lit up.

align [a-line] *v* bring (a person or group) into agreement with the policy of another; place in a line. **alignment** *n*

alike *adj* like, similar. ▶ *adv* in the same way.

alimentary *adj* of nutrition. **alimentary canal** food passage in the body.

alimony *n* allowance paid under a court order to a separated or divorced spouse.

A-line *adj* (of a skirt) slightly flared.

aliquot *Maths* ▸ *adj* of or denoting an exact divisor of a number. ▸ *n* exact divisor.

alive *adj* living, in existence; lively. **alive to** aware of. **alive with** swarming with.

alkali [alk-a-lie] *n* substance which combines with acid and neutralizes it to form a salt. **alkaline** *adj* **alkalinity** *n* **alkaloid** *n* any of a group of organic compounds containing nitrogen.

all *adj* whole quantity or number (of). ▸ *adv* wholly, entirely; (in the score of games) each. **give one's all** make the greatest possible effort. **all in** *adj* exhausted; (of wrestling) with no style forbidden. ▸ *adv* with all expenses included.

all right *adj* adequate, satisfactory; unharmed. ▸ *interj* expression of approval or agreement.

all-rounder *n* person with ability in many fields.

Allah *n* name of God in Islam.

allay *v* reduce (fear or anger).

allege *v* state without proof. **alleged** *adj* **allegedly** *adv* **allegation** *n* unproved accusation.

allegiance *n* loyalty to a person, country, or cause.

allegory *n, pl* **-ries.** story with an underlying meaning as well as the literal one. **allegorical** *adj*

allegretto *n, pl* **-tos,** *adv Music* (piece to be played) fairly quickly or briskly.

allegro *n, pl* **-gros,** *adv Music* (piece to be played) in a brisk lively manner.

alleluia *interj* same as HALLELUJAH.

allergy *n, pl* **-gies.** extreme sensitivity to a substance, which causes the body to react to it. **allergic** *adj* having or caused by an allergy. **allergen** *n* substance capable of causing an allergic reaction.

alleviate *v* lessen (pain or suffering). **alleviation** *n*

alley *n* narrow street or path; long narrow enclosure in which tenpin bowling or skittles is played.

alliance *n* state of being allied; formal relationship between countries or groups for a shared purpose.

alligator *n* reptile of the crocodile family, found in the southern US and China.

alliteration *n* use of the same sound at the start of words occurring together, e.g. *moody music.* **alliterative** *adj*

allocate *v* assign to someone or for a particular purpose. **allocation** *n*

allot *v* **-lotting, -lotted.** assign as a share or for a particular purpose. **allotment** *n* distribution; portion allotted; small piece of public land rented to grow vegetables on.

allotrope *n* any of two or more physical forms in which an element can exist.

allow *v* permit; set aside; acknowledge (a point or claim). **allow for** *v* take into account. **allowable** *adj* **allowance** *n* amount of money given at regular intervals; amount permitted. **make allowances for** treat or judge (someone) less severely because he or she has special problems; take into account.

alloy *n* mixture of two or more metals. ▸ *v* mix (metals).

allspice *n* spice made from the berries of a tropical American tree.

allude *v* (foll. by *to*) refer indirectly to. **allusion** *n* indirect reference. **allusive** *adj*

allure *n* attractiveness. ▸ *v* entice or attract. **alluring** *adj*

alluvium *n* fertile soil deposited by flowing water. **alluvial** *adj*

ally n, pl **-lies.** country, person, or group with an agreement to support another. ▶ v **-lying, -lied.**
ally oneself with join as an ally.
allied adj

alma mater n school, university, or college that one attended.

almanac n yearly calendar with detailed information on anniversaries, phases of the moon, etc.

almighty adj having absolute power; Informal very great. ▶ n **the Almighty** God.

almond n edible oval-shaped nut which grows on a small tree.

almoner n Brit formerly, a hospital social worker.

almost adv very nearly.

alms [ahmz] pl n Old-fashioned gifts to the poor.

aloe n plant with fleshy spiny leaves. ▶ pl bitter drug made from aloe leaves.

aloft adv in the air; in a ship's rigging.

alone adj, adv without anyone or anything else.

along prep over part or all the length of. ▶ adv forward; in company with others. **alongside** prep, adv beside (something).

aloof adj distant or haughty in manner. **aloofness** n

alopecia [al-loh-pee-sha] n loss of hair.

aloud adv in an audible voice.

alpaca n Peruvian llama; wool or cloth made from its hair.

alpenstock n iron-tipped stick used by climbers.

alphabet n set of letters used in writing a language. **alphabetical** adj in the conventional order of the letters of an alphabet. **alphabetically** adv **alphabetize** v put in alphabetical order.

alpine adj of high mountains; (A-)

of the Alps. ▶ n mountain plant.

already adv before the present time; sooner than expected.

alright adj, interj all right.

Alsatian n large wolflike dog.

also adv in addition, too. **also-ran** n loser in a race, competition, or election.

altar n table used for Communion in Christian churches; raised structure on which sacrifices are offered and religious rites are performed. **altarpiece** n work of art above and behind the altar in some Christian churches.

alter v make or become different. **alteration** n

altercation n heated argument.

alter ego n second self; very close friend.

alternate v (cause to) occur by turns. ▶ adj occurring by turns; every second (one) of a series. **alternately** adv **alternation** n **alternator** n electric generator for producing alternating current. **alternating current** electric current that reverses direction at frequent regular intervals.

alternative n one of two choices. ▶ adj able to be done or used instead of something else; (of medicine, lifestyle, etc.) not conventional. **alternatively** adv

although conj despite the fact that.

altimeter [al-**tim**-it-er] n instrument that measures altitude.

altitude n height above sea level.

alto n, pl **-tos.** Music short for CONTRALTO; (singer with) the highest adult male voice; instrument with the second-highest pitch in its group.

altogether adv entirely; on the whole; in total.

altruism n unselfish concern for the welfare of others. **altruistic** adj **altruistically** adv

aluminium n Chem light silvery-white metal that does not rust.

alumnus [al-lumm-nuss] n, pl -ni [-nie] graduate of a college. **alumna** [al-lumm-na] n fem, pl -nae [-nee]

always adv at all times; for ever.

alyssum n garden plant with small yellow or white flowers.

am v see BE.

AM amplitude modulation; (in Britain) Member of the National Assembly for Wales.

a.m. ante meridiem: before noon.

amalgam n blend or combination; alloy of mercury and another metal.

amalgamate v combine or unite. **amalgamation** n

amandla [ah-mand-lah] n S Afr political slogan calling for power to the Black population.

amanuensis [am-man-yew-en-siss] n, pl -ses [-seez] person who writes from dictation.

amaranth n imaginary flower that never fades; lily-like plant with red, green, or purple flowers.

amaryllis n lily-like plant with large red, pink, or white flowers.

amass v collect or accumulate.

amateur n person who engages in a sport or activity as a pastime rather than as a profession; person unskilled in something. ▶ adj not professional. **amateurish** adj lacking skill. **amateurishly** adv

amatory adj relating to romantic or sexual love.

amaze v surprise greatly, astound. **amazing** adj **amazingly** adv **amazement** n

Amazon n strong and powerful woman; legendary female warrior. **Amazonian** adj

ambassador n senior diplomat who represents his or her country in another country. **ambassadorial** adj

amber n clear yellowish fossil resin. ▶ adj brownish-yellow.

ambergris [am-ber-greece] n waxy substance secreted by the sperm whale, used in making perfumes.

ambidextrous adj able to use both hands with equal ease.

ambience n atmosphere of a place.

ambient adj surrounding.

ambiguous adj having more than one possible meaning. **ambiguously** adv **ambiguity** n

ambit n limits or boundary.

ambition n desire for success; something so desired, goal. **ambitious** adj **ambitiously** adv

ambivalence n state of feeling two conflicting emotions at the same time. **ambivalent** adj **ambivalently** adv

amble v walk at a leisurely pace. ▶ n leisurely walk or pace.

ambrosia n Myth food of the gods. **ambrosial** adj

ambulance n motor vehicle designed to carry sick or injured people.

ambush n act of waiting in a concealed position to make a surprise attack; attack from a concealed position. ▶ v attack from a concealed position.

ameliorate [am-meal-yor-rate] v make (something) better. **amelioration** n

amen interj so be it: used at the end of a prayer.

amenable adj likely or willing to cooperate.

amend v make small changes to correct or improve (something). **amendment** n

amends pl n **make amends for** compensate for.

amenity n, pl -ties. useful or enjoyable feature.

American adj of the United States of America or the American continent. ▶ n person from America or the American continent. **Americanism** n expression or custom characteristic of Americans.

amethyst [am-myth-ist] n bluish-violet variety of quartz used as a gemstone.

amiable adj friendly, pleasant-natured. **amiably** adv **amiability** n

amicable adj friendly. **amicably** adv

amid, amidst prep in the middle of, among. **amidships** adv at or towards the middle of a ship.

amino acid [am-**mean**-oh] n organic compound found in protein.

amiss adv wrongly, badly. ▶ adj wrong, faulty. **take something amiss** be offended by something.

amity n friendship.

ammeter n instrument for measuring electric current.

ammonia n strong-smelling alkaline gas containing hydrogen and nitrogen; solution of this in water.

ammonite n fossilized spiral shell of an extinct sea creature.

ammunition n bullets, bombs, and shells that can be fired from or as a weapon; facts that can be used in an argument.

amnesia n loss of memory. **amnesiac** n

amnesty n, pl -**ties.** general pardon for offences against a government.

amniocentesis n, pl -**ses.** removal of some amniotic fluid to test for possible abnormalities in a fetus.

amniotic fluid n fluid surrounding a fetus in the womb.

amoeba [am-**mee**-ba] n, pl -**bae, -bas.** microscopic single-celled animal able to change its shape.

amok [a-**muck** or a-**mock**] adv **run amok** run about in a violent frenzy.

among, amongst prep in the midst of; in the group or number of; to each of, e.g. divide it among yourselves.

amoral [aim-**mor**-ral] adj without moral standards. **amorality** n

amorous adj feeling, showing, or relating to sexual love. **amorously** adv

amorphous adj without distinct shape.

amortize v pay off (a debt) gradually by periodic transfers to a sinking fund.

amount n extent or quantity. ▶ v (foll. by to) be equal or add up to.

amour n (secret) love affair.

amp n ampere; Informal amplifier.

ampere [am-**pair**] n basic unit of electric current.

ampersand n the character (&), meaning and.

amphetamine [am-**fet**-am-mean] n drug used as a stimulant.

amphibian n animal that lives on land but breeds in water; vehicle that can travel on both land and water. **amphibious** adj living or operating both on land and in water.

amphitheatre n open oval or circular building with tiers of seats rising round an arena.

amphora [am-**for**-ra] n, pl -**phorae.** two-handled ancient Greek or Roman jar.

ample adj more than sufficient; large. **amply** adv

amplifier n device used to amplify a current or sound signal.

amplify v -**fying, -fied.** increase the strength of (a current or sound signal); explain in more detail; increase the size or effect of. **amplification** n

amplitude n greatness of extent.

ampoule n small sealed glass vessel containing liquid for injection.

amputate v cut off (a limb or part of a limb) for medical reasons. **amputation** n

amuck adv same as AMOK.

amulet n something carried or worn as a protection against evil.

amuse v cause to laugh or smile; entertain or divert. **amusing** adj **amusement** n state of being amused; something that amuses.

an adj form of **a** used before vowels, and sometimes before h.

anabolic steroid n synthetic steroid hormone used to stimulate muscle and bone growth.

anachronism [an-**nak**-kron-iz-zum] n person or thing placed in the wrong historical period or seeming to belong to another time. **anachronistic** adj

anaconda n large S American snake which kills by constriction.

anaemia [an-**neem**-ee-a] n deficiency in the number of red blood cells. **anaemic** adj having anaemia; pale and sickly; lacking vitality.

anaesthetic [an-niss-**thet**-ik] n, adj (substance) causing loss of bodily feeling. **anaesthesia** [an-niss-**theez**-ee-a] n loss of bodily feeling. **anaesthetist** [an-**neess**-thet-ist] n doctor trained to administer anaesthetics. **anaesthetize** v

anagram n word or phrase made by rearranging the letters of another word or phrase.

anal [**ain**-al] adj of the anus.

analgesic [an-nal-**jeez**-ik] n, adj (drug) relieving pain. **analgesia** n absence of pain.

analogous adj similar in some respects.

analogue n something that is similar in some respects to

something else. ▶ adj displaying information by means of a dial.

analogy n, pl **-gies.** similarity in some respects; comparison made to show such a similarity.

analogical adj

analysis n, pl **-ses.** separation of a whole into its parts for study and interpretation; psychoanalysis.

analyse v make an analysis of (something); psychoanalyse.

analyst n person skilled in analysis. **analytical, analytic** adj **analytically** adv

anarchism n doctrine advocating the abolition of government.

anarchist n person who advocates the abolition of government; person who causes disorder. **anarchistic** adj

anarchy [an-**ark**-ee] n lawlessness and disorder; lack of government in a state. **anarchic** adj

anathema [an-**nath**-im-a] n detested person or thing.

anatomy n, pl **-mies.** science of the structure of the body; physical structure; person's body; detailed analysis. **anatomical** adj **anatomically** adv **anatomist** n expert in anatomy.

ANC African National Congress.

ancestor n person from whom one is descended; forerunner. **ancestral** adj **ancestry** n lineage or descent.

anchor n heavy hooked device attached to a boat by a cable and dropped overboard to fasten the ship to the sea bottom. ▶ v fasten with or as if with an anchor. **anchorage** n place where boats can be anchored. **anchorman, anchorwoman** n broadcaster in a central studio who links up and presents items from outside camera units and other studios; last person to compete in a relay team.

anchorite n religious recluse.

anchovy [an-**chov**-ee] n, pl **-vies**. small strong-tasting fish.

ancient adj dating from very long ago; very old. **ancients** pl n people who lived very long ago.

ancillary adj supporting the main work of an organization; used as an extra or supplement.

and conj in addition to; as a consequence; then, afterwards.

andante [an-**dan**-tay] n, adv Music (piece to be played) moderately slowly.

andiron n iron stand for supporting logs in a fireplace.

androgynous adj having both male and female characteristics.

android n robot resembling a human.

anecdote n short amusing account of an incident. **anecdotal** adj

anemometer n instrument for recording wind speed.

anemone [an-**nem**-on-ee] n plant with white, purple, or red flowers.

aneroid barometer n device for measuring air pressure, consisting of a partially evacuated chamber in which variations in pressure cause a pointer on the lid to move.

aneurysm, aneurism [an-new-**riz**-zum] n permanent swelling of a blood vessel.

anew adv once more; in a different way.

angel n spiritual being believed to be an attendant or messenger of God; person who is kind, pure, or beautiful. **angelic** adj **angelically** adv

angelica n aromatic plant; its candied stalks, used in cookery.

Angelus [an-**jell**-uss] n (in the Roman Catholic Church) prayers recited in the morning, at midday, and in the evening; bell signalling

the times of these prayers.

anger n fierce displeasure or extreme annoyance. ▸ v make (someone) angry.

angina [an-**jine**-a] n heart disorder causing sudden severe chest pains (also **angina pectoris**).

angle[1] n space between or shape formed by two lines or surfaces that meet; divergence between these, measured in degrees; corner; point of view. ▸ v bend or place (something) at an angle.

angle[2] v fish with a hook and line; (foll. by for) try to get by hinting. **angling** n

angler n person who fishes with a hook and line.

Anglican n, adj (member) of the Church of England. **Anglicanism** n

anglicize v make or become English in outlook, form, etc.

Anglo- combining form English, e.g. Anglo-Scottish; British, e.g. Anglo-American.

Anglo-Saxon n member of any of the W Germanic tribes that settled in England from the fifth century AD; language of the Anglo-Saxons. ▸ adj of the Anglo-Saxons or their language.

angora n variety of goat, cat, or rabbit with long silky hair; hair of the angora goat or rabbit; cloth made from this hair.

Angostura Bitters pl n ® bitter tonic, used as a flavouring in alcoholic drinks.

angry adj **-grier, -griest**. full of anger; inflamed, e.g. an angry wound. **angrily** adv

angst n feeling of anxiety.

angstrom n unit of length used to measure wavelengths.

anguish n great mental pain. **anguished** adj

angular adj (of a person) lean and bony; having angles; measured by an angle. **angularity** n

anhydrous adj Chem containing no water.

aniline n colourless oily liquid obtained from coal tar and used for making dyes, plastics, and explosives.

animal n living creature with specialized sense organs and capable of voluntary motion, esp. one other than a human being; quadruped. ▶ adj of animals; sensual, physical.

animate v give life to; make lively; make a cartoon film of. ▶ adj having life. **animated** adj **animation** n technique of making cartoon films; liveliness and enthusiasm. **animator** n

animism n belief that natural objects possess souls. **animist** n, adj **animistic** adj

animosity n, pl -ties. hostility, hatred.

animus n hatred, animosity.

anion [an-eye-on] n ion with negative charge.

anise [an-niss] n plant with liquorice-flavoured seeds.

aniseed n liquorice-flavoured seeds of the anise plant.

ankle n joint between the foot and leg. **anklet** n ornamental chain worn round the ankle.

annals pl n yearly records of events.

anneal v toughen (metal or glass) by heating and slow cooling.

annelid n worm with a segmented body, such as an earthworm.

annex v seize (territory); take (something) without permission; join or add (something) to something larger. **annexation** n

annexe n extension to a building; nearby building used as an extension.

annihilate v destroy utterly. **annihilation** n

anniversary n, pl -ries. date on which something occurred in a previous year; celebration of this.

anno Domini [an-no dom-in-eye] adv Latin (indicating years numbered from the supposed year of the birth of Christ) in the year of our Lord.

annotate v add notes to (a written work). **annotation** n

announce v make known publicly; proclaim. **announcement** n **announcer** n person who introduces radio or television programmes.

annoy v irritate or displease. **annoyance** n

annual adj happening once a year; lasting for a year. ▶ n plant that completes its life cycle in a year; book published once every year. **annually** adv

annuity n, pl -ties. fixed sum paid every year.

annul v -nulling, -nulled. declare (something, esp. a marriage) invalid. **annulment** n

annular [an-new-lar] adj ring-shaped.

Annunciation n Christianity angel Gabriel's announcement to the Virgin Mary of her conception of Christ.

anode n Electricity positive electrode in a battery, valve, etc. **anodize** v coat (metal) with a protective oxide film by electrolysis.

anodyne n something that relieves pain or distress. ▶ adj relieving pain or distress.

anoint v smear with oil as a sign of consecration.

anomaly [an-nom-a-lee] n, pl -lies. something that deviates from the normal, irregularity. **anomalous** adj

anon adv Obs in a short time, soon.

anon. anonymous.

anonymous *adj* by someone whose name is unknown or withheld; having no known name. **anonymously** *adv* **anonymity** *n*

anorak *n* light waterproof hooded jacket.

anorexia *n* psychological disorder characterized by fear of becoming fat and refusal to eat (also **anorexia nervosa**). **anorexic** *adj, n*

another *adj, pron* one more; different (one).

answer *n* reply to a question, request, letter, etc.; solution to a problem; reaction or response. ▶ *v* give an answer (to); be responsible to (a person); respond or react. **answerable** *adj* (foll. by *for* or *to*) responsible for or accountable to. **answering machine** device for answering a telephone automatically and recording messages.

ant *n* small insect living in highly organized colonies. **anteater** *n* mammal which feeds on ants by means of a long snout. **ant hill** mound built by ants around their nest.

antacid *n* substance that counteracts acidity, esp. in the stomach.

antagonist *n* opponent or adversary. **antagonism** *n* open opposition or hostility. **antagonistic** *adj* **antagonize** *v* arouse hostility in, annoy.

Antarctic *n* the **Antarctic** area around the South Pole. ▶ *adj* of this region.

ante *n* player's stake in poker. ▶ *v* **-teing, -ted** or **-teed.** place (one's stake) in poker.

ante- *prefix* before in time or position, e.g. *antedate; antechamber.*

antecedent *n* event or circumstance happening or existing before another. ▶ *adj* preceding, prior.

antedate *v* precede in time.

antediluvian *adj* of the time before the biblical Flood; old-fashioned.

antelope *n* deerlike mammal with long legs and horns.

antenatal *adj* during pregnancy, before birth.

antenna *n, pl* **-nae.** insect's feeler; (*pl* **-nas**) aerial.

anterior *adj* to the front; earlier.

anteroom *n* small room leading into a larger one, often used as a waiting room.

anthem *n* song of loyalty, esp. to a country; piece of choral music, usu. set to words from the Bible.

anther *n* part of a flower's stamen containing pollen.

anthology *n, pl* **-gies.** collection of poems or other literary pieces by various authors. **anthologist** *n*

anthracite *n* hard coal burning slowly with little smoke or flame but intense heat.

anthrax *n* dangerous disease of cattle and sheep, communicable to humans.

anthropoid *adj* like a human. ▶ *n* ape, such as a chimpanzee, that resembles a human.

anthropology *n* study of human origins, institutions, and beliefs. **anthropological** *adj* **anthropologist** *n*

anthropomorphic *adj* attributing human form or personality to a god, animal, or object. **anthropomorphism** *n*

anti- *prefix* against, opposed to, e.g. *anti-war;* opposite to, e.g. *anticlimax;* counteracting, e.g. *antifreeze.*

anti-aircraft *adj* for defence against aircraft attack.

antibiotic n chemical substance capable of destroying bacteria. ▶ adj of antibiotics.

antibody n, pl **-bodies.** protein produced in the blood, which destroys bacteria.

anticipate v foresee and act in advance of; look forward to. **anticipation** n **anticipatory** adj

anticlimax n disappointing conclusion to a series of events.

anticlockwise adv, adj in the opposite direction to the rotation of the hands of a clock.

antics pl n absurd acts or postures.

anticyclone n area of moving air of high pressure in which the winds rotate outwards.

antidote n substance that counteracts a poison.

antifreeze n liquid added to water to lower its freezing point, used esp. in car radiators.

antigen [an-tee-jen] n substance, usu. a toxin, causing the blood to produce antibodies.

antihero n, pl **-roes.** central character in a book, film, etc., who lacks the traditional heroic virtues.

antihistamine n drug used to treat allergies.

antimacassar n cloth put over a chair-back to prevent soiling.

antimony n Chem brittle silvery-white metallic element.

antipathy [an-tip-a-thee] n dislike, hostility. **antipathetic** adj

antiperspirant n substance used to reduce or prevent sweating.

antiphon n hymn sung in alternate parts by two groups of singers. **antiphonal** adj

antipodes [an-tip-pod-deez] pl n any two places diametrically opposite one another on the earth's surface. **the Antipodes** Australia and New Zealand.

antipodean adj

antipyretic adj reducing fever. ▶ n drug that reduces fever.

antiquary n, pl **-quaries.** student or collector of antiques or ancient works of art. **antiquarian** adj of or relating to antiquities or rare books. ▶ n antiquary.

antiquated adj out-of-date.

antique n object of an earlier period, valued for its beauty, workmanship, or age. ▶ adj made in an earlier period; old-fashioned.

antiquity n great age; ancient times. **antiquities** pl n objects dating from ancient times.

antiracism n policy of challenging racism and promoting racial tolerance.

antirrhinum n two-lipped flower of various colours.

anti-Semitism n discrimination against Jews. **anti-Semitic** adj

antiseptic adj preventing infection by killing germs. ▶ n antiseptic substance.

antisocial adj avoiding the company of other people; (of behaviour) harmful to society.

antistatic adj reducing the effects of static electricity.

antithesis [an-tith-iss-iss] n, pl **-ses** [-seez] exact opposite; placing together of contrasting ideas or words to produce an effect of balance. **antithetical** adj

antitoxin n (serum containing) an antibody that acts against a toxin.

antitrust adj Aust & S Afr (of laws) opposing business monopolies.

antler n branched horn of male deer.

antonym n word that means the opposite of another.

anus [ain-uss] n opening at the end of the alimentary canal, through which faeces are discharged.

anvil n heavy iron block on which metals are hammered into particular shapes.

anxiety n, pl -ties. state of being anxious.

anxious adj worried and tense; intensely desiring. **anxiously** adv

any adj, pron one or some, no matter which. ▶ adv at all, e.g. it isn't any worse. **anybody** pron anyone. **anyhow** adv anyway. **anyone** pron any person; person of any importance. **anything** pron anyway adv at any rate, nevertheless; in any manner. **anywhere** adv in, at, or to any place.

Anzac n (in World War 1) a soldier serving with the Australian and New Zealand Army Corps. **Anzac Day** 25th April, a public holiday in Australia and New Zealand commemorating the Anzac landing at Gallipoli in 1915.

AOB (on the agenda for a meeting) any other business.

aorta [eh-or-ta] n main artery of the body, carrying oxygen-rich blood from the heart.

apace adv Lit swiftly.

apart adv to or in pieces; to or at a distance; individual, distinct.

apartheid n former official government policy of racial segregation in S Africa.

apartment n room in a building; flat.

apathy n lack of interest or enthusiasm. **apathetic** adj

ape n tailless monkey such as the chimpanzee or gorilla; stupid, clumsy, or ugly man. ▶ v imitate.

aperient [ap-peer-ee-ent] adj having a mild laxative effect. ▶ n mild laxative.

aperitif [ap-per-rit-teef] n alcoholic drink taken before a meal.

aperture n opening or hole.

apex n highest point.

APEX Brit, NZ & S Afr Advance Purchase Excursion: reduced fare for journeys booked a specified period in advance.

aphasia n disorder of the central nervous system that affects the ability to speak and understand words.

aphid [eh-fid], **aphis** [eh-fiss] n small insect which sucks the sap from plants.

aphorism n short clever saying expressing a general truth.

aphrodisiac [af-roh-diz-zee-ak] n substance that arouses sexual desire. ▶ adj arousing sexual desire.

apiary n, pl -ries. place where bees are kept.

apiculture n breeding and care of bees.

apiece adv each.

aplomb n calm self-possession.

apocalypse n end of the world; event of great destruction. **the Apocalypse** book of Revelation, the last book of the New Testament. **apocalyptic** adj

Apocrypha [ap-pok-rif-fa] pl n **the Apocrypha** collective name for the 14 books of the Old Testament which are not accepted as part of the Hebrew scriptures.

apocryphal [ap-pok-rif-al] adj (of a story) of questionable authenticity.

apogee [ap-oh-jee] n point of the moon's or a satellite's orbit that is farthest from the earth; highest point.

apology n, pl -gies. expression of regret for wrongdoing; (foll. by for) poor example (of). **apologetic** adj showing or expressing regret. **apologetically** adv **apologetics** n branch of theology concerned with the reasoned defence of Christianity.

apologist n person who formally

defends a cause. **apologize** v make an apology.

apoplexy n Med stroke. **apoplectic** adj of apoplexy; Informal furious.

apostasy [ap-**poss**-stass-ee] n, pl **-sies**. abandonment of one's religious faith or other belief. **apostate** n, adj

a posteriori [eh poss-steer-ee-**or**-rye] adj involving reasoning from effect to cause.

Apostle n one of the twelve disciples chosen by Christ to preach his gospel; (**a-**) ardent supporter of a cause or movement. **apostolic** adj

apostrophe [ap-**poss**-trof-fee] n punctuation mark (') showing the omission of a letter or letters in a word, e.g. don't, or forming the possessive, e.g. Jill's car; digression from a speech to address an imaginary or absent person or thing.

apothecary n, pl -caries. Obs chemist.

apotheosis [ap-poth-ee-**oh**-siss], pl **-ses** [-seez] perfect example; elevation to the rank of a god.

appal v -palling, -palled. dismay, terrify. **appalling** adj dreadful, terrible.

apparatus n equipment for a particular purpose.

apparel n Old-fashioned clothing.

apparent adj readily seen, obvious; seeming as opposed to real. **apparently** adv

apparition n ghost or ghostlike figure.

appeal v make an earnest request; attract, please, or interest; request a review of a lower court's decision by a higher court. ▶ n earnest request; attractiveness; request for a review of a lower court's decision by a higher court.

appealing adj

appear v become visible or present; seem; be seen in public. **appearance** n appearing; outward aspect.

appease v pacify (a person) by yielding to his or her demands; satisfy or relieve (a feeling). **appeasement** n

appellant n person who makes an appeal to a higher court.

appellation n Formal name, title.

append v join on, add. **appendage** n thing joined on or added.

appendicitis n inflammation of the appendix.

appendix n, pl -dices, -dixes. separate additional material at the end of a book; Anat short closed tube attached to the large intestine.

appertain v (foll. by to) belong to; be connected with.

appetite n desire for food or drink; liking or willingness. **appetizer** n thing eaten or drunk to stimulate the appetite. **appetizing** adj stimulating the appetite.

applaud v show approval of by clapping one's hands; approve strongly. **applause** n approval shown by clapping one's hands.

apple n round firm fleshy fruit that grows on trees. **in apple-pie order** Informal very tidy.

appliance n device with a specific function.

applicable adj relevant, appropriate. **applicability** n

applicant n person who applies for something.

application n formal request; act of applying something to a particular use; diligent effort; act of putting something onto a surface.

appliqué [ap-**plee**-kay] n kind of

decoration in which one material is cut out and attached to another.

apply v **-plying, -plied.** make a formal request; put to practical use; put onto a surface; be relevant or appropriate. **apply oneself** concentrate one's efforts. **applied** adj (of a skill, science, etc.) put to practical use.

appoint v assign to a job or position; fix or decide, e.g. *appoint a time*; equip or furnish. **appointment** n arrangement to meet a person; act of placing someone in a job; the job itself. ▶ pl fixtures or fittings.

apportion v divide out in shares.

apposite adj suitable, apt. **apposition** n grammatical construction in which two nouns or phrases referring to the same thing are placed one after another without a conjunction, e.g. *my son the doctor*.

appraise v estimate the value or quality of. **appraisal** n

appreciate v value highly; be aware of and understand; be grateful for; rise in value. **appreciable** adj enough to be noticed. **appreciably** adv **appreciation** n **appreciative** adj feeling or showing appreciation.

apprehend v arrest and take into custody; grasp (something) mentally. **apprehension** n dread, anxiety; arrest; understanding. **apprehensive** adj fearful or anxious.

apprentice n someone working for a skilled person for a fixed period in order to learn his or her trade. ▶ v take or place (someone) as an apprentice. **apprenticeship** n

apprise v make aware (of).

appro n on appro Brit, Austral, NZ & S Afr informal on approval.

approach v come near or nearer

(to); make a proposal or suggestion to; begin to deal with (a matter). ▶ n approaching or means of approaching; approximation. **approachable** adj **approach road** smaller road leading into a major road.

approbation n approval.

appropriate adj suitable, fitting. ▶ v take for oneself; put aside for a particular purpose. **appropriately** adv **appropriateness** n **appropriation** n

approve v consider good or right; authorize, agree to. **approval** n consent; favourable opinion. **on approval** (of goods) with an option to be returned without payment if unsatisfactory.

approx. approximate(ly).

approximate adj almost but not quite exact. ▶ v (foll. by *to*) come close to; be almost the same as. **approximately** adv **approximation** n

appurtenances pl n minor or additional features.

Apr. April.

après-ski [ap-ray-skee] n social activities after a day's skiing.

apricot n yellowish-orange juicy fruit like a small peach. ▶ adj yellowish-orange.

April n fourth month of the year. **April fool** victim of a practical joke played on April 1 (**April Fools' Day**).

a priori [eh pry-or-rye] adj involving reasoning from cause to effect.

apron n garment worn over the front of the body to protect the clothes; area at an airport or hangar for manoeuvring and loading aircraft; part of a stage in front of the curtains.

apropos [ap-prop-poh] adj, adv appropriate(ly). **apropos of** with regard to.

apse n arched or domed recess, esp. in a church.

apt adj having a specified tendency; suitable; quick to learn. **aptly** adv **aptness** n **aptitude** n natural ability.

aqualung n mouthpiece attached to air cylinders, worn for underwater swimming.

aquamarine n greenish-blue gemstone. ▶ adj greenish-blue.

aquaplane n board on which a person stands to be towed by a motorboat. ▶ v ride on an aquaplane; (of a motor vehicle) skim uncontrollably on a thin film of water.

aquarium n, pl **aquariums**, **aquaria.** tank in which fish and other underwater creatures are kept; building containing such tanks.

aquatic adj living in or near water; done in or on water. **aquatics** pl n water sports.

aquatint n print like a watercolour, produced by etching copper.

aqua vitae [ak-wa **vee**-tie] n Obs brandy.

aqueduct n structure carrying water across a valley or river.

aqueous adj of, like, or containing water.

aquiline adj (of a nose) curved like an eagle's beak; of or like an eagle.

Arab n member of a Semitic people originally from Arabia. ▶ adj of the Arabs. **Arabic** n language of the Arabs. ▶ adj of Arabic, Arabs, or Arabia.

arabesque [ar-ab-**besk**] n ballet position in which one leg is raised behind and the arms are extended; elaborate ornamental design.

arable adj suitable for growing crops on.

arachnid [ar-**rak**-nid] n eight-legged invertebrate, such as a spider, scorpion, tick, or mite.

Aran adj (of sweaters etc.) knitted in a complicated pattern traditional to the Aran Islands, usu. with natural unbleached wool.

arbiter n person empowered to judge in a dispute; person with influential opinions about something.

arbitrary adj based on personal choice or chance, rather than reason. **arbitrarily** adv

arbitration n hearing and settling of a dispute by an impartial referee chosen by both sides. **arbitrate** v **arbitrator** n

arboreal adj of or living in trees.

arboretum [ahr-bore-**ee**-tum] n, pl **-ta.** place where rare trees or shrubs are cultivated.

arboriculture n cultivation of trees or shrubs.

arbour n glade sheltered by trees.

arc n part of a circle or other curve; luminous discharge of electricity across a small gap between two electrodes. ▶ v form an arc.

arcade n covered passageway lined with shops; set of arches and their supporting columns.

arcane adj mysterious and secret.

arch[1] n curved structure supporting a bridge or roof; something curved; curved lower part of the foot. ▶ v (cause to) form an arch. **archway** n passageway under an arch.

arch[2] adj superior, knowing; coyly playful. **archly** adv **archness** n

arch- combining form chief, principal, e.g. archenemy.

archaeology n study of ancient cultures from their physical remains. **archaeological** adj **archaeologist** n

archaic [ark-**kay**-ik] *adj* ancient; out-of-date. **archaism** [ark-kay-iz-zum] *n* archaic word or phrase.

archangel [ark-ain-jell] *n* chief angel.

archbishop *n* chief bishop.

archdeacon *n* priest ranking just below a bishop.

archdiocese *n* diocese of an archbishop.

archer *n* person who shoots with a bow and arrow. **archery** *n*

archetype [ark-ee-type] *n* perfect specimen; original model. **archetypal** *adj*

archipelago [ark-ee-pel-a-go] *n, pl* **-gos, -goes.** group of islands; sea full of small islands.

architect *n* person qualified to design and supervise the construction of buildings. **architecture** *n* style in which a building is designed and built; designing and construction of buildings. **architectural** *adj*

architrave *n Archit* beam that rests on columns; moulding round a doorway or window.

archive [ark-ive] *n* (often *pl*) collection of records or documents; place where these are kept. **archival** *adj* **archivist** [ark-iv-ist] *n* person in charge of archives.

Arctic *n* **the Arctic** area around the North Pole. ▶ *adj* of this region; **(a-)** *Informal* very cold.

ardent *adj* passionate; eager, zealous. **ardently** *adv* **ardour** *n* passion; enthusiasm, zeal.

arduous *adj* hard to accomplish, strenuous. **arduously** *adv*

are[1] *v* see BE.

are[2] *n* unit of measure, 100 square metres.

area *n* part or region; size of a two-dimensional surface; subject field.

arena *n* seated enclosure for sports events; area of a Roman amphitheatre where gladiators fought; sphere of intense activity.

aren't are not.

areola *n, pl* **-lae, -las.** small circular area, such as the coloured ring around the human nipple.

argon *n Chem* inert gas found in the air.

argot [ahr-go] *n* slang or jargon.

argue *v* **-guing, -gued.** try to prove by giving reasons; debate; quarrel, dispute. **arguable** *adj* **arguably** *adv* **argument** *n* quarrel; discussion; point presented for or against something. **argumentation** *n* process of reasoning methodically. **argumentative** *adj* given to arguing.

argy-bargy *n, pl* **-bargies.** *Informal* squabbling argument.

aria [ah-ree-a] *n* elaborate song for solo voice, esp. one from an opera.

arid *adj* parched, dry; uninteresting. **aridity** *n*

aright *adv* rightly.

arise *v* **arising, arose, arisen.** come about; come into notice; get up.

aristocracy *n, pl* **-cies.** highest social class. **aristocrat** *n* member of the aristocracy. **aristocratic** *adj*

arithmetic *n* calculation by or of numbers. ▶ *adj* of arithmetic. **arithmetical** *adj* **arithmetically** *adv*

ark *n Old Testament* boat built by Noah, which survived the Flood; **(A-)** *Judaism* chest containing the writings of Jewish Law.

arm[1] *n* either of the upper limbs from the shoulder to the wrist; sleeve of a garment; side of a chair. **armful** *n* as much as can be held in the arms. **armchair** *n* upholstered chair with side supports for the arms. **armhole** n opening in a garment through which the arm passes. **armpit** n hollow under the arm at the shoulder.

arm² v supply with weapons; prepare (a bomb etc.) for use. **arms** pl n weapons; military exploits; heraldic emblem.

armada n large number of warships.

armadillo n, pl -**los**. small S American mammal covered in strong bony plates.

Armageddon n New Testament final battle between good and evil at the end of the world; catastrophic conflict.

armament n military weapons; preparation for war.

armature n revolving structure in an electric motor or generator, wound with coils carrying the current.

armistice [arm-miss-stiss] n agreed suspension of fighting.

armour n metal clothing formerly worn to protect the body in battle; metal plating of tanks, warships, etc. **armourer** n maker, repairer, or keeper of arms or armour. **armoury** n place where weapons are stored.

army n, pl **armies**. military land forces of a nation; great number.

aroma n pleasant smell. **aromatic** adj **aromatherapy** n massage with fragrant oils to relieve tension.

arose v past tense of ARISE.

around prep, adv on all sides (of); from place to place (in); somewhere in or near; approximately.

arouse v stimulate, make active; awaken.

arpeggio [arp-**pej**-ee-oh] n, pl -**gios**. Music notes of a chord played or sung in quick succession.

arr. arranged (by); arrival; arrive(d).

arraign [ar-**rain**] v bring (a prisoner) before a court to answer a charge; accuse. **arraignment** n

arrange v plan; agree; put in order; adapt (music) for performance in a certain way. **arrangement** n

arrant adj utter, downright.

arras n tapestry wall-hanging.

array n impressive display or collection; orderly arrangement, esp. of troops; Poetic rich clothing. ▶ v arrange in order; dress in rich clothing.

arrears pl n money owed. **in arrears** late in paying a debt.

arrest v take (a person) into custody; stop the movement or development of; catch and hold (the attention). ▶ n act of taking a person into custody; slowing or stopping. **arresting** adj attracting attention, striking.

arrive v reach a place or destination; happen; come; Informal be born; Informal attain success. **arrival** n arriving; person or thing that has just arrived.

arrogant adj proud and overbearing. **arrogantly** adv **arrogance** n

arrogate v claim or seize without justification.

arrow n pointed shaft shot from a bow; arrow-shaped sign or symbol used to show direction. **arrowhead** n pointed tip of an arrow.

arrowroot n nutritious starch obtained from the root of a W Indian plant.

arsenal n place where arms and ammunition are made or stored.

arsenic n toxic grey element; highly poisonous compound of this. **arsenical** adj

arson n crime of intentionally

setting property on fire. **arsonist** n

art n creation of works of beauty, esp. paintings or sculpture; works of art collectively; skill. ▶ pl nonscientific branches of knowledge. **artist** n person who produces works of art, esp. paintings or sculpture; person skilled at something; artiste. **artiste** n professional entertainer such as a singer or dancer. **artistic** adj **artistically** adv **artistry** n artistic skill. **arty** adj **artier, artiest.** Informal having an affected interest in art.

artefact n something made by human beings.

arteriosclerosis [art-ear-ee-oh-skler-**oh**-siss] n hardening of the arteries.

artery n, pl -**teries.** one of the tubes carrying blood from the heart; major road or means of communication. **arterial** adj of an artery; (of a route) major.

artesian well [art-**teez**-yan] n well bored vertically so that the water is forced to the surface by natural pressure.

Artex n ® Brit textured plaster-like covering for ceilings and walls.

artful adj cunning, wily. **artfully** adv **artfulness** n

arthritis n painful inflammation of a joint or joints. **arthritic** adj, n

arthropod n animal, such as a spider or insect, with jointed limbs and a segmented body.

artichoke n flower head of a thistle-like plant, cooked as a vegetable.

article n written piece in a magazine or newspaper; item or object; clause in a document; Grammar any of the words the, a, or an.

articled adj bound (as an apprentice) by a written contract.

articulate adj able to express oneself clearly and coherently; (of speech) clear, distinct; Zool having joints. ▶ v speak or say clearly and coherently. **articulately** adv **articulated** adj jointed.

articulated vehicle large vehicle in two separate sections joined by a pivoted bar. **articulation** n

artifice n clever trick; cleverness, skill. **artificer** [art-**tiff**-iss-er] n craftsman.

artificial adj man-made, not occurring naturally; made in imitation of something natural; not sincere. **artificial insemination** introduction of semen into the womb by means other than sexual intercourse. **artificial intelligence** branch of computer science aiming to produce machines which can imitate intelligent human behaviour. **artificial respiration** method of restarting a person's breathing after it has stopped. **artificially** adv **artificiality** n

artillery n large-calibre guns; branch of the army who use these.

artisan n skilled worker, craftsman.

artless adj free from deceit or cunning; natural, unpretentious. **artlessly** adv

arum lily [**air**-rum] n plant with a white funnel-shaped leaf surrounding a spike of flowers.

arvie n S Afr informal afternoon.

as conj while, when; in the way that; that which, e.g. do as you are told; since, seeing that; for instance. ▶ adv, conj used to indicate amount or extent in comparisons, e.g. he is as tall as you. ▶ prep in the role of, being, e.g. as a mother, I am concerned.

asafoetida n strong-smelling plant resin used as a spice in Eastern cookery.

a.s.a.p. as soon as possible.

asbestos n fibrous mineral which does not burn. **asbestosis** n lung disease caused by inhalation of asbestos fibre.

ascend v go or move up. **ascent** n ascending; upward slope. **ascendant** adj dominant or influential. ► n **in the ascendant** increasing in power or influence. **ascendancy** n condition of being dominant. **the Ascension** Christianity passing of Jesus Christ from earth into heaven.

ascertain v find out definitely. **ascertainable** adj **ascertainment** n

ascetic [ass-set-tik] n, adj (person) abstaining from worldly pleasures and comforts. **asceticism** n

ascorbic acid [ass-core-bik] n vitamin C.

ascribe v attribute, as to a particular origin. **ascription** n

aseptic [eh-sep-tik] adj free from harmful bacteria.

asexual [eh-sex-yew-al] adj without sex. **asexually** adv

ash[1] n powdery substance left when something is burnt. ► pl remains after burning, esp. of a human body after cremation. **the Ashes** cricket trophy competed for in test matches by England and Australia. **ashen** adj pale with shock. **ashtray** n receptacle for tobacco ash and cigarette butts. **Ash Wednesday** first day of Lent.

ash[2] n tree with grey bark.

ashamed adj feeling shame.

ashlar n square block of hewn stone used in building.

ashore adv towards or on land.

ashram n religious retreat where a Hindu holy man lives.

Asian adj of the continent of Asia or any of its peoples or languages. ► n person from Asia or a descendant of one.

aside adv to one side; out of other people's hearing, e.g. he took me aside to tell me his plans. ► n remark not meant to be heard by everyone present.

asinine adj stupid, idiotic.

ask v say or write (something) in a form that requires an answer; make a request or demand; invite.

askance [ass-kanss] adv **look askance at** look at with an oblique glance; regard with suspicion.

askew adv, adj to one side, crooked.

aslant adv, prep at a slant (to), slanting (across).

asleep adj sleeping; (of limbs) numb.

asp n small poisonous snake.

asparagus n plant whose shoots are cooked as a vegetable.

aspect n feature or element; position facing a particular direction; appearance or look.

aspen n kind of poplar tree.

asperity n roughness of temper.

aspersion n **cast aspersions on** make derogatory remarks about.

asphalt n black hard tarlike substance used for road surfaces etc.

asphodel n plant with clusters of yellow or white flowers.

asphyxia [ass-fix-ee-a] n suffocation. **asphyxiate** v suffocate. **asphyxiation** n

aspic n savoury jelly used to coat meat, eggs, fish, etc.

aspidistra n plant with long tapered leaves.

aspirate Phonetics ► v pronounce with an h sound. ► n h sound.

aspire v (foll. by to) yearn (for), hope (to do or be). **aspirant** n person who aspires. **aspiration** n strong desire or aim.

aspirin n drug used to relieve pain

and fever; tablet of this.

ass n donkey; stupid person.

assagai n same as ASSEGAI.

assail v attack violently. **assailant** n

assassin n person who murders a prominent person. **assassinate** v murder (a prominent person). **assassination** n

assault n violent attack. ▶ v attack violently. **assault course** series of obstacles used in military training.

assay n analysis of a substance, esp. a metal, to ascertain its purity. ▶ v make such an analysis.

assegai [ass-a-guy] n slender spear used in S Africa.

assemble v collect or congregate; put together the parts of (a machine). **assemblage** n collection or group; assembling. **assembly** n, pl -blies. assembled group; assembling. **assembly line** sequence of machines and workers in a factory assembling a product.

assent n agreement or consent. ▶ v agree or consent.

assert v declare forcefully; insist upon (one's rights etc.). **assert oneself** put oneself forward forcefully. **assertion** n **assertive** adj **assertively** adv

assess v judge the worth or importance of; estimate the value of (income or property) for taxation purposes. **assessment** n **assessor** n

asset n valuable or useful person or thing. ▶ pl property that a person or firm can sell, esp. to pay debts.

asseverate v declare solemnly.

assiduous adj hard-working. **assiduously** adv **assiduity** n

assign v appoint (someone) to a job or task; allot (a task); attribute. **assignation** n assigning; secret arrangement to meet.

assignment n task assigned; assigning.

assimilate v learn and understand (information); absorb or be absorbed or incorporated. **assimilable** adj **assimilation** n

assist v give help or support. **assistance** n **assistant** n helper. ▶ adj junior or deputy.

assizes pl n Brit court sessions formerly held in each county of England and Wales.

associate v connect in the mind; mix socially. ▶ n partner in business; friend or companion. ▶ adj having partial rights or subordinate status, e.g. associate member. **association** n society or club; associating.

assonance n rhyming of vowel sounds but not consonants, as in time and light.

assorted adj consisting of various types mixed together. **assortment** n assorted mixture.

assuage [ass-wage] v relieve (pain, grief, thirst, etc.).

assume v take to be true without proof; take upon oneself, e.g. he assumed command; pretend, e.g. I assumed indifference. **assumption** n thing assumed; assuming.

assure v promise or guarantee; convince; make (something) certain; insure against loss of life. **assured** adj confident; certain to happen. **assuredly** adv definitely. **assurance** n assuring or being assured.

astatine n Chem radioactive nonmetallic element.

aster n plant with daisy-like flowers.

asterisk n star-shaped symbol (*) used in printing or writing to indicate a footnote etc. ▶ v mark with an asterisk.

astern adv at or towards the stern of a ship; backwards.

asteroid n any of the small planets that orbit the sun between Mars and Jupiter.

asthma [ass-ma] n illness causing difficulty in breathing. **asthmatic** adj, n

astigmatism [eh-stig-mat-tiz-zum] n inability of a lens, esp. of the eye, to focus properly.

astir adj Old-fashioned out of bed; in motion.

astonish v surprise greatly. **astonishment** n

astound v overwhelm with amazement. **astounding** adj

astrakhan n dark curly fleece of lambs from Astrakhan in Russia; fabric resembling this.

astral adj of stars; of the spirit world.

astray adv off the right path.

astride adv, prep with a leg on either side (of).

astringent adj causing contraction of body tissue; checking the flow of blood from a cut; severe or harsh. ▸ n astringent substance. **astringency** n

astrolabe n instrument formerly used to measure the altitude of stars and planets.

astrology n study of the alleged influence of the stars, planets, and moon on human affairs. **astrologer** n **astrological** adj

astronaut n person trained for travelling in space.

astronautics n science and technology of space flight. **astronautical** adj

astronomy n scientific study of heavenly bodies. **astronomer** n **astronomical** adj very large; of astronomy. **astronomically** adv

astrophysics n science of the physical and chemical properties of stars, planets, etc. **astrophysical** adj **astrophysicist** n

astute adj perceptive or shrewd. **astutely** adv **astuteness** n

asunder adv Obs or poetic into parts or pieces.

asylum n refuge or sanctuary; old name for a mental hospital.

asymmetry n lack of symmetry. **asymmetrical, asymmetric** adj

asymptote [ass-im-tote] n straight line closely approached but never met by a curve.

at prep indicating position in space or time, movement towards an object, etc., e.g. at midnight; throwing stones at windows.

atavism [at-a-viz-zum] n recurrence of a trait present in distant ancestors. **atavistic** adj

ate v past tense of EAT.

atheism [aith-ee-iz-zum] n belief that there is no God. **atheist** n **atheistic** adj

atherosclerosis n, pl **-ses.** disease in which deposits of fat cause the walls of the arteries to thicken.

athlete n person trained in or good at athletics. **athletic** adj physically fit or strong; of an athlete or athletics. **athletics** pl n track-and-field sports such as running, jumping, throwing, etc. **athletically** adv **athleticism** n

athwart prep across. ▸ adv transversely.

atlas n book of maps.

atmosphere n mass of gases surrounding a heavenly body, esp. the earth; prevailing tone or mood (of a place etc.); unit of pressure. **atmospheric** adj **atmospherics** pl n radio interference due to electrical disturbance in the atmosphere.

atoll n ring-shaped coral reef enclosing a lagoon.

atom n smallest unit of matter which can take part in a chemical reaction; very small amount.

atom bomb same as ATOMIC BOMB.

atomic *adj* of or using atomic bombs or atomic energy; of atoms. **atomic bomb** bomb in which the energy is provided by nuclear fission. **atomic energy** nuclear energy. **atomic number** number of protons in the nucleus of an atom. **atomic weight** ratio of the mass per atom of an element to one twelfth of the mass of a carbon atom.

atomize *v* reduce to atoms or small particles.

atomizer *n* device for discharging a liquid in a fine spray.

atonal [eh-tone-al] *adj* (of music) not written in an established key.

atone *v* make amends (for sin or wrongdoing). **atonement** *n*

atop *prep* Lit on top of.

atrium *n, pl* **atria.** upper chamber of either half of the heart; central hall extending through several storeys of a modern building; main courtyard of an ancient Roman house.

atrocious *adj* extremely cruel or wicked; horrifying or shocking; Informal very bad. **atrociously** *adv* **atrocity** *n* wickedness; (*pl* **-ties**) act of cruelty.

atrophy [at-trof-fee] *n, pl* **-phies.** wasting away of an organ or part. ▶ *v* **-phying, -phied.** (cause to) waste away.

attach *v* join, fasten, or connect; attribute or ascribe. **attached** *adj* (foll. by *to*) fond of. **attachment** *n*

attaché [at-tash-shay] *n* specialist attached to a diplomatic mission. **attaché case** flat rectangular briefcase for papers.

attack *v* launch a physical assault (against); criticize; set about (a job or problem) with vigour; affect adversely. ▶ *n* act of attacking; sudden bout of illness. **attacker** *n*

attain *v* achieve or accomplish (a task or aim); reach. **attainable** *adj* **attainment** *n* accomplishment.

attar *n* fragrant oil made from roses.

attempt *v* try, make an effort. ▶ *n* effort or endeavour.

attend *v* be present at; go regularly to a school, college, etc.; look after; pay attention; apply oneself (to). **attendance** *n* attending; number attending. **attendant** *n* person who assists, guides, or provides a service. ▶ *adj* accompanying. **attention** *n* concentrated direction of the mind; consideration; care; alert position in military drill. **attentive** *adj* giving attention; considerately helpful. **attentively** *adv* **attentiveness** *n*

attenuated *adj* weakened; thin and extended. **attenuation** *n*

attest *v* affirm the truth of, be proof of. **attestation** *n*

attic *n* space or room within the roof of a house.

attire *n* Formal fine or formal clothes.

attired *adj* dressed in a specified way.

attitude *n* way of thinking and behaving; posture of the body.

attorney *n* person legally appointed to act for another; US & S Afr lawyer.

attract *v* arouse the interest or admiration of; draw (something) closer by exerting a force on it. **attraction** *n* power to attract; something that attracts. **attractive** *adj* **attractively** *adv* **attractiveness** *n*

attribute *v* (usu. foll. by *to*) regard as belonging to or produced by. ▶ *n* quality or feature representative of a person or thing. **attributable** *adj*

attribution n **attributive** adj
Grammar (of an adjective)
preceding the noun modified.

attrition n constant wearing down
to weaken or destroy.

attune v adjust or accustom (a
person or thing).

atypical [eh-**tip**-ik-al] adj not
typical.

Au Chem gold.

aubergine [oh-bur-zheen] n Brit
dark purple tropical fruit, cooked
and eaten as a vegetable.

aubrietia [aw-bree-sha] n trailing
plant with purple flowers.

auburn adj (of hair) reddish-brown.

auction n public sale in which
articles are sold to the highest
bidder. ▶ v sell by auction.
auctioneer n person who
conducts an auction.

audacious adj recklessly bold or
daring; impudent. **audaciously**
adv **audacity** n

audible adj loud enough to be
heard. **audibly** adv **audibility** n

audience n group of spectators or
listeners; formal interview.

audio adj of sound or hearing; of
or for the transmission or
reproduction of sound. **audio
typist** typist trained to type from
a dictating machine. **audiovisual**
adj (esp. of teaching aids)
involving both sight and hearing.

audit n official examination of
business accounts. ▶ v **auditing,
audited.** examine (business
accounts) officially. **auditor** n

audition n test of a performer's
ability for a particular role or job.
▶ v test or be tested in an audition.

auditorium n, pl **-toriums, -toria.**
area of a concert hall or theatre
where the audience sits.

auditory adj of or relating to
hearing.

au fait [oh **fay**] adj French fully

informed; expert.

Aug. August.

auger n tool for boring holes.

aught pron Obs anything whatever.

augment v increase or enlarge.
augmentation n

au gratin [oh **grat**-tan] adj
covered and cooked with
breadcrumbs and sometimes
cheese.

augur v be a sign of (future
events). **augury** n foretelling of
the future; (pl **-ries**) omen.

august [aw-**gust**] adj dignified and
imposing.

August n eighth month of the year.

auk n northern sea bird with short
wings and black-and-white
plumage.

aunt n father's or mother's sister;
uncle's wife. **auntie, aunty** n, pl
aunties. Informal aunt. **Aunt Sally**
Brit, NZ & S Afr figure used in
fairgrounds as a target; target of
abuse or criticism.

au pair n young foreign woman
who does housework in return for
board and lodging.

aura n distinctive air or quality of a
person or thing.

aural adj of or using the ears or
hearing.

aureole, aureola n halo.

au revoir [oh riv-**vwahr**] interj
French goodbye.

auricle n upper chamber of the
heart; outer part of the ear.
auricular adj

aurochs n, pl **aurochs.** recently
extinct European wild ox.

aurora n, pl **-ras, -rae.** bands of
light sometimes seen in the sky in
polar regions. **aurora australis**
aurora seen near the South Pole.
aurora borealis aurora seen near
the North Pole.

auscultation n listening to the
internal sounds of the body, usu.

with a stethoscope, to help with diagnosis.

auspices [aw-spiss-siz] *pl n* **under the auspices of** with the support and approval of.

auspicious *adj* showing signs of future success, favourable. **auspiciously** *adv*

Aussie *n, adj Informal* Australian.

Aust. Australia(n).

austere *adj* stern or severe; ascetic or self-disciplined; severely simple or plain. **austerely** *adv* **austerity** *n*

Australasian *n, adj* (person) from Australia, New Zealand, and neighbouring islands.

Australia Day *n Aust* public holiday on 26th January.

Australian *n, adj* (person) from Australia.

autarchy [aw-tar-kee] *n* absolute power or autocracy.

autarky [aw-tar-kee] *n* policy of economic self-sufficiency.

authentic *adj* known to be real, genuine. **authentically** *adv* **authenticity** *n* **authenticate** *v* establish as genuine. **authentication** *n*

author *n* writer of a book etc.; originator or creator. **authorship** *n*

authority *n, pl* **-ties.** power to command or control others; (often *pl*) person or group having this power; expert in a particular field. **authoritarian** *n, adj* (person) insisting on strict obedience to authority. **authoritative** *adj* recognized as being reliable; possessing authority. **authoritatively** *adv* **authorize** *v* give authority to; give permission for. **authorization** *n*

autism *n Psychiatry* disorder, usu. of children, characterized by lack of response to people and limited ability to communicate. **autistic**

adj

auto- *combining form* self-, e.g. *autobiography.*

autobiography *n, pl* **-phies.** account of a person's life written by that person. **autobiographical** *adj* **autobiographically** *adv*

autocrat *n* ruler with absolute authority; dictatorial person. **autocratic** *adj* **autocratically** *adv* **autocracy** *n* government by an autocrat.

autocross *n* motor-racing over a rough course.

Autocue *n* ® electronic television prompting device displaying a speaker's script, unseen by the audience.

autogiro, autogyro *n, pl* **-ros.** self-propelled aircraft resembling a helicopter but with an unpowered rotor.

autograph *n* handwritten signature of a (famous) person. ▶ *v* write one's signature on or in.

automat *n US* vending machine.

automate *v* make (a manufacturing process) automatic. **automation** *n*

automatic *adj* (of a device) operating mechanically by itself; (of a process) performed by automatic equipment; done without conscious thought; (of a firearm) self-loading. ▶ *n* self-loading firearm; vehicle with automatic transmission. **automatically** *adv*

automaton *n* robot; person who acts mechanically.

automobile *n US* motor car.

autonomy *n* self-government. **autonomous** *adj*

autopsy *n, pl* **-sies.** examination of a corpse to determine the cause of death.

autosuggestion *n* process in which a person unconsciously

autumn

influences his or her own
behaviour or beliefs.
autumn n season between summer
and winter. **autumnal** adj
auxiliary adj secondary or
supplementary; supporting. ▶ n, pl
-ries. person or thing that
supplements or supports.
auxiliary verb verb used to form
the tense, voice, or mood of
another, such as will in I will go.
avail v be of use or advantage (to).
▶ n use or advantage, esp. in to no
avail. **avail oneself of** make use
of.
available adj obtainable or
accessible. **availability** n
avalanche n mass of snow or ice
falling down a mountain; sudden
overwhelming quantity of
anything.
avant-garde [av-ong-**gard**] n
group of innovators, esp. in the
arts. ▶ adj innovative and
progressive.
avarice [av-a-riss] n greed for
wealth. **avaricious** adj
avast interj Naut stop.
avatar n Hinduism appearance of a
god in animal or human form.
Ave. Avenue.
avenge v take revenge in
retaliation for (harm done) or on
behalf of (a person harmed).
avenger n
avenue n wide street; road
between two rows of trees; way of
approach.
aver [av-**vur**] v **averring, averred.**
state to be true.
average n typical or normal
amount or quality; result obtained
by adding quantities together and
dividing the total by the number
of quantities. ▶ adj usual or typical;
calculated as an average. ▶ v
calculate the average of; amount
to as an average.

averse adj (usu. foll. by to)
disinclined or unwilling. **aversion**
n strong dislike; person or thing
disliked.
avert v turn away; ward off.
aviary n, pl **aviaries.** large cage or
enclosure for birds.
aviation n art of flying aircraft.
aviator n
avid adj keen or enthusiastic;
greedy (for). **avidly** adv **avidity** n
avocado n, pl **-dos.** pear-shaped
tropical fruit with a leathery green
skin and yellowish-green flesh.
avocation n Old-fashioned
occupation; hobby.
avocet n long-legged wading bird
with a long slender
upward-curving bill.
avoid v prevent from happening;
refrain from; keep away from.
avoidable adj **avoidance** n
avoirdupois [av-er-de-**poise**] n
system of weights based on
pounds and ounces.
avow v state or affirm; admit
openly. **avowal** n **avowed** adj
avowedly adv
avuncular adj (of a man) friendly,
helpful, and caring towards
someone younger.
await v wait for; be in store for.
awake v **awaking, awoke,
awoken.** emerge or rouse from
sleep; (cause to) become alert.
▶ adj not sleeping; alert.
awaken v awake.
award v give (something, such as
a prize) formally. ▶ n something
awarded, such as a prize.
aware adj having knowledge,
informed. **awareness** n
awash adj washed over by water.
away adv from a place, e.g. go
away; to another place, e.g. put
that gun away; out of existence,
e.g. fade away; continuously, e.g.
laughing away. ▶ adj not present;

distant, e.g. *two miles away*; *Sport* played on an opponent's ground.

awe *n* wonder and respect mixed with dread. ▶ *v* fill with awe.

awesome *adj* inspiring awe; *Slang* excellent or outstanding.

awestruck *adj* filled with awe.

awful *adj* very bad or unpleasant; *Informal* very great; *Obs* inspiring awe. **awfully** *adv* in an unpleasant way; *Informal* very.

awhile *adv* for a brief time.

awkward *adj* clumsy or ungainly; embarrassed; difficult to use or handle; inconvenient. **awkwardly** *adv* **awkwardness** *n*

awl *n* pointed tool for piercing wood, leather, etc.

awning *n* canvas roof supported by a frame to give protection against the weather.

awoke *v* past tense of AWAKE. **awoken** *v* past participle of AWAKE.

AWOL *adj Mil* absent without leave.

awry [a-rye] *adv, adj* with a twist to one side, askew; amiss.

axe *n* tool with a sharp blade for felling trees or chopping wood; *Informal* dismissal from employment etc. ▶ *v Informal* dismiss (employees), restrict (expenditure), or terminate (a project).

axil *n* angle where the stalk of a leaf joins a stem.

axiom *n* generally accepted principle; self-evident statement. **axiomatic** *adj* self-evident.

axis *n, pl* **axes**. (imaginary) line round which a body can rotate or about which an object or geometrical figure is symmetrical; one of two fixed lines on a graph, against which quantities or positions are measured. **axial** *adj*

axle *n* shaft on which a wheel or pair of wheels turns.

axolotl *n* aquatic salamander of

central America.

ayatollah *n* Islamic religious leader in Iran.

aye, ay *interj* yes. ▶ *n* affirmative vote or voter.

azalea [az-zale-ya] *n* garden shrub grown for its showy flowers.

azimuth *n* arc of the sky between the zenith and the horizon; horizontal angle of a bearing measured clockwise from the north.

azure *adj, n* (of) the colour of a clear blue sky.

── B b ──

BA Bachelor of Arts.

baa *v* **baaing, baaed**. make the characteristic bleating sound of a sheep. ▶ *n* cry made by a sheep.

babble *v* talk excitedly or foolishly; (of streams) make a low murmuring sound. ▶ *n* muddled or foolish speech.

babe *n* baby.

babel *n* confused mixture of noises or voices.

baboon *n* large monkey with a pointed face and a long tail.

baby *n, pl* **-bies**. very young child or animal; *Slang* sweetheart. ▶ *adj* comparatively small of its type. **babyish** *adj* **baby-sit** *v* take care of a child while the parents are out. **baby-sitter** *n*

baccarat [back-a-rah] *n* card game involving gambling.

bacchanalia [back-a-nail-ee-a] *n* wild drunken party or orgy.

bach [batch] *NZ v* in small holiday cottage. ▶ *v* look after oneself when one's spouse is away.

bachelor *n* unmarried man; person who holds the lowest university or college degree.

bacillus [bass-**ill**-luss] *n, pl* **-li** [-lie] rod-shaped bacterium.

back *n* rear part of the human body, from the neck to the pelvis; part or side of an object opposite the front; part of anything less often seen or used; *Ball games* defensive player or position. ▶ *v* (cause to) move backwards; provide money for (a person or enterprise); bet on the success of; (foll. by *onto*) have the back facing towards. ▶ *adj* situated behind; owing from an earlier date. ▶ *adv* at, to, or towards the rear; to or towards the original starting point or condition.
backer *n* person who gives financial support. **backing** *n* support; musical accompaniment for a pop singer. **backward** *adj* directed towards the rear; retarded in physical, material, or intellectual development.
backwardness *n* **backwards** *adv* towards the rear; with the back foremost; in the reverse of the usual direction. **back up** *v* support. **backup** *n* support or reinforcement; reserve or substitute.

backbencher *n* Member of Parliament who does not hold office in the government or opposition.

backbiting *n* spiteful talk about an absent person.

backbone *n* spinal column; strength of character.

backchat *n Informal* impudent replies.

backcloth, backdrop *n* painted curtain at the back of a stage set.

backdate *v* make (a document) effective from a date earlier than its completion.

backfire *v* (of a plan) fail to have the desired effect; (of an engine) make a loud noise like an explosion.

backgammon *n* game played with counters and dice.

background *n* events or circumstances that help to explain something; person's social class, education, or experience; part of a scene or picture furthest from the viewer.

backhand *n Tennis etc.* stroke played with the back of the hand facing the direction of the stroke.
backhanded *adj* ambiguous or implying criticism, e.g. *a backhanded compliment.*
backhander *n Slang* bribe.

backlash *n* sudden and adverse reaction.

backlog *n* accumulation of things to be dealt with.

backpack *n* large pack carried on the back.

backside *n Informal* buttocks.

backslide *v* relapse into former bad habits. **backslider** *n*

backstage *adv, adj* behind the stage in a theatre.

backstroke *n* swimming stroke performed on the back.

backtrack *v* return by the same route by which one has come; retract or reverse one's opinion or policy.

backwash *n* water washed backwards by the motion of a boat; repercussion.

backwater *n* isolated or backward place or condition.

backwoods *pl n* remote sparsely populated area.

bacon *n* salted or smoked pig meat.

bacteria *pl n, sing* **-rium.** large group of microorganisms, many of which cause disease. **bacterial** *adj* **bacteriology** *n* study of bacteria. **bacteriologist** *n*

bad *adj* **worse, worst.** of poor

quality; lacking skill or talent; harmful; immoral or evil; naughty or mischievous; rotten or decayed; unpleasant. **badly** adv **badness** n

bade v a past tense of BID.

badge n emblem worn to show membership, rank, etc.

badger n nocturnal burrowing mammal of Europe, Asia, and N America with a black and white head. ▸ v pester or harass.

badinage [bad-in-nahzh] n playful and witty conversation.

badminton n game played with rackets and a shuttlecock, which is hit back and forth over a high net.

Bafana bafana [bah-fan-na] pl n S Afr South African national soccer team.

baffle v perplex or puzzle. ▸ n device to limit or regulate the flow of fluid, light, or sound. **bafflement** n

bag n flexible container with an opening at one end; handbag or piece of luggage. ▸ v **bagging, bagged.** put into a bag; succeed in capturing, killing or scoring. **baggy** adj (of clothes) hanging loosely.

bagatelle n something of little value; board game in which balls are struck into holes.

bagel n hard ring-shaped bread roll.

baggage n suitcases packed for a journey.

bagpipes pl n musical wind instrument with reed pipes and an inflatable bag.

bail¹ n Law money deposited with a court as security for a person's reappearance in court. ▸ v pay bail for (a person).

bail², **bale** v (foll. by out) remove (water) from (a boat); Informal help (a person or organization) out of a predicament; make an emergency parachute jump from an aircraft.

bail³ n Cricket either of two wooden bars across the tops of the stumps.

bailey n outermost wall or court of a castle.

bailiff n sheriff's officer who serves writs and summonses; landlord's agent.

bairn n Scot child.

bait n piece of food on a hook or in a trap to attract fish or animals. ▸ v put a piece of food on or in (a hook or trap); persecute or tease.

baize n woollen fabric used to cover billiard and card tables.

bake v cook by dry heat as in an oven; make or become hardened by heat. **baking powder** powdered mixture containing sodium bicarbonate, used as a raising agent in baking.

baker n person whose business is to make or sell bread, cakes, etc. **baker's dozen** thirteen. **bakery** n, pl **-ries.** place where bread, cakes, etc. are baked or sold.

bakkie n S Afr small truck.

Balaclava, Balaclava helmet n close-fitting woollen hood that covers the ears and neck.

balalaika n guitar-like musical instrument with a triangular body.

balance n state in which a weight or amount is evenly distributed; amount that remains, e.g. *the balance of what you owe;* weighing device; difference between the credits and debits of an account. ▸ v weigh in a balance; make or remain steady; consider or compare; compare or equalize the money going into or coming out of an account.

balcony n, pl **-nies.** platform on the outside of a building with a rail along the outer edge; upper tier of seats in a theatre or cinema.

bald *adj* having little or no hair on the scalp; plain or blunt; (of a tyre) having a worn tread.
balding *adj* becoming bald.
baldness *n*

balderdash *n* stupid talk.

bale¹ *n* large bundle of hay or goods tightly bound together. ▸ *v* make or put into bales.

bale² *v* same as BAIL².

baleful *adj* vindictive or menacing.
balefully *adv*

balk, baulk *v* be reluctant to (do something); thwart or hinder.

Balkan *adj* of any of the countries of the Balkan Peninsula: Romania, Bulgaria, Albania, Greece, the former Yugoslavia, and the European part of Turkey.

ball¹ *n* round or nearly round object, esp. one used in games; single delivery of the ball in a game. ▸ *v* form into a ball. **ball bearings** steel balls between moving parts of a machine to reduce friction. **ball cock** device with a floating ball and a valve for regulating the flow of water.
ballpoint, ballpoint pen *n* pen with a tiny ball bearing as a writing point.

ball² *n* formal social function for dancing. **ballroom** *n*

ballad *n* narrative poem or song; slow sentimental song.

ballast *n* substance, such as sand, used to stabilize a ship when it is not carrying cargo.

ballet *n* classical style of expressive dancing based on conventional steps; theatrical performance of this. **ballerina** *n* female ballet dancer.

ballistics *n* study of the flight of projectiles, such as bullets.
ballistic missile missile guided automatically in flight but which

falls freely at its target.

balloon *n* inflatable rubber bag used as a plaything or decoration; large bag inflated with air or gas, designed to float in the atmosphere with passengers in a basket underneath. ▸ *v* fly in a balloon; swell or increase rapidly in size. **balloonist** *n*

ballot *n* method of voting; actual vote or paper indicating a person's choice. ▸ *v* -loting, -loted. vote or ask for a vote from.

ballyhoo *n* exaggerated fuss.

balm *n* aromatic substance used for healing and soothing; anything that comforts or soothes.

balmy *adj* **balmier, balmiest.** (of weather) mild and pleasant.

baloney *n Informal* nonsense.

balsa [bawl-sa] *n* very light wood from a tropical American tree.

balsam *n* soothing ointment; flowering plant.

baluster *n* set of posts supporting a rail.

balustrade *n* ornamental rail supported by balusters.

bamboo *n* tall treelike tropical grass with hollow stems.

bamboozle *v Informal* cheat or mislead; confuse, puzzle.

ban *v* **banning, banned.** prohibit or forbid officially. ▸ *n* official prohibition.

banal [ban-nahl] *adj* ordinary and unoriginal. **banality** *n*

banana *n* yellow crescent-shaped fruit.

band¹ *n* group of musicians playing together; group of people having a common purpose. **bandsman** *n* **bandstand** *n* roofed outdoor platform for a band. **band together** *v* unite.

band² *n* strip of some material, used to hold objects; *Physics* range of frequencies or wavelengths between two limits.

bandage n piece of material used to cover a wound or wrap an injured limb. ▶ v cover with a bandage.

bandanna, bandana n large brightly coloured handkerchief or neckerchief.

B & B bed and breakfast.

bandit n robber, esp. a member of an armed gang. **banditry** n

bandolier n shoulder belt for holding cartridges.

bandwagon n **jump, climb on the bandwagon** join a party or movement that seems assured of success.

bandy adj -dier, -diest. (also **bandy-legged**) having legs curved outwards at the knees. ▶ v -dying, -died. exchange (words) in a heated manner; use (a name, term, etc.) frequently.

bane n person or thing that causes misery or distress. **baneful** adj

bang n short loud explosive noise; hard blow or loud knock. ▶ v hit or knock, esp. with a loud noise; close (a door) noisily. ▶ adv precisely; with a sudden impact.

banger n Informal, Brit & Aust old decrepit car; Slang sausage; firework that explodes loudly.

bangle n bracelet worn round the arm or the ankle.

banish v send (someone) into exile; drive away. **banishment** n

banisters pl n railing supported by posts on a staircase.

banjo n, pl **-jos, -joes**. guitar-like musical instrument with a circular body.

bank[1] n institution offering services such as the safekeeping and lending of money; any supply, store, or reserve. ▶ v deposit (cash or cheques) in a bank. **banking** n **banknote** n piece of paper

money. **bank on** v rely on.

bank[2] n raised mass, esp. of earth; sloping ground at the side of a river. ▶ v form into a bank; cause (an aircraft) or (of an aircraft) to tip to one side on turning.

bank[3] n arrangement of switches, keys, oars, etc. in a row or in tiers.

banker n manager or owner of a bank.

bankrupt n person declared by a court to be unable to pay his or her debts. ▶ adj financially ruined. ▶ v make bankrupt. **bankruptcy** n

banksia n Australian evergreen tree or shrub.

banner n long strip of cloth displaying a slogan, advertisement, etc.; placard carried in a demonstration or procession.

bannisters pl n same as BANISTERS.

banns pl n public declaration, esp. in a church, of an intended marriage.

banquet n elaborate formal dinner.

banshee n (in Irish folklore) female spirit whose wailing warns of a coming death.

bantam n small breed of chicken. **bantamweight** n boxer weighing up to 118lb (professional) or 54kg (amateur).

banter v tease jokingly. ▶ n teasing or joking conversation.

Bantu n group of languages of Africa.

baptism n Christian religious ceremony in which a person is immersed in or sprinkled with water as a sign of being cleansed from sin and accepted into the Church. **baptismal** adj **baptize** v perform baptism on.

Baptist n member of a Protestant denomination that believes in adult baptism by immersion.

bar[1] n rigid length of metal, wood,

etc.; solid, usu. rectangular block, of any material; anything that obstructs or prevents; counter or room where drinks are served; heating element in an electric fire; *Music* group of beats repeated throughout a piece of music. ▶ *v* **barring, barred.** secure with a bar; obstruct; ban or forbid. ▶ *prep* (also **barring**) except for. **the Bar** barristers collectively. **barman, barmaid** *n*

bar[2] *n* unit of atmospheric pressure.

barb *n* cutting remark; point facing in the opposite direction to the main point of a fish-hook etc. **barbed** *adj* **barbed wire** strong wire with protruding sharp points.

barbarian *n* member of a primitive or uncivilized people. **barbaric** *adj* cruel or brutal. **barbarism** *n* condition of being backward or ignorant. **barbarity** *n* state of being barbaric or barbarous; (*pl* **-ties**) vicious act. **barbarous** *adj* uncivilized; brutal or cruel.

barbecue *n* grill on which food is cooked over hot charcoal, usu. outdoors; outdoor party at which barbecued food is served. ▶ *v* cook (food) on a barbecue.

barber *n* person who cuts men's hair and shaves beards.

barbiturate *n* drug used as a sedative.

bar code *n* arrangement of numbers and parallel lines on a package, which can be electronically scanned at a checkout to give the price of the goods.

bard *n Lit* poet.

bare *adj* unclothed, naked; without the natural or usual covering; unembellished, simple; just sufficient. ▶ *v* uncover. **barely** *adv* only just. **bareness** *n*

bareback *adj, adv* (of horse-riding)

without a saddle.

barefaced *adj* shameless or obvious.

bargain *n* agreement establishing what each party will give, receive, or perform in a transaction; something bought or offered at a low price. ▶ *v* negotiate the terms of an agreement. **bargain for** *v* anticipate or take into account.

barge *n* flat-bottomed boat used to transport freight. ▶ *v Informal* push violently. **barge in, into** *v* interrupt rudely.

baritone *n* (singer with) the second lowest adult male voice.

barium *n Chem* soft white metallic element.

bark[1] *n* loud harsh cry of a dog. ▶ *v* (of a dog) make its typical cry; shout in an angry tone.

bark[2] *n* tough outer layer of a tree.

barley *n* tall grasslike plant cultivated for grain.

barmy *adj* **-mier, -miest.** *Slang* insane.

barn *n* large building on a farm used for storing grain.

barnacle *n* shellfish that lives attached to rocks, ship bottoms, etc.

barney *n Informal* noisy fight or argument.

barometer *n* instrument for measuring atmospheric pressure. **barometric** *adj*

baron *n* member of the lowest rank of nobility; powerful businessman. **baroness** *n* **baronial** *adj*

baronet *n* commoner who holds the lowest hereditary British title.

baroque [bar-**rock**] *n* highly ornate style of art, architecture, or music from the late 16th to the early 18th century. ▶ *adj* ornate in style.

barque [bark] *n* sailing ship, esp. one with three masts.

barrack v criticize loudly or shout against (a team or speaker).

barracks pl n building used to accommodate military personnel.

barracuda n tropical sea fish.

barrage [bar-rahzh] n continuous delivery of questions, complaints, etc.; continuous artillery fire; artificial barrier across a river to control the water level.

barramundi n edible Australian fish.

barrel n cylindrical container with rounded sides and flat ends; tube in a firearm through which the bullet is fired. **barrel organ** musical instrument played by turning a handle.

barren adj (of a woman or female animal) incapable of producing offspring; (of land) unable to support the growth of crops, fruit, etc. **barrenness** n

barricade n barrier, esp. one erected hastily for defence. ▶ v erect a barricade across (an entrance).

barrier n anything that prevents access, progress, or union.

barrister n Brit, Aust & NZ lawyer qualified to plead in a higher court.

barrow[1] n wheelbarrow; movable stall used by street traders.

barrow[2] n mound of earth over a prehistoric tomb.

barter v trade (goods) in exchange for other goods. ▶ n trade by the exchange of goods.

basalt [bass-awlt] n dark volcanic rock. **basaltic** adj

base[1] n bottom or supporting part of anything; fundamental part; centre of operations, organization, or supply; starting point. ▶ v (foll. by on or upon) use as a basis (for); (foll. by at or in) to station or place. **baseless** adj

base[2] adj dishonourable or immoral; of inferior quality or value. **baseness** n

baseball n team game in which runs are scored by hitting a ball with a bat then running round four bases; ball used for this.

basement n partly or wholly underground storey of a building.

bash Informal ▶ v hit violently or forcefully. ▶ n heavy blow; party.

bashful adj shy or modest. **bashfully** adv **bashfulness** n

basic adj of or forming a base or basis; elementary or simple. **basics** pl n fundamental principles, facts, etc. **basically** adv

BASIC n computer programming language that uses common English words.

basil n aromatic herb used in cooking.

basilica n rectangular church with a rounded end and two aisles.

basilisk n legendary serpent said to kill by its breath or glance.

basin n round open container; sink for washing the hands and face; sheltered area of water where boats may be moored; catchment area of a particular river.

basis n, pl **-ses**, fundamental principles etc. from which something is started or developed.

bask v lie in or be exposed to something, esp. pleasant warmth.

basket n container made of interwoven strips of wood or cane. **basketwork** n

basketball n team game in which points are scored by throwing the ball through a high horizontal hoop; ball used for this.

Basque n, adj (member or language) of a people living in the W Pyrenees in France and Spain.

bas-relief n sculpture in which the figures project slightly from the background.

bass¹ [base] n (singer with) the lowest adult male voice. ▸ adj of the lowest range of musical notes.

bass² n edible sea fish.

basset hound n smooth-haired dog with short legs and long ears.

bassoon n low-pitched woodwind instrument.

baste¹ v moisten (meat) during cooking with hot fat.

baste² v sew with loose temporary stitches.

bastion n projecting part of a fortification; thing or person regarded as defending a principle.

bat¹ n any of various types of club used to hit the ball in certain sports. ▸ v **batting, batted**. strike with or as if with a bat. **batsman** n Cricket person who bats or specializes in batting.

bat² n nocturnal mouselike flying animal.

batch n group of people or things dealt with at the same time.

bated adj **with bated breath** in suspense or fear.

bath n large container in which to wash the body; act of washing in such a container. ▸ pl public swimming pool. ▸ v wash in a bath. **bathroom** n room with a bath, sink, and usu. a toilet. **Bath chair** n wheelchair for an invalid.

bathe v swim in open water for pleasure; apply liquid to (the skin or a wound) in order to cleanse or soothe; (foll. by in) fill (with), e.g. bathed in sunlight. **bather** n

bathos [bay-thoss] n sudden ludicrous change in speech or writing from a serious subject to a trivial one.

batik [bat-teek] n process of printing fabric using wax to cover areas not to be dyed; fabric printed in this way.

batman n officer's servant in the armed forces.

baton n thin stick used by the conductor of an orchestra; short bar transferred in a relay race; police officer's truncheon.

battalion n army unit consisting of three or more companies.

batten n strip of wood fixed to something, esp. to hold it in place. **batten down** v secure with battens.

batter¹ v hit repeatedly. **battering ram** large beam used to break down fortifications.

batter² n mixture of flour, eggs, and milk, used in cooking.

battery n, pl **-teries**. device that produces electricity in a torch, radio, etc.; group of heavy guns operating as a single unit. ▸ adj kept in series of cages for intensive rearing.

battle n fight between large armed forces; conflict or struggle. ▸ v struggle.

battle-axe n Informal domineering woman; (formerly) large heavy axe.

battlement n wall with gaps along the top for firing through.

battleship n large heavily armoured warship.

batty adj **-tier, -tiest**. Slang eccentric or crazy.

bauble n trinket of little value.

bauera n small evergreen Australian shrub.

baulk v same as BALK.

bauxite n claylike substance that is the chief source of aluminium.

bawdy adj **bawdier, bawdiest**. (of writing etc.) containing humorous references to sex.

bawl v shout or weep noisily.

bay¹ n stretch of coastline that curves inwards.

bay² n recess in a wall; area set aside for a particular purpose, e.g.

loading bay.

bay³ v howl in deep prolonged tones.

bay⁴ n Mediterranean laurel tree. **bay leaf** its dried leaf, used in cooking.

bay⁵ adj, n reddish-brown (horse).

bayonet n sharp blade that can be fixed to the end of a rifle. ▶ v **-neting, -neted.** stab with a bayonet.

bazaar n sale in aid of charity; market area, esp. in Eastern countries.

bazooka n portable rocket launcher that fires an armour-piercing projectile.

BBC British Broadcasting Corporation.

BC before Christ.

BCG antituberculosis vaccine.

be v, present sing 1st person **am.** 2nd person **are.** 3rd person **is.** present pl **are.** past sing 1st person **was.** 2nd person **were.** 3rd person **was.** past pl **were.** past participle **being.** past participle **been.** exist or live; used as a linking between the subject of a sentence and its complement, e.g. *John is a musician;* forms the progressive present tense, e.g. *the man is running;* forms the passive voice of all transitive verbs, e.g. *a good film is being shown on television tonight.*

beach n area of sand or pebbles on a shore. ▶ v run or haul (a boat) onto a beach. **beachhead** n beach captured by an attacking army on which troops can be landed.

beacon n fire or light on a hill or tower, used as a warning.

bead n small piece of plastic, wood, etc., pierced for threading on a string to form a necklace etc.; small drop of moisture.

beaded adj **beading** n strip of moulding used for edging furniture. **beady** adj small, round, and glittering, e.g. *beady eyes.*

beagle n small hound with short legs and drooping ears.

beak¹ n projecting horny jaws of a bird; Slang nose. **beaky** adj

beak² n Brit, Aust & NZ slang judge, magistrate, or headmaster.

beaker n large drinking cup; lipped glass container used in laboratories.

beam n broad smile; ray of light; narrow flow of electromagnetic radiation or particles; long thick piece of wood, metal, etc., used in building. ▶ v smile broadly; divert or aim (a radio signal, light, etc.) in a certain direction.

bean n seed or pod of various plants, eaten as a vegetable or used to make coffee etc.

beanie n close-fitting woollen hat.

bear¹ v **bearing, bore, borne.** support or hold up; bring, e.g. *to bear gifts;* (passive **born**) give birth to; tolerate or endure; hold in the mind. **bearable** adj **bear out** v show to be truthful.

bear² n large heavy mammal with a shaggy coat. **bearskin** n tall fur helmet worn by some British soldiers.

beard n hair growing on the lower parts of a man's face. **bearded** adj

bearer n person who carries, presents, or upholds something.

bearing n relevance (to); person's general social conduct; part of a machine that supports another part, esp. one that reduces friction. ▶ pl sense of one's own relative position.

beast n large wild animal; brutal or uncivilized person. **beastly** adj unpleasant or disagreeable.

beat v **beating, beat, beaten** or

beat. hit hard and repeatedly; move (wings) up and down; throb rhythmically; stir or mix vigorously; overcome or defeat. ▶ n regular throb; assigned route, as of a policeman; basic rhythmic unit in a piece of music. **beat up** v injure (someone) by repeated blows or kicks.

beatify [bee-**at**-if-fie] v **-fying, -fied.** RC Church declare (a dead person) to be among the blessed in heaven: the first step towards canonization. **beatific** adj displaying great happiness. **beatification** n **beatitude** n Christianity any of the blessings on the poor, meek, etc., in the Sermon on the Mount.

beau [boh] n, pl **beaux, beaus.** boyfriend or admirer; man greatly concerned with his appearance.

Beaufort scale n scale for measuring wind speeds.

beautician n person who gives beauty treatments professionally.

beautiful adj very attractive to look at; very pleasant. **beautifully** adv

beautify v **-fying, -fied.** make beautiful. **beautification** n

beauty n, pl **-ties.** combination of all the qualities of a person or thing that delight the senses and mind; very attractive woman; Informal something outstanding of its kind.

beaver n amphibious rodent with a big flat tail. **beaver away** v work industriously.

becalmed adj (of a sailing ship) motionless through lack of wind.

became v past tense of BECOME.

because conj on account of the fact that. **because of** on account of.

beck¹ n at someone's beck and call having to be constantly available to do as someone asks.

beck² n N English stream.

beckon v summon with a gesture.

become v **-coming, -came, -come.** come to be; (foll. by of) happen to; suit. **becoming** adj attractive or pleasing; appropriate or proper.

bed n piece of furniture on which to sleep; garden plot; bottom of a river, lake, or sea; layer of rock. **go to bed with** have sexual intercourse with. **bed down** v go to or put into a place to sleep or rest. **bedpan** n shallow bowl used as a toilet by bedridden people. **bedridden** adj confined to bed because of illness or old age. **bedrock** n solid rock beneath the surface soil; basic facts or principles. **bedroom** n **bedsit, bedsitter** n furnished sitting room with a bed.

bedding n sheets and covers that are used on a bed.

bedevil v **-illing, -illed.** harass, confuse, or torment.

bedlam n noisy confused situation.

bedraggled adj untidy, wet, or dirty.

bee n insect that makes wax and honey. **beehive** n structure in which bees live. **beeswax** n wax secreted by bees, used in polishes etc.

beech n tree with a smooth greyish bark.

beef n flesh of a cow, bull, or ox. **beefy** adj like beef; Informal strong and muscular. **beefburger** n flat grilled or fried cake of minced beef. **beefeater** n yeoman warder at the Tower of London.

been v past participle of BE.

beep n high-pitched sound, like that of a car horn. ▶ v (cause to) make this noise.

beer n alcoholic drink brewed from malt and hops. **beery** adj

beet n plant with an edible root and leaves. **beetroot** n type of beet plant with a dark red root.

beetle n insect with a hard wing cover on its back.

befall v Old-fashioned happen to (someone).

befit v be appropriate or suitable for. **befitting** adj

before conj, prep, adv indicating something earlier in time, in front of, or preferred to, e.g. before the war; brought before a judge; death before dishonour. **beforehand** adv in advance.

befriend v become friends with.

beg v **begging, begged.** solicit (for money or food), esp. in the street; ask formally or humbly.

began v past tense of BEGIN.

beget v **-getting, -got** or **-gat, -gotten** or **-got.** Old-fashioned cause or create; father.

beggar n person who lives by begging. **beggarly** adj

begin v **-ginning, -gan, -gun.** start; bring or come into being. **beginner** n person who has just started learning to do something. **beginning** n

begonia n tropical plant with waxy flowers.

begrudge v envy (someone) the possession of something; give or allow unwillingly.

beguile [big-**gile**] v cheat or mislead; charm or amuse. **beguiling** adj

begun v past participle of BEGIN.

behalf n **on behalf of** in the interest of or for the benefit of.

behave v act or function in a particular way; conduct (oneself) properly.

behaviour n manner of behaving.

behead v remove the head from.

beheld v past of BEHOLD.

behest n order or earnest request.

behind prep, adv indicating position to the rear, lateness, responsibility, etc., e.g. behind the wall; behind schedule; the reasons behind her departure. ▸ n Informal buttocks.

behold v **-holding, -held.** Old-fashioned look (at). **beholder** n

beholden adj indebted or obliged.

behove v Old-fashioned be necessary or fitting for.

beige adj pale brown.

being n state or fact of existing; something that exists or is thought to exist; human being. ▸ v present participle of BE.

belabour v attack verbally or physically.

belated adj late or too late. **belatedly** adv

belch v expel wind from the stomach noisily through the mouth; expel or be expelled forcefully, e.g. smoke belched from the factory. ▸ n act of belching.

beleaguered adj struggling against difficulties or criticism; besieged by an enemy.

belfry n, pl **-fries.** part of a tower where bells are hung.

belgium sausage n NZ large smooth bland sausage.

belie v show to be untrue.

belief n faith or confidence; opinion; principle accepted as true, often without proof.

believe v accept as true or real; think, assume, or suppose. **believable** adj **believer** n **believe in** be convinced of the truth or existence of.

Belisha beacon [bill-**lee**-sha] n Brit flashing orange globe mounted on a post, marking a pedestrian crossing.

belittle v treat as having little value or importance.

bell n hollow, usu. metal,

cup-shaped instrument that emits a ringing sound when struck; device that rings or buzzes as a signal.

belladonna n (drug obtained from) deadly nightshade.

belle n beautiful woman, esp. the most attractive woman at a function.

bellicose adj warlike and aggressive.

belligerent adj hostile and aggressive; engaged in war. ▶ n person or country engaged in war. **belligerence** n

bellow v make a low deep cry like that of a bull; shout in anger. ▶ n loud deep roar.

bellows pl n instrument for pumping a stream of air into something.

belly n, pl **-lies.** part of the body of a vertebrate which contains the intestines; stomach; front, lower, or inner part of something. ▶ v **-lying, -lied.** (cause to) swell out. **bellyful** n Slang more than one can tolerate.

belong v (foll. by to) be the property of; (foll. by to) be a part or member of. **belongings** pl n personal possessions.

beloved adj dearly loved. ▶ n person dearly loved.

below prep, adv at or to a position lower than, under.

belt n band of cloth, leather, etc., worn usu. around the waist; long narrow area, e.g. a belt of trees; circular strip of rubber that drives moving parts in a machine. ▶ v fasten with a belt; Slang hit very hard; Slang move very fast.

bemoan v express sorrow or dissatisfaction about.

bemused adj puzzled or confused.

bench n long seat; long narrow work table. **the bench** judge or

magistrate sitting in court, or judges and magistrates collectively. **benchmark** n criterion by which to measure something.

bend v bending, bent. (cause to) form a curve; (often foll. by down etc.) incline the body. ▶ n curved part. ▶ pl Informal decompression sickness. **bendy** adj

beneath adv, prep below; not worthy of.

Benedictine adj of an order of Christian monks and nuns founded by Saint Benedict.

benediction n prayer for divine blessing.

benefactor, benefactress n someone who supports a person or institution by giving money. **benefaction** n

beneficent [bin-**eff**-iss-ent] adj charitable or generous. **beneficence** n

beneficial adj helpful or advantageous.

beneficiary n, pl **-ciaries.** person who gains or benefits.

benefit n something that improves or promotes; advantage or sake, e.g. I'm doing this for your benefit; payment made by a government to a poor, ill, or unemployed person. ▶ v **-fiting, -fited.** do or receive good.

benevolence n inclination to do good; act of kindness. **benevolent** adj **benevolently** adv

benighted adj ignorant or uncultured.

benign [bin-**nine**] adj showing kindliness; (of a tumour) not threatening to life. **benignly** adv

bent v past of BEND. ▶ adj curved; Slang dishonest or corrupt. ▶ n personal inclination or aptitude. **bent on** determined to pursue (a course of action).

bento, bento box n thin lightweight box divided into compartments, which contain small separate dishes comprising a Japanese meal.

benzene n flammable poisonous liquid used as a solvent, insecticide, etc.

bequeath v dispose of (property) as in a will. **bequest** n legal gift of money or property by someone who has died.

berate v scold harshly.

bereaved adj having recently lost a close friend or relative through death. **bereavement** n

bereft adj (foll. by of) deprived.

beret [ber-ray] n round flat close-fitting brimless cap.

berg[1] n iceberg.

berg[2] n S Afr mountain.

bergamot n small Asian tree, the fruit of which yields an oil used in perfumery.

beri-beri n disease caused by vitamin B deficiency.

berk n Brit, Aust & NZ slang stupid person.

berm n NZ narrow grass strip between the road and the footpath in a residential area.

berry n, pl **-ries.** small soft stoneless fruit.

berserk adj **go berserk** become violent or destructive.

berth n bunk in a ship or train; place assigned to a ship at a mooring. ▸ v dock (a ship).

beryl n hard transparent mineral.

beryllium n Chem toxic silvery-white metallic element.

beseech v **-seeching, -sought** or **-seeched.** ask earnestly.

beset v trouble or harass constantly.

beside prep at, by, or to the side of; as compared with. **beside oneself** overwhelmed or

overwrought. **besides** adv, prep in addition.

besiege v surround with military forces; overwhelm, as with requests.

besotted adj infatuated.

besought v a past of BESEECH.

bespeak v indicate or suggest. **bespoke** adj (esp. of a suit) made to the customer's specifications.

best adj most excellent of a particular group etc. ▸ adv in a manner surpassing all others. ▸ n most outstanding or excellent person, thing, or group in a category. **best man** groom's attendant at a wedding.

bestseller n book or other product that has sold in great numbers.

bestial adj brutal or savage; of or like a beast. **bestiality** n

bestir v cause (oneself) to become active.

bestow v present (a gift) or confer (an honour). **bestowal** n

bestride v have or put a leg on either side of.

bet n the act of staking a sum of money or other stake on the outcome of an event; stake risked. ▸ v **betting, bet** or **betted.** make or place (a bet); Informal predict.

betel [bee-tl] n Asian climbing plant, the leaves and nuts of which can be chewed.

bête noire [bet nwahr] n, pl **bêtes noires.** person or thing that one particularly dislikes.

betide v happen (to).

betoken v indicate or signify.

betray v hand over or expose (one's nation, friend, etc.) treacherously to an enemy; disclose (a secret or confidence) treacherously; reveal unintentionally. **betrayal** n **betrayer** n

betrothed adj engaged to be married. **betrothal** n

better adj more excellent than others; improved or fully recovered in health. ▶ adv in a more excellent manner; in or to a greater degree. ▶ pl n one's superiors. ▶ v improve upon.

between prep, adv indicating position in the middle, alternatives, etc.

betwixt prep, adv Old-fashioned between.

bevel n slanting edge. ▶ v -elling, -elled. cut a bevel on (a piece of timber etc.).

beverage n drink.

bevy n, pl **bevies**. flock or group.

bewail v express sorrow over.

beware v be on one's guard (against).

bewilder v confuse utterly. **bewildering** adj **bewilderment** n

bewitch v attract and fascinate; cast a spell over. **bewitching** adj

beyond prep at or to a point on the other side of; outside the limits or scope of. ▶ adv at or to the far side of something.

bi- combining form two or twice, e.g. bifocal; biweekly.

biannual adj occurring twice a year. **biannually** adv

bias n mental tendency, esp. prejudice; diagonal cut across the weave of a fabric; Bowls bulge or weight on one side of a bowl that causes it to roll in a curve. ▶ v -asing, -ased or -assing, -assed. cause to have a bias. **biased**, **biassed** adj

bib n piece of cloth or plastic worn to protect a young child's clothes when eating; upper front part of dungarees etc.

Bible n sacred writings of the Christian religion; (**b-**) book regarded as authoritative. **biblical** adj

bibliography n, pl **-phies**. list of books on a subject; list of sources used in a book etc. **bibliographer** n

bibliophile n person who collects or is fond of books.

bibulous adj addicted to alcohol.

bicarbonate n salt of carbonic acid. **bicarbonate of soda** powder used in baking or as medicine.

bicentenary n, pl **-naries**. 200th anniversary.

biceps n muscle with two origins, esp. the muscle that flexes the forearm.

bicker v argue over petty matters.

bicycle n vehicle with two wheels, one behind the other, pedalled by the rider.

bid v **bidding**, **bade**, **bidden**. say (a greeting); command; (past **bid**) offer (an amount) in an attempt to buy something. ▶ n offer of a specified amount; attempt. **bidder** n **biddable** adj obedient. **bidding** n command.

biddy-bid, **biddy-biddy** n, pl **-bids** **-biddies**. NZ low-growing plant with hooked burrs.

bide v bide one's time wait patiently for an opportunity.

bidet [bee-day] n low basin for washing the genital area.

biennial adj occurring every two years. ▶ n plant that completes its life cycle in two years.

bier n stand on which a corpse or coffin rests before burial.

bifocals pl n spectacles with lenses permitting near and distant vision.

big adj **bigger**, **biggest**. of considerable size, height, number, or capacity; important through having power, wealth, etc.; elder; generous. ▶ adv on a grand scale.

bighead n Informal conceited

person. **big-headed** adj **big shot, bigwig** n Informal important person.

bigamy n crime of marrying a person while still legally married to someone else. **bigamist** n **bigamous** adj

bigot n person who is intolerant, esp. regarding religion or race. **bigoted** adj **bigotry** n

bijou [bee-zhoo] adj (of a house) small but elegant.

bike n Informal bicycle or motorcycle.

bikini n woman's brief two-piece swimming costume.

bilateral adj affecting or undertaken by two parties.

bilberry n bluish-black edible berry.

bilby n, pl -bies. Australian marsupial with long pointed ears and grey fur.

bile n bitter yellow fluid secreted by the liver.

bilge n Informal nonsense; ship's bottom.

bilingual adj involving or using two languages.

bilious adj sick, nauseous.

bill[1] n statement of money owed for goods or services supplied; draft of a proposed new law; poster; Chiefly US & Canadian piece of paper money; list of events, such as a theatre programme. ▶ v send or present a bill to; advertise by posters.

bill[2] n bird's beak.

billabong n Aust stagnant pool in an intermittent stream.

billet v -leting, -leted. assign a lodging to (a soldier). ▶ n accommodation for a soldier in civil lodgings.

billet-doux [bill-ee-doo] n, pl billets-doux. love letter.

billhook n tool with a hooked blade, used for chopping etc.

billiards n game played on a table with balls and a cue.

billion n one thousand million; formerly, one million million. **billionth** adj

billow n large sea wave. ▶ v rise up or swell out. **billowy, billowing** adj

billy, billycan n, pl -lies, -lycans. metal can or pot for cooking on a camp fire.

biltong n S Afr strips of dried meat.

bimbo n Slang attractive but empty-headed young person, esp. a woman.

bin n container for rubbish or for storing grain, coal, etc.

binary adj composed of two parts; Maths, computers of or in a counting system with only two digits, 0 and 1.

bind v binding, bound. make secure with or as if with a rope; place (someone) under obligation; enclose and fasten (the pages of a book) between covers. ▶ n Informal annoying situation. **binder** n firm cover for holding loose sheets of paper together. **binding** n anything that binds or fastens; book cover.

bindweed n plant that twines around a support.

binge n Informal bout of excessive indulgence, esp. in drink.

bingo n gambling game in which numbers are called out and covered by the players on their individual cards.

binoculars pl n optical instrument consisting of two small telescopes joined together.

binomial n, adj (mathematical expression) consisting of two terms.

bio- combining form life or living organisms, e.g. biology.

biochemistry n study of the

chemistry of living things.
biochemist n

biodegradable adj capable of being decomposed by natural means.

biodiversity n existence of a wide variety of species in their natural environment.

biographer n person who writes an account of another person's life.

biography n, pl -**phies**. account of a person's life by another person. **biographical** adj

biological adj of or relating to biology.

biology n study of living organisms. **biologist** n

bionic adj having a part of the body that is operated electronically.

biopsy n, pl -**sies**. examination of tissue from a living body.

biotechnology n use of microorganisms, such as cells or bacteria, in industry and technology.

bioterrorism n use of viruses, bacteria, etc., by terrorists. **bioterrorist** n

biped [bye-ped] n animal with two feet.

biplane n aeroplane with two sets of wings, one above the other.

birch n tree with thin peeling bark; birch rod or twigs used, esp. formerly, for flogging offenders.

bird n creature with feathers and wings, most types of which can fly; Slang young woman.

birdie n Golf score of one stroke under par for a hole.

biretta n stiff square cap worn by the Catholic clergy.

Biro n ® ballpoint pen.

birth n process of bearing young; childbirth; act of being born; ancestry. **give birth to** bear (offspring). **birth control** any method of contraception.

birthday n anniversary of the day of one's birth. **birthmark** n blemish on the skin formed before birth. **birthright** n privileges or possessions that someone is entitled to as soon as he or she is born.

biscuit n small flat dry sweet or plain cake.

bisect v divide into two equal parts.

bisexual adj sexually attracted to both men and women. **bisexuality** n

bishop n clergyman who governs a diocese; chessman which is moved diagonally. **bishopric** n diocese or office of a bishop.

bismuth n Chem pinkish-white metallic element.

bison n, pl -**son**. large hairy animal of the cattle family, native to N America and Europe.

bistro n, pl -**tros**. small restaurant.

bit[1] n small piece, portion, or quantity. **a bit** rather, somewhat. **bit by bit** gradually.

bit[2] n metal mouthpiece on a bridle; cutting or drilling part of a tool.

bit[3] v past tense of BITE.

bit[4] n Maths, computers single digit of binary notation, either 0 or 1.

bitch n female dog, fox, or wolf. **bite** v **biting**, **bit**, **bitten**. grip, tear, or puncture the skin, as with the teeth or jaws; take firm hold of or act effectively upon. ▶ n act of biting; wound or sting inflicted by biting; snack. **biter** n **biting** adj piercing or keen; sarcastic.

bitter adj having a sharp unpleasant taste; showing or caused by hostility or resentment; extremely cold. ▶ n beer with a slightly bitter taste. ▶ pl bitter-tasting alcoholic drink. **bitterly** adv **bitterness** n

bittern n wading marsh bird with a booming call.

bitumen n black sticky substance obtained from tar or petrol.

bivalve n, adj (marine mollusc) with two hinged segments to its shell.

bivouac n temporary camp in the open air. ▶ v **-acking, -acked.** camp in a bivouac.

bizarre adj odd or unusual.

blab v **blabbing, blabbed.** reveal (secrets) indiscreetly.

black adj of the darkest colour, like coal; (**B-**) dark-skinned; without hope; angry or resentful, e.g. **black looks**; unpleasant in a macabre manner, e.g. **black comedy.** ▶ n darkest colour; (**B-**) member of a dark-skinned people; complete darkness. ▶ v make black; (of trade unionists) boycott (goods or people). **blackness** n **blacken** v make or become black; defame or slander. **black magic** magic used for evil purposes. **black market** illegal trade in goods or currencies. **black sheep** person who is regarded as a disgrace by his or her family. **black spot** place on a road where accidents frequently occur.

blackball v exclude from a group. ▶ n NZ hard boiled sweet with black-and-white stripes.

blackberry n small blackish edible fruit.

blackbird n common European thrush.

blackboard n hard black surface used for writing on with chalk.

blackcurrant n very small blackish edible fruit that grows in bunches.

blackguard [blag-gard] n unprincipled person.

blackhead n black-tipped plug of fatty matter clogging a skin pore.

blackleg n person who continues to work during a strike.

blacklist n list of people or organizations considered untrustworthy etc.

blackmail n act of attempting to extort money by threats. ▶ v (attempt to) obtain money by blackmail.

blackout n extinguishing of all light as a precaution against an air attack; momentary loss of consciousness or memory. **black out** v extinguish (lights); lose consciousness or memory temporarily.

blacksmith n person who works iron with a furnace, anvil, etc.

bladder n sac in the body where urine is held; hollow bag which may be filled with air or liquid.

blade n cutting edge of a weapon or tool; thin flattish part of a propeller, oar, etc.; leaf of grass.

blame v consider (someone) responsible for. ▶ n responsibility for something that is wrong. **blameless** adj **blameworthy** adj deserving blame.

blanch v become white or pale; prepare (vegetables etc.) by plunging them in boiling water.

blancmange [blam-monzh] n jelly-like dessert made with milk.

bland adj dull and uninteresting. **blandly** adv

blandishments pl n flattery intended to coax or persuade.

blank adj not written on; showing no interest or expression. ▶ n empty space; cartridge containing no bullet. **blankly** adv **blank verse** unrhymed verse.

blanket n large thick cloth used as covering for a bed; concealing cover, as of snow. ▶ v cover as with a blanket.

blare v sound loudly and harshly. ▶ n loud harsh noise.

blarney n flattering talk.

blasé [**blah-zay**] adj indifferent or bored through familiarity.

blaspheme v speak disrespectfully of (God or sacred things). **blasphemy** n **blasphemous** adj **blasphemer** n

blast n explosion; sudden strong gust of air or wind; sudden loud sound, as of a trumpet. ▶ v blow up (a rock etc.) with explosives. **blatant** adj glaringly obvious. **blatantly** adv

blaze[1] n strong fire or flame; very bright light. ▶ v burn or shine brightly.

blaze[2] n mark made on a tree to indicate a route.

blazer n lightweight jacket, often in the colours of a school etc.

blazon v proclaim publicly.

bleach v make or become white or colourless. ▶ n bleaching agent.

bleak adj exposed and barren; offering little hope.

bleary adj **-rier, -riest.** with eyes dimmed, as by tears or tiredness. **blearily** adv

bleat v (of a sheep, goat, or calf) utter its plaintive cry. ▶ n cry of sheep, goats, and calves.

bleed v **bleeding, bled.** lose or emit blood; draw blood from (a person or animal); Informal obtain money by extortion.

bleep n short high-pitched signal made by an electrical device. ▶ v make a bleeping sound. **bleeper** n small portable radio receiver that makes a bleeping signal.

blemish n defect or stain. ▶ v spoil or tarnish.

blench v shy away, as in fear.

blend v mix or mingle (components or ingredients); look good together. ▶ n mixture.

blender n electrical appliance for puréeing vegetables etc.

bless v make holy by means of a religious rite; call upon God to protect; endow with health, talent, etc. **blessed** adj holy.

blessing n invoking of divine aid; approval; happy event.

blether Scot ▶ v talk, esp. foolishly or at length. ▶ n conversation.

blew v past tense of BLOW[1].

blight n person or thing that spoils or prevents growth; withering plant disease. ▶ v frustrate or disappoint.

blighter n Informal irritating person.

blimp n small airship.

blind adj unable to see; unable or unwilling to understand; not determined by reason, e.g. blind hatred. ▶ v deprive of sight; deprive of good sense, reason, or judgment. ▶ n covering for a window; something that serves to conceal the truth. **blindly** adv **blindness** n

blindfold v prevent (a person) from seeing by covering the eyes. ▶ n piece of cloth used to cover the eyes.

blink v close and immediately reopen (the eyes); shine intermittently. ▶ n act of blinking. **on the blink** Slang not working properly.

blinkers pl n leather flaps on a horse's bridle to prevent sideways vision.

blip n spot of light on a radar screen indicating the position of an object.

bliss n perfect happiness. **blissful** adj **blissfully** adv

blister n small bubble on the skin; swelling, as on a painted surface. ▶ v (cause to) have blisters. **blistering** adj (of weather) very hot; (of criticism) extremely harsh.

blithe adj casual and indifferent.

blithely adv

blitz n violent and sustained attack by aircraft; intensive attack or concerted effort. ▸ v attack suddenly and intensively.

blizzard n blinding storm of wind and snow.

bloat v cause to swell, as with liquid or air.

bloater n Brit salted smoked herring.

blob n soft mass or drop; indistinct or shapeless form.

bloc n people or countries combined by a common interest.

block n large solid piece of wood, stone, etc.; large building of offices, flats, etc.; group of buildings enclosed by intersecting streets; obstruction or hindrance; Slang person's head. ▸ v obstruct or impede by introducing an obstacle. **blockage** n **blockhead** n stupid person. **block letter** plain capital letter.

blockade n sealing off of a place to prevent the passage of goods. ▸ v impose a blockade on.

bloke n Informal man.

blonde, (masc) **blond** adj, n fair-haired (person).

blood n red fluid that flows around the body; race or kinship. **in cold blood** done deliberately. **bloodless** adj **blood bath** massacre. **bloodhound** n large dog formerly used for tracking. **bloodshed** n slaughter or killing. **bloodshot** adj (of an eye) inflamed. **blood sport** sport involving the killing of animals. **bloodstream** n flow of blood round the body. **bloodsucker** n animal that sucks blood; Informal person who extorts money from other people. **bloodthirsty** adj taking pleasure in violence.

bloody adj covered with blood; marked by much killing. ▸ v stain with blood.

bloom n blossom on a flowering plant; youthful or healthy glow. ▸ v bear flowers; be in a healthy, glowing condition.

bloomer n Brit informal stupid mistake.

bloomers pl n woman's baggy knickers.

blooper n Chiefly US informal stupid mistake.

blossom n flowers of a plant. ▸ v (of plants) flower; come to a promising stage.

blot n spot or stain; something that spoils. ▸ v **blotting, blotted.** cause a blemish in or on; soak up (ink) by using blotting paper. **blotter** n **blot out** v darken or hide completely. **blotting paper** soft absorbent paper for soaking up ink.

blotch n discoloured area or stain. **blotchy** adj

blotto adj Brit, Aust & NZ slang extremely drunk.

blouse n woman's shirtlike garment.

blow¹ v **blowing, blew, blown.** (of air, the wind, etc.) move; move or be carried as if by the wind; expel (air etc.) through the mouth or nose; cause (a musical instrument) to sound by forcing air into it; burn out (a fuse etc.); Slang spend (money) freely. **blower** n **blowy** adj windy. **blow-dry** v style (the hair) with a hand-held dryer. **blowout** n sudden loss of air in a tyre; escape of oil or gas from a well; Slang filling meal. **blow up** v explode; fill with air; Informal lose one's temper; Informal enlarge (a photograph).

blow² n hard hit; sudden setback; attacking action.

blown v past participle of BLOW¹.

blowsy *adj* fat, untidy, and red-faced.

blubber *n* fat of whales, seals, etc. ▶ *v* sob without restraint.

bludge *Informal* ▶ *v Aust & NZ* evade work; *Aust & NZ* scrounge. ▶ *n Aust* easy task. **bludger** *n* person who scrounges.

bludgeon *n* short thick club. ▶ *v* hit with a bludgeon; force or bully.

blue *n* colour of a clear unclouded sky. ▶ *pl* feeling of depression; type of folk music of Black American origin. ▶ *adj* **bluer, bluest.** of the colour blue; depressed; pornographic. **out of the blue** unexpectedly. **bluish** *adj* **bluebell** *n* flower with blue bell-shaped flowers. **bluebottle** *n* large fly with a dark-blue body. **blue-collar** *adj* denoting manual industrial workers. **blueprint** *n* photographic print of a plan; description of how a plan is expected to work.

bluff[1] *v* pretend to be confident in order to influence (someone). ▶ *n* act of bluffing.

bluff[2] *n* steep cliff or bank. ▶ *adj* good-naturedly frank and hearty.

blunder *n* clumsy mistake. ▶ *v* make a blunder; act clumsily.

blunderbuss *n* obsolete gun with a wide flared muzzle.

blunt *adj* not having a sharp edge or point; (of people, speech, etc.) straightforward or uncomplicated. ▶ *v* make less sharp. **bluntly** *adv*

blur *v* **blurring, blurred.** make or become vague or less distinct. ▶ *n* something vague, hazy, or indistinct. **blurry** *adj*

blurb *n* promotional description, as on the jacket of a book.

blurt *v* (foll. by *out*) utter suddenly and involuntarily.

blush *v* become red in the face, esp. from embarrassment or shame. ▶ *n* reddening of the face.

bluster *v* speak loudly or in a bullying way. ▶ *n* empty threats or protests. **blustery** *adj* (of weather) rough and windy.

BMA British Medical Association.

BO *Informal* body odour.

boa *n* large nonvenomous snake; long scarf of fur or feathers. **boa constrictor** large snake that kills its prey by crushing.

boar *n* uncastrated male pig; wild pig.

board *n* long flat piece of sawn timber; smaller flat piece of rigid material for a specific purpose, e.g. *ironing board; chess board;* group of people who administer a company, trust, etc.; meals provided for money. ▶ *v* go aboard (a train, aeroplane, etc.); cover with boards; receive meals and lodgings in return for money. **on board** on or in a ship, aeroplane, etc. **boarder** *n* person who pays rent in return for accommodation in someone else's home; *Brit* pupil who lives at school during the school term. **boarding house** private house that provides meals and accommodation for paying guests. **boardroom** *n* room where the board of a company meets.

boast *v* speak too proudly about one's talents etc.; possess (something to be proud of). ▶ *n* bragging statement. **boastful** *adj*

boat *n* small vehicle for travelling across water. **boater** *n* flat straw hat. **boating** *n*

boatswain *n* same as BOSUN.

bob[1] *v* **bobbing, bobbed.** move up and down repeatedly. ▶ *n* short abrupt movement.

bob[2] *n* hairstyle in which the hair is cut short evenly all round the head. ▶ *v* **bobbing, bobbed.** cut (the hair) in a bob.

bobbin n reel on which thread is wound.

bobble n small ball of material, usu. for decoration.

bobby n, pl -bies. Brit informal policeman.

bobotie [ba-boot-ee] n S Afr dish of curried mince.

bobsleigh n sledge for racing down an icy track. ▶ v ride on a bobsleigh.

bode v be an omen of (good or ill).

bodice n upper part of a dress.

bodkin n blunt large-eyed needle.

body n, pl bodies. entire physical structure of an animal or human; trunk or torso; corpse; group regarded as a single entity; main part of anything; woman's one-piece undergarment. **bodily** adj relating to the body. ▶ adv by taking hold of the body.

body-board n small polystyrene surfboard. **body-boarder** n

bodyguard n person or group of people employed to protect someone. **bodywork** n outer shell of a motor vehicle.

Boer n descendant of the Dutch settlers in S Africa. **boerewors** n S Afr spiced sausage.

boffin n Brit, Austral, NZ & S Afr informal scientist or expert.

bog n wet spongy ground; Slang toilet. **boggy** adj **bog down** v **bogging, bogged.** impede physically or mentally.

bogan n Aust dated & NZ slang youth who dresses and behaves rebelliously.

bogey, bogy n something that worries or annoys; Golf score of one stroke over par on a hole.

boggle v be surprised, confused, or alarmed.

bogong, bugong n large nocturnal Australian moth.

bogus adj not genuine.

bogy n, pl -gies. same as BOGEY.

bohemian n, adj (person) leading an unconventional life.

boil¹ v (cause to) change from a liquid to a vapour so quickly that bubbles are formed; cook by the process of boiling. ▶ n state or action of boiling. **boiler** n piece of equipment which provides hot water.

boil² n red pus-filled swelling on the skin.

boisterous adj noisy and lively. **boisterously** adv

bold adj confident and fearless; immodest or impudent. **boldly** adv **boldness** n

bole n tree trunk.

bolero n, pl -ros. (music for) traditional Spanish dance; short open jacket.

bollard n short thick post used to prevent the passage of motor vehicles.

boloney n same as BALONEY.

Bolshevik n (formerly) Russian Communist. **bolshie, bolshy** adj Informal difficult or rebellious.

bolster v support or strengthen. ▶ n long narrow pillow.

bolt¹ n sliding metal bar for fastening a door etc.; metal pin which screws into a nut; flash (of lightning). ▶ v run away suddenly; fasten with a bolt; eat hurriedly. **bolt upright** stiff and rigid. **bolt hole** place of escape.

bomb n container fitted with explosive material; Slang large amount of money. ▶ v attack with bombs; move very quickly. **the bomb** nuclear bomb. **bomber** n aircraft that drops bombs; person who throws or puts a bomb in a particular place. **bomb out** v Aust, NZ & S Afr informal fail disastrously. **bombshell** n shocking or unwelcome surprise.

bombard v attack with heavy gunfire or bombs; attack verbally, esp. with questions. **bombardment** n

bombast n pompous language. **bombastic** adj

bona fide [bone-a fide-ee] adj genuine.

bonanza n sudden good luck or wealth.

bond n something that binds, fastens or holds together; something that unites people; written or spoken agreement; Finance certificate of debt issued to raise funds; S Afr conditional pledging of property, esp. a house, as security for the repayment of a loan. ▶ pl something that restrains or imprisons. ▶ v bind. **bonded** adj

bondage n slavery.

bone n any of the hard parts in the body that form the skeleton. ▶ v remove the bones from (meat for cooking etc.). **boneless** adj **bony** adj having many bones; thin or emaciated. **bone-dry** adj completely dry. **bone-idle** adj extremely lazy.

bonfire n large outdoor fire.

bongo n, pl -gos, -goes. small drum played with the fingers.

bonhomie [bon-om-ee] n cheerful friendliness.

bonk v Informal have sex with; hit.

bonnet n metal cover over a vehicle's engine; hat which ties under the chin.

bonny adj -nier, -niest. Scot beautiful.

bonsai n, pl -sai. ornamental miniature tree or shrub.

bonus n something given, paid, or received above what is due or expected.

boo interj shout of disapproval. ▶ v

booing, booed. shout 'boo' to show disapproval.

boob Slang ▶ n foolish mistake.

booby n, pl -bies. foolish person. **booby prize** prize given for the lowest score in a competition. **booby trap** hidden bomb primed to be set off by an unsuspecting victim; trap for an unsuspecting person, intended as a joke.

boogie v Informal dance to fast pop music.

book n number of pages bound together between covers; long written work; number of tickets, stamps, etc. fastened together. ▶ v record of transactions of a business or society. ▶ v reserve (a place, passage, etc.) in advance; record the name of (a person) who has committed an offence. **booklet** n thin book with paper covers.

book-keeping n systematic recording of business transactions.

bookmaker n person whose occupation is taking bets.

bookmark n person whose occupation is taking bets; Computers marker on a website that enables the user to return to it quickly and easily. ▶ v Computers identify and store (a website) so that one can return to it quickly and easily.

bookworm n person devoted to reading.

boom¹ v make a loud deep echoing sound; prosper vigorously and rapidly. ▶ n loud deep echoing sound; period of high economic growth.

boom² n pole to which the foot of a sail is attached; pole carrying an overhead microphone; barrier across a waterway.

boomerang n curved wooden missile which can be made to

return to the thrower. ▶ v (of a plan) recoil unexpectedly.

boon n something helpful or beneficial.

boor n rude or insensitive person. **boorish** adj

boost n encouragement or help; increase. ▶ v improve; increase. **booster** n small additional injection of a vaccine.

boot[1] n outer covering for the foot that extends above the ankle; space in a car for luggage; *Informal* kick. ▶ v *Informal* kick; start up (a computer). **bootee** n baby's soft shoe. **boot camp** centre for young offenders, with strict discipline and hard physical exercise.

boot[2] n **to boot** in addition.

booth n small partly enclosed cubicle; stall at a fair or market.

bootleg adj produced, distributed, or sold illicitly. ▶ v **-legging, -legged.** make, carry, or sell (illicit goods). **bootlegger** n

booty n, pl **-ties.** valuable articles obtained as plunder.

booze v, n *Informal* (consume) alcoholic drink. **boozy** adj **boozer** n *Informal* person who is fond of drinking; *Brit, Aust & NZ* pub. **booze-up** n *Informal* drinking spree.

bop v **bopping, bopped.** *Informal* dance to pop music.

bora n *Aust* Aboriginal ceremony.

borax n white mineral used in making glass.

border n dividing line between political or geographical regions; band around or along the edge of something. ▶ v provide with a border; be nearly the same as, e.g. *resentment that borders on hatred*.

bore[1] v make (a hole) with a drill etc. ▶ n (diameter of) the hollow

of a gun barrel or other tube.

bore[2] v make weary by being dull or repetitious. ▶ n dull or repetitious person or thing. **bored** adj **boredom** n

bore[3] n high wave in a narrow estuary, caused by the tide.

bore[4] v past tense of BEAR[1].

born v a past participle of BEAR[1]. ▶ adj possessing certain qualities from birth, e.g. *a born musician*.

borne v a past participle of BEAR[1].

boron n *Chem* element used in hardening steel.

borough n *Chiefly Brit* town or district with its own council.

borrow v obtain (something) temporarily; adopt (ideas etc.) from another source. **borrower** n

borstal n (formerly in Britain) prison for young criminals.

borzoi n tall dog with a long silky coat.

bosh n *Brit, Aust & NZ informal* empty talk, nonsense.

bosom n chest of a person, esp. the female breasts. ▶ adj very dear, e.g. *a bosom friend*.

boss[1] n person in charge of or employing others. ▶ v **boss around, about** be domineering towards. **bossy** adj

boss[2] n raised knob or stud.

bosun n officer responsible for the maintenance of a ship.

botany n study of plants. **botanical, botanic** adj **botanist** n

botch v spoil through clumsiness. ▶ n (also **botch-up**) badly done piece of work or repair.

both adj, pron two considered together.

bother v take the time or trouble; give annoyance or trouble to; pester. ▶ n trouble, fuss, or difficulty. **bothersome** adj

bottle n container for holding liquids; *Brit informal* courage. ▶ v put in a bottle. **bottleneck** *n* narrow stretch of road where traffic is held up. **bottle shop** *Aust & NZ* shop licensed to sell alcohol for drinking elsewhere. **bottle store** *S Afr* shop licensed to sell alcohol for drinking elsewhere. **bottle up** *v* restrain (powerful emotion).

bottom *n* lowest, deepest, or farthest removed part of a thing; buttocks. ▶ *adj* lowest or last. **bottomless** *adj*

botulism *n* serious food poisoning.

boudoir [boo-dwahr] *n* woman's bedroom or private sitting room.

bougainvillea *n* climbing plant with red or purple flowers.

bough *n* large branch of a tree.

bought *v* past of BUY.

boulder *n* large rounded rock.

boulevard *n* wide, usu. tree-lined, street.

bounce *v* (of a ball etc.) rebound from an impact; *Slang* (of a cheque) be returned uncashed owing to a lack of funds in the account. ▶ *n* act of rebounding; springiness; *Informal* vitality or vigour. **bouncer** *n* person employed at a disco etc. to remove unwanted people.

bouncing *adj* vigorous and robust.

bound¹ *v* past of BIND. ▶ *adj* destined or certain; compelled or obliged.

bound² *v* move forwards by jumps. ▶ *n* jump upwards or forwards.

bound³ *v* form a boundary of. ▶ *n* limit. **boundary** *n* dividing line that indicates the farthest limit.

bound⁴ *adj* going or intending to go towards, e.g. *homeward bound*.

bounty *n*, *pl* **-ties**. generosity; generous gift or reward. **bountiful, bounteous** *adj*

bouquet *n* bunch of flowers; aroma of wine.

bourbon [bur-bn] *n* whiskey made from maize.

bourgeois [boor-zhwah] *adj, n Offens* middle-class (person).

bout *n* period of activity or illness; boxing or wrestling match.

boutique *n* small clothes shop.

bovine *adj* relating to cattle; rather slow and stupid.

bow¹ [rhymes with **now**] *v* lower (one's head) or bend (one's knee or body) as a sign of respect or shame; comply or accept. ▶ *n* movement made when bowing.

bow² [rhymes with **go**] *n* knot with two loops and loose ends; weapon for shooting arrows; long stick stretched with horsehair for playing stringed instruments. **bow-legged** *adj* having legs that curve outwards at the knees.

bow³ [rhymes with **now**] *n* front end of a ship.

bowdlerize *v* remove words regarded as indecent from (a play, novel, etc.).

bowel *n* intestine, esp. the large intestine. ▶ *pl* innermost part.

bower *n* shady leafy shelter.

bowl¹ *n* round container with an open top; hollow part of an object.

bowl² *n* large heavy ball. ▶ *pl* game played on smooth grass with wooden bowls. ▶ *v Cricket* send (a ball) towards the batsman. **bowling** *n* game in which bowls are rolled at a group of pins.

bowler¹ *n Cricket* player who sends (a ball) towards the batsman; person who plays bowls or bowling.

bowler² *n* stiff felt hat with a rounded crown.

box¹ *n* container with a firm flat base and sides; separate compartment in a theatre, stable, etc. ▶ *v* put into a box. **the box** *Informal* television. **box office**

box 61 **brandy**

place where theatre or cinema tickets are sold.

box² v fight (an opponent) in a boxing match. **boxer** n person who participates in the sport of boxing; medium-sized dog with smooth hair and a short nose. **boxer shorts, boxers** pl n men's underpants shaped like shorts but with a front opening. **boxing** n sport of fighting with the fists.

box¹ n evergreen tree with shiny leaves.

boy n male child. **boyish** adj **boyhood** n **boyfriend** n male friend with whom a person is romantically or sexually involved.

boycott v refuse to deal with (an organization or country). ▶ n instance of boycotting.

bra n woman's undergarment for supporting the breasts.

braaivleis [brye-flayss], braai S Afr ▶ n grill on which food is cooked over hot charcoal, usu. outdoors; outdoor party at which food like this is served. ▶ v cook (food) on in this way.

brace n object fastened to something to straighten or support it; pair, esp. of game birds. ▶ pl straps worn over the shoulders to hold up trousers. ▶ v steady or prepare (oneself) for something unpleasant; strengthen or fit with a brace. **bracing** adj refreshing and invigorating.

bracelet n ornamental chain or band for the wrist.

bracken n large fern.

bracket n pair of characters used to enclose a section of writing; group falling within certain defined limits; support fixed to a wall. ▶ v **-eting, -eted.** put in brackets; class together.

brackish adj (of water) slightly salty.

bract n leaf at the base of a flower.

brag v **bragging, bragged.** speak arrogantly and boastfully. **braggart** n

braid v interweave (hair, thread, etc.). ▶ n length of hair etc. that has been braided; narrow ornamental tape of woven fabric etc.

Braille n system of writing for the blind, consisting of raised dots interpreted by touch.

brain n soft mass of nervous tissue in the head; intellectual ability. ▶ v hit (someone) hard on the head. **brainless** adj stupid. **brainy** adj Informal clever. **brainchild** n idea produced by creative thought. **brain up** v Brit make (something) more intellectually advanced or sophisticated. **brainwash** v cause (a person) to alter his or her beliefs, esp. by methods based on isolation, sleeplessness, etc. **brainwave** n sudden idea.

braise v cook slowly in a covered pan with a little liquid.

brake n device for slowing or stopping a vehicle. ▶ v slow down or stop by using a brake.

bramble n prickly shrub that produces blackberries.

bran n husks of cereal grain.

branch n secondary stem of a tree; offshoot or subsidiary part of something larger or more complex. ▶ v (of stems, roots, etc.) divide, then develop in different directions. **branch out** v expand one's interests.

brand n particular product; particular kind or variety; identifying mark burnt onto the skin of an animal. ▶ v mark with a brand; denounce as being. **brand-new** adj absolutely new.

brandish v wave (a weapon etc.) in a threatening way.

brandy n, pl **-dies.** alcoholic spirit

distilled from wine.

brash adj offensively loud, showy, or self-confident. **brashness** n

brass n alloy of copper and zinc; family of wind instruments made of brass; N English dialect money. **brassy** adj brazen or flashy; like brass, esp. in colour.

brassiere n bra.

brat n unruly child.

bravado n showy display of self-confidence.

brave adj having or showing courage, resolution, and daring. ▶ n Native American warrior. ▶ v confront with resolution or courage. **bravery** n

bravo interj well done!

brawl n noisy fight. ▶ v fight noisily.

brawn n physical strength; pressed meat from the head of a pig or calf. **brawny** adj

bray v (of a donkey) utter its loud harsh sound. ▶ n donkey's loud harsh sound.

brazen adj shameless and bold. ▶ v **brazenly** adv

brazier [bray-zee-er] n portable container for burning charcoal or coal.

breach n breaking of a promise, obligation, etc.; gap or break. ▶ v break (a promise, law, etc.); make a gap in.

bread n food made by baking a mixture of flour and water or milk; Slang money. **breadwinner** n person whose earnings support a family.

breadth n extent of something from side to side.

break v breaking, broke, broken. separate or become separated into two or more pieces; damage or become damaged so as to be inoperative; fail to observe (an agreement etc.); disclose or be disclosed, e.g. he broke the news; bring or come to an end, e.g. the good weather broke at last; weaken or be weakened, as in spirit; improve on or surpass, e.g. break a record; (of the male voice) become permanently deeper at puberty. ▶ n act or result of breaking; gap or interruption in continuity; Informal fortunate opportunity. **break even** make neither a profit nor a loss. **breakable** adj **breakage** n **breaker** n large wave. **break down** v cease to function; yield to strong emotion. **breakdown** n act or instance of breaking down; nervous breakdown. **break-in** n illegal entering of a building, esp. by thieves. **breakneck** adj fast and dangerous. **break off** v sever or detach; end (a relationship etc.). **break out** v begin or arise suddenly. **breakthrough** n important development or discovery. **break up** v (cause to) separate; come to an end; (of a school) close for the holidays.

breakwater n wall that extends into the sea to protect a harbour or beach from the force of waves.

breakfast v, n (eat) the first meal of the day.

bream n freshwater fish with silvery scales; food fish of European seas.

breast n either of the two soft fleshy milk-secreting glands on a woman's chest; chest. **breastbone** n long flat bone in the front of the body, to which most of the ribs are attached. **breaststroke** n swimming stroke in which the arms are extended in front of the head and swept back on either side.

breath n taking in and letting out of air during breathing; air taken in and let out during breathing.

breathless adj **breathtaking** adj causing awe or excitement.

breathe v take in oxygen and give out carbon dioxide; whisper.

breather n Informal short rest.

breathing n

Breathalyser n ® device for estimating the amount of alcohol in the breath. **breathalyse** v

bred v past of BREED.

breech n buttocks; back part of gun where bullet or shell is loaded. **breech birth** birth of a baby with the feet or buttocks appearing first.

breeches pl n trousers extending to just below the knee.

breed v **breeding, bred.** produce new or improved strains of (domestic animals or plants); bear (offspring); produce or be produced, e.g. breed trouble. ▶ n group of animals etc. within a species that have certain clearly defined characteristics; kind or sort. **breeder** n **breeding** n result of good upbringing or training.

breeze n gentle wind. ▶ v move quickly or casually. **breezy** adj windy; casual or carefree.

brethren pl n Old-fashioned (used in religious contexts) brothers.

brevity n shortness.

brew v make (beer etc.) by steeping, boiling, and fermentation; prepare (a drink) by infusing; be about to happen or forming. ▶ n beverage produced by brewing.

brewer n person or company that brews beer. **brewery** n, pl -eries. place where beer etc. is brewed.

briar[1], **brier** n European shrub with a hard woody root; tobacco pipe made from this root.

briar[2] n same as BRIER[1].

bribe v offer or give something to someone to gain favour, influence, etc. ▶ n something given or offered as a bribe. **bribery** n

bric-a-brac n miscellaneous small ornamental objects.

brick n (rectangular block of) baked clay used in building. ▶ v (foll. by up or over) build, enclose, or fill with bricks. **bricklayer** n person who builds with bricks.

bride n woman who has just been or is about to be married. **bridal** adj **bridegroom** n man who has just been or is about to be married. **bridesmaid** n girl or woman who attends a bride at her wedding.

bridge[1] n structure for crossing a river etc.; platform from which a ship is steered or controlled; upper part of the nose; piece of wood supporting the strings of a violin etc. ▶ v build a bridge over (something). **bridgehead** n fortified position at the end of a bridge nearest the enemy.

bridge[2] n card game based on whist, played between two pairs.

bridle n headgear for controlling a horse. ▶ v show anger or indignation. **bridle path** path suitable for riding horses.

brief adj short in duration. ▶ n condensed statement or written synopsis; (also **briefing**) set of instructions. ▶ pl men's or women's underpants. ▶ v give information and instructions to (a person). **briefly** adv **briefcase** n small flat case for carrying papers, books, etc.

brier[1], **briar** n wild rose with long thorny stems.

brier[2] n same as BRIAR[1].

brig n two-masted square-rigged ship.

brigade n army unit smaller than a division; group of people

organized for a certain task.
brigadier n high-ranking army officer.
brigalow n Aust type of acacia tree.
brigand n Lit bandit.
brigantine n two-masted sailing ship.
bright adj emitting or reflecting much light; (of colours) intense; clever. **brightly** adv **brightness** n **brighten** v
brilliant adj shining with light; splendid; extremely clever. **brilliance, brilliancy** n
brim n upper rim of a cup etc.; projecting edge of a hat. ▶ v **brimming, brimmed.** be full to the brim.
brimstone n Obs sulphur.
brine n salt water. **briny** adj very salty. **the briny** Informal the sea.
bring v **bringing, brought.** carry, convey, or take to a designated place or person; cause to happen, Law put forward (charges) officially. **bring about** v cause to happen. **bring off** v succeed in achieving. **bring out** v publish or have (a book) published; reveal or cause to be seen. **bring up** v rear (a child); mention; vomit (food).
brinjal n S Afr dark purple tropical fruit, cooked and eaten as a vegetable.
brink n edge of a steep place.
brisk adj lively and quick. **briskly** adv
brisket n beef from the breast of a cow.
bristle n short stiff hair. ▶ v (cause to) stand up like bristles; show anger. **bristly** adj
Brit n Informal British person.
British adj of Great Britain or the British Commonwealth. ▶ pl n people of Great Britain.
brittle adj hard but easily broken. **brittleness** n

broach v introduce (a topic) for discussion; open (a bottle or barrel).
broad adj having great breadth or width; not detailed; extensive, e.g. broad support; strongly marked, e.g. a broad American accent. **broadly** adv **broaden** v
broadband n telecommunication transmission technique using a wide range of frequencies. **broad bean** thick flat edible bean. **broad-minded** adj tolerant.
broadside n strong verbal or written attack; Naval firing of all the guns on one side of a ship at once.
broadcast n programme or announcement on radio or television. ▶ v transmit (a programme or announcement) on radio or television; make widely known. **broadcaster** n **broadcasting** n
brocade n rich fabric woven with a raised design.
broccoli n type of cabbage with greenish flower heads.
brochure n booklet that contains information about a product or service.
broekies [brook-eez] pl n S Afr informal underpants.
brogue[1] n sturdy walking shoe.
brogue[2] n strong accent, esp. Irish.
broil v Aust, NZ, US & Canadian cook by direct heat under a grill.
broke v past tense of BREAK. ▶ adj Informal having no money.
broken v past participle of BREAK. ▶ adj fractured or smashed; (of the speech of a foreigner) noticeably imperfect, e.g. broken English. **brokenhearted** adj overwhelmed by grief.
broker n agent who buys or sells goods, securities, etc.
brolga n large grey Australian

crane with a trumpeting call (also **native companion**).

brolly n, pl **-lies**. Informal umbrella.

bromide n chemical compound used in medicine and photography.

bromine n Chem dark red liquid element that gives off a pungent vapour.

bronchial [bronk-ee-al] adj of the bronchi.

bronchitis [bronk-**eye**-tiss] n inflammation of the bronchi.

bronchus [bronk-uss] n, pl **bronchi** [bronk-eye] either of the two branches of the windpipe.

bronco n, pl **-cos**. (in the US) wild or partially tamed pony.

brontosaurus n very large plant-eating four-footed dinosaur.

bronze n alloy of copper and tin; statue, medal, etc. made of bronze. ▶ adj made of, or coloured like, bronze. ▶ v (esp. of the skin) make or become brown. **Bronze Age** era when bronze tools and weapons were used.

brooch n ornament with a pin, worn fastened to clothes.

brood n number of birds produced at one hatching; all the children of a family. ▶ v think long and unhappily. **broody** adj moody and sullen; Informal (of a woman) wishing to have a baby.

brook[1] n small stream.

brook[2] v bear or tolerate.

broom n long-handled sweeping brush; yellow-flowered shrub. **broomstick** n handle of a broom.

broth n soup, usu. containing vegetables.

brothel n house where men pay to have sex with prostitutes.

brother n boy or man with the same parents as another person; member of a male religious order. **brotherly** adj brotherhood n

fellowship; association, such as a trade union. **brother-in-law** n, pl **brothers-in-law.** brother of one's husband or wife; husband of one's sister.

brought v past of BRING.

brow n part of the face from the eyes to the hairline; eyebrow; top of a hill.

browbeat v frighten (someone) with threats.

brown n colour of earth or wood. ▶ adj of the colour brown. ▶ v make or become brown.

brownish adj **browned-off** adj Informal bored and depressed.

Brownie Guide, Brownie n junior Guide.

browse v look through (a book or articles for sale) in a casual manner; nibble on young shoots or leaves. ▶ n instance of browsing. **browser** n Computers software package that enables a user to read hypertext, esp. on the Internet.

bruise n discoloured area on the skin caused by an injury. ▶ v cause a bruise on. **bruiser** n strong tough person.

brumby n, pl **-bies**. Aust wild horse; unruly person.

brunch n Informal breakfast and lunch combined.

brunette n girl or woman with dark brown hair.

brunt n main force or shock of a blow, attack, etc.

brush[1] n device made of bristles, wires, etc. used for cleaning, painting, etc.; brief unpleasant encounter; fox's tail. ▶ v clean, scrub, or paint with a brush; touch lightly and briefly. **brush off** v Slang dismiss or ignore (someone). **brush up** v refresh one's knowledge of (a subject).

brush[2] n thick growth of shrubs.

brusque adj blunt or curt in manner or speech. **brusquely** adv **brusqueness** n

Brussels sprout n vegetable like a tiny cabbage.

brute n brutal person; animal other than man. ▶ adj wholly instinctive or physical, like an animal; without reason. **brutish** adj of or like an animal. **brutal** adj cruel and vicious; extremely honest in speech or manner. **brutally** adv **brutality** n **brutalize** v

BSc Bachelor of Science.

BSE bovine spongiform encephalopathy: fatal virus disease of cattle.

BST British Summer Time.

bubble n ball of air in a liquid or solid. ▶ v form bubbles; move or flow with a gurgling sound. **bubbly** adj excited and lively; full of bubbles. **bubble over** v express an emotion freely.

bubonic plague [bew-bonn-ik] n acute infectious disease characterized by swellings.

buccaneer n Hist pirate.

buck[1] n male of the goat, hare, kangaroo, rabbit, and reindeer. ▶ v (of a horse etc.) jump with legs stiff and back arched. **buck up** v make or become more cheerful.

buck[2] n US, Canadian, Aust & NZ slang dollar; S Afr rand.

buck[3] n **pass the buck** Informal shift blame or responsibility onto someone else.

bucket n open-topped round container with a handle. ▶ v **-eting, -eted.** rain heavily. **bucketful** n

buckle n clasp for fastening a belt or strap. ▶ v fasten or be fastened with a buckle; (cause to) bend out of shape through pressure or heat. **buckle down** v Informal apply

oneself with determination.

buckshee adj Slang free.

buckteeth pl n projecting upper front teeth. **buck-toothed** adj

buckwheat n small black grain used for making flour.

bucolic [bew-koll-ik] adj of the countryside or country life.

bud n swelling on a tree or plant that develops into a leaf or flower. ▶ v **budding, budded.** produce buds. **budding** adj beginning to develop or grow.

Buddhism n eastern religion founded by Buddha. **Buddhist** n, adj

buddleia n shrub with long spikes of purple flowers.

buddy n, pl **-dies.** Informal friend.

budge v move slightly.

budgerigar n small cage bird bred in many different-coloured varieties.

budget n financial plan for a period of time; money allocated for a specific purpose. ▶ v **-eting, -eted.** plan the expenditure of (money or time). ▶ adj cheap. **budgetary** adj

budgie n Informal short for BUDGERIGAR.

buff[1] adj dull yellowish-brown. ▶ v clean or polish with soft material.

buff[2] n Informal expert on or devotee of a given subject.

buffalo n type of cattle; US bison.

buffer n something that lessens shock or protects from damaging impact, circumstances, etc.

buffet[1] [boof-ay or buff-ay] n counter where drinks and snacks are served.

buffet[2] [buff-it] v **-feting, -feted.** knock against or about.

buffoon n clown or fool. **buffoonery** n

bug n small insect; Informal minor illness; small mistake in a computer program; concealed microphone; *Aust* flattish edible shellfish. ▶ v **bugging, bugged.** *Informal* irritate (someone); conceal a microphone in (a room or phone).

bugbear n thing that causes obsessive anxiety.

bugle n instrument like a small trumpet. **bugler** n

build v **building, built.** make, construct, or form by joining parts or materials. ▶ n shape of the body. **builder** n **building** n structure with walls and a roof. **building society** organization where money can be borrowed or invested. **build-up** n gradual increase.

built v past of BUILD. **built-up** adj having many buildings.

bulb n same as LIGHT BULB; onion-shaped root which grows into a flower or plant. **bulbous** adj round and fat.

bulge n swelling on a normally flat surface; sudden increase in number. ▶ v swell outwards. **bulging** adj

bulimia n disorder characterized by compulsive overeating followed by vomiting. **bulimic** adj, n

bulk n size or volume, esp. when great; main part. **in bulk** in large quantities. **bulky** adj

bulkhead n partition in a ship or aeroplane.

bull[1] n male of some animals, such as cattle, elephants, and whales. **bullock** n castrated bull. **bulldog** n thickset dog with a broad head and a muscular body. **bulldozer** n powerful tractor for moving earth. **bulldoze** v **bullfight** n public show in which a matador kills a bull. **bull's-eye** n central disc of a target. **bullswool** n *Aust dated & NZ slang* nonsense.

bull[2] n *Informal* complete nonsense.

bull[3] n papal decree.

bullet n small piece of metal fired from a gun.

bulletin n short official report or announcement.

bullion n gold or silver in the form of bars.

bully n, pl **-lies.** person who hurts, persecutes, or intimidates a weaker person. ▶ v **-lying, -lied.** hurt, intimidate, or persecute (a weaker person).

bulrush n tall stiff reed.

bulwark n wall used as a fortification; person or thing acting as a defence.

bum[1] n *Slang* buttocks or anus.

bum[2] *Informal* ▶ n disreputable idler. ▶ adj of poor quality.

bumble v speak, do, or move in a clumsy way. **bumbling** adj, n

bumblebee n large hairy bee.

bumf, bumph n *Informal* official documents or forms.

bump v knock or strike with a jolt; travel in jerks and jolts. ▶ n dull thud from an impact or collision; raised uneven part. **bumpy** adj **bump off** v *Informal* murder.

bumper[1] n bar on the front and back of a vehicle to protect against damage.

bumper[2] adj unusually large or abundant.

bumph n same as BUMF.

bumpkin n awkward simple country person.

bumptious adj offensively self-assertive.

bun n small sweet bread roll or cake; hair gathered into a bun shape at the back of the head.

bunch n number of things growing, fastened, or grouped together. ▶ v group or be grouped together in a bunch.

bundle n number of things

gathered loosely together. ▶ v cause to go roughly or unceremoniously. **bundle up** v make into a bundle.

bung n stopper for a cask etc. ▶ v (foll. by *up*) *Informal* close with a bung; *Brit slang* throw (something) somewhere in a careless manner.

bungalow n one-storey house.

bungee jumping, bungy jumping n sport of leaping from a high bridge, tower, etc., to which one is connected by a rubber rope.

bungle v spoil through incompetence. **bungler** n **bungling** adj, n

bunion n inflamed swelling on the big toe.

bunk[1] n narrow shelflike bed. **bunk bed** one of a pair of beds constructed one above the other.

bunk[2] n same as BUNKUM.

bunk[3] *Slang* ▶ n *Brit* **do a bunk** make a hurried and secret departure. ▶ v *Brit, NZ & S Afr* be absent without permission.

bunker n sand-filled hollow forming an obstacle on a golf course; underground shelter; large storage container for coal etc.

bunkum n nonsense.

bunny n, pl **-nies.** child's word for a rabbit.

Bunsen burner n gas burner used in laboratories.

bunting n decorative flags.

bunyip n *Aust* legendary monster said to live in swamps and lakes.

buoy n floating marker anchored in the sea. ▶ v prevent from sinking; encourage or hearten. **buoyant** adj able to float; cheerful or resilient. **buoyancy** n

bur n same as BURR[1].

burble v make a bubbling sound; talk quickly and excitedly.

burden[1] n heavy load; something

difficult to cope with. ▶ v put a burden on; oppress. **burdensome** adj

burden[2] n theme of a speech etc.

bureau n, pl **-reaus, -reaux.** office that provides a service; writing desk with shelves and drawers.

bureaucracy n, pl **-cies.** administrative system based on complex rules and procedures; excessive adherence to complex procedures. **bureaucrat** n **bureaucratic** adj

burgeon v develop or grow rapidly.

burgh n Scottish borough.

burglar n person who enters a building to commit a crime, esp. theft. **burglary** n **burgle** v

Burgundy n type of French wine. **burgundy** adj dark-purplish red.

burial n burying of a dead body.

burlesque n artistic work which satirizes a subject by caricature.

burly adj **-lier, -liest.** (of a person) broad and strong.

burn[1] v **burning, burnt** or **burned.** be or set on fire; destroy or be destroyed by fire; damage, injure, or mark by heat; feel strong emotion; record data on (a compact disc). ▶ n injury or mark caused by fire or exposure to heat. **burning** adj intense; urgent or crucial.

burn[2] n *Scot* small stream.

burnish v make smooth and shiny by rubbing.

burp v, n *Informal* belch.

burr[1] n head of a plant with prickles or hooks.

burr[2] n soft trilling sound given to the letter r in some dialects; whirring sound.

burrow n hole dug in the ground by a rabbit etc. ▶ v dig holes in the ground.

bursar n treasurer of a school, college, or university. **bursary** n scholarship.

burst v **bursting, burst.** (cause to) break open or apart noisily and suddenly; come or go suddenly and forcibly; be full to the point of breaking open. ▶ n instance of breaking open suddenly; sudden outbreak or occurrence. **burst into** v give vent to (an emotion) suddenly.

bury v **burying, buried.** place in a grave; place in the earth and cover with soil; conceal or hide.

bus n large motor vehicle for carrying passengers. ▶ v **bussing, bussed.** travel or transport by bus.

busby n, pl **-bies.** tall fur hat worn by some soldiers.

bush n dense woody plant, smaller than a tree; wild uncultivated part of a country. **bushy** adj (of hair) thick and shaggy. **bushbaby** n small African tree-living mammal with large eyes.

bushel n obsolete unit of measure equal to 8 gallons (36.4 litres).

business n purchase and sale of goods and services; commercial establishment; trade or profession; proper concern or responsibility; affair, e.g. *it's a dreadful business.* **businesslike** adj efficient and methodical. **businessman, businesswoman** n

busker n street entertainer. **busk** v act as a busker.

bust[1] n woman's bosom; sculpture of the head and shoulders.

bust[2] Informal ▶ v **busting, bust** or **busted.** burst or break; (of the police) raid (a place) or arrest (someone). ▶ adj broken. **go bust** become bankrupt.

bustle[1] v hurry with a show of activity or energy. ▶ n energetic and noisy activity. **bustling** adj

bustle[2] n cushion or framework formerly worn under the back of a woman's skirt to hold it out.

busy adj **busier, busiest.** actively employed; crowded or full of activity. ▶ v **busying, busied.** keep (someone, esp. oneself) busy.

busily adv **busybody** n meddlesome or nosy person.

but conj contrary to expectation; in contrast; other than; without it happening. ▶ prep except. ▶ adv only. **but for** were it not for.

butane n gas used for fuel.

butch adj Slang markedly or aggressively masculine.

butcher n person who slaughters animals or sells their meat; brutal murderer. ▶ v kill and prepare (animals) for meat; kill (people) brutally or indiscriminately. **butchery** n

butler n chief male servant.

butt[1] n thicker end of something; unused end of a cigar or cigarette; slang buttocks.

butt[2] n person or thing that is the target of ridicule.

butt[3] v strike with the head or horns. **butt in** v interrupt a conversation.

butt[4] n large cask.

butter n edible fatty solid made by churning cream. ▶ v put butter on. **buttery** adj **butter up** v flatter.

butter bean n large pale flat edible bean.

buttercup n small yellow flower.

butterfingers n Informal person who drops things by mistake.

butterfly n insect with brightly coloured wings; swimming stroke in which both arms move together in a forward circular action.

buttermilk n sourish milk that remains after the butter has been separated from milk.

butterscotch n kind of hard brittle toffee.

buttock n either of the two fleshy masses that form the human rump.

button n small disc or knob sewn to clothing, which can be passed through a slit in another piece of fabric to fasten them; knob that operates a piece of equipment when pressed. ▶ v fasten with buttons. **buttonhole** n slit in a garment through which a button is passed; flower worn on a lapel. ▶ v detain (someone) in conversation.

buttress n structure to support a wall. ▶ v support with, or as if with, a buttress.

buxom adj (of a woman) healthily plump and full-bosomed.

buy v **buying, bought.** acquire by paying money for; Slang accept as true. ▶ n thing acquired through payment. **buyer** n customer; person employed to buy merchandise.

buzz n rapidly vibrating humming sound; Informal sense of excitement. ▶ v make a humming sound; be filled with an air of excitement. **buzzer** n **buzz around** v move around quickly and busily. **buzz word** jargon word which becomes fashionably popular.

buzzard n bird of prey of the hawk family.

by prep indicating the doer of an action, nearness, movement past, time before or during which, etc., e.g. bitten by a dog; down by the river; driving by the school; in bed by midnight. ▶ adv near; past. **by and by** eventually. **by and large** in general.

bye, bye-bye interj Informal goodbye.

by-election n election held during parliament to fill a vacant seat.

bygone adj past or former.

bylaw, bye-law n rule made by a local authority.

BYO, BYOG n Aust & NZ unlicensed restaurant at which diners may bring their own alcoholic drink.

bypass n main road built to avoid a city; operation to divert blood flow away from a damaged part of the heart. ▶ v go round or avoid.

by-product n secondary or incidental product of a process.

byre n Brit shelter for cows.

bystander n person present but not involved.

byte n Computers group of bits processed as one unit of data.

byway n minor road.

byword n person or thing regarded as a perfect example of something.

C c

C Chem carbon; Celsius; centigrade; century.

c. circa.

cab n taxi; enclosed driver's compartment on a train, truck, etc. **cabbie, cabby** n, pl **-bies.** Informal taxi driver.

cabal [kab-bal] n small group of political plotters; secret plot.

cabaret [kab-a-ray] n dancing and singing show in a nightclub.

cabbage n vegetable with a large head of green leaves. **cabbage tree** NZ palm-like tree with a bare trunk and spiky leaves.

caber n tree trunk tossed in competition at Highland games.

cabin n compartment in a ship or aircraft; small hut. **cabin cruiser** motorboat with a cabin.

cabinet n piece of furniture with

drawers or shelves; (C-) committee of senior government ministers.

cabinet-maker n person who makes fine furniture.

cable n strong thick rope; bundle of wires that carries electricity or electronic signals; telegram sent abroad. ▶ v send (someone) a message by cable. **cable car** vehicle pulled up a steep slope by a moving cable. **cable television** television service conveyed by cable to subscribers.

caboodle n **the whole caboodle** Informal the whole lot.

cabriolet [kab-ree-oh-lay] n small horse-drawn carriage with a folding hood.

cacao [kak-kah-oh] n tropical tree with seed pods from which chocolate and cocoa are made.

cache [kash] n hidden store of weapons or treasure.

cachet [kash-shay] n prestige, distinction.

cack-handed adj Informal clumsy.

cackle v laugh shrilly; (of a hen) squawk with shrill broken notes. ▶ n cackling noise.

cacophony [kak-koff-on-ee] n harsh discordant sound. **cacophonous** adj

cactus n, pl -tuses, -ti. fleshy desert plant with spines but no leaves.

cad n Old-fashioned dishonourable man. **caddish** adj

cadaver [kad-dav-ver] n corpse. **cadaverous** adj pale, thin, and haggard.

caddie, caddy n, pl -dies. person who carries a golfer's clubs. ▶ v -dying, -died. act as a caddie.

caddis fly n insect whose larva (**caddis worm**) lives underwater in a protective case of sand and stones.

caddy n, pl -dies. small container for tea.

cadence [kade-enss] n rise and fall in the pitch of the voice; close of a musical phrase.

cadenza n complex solo passage in a piece of music.

cadet n young person training for the armed forces or police.

cadge v Informal get (something) by taking advantage of someone's generosity. **cadger** n

cadmium n Chem bluish-white metallic element used in alloys.

cadre [kah-der] n small group of people selected and trained to form the core of a political organization or military unit.

caecum [seek-um] n, pl -ca [-ka] pouch at the beginning of the large intestine.

Caesarean section [see-zair-ee-an] n surgical incision into the womb to deliver a baby.

caesium n Chem silvery-white metallic element used in photocells.

café n small or inexpensive restaurant serving light refreshments; S Afr corner shop or grocer. **cafeteria** n self-service restaurant.

caffeine n stimulant found in tea and coffee.

caftan n same as KAFTAN.

cage n enclosure of bars or wires, for keeping animals or birds; enclosed platform of a lift in a mine. **caged** adj kept in a cage.

cagey adj cagier, cagiest. Informal reluctant to give details.

cagoule n Brit lightweight hooded waterproof jacket.

cahoots pl n **in cahoots** Informal conspiring together.

cairn n mound of stones erected as a memorial or marker.

cajole v persuade by flattery. **cajolery** n

cake n sweet food baked from a mixture of flour, eggs, etc.; flat compact mass of something, such as soap. ▶ v form into a hardened mass or crust.

calamine n pink powder consisting chiefly of zinc oxide, used in skin lotions and ointments.

calamity n, pl **-ties.** disaster. **calamitous** adj

calcify v **-fying, -fied.** harden by the depositing of calcium salts. **calcification** n

calcium n Chem silvery-white metallic element found in bones, teeth, limestone, and chalk.

calculate v solve or find out by a mathematical procedure or by reasoning; aim to have a particular effect. **calculable** adj **calculating** adj selfishly scheming. **calculation** n **calculator** n small electronic device for making calculations.

calculus n, pl **-luses.** branch of mathematics dealing with infinitesimal changes to a variable number or quantity; Pathology hard deposit in kidney or bladder.

Caledonian adj Scottish.

calendar n chart showing a year divided up into months, weeks, and days; system for determining the beginning, length, and division of years; schedule of events or appointments.

calendula n marigold.

calf[1] n, pl **calves.** young cow, bull, elephant, whale, or seal; leather made from calf skin. **calve** v give birth to a calf.

calf[2] n, pl **calves.** back of the leg between the ankle and knee.

calibre n person's ability or worth; diameter of the bore of a gun or of a shell or bullet. **calibrate** v mark the scale or check the accuracy of (a measuring instrument). **calibration** n

calico n, pl **-coes.** white cotton fabric.

caliph n Hist Muslim ruler.

call v name; shout to attract attention; telephone; summon; (often foll. by on) visit; arrange (a meeting, strike, etc.). ▶ n cry, shout; animal's or bird's cry; telephone communication; short visit; summons, invitation; need, demand. **caller** n **calling** n vocation, profession. **call box** kiosk for a public telephone. **call centre** office where staff carry out an organization's telephone transactions. **call for** v require. **call off** v cancel. **call up** v summon to serve in the armed forces; cause one to remember.

calligraphy n (art of) beautiful handwriting. **calligrapher** n

calliper n metal splint for supporting the leg; instrument for measuring diameters.

callisthenics pl n light keep-fit exercises.

callous adj showing no concern for other people's feelings. **calloused** adj (of skin) thickened and hardened. **callously** adv **callousness** n

callow adj young and inexperienced.

callus n, pl **-luses.** area of thick hardened skin.

calm adj not agitated or excited; not ruffled by the wind; windless. ▶ n peaceful state. ▶ v (often foll. by down) make or become calm. **calmly** adv **calmness** n

calorie n unit of measurement for the energy value of food; unit of heat. **calorific** adj of calories or heat.

calumny n, pl **-nies.** false or malicious statement.

calypso n, pl **-sos.** West Indian song with improvised topical lyrics.

calyx n, pl **calyxes, calyces.** outer leaves that protect a flower bud.

cam n device that converts a circular motion to a to-and-fro motion. **camshaft** n part of an engine consisting of a rod to which cams are fixed.

camaraderie n comradeship.

camber n slight upward curve to the centre of a surface.

cambric n fine white linen fabric.

camcorder n combined portable video camera and recorder.

came v past tense of COME.

camel n humped mammal that can survive long periods without food or water in desert regions.

camellia [kam-**meal**-ya] n evergreen ornamental shrub with white, pink, or red flowers.

Camembert [**kam**-mem-bare] n soft creamy French cheese.

cameo n, pl **cameos.** brooch or ring with a profile head carved in relief; small part in a film or play performed by a well-known actor or actress.

camera n apparatus used for taking photographs or pictures for television or cinema. **in camera** in private session. **cameraman** n man who operates a camera for television or cinema.

camiknickers pl n Brit woman's undergarment consisting of knickers attached to a camisole.

camisole n woman's bodice-like garment.

camomile n aromatic plant, used to make herbal tea.

camouflage [kam-moo-flahzh] n use of natural surroundings or artificial aids to conceal or disguise something. ▶ v conceal by camouflage.

camp[1] n (place for) temporary lodgings consisting of tents, huts, or cabins; group supporting a particular doctrine. ▶ v stay in a camp. **camper** n

camp[2] adj Informal effeminate or homosexual; consciously artificial or affected. **camp it up** Informal behave in a camp way.

campaign n series of coordinated activities designed to achieve a goal. ▶ v take part in a campaign.

campanology n art of ringing bells.

campanula n plant with blue or white bell-shaped flowers.

camphor n aromatic crystalline substance used medicinally and in mothballs.

campion n red, pink, or white wild flower.

campus n, pl **-puses.** grounds of a university or college.

can[1] v, past **could.** be able to; be allowed to.

can[2] n metal container for food or liquids. ▶ v **canning, canned.** put (something) into a can. **canned** adj preserved in a can; (of music) prerecorded. **cannery** n, pl factory where food is canned.

canal n artificial waterway; passage in the body.

canapé [kan-nap-pay] n small piece of bread or toast with a savoury topping.

canary n, pl **-ries.** small yellow songbird often kept as a pet.

canasta n card game like rummy, played with two packs.

cancan n lively high-kicking dance performed by a female group.

cancel v **-celling, -celled.** stop (something that has been arranged) from taking place; mark (a cheque or stamp) with an official stamp to prevent further use. **cancellation** n **cancel out** v counterbalance, neutralize.

cancer n serious disease resulting from a malignant growth or tumour; malignant growth or tumour. **cancerous** adj

candela [kan-dee-la] n unit of luminous intensity.

candelabrum n, pl **-bra.** large branched candle holder.

candid adj honest and straightforward. **candidly** adv

candidate n person seeking a job or position; person taking an examination. **candidacy, candidature** n

candle n stick of wax enclosing a wick, which is burned to produce light. **candlestick** n holder for a candle. **candlewick** n cotton fabric with a tufted surface.

candour n honesty and straightforwardness.

candy n, pl **-dies.** US sweet or sweets. **candied** adj coated with sugar. **candyfloss** n light fluffy mass of spun sugar on a stick. **candy-striped** adj having coloured stripes on a white background.

cane n stem of the bamboo or similar plant; flexible rod used to beat someone; slender walking stick. ▶ v beat with a cane.

canine adj of or like a dog. ▶ n sharp pointed tooth between the incisors and the molars.

canister n metal container.

canker n ulceration, ulcerous disease; something evil that spreads and corrupts.

cannabis n Asian plant with tough fibres; drug obtained from the dried leaves and flowers of this plant, which can be smoked or chewed.

cannelloni pl n tubular pieces of pasta filled with meat etc.

cannibal n person who eats human flesh; animal that eats others of its own kind. **cannibalism** n **cannibalize** v use parts from (one machine) to repair another.

cannon n large gun on wheels;

billiard stroke in which the cue ball hits two balls successively. **cannonade** n continuous heavy gunfire. **cannonball** n heavy metal ball fired from a cannon.

cannon into v collide with.

cannot can not.

canny adj **-nier, -niest.** shrewd, cautious. **cannily** adv

canoe n light narrow open boat propelled by a paddle or paddles. **canoeing** n sport of rowing in a canoe. **canoeist** n

canon[1] n priest serving in a cathedral.

canon[2] n Church decree regulating morals or religious practices; general rule or standard; list of the works of an author that are accepted as authentic. **canonical** adj **canonize** v declare (a person) officially to be a saint. **canonization** n

canoodle v Slang kiss and cuddle.

canopy n, pl **-pies.** covering above a bed, door, etc; any large or wide covering. **canopied** adj covered with a canopy.

cant[1] n insincere talk; specialized vocabulary of a particular group.

cant[2] n tilted position. ▶ v tilt, overturn.

can't can not.

cantaloupe, cantaloup n kind of melon with sweet orange flesh.

cantankerous adj quarrelsome, bad-tempered.

cantata n musical work consisting of arias, duets, and choruses.

canteen n restaurant attached to a workplace or school; box containing a set of cutlery.

canter n horse's gait between a trot and a gallop. ▶ v move at a canter.

canticle n short hymn with words from the Bible.

cantilever n beam or girder fixed

at one end only.

canto n, pl **-tos.** main division of a long poem.

canton n political division of a country, esp. Switzerland.

cantor n man employed to lead services in a synagogue.

canvas n heavy coarse cloth used for sails and tents, and for oil painting; oil painting on canvas.

canvass v try to get votes or support (from); find out the opinions of (people) by conducting a survey. ▶ n canvassing.

canyon n deep narrow valley.

cap n soft close-fitting covering for the head; small lid; small explosive device used in a toy gun. ▶ v **capping, capped.** cover or top with something; select (a player) for a national team; impose an upper limit on (a tax); outdo, excel.

capable adj (foll. by of) having the ability (for); competent and efficient. **capably** adv **capability** n, pl **-ties.**

capacity n, pl **-ties.** ability to contain, absorb, or hold; maximum that can be contained or produced; physical or mental ability; position, function. **capacious** adj roomy. **capacitance** n (measure of) the ability of a system to store electrical charge. **capacitor** n device for storing electrical charge.

caparisoned adj magnificently decorated.

cape[1] n short cloak.

cape[2] n large piece of land that juts out into the sea.

caper n high-spirited prank. ▶ v skip about.

capercaillie, capercailzie [kap-per-**kale**-yee] n large black European grouse.

capers pl n pickled flower buds of a Mediterranean shrub used in sauces.

capillary n, pl **-laries.** very fine blood vessel.

capital[1] n chief city of a country; accumulated wealth; wealth used to produce more wealth; large letter, as used at the beginning of a name or sentence. ▶ adj involving or punishable by death; Old-fashioned excellent. **capitalize** v write or print (words) in capitals; convert into or provide with capital. **capitalize on** v take advantage of (a situation).

capital[2] n top part of a pillar.

capitalism n economic system based on the private ownership of industry. **capitalist** adj of capitalists or capitalism; supporting capitalism. ▶ n supporter of capitalism; person who owns a business.

capitation n tax of a fixed amount per person.

capitulate v surrender on agreed terms. **capitulation** n

capon n castrated cock fowl fattened for eating.

cappuccino [kap-poo-**cheen**-oh] n, pl **-nos.** coffee with steamed milk, sprinkled with powdered chocolate.

caprice [kap-**reess**] n sudden change of attitude. **capricious** adj tending to have sudden changes of attitude. **capriciously** adv

capsicum n kind of pepper used as a vegetable or as a spice.

capsize v (of a boat) overturn accidentally.

capstan n rotating cylinder round which a ship's rope is wound.

capsule n soluble gelatine case containing a dose of medicine; plant's seed case; detachable crew compartment of a spacecraft.

captain n commander of a ship or

civil aircraft; middle-ranking naval officer; junior officer in the army; leader of a team or group. ▶ v be captain of. **captaincy** n

caption n title or explanation accompanying an illustration. ▶ v provide with a caption.

captious adj tending to make trivial criticisms.

captivate v attract and hold the attention of. **captivating** adj

captive n person kept in confinement. ▶ adj kept in confinement; (of an audience) unable to leave. **captivity** n

captor n person who captures a person or animal.

capture v take by force; succeed in representing (something elusive) artistically. ▶ n capturing.

car n motor vehicle designed to carry a small number of people; passenger compartment of a cable car, lift, etc.; US railway carriage. **car park** area or building reserved for parking cars.

carafe [kar-raff] n glass bottle for serving water or wine.

caramel n chewy sweet made from sugar and milk; burnt sugar, used for colouring and flavouring food. **caramelize** v turn into caramel.

carapace n hard upper shell of tortoises and crustaceans.

carat n unit of weight of precious stones; measure of the purity of gold in an alloy.

caravan n large enclosed vehicle for living in, designed to be towed by a car or horse; group travelling together in Eastern countries.

caraway n plant whose seeds are used as a spice.

carbide n compound of carbon with a metal.

carbine n light automatic rifle.

carbohydrate n any of a large group of energy-producing compounds in food, such as sugars and starches.

carbolic acid n disinfectant derived from coal tar.

carbon n nonmetallic element occurring as charcoal, graphite, and diamond, found in all organic matter. **carbonate** n salt or ester of carbonic acid. **carbonated** adj (of a drink) containing carbon dioxide. **carbonize** v turn into carbon as a result of heating; coat with carbon. **carbon copy** copy made with carbon paper; very similar person or thing. **carbon dioxide** colourless gas exhaled by people and animals. **carbonic acid** weak acid formed from carbon dioxide and water. **carbon paper** paper coated on one side with a dark waxy pigment, used to make a copy of something as it is typed or written.

Carborundum n ® compound of silicon and carbon, used for grinding and polishing.

carbuncle n inflamed boil.

carburettor n device which mixes petrol and air in an internal-combustion engine.

carcass, carcase n dead body of an animal.

carcinogen n substance that produces cancer. **carcinogenic** adj **carcinoma** n malignant tumour.

card n piece of thick stiff paper or cardboard used for identification, reference, or sending greetings or messages; one of a set of cards with a printed pattern, used for playing games; small rectangle of stiff plastic with identifying numbers for use as a credit card, cheque card, or charge card; Old-fashioned witty or eccentric person. ▶ pl any card game, or card games in general.

cardboard n thin stiff board made from paper pulp. **cardsharp** n professional card player who cheats.

cardiac adj of the heart.

cardiogram n electrocardiogram.

cardiograph n electrocardiograph.

cardiology n study of the heart and its diseases. **cardiologist** n

cardiovascular adj of the heart and the blood vessels.

cardigan n knitted jacket.

cardinal n any of the high-ranking clergymen of the RC Church who elect the Pope and act as his counsellors. ▶ adj fundamentally important. **cardinal number** number denoting quantity but not order in a group, for example four as distinct from fourth. **cardinal points** the four main points of the compass.

care v be concerned; like (to do something); (foll. by for) like, be fond of; (foll. by for) look after. ▶ n careful attention, caution; protection, charge; trouble; worry. **careful** adj **carefully** adv **carefulness** n **careless** adj **carelessly** adv **carelessness** n

careen v tilt over to one side.

career n series of jobs in a profession or occupation that a person has through their life; part of a person's life spent in a particular occupation. ▶ v rush in an uncontrolled way. **careerist** n person who seeks advancement by any possible means.

carefree adj without worry or responsibility.

caress n gentle affectionate touch or embrace. ▶ v touch gently and affectionately.

caret [kar-rett] n symbol (∧) indicating a place in written or printed matter where something is to be inserted.

caretaker n person employed to look after a place.

careworn adj showing signs of worry.

cargo n, pl **-goes.** goods carried by a ship, aircraft, etc. **cargo pants, trousers** loose trousers with a large pocket on the outside of each leg.

caribou n, pl **-bou** or **-bous.** large N American reindeer.

caricature n drawing or description of a person that exaggerates features for comic effect. ▶ v make a caricature of.

caries [care-reez] n tooth decay.

carillon [kar-**rill**-yon] n set of bells played by keyboard or mechanically; tune played on such bells.

cark v **cark it** Aust & NZ slang die.

carmine adj vivid red.

carnage n extensive slaughter of people.

carnal adj of a sexual or sensual nature. **carnal knowledge** sexual intercourse.

carnation n cultivated plant with fragrant white, pink, or red flowers.

carnival n festive period with processions, music, and dancing in the street.

carnivore n meat-eating animal. **carnivorous** adj

carob n pod of a Mediterranean tree, used as a chocolate substitute.

carol n joyful Christmas hymn. ▶ v **-olling, -olled.** sing carols; sing joyfully.

carotid adj, n (of) either of the two arteries supplying blood to the head.

carouse v have a merry drinking party.

carousel [kar-roo-**sell**] n revolving conveyor belt for luggage or photographic slides; US merry-go-round.

carp [1] *n* large freshwater fish.

carp [2] *v* complain, find fault.

carpel *n* female reproductive organ of a flowering plant.

carpenter *n* person who makes or repairs wooden structures. **carpentry** *n*

carpet *n* heavy fabric for covering floors. ▶ *v* **carpeting, carpeted.** cover with a carpet. **on the carpet** *Informal* being reprimanded.

carpus *n, pl* **-pi.** set of eight bones of the wrist.

carriage *n* one of the sections of a train for passengers; way a person holds his or her head and body; four-wheeled horse-drawn vehicle; moving part of a machine that supports and shifts another part; charge made for conveying goods. **carriageway** *n Brit* part of a road along which traffic passes in one direction.

carrier *n* person or thing that carries something; person or animal that does not suffer from a disease but can transmit it to others. **carrier pigeon** homing pigeon used for carrying messages.

carrion *n* dead and rotting flesh.

carrot *n* long tapering orange root vegetable; something offered as an incentive. **carroty** *adj* (of hair) reddish-orange.

carry *v* **-rying, -ried.** take from one place to another; have with one habitually, in one's pocket etc.; transmit (a disease); have as a factor or result; hold (one's head or body) in a specified manner; secure the adoption of (a bill or motion); (of sound) travel a certain distance. **carry on** *v* continue; *Informal* cause a fuss. **carry out** *v* follow, accomplish.

cart *n* open two-wheeled horse-drawn vehicle for carrying goods or passengers. ▶ *v* carry, usu. with some effort. **carthorse** *n* large heavily built horse.

cartwheel *n* sideways somersault supported by the hands with legs outstretched; large spoked wheel of a cart.

carte blanche [kaht blahntsh] *n French* complete authority.

cartel *n* association of competing firms formed to fix prices.

cartilage *n* strong flexible tissue forming part of the skeleton. **cartilaginous** *adj*

cartography *n* map making. **cartographer** *n* **cartographic** *adj*

carton *n* container made of cardboard or waxed paper.

cartoon *n* humorous or satirical drawing; sequence of these telling a story; film made by photographing a series of drawings which give the illusion of movement when projected. **cartoonist** *n*

cartridge *n* casing containing an explosive charge and bullet for a gun; part of the pick-up of a record player that converts the movements of the stylus into electrical signals; sealed container of film, tape, etc. **cartridge paper** strong thick drawing paper.

carve *v* cut to form an object; form (an object or design) by cutting; slice (cooked meat). **carving** *n*

caryatid [kar-ree-at-id] *n* supporting column in the shape of a female figure.

Casanova *n* promiscuous man.

casbah *n* citadel of a N African city.

cascade *n* waterfall; something flowing or falling like a waterfall. ▶ *v* flow or fall in a cascade.

case [1] *n* instance, example; condition, state of affairs; set of arguments supporting an action or cause; person or problem dealt with by a doctor, social worker, or solicitor; action, lawsuit; *Grammar* form of a noun, pronoun, or adjective showing its relation to other words in the sentence. **in case** so as to allow for the possibility of.

case² *n* container, protective covering. ▶ *v Slang* inspect (a building) with the intention of burgling it. **case-hardened** *adj* having been made callous by experience.

casement *n* window that is hinged on one side.

cash *n* banknotes and coins. ▶ *v* obtain cash for. **cash in on** *v Informal* gain profit or advantage from. **cash register** till that displays and adds the prices of the goods sold.

cashew *n* edible kidney-shaped nut.

cashier¹ *n* person responsible for handling cash in a bank, shop, etc.

cashier² *v* dismiss with dishonour from the armed forces.

cashmere *n* fine soft wool obtained from goats.

casing *n* protective case, covering.

casino *n, pl* **-nos.** public building or room where gambling games are played.

cask *n* barrel used to hold alcoholic drink; *Aust* cubic carton containing wine, with a tap for dispensing.

casket *n* small box for valuables; *US* coffin.

cassava *n* starch obtained from the roots of a tropical American plant, used to make tapioca.

casserole *n* covered dish in which food is cooked slowly, usu. in an oven; dish cooked in this way. ▶ *v* cook in a casserole.

cassette *n* plastic case containing a reel of film or magnetic tape.

cassock *n* long tunic, usu. black, worn by priests.

cassowary *n, pl* **-waries.** large flightless bird of Australia and New Guinea.

cast *n* actors in a play or film collectively; object shaped by a mould while molten; mould used to shape such an object; rigid plaster-of-Paris casing for immobilizing broken bones while they heal; sort, kind; slight squint in the eye. ▶ *v* **casting, cast.** select (an actor) to play a part in a play or film; give (a vote); let fall, shed; shape (molten material) in a mould; throw with force; direct (a glance). **castaway** *n* shipwrecked person. **casting vote** deciding vote used by the chairperson of a meeting when the votes on each side are equal. **cast-iron** *adj* made of a hard but brittle type of iron; definite, unchallengeable. **cast-off** *adj, n* discarded (person or thing).

castanets *pl n* musical instrument, used by Spanish dancers, consisting of curved pieces of hollow wood clicked together in the hand.

caste *n* any of the hereditary classes into which Hindu society is divided; social rank.

castellated *adj* having battlements.

caster sugar finely ground white sugar.

castigate *v* reprimand severely. **castigation** *n*

castle *n* large fortified building, often built as a ruler's residence; rook in chess.

castor *n* small swivelling wheel fixed to the bottom of a piece of furniture for easy moving.

castor oil oil obtained from an Indian plant, used as a lubricant and purgative.

castrate *v* remove the testicles of;

deprive of vigour or masculinity. **castration** n

casual adj careless, nonchalant; (of work or workers) occasional or not permanent; for informal wear; happening by chance. **casually** adv

casualty n, pl **-ties.** person killed or injured in an accident or war; person or thing that has suffered as the result of something.

casuarina [kass-yew-a-**reen**-a] n Australian tree with jointed green branches.

casuistry n reasoning that is misleading or oversubtle.

cat n small domesticated furry mammal; related wild mammal, such as the lion or tiger. **catty** adj Informal spiteful. **catkin** n drooping flower spike of certain trees. **catcall** n derisive whistle or cry. **catgut** n strong cord used to string musical instruments and sports rackets. **catnap** n, v doze. **Catseyes** pl n ® glass reflectors set in the road to indicate traffic lanes. **cat's paw** person used by another to do unpleasant things for him or her. **catwalk** n narrow pathway or platform.

cataclysm [kat-a-kliz-zum] n violent upheaval; disaster, such as an earthquake. **cataclysmic** adj

catacombs [kat-a-koomz] pl n underground burial place consisting of tunnels with recesses for tombs.

catafalque [kat-a-falk] n raised platform on which a body lies in state before or during a funeral.

catalepsy n trancelike state in which the body is rigid. **cataleptic** adj

catalogue n book containing details of items for sale; systematic list of items. ▶ v make a systematic list of.

catalyst n substance that speeds up a chemical reaction without itself changing. **catalyse** v speed up (a chemical reaction) by a catalyst. **catalysis** n **catalytic** adj

catamaran n boat with twin parallel hulls.

catapult n Y-shaped device with a loop of elastic, used by children for firing stones. ▶ v shoot forwards or upwards violently.

cataract n eye disease in which the lens becomes opaque; opaque area of an eye; large waterfall.

catarrh [kat-**tar**] n excessive mucus in the nose and throat, during or following a cold. **catarrhal** adj

catastrophe [kat-**ass**-trof-fee] n great and sudden disaster. **catastrophic** adj

catch v **catching, caught.** seize, capture; surprise in an act, e.g. two boys were caught stealing; be in time for (a bus, train, etc.); see or hear; be infected with (an illness); entangle; understand, make out. ▶ n device for fastening a door, window, etc.; Informal concealed or unforeseen drawback. **catch it** Informal be punished. **catching** adj infectious. **catchy** adj (of a tune) pleasant and easily remembered. **catchment area** area served by a particular school or hospital; area of land draining into a river, basin, or reservoir. **catch on** v Informal become popular; understand. **catch out** v Informal trap (someone) in an error or lie. **catch phrase** well-known phrase associated with a particular entertainer. **catch 22** inescapable dilemma. **catchword** n well-known and frequently used phrase.

catechism [kat-ti-**kiz**-zum] n instruction on the doctrine of a

Christian Church in a series of questions and answers.

category n, pl **-ries.** class, group.

categorical adj absolutely clear and certain. **categorically** adv

categorize v put in a category. **categorization** n

cater v provide what is needed or wanted, esp. food or services. **caterer** n

caterpillar n wormlike larva of a moth or butterfly; ® endless track, driven by cogged wheels, used to propel a heavy vehicle.

caterwaul v wail, yowl.

catharsis [kath-thar-siss] n, pl **-ses.** relief of strong suppressed emotions. **cathartic** adj

cathedral n principal church of a diocese.

Catherine wheel n rotating firework.

catheter [kath-it-er] n tube inserted into a body cavity to drain fluid.

cathode n negative electrode, by which electrons leave a circuit. **cathode rays** stream of electrons from a cathode in a vacuum tube.

catholic adj (of tastes or interests) covering a wide range. ▶ n, adj (C-) (member) of the Roman Catholic Church. **Catholicism** n

cation [kat-eye-on] n positively charged ion.

cattle pl n domesticated cows and bulls.

Caucasian n, adj (member) of the light-skinned racial group of humankind.

caucus n, pl **-cuses.** local committee or faction of a political party; political meeting to decide future plans.

caught v past of CATCH.

cauldron n large pot used for boiling.

cauliflower n vegetable with a

large head of white flower buds surrounded by green leaves.

caulk v fill in (cracks) with paste etc.

causal adj of or being a cause. **causally** adv **causation, causality** n relationship of cause and effect.

cause n something that produces a particular effect; (foll. by for) reason, motive; aim or principle supported by a person or group. ▶ v be the cause of.

cause célèbre [kawz sill-**leb**-ra] n, pl **causes célèbres** [kawz sill-**leb**-ra] controversial legal case or issue.

causeway n raised path or road across water or marshland.

caustic adj capable of burning by chemical action; bitter and sarcastic. **caustically** adv

cauterize v burn (a wound) with heat or a caustic agent to prevent infection.

caution n care, esp. in the face of danger; warning. ▶ v warn, advise. **cautionary** adj warning. **cautious** adj showing caution. **cautiously** adv

cavalcade n procession of people on horseback or in cars.

cavalier adj showing haughty disregard. ▶ n (C-) supporter of Charles I in the English Civil War.

cavalry n, pl **-ries.** part of the army orig. on horseback, but now often using fast armoured vehicles.

cave n hollow in the side of a hill or cliff. **caving** n sport of exploring caves. **cave in** v collapse inwards; Informal yield under pressure. **caveman** n prehistoric cave dweller.

caveat [kav-vee-at] n warning.

cavern n large cave. **cavernous** adj

caviar, caviare n salted sturgeon roe, regarded as a delicacy.

cavil v **-illing, -illed.** make petty

objections. ▶ *n* petty objection.
cavity *n, pl* **-ties.** hollow space; decayed area on a tooth.
cavort *v* skip about.
caw *n* cry of a crow, rook, or raven. ▶ *v* make this cry.
cayenne pepper, cayenne *n* hot red spice made from capsicum seeds.
cayman *n, pl* **-mans.** S American reptile similar to an alligator.
CB Citizens' Band.
CBE (in Britain) Commander of the Order of the British Empire.
CBI Confederation of British Industry.
cc cubic centimetre; carbon copy.
CD compact disc.
CD-ROM compact disc read-only memory.
cease *v* bring or come to an end. **ceaseless** *adj* **ceaselessly** *adv* **ceasefire** *n* temporary truce.
cedar *n* evergreen coniferous tree; its wood.
cede *v* surrender (territory or legal rights).
cedilla *n* character (¸) placed under a *c* in some languages, to show that it is pronounced *s*, not *k*.
ceilidh [kay-lee] *n* informal social gathering for singing and dancing, esp. in Scotland.
ceiling *n* inner upper surface of a room; upper limit set on something.
celandine *n* wild plant with yellow flowers.
celebrate *v* hold festivities to mark (a happy event, anniversary, etc.); perform (a religious ceremony). **celebrated** *adj* well known. **celebration** *n* **celebrant** *n* person who performs a religious ceremony. **celebrity** *n, pl* **-rities.** famous person; state of being famous.
celeriac [sill-ler-ee-ak] *n* variety of

celery with a large turnip-like root.
celerity [sill-ler-rit-tee] *n* swiftness.
celery *n* vegetable with long green crisp edible stalks.
celestial *adj* heavenly, divine; of the sky.
celibate *adj* unmarried or abstaining from sex, esp. because of a religious vow of chastity. ▶ *n* celibate person. **celibacy** *n*
cell *n* smallest unit of an organism that is able to function independently; small room for a prisoner, monk, or nun; small compartment of a honeycomb etc.; small group operating as the core of a larger organization; device that produces electrical energy by chemical reaction.
cellular *adj* of or consisting of cells.
cellar *n* underground room for storage; stock of wine.
cello [chell-oh] *n, pl* **-los.** large low-pitched instrument of the violin family. **cellist** *n*
Cellophane *n* ® thin transparent cellulose sheeting used as wrapping.
celluloid *n* kind of plastic used to make toys and, formerly, photographic film.
cellulose *n* main constituent of plant cell walls, used in making paper, plastics, etc.
Celsius *adj* of the temperature scale in which water freezes at 0° and boils at 100°.
Celt [kelt] *n* person from Scotland, Ireland, Wales, Cornwall, or Brittany.
Celtic [kel-tik *or* sel-tik] *n* group of languages including Gaelic and Welsh. ▶ *adj* of the Celts or the Celtic languages.
cement *n* fine grey powder mixed with water and sand to make mortar or concrete; something that unites, binds, or joins;

material used to fill teeth. ▶ v join, bind, or cover with cement; make (a relationship) stronger.

cemetery n, pl **-teries**. place where dead people are buried.

cenotaph n monument honouring soldiers who died in a war.

censer n container for burning incense.

censor n person authorized to examine films, books, etc., to ban or cut anything considered obscene or objectionable. ▶ v ban or cut parts of (a film, book, etc.). **censorship** n **censorious** adj harshly critical.

censure n severe disapproval. ▶ v criticize severely.

census n, pl **-suses**. official count of a population.

cent n hundredth part of a monetary unit such as the dollar or euro.

centaur n mythical creature with the head, arms, and torso of a man, and the lower body and legs of a horse.

centenary [sen-**teen**-a-ree] n Chiefly Brit pl **-naries**. 100th anniversary or its celebration. **centenarian** n person at least 100 years old.

centennial n 100th anniversary or its celebration.

centi- prefix one hundredth.

centigrade adj same as CELSIUS.

centigram, **centigramme** n one hundredth of a gram.

centilitre n one hundredth of a litre.

centimetre n one hundredth of a metre.

centipede n small wormlike creature with many legs.

central adj of, at, or forming the centre; main, principal. **centrally** adv **centrality** n **centralism** n principle of central control of a

country or organization. **centralize** v bring under central control. **centralization** n **central heating** system for heating a building from one central source of heat.

centre n middle point or part; place for a specified activity; political party or group favouring moderation; Sport player who plays in the middle of the field. ▶ v put in the centre of something. **centrist** n person favouring political moderation. **centre on** v have as a centre or main theme.

centrifugal adj moving away from a centre. **centrifuge** n machine that separates substances by centrifugal force.

centripetal adj moving towards a centre.

centurion n (in ancient Rome) officer commanding 100 men.

century n, pl **-ries**. period of 100 years; cricket score of 100 runs.

CEO chief executive officer.

cephalopod [seff-a-loh-pod] n sea mollusc with a head and tentacles, such as the octopus.

ceramic n hard brittle material made by heating clay to a very high temperature; object made of this. ▶ pl art of producing ceramic objects. ▶ adj made of ceramic.

cereal n grass plant with edible grain, such as oat or wheat; this grain; breakfast food made from this grain, eaten mixed with milk.

cerebral [ser-rib-ral or ser-reeb-ral] adj of the brain; intellectual.

cerebrum [serr-rib-rum] n, pl **-brums, -bra** [-bra] main part of the brain.

ceremony n, pl **-nies**. formal act or ritual; formally polite behaviour. **ceremonial** adj, n **ceremonially** adv **ceremonious** adj excessively polite or formal. **ceremoniously** adv

cerise [ser-reess] adj cherry-red.

certain adj positive and confident; definite; some but not much. **certainly** adv **certainty** n state of being sure; (pl **-ties**) something that is inevitable.

certificate n official document stating the details of a birth, academic course, etc.

certify v **-fying, -fied.** confirm, attest to; guarantee; declare legally insane. **certifiable** adj considered legally insane. **certification** n

certitude n confidence, certainty.

cervix n, pl **cervixes, cervices.** narrow entrance of the womb; neck. **cervical** adj

cessation n ceasing.

cesspit, cesspool n covered tank or pit for sewage.

cetacean [sit-tay-shun] n fish-shaped sea mammal such as a whale or dolphin.

cf compare.

CFC chlorofluorocarbon.

CGI computer-generated image(s).

ch. chapter; church.

chafe v make sore or worn by rubbing; be annoyed or impatient.

chaff¹ n grain husks.

chaff² v Old-fashioned tease good-naturedly.

chaffinch n small European songbird.

chagrin [shag-grin] n annoyance and disappointment. **chagrined** adj annoyed and disappointed.

chain n flexible length of connected metal links; series of connected facts or events; group of shops, hotels, etc. owned by one firm. ▶ v restrict or fasten with or as if with a chain. **chain reaction** series of events, each of which causes the next.

chain-smoke v smoke (cigarettes) continuously. **chain smoker**

chair n seat with a back, for one person; official position of authority; person holding this; professorship. ▶ v preside over (a meeting). **chairlift** series of chairs suspended from a moving cable for carrying people up a slope. **chairman, chairwoman** n person in charge of a company's board of directors or a meeting (also **chairperson**).

chaise [shaze] n Hist light horse-drawn carriage.

chaise longue [long] n couch with a back and a single armrest.

chalcedony [kal-sed-don-ee] n, pl **-nies.** variety of quartz.

chalet n kind of Swiss wooden house with a sharply sloping roof; similar house, used as a holiday home.

chalice n large goblet.

chalk n soft white rock consisting of calcium carbonate; piece of chalk, often coloured, used for drawing and writing on blackboards. ▶ v draw or mark with chalk. **chalky** adj

challenge n demanding or stimulating situation; call to take part in a contest or fight; questioning of a statement of fact; demand by a sentry for identification or a password. ▶ v issue a challenge to. **challenged** adj disabled as specified, e.g. physically challenged. **challenger** n

chamber n hall used for formal meetings; legislative or judicial assembly; Old-fashioned bedroom; compartment, cavity. ▶ pl set of rooms used as offices by a barrister. **chambermaid** n woman employed to clean bedrooms in a hotel. **chamber music** classical music to be performed by a small group of musicians. **chamber pot** bowl for urine, formerly used in bedrooms.

chamberlain *n Hist* officer who managed the household of a king or nobleman.

chameleon [kam-**meal**-yon] *n* small lizard that changes colour to blend in with its surroundings.

chamfer [**cham**-fer] *v* bevel the edge of.

chamois [**sham**-wah] *n, pl* **-ois**. small mountain antelope; [**sham**-ee] soft suede leather; piece of this, used for cleaning or polishing.

chamomile [**kam**-mo-mile] *n* same as CAMOMILE.

champ[1] *v* chew noisily. **champ at the bit** *Informal* be impatient to do something.

champ[2] *n* short for CHAMPION.

champagne *n* sparkling white French wine.

champion *n* overall winner of a competition; (foll. by *of*) someone who defends a person or cause. ▸ *v* support. ▸ *adj Dialect* excellent. **championship** *n*

chance *n* likelihood, probability; opportunity to do something; risk, gamble; unpredictable element that causes things to happen one way rather than another. ▸ *v* risk, hazard. **chancy** *adj* uncertain, risky.

chancel *n* part of a church containing the altar and choir.

chancellor *n* head of government in some European countries; honorary head of a university. **chancellorship** *n*

Chancery *n* division of the British High Court of Justice.

chandelier [shan-dill-**eer**] *n* ornamental light with branches and holders for several candles or bulbs.

chandler *n* dealer, esp. in ships' supplies.

change *n* becoming different; variety or novelty; different set, esp. of clothes; balance received when the amount paid is more than the cost of a purchase; coins of low value. ▸ *v* make or become different; give and receive (something) in return; exchange (money) for its equivalent in a smaller denomination or different currency; put on other clothes; leave one vehicle and board another. **changeable** *adj* changing often. **changeling** *n* child believed to have been exchanged by fairies for another.

channel *n* band of broadcasting frequencies; means of access or communication; broad strait connecting two areas of sea; bed or course of a river, stream, or canal; groove. ▸ *v* **-nelling, -nelled.** direct or convey through a channel.

chant *v* utter or sing (a slogan or psalm). ▸ *n* rhythmic or repetitious slogan; psalm that has a short simple melody with several words sung on one note.

chanter *n* (on bagpipes) pipe on which the melody is played.

chaos *n* complete disorder or confusion. **chaotic** *adj* **chaotically** *adv*

chap *n Informal* man or boy.

chapati, chapatti *n* (in Indian cookery) flat thin unleavened bread.

chapel *n* place of worship with its own altar, within a church; similar place of worship in a large house or institution; Nonconformist place of worship.

chaperone [**shap**-per-rone] *n* older person who accompanies and supervises a young person or young people on a social occasion. ▶ v act as a chaperone to.

chaplain n clergyman attached to a chapel, military body, or institution. **chaplaincy** n, pl **-cies.**

chaplet n garland for the head.

chapped adj (of the skin) raw and cracked, through exposure to cold.

chapter n division of a book; period in a life or history; branch of a society or club.

char[1] v **charring, charred.** blacken by partial burning.

char[2] Brit informal ▶ n charwoman. ▶ v **charring, charred.** clean other people's houses as a job.

char[3] n Brit old-fashioned slang tea.

charabanc [shar-rab-bang] n Old-fashioned coach for sightseeing.

character n combination of qualities distinguishing a person, group, or place; reputation, esp. good reputation; person represented in a play, film, or story; unusual or amusing person; letter, numeral, or symbol used in writing or printing. **characteristic** n distinguishing feature or quality. ▶ adj typical. **characteristically** adv **characterize** v be a characteristic of; (foll. by as) describe. **characterization** n

charade [shar-rahd] n absurd pretence. ▶ pl game in which two teams act out a word or phrase, which the other team has to guess.

charcoal n black substance formed by partially burning wood.

charge v ask as a price; enter a debit against a person's account for (a purchase); accuse formally; make a rush at or sudden attack upon; fill (a glass); fill (a battery) with electricity; command, assign. ▶ n price charged; formal accusation; attack; command, exhortation; custody,

guardianship; person or thing entrusted to someone's care; amount of electricity stored in a battery. **in charge of** in control of. **chargeable** adj **charger** n device for charging an accumulator; (in the Middle Ages) warhorse.

chargé d'affaires [shar-zhay daf-fair] n, pl **chargés d'affaires.** head of a diplomatic mission in the absence of an ambassador or in a small mission.

chariot n two-wheeled horse-drawn vehicle used in ancient times in wars and races. **charioteer** n chariot driver.

charisma [kar-rizz-ma] n person's power to attract or influence people. **charismatic** [kar-rizz-mat-ik] adj

charity n, pl **-ties.** organization that gives help, such as money or food, to those in need; giving of help to those in need; help given to those in need; kindly attitude towards people. **charitable** adj **charitably** adv

charlady n Brit informal same as CHARWOMAN.

charlatan [shar-lat-tan] n person who claims expertise that he or she does not have.

charleston n lively dance of the 1920s.

charm n attractive quality; trinket worn on a bracelet; magic spell. ▶ v attract, delight; influence by personal charm; protect or influence as if by magic. **charmer** n **charming** adj attractive.

charnel house n Hist building or vault for the bones of the dead.

chart n graph, table, or diagram showing information; map of the sea or stars. ▶ v plot the course of; make a chart of. **the charts** Informal weekly lists of the bestselling pop records.

charter n document granting or demanding certain rights; fundamental principles of an organization; hire of transport for private use. ▶ v hire by charter; grant a charter to. **chartered** adj officially qualified to practise a profession.

chartreuse [shar-**trerz**] n sweet-smelling green or yellow liqueur.

charwoman n woman whose job is to clean other people's homes.

chary [**chair**-ee] adj -rier, -riest. wary, careful.

chase[1] v run after quickly in order to catch or drive away; Informal rush, run; Informal try energetically to obtain. ▶ n chasing, pursuit. **chaser** n milder drink drunk after another stronger one.

chase[2] v engrave or emboss (metal).

chasm [kaz-zum] n deep crack in the earth.

chassis [**shass**-ee] n, pl -sis. frame, wheels, and mechanical parts of a vehicle.

chaste adj abstaining from sex outside marriage or altogether; (of style) simple. **chastely** adv **chastity** n

chasten [**chase**-en] v subdue by criticism.

chastise v scold severely; punish by beating. **chastisement** n

chat n informal conversation. ▶ v chatting, chatted. have an informal conversation. **chatty** adj **chatroom** n site on the Internet where users have group discussions by e-mail.

chateau [shat-toe] n, pl -teaux, -teaus. French castle.

chatelaine [shat-tell-lane] n (formerly) mistress of a large house or castle.

chattels pl n possessions.

chatter v speak quickly and continuously about unimportant things; (of the teeth) rattle with cold or fear. ▶ n idle talk. **chatterbox** n person who chatters a lot.

chauffeur n person employed to drive a car for someone.

chauvinism [**show**-vin-iz-zum] n irrational belief that one's own country, race, group, or sex is superior. **chauvinist** n, adj **chauvinistic** adj

cheap adj costing relatively little; of poor quality; not valued highly; mean, despicable. **cheaply** adv **cheapen** v lower the reputation of; reduce the price of. **cheapskate** n Informal miserly person.

cheat v act dishonestly to gain profit or advantage. ▶ n person who cheats; fraud, deception.

check v examine, investigate; slow the growth or progress of; correspond, agree. ▶ n test to ensure accuracy or progress; break in progress; US cheque; pattern of squares or crossed lines; Chess position of a king under attack. **check in** v register one's arrival. **checkmate** n Chess winning position in which an opponent's king is under attack and unable to escape; utter defeat. ▶ v Chess place the king of (one's opponent) in checkmate; thwart, defeat. **check out** v pay the bill and leave a hotel; examine, investigate; Informal have a look at. **checkout** n counter in a supermarket, where customers pay. **checkup** n thorough medical examination.

Cheddar n firm orange or yellowy-white cheese.

cheek n either side of the face below the eye; Informal

impudence, boldness. ▷ v *Brit, Aust & NZ informal* speak impudently to. **cheeky** adj impudent, disrespectful. **cheekily** adv **cheekiness** n

cheep n young bird's high-pitched cry. ▷ v utter a cheep.

cheer v applaud or encourage with shouts; make or become happy. ▷ n shout of applause or encouragement. **cheerful** adj **cheerfully** adv **cheerfulness** n **cheerless** adj dreary, gloomy. **cheery** adj **cheerily** adv

cheerio interj *Informal* goodbye. ▷ n *Aust & NZ* small red cocktail sausage.

cheese n food made from coagulated milk curd; block of this. **cheesy** adj **cheeseburger** n hamburger topped with melted cheese. **cheesecake** n dessert with a biscuit-crumb base covered with a sweet cream-cheese mixture. **cheesecloth** n light cotton cloth. **cheesed off** bored, annoyed.

cheetah n large fast-running spotted African wild cat.

chef n cook in a restaurant.

chef-d'oeuvre [shay-**durv**] n, pl **chefs-d'oeuvre**. masterpiece.

chemical n substance used in or resulting from a reaction involving changes to atoms or molecules. ▷ adj of chemistry or chemicals. **chemically** adv

chemise [shem-**meez**] n *Old-fashioned* woman's loose-fitting slip.

chemistry n science of the composition, properties, and reactions of substances. **chemist** n shop selling medicines and cosmetics; qualified dispenser of prescribed medicines; specialist in chemistry.

chemotherapy n treatment of

disease, often cancer, using chemicals.

chenille [shen-**neel**] n (fabric of) thick tufty yarn.

cheque n written order to one's bank to pay money from one's account. **cheque card** *Brit* plastic card issued by a bank guaranteeing payment of a customer's cheques.

chequer n piece used in Chinese chequers. ▷ pl game of draughts. **chequered** adj marked by varied fortunes; having a pattern of squares.

cherish v cling to (an idea or feeling); care for.

cheroot [sher-**root**] n cigar with both ends cut flat.

cherry n, pl -**ries**. small red or black fruit with a stone; tree on which it grows. ▷ adj deep red.

cherub n, pl -**ubs**, -**ubim**. angel, often represented as a winged child; sweet child. **cherubic** [cher-**rew-bik**] adj

chervil n aniseed-flavoured herb.

chess n game for two players with 16 pieces each, played on a chequered board of 64 squares. **chessman** n piece used in chess.

chest n front of the body, from neck to waist; large strong box. **chest of drawers** piece of furniture consisting of drawers in a frame.

chesterfield n couch with high padded sides and back.

chestnut n reddish-brown edible nut; tree on which it grows; reddish-brown horse; *Informal* old joke. ▷ adj (of hair or a horse) reddish-brown.

chevron [shev-ron] n V-shaped pattern, esp. on the sleeve of a military uniform to indicate rank.

chew v grind (food) between the teeth. **chewy** adj requiring a lot

of chewing. **chewing gum**
flavoured gum to be chewed but
not swallowed.

chianti [kee-**ant**-ee] *n* dry red
Italian wine.

chiaroscuro [kee-ah-roh-**skew**-roh]
n, pl **-ros.** distribution of light and
shade in a picture.

chic [**sheek**] *adj* stylish, elegant. ▶ *n*
stylishness, elegance.

chicane [shik-**kane**] *n* obstacle in a
motor-racing circuit.

chicanery *n* trickery, deception.

chick *n* baby bird. **chickpea** *n*
edible yellow pealike seed.
chickweed *n* weed with small
white flowers.

chicken *n* domestic fowl; its flesh,
used as food; *Slang* coward. ▶ *adj
Slang* cowardly. **chicken feed**
Slang trifling amount of money.
chicken out *v Informal* fail to do
something through cowardice.
chickenpox *n* infectious disease
with an itchy rash.

chicory *n, pl* **-ries.** plant whose
leaves are used in salads; root of
this plant, used as a coffee
substitute.

chide *v* **chiding, chided** or **chid,
chid** or **chidden.** rebuke, scold.

chief *n* head of a group of people.
▶ *adj* most important. **chiefly** *adv*
especially; mainly. **chieftain** *n*
leader of a tribe.

chiffon [**shif**-fon] *n* fine
see-through fabric.

chignon [**sheen**-yon] *n* knot of hair
pinned up at the back of the head.

chihuahua [chee-**wah**-wah] *n* tiny
short-haired dog.

chilblain *n* inflammation of the
fingers or toes, caused by
exposure to cold.

child *n, pl* **children.** young human
being, boy or girl; son or
daughter. **childhood** *n* **childish**
adj immature, silly; or like a

child. **childishly** *adv* **childless** *adj*
childlike *adj* innocent, trustful.
childbirth *n* giving birth to a
child. **child's play** easy task.

chill *n* feverish cold; moderate
coldness. ▶ *v* make (something)
cool or cold; cause (someone) to
feel cold or frightened. ▶ *adj*
unpleasantly cold. **chilly** *adj*
moderately cold; unfriendly.
chilly-bin *n NZ informal* insulated
container for carrying food and
drink. **chilliness** *n* **chill (out)** *v
Informal* relax. **chill-out** *adj
Informal* suitable for relaxation,
esp. after energetic activity, e.g. *a
chill-out area.*

chilli, chili *n* small red or green
hot-tasting capsicum pod, used in
cooking; (also **chilli con carne**)
hot-tasting Mexican dish of meat,
onions, beans, and chilli powder.

chime *n* musical ringing sound of a
bell or clock. ▶ *v* make a musical
ringing sound; indicate (the time)
by chiming; (foll. by *with*) be
consistent with.

chimera [kime-**meer**-a] *n*
unrealistic hope or idea; fabled
monster with a lion's head, goat's
body, and serpent's tail.

chimney *n* hollow vertical structure
for carrying away smoke from a
fire. **chimney pot** short pipe on
the top of a chimney. **chimney
sweep** person who cleans soot
from chimneys.

chimp *n Informal* short for
CHIMPANZEE.

chimpanzee *n* intelligent black
African ape.

chin *n* part of the face below the
mouth. **chinwag** [*n Brit, Aust & NZ
informal* chat.

china *n* fine earthenware or
porcelain; dishes or ornaments
made of this; *Brit, Aust, NZ & S Afr
informal* friend.

chinchilla n S American rodent bred for its soft grey fur; its fur.

chine n cut of meat including part of the backbone.

Chinese adj of China. ▸ n, pl **-nese.** person from China; any of the languages of China.

chink[1] n small narrow opening.

chink[2] v, n (make) a light ringing sound.

chintz n printed cotton fabric with a glazed finish.

chip n strip of potato, fried in deep fat; tiny wafer of semiconductor material forming an integrated circuit; counter used to represent money in gambling games; small piece removed by chopping, breaking, etc.; mark left where a small piece has been broken off something. ▸ v **chipping, chipped.** break small pieces from. **have a chip on one's shoulder** Informal bear a grudge. **chip in** v Informal contribute (money); interrupt with a remark. **chippie** n Brit, Aust & NZ informal carpenter.

chipboard n thin board made of compressed wood particles.

chipmunk n small squirrel-like N American rodent with a striped back.

chiropodist [kir-rop-pod-ist] n person who treats minor foot complaints. **chiropody** n

chiropractic [kire-oh-prak-tik] n system of treating bodily disorders by manipulation of the spine. **chiropractor** n

chirp v (of a bird or insect) make a short high-pitched sound. ▸ n chirping sound. **chirpy** adj Informal lively and cheerful.

chisel n metal tool with a sharp end for shaping wood or stone. ▸ v **-elling, -elled.** carve or form with a chisel.

chit[1] n short official note, such as a receipt.

chit[2] n Brit, Aust & NZ old-fashioned pert or impudent girl.

chitchat n chat, gossip.

chitterlings pl n pig's intestines cooked as food.

chivalry n courteous behaviour, esp. by men towards women; medieval system and principles of knighthood. **chivalrous** adj

chives pl n herb with a mild onion flavour.

chivvy v **-vying, -vied.** Informal harass, nag.

chlorine n strong-smelling greenish-yellow gaseous element, used to disinfect water. **chlorinate** v disinfect (water) with chlorine. **chlorination** n **chloride** n compound of chlorine and another substance.

chlorofluorocarbon n any of various gaseous compounds of carbon, hydrogen, chlorine, and fluorine, used in refrigerators and aerosol propellants, some of which break down the ozone in the atmosphere.

chloroform n strong-smelling liquid formerly used as an anaesthetic.

chlorophyll n green colouring matter of plants, which enables them to convert sunlight into energy.

chock n block or wedge used to prevent a heavy object from moving. **chock-full, chock-a-block** adj completely full.

chocolate n sweet food made from cacao seeds; sweet or drink made from this. ▸ adj dark brown.

choice n choosing; opportunity or power of choosing; person or thing chosen or that may be chosen; alternative action or possibility. ▸ adj of high quality.

choir n organized group of singers,

esp. in church; part of a church occupied by the choir.

choke v hinder or stop the breathing of (a person) by strangling or smothering; have trouble in breathing; block, clog up. ▶ n device controlling the amount of air that is mixed with the fuel in a petrol engine.

choker n tight-fitting necklace.

choke back v suppress (tears or anger).

cholera [kol-ler-a] n serious infectious disease causing severe vomiting and diarrhoea.

choleric [kol-ler-ik] adj bad-tempered.

cholesterol [kol-lest-er-oll] n fatty substance found in animal tissue, an excess of which can cause heart disease.

chomp v chew noisily.

chook n Aust & NZ hen or chicken.

choose v choosing, chose, chosen. select from a number of alternatives; decide (to do something) because one wants to.

choosy adj Informal fussy, hard to please.

chop¹ v chopping, chopped. cut with a blow from an axe or knife; cut into pieces; dispense with; Boxing, karate hit (an opponent) with a short sharp blow. ▶ n cutting or sharp blow; slice of lamb or pork, usu. with a rib.

chopper n Informal helicopter; small axe. **choppy** adj (of the sea) fairly rough.

chop² v chopping, chopped. **chop and change** change one's mind repeatedly.

chops pl n Brit, Aust & NZ informal jaws, cheeks.

chopsticks pl n pair of thin sticks used to eat Chinese food.

chop suey n Chinese dish of chopped meat and vegetables in a sauce.

choral adj of a choir.

chorale [kor-rahl] n slow stately hymn tune.

chord¹ n Maths straight line joining two points on a curve.

chord² n simultaneous sounding of three or more musical notes.

chore n routine task.

choreography n composition of steps and movements for dancing. **choreographer** n **choreographic** adj

chorister n singer in a choir.

chortle v chuckle in amusement. ▶ n amused chuckle.

chorus n, pl -ruses. large choir; part of a song repeated after each verse; something expressed by many people at once; group of singers or dancers who perform together in a show. ▶ v chorusing, chorused. sing or say together. **in chorus** in unison.

chose v past tense of CHOOSE.

chosen v past participle of CHOOSE.

choux pastry [shoo] n very light pastry made with eggs.

chow n thick-coated dog with a curled tail, orig. from China.

chowder n thick soup containing clams or fish.

chow mein n Chinese-American dish of chopped meat or vegetables fried with noodles.

Christ n Jesus of Nazareth, regarded by Christians as the Messiah.

christen v baptize; give a name to; Informal use for the first time. **christening** n

Christendom n all Christian people or countries.

Christian n person who believes in and follows Christ. ▶ adj of Christ or Christianity; kind, good.

Christianity n religion based on the life and teachings of Christ.

Christian name personal name given to Christians at baptism; loosely used to mean a person's first name. **Christian Science** religious system which emphasizes spiritual healing.

Christmas n annual festival on Dec. 25 commemorating the birth of Christ; period around this time. **Christmassy** adj **Christmas Day** Dec. 25. **Christmas Eve** Dec. 24. **Christmas tree** evergreen tree or imitation of one, decorated as part of Christmas celebrations.

chromatic adj of colour or colours; Music (of a scale) proceeding by semitones.

chromatography n separation and analysis of the components of a substance by slowly passing it through an adsorbing material.

chromium, chrome n Chem grey metallic element used in steel alloys and for electroplating.

chromosome n microscopic gene-carrying body in the nucleus of a cell.

chronic adj (of an illness) lasting a long time; habitual, e.g. chronic drinking; Brit, Aust & NZ informal of poor quality. **chronically** adv

chronicle n record of events in order of occurrence. ▶ v record in or as if in a chronicle. **chronicler** n

chronology n, pl -gies. arrangement or list of events in order of occurrence. **chronological** adj **chronologically** adv

chronometer n timepiece designed to be accurate in all conditions.

chrysalis [kriss-a-liss] n insect in the stage between larva and adult, when it is in a cocoon.

chrysanthemum n garden flower with a large head made up of thin petals.

chub n European freshwater fish of the carp family.

chubby adj **-bier, -biest.** plump and round.

chuck[1] v Informal throw; Informal give up, reject; touch (someone) affectionately under the chin; Aust & NZ informal vomit.

chuck[2] n cut of beef from the neck to the shoulder; device that holds a workpiece in a lathe or a tool in a drill.

chuckle v laugh softly. ▶ n soft laugh.

chuffed adj informal very pleased.

chug n short dull sound like the noise of an engine. ▶ v **chugging, chugged.** operate or move with this sound.

chukka n period of play in polo.

chum Informal ▶ n close friend. ▶ v **chumming, chummed. chum up with** form a close friendship with. **chummy** adj

chump n Informal stupid person; thick piece of meat.

chunk n thick solid piece; considerable amount. **chunky** adj (of a person) broad and heavy; (of an object) large and thick.

church n building for public Christian worship; particular Christian denomination; (C-) Christians collectively; clergy. **churchgoer** n person who attends church regularly. **churchwarden** n member of a congregation who assists the vicar. **churchyard** n grounds round a church, used as a graveyard.

churlish adj surly and rude.

churn n machine in which cream is shaken to make butter; large container for milk. ▶ v stir (cream) vigorously to make butter; move about violently. **churn out** v Informal produce (things) rapidly in large numbers.

chute¹ [shoot] n steep slope down which things may be slid.

chute² n Informal short for PARACHUTE.

chutney n pickle made from fruit, vinegar, spices, and sugar.

CIA (in the US) Central Intelligence Agency.

cicada [sik-kah-da] n large insect that makes a high-pitched drone.

cicatrix [sik-a-trix] n, pl -trices. scar.

CID (in Britain) Criminal Investigation Department.

cider n alcoholic drink made from fermented apple juice.

cigar n roll of cured tobacco leaves for smoking.

cigarette n thin roll of shredded tobacco in thin paper, for smoking.

cinch [sinch] n Informal easy task.

cinder n piece of material that will not burn, left after burning coal.

cine camera n camera for taking moving pictures.

cinema n place for showing films; films collectively. **cinematic** adj **cinematography** n technique of making films. **cinematographer** n

cineraria n garden plant with daisy-like flowers.

cinnamon n spice obtained from the bark of an Asian tree.

cipher [sife-er] n system of secret writing; unimportant person.

circa [sir-ka] prep Latin approximately, about.

circle n perfectly round geometric figure, line, or shape; group of people sharing an interest or activity; Theatre section of seats above the main level of the auditorium. ▶ v move in a circle (round); enclose in a circle.

circlet n circular ornament worn on the head.

circuit n complete route or course, esp. a circular one; complete path through which an electric current can flow; periodical journey round a district, as made by judges; motor-racing track. **circuitous** [sir-kew-it-uss] adj indirect and lengthy; deliberately indirect. **circuitry** [sir-kit-tree] n electrical circuit(s).

circular adj in the shape of a circle; moving in a circle. ▶ n letter for general distribution. **circularity** n

circulate v send, go, or pass from place to place or person to person. **circulation** n flow of blood around the body; number of copies of a newspaper or magazine sold; sending or moving round. **circulatory** adj

circumcise v remove the foreskin of. **circumcision** n

circumference n boundary of a specified area or shape, esp. of a circle; distance round this.

circumflex n mark (^) over a vowel to show that it is pronounced in a particular way.

circumlocution n indirect way of saying something.

circumnavigate v sail right round. **circumnavigation** n

circumscribe v limit, restrict; draw a line round. **circumscription** n

circumspect adj cautious and careful not to take risks. **circumspectly** adv **circumspection** n

circumstance n (usu. pl) occurrence or condition that accompanies or influences a person or event. **circumstantial** adj (of evidence) strongly suggesting something but not proving it; very detailed.

circumvent v avoid or get round (a rule etc.). **circumvention** n

circus n, pl -cuses. (performance given by) a travelling company of acrobats, clowns, performing animals, etc.

cirrhosis [sir-roh-siss] n serious liver disease, often caused by drinking too much alcohol.

cirrus n, pl **-ri.** high wispy cloud.

cistern n water tank, esp. one that holds water for flushing a toilet.

citadel n fortress in a city.

cite v refer to; bring forward as proof. **citation** n

citizen n native or naturalized member of a state or nation; inhabitant of a city or town. **citizenship** n **Citizens' Band** range of radio frequencies for private communication by the public.

citric acid n weak acid found in citrus fruits.

citrus fruit n juicy sharp-tasting fruit such as an orange or lemon.

city n, pl **-ties.** large or important town. **the City** Brit area of London as a financial centre.

civet [**siv-vit**] n spotted catlike African mammal; musky fluid from its glands used in perfume.

civic adj of a city or citizens. **civics** n study of the rights and responsibilities of citizenship.

civil adj relating to the citizens of a state as opposed to the armed forces or the Church; polite; courteous. **civilly** adv **civility** n polite or courteous behaviour. **civilian** n, adj (person) not belonging to the armed forces. **civil service** service responsible for the administration of the government. **civil servant** member of the civil service. **civil war** war between people of the same country.

civilize v refine or educate (a person); make (a place) more pleasant or more acceptable. **civilization** n high level of human cultural and social development; particular society which has reached this level.

civvies pl n Brit, Aust & NZ slang

ordinary clothes that are not part of a uniform.

clack n sound made by two hard objects striking each other. ▶ v make this sound.

clad v a past of **clothe.**

cladding n material used to cover the outside of a building.

claim v assert as a fact; demand as a right; need, require. ▶ n assertion that something is true; assertion of a right; something claimed as a right. **claimant** n

clairvoyance n power of perceiving things beyond the natural range of the senses. **clairvoyant** n, adj

clam n edible shellfish with a hinged shell. ▶ v **clamming, clammed. clam up** Informal stop talking, esp. through nervousness.

clamber v climb awkwardly.

clammy adj **-mier, -miest.** unpleasantly moist and sticky.

clamour n loud protest; loud persistent noise or outcry. ▶ v make a loud noise or outcry. **clamorous** adj **clamour for** v demand noisily.

clamp n tool with movable jaws for holding things together tightly. ▶ v fasten with a clamp. **clamp down on** v become stricter about; suppress.

clan n group of families with a common ancestor, esp. among Scottish Highlanders; close group. **clannish** adj (of a group) tending to exclude outsiders.

clandestine adj secret and concealed.

clang v make a loud ringing metallic sound. ▶ n ringing metallic sound.

clanger n Informal obvious mistake.

clangour n loud continuous clanging sound.

clank n harsh metallic sound. ▶ v

make such a sound.

clap v **clapping, clapped.** applaud by hitting the palms of one's hands sharply together; put quickly or forcibly. ▸ n act or sound of clapping; sudden loud noise, e.g. a clap of thunder.

clapped out Slang worn out, dilapidated.

clapper n piece of metal inside a bell, which causes it to sound when struck against the side.

clapperboard n pair of hinged boards clapped together during filming to help in synchronizing sound and picture.

claptrap n Informal foolish or pretentious talk.

claret [klar-et] n dry red wine from Bordeaux.

clarify v **-fying, -fied.** make (a matter) clear and unambiguous. **clarification** n

clarinet n keyed woodwind instrument with a single reed. **clarinettist** n

clarion n obsolete high-pitched trumpet; its sound. **clarion call** strong encouragement to do something.

clarity n clearness.

clash v come into conflict; (of events) happen at the same time; (of colours) look unattractive together; (of objects) make a loud harsh sound by being hit together. ▸ n fight, argument; fact of two events happening at the same time.

clasp n device for fastening things; firm grasp or embrace. ▸ v grasp or embrace firmly; fasten with a clasp.

class n group of people sharing a similar social position; system of dividing society into such groups; group of people or things sharing a common characteristic; group of

pupils or students taught together; standard of quality; Informal elegance or excellence, e.g. a touch of class. ▸ v place in a class.

classic adj being a typical example of something; of lasting interest because of excellence; attractive because of simplicity of form. ▸ n author, artist, or work of art of recognized excellence. ▸ pl study of ancient Greek and Roman literature and culture. **classical** adj of or in a restrained conservative style; denoting serious art music; of or influenced by ancient Greek and Roman culture. **classically** adv **classicism** n artistic style showing emotional restraint and regularity of form. **classicist** n

classify v **-fying, -fied.** divide into groups with similar characteristics; declare (information) to be officially secret. **classifiable** adj **classification** n

classy adj **classier, classiest.** Informal stylish and elegant.

clatter v, n (make) a rattling noise.

clause n section of a legal document; part of a sentence, containing a verb.

claustrophobia n abnormal fear of confined spaces. **claustrophobic** adj

clavichord n early keyboard instrument.

clavicle n same as COLLARBONE.

claw n sharp hooked nail of a bird or beast; similar part, such as a crab's pincer. ▸ v tear with claws or nails.

clay n fine-grained earth, soft when moist and hardening when baked, used to make bricks and pottery. **clayey** adj **clay pigeon** baked clay disc hurled into the air as a target for shooting.

claymore n large two-edged sword formerly used by Scottish Highlanders.

clean adj free from dirt or impurities; not yet used; morally acceptable, inoffensive; (of a reputation or record) free from dishonesty or corruption; complete, e.g. a clean break; smooth and regular. ▶ v make (something) free from dirt. ▶ adv Not standard completely, e.g. I clean forgot. **come clean** Informal reveal or admit something. **cleaner** n **cleanly** adv **cleanliness** n

cleanse v make clean. **cleanser** n

clear adj free from doubt or confusion; easy to see or hear; able to be seen through; free of obstruction; (of weather) free from clouds; (of skin) without blemish. ▶ adv out of the way. ▶ v make or become clear; pass by or over (something) without contact; prove (someone) innocent of a crime or mistake; make as profit. **clearly** adv **clearance** n clearing; official permission. **clearing** n treeless area in a wood. **clear off** v Brit, Aust & NZ informal go away. **clear out** v remove and sort the contents of; Brit, Aust & NZ informal go away. **clear-sighted** adj having good judgment. **clearway** n stretch of road on which motorists may stop in an emergency.

cleat n wedge; piece of wood, metal, or plastic with two projecting ends round which ropes are fastened.

cleave¹ v **cleaving, cleft, cleaved** or **clove, cleft, cleaved** or **cloven.** split apart. **cleavage** n space between a woman's breasts, as revealed by a low-cut dress; division, split.

cleave² v cling or stick.

cleaver n butcher's heavy knife with a square blade.

clef n Music symbol at the beginning of a stave to show the pitch.

cleft n narrow opening or crack. ▶ v a past of CLEAVE¹. **in a cleft stick** in a very difficult position.

clematis n climbing plant with large colourful flowers.

clement adj (of weather) mild. **clemency** n kind or lenient treatment.

clementine n small orange citrus fruit.

clench v close or squeeze (one's teeth or fist) tightly; grasp firmly.

clerestory [clear-store-ee] n, pl **-ries.** row of windows at the top of a wall above an adjoining roof.

clergy n priests and ministers as a group. **clergyman** n

cleric n member of the clergy.

clerical adj of clerks or office work; of the clergy.

clerk n employee in an office, bank, or court who keeps records, files, and accounts.

clever adj intelligent, quick at learning; showing skill. **cleverly** adv **cleverness** n

cliché [klee-shay] n expression or idea that is no longer effective because of overuse. **clichéd** adj

click n short sharp sound. ▶ v make this sound; Informal (of two people) get on well together; Informal become suddenly clear; Computers press and release (a button or a mouse); Slang be a success.

client n person who uses the services of a professional person or company. **clientele** [klee-on-**tell**] n clients collectively.

cliff n steep rock face, esp. along the sea shore. **cliffhanger** n film, game, etc., that is tense and exciting because its outcome is uncertain.

climate n typical weather conditions of an area. **climatic** adj

climax n most intense point of an experience, series of events, or story; same as ORGASM. **climactic** adj

climb v go up, ascend; rise to a higher point or intensity. ▶ n climbing; place to be climbed. **climber** n **climb down** v retreat from an opinion or position.

clime n Poetic place or its climate.

clinch v settle (an argument or agreement) decisively. **clincher** n Informal something decisive.

cling v **clinging, clung**. hold tightly or stick closely. **clingfilm** n thin polythene material for wrapping food.

clinic n building where outpatients receive medical treatment or advice; private or specialized hospital. **clinical** adj of a clinic; logical and unemotional. **clinically** adv

clink[1] v, n (make) a light sharp metallic sound.

clink[2] n Brit, Aust & NZ slang prison.

clinker n fused coal left over in a fire or furnace.

clinker-built adj (of a boat) made of overlapping planks.

clip[1] v **clipping, clipped**. cut with shears or scissors; Informal hit sharply. ▶ n short extract of a film; Informal sharp blow. **clippers** pl n tool for clipping. **clipping** n something cut out, esp. an article from a newspaper.

clip[2] n device for attaching or holding things together. ▶ v **clipping, clipped**. attach or hold together with a clip.

clipper n fast commercial sailing ship.

clique [kleek] n small exclusive group.

clitoris [klit-or-iss] n small sexually sensitive organ at the front of the vulva. **clitoral** adj

cloak n loose sleeveless outer garment. ▶ v cover or conceal. **cloakroom** n room where coats may be left temporarily.

clobber[1] v Informal hit; defeat utterly.

clobber[2] n Brit, Aust & NZ informal belongings, esp. clothes.

cloche [klosh] n cover to protect young plants; woman's close-fitting hat.

clock n instrument for showing the time; device with a dial for recording or measuring. **clockwise** adv, adj in the direction in which the hands of a clock rotate. **clock in** or **on, out** or **off** v register arrival at or departure from work on an automatic time recorder. **clock up** v reach (a total). **clockwork** n mechanism similar to the kind in a clock, used in wind-up toys.

clod n lump of earth; Brit, Aust & NZ stupid person.

clog v **clogging, clogged**. obstruct. ▶ n wooden or wooden-soled shoe.

cloister n covered pillared arcade, usu. in a monastery. **cloistered** adj sheltered.

clone n animal or plant produced artificially from the cells of another animal or plant, and identical to the original; Informal person who closely resembles another. ▶ v produce as a clone.

close[1] v [rhymes with **nose**] shut; prevent access to; end, terminate; bring or come nearer together. ▶ n end, conclusion; [rhymes with **dose**] street closed at one end; [rhymes with **dose**] Brit courtyard, quadrangle. **closed shop** place of work in which all workers must belong to a particular trade union.

close² adj [rhymes with **dose**] near; intimate; careful, thorough; compact, dense; oppressive, stifling; secretive. ▶ adv closely, tightly. **closely** adv **closeness** n

close season period when it is illegal to kill certain game or fish.

close shave Informal narrow escape. **close-up** n photograph or film taken at close range.

closet n US cupboard; small private room. ▶ adj private, secret. ▶ v **closeting, closeted**. shut (oneself) away in private.

closure n closing.

clot n soft thick lump formed from liquid; Brit, Aust & NZ informal stupid person. ▶ v **clotting, clotted**. form soft thick lumps.

cloth n (piece of) woven fabric.

clothe v **clothing, clothed** or **clad**. put clothes on; provide with clothes. **clothes** pl n articles of dress; bed coverings. **clothing** n clothes collectively.

cloud n mass of condensed water vapour floating in the sky; floating mass of smoke, dust, etc. ▶ v (foll. by over) become cloudy; confuse; make gloomy or depressed. **cloudless** adj **cloudy** adj having a lot of clouds; (of liquid) not clear. **cloudburst** n heavy fall of rain.

clout Informal ▶ n hard blow; power, influence. ▶ v hit hard.

clove¹ n dried flower bud of a tropical tree, used as a spice.

clove² n segment of a bulb of garlic.

clove³ v a past tense of CLEAVE¹. **clove hitch** knot used to fasten a rope to a spar.

cloven v a past participle of CLEAVE¹. **cloven hoof** divided hoof of a cow, goat, etc.

clover n plant with three-lobed

leaves. **in clover** in luxury.

clown n comic entertainer in a circus; amusing person; stupid person. ▶ v behave foolishly; perform as a clown. **clownish** adj

club n association of people with common interests; building used by such a group; thick stick used as a weapon; stick with a curved end used to hit the ball in golf; playing card with black three-leaved symbols. ▶ v **clubbing, clubbed**. hit with a club. **club together** v combine resources for a common purpose.

club foot n deformity of the foot causing inability to put the foot flat on the ground.

cluck n low clicking noise made by a hen. ▶ v make this noise.

clue n something that helps to solve a mystery or puzzle. **not have a clue** to be completely baffled. **clueless** adj stupid.

clump n small group of things or people; dull heavy tread. ▶ v walk heavily; form into clumps.

clumsy adj **-sier, -siest**. lacking skill or physical coordination; badly made or done. **clumsily** adv **clumsiness** n

clung v past of CLING.

clunk n dull metallic sound. ▶ v make such a sound.

cluster n small close group. ▶ v gather in clusters.

clutch¹ v grasp tightly; (foll. by at) try to get hold of. ▶ n device enabling two revolving shafts to be connected and disconnected, esp. in a motor vehicle; tight grasp.

clutch² n set of eggs laid at the same time.

clutter v scatter objects about (a place) untidily. ▶ n untidy mess.

cm centimetre.

CND Campaign for Nuclear

Disarmament.

CO Commanding Officer.

Co. Company; County.

co- prefix together, joint, or jointly, e.g. coproduction.

c/o care of; Book-keeping carried over.

coach n long-distance bus; railway carriage; large four-wheeled horse-drawn carriage; trainer, instructor. ▸ v train, teach.

coagulate [koh-**ag**-yew-late] v change from a liquid to a semisolid mass. **coagulation** n **coagulant** n substance causing coagulation.

coal n black rock consisting mainly of carbon, used as fuel. **coalfield** n area with coal under the ground.

coalesce [koh-a-**less**] v come together, merge. **coalescence** n

coalition [koh-a-**lish**-un] n temporary alliance, esp. between political parties.

coarse adj rough in texture; unrefined, indecent. **coarsely** adv **coarseness** n **coarsen** v **coarse fish** any freshwater fish not of the salmon family.

coast n place where the land meets the sea. ▸ v move by momentum, without the use of power. **coastal** adj **coaster** n small mat placed under a glass. **coastguard** n organization that aids ships and swimmers in trouble and prevents smuggling; member of this. **coastline** n outline of a coast.

coat n outer garment with long sleeves; animal's fur or hair; covering layer, e.g. a coat of paint. ▸ v cover with a layer. **coating** n covering layer. **coat of arms** heraldic emblem of a family or institution.

coax v persuade gently; obtain by persistent coaxing.

coaxial [koh-**ax**-ee-al] adj (of a cable) transmitting by means of two concentric conductors separated by an insulator.

cob n stalk of an ear of maize; thickset type of horse; round loaf of bread; male swan.

cobalt n Chem brittle silvery-white metallic element.

cobber n Aust & old-fashioned NZ informal friend.

cobble n cobblestone. **cobblestone** n rounded stone used for paving. **cobble together** v put together clumsily.

cobbler n shoe mender.

cobra n venomous hooded snake of Asia and Africa.

cobweb n spider's web.

cocaine n addictive drug used as a narcotic and as an anaesthetic.

coccyx [kok-six] n, pl **coccyges** [kok-**sije**-eez] bone at the base of the spinal column.

cochineal n red dye obtained from a Mexican insect, used for food colouring.

cock n male bird, esp. of domestic fowl; stopcock. ▸ v draw back (the hammer of a gun) to firing position; lift and turn (part of the body). **cockerel** n young domestic cock. **cock-a-hoop** adj Brit, Aust & NZ in high spirits. **cock-and-bull story** highly improbable story.

cockade n feather or rosette worn on a hat as a badge.

cockatoo n crested parrot of Australia or the East Indies.

cocker spaniel n small spaniel.

cockeyed adj Informal crooked, askew; foolish, absurd.

cockie, cocky n, pl **-kies**. Aust & NZ informal farmer.

cockle n edible shellfish.

Cockney n native of the East End of London; London dialect.

cockpit n pilot's compartment in an aircraft; driver's compartment in a racing car.

cockroach n beetle-like insect which is a household pest.

cocksure adj overconfident, arrogant.

cocktail n mixed alcoholic drink; appetizer of seafood or mixed fruits.

cocky adj **cockier, cockiest.** conceited and overconfident. **cockily** adv **cockiness** n

cocoa n powder made from the seed of the cacao tree; drink made from this powder.

coconut n large hard fruit of a type of palm tree; edible flesh of this fruit.

cocoon n silky protective covering of a silkworm; protective covering. ▶ v wrap up tightly for protection.

cod n large food fish of the North Atlantic.

COD cash on delivery.

coda n final part of a musical composition.

coddle v pamper, overprotect.

code n system of letters, symbols, or prearranged signals by which messages can be communicated secretly or briefly; set of principles or rules. ▶ v put into code. **codify** v **-fying, -fied.** organize (rules or procedures) systematically. **codification** n

codeine [kode-een] n drug used as a painkiller.

codex n, pl **codices.** volume of manuscripts of an ancient text.

codger n Brit, Aust & NZ informal old man.

codicil [kode-iss-ill] n addition to a will.

coeducation n education of boys and girls together. **coeducational** adj

coefficient n Maths number or

constant placed before and multiplying a quantity.

coelacanth [seel-a-kanth] n primitive marine fish.

coeliac disease [seel-ee-ak] n disease which hampers digestion of food.

coerce [koh-urss] v compel, force. **coercion** n **coercive** adj

coeval [koh-eev-al] adj, n contemporary.

coexist v exist together, esp. peacefully despite differences. **coexistence** n

C of E Church of England.

coffee n drink made from the roasted and ground seeds of a tropical shrub; beanlike seeds of this shrub. ▶ adj medium-brown. **coffee bar** café, snack bar. **coffee table** small low table.

coffer n chest for valuables. ▶ pl store of money.

coffin n box in which a corpse is buried or cremated.

cog n one of the teeth on the rim of a gearwheel; unimportant person in a big organization.

cogent [koh-jent] adj forcefully convincing. **cogency** n

cogitate [koj-it-tate] v think deeply about. **cogitation** n

cognac [kon-yak] n French brandy.

cognate adj derived from a common original form.

cognition n act or experience of knowing or acquiring knowledge. **cognitive** adj

cognizance n knowledge, understanding. **cognizant** adj

cognoscenti [kon-yo-shen-tee] pl n connoisseurs.

cohabit v live together as husband and wife without being married. **cohabitation** n

cohere v hold or stick together; be logically connected or consistent.

coherent adj logical and

consistent; capable of intelligible speech. **coherence** n **coherently** adv

cohesion n sticking together.

cohesive adj sticking together to form a whole.

cohort n band of associates; tenth part of an ancient Roman legion.

coiffure n hairstyle. **coiffeur, coiffeuse** n hairdresser.

coil v wind in loops; move in a winding course. ▶ n something coiled; single loop of this; coil-shaped contraceptive device inserted in the womb.

coin n piece of metal money; metal currency collectively. ▶ v invent (a word or phrase). **coin it in** Informal earn money quickly.

coinage n coins collectively; word or phrase coined; coining.

coincide v happen at the same time; agree or correspond exactly. **coincidence** n occurrence of simultaneous or apparently connected events; coinciding. **coincident** adj in agreement. **coincidental** adj resulting from coincidence. **coincidentally** adv

coir n coconut fibre, used for matting.

coitus [koh-it-uss], **coition** [koh-ish-un] n sexual intercourse. **coital** adj

coke[1] n solid fuel left after gas has been distilled from coal.

coke[2] n Slang cocaine.

col n high mountain pass.

cola n dark brown fizzy soft drink.

colander n perforated bowl for straining or rinsing foods.

cold adj lacking heat; lacking affection or enthusiasm; (of a colour) giving an impression of coldness; Slang unconscious, e.g. out cold. ▶ n lack of heat; mild illness causing a runny nose, sneezing, and coughing. **coldly**

adv **coldness** n **cold-blooded** adj cruel, unfeeling; having a body temperature that varies according to the surrounding temperature. **cold cream** creamy preparation for softening and cleansing the skin. **cold feet** Slang nervousness, fear. **cold-shoulder** v treat with indifference. **cold war** political hostility between countries without actual warfare.

coleslaw n salad dish of shredded raw cabbage in a dressing.

coley n codlike food fish of the N Atlantic.

colic n severe pains in the stomach and bowels. **colicky** adj

colitis [koh-lie-tiss] n inflammation of the colon.

collaborate v work with another on a project; cooperate with an enemy invader. **collaboration** n **collaborative** adj **collaborator** n

collage [kol-lahzh] n art form in which various materials or objects are glued onto a surface; picture made in this way.

collapse v fall down suddenly; fail completely; fold compactly. ▶ n collapsing; sudden failure or breakdown. **collapsible** adj

collar n part of a garment round the neck; band put round an animal's neck; cut of meat from an animal's neck. ▶ v Brit, Aust & NZ informal seize, arrest; catch in order to speak to. **collarbone** n bone joining the shoulder blade to the breastbone.

collate v gather together, examine, and put in order. **collation** n collating; light meal.

collateral n security pledged for the repayment of a loan.

colleague n fellow worker, esp. in a profession.

collect[1] v gather together; accumulate (stamps etc.) as a hobby; fetch. **collected** adj calm and controlled. **collection** n things collected; collecting; sum of money collected. **collector** n

collect[2] n short prayer.

collective adj of or done by a group. ▶ n group of people working together on an enterprise and sharing the benefits from it. **collectively** adv

colleen n Irish girl.

college n place of higher education; group of people of the same profession or with special duties. **collegiate** adj

collide v crash together violently; have an argument. **collision** n

collie n silky-haired sheepdog.

collier n coal miner; coal ship. **colliery** n, pl **-lieries**. coal mine.

collocate v (of words) occur together regularly. **collocation** n

colloid n suspension of particles in a solution.

colloquial adj suitable for informal speech or writing. **colloquialism** n colloquial word or phrase.

collusion n secret or illegal cooperation. **collude** v act in collusion.

collywobbles pl n Slang nervousness.

cologne n mild perfume.

colon[1] n punctuation mark (:).

colon[2] n part of the large intestine connected to the rectum.

colonel n senior commissioned army or air-force officer.

colonnade n row of columns.

colony n, pl **-nies**. group of people who settle in a new country but remain under the rule of their homeland; territory occupied by a colony; group of people or animals of the same kind living together. **colonial** adj, n (inhabitant) of a colony. **colonialism** n policy of acquiring

and maintaining colonies. **colonist** n settler in a colony. **colonize** v make into a colony. **colonization** n

Colorado beetle n black-and-yellow beetle that is a serious pest of potatoes.

coloration n arrangement of colours.

colossal adj very large.

colossus n, pl **-si, -suses**. huge statue; huge or important person or thing.

colostomy n, pl **-mies**. operation to form an opening from the colon onto the surface of the body, for emptying the bowel.

colour n appearance of things as a result of reflecting light; substance that gives colour; complexion. ▶ pl flag of a country or regiment; Sport badge or symbol denoting membership of a team. ▶ v apply colour to; influence (someone's judgment); blush. **coloured** adj having colour; (**C-**) (in S Africa) of mixed White and non-White parentage. **colourful** adj with bright or varied colours; vivid, distinctive. **colourfully** adv **colourless** adj **colour-blind** adj unable to distinguish between certain colours.

colt n young male horse.

columbine n garden flower with five petals.

column n pillar; vertical division of a newspaper page; regular feature in a newspaper; vertical arrangement of numbers; narrow formation of troops. **columnist** n journalist who writes a regular feature in a newspaper.

coma n state of deep unconsciousness. **comatose** adj in a coma; sound asleep.

comb n toothed implement for arranging the hair; cock's crest;

honeycomb. ▶ v use a comb on; search with great care.

combat n, v **-bating, -bated.** fight, struggle. **combatant** n **combative** adj

combine v join together. ▶ n association of people or firms for a common purpose. **combination** n combining; people or things combined; set of numbers that opens a special lock. ▶ pl Brit old-fashioned undergarment with long sleeves and long legs. **combine harvester** machine that reaps and threshes grain in one process.

combustion n process of burning. **combustible** adj burning easily.

come v **coming, came, come.** move towards a place, arrive; occur; reach a specified point or condition; be produced; (foll. by from) be born in; become, e.g. a dream come true. **come across** v meet or find by accident; (often foll. by as) give an impression of (being). **comeback** n Informal return to a former position; retort. **comedown** n decline in status; disappointment. **comeuppance** n Informal deserved punishment.

comedy n, pl **-dies.** humorous play, film, or programme. **comedian, comedienne** n entertainer who tells jokes; person who performs in comedy.

comely adj **-lier, -liest.** Old-fashioned nice-looking.

comestibles pl n Formal food.

comet n heavenly body with a long luminous tail.

comfit n Old-fashioned sugar-coated sweet.

comfort n physical ease or wellbeing; consolation; means of consolation. ▶ v soothe, console. **comfortable** adj giving comfort; free from pain; Informal well-off

financially. **comfortably** adv **comforter** n

comfrey n tall plant with bell-shaped flowers.

comfy adj **-fier, -fiest.** Informal comfortable.

comic adj humorous, funny; of comedy. ▶ n comedian; magazine containing strip cartoons. **comical** adj amusing. **comically** adv

comma n punctuation mark (,).

command v order; have authority over; deserve and get; look down over. ▶ n authoritative instruction that something must be done; authority to command; knowledge; military or naval unit with a specific function. **commandant** n officer commanding a military group. **commandeer** v seize for military use. **commandment** n command from God.

commander n military officer in command of a group or operation; middle-ranking naval officer. **commander-in-chief** n, pl **commanders-in-chief.** supreme commander of a nation's armed forces.

commando n, pl **-dos, -does.** (member of) a military unit trained for swift raids in enemy territory.

commemorate v honour the memory of. **commemoration** n **commemorative** adj

commence v begin. **commencement** n

commend v praise; recommend. **commendable** adj **commendably** adv **commendation** n

commensurable adj measurable by the same standards. **commensurate** adj corresponding in degree, size, or value.

comment n remark; talk, gossip; explanatory note. ▶ v make a comment. **commentary** n, pl **-taries.** spoken accompaniment to a broadcast or film; explanatory notes. **commentate** v provide a commentary. **commentator** n

commerce n buying and selling, trade. **commercial** adj of commerce; (of television or radio) paid for by advertisers; having profit as the main aim. ▸ n television or radio advertisement. **commercialize** v make commercial. **commercialization** n

commiserate v (foll. by with) express sympathy (for). **commiseration** n

commissar n (formerly) official responsible for political education in Communist countries.

commissariat n Brit, Aust & NZ military department in charge of food supplies.

commission n piece of work that an artist is asked to do; duty, task; percentage paid to a salesperson for each sale made; group of people appointed to perform certain duties; committing of a crime; Mil rank or authority officially given to an officer. ▸ v place an order for; Mil give a commission to; grant authority to. **out of commission** not in working order. **commissioner** n appointed official in a government department; member of a commission.

commissionaire n uniformed doorman at a hotel, theatre, etc.

commit v -mitting, -mitted. perform (a crime or error); pledge (oneself) to a course of action; send (someone) to prison or hospital. **committal** n sending someone to prison or hospital. **commitment** n dedication to a cause; responsibility that restricts freedom of action.

committee n group of people appointed to perform a specified service or function.

commode n seat with a hinged flap concealing a chamber pot; chest of drawers.

commodious adj roomy.

commodity n, pl -ities. something that can be bought or sold.

commodore n senior commissioned officer in the navy.

common adj occurring often; belonging to two or more people; public, general; lacking in taste or manners. ▸ n area of grassy land belonging to a community. **House of Commons, the Commons** lower chamber of the British parliament. **commonly** adv **commoner** n person who does not belong to the nobility. **common-law** adj (of a relationship) regarded as a marriage through being long-standing. **Common Market** former name for EUROPEAN UNION. **commonplace** adj ordinary, everyday. ▸ n trite remark. **common sense** good practical understanding.

commonwealth n state or nation viewed politically; (C-) association of independent states that used to be ruled by Britain.

commotion n noisy disturbance.

commune[1] n group of people who live together and share everything. **communal** adj shared. **communally** adv

commune[2] v (foll. by with) feel very close (to), e.g. communing with nature. **communion** n sharing of thoughts or feelings; (C-) Christian ritual of sharing consecrated bread and wine; religious group with shared beliefs and practices.

communicate v make known or

share (information, thoughts, or feelings). **communicable** adj (of a disease) able to be passed on. **communicant** n person who receives Communion. **communicating** adj (of a door) joining two rooms. **communication** n communicating; thing communicated. ▶ pl means of travelling or sending messages. **communicative** adj talking freely.

communiqué [kom-mune-ik-kay] n official announcement.

communism n belief that all property and means of production should be shared by the community; (C-) system of state control of the economy and society in some countries. **communist** n, adj

community n, pl -ties. all the people living in one district; group with shared origins or interests; the public, society. **community centre** building used by a community for activities.

commute v travel daily to and from work; reduce (a sentence) to a less severe one. **commutator** n device used to change alternating electric current into direct current. **commuter** n person who commutes to and from work.

compact[1] adj closely packed; neatly arranged; concise, brief. ▶ n small flat case containing a mirror and face powder. ▶ v pack closely together. **compactly** adv **compactness** n **compact disc** small digital audio disc on which the sound is read by an optical laser system.

compact[2] n contract, agreement.

companion n person who associates with or accompanies someone. **companionable** adj friendly. **companionship** n **companionway** n ladder linking

the decks of a ship.

company n, pl -nies. business organization; group of actors; fact of being with someone; guest or guests.

compare v examine (things) and point out the resemblances or differences; (foll. by to) declare to be (like); (foll. by with) be worthy of comparison. **comparable** adj **comparability** n **comparative** adj relative; involving comparison; Grammar denoting the form of an adjective or adverb indicating more. ▶ n Grammar comparative form of a word. **comparatively** adv **comparison** n comparing; similarity or equivalence.

compartment n section of a railway carriage; separate section.

compass n instrument for showing direction, with a needle that points north; limits, range. ▶ pl hinged instrument for drawing circles.

compassion n pity, sympathy. **compassionate** adj

compatible adj able to exist, work, or be used together. **compatibility** n

compatriot n fellow countryman or countrywoman.

compel v -pelling, -pelled. force (to be or do).

compendium n, pl -diums, -dia. selection of board games in one box. **compendious** adj brief but comprehensive.

compensate v make amends to (someone), esp. for injury or loss; (foll. by for) cancel out (a bad effect). **compensation** n payment to make up for loss or injury. **compensatory** adj

compere n person who presents a stage, radio, or television show. ▶ v be the compere of.

compete v try to win or achieve (a

prize, profit, etc.). **competition** n competing; event in which people compete; people against whom one competes. **competitive** adj **competitor** n

competent adj having the skill or knowledge to do something well. **competently** adv **competence** n

compile v collect and arrange (information), esp. to make a book. **compilation** n **compiler** n

complacent adj self-satisfied. **complacently** adv **complacency** n

complain v express resentment or displeasure; (foll. by of) say that one is suffering from (an illness). **complaint** n complaining; mild illness. **complainant** n Law plaintiff.

complaisant [kom-**play**-zant] adj willing to please. **complaisance** n

complement n thing that completes something; complete amount or number; Grammar word or words added to a verb to complete the meaning. ▶ v make complete. **complementary** adj

complete adj thorough, absolute; finished; having all the necessary parts. ▶ v finish; make whole or perfect. **completely** adv **completeness** n **completion** n finishing.

complex adj made up of parts; complicated. ▶ n whole made up of parts; group of unconscious feelings that influences behaviour. **complexity** n

complexion n skin of the face; character, nature.

compliance n complying; tendency to do what others want. **compliant** adj

complicate v make or become complex or difficult to deal with. **complication** n

complicity n fact of being an accomplice in a crime.

compliment n expression of praise. ▶ pl formal greetings. ▶ v praise. **complimentary** adj expressing praise; free of charge.

compline n last service of the day in the Roman Catholic Church.

comply v -plying, -plied. (foll. by with) act in accordance (with).

component n, adj (being) part of a whole.

comport v Formal behave (oneself) in a specified way.

compose v put together; be the component parts of; create (a piece of music or writing); calm (oneself); arrange artistically. **composer** n person who writes music.

composite n, adj (something) made up of separate parts.

composition n way that something is put together or arranged; work of art, esp. a musical one; essay; composing.

compositor n person who arranges type for printing.

compos mentis adj Latin sane.

compost n decayed plants used as a fertilizer.

composure n calmness.

compote n fruit stewed with sugar.

compound[1] n, adj (thing, esp. chemical) made up of two or more combined parts or elements. ▶ v combine or make by combining; intensify, make worse.

compound[2] n fenced enclosure containing buildings.

comprehend v understand. **comprehensible** adj **comprehension** n **comprehensive** adj of broad scope, fully inclusive. ▶ n Brit comprehensive school.

comprehensive school Brit secondary school for children of all abilities.

compress v [kum-**press**] squeeze together; make shorter. ▶ n [kom-press] pad applied to stop bleeding or cool inflammation.

compression n **compressor** n machine that compresses gas or air.

comprise v be made up of or make up.

compromise [kom-prom-mize] n settlement reached by concessions on each side. ▶ v settle a dispute by making concessions; put in a dishonourable position.

comptroller n (in titles) financial controller.

compulsion n irresistible urge; forcing by threats or violence. **compulsive** adj **compulsively** adv **compulsory** adj required by rules or laws.

compunction n feeling of guilt or shame.

compute v calculate, esp. using a computer. **computation** n

computer n electronic machine that stores and processes data. **computerize** v adapt (a system) to be handled by computer; store or process in a computer. **computerization** n

comrade n fellow member of a union or socialist political party; companion. **comradeship** n

con[1] Informal ▶ n short for CONFIDENCE TRICK. ▶ v conning, conned. deceive, swindle.

con[2] n pros and cons see PRO[1].

concatenation n series of linked events.

concave adj curving inwards.

conceal v cover and hide; keep secret. **concealment** n

concede v admit to be true; acknowledge defeat in a (contest or argument); grant as a right.

conceit n too high an opinion of oneself; far-fetched or clever comparison. **conceited** adj

conceive v imagine, think; form in

the mind; become pregnant.

conceivable adj imaginable, possible. **conceivably** adv

concentrate v fix one's attention or efforts on something; bring or come together in large numbers in one place; make (a liquid) stronger by removing water from it. ▶ n concentrated liquid.

concentration n concentrating; proportion of a substance in a mixture or solution.

concentration camp prison camp for civilian prisoners, esp. in Nazi Germany.

concentric adj having the same centre.

concept n abstract or general idea. **conceptual** adj of or based on concepts. **conceptualize** v form a concept of.

conception n general idea; becoming pregnant.

concern n anxiety, worry; something that is of importance to someone; business, firm. ▶ v worry (someone); involve (oneself); be relevant or important to. **concerned** adj interested, involved; anxious, worried. **concerning** prep about, regarding.

concert n musical entertainment. **in concert** working together; (of musicians) performing live. **concerted** adj done together.

concertina n small musical instrument similar to an accordion. ▶ v -naing, -naed. collapse or fold up like a concertina.

concerto [kon-chair-toe] n, pl -tos, -ti. large-scale composition for a solo instrument and orchestra.

concession n grant of rights, land, or property; reduction in price for a specified category of people; conceding; thing conceded. **concessionary** adj

conch n shellfish with a large spiral shell; its shell.

concierge [kon-see-airzh] n (in France) caretaker in a block of flats.

conciliate v try to end a disagreement (with). **conciliation** n **conciliator** n

conciliatory adj intended to end a disagreement.

concise adj brief and to the point. **concisely** adv **concision**, **conciseness** n

conclave n secret meeting; private meeting of cardinals to elect a new pope.

conclude v decide by reasoning; end, finish; arrange or settle finally. **conclusion** n decision based on reasoning; ending; final arrangement or settlement. **conclusive** adj ending doubt, convincing. **conclusively** adv

concoct v make up (a story or plan); make by combining ingredients. **concoction** n

concomitant adj existing along with something else.

concord n state of peaceful agreement, harmony. **concordance** n similarity or consistency; index of words in a book. **concordant** adj agreeing.

concourse n large open public place where people can gather; large crowd.

concrete n mixture of cement, sand, stone, and water, used in building. ▶ adj made of concrete; particular, specific; real or solid, not abstract.

concubine [kon-kew-bine] n Hist woman living in a man's house but not married to him and kept for his sexual pleasure.

concupiscence [kon-kew-piss-enss] n Formal lust.

concur v -curring, -curred. agree. **concurrence** n **concurrent** adj

happening at the same time or place. **concurrently** adv at the same time.

concussion n period of unconsciousness caused by a blow to the head. **concussed** adj having concussion.

condemn v express disapproval of; sentence, e.g. he was condemned to death; force into an unpleasant situation; declare unfit for use. **condemnation** n **condemnatory** adj

condense v make shorter; turn from gas into liquid. **condensation** n **condenser** n Electricity capacitor.

condescend v behave patronizingly towards someone; agree to do something, but as if doing someone a favour. **condescension** n

condiment n seasoning for food, such as salt or pepper.

condition n particular state of being; necessary requirement for something else to happen; restriction, qualification; state of health, physical fitness; medical problem. ▶ pl circumstances. ▶ v train or influence to behave in a particular way; treat with conditioner; control. **on condition that** only if. **conditional** adj depending on circumstances. **conditioner** n thick liquid used when washing to make hair or clothes feel softer.

condolence n sympathy. ▶ pl expression of sympathy.

condom n rubber sheath worn on the penis or in the vagina during sexual intercourse to prevent conception or infection.

condominium n Aust, US & Canadian block of flats in which each flat is owned by the occupant.

condone v overlook or forgive (wrongdoing).

condor n large vulture of S America.

conducive adj (foll. by to) likely to lead (to).

conduct n management of an activity; behaviour. ▶ v carry out (a task); behave (oneself); direct (musicians) by moving the hands or a baton; lead, guide; transmit (heat or electricity). **conduction** n transmission of heat or electricity. **conductivity** n ability to transmit heat or electricity. **conductive** adj **conductor** n person who conducts musicians; (fem **conductress**) official on a bus who collects fares; something that conducts heat or electricity.

conduit [kon-dew-it] n channel or tube for fluid or cables.

cone n object with a circular base, tapering to a point; cone-shaped ice-cream wafer; Brit, Aust & NZ plastic cone used as a traffic marker on the roads; scaly fruit of a conifer tree.

coney n same as CONY.

confab n Informal conversation (also **confabulation**).

confection n any sweet food; Old-fashioned elaborate article of clothing. **confectioner** n maker or seller of confectionery. **confectionery** n sweets.

confederate n member of a confederacy; accomplice. ▶ adj united, allied. ▶ v unite in a confederacy. **confederacy** n, pl **-cies.** union of states or people for a common purpose. **confederation** n alliance of political units.

confer v -**ferring, -ferred.** discuss together; grant, give. **conferment** n granting, giving.

conference n meeting for discussion.

confess v admit (a fault or crime); admit to be true; declare (one's sins) to God or a priest, in hope of forgiveness. **confession** n something confessed; confessing. **confessional** n small stall in which a priest hears confessions. **confessor** n priest who hears confessions.

confetti n small pieces of coloured paper thrown at weddings.

confidant n person confided in. **confidante** n fem

confide v tell someone (a secret); entrust.

confidence n trust; self-assurance; something confided. **confidence trick** swindle involving gaining a person's trust in order to cheat him or her. **in confidence** as a secret.

confident adj sure, esp. of oneself. **confidently** adv **confidential** adj private, secret; entrusted with someone's secret affairs. **confidentially** adv **confidentiality** n

configuration n arrangement of parts.

confine v keep within bounds; restrict the free movement of. **confines** pl n boundaries, limits. **confinement** n being confined; period of childbirth.

confirm v prove to be true; reaffirm, strengthen; administer the rite of confirmation to. **confirmation** n confirming; something that confirms; Christianity rite that admits a baptized person to full church membership. **confirmed** adj firmly established in a habit or condition.

confiscate v seize (property) by authority. **confiscation** n

conflagration n large destructive fire.

conflate v combine or blend into a whole. **conflation** n

conflict n disagreement; struggle or fight. ▶ v be incompatible.

confluence n place where two rivers join.

conform v comply with accepted standards or customs; (foll. by to or with) be like or in accordance with. **conformist** n, adj (person) complying with accepted standards or customs. **conformity** n compliance with accepted standards or customs.

confound v astound, bewilder; confuse. **confounded** adj Old-fashioned damned.

confront v come face to face with. **confrontation** n serious argument.

confuse v mix up; perplex, disconcert; make unclear. **confusion** n

confute v prove wrong.

conga n dance performed by a number of people in single file; large single-headed drum played with the hands.

congeal v (of a liquid) become thick and sticky.

congenial adj pleasant, agreeable; having similar interests and attitudes. **congeniality** n

congenital adj (of a condition) existing from birth. **congenitally** adv

conger n large sea eel.

congested adj crowded to excess. **congestion** n

conglomerate n large corporation made up of many companies; thing made up of several different elements. ▶ v form into a mass. ▶ adj made up of several different elements. **conglomeration** n

congratulate v express one's pleasure to (someone) at his or her good fortune or success. **congratulations** pl n, interj **congratulatory** adj

congregate v gather together in a crowd. **congregation** n people who attend a church.

congregational adj **Congregationalism** n Protestant denomination in which each church is self-governing. **Congregationalist** adj, n

congress n formal meeting for discussion; (C-) federal parliament of the US. **congressional** adj **Congressman, Congresswoman** n member of Congress.

congruent adj similar, corresponding; Geom identical in shape and size. **congruence** n

conical adj cone-shaped.

conifer n cone-bearing tree, such as the fir or pine. **coniferous** adj

conjecture n, v guess. **conjectural** adj

conjugal adj of marriage.

conjugate v give the inflections of (a verb). **conjugation** n complete set of inflections of a verb.

conjunction n combination; simultaneous occurrence of events; part of speech joining words, phrases, or clauses.

conjunctivitis n inflammation of the membrane covering the eyeball and inner eyelid. **conjunctiva** n this membrane.

conjure v perform tricks that appear to be magic. **conjuror** n **conjure up** v produce as if by magic.

conk n Brit, Aust & NZ slang nose.

conker n Informal nut of the horse chestnut.

conk out v Informal (of a machine) break down.

connect v join together; associate in the mind. **connection, connexion** n relationship, association; link or bond; opportunity to transfer from one public vehicle to another; influential acquaintance. **connective** adj

conning tower n raised observation tower containing the periscope on a submarine.

connive v (foll. by at) allow (wrongdoing) by ignoring it; conspire. **connivance** n

connoisseur [kon-noss-**sir**] n person with special knowledge of the arts, food, or drink.

connotation n associated idea conveyed by a word. **connote** v

connubial adj Formal of marriage.

conquer v defeat; overcome (a difficulty); take (a place) by force. **conqueror** n **conquest** n conquering; person or thing conquered.

conscience n sense of right or wrong as regards thoughts and actions.

conscientious adj painstaking. **conscientiously** adv **conscientious objector** person who refuses to serve in the armed forces on moral or religious grounds.

conscious adj alert and awake; aware; deliberate, intentional. **consciously** adv **consciousness** n

conscript n person enrolled for compulsory military service. ▶ v enrol (someone) for compulsory military service. **conscription** n

consecrate v make sacred; dedicate to a specific purpose. **consecration** n

consecutive adj in unbroken succession. **consecutively** adv

consensus n general agreement.

consent n agreement, permission. ▶ v (foll. by to) permit, agree to. **consequence** n result, effect; importance. **consequent** adj

resulting. **consequently** adv as a result, therefore. **consequential** adj important.

conservative adj opposing change; moderate, cautious; conventional in style; (C-) of the Conservative Party, the British right-wing political party which believes in private enterprise and capitalism. ▶ n conservative person; (C-) supporter or member of the Conservative Party. **conservatism** n

conservatoire [kon-**serv**-a-twahr] n school of music.

conservatory n, pl **-ries.** room with glass walls and a glass roof, attached to a house; Chiefly US conservatoire.

conserve v protect from harm, decay, or loss; preserve (fruit) with sugar. ▶ n jam containing large pieces of fruit. **conservancy** n environmental conservation. **conservation** n protection of natural resources and the environment; conserving. **conservationist** n

consider v regard as; think about; be considerate of; discuss; look at. **considerable** adj large in amount or degree. **considerably** adv **considerate** adj thoughtful towards others. **considerately** adv **consideration** n careful thought; fact that should be considered; thoughtfulness; payment for a service. **considering** prep taking a (specified fact) into account.

consign v put somewhere; send (goods). **consignment** n shipment of goods.

consist v **consist of** be made up of. **consist in** have as its main or only feature.

consistent adj unchanging, constant; (foll. by with) in

agreement. **consistently** adv
consistency n, pl **-cies.** being
consistent; degree of thickness or
smoothness.

console[1] v comfort in distress.
consolation n consoling; person
or thing that consoles.

console[2] n panel of controls for
electronic equipment; cabinet for
a television or audio equipment;
ornamental wall bracket; part of
an organ containing the pedals,
stops, and keys.

consolidate v make or become
stronger or more stable; combine
into a whole. **consolidation** n

consommé [kon-**som**-may] n thin
clear meat soup.

consonant n speech sound made
by partially or completely blocking
the breath stream, such as b or f;
letter representing this. ▶ adj (foll.
by with) agreeing (with).
consonance n agreement,
harmony.

consort v (foll. by with) keep
company (with). ▶ n husband or
wife of a monarch.

consortium n, pl **-tia.** association
of business firms.

conspectus n Formal survey or
summary.

conspicuous adj clearly visible;
noteworthy, striking.
conspicuously adv

conspire v plan a crime together
in secret; act together as if by
design. **conspiracy** n conspiring;
(pl **-cies**) plan made by conspiring.
conspirator n **conspiratorial** adj

constable n police officer of the
lowest rank. **constabulary** n, pl
-laries. police force of an area.

constant adj continuous;
unchanging; faithful. ▶ n
unvarying quantity; something
that stays the same. **constantly**
adv **constancy** n

constellation n group of stars.

consternation n anxiety or dismay.

constipation n difficulty in
defecating. **constipated** adj
having constipation.

constituent n member of a
constituency; component part.
▶ adj forming part of a whole.
constituency n, pl **-cies.** area
represented by a Member of
Parliament; voters in such an area.

constitute v form, make up.

constitution n principles on which
a state is governed; physical
condition; structure.
constitutional adj of a
constitution; in accordance with a
political constitution. ▶ n walk
taken for exercise.
constitutionally adv

constrain v compel, force; limit,
restrict. **constraint** n

constrict v make narrower by
squeezing. **constriction** n
constrictive adj **constrictor** n
large snake that squeezes its prey
to death; muscle that compresses
an organ.

construct v build or put together.
construction n constructing; thing
constructed; interpretation;
Grammar way in which words are
arranged in a sentence, clause, or
phrase. **constructive** adj (of
advice, criticism, etc.) useful and
helpful. **constructively** adv

construe v **-struing, -strued.**
interpret.

consul n official representing a
state in a foreign country; one of
the two chief magistrates in
ancient Rome. **consular** adj
consulate n workplace or position
of a consul. **consulship** n

consult v go to for advice or
information. **consultant** n
specialist doctor with a senior
position in a hospital; specialist

who gives professional advice.
consultancy n, pl **-cies.** work or
position of a consultant.
consultation n (meeting for)
consulting. **consultative** adj
giving advice.
consume v eat or drink; use up;
destroy; obsess. **consumption** n
amount consumed; consuming;
Old-fashioned tuberculosis.
consumptive n, adj Old-fashioned
(person) having tuberculosis.
consumer n person who buys
goods or uses services.
consummate [kon-**sum**-mate] v
make (a marriage) legal by sexual
intercourse; complete or fulfil.
▶ adj [kon-**sum**-mit] supremely
skilled; complete, extreme.
consummation n
cont. continued.
contact n communicating;
touching; useful acquaintance;
connection between two electrical
conductors in a circuit. ▶ v get in
touch with. **contact lens** lens
placed on the eyeball to correct
defective vision.
contagion n passing on of disease
by contact; disease spread by
contact; spreading of a harmful
influence. **contagious** adj
spreading by contact, catching.
contain v hold or be capable of
holding; consist of; control,
restrain. **container** n object used
to hold or store things in; large
standard-sized box for
transporting cargo by truck or
ship. **containment** n prevention
of the spread of something
harmful.
contaminate v make impure,
pollute; make radioactive.
contaminant n contaminating
substance. **contamination** n
contemplate v think deeply;
consider as a possibility; gaze at.

contemplation n **contemplative**
adj
contemporary adj present-day,
modern; living or occurring at the
same time. ▶ n, pl **-raries.** person
or thing living or occurring at the
same time as another.
contemporaneous adj happening
at the same time.
contempt n dislike and disregard;
open disrespect for the authority
of a court. **contemptible** adj
deserving contempt.
contemptuous adj showing
contempt. **contemptuously** adv
contend v (foll. by with) deal with;
state, assert; compete.
contender n competitor, esp. a
strong one.
content[1] n meaning or substance
of a piece of writing; amount of a
substance in a mixture. ▶ pl what
something contains; list of
chapters at the front of a book.
content[2] adj satisfied with things
as they are. ▶ v make (someone)
content. ▶ n happiness and
satisfaction. **contented** adj
contentment n
contention n disagreement or
dispute; point asserted in
argument. **contentious** adj
causing disagreement;
quarrelsome.
contest n competition or struggle.
▶ v dispute, object to; fight or
compete for. **contestant** n
context n circumstances of an
event or fact; words before and
after a word or sentence that help
make its meaning clear.
contextual adj
contiguous adj very near or
touching.
continent[1] n one of the earth's
large masses of land. **the
Continent** mainland of Europe.
continental adj **continental**

breakfast light breakfast of coffee and rolls.

continent[2] adj able to control one's bladder and bowels; sexually restrained. **continence** n

contingent n group of people that represents or is part of a larger group. ▶ adj (foll. by on) dependent on (something uncertain). **contingency** n, pl **-cies.** something that may happen.

continue v **-tinuing, -tinued.** (cause to) remain in a condition or place; carry on (doing something); resume. **continual** adj constant; recurring frequently. **continually** adv **continuance** n continuing. **continuation** n continuing; part added. **continuity** n, pl smooth development or sequence. **continuous** adj continuing uninterrupted. **continuously** adv

continuo n, pl **-tinuos.** Music continuous bass part, usu. played on a keyboard instrument.

continuum n, pl **-tinua, -tinuums.** continuous series.

contort v twist out of shape. **contortion** n **contortionist** n performer who contorts his or her body to entertain.

contour n outline; (also **contour line**) line on a map joining places of the same height.

contra- prefix against or contrasting, e.g. contraflow.

contraband n, adj smuggled (goods).

contraception n prevention of pregnancy by artificial means. **contraceptive** n device used or pill taken to prevent pregnancy. ▶ adj preventing pregnancy.

contract n (document setting out) a formal agreement. ▶ v make a formal agreement (to do something); make or become smaller or shorter; catch (an illness). **contraction** n **contractor** n firm that supplies materials or labour. **contractual** adj

contradict v declare the opposite of (a statement) to be true; be at variance with. **contradiction** n **contradictory** adj

contraflow n flow of traffic going alongside but in an opposite direction to the usual flow.

contralto n, pl **-tos.** (singer with) the lowest female voice.

contraption n strange-looking device.

contrapuntal adj Music of or in counterpoint.

contrary n complete opposite. ▶ adj opposed, completely different; perverse, obstinate. ▶ adv in opposition. **contrarily** adv **contrariness** n **contrariwise** adv

contrast n obvious difference; person or thing very different from another. ▶ v compare in order to show differences; (foll. by with) be very different (from).

contravene v break (a rule or law). **contravention** n

contretemps [kon-tra-tahn] n, pl **-temps.** embarrassing minor disagreement.

contribute v give for a common purpose or fund; (foll. by to) be partly responsible (for). **contribution** n **contributor** n **contributory** adj

contrite adj sorry and apologetic. **contritely** adv **contrition** n

contrive v make happen; devise or construct. **contrivance** n device; plan; contriving. **contrived** adj planned or artificial.

control n power to direct something; curb or check. ▶ pl instruments used to operate a machine. ▶ v **-trolling, -trolled.** have power over; limit, restrain;

regulate, operate. **controllable** adj **controller** n

controversy n, pl **-sies.** fierce argument or debate. **controversial** adj causing controversy.

contumely [kon-tume-mill-ee] n Lit scornful or insulting treatment.

contusion n Formal bruise.

conundrum n riddle.

conurbation n large urban area formed by the growth and merging of towns.

convalesce v recover after an illness or operation. **convalescence** n **convalescent** n, adj

convection n transmission of heat in liquids or gases by the circulation of currents. **convector** n heater that gives out hot air.

convene v gather or summon for a formal meeting. **convener, convenor** n person who calls a meeting.

convenient adj suitable or opportune; easy to use; nearby. **conveniently** adv **convenience** n quality of being convenient; useful object; Euphemistic public toilet.

convent n building where nuns live; school run by nuns.

convention n widely accepted view of proper behaviour; assembly or meeting; formal agreement. **conventional** adj (unthinkingly) following the accepted customs; customary; (of weapons or warfare) not nuclear. **conventionally** adv **conventionality** n

converge v meet or join. **convergence** n

conversant adj **conversant with** having knowledge or experience of.

conversation n informal talk. **conversational** adj

conversationalist n person with a specified ability at conversation.

converse[1] v have a conversation.

converse[2] adj, n opposite or contrary. **conversely** adv

convert v change in form, character, or function; cause to change in opinion or belief. ▶ n person who has converted to a different belief or religion. **conversion** n (thing resulting from) converting; Rugby score made after a try by kicking the ball over the crossbar.

convertible adj capable of being converted. ▶ n car with a folding or removable roof.

convex adj curving outwards.

convey v communicate (information); carry, transport. **conveyance** n Old-fashioned vehicle; transfer of the legal title to property. **conveyancing** n branch of law dealing with the transfer of ownership of property. **conveyor belt** continuous moving belt for transporting things, esp. in a factory.

convict v declare guilty. ▶ n person serving a prison sentence. **conviction** n firm belief; instance of being convicted.

convince v persuade by argument or evidence. **convincing** adj **convincingly** adv

convivial adj sociable, lively. **conviviality** n

convocation n calling together; large formal meeting. **convoke** v call together.

convoluted adj coiled, twisted; (of an argument or sentence) complex and hard to understand. **convolution** n

convolvulus n twining plant with funnel-shaped flowers.

convoy n group of vehicles or ships travelling together.

convulse v (of part of the body) undergo violent spasms; *Informal* (be) overcome with laughter. **convulsion** n violent muscular spasm. ▶ *pl* uncontrollable laughter. **convulsive** *adj*

cony n, *pl* **conies** *Brit* rabbit; rabbit fur.

coo v **cooing, cooed.** (of a dove or pigeon) make a soft murmuring sound.

cooee *interj Brit, Aust & NZ* call to attract attention.

cook v prepare (food) by heating; (of food) be cooked. ▶ n person who cooks food. **cook the books** falsify accounts. **cooker** n *Chiefly Brit* apparatus for cooking heated by gas or electricity; *Chiefly Brit* apple suitable for cooking. **cookery** n art of cooking. **cookie** n *US* biscuit. **cook up** v *Informal* devise (a story or scheme).

cool *adj* moderately cold; calm and unemotional; indifferent or unfriendly; *Informal* sophisticated or excellent; *Informal* (of a large sum of money) without exaggeration, e.g. *a cool million.* ▶ v make or become cool. ▶ n coolness; *Slang* calmness, composure. **coolly** *adv* **coolness** n **coolant** n fluid used to cool machinery while it is working. **cool drink** *S Afr* nonalcoholic drink. **cooler** n container for making or keeping things cool.

coolibah n Australian eucalypt that grows beside rivers.

coomb, coombe n *S English* short valley or deep hollow.

coop¹ n cage or pen for poultry. **coop up** v confine in a restricted place.

coop² [koh-op] n *Brit, US & Aust* (shop run by) a cooperative society.

cooper n person who makes or repairs barrels.

cooperate v work or act together. **cooperation** n **cooperative** *adj* willing to cooperate; (of an enterprise) owned and managed collectively. ▶ n cooperative organization.

coopt [koh-opt] v add (someone) to a group by the agreement of the existing members.

coordinate v bring together and cause to work together efficiently. ▶ n *Maths* any of a set of numbers defining the location of a point. ▶ *pl* clothes designed to be worn together. **coordination** n **coordinator** n

coot n small black water bird.

cop *Slang* ▶ n policeman. ▶ v **copping, copped.** take or seize. **cop it** get into trouble or be punished. **cop out** v avoid taking responsibility or committing oneself.

cope¹ v (often foll. by *with*) deal successfully (with).

cope² n large ceremonial cloak worn by some Christian priests.

coping n sloping top row of a wall.

copious [kope-ee-uss] *adj* abundant, plentiful. **copiously** *adv*

copper¹ n soft reddish-brown metal; copper or bronze coin. **copper-bottomed** *adj* financially reliable. **copperplate** n fine handwriting style.

copper² n *Brit slang* policeman.

coppice, copse n small group of trees growing close together.

copra n dried oil-yielding kernel of the coconut.

copulate v have sexual intercourse. **copulation** n

copy n, *pl* **copies.** thing made to look exactly like another; single specimen of a book etc.; material for printing. ▶ v **copying, copied.** make a copy of; act or try to be like. **copyright** n exclusive legal right to reproduce and control a book, work of art, etc. ▶ v take out a copyright on. ▶ adj protected by copyright.

copywriter n person who writes advertising copy.

coquette n woman who flirts. **coquettish** adj

coracle n small round boat of wicker covered with skins.

coral n hard substance formed from the skeletons of very small sea animals. ▶ adj orange-pink.

cor anglais n, pl **cors anglais.** woodwind instrument similar to the oboe.

cord n thin rope or thick string; cordlike structure in the body; corduroy. ▶ pl corduroy trousers.

cordial adj warm and friendly. ▶ n drink with a fruit base. **cordially** adv **cordiality** n

cordite n explosive used in guns and bombs.

cordon n chain of police, soldiers, etc., guarding an area. **cordon off** v form a cordon round.

cordon bleu [bluh] adj (of cookery or cooks) of the highest standard.

corduroy n cotton fabric with a velvety ribbed surface.

core n central part of certain fruits, containing the seeds; central or essential part. ▶ v remove the core from.

co-respondent n Brit, Aust & NZ person with whom someone being sued for divorce is claimed to have committed adultery.

corgi n short-legged sturdy dog.

coriander n plant grown for its aromatic seeds and leaves.

cork n thick light bark of a Mediterranean oak; piece of this used as a stopper. ▶ v seal with a cork. **corkage** n restaurant's charge for serving wine bought

elsewhere. **corkscrew** n spiral metal tool for pulling corks from bottles.

corm n bulblike underground stem of certain plants.

cormorant n large dark-coloured long-necked sea bird.

corn[1] n cereal plant such as wheat or oats; grain of such plants; US, Canadian, Aust & NZ maize; Slang something unoriginal or oversentimental. **corny** adj Slang unoriginal or oversentimental. **cornflakes** pl n breakfast cereal made from toasted maize. **cornflour** n Chiefly Brit fine maize flour; NZ fine wheat flour. **cornflower** n plant with blue flowers.

corn[2] n painful hard skin on the toe.

cornea [korn-ee-a] n, pl **-neas, -neae.** transparent membrane covering the eyeball. **corneal** adj

corned beef n beef preserved in salt.

corner n area or angle where two converging lines or surfaces meet; place where two streets meet; remote place; Sport free kick or shot from the corner of the field. ▶ v force into a difficult or inescapable position; (of a vehicle) turn a corner; obtain a monopoly of. **cornerstone** n indispensable part or basis.

cornet n brass instrument similar to the trumpet; cone-shaped ice-cream wafer.

cornice n decorative moulding round the top of a wall.

corn on the cob n corn cooked and eaten on the cob.

cornucopia [korn-yew-**kope**-ee-a] n great abundance; symbol of plenty, consisting of a horn overflowing with fruit and flowers.

corolla n petals of a flower collectively.

corollary n, pl **-laries.** idea, fact, or proposition which is the natural result of something else.

corona n, pl **-nas, -nae.** ring of light round the moon or sun.

coronary [kor-ron-a-ree] adj of the arteries surrounding the heart. ▶ n, pl **-naries.** coronary thrombosis. **coronary thrombosis** condition in which the flow of blood to the heart is blocked by a blood clot.

coronation n ceremony of crowning a monarch.

coroner n Brit, Aust & NZ official responsible for the investigation of violent, sudden, or suspicious deaths.

coronet n small crown.

corpora n plural of CORPUS.

corporal[1] n noncommissioned officer in an army.

corporal[2] adj of the body. **corporal punishment** physical punishment, such as caning.

corporation n large business or company; city or town council. **corporate** adj of business corporations; shared by a group.

corporeal [kore-pore-ee-al] adj physical or tangible.

corps [kore] n, pl **corps.** military unit with a specific function; organized body of people.

corpse n dead body.

corpulent adj fat or plump. **corpulence** n

corpus n, pl **corpora.** collection of writings, esp. by a single author.

corpuscle n red or white blood cell.

corral US ▶ n enclosure for cattle or horses. ▶ v **-ralling, -ralled.** put in a corral.

correct adj free from error, true; in accordance with accepted standards. ▶ v put right; indicate the errors in; rebuke or punish. **correctly** adv **correctness** n **correction** n correcting; alteration

correcting something. **corrective** adj intended to put right something wrong.

correlate v place or be placed in a mutual relationship. **correlation** n

correspond v be consistent or compatible with); (be the same or similar; communicate by letter. **corresponding** adj **correspondingly** adv **correspondence** n communication by letters; letters so exchanged; relationship or similarity. **correspondent** n person employed by a newspaper etc. to report on a special subject or from a foreign country; letter writer.

corridor n passage in a building or train; strip of land or airspace providing access through foreign territory.

corrigendum [kor-rij-**end**-um] n, pl **-da.** error to be corrected.

corroborate v support (a fact or opinion) by giving proof. **corroboration** n **corroborative** adj

corroboree n Aust Aboriginal gathering or dance.

corrode v eat or be eaten away by chemical action or rust. **corrosion** n **corrosive** adj

corrugated adj folded into alternate grooves and ridges.

corrupt adj open to or involving bribery; morally depraved; (of a text or data) unreliable through errors or alterations. ▶ v make corrupt. **corruptly** adv **corruption** n **corruptible** adj

corsage [kor-**sahzh**] n small bouquet worn on the bodice of a dress.

corsair n pirate; pirate ship.

corset n women's close-fitting undergarment worn to shape the torso.

cortege [kor-**tayzh**] n funeral procession.

cortex n, pl **-tices.** Anat outer layer of the brain or other internal organ. **cortical** adj

cortisone n steroid hormone used to treat various diseases.

corundum n hard mineral used as an abrasive.

coruscate v Formal sparkle.

corvette n lightly armed escort warship.

cos Maths cosine.

cosh n Brit heavy blunt weapon. ▶ v hit with a cosh.

cosine [koh-sine] n (in trigonometry) ratio of the length of the adjacent side to that of the hypotenuse in a right-angled triangle.

cosmetic n preparation used to improve the appearance of a person's skin. ▶ adj improving the appearance only.

cosmic adj of the whole universe. **cosmic rays** electromagnetic radiation from outer space.

cosmonaut n Russian name for an astronaut.

cosmopolitan adj composed of people or elements from many countries; having lived and travelled in many countries. ▶ n cosmopolitan person. **cosmopolitanism** n

cosmos n the universe. **cosmology** n study of the origin and nature of the universe. **cosmological** adj

Cossack n member of a S Russian people famous as horsemen and dancers.

cosset v **cosseting, cosseted.** pamper.

cost n amount of money, time, labour, etc., required for something. ▶ pl expenses of a lawsuit. ▶ v **costing, cost.** have as its cost; involve the loss or sacrifice of; (past **costed**) estimate

the cost of. **costly** adj expensive; involving great loss or sacrifice. **costliness** n

costermonger n Brit person who sells fruit and vegetables from a street barrow.

costume n style of dress of a particular place or time, or for a particular activity; clothes worn by an actor or performer. **costumier** n maker or seller of costumes. **costume jewellery** inexpensive artificial jewellery.

cosy adj **-sier, -siest.** warm and snug; intimate, friendly. ▶ n cover for keeping things warm, e.g. a tea cosy. **cosily** adv **cosiness** n

cot n baby's bed with high sides; small portable bed. **cot death** unexplained death of a baby while asleep.

cote n shelter for birds or animals.

coterie [kote-er-ee] n exclusive group, clique.

cotoneaster [kot-tone-ee-ass-ter] n garden shrub with red berries.

cottage n small house in the country. **cottage cheese** soft mild white cheese. **cottage industry** craft industry in which employees work at home. **cottage pie** dish of minced meat topped with mashed potato.

cotter n pin or wedge used to secure machine parts.

cotton n white downy fibre covering the seeds of a tropical plant; cloth or thread made from this. **cottony** adj **cotton on (to)** v Informal understand. **cotton wool** fluffy cotton used for surgical dressings etc.

cotyledon [kot-ill-ee-don] n first leaf of a plant embryo.

couch n piece of upholstered furniture for seating more than one person. ▶ v express in a particular way. **couch potato**

Slang lazy person whose only hobby is watching television.

couchette [koo-**shett**] *n* bed converted from seats on a train or ship.

couch grass *n* quickly spreading grassy weed.

cougar *n* puma.

cough *v* expel air from the lungs abruptly and noisily. ▶ *n* act or sound of coughing; illness which causes coughing.

could *v* past tense of CAN[1].

couldn't could not.

coulomb [koo-lom] *n* SI unit of electric charge.

coulter *n* blade at the front of a ploughshare.

council *n* group meeting for discussion or consultation; local governing body of a town or region. ▶ *adj* of or by a council.

councillor *n* member of a council.

council tax (in Britain) tax based on the value of property, to fund local services.

counsel *n* advice or guidance; barrister or barristers. ▶ *v* **-selling, -selled.** give guidance to; urge, recommend. **counsellor** *n*

count[1] *v* say numbers in order; find the total of; be important; regard as; take into account. ▶ *n* counting; number reached by counting; *Law* one of a number of charges. **countless** *adj* too many to count. **count on** *v* rely or depend on.

count[2] *n* European nobleman.

countdown *n* counting backwards to zero of the seconds before an event.

countenance *n* (expression of) the face. ▶ *v* allow or tolerate.

counter[1] *n* long flat surface in a bank or shop, on which business is transacted; small flat disc used in board games.

counter[2] *v* oppose, retaliate against. ▶ *adv* in the opposite direction; in direct contrast. ▶ *n* opposing or retaliatory action.

counter- *prefix* opposite, against, e.g. *counterattack*; complementary, corresponding, e.g. *counterpart*.

counteract *v* act against or neutralize. **counteraction** *n*

counterattack *n, v* attack in response to an attack.

counterbalance *n* weight or force balancing or neutralizing another. ▶ *v* act as a counterbalance to.

counterblast *n* aggressive response to a verbal attack.

counterfeit *adj* fake, forged. ▶ *n* fake, forgery. ▶ *v* fake, forge.

counterfoil *n* part of a cheque or receipt kept as a record.

countermand *v* cancel (a previous order).

counterpane *n* bed covering.

counterpart *n* person or thing complementary to or corresponding to another.

counterpoint *n Music* technique of combining melodies.

counterpoise *n, v* counterbalance.

counterproductive *adj* having an effect opposite to the one intended.

countersign *v* sign (a document already signed by someone) as confirmation.

countersink *v* drive (a screw) into a shaped hole so that its head is below the surface.

countertenor *n* male alto.

countess *n* woman holding the rank of count or earl; wife or widow of a count or earl.

country *n, pl* **-tries.** nation; nation's territory; nation's people; part of the land away from cities. **countrified** *adj* rustic in manner or appearance. **country and western, country music** popular music based on American White folk music. **countryman, countrywoman** n person from one's native land; Brit, Aust & NZ person who lives in the country. **countryside** n land away from cities.

county n, pl **-ties.** (in some countries) division of a country.

coup [koo] n successful action; coup d'état.

coup de grâce [koo de grahss] n final or decisive action.

coup d'état [koo day-tah] n sudden violent overthrow of a government.

coupé [koo-pay] n sports car with two doors and a sloping fixed roof.

couple n two people who are married or romantically involved; two partners in a dance or game. ▶ v connect, associate. **a couple** pair; Informal small number. **couplet** n two consecutive lines of verse, usu. rhyming and of the same metre. **coupling** n device for connecting things, such as railway carriages.

coupon n piece of paper entitling the holder to a discount or gift; detachable order form; football pools entry form.

courage n ability to face danger or pain without fear. **courageous** adj **courageously** adv

courgette n type of small vegetable marrow.

courier n person employed to look after holiday-makers; person employed to deliver urgent messages.

course n series of lessons or medical treatment; route or direction taken; area where golf is played or a race is run; any of the successive parts of a meal; mode of conduct or action; natural development of events. ▶ v (of

liquid) run swiftly. **of course** as expected, naturally.

court n body which decides legal cases; place where it meets; marked area for playing a racket game; courtyard; residence, household, or retinue of a sovereign. ▶ v Old-fashioned try to gain the love of; try to win the favour of; invite, e.g. to court disaster. **courtier** n attendant at a royal court. **courtly** adj ceremoniously polite. **courtliness** n **courtship** n courting of an intended spouse or mate. **court martial** n, pl **courts martial**. court for trying naval or military offences. **court shoe** woman's low-cut shoe without straps or laces. **courtyard** n paved space enclosed by buildings or walls.

courtesan [kor-tiz-zan] n Hist mistress or high-class prostitute.

courtesy n politeness, good manners; (pl **-sies**) courteous act. **(by) courtesy of** by permission of. **courteous** adj polite. **courteously** adv

cousin n child of one's uncle or aunt.

couture [koo-toor] n high-fashion designing and dressmaking. **couturier** n person who designs women's fashion clothes.

cove n small bay or inlet.

coven [kuv-ven] n meeting of witches.

covenant [kuv-ven-ant] n contract; Chiefly Brit formal agreement to make an annual (charitable) payment. ▶ v agree by a covenant.

Coventry n **send someone to Coventry** punish someone by refusing to speak to them.

cover v place something over, to protect or conceal; extend over or lie on the surface of; travel over; insure against loss or risk; include;

report (an event) for a newspaper; be enough to pay for. ▶ *n* anything that covers; outside of a book or magazine; insurance; shelter or protection. **coverage** *n* amount or extent covered. **coverlet** *n* bed cover.

covert *adj* concealed, secret. ▶ *n* thicket giving shelter to game birds or animals. **covertly** *adv*

covet *v* **coveting, coveted.** long to possess (what belongs to someone else). **covetous** *adj* **covetousness** *n*

covey [kuv-vee] *n* small flock of grouse or partridge.

cow[1] *n* mature female of cattle and of certain other mammals, such as the elephant or seal. **cowboy** *n* (in the US) ranch worker who herds and tends cattle, usu. on horseback; *Informal* irresponsible or unscrupulous worker.

cow[2] *v* intimidate, subdue.

coward *n* person who lacks courage. **cowardly** *adj* **cowardice** *n* lack of courage.

cower *v* cringe in fear.

cowl *n* loose hood; monk's hooded robe; cover on a chimney to increase ventilation.

cowling *n* cover on an engine.

cowrie *n* brightly-marked sea shell.

cowslip *n* small yellow wild European flower.

cox *n* coxswain. ▶ *v* act as cox of (a boat).

coxswain [kok-sn] *n* person who steers a rowing boat.

coy *adj* affectedly shy or modest. **coyly** *adv* **coyness** *n*

coyote [koy-ote-ee] *n* prairie wolf of N America.

coypu *n* beaver-like aquatic rodent native to S America, bred for its fur.

cozen *v Lit* cheat, trick.

CPU *Computers* central processing

unit.

crab *n* edible shellfish with ten legs, the first pair modified into pincers.

crab apple *n* small sour apple.

crabbed *adj* (of handwriting) hard to read; (also **crabby**) bad-tempered.

crack *v* break or split partially; (cause to) make a sharp noise; break down or yield under strain; hit suddenly; solve (a code or problem); tell (a joke). ▶ *n* sudden sharp noise; narrow gap; sharp blow; *Informal* gibe, joke; *Slang* highly addictive form of cocaine. ▶ *adj Informal* first-rate, excellent, e.g. *a crack shot.* **cracking** *adj* very good. **crackdown** *n* severe disciplinary measures. **crack down on** *v* take severe measures against.

cracker *n* thin dry biscuit; decorated cardboard tube, pulled apart with a bang, containing a paper hat and a joke or toy; small explosive firework; *Slang* outstanding thing or person. **crackers** *adj Slang* insane.

crackle *v* make small sharp popping noises. ▶ *n* crackling sound. **crackling** *n* crackle; crisp skin of roast pork.

crackpot *n, adj Informal* eccentric (person).

cradle *n* baby's bed on rockers; place where something originates; supporting structure. ▶ *v* hold gently as if in a cradle.

craft *n* occupation requiring skill with the hands; skill or ability; (*pl* **craft**) boat, ship, aircraft, or spaceship. **crafty** *adj* skilled in deception. **craftily** *adv* **craftiness** *n* **craftsman, craftswoman** *n* skilled worker. **craftsmanship** *n*

crag *n* steep rugged rock. **craggy** *adj*

cram v **cramming, crammed.** force into too small a space; fill too full; study hard just before an examination.

cramp[1] n painful muscular contraction; clamp for holding masonry or timber together.

cramp[2] v confine, restrict.

crampon n spiked plate strapped to a boot for climbing on ice.

cranberry n sour edible red berry.

crane n machine for lifting and moving heavy weights; large wading bird with a long neck and legs. ▶ v stretch (one's neck) to see something.

crane fly n long-legged insect with slender wings.

cranium n, pl **-niums, -nia.** Anat skull. **cranial** adj

crank n arm projecting at right angles from a shaft, for transmitting or converting motion; Informal eccentric person. ▶ v start (an engine) with a crank. **cranky** adj Informal eccentric; bad-tempered. **crankshaft** n shaft driven by a crank.

cranny n, pl **-nies.** narrow opening.

crape n same as CREPE.

craps n gambling game played with two dice.

crash n collision involving a vehicle or vehicles; sudden loud smashing noise; financial collapse. ▶ v (cause to) collide violently with a vehicle, a stationary object, or the ground; (cause to) make a loud smashing noise; (cause to) fall with a crash; collapse or fail financially. **crash course** short, very intensive course in a particular subject. **crash helmet** protective helmet worn by a motorcyclist. **crash-land** v (of an aircraft) land in an emergency, causing damage. **crash-landing** n

crass adj stupid and insensitive. **crassly** adv **crassness** n

crate n large wooden container for packing goods.

crater n very large hole in the ground or in the surface of the moon.

cravat n man's scarf worn like a tie.

crave v desire intensely; beg or plead for. **craving** n

craven adj cowardly.

crawfish n same as CRAYFISH.

crawl v move on one's hands and knees; move very slowly; (foll. by to) flatter in order to gain some advantage; feel as if covered with crawling creatures. ▶ n crawling motion or pace; overarm swimming stroke. **crawler** n

crayfish n edible shellfish like a lobster.

crayon v, n (draw or colour with) a stick or pencil of coloured wax or clay.

craze n short-lived fashion or enthusiasm. **crazed** adj wild and uncontrolled; (of porcelain) having fine cracks.

crazy adj ridiculous; (foll. by about) very fond (of); insane. **craziness** n **crazy paving** paving made of irregularly shaped slabs of stone.

creak v, n (make) a harsh squeaking sound. **creaky** adj

cream n fatty part of milk; food or cosmetic resembling cream in consistency; best part (of something). ▶ adj yellowish-white. ▶ v beat to a creamy consistency. **creamy** adj **cream cheese** rich soft white cheese. **cream off** v take the best part from.

crease n line made by folding or pressing; Cricket line marking the bowler's and batsman's positions. ▶ v crush or line.

create v make, cause to exist; appoint to a new rank or position; Slang make an angry fuss. **creation** n **creative** adj

imaginative or inventive.
creativity n **creator** n
creature n animal, person, or
other being.
crèche n place where small
children are looked after while
their parents are working,
shopping, etc.
credence n belief in the truth or
accuracy of a statement.
credentials pl n document giving
evidence of a person's identity or
qualifications.
credible adj believable;
trustworthy. **credibly** adv
credibility n
credit n system of allowing
customers to receive goods and
pay later; reputation for
trustworthiness in paying debts;
money at one's disposal in a bank
account; side of an account book
on which such sums are entered;
(source or cause of) praise or
approval; influence or reputation
based on the good opinion of
others; belief or trust. ▶ pl list of
people responsible for the
production of a film, programme,
or record. ▶ v **crediting, credited.**
enter as a credit in an account;
(foll. by with) attribute (to);
believe. **creditable** adj
praiseworthy. **creditably** adv
creditor n person to whom
money is owed. **credit card** card
allowing a person to buy on credit.
credulous adj too willing to
believe. **credulity** n
creed n statement or system of
(Christian) beliefs or principles.
creek n narrow inlet or bay; Aust,
NZ, US & Canadian small stream.
creel n wicker basket used by
anglers.
creep v **creeping, crept.** move
quietly and cautiously; crawl with
the body near to the ground; (of

a plant) grow along the ground or
over rocks. ▶ n Slang obnoxious or
servile person. **give one the
creeps** Informal make one feel fear
or disgust. **creeper** n creeping
plant. **creepy** adj Informal causing
a feeling of fear or disgust.
cremate v burn (a corpse) to ash.
cremation n **crematorium** n
building where corpses are
cremated.
crenellated adj having battlements.
creole n language developed from
a mixture of languages; (C-)
native-born W Indian or Latin
American of mixed European and
African descent.
creosote n dark oily liquid made
from coal tar and used for
preserving wood. ▶ v treat with
creosote.
crepe [krayp] n fabric or rubber
with a crinkled texture; very thin
pancake. **crepe paper** paper with
a crinkled texture.
crept v past of CREEP.
crepuscular adj Lit of or like
twilight.
crescendo [krish-**end**-oh] n, pl
-dos. gradual increase in loudness,
esp. in music.
crescent n (curved shape of) the
moon as seen in its first or last
quarter; crescent-shaped street.
cress n plant with strong-tasting
leaves, used in salads.
crest n top of a mountain, hill, or
wave; tuft or growth on a bird's
or animal's head; heraldic design
used on a coat of arms and
elsewhere. **crested** adj
crestfallen adj disheartened.
cretin n Informal stupid person;
Obs person afflicted with physical
and mental retardation caused by
a thyroid deficiency. **cretinous** adj
crevasse n deep open crack in a
glacier.

crevice n narrow crack or gap in rock.

crew n people who work on a ship or aircraft; group of people working together; *Informal* any group of people. ▶ v serve as a crew member (on). **crew cut** man's closely cropped haircut.

crewel n fine worsted yarn used in embroidery.

crib n piece of writing stolen from elsewhere; translation or list of answers used by students, often illicitly; baby's cradle; rack for fodder; short for CRIBBAGE. ▶ v **cribbing, cribbed.** copy (someone's work) dishonestly. **crib-wall** n NZ retaining wall built against an earth bank.

cribbage n card game for two to four players.

crick n muscle spasm or cramp in the back or neck. ▶ v cause a crick in.

cricket[1] n outdoor game played with bats, a ball, and wickets by two teams of eleven. **cricketer** n

cricket[2] n chirping insect like a grasshopper.

crime n unlawful act; unlawful acts collectively. **criminal** n person guilty of a crime. ▶ adj of crime; *Informal* deplorable. **criminally** adv **criminality** n **criminology** n study of crime. **criminologist** n

crimp v fold or press into ridges.

crimson adj deep purplish-red.

cringe v flinch in fear; behave in a submissive or timid way.

crinkle v, n wrinkle, crease, or fold.

crinoline n hooped petticoat.

cripple n person who is lame or disabled. ▶ v make lame or disabled; damage (something).

crisis n, pl **-ses.** crucial stage, turning point; time of extreme trouble.

crisp adj fresh and firm; dry and brittle; clean and neat; (of weather) cold but invigorating; lively or brisk. ▶ n Brit very thin slice of potato fried till crunchy. **crisply** adv **crispness** n **crispy** adj hard and crunchy. **crispbread** n thin dry biscuit.

crisscross v move in or mark with a crosswise pattern. ▶ adj (of lines) crossing in different directions.

criterion n, pl **-ria.** standard of judgment.

critic n professional judge of any of the arts; person who finds fault. **critical** adj very important or dangerous; fault-finding; able to examine and judge carefully; of a critic or criticism. **critically** adv **criticism** n fault-finding; analysis of a book, work of art, etc. **criticize** v find fault with. **critique** n critical essay.

croak v (of a frog or crow) give a low hoarse cry; utter or speak with a croak. ▶ n low hoarse sound. **croaky** adj hoarse.

crochet [kroh-shay] v **-cheting, -cheted.** make by looping and intertwining yarn with a hooked needle. ▶ n work made in this way.

crock[1] n earthenware pot or jar. **crockery** n dishes.

crock[2] n Brit, Aust & NZ informal old or decrepit person or thing.

crocodile n large amphibious tropical reptile; Brit, Aust & NZ line of people, esp. schoolchildren, walking two by two. **crocodile tears** insincere show of grief.

crocus n, pl **-cuses.** small plant with yellow, white, or purple flowers in spring.

croft n small farm worked by one family in Scotland. **crofter** n

croissant [krwah-son] n rich flaky crescent-shaped roll.

cromlech n Brit circle of prehistoric standing stones.

crone n witchlike old woman.

crony n, pl **-nies**. close friend.

crook n Informal criminal; bent or curved part; hooked pole. ▶ adj Aust & NZ slang unwell, injured **go crook** Aust & NZ slang become angry. **crooked** adj bent or twisted; set at an angle; Informal dishonest.

croon v sing, hum, or speak in a soft low tone.

crooner n male singer of sentimental ballads.

crop n cultivated plant; season's total yield of produce; group of things appearing at one time; (handle of) a whip; pouch in a bird's gullet; very short haircut. ▶ v **cropping, cropped.** cut very short; produce or harvest as a crop; (of animals) feed on (grass). **cropper** n **come a cropper** Informal have a disastrous failure or heavy fall. **crop up** v Informal happen unexpectedly.

croquet [kroh-kay] n game played on a lawn in which balls are hit through hoops.

croquette [kroh-kett] n fried cake of potato, meat, or fish.

crosier n same as CROZIER.

cross v move or go across (something); meet and pass; (with out) delete with a cross or lines; place (one's arms or legs) crosswise. ▶ n structure, symbol, or mark of two intersecting lines; such a structure of wood as a means of execution; representation of the Cross as an emblem of Christianity; mixture of two things. ▶ adj angry, annoyed. **the Cross** Christianity the cross on which Christ was crucified. **crossing** n place where a street may be crossed safely; place where one thing crosses another; journey across water. **crossly** adv

crossbar n horizontal bar across goalposts or on a bicycle.

crossbow n weapon consisting of a bow fixed across a wooden stock. **crossbred** adj bred from two different types of animal or plant. **crossbreed** n crossbred animal or plant. **cross-check** v check using a different method. **cross-country** adj, adv by way of open country or fields. **cross-examine** v Law question (a witness for the opposing side) to check his or her testimony. **cross-examination** n **cross-eyed** adj with eyes looking towards each other. **cross-fertilize** v fertilize (an animal or plant) from one of a different kind. **cross-fertilization** n **crossfire** n gunfire crossing another line of fire. **cross-purposes** pl n **at cross-purposes** misunderstanding each other. **cross-reference** n reference within a text to another part. **crossroads** n place where roads intersect. **cross section** (diagram of) a surface made by cutting across something; representative sample. **crosswise** adj, adv across; in the shape of a cross. **crossword puzzle, crossword** n puzzle in which words suggested by clues are written into a grid of squares.

crotch n part of the body between the tops of the legs.

crotchet n musical note half the length of a minim.

crotchety adj Informal bad-tempered.

crouch v bend low with the legs and body close. ▶ n this position.

croup[1] [kroop] n throat disease of children, with a cough.

croup[2] [kroop] n hind quarters of a horse.

croupier [kroop-ee-ay] n person

who collects bets and pays out winnings at a gambling table in a casino.

crouton n small piece of fried or toasted bread served in soup.

crow[1] n large black bird with a harsh call. **as the crow flies** in a straight line. **crow's feet** wrinkles at the corners of the eyes. **crow's nest** lookout platform at the top of a ship's mast.

crow[2] v (of a cock) make a shrill squawking sound; boast or gloat.

crowbar n iron bar used as a lever.

crowd n large group of people or things; particular group of people. ▶ v gather together in large numbers; press together in a confined space; fill or occupy fully.

crown n monarch's headdress of gold and jewels; wreath for the head, given as an honour; top of the head or of a hill; artificial cover for a broken or decayed tooth; former British coin worth 25 pence. ▶ v put a crown on the head of (someone) to proclaim him or her monarch; put on or form the top of; put the finishing touch to (a series of events); Informal hit on the head. **the Crown** power of the monarchy. **crown court** local criminal court in England and Wales. **crown prince, crown princess** heir to a throne.

crozier n bishop's hooked staff.

crucial adj very important. **crucially** adv

crucible n pot in which metals are melted.

crucify v -fying, -fied. put to death by fastening to a cross. **crucifix** n model of Christ on the Cross. **crucifixion** n crucifying. **the Crucifixion** Christianity crucifying of Christ. **cruciform** adj cross-shaped.

crude adj rough and simple; tasteless, vulgar; in a natural or unrefined state. **crudely** adv **crudity** n

cruel adj delighting in others' pain; causing pain or suffering. **cruelly** adv **cruelty** n

cruet n small container for salt, pepper, etc., at table.

cruise n sail for pleasure. ▶ v sail from place to place for pleasure; (of a vehicle) travel at a moderate and economical speed. **cruiser** n fast warship; motorboat with a cabin. **cruise missile** low-flying guided missile.

crumb n small fragment of bread or other dry food; small amount.

crumble v break into fragments; fall apart or decay. ▶ n pudding of stewed fruit with a crumbly topping. **crumbly** adj

crummy adj -mier, -miest. Slang of poor quality.

crumpet n round soft yeast cake, eaten buttered; Brit, Aust & NZ slang sexually attractive women collectively.

crumple v crush, crease; collapse, esp. from shock. **crumpled** adj

crunch v bite or chew with a noisy crushing sound; make a crisp or brittle sound. ▶ n crunching sound; Informal critical moment. **crunchy** adj

crupper n strap that passes from the back of a saddle under a horse's tail.

crusade n medieval Christian war to recover the Holy Land from the Muslims; vigorous campaign in favour of a cause. ▶ v take part in a crusade.

crusader n person who took part in the medieval Christian war to recover the Holy Land from the Muslims; person who campaigns vigorously in favour of a cause.

crush v compress so as to injure, break, or crumple; break into small pieces; defeat or humiliate utterly. ▶ n dense crowd; *Informal* infatuation; drink made by crushing fruit.

crust n hard outer part of something, esp. bread. ▶ v cover with or form a crust. **crusty** adj having a crust; irritable.

crustacean n hard-shelled, usu. aquatic animal with several pairs of legs, such as the crab or lobster.

crutch n long sticklike support with a rest for the armpit, used by a lame person; person or thing that gives support; crotch.

crux n, pl **cruxes**. crucial or decisive point.

cry v **crying, cried.** shed tears; call or utter loudly. ▶ n, pl **cries.** fit of weeping; loud utterance; urgent appeal, e.g. a cry for help. **crybaby** n person, esp. a child, who cries too readily. **cry off** v *Informal* withdraw from an arrangement. **cry out for** v need urgently.

cryogenics n branch of physics concerned with very low temperatures. **cryogenic** adj

crypt n vault under a church, esp. one used as a burial place.

cryptic adj obscure in meaning, secret. **cryptically** adv **cryptography** n art of writing in and deciphering codes.

crystal n (single grain of) a symmetrically shaped solid formed naturally by some substances; very clear and brilliant glass, usu. with the surface cut in many planes; tumblers, vases, etc., made of crystal. ▶ adj bright and clear. **crystalline** adj of or like crystal or crystals; clear. **crystallize** v make or become definite; form into crystals. **crystallization** n

cu. cubic.

cub n young wild animal such as a bear or fox; (C-) Cub Scout. ▶ v **cubbing, cubbed.** give birth to cubs. **Cub Scout** member of a junior branch of the Scout Association.

cubbyhole n small enclosed space or room.

cube n object with six equal square sides; number resulting from multiplying a number by itself twice. ▶ v cut into cubes; find the cube of (a number). **cubic** adj having three dimensions; cube-shaped. **cubism** n style of art in which objects are represented by geometrical shapes. **cubist** adj, n **cube root** number whose cube is a given number.

cubicle n enclosed part of a large room, screened for privacy.

cuckold n man whose wife has been unfaithful. ▶ v be unfaithful to (one's husband).

cuckoo n migratory bird with a characteristic two-note call, which lays its eggs in the nests of other birds. ▶ adj *Informal* insane or foolish.

cucumber n long green-skinned fleshy fruit used in salads.

cud n partially digested food which a ruminant brings back into its mouth to chew again. **chew the cud** think deeply.

cuddle v, n hug. **cuddly** adj

cudgel n short thick stick used as a weapon.

cue[1] n signal to an actor or musician to begin speaking or playing; signal or reminder. ▶ v **cueing, cued.** give a cue to.

cue[2] n long tapering stick used in billiards, snooker, or pool. ▶ v **cueing, cued.** hit (a ball) with a cue.

cuff[1] n end of a sleeve. **off the cuff** Informal without preparation. **cuff link** one of a pair of decorative fastenings for shirt cuffs.

cuff[2] Brit, Aust & NZ ▶ v hit with an open hand. ▶ n blow with an open hand.

cuisine [quiz-zeen] n style of cooking.

cul-de-sac n road with one end blocked off.

culinary adj of kitchens or cookery.

cull v choose, gather; remove or kill (inferior or surplus animals) from a herd. ▶ n culling.

culminate v reach the highest point or climax. **culmination** n

culottes pl n women's knee-length trousers cut to look like a skirt.

culpable adj deserving blame. **culpability** n

culprit n person guilty of an offence or misdeed.

cult n specific system of worship; devotion to a person, idea, or activity; popular fashion.

cultivate v prepare (land) to grow crops; grow (plants); develop or improve (something); try to develop a friendship with (someone). **cultivated** adj well-educated. **cultivation** n

culture n ideas, customs, and art of a particular society; particular society; developed understanding of the arts; cultivation of plants or rearing of animals; growth of bacteria for study. **cultural** adj **cultured** adj showing good taste or manners. **cultured pearl** pearl artificially grown in an oyster shell.

culvert n drain under a road or railway.

cumbersome adj awkward because of size or shape.

cumin, cummin n sweet-smelling seeds of a Mediterranean plant, used in cooking.

cummerbund n wide sash worn round the waist.

cumulative adj increasing steadily.

cumulus [kew-myew-luss] n, pl **-li**. thick white or dark grey cloud.

cuneiform [kew-nif-form] n, adj (written in) an ancient system of writing using wedge-shaped characters.

cunning adj clever at deceiving; ingenious. ▶ n cleverness at deceiving; ingenuity. **cunningly** adv

cup n small bowl-shaped drinking container with a handle; contents of a cup; (competition with) a cup-shaped trophy given as a prize; hollow rounded shape. ▶ v **cupping, cupped.** form (one's hands) into the shape of a cup; hold in cupped hands. **cupful** n

cupboard n piece of furniture or alcove with a door, for storage.

cupidity [kew-pid-it-ee] n greed for money or possessions.

cupola [kew-pol-la] n domed roof or ceiling.

cur n Lit mongrel dog; contemptible person.

curaçao [kew-rah-so] n orange-flavoured liqueur.

curare [kew-rah-ree] n poisonous resin of a S American tree, used as a muscle relaxant in medicine.

curate n clergyman who assists a parish priest. **curacy** [kew-rah-see] n, pl **-cies.** work or position of a curate.

curative adj, n (something) able to cure.

curator n person in charge of a museum or art gallery. **curatorship** n

curb n something that restrains. ▶ v control, restrain.

curd n coagulated milk, used to make cheese. **curdle** v turn into curd, coagulate.

cure v get rid of (an illness or problem); make (someone) well again; preserve by salting, smoking, or drying. ▶ n (treatment causing) curing of an illness or person; remedy or solution. **curable** adj

curette n surgical instrument for scraping tissue from body cavities. ▶ v scrape with a curette. **curettage** n

curfew n law ordering people to stay inside their homes after a specific time at night; time set as a deadline by such a law.

curie n standard unit of radioactivity.

curio n, pl **-rios**. rare or unusual object valued as a collector's item.

curious adj eager to learn or know; eager to find out private details; unusual or peculiar. **curiously** adv **curiosity** n eagerness to know or find out; (pl **-ties**) rare or unusual object.

curl n curved piece of hair; curved spiral shape. ▶ v make (hair) into curls or (of hair) grow in curls; make into a curved spiral shape. **curly** adj **curling** n game like bowls, played with heavy stones on ice.

curlew n long-billed wading bird.

curmudgeon n bad-tempered person.

currant n small dried grape; small round berry, such as a redcurrant.

currawong n Australian songbird.

current adj of the immediate present; most recent, up-to-date; commonly accepted. ▶ n flow of water or air in one direction; flow of electricity; general trend. **currently** adv **currency** n, pl **-cies**. money in use in a particular country; general acceptance or use.

curriculum n, pl **-la, -lums**. all the courses of study offered by a school or college. **curriculum vitae** [vee-tie] outline of someone's educational and professional history, prepared for job applications.

curry[1] n, pl **-ries**. Indian dish of meat or vegetables in a hot spicy sauce. ▶ v **-rying, -ried**. prepare (food) with curry powder. **curry powder** mixture of spices for making curry.

curry[2] v **-rying, -ried**. groom (a horse). **curry favour** ingratiate oneself with an important person. **curry comb** ridged comb for grooming a horse.

curse v swear (at); ask a supernatural power to cause harm to. ▶ n swearword; (result of) a call to a supernatural power to cause harm to someone; something causing trouble or harm. **cursed** adj

cursive adj, n (handwriting) done with joined letters.

cursor n movable point of light that shows a specific position on a visual display unit.

cursory adj quick and superficial. **cursorily** adv

curt adj brief and rather rude. **curtly** adv **curtness** n

curtail v cut short; restrict. **curtailment** n

curtain n piece of cloth hung at a window or opening as a screen; hanging cloth separating the audience and the stage in a theatre; fall or closing of the curtain at the end, or the rise or opening of the curtain at the start of a theatrical performance; something forming a barrier or screen. ▶ v provide with curtains; (foll. by off) separate by a curtain.

curtsy, curtsey n, pl **-sies, -seys**. woman's gesture of respect made by bending the knees and bowing the head. ▶ *v* **-sying, -sied** or **-seying, -seyed.** make a curtsy.

curve *n* continuously bending line with no straight parts. ▶ *v* form or move in a curve. **curvy** *adj*

curvaceous *adj Informal* (of a woman) having a shapely body.

curvature *n* curved shape.

curvilinear *adj* consisting of or bounded by a curve.

cuscus *n, pl* **-cuses.** large Australian nocturnal possum.

cushion *n* bag filled with soft material, to make a seat more comfortable; something that provides comfort or absorbs shock. ▶ *v* lessen the effects of; protect from injury or shock.

cushy *adj* **cushier, cushiest.** *Informal* easy.

cusp *n* pointed end, esp. on a tooth; *Astrol* division between houses or signs of the zodiac.

cuss *Informal* ▶ *n* curse, oath; annoying person. ▶ *v* swear (at). **cussed** [kuss-id] *adj Informal* obstinate.

custard *n* sweet yellow sauce made from milk and eggs.

custody *n* protective care; imprisonment prior to being tried. **custodial** *adj* **custodian** *n* person in charge of a public building.

custom *n* long-established activity or action; usual habit; regular use of a shop or business. ▶ *pl* duty charged on imports or exports; government department which collects these; area at a port, airport, or border where baggage and freight are examined for dutiable goods. **customary** *adj* usual; established by custom. **customarily** *adv* **custom-built, custom-made** *adj* made to the specifications of an individual customer.

customer *n* person who buys

goods or services.

cut *v* **cutting, cut.** open up, penetrate, wound, or divide with a sharp instrument; divide; trim or shape by cutting; abridge, shorten; reduce, restrict; *Informal* hurt the feelings of; pretend not to recognize. ▶ *n* stroke or incision made by cutting; piece cut off; reduction; deletion in a text, film, or play; *Informal* share, esp. of profits; style in which hair or a garment is cut. **cut in** *v* interrupt; obstruct another vehicle in overtaking it.

cutaneous [kew-**tane**-ee-uss] *adj* of the skin.

cute *adj* appealing or attractive; *Informal* clever or shrewd. **cutely** *adv* **cuteness** *n*

cuticle *n* skin at the base of a fingernail or toenail.

cutlass *n* curved one-edged sword formerly used by sailors.

cutlery *n* knives, forks, and spoons. **cutler** *n* maker of cutlery.

cutlet *n* small piece of meat like a chop; flat croquette of chopped meat or fish.

cutter *n* person or tool that cuts; any of various small fast boats.

cut-throat *adj* fierce or relentless. ▶ *n* murderer.

cutting *n* article cut from a newspaper or magazine; piece cut from a plant from which to grow a new plant; passage cut through high ground for a road or railway. ▶ *adj* (of a remark) hurtful.

cuttlefish *n* squidlike sea mollusc.

CV curriculum vitae.

cwt hundredweight.

cyanide *n* extremely poisonous chemical compound.

cyber- *combining form* computers, e.g. *cyberspace.*

cybernetics *n* branch of science in which electronic and mechanical systems are studied and compared to biological systems.

cyberspace n place said to contain all the data stored in computers.

cyclamen [**sik**-la-men] n plant with red, pink, or white flowers.

cycle v ride a bicycle. ▶ n Brit, Aust & NZ bicycle; US motorcycle; complete series of recurring events; time taken for one such series. **cyclical, cyclic** adj occurring in cycles. **cyclist** n person who rides a bicycle.

cyclone n violent wind moving round a central area.

cyclotron n apparatus that accelerates charged particles by means of a strong vertical magnetic field.

cygnet n young swan.

cylinder n solid or hollow body with straight sides and circular ends; chamber within which the piston moves in an internal-combustion engine. **cylindrical** adj

cymbal n percussion instrument consisting of a brass plate which is struck against another or hit with a stick.

cynic [**sin**-ik] n person who believes that people act selfishly. **cynical** adj **cynically** adv **cynicism** n

cynosure [**sin**-oh-zyure] n centre of attention.

cypher n same as CIPHER.

cypress n evergreen tree with dark green leaves.

cyst [sist] n (abnormal) sac in the body containing fluid or soft matter. **cystic** adj **cystitis** [siss-**tite**-iss] n inflammation of the bladder.

cytology [site-ol-a-jee] n study of plant and animal cells. **cytological** adj **cytologist** n

czar [zahr] n same as TSAR.

—— D d ——

d Physics density.

D Chem deuterium.

d. (before decimalization) penny; died.

dab[1] v **dabbing, dabbed.** pat lightly; apply with short tapping strokes. ▶ n small amount of something soft or moist; light stroke or tap. **dab hand** Informal person who is particularly good at something.

dab[2] n small European flatfish with rough scales.

dabble v be involved in something superficially; splash about. **dabbler** n

dace n small European freshwater fish.

dachshund n dog with a long body and short legs.

dad n Informal father.

daddy n, pl **-dies.** Informal father.

daddy-longlegs n Brit crane fly; US & Canadian small web-spinning spider with long legs.

dado [**day**-doe] n, pl **-does, -dos.** lower part of an interior wall, below a rail, decorated differently from the upper part.

daffodil n yellow trumpet-shaped flower that blooms in spring.

daft adj Informal foolish or crazy.

dag NZ ▶ n dried dung on a sheep's rear; Informal amusing person. ▶ pl n **rattle one's dags** Informal hurry up. ▶ v remove the dags from a sheep. **daggy** adj Informal amusing.

dagga n S Afr informal cannabis.

dagger n short knifelike weapon with a pointed blade.

daguerreotype [dag-**gair**-oh-type] n type of early photograph produced on chemically treated silver.

dahlia [**day**-lya] n brightly coloured garden flower.

daily adj occurring every day or every weekday. ▶ adv every day. ▶ n, pl **-lies.** daily newspaper; Brit informal person who cleans other people's houses.

dainty adj **-tier, -tiest.** delicate or elegant. **daintily** adv

daiquiri [**dak**-eer-ee] n iced drink containing rum, lime juice, and sugar.

dairy n, pl **dairies.** place for the processing or sale of milk and its products; NZ small shop selling groceries and other items outside normal trading hours. ▶ adj of milk or its products.

dais [**day**-iss or **dayss**] n raised platform in a hall, used by a speaker.

daisy n, pl **-sies.** small wild flower with a yellow centre and white petals. **daisy wheel** flat disc in a word processor with radiating spokes for printing letters.

Dalai Lama n chief lama and (until 1959) ruler of Tibet.

dale n (esp. in N England) valley.

dally v **-lying, -lied.** waste time; (foll. by with) deal frivolously (with). **dalliance** n flirtation.

Dalmatian n large dog with a white coat and black spots.

dam¹ n barrier built across a river to create a lake; lake created by this. ▶ v **damming, dammed.** build a dam across (a river).

dam² n mother of an animal such as a sheep or horse.

damage v harm, spoil. ▶ n harm to a person or thing; Informal cost, e.g. what's the damage? ▶ pl money awarded as compensation for injury or loss.

damask n fabric with a pattern woven into it, used for tablecloths etc.

dame n Chiefly US & Canadian slang woman; (**D-**) title of a woman who has been awarded the OBE or another order of chivalry.

damn interj Slang exclamation of annoyance. ▶ adv, adj (also **damned**) Slang extreme(ly). ▶ v condemn as bad or worthless; (of God) condemn to hell. **damnable** adj annoying. **damnably** adv **damnation** interj, n **damning** adj proving or suggesting guilt, e.g. a damning report.

damp adj slightly wet. ▶ n slight wetness, moisture. ▶ v (also **dampen**) make damp; (foll. by down) reduce the intensity of (feelings or actions). **damply** adv **dampness** n **damper** n movable plate to regulate the draught in a fire; pad in a piano that deadens the vibration of each string. **put a damper on** have a depressing or inhibiting effect on.

damsel n Old-fashioned young woman.

damson n small blue-black plumlike fruit.

dance v move the feet and body rhythmically in time to music; perform (a particular dance); skip or leap; move rhythmically. ▶ n series of steps and movements in time to music; social meeting arranged for dancing. **dancer** n

D and C n Med dilatation and curettage: a minor operation in which the neck of the womb is stretched and the lining of the womb scraped, to clear the womb or remove tissue for diagnosis.

dandelion n yellow-flowered wild plant.

dander n **get one's dander up** Slang become angry.

dandle v move (a child) up and down on one's knee.

dandruff n loose scales of dry dead skin shed from the scalp.

dandy n, pl **-dies**. man who is overconcerned with the elegance of his appearance. ▸ adj **-dier, -diest.** Informal very good. **dandified** adj

danger n possibility of being injured or killed; person or thing that may cause injury or harm; likelihood that something unpleasant will happen. **dangerous** adj **dangerously** adv

dangle v hang loosely; display as an enticement.

dank adj unpleasantly damp and chilly.

dapper adj (of a man) neat in appearance.

dappled adj marked with spots of a different colour. **dapple-grey** n horse with a grey coat and darker coloured spots.

dare v be courageous enough to try (to do something); challenge to do something risky. ▸ n challenge to do something risky. **daring** adj willing to take risks. ▸ n courage to do dangerous things. **daringly** adv **daredevil** adj, n recklessly bold (person).

dark adj having little or no light; (of a colour) reflecting little light; (of hair or skin) brown or black; gloomy; sad; sinister; evil; secret, e.g. keep it dark. ▸ n absence of light; night. **darkly** adv **darkness** n **darken** v **dark horse** person about whom little is known.

darkroom n darkened room for processing photographic film.

darling n much-loved person; favourite. ▸ adj much-loved.

darn¹ v mend (a garment) with a series of interwoven stitches. ▸ n patch of darned work.

darn² interj, adv, adj, v Euphemistic damn.

dart n small narrow pointed missile that is thrown or shot, esp. in the game of darts; sudden quick movement; tapered tuck made in dressmaking. ▸ pl game in which darts are thrown at a circular numbered board. ▸ v move or dart quickly and suddenly.

Darwinism n theory of the origin of animal and plant species by evolution. **Darwinian, Darwinist** adj, n

dash v move quickly; hurl or crash; frustrate (someone's hopes). ▸ n sudden quick movement; small amount; mixture of style and courage; punctuation mark (–) indicating a change of subject; longer symbol used in Morse code. **dashing** adj stylish and attractive. **dashboard** n instrument panel in a vehicle.

dassie n S Afr type of hoofed rodent-like animal (also **hyrax**).

dastardly adj wicked and cowardly.

data n information consisting of observations, measurements, or facts; numbers, digits, etc., stored by a computer. **data base** store of information that can be easily handled by a computer. **data capture** process for converting information into a form that can be handled by a computer. **data processing** series of operations performed on data, esp. by a computer, to extract or interpret information.

date¹ n specified day of the month; particular day or year when an event happened; Informal appointment, esp. with a person to whom one is sexually attracted; Informal person with whom one has a date. ▸ v mark with the date; assign a date of occurrence to; become old-fashioned; (foll. by *from*) originate from. **dated** *adj* old-fashioned.

date² *n* dark-brown sweet-tasting fruit of the date palm. **date palm** tall palm grown in tropical regions for its fruit.

dative *n* (in certain languages) the form of the noun that expresses the indirect object.

datum *n, pl* **data.** single piece of information in the form of a fact or statistic.

daub *v* smear or spread quickly or clumsily.

daughter *n* female child; woman who comes from a certain place or is connected with a certain thing. **daughterly** *adj* **daughter-in-law** *n, pl* **daughters-in-law.** son's wife.

daunting *adj* intimidating or worrying. **dauntless** *adj* fearless.

dauphin [doe-fan] *n* (formerly) eldest son of the king of France.

davenport *n Chiefly Brit* small writing table with drawers; *Aust, US & Canadian* large couch.

davit [dav-vit] *n* crane, usu. one of a pair, at a ship's side, for lowering and hoisting a lifeboat.

Davy lamp *n* miner's lamp designed to prevent it from igniting gas.

dawdle *v* walk slowly, lag behind.

dawn *n* daybreak; beginning (of something). ▸ *v* begin to grow light; begin to develop or appear; (foll. by *on*) become apparent (to).

day *n* period of 24 hours; period of light between sunrise and sunset; part of a day occupied with regular activity, esp. work; period or point in time; time of success. **daybreak** *n* time in the morning when light first appears. **daydream** *n* pleasant fantasy indulged in while awake. ▸ *v*

indulge in idle fantasy. **daydreamer** *n* **daylight** *n* light from the sun. **day release** *Brit* system in which workers go to college one day a week. **day-to-day** *adj* routine.

daze *v* stun, by a blow or shock. ▸ *n* state of confusion or shock.

dazzle *v* impress greatly; blind temporarily by sudden excessive light. ▸ *n* bright light that dazzles. **dazzling** *adj* **dazzlingly** *adv*

dB, db decibel(s).

DC direct current.

DD Doctor of Divinity.

D-day *n* day selected for the start of some operation, orig. the Allied invasion of Europe in 1944.

DDT *n* kind of insecticide.

de- *prefix* indicating: removal, e.g. *dethrone*; reversal, e.g. *declassify*; departure, e.g. *decamp*.

deacon *n Christianity* ordained minister ranking immediately below a priest; (in some Protestant churches) lay official who assists the minister.

dead *adj* no longer alive; no longer in use; numb, e.g. *my leg has gone dead*; complete, absolute, e.g. *dead silence*; *Informal* very tired; (of a place) lacking activity. ▸ *n* period during which coldness or darkness is most intense, e.g. *in the dead of night*. ▸ *adv* extremely; suddenly, e.g. *I stopped dead*. **the dead** dead people. **dead set** firmly decided. **deadbeat** *n Informal* lazy useless person. **dead beat** *Informal* exhausted. **dead end** road with one end blocked off; situation in which further progress is impossible. **dead heat** tie for first place between two participants in a contest. **deadline** *n* time limit. **deadlock** *n* point in a dispute at which no agreement can be reached.

deadlocked adj **deadpan** adj, adv showing no emotion or expression. **dead reckoning** method of establishing one's position using the distance and direction travelled. **dead weight** heavy weight.

deaden v make less intense.

deadly adj -lier, -liest. likely to cause death; Informal extremely boring. ▶ adv extremely. **deadly nightshade** plant with poisonous black berries.

deaf adj unable to hear. **deaf to** refusing to listen to or take notice of. **deafen** v make deaf, esp. temporarily. **deafness** n

deal¹ n agreement or transaction; kind of treatment, e.g. a fair deal; large amount. ▶ v **dealing, dealt** [delt] inflict (a blow) on; Cards give out (cards) to the players. **dealer** n **dealings** pl n transactions or business relations. **deal in** v buy or sell (goods). **deal out** v distribute. **deal with** v take action on; be concerned with.

deal² n plank of fir or pine wood.

dean n chief administrative official of a college or university faculty; chief administrator of a cathedral. **deanery** n, pl **-eries.** office or residence of a dean; parishes of a dean.

dear n someone regarded with affection. ▶ adj much-loved; costly. **dearly** adv **dearness** n

dearth [dirth] n inadequate amount, scarcity.

death n permanent end of life in a person or animal; instance of this; ending, destruction. **deathly** adj, adv like death, e.g. a deathly silence; deathly pale. **death duty** (in Britain) former name for INHERITANCE TAX. **death's-head** n human skull or a representation of one. **death trap** place or vehicle

considered very unsafe. **deathwatch beetle** beetle that bores into wood and makes a tapping sound.

deb n Informal debutante.

debacle [day-bah-kl] n disastrous failure.

debar v prevent, bar.

debase v lower in value, quality, or character. **debasement** n

debate n discussion. ▶ v discuss formally; consider (a course of action). **debatable** adj not absolutely certain.

debauch [dib-bawch] v make (someone) bad or corrupt, esp. sexually. **debauched** adj immoral, sexually corrupt. **debauchery** n

debenture n long-term bond bearing fixed interest, issued by a company or a government agency.

debilitate v weaken, make feeble. **debilitation** n **debility** n weakness, infirmity.

debit n acknowledgment of a sum owing by entry on the left side of an account. ▶ v **debiting, debited.** charge (an account) with a debt.

debonair adj (of a man) charming and refined.

debouch v move out from a narrow place to a wider one.

debrief v receive a report from (a soldier, diplomat, etc.) after an event. **debriefing** n

debris [deb-ree] n fragments of something destroyed.

debt n something owed, esp. money. **in debt** owing money. **debtor** n

debunk v Informal expose the falseness of.

debut [day-byoo] n first public appearance of a performer. **debutante** [day-byoo-tont] n young upper-class woman being formally presented to society.

Dec. December.

decade n period of ten years.

decadence n deterioration in morality or culture. **decadent** adj

decaffeinated [dee-**kaf**-fin-ate-id] adj (of coffee, tea, or cola) with caffeine removed.

decagon n geometric figure with ten faces.

decahedron [deca-a-**heed**-ron] n solid figure with ten sides.

Decalogue n the Ten Commandments.

decamp v depart secretly or suddenly.

decant v pour (a liquid) from one container to another; Chiefly Brit rehouse (people) while their homes are being renovated.

decanter n stoppered bottle for wine or spirits.

decapitate v behead. **decapitation** n

decathlon n athletic contest with ten events.

decay v become weaker or more corrupt; rot. ▶ n process of decaying; state brought about by this process.

decease n Formal death. **deceased** adj Formal dead. **the deceased** dead person.

deceive v mislead by lying; be unfaithful to (one's sexual partner). **deceiver** n **deceit** n behaviour intended to deceive. **deceitful** adj

decelerate v slow down. **deceleration** n

December n twelfth month of the year.

decent adj (of a person) polite and morally acceptable; fitting or proper; conforming to conventions of sexual behaviour; Informal kind. **decently** adv **decency** n

decentralize v reorganize into smaller local units.

decentralization n

deception n deceiving; something that deceives, trick. **deceptive** adj likely or designed to deceive. **deceptively** adv **deceptiveness** n

deci- combining form one tenth.

decibel n unit for measuring the intensity of sound.

decide v (cause to) reach a decision; settle (a contest or question). **decided** adj unmistakable; determined. **decidedly** adv

deciduous adj (of a tree) shedding its leaves annually.

decimal n fraction written in the form of a dot followed by one or more numbers. ▶ adj relating to or using powers of ten; expressed as a decimal. **decimalization** n **decimal currency** system of currency in which the units are parts or powers of ten. **decimal point** dot between the unit and the fraction of a number in the decimal system. **decimal system** number system with a base of ten, in which numbers are expressed by combinations of the digits 0 to 9.

decimate v destroy or kill a large proportion of. **decimation** n

decipher v work out the meaning of (something illegible or in code). **decipherable** adj

decision n judgment, conclusion, or resolution; act of making up one's mind; firmness of purpose. **decisive** adj having a definite influence; having the ability to make quick decisions. **decisively** adv **decisiveness** n

deck n area of a ship that forms a floor; similar area in a bus; platform that supports the turntable and pick-up of a record player. **deck chair** folding chair made of canvas over a wooden frame. **deck out** v decorate.

declaim v speak loudly and
dramatically; protest loudly.
declamation n **declamatory** adj

declare v state firmly and
forcefully; announce officially;
acknowledge for tax purposes.
declaration n **declaratory** adj

declension n Grammar changes in
the form of nouns, pronouns, or
adjectives to show case, number,
and gender.

decline v become smaller, weaker,
or less important; refuse politely
to accept or do; Grammar list the
inflections of (a noun, pronoun, or
adjective). ▶ n gradual weakening
or loss.

declivity n, pl **-ties.** downward
slope.

declutch v disengage the clutch of
a motor vehicle.

decoct v extract the essence from
(a substance) by boiling.
decoction n

decode v convert from code into
ordinary language. **decoder** n

décolleté [day-kol-tay] adj (of a
woman's garment) low-cut.

decommission v dismantle (a
nuclear reactor, weapon, etc.)
which is no longer needed.

decompose v be broken down
through chemical or bacterial
action. **decomposition** n

decompress v free from pressure;
return (a diver) to normal
atmospheric pressure.
decompression n **decompression
sickness** severe pain and difficulty
in breathing, caused by a sudden
change in atmospheric pressure.

decongestant n medicine that
relieves nasal congestion.

decontaminate v make safe by
removing poisons, radioactivity,
etc. **decontamination** n

decor [day-core] n style in which a

room or house is decorated.

decorate v make more attractive
by adding something ornamental;
paint or wallpaper; award a
(military) medal to. **decoration** n
decorative adj **decorator** n

decorous [dek-a-russ] adj polite,
calm, and sensible in behaviour.
decorously adv

decorum [dik-core-um] n polite
and socially correct behaviour.

decoy n person or thing used to
lure someone into danger;
dummy bird or animal, used to
lure game within shooting range.
▶ v lure away by means of a trick.

decrease v make or become less.
▶ n lessening, reduction; amount
by which something has
decreased.

decree n law made by someone in
authority; court judgment. ▶ v
order by decree.

decrepit adj weakened or worn
out by age or long use.
decrepitude n

decry v **-crying, -cried.** express
disapproval of.

dedicate v commit (oneself or
one's time) wholly to a special
purpose or cause; inscribe or
address (a book etc.) to someone
as a tribute. **dedicated** adj
devoted to a particular purpose or
cause. **dedication** n

deduce v reach (a conclusion) by
reasoning from evidence.
deducible adj

deduct v subtract.

deduction n deducting; something
that is deducted; deducing;
conclusion reached by deducing.
deductive adj

deed n something that is done;
legal document.

deem v consider, judge.

deep adj extending or situated far
down, inwards, backwards, or

sideways; of a specified dimension downwards, inwards, or backwards; difficult to understand; of great intensity; (foll. by *in*) absorbed in (an activity); (of a colour) strong or dark; low in pitch. **the deep** *Poetic* the sea. **deeply** *adv* profoundly or intensely (also **deep down**). **deepen** *v* **deep-freeze** *n* same as FREEZER.

deer *n, pl* **deer.** large wild animal, the male of which has antlers. **deerstalker** *n* cloth hat with peaks at the back and front and earflaps.

deface *v* deliberately spoil the appearance of. **defacement** *n*

de facto *adv* in fact. ▶ *adj* existing in fact, whether legally recognized or not.

defame *v* attack the good reputation of. **defamation** *n* **defamatory** [dif-fam-a-tree] *adj*

default *n* failure to do something; *Computers* instruction to a computer to select a particular option unless the user specifies otherwise. ▶ *v* fail to fulfil an obligation. **in default of** in the absence of. **defaulter** *n*

defeat *v* win a victory over; thwart, frustrate. ▶ *n* defeating. **defeatism** *n* ready acceptance or expectation of defeat. **defeatist** *adj, n*

defecate *v* discharge waste from the body through the anus. **defecation** *n*

defect *n* imperfection, blemish. ▶ *v* desert one's cause or country to join the opposing forces. **defective** *adj* imperfect, faulty. **defection** *n* **defector** *n*

defence *n* resistance against attack; argument in support of something; country's military resources; defendant's case in a court of law. **defenceless** *adj*

defend *v* protect from harm or danger; support in the face of criticism; represent (a defendant) in court. **defendant** *n* person accused of a crime. **defensible** *adj* capable of being defended because believed to be right. **defensibility** *n* **defensive** *adj* intended for defence; overanxious to protect oneself against (threatened) criticism. **defensively** *adv*

defender *n* person who supports someone or something in the face of criticism; player whose chief task is to stop the opposition scoring.

defer[1] *v* **-ferring, -ferred.** delay (something) until a future time. **deferment, deferral** *n*

defer[2] *v* **-ferring, -ferred.** (foll. by *to*) comply with the wishes (of). **deference** *n* polite and respectful behaviour. **deferential** *adj* **deferentially** *adv*

defiance *n* see DEFY.

deficient *adj* lacking some essential thing or quality; inadequate in quality or quantity. **deficiency** *n* state of being deficient; lack, shortage.

deficit *n* amount by which a sum of money is too small.

defile[1] *v* treat (something sacred or important) without respect. **defilement** *n*

defile[2] *n* narrow valley or pass.

define *v* state precisely the meaning of; show clearly the outline of. **definable** *adj* **definite** *adj* firm, clear, and precise; having precise limits; known for certain. **definitely** *adv* **definition** *n* statement of the meaning of a word or phrase; quality of being clear and distinct. **definitive** *adj* providing an unquestionable conclusion; being the best example of something.

deflate v (cause to) collapse through the release of air; take away the self-esteem or conceit from; *Economics* cause deflation of (an economy). **deflation** n *Economics* reduction in economic activity resulting in lower output and investment; feeling of sadness following excitement.
deflationary adj

deflect v (cause to) turn aside from a course. **deflection** n **deflector** n

deflower v *Lit* deprive (a woman) of her virginity.

defoliate v deprive (a plant) of its leaves. **defoliant** n **defoliation** n

deforestation n destruction of all the trees in an area.

deform v put out of shape or spoil the appearance of. **deformation** n **deformity** n

defraud v cheat out of money, property, etc.

defray v provide money for (costs or expenses).

defrock v deprive (a priest) of priestly status.

defrost v make or become free of ice; thaw (frozen food) by removing it from a freezer.

deft adj quick and skilful in movement. **deftly** adv **deftness** n

defunct adj no longer existing or operative.

defuse v remove the fuse of (an explosive device); remove the tension from (a situation).

defy v -fying, -fied. resist openly and boldly; make impossible, e.g. *the condition of the refugees defied description.* **defiance** n **defiant** adj

degenerate adj having deteriorated to a lower mental, moral, or physical level. ▸ n degenerate person. ▸ v become degenerate. **degeneracy** n

degenerate behaviour.
degeneration n

degrade v reduce to dishonour or disgrace; reduce in status or quality; *Chem* decompose into smaller molecules. **degradation** n

degree n stage in a scale of relative amount or intensity; academic award given by a university or college on successful completion of a course; unit of measurement for temperature, angles, or latitude and longitude.

dehumanize v deprive of human qualities; make (an activity) mechanical or routine.
dehumanization n

dehydrate v remove water from (food) to preserve it. **be dehydrated** become weak through losing too much water from the body. **dehydration** n

de-ice v free of ice. **de-icer** n

deify [day-if-fie] v -fying, -fied. treat or worship as a god.
deification n

deign [dane] v agree (to do something), but as if doing someone a favour.

deity [dee-it-ee or day-it-ee] n, pl -ties. god or goddess; state of being divine.

déjà vu [day-zhah voo] n feeling of having experienced before something that is actually happening now.

dejected adj unhappy. **dejectedly** adv **dejection** n

de jure adv, adj according to law.

dekko n *Brit, Aust & NZ slang* have a dekko have a look.

delay v put off to a later time; slow up or cause to be late. ▸ n act of delaying; interval of time between events.

delectable adj delightful, very attractive. **delectation** n *Formal* great pleasure.

delegate n person chosen to represent others, esp. at a meeting. ▶ v entrust (duties or powers) to someone; appoint as a delegate. **delegation** n group chosen to represent others; delegating.

delete v remove (something written or printed). **deletion** n

deleterious [del-it-eer-ee-uss] adj harmful, injurious.

deliberate adj planned in advance, intentional; careful and unhurried. ▶ v think something over. **deliberately** adv **deliberation** n **deliberative** adj

delicate adj fine or subtle in quality or workmanship; having a fragile beauty; (of a taste etc.) pleasantly subtle; easily damaged; requiring tact. **delicately** adv **delicacy** n being delicate; (pl -cies) something particularly good to eat.

delicatessen n shop selling imported or unusual foods, often already cooked or prepared.

delicious adj very appealing to taste or smell. **deliciously** adv

delight n (source of) great pleasure. ▶ v please greatly; (foll. by in) take great pleasure (in). **delightful** adj **delightfully** adv

delimit v mark or lay down the limits of. **delimitation** n

delineate [dill-lin-ee-ate] v show by drawing; describe in words. **delineation** n

delinquent n someone, esp. a young person, who repeatedly breaks the law. ▶ adj repeatedly breaking the law. **delinquency** n

delirium n state of excitement and mental confusion, often with hallucinations; great excitement. **delirious** adj **deliriously** adv

deliver v carry (goods etc.) to a destination; hand over; aid in the birth of; present (a lecture or speech); release or rescue; strike (a blow). **deliverance** n rescue from captivity or evil. **delivery** n, pl **-eries**. delivering; something that is delivered; act of giving birth to a baby; style in public speaking.

dell n Chiefly Brit small wooded hollow.

Delphic adj ambiguous, like the ancient Greek oracle at Delphi.

delphinium n large garden plant with blue flowers.

delta n fourth letter in the Greek alphabet; flat area at the mouth of some rivers where the main stream splits up into several branches.

delude v deceive.

deluge [del-lyooj] n great flood; torrential rain; overwhelming number. ▶ v flood; overwhelm.

delusion n mistaken idea or belief; state of being deluded. **delusive** adj

de luxe adj rich or sumptuous; superior in quality.

delve v research deeply (for information).

demagogue n political agitator who appeals to the prejudice and passions of the mob. **demagogic** adj **demagogy** n

demand v request forcefully; require as just, urgent, etc.; claim as a right. ▶ n forceful request; Economics willingness and ability to purchase goods and services; something that requires special effort or sacrifice. **demanding** adj requiring a lot of time or effort.

demarcation n Formal establishing limits or boundaries, esp. between the work performed by different trade unions.

demean v **demean oneself** do something unworthy of one's status or character.

demeanour n way a person behaves.

demented adj mad. **dementedly** adv **dementia** [dim-men-sha] n state of serious mental deterioration.

demerara sugar n brown crystallized cane sugar.

demerit n fault, disadvantage.

demesne [dim-mane] n land surrounding a house; Law possession of one's own property or land.

demi- combining form half.

demijohn n large bottle with a short neck, often encased in wicker.

demilitarize v remove the military forces from. **demilitarization** n

demimonde n (esp. in the 19th century) class of women considered to be outside respectable society because of promiscuity; group considered not wholly respectable.

demise n eventual failure (of something successful); Formal death.

demo n, pl **demos**. Informal demonstration, organized expression of public opinion.

demob v Brit, Aust & NZ informal demobilize.

demobilize v release from the armed forces. **demobilization** n

democracy n, pl **-cies**. government by the people or their elected representatives; state governed in this way. **democrat** n advocate of democracy; (D-) member or supporter of the Democratic Party in the US. **democratic** adj of democracy; upholding democracy; (D-) of the Democratic Party, the more liberal of the two main political parties in the US. **democratically** adv

demography n study of

population statistics, such as births and deaths. **demographer** n **demographic** adj

demolish v knock down or destroy (a building); disprove (an argument). **demolition** n

demon n evil spirit; person who does something with great energy or skill. **demonic** adj evil. **demoniac, demoniacal** adj appearing to be possessed by a devil; frenzied. **demonology** n study of demons.

demonstrate v show or prove by reasoning or evidence; display and explain the workings of; reveal the existence of; show support or opposition by public parades or rallies. **demonstrable** adj able to be proved. **demonstrably** adv **demonstration** n organized expression of public opinion; explanation or display of how something works; proof. **demonstrative** adj tending to show one's feelings unreservedly. **demonstratively** adv **demonstrator** n person who demonstrates how a device or machine works; person who takes part in a public demonstration.

demoralize v undermine the morale of. **demoralization** n

demote v reduce in status or rank. **demotion** n

demur v -murring, -murred. show reluctance. ▶ n without demur without objecting.

demure adj quiet, reserved, and rather shy. **demurely** adv

den n home of a wild animal; small secluded room in a home; place where people indulge in criminal or immoral activities.

denationalize v transfer (an industry) from public to private ownership. **denationalization** n

denature v change the nature of;

make (alcohol) unfit to drink.

denier [den-yer] n unit of weight used to measure the fineness of nylon or silk.

denigrate v criticize unfairly. **denigration** n

denim n hard-wearing cotton fabric, usu. blue. ▶ pl jeans made of denim.

denizen n inhabitant.

denominate v give a specific name to.

denomination n group having a distinctive interpretation of a religious faith; unit in a system of weights, values, or measures. **denominational** adj

denominator n number below the line in a fraction.

denote v be a sign of; have as a literal meaning. **denotation** n

denouement [day-noo-mon] n final outcome or solution in a play or book.

denounce v speak vehemently against; give information against. **denunciation** n open condemnation.

dense adj closely packed; difficult to see through; stupid. **densely** adv **density** n, pl **-ties**. degree to which something is filled or occupied; measure of the compactness of a substance, expressed as its mass per unit volume.

dent n hollow in the surface of something, made by hitting it. ▶ v make a dent in.

dental adj of teeth or dentistry. **dental floss** waxed thread used to remove food particles from between the teeth. **dentine** [den-teen] n hard dense tissue forming the bulk of a tooth. **denture** n false tooth.

dentist n person qualified to practise dentistry. **dentistry** n

branch of medicine concerned with the teeth and gums.

denude v remove the covering or protection from.

deny v **-nying, -nied.** declare to be untrue; refuse to give or allow; refuse to acknowledge. **deniable** adj **denial** n statement that something is not true; rejection of a request.

deodorant n substance applied to the body to mask the smell of perspiration.

deodorize v remove or disguise the smell of.

depart v leave; differ, deviate. **departed** adj Euphemistic dead. **the departed** Euphemistic dead person. **departure** n

department n specialized division of a large organization; major subdivision of the administration of a government. **departmental** adj **department store** large shop selling many kinds of goods.

depend v (foll. by on) put trust (in); be influenced or determined (by); rely (on) for income or support. **dependable** adj **dependably** adv **dependability** n **dependant** n person who depends on another for financial support. **dependence** n state of being dependent. **dependency** n, pl **-cies.** country controlled by another country; overreliance on another person or on a drug. **dependent** adj depending on someone or something.

depict v produce a picture of; describe in words. **depiction** n

depilatory [dip-pill-a-tree] n, pl **-tories,** adj (substance) designed to remove unwanted hair.

deplete v use up; reduce in number. **depletion** n

deplore v condemn strongly. **deplorable** adj very bad or unpleasant.

deploy v organize (troops or resources) into a position ready for immediate action. **deployment** n

depopulate v reduce the population of a. **depopulation** n

deport v remove forcibly from a country. **deport oneself** behave in a specified way. **deportation** n **deportee** n

deportment n way in which a person moves or stands.

depose v remove from an office or position of power; Law testify on oath.

deposit v put down; entrust for safekeeping, esp. to a bank; lay down naturally. ▶ n sum of money paid into a bank account; money given in part payment for goods or services; accumulation of sediments, minerals, etc.

depositary n person to whom something is entrusted for safety.

depositor n **depository** n store for furniture etc.

deposition n Law sworn statement of a witness used in court in his or her absence; deposing; depositing; something deposited.

depot [dep-oh] n building where goods or vehicles are kept when not in use; NZ & US bus or railway station.

depraved adj morally bad. **depravity** n

deprecate v express disapproval of. **deprecation** n **deprecatory** adj

depreciate v decline in value or price; criticize. **depreciation** n

depredation n plundering.

depress v make sad; lower (prices or wages); push down.

depressing adj **depressingly** adv **depressant** n, adj (drug) able to reduce nervous activity.

depression n mental state in which a person has feelings of gloom and inadequacy; economic condition in which there is high unemployment and low output and investment; area of low air pressure; sunken place.

depressive adj tending to cause depression. ▶ n person who suffers from depression.

deprive v (foll. by of) prevent from (having or enjoying). **deprivation** n **deprived** adj lacking adequate living conditions, education, etc.

depth n distance downwards, backwards, or inwards; intensity of emotion; profundity of character or thought. **depth charge** bomb used to attack submarines by exploding at a preset depth of water.

depute v appoint (someone) to act on one's behalf. **deputation** n body of people appointed to represent others.

deputy n, pl -ties. person appointed to act on behalf of another. **deputize** v act as deputy.

derail v cause (a train) to go off the rails. **derailment** n

deranged adj insane or uncontrolled; in a state of disorder. **derangement** n

derby [dah-bee] n, pl -bies. sporting event between teams from the same area. ▶ n any of various horse races.

deregulate v remove regulations or controls from. **deregulation** n

derelict adj unused and falling into ruins. ▶ n social outcast, vagrant. **dereliction** n state of being abandoned. **dereliction of duty** failure to do one's duty.

deride v treat with contempt or ridicule. **derision** n **derisive** adj mocking, scornful. **derisory** adj too small or inadequate to be considered seriously.

de rigueur [de rig-**gur**] *adj* required by fashion.

derive *v* (foll. by *from*) take or develop (from). **derivation** *n* **derivative** *adj* word, idea, etc., derived from another.

dermatitis *n* inflammation of the skin.

dermatology *n* branch of medicine concerned with the skin. **dermatologist** *n*

derogatory [dir-**rog**-a-tree] *adj* intentionally offensive.

derrick *n* simple crane; framework erected over an oil well.

derv *n Brit* diesel oil, when used for road transport.

dervish *n* member of a Muslim religious order noted for a frenzied whirling dance.

descant *n Music* tune played or sung above a basic melody.

descend *v* move down (a slope etc.); move to a lower level, pitch, etc.; (foll. by *to*) stoop to (unworthy behaviour); (foll. by *on*) visit unexpectedly. **be descended from** be connected by a blood relationship to. **descendant** *n* person or animal descended from an individual, race, or species. **descendent** *adj* descending. **descent** *n* descending; downward slope; derivation from an ancestor.

describe *v* give an account of (something or someone) in words; trace the outline of (a circle etc.). **description** *n* statement that describes something or someone; sort, e.g. *flowers of every description*. **descriptive** *adj* **descriptively** *adv*

descry *v* **-scrying, -scried.** catch sight of; discover by looking carefully.

desecrate *v* damage or insult (something sacred). **desecration** *n*

desegregate *v* end racial

segregation in. **desegregation** *n*

deselect *v Brit politics* refuse to select (an MP) for re-election. **deselection** *n*

desert[1] *n* region with little or no vegetation because of low rainfall.

desert[2] *v* abandon (a person or place) without intending to return; *Mil* leave (a post or duty) with no intention of returning. **deserter** *n* **desertion** *n*

deserts *pl n* **get one's just deserts** get the punishment one deserves.

deserve *v* be entitled to or worthy of. **deserved** *adj* rightfully earned. **deservedly** *adv* **deserving** *adj* worthy of help, praise, or reward.

deshabille [day-zab-**beel**] *n* state of being partly dressed.

desiccate *v* remove most of the water from. **desiccation** *n*

design *v* work out the structure or form of (something), by making a sketch or plans; plan and make artistically; intend for a specific purpose. ▶ *n* preliminary drawing; arrangement or features of an artistic or decorative work; art of designing; intention, e.g. *by design*. **designedly** [dee-**zine**-id-lee] *adv* intentionally.

designer *n* person who draws up original sketches or plans from which things are made. ▶ *adj* designed by a well-known designer. **designing** *adj* cunning and scheming.

designate [dez-**zig**-nate] *v* give a name to; select (someone) for an office or duty. ▶ *adj* appointed but not yet in office. **designation** *n* name.

desire *v* want very much. ▶ *n* wish, longing; sexual appetite; person or thing desired. **desirable** *adj* worth having; arousing sexual desire. **desirability** n **desirous of** having a desire for.

desist v (foll. by from) stop (doing something).

desk n piece of furniture with a writing surface and drawers; service counter in a public building; section of a newspaper covering a specific subject, e.g. the sports desk. **desktop** adj (of a computer) small enough to use at a desk.

desolate adj uninhabited and bleak; very sad. ▶ v deprive of inhabitants; make (someone) very sad. **desolation** n

despair n total loss of hope. ▶ v lose hope.

despatch v, n same as DISPATCH.

desperado n, pl **-does, -dos.** reckless person ready to commit any violent illegal act.

desperate adj in despair and reckless; (of an action) undertaken as a last resort; having a strong need or desire. **desperately** adv **desperation** n

despise v regard with contempt. **despicable** adj deserving contempt. **despicably** adv

despite prep in spite of.

despoil v Formal plunder. **despoliation** n

despondent adj unhappy. **despondently** adv **despondency** n

despot n person in power who acts unfairly or cruelly. **despotic** adj **despotism** n unfair or cruel government or behaviour.

dessert n sweet course served at the end of a meal. **dessertspoon** n spoon between a tablespoon and a teaspoon in size.

destination n place to which someone or something is going.

destined adj certain to be or to do something.

destiny n, pl **-nies.** future marked

out for a person or thing; the power that predetermines the course of events.

destitute adj having no money or possessions. **destitution** n

destroy v ruin, demolish; put an end to; kill (an animal).

destroyer n small heavily armed warship; person or thing that destroys.

destruction n destroying; cause of ruin. **destructive** adj (capable of) causing destruction. **destructively** adv

desuetude [diss-syoo-it-tude] n condition of not being in use.

desultory [dez-zl-tree] adj jumping from one thing to another, disconnected; random. **desultorily** adv

detach v disengage and separate. **detachable** adj **detached** adj Brit, Aust & S Afr (of a house) not joined to another house; showing no emotional involvement. **detachment** n lack of emotional involvement; small group of soldiers.

detail n individual piece of information; unimportant item; small individual features of something, considered collectively; Chiefly mil (personnel assigned) a specific duty. ▶ v list fully.

detain v delay (someone); hold (someone) in custody. **detainee** n

detect v notice; discover, find. **detectable** adj **detection** n **detective** n policeman or private agent who investigates crime. **detector** n instrument used to find something.

detente [day-tont] n easing of tension between nations.

detention n imprisonment; form of punishment in which a pupil is detained after school.

deter v **-terring, -terred.**

discourage (someone) from doing something by instilling fear or doubt. **deterrent** n something that deters; weapon, esp. nuclear, intended to deter attack. ▶ adj tending to deter.

detergent n chemical substance for washing clothes or dishes.

deteriorate v become worse. **deterioration** n

determine v settle (an argument or a question) conclusively; find out the facts about; make a firm decision (to do something). **determinant** n factor that determines. **determinate** adj definitely limited or fixed. **determination** n being determined or resolute. **determined** adj firmly decided, unable to be dissuaded. **determinedly** adv **determiner** n Grammar word that determines the object to which a noun phrase refers, e.g. all. **determinism** n theory that human choice is not free, but decided by past events. **determinist** n, adj

detest v dislike intensely. **detestable** adj **detestation** n

dethrone v remove from a throne or position of power.

detonate v explode. **detonation** n **detonator** n small amount of explosive, or a device, used to set off an explosion.

detour n route that is not the most direct one.

detract v (foll. by from) make (something) seem less good. **detractor** n

detriment n disadvantage or damage. **detrimental** adj **detrimentally** adv

detritus [dit-**trite**-uss] n loose mass of stones and silt worn away from rocks; debris.

de trop [de **troh**] adj French

unwanted, unwelcome.

deuce [dyewss] n Tennis score of forty all; playing card with two symbols or dice with two spots.

deuterium n isotope of hydrogen twice as heavy as the normal atom.

Deutschmark [doytch-mark], **Deutsche Mark** [doytch-a] n former monetary unit of Germany.

devalue v -valuing, -valued. reduce the exchange value of (a currency); reduce the value of (something or someone). **devaluation** n

devastate v destroy. **devastated** adj shocked and extremely upset. **devastation** n

develop v grow or bring to a later, more elaborate, or more advanced stage; come or bring into existence; build houses or factories on (an area of land); produce (photographs) by making negatives or prints from a film. **developer** n person who develops property; chemical used to develop photographs or films. **development** n developing **country** poor or nonindustrial country that is trying to develop its resources by industrialization.

deviate v differ from others in belief or thought; depart from one's previous behaviour. **deviation** n **deviant** n, adj (person) deviating from what is considered acceptable behaviour. **deviance** n

device n machine or tool used for a specific task; scheme or plan.

devil n evil spirit; evil person; person, e.g. poor devil; daring person, e.g. be a devil; Informal something difficult or annoying, e.g. a devil of a long time. ▶ v -illing, -illed. prepare (food) with a highly flavoured spiced mixture. **the Devil** Theology chief spirit of

evil and enemy of God. **devilish**
adj cruel or unpleasant. ▶ adv (also
devilishly) Informal extremely.

devilment n mischievous conduct.

devilry n mischievousness.

devil-may-care adj carefree and
cheerful. **devil's advocate** person
who takes an opposing or
unpopular point of view for the
sake of argument.

devious adj insincere and
dishonest; indirect. **deviously** adv
deviousness n

devise v work out (something) in
one's mind.

devoid adj (foll. by of) completely
lacking in.

devolve v (foll. by on or to) pass
(power or duties) or (of power or
duties) be passed to a successor
or substitute. **devolution** n
transfer of authority from a central
government to regional
governments.

devote v apply or dedicate to a
particular purpose. **devoted** adj
showing loyalty or devotion.
devotedly adv **devotee** n person
who is very enthusiastic about
something; zealous follower of a
religion. **devotion** n strong
affection for or loyalty to someone
or something; religious zeal. ▶ pl
prayers. **devotional** adj

devour v eat greedily; (of an
emotion) engulf and destroy; read
eagerly.

devout adj deeply religious.
devoutly adv

dew n drops of water that form on
the ground at night from vapour
in the air. **dewy** adj

dewlap n loose fold of skin
hanging under the throat in dogs,
cattle, etc.

dexterity n skill in using one's
hands; mental quickness.
dexterous adj **dexterously** adv

dextrose n glucose occurring in
fruit, honey, and the blood of
animals.

DH (in Britain) Department of
Health.

DI donor insemination: method of
making a woman pregnant by
transferring sperm from a man
other than her regular partner
using artificial means.

diabetes [die-a-beet-eez] n
disorder in which an abnormal
amount of urine containing an
excess of sugar is excreted.
diabetic n, adj

diabolic adj of the Devil.
diabolism n witchcraft, devil
worship.

diabolical adj Informal extremely
bad. **diabolically** adv

diaconate n position or period of
office of a deacon.

diacritic n sign above or below a
character to indicate phonetic
value or stress.

diadem n Old-fashioned crown.

diaeresis n, pl **-ses** mark (¨)
placed over a vowel to show that
it is pronounced separately from
the preceding one, for example in
Noël.

diagnosis [die-ag-no-siss] n, pl **-ses**
[-seez] discovery and identification
of diseases from the examination
of symptoms. **diagnose** v
diagnostic adj

diagonal adj from corner to
corner; slanting. ▶ n diagonal line.
diagonally adv

diagram n sketch showing the
form or workings of something.
diagrammatic adj

dial n face of a clock or watch;
graduated disc on a measuring
instrument; control on a radio or
television set used to change the
station; numbered disc on the
front of some telephones. ▶ v

dialling, dialled. operate the dial or buttons on a telephone in order to contact (a number).

dialect n form of a language spoken in a particular area. **dialectal** adj

dialectic n logical debate by question and answer to resolve differences between two views. **dialectical** adj

dialogue n conversation between two people, esp. in a book, film, or play; discussion between representatives of two nations or groups. **dialogue box** n small window that may open on a computer screen to prompt the user to enter information or select an option.

dialysis [die-al-iss-iss] n Med filtering of blood through a membrane to remove waste products.

diamanté [die-a-man-tee] adj decorated with artificial jewels or sequins.

diameter n (length of) a straight line through the centre of a circle or sphere. **diametric, diametrical** adj of a diameter; completely opposed, e.g. the diametric opposite. **diametrically** adv

diamond n exceptionally hard, usu. colourless, precious stone; Geom figure with four sides of equal length forming two acute and two obtuse angles; playing card marked with red diamond-shaped symbols. **diamond wedding** sixtieth anniversary of a wedding.

diaper n US nappy.

diaphanous [die-af-fan-ous] adj fine and almost transparent.

diaphragm [die-a-fram] n muscular partition that separates the abdominal cavity and chest cavity; contraceptive device placed over

the neck of the womb.

diarrhoea [die-a-ree-a] n frequent discharge of abnormally liquid faeces.

diary n, pl -ries. (book for) a record of daily events, appointments, or observations. **diarist** n

diatribe n bitter critical attack.

dibble n small hand tool used to make holes in the ground for seeds or plants.

dice n, pl dice. small cube each of whose sides has a different number of spots (1 to 6), used in games of chance. ▶ v cut (food) into small cubes. **dice with death** take a risk. **dicey** adj Informal dangerous or risky.

dichotomy [die-kot-a-mee] n, pl -mies. division into two opposed groups or parts.

dicky[1] n, pl dickies. false shirt front. **dicky-bird** n child's word for a bird.

dicky[2] adj dickier, dickiest. Informal shaky or weak.

Dictaphone n ® tape recorder for recording dictation for subsequent typing.

dictate v say aloud for someone else to write down; (foll. by to) seek to impose one's will on (other people). ▶ n authoritative command; guiding principle. **dictation** n **dictator** n ruler who has complete power; person in power who acts unfairly or cruelly. **dictatorship** n **dictatorial** adj like a dictator.

diction n manner of pronouncing words and sounds.

dictionary n, pl -aries. book consisting of an alphabetical list of words with their meanings; alphabetically ordered reference book of terms relating to a particular subject.

dictum *n, pl* **-tums, -ta.** formal statement; popular saying.

did *v* past tense of DO.

didactic *adj* intended to instruct. **didactically** *adv*

diddle *v Informal* swindle.

didgeridoo *n* Australian musical instrument made from a long hollow piece of wood.

didn't did not.

die¹ *v* dying, died. (of a person, animal, or plant) cease all biological activity permanently; (of something inanimate) cease to exist or function. **be dying for, to do something** *Informal* be eager for or to do something. **die-hard** *n* person who resists change.

die² *n* shaped block used to cut or form metal.

dieresis [die-air-iss-iss] *n, pl* **-ses** [-seez] same as DIAERESIS.

diesel *n* diesel engine; vehicle driven by a diesel engine; diesel oil. **diesel engine** internal-combustion engine in which oil is ignited by compression. **diesel oil** fuel obtained from petroleum distillation.

diet¹ *n* food that a person or animal regularly eats; specific range of foods, to control weight or for health reasons. ▶ *v* follow a special diet so as to lose weight. ▶ *adj* (of food) suitable for a weight-reduction diet. **dietary** *adj* **dietary fibre** fibrous substances in fruit and vegetables that aid digestion. **dieter** *n* **dietetic** *adj* prepared for special dietary requirements. **dietetics** *n* study of diet and nutrition. **dietician** *n* person who specializes in dietetics.

diet² *n* parliament of some countries.

differ *v* be unlike; disagree.

different *adj* unlike; unusual.

difference *n* state of being unlike; disagreement; remainder left after subtraction. **differently** *adv*

differential *adj* of or using a difference; *Maths* involving differentials. ▶ *n* factor that differentiates between two comparable things; *Maths* tiny difference between values in a scale; difference between rates of pay for different types of work. **differential calculus** branch of calculus concerned with derivatives and differentials. **differentiate** *v* perceive or show the difference (between); make (one thing) distinct from other such things. **differentiation** *n*

difficult *adj* requiring effort or skill to do or understand; not easily pleased. **difficulty** *n*

diffident *adj* lacking self-confidence. **diffidence** *n* **diffidently** *adv*

diffraction *n Physics* deviation in the direction of a wave at the edge of an obstacle in its path; formation of light and dark fringes by the passage of light through a small aperture.

diffuse *v* spread over a wide area. ▶ *adj* widely spread; lacking concision. **diffusion** *n*

dig *v* digging, dug. cut into, break up, and turn over or remove (earth), esp. with a spade; (foll. by *out* or *up*) find by effort or searching; (foll. by *in* or *into*) thrust or jab. ▶ *n* digging; archaeological excavation; thrust or poke; spiteful remark. ▶ *pl Brit, Aust & S Afr informal* lodgings. **digger** *n* machine used for digging.

digest *v* subject to a process of digestion; absorb mentally. ▶ *n* shortened version of a book,

report, or article. **digestible** adj
digestion n (body's system for)
breaking down food into easily
absorbed substances. **digestive**
adj **digestive biscuit** biscuit
made from wholemeal flour.

digit [dij-it] n finger or toe;
numeral from 0 to 9. **digital** adj
displaying information as numbers
rather than with hands and a dial,
e.g. a digital clock. **digital
recording** sound-recording
process that converts audio or
analogue signals into a series of
pulses. **digital television**
television in which the picture is
transmitted in digital form and
then decoded. **digitally** adv

digitalis n drug made from
foxglove leaves, used as a heart
stimulant.

dignity n, pl -ties. serious, calm,
and controlled behaviour or
manner; quality of being worthy
of respect; sense of
self-importance. **dignify** v add
distinction to. **dignitary** n person
of high official position.

digress v depart from the main
subject in speech or writing.
digression n

dike n same as DYKE.

dilapidated adj (of a building)
having fallen into ruin.
dilapidation n

dilate v make or become wider or
larger. **dilation, dilatation** n

dilatory [dill-a-tree] adj tending or
intended to waste time.

dildo n, pl -dos. object used as a
substitute for an erect penis.

dilemma n situation offering a
choice between two equally
undesirable alternatives.

dilettante [dill-it-tan-tee] n, pl
-tantes, -tanti. person whose
interest in a subject is superficial
rather than serious. **dilettantism** n

diligent adj careful and persevering
in carrying out duties; carried out
with care and perseverance.
diligently adv **diligence** n

dill n sweet-smelling herb.

dilly-dally v -lying, -lied. Brit, Aust
& NZ informal dawdle, waste time.

dilute v make (a liquid) less
concentrated, esp. by adding
water; make (a quality etc.)
weaker in force. **dilution** n

diluvial, diluvian adj of a flood,
esp. the great Flood described in
the Old Testament.

dim adj dimmer, dimmest. badly
lit; not clearly seen; unintelligent.
▶ v dimming, dimmed. make or
become dim. **take a dim view of**
disapprove of. **dimly** adv
dimness n **dimmer** n device for
dimming an electric light.

dime n coin of the US and
Canada, worth ten cents.

dimension n measurement of the
size of something in a particular
direction; aspect, factor.

diminish v make or become
smaller, fewer, or less. **diminution**
n **diminutive** adj very small. ▶ n
word or affix which implies
smallness or unimportance.

diminuendo n Music gradual
decrease in loudness.

dimple n small natural dent, esp.
in the cheeks or chin. ▶ v produce
dimples by smiling.

din n loud unpleasant confused
noise. ▶ v dinning, dinned. (foll.
by into) instil (something) into
someone by constant repetition.

dinar [dee-nahr] n monetary unit
of various Balkan, Middle Eastern,
and North African countries.

dine v eat dinner. **diner** n person
eating a meal; Chiefly US small
cheap restaurant. **dining car**
railway coach where meals are
served. **dining room** room where

meals are eaten.

ding n Aust dated & NZ informal small dent in a vehicle.

ding-dong n sound of a bell; Informal lively quarrel or fight.

dinghy [ding-ee] n, pl -ghies. small boat, powered by sails, oars, or a motor.

dingo n, pl -goes. Australian wild dog.

dingy [din-jee] adj -gier, -giest. Brit, Aust & NZ dull and drab. **dinginess** n

dinkum adj Aust & NZ informal genuine or right.

dinky adj -kier, -kiest. Brit, Aust & NZ informal small and neat.

dinky-di adj Aust informal typical.

dinner n main meal of the day, eaten either in the evening or at midday. **dinner jacket** man's semiformal black evening jacket.

dinosaur n type of extinct prehistoric reptile, many of which were of gigantic size.

dint n by dint of by means of.

diocese [die-a-siss] n district over which a bishop has control. **diocesan** adj

diode n semiconductor device for converting alternating current to direct current.

dioptre [die-op-ter] n unit for measuring the refractive power of a lens.

dioxide n oxide containing two oxygen atoms per molecule.

dip v dipping, dipped. plunge quickly or briefly into a liquid; slope downwards; switch (car headlights) from the main to the lower beam; lower briefly. ▶ n dipping; brief swim; liquid chemical in which farm animals are dipped to rid them of insects; depression in a landscape; creamy mixture into which pieces of food are dipped before being eaten.

dip into v read passages at random from (a book or journal).

diphtheria [dif-theer-ya] n contagious disease producing fever and difficulty in breathing and swallowing.

diphthong n union of two vowel sounds in a single compound sound.

diploma n qualification awarded by a college on successful completion of a course.

diplomacy n conduct of the relations between nations by peaceful means; tact or skill in dealing with people. **diplomat** n official engaged in diplomacy. **diplomatic** adj of diplomacy; tactful in dealing with people. **diplomatically** adv

dipper n ladle used for dipping; (also **ousel, ouzel**) European songbird that lives by a river.

dipsomania n compulsive craving for alcohol. **dipsomaniac** n, adj

diptych [dip-tik] n painting on two hinged panels.

dire adj disastrous, urgent, or terrible.

direct adj (of a route) shortest, straight; without anyone or anything intervening; likely to have an immediate effect; honest, frank. ▶ adv in a direct manner. ▶ v lead and organize; tell (someone) to do something; tell (someone) the way to a place; address (a letter, package, remark, etc.); provide guidance to (actors, cameramen, etc.) in (a play or film). **directly** adv in a direct manner; at once. ▶ conj as soon as. **directness** n **direct current** electric current that flows in one direction only.

direction n course or line along which a person or thing moves, points, or lies; management or guidance. ▶ *pl* instructions for doing something or for reaching a place. **directional** *adj*

directive *n* instruction, order.

director *n* person or thing that directs or controls; member of the governing board of a business etc.; person responsible for the artistic and technical aspects of the making of a film etc. **directorial** *adj* **directorship** *n* **directorate** *n* board of directors; position of director.

directory *n, pl* **-tories.** book listing names, addresses, and telephone numbers; *Computers* area of a disk containing the names and locations of the files it currently holds.

dirge *n* slow sad song of mourning.

dirigible [dir-rij-jib-bl] *adj* able to be steered. ▶ *n* airship.

dirk *n* dagger, formerly worn by Scottish Highlanders.

dirndl *n* full gathered skirt originating from Tyrolean peasant wear.

dirt *n* unclean substance, filth; earth, soil; obscene speech or writing; *Informal* harmful gossip. **dirt track** racetrack made of packed earth or cinders.

dirty *adj* **dirtier, dirtiest.** covered or marked with dirt; unfair or dishonest; obscene; displaying dislike or anger, e.g. *a dirty look.* ▶ *v* **dirtying, dirtied.** make dirty. **dirtiness** *n*

dis- *prefix* indicating: reversal, e.g. *disconnect;* negation or lack, e.g. *dissimilar; disgrace;* removal or release, e.g. *disembowel.*

disable *v* make ineffective, unfit, or incapable. **disabled** *adj* lacking a physical power, such as the ability to walk. **disablement** *n* **disability** *n, pl* **-ties.** condition of being disabled; something that

disables someone.

disabuse *v* (foll. by *of*) rid (someone) of a mistaken idea.

disadvantage *n* unfavourable or harmful circumstance. **disadvantageous** *adj* **disadvantaged** *adj* socially or economically deprived.

disaffected *adj* having lost loyalty to or affection for someone or something. **disaffection** *n*

disagree *v* **-greeing, -greed.** argue or have different opinions; be different, conflict; (foll. by *with*) cause physical discomfort (to), e.g. *curry disagrees with me.* **disagreement** *n* **disagreeable** *adj* unpleasant; (of a person) unfriendly or unhelpful. **disagreeably** *adv*

disallow *v* reject as untrue or invalid.

disappear *v* cease to be visible; cease to exist. **disappearance** *n*

disappoint *v* fail to meet the expectations or hopes of. **disappointment** *n* feeling of being disappointed; person or thing that disappoints.

disapprobation *n* disapproval.

disapprove *v* (foll. by *of*) consider wrong or bad. **disapproval** *n*

disarm *v* deprive of weapons; win the confidence or affection of; (of a country) decrease the size of one's armed forces. **disarmament** *n* **disarming** *adj* removing hostility or suspicion. **disarmingly** *adv*

disarrange *v* throw into disorder.

disarray *n* confusion and lack of discipline; extreme untidiness.

disaster *n* occurrence that causes great distress or destruction; project etc. that fails. **disastrous** *adj* **disastrously** *adv*

disavow *v* deny connection with or responsibility for. **disavowal** *n*

disband v (cause to) cease to function as a group.

disbelieve v reject as false; (foll. by *in*) have no faith (in). **disbelief** n

disburse v pay out. **disbursement** n

disc n flat circular object; gramophone record; *Anat* circular flat structure in the body, esp. between the vertebrae; *Computers* same as DISK. **disc jockey** person who introduces and plays pop records on a radio programme or at a disco.

discard v get rid of (something or someone) as useless or undesirable.

discern v see or be aware of (something) clearly. **discernible** adj **discerning** adj having good judgment. **discernment** n

discharge v release, allow to go; dismiss (someone) from duty or employment; fire (a gun); pour forth, send out; meet the demands of (a duty or responsibility); relieve oneself of (a debt). ▶ n substance that comes out from a place; discharging.

disciple [diss-**sipe**-pl] n follower of the doctrines of a teacher, esp. Jesus Christ.

discipline n practice of imposing strict rules of behaviour; area of academic study. ▶ v attempt to improve the behaviour of (oneself or another) by training or rules; punish. **disciplined** adj able to behave and work in a controlled way. **disciplinarian** n person who practises strict discipline. **disciplinary** adj

disclaimer n statement denying responsibility. **disclaim** v

disclose v make known; allow to be seen. **disclosure** n

disco n, pl **-cos**. nightclub where people dance to amplified pop

records; occasion at which people dance to amplified pop records; mobile equipment for providing music for a disco.

discolour v change in colour, fade. **discoloration** n

discomfit v make uneasy or confused. **discomfiture** n

discomfort n inconvenience, distress, or mild pain.

discommode v cause inconvenience to.

disconcert v embarrass or upset.

disconnect v undo or break the connection between (two things); stop the supply of electricity or gas of. **disconnected** adj (of speech or ideas) not logically connected. **disconnection** n

disconsolate adj sad beyond comfort. **disconsolately** adv

discontent n lack of contentment. **discontented** adj

discontinue v come or bring to an end. **discontinuous** adj characterized by interruptions. **discontinuity** n

discord n lack of agreement or harmony between people; harsh confused sounds. **discordant** adj **discordance** n

discotheque n same as DISCO.

discount v take no account of (something) because it is considered to be unreliable, prejudiced, or irrelevant; deduct (an amount) from the price of something. ▶ n deduction from the full price of something.

discourage v deprive of the will to persist in something; oppose by expressing disapproval. **discouragement** n

discourse n conversation; formal treatment of a subject in speech or writing. ▶ v (foll. by *on*) speak or write (about) at length.

discourteous adj showing bad

manners. **discourtesy** n

discover v be the first to find or to find out about; learn about for the first time; find after study or search. **discoverer** n **discovery** n, pl **-eries.** discovering; person, place, or thing that has been discovered.

discredit v damage the reputation of; cause (an idea) to be disbelieved or distrusted. ▶ n damage to someone's reputation. **discreditable** adj bringing shame.

discreet adj careful to avoid embarrassment, esp. by keeping confidences secret; unobtrusive. **discreetly** adv

discrepancy n, pl **-cies.** conflict or variation between facts, figures, or claims.

discrete adj separate, distinct.

discretion n quality of behaving in a discreet way; freedom or authority to make judgments and decide what to do. **discretionary** adj

discriminate v (foll. by against or in favour of) single out (a particular person or group) for worse or better treatment than others; (foll. by between) recognize or understand the difference (between). **discriminating** adj showing good taste and judgment. **discrimination** n **discriminatory** adj based on prejudice.

discursive adj passing from one topic to another.

discus n heavy disc-shaped object thrown in sports competitions.

discuss v consider (something) by talking it over; treat (a subject) in speech or writing. **discussion** n

disdain n feeling of superiority and dislike. ▶ v refuse with disdain. **disdainful** adj **disdainfully** adv

disease n illness, sickness.

diseased adj

disembark v get off a ship, aircraft, or bus. **disembarkation** n

disembodied adj lacking a body; seeming not to be attached to or coming from anyone.

disembowel v -elling, -elled. remove the entrails of.

disenchanted adj disappointed and disillusioned. **disenchantment** n

disenfranchise v deprive (someone) of the right to vote or of other rights of citizenship.

disengage v release from a connection. **disengagement** n

disentangle v release from entanglement or confusion.

disfavour n disapproval or dislike.

disfigure v spoil the appearance of. **disfigurement** n

disfranchise v same as DISENFRANCHISE.

disgorge v empty out, discharge.

disgrace n condition of shame, loss of reputation, or dishonour; shameful person or thing. ▶ v bring shame upon (oneself or others). **disgraceful** adj **disgracefully** adv

disgruntled adj sulky or discontented. **disgruntlement** n

disguise v change the appearance or manner in order to conceal the identity of (someone or something); misrepresent (something) in order to obscure its actual nature or meaning. ▶ n mask, costume, or manner that disguises; state of being disguised.

disgust n great loathing or distaste. ▶ v sicken, fill with loathing.

dish n shallow container used for holding or serving food; particular kind of food; short for DISH AERIAL; Informal attractive person. **dish aerial** aerial consisting of a

concave disc-shaped reflector, used esp. for satellite television.
dishcloth n cloth for washing dishes. **dish out** v Informal distribute. **dish up** v Informal serve (food).
dishabille [diss-a-beel] n same as DESHABILLE.
dishearten v weaken or destroy the hope, courage, or enthusiasm of.
dishevelled adj (of a person's hair, clothes, or general appearance) disordered and untidy.
dishonest adj not honest or fair. **dishonestly** adv **dishonesty** n
dishonour v treat with disrespect. ▶ n lack of respect; state of shame or disgrace; something that causes a loss of honour. **dishonourable** adj **dishonourably** adv
disillusion v destroy the illusions or false ideas of. ▶ n (also **disillusionment**) state of being disillusioned.
disincentive n something that acts as a deterrent.
disinclined adj unwilling, reluctant. **disinclination** n
disinfect v rid of harmful germs, chemically. **disinfectant** n substance that destroys harmful germs. **disinfection** n
disinformation n false information intended to mislead.
disingenuous adj not sincere. **disingenuously** adv
disinherit v Law deprive (an heir) of inheritance. **disinheritance** n
disintegrate v break up. **disintegration** n
disinter v -terring, -terred. dig up; reveal, make known.
disinterested adj free from bias or involvement. **disinterest** n
disjointed adj having no coherence, disconnected.
disk n Computers storage device,

consisting of a stack of plates coated with a magnetic layer, which rotates rapidly as a single unit.
dislike v consider unpleasant or disagreeable. ▶ n feeling of not liking something or someone.
dislocate v displace (a bone or joint) from its normal position; disrupt or shift out of place. **dislocation** n
dislodge v remove (something) from a previously fixed position.
disloyal adj not loyal, deserting one's allegiance. **disloyalty** n
dismal adj gloomy and depressing; Informal of poor quality. **dismally** adv
dismantle v take apart piece by piece.
dismay v fill with alarm or depression. ▶ n alarm mixed with sadness.
dismember v remove the limbs of; cut to pieces. **dismemberment** n
dismiss v remove (an employee) from a job; allow (someone) to leave; put out of one's mind; (of a judge) state that (a case) will not be brought to trial. **dismissal** n **dismissive** adj scornful, contemptuous.
dismount v get off a horse or bicycle.
disobey v neglect or refuse to obey. **disobedient** adj **disobedience** n
disobliging adj unwilling to help.
disorder n state of untidiness and disorganization; public violence or rioting; illness. **disordered** adj untidy. **disorderly** adj untidy and disorganized; uncontrolled, unruly.
disorganize v disrupt the arrangement or system of. **disorganization** n
disorientate, disorient v cause (someone) to lose his or her

bearings. **disorientation** n

disown v deny any connection with (someone).

disparage v speak contemptuously of. **disparagement** n

disparate adj completely different. **disparity** n

dispassionate adj not influenced by emotion. **dispassionately** adv

dispatch v send off to a destination or to perform a task; carry out (a duty or a task) with speed; Old-fashioned kill. ▶ n official communication or report, sent in haste; report sent to a newspaper by a correspondent. **dispatch rider** Brit, Aust & NZ motorcyclist who carries dispatches.

dispel v -pelling, -pelled. destroy or remove.

dispense v distribute in portions; prepare and distribute (medicine); administer (the law etc.). **dispensable** adj not essential. **dispensation** n dispensing; exemption from an obligation. **dispenser** n **dispensary** n, pl -saries. place where medicine is dispensed. **dispense with** v do away with; manage without.

disperse v scatter over a wide area; (cause to) leave a gathering. **dispersal, dispersion** n

dispirit v make downhearted.

displace v move from the usual location; remove from office. **displacement** n **displaced person** person forced from his or her home or country, esp. by war.

display v make visible or noticeable. ▶ n displaying; something displayed; exhibition.

displease v annoy or upset. **displeasure** n

disport v **disport oneself** indulge oneself in pleasure.

dispose v place in a certain order.

disposed adj willing or eager; having an attitude as specified, e.g. he felt well disposed towards her. **disposable** adj designed to be thrown away after use; available for use, e.g. disposable income. **disposal** n getting rid of something. **at one's disposal** available for use. **disposition** n person's usual temperament; desire or tendency to do something; arrangement. **dispose of** v throw away, get rid of; deal with (a problem etc.); kill.

dispossess v (foll. by of) deprive (someone) of (a possession). **dispossession** n

disproportion n lack of proportion or equality. **disproportionate** adj out of proportion. **disproportionately** adv

disprove v show (an assertion or claim) to be incorrect.

dispute n disagreement, argument. ▶ v argue about (something); doubt the validity of; fight over possession of.

disqualify v stop (someone) officially from taking part in something for wrongdoing. **disqualification** n

disquiet n feeling of anxiety. ▶ v make (someone) anxious. **disquietude** n

disregard v give little or no attention to. ▶ n lack of attention or respect.

disrepair n condition of being worn out or in poor working order.

disrepute n loss or lack of good reputation. **disreputable** adj having or causing a bad reputation.

disrespect n lack of respect. **disrespectful** adj **disrespectfully** adv

disrobe v undress.

disrupt v interrupt the progress of. **disruption** n **disruptive** adj

dissatisfied adj not pleased or contented. **dissatisfaction** n

dissect v cut open (a corpse) to examine it; examine critically and minutely. **dissection** n

dissemble v conceal one's real motives or emotions by pretence.

disseminate v spread (information). **dissemination** n

dissent v disagree; Christianity reject the doctrines of an established church. ▶ n disagreement; Christianity separation from an established church. **dissension** n **dissenter** n

dissertation n written thesis, usu. required for a higher university degree; long formal speech.

disservice n harmful action.

dissident n person who disagrees with and criticizes the government. ▶ adj disagreeing with the government. **dissidence** n

dissimilar adj not alike, different. **dissimilarity** n

dissimulate v conceal one's real feelings by pretence. **dissimulation** n

dissipate v waste or squander; scatter, disappear. **dissipated** adj showing signs of overindulgence in alcohol and other physical pleasures. **dissipation** n

dissociate v regard or treat as separate. **dissociate oneself from** deny or break an association with. **dissociation** n

dissolute adj leading an immoral life.

dissolution n official breaking up of an organization or institution, such as Parliament; official ending of a formal agreement, such as a marriage.

dissolve v (cause to) become liquid; break up or end officially; break down emotionally, e.g. she dissolved into tears.

dissonance n lack of agreement or harmony. **dissonant** adj

dissuade v deter (someone) by persuasion from doing something. **dissuasion** n

distaff n rod on which wool etc. is wound for spinning. **distaff side** female side of a family.

distance n space between two points; state of being apart; remoteness in manner. **the distance** most distant part of the visible scene. **distance oneself from** separate oneself mentally from. **distant** adj far apart; separated by a specified distance; remote in manner. **distantly** adv

distaste n dislike, disgust. **distasteful** adj unpleasant, offensive.

distemper¹ n highly contagious viral disease of dogs.

distemper² n paint mixed with water, glue, etc., used for painting walls.

distend v (of part of the body) swell. **distension** n

distil v -tilling, -tilled. subject to or obtain by distillation; give off (a substance) in drops; extract the essence of. **distillation** n process of evaporating a liquid and condensing its vapour; (also **distillate** n concentrated essence.

distiller n person or company that makes strong alcoholic drink, esp. whisky. **distillery** n, pl -leries. place where a strong alcoholic drink, esp. whisky, is made.

distinct adj not the same; easily sensed or understood; clear and definite. **distinctly** adv **distinction** n act of distinguishing; distinguishing feature; state of being different; special honour,

recognition, or fame. **distinctive** adj easily recognizable.
distinctively adv **distinctiveness** n
distinguish v (usu. foll. by between) make, show, or recognize a difference (between); be a distinctive feature of; make out by hearing, seeing, etc.
distinguishable adj **distinguished** adj dignified in appearance; highly respected.
distort v misrepresent (the truth or facts); twist out of shape.
distortion n
distract v draw the attention of (a person) away from something; entertain. **distracted** adj unable to concentrate, preoccupied.
distraction n
distrait [diss-**tray**] adj absent-minded or preoccupied.
distraught [diss-**trawt**] adj extremely anxious or agitated.
distress n extreme unhappiness; great physical pain; poverty. ▶ v upset badly. **distressed** adj extremely upset; in financial difficulties. **distressing** adj **distressingly** adv
distribute v hand out or deliver; share out. **distribution** n distributing; arrangement or spread. **distributor** n wholesaler who distributes goods to retailers in a specific area; device in a petrol engine that sends the electric current to the spark plugs.
distributive adj
district n area of land regarded as an administrative or geographical unit. **district court judge** Aust & NZ judge presiding over a lower court.
distrust v regard as untrustworthy. ▶ n feeling of suspicion or doubt.
distrustful adj
disturb v intrude on; worry, make anxious; change the position or

shape of. **disturbance** n
disturbing adj **disturbingly** adv
disturbed adj Psychiatry emotionally upset or maladjusted.
disunite v cause disagreement among. **disunity** n
disuse n state of being no longer used. **disused** adj
ditch n narrow channel dug in the earth for drainage or irrigation. ▶ v Slang abandon.
dither v be uncertain or indecisive. ▶ n state of indecision or agitation.
ditherer n **dithery** adj
ditto n, pl **-tos.** the same. ▶ adv in the same way.
ditty n, pl **-ties.** short simple poem or song.
diuretic [die-yoor-**et**-ik] n drug that increases the flow of urine.
diurnal [die-**urn**-al] adj happening during the day or daily.
diva n distinguished female singer.
divan n low backless bed; backless sofa or couch.
dive v **diving, dived.** plunge headfirst into water; (of a submarine or diver) submerge under water; fly in a steep nose-down descending path; move quickly in a specified direction; (foll. by in or into) start doing (something) enthusiastically. ▶ n diving; steep nose-down descent; Slang disreputable bar or club. **diver** n person who works or explores underwater; person who dives for sport. **dive bomber** military aircraft designed to release bombs during a dive.
diverge v separate and go in different directions; deviate (from a prescribed course). **divergence** n **divergent** adj
divers adj Old-fashioned various.
diverse adj having variety, assorted; different in kind.
diversity n, pl **-ties.** quality of

being different or varied; range of difference. **diversify** v **-fying, -fied. diversification** n

divert v change the direction of; entertain; distract the attention of. **diversion** n official detour used by traffic when a main route is closed; something that distracts someone's attention; diverting; amusing pastime. **diversionary** adj

divest v strip (of clothes); deprive (of a role or function).

divide v separate into parts; share or be shared out in parts; (cause to) disagree; keep apart, be a boundary between; calculate how many times (one number) can be contained in (another). ▶ n division, split. **dividend** n sum of money representing part of the profit made, paid by a company to its shareholders; extra benefit. **divider** n screen used to divide a room into separate areas. ▶ pl compasses with two pointed arms, used for measuring or dividing lines.

divine adj of God or a god; godlike; Informal splendid. ▶ v discover (something) by intuition or guessing. **divinely** adv **divination** n art of discovering future events, as though by supernatural powers. **divinity** n study of religion; (pl **-ties**) god; state of being divine. **divining rod** forked twig said to move when held over ground in which water or metal is to be found.

division n dividing, sharing out; one of the parts into which something is divided; mathematical operation of dividing; difference of opinion. **divisional** adj of a division in an organization. **divisible** adj **divisibility** n **divisive** adj tending to cause disagreement. **divisor** n

number to be divided into another number.

divorce n legal ending of a marriage; any separation, esp. a permanent one. ▶ v legally end one's marriage (to); separate, consider separately. **divorcée**, (masc) **divorcé** n person who is divorced.

divulge v make known, disclose. ▶ n

Dixie n southern states of the US (also **Dixieland**).

DIY Brit, Aust & NZ do-it-yourself.

dizzy adj **-zier, -ziest.** having or causing a whirling sensation; mentally confused. ▶ v **-zying, -zied.** make dizzy. **dizzily** adv **dizziness** n

DJ disc jockey; Brit dinner jacket.

DNA n deoxyribonucleic acid, the main constituent of the chromosomes of all living things.

do v **does, doing, did, done.** perform or complete (a deed or action); be adequate, e.g. that one will do; suit or improve, e.g. that style does nothing for you; find the answer to (a problem or puzzle); cause; produce, e.g. it does no harm to think about; give, grant, e.g. do me a favour; work at, as a course of study or a job; used to form questions, e.g. how do you know?; used to intensify positive statements and commands, e.g. I do like port; do go on; used to form negative statements and commands, e.g. I do not know her well; do not get up; used to replace an earlier verb, e.g. he gets paid more than I do. ▶ n, pl **dos, do's.** Informal party, celebration. **do away with** v get rid of. **do-it-yourself** n constructing and repairing things oneself. **do up** v fasten; decorate and repair. **do with** v find useful or benefit from, e.g. I could do with a rest. **do**

without v manage without.

Doberman pinscher, Doberman n large dog with a black-and-tan coat.

dob in v **dobbing, dobbed.** Aust & NZ informal inform against; contribute to a fund.

DOC (in New Zealand) Department of Conservation.

docile adj (of a person or animal) easily controlled. **docilely** adv **docility** n

dock[1] n enclosed area of water where ships are loaded, unloaded, or repaired. ▶ v bring or be brought into dock; link (two spacecraft) or (of two spacecraft) be linked together in space.

docker n Brit person employed to load and unload ships. **dockyard** n place where ships are built or repaired.

dock[2] v deduct money from (a person's wages); remove part of (an animal's tail) by cutting through the bone.

dock[3] n enclosed space in a court of law where the accused person sits or stands.

dock[4] n weed with broad leaves.

docket n label on a package or other delivery, stating contents, delivery instructions, etc.

doctor n person licensed to practise medicine; person who has been awarded a doctorate. ▶ v alter in order to deceive; poison or drug (food or drink); Informal castrate (an animal). **doctoral** adj **doctorate** n highest academic degree in any field of knowledge.

doctrine n body of teachings of a religious, political, or philosophical group; principle or body of principles that is taught or advocated. **doctrinal** adj of doctrines. **doctrinaire** adj stubbornly insistent on the application of a theory without regard to practicality.

document n piece of paper providing an official record of something. ▶ v record or report (something) in detail; support (a claim) with evidence. **documentation** n

documentary n, pl **-ries.** film or television programme presenting the facts about a particular subject. ▶ adj (of evidence) based on documents.

docu-soap n television documentary series presenting the lives of the people filmed as entertainment.

dodder v move unsteadily. **doddery** adj

dodecagon [doe-deck-a-gon] n geometric figure with twelve sides.

dodge v avoid (a blow, being seen, etc.) by moving suddenly; evade by cleverness or trickery. ▶ n cunning or deceitful trick. **dodgy** adj **dodgier, dodgiest.** Informal dangerous, risky; untrustworthy.

Dodgem n ® small electric car driven and bumped against similar cars in a rink at a funfair.

dodger n person who evades a responsibility or duty.

dodo n, pl **dodos, dodoes.** large flightless extinct bird.

doe n female deer, hare, or rabbit.

does v third person singular of the present tense of DO.

doesn't does not.

doff v take off or lift (one's hat) in polite greeting.

dog n domesticated four-legged mammal of many different breeds; related wild mammal, such as the dingo or coyote; male animal of the dog family; Informal person, e.g. you lucky dog! ▶ v **dogging, dogged.** follow (someone) closely; trouble, plague. **go to the dogs**

Informal go to ruin physically or morally. **let sleeping dogs lie** leave things undisturbed. **doggy, doggie** *n, pl* **-gies.** child's word for a dog. **dogcart** *n* light horse-drawn two-wheeled cart.

dog collar collar for a dog; *Informal* white collar fastened at the back, worn by members of the clergy. **dog-eared** *adj* (of a book) having pages folded down at the corner; shabby, worn.

dogfight *n* close-quarters combat between fighter aircraft. **dogfish** *n* small shark. **doghouse** *n US* kennel. **in the doghouse** *Informal* in disgrace. **dogleg** *n* sharp bend. **dog-roll** *n NZ* sausage-shaped roll of meat processed as dog food. **dog rose** wild rose with pink or white flowers. **dog-tired** *adj Informal* exhausted.

doge [doje] *n* (formerly) chief magistrate of Venice or Genoa.

dogged [dog-gid] *adj* obstinately determined. **doggedly** *adv* **doggedness** *n*

doggerel *n* poorly written poetry, usu. comic.

doggo *adv* **lie doggo** *Informal* hide and keep quiet.

dogma *n* doctrine or system of doctrines proclaimed by authority as true. **dogmatic** *adj* stating one's opinions forcefully or arrogantly. **dogmatically** *adv* **dogmatism** *n*

dogsbody *n, pl* **-bodies.** *Informal* person who carries out boring tasks for others.

doily *n, pl* **-lies.** decorative lacy paper mat, laid on a plate.

doldrums *pl n* depressed state of mind; state of inactivity.

dole *n Brit, Aust & NZ informal* money received from the state while unemployed. ▶ *v* (foll. by

out) distribute in small quantities.

doleful *adj* dreary, unhappy. **dolefully** *adv*

doll *n* small model of a human being, used as a toy; *Slang* pretty girl or young woman.

dollar *n* standard monetary unit of many countries.

dollop *n Informal* lump (of food).

dolly *n, pl* **-lies.** child's word for a doll; wheeled support on which a camera may be moved.

dolman sleeve *n* sleeve that is very wide at the armhole, tapering to a tight wrist.

dolmen *n* prehistoric monument consisting of a horizontal stone supported by vertical stones.

dolomite *n* mineral consisting of calcium magnesium carbonate.

dolorous *adj* sad, mournful.

dolphin *n* sea mammal of the whale family, with a beaklike snout. **dolphinarium** *n* aquarium for dolphins.

dolt *n* stupid person. **doltish** *adj*

domain *n* field of knowledge or activity; land under one ruler or government; *Computers* group of computers with the same name on the Internet; *NZ* public park.

dome *n* rounded roof built on a circular base; something shaped like this. **domed** *adj*

domestic *adj* of one's own country or a specific country; of the home or family; enjoying running a home; (of an animal) kept as a pet or to produce food. ▶ *n* person whose job is to do housework in someone else's house. **domestically** *adv* **domesticity** *n* **domesticate** *v* bring or keep (a wild animal or plant) under control or cultivation; accustom (someone) to home life. **domestication** *n* **domestic science** study of household skills.

domicile [dom-miss-ile] n place where one lives.

dominant adj having authority or influence; main, chief. **dominance** n

dominate v control or govern; tower above (surroundings); be very significant in. **domination** n

domineering adj forceful and arrogant.

Dominican n, adj (friar or nun) of an order founded by Saint Dominic.

dominion n control or authority; land governed by one ruler or government; (formerly) self-governing division of the British Empire.

domino n, pl **-noes**. small rectangular block marked with dots, used in dominoes. ▶ pl game in which dominoes with matching halves are laid together.

don[1] v **donning, donned.** put on (clothing).

don[2] n Brit member of the teaching staff at a university or college; Spanish gentleman or nobleman. **donnish** adj serious and academic.

donate v give, esp. to a charity or organization. **donation** n donating; thing donated. **donor** n Med person who gives blood or organs for use in the treatment of another person; person who makes a donation.

done v past participle of DO.

doner kebab n see KEBAB.

donga [dong-ga] n S Afr, Aust & NZ steep-sided gully created by soil erosion.

donkey n long-eared member of the horse family. **donkey jacket** Brit, Aust & NZ man's long thick jacket with a waterproof panel across the shoulders. **donkey's years** Informal long time. **donkey-work** n tedious hard work.

don't do not.

doodle v scribble or draw aimlessly. ▶ n shape or picture drawn aimlessly.

doom n death or a terrible fate. ▶ v destine or condemn to death or a terrible fate. **doomsday** n Christianity day on which the Last Judgment will occur; any dreaded day.

door n hinged or sliding panel for closing the entrance to a building, room, etc.; entrance. **doormat** n mat for wiping dirt from shoes before going indoors; Informal person who offers little resistance to ill-treatment. **doorway** n opening into a building or room.

dope n Slang illegal drug, usu. cannabis; medicine, drug; Informal stupid person. ▶ v give a drug to, esp. in order to improve performance in a race. **dopey, dopy** adj half-asleep, drowsy; Slang silly.

dork n Slang stupid person.

dormant adj temporarily quiet, inactive, or not being used. **dormancy** n

dormer, dormer window n window that sticks out from a sloping roof.

dormitory n, pl **-ries.** large room, esp. at a school, containing several beds.

dormouse n, pl **-mice.** small mouselike rodent with a furry tail.

dorp n S Afr small town.

dorsal adj of or on the back.

dory, John Dory n, pl **-ries.** spiny-finned edible sea fish.

dose n specific quantity of a medicine taken at one time; Informal something unpleasant to experience. ▶ v give a dose to. **dosage** n size of a dose.

doss v **doss down** slang sleep in an uncomfortable place.

dosshouse n Brit & S Afr slang cheap lodging house for homeless people.

dossier [doss-ee-ay] n collection of documents about a subject or person.

dot n small round mark; shorter symbol used in Morse code. ▶ v **dotting, dotted.** mark with a dot; scatter, spread around. **on the dot** at exactly the arranged time. **dotty** adj Slang rather eccentric. **dotcom, dot.com** n company that does most of its business on the Internet.

dote v **dote on** love to an excessive degree. **dotage** n weakness as a result of old age.

double adj as much again in number, amount, size, etc.; composed of two equal or similar parts; designed for two users, e.g. double room; folded in two. ▶ adv twice over. ▶ n twice the number, amount, size, etc.; person who looks almost exactly like another. ▶ pl game between two pairs of players. ▶ v make or become twice as much or as many; bend or fold (material etc.); play two parts; turn sharply. **at, on the double** quickly or immediately. **doubly** adv **double agent** spy employed by two enemy countries at the same time. **double bass** stringed instrument, largest and lowest member of the violin family. **double chin** fold of fat under the chin. **double cream** Brit thick cream with a high fat content. **double-cross** v cheat or betray. ▶ n double-crossing. **double-dealing** n treacherous or deceitful behaviour. **double-decker** n bus with two passenger decks one on top of the other. **double Dutch** Informal incomprehensible talk, gibberish.

double glazing two panes of glass in a window, fitted to reduce heat loss. **double talk** deceptive or ambiguous talk. **double whammy** Informal devastating setback made up of two elements.

double entendre [doob-bl on-**tond**-ra] n word or phrase that can be interpreted in two ways, one of which is rude.

doublet [dub-lit] n Hist man's close-fitting jacket, with or without sleeves.

doubloon n former Spanish gold coin.

doubt n uncertainty about the truth, facts, or existence of something; unresolved difficulty or point. ▶ v question the truth of; distrust or be suspicious of (someone). **doubter** n **doubtful** adj unlikely; feeling doubt. **doubtfully** adv **doubtless** adv probably or certainly.

douche [doosh] n (instrument for applying) a stream of water directed onto or into the body for cleansing or medical purposes. ▶ v cleanse or treat by means of a douche.

dough n thick mixture of flour and water or milk, used for making bread etc.; Slang money. **doughnut** n small cake of sweetened dough fried in deep fat. **doughty** [dowt-ee] adj -tier, -tiest. Old-fashioned brave and determined.

dour [doo-er] adj sullen and unfriendly. **dourness** n

douse [rhymes with **mouse**] v drench with water or other liquid; put out (a light).

dove n bird with a heavy body, small head, and short legs; Politics person opposed to war. **dovecote, dovecot** n structure for housing pigeons. **dovetail** n joint

containing wedge-shaped tenons.
▶ v fit together neatly.

dowager n widow possessing property or a title obtained from her husband.

dowdy adj **-dier, -diest.** dull and old-fashioned. **dowdiness** n

dowel n wooden or metal peg that fits into two corresponding holes to join two adjacent parts.

dower n life interest in a part of her husband's estate allotted to a widow by law.

down¹ prep, adv indicating movement to or position in a lower place. ▶ adv indicating completion of an action, lessening of intensity, etc., e.g. calm down. ▶ adj depressed, unhappy. ▶ v Informal drink quickly. **have a down on** Informal feel hostile towards. **down under** Informal (in or to) Australia or New Zealand. **downward** adj, adv (descending) from a higher to a lower level, condition, or position. **downwards** adv from a higher to a lower level, condition, or position. **down-and-out** n person who is homeless and destitute. ▶ adj without any means of support. **down-to-earth** adj sensible or practical.

down² n soft fine feathers. **downy** adj

downbeat adj Informal gloomy; Brit, Aust & NZ relaxed.

downcast adj sad, dejected; (of the eyes) directed downwards.

downfall n (cause of) a sudden loss of position or reputation.

downgrade v reduce in importance or value.

downhearted adj sad and discouraged.

downhill adj going or sloping down. ▶ adv towards the bottom of a hill.

download v transfer (data) from the memory of one computer to that of another.

downpour n heavy fall of rain.

downright adj, adv extreme(ly).

downs pl n low grassy hills, esp. in S England.

Down's syndrome n genetic disorder characterized by a flat face, slanting eyes, and mental retardation.

downstairs adv to or on a lower floor. ▶ n lower or ground floor.

downtrodden adj oppressed and lacking the will to resist.

dowry n, pl **-ries.** property brought by a woman to her husband at marriage.

dowse [rhymes with **cows**] v search for underground water or minerals using a divining rod.

doxology n, pl **-gies.** short hymn of praise to God.

doyen [doy-en] n senior member of a group, profession, or society. **doyenne** [doy-en] n fem

doze v sleep lightly or briefly. ▶ n short sleep. **dozy** adj **dozier, doziest.** feeling sleepy; Informal stupid. **doze off** v fall into a light sleep.

dozen adj, n twelve. **dozenth** adj

DPB (in New Zealand) Domestic Purposes Benefit.

DPP (in Britain) Director of Public Prosecutions.

Dr Doctor; Drive.

drab adj **drabber, drabbest.** dull and dreary. **drabness** n

drachm [dram] n Brit one eighth of a fluid ounce.

drachma n, pl **-mas, -mae.** former monetary unit of Greece.

draconian adj severe, harsh.

draft n plan, sketch, or drawing of something; preliminary outline of a book, speech, etc.; written order for payment of money by a bank;

US & Aust selection for compulsory military service. ▶ *v* draw up an outline or plan of; send (people) from one place to another to do a specific job; *US & Aust* select for compulsory military service.

drag *v* **dragging, dragged.** pull with force, esp. along the ground; trail on the ground; persuade or force (oneself or someone else) to go somewhere; (foll. by *on* or *out*) last or be prolonged tediously; search (a river) with a dragnet or hook; *Computers* move (an image) on the screen by use of the mouse. ▶ *n* person or thing that slows up progress; *Informal* tedious thing or person; *Slang* women's clothes worn by a man. **dragnet** *n* net used to scour the bottom of a pond or river to search for something. **drag race** race in which specially built cars or motorcycles are timed over a measured course.

dragon *n* mythical fire-breathing monster like a huge lizard; *Informal* fierce woman. **dragonfly** *n* brightly coloured insect with a long slender body and two pairs of wings.

dragoon *n* heavily armed cavalryman. ▶ *v* coerce, force.

drain *n* pipe or channel that carries off water or sewage; cause of a continuous reduction in energy or resources. ▶ *v* draw off or remove liquid from; flow away or filter off; drink the entire contents of (a glass or cup); make constant demands on (energy or resources), exhaust. **drainage** *n* system of drains; process or method of draining.

drake *n* male duck.

dram *n* small amount of a strong alcoholic drink, esp. whisky; one

sixteenth of an ounce.

drama *n* serious play for theatre, television, or radio; writing, producing, or acting in plays; situation that is exciting or highly emotional. **dramatic** *adj* of or like drama; behaving flamboyantly. **dramatically** *adv* **dramatist** *n* person who writes plays. **dramatize** *v* rewrite (a book) in the form of a play; express (something) in a dramatic or exaggerated way. **dramatization** *n*

drank *v* past tense of DRINK.

drape *v* cover with material, usu. in folds; place casually. ▶ *n Aust, US & Canadian* piece of cloth hung at a window or opening as a screen. **drapery** *n, pl* **-peries.** fabric or clothing arranged and draped; fabrics and cloth collectively.

draper *n Brit* person who sells fabrics and sewing materials.

drastic *adj* strong and severe.

draught *n* current of cold air, esp. in an enclosed space; portion of liquid to be drunk, esp. medicine; gulp or swallow; one of the flat discs used in the game of draughts. ▶ *pl* game for two players using a chessboard and twelve draughts each. ▶ *adj* (of an animal) used for pulling heavy loads. **draughty** *adj* exposed to draughts of air. **draughtsman** *n* person employed to prepare detailed scale drawings of machinery, buildings, etc. **draughtsmanship** *n* **draught beer** beer stored in a cask.

draw *v* **drawing, drew, drawn.** sketch (a figure, picture, etc.) with a pencil or pen; pull (a person or thing) closer to or further away from a place; move in a specified direction, e.g. *the car drew near;* take from a source, e.g. *draw* money from bank accounts; attract, interest; formulate or decide, e.g. to draw conclusions; (of two teams or contestants) finish a game with an equal number of points. ▶ n raffle or lottery; contest or game ending in a tie; event, act, etc., that attracts a large audience. **drawing** n picture or plan made by means of lines on a surface; art of making drawings. **drawing pin** short tack with a broad smooth head. **drawing room** Old-fashioned room where visitors are received and entertained.

drawback n disadvantage.

drawbridge n bridge that may be raised to prevent access or to enable vessels to pass. **draw out** v encourage (someone) to talk freely; make longer. **drawstring** n cord run through a hem around an opening, so that when it is pulled tighter, the opening closes. **draw up** v prepare and write out (a contract); (of a vehicle) come to a stop.

drawer n sliding box-shaped part of a piece of furniture, used for storage. ▶ pl Old-fashioned undergarment worn on the lower part of the body.

drawl v speak slowly, with long vowel sounds. ▶ n drawling manner of speech.

drawn v past participle of DRAW. ▶ adj haggard, tired, or tense in appearance.

dray n low cart used for carrying heavy loads.

dread v anticipate with apprehension or fear. ▶ n great fear. **dreadful** adj very disagreeable or shocking; extreme. **dreadfully** adv

dreadlocks pl n hair worn in the Rastafarian style of tightly twisted strands.

dream n imagined series of events experienced in the mind while asleep; cherished hope; Informal wonderful person or thing. ▶ v dreaming, dreamed or dreamt. see imaginary pictures in the mind while asleep; (often foll. by of or about) have an image (of) or fantasy (about); (foll. by of) consider the possibility (of). ▶ adj ideal, e.g. a dream house. **dreamer** n **dreamy** adj vague or impractical; Informal wonderful. **dreamily** adv

dreary adj drearier, dreariest. dull, boring. **drearily** adv **dreariness** n

dredge[1] v clear or search (a river bed or harbour) by removing silt or mud. **dredger** n boat fitted with machinery for dredging.

dredge[2] v sprinkle (food) with flour etc.

dregs pl n solid particles that settle at the bottom of some liquids; most despised elements.

drench v make completely wet.

dress n one-piece garment for a woman or girl, consisting of a skirt and bodice and sometimes sleeves; complete style of clothing. ▶ v put clothes on; put on formal clothes; apply a protective covering to (a wound); arrange or prepare. **dressing** n sauce for salad; covering for a wound. **dressing-down** n Informal severe scolding. **dressing gown** coat-shaped garment worn over pyjamas or nightdress. **dressing room** room used for changing clothes, esp. backstage in a theatre. **dressy** adj (of clothes) elegant. **dress circle** first gallery in a theatre. **dressmaker** n person who makes women's clothes. **dressmaking** n **dress rehearsal** last rehearsal of a play or show, using costumes, lighting, etc.

dressage [dress-ahzh] n training of a horse to perform manoeuvres in response to the rider's body signals.

dresser[1] n piece of furniture with shelves and with cupboards, for storing or displaying dishes.

dresser[2] n Theatre person employed to assist actors with their costumes.

drew v past tense of DRAW.

drey n squirrel's nest.

dribble v (allow to) flow in drops; allow saliva to trickle from the mouth; Sport propel (a ball) by repeatedly tapping it with the foot, hand, or a stick. ▶ n small quantity of liquid falling in drops. **dribbler** n

dried v past of DRY.

drier[1] adj a comparative of DRY.

drier[2] n same as DRYER.

driest adj a superlative of DRY.

drift v be carried along by currents of air or water; move aimlessly from one place or activity to another. ▶ n something piled up by the wind or current, such as a snowdrift; general movement or development; point, meaning, e.g. catch my drift? **drifter** n person who moves aimlessly from place to place or job to job. **driftwood** n wood floating on or washed ashore by the sea.

drill[1] n tool or machine for boring holes; strict and often repetitious training; Informal correct procedure. ▶ v bore a hole in (something) with or as if with a drill; teach by rigorous exercises or training.

drill[2] n machine for sowing seed in rows; small furrow for seed.

drill[3] n hard-wearing cotton cloth.

drily adv see DRY.

drink v drinking, drank, drunk. swallow (a liquid); consume alcohol, esp. to excess. ▶ n (portion of) a liquid suitable for drinking; alcohol, or its habitual or excessive consumption. **drinkable** adj **drinker** n **drink in** v pay close attention to. **drink to** v drink a toast to.

drip v dripping, dripped. (let) fall in drops. ▶ n falling of drops of liquid; sound made by falling drops; Informal weak dull person; Med device by which a solution is passed in small drops through a tube into a vein. **drip-dry** adj denoting clothing that will dry free of creases if hung up when wet.

dripping n fat that comes from meat while it is being roasted or fried.

drive v driving, drove, driven. guide the movement of (a vehicle); transport in a vehicle; goad into a specified state; push or propel; Sport hit (a ball) very hard and straight. ▶ n journey by car, van, etc.; (also driveway) path for vehicles connecting a building to a public road; united effort towards a common goal; energy and ambition; Psychol motive or interest, e.g. sex drive; means by which power is transmitted in a mechanism. **drive at** v Informal intend or mean, e.g. what was he driving at? **drive-in** adj, n (denoting) a cinema, restaurant, etc., used by people in their cars.

drivel n foolish talk. ▶ v -elling, -elled. speak foolishly.

driver n person who drives a vehicle.

drizzle n very light rain. ▶ v rain lightly. **drizzly** adj

droll adj quaintly amusing. **drolly**

adv **drollery** n

dromedary [drom-mid-er-ee] n, pl **-daries**. camel with a single hump.

drone¹ n male bee.

drone² v, n (make) a monotonous low dull sound. **drone on** v talk for a long time in a monotonous tone.

drool v (foll. by over) show excessive enthusiasm (for); allow saliva to flow from the mouth.

droop v hang downwards loosely. **droopy** adj

drop v **dropping, dropped.** (allow to) fall vertically; decrease in amount, strength, or value; mention (a hint or name) casually; discontinue. ▶ n small quantity of liquid forming a round shape; any small quantity of liquid; decrease in amount, strength, or value; vertical distance that something may fall. ▶ pl liquid medication applied in small drops. **droplet** n **droppings** pl n faeces of certain animals, such as rabbits or birds. **drop in, by** v pay someone a casual visit. **drop off** v Informal fall asleep; grow smaller or less. **dropout** n person who rejects conventional society; person who does not complete a course of study. **drop out (of)** v abandon or withdraw from (a school, job, etc.).

dropsy n illness in which watery fluid collects in the body.

dross n scum formed on the surfaces of molten metals; anything worthless.

drought n prolonged shortage of rainfall.

drove¹ v past tense of DRIVE.

drove² n very large group, esp. of people. **drover** n person who drives sheep or cattle.

drown v die or kill by immersion in liquid; forget (one's sorrows)

temporarily by drinking alcohol; drench thoroughly; make (a sound) inaudible by being louder.

drowse v be sleepy, dull, or sluggish. **drowsy** adj **drowsily** adv **drowsiness** n

drubbing n utter defeat in a contest etc.

drudge n person who works hard at uninteresting tasks. **drudgery** n

drug n substance used in the treatment or prevention of disease; chemical substance, esp. a narcotic, taken for the effects it produces. ▶ v **drugging, drugged.** give a drug to (a person or animal) to cause sleepiness or unconsciousness; mix a drug with (food or drink). **drugstore** n US pharmacy where a wide range of goods are available.

Druid n member of an ancient order of Celtic priests. **Druidic, Druidical** adj

drum n percussion instrument sounded by striking a membrane stretched across the opening of a hollow cylinder; cylindrical object or container. ▶ v **drumming, drummed.** play (music) on a drum; tap rhythmically or regularly. **drum into** v instil into (someone) by constant repetition. **drumstick** n stick used for playing a drum; lower joint of the leg of a cooked chicken etc. **drum up** v obtain (support or business) by making requests or canvassing.

drummer n person who plays a drum or drums.

drunk v past participle of DRINK. ▶ adj intoxicated with alcohol to the extent of losing control over normal functions; overwhelmed by a strong influence or emotion. ▶ n person who is drunk or who frequently gets drunk. **drunkard** n person who frequently gets drunk. **drunken** *adj* drunk or frequently drunk; caused by or relating to alcoholic intoxication. **drunkenly** *adv* **drunkenness** *n*

dry *adj* **drier, driest** or **dryer, dryest.** lacking moisture; having little or no rainfall; *Informal* thirsty; (of wine) not sweet; uninteresting; (of humour) subtle and sarcastic; prohibiting the sale of alcohol, e.g. *a dry town.* ▸ *v* **drying, dried.** make or become dry; preserve (food) by removing the moisture. **drily, dryly** *adv* **dryness** *n* **dryer** *n* apparatus for removing moisture. **dry-clean** *v* clean (clothes etc.) with chemicals rather than water. **dry-cleaner** *n* **dry-cleaning** *n* **dry out** *v* make or become dry; (cause to) undergo treatment for alcoholism. **dry rot** crumbling and drying of timber, caused by certain fungi. **dry run** *Informal* rehearsal. **dry stock** *NZ* cattle raised for meat.

dryad *n* wood nymph.

DSS (in Britain) Department of Social Security.

dual *adj* having two parts, functions, or aspects. **duality** *n* **dual carriageway** *Brit, Aust & NZ* road on which traffic travelling in opposite directions is separated by a central strip of grass or concrete.

dub¹ *v* **dubbing, dubbed.** give (a person or place) a name or nickname.

dub² *v* **dubbing, dubbed.** provide (a film) with a new soundtrack, esp. in a different language; provide (a film or tape) with a soundtrack.

dubbin *n* *Brit* thick grease applied to leather to soften and waterproof it.

dubious [dew-bee-uss] *adj* feeling or causing doubt. **dubiously** *adv* **dubiety** [dew-by-it-ee] *n*

ducal [duke-al] *adj* of a duke.

ducat [duck-it] *n* former European gold or silver coin.

duchess *n* woman who holds the rank of duke; wife or widow of a duke.

duchesse *n* *NZ* dressing table with a mirror.

duchy *n*, *pl* **duchies.** territory of a duke or duchess.

duck¹ *n* water bird with short legs, webbed feet, and a broad blunt bill; its flesh, used as food; female of this bird; *Cricket* score of nothing. **duckling** *n* baby duck.

duck² *v* move (the head or body) quickly downwards, to avoid being seen or to dodge a blow; plunge suddenly under water; *Informal* dodge (a duty or responsibility).

duct *n* tube, pipe, or channel through which liquid or gas is conveyed; bodily passage conveying secretions or excretions. **ductile** *adj* (of a metal) able to be shaped into sheets or wires.

dud *Informal* ▸ *n* ineffectual person or thing. ▸ *adj* bad or useless.

dude *n* *US informal* man; *Old-fashioned* dandy; any person.

dudgeon *n* **in high dudgeon** angry, resentful.

due *adj* expected or scheduled to be present or arrive; owed as a debt; fitting, proper. ▸ *n* something that is owed or required. ▸ *pl* charges for membership of a club or organization. ▸ *adv* directly or exactly, e.g. *due south.* **due to** attributable to or caused by.

duel *n* formal fight with deadly weapons between two people, to settle a quarrel. ▸ *v* **duelling, duelled.** fight in a duel. **duellist** *n*

duet *n* piece of music for two performers.

duff adj Chiefly Brit broken or useless. **duff up** v Brit informal beat (someone) severely.

duffel, duffle n short for DUFFEL COAT. **duffel bag** cylindrical canvas bag fastened with a drawstring. **duffel coat** wool coat with toggle fastenings, usu. with a hood.

duffer n Informal dull or incompetent person.

dug[1] v past of DIG.

dug[2] n teat or udder.

dugong n whalelike mammal of tropical waters.

dugout n Brit (at a sports ground) covered bench where managers and substitutes sit; canoe made by hollowing out a log; Mil covered excavation to provide shelter.

duke n nobleman of the highest rank; prince or ruler of a small principality or duchy. **dukedom** n

dulcet [dull-sit] adj (of a sound) soothing or pleasant.

dulcimer n tuned percussion instrument consisting of a set of strings stretched over a sounding board and struck with hammers.

dull adj not interesting; (of an ache) not acute; (of weather) not bright or clear; lacking in spirit; not very intelligent; (of a blade) not sharp. ▶ v make or become dull. **dullness** n **dully** adv **dullard** n dull or stupid person.

duly adv in a proper manner; at the proper time.

dumb adj lacking the power to speak; silent; Informal stupid. **dumbly** adv **dumbness** n **dumbbell** n short bar with a heavy ball or disc at each end, used for physical exercise. **dumbfounded** adj speechless with astonishment. **dumb down** make less intellectually demanding or sophisticated. **dumb show**

meaningful gestures without speech.

dumdum n soft-nosed bullet that expands on impact and causes serious wounds.

dummy n, pl -mies. figure representing the human form, used for displaying clothes etc.; copy of an object, often lacking some essential feature of the original; rubber teat for a baby to suck; Slang stupid person. ▶ adj imitation, substitute. **dummy run** rehearsal.

dump v drop or let fall in a careless manner; Informal get rid of (someone or something no longer wanted). ▶ n place where waste materials are left; Informal dirty unattractive place; Mil place where weapons or supplies are stored. **down in the dumps** Informal depressed and miserable.

dumpling n small ball of dough cooked and served with stew; round pastry case filled with fruit.

dumpy adj dumpier, dumpiest. short and plump.

dun adj brownish-grey.

dunce n person who is stupid or slow to learn.

dunderhead n slow-witted person.

dune n mound or ridge of drifted sand.

dung n faeces from animals such as cattle.

dungarees pl n trousers with a bib attached.

dungeon n underground prison cell.

dunk v dip (a biscuit or bread) in a drink or soup before eating it; put (something) in liquid.

dunny n, pl -nies. Aust & old-fashioned NZ informal toilet.

duo n, pl duos. pair of performers; Informal pair of closely connected people.

duodenum [dew-oh-**deen**-um] n,
pl **-na, -nums.** first part of the
small intestine, just below the
stomach. **duodenal** adj

dupe v deceive or cheat. ▶
person who is easily deceived.

duple adj Music having two beats
in a bar.

duplex n Chiefly US apartment on
two floors.

duplicate adj copied exactly from
an original. ▶ n exact copy. ▶ v
make an exact copy of; do again
(something that has already been
done). **duplication** n **duplicator** n

duplicity n deceitful behaviour.

durable adj long-lasting.
durability n **durable goods,
durables** pl n goods that require
infrequent replacement.

duration n length of time that
something lasts.

duress n compulsion by use of
force or threats.

during prep throughout or within
the limit of (a period of time).

dusk n time just before nightfall,
when it is almost dark. **dusky** adj
dark in colour; shadowy.

dust n small dry particles of earth,
sand, or the like. ▶ v remove dust
from (furniture) by wiping;
sprinkle (something) with a
powdery substance. **duster** n
cloth used for dusting. **dusty** adj
covered with dust. **dustbin** n
large container for household
rubbish. **dust bowl** dry area in
which the surface soil is exposed
to wind erosion. **dust jacket**
removable paper cover used to
protect a book. **dustman** n Brit
man whose job is to collect
household rubbish. **dustpan** n
short-handled shovel into which
dust is swept from floors.

Dutch adj of the Netherlands. **go
Dutch** Informal share the expenses

on an outing. **Dutch courage**
false courage gained from
drinking alcohol.

duty n, pl **-ties.** work or a task
performed as part of one's job;
task that a person feels morally
bound to do; government tax on
imports. **on duty** at work.

dutiable adj (of goods) requiring
payment of duty. **dutiful** adj
doing what is expected. **dutifully**
adv

duvet [**doo**-vay] n kind of quilt
used in bed instead of a top sheet
and blankets.

DVD Digital Versatile (or Video)
Disk.

DVT deep-vein thrombosis.

dwang n NZ & S Afr short piece of
wood inserted in a timber-framed
wall.

dwarf n, pl dwarfs, dwarves.
person who is smaller than
average; (in folklore) small ugly
manlike creature, often possessing
magical powers. ▶ adj (of an
animal or plant) much smaller
than the usual size for the species.
▶ v cause (someone or something)
to seem small by being much
larger.

dwell v dwelling, dwelt or
dwelled. live, reside. **dwelling** n
place of residence. **dwell on,
upon** v think, speak, or write at
length about.

dweller n person who lives in a
specified place, e.g. city dweller.

dwindle v grow less in size,
strength, or number.

dye n colouring substance; colour
produced by dyeing. ▶ v dyeing,
dyed. colour (hair or fabric) by
applying a dye. **dyer** n
dyed-in-the-wool adj
uncompromising or unchanging in
opinion.

dying v present participle of DIE[1].

dyke *n* wall built to prevent flooding.

dynamic *adj* full of energy, ambition, and new ideas; *Physics* of energy or forces that produce motion. **dynamically** *adv*

dynamism *n* great energy and enthusiasm.

dynamics *n* branch of mechanics concerned with the forces that change or produce the motions of bodies. ▶ *pl* forces that produce change in a system.

dynamite *n* explosive made of nitroglycerine; *Informal* dangerous or exciting person or thing. ▶ *v* blow (something) up with dynamite.

dynamo *n, pl* **-mos.** device for converting mechanical energy into electrical energy.

dynasty *n, pl* **-ties.** sequence of hereditary rulers. **dynastic** *adj*

dysentery *n* infection of the intestine causing severe diarrhoea.

dysfunction *n Med* disturbance or abnormality in the function of an organ or part. **dysfunctional** *adj*

dyslexia *n* disorder causing impaired ability to read. **dyslexic** *adj*

dysmenorrhoea *n* painful menstruation.

dyspepsia *n* indigestion. **dyspeptic** *adj*

dystrophy [diss-trof-fee] *n* see MUSCULAR DYSTROPHY.

E e

E East(ern). *n, pl* **Es** *or* **E's.** *Slang* ecstasy (the drug).

e- *prefix* electronic, e.g. *e-mail.*

each *adj, pron* every (one) taken separately.

eager *adj* showing or feeling great desire, keen. **eagerly** *adv* **eagerness** *n*

eagle *n* large bird of prey with keen eyesight; *Golf* score of two strokes under par for a hole.

eaglet *n* young eagle.

ear[1] *n* organ of hearing, esp. the external part of it; sensitivity to musical or other sounds. **earache** *n* pain in the ear. **earbash** *v Aust & NZ informal* talk incessantly. **earbashing** *n* **eardrum** *n* thin piece of skin inside the ear which enables one to hear sounds. **earmark** *v* set (something) aside for a specific purpose. **earphone** *n* receiver for a radio etc., held to or put in the ear. **earring** *n* ornament for the lobe of the ear. **earshot** *n* hearing range.

ear[2] *n* head of corn.

earl *n* British nobleman ranking next below a marquess. **earldom** *n*

early *adj, adv* **-lier, -liest.** before the expected or usual time; in the first part of a period; in a period far back in time.

earn *v* obtain by work or merit; (of investments etc.) gain (interest). **earnings** *pl n* money earned.

earnest[1] *adj* serious and sincere. **in earnest** seriously. **earnestly** *adv* **earnestness** *n*

earnest[2] *n* part payment given in advance, esp. to confirm a contract.

earth *n* planet that we live on; land, the ground; soil; fox's hole; wire connecting an electrical apparatus with the earth. ▶ *v* connect (a circuit) to earth.

earthen *adj* made of baked clay or earth. **earthenware** *n* pottery made of baked clay. **earthly** *adj* conceivable or possible. **earthy** *adj* coarse or crude; of or like earth. **earthquake** *n* violent vibration of the earth's surface.

earthwork n fortification made of earth. **earthworm** n worm which burrows in the soil.

earwig n small insect with a pincer-like tail.

ease n freedom from difficulty, discomfort, or worry; rest or leisure. ▶ v give bodily or mental ease to; lessen (severity, tension, pain, etc.); move carefully or gradually.

easel n frame to support an artist's canvas or a blackboard.

east n (direction towards) the part of the horizon where the sun rises; region lying in this direction. ▶ adj to or in the east; (of a wind) from the east. ▶ adv in, to, or towards the east. **easterly** adj **eastern** adj **eastward** adj, adv **eastwards** adv

Easter n Christian spring festival commemorating the Resurrection of Jesus Christ. **Easter egg** chocolate egg given at Easter.

easy adj **easier, easiest.** not needing much work or effort; free from pain, care, or anxiety; easy-going. **easily** adv **easiness** n **easy chair** comfortable armchair. **easy-going** adj relaxed in attitude, tolerant.

eat v **eating, ate, eaten.** take (food) into the mouth and swallow it; have a meal; (foll. by away or up) destroy. **eatable** adj fit or suitable for eating.

eau de Cologne [oh de kol-**lone**] n French light perfume.

eaves pl n overhanging edges of a roof.

eavesdrop v **-dropping, -dropped.** listen secretly to a private conversation. **eavesdropper** n **eavesdropping** n

ebb v (of tide water) flow back; fall away or decline. ▶ n flowing back of the tide. **at a low ebb** in a state of weakness.

ebony n, pl **-onies.** hard black wood. ▶ adj deep black.

ebullient adj full of enthusiasm or excitement. **ebullience** n

EC European Commission; European Community: a former name for the European Union.

eccentric adj odd or unconventional; (of circles) not having the same centre. ▶ n eccentric person. **eccentrically** adv **eccentricity** n

ecclesiastic n member of the clergy. ▶ adj (also **ecclesiastical**) of the Christian Church or clergy.

ECG electrocardiogram.

echelon [**esh**-a-lon] n level of power or responsibility; Mil formation in which units follow one another but are spaced out sideways to allow each a line of fire ahead.

echidna [ik-**kid**-na] n, pl **-nas, -nae** [-nee] Australian spiny egg-laying mammal (also **spiny anteater**).

echo n, pl **-oes.** repetition of sounds by reflection of sound waves off a surface; close imitation. ▶ v **-oing, -oed.** repeat or be repeated as an echo; imitate (what someone else has said). **echo sounder** sonar.

éclair n finger-shaped pastry filled with cream and covered with chocolate.

éclat [ake-**lah**] n brilliant success; splendour.

eclectic adj selecting from various styles, ideas, or sources. **eclecticism** n

eclipse n temporary obscuring of one star or planet by another. ▶ v surpass or outclass. **ecliptic** n apparent path of the sun.

ecological adj of ecology; intended to protect the environment. **ecologically** adv **ecology** n study of the relationships between living things and their environment. **ecologist** n

e-commerce, ecommerce n business transactions done on the Internet.

economy n, pl **-mies.** system of interrelationship of money, industry, and employment in a country; careful use of money or resources to avoid waste. **economic** adj of economics; profitable; Informal inexpensive or cheap. **economics** n social science concerned with the production and consumption of goods and services. ▶ pl financial aspects. **economical** adj not wasteful, thrifty. **economically** adv **economist** n specialist in economics. **economize** v reduce expense or waste.

ecosystem n system involving interactions between a community and its environment.

ecru adj pale creamy-brown.

ecstasy n state of intense delight; Slang powerful drug that can produce hallucinations. **ecstatic** adj **ecstatically** adv

ectoplasm n Spiritualism substance that supposedly is emitted from the body of a medium during a trance.

ecumenical adj of the Christian Church throughout the world, esp. with regard to its unity.

eczema [ek-sim-a] n skin disease causing intense itching.

Edam n round Dutch cheese with a red waxy cover.

eddy n, pl **eddies.** circular movement of air, water, etc. ▶ v **eddying, eddied.** move with a circular motion.

edelweiss [ade-el-vice] n alpine plant with white flowers.

Eden n Bible garden in which

Adam and Eve were placed at the Creation.

edge n border or line where something ends or begins; cutting side of a blade; sharpness of tone. ▶ v provide an edge or border for; push (one's way) gradually. **have the edge on** have an advantage over. **on edge** nervous or irritable. **edgeways** adv with the edge forwards or uppermost. **edging** n anything placed along an edge to finish it. **edgy** adj nervous or irritable.

edible adj fit to be eaten. **edibility** n

edict [ee-dikt] n order issued by an authority.

edifice [ed-if-iss] n large building.

edify [ed-if-fie] v **-fying, -fied.** improve morally by instruction. **edification** n

edit v prepare (a book, film, etc.) for publication or broadcast. **edition** n number of copies of a new publication printed at one time. **editor** n person who edits; person in charge of one section of a newspaper or magazine. **editorial** n newspaper article stating the opinion of the editor. ▶ adj of editing or editors.

educate v teach; provide schooling for. **education** n **educational** adj **educationally** adv **educationalist** n expert in the theory of education. **educative** adj educating.

Edwardian adj of the reign of King Edward VII of Great Britain and Ireland (1901–10).

EEG electroencephalogram.

eel n snakelike fish.

eerie adj **eerier, eeriest.** uncannily frightening or disturbing. **eerily** adv

efface v remove by rubbing; make (oneself) inconspicuous.

effacement n

effect n change or result caused by someone or something; condition of being operative, e.g. *the law comes into effect next month*; overall impression. ▸ *pl* personal belongings; lighting, sounds, etc. to accompany a film or a broadcast. ▸ v cause to happen, accomplish. **effective** *adj* producing a desired result; operative; impressive. **effectively** *adv* **effectual** *adj* producing the intended result. **effectually** *adv*

effeminate *adj* (of a man) displaying characteristics thought to be typical of a woman. **effeminacy** n

effervescent *adj* (of a liquid) giving off bubbles of gas; (of a person) lively and enthusiastic. **effervescence** n

effete [if-**feet**] *adj* powerless, feeble.

efficacious *adj* producing the intended result. **efficacy** n

efficient *adj* functioning effectively with little waste of effort. **efficiently** *adv* **efficiency** n

effigy [**ef**-fij-ee] n, *pl* **-gies**. image or likeness of a person.

efflorescence n flowering.

effluent n liquid discharged as waste.

effluvium n, *pl* **-via**. unpleasant smell, as of decaying matter or gaseous waste.

effort n physical or mental exertion; attempt. **effortless** *adj*

effrontery n brazen impudence.

effusion n unrestrained outburst. **effusive** *adj* openly emotional, demonstrative. **effusively** *adv*

EFTA European Free Trade Association.

e.g. for example.

egalitarian *adj* upholding the equality of all people. ▸ n person who holds egalitarian beliefs. **egalitarianism** n

egg[1] n oval or round object laid by the females of birds and other creatures, containing a developing embryo; hen's egg used as food; (also **egg cell**) ovum. **egghead** n *Informal* intellectual person.

eggplant n *US, Canadian, Aust & NZ* dark purple tropical fruit, cooked and eaten as a vegetable.

egg[2] v **egg on** encourage or incite, esp. to do wrong.

ego n, *pl* **egos**. the conscious mind of an individual; self-esteem. **egoism, egotism** n excessive concern for one's own interests; excessively high opinion of oneself. **egotist, egoist** n **egotistic, egoistic** *adj* **egocentric** *adj* self-centred.

egregious [ig-**greej**-uss] *adj* outstandingly bad.

egress [**ee**-gress] n departure; way out.

egret [**ee**-grit] n lesser white heron.

Egyptology n study of the culture of ancient Egypt.

eider n Arctic duck. **eiderdown** n quilt (orig. stuffed with eider feathers).

eight *adj, n* one more than seven. ▸ n eight-oared boat; its crew. **eighth** *adj, n* (of) number eight in a series. **eighteen** *adj, n* eight and ten. **eighteenth** *adj, n* **eighty** *adj, n* eight times ten. **eightieth** *adj, n*

eisteddfod [ice-**sted**-fod] n Welsh festival with competitions in music and other performing arts.

either *adj, pron* one or the other (of two); each of two. ▸ *conj* used preceding two or more possibilities joined by *or*. ▸ *adv* likewise, e.g. *I don't eat meat and he doesn't either.*

ejaculate v eject (semen); utter

abruptly. **ejaculation** n

eject v force out, expel. **ejection** n **ejector** n

eke out v make (a supply) last by frugal use; make (a living) with difficulty.

elaborate adj with a lot of fine detail. ▶ v expand upon. **elaboration** n

élan [ale-**an**] n style and vigour.

eland [**eel**-and] n large antelope of southern Africa.

elapse v (of time) pass by.

elastic adj resuming normal shape after distortion; adapting easily to change. ▶ n tape or fabric containing interwoven strands of flexible rubber. **elasticity** n

elated adj extremely happy and excited. **elation** n

elbow n joint between the upper arm and the forearm. ▶ v shove or strike with the elbow. **elbow grease** vigorous physical labour. **elbow room** sufficient room to move freely.

elder[1] adj older. ▶ n older person; (in certain Protestant Churches) lay officer. **elderly** adj (fairly) old. **eldest** adj oldest.

elder[2] n small tree with white flowers and black berries.

El Dorado [el dor-**rah**-doe] n fictitious country rich in gold.

eldritch adj Scot weird, uncanny.

elect v choose by voting; decide (to do something). ▶ adj appointed but not yet in office, e.g. president elect. **election** n choosing of representatives by voting; act of choosing. **electioneering** n active participation in a political campaign. **elective** adj chosen by election; optional. **elector** n someone who has the right to vote in an election. **electoral** adj **electorate** n people who have the

right to vote.

electricity n form of energy associated with stationary or moving electrons or other charged particles; electric current or charge. **electric** adj produced by, transmitting, or powered by electricity; exciting or tense. **electrical** adj using or concerning electricity. **electrician** n person trained to install and repair electrical equipment. **electrics** pl n Brit electric appliances. **electric chair** US chair in which criminals who have been sentenced to death are electrocuted.

electrify v **-fying, -fied.** adapt for operation by electric power; charge with electricity; startle or excite intensely. **electrification** n

electro- combining form operated by or caused by electricity.

electrocardiograph n instrument for recording the electrical activity of the heart. **electrocardiogram** n tracing produced by this.

electrocute v kill or injure by electricity. **electrocution** n

electrode n conductor through which an electric current enters or leaves a battery, vacuum tube, etc.

electrodynamics n branch of physics concerned with the interactions between electrical and mechanical forces.

electroencephalograph [ill-lek-tro-en-**sef**-a-loh-graf] n instrument for recording the electrical activity of the brain. **electroencephalogram** n tracing produced by this.

electrolysis [ill-lek-**troll**-iss-iss] n conduction of electricity by an electrolyte, esp. to induce chemical change; destruction of living tissue such as hair roots by an electric current.

electrolyte n solution or molten

substance that conducts electricity. **electrolytic** adj

electromagnet n magnet containing a coil of wire through which an electric current is passed. **electromagnetic** adj of or operated by an electomagnet. **electromagnetism** n

electron n elementary particle in all atoms that has a negative electrical charge. **electron microscope** microscope that uses electrons, rather than light, to produce a magnified image. **electronvolt** n unit of energy used in nuclear physics.

electronic adj (of a device) dependent on the action of electrons; (of a process) using electronic devices. **electronic mail** see E-MAIL. **electronics** n technology concerned with the development of electronic devices and circuits.

electroplate v coat with silver etc. by electrolysis.

elegant adj pleasing or graceful in dress, style, or design. **elegance** n

elegy [el-lij-ee] n, pl -gies. mournful poem, esp. a lament for the dead. **elegiac** adj mournful or plaintive.

element n component part; substance that cannot be separated into other substances by ordinary chemical techniques; section of people within a larger group, e.g. *the rowdy element;* heating wire in an electric kettle, stove, etc. ▶ pl basic principles of something; weather conditions, esp. wind, rain, and cold. **in one's element** in a situation where one is happiest. **elemental** adj of primitive natural forces or passions. **elementary** adj simple and straightforward.

elephant n huge four-footed thick-skinned animal with ivory tusks and a long trunk. **elephantine** adj unwieldy, clumsy. **elephantiasis** [el-lee-fan-tie-a-siss] n disease with hardening of the skin and enlargement of the legs etc.

elevate v raise in rank or status; lift up. **elevation** n raising; height above sea level; scale drawing of one side of a building. **elevator** n Aust, US & Canadian lift for carrying people.

eleven adj, n one more than ten. ▶ n Sport team of eleven people. **eleventh** adj, n (of) number eleven in a series. **elevenses** n Brit & S Afr informal mid-morning snack.

elf n, pl **elves.** (in folklore) small mischievous fairy. **elfin** adj small and delicate.

elicit v bring about (a response or reaction); find out (information) by careful questioning.

elide v omit (a vowel or syllable) from a spoken word. **elision** n

eligible adj meeting the requirements or qualifications needed; desirable as a spouse. **eligibility** n

eliminate v get rid of. **elimination** n

elite [ill-eet] n most powerful, rich, or gifted members of a group. **elitism** n belief that society should be governed by a small group of superior people. **elitist** n, adj

elixir [ill-ix-er] n imaginary liquid that can prolong life or turn base metals into gold.

Elizabethan adj of the reign of Elizabeth I of England (1558–1603).

elk n large deer of N Europe and Asia.

ellipse n oval shape. **elliptical** adj oval-shaped; (of speech or writing) obscure or ambiguous.

ellipsis n, pl **-ses.** omission of letters or words in a sentence.

elm n tree with serrated leaves.

elocution n art of speaking clearly in public.

elongate [eel-long-gate] v make or become longer. **elongation** n

elope v (of two people) run away secretly to get married. **elopement** n

eloquence n fluent powerful use of language. **eloquent** adj **eloquently** adv

else adv in addition or more, e.g. what else can I do?; other or different, e.g. it was unlike anything else that had happened. **elsewhere** adv in or to another place.

elucidate v make (something difficult) clear. **elucidation** n

elude v escape from by cleverness or quickness; baffle. **elusive** adj difficult to catch or remember.

elver n young eel.

elves n plural of ELF.

emaciated [im-mace-ee-ate-id] adj abnormally thin. **emaciation** n

e-mail, email n (also **electronic mail**) sending of messages between computer terminals. ▶ v communicate in this way.

emanate [em-a-nate] v issue, proceed from a source. **emanation** n

emancipate v free from social, political, or legal restraints. **emancipation** n

emasculate v deprive of power. **emasculation** n

embalm v preserve (a corpse) from decay by the use of chemicals etc.

embankment n man-made ridge that carries a road or railway or holds back water.

embargo n, pl **-goes.** order by a government prohibiting trade with a country. ▶ v **-going, -goed.** put an embargo on.

embark v board a ship or aircraft; (foll. by on) begin (a new project). **embarkation** n

embarrass v cause to feel self-conscious or ashamed. **embarrassed** adj **embarrassing** adj **embarrassment** n

embassy n, pl **-sies.** offices or official residence of an ambassador; ambassador and his staff.

embattled adj having a lot of difficulties.

embed v **-bedding, -bedded.** fix firmly in something solid.

embellish v decorate; embroider (a story). **embellishment** n

ember n glowing piece of wood or coal in a dying fire.

embezzle v steal money that has been entrusted to one. **embezzlement** n **embezzler** n

embittered adj feeling anger as a result of misfortune.

emblazon v decorate with bright colours; proclaim or publicize.

emblem n object or design that symbolizes a quality, type, or group. **emblematic** adj

embody v **-bodying, -bodied.** be an example or expression of; comprise, include. **embodiment** n

embolden v encourage (someone).

embolism n blocking of a blood vessel by a blood clot or air bubble.

embossed adj (of a design or pattern) standing out from a surface.

embrace v clasp in the arms, hug; accept (an idea) eagerly; comprise. ▶ n act of embracing.

embrasure n door or window having splayed sides so that the opening is larger on the inside; opening like this in a fortified wall, for shooting through.

embrocation n lotion for rubbing into the skin to relieve pain.

embroider v decorate with needlework; make (a story) more interesting with fictitious detail. **embroidery** n

embroil v involve (a person) in problems.

embryo [em-bree-oh] n, pl **-bryos.** unborn creature in the early stages of development; something at an undeveloped stage. **embryonic** adj at an early stage. **embryology** n

emend v remove errors from. **emendation** n

emerald n bright green precious stone. ▶ adj bright green.

emerge v come into view; (foll. by from) come out of; become known. **emergence** n **emergent** adj

emergency n, pl **-cies.** sudden unforeseen occurrence needing immediate action.

emeritus [im-mer-rit-uss] adj retired, but retaining an honorary title, e.g. emeritus professor.

emery n hard mineral used for smoothing and polishing. **emery board** cardboard strip coated with crushed emery, for filing the nails.

emetic [im-met-ik] n substance that causes vomiting. ▶ adj causing vomiting.

emigrate v go and settle in another country. **emigrant** n **emigration** n

émigré [em-mig-gray] n someone who has left his native country for political reasons.

eminent adj distinguished, well-known. **eminently** adv **eminence** n position of superiority or fame; (**E-**) title of a cardinal.

emir [em-meer] n Muslim ruler. **emirate** n his country.

emissary n, pl **-saries.** agent sent on a mission by a government.

emit v emitting, emitted. give out (heat, light, or a smell); utter. **emission** n

emollient adj softening, soothing. ▶ n substance which softens or soothes the skin.

emolument n formal fees or wages from employment.

emoticon [i-mote-i-kon] n Computers same as SMILEY.

emotion n strong feeling. **emotional** adj readily affected by or appealing to the emotions. **emotionally** adv **emotive** adj tending to arouse emotion.

empathy n ability to understand someone else's feelings as if they were one's own.

emperor n ruler of an empire. **empress** n fem

emphasis n, pl **-ses.** special importance or significance; stress on a word or phrase in speech. **emphasize** v **emphatic** adj showing emphasis. **emphatically** adv

emphysema [em-fiss-see-ma] n condition in which the air sacs of the lungs are grossly enlarged, causing breathlessness.

empire n group of territories under the rule of one state or person; large organization that is directed by one person or group.

empirical adj relying on experiment or experience, not on theory. **empirically** adv **empiricism** n doctrine that all knowledge derives from experience. **empiricist** n

emplacement n prepared position for a gun.

employ v hire (a person); provide work or occupation for; use. ▶ n in the employ of doing regular paid work for. **employee** n

employment n state of being employed; work done by a person to earn money.

employer n person or organization that employs someone.

emporium n, pl **-riums, -ria.** Old-fashioned large general shop.

empower v enable, authorize.

empress n see EMPEROR.

empty adj **-tier, -tiest.** containing nothing; unoccupied; without purpose or value; (of words) insincere. ▶ v **-tying, -tied.** make or become empty. **empties** pl n empty boxes, bottles, etc. **emptiness** n

emu n large Australian flightless bird with long legs.

emulate v attempt to equal or surpass by imitating. **emulation** n

emulsion n light-sensitive coating on photographic film; type of water-based paint. ▶ v paint with emulsion paint. **emulsify** v (of two liquids) join together or join (two liquids) together. **emulsifier** n

enable v provide (a person) with the means, opportunity, or authority (to do something).

enact v establish by law; perform (a story or play) by acting. **enactment** n

enamel n glasslike coating applied to metal etc. to preserve the surface; hard white coating on a tooth. ▶ v **-elling, -elled.** cover with enamel.

enamoured adj inspired with love.

en bloc adv French as a whole, all together.

encamp v set up in a camp. **encampment** n

encapsulate v summarize; enclose as in a capsule.

encephalitis [en-sef-a-**lite**-iss] n inflammation of the brain.

encephalogram n short for ELECTROENCEPHALOGRAM.

enchant v delight and fascinate. **enchantment** n **enchanter** n **enchantress** n fem

encircle v form a circle around. **encirclement** n

enclave n part of a country entirely surrounded by foreign territory.

enclose v surround completely; include along with something else. **enclosure** n

encomium n, pl **-miums, -mia.** formal expression of praise.

encompass v surround; include comprehensively.

encore interj again, once more. ▶ n extra performance due to enthusiastic demand.

encounter v meet unexpectedly; be faced with. ▶ n unexpected meeting; game or battle.

encourage v inspire with confidence; spur on. **encouragement** n

encroach v intrude gradually on a person's rights or land. **encroachment** n

encrust v cover with a layer of something.

encumber v hinder or impede. **encumbrance** n something that impedes or is burdensome.

encyclical [en-**sik**-lik-kl] n letter sent by the Pope to all bishops.

encyclopedia, encyclopaedia n book or set of books containing facts about many subjects, usu. in alphabetical order. **encyclopedic, encyclopaedic** adj

end n furthest point or part; limit; last part of something; fragment; death or destruction; purpose; Sport either of the two defended areas of a playing field. ▶ v bring or come to a finish. **make ends meet** have just enough money for one's needs. **ending** n **endless**

adj **endways** *adv* having the end forwards or upwards.

endanger *v* put in danger.

endear *v* cause to be liked. **endearing** *adj* **endearment** *n* affectionate word or phrase.

endeavour *v* try. ▶ *n* effort.

endemic *adj* present within a localized area or peculiar to a particular group of people.

endive *n* curly-leaved plant used in salads.

endocrine *adj* relating to the glands which secrete hormones directly into the bloodstream.

endogenous [en-**dodge**-in-uss] *adj* originating from within.

endorse *v* give approval to; sign the back of (a cheque); record a conviction on (a driving licence). **endorsement** *n*

endow *v* provide permanent income for. **endowed with** provided with. **endowment** *n*

endure *v* bear (hardship) patiently; last for a long time. **endurable** *adj* **endurance** *n* act or power of enduring.

enema [en-im-a] *n* medicine injected into the rectum to empty the bowels.

enemy *n, pl* **-mies.** hostile person or nation, opponent.

energy *n, pl* **-gies.** capacity for intense activity; capacity to do work and overcome resistance; source of power, such as electricity. **energetic** *adj* **energetically** *adv* **energize** *v* give vigour to.

enervate *v* deprive of strength or vitality. **enervation** *n*

enfant terrible [on-fon ter-**reeb**-la] *n, pl* **enfants terribles.** *French* clever but unconventional or indiscreet person.

enfeeble *v* weaken.

enfold *v* cover by wrapping

something around; embrace.

enforce *v* impose obedience (to a law etc.); impose (a condition). **enforceable** *adj* **enforcement** *n*

enfranchise *v* grant (a person) the right to vote. **enfranchisement** *n*

engage *v* take part, participate; involve (a person or his or her attention) intensely; employ (a person); begin a battle with; bring (a mechanism) into operation. **engaged** *adj* pledged to be married; in use. **engagement** *n* **engaging** *adj* charming.

engender *v* produce, cause to occur.

engine *n* any machine which converts energy into mechanical work; railway locomotive.

engineer *n* person trained in any branch of engineering. ▶ *v* plan in a clever manner; design or construct as an engineer.

engineering *n* profession of applying scientific principles to the design and construction of engines, cars, buildings, or machines.

English *n* official language of Britain, Ireland, Australia, New Zealand, South Africa, Canada, the US, and several other countries. ▶ *adj* relating to England. **the English** the people of England.

engrave *v* carve (a design) onto a hard surface; fix deeply in the mind. **engraver** *n* **engraving** *n* print made from an engraved plate.

engross [en-**groce**] *v* occupy the attention of (a person) completely.

engulf *v* cover or surround completely.

enhance *v* increase in quality, value, or attractiveness. **enhancement** *n*

enigma *n* puzzling thing or person. **enigmatic** *adj* **enigmatically** *adv*

enjoin v order (someone) to do something.

enjoy v take joy in; have the benefit of; experience. **enjoyable** adj **enjoyment** n

enlarge v make or grow larger; (foll. by on) speak or write about in greater detail. **enlargement** n

enlighten v give information to. **enlightenment** n

enlist v enter the armed forces; obtain the support of. **enlistment** n

enliven v make lively or cheerful.

en masse [on **mass**] adv French in a group, all together.

enmeshed adj deeply involved.

enmity n, pl **-ties.** ill will, hatred.

ennoble v make noble, elevate.

ennui [on-**nwee**] n boredom, dissatisfaction.

enormous adj very big, vast. **enormity** n, pl **-ties.** great wickedness; gross offence; Informal great size.

enough adj as much or as many as necessary. ▶ n sufficient quantity. ▶ adv sufficiently; fairly or quite, e.g. that's a common enough experience.

en passant [on **pass**-on] adv French in passing, by the way.

enquire v same as INQUIRE. **enquiry** n

enraptured adj filled with delight and fascination.

enrich v improve in quality; make wealthy or wealthier.

enrol v -**rolling,** -**rolled.** (cause to) become a member. **enrolment** n

en route adv French on the way.

ensconce v settle firmly or comfortably.

ensemble [on-**som**-bl] n all the parts of something taken together; complete outfit of clothes; company of actors or musicians; Music group of musicians playing together.

enshrine v cherish or treasure.

ensign n naval flag; banner; US naval officer.

enslave v make a slave of (someone). **enslavement** n

ensnare v catch in or as if in a snare.

ensue v come next, result.

en suite adv French connected to a bedroom and entered directly from it.

ensure v make certain or sure; make safe or protect.

entail v bring about or impose inevitably.

entangle v catch or involve in or as if in a tangle. **entanglement** n

entente [on-**tont**] n friendly understanding between nations.

enter v come or go in; join; become involved in, take part in; record (an item) in a journal etc.; begin. **entrance** n way into a place; act of entering; right of entering. **entrant** n person who enters a university, contest, etc. **entry** n, pl **-tries.** entrance; entering; item entered in a journal etc.

enteric [en-**ter**-ik] adj intestinal. **enteritis** [en-ter-**rite**-iss] n inflammation of the intestine, causing diarrhoea.

enterprise n company or firm; bold or difficult undertaking; boldness and energy. **enterprising** adj full of boldness and initiative.

entertain v amuse; receive as a guest; consider (an idea). **entertainer** n **entertainment** n

enthral [en-**thrawl**] v -**thralling,** -**thralled.** hold the attention of. **enthralling** adj

enthusiasm n ardent interest, eagerness. **enthuse** v (cause to) show enthusiasm. **enthusiast** n

ardent supporter of something. **enthusiastic** *adj* **enthusiastically** *adv*

entice *v* attract by exciting hope or desire; tempt. **enticement** *n*

entire *adj* including every detail, part, or aspect of something. **entirely** *adv* **entirety** *n*

entitle *v* give a right to; give a title to. **entitlement** *n*

entity *n, pl* **-ties.** separate distinct thing.

entomology *n* study of insects. **entomological** *adj* **entomologist** *n*

entourage [on-toor-ahzh] *n* group of people who assist an important person.

entrails *pl n* intestines; innermost parts of something.

entrance[1] *n* see ENTER.

entrance[2] *v* delight; put into a trance.

entreat *v* ask earnestly. **entreaty** *n, pl* **-ties.** earnest request.

entrée [on-tray] *n* dish served before a main course; main course; right of admission.

entrench *v* establish firmly; establish in a fortified position with trenches. **entrenchment** *n*

entrepreneur *n* business person who attempts to make a profit by risk and initiative.

entropy [en-trop-ee] *n* lack of organization.

entrust *v* put into the care or protection of.

entwine *v* twist together or around.

E number *n* any of a series of numbers with the prefix E indicating a specific food additive recognized by the EU.

enumerate *v* name one by one. **enumeration** *n*

enunciate *v* pronounce clearly; state precisely or formally. **enunciation** *n*

envelop *v* **enveloping, enveloped.**

wrap up, enclose. **envelopment** *n*

envelope *n* folded gummed paper cover for a letter.

environment [en-vire-on-ment] *n* external conditions and surroundings in which people, animals, or plants live. **environmental** *adj* **environmentalist** *n* person concerned with the protection of the natural environment.

environs *pl n* surrounding area, esp. of a town.

envisage *v* conceive of as a possibility.

envoy *n* messenger; diplomat ranking below an ambassador.

envy *n* feeling of discontent aroused by another's good fortune. ▶ *v* **-vying, -vied.** grudge (another's good fortune, success, or qualities). **enviable** *adj* arousing envy, fortunate. **envious** *adj* full of envy.

enzyme *n* any of a group of complex proteins that act as catalysts in specific biochemical reactions.

Eolithic *adj* of the early part of the Stone Age.

epaulette *n* shoulder ornament on a uniform.

ephemeral *adj* short-lived.

epic *n* long poem, book, or film about heroic events or actions. ▶ *adj* very impressive or ambitious.

epicentre *n* point on the earth's surface immediately above the origin of an earthquake.

epicure *n* person who enjoys good food and drink. **epicurean** *adj* devoted to sensual pleasures, esp. food and drink. ▶ *n* **epicure.**

epidemic *n* widespread occurrence of a disease; rapid spread of something.

epidermis *n* outer layer of the skin.

epidural [ep-pid-**dure**-al] *adj, n* (of)

epiglottis n thin flap that covers the opening of the larynx during swallowing.

epigram n short witty remark or poem. **epigrammatic** adj

epigraph n quotation at the start of a book; inscription.

epilepsy n disorder of the nervous system causing loss of consciousness and sometimes convulsions. **epileptic** adj of or having epilepsy. ▶ n person who has epilepsy.

epilogue n short speech or poem at the end of a literary work, esp. a play.

Epiphany n Christian festival held on January 6 commemorating the manifestation of Christ to the Magi.

episcopal [ip-**piss**-kop-al] adj of or governed by bishops.

episcopalian adj advocating Church government by bishops. ▶ n advocate of such Church government.

episode n incident in a series of incidents; section of a serialized book, television programme, etc. **episodic** adj occurring at irregular intervals.

epistemology [ip-iss-stem-**ol**-a-jee] n study of the source, nature, and limitations of knowledge. **epistemological** adj

epistle n letter, esp. of an apostle. **epistolary** adj

epitaph n commemorative inscription on a tomb; commemorative speech or passage.

epithet n descriptive word or name.

epitome [ip-**pit**-a-mee] n typical example. **epitomize** v be the epitome of.

epoch [**ee**-pok] n period of notable events. **epoch-making** adj extremely important.

eponymous [ip-**pon**-im-uss] adj after whom a book, play, etc. is named.

equable [**ek**-wab-bl] adj even-tempered. **equably** adv

equal adj identical in size, quantity, degree, etc.; having identical rights or status; evenly balanced; (foll. by to) having the necessary ability (for). ▶ n person or thing equal to another. ▶ v **equalling, equalled.** be equal to. **equally** adv **equality** n state of being equal. **equalize** v make or become equal; reach the same score as one's opponent.

equalization n **equal opportunity** nondiscrimination as to sex, race, etc. in employment.

equanimity n calmness of mind.

equate v make or regard as equivalent. **equation** n mathematical statement that two expressions are equal; act of equating.

equator n imaginary circle round the earth, equidistant from the poles. **equatorial** adj

equerry [**ek**-kwer-ee] n, pl **-ries.** Brit officer who acts as an attendant to a member of a royal family.

equestrian adj of horses and riding.

equidistant adj equally distant.

equilateral adj having equal sides.

equilibrium n, pl **-ria.** steadiness or stability.

equine adj of or like a horse.

equinox n time of year when day and night are of equal length. **equinoctial** adj

equip v **equipping, equipped.** provide with supplies, components, etc. **equipment** n set of tools or devices used for a particular purpose; act of equipping.

equipoise n perfect balance.

equity n, pl **-ties.** fairness; legal system, founded on the principles of natural justice, that supplements common law. ▶ pl interest of ordinary shareholders in a company. **equitable** adj fair and reasonable. **equitably** adv

equivalent adj equal in value; having the same meaning or result. ▶ n something that is equivalent. **equivalence** n

equivocal adj ambiguous; deliberately misleading; of doubtful character or sincerity. **equivocally** adv **equivocate** v use vague or ambiguous language to mislead people. **equivocation** n

ER Queen Elizabeth.

era n period of time considered as distinctive.

eradicate v destroy completely. **eradication** n

erase v rub out; remove sound or information from (a magnetic tape or disk). **eraser** n object for erasing something written. **erasure** n erasing; place or mark where something has been erased.

ere prep, conj Poetic before.

erect v build; found or form. ▶ adj upright; (of the penis, clitoris, or nipples) rigid as a result of sexual excitement. **erectile** adj capable of becoming erect from sexual excitement. **erection** n

erg n unit of work or energy.

ergonomics n study of the relationship between workers and their environment. **ergonomic** adj

ergot n fungal disease of cereal; dried fungus used in medicine.

ermine n stoat in northern regions; its white winter fur.

erode v wear away. **erosion** n

erogenous [ir-roj-in-uss] adj sensitive to sexual stimulation.

erotic adj relating to sexual pleasure or desire. **eroticism** n

erotica n sexual literature or art.

err v make a mistake. **erratum** n, pl **-ta.** error in writing or printing. **erroneous** adj incorrect, mistaken.

errand n short trip to do something for someone.

errant adj behaving in a manner considered to be unacceptable.

erratic adj irregular or unpredictable. **erratically** adv

error n mistake, inaccuracy, or misjudgment.

ersatz [air-zats] adj made in imitation, e.g. ersatz coffee.

erstwhile adj former.

erudite adj having great academic knowledge. **erudition** n

erupt v eject (steam, water, or volcanic material) violently; burst forth suddenly and violently; (of a blemish) appear on the skin. **eruption** n

erysipelas [err-riss-sip-pel-ass] n acute skin infection causing purplish patches.

escalate v increase in extent or intensity. **escalation** n

escalator n moving staircase.

escalope [ess-kal-lop] n thin slice of meat, esp. veal.

escapade n mischievous adventure.

escape v get free (of); avoid, e.g. escape attention; (of a gas, liquid, etc.) leak gradually. ▶ n act of escaping; means of relaxation. **escapee** n person who has escaped. **escapism** n taking refuge in fantasy to avoid unpleasant reality. **escapologist** n entertainer who specializes in freeing himself from confinement. **escapology** n

escarpment n steep face of a ridge or mountain.

eschew [iss-chew] v abstain from, avoid.

escort n people or vehicles accompanying another person for protection or as an honour; person who accompanies a person of the opposite sex to a social event. ▶ v act as an escort to.

escudo [ess-kyoo-doe] n, pl **-dos**. former monetary unit of Portugal.

escutcheon n shield with a coat of arms. **blot on one's escutcheon** stain on one's honour.

Eskimo n Offens a former name for a member of the aboriginal race inhabiting N Canada, Greenland, Alaska, and E Siberia. This term may cause offence. It is often better to use the term Inuit.; their language.

esoteric [ee-so-**ter**-rik] adj understood by only a small number of people with special knowledge.

ESP extrasensory perception.

esp. especially.

espadrille [ess-pad-drill] n light canvas shoe with a braided cord sole.

espalier [ess-**pal**-yer] n shrub or fruit tree trained to grow flat; trellis for this.

esparto n, pl **-tos.** grass of S Europe and N Africa used for making rope etc.

especial adj Formal special.

especially adv particularly.

Esperanto n universal artificial language.

espionage [ess-pyon-ahzh] n spying.

esplanade n wide open road used as a public promenade.

espouse v adopt or give support to (a cause etc.). **espousal** n

espresso n, pl **-sos.** strong coffee made by forcing steam or boiling water through ground coffee beans.

esprit [ess-**pree**] n spirit, liveliness,

or wit. **esprit de corps** [de core] pride in and loyalty to a group.

espy v espying, espied. catch sight of.

Esq. esquire.

esquire n courtesy title placed after a man's name.

essay n short literary composition; short piece of writing on a subject done as an exercise by a student. ▶ v attempt. **essayist** n

essence n most important feature of a thing which determines its identity; concentrated liquid used to flavour food. **essential** adj vitally important; basic or fundamental. ▶ n something fundamental or indispensable. **essentially** adv

establish v set up on a permanent basis; make secure or permanent in a certain place, job, etc.; prove; cause to be accepted.

establishment n act of establishing; commercial or other institution. **the Establishment** group of people having authority within a society.

estate n landed property; large area of property development, esp. of new houses or factories; property of a deceased person. **estate agent** agent concerned with the valuation, lease, and sale of property. **estate car** car with a rear door and luggage space behind the rear seats.

esteem n high regard. ▶ v think highly of; judge or consider.

ester n Chem compound produced by the reaction between an acid and an alcohol.

estimate v calculate roughly; form an opinion about. ▶ n approximate calculation; statement from a workman etc. of the likely charge for a job; opinion. **estimable** adj worthy of respect. **estimation** n considered opinion.

estranged adj no longer living with one's spouse. **estrangement** n

estuary n, pl **-aries.** mouth of a river.

ETA estimated time of arrival.

et al. and elsewhere.

etc. et cetera.

et cetera [et **set**-ra] Latin the rest, and others; or the like. **etceteras** pl n miscellaneous extra things or people.

etch v wear away or cut the surface of (metal, glass, etc.) with acid; imprint vividly (on someone's mind). **etching** n

eternal adj without beginning or end; unchanging. **eternally** adv **eternity** n infinite time; timeless existence after death. **eternity ring** ring given as a token of lasting affection.

ether n colourless sweet-smelling liquid used as an anaesthetic; region above the clouds. **ethereal** [eth-**eer**-ee-al] adj extremely delicate.

ethic n moral principle. **ethical** adj **ethically** adv **ethics** n code of behaviour; study of morals.

ethnic adj relating to a people or group that shares a culture, religion, or language; belonging or relating to such a group, esp. one that is a minority group in a particular place. **ethnic cleansing** practice, by the dominant ethnic group in an area, of removing other ethnic groups by expulsion or extermination. **ethnology** n study of human races. **ethnological** adj **ethnologist** n

ethos [**eeth**-oss] n distinctive spirit and attitudes of a people, culture, etc.

ethyl [**eeth**-ile] adj of, consisting of, or containing the hydrocarbon

group C_2H_5. **ethylene** n poisonous gas used as an anaesthetic and as fuel.

etiolate [**ee**-tee-oh-late] v become pale and weak; Botany whiten through lack of sunlight.

etiology n study of the causes of diseases.

etiquette n conventional code of conduct.

étude [ay-**tewd**] n short musical composition for a solo instrument, esp. intended as a technical exercise.

etymology n, pl **-gies.** study of the sources and development of words. **etymological** adj

EU European Union.

eucalyptus, eucalypt n tree, mainly grown in Australia, that provides timber, gum, and medicinal oil from the leaves.

Eucharist [**yew**-kar-ist] n Christian sacrament commemorating Christ's Last Supper; consecrated elements of bread and wine. **Eucharistic** adj

eugenics [yew-**jen**-iks] n study of methods of improving the human race.

eulogy n, pl **-gies.** speech or writing in praise of a person. **eulogize** v praise (a person or thing) highly in speech or writing. **eulogistic** adj

eunuch n castrated man, esp. (formerly) a guard in a harem.

euphemism n inoffensive word or phrase substituted for one considered offensive or upsetting. **euphemistic** adj **euphemistically** adv

euphony n, pl **-nies.** pleasing sound. **euphonious** adj pleasing to the ear. **euphonium** n brass musical instrument, tenor tuba.

euphoria n sense of elation. **euphoric** adj

Eurasian adj of Europe and Asia; of mixed European and Asian parentage. ▶ n person of Eurasian parentage.

eureka [yew-reek-a] interj exclamation of triumph at finding something.

euro n, pl **euros**. unit of the single currency of the European Union.

European n, adj (person) from Europe. **European Union** economic and political association of a number of European nations.

Eustachian tube n passage leading from the ear to the throat.

euthanasia n act of killing someone painlessly, esp. to relieve his or her suffering.

evacuate v send (someone) away from a place of danger; empty. **evacuation** n **evacuee** n

evade v get away from or avoid; elude. **evasion** n **evasive** adj not straightforward. **evasively** adv

evaluate v find or judge the value of. **evaluation** n

evanescent adj quickly fading away. **evanescence** n

evangelical adj of or according to gospel teaching; of certain Protestant sects which maintain the doctrine of salvation by faith. ▶ n member of an evangelical sect. **evangelicalism** n

evangelist n writer of one of the four gospels; travelling preacher. **evangelism** n teaching and spreading of the Christian gospel. **evangelize** v preach the gospel. **evangelization** n

evaporate v change from a liquid or solid to a vapour; disappear. **evaporation** n **evaporated milk** thick unsweetened tinned milk.

eve n evening or day before some special event; period immediately before an event. **evensong** n evening prayer.

even adj flat or smooth; (foll. by with) on the same level (as); constant; calm; equally balanced; divisible by two. ▶ adv equally; simply; nevertheless. ▶ v make even.

evening n end of the day or early part of the night. ▶ adj of or in the evening.

event n anything that takes place; planned and organized occasion; contest in a sporting programme. **eventful** adj full of exciting incidents.

eventing n Brit, Aust & NZ riding competitions, usu. involving cross-country, jumping, and dressage.

eventual adj ultimate. **eventuality** n possible event.

eventually adv at the end of a situation or process.

ever adv at any time; always. **evergreen** n, adj (tree or shrub) having leaves throughout the year. **everlasting** adj **evermore** adv for all time to come.

every adj each without exception; all possible. **everybody** pron every person. **everyday** adj usual or ordinary. **everyone** pron every person. **everything** pron **everywhere** adv in all places.

evict v legally expel (someone) from his or her home. **eviction** n

evidence n ground for belief; matter produced before a law court to prove or disprove a point; sign, indication. ▶ v demonstrate, prove. **in evidence** conspicuous. **evident** adj easily seen or understood. **evidently** adv **evidential** adj of, serving as, or based on evidence.

evil n wickedness; wicked deed. ▶ adj harmful; morally bad; very unpleasant. **evilly** adv **evildoer** n wicked person.

evince v make evident.

eviscerate v disembowel.
evisceration n

evoke v call or summon up (a memory, feeling, etc.). **evocation** n **evocative** adj

evolve v develop gradually; (of an animal or plant species) undergo evolution. **evolution** n gradual change in the characteristics of living things over successive generations, esp. to a more complex form. **evolutionary** adj

ewe n female sheep.

ewer n large jug with a wide mouth.

ex n Informal former wife or husband.

ex- prefix out of, outside, from, e.g. exodus; former, e.g. ex-wife.

exacerbate [ig-zass-er-bate] v make (pain, emotion, or a situation) worse. **exacerbation** n

exact adj correct and complete in every detail; precise, as opposed to approximate. ▶ v demand (payment or obedience). **exactly** adv precisely, in every respect. **exactness, exactitude** n **exacting** adj making rigorous or excessive demands.

exaggerate v regard or represent as greater than is true; make greater or more noticeable. **exaggeratedly** adv **exaggeration** n

exalt v praise highly; raise to a higher rank. **exalted** adj **exaltation** n

exam n short for EXAMINATION.

examine v look at closely; test the knowledge of; ask questions of. **examination** n examining; test of a candidate's knowledge or skill. **examinee** n **examiner** n

example n specimen typical of its group; person or thing worthy of imitation; punishment regarded as a warning to others.

exasperate v cause great irritation to. **exasperation** n

excavate v unearth buried objects from (a piece of land) methodically to learn about the past; make (a hole) in solid matter by digging. **excavation** n **excavator** n large machine used for digging.

exceed v be greater than; go beyond (a limit). **exceedingly** adv very.

excel v -celling, -celled. be superior to; be outstandingly good at something.

Excellency n title used to address a high-ranking official, such as an ambassador.

excellent adj exceptionally good. **excellence** n

except prep (sometimes foll. by for) other than, not including. ▶ v not include. **except that** but for the fact that. **excepting** prep except. **exception** n excepting; thing that is excluded from or does not conform to the general rule. **exceptional** adj not ordinary; much above the average.

excerpt n passage taken from a book, speech, etc.

excess n state or act of exceeding the permitted limits; immoderate amount; amount by which a thing exceeds the permitted limits. **excessive** adj **excessively** adv

exchange v give or receive (something) in return for something else. ▶ n act of exchanging; thing given or received in place of another; centre in which telephone lines are interconnected; Finance place where securities or commodities are traded; transfer of sums of money of equal value between different currencies.

exchangeable adj

Exchequer n Brit government department in charge of state money.

excise[1] n tax on goods produced for the home market.

excise[2] v cut out or away. **excision** n

excite v arouse to strong emotion; arouse or evoke (an emotion); arouse sexually. **excitement** n **excitable** adj easily excited. **excitability** n

exclaim v speak suddenly, cry out. **exclamation** n **exclamation mark** punctuation mark (!) used after exclamations. **exclamatory** adj

exclude v keep out, leave out; leave out of consideration. **exclusion** n **exclusive** adj excluding everything else; not shared; catering for a privileged minority. ▶ n story reported in only one newspaper. **exclusively** adv **exclusivity, exclusiveness** n

excommunicate v exclude from membership and the sacraments of the Church. **excommunication** n

excoriate v censure severely; strip skin from. **excoriation** n

excrement n waste matter discharged from the body.

excrescence n lump or growth on the surface of an animal or plant.

excrete v discharge (waste matter) from the body. **excretion** n **excreta** [ik-skree-ta] n excrement. **excretory** adj

excruciating adj agonizing; hard to bear. **excruciatingly** adv

exculpate v free from blame or guilt.

excursion n short journey, esp. for pleasure.

excuse n explanation offered to justify (a fault etc.). ▶ v put forward a reason or justification

for (a fault etc.); forgive (a person) or overlook (a fault etc.); make allowances for; exempt; allow to leave. **excusable** adj

ex-directory adj not listed in a telephone directory by request.

execrable [eks-sik-rab-bl] adj of very poor quality.

execute v put (a condemned person) to death; carry out or accomplish; produce (a work of art); render (a legal document) effective, as by signing. **execution** n **executioner** n

executive n person or group in an administrative position; branch of government responsible for carrying out laws etc. ▶ adj having the function of carrying out plans, orders, laws, etc.

executor, executrix n person appointed to perform the instructions of a will.

exegesis [eks-sij-jee-siss] n, pl **-ses** [-seez] explanation of a text, esp. of the Bible.

exemplar n person or thing to be copied, model; example. **exemplary** adj being a good example; serving as a warning.

exemplify v -fying, -fied. show an example of; be an example of. **exemplification** n

exempt adj not subject to an obligation etc. ▶ v release from an obligation etc. **exemption** n

exequies [eks-sik-wiz] pl n funeral rites.

exercise n activity to train the body or mind; set of movements or tasks designed to improve or test a person's ability; performance of a function. ▶ v make use of, e.g. to exercise one's rights; take exercise or perform exercises.

exert v use (influence, authority, etc.) forcefully or effectively.

exert oneself make a special effort. **exertion** n

exeunt [eks-see-unt] Latin they go out: used as a stage direction.

ex gratia [eks gray-sha] adj given as a favour where no legal obligation exists.

exhale v breathe out. **exhalation** n

exhaust v tire out; use up; discuss (a subject) thoroughly. ▶ n gases ejected from an engine as waste products; pipe through which an engine's exhaust fumes pass. **exhaustion** n extreme tiredness; exhausting. **exhaustive** adj comprehensive. **exhaustively** adv

exhibit v display to the public; show (a quality or feeling). ▶ n object exhibited to the public; Law document or object produced in court as evidence. **exhibitor** n **exhibition** n public display of art, skills, etc.; exhibiting. **exhibitionism** n compulsive desire to draw attention to oneself; compulsive desire to display one's genitals in public. **exhibitionist** n

exhilarate v make lively and cheerful. **exhilaration** n

exhort v urge earnestly. **exhortation** n

exhume [ig-**zyume**] v dig up (something buried, esp. a corpse). **exhumation** n

exigency n, pl -cies. urgent demand or need. **exigent** adj

exiguous adj scanty or meagre.

exile n prolonged, usu. enforced, absence from one's country; person banished or living away from his or her country. ▶ v expel from one's country.

exist v have being or reality; eke out a living; live. **existence** n **existent** adj

existential adj of or relating to existence, esp. human existence. **existentialism** n philosophical

movement stressing the personal experience and responsibility of the individual, who is seen as a free agent. **existentialist** adj, n

exit n way out; going out; actor's going off stage. ▶ v go out; go offstage: used as a stage direction.

exocrine adj relating to a gland, such as the sweat gland, that secretes externally through a duct.

exodus [**eks**-so-duss] n departure of a large number of people.

ex officio [eks off-**fish**-ee-oh] adv, adj Latin by right of position or office.

exonerate v free from blame or a criminal charge. **exoneration** n

exorbitant adj (of prices, demands, etc.) excessive, immoderate. **exorbitantly** adv

exorcize v expel (evil spirits) by prayers and religious rites. **exorcism** n **exorcist** n

exotic adj having a strange allure or beauty; originating in a foreign country. ▶ n non-native plant. **exotically** adv **exotica** pl n (collection of) exotic objects.

expand v make or become larger; spread out; (foll. by on) enlarge (on); become more relaxed, friendly, and talkative. **expansion** n **expanse** n uninterrupted wide area. **expansive** adj wide or extensive; friendly and talkative.

expat adj, n short for EXPATRIATE.

expatiate [iks-**pay**-shee-ate] v (foll. by on) speak or write at great length (on).

expatriate [eks-**pat**-ree-it] adj living outside one's native country. ▶ n person living outside his or her native country. **expatriation** n

expect v regard as probable; look forward to, await; require as an obligation. **expectancy** n something expected on the basis

of an average, e.g. *life expectancy*; feeling of anticipation. **expectant** *adj* expecting or hopeful; pregnant. **expectantly** *adv*
expectation *n* act or state of expecting; something looked forward to; attitude of anticipation or hope.
expectorant *n* medicine that helps to bring up phlegm from the respiratory passages.
expectorate *v* spit out (phlegm etc.). **expectoration** *n*
expedient *n* something that achieves a particular purpose. ▶ *adj* suitable to the circumstances, appropriate. **expediency** *n*
expedite *v* hasten the progress of.
expedition *n* organized journey, esp. for exploration; people and equipment comprising an expedition; pleasure trip or excursion. **expeditionary** *adj* relating to an expedition, esp. a military one. **expeditious** *adj* done quickly and efficiently.
expel *v* **-pelling, -pelled.** drive out with force; dismiss from a school etc. permanently. **expulsion** *n*
expend *v* spend, use up.
expendable *adj* able to be sacrificed to achieve an objective. **expenditure** *n* something expended, esp. money; amount expended.
expense *n* cost; (cause of) spending. ▶ *pl* charges, outlay incurred.
expensive *adj* high-priced.
experience *n* direct personal participation; particular incident, feeling, etc. that a person has undergone; accumulated knowledge. ▶ *v* participate in; be affected by (an emotion).
experienced *adj* skilful from extensive participation.
experiment *n* test to provide

evidence to prove or disprove a theory; attempt at something new. ▶ *v* carry out an experiment. **experimental** *adj* **experimentally** *adv* **experimentation** *n*
expert *n* person with extensive skill or knowledge in a particular field. ▶ *adj* skilful or knowledgeable. **expertise** [eks-per-**teez**] *n* special skill or knowledge.
expiate *v* make amends for. **expiation** *n*
expire *v* finish or run out; breathe out; *Lit* die. **expiration** *n* **expiry** *n* end, esp. of a contract period.
explain *v* make clear and intelligible; account for. **explanation** *n* **explanatory** *adj*
expletive *n* swearword.
explicable *adj* able to be explained. **explicate** *v Formal* explain. **explication** *n*
explicit *adj* precisely and clearly expressed; shown in realistic detail. **explicitly** *adv*
explode *v* burst with great violence, blow up; react suddenly with emotion; increase rapidly; show (a theory etc.) to be baseless. **explosion** *n* **explosive** *adj* tending to explode. ▶ *n* substance that causes explosions.
exploit *v* take advantage of for one's own purposes; make the best use of. ▶ *n* notable feat or deed. **exploitation** *n* **exploiter** *n*
explore *v* investigate; travel into (unfamiliar regions), esp. for scientific purposes. **exploration** *n* **exploratory** *adj* **explorer** *n*
expo *n, pl* **expos.** *Informal* exposition, large public exhibition.
exponent *n* person who advocates an idea, cause, etc.; skilful performer, esp. a musician.
exponential *adj Informal* very rapid. **exponentially** *adv*

export n selling or shipping of goods to a foreign country; product shipped or sold to a foreign country. ▶ v sell or ship (goods) to a foreign country. **exporter** n

expose v uncover or reveal; make vulnerable, leave unprotected; subject (a photographic film) to light. **expose oneself** display one's sexual organs in public. **exposure** n exposing; lack of shelter from the weather, esp. the cold; appearance before the public, as on television.

exposé [iks-pose-ay] n bringing of a crime, scandal, etc. to public notice.

exposition n see EXPOUND.

expostulate v (foll. by with) reason (with), esp. to dissuade.

expound v explain in detail. **exposition** n explanation; large public exhibition.

express v put into words; show (an emotion); indicate by a symbol or formula; squeeze out (juice etc.). ▶ adj explicitly stated; (of a purpose) particular; of or for rapid transportation of people, mail, etc. ▶ n fast train or bus stopping at only a few stations. ▶ adv by express delivery. **expression** n expressing; word or phrase; showing or communication of emotion; look on the face that indicates mood; Maths variable, function, or some combination of these. **expressionless** adj **expressive** adj

expressionism n early 20th-century artistic movement which sought to express emotions rather than represent the physical world. **expressionist** n, adj

expropriate v deprive an owner of (property). **expropriation** n

expunge v delete, erase, blot out.

expurgate v remove objectionable parts from (a book etc.).

exquisite adj of extreme beauty or delicacy; intense in feeling. **exquisitely** adv

extant adj still existing.

extemporize v speak, perform, or compose without preparation.

extend v draw out or be drawn out, stretch; last for a certain time; (foll. by to) include; increase in size or scope; offer, e.g. extend one's sympathy. **extendable** adj **extension** n room or rooms added to an existing building; additional telephone connected to the same line as another; extending. **extensive** adj having a large extent, widespread. **extensor** n muscle that extends a part of the body. **extent** n range over which something extends, area.

extenuate v make (an offence or fault) less blameworthy. **extenuation** n

exterior n part or surface on the outside; outward appearance. ▶ adj of, on, or coming from the outside.

exterminate v destroy (animals or people) completely. **extermination** n **exterminator** n

external adj of, situated on, or coming from the outside. **externally** adv

extinct adj having died out; (of a volcano) no longer liable to erupt. **extinction** n

extinguish v put out (a fire or light); remove or destroy entirely. **extinguisher** n device for extinguishing a fire or light.

extirpate v destroy utterly.

extol v -tolling, -tolled. praise highly.

extort v get (something) by force or threats. **extortion** n

extortionate adj (of prices) excessive.

extra adj more than is usual, expected or needed. ▶ n additional person or thing; something for which an additional charge is made; Films actor hired for crowd scenes. ▶ adv unusually or exceptionally.

extra- prefix outside or beyond an area or scope, e.g. extrasensory; extraterritorial.

extract v pull out by force; remove; derive; copy out (an article, passage, etc.) from a publication. ▶ n something extracted, such as a passage from a book etc.; preparation containing the concentrated essence of a substance, e.g. beef extract. **extraction** n **extractor** n

extradite v send (an accused person) back to his or her own country for trial. **extradition** n

extramural adj connected with but outside the normal courses of a university or college.

extraneous [iks-train-ee-uss] adj irrelevant.

extraordinary adj very unusual; (of a meeting) specially arranged to deal with a particular subject. **extraordinarily** adv

extrapolate v infer (something not known) from the known facts; Maths estimate (a value of a function or measurement) beyond the known values by the extension of a curve. **extrapolation** n

extrasensory adj **extrasensory perception** supposed ability to obtain information other than through the normal senses.

extravagant adj spending money excessively; going beyond reasonable limits. **extravagance** n **extravaganza** n elaborate and lavish entertainment, display, etc.

extreme adj of a high or the highest degree or intensity; severe; immoderate; farthest or outermost. ▶ n either of the two limits of a scale or range. **extremely** adv **extreme sport** sport with a high risk of injury or death. **extremist** n person who favours immoderate methods. ▶ adj holding extreme opinions. **extremity** n, pl -ties. farthest point; extreme condition, as of misfortune. ▶ pl hands and feet.

extricate v free from complication or difficulty. **extrication** n

extrovert adj lively and outgoing; concerned more with external reality than inner feelings. ▶ n extrovert person.

extrude v squeeze or force out. **extrusion** n

exuberant adj high-spirited; growing luxuriantly. **exuberance** n

exude v (of a liquid or smell) seep or flow out slowly and steadily; make apparent by mood or behaviour, e.g. exude confidence.

exult v be joyful or jubilant. **exultation** n **exultant** adj

eye n organ of sight; ability to judge or appreciate, e.g. a good eye for detail; one end of a sewing needle; dark spot on a potato from which a stem grows. ▶ v eyeing or eying, eyed. look at carefully or warily. **eyeless** adj **eyelet** n small hole for a lace or cord to be passed through; ring that strengthens this. **eyeball** n ball-shaped part of the eye. **eyebrow** n line of hair on the bony ridge above the eye. **eyeglass** n lens for aiding defective vision. **eyelash** n short hair that grows out from the eyelid. **eyelid** n fold of skin that covers the eye when it is closed. **eyeliner** n cosmetic used to outline the eyes. **eye-opener** n Informal something startling or revealing. **eye shadow** coloured cosmetic worn on the upper eyelids. **eyesight** n ability to see. **eyesore** n ugly object. **eye tooth** canine tooth. **eyewitness** n person who was present at an event and can describe what happened.

eyrie n nest of an eagle; high isolated place.

F f

f Music forte.

F Fahrenheit; farad.

FA Football Association (of England).

fable n story with a moral; false or fictitious account; legend. **fabled** adj made famous in legend.

fabric n knitted or woven cloth; framework or structure.

fabricate v make up (a story or lie); make or build. **fabrication** n

fabulous adj Informal excellent; astounding; told of in fables. **fabulously** adv

facade [fas-**sahd**] n front of a building; (false) outward appearance.

face n front of the head; facial expression; distorted expression; outward appearance; front or main side; dial of a clock; dignity, self-respect. ▶ v look or turn towards; be opposite; be confronted by; provide with a surface. **faceless** adj impersonal, anonymous. **face-lift** n operation to tighten facial skin, to remove wrinkles. **face-saving** adj maintaining dignity or self-respect. **face up to** v accept (an unpleasant fact or reality). **face**

value apparent worth or meaning.

facet n aspect; surface of a cut gem.

facetious [fas-**see**-shuss] adj funny or trying to be funny, esp. at inappropriate times.

facia n, pl **-ciae**. same as FASCIA.

facial adj of the face. ▶ n beauty treatment for the face.

facile [fas-**sile**] adj (of a remark, argument, etc.) superficial and showing lack of real thought.

facilitate v make easy. **facilitation** n

facility n, pl **-ties**. skill; easiness. ▶ pl means or equipment for an activity.

facing n lining or covering for decoration or reinforcement. ▶ pl contrasting collar and cuffs on a jacket.

facsimile [fak-**sim**-ill-ee] n exact copy.

fact n event or thing known to have happened or existed; provable truth. **facts of life** details of sex and reproduction. **factual** adj

faction n (dissenting) minority group within a larger body; dissension. **factious** adj of or producing factions.

factitious adj artificial.

factor n element contributing to a result; Maths one of the integers multiplied together to give a given number; Scot property manager. **factorial** n product of all the integers from one to a given number. **factorize** v calculate the factors of (a number).

factory n, pl **-ries**. building where goods are manufactured.

factotum n person employed to do all sorts of work.

faculty n, pl **-ties**. physical or mental ability; department in a university or college.

fad n short-lived fashion; whim. **faddy, faddish** adj

fade v (cause to) lose brightness, colour, or strength; vanish slowly.

faeces [fee-seez] pl n waste matter discharged from the anus. **faecal [fee-kl]** adj

fag[1] n Informal boring task; Brit young public schoolboy who does menial chores for a senior boy. ► v Brit do menial chores in a public school.

fag[2] n Brit slang cigarette. **fag end** last and worst part; Slang cigarette stub.

faggot n Brit, Aust & NZ ball of chopped liver, herbs, and bread; bundle of sticks for fuel.

Fahrenheit [far-ren-hite] adj of a temperature scale with the freezing point of water at 32° and the boiling point at 212°.

faïence [fie-ence] n tin-glazed earthenware.

fail v be unsuccessful; stop operating; be or judge to be below the required standard in a test; disappoint or be useless to (someone); neglect or be unable to do (something); go bankrupt. ► n instance of not passing an exam or test. **without fail** regularly; definitely. **failing** n weak point. ► prep in the absence of. **failure** n act or instance of failing; unsuccessful person or thing.

fain adv Obs gladly.

faint adj lacking clarity, brightness, or volume; feeling dizzy or weak; lacking conviction or force. ► v lose consciousness temporarily. ► n temporary loss of consciousness.

fair[1] adj unbiased and reasonable; light in colour; beautiful; quite good, e.g. a fair attempt; quite large, e.g. a fair amount of money; (of weather) fine. ► adv fairly.

fairly adv moderately; to a great degree or extent; as deserved, reasonably. **fairness** n **fairway** n Golf smooth area between the tee and the green.

fair[2] n travelling entertainment with sideshows, rides, and amusements; exhibition of commercial or industrial products. **fairground** n open space used for a fair.

Fair Isle n intricate multicoloured knitted pattern.

fairy n, pl **fairies**. imaginary small creature with magic powers. **fairy godmother** person who helps in time of trouble. **fairyland** n **fairy lights** small coloured electric bulbs used as decoration. **fairy tale, story** story about fairies or magic; unbelievable story or explanation.

fait accompli [fate ak-kom-plee] n French something already done that cannot be altered.

faith n strong belief, esp. without proof; religion; complete confidence or trust; allegiance to a person or cause. **faithful** adj loyal; consistently reliable; accurate in detail. **faithfully** adv **faithless** adj disloyal or dishonest.

fake v cause something not genuine to appear real or more valuable by fraud; pretend to have (an illness, emotion, etc.). ► n person, thing, or act that is not genuine. ► adj not genuine.

fakir [fay-keer] n Muslim who spurns worldly possessions; Hindu holy man.

falcon n small bird of prey. **falconry** n art of training falcons; sport of hunting with falcons. **falconer** n

fall v **falling, fell, fallen**. drop from a higher to a lower place through the force of gravity; collapse to the ground; decrease in number or quality; pass into a specified condition; occur. ▸ n falling; thing or amount that falls; decrease in value or number; decline in power or influence; *US* autumn. ▸ pl waterfall. **fall for** v *Informal* fall in love with; be deceived by (a lie or trick). **fall guy** *Informal* victim of a confidence trick; scapegoat. **fallout** n radioactive particles spread as a result of a nuclear explosion.

fallacy n, pl **-cies.** false belief; unsound reasoning. **fallacious** adj

fallible adj (of a person) liable to make mistakes. **fallibility** n

Fallopian tube n either of a pair of tubes through which egg cells pass from the ovary to the womb.

fallow adj (of land) ploughed but left unseeded to regain fertility.

false adj not true or correct; artificial, fake; deceptive, e.g. *false promises.* **falsely** adv **falseness** n **falsity** n **falsehood** n quality of being untrue; lie.

falsetto n, pl **-tos.** voice pitched higher than one's natural range.

falsify v **-fying, -fied.** alter fraudulently. **falsification** n

falter v be hesitant, weak, or unsure; lose power momentarily; utter hesitantly; move unsteadily.

fame n state of being widely known or recognized. **famed** adj famous.

familiar adj well-known; intimate, friendly; too friendly. ▸ n demon supposed to attend to a witch; friend. **familiarly** adv **familiarity** n **familiarize** v acquaint fully with a particular subject. **familiarization** n

family n, pl **-lies.** group of parents and their children; one's spouse and children; group descended from a common ancestor; group of related objects or beings. ▸ adj suitable for parents and children

together. **familial** adj **family planning** control of the number of children in a family by the use of contraception.

famine n severe shortage of food.

famished adj very hungry.

famous adj very well-known. **famously** adv *Informal* excellently.

fan¹ n hand-held or mechanical object used to create a current of air for ventilation or cooling. ▸ v fanning, fanned. blow or cool with a fan; spread out like a fan. **fan belt** belt that drives a cooling fan in a car engine. **fantail** n small New Zealand bird with a tail like a fan.

fan² n *Informal* devotee of a pop star, sport, or hobby.

fanatic n person who is excessively enthusiastic about something. **fanatical** adj **fanatically** adv **fanaticism** n

fancy adj **-cier, -ciest.** elaborate, not plain; (of prices) higher than usual. ▸ n, pl **-cies.** sudden irrational liking or desire; uncontrolled imagination. ▸ v **-cying, -cied.** *Informal* be sexually attracted to; *Informal* have a wish for; picture in the imagination; suppose. **fancy oneself** *Informal* have a high opinion of oneself. **fanciful** adj not based on fact; excessively elaborate. **fancifully** adv **fancy dress** party costume representing a historical figure, animal, etc. **fancy-free** adj not in love.

fandango n, pl **-gos.** lively Spanish dance.

fanfare n short loud tune played on brass instruments.

fang n snake's tooth which injects poison; long pointed tooth.

fantasia n musical composition of an improvised nature.

fantastic adj *Informal* very good;

unrealistic or absurd; strange or difficult to believe. **fantastically** adv

fantasy n, pl -**sies**. far-fetched notion; imagination unrestricted by reality; daydream; fiction with a large fantasy content. **fantasize** v indulge in daydreams.

FAQ Computers frequently asked question or questions.

far adv **farther** or **further**, **farthest** or **furthest**. at, to, or from a great distance; at or to a remote time; very much. ▶ adj remote in space or time. **Far East** East Asia. **far-fetched** adj hard to believe.

farad n unit of electrical capacitance.

farce n boisterous comedy; ludicrous situation. **farcical** adj ludicrous. **farcically** adv

fare n charge for a passenger's journey; passenger; food provided. ▶ v get on (as specified), e.g. we fared badly.

farewell interj goodbye. ▶ n act of saying goodbye and leaving. ▶ v NZ say goodbye.

farinaceous adj containing starch or having a starchy texture.

farm n area of land for growing crops or rearing livestock; area of land or water for growing or rearing a specified animal or plant, e.g. fish farm. ▶ v cultivate (land); rear (stock). **farmhouse** n **farm out** v send (work) to be done by others. **farmstead** n farm and its buildings. **farmyard** n

farmer n person who owns or runs a farm.

farrago [far-**rah**-go] n, pl -**gos**, -**goes**. jumbled mixture of things.

farrier n person who shoes horses.

farrow n litter of piglets. ▶ v (of a sow) give birth.

farther, **farthest** adv, adj see FAR.

farthing n former British coin

equivalent to a quarter of a penny.

fascia [**fay**-shya] n, pl -**ciae**, -**cias**. outer surface of a dashboard; flat surface above a shop window.

fascinate v attract and interest strongly; make motionless from fear or awe. **fascinating** adj **fascination** n

fascism [**fash**-iz-zum] n right-wing totalitarian political system characterized by state control and extreme nationalism. **fascist** adj, n

fashion n style in clothes, hairstyle, etc., popular at a particular time; way something happens or is done. ▶ v form or make into a particular shape. **fashionable** adj currently popular. **fashionably** adv

fast[1] adj (capable of) acting or moving quickly; done in or lasting a short time; adapted to or allowing rapid movement; (of a clock or watch) showing a time later than the correct time; dissipated; firmly fixed, fastened, or shut. ▶ adv quickly; soundly, deeply, e.g. fast asleep; tightly and firmly. **fast food** food, such as hamburgers, prepared and served very quickly. **fast-track** adj taking the quickest but most competitive route to success, e.g. fast-track executives. ▶ v speed up the progress of (a project or person).

fast[2] v go without food, esp. for religious reasons. ▶ n period of fasting.

fasten v make or become firmly fixed or joined; close by fixing in place or locking; (foll. by on) direct (one's attention) towards. **fastener**, **fastening** n device that fastens.

fastidious adj very fussy about details; excessively concerned with cleanliness. **fastidiously** adv **fastidiousness** n

fastness n fortress, safe place.

fat adj **fatter, fattest.** having excess flesh on the body; (of meat) containing a lot of fat; thick; profitable. ▶ n extra flesh on the body; oily substance obtained from animals or plants. **fatness** n

fatten v (cause to) become fat. **fatty** adj containing fat. **fathead** n Informal stupid person.

fat-headed adj

fatal adj causing death or ruin. **fatally** adv **fatality** n, pl **-ties.** death caused by an accident or disaster.

fatalism n belief that all events are predetermined and people are powerless to change their destinies. **fatalist** n **fatalistic** adj

fate n power supposed to predetermine events; inevitable fortune that befalls a person or thing. **fated** adj destined; doomed to death or destruction. **fateful** adj having important, usu. disastrous, consequences.

father n male parent; person who founds a line or family; man who starts, creates, or invents something; (F-) God; (F-) title of some priests. ▶ v be the father of (offspring). **fatherhood** n **fatherless** adj **fatherly** adj **father-in-law** n, pl **fathers-in-law.** father of one's husband or wife. **fatherland** n one's native country.

fathom n unit of length, used in navigation, equal to six feet (1.83 metres). ▶ v understand. **fathomable** adj **fathomless** adj too deep or difficult to fathom.

fatigue [fat-**eeg**] n extreme physical or mental tiredness; weakening of a material due to stress; soldier's nonmilitary duty. ▶ v tire out.

fatuous adj foolish. **fatuously** adv **fatuity** n

faucet [**faw**-set] n US tap.

fault n responsibility for something wrong; defect or flaw; mistake or error; Geology break in layers of rock; Tennis, squash, etc. invalid serve. ▶ v criticize or blame. **at fault** guilty of error. **find fault with** seek out minor imperfections in. **to a fault** excessively. **faulty** adj **faultless** adj **faultlessly** adv

faun n (in Roman legend) creature with a human face and torso and a goat's horns and legs.

fauna n, pl **-nas, -nae.** animals of a given place or time.

faux pas [foe **pah**] n, pl **faux pas.** social blunder.

favour n approving attitude; act of goodwill or generosity; partiality. ▶ v prefer; regard or treat with especial kindness; support or advocate.

favourable adj encouraging or advantageous; giving consent; useful or beneficial. **favourably** adv

favourite adj most liked. ▶ n preferred person or thing; Sport competitor expected to win. **favouritism** n practice of giving special treatment to a person or group.

fawn[1] n young deer. ▶ adj light yellowish-brown.

fawn[2] v (foll. by on) seek attention from (someone) by insincere flattery; (of a dog) try to please by a show of extreme affection.

fax n electronic system for sending facsimiles of documents by telephone; document sent by this system. ▶ v send (a document) by this system.

FBI US Federal Bureau of Investigation.

FC (in Britain) Football Club.

Fe Chem iron.

fealty n (in feudal society) subordinate's loyalty to his ruler or lord.

fear n distress or alarm caused by impending danger or pain; something that causes distress. ▶ v be afraid of (something or someone). **fear for** feel anxiety about something. **fearful** adj feeling fear; causing fear; Informal very unpleasant. **fearfully** adv **fearless** adj **fearlessly** adv **fearsome** adj terrifying.

feasible adj able to be done, possible. **feasibly** adv **feasibility** n

feast n lavish meal; something extremely pleasing; annual religious celebration. ▶ v eat a feast; give a feast to; (foll. by on) eat a large amount of.

feat n remarkable, skilful, or daring action.

feather n one of the barbed shafts forming the plumage of birds. ▶ v fit or cover with feathers; turn (an oar) edgeways. **feather in one's cap** achievement one can be pleased with. **feather one's nest** make one's life comfortable. **feathered** adj **feathery** adj **featherweight** n boxer weighing up to 126lb (professional) or 57kg (amateur); insignificant person or thing.

feature n part of the face, such as the eyes; prominent or distinctive part; special article in a newspaper or magazine; main film in a cinema programme. ▶ v have as a feature or be a feature in; give prominence to. **featureless** adj

Feb. February.

febrile [fee-brile] adj feverish.

February n second month of the year.

feckless adj ineffectual or irresponsible.

fecund adj fertile. **fecundity** n

fed v past of FEED. **fed up** Informal bored, dissatisfied.

federal adj of a system in which power is divided between one central government and several regional governments; of the central government of a federation. **federalism** n **federalist** n **federate** v unite in a federation. **federation** n union of several states, provinces, etc.; association.

fedora [fid-or-a] n man's soft hat with a brim.

fee n charge paid to be allowed to do something; payment for professional services.

feeble adj lacking physical or mental power; unconvincing. **feebleness** n **feebly** adv **feeble-minded** adj unable to think or understand effectively.

feed v feeding, fed. give food to; give (something) as food; eat; supply or prepare food for; supply (what is needed). ▶ n act of feeding; food, esp. for babies or animals; Informal meal. **feeder** n road or railway line linking outlying areas to the main traffic network. **feedback** n information received in response to something done; return of part of the output of an electrical circuit or loudspeaker to its source.

feel v feeling, felt. have a physical or emotional sensation of; become aware of or examine by touch; believe. ▶ n act of feeling; impression; way something feels; sense of touch; instinctive aptitude. **feeler** n organ of touch in some animals; remark made to test others' opinion. **feeling** n emotional reaction; intuitive understanding; opinion; sympathy, understanding; ability to experience physical sensations; sensation experienced. ▶ pl emotional sensitivities. **feel like** wish for, want.

feet n plural of FOOT.

feign [fane] v pretend.

feint[1] [faint] n sham attack or blow meant to distract an opponent. ► v make a feint.

feint[2] [faint] n narrow lines on ruled paper.

feldspar n hard mineral that is the main constituent of igneous rocks.

felicity n happiness; (pl **-ties**) appropriate expression or style. **felicitations** pl n congratulations. **felicitous** adj

feline adj of cats; catlike. ► n member of the cat family.

fell[1] v past tense of FALL.

fell[2] v cut down (a tree); knock down.

fell[3] adj **in one fell swoop** in a single action or occurrence.

fell[4] n Scot & N English mountain, hill, or moor.

felloe n (segment of) the rim of a wheel.

fellow n man or boy; comrade or associate; person in the same group or condition; member of a learned society or the governing body of a college. ► adj in the same group or condition. **fellowship** n sharing of aims or interests; group with shared aims or interests; feeling of friendliness; paid research post in a college or university.

felon n Criminal law (formerly) person guilty of a felony. **felony** n, pl **-nies**. serious crime. **felonious** adj

felspar n same as FELDSPAR.

felt[1] v past of FEEL.

felt[2] n matted fabric made by bonding fibres by pressure. **felt-tip pen** pen with a writing point made from pressed fibres. **fem.** feminine.

female adj of the sex which bears offspring; (of plants) producing fruits. ► n female person or animal.

feminine adj having qualities traditionally regarded as suitable for, or typical of, women; of women; belonging to a particular class of grammatical inflection in some languages. **femininity** n **feminism** n advocacy of equal rights for women. **feminist** n, adj

femme fatale [fam fat-**tahl**], n, pl **femmes fatales**. alluring woman who leads men into dangerous situations by her charm.

femur [**fee**-mer] n thighbone. **femoral** adj of the thigh.

fen n Brit low-lying flat marshy land.

fence n barrier of posts linked by wire or wood, enclosing an area; Slang dealer in stolen property. ► v enclose with or as if with a fence; fight with swords as a sport; avoid a question. **fencing** n sport of fighting with swords; material for making fences. **fencer** n

fend v **fend for oneself** provide for oneself. **fend off** v defend oneself against (verbal or physical attack).

fender n low metal frame in front of a fireplace; soft but solid object hung over a ship's side to prevent damage when docking; Chiefly US wing of a car.

feng shui [fung **shway**] n Chinese art of deciding the best design of a building, etc., in order to bring good luck.

fennel n fragrant plant whose seeds, leaves, and root are used in cookery.

fenugreek n Mediterranean plant grown for its heavily scented seeds.

feral adj wild.

ferment n commotion, unrest. ► v undergo or cause to undergo fermentation. **fermentation** n reaction in which an organic molecule splits into simpler substances, esp. the conversion of sugar to alcohol.

fern n flowerless plant with fine fronds.

ferocious adj savagely fierce or cruel. **ferocity** n

ferret n tamed polecat used to catch rabbits or rats. ▸ v **ferreting, ferreted.** hunt with ferrets; search around. **ferret out** v find by searching.

ferric, ferrous adj of or containing iron.

Ferris wheel n large vertical fairground wheel with hanging seats for riding in.

ferry n, pl **-ries.** boat for transporting people and vehicles. ▸ v **-rying, -ried.** carry by ferry; convey (goods or people). **ferryman** n

fertile adj capable of producing young, crops, or vegetation; highly productive, e.g. a fertile mind. **fertility** n **fertilize** v provide (an animal or plant) with sperm or pollen to bring about fertilization; supply (soil) with nutrients. **fertilization** n

fertilizer n substance added to the soil to increase its productivity.

fervent, fervid adj intensely passionate and sincere. **fervently** adv **fervour** n intensity of feeling.

fescue n pasture and lawn grass with stiff narrow leaves.

fester v grow worse and increasingly hostile; (of a wound) form pus; rot and decay.

festival n organized series of special events or performances; day or period of celebration. **festive** adj of or like a celebration. **festivity** n, pl **-ties.** happy celebration. ▸ pl celebrations.

festoon v hang decorations in loops.

feta n white salty Greek cheese.

fetch v go after and bring back; be sold for; Informal deal (a blow). **fetching** adj attractive. **fetch up** v Informal arrive or end up.

fete [fate] n gala, bazaar, etc., usu. held outdoors. ▸ v honour or entertain regally.

fetid adj stinking.

fetish n form of behaviour in which sexual pleasure is derived from looking at or handling an inanimate object; thing with which one is excessively concerned; object believed to have magical powers. **fetishism** n **fetishist** n

fetlock n projection behind and above a horse's hoof.

fetter n chain or shackle for the foot. ▸ pl restrictions. ▸ v restrict; bind in fetters.

fettle n state of health or spirits.

fetus [fee-tuss] n, pl **-tuses.** embryo of a mammal in the later stages of development. **fetal** adj

feu n (in Scotland) right of use of land in return for a fixed annual payment.

feud n long bitter hostility between two people or groups. ▸ v carry on a feud.

feudalism n medieval system in which people held land from a lord, and in return worked and fought for him. **feudal** adj of or like feudalism.

fever n (illness causing) high body temperature; nervous excitement. **fevered** adj **feverish** adj suffering from fever; in a state of nervous excitement. **feverishly** adv

few adj not many. **a few** small number. **quite a few, a good few** several.

fey adj whimsically strange; having the ability to look into the future.

fez n, pl **fezzes.** brimless tasselled cap, orig. from Turkey.

ff Music fortissimo.

fiancé [fee-on-say] n man engaged to be married. **fiancée** n fem

fiasco n, pl **-cos, -coes.** ridiculous or humiliating failure.

fiat [fee-at] n arbitrary order; official permission.

fib n trivial lie. ▶ v **fibbing, fibbed.** tell a lie. **fibber** n

fibre n thread that can be spun into yarn; threadlike animal or plant tissue; fibrous material in food; strength of character; essential substance or nature. **fibrous** adj **fibreglass** n material made of fine glass fibres. **fibre optics** transmission of information by light along very thin flexible fibres of glass.

fibro n Aust mixture of cement and asbestos fibre, used in sheets for building (also **fibrocement**).

fibroid [fibe-royd] n benign tumour composed of fibrous connective tissue. **fibrositis** [fibe-roh-site-iss] n inflammation of the tissues of muscle sheaths.

fibula n, pl **-lae, -las.** slender outer bone of the lower leg.

fiche [feesh] n sheet of film for storing publications in miniaturized form.

fickle adj changeable, inconstant. **fickleness** n

fiction n literary works of the imagination, such as novels; invented story. **fictional** adj **fictionalize** v turn into fiction. **fictitious** adj not genuine; of or in fiction.

fiddle n violin; Informal dishonest action or scheme. ▶ v play the violin; falsify (accounts); move or touch something restlessly. **fiddling** adj trivial. **fiddly** adj awkward to do or use.

fiddlesticks interj expression of annoyance or disagreement.

fidelity n faithfulness; accuracy in detail; quality of sound reproduction.

fidget v move about restlessly. ▶ n person who fidgets. ▶ pl restlessness. **fidgety** adj

fiduciary [fid-yew-she-er-ee] Law n, pl **-aries.** person bound to act for someone else's benefit, as a trustee. ▶ adj of a trust or trustee.

fief [feef] n Hist land granted by a lord in return for war service.

field n enclosed piece of agricultural land; marked off area for sports; area rich in a specified natural resource; sphere of knowledge or activity; place away from the laboratory or classroom where practical work is done. ▶ v Sport catch and return (a ball); deal with (a question) successfully. **fielder** n Sport player whose task is to field the ball. **field day** day or time of exciting activity. **field events** throwing and jumping events in athletics. **fieldfare** n type of large Old World thrush. **field glasses** binoculars. **field marshal** army officer of the highest rank. **field sports** hunting, shooting, and fishing. **fieldwork** n investigation made in the field as opposed to the classroom or the laboratory.

fiend [feend] n evil spirit; cruel or wicked person; Informal person devoted to something, e.g. fitness fiend. **fiendish** adj **fiendishly** adv

fierce adj wild or aggressive; intense or strong. **fiercely** adv **fierceness** n

fiery adj **fierier, fieriest.** consisting of or like fire; easily angered; (of food) very spicy.

fiesta n religious festival, carnival.

fife n small high-pitched flute.

fifteen adj, n five and ten.
fifteenth adj, n

fifth adj, n (of) number five in a series. **fifth column** group secretly helping the enemy.

fifty adj, n, pl **-ties.** five times ten. **fiftieth** adj, n

fig n soft pear-shaped fruit; tree bearing it.

fight v **fighting, fought.** struggle (against) in battle or physical combat; struggle to overcome someone or obtain something; carry on (a battle or contest); make (one's way) somewhere with difficulty. ▶ n aggressive conflict between two (groups of) people; quarrel or contest; resistance; boxing match. **fighter** n boxer; determined person; aircraft designed to destroy other aircraft. **fight off** v drive away (an attacker); struggle to avoid.

figment n **figment of one's imagination** imaginary thing.

figure n numerical symbol; amount expressed in numbers; bodily shape; well-known person; representation in painting or sculpture of a human form; *Maths* any combination of lines, planes, points, or curves. ▶ v consider, conclude; (usu. foll. by *in*) be included (in). **figure of speech** expression in which words do not have their literal meaning. **figurative** adj (of language) abstract, imaginative, or symbolic. **figuratively** adv **figurine** n statuette. **figurehead** n nominal leader; carved bust at the bow of a ship. **figure out** v solve or understand.

filament n fine wire in a light bulb that gives out light; fine thread.

filbert n hazelnut.

filch v steal (small amounts).

file[1] n box or folder used to keep documents in order; documents in a file; information about a person or subject; line of people one behind the other; *Computers* organized collection of related material. ▶ v place (a document) in a file; place (a legal document) on official record; bring a lawsuit, esp. for divorce; walk or march in a line.

file[2] n tool with a roughened blade for smoothing or shaping. ▶ v shape or smooth with a file. **filings** pl n shavings removed by a file.

filial adj of or befitting a son or daughter.

filibuster n obstruction of legislation by making long speeches; person who filibusters. ▶ v obstruct (legislation) with such delaying tactics.

filigree n delicate ornamental work of gold or silver wire. ▶ adj made of filigree.

fill v make or become full; occupy completely; plug (a gap); satisfy (a need); hold and perform the duties of (a position); appoint to (a job or position). **one's fill** sufficient for one's needs or wants. **filler** n substance that fills a gap or increases bulk. **filling** n substance that fills a gap or cavity, esp. in a tooth. ▶ adj (of food) substantial and satisfying. **filling station** *Chiefly Brit* garage selling petrol, oil, etc.

fillet n boneless piece of meat or fish. ▶ v **filleting, filleted.** remove the bones from.

fillip n something that adds stimulation or enjoyment.

filly n, pl **-lies.** young female horse.

film n sequence of images projected on a screen, creating the illusion of movement; story told in such a sequence of images;

thin strip of light-sensitive cellulose used to make photographic negatives and transparencies; thin sheet or layer. ▶ *v* photograph with a movie or video camera; make a film of (a scene, story, etc.); cover or become covered with a thin layer. ▶ *adj* connected with films or the cinema. **filmy** *adj* very thin, delicate. **film strip** set of pictures on a strip of film, projected separately as slides.

filter *n* material or device permitting fluid to pass but retaining solid particles; device that blocks certain frequencies of sound or light; *Brit* traffic signal that allows vehicles to turn either left or right while the main signals are at red. ▶ *v* remove impurities from (a substance) with a filter; pass slowly or faintly.

filth *n* disgusting dirt; offensive material or language. **filthy** *adj* **filthiness** *n*

filtrate *n* filtered gas or liquid. ▶ *v* remove impurities with a filter. **filtration** *n*

fin *n* projection from a fish's body enabling it to balance and swim; vertical tailplane of an aircraft.

finagle [fin-**nay**-gl] *v* get or achieve by craftiness or trickery.

final *adj* at the end; having no possibility of further change, action, or discussion. ▶ *n* deciding contest between winners of previous rounds in a competition. ▶ *pl Brit & S Afr* last examinations in an educational course. **finally** *adv* **finality** *n* **finalist** *n* competitor in a final. **finalize** *v* put into final form. **finale** [fin-**nah**-lee] *n* concluding part of a dramatic performance or musical work.

finance *v* provide or obtain funds

for. ▶ *n* management of money, loans, or credits; (provision of) funds. ▶ *pl* money resources. **financial** *adj* **financially** *adv* **financier** *n* person involved in large-scale financial business. **financial year** twelve-month period used for financial calculations.

finch *n, pl* **finches.** small songbird with a short strong beak.

find *v* **finding, found.** discover by chance; discover by search or effort; become aware of; consider to have a particular quality; experience (a particular feeling); *Law* pronounce (the defendant) guilty or not guilty; provide, esp. with difficulty. ▶ *n* person or thing found, esp. when valuable. **finder** *n* **finding** *n* conclusion from an investigation. **find out** *v* gain knowledge of; detect (a crime, deception, etc.).

fine¹ *adj* very good; (of weather) clear and dry; in good health; satisfactory; of delicate workmanship; thin or slender; subtle or abstruse, e.g. a fine distinction. **finely** *adv* **fineness** *n* **finery** *n* showy clothing. **fine art** art produced to appeal to the sense of beauty. **fine-tune** *v* make small adjustments to (something) so that it works really well.

fine² *n* payment imposed as a penalty. ▶ *v* impose a fine on.

finesse [fin-**ness**] *n* delicate skill; subtlety and tact.

finger *n* one of the four long jointed parts of the hand; part of a glove that covers a finger; quantity of liquid in a glass as deep as a finger is wide. ▶ *v* touch or handle with the fingers. **fingering** *n* technique of using the fingers in playing a musical instrument. **fingerboard** *n* part of

a stringed instrument against which the strings are pressed.
fingerprint *n* impression of the ridges on the tip of the finger. ▶ *v* take the fingerprints of (someone).
finger stall cover to protect an injured finger.

finicky *adj* excessively particular, fussy; overelaborate.

finish *v* bring to an end, stop; use up; bring to a desired or completed condition; put a surface texture on (wood, cloth, or metal); defeat or destroy. ▶ *n* end, last part; death or defeat; surface texture.

finite *adj* having limits in space, time, or size.

fiord *n* same as FJORD.

fir *n* pyramid-shaped tree with needle-like leaves and erect cones.

fire *n* state of combustion producing heat, flames, and smoke; *Brit* burning coal or wood, or a gas or electric device, used to heat a room; uncontrolled destructive burning; shooting of guns; intense passion, ardour. ▶ *v* operate (a weapon) so that a bullet or missile is released; *Informal* dismiss from employment; bake (ceramics etc.) in a kiln; excite. **firearm** *n* rifle, pistol, or shotgun. **firebrand** *n* person who causes unrest. **firebreak** *n* strip of cleared land to stop the advance of a fire. **fire brigade** organized body of people whose job is to put out fires. **firedamp** *n* explosive gas, composed mainly of methane, formed in mines. **fire drill** rehearsal of procedures for escape from a fire. **fire engine** vehicle with apparatus for extinguishing fires. **fire escape** metal staircase or ladder down the outside of a building for escape in the event of fire. **firefighter** *n*

member of a fire brigade. **firefly** *n*, *pl* **-flies**. beetle that glows in the dark. **fireguard** *n* protective grating in front of a fire. **fire irons** tongs, poker, and shovel for tending a domestic fire. **fireplace** *n* recess in a room for a fire. **fire power** *Mil* amount a weapon or unit can fire. **fire station** building where firefighters are stationed. **firewall** *n Computers* computer that prevents unauthorized access to a computer network from the Internet. **firework** *n* device containing chemicals that is ignited to produce spectacular explosions and coloured sparks. ▶ *pl* show of fireworks; *Informal* outburst of temper. **firing squad** group of soldiers ordered to execute an offender by shooting.

firm¹ *adj* not soft or yielding; securely in position; definite; having determination or strength. ▶ *adv* in an unyielding manner, e.g. **hold firm**. ▶ *v* make or become firm. **firmly** *adv* **firmness** *n*

firm² *n* business company.

firmament *n Lit* sky or the heavens.

first *adj* earliest in time or order; graded or ranked above all others. ▶ *n* person or thing coming before all others; outset or beginning; first-class honours degree at university; lowest forward gear in a motor vehicle. ▶ *adv* before anything else; for the first time. **firstly** *adv* **first aid** immediate medical assistance given in an emergency. **first-class** *adj* of the highest class or grade; excellent. **first-hand** *adj, adv* (obtained) directly from the original source. **first mate** officer of a merchant ship second in command to the captain. **first person** *Grammar* category of verbs and pronouns used by a speaker to refer to himself or herself. **first-rate** adj excellent. **first-strike** adj (of a nuclear missile) for use in an opening attack to destroy enemy weapons.

firth n narrow inlet of the sea, esp. in Scotland.

fiscal adj of government finances, esp. taxes.

fish n, pl **fish, fishes**. cold-blooded vertebrate with gills, that lives in water; its flesh as food. ▶ v try to catch fish; fish in (a particular area of water); (foll. by *for*) grope for and find with difficulty; (foll. by *for*) seek indirectly. **fisherman** n person who catches fish for a living or for pleasure. **fishery** n, pl **-eries**. area of the sea used for fishing. **fishy** adj of or like fish; *Informal* suspicious or questionable. **fishfinger** n oblong piece of fish covered in breadcrumbs. **fishmeal** dried ground fish used as animal feed or fertilizer. **fishmonger** n seller of fish. **fishnet** n open mesh fabric resembling netting. **fishwife** n, pl **-wives**. coarse scolding woman.

fishplate n metal plate holding rails together.

fission n splitting; *Biol* asexual reproduction involving a division into two or more equal parts; splitting of an atomic nucleus with the release of a large amount of energy. **fissionable** adj **fissile** adj capable of undergoing nuclear fission; tending to split.

fissure [**fish-er**] n long narrow cleft or crack.

fist n clenched hand. **fisticuffs** pl n fighting with the fists.

fit[1] v **fitting, fitted**. be appropriate or suitable for; be of the correct size or shape (for); adjust so as to make appropriate; try (clothes) on and note any adjustments needed;

make competent or ready; correspond with the facts or circumstances. ▶ adj appropriate; in good health; worthy or deserving. ▶ n way in which something fits. **fitness** n **fitter** n person skilled in the installation and adjustment of machinery; person who fits garments. **fitting** adj appropriate, suitable. ▶ n accessory or part; trying on of clothes for size. ▶ pl furnishings and accessories in a building. **fitment** n detachable part of the furnishings of a room. **fit in** v give a place or time to; belong or conform. **fit out** v provide with the necessary equipment.

fit[2] n sudden attack or convulsion, such as an epileptic seizure; sudden short burst or spell. **fitful** adj occurring in irregular spells. **fitfully** adv

five adj, n one more than four. **fiver** n *Informal* five-pound note. **fives** n ball game resembling squash but played with bats or the hands.

fix v make or become firm, stable, or secure; repair; place permanently; settle definitely; direct (the eyes etc.) steadily; *Informal* unfairly influence the outcome of. ▶ n *Informal* difficult situation; ascertaining of the position of a ship by radar etc.; *Slang* injection of a narcotic drug. **fixed** adj **fixedly** adv steadily. **fixer** n solution used to make a photographic image permanent; *Slang* person who arranges things. **fix up** v arrange; provide (with).

fixation n obsessive interest in something. **fixated** adj obsessed.

fixative n liquid used to preserve or hold things in place.

fixture n permanently fitted piece of household equipment; person whose presence seems permanent; sports match or the date fixed for it.

fizz v make a hissing or bubbling noise; give off small bubbles. ▶ n hissing or bubbling noise; releasing of small bubbles of gas by a liquid; effervescent drink. **fizzy** adj

fizzle v make a weak hissing or bubbling sound. **fizzle out** v Informal come to nothing, fail.

fjord [fee-ord] n long narrow inlet of the sea between cliffs, esp. in Norway.

flab n Informal unsightly body fat.

flabbergasted adj completely astonished.

flabby adj -bier, -biest. having flabby flesh; loose or limp.

flaccid [flas-sid] adj soft and limp. **flaccidity** n

flag[1] n piece of cloth attached to a pole as an emblem or signal. ▶ v **flagging, flagged.** mark with a flag or sticker; (often foll. by down) signal (a vehicle) to stop by waving the arm. **flag day** Brit day on which small stickers are sold in the streets for charity. **flagpole, flagstaff** n pole for a flag. **flagship** n admiral's ship; most important product of an organization.

flag[2] v **flagging, flagged.** lose enthusiasm or vigour.

flag[3], **flagstone** n flat paving-stone. **flagged** adj paved with flagstones.

flagellate [flaj-a-late] v whip, esp. in religious penance or for sexual pleasure. **flagellation** n **flagellant** n person who whips himself or herself.

flageolet [flaj-a-let] n small instrument like a recorder.

flagon n wide bottle for wine or cider; narrow-necked jug for liquid.

flagrant [flayg-rant] adj openly outrageous. **flagrantly** adv

flail v wave about wildly; beat or thrash. ▶ n tool formerly used for threshing grain by hand.

flair n natural ability; stylishness.

flak n anti-aircraft fire; Informal severe criticism.

flake[1] n small thin piece, esp. chipped off something; Aust & NZ informal unreliable person. ▶ v peel off in flakes. **flaky** adj **flake out** v Informal collapse or fall asleep from exhaustion.

flake[2] n (in Australia) the commercial name for the meat of the gummy shark.

flambé [flahm-bay] v **flambéing, flambéed.** cook or serve (food) in flaming brandy.

flamboyant adj behaving in a very noticeable, extravagant way; very bright and showy. **flamboyance** n

flame n luminous burning gas coming from burning material. ▶ v burn brightly; become bright red. **old flame** Informal former sweetheart.

flamenco n, pl -cos. rhythmical Spanish dance accompanied by a guitar and vocalist; music for this dance.

flamingo n, pl -gos, -goes. large pink wading bird with a long neck and legs.

flammable adj easily set on fire. **flammability** n

flan n open sweet or savoury tart.

flange n projecting rim or collar.

flank n part of the side between the hips and ribs; side of a body of troops. ▶ v be at or move along the side of.

flannel n Brit small piece of cloth for washing the face; soft woollen fabric for clothing; Informal evasive talk. ▶ pl trousers made of flannel. ▶ v **-nelling, -nelled.** Informal talk evasively. **flannelette** n cotton imitation of flannel.

flap v **flapping, flapped.** move back and forwards or up and down. ▶ n action or sound of flapping; piece of something attached by one edge only; Informal state of excitement or panic.

flapjack n chewy biscuit made with oats.

flare v blaze with a sudden unsteady flame; Informal (of temper, violence, or trouble) break out suddenly; (of a skirt or trousers) become wider towards the hem. ▶ n sudden unsteady flame; signal light. ▶ pl flared trousers. **flared** adj (of a skirt or trousers) becoming wider towards the hem.

flash n sudden burst of light or flame; sudden occurrence of intuition or emotion; very short time; brief unscheduled news announcement; Photog small bulb that produces an intense flash of light. ▶ adj (also **flashy**) vulgarly showy. ▶ v (cause to) burst into flame; (cause to) emit light suddenly or intermittently; move very fast; come rapidly (to mind or view); Informal display ostentatiously; Slang expose oneself indecently. **flasher** n Slang man who exposes himself indecently. **flashback** n scene in a book, play, or film, that shows earlier events. **flash flood** sudden short-lived flood. **flashlight** n US torch. **flash point** critical point beyond which a situation will inevitably erupt into violence; lowest temperature at which vapour given off by a liquid can ignite.

flashing n watertight material used to cover joins in a roof.

flask n same as VACUUM FLASK; flat bottle for carrying alcoholic drink in the pocket; narrow-necked bottle.

flat[1] adj **flatter, flattest.** level and horizontal; even and smooth; (of a tyre) deflated; outright; fixed; without variation or emotion; (of a drink) no longer fizzy; (of a battery) with no electrical charge; Music below the true pitch. ▶ adv in or into a flat position; completely or absolutely; exactly; Music too low in pitch. ▶ n Music symbol lowering the pitch of a note by a semitone; mud bank exposed at low tide. **flat out** with maximum speed or effort. **flatly** adv **flatness** n **flatten** v **flatfish** n sea fish, such as the sole, which has a flat body. **flat racing** horse racing over level ground with no jumps.

flat[2] n set of rooms for living in which are part of a larger building. ▶ v **flatting, flatted.** Aust & NZ live in a flat. **flatlet** n Brit, Aust & S Afr small flat. **flatmate** n person with whom one shares a flat.

flatter v praise insincerely; show to advantage; (of a person) appear more attractive in a picture than in reality. **flatterer** n **flattery** n

flattie n NZ & S Afr informal flat tyre.

flatulent adj suffering from or caused by too much gas in the intestines. **flatulence** n

flaunt v display (oneself or one's possessions) arrogantly.

flautist n flute player.

flavour n distinctive taste; distinctive characteristic or quality. ▶ v give flavour to. **flavouring** n substance used to flavour food. **flavourless** adj

flaw n imperfection or blemish; mistake that makes a plan or argument invalid. **flawed** adj **flawless** adj

flax n plant grown for its stem fibres and seeds; its fibres, spun into linen thread. **flaxen** adj (of hair) pale yellow.

flay v strip the skin off; criticize severely.

flea n small wingless jumping bloodsucking insect. **flea market** market for cheap goods. **fleapit** n Informal shabby cinema or theatre.

fleck n small mark, streak, or speck. ▶ v speckle.

fled v past of FLEE.

fledged adj (of young birds) able to fly; (of people) fully trained. **fledgling, fledgeling** n young bird. ▶ adj new or inexperienced.

flee v **fleeing, fled.** run away (from).

fleece n sheep's coat of wool; sheepskin used as a lining for coats etc.; warm polyester fabric; Brit jacket or top made of this fabric. ▶ v defraud or overcharge. **fleecy** adj made of or like fleece.

fleet[1] n number of warships organized as a unit; number of vehicles under the same ownership.

fleet[2] adj swift in movement. **fleeting** adj rapid and soon passing. **fleetingly** adv

flesh n soft part of a human or animal body; Informal excess fat; meat of animals as opposed to fish or fowl; thick soft part of a fruit or vegetable; human body as opposed to the soul. **in the flesh** in person, actually present. **one's own flesh and blood** one's family. **flesh-coloured** adj yellowish-pink. **fleshly** adj carnal; worldly. **fleshy** adj plump; like flesh. **flesh wound** wound affecting only the

superficial tissue.

fleur-de-lys, fleur-de-lis [flur-de-lee] n, pl **fleurs-de-lys, fleurs-de-lis.** heraldic lily with three petals.

flew v past tense of FLY[1].

flex n flexible insulated electric cable. ▶ v bend. **flexible** adj easily bent; adaptable. **flexibly** adv **flexibility** n **flexitime, flextime** n system permitting variation in starting and finishing times of work.

flick v touch or move with the finger or hand in a quick movement; move with a short sudden movement, often repeatedly. ▶ n tap or quick stroke. ▶ pl Slang the cinema. **flick knife** knife with a spring-loaded blade which shoots out when a button is pressed. **flick through** v look at (a book or magazine) quickly or idly.

flicker v shine unsteadily or intermittently; move quickly to and fro. ▶ n unsteady brief light; brief faint indication.

flier n see FLY[1].

flight[1] n journey by air; act or manner of flying through the air; group of birds or aircraft flying together; aircraft flying on a scheduled journey; set of stairs between two landings; stabilizing feathers or plastic fins on an arrow or dart. **flightless** adj (of certain birds or insects) unable to fly. **flight attendant** person who looks after passengers on an aircraft. **flight deck** crew compartment in an airliner; runway deck on an aircraft carrier. **flight recorder** electronic device in an aircraft storing information about its flight.

flight[2] n act of running away.

flighty adj **flightier, flightiest.** frivolous and fickle.

flimsy adj **-sier, -siest.** not strong or substantial; thin; not very convincing. **flimsily** adv **flimsiness** n

flinch v draw back or wince, as from pain. **flinch from** v shrink from or avoid.

fling v **flinging, flung.** throw, send, or move forcefully or hurriedly. ▶ n spell of self-indulgent enjoyment; brief romantic or sexual relationship. **fling oneself into** (start to) do with great vigour.

flint n hard grey stone; piece of this; small piece of an iron alloy, used in cigarette lighters. **flinty** adj cruel; of or like flint.

flip v **flipping, flipped.** throw (something small or light) carelessly; turn (something) over; (also **flip one's lid**) Slang fly into an emotional state. ▶ n snap or tap. ▶ adj Informal flippant.

flipper n limb of a sea animal adapted for swimming; one of a pair of paddle-like rubber devices worn on the feet to help in swimming. **flip-flop** n Brit & S Afr rubber-soled sandal held on by a thong between the big toe and the next toe. **flip through** v look at (a book or magazine) quickly or idly.

flippant adj treating serious things lightly. **flippancy** n

flirt v behave as if sexually attracted to someone; consider lightly, toy (with). ▶ n person who flirts. **flirtation** n **flirtatious** adj

flit v **flitting, flitted.** move lightly and rapidly; Scot move house; Informal depart hurriedly and secretly. ▶ n act of flitting.

float v rest on the surface of a liquid; move lightly and freely; move about aimlessly; launch (a company); offer for sale on the stock market; allow (a currency) to fluctuate against other currencies. ▶ n light object used to help someone or something float; indicator on a fishing line that moves when a fish bites; decorated truck in a procession; Brit small delivery vehicle; sum of money used for minor expenses or to provide change. **floating** adj moving about, changing, e.g. *floating population*; (of a voter) not committed to one party.

flock[1] n number of animals of one kind together; large group of people; Christianity congregation. ▶ v gather in a crowd.

flock[2] n wool or cotton waste used as stuffing. ▶ adj (of wallpaper) with a velvety raised pattern.

floe n sheet of floating ice.

flog v **flogging, flogged.** beat with a whip or stick; (sometimes foll. by off) Brit, NZ & S Afr informal sell; NZ informal steal. **flogging** n

flood n overflow of water onto a normally dry area; large amount of water; rising of the tide. ▶ v cover or become covered with water; fill to overflowing; come in large numbers or quantities. **floodgate** n gate used to control the flow of water. **floodlight** n lamp that casts a broad intense beam of light. ▶ v **-lighting, -lit.** illuminate by floodlight.

floor n lower surface of a room; level of a building; flat bottom surface; (right to speak in) a legislative hall. ▶ v knock down; Informal disconcert or defeat. **floored** adj covered with a floor. **flooring** n material for floors. **floor show** entertainment in a nightclub.

floozy n, pl **-zies.** Old-fashioned slang disreputable woman.

flop v **flopping, flopped.** bend, fall, or collapse loosely or carelessly; *Informal* fail. ▶ *n Informal* failure; flopping movement.

floppy *adj* hanging downwards, loose. **floppy disk** *Computers* flexible magnetic disk that stores information.

flora *n* plants of a given place or time.

floral *adj* consisting of or decorated with flowers.

floret *n* small flower forming part of a composite flower head.

floribunda *n* type of rose whose flowers grow in large clusters.

florid *adj* with a red or flushed complexion; ornate.

florin *n* former British and Australian coin.

florist *n* seller of flowers.

floss *n* fine silky fibres.

flotation *n* launching or financing of a business enterprise.

flotilla *n* small fleet or fleet of small ships.

flotsam *n* floating wreckage. **flotsam and jetsam** odds and ends; *Brit* homeless or vagrant people.

flounce[1] *v* go with emphatic movements. ▶ *n* flouncing movement.

flounce[2] *n* ornamental frill on a garment.

flounder[1] *v* move with difficulty, as in mud; behave or speak in a bungling or hesitating manner.

flounder[2] *n* edible flatfish.

flour *n* powder made by grinding grain, esp. wheat. ▶ *v* sprinkle with flour. **floury** *adj*

flourish *v* be active, successful, or widespread; be at the peak of development; wave (something) dramatically. ▶ *n* dramatic waving motion; ornamental curly line in writing. **flourishing** *adj*

flout *v* deliberately disobey (a rule, law, etc.).

flow *v* (of liquid) move in a stream; (of blood or electricity) circulate; proceed smoothly; hang loosely; be abundant. ▶ *n* act, rate, or manner of flowing; continuous stream or discharge. **flow chart** diagram showing a sequence of operations in a process.

flower *n* part of a plant that produces seeds; plant grown for its colourful flowers; best or finest part. ▶ *v* produce flowers, bloom; reach full growth or maturity. **in flower** with flowers open.

flowered *adj* decorated with a floral design. **flowery** *adj* decorated with a floral design; (of language or style) elaborate.

flowerbed *n* piece of ground for growing flowers.

flown *v* past participle of FLY[1].

fl. oz. fluid ounce(s).

flu *n* short for INFLUENZA.

fluctuate *v* change frequently and erratically. **fluctuation** *n*

flue *n* passage or pipe for smoke or hot air.

fluent *adj* able to speak or write with ease; spoken or written with ease. **fluently** *adv* **fluency** *n*

fluff *n* soft fibres; *Brit, Aust & NZ informal* mistake. ▶ *v* make or become soft and puffy; *Informal* make a mistake. **fluffy** *adj*

fluid *n* substance able to flow and change its shape; a liquid or a gas. ▶ *adj* able to flow or change shape easily. **fluidity** *n* **fluid ounce** *Brit* one twentieth of a pint (28.4 ml).

fluke[1] *n* accidental stroke of luck.

fluke[2] *n* flat triangular point of an anchor; lobe of a whale's tail.

fluke[3] *n* parasitic worm.

flume *n* narrow sloping channel for water; enclosed water slide at a swimming pool.

flummox *v* puzzle or confuse.

flung v past of FLING.

flunk v US, Aust, NZ & S Afr informal fail.

flunky, flunkey n, pl **flunkies, flunkeys**. servile person; manservant who wears a livery.

fluorescence n emission of light from a substance bombarded by particles, such as electrons, or by radiation. **fluoresce** v exhibit fluorescence.

fluorescent adj of or resembling fluorescence.

fluoride n compound containing fluorine. **fluoridate** v add fluoride to (water) as protection against tooth decay. **fluoridation** n

fluorine n Chem toxic yellow gas, most reactive of all the elements.

flurry n, pl **-ries**. sudden commotion; gust of rain or wind or fall of snow. ▶ v **-rying, -ried**. confuse.

flush¹ v blush or cause to blush; send water through (a toilet or pipe) so as to clean it; elate. ▶ n blush; rush of water; excitement or elation.

flush² adj level with the surrounding surface; Informal having plenty of money.

flush³ v drive out of a hiding place.

flush⁴ n (in card games) hand all of one suit.

fluster v make nervous or upset. ▶ n nervous or upset state.

flute n wind instrument consisting of a tube with sound holes and a mouth hole in the side; tall narrow wineglass. **fluted** adj having decorative grooves.

flutter v wave rapidly; flap the wings; move quickly and irregularly; (of the heart) beat abnormally quickly. ▶ n flapping movement; nervous agitation; Informal small bet; abnormally fast heartbeat.

fluvial adj of rivers.

flux n constant change or instability; flow or discharge; substance mixed with metal to assist in fusion.

fly¹ v **flying, flew, flown**. move through the air on wings or in an aircraft; control the flight of; float, flutter, display, or be displayed in the air; transport or be transported by air; move quickly or suddenly; (of time) pass rapidly; flee. ▶ n, pl **flies**. (often pl) Brit fastening at the front of trousers; flap forming the entrance to a tent. ▶ pl space above a stage, used for storage. **flyer, flier** n small advertising leaflet; aviator. **flying fox** Aust & NZ platform suspended from an overhead cable, used for transporting people or materials. **flyleaf** n blank leaf at the beginning or end of a book. **flyover** n road passing over another by a bridge. **flywheel** n heavy wheel regulating the speed of a machine.

fly² n, pl **flies**. two-winged insect. **flycatcher** n small insect-eating songbird. **fly-fishing** n fishing with an artificial fly as a lure. **flypaper** n paper with a sticky poisonous coating, used to kill flies. **flyweight** n boxer weighing up to 112lb (professional) or 51kg (amateur).

fly³ adj Slang sharp and cunning.

flying adj hurried and brief. **flying boat** aircraft fitted with floats instead of landing wheels. **flying colours** conspicuous success. **flying fish** fish with winglike fins used for gliding above the water. **flying fox** large fruit-eating bat. **flying saucer** unidentified disc-shaped flying object, supposedly from outer space.

flying squad small group of police, soldiers, etc., ready to act quickly. **flying start** very good start.

FM frequency modulation.

foal n young of a horse or related animal. ▶ v give birth to a foal.

foam n mass of small bubbles on a liquid; frothy saliva; light spongelike solid used for insulation, packing, etc. ▶ v produce foam. **foamy** adj

fob n short watch chain; small pocket in a waistcoat.

fob off v fobbing, fobbed. pretend to satisfy (a person) with lies or excuses; sell or pass off (inferior goods) as valuable.

fo'c's'le n same as FORECASTLE.

focus v, pl -cuses, -ci [-sye] point at which light or sound waves converge; state of an optical image when it is clearly defined; state of an instrument producing such an image; centre of interest or activity. ▶ v -cusing, -cused or -cussing, -cussed. bring or come into focus; concentrate (on). **focal** adj or at a focus. **focus group** group of people gathered by a market-research company to discuss and assess a product or service.

fodder n feed for livestock.

foe n enemy, opponent.

foetid adj same as FETID.

foetus n, pl -tuses. same as FETUS.

fog n mass of condensed water vapour in the lower air, often greatly reducing visibility. ▶ v fogging, fogged. cover with steam. **foggy** adj **foghorn** n large horn sounded to warn ships in fog.

fogey, fogy n, pl -geys, -gies. old-fashioned person.

foible n minor weakness or slight peculiarity.

foil[1] v ruin (someone's plan).

foil[2] n metal in a thin sheet, esp. for wrapping food; anything which sets off another thing to advantage.

foil[3] n light slender flexible sword tipped with a button.

foist v (foll. by on or upon) force or impose on.

fold[1] v bend so that one part covers another; interlace (the arms); clasp (in the arms); Cooking mix gently; Informal fail or go bankrupt. ▶ n folded piece or part; mark, crease, or hollow made by folding. **folder** n piece of folded cardboard for holding loose papers.

fold[2] n Brit, Aust & S Afr enclosure for sheep; church or its members.

foliage n leaves. **foliation** n process of producing leaves.

folio n, pl -lios. sheet of paper folded in half to make two leaves of a book; book made up of such sheets; page number.

folk n people in general; race of people. ▶ pl relatives. **folksy** adj simple and unpretentious. **folk dance** traditional country dance. **folklore** n traditional beliefs and stories of a people. **folk song** song handed down among the common people; modern song like this. **folk singer**

follicle n small cavity in the body, esp. one from which a hair grows.

follow v go or come after; be a logical or natural consequence of; keep to the course or track of; act in accordance with; accept the ideas or beliefs of; understand; have a keen interest in. **follower** n disciple or supporter. **following** adj about to be mentioned; next in time. ▶ n group of supporters. ▶ prep as a result of. **follow up** v investigate; do a second, often

similar, thing after (a first).
follow-up n something done to reinforce an initial action.

folly n, pl **-lies** foolishness; foolish action or idea; useless extravagant building.

foment [foam-**ent**] v encourage or stir up (trouble).

fond adj tender, loving; unlikely to be realized, e.g. a fond hope. **fond of** having a liking for. **fondly** adv **fondness** n

fondant n (sweet made from) flavoured paste of sugar and water.

fondle v caress.

fondue n Swiss dish of a hot melted cheese sauce into which pieces of bread are dipped.

font[1] n bowl in a church for baptismal water.

font[2] n set of printing type of one style and size.

fontanelle n soft membranous gap between the bones of a baby's skull.

food n what one eats, solid nourishment. **foodie** n Informal gourmet. **foodstuff** n substance used as food.

fool[1] n person lacking sense or judgment; person made to appear ridiculous; Hist jester, clown. ▶ v deceive (someone). **foolish** adj unwise, silly, or absurd. **foolishly** adv **foolishness** n **foolery** n foolish behaviour. **fool around** v act or play irresponsibly or aimlessly. **foolproof** adj unable to fail.

fool[2] n dessert of puréed fruit mixed with cream.

foolhardy adj recklessly adventurous. **foolhardiness** n

foolscap n size of paper, 34.3 × 43.2 centimetres.

foot n, pl **feet**. part of the leg below the ankle; unit of length of twelve inches (0.3048 metre);

lowest part of anything; unit of poetic rhythm. **foot it** Informal walk. **foot the bill** pay the entire cost. **footage** n amount of film used. **foot-and-mouth disease** infectious viral disease of sheep, cattle, etc. **footbridge** n bridge for pedestrians. **football** n sound of a footstep. **foothills** pl n hills at the foot of a mountain.

foothold n secure position from which progress may be made; small place giving a secure grip for the foot. **footlights** pl n lights across the front of a stage.

footloose adj free from ties.

footman n male servant in uniform. **footnote** n note printed at the foot of a page. **footpath** n narrow path for walkers only; Aust raised space alongside a road, for pedestrians. **footplate** n platform in the cab of a locomotive for the driver. **footprint** n mark left by a foot. **footstep** n step in walking; sound made by walking.

footstool n low stool used to rest the feet on while sitting.

footwear n anything worn to cover the feet. **footwork** n skilful use of the feet, as in sport or dancing.

football n game played by two teams of eleven players kicking a ball in an attempt to score goals; any of various similar games, such as rugby; ball used for this. **footballer** n **football pools** form of gambling on the results of soccer matches.

footing n basis or foundation; relationship between people; secure grip by or for the feet.

footling adj Chiefly Brit informal trivial.

footsie n Informal flirtation involving the touching together of feet.

fop n man excessively concerned with fashion. **foppery** n **foppish** adj

for prep indicating a person intended to benefit from or receive something, span of time or distance, person or thing represented by someone, etc., e.g. a gift for you; for five miles; playing for his country. ▶ conj because. **for it** Informal liable for punishment or blame.

forage v search about (for). ▶ n food for cattle or horses.

foray n brief raid or attack; first attempt or new undertaking.

forbear v cease or refrain (from doing something). **forbearance** n tolerance, patience.

forbid v prohibit, refuse to allow. **forbidden** adj **forbidding** adj severe, threatening.

force n strength or power; compulsion; Physics influence tending to produce a change in a physical system; mental or moral strength; person or thing with strength or influence; vehemence or intensity; group of people organized for a particular task or duty. ▶ v compel, make (someone) do something; acquire or produce through effort, strength, etc.; propel or drive; break open; impose or inflict; cause to grow at an increased rate. **in force** having legal validity; in great numbers.

forced adj compulsory; false or unnatural; due to an emergency.

forceful adj emphatic and confident; effective. **forcefully** adv **forcible** adj involving physical force or violence; strong and emphatic. **forcibly** adv

forceps pl n surgical pincers.

ford n shallow place where a river may be crossed. ▶ v cross (a river) at a ford.

fore adj in, at, or towards the front. ▶ n front part. **to the fore** in a conspicuous position.

fore- prefix before in time or rank, e.g. forefather; at the front, e.g. forecourt.

fore-and-aft adj located at both ends of a ship.

forearm[1] n arm from the wrist to the elbow.

forearm[2] v prepare beforehand.

forebear n ancestor.

foreboding n feeling that something bad is about to happen.

forecast v **-casting, -cast** or **-casted.** predict (weather, events, etc.). ▶ n prediction.

forecastle [foke-sl] n raised front part of a ship.

foreclose v take possession of (property bought with borrowed money which has not been repaid). **foreclosure** n

forecourt n courtyard or open space in front of a building.

forefather n ancestor.

forefinger n finger next to the thumb.

forefront n most active or prominent position; very front.

foregather v meet together or assemble.

forego v same as FORGO.

foregoing adj going before, preceding. **foregone conclusion** inevitable result.

foreground n part of a view, esp. in a picture, nearest the observer.

forehand n Tennis etc. stroke played with the palm of the hand facing forward.

forehead n part of the face above the eyebrows.

foreign adj not of, or in, one's own country; relating to or connected with other countries; unfamiliar, strange; in an abnormal place or position, e.g.

foreign matter. **foreigner** n

forelock n lock of hair over the forehead.

foreman n person in charge of a group of workers; leader of a jury.

foremast n mast nearest the bow of a ship.

foremost adj, adv first in time, place, or importance.

forename n first name.

forenoon n Chiefly US & Canadian morning.

forensic adj used in or connected with courts of law. **forensic medicine** use of medical knowledge for the purposes of the law.

foreplay n sexual stimulation before intercourse.

forerunner n person or thing that goes before, precursor.

foresee v see or know beforehand. **foreseeable** adj

foreshadow v show or indicate beforehand.

foreshore n part of the shore between high- and low-tide marks.

foreshorten v represent (an object) in a picture as shorter than it really is, in accordance with perspective.

foresight n ability to anticipate and provide for future needs.

foreskin n fold of skin covering the tip of the penis.

forest n large area with a thick growth of trees. **forested** adj **forestry** n science of planting and caring for trees; management of forests. **forester** n person skilled in forestry.

forestall v prevent or guard against in advance.

foretaste n early limited experience of something to come.

foretell v tell or indicate beforehand.

forethought n thoughtful

planning for future events.

forever, for ever adv without end; at all times; *Informal* for a long time.

forewarn v warn beforehand.

foreword n introduction to a book.

forfeit [for-fit] n thing lost or given up as a penalty for a fault or mistake. ▶ v lose as a forfeit. ▶ adj lost as a forfeit. **forfeiture** n

forge[1] n place where metal is worked, smithy; furnace for melting metal. ▶ v make a fraudulent imitation of (something); shape (metal) by heating and hammering it; create (an alliance etc.).

forge[2] v advance steadily. **forge ahead** increase speed or take the lead.

forger n person who makes an illegal copy of something.

forgery n, pl **-ries.** illegal copy of something; crime of making an illegal copy.

forget v **-getting, -got, -gotten.** fail to remember; neglect; leave behind by mistake. **forgetful** adj tending to forget. **forgetfulness** n **forget-me-not** n plant with clusters of small blue flowers.

forgive v **-giving, -gave, -given.** cease to blame or hold resentment against, pardon. **forgiveness** n

forgo v do without or give up.

forgot v past tense of FORGET.

forgotten v past participle of FORGET.

fork n tool for eating food, with prongs and a handle; large similarly-shaped tool for digging or lifting; point where a road, river, etc. divides into branches; one of the branches. ▶ v pick up, dig, etc. with a fork; branch; take one or other branch at a fork in the road. **forked** adj **fork-lift**

truck vehicle with a forklike device at the front which can be raised or lowered to move loads. **fork out** v *Informal* pay.

forlorn adj lonely and unhappy. **forlorn hope** hopeless enterprise. **forlornly** adv

form n shape or appearance; mode in which something appears; type or kind; printed document with spaces for details; physical or mental condition; previous record of an athlete, racehorse, etc.; class in school. ▶ v give a (particular) shape to or take a (particular) shape; come or bring into existence; make or be made; train; acquire or develop. **formless** adj

formal adj of or characterized by established conventions of ceremony and behaviour; of or for formal occasions; stiff in manner; organized; symmetrical. **formally** adv **formality** n, pl **-ties.** requirement of custom or etiquette; necessary procedure without real importance.

formalize v make official or formal.

formaldehyde [for-**mal**-de-hide] n colourless pungent gas used to make formalin. **formalin** n solution of formaldehyde in water, used as a disinfectant or a preservative for biological specimens.

format n style in which something is arranged. ▶ v **-matting, -matted.** arrange in a format.

formation n forming; thing formed; structure or shape; arrangement of people or things acting as a unit.

formative adj of or relating to development; shaping.

former adj of an earlier time, previous. **the former** first mentioned of two. **formerly** adv

Formica n ® kind of laminated

sheet used to make heat-resistant surfaces.

formic acid n acid derived from ants.

formidable adj frightening because difficult to overcome or manage; extremely impressive. **formidably** adv

formula n, pl **-las, -lae.** group of numbers, letters, or symbols expressing a scientific or mathematical rule; method or rule for doing or producing something; set form of words used in religion, law, etc.; specific category of car in motor racing. **formulaic** adj **formulate** v plan or describe precisely and clearly. **formulation** n

fornicate v have sexual intercourse without being married. **fornication** n **fornicator** n

forsake v **-saking, -sook, -saken.** withdraw support or friendship from; give up, renounce.

forsooth adv *Obs* indeed.

forswear v **-swearing, -swore, -sworn.** renounce or reject.

forsythia [for-**syth**-ee-a] n shrub with yellow flowers in spring.

fort n fortified building or place. **hold the fort** *Informal* keep things going during someone's absence.

forte[1] [for-tay] n thing at which a person excels.

forte[2] [for-tay] adv *Music* loudly.

forth adv forwards, out, or away.

forthcoming adj about to appear or happen; available; (of a person) communicative.

forthright adj direct and outspoken.

forthwith adv at once.

fortieth adj, n see FORTY.

fortify v **-fying, -fied.** make (a place) defensible, as by building walls; strengthen; add vitamins etc. to (food); add alcohol to

(wine) to make sherry or port.
fortification n

fortissimo adv Music very loudly.

fortitude n courage in adversity or pain.

fortnight n two weeks.
fortnightly adv, adj

FORTRAN n Computers programming language for mathematical and scientific purposes.

fortress n large fort or fortified town.

fortuitous [for-**tyew**-it-uss] adj happening by (lucky) chance.
fortuitously adv

fortunate adj having good luck; occurring by good luck.
fortunately adv

fortune n luck, esp. when favourable; power regarded as influencing human destiny; wealth, large sum of money. ▶ pl person's destiny. **fortune-teller** n person who claims to predict the future of others.

forty adj, n, pl **-ties**. four times ten. **fortieth** adj, n

forum n meeting or medium for open discussion or debate.

forward adj directed or moving ahead; in, at, or near the front; presumptuous; well developed or advanced; relating to the future. ▶ n attacking player in various team games, such as soccer or hockey. ▶ adv forwards. ▶ v send (a letter etc.) on to an ultimate destination; advance or promote.
forwards adv towards or at a place further ahead in space or time; towards the front.

fossick v Aust & NZ search, esp. for gold or precious stones.

fossil n hardened remains of a prehistoric animal or plant preserved in rock. **fossilize** v turn into a fossil; become out-of-date

or inflexible.

foster v promote the growth or development of; bring up (a child not one's own). ▶ adj of or involved in fostering a child, e.g. foster parents.

fought v past of FIGHT.

foul adj loathsome or offensive; stinking or dirty; (of language) obscene or vulgar; unfair. ▶ n Sport violation of the rules. ▶ v make dirty or polluted; make or become entangled or clogged; Sport commit a foul against (an opponent). **fall foul of** come into conflict with. **foul-mouthed** adj habitually using foul language. **foul play** unfair conduct, esp. involving violence.

found[1] v past of FIND.

found[2] v establish or bring into being; lay the foundation of; (foll. by on or upon) have a basis (in). **founder** n

found[3] v cast (metal or glass) by melting and setting in a mould; make (articles) by this method.

foundation n basis or base; part of a building or wall below the ground; act of founding; institution supported by an endowment; cosmetic used as a base for make-up.

founder v break down or fail; (of a ship) sink; stumble or fall.

foundling n Chiefly Brit abandoned baby.

foundry n, pl **-ries**. place where metal is melted and cast.

fount[1] n Lit fountain; source.

fount[2] n set of printing type of one style and size.

fountain n jet of water; structure from which such a jet spurts; source. **fountainhead** n original source. **fountain pen** pen supplied with ink from a container inside it.

four adj, n one more than three. ▶ n (crew of) four-oared rowing boat. **on all fours** on hands and knees. **four-letter word** short obscene word referring to sex or excrement. **four-poster** n bed with four posts supporting a canopy. **foursome** n group of four people.

fourteen adj, n four and ten. **fourteenth** adj, n

fourth adj, n (of) number four in a series. ▶ n quarter. **fourth dimension** time. **fourth estate** the press.

fowl n domestic cock or hen; any bird used for food or hunted as game.

fox n reddish-brown bushy-tailed animal of the dog family; its fur; cunning person. ▶ v Informal perplex or deceive. **foxy** adj of or like a fox, esp. in craftiness. **foxglove** n tall plant with purple or white flowers. **foxhole** n Mil small pit dug for protection. **foxhound** n dog bred for hunting foxes. **fox terrier** small short-haired terrier. **foxtrot** n ballroom dance with slow and quick steps; music for this.

foyer [foy-ay] n entrance hall in a theatre, cinema, or hotel.

fracas [frak-ah] n, pl **-cas.** noisy quarrel.

fraction n numerical quantity that is not a whole number; fragment; piece; Chem substance separated by distillation. **fractional** adj **fractionally** adv

fractious adj easily upset and angered.

fracture n breaking, esp. of a bone. ▶ v break.

fragile adj easily broken or damaged; in a weakened physical state. **fragility** n

fragment n piece broken off;

incomplete piece. ▶ v break into pieces. **fragmentary** adj **fragmentation** n

fragrant adj sweet-smelling. **fragrance** n pleasant smell; perfume, scent.

frail adj physically weak; easily damaged. **frailty**, pl **-ties.** physical or moral weakness.

frame n structure giving shape or support; enclosing case or border, as round a picture; person's build; individual exposure on a strip of film; individual game of snooker in a match. ▶ v put together, construct; put into words; put into a frame; Slang incriminate (a person) on a false charge. **frame of mind** mood or attitude. **frame-up** n Slang false incrimination. **framework** n supporting structure.

franc n monetary unit of Switzerland, various African countries, and formerly of France and Belgium.

franchise n right to vote; authorization to sell a company's goods.

Franciscan n, adj (friar or nun) of the order founded by St. Francis of Assisi.

francium n Chem radioactive metallic element.

Franco- combining form of France or the French.

frangipani [fran-jee-pah-nee] n Australian evergreen tree with large yellow fragrant flowers; tropical shrub with fragrant white or pink flowers.

frank adj honest and straightforward in speech or attitude. ▶ n official mark on a letter permitting delivery. ▶ v put such a mark on (a letter). **frankly** adv **frankness** n

frankfurter n smoked sausage.

frankincense n aromatic gum resin burned as incense.

frantic adj distracted with rage, grief, joy, etc.; hurried and disorganized. **frantically** adv

fraternal adj of a brother, brotherly. **fraternally** adv

fraternity n group of people with shared interests, aims, etc.; brotherhood; US male social club at college. **fraternize** v associate on friendly terms. **fraternization** n crime of killing one's brother; person who does this.

Frau [rhymes with **how**] n, pl **Fraus, Frauen.** German title, equivalent to Mrs. **Fräulein** [froy-line] n, pl **-leins, -lein.** German title, equivalent to Miss.

fraud n (criminal) deception, swindle; person who acts in a deceitful way. **fraudulent** adj **fraudulence** n

fraught [frawt] adj tense or anxious. **fraught with** involving, filled with.

fray[1] n Brit, Aust & NZ noisy quarrel or conflict.

fray[2] v make or become ragged at the edge; become strained.

frazzle n Informal exhausted state.

freak n abnormal person or thing; person who is excessively enthusiastic about something. ▶ adj abnormal. **freakish** adj **freak out** v Informal (cause) to be in a heightened emotional state.

freckle n small brown spot on the skin. **freckled** adj marked with freckles.

free adj **freer, freest.** able to act at will, not compelled or restrained; not subject (to); provided without charge; not in use; (of a person) not busy; not fixed or joined. ▶ v **freeing, freed.** release, liberate; remove

(obstacles, pain, etc.) from; make available or usable. **a free hand** unrestricted freedom to act.

freely adv **free fall** part of a parachute descent before the parachute opens. **free-for-all** n Informal brawl. **freehand** adj drawn without guiding instruments. **freehold** n tenure of land for life without restrictions. **freeholder** n **free house** Brit public house not bound to sell only one brewer's products. **freelance** adj, n (of) a self-employed person doing specific pieces of work for various employers. **freeloader** n Slang habitual scrounger. **free-range** adj kept or produced in natural conditions. **freeway** n US & Aust motorway. **freewheel** v travel downhill on a bicycle without pedalling.

-free combining form without, e.g. a trouble-free journey.

freedom n being free; right or privilege of unlimited access, e.g. the freedom of the city.

Freemason n member of a secret fraternity pledged to help each other.

freesia n plant with fragrant tubular flowers.

freeze v **freezing, froze, frozen.** change from a liquid to a solid by the reduction of temperature, as water to ice; preserve (food etc.) by extreme cold; (cause to) be very cold; become motionless with fear, shock, etc.; fix (prices or wages) at a particular level; ban the exchange or collection of (loans, assets, etc.). ▶ n period of very cold weather; freezing of prices or wages. **freezer** n insulated cabinet for cold-storage of perishable foods. **freeze-dry** v preserve (food) by rapid freezing and drying in a vacuum. **freezing** *adj Informal* very cold.

freight [frate] *n* commercial transport of goods; cargo transported; cost of this. ▶ *v* send by freight. **freighter** *n* ship or aircraft for transporting goods.

French *n* language of France, also spoken in parts of Belgium, Canada, and Switzerland. ▶ *adj* of France, its people, or their language. **French bread** white bread in a long thin crusty loaf. **French dressing** salad dressing of oil and vinegar. **French fries** potato chips. **French horn** brass wind instrument with a coiled tube. **French polish** shellac varnish for wood. **French window** window extending to floor level, used as a door.

frenetic [frin-net-ik] *adj* uncontrolled, excited. **frenetically** *adv*

frenzy *n, pl* -zies. violent mental derangement; wild excitement. **frenzied** *adj* **frenziedly** *adv*

frequent *adj* happening often; habitual. ▶ *v* visit habitually. **frequently** *adv* **frequency** *n, pl* -cies. rate of occurrence; *Physics* number of times a wave repeats itself in a given time.

fresco *n, pl* -coes, -cos. watercolour painting done on wet plaster on a wall.

fresh *adj* newly made, acquired, etc.; novel, original; further, additional; (of food) not preserved; (of water) not salty; (of weather) brisk or invigorating; not tired. **freshly** *adv* **freshness** *n* **freshen** *v* make or become fresh or fresher. **fresher**, (*US*) **freshman** *n Brit & US* first-year student.

fret[1] *v* **fretting, fretted.** be worried. **fretful** *adj* irritable.

fret[2] *n* small bar on the

fingerboard of a guitar etc.

fretwork *n* decorative carving in wood. **fretsaw** *n* fine saw with a narrow blade, used for fretwork.

Freudian [froy-dee-an] *adj* of or relating to the psychoanalyst Sigmund Freud or his theories.

friable *adj* easily crumbled.

friar *n* member of a male Roman Catholic religious order. **friary** *n, pl* -ries. house of friars.

fricassee *n* stewed meat served in a thick white sauce.

friction *n* resistance met with by a body moving over another; rubbing; clash of wills or personalities. **frictional** *adj*

Friday *n* sixth day of the week. **Good Friday** Friday before Easter.

fridge *n* apparatus in which food and drinks are kept cool.

fried *v* past of FRY[1].

friend *n* person whom one knows well and likes; supporter or ally; (F-) Quaker. **friendly** *adj* showing or expressing liking; not hostile, on the same side. ▶ *n, pl* -lies. *Sport* match played for its own sake and not as part of a competition. **-friendly** *combining form* good or easy for the person or thing specified, e.g. *user-friendly*. **friendly society** (in Britain) association of people who pay regular dues in return for pensions, sickness benefits, etc. **friendliness** *n* **friendless** *adj* **friendship** *n*

Friesian [free-zhan] *n* breed of black-and-white dairy cattle.

frieze [freeze] *n* ornamental band on a wall.

frigate [frig-it] *n* medium-sized fast warship.

fright *n* sudden fear or alarm; sudden alarming shock. **frightful** *adj* horrifying; *Informal* very great. **frightfully** *adv*

frighten v scare or terrify; force (someone) to do something from fear. **frightening** adj

frigid [frij-id] adj (of a woman) sexually unresponsive; very cold; excessively formal. **frigidity** n

frill n gathered strip of fabric attached to one edge. ▶ pl superfluous decorations or details. **frilled** adj **frilly** adj

fringe n hair cut short and hanging over the forehead; ornamental edge of hanging threads, tassels, etc.; outer edge; less important parts of an activity or group. ▶ v decorate with a fringe. ▶ adj (of theatre) unofficial or unconventional. **fringed** adj **fringe benefit** benefit given in addition to a regular salary.

frippery n, pl **-peries.** useless ornamentation; trivia.

frisk v move or leap playfully; Informal search (a person) for concealed weapons etc. **frisky** adj lively or high-spirited.

frisson [frees-sonn] n shiver of fear or excitement.

fritter n piece of food fried in batter.

fritter away v waste.

frivolous adj not serious or sensible; enjoyable but trivial. **frivolity** n

frizz v form (hair) into stiff wiry curls. **frizzy** adj

frizzle v cook or heat until crisp and shrivelled.

frock n dress. **frock coat** man's skirted coat as worn in the 19th century.

frog n smooth-skinned tailless amphibian with long back legs used for jumping. **frog in one's throat** phlegm on the vocal cords, hindering speech. **frogman** n swimmer with a rubber suit and breathing equipment for working underwater. **frogspawn** n jelly-like substance containing frog's eggs.

frolic v **-icking, -icked.** run and play in a lively way. ▶ n lively and merry behaviour. **frolicsome** adj playful.

from prep indicating the point of departure, source, distance, cause, change of state, etc.

frond n long leaf or leaflike part of a fern, palm, or seaweed.

front n fore part; position directly before or ahead; battle line or area; Meteorol dividing line between two different air masses; outward appearance; Informal cover for another, usu. criminal, activity; particular field of activity, e.g. on the economic front. ▶ adj of or at the front. ▶ v face (onto); be the presenter of (a television show). **frontal** adj **frontage** n facade of a building. **front bench** (in Britain) parliamentary leaders of the government or opposition. **front-bencher** n **frontrunner** n Informal person regarded as most likely to win a race, election, etc.

frontier n area of a country bordering on another.

frontispiece n illustration facing the title page of a book.

frost n white frozen dew or mist; atmospheric temperature below freezing point. ▶ v become covered with frost. **frosted** adj (of glass) having a rough surface to make it opaque. **frosting** n Chiefly US sugar icing. **frosty** adj characterized or covered by frost; unfriendly. **frostily** adv **frostiness** n **frostbite** n destruction of tissue, esp. of the fingers or ears, by cold. **frostbitten** adj

froth n mass of small bubbles. ▶ v foam. **frothy** adj

frown v wrinkle one's brows in worry, anger, or thought; look disapprovingly (on). ▶ n frowning expression.

frowsty adj Brit stale or musty.

frowzy, frowsy adj -zier, -ziest or -sier, -siest. dirty or unkempt.

froze v past tense of FREEZE. **frozen** v past participle of FREEZE.

frugal adj thrifty, sparing; meagre and inexpensive. **frugally** adv **frugality** n

fruit n part of a plant containing seeds, esp. if edible; any plant product useful to humans; (often pl) result of an action or effort. ▶ v bear fruit. **fruiterer** n person who sells fruit. **fruitful** adj useful or productive. **fruitfully** adv **fruitless** adj useless or unproductive. **fruitlessly** adv **fruity** adj of or like fruit; (of a voice) mellow; (of a remark) bawdy. **fruit machine** coin-operated gambling machine.

fruition [froo-**ish**-on] n fulfilment of something worked for or desired.

frump n dowdy woman. **frumpy** adj

frustrate v upset or anger; hinder or prevent. **frustrated** adj **frustrating** adj **frustration** n

fry[1] v frying, fried. cook or be cooked in fat or oil. ▶ n, pl **fries**. (also **fry-up**) dish of fried food. ▶ pl potato chips.

fry[2] pl n young fishes. **small fry** young or insignificant people.

ft. foot; feet.

fuchsia [fyew-sha] n ornamental shrub with hanging flowers.

fuddle v cause to be intoxicated or confused. **fuddled** adj

fuddy-duddy n, pl -dies. Informal old-fashioned (person).

fudge[1] n soft caramel-like sweet.

fudge[2] v avoid making a firm statement or decision.

fuel n substance burned or treated to produce heat or power; something that intensifies (a feeling etc.). ▶ v **fuelling, fuelled.** provide with fuel.

fug n hot stale atmosphere. **fuggy** adj

fugitive [fyew-jit-iv] n person who flees, esp. from arrest or pursuit. ▶ adj fleeing; transient.

fugue [fyewg] n musical composition in which a theme is repeated in different parts.

fulcrum n, pl -crums, -cra. pivot about which a lever turns.

fulfil v -filling, -filled. bring about the achievement of (a desire or promise); carry out (a request or order); do what is required. **fulfilment** n **fulfil oneself** v achieve one's potential.

full adj containing as much or as many as possible; abundant in supply; having had enough to eat; plump; complete, whole; (of a garment) of ample cut; (of a sound or flavour) rich and strong. ▶ adv completely; directly; very. **fully** adv **fullness** n **in full** without shortening. **full-blooded** adj vigorous or enthusiastic. **full-blown** adj fully developed. **full moon** phase of the moon when it is visible as a fully illuminated disc. **full-scale** adj (of a plan) of actual size; using all resources. **full stop** punctuation mark (.) at the end of a sentence and after abbreviations.

fulmar n Arctic sea bird.

fulminate v (foll. by against) criticize or denounce angrily.

fulsome adj distastefully excessive or insincere.

fumble v handle awkwardly; say awkwardly. ▶ n act of fumbling.

fume v be very angry; give out smoke or vapour. ▶ pl n pungent smoke or vapour.

fumigate [fyew-mig-gate] v disinfect with fumes. **fumigation** n

fun n enjoyment or amusement. **make fun of** mock or tease.

funny adj comical, humorous; odd. **funny bone** part of the elbow where the nerve is near the surface. **funnily** adv

function n purpose something exists for; way something works; large or formal social event; Maths quantity whose value depends on the varying value of another; sequence of operations performed by a computer at a key stroke. ▶ v operate or work; (foll. by as) fill the role of. **functional** adj of or as a function; practical rather than decorative; in working order. **functionally** adv **functionary** n, pl -aries. official.

fund n stock of money for a special purpose; supply or store. ▶ pl money resources. ▶ v provide money to. **funding** n

fundamental adj essential or primary; basic. ▶ n basic rule or fact. **fundamentally** adv **fundamentalism** n literal or strict interpretation of a religion. **fundamentalist** n, adj

fundi n S Afr expert or boffin.

funeral n ceremony of burying or cremating a dead person. **funerary** adj of or for a funeral. **funereal** [fyew-neer-ee-al] adj gloomy or sombre.

funfair n entertainment with machines to ride on and stalls.

fungus n, pl -gi, -guses. plant without leaves, flowers, or roots, such as a mushroom or mould. **fungal, fungous** adj **fungicide** n substance that destroys fungi.

funicular n cable railway on a mountainside or cliff.

funk[1] n style of dance music with a strong beat. **funky** adj (of music) having a strong beat.

funk[2] Informal ▶ n nervous or fearful state. ▶ v avoid (doing something) through fear.

funnel n cone-shaped tube for pouring liquids into a narrow opening; chimney of a ship or locomotive. ▶ v -nelling, -nelled. (cause to) move through or as if through a funnel.

fur n soft hair of a mammal; animal skin with the fur left on; garment made of this; whitish coating on the tongue or inside a kettle. ▶ v cover or become covered with fur. **furry** adj **furrier** n dealer in furs.

furbish v smarten up.

furious adj very angry; violent or unrestrained. **furiously** adv

furl v roll up and fasten (a sail, umbrella, or flag).

furlong n unit of length equal to 220 yards (201.168 metres).

furlough [fur-loh] n leave of absence.

furnace n enclosed chamber containing a very hot fire.

furnish v provide (a house or room) with furniture; supply, provide. **furnishings** pl n furniture, carpets, and fittings. **furniture** n large movable articles such as chairs and wardrobes.

furore [fyew-ror-ee] n very excited or angry reaction.

furrow n trench made by a plough; groove, esp. a wrinkle on the forehead. ▶ v make or become wrinkled; make furrows in.

further adv in addition; to a greater distance or extent. ▶ adj additional; more distant. ▶ v assist the progress of. **further education** Brit education beyond school other than at a university. **furthest** adv to the greatest

distance or extent. ▶ adj most distant. **furtherance** n
furthermore adv besides.
furthermost adj most distant.
furtive adj sly and secretive.
furtively adv
fury n, pl **-ries**. wild anger; uncontrolled violence.
furze n gorse.
fuse[1] n cord containing an explosive for detonating a bomb.
fuse[2] n safety device for electric circuits, containing a wire that melts and breaks the connection when the circuit is overloaded. ▶ v (cause to) fail as a result of a blown fuse; join or combine; unite by melting; melt with heat.
fuselage [**fyew-zill-lahzh**] n body of an aircraft.
fusilier [fyew-zill-**leer**] n soldier of certain regiments.
fusillade [fyew-zill-**lade**] n continuous discharge of firearms; outburst of criticism, questions, etc.
fusion n melting; product of fusing; combination of the nucleus of two atoms with the release of energy; something new created by a mixture of qualities, ideas, or things; popular music blending styles, esp. jazz and funk. ▶ adj of a style of cooking that combines traditional Western techniques and ingredients with those used in Eastern cuisine.
fuss n needless activity or worry; complaint or objection; great display of attention. ▶ v make a fuss. **fussy** adj inclined to fuss; overparticular; overelaborate.
fussily adv **fussiness** n
fusty adj **-tier, -tiest.** stale-smelling; behind the times.
fustiness n
futile adj unsuccessful or useless.
futility n
futon [**foo-tonn**] n Japanese-style

bed.
future n time to come; what will happen; prospects. ▶ adj yet to come or be; of or relating to time to come; (of a verb tense) indicating that the action specified has not yet taken place. **futuristic** adj of a design appearing to belong to some future time.
fuzz[1] n mass of fine or curly hairs or fibres. **fuzzy** adj of, like, or covered with fuzz; blurred or indistinct; (of hair) tightly curled.
fuzzily adv **fuzziness** n
fuzz[2] n Slang police.

G g

g gram(s); (acceleration due to) gravity.
gab n, v **gabbing, gabbed.** Informal talk or chatter. **gift of the gab** eloquence. **gabby** adj **-bier, -biest.** Informal talkative.
gabardine, gaberdine n strong twill cloth used esp. for raincoats.
gabble v speak rapidly and indistinctly. ▶ n rapid indistinct speech.
gable n triangular upper part of a wall between sloping roofs.
gabled adj
gad v **gadding, gadded. gad about, around** go around in search of pleasure. **gadabout** n pleasure-seeker.
gadfly n fly that bites cattle; constantly annoying person.
gadget n small mechanical device or appliance. **gadgetry** n gadgets.
Gael [gayl] n speaker of Gaelic.
Gaelic [**gal**-lik or **gay**-lik] n any of the Celtic languages of Ireland and the Scottish Highlands. ▶ adj of the Gaels or their language.
gaff[1] n stick with an iron hook for

landing large fish.

gaff² n **blow the gaff** Slang divulge a secret.

gaffe n social blunder.

gaffer n Brit informal foreman or boss; Informal old man; senior electrician on a TV or film set.

gag¹ v **gagging, gagged.** choke or retch; stop up the mouth of (a person) with cloth etc.; deprive of free speech. ▶ n cloth etc. put into or tied across the mouth.

gag² n Informal joke.

gaga [gah-gah] adj Slang senile.

gaggle n Informal disorderly crowd; flock of geese.

gaiety n cheerfulness; merrymaking. **gaily** adv merrily; colourfully.

gain v acquire or obtain; increase or improve; reach; (of a watch or clock) be or become too fast. ▶ n profit or advantage; increase or improvement. **gainful** adj useful or profitable. **gainfully** adv **gain on, upon** v get nearer to or catch up with.

gainsay v **-saying, -said.** deny or contradict.

gait n manner of walking.

gaiter n cloth or leather covering for the lower leg.

gala [gah-la] n festival; competitive sporting event.

galaxy n, pl **-axies.** system of stars; gathering of famous people. **galactic** adj

gale n strong wind; Informal loud outburst.

gall¹ [gawl] n Informal impudence; bitter feeling. **gall bladder** sac attached to the liver, storing bile. **gallstone** n hard mass formed in the gall bladder or its ducts.

gall² [gawl] v annoy; make sore by rubbing.

gall³ [gawl] n abnormal outgrowth on a tree or plant.

gallant adj brave and noble; (of a man) attentive to women. **gallantly** adv **gallantry** n showy, attentive treatment of women; bravery.

galleon n large three-masted sailing ship of the 15th–17th centuries.

gallery n, pl **-ries.** room or building for displaying works of art; balcony in a church, theatre, etc.; passage in a mine; long narrow room for a specific purpose, e.g. shooting gallery.

galley n kitchen of a ship or aircraft; Hist ship propelled by oars, usu. rowed by slaves. **galley slave** Hist slave forced to row in a galley; Informal drudge.

Gallic adj French; of ancient Gaul.

gallium n Chem soft grey metallic element used in semiconductors.

gallivant v go about in search of pleasure.

gallon n liquid measure of eight pints, equal to 4.55 litres.

gallop n horse's fastest pace; galloping. ▶ v galloping, galloped. go or ride at a gallop; move or progress rapidly.

gallows n wooden structure used for hanging criminals.

Gallup poll n public opinion poll carried out by questioning a cross section of the population.

galore adv in abundance.

galoshes pl n Brit, Aust & NZ waterproof overshoes.

galumph v Brit, Aust & NZ informal leap or move about clumsily.

galvanic adj of or producing an electric current generated by chemical means; Informal stimulating or startling. **galvanize** v stimulate into action; coat (metal) with zinc.

gambit n opening line or move intended to secure an advantage;

Chess opening move involving the sacrifice of a pawn.

gamble v play games of chance to win money; act on the expectation of something. ▶ n risky undertaking; bet or wager. **gambler** n **gambling** n

gamboge [gam-**boje**] n gum resin used as a yellow pigment and purgative.

gambol v **-bolling, -bolled.** jump about playfully, frolic. ▶ n frolic.

game¹ n amusement or pastime; contest for amusement; single period of play in a contest; animals or birds hunted for sport or food; their flesh; scheme or trick. ▶ v gamble. ▶ adj brave; willing. **gamely** adv **gaming** n gambling. **gamekeeper** n Brit, Aust & S Afr person employed to breed game and prevent poaching. **gamesmanship** n art of winning by cunning practices without actually cheating.

game² adj Brit, Aust & NZ lame, crippled.

gamete n Biol reproductive cell.

gamine [gam-**een**] n slim boyish young woman.

gamma n third letter of the Greek alphabet. **gamma ray** electromagnetic ray of shorter wavelength and higher energy than an x-ray.

gammon n cured or smoked ham.

gammy adj **-mier, -miest.** same as GAME².

gamut n whole range or scale (of music, emotions, etc.).

gander n male goose; Informal quick look.

gang n (criminal) group; organized group of workmen. **gangland** n criminal underworld. **gang up** v form an alliance (against).

gangling adj lanky and awkward.

ganglion n group of nerve cells;

small harmless tumour.

gangplank n portable bridge for boarding or leaving a ship.

gangrene n decay of body tissue as a result of disease or injury. **gangrenous** adj

gangsta rap n style of music portraying life in Black ghettos in the US.

gangster n member of a criminal gang.

gangway n passage between rows of seats; gangplank.

gannet n large sea bird; Brit slang greedy person.

gantry n, pl **-tries.** structure supporting something such as a crane or rocket.

gaol [jayl] n same as JAIL.

gap n break or opening; interruption or interval; divergence or difference. **gappy** adj

gape v stare in wonder; open the mouth wide; be or become wide open. **gaping** adj

garage n building used to house cars; place for the refuelling, sale, and repair of cars. ▶ v put or keep a car in a garage.

garb n clothes. ▶ v clothe.

garbage n rubbish.

garbled adj (of a story etc.) jumbled and confused.

garden n piece of land for growing flowers, fruit, or vegetables. ▶ pl ornamental park. ▶ v cultivate a garden. **gardener** n **gardening** n **garden centre** place selling plants and gardening equipment.

gardenia [gar-**deen**-ya] n large fragrant white waxy flower; shrub bearing this.

gargantuan adj huge.

gargle v wash the throat with (a liquid) by breathing out slowly through the liquid. ▶ n liquid used for gargling.

gargoyle n waterspout carved in the form of a grotesque face, esp. on a church.

garish adj crudely bright or colourful. **garishly** adv **garishness** n

garland n wreath of flowers worn or hung as a decoration. ▶ v decorate with garlands.

garlic n pungent bulb of a plant of the onion family, used in cooking.

garment n article of clothing. ▶ pl clothes.

garner v collect or store.

garnet n red semiprecious stone.

garnish v decorate (food). ▶ n decoration for food.

garret n attic in a house.

garrison n troops stationed in a town or fort; fortified place. ▶ v station troops in.

garrotte, garotte n Spanish method of execution by strangling; cord or wire used for this. ▶ v kill by this method.

garrulous adj talkative.

garter n band worn round the leg to hold up a sock or stocking.

gas n, pl **gases, gasses.** airlike substance that is not liquid or solid; fossil fuel in the form of a gas, used for heating; gaseous anaesthetic; Chiefly US petrol. ▶ v **gassing, gassed.** poison or render unconscious with gas; Informal talk idly or boastfully. **gassy** adj filled with gas. **gaseous** adj of or like gas. **gasbag** n Informal person who talks too much. **gas chamber** airtight room which is filled with poison gas to kill people or animals. **gasholder, gasometer** [gas-som-it-er] n large tank for storing gas. **gas mask** mask with a chemical filter to protect the wearer against poison gas.

gash v make a long deep cut in.

▶ n long deep cut.

gasket n piece of rubber etc. placed between the faces of a metal joint to act as a seal.

gasoline n US petrol.

gasp v draw in breath sharply or with difficulty; utter breathlessly. ▶ n convulsive intake of breath.

gastric adj of the stomach. **gastritis** n inflammation of the stomach lining. **gastroenteritis** n inflammation of the stomach and intestines.

gastronomy n art of good eating. **gastronomic** adj

gastropod n mollusc, such as a snail, with a single flattened muscular foot.

gate n movable barrier, usu. hinged, in a wall or fence; opening with a gate; any entrance or way in; (entrance money paid by) those attending a sporting event. **gate-crash** v enter (a party) uninvited. **gatehouse** n building at or above a gateway. **gateway** n entrance with a gate; means of access, e.g. London's gateway to Scotland.

gâteau [gat-toe] n, pl -teaux [-toes] rich elaborate cake.

gather v assemble; collect gradually; increase gradually; learn from information given; pick or harvest; draw (material) into small tucks or folds. **gathers** pl n gathered folds in material. **gathering** n assembly.

gauche [gohsh] adj socially awkward. **gaucheness** n

gaucho [gow-choh] n, pl -chos. S American cowboy.

gaudy adj gaudier, gaudiest. vulgarly bright or colourful. **gaudily** adv **gaudiness** n

gauge [gayj] v estimate or judge; measure the amount or condition of. ▶ n measuring instrument;

scale or standard of measurement; distance between the rails of a railway track.

gaunt *adj* lean and haggard. **gauntness** *n*

gauntlet¹ *n* heavy glove with a long cuff. **throw down the gauntlet** offer a challenge.

gauntlet² *n* **run the gauntlet** be exposed to criticism or unpleasant treatment.

gauze *n* transparent loosely-woven fabric, often used for surgical dressings. **gauzy** *adj*

gave *v* past tense of GIVE.

gavel [gav-el] *n* small hammer banged on a table by a judge, auctioneer, or chairman to call for attention.

gavotte *n* old formal dance; music for this.

gawk *v* stare stupidly. **gawky** *adj* clumsy or awkward. **gawkiness** *n*

gawp *v Slang* stare stupidly.

gay *adj* homosexual; carefree and merry; colourful. ▶ *n* homosexual. **gayness** *n* homosexuality.

gaze *v* look fixedly. ▶ *n* fixed look.

gazebo [gaz-zee-boh] *n, pl* -**bos**, -**boes**. summerhouse with a good view.

gazelle *n* small graceful antelope.

gazette *n* official publication containing announcements. **gazetteer** *n* (part of) a book that lists and describes places.

gazump *v Brit & Aust* raise the price of a property after verbally agreeing with it (a prospective buyer).

GB Great Britain.

GBH (in Britain) grievous bodily harm.

GCE (in Britain) General Certificate of Education.

GCSE (in Britain) General Certificate of Secondary Education.

gear *n* set of toothed wheels

connecting with another or with a rack to change the direction or speed of transmitted motion; mechanism for transmitting motion by gears; setting of a gear to suit engine speed, e.g. *first gear;* clothing or belongings; equipment. ▶ *v* prepare or organize for something. **in, out of gear** with the gear mechanism engaged or disengaged. **gearbox** *n* case enclosing a set of gears in a motor vehicle. **gear up** *v* prepare for an activity.

gecko *n, pl* **geckos, geckoes.** small tropical lizard.

geek *n Informal* boring, unattractive person. **geeky** *adj*

geelbek *n S Afr* edible marine fish.

geese *n* plural of GOOSE.

geezer *n Brit, Aust & NZ informal* man.

Geiger counter [guy-ger] *n* instrument for detecting and measuring radiation.

geisha [gay-sha] *n, pl* -**sha**, -**shas.** (in Japan) professional female companion for men.

gel [jell] *n* jelly-like substance, esp. one used to secure a hairstyle. ▶ *v* **gelling, gelled.** form a gel; *Informal* take on a definite form.

gelatine [jel-at-teen], **gelatin** *n* substance made by boiling animal bones; edible jelly made of this. **gelatinous** [jel-at-in-uss] *adj* of or like jelly.

geld *v* castrate.

gelding *n* castrated horse.

gelignite *n* type of dynamite used for blasting.

gem *n* precious stone or jewel; highly valued person or thing.

gen *n Informal* information. **gen up on** *v* **genning, genned.** *Brit informal* make or become fully informed about.

gendarme [zhohn-darm] *n*

member of the French police force.

gender *n* state of being male or female; *Grammar* classification of nouns in certain languages as masculine, feminine, or neuter.

gene [jean] *n* part of a cell which determines inherited characteristics.

genealogy [jean-ee-al-a-gee] *n, pl* **-gies.** (study of) the history and descent of a family or families. **genealogical** *adj* **genealogist** *n*

genera [jen-er-a] *n* plural of GENUS.

general *adj* common or widespread; of or affecting all or most; not specific; including or dealing with various or miscellaneous items; highest in authority or rank, e.g. *general manager.* ▶ *n* very senior army officer. **in general** mostly or usually. **generally** *adv* **generality** *n, pl* **-ties.** general principle; state of being general. **generalize** *v* draw general conclusions; speak in generalities; make widely known or used. **generalization** *n*

general election election in which representatives are chosen for every constituency. **general practitioner** nonspecialist doctor serving a local area.

generate *v* produce or bring into being. **generative** *adj* capable of producing. **generator** *n* machine for converting mechanical energy into electrical energy.

generation *n* all the people born about the same time; average time between two generations (about 30 years); generating.

generic [jin-ner-ik] *adj* of a class, group, or genus. **generically** *adv*

generous *adj* free in giving; free from pettiness; plentiful. **generously** *adv* **generosity** *n*

genesis [jen-iss-iss] *n, pl* **-eses** [-iss-eez] beginning or origin.

genetic [jin-net-tik] *adj* of genes or

genetics. **genetics** *n* study of heredity and variation in organisms. **geneticist** *n* **genetic engineering** alteration of the genetic structure of an organism for a particular purpose. **genetic fingerprinting** use of a person's unique DNA pattern as a means of identification.

genial [jean-ee-al] *adj* cheerful and friendly. **genially** *adv* **geniality** *n*

genie [jean-ee] *n* (in fairy tales) servant who appears by magic and grants wishes.

genital *adj* of the sexual organs or reproduction. **genitals, genitalia** [jen-it-ail-ya] *pl n* external sexual organs.

genitive *n* grammatical case indicating possession or association.

genius [jean-yuss] *n* (person with) exceptional ability in a particular field.

genocide [jen-no-side] *n* murder of a race of people.

genre [zhohn-ra] *n* style of literary, musical, or artistic work.

gent *n Brit, Aust & NZ informal* gentleman. **gents** *n* men's public toilet.

genteel *adj* affectedly proper and polite. **genteelly** *adv*

gentian [jen-shun] *n* mountain plant with deep blue flowers.

gentile *adj, n* non-Jewish (person).

gentle *adj* mild or kindly; not rough or severe; gradual; easily controlled, tame. **gentleness** *n* **gently** *adv* **gentleman** *n* polite well-bred man; man of high social position; polite name for a man. **gentlemanly** *adj* **gentlewoman** *n fem*

gentry *n* people just below the nobility in social rank.

gentrification *n* taking-over of a traditionally working-class area by middle-class incomers. **gentrify** v

genuflect v bend the knee as a sign of reverence or deference. **genuflection, genuflexion** n

genuine adj not fake, authentic; sincere. **genuinely** adv **genuineness** n

genus [jean-uss] n, pl **genera**. group into which a family of animals or plants is divided; kind, type.

geocentric adj having the earth as a centre; measured as from the earth's centre.

geography n study of the earth's physical features, climate, population, etc. **geographer** n **geographical, geographic** adj **geographically** adv

geology n study of the earth's origin, structure, and composition. **geological** adj **geologically** adv **geologist** n

geometry n branch of mathematics dealing with points, lines, curves, and surfaces. **geometric, geometrical** adj **geometrically** adv

Geordie n person from, or dialect of, Tyneside, an area of NE England.

Georgian adj of the time of any of the four kings of Britain called George, esp. 1714–1830.

geostationary adj (of a satellite) orbiting so as to remain over the same point of the earth's surface.

geothermal adj of or using the heat in the earth's interior.

geranium n cultivated plant with red, pink, or white flowers.

gerbil [jer-bill] n burrowing desert rodent of Asia and Africa.

geriatrics n branch of medicine dealing with old age and its diseases. **geriatric** adj, n old (person).

germ n microbe, esp. one causing

disease; beginning from which something may develop; simple structure that can develop into a complete organism.

German n language of Germany, Austria, and part of Switzerland; person from Germany. ▶ adj of Germany or its language. **Germanic** adj **German measles** contagious disease accompanied by a cough, sore throat, and red spots. **German shepherd dog** Alsatian.

germane adj **germane to** relevant to.

germanium n Chem brittle grey element that is a semiconductor.

germinate v (cause to) sprout or begin to grow. **germination** n **germinal** adj of or in the earliest stage of development.

gerrymandering n alteration of voting constituencies in order to give an unfair advantage to one party.

gerund [jer-rund] n noun formed from a verb, such as *living*.

Gestapo n secret state police of Nazi Germany.

gestation n (period of) carrying of young in the womb between conception and birth; developing of a plan or idea in the mind.

gesticulate v make expressive movements with the hands and arms. **gesticulation** n

gesture n movement to convey meaning; thing said or done to show one's feelings. ▶ v gesticulate.

get v **getting, got**. obtain or receive; bring or fetch; contract (an illness); (cause to) become as specified, e.g. *get wet*; understand; (often foll. by *to*) come (to) or arrive (at); go on board (a plane, bus, etc.); *Informal* annoy. **get across** v (cause to) be understood. **get at** v gain access

to; imply or mean; criticize.
getaway *adj, n* (used in) escape.
get by *v* manage in spite of
difficulties. **get off** *v* (cause to)
avoid the consequences of, or
punishment for, an action. **get
off with** *v Informal* start a
romantic or sexual relationship
with. **get over** *v* recover from.
get through *v* (cause to) succeed;
use up (money or supplies). **get
through to** *v* make a (person)
understand; contact by telephone.
get-up *n Informal* costume. **get
up to** *v* be involved in.

geyser [geez-er] *n* spring that
discharges steam and hot water;
Brit & S Afr domestic gas water
heater.

ghastly *adj* **-lier, -liest.** *Informal*
unpleasant; deathly pale; *Informal*
unwell; *Informal* horrible.
ghastliness *n*

ghat *n* (in India) steps leading
down to a river; mountain pass.

ghee [gee] *n* (in Indian cookery)
clarified butter.

gherkin *n* small pickled cucumber.

ghetto *n, pl* **-tos, -toes.** slum area
inhabited by a deprived minority.
ghetto-blaster *n Informal* large
portable cassette recorder or CD
player.

ghillie *n* same as GILLIE.

ghost *n* disembodied spirit of a
dead person; faint trace. ▸ *v*
ghostwrite. **ghostly** *adj* **ghost
town** deserted town. **ghostwriter**
n writer of a book or article on
behalf of another person who is
credited as the author.

ghoul [gool] *n* person with morbid
interests; demon that eats corpses.
ghoulish *adj*

GI *n Informal* US soldier.

giant *n* mythical being of
superhuman size; very large
person or thing. ▸ *adj* huge.

gibber¹ [jib-ber] *v* speak or utter
rapidly and unintelligibly.
gibberish *n* rapid unintelligible
talk.

gibber² [gib-ber] *n Aust* boulder;
barren land covered with stones.

gibbet [jib-bit] *n* gallows for
displaying executed criminals.

gibbon [gib-bon] *n* agile
tree-dwelling ape of S Asia.

gibbous *adj* (of the moon) more
than half but less than fully
illuminated.

gibe [jibe] *v, n* same as JIBE¹.

giblets [jib-lets] *pl n* gizzard, liver,
heart, and neck of a fowl.

gidday, g'day *interj Aust & NZ*
expression of greeting.

giddy *adj* **-dier, -diest.** having or
causing a feeling of dizziness.
giddily *adv* **giddiness** *n*

gift *n* present; natural talent. ▸ *v*
make a present of. **gifted** *adj*
talented.

gig¹ *n* single performance by pop
or jazz musicians. ▸ *v* **gigging,
gigged.** play a gig or gigs.

gig² *n* light two-wheeled
horse-drawn carriage.

gigantic *adj* enormous.

giggle *v* laugh nervously or
foolishly. ▸ *n* such a laugh. **giggly**
adj

gigolo [jig-a-lo] *n, pl* **-los.** man
paid by an older woman to be her
escort or lover.

gigot *n Chiefly Brit* leg of lamb or
mutton.

gild *v* **gilding, gilded** or **gilt.** put a
thin layer of gold on; make falsely
attractive.

gill¹ [jill] *n* liquid measure of quarter
of a pint, equal to 0.142 litres.

gillie *n* (in Scotland) attendant for
hunting or fishing.

gills [gillz] *pl n* breathing organs in
fish and other water creatures.

gilt *adj* covered with a thin layer of

gold. ▶ n thin layer of gold used as decoration. **gilt-edged** adj denoting government stocks on which interest payments and final repayments are guaranteed.

gimbals pl n set of pivoted rings which allow nautical instruments to remain horizontal at sea.

gimcrack [jim-krak] adj showy but cheap; shoddy.

gimlet [gim-let] n small tool with a screwlike tip for boring holes in wood. **gimlet-eyed** adj having a piercing glance.

gimmick n something designed to attract attention or publicity. **gimmickry** n **gimmicky** adj

gin[1] n spirit flavoured with juniper berries.

gin[2] n wire noose used to trap small animals; machine for separating seeds from raw cotton.

ginger n root of a tropical plant, used as a spice; light orange-brown colour. **gingery** adj **ginger ale, beer** fizzy ginger-flavoured soft drink. **gingerbread** n moist cake flavoured with ginger. **ginger group** Brit, Aust & NZ group within a larger group that agitates for a more active policy. **ginger nut, snap** crisp ginger-flavoured biscuit.

gingerly adv cautiously.

gingham n cotton cloth, usu. checked or striped.

gingivitis [jin-jiv-vite-iss] n inflammation of the gums.

ginkgo [gink-go] n, pl **-goes**. ornamental Chinese tree.

ginseng [jin-seng] n (root of) a plant believed to have tonic and energy-giving properties.

Gipsy n, pl **-sies**. same as GYPSY.

giraffe n African ruminant mammal with a spotted yellow skin and long neck and legs.

gird v **girding, girded** or **girt**. put a belt round; secure in or as if with a belt; surround. **gird (up) one's loins** prepare for action.

girder n large metal beam.

girdle[1] n woman's elastic corset; belt; Anat encircling structure or part. ▶ v surround or encircle.

girdle[2] n Scot griddle.

girl n female child; young woman; girlfriend; Informal any woman. **girlhood** n **girlish** adj **girlie, girly** adj Informal featuring photographs of naked or scantily clad women. **girlfriend** n girl or woman with whom a person is romantically or sexually involved; female friend.

giro [jire-oh] n, pl **-ros**. (in some countries) system of transferring money within a post office or bank directly from one account to another; Brit informal social security payment by giro cheque.

girt v a past of GIRD.

girth n measurement round something; band round a horse to hold the saddle in position.

gist [jist] n substance or main point of a matter.

give v **giving, gave, given**. present (something) to another person; impart; administer; utter or emit; sacrifice or devote; organize or host; yield or break under pressure. ▶ n resilience or elasticity. **give away** v donate as a gift; reveal. **giveaway** n something that reveals hidden feelings or intentions. ▶ adj very cheap or free. **give in** v admit defeat. **give off** v emit. **give out** v distribute; emit; come to an end or fail. **give over** v set aside for a specific purpose; Informal cease. **give up** v abandon; acknowledge defeat.

gizzard n part of a bird's stomach.

glacé [glass-say] adj preserved in a

thick sugary syrup.

glacier *n* slow-moving mass of ice formed by accumulated snow. **glacial** *adj* of ice or glaciers; very cold; unfriendly. **glaciated** *adj* covered with or affected by glaciers. **glaciation** *n*

glad *adj* **gladder, gladdest.** pleased and happy; causing happiness. **glad to** very willing to (do something). **the glad eye** *Chiefly Brit informal* inviting or seductive glance. **gladly** *adv* **gladness** *n* **gladden** *v* make glad. **glad rags** *Informal* best clothes.

glade *n* open space in a forest.

gladiator *n* (in ancient Rome) man trained to fight in arenas to provide entertainment.

gladiolus *n, pl* **-lus, -li, -luses.** garden plant with sword-shaped leaves.

gladwrap *Aust, NZ & S Afr* ▶ *n* ® thin polythene material for wrapping food. ▶ *v* wrap in gladwrap.

glamour *n* alluring charm or fascination. **glamorous** *adj* alluring. **glamorize** *v*

glance *v* look rapidly or briefly; glint or gleam. ▶ *n* brief look. **glancing** *adj* hitting at an oblique angle. **glance off** *v* strike and be deflected off (an object) at an oblique angle.

gland *n* organ that produces and secretes substances in the body. **glandular** *adj*

glare *v* stare angrily; be unpleasantly bright. ▶ *n* angry stare; unpleasant brightness. **glaring** *adj* conspicuous; unpleasantly bright. **glaringly** *adv*

glass *n* hard brittle, usu. transparent substance consisting of metal silicates or similar compounds; tumbler; its contents; objects made of glass; mirror;

barometer. ▶ *pl* spectacles. **glassy** *adj* like glass; expressionless.

glasshouse *n* greenhouse; *Brit informal* army prison.

glaucoma *n* eye disease.

glaze *v* fit or cover with glass; cover with a protective shiny coating. ▶ *n* transparent coating; substance used for this. **glazier** *n* person who fits windows with glass.

gleam *n* small beam or glow of light; brief or faint indication. ▶ *v* emit a gleam. **gleaming** *adj*

glean *v* gather (facts etc.) bit by bit; gather (the useful remnants of a crop) after harvesting. **gleaner** *n*

glee *n* triumph and delight. **gleeful** *adj* **gleefully** *adv*

glen *n* deep narrow valley, esp. in Scotland.

glib *adj* **glibber, glibbest.** fluent but insincere or superficial. **glibly** *adv* **glibness** *n*

glide *v* move easily and smoothly; (of an aircraft) move without the use of engines. ▶ *n* smooth easy movement. **glider** *n* aircraft without an engine which floats on air currents. **gliding** *n* sport of flying gliders.

glimmer *v* shine faintly, flicker. ▶ *n* faint gleam; faint indication.

glimpse *n* brief or incomplete view. ▶ *v* catch a glimpse of.

glint *v* gleam brightly. ▶ *n* bright gleam.

glissando *n* *Music* slide between two notes in which all intermediate notes are played.

glisten *v* gleam by reflecting light.

glitch *n* small problem that stops something from working properly.

glitter *v* shine with bright flashes; be showy. ▶ *n* sparkle or brilliance; tiny pieces of shiny decorative material.

gloaming *n* *Scot poetic* twilight.

gloat v (often foll. by over) regard one's own good fortune or the misfortune of others with smug or malicious pleasure.

glob n rounded mass of thick fluid.

globe n sphere with a map of the earth on it; spherical object; S Afr light bulb. **the globe** the earth. **global** adj worldwide; total or comprehensive. **globalization** n process by which a company, etc., expands to operate internationally. **global warming** increase in the overall temperature worldwide believed to be caused by the greenhouse effect. **globally** adv **globetrotter** n habitual worldwide traveller. **globetrotting** n, adj

globule n small round drop. **globular** adj

glockenspiel n percussion instrument consisting of small metal bars played with hammers.

gloom n melancholy or depression; darkness. **gloomy** adj **gloomier, gloomiest. gloomily** adv

glory n, pl **-ries.** praise or honour; splendour; praiseworthy thing. ▸ v **-rying, -ried.** (foll. by in) triumph or exalt. **glorify** v make (something) seem more worthy than it is; praise. **glorification** n **glorious** adj brilliantly beautiful; delightful; full of or conferring glory. **gloriously** adv **glory hole** Informal untidy cupboard or storeroom.

gloss[1] n surface shine or lustre; paint or cosmetic giving a shiny finish. **glossy** adj **-sier, -siest.** smooth and shiny; (of a magazine) printed on shiny paper. **glossily** adv **glossiness** n **gloss over** v (try to) cover up or pass over (a fault or error).

gloss[2] n explanatory comment added to the text of a book. ▸ v add glosses to.

glossary n, pl **-ries.** list of special or technical words with definitions.

glottal adj of the glottis.

glottis n, pl **-tises, -tides.** vocal cords and the space between them.

glove n covering for the hand with individual sheaths for each finger and the thumb. **gloved** adj covered by a glove or gloves. **glove compartment** or **box** small storage area in the dashboard of a car.

glow v emit light and heat without flames; shine; have a feeling of wellbeing or satisfaction; (of a colour) look warm; be hot. ▸ n glowing light; warmth of colour; feeling of wellbeing. **glow-worm** n insect giving out a green light.

glower [rhymes with **power**] v, n scowl.

gloxinia n tropical plant with large bell-shaped flowers.

glucose n kind of sugar found in fruit.

glue n natural or synthetic sticky substance used as an adhesive. ▸ v gluing or glueing, glued. fasten with glue; (foll. by to) pay full attention to, e.g. her eyes were glued to the TV. **gluey** adj **glue-sniffing** n inhaling of glue fumes for intoxicating or hallucinatory effects.

glum adj **glummer, glummest.** sullen or gloomy. **glumly** adv

glut n excessive supply. ▸ v **glutting, glutted.** oversupply.

gluten [gloo-ten] n protein found in cereal grain.

glutinous [gloo-tin-uss] adj sticky or gluey.

glutton n greedy person; person with a greedy capacity for something. **gluttonous** adj **gluttony** n

glycerine, glycerin n colourless

sweet liquid used widely in chemistry and industry.

glycerol [**gliss**-ser-ol] n technical name for GLYCERINE.

gm gram.

GM genetically modified.

GMO genetically modified organism.

GMT Greenwich Mean Time.

gnarled adj rough, twisted, and knobbly.

gnash v grind (the teeth) together in anger or pain.

gnat n small biting two-winged fly.

gnaw v gnawing, gnawed, gnawed or gnawn. bite or chew steadily; (foll. by at) cause constant distress (to).

gneiss n coarse-grained metamorphic rock.

gnome n imaginary creature like a little old man.

gnomic [**no**-mik] adj of pithy sayings.

Gnosticism n religious movement believing in intuitive spiritual knowledge. **Gnostic** n, adj

gnu [noo] n oxlike S African antelope.

go v going, went, gone. move to or from a place; be in regular attendance at; depart; be, do, or become as specified; be allotted to a specific purpose or recipient; blend or harmonize; fail or break down; elapse; be got rid of; attend; be acceptable. ▶ n attempt; verbal attack; turn. **make a go of** be successful at. **go back on** break (a promise etc.). **go-between** n intermediary. **go for** v Informal choose; attack; apply to equally. **go-getter** n energetically ambitious person. **go-go dancer** scantily dressed erotic dancer. **go off** v explode; ring or sound; Informal become stale or rotten; Informal stop liking. **go out** v go to entertainments or social functions; be romantically involved (with); be extinguished. **go over** v examine or check. **go-slow** n deliberate slowing of work-rate as an industrial protest. **go through** v suffer or undergo; examine or search.

goad v provoke (someone) to take some kind of action, usu. in anger. ▶ n spur or provocation; spiked stick for driving cattle.

goal n Sport posts through which the ball or puck has to be propelled to score; score made in this way; aim or purpose. **goalie** n Informal goalkeeper. **goalkeeper** n player whose task is to stop shots entering the goal. **goalpost** n one of the two posts marking the limit of a goal. **move the goalposts** change the aims of an activity to ensure the desired result.

goanna n large Australian lizard.

goat n sure-footed ruminant animal with horns. **get someone's goat** Slang annoy someone. **goatee** n pointed tuftlike beard.

gob n lump of a soft substance; Brit, Aust & NZ slang mouth.

gobbet n lump, esp. of food.

gobble[1] v eat hastily and greedily.

gobble[2] n rapid gurgling cry of the male turkey. ▶ v make this noise.

gobbledegook, gobbledygook n unintelligible (official) language or jargon.

goblet n drinking cup without handles.

goblin n (in folklore) small malevolent creature.

goby n, pl -by, -bies. small spiny-finned fish.

god n spirit or being worshipped as having supernatural power;

object of worship, idol; (**G-**) (in monotheistic religions) the Supreme Being, creator and ruler of the universe. **the gods** top balcony in a theatre. **goddess** n fem adj. **godly** adj devout or pious. **godliness** n

god-fearing adj pious and devout. **godforsaken** adj desolate or dismal. **godsend** n something unexpected but welcome.

godetia n plant with showy flowers.

godparent n person who promises at a child's baptism to bring the child up as a Christian. **godchild** n child for whom a person stands as godparent. **goddaughter** n **godfather** n male godparent; head of a criminal, esp. Mafia, organization. **godmother** n **godson** n

gogga n S Afr informal any small insect.

goggle v (of the eyes) bulge; stare. **goggles** pl n protective spectacles.

going n condition of the ground for walking or riding over; speed or progress; departure. ▶ adj thriving; current or accepted. **going-over** n, pl **goings-over**. Informal investigation or examination; scolding or thrashing. **goings-on** pl n mysterious or unacceptable events.

goitre [goy-ter] n swelling of the thyroid gland in the neck.

go-kart n small low-powered racing car.

gold n yellow precious metal; coins or articles made of this; colour of gold. ▶ adj made of gold; gold-coloured. **goldcrest** n small bird with a yellow crown.

gold-digger n Informal woman who uses her sexual attractions to get money from a man.

goldfinch n kind of finch, the

male of which has yellow-and-black wings. **goldfish** n orange fish kept in ponds or aquariums. **gold leaf** thin gold sheet used for gilding. **gold medal** medal given to the winner of a competition or race.

golden adj made of gold; gold-coloured; very successful or promising. **golden eagle** large mountain eagle of the N hemisphere. **golden handshake** Informal payment to a departing employee. **golden rule** important principle. **golden wedding** fiftieth wedding anniversary.

golf n outdoor game in which a ball is struck with clubs into a series of holes. ▶ v play golf. **golfer** n

golliwog n soft black-faced doll.

gonad n organ producing reproductive cells, such as a testicle or ovary.

gondola n long narrow boat used in Venice; suspended cabin of a cable car, airship, etc. **gondolier** n person who propels a gondola.

gone v past participle of GO. **goner** n Informal person or thing beyond help or recovery.

gong n rimmed metal disc that produces a note when struck; Slang medal.

gonorrhoea [gon-or-**ree**-a] n venereal disease with a discharge from the genitals.

good adj **better, best**. giving pleasure; morally excellent; beneficial; kindly; talented; well-behaved; valid; reliable; complete or full. ▶ n benefit; positive moral qualities. ▶ pl merchandise; property. **as good as** virtually. **for good** permanently. **goodness** n **goodly** adj considerable. **goody** n Informal hero in a book or film;

enjoyable thing. **goody-goody** adj, n smugly virtuous (person).

good-for-nothing adj, n irresponsible or worthless (person).

Good Samaritan person who helps another in distress.

goodwill n kindly feeling; value of a business in reputation etc. over and above its tangible assets.

goodbye interj, n expression used on parting.

gooey adj **gooier, gooiest.** Informal sticky and soft.

goof Informal ▶ n mistake. ▶ v make a mistake.

googly n, pl **-lies.** Cricket ball that spins unexpectedly from off to leg on the bounce.

goon n Informal stupid person; Chiefly US hired thug.

goose n, pl **geese.** web-footed bird like a large duck; female of this bird. **goose flesh, pimples** bumpy condition of the skin and bristling of the hair due to cold or fright. **goose step** march step in which the leg is raised rigidly.

gooseberry n edible yellowy-green berry; Brit informal unwanted third person accompanying a couple.

gopher [go-fer] n American burrowing rodent.

gore[1] n blood from a wound.

gore[2] v pierce with horns.

gorge n deep narrow valley. ▶ v eat greedily. **make one's gorge rise** cause feelings of disgust or nausea.

gorgeous adj strikingly beautiful or attractive; Informal very pleasant. **gorgeously** adv

gorgon n terrifying or repulsive woman.

Gorgonzola n sharp-flavoured blue-veined Italian cheese.

gorilla n largest of the apes, found in Africa.

gormless adj Informal stupid.

gorse n prickly yellow-flowered shrub.

gory adj **gorier, goriest.** horrific or bloodthirsty; involving bloodshed.

goshawk n large hawk.

gosling n young goose.

gospel n **(G-)** any of the first four books of the New Testament; unquestionable truth; Black religious music originating in the churches of the Southern US.

gossamer n very fine fabric; filmy cobweb.

gossip n idle talk, esp. about other people; person who engages in gossip. ▶ v **gossiping, gossiped.** engage in gossip. **gossipy** adj

got v past of GET. **have got** possess. **have got to** need or be required to.

Gothic adj (of architecture) of or in the style common in Europe from the 12th–16th centuries, with pointed arches; or in an 18th-century literary style characterized by gloom and the supernatural; (of print) using a heavy ornate typeface.

gouache n (painting using) watercolours mixed with glue.

Gouda n mild-flavoured Dutch cheese.

gouge [gowj] v scoop or force out; cut (a hole or groove) in (something). ▶ n hole or groove; chisel with a curved cutting edge.

goulash [goo-lash] n rich stew seasoned with paprika.

gourd [goord] n fleshy fruit of a climbing plant; its dried shell, used as a container.

gourmand [goor-mand] n person who is very keen on food and drink.

gourmet [goor-may] n connoisseur of food and drink.

gout [gowt] n disease causing inflammation of the joints.

govern v rule, direct, or control; exercise restraint over (temper etc.). **governable** adj

governance n governing.

governess n woman teacher in a private household. **governor** n official governing a province or state; senior administrator of a society, institution, or prison. **governor general** representative of the Crown in a Commonwealth country.

government n executive policy-making body of a state; exercise of political authority over a country or state; system by which a country or state is ruled. **governmental** adj

gown n woman's long formal dress; surgeon's overall; official robe worn by judges, clergymen, etc.

goy n, pl **goyim, goys.** Slang Jewish word for a non-Jew.

GP general practitioner.

GPS Global Positioning System: a satellite-based navigation system.

grab v **grabbing, grabbed.** grasp suddenly, snatch. ▶ n sudden snatch; mechanical device for gripping.

grace n beauty and elegance; polite, kind behaviour; goodwill or favour; delay granted; short prayer of thanks for a meal; (**G-**) title of a duke, duchess, or archbishop. ▶ v add grace to. **graceful** adj **gracefully** adv **graceless** adj **gracious** adj kind and courteous; condescendingly polite; elegant. **graciously** adv **grace note** Music note ornamenting a melody.

grade n place on a scale of quality, rank, or size; mark or rating; US, Aust & S Afr class in school. ▶ v arrange in grades; assign a grade to. **make the grade** succeed. **gradation** n (stage in) a series of

degrees or steps; arrangement in stages.

gradient n (degree of) slope.

gradual adj occurring, developing, or moving in small stages. **gradually** adv

graduate v receive a degree or diploma; group by type or quality; mark (a container etc.) with units of measurement. ▶ n holder of a degree. **graduation** n

graffiti [graf-**fee**-tee] pl n words or drawings scribbled or sprayed on walls etc.

graft[1] n surgical transplant of skin or tissue; shoot of a plant set in the stalk of another. ▶ v transplant (living tissue) surgically; insert (a plant shoot) in another stalk.

graft[2] Brit informal ▶ n hard work; obtaining of money by misusing one's position. ▶ v work hard. **grafter** n

grail n same as HOLY GRAIL.

grain n seedlike fruit of a cereal plant; cereal plants in general; small hard particle; very small amount; arrangement of fibres, as in wood; texture or pattern resulting from this. **go against the grain** be contrary to one's natural inclination. **grainy** adj

gram, gramme n metric unit of mass equal to one thousandth of a kilogram.

grammar n branch of linguistics dealing with the form, function, and order of words; use of words; book on the rules of grammar. **grammarian** n **grammatical** adj according to the rules of grammar. **grammatically** adv **grammar school** Brit esp. formerly, a secondary school providing an education with a strong academic bias.

gramophone n old-fashioned type of record player.

grampus n, pl **-puses.** dolphin-like mammal.

gran n Brit, Aust & NZ informal grandmother.

granary n, pl **-ries.** storehouse for grain.

grand adj large or impressive, imposing; dignified or haughty; Informal excellent; (of a total) final. ▶ n Slang thousand pounds or dollars; grand piano. **grandchild** n child of one's child. **granddaughter** n female grandchild. **grandfather** n male grandparent. **grandfather clock** tall standing clock with a pendulum and wooden case. **grandmother** n female grandparent. **grandparent** n parent of one's parent. **grand piano** large harp-shaped piano with the strings set horizontally. **grand slam** winning of all the games or major tournaments in a sport in one season. **grandson** n male grandchild. **grandstand** n terraced block of seats giving the best view at a sports ground.

grandee n person of high station.

grandeur n magnificence; nobility or dignity.

grandiloquent adj using pompous language. **grandiloquence** n

grandiose adj imposing; pretentiously grand. **grandiosity** n

grange n Brit country house with farm buildings.

granite [gran-nit] n very hard igneous rock often used in building.

granny, grannie n, pl **-nies.** Informal grandmother. **granny flat** flat in or added to a house, suitable for an elderly parent.

grant v consent to fulfil (a request); give formally; admit. ▶ n sum of money provided by a government for a specific purpose,

such as education. **take for granted** accept as true without proof; take advantage of without due appreciation.

granule n small grain. **granular** adj of or like grains. **granulated** adj (of sugar) in the form of coarse grains.

grape n small juicy green or purple berry, eaten raw or used to produce wine, raisins, currants, or sultanas. **grapevine** n grape-bearing vine; Informal unofficial way of spreading news.

grapefruit n large round yellow citrus fruit.

graph n drawing showing the relation of different numbers or quantities plotted against a set of axes.

graphic adj vividly descriptive; of or using drawing, painting, etc. **graphics** pl n diagrams, graphs, etc., esp. as used on a television programme or computer screen. **graphically** adv

graphite n soft black form of carbon, used in pencil leads.

graphology n study of handwriting. **graphologist** n

grapnel n device with several hooks, used to grasp or secure things.

grapple v try to cope with (something difficult); come to grips with (a person). **grappling iron** grapnel.

grasp v grip something firmly; understand; try to seize. ▶ n grip or clasp; understanding; total rule or possession. **grasping** adj greedy or avaricious.

grass n common type of plant with jointed stems and long narrow leaves, including cereals and bamboo; lawn; pasture land; Slang marijuana; Brit slang person who informs, esp. on criminals. ▶ v

cover with grass; (often foll. by
on) *Brit slang* inform on. **grassy**
adj **-sier, -siest. grasshopper** *n*
jumping insect with long hind
legs. **grass roots** ordinary
members of a group, as distinct
from its leaders; essentials.
grassroots *adj*

grate¹ *v* rub into small bits on a
rough surface; scrape with a harsh
rasping noise; annoy. **grater** *n*
grating *adj* harsh or rasping;
annoying.

grate² *n* framework of metal bars
for holding fuel in a fireplace.
grating *n* framework of metal bars
covering an opening.

grateful *adj* feeling or showing
gratitude. **gratefully** *adv*

gratify *v* **-fying, -fied.** satisfy or
please; indulge (a desire or whim).
gratification *n*

gratis *adv, adj* free, for nothing.

gratitude *n* feeling of being
thankful for a favour or gift.

gratuitous *adj* unjustified, e.g.
gratuitous violence; given free.
gratuitously *adv*

gratuity *n, pl* **-ties.** money given
for services rendered, tip.

grave¹ *n* hole for burying a corpse.
gravestone *n* stone marking a
grave. **graveyard** *n* cemetery.

grave² *adj* causing concern; serious
and solemn. **gravely** *adv*

grave³ [rhymes with **halve**] *adj* (of an
accent (ˋ) over a vowel to indicate
a special pronunciation.

gravel *n* mixture of small stones
and coarse sand. **gravelled** *adj*
covered with gravel. **gravelly** *adj*
covered with gravel;
rough-sounding.

graven *adj* carved or engraved.

gravid [**grav**-id] *adj Med* pregnant.

gravitate *v* be influenced or drawn
towards; *Physics* move by gravity.
gravitation *n* **gravitational** *adj*

gravity *n, pl* **-ties.** force of
attraction of one object for
another, esp. of objects to the
earth; seriousness or importance;
solemnity.

gravy *n, pl* **-vies.** juices from meat
in cooking; sauce made from
these.

gray *adj Chiefly US* grey.

grayling *n* fish of the salmon
family.

graze¹ *v* feed on grass.

graze² *v* scratch or scrape the skin;
touch lightly in passing. ▶ *n* slight
scratch or scrape.

grease *n* soft melted animal fat;
any thick oily substance. ▶ *v* apply
grease to. **greasy** *adj* **greasier,
greasiest.** covered with or
containing grease. **greasiness** *n*
greasepaint *n* theatrical make-up.

great *adj* large in size or number;
important; pre-eminent; *Informal*
excellent. **great-** *prefix* one
generation older or younger than,
e.g. *great-grandfather.* **greatly** *adv*
greatness *n* **greatcoat** *n* heavy
overcoat. **Great Dane** very large
dog with short smooth hair.

greave *n* piece of armour for the
shin.

grebe *n* diving water bird.

Grecian [**gree**-shan] *adj* of ancient
Greece.

greed *n* excessive desire for food,
wealth, etc. **greedy** *adj* **greedily**
adv **greediness** *n*

Greek *n* language of Greece;
person from Greece. ▶ *adj* of
Greece, the Greeks, or the Greek
language.

green *adj* of a colour between blue
and yellow; characterized by
green plants or foliage; **(G-)** of or
concerned with environmental
issues; unripe; envious or jealous;
immature or gullible. ▶ *n* colour
between blue and yellow; area of

grass kept for a special purpose; **(G-)** person concerned with environmental issues. ▶ *pl* green vegetables. ▶ *v* make or become green. **greenness** *n* **greenish, greeny** *adj* **greenery** *n* vegetation. **green belt** protected area of open country around a town. **greenfinch** *n* European finch with dull green plumage in the male. **green fingers** skill in gardening. **greenfly** *n* green aphid, a common garden pest. **greengage** *n* sweet green plum. **greengrocer** *n Brit* shopkeeper selling vegetables and fruit. **greenhorn** *n Chiefly US* novice. **greenhouse** *n* glass building for rearing plants. **greenhouse effect** rise in the temperature of the earth caused by heat absorbed from the sun being unable to leave the atmosphere. **green light** signal to go; permission to proceed with something. **greenshank** *n* large European sandpiper. **greenstone** *n NZ* type of green jade used for Maori ornaments.

greet *v* meet with expressions of welcome; receive in a specified manner; be immediately noticeable to. **greeting** *n*

gregarious *adj* fond of company; (of animals) living in flocks or herds.

gremlin *n* imaginary being blamed for mechanical malfunctions.

grenade *n* small bomb thrown by hand or fired from a rifle. **grenadier** *n* soldier of a regiment formerly trained to throw grenades.

grenadine [gren-a-**deen**] *n* syrup made from pomegranates.

grevillea *n* any of various Australian evergreen trees and shrubs.

grew *v* past tense of GROW.

grey *adj* of a colour between black and white; (of hair) partly turned white; dismal or dark; dull or boring. ▶ *n* grey colour; grey or white horse. **greying** *adj* (of hair) turning grey. **greyish** *adj* **greyness** *n* **grey matter** *Informal* brains.

greyhound *n* swift slender dog used in racing.

grid *n* network of horizontal and vertical lines, bars, etc.; national network of electricity supply cables.

griddle *n* flat iron plate for cooking.

gridiron *n* frame of metal bars for grilling food; American football pitch.

gridlock *n* situation where traffic is not moving; point in a dispute at which no agreement can be reached. **gridlocked** *adj*

grief *n* deep sadness. **grieve** *v* (cause to) feel grief. **grievance** *n* real or imaginary cause for complaint. **grievous** *adj* very severe or painful; very serious.

griffin *n* mythical monster with an eagle's head and wings and a lion's body.

grill *n* device on a cooker that radiates heat downwards; grilled food; gridiron. ▶ *v* cook under a grill; question relentlessly. **grilling** *n* relentless questioning.

grille, grill *n* grating over an opening.

grilse [grillss] *n* salmon on its first return from the sea to fresh water.

grim *adj* grimmer, grimmest. stern; harsh or forbidding; very unpleasant. **grimly** *adv* **grimness** *n*

grimace *n* ugly or distorted facial expression of pain, disgust, etc. ▶ *v* make a grimace.

grime *n* ingrained dirt. ▶ *v* make very dirty. **grimy** *adj*

grin v **grinning, grinned.** smile broadly, showing the teeth. ▶ n broad smile.

grind v **grinding, ground.** crush or rub to a powder; smooth or sharpen by friction; scrape together with a harsh noise; oppress. ▶ n *Informal* hard work; act or sound of grinding. **grind out** v produce in a routine or uninspired manner. **grindstone** n stone used for grinding.

grip n firm hold or grasp; way in which something is grasped; mastery or understanding; *US* travelling bag; handle. ▶ v **gripping, gripped.** grasp or hold tightly; hold the interest or attention of. **gripping** adj

gripe v *Informal* complain persistently. ▶ n *Informal* complaint; sudden intense bowel pain.

grisly adj **-lier, -liest.** horrifying or ghastly.

grist n grain for grinding. **grist to one's mill** something which can be turned to advantage.

gristle n tough stringy animal tissue found in meat. **gristly** adj

grit n rough particles of sand; courage. ▶ pl coarsely ground grain. ▶ v **gritting, gritted.** spread grit on (an icy road etc.); clench or grind (the teeth). **gritty** adj **-tier, -tiest. grittiness** n

grizzle v *Brit, Aust & NZ informal* whine or complain.

grizzled adj grey-haired.

grizzly n, pl **-zlies.** large American bear (also **grizzly bear**).

groan n deep sound of grief or pain; *Informal* complaint. ▶ v utter a groan; *Informal* complain.

groat n *Hist* fourpenny piece.

grocer n shopkeeper selling foodstuffs. **grocery** n, pl **-ceries.** business or premises of a grocer.

▶ pl goods sold by a grocer.

grog n *Brit, Aust & NZ* spirit, usu. rum, and water.

groggy adj **-gier, -giest.** *Informal* faint, shaky, or dizzy.

groin n place where the legs join the abdomen.

grommet n ring or eyelet; *Med* tube inserted in the ear to drain fluid from the middle ear.

groom n person who looks after horses; bridegroom; officer in a royal household. ▶ v make or keep one's clothes and appearance neat and tidy; brush or clean a horse; train (someone) for a future role.

groove n long narrow channel in a surface.

grope v feel about or search uncertainly; *Slang* fondle (someone) in a rough sexual way. **groping** n

gross adj flagrant; vulgar; *Slang* disgusting or repulsive; repulsively fat; total, without deductions. ▶ n twelve dozen. ▶ v make as total revenue before deductions. **grossly** adv **grossness** n

grotesque [grow-**tesk**] adj strangely distorted; absurd. ▶ n grotesque person or thing; artistic style mixing distorted human, animal, and plant forms. **grotesquely** adv

grotto n, pl **-toes, -tos.** small picturesque cave.

grotty adj **-tier, -tiest.** *Informal* nasty or in bad condition.

grouch *Informal* ▶ v grumble or complain. ▶ n person who is always complaining; persistent complaint. **grouchy** adj

ground[1] n surface of the earth; soil; area used for a specific purpose, e.g. *rugby ground*; position in an argument or controversy. ▶ pl enclosed land round a house; reason or motive;

coffee dregs. ▶ v base or establish; instruct in the basics; ban an aircraft or pilot from flying; run (a ship) aground. **groundless** adj without reason. **grounding** n basic knowledge of a subject. **ground-breaking** adj innovative. **ground floor** floor of a building level with the ground. **groundnut** n peanut. **groundsheet** n waterproof sheet put on the ground under a tent. **groundsman** n person employed to maintain a sports ground or park. **groundswell** n rapidly developing general feeling or opinion. **groundwork** n preliminary work.

ground[2] v past of GRIND.

group n number of people or things regarded as a unit; small band of musicians or singers. ▶ v place or form into a group.

grouse[1] n stocky game bird; its flesh.

grouse[2] v grumble or complain. ▶ n complaint.

grout n thin mortar. ▶ v fill up with grout.

grove n small group of trees.

grovel [grov-el] v -elling, -elled. behave humbly in order to win a superior's favour; crawl on the floor.

grow v growing, grew, grown. develop physically; (of a plant) exist; cultivate (plants); increase in size or degree; originate, e.g. it was growing dark. **growth** n growing; increase; something grown or growing; tumour. **grown-up** adj, n adult. **grow up** v mature.

growl v make a low rumbling sound; utter with a growl. ▶ n growling sound.

groyne n wall built out from the shore to control erosion.

grub n legless insect larva; Slang food. ▶ v grubbing, grubbed. search carefully for something by digging or by moving things about; dig up the surface of (soil). **grubby** adj -bier, -biest. dirty. **grubbiness** n

grudge v be unwilling to give or allow. ▶ n resentment.

gruel n thin porridge.

gruelling adj exhausting or severe.

gruesome adj causing horror and disgust.

gruff adj rough or surly in manner or voice. **gruffly** adv **gruffness** n

grumble v complain; rumble. ▶ n complaint; rumble. **grumbler** n **grumbling** adj, n

grumpy adj grumpier, grumpiest. bad-tempered. **grumpily** adv **grumpiness** n

grunge n style of rock music with a fuzzy guitar sound; deliberately untidy and uncoordinated fashion style.

grunt v make a low short gruff sound, like a pig. ▶ n pig's sound; gruff noise.

Gruyère [grew-yair] n hard yellow Swiss cheese with holes.

gryphon n same as GRIFFIN.

GST (in Australia, New Zealand, and Canada) Goods and Services Tax.

G-string n small strip of cloth covering the genitals and attached to a waistband.

GT gran turismo, used of a sports car.

guano [gwah-no] n dried sea-bird manure, used as fertilizer.

guarantee n formal assurance, esp. in writing, that a product will meet certain standards; something that makes a specified condition or outcome certain. ▶ v -teeing, -teed. give a guarantee; secure against risk etc.; ensure.

guarantor n person who gives or is bound by a guarantee.

guard v watch over to protect or to prevent escape. ▶ n person or group that guards; official in charge of a train; protection; screen for enclosing anything dangerous; posture of defence in sports such as boxing or fencing. ▶ pl (G-) regiment with ceremonial duties. **guarded** adj cautious or noncommittal. **guardedly** adv **guard against** v take precautions against. **guardsman** n member of the Guards.

guardian n keeper or protector; person legally responsible for a child, mentally ill person, etc. **guardianship** n

guava [gwah-va] n yellow-skinned tropical American fruit.

gudgeon n small freshwater fish.

Guernsey [gurn-zee] n breed of dairy cattle.

guerrilla, guerilla n member of an unofficial armed force fighting regular forces.

guess v estimate or draw a conclusion without proper knowledge; estimate correctly by guessing; suppose. ▶ n estimate or conclusion reached by guessing. **guesswork** n process or results of guessing.

guest n person entertained at another's house or at another's expense; invited performer or speaker; customer at a hotel or restaurant. ▶ v appear as a visiting player or performer. **guesthouse** n boarding house.

guff n Brit, Aust & NZ slang nonsense.

guffaw n crude noisy laugh. ▶ v laugh in this way.

guide n person who conducts tour expeditions; person who shows the way; book of instruction or information; model for behaviour; something used to gauge something or to help in planning one's actions; (G-) member of an organization for girls equivalent to the Scouts. ▶ v act as a guide for; control, supervise, or influence. **guidance** n leadership, instruction, or advice. **guided missile** missile whose flight is controlled electronically. **guide dog** dog trained to lead a blind person. **guideline** n set principle for doing something.

guild n organization or club; Hist society of men in the same trade or craft.

guilder n former monetary unit of the Netherlands.

guile [gile] n cunning or deceit. **guileful** adj **guileless** adj

guillemot [gil-lee-mot] n black-and-white diving sea bird of N hemisphere.

guillotine n machine for beheading people; device for cutting paper or sheet metal; method of preventing lengthy debate in parliament by fixing a time for taking the vote. ▶ v behead by guillotine; limit debate by the guillotine.

guilt n fact or state of having done wrong; remorse for wrongdoing. **guiltless** adj innocent. **guilty** adj responsible for an offence or misdeed; feeling or showing guilt. **guiltily** adv

guinea n former British monetary unit worth 21 shillings (1.05 pounds); former gold coin of this value. **guinea fowl** wild bird related to the pheasant. **guinea pig** tailless S American rodent, commonly kept as a pet; Informal person used for experimentation.

guise [rhymes with size] n false appearance; external appearance.

guitar n stringed instrument with a flat back and a long neck, played by plucking or strumming. **guitarist** n

gulch n US deep narrow valley.

gulf n large deep bay; chasm; large difference in opinion or understanding.

gull n long-winged sea bird.

gullet n muscular tube through which food passes from the mouth to the stomach.

gullible adj easily tricked. **gullibility** n

gully n, pl **-lies.** channel cut by running water.

gulp v swallow hastily; gasp. ▶ n gulping; thing gulped.

gum[1] n firm flesh in which the teeth are set. **gummy** adj **-mier, -miest.** toothless.

gum[2] n sticky substance obtained from certain trees; adhesive; chewing gum; gumdrop; gum tree. ▶ v **gumming, gummed.** stick with gum. **gummy** adj **-mier, -miest. gumboots** pl n Chiefly Brit Wellington boots. **gumdrop** n hard jelly-like sweet. **gum tree** eucalypt tree.

gumption n Informal resourcefulness; courage.

gun n weapon with a metal tube from which missiles are fired by explosion; device from which a substance is ejected under pressure. ▶ v **gunning, gunned.** cause (an engine) to run at high speed. **jump the gun** act prematurely. **gunner** n artillery soldier. **gunnery** n use or science of large guns. **gunboat** n small warship. **gun dog** dog used to retrieve game. **gun down** v shoot (a person). **gun for** v seek or pursue vigorously. **gunman** n armed criminal. **gunmetal** n alloy of copper, tin, and zinc. ▶ adj dark grey. **gunpowder** n explosive mixture of potassium nitrate, sulphur, and charcoal. **gunrunning** n smuggling of guns and ammunition. **gunrunner** n **gunshot** n shot or range of a gun.

gunge n Informal sticky unpleasant substance. **gungy** adj **-gier, -giest.**

gunny n strong coarse fabric used for sacks.

gunwale, gunnel [gun-nel] n top of a ship's side.

gunyah n Aust hut or shelter in the bush.

guppy n, pl **-pies.** small colourful aquarium fish.

gurgle v, n (make) a bubbling noise.

Gurkha n person, esp. a soldier, belonging to a Hindu people of Nepal.

guru n Hindu or Sikh religious teacher or leader; leader, adviser, or expert.

gush v flow out suddenly and profusely; express admiration effusively. ▶ n sudden copious flow; sudden surge of strong feeling. **gusher** n spurting oil well.

gusset n piece of material sewn into a garment to strengthen it.

gust n sudden blast of wind. ▶ v blow in gusts. **gusty** adj

gusto n enjoyment or zest.

gut n intestine; Informal fat stomach; short for CATGUT. ▶ pl internal organs; Informal courage. ▶ v **gutting, gutted.** remove the guts from; (of a fire) destroy the inside of (a building). ▶ adj basic or instinctive, e.g. a gut reaction. **gutsy** adj **-sier, -siest.** Informal courageous; vigorous or robust, e.g. a gutsy performance. **gutted** adj Brit, Aust & NZ informal disappointed and upset.

gutta-percha n whitish rubbery substance obtained from an Asian tree.

gutter *n* shallow channel for carrying away water from a roof or roadside. ▶ *v* (of a candle) burn unsteadily, with wax running down the sides. **the gutter** degraded or criminal environment. **guttering** *n* material for gutters. **gutter press** newspapers that rely on sensationalism. **guttersnipe** *n* *Brit* neglected slum child.

guttural *adj* (of a sound) produced at the back of the throat; (of a voice) harsh-sounding.

guy¹ *n* *Informal* man or boy; effigy of Guy Fawkes burnt on Nov. 5th (**Guy Fawkes Day**).

guy² *n* rope or chain to steady or secure something. **guy rope**

guzzle *v* eat or drink greedily.

gybe [**jibe**] *v* (of a fore-and-aft sail) swing suddenly from one side to the other; (of a boat) change course by letting the sail gybe.

gym *n* gymnasium; gymnastics.

gymkhana [jim-**kah**-na] *n* horse-riding competition.

gymnasium *n* large room with equipment for physical training. **gymnast** *n* expert in gymnastics. **gymnastic** *adj* **gymnastics** *pl n* exercises to develop strength and agility.

gynaecology [guy-nee-**kol**-la-jee] *n* branch of medicine dealing with diseases and conditions specific to women. **gynaecological** *adj* **gynaecologist** *n*

gypsophila *n* garden plant with small white flowers.

gypsum *n* chalklike mineral used to make plaster of Paris.

Gypsy *n, pl* **-sies.** member of a travelling people found throughout Europe.

gyrate [jire-**rate**] *v* rotate or spiral about a point or axis. **gyration** *n* **gyratory** *adj* gyrating.

gyrocompass *n* compass using a gyroscope.

gyroscope [**jire**-oh-skohp] *n* disc rotating on an axis that can turn in any direction, so the disc maintains the same position regardless of the movement of the surrounding structure. **gyroscopic** *adj*

H h

H *Chem* hydrogen.

habeas corpus [**hay**-bee-ass **kor**-puss] *n* writ ordering a prisoner to be brought before a court.

haberdasher *n* *Brit, Aust & NZ* dealer in small articles used for sewing. **haberdashery** *n*

habit *n* established way of behaving; addiction to a drug; costume of a monk or nun.

habitable *adj* fit to be lived in.

habitation *n* (occupation of) a dwelling place.

habitat *n* natural home of an animal or plant.

habitual *adj* done regularly and repeatedly. **habitually** *adv*

habituate *v* accustom.

habituation *n* **habitué** [hab-**it**-yew-ay] *n* frequent visitor to a place.

hacienda [hass-ee-**end**-a] *n* ranch or large estate in Latin America.

hack¹ *v* cut or chop violently; *Brit & NZ informal* tolerate.

hack² *n* (inferior) writer or journalist; horse kept for riding.

hacker *n* *Slang* computer enthusiast, esp. one who breaks into the computer system of a company or government.

hackles *pl n* **make one's hackles rise** make one feel angry or hostile.

hackney n Brit taxi.

hackneyed adj (of a word or phrase) unoriginal and overused.

hacksaw n small saw for cutting metal.

had v past of HAVE.

haddock n edible sea fish of N Atlantic.

Hades [hay-deez] n Greek myth underworld home of the dead.

hadj n same as HAJJ.

haematology n study of blood and its diseases.

haemoglobin [hee-moh-**globe**-in] n protein found in red blood cells which carries oxygen.

haemophilia [hee-moh-**fill**-lee-a] n hereditary illness in which the blood does not clot. **haemophiliac** n

haemorrhage [hem-or-ij] n heavy bleeding. ▷ v bleed heavily.

haemorrhoids [hem-or-oydz] pl n swollen veins in the anus (also **piles**).

hafnium n Chem metallic element found in zirconium ores.

haft n handle of an axe, knife, or dagger.

hag n ugly old woman. **hag-ridden** adj distressed or worried.

haggard adj looking tired and ill.

haggis n Scottish dish made from sheep's offal, oatmeal, suet, and seasonings, boiled in a bag made from the sheep's stomach.

haggle v bargain or wrangle over a price.

hagiography n, pl -**phies**. writing about the lives of the saints.

hail[1] n (shower of) small pellets of ice; large number of insults, missiles, blows, etc. ▷ v fall as or like hail. **hailstone** n

hail[2] v call out to, greet; stop (a taxi) by waving; acknowledge publicly. **hail from** v come

originally from.

hair n threadlike growth on the skin; such growths collectively, esp. on the head. **hairy** adj covered with hair; Slang dangerous or exciting. **hairiness** n **hairclip** n small bent metal hairpin. **hairdo** n Informal hairstyle. **hairdresser** n person who cuts and styles hair. **hairgrip** n Brit same as HAIRCLIP. **hairline** n edge of hair at the top of the forehead. ▷ adj very fine or narrow. **hairpin** n U-shaped wire used to hold the hair in place. **hairpin bend** very sharp bend in a road. **hair-raising** adj frightening or exciting. **hair-splitting** n, adj making petty distinctions. **hairstyle** n cut and arrangement of a person's hair.

hajj n pilgrimage a Muslim makes to Mecca.

haka n NZ ceremonial Maori dance with chanting; similar dance performed by a sports team before a match.

hake n edible sea fish of N hemisphere.

hakea [hah-kee-a] n Australian tree or shrub with hard woody fruit.

halal n meat from animals slaughtered according to Muslim law.

halberd n Hist spear with an axe blade.

halcyon [hal-see-on] adj peaceful and happy. **halcyon days** time of peace and happiness.

hale adj healthy, robust.

half n, pl **halves**. either of two equal parts; Informal half-pint of beer etc.; half-price ticket. ▷ adj denoting one of two equal parts. ▷ adv to the extent of half; partially. **half-baked** adj Informal not properly thought out.

half-brother, half-sister n brother

or sister related through one parent only. **half-cocked** adj **go off half-cocked, (at) half-cock** fail because of inadequate preparation. **half-hearted** adj unenthusiastic. **half-life** n time taken for half the atoms in radioactive material to decay. **half-nelson** n wrestling hold in which one wrestler's arm is pinned behind his back by his opponent. **half-pie** adj NZ informal incomplete. **half-pipe** n large U-shaped ramp used for skateboarding, snowboarding, etc. **half-timbered** adj (of a house) having an exposed wooden frame filled in with plaster. **half-time** n Sport short rest period between two halves of a game. **halftone** n illustration showing lights and shadows by means of very small dots. **halfway** adv, adj at or to half the distance. **halfwit** n foolish or stupid person.

halfpenny [hayp-nee] n former British coin worth half an old penny.

halibut n large edible flatfish of N Atlantic.

halitosis n unpleasant-smelling breath.

hall n (also **hallway**) entrance passage; large room or building for public meetings, dances, etc.; Brit large country house.

hallelujah [hal-ee-loo-ya] interj exclamation of praise to God.

hallmark n typical feature; mark indicating the standard of tested gold and silver. ▸ v stamp with a hallmark.

hallo interj same as HELLO.

hallowed adj regarded as holy.

Halloween, Hallowe'en n October 31, celebrated by children by dressing up as ghosts, witches, etc.

hallucinate v seem to see something that is not really there. **hallucination** n **hallucinatory** adj **hallucinogen** n drug that causes hallucinations. **hallucinogenic** adj

halo [hay-loh] n, pl -loes, -los. ring of light round the head of a sacred figure; circle of refracted light round the sun or moon.

halogen [hal-oh-jen] n Chem any of a group of nonmetallic elements including chlorine and iodine.

halt v come or bring to a stop. ▸ n temporary stop; minor railway station without a building. **halting** adj hesitant, uncertain.

halter n strap round a horse's head with a rope to lead it with. **halterneck** n woman's top or dress with a strap fastened at the back of the neck.

halve v divide in half; reduce by half.

halves n plural of HALF.

halyard n rope for raising a ship's sail or flag.

ham¹ n smoked or salted meat from a pig's thigh. **ham-fisted** adj clumsy.

ham² Informal ▸ n amateur radio operator; actor who overacts. ▸ v **hamming, hammed. ham it up** overact.

hamburger n minced beef shaped into a flat disc, cooked and usu. served in a bread roll.

hamlet n small village.

hammer n tool with a heavy metal head and a wooden handle, used to drive in nails etc.; part of a gun which causes the bullet to be fired; heavy metal ball on a wire, thrown as a sport; auctioneer's mallet; striking mechanism in a piano. ▸ v hit (as if) with a hammer; Informal punish or defeat utterly. **go at it hammer and**

tongs do something, esp. argue, very vigorously. **hammerhead** n shark with a wide flattened head.

hammer toe condition in which a toe is permanently bent at the joint.

hammock n hanging bed made of canvas or net.

hamper¹ v make it difficult for (someone or something) to move or progress.

hamper² n large basket with a lid; selection of food and drink packed as a gift.

hamster n small rodent with a short tail and cheek pouches.

hamstring n tendon at the back of the knee. ▶ v make it difficult for (someone) to take any action.

hand n part of the body at the end of the arm, consisting of a palm, four fingers, and a thumb; style of handwriting; round of applause; manual worker; pointer on a dial, esp. on a clock; cards dealt to a player in a card game; unit of length of four inches (10.16 centimetres) used to measure horses. ▶ v pass, give. **have a hand in** be involved in. **lend a hand** help. **out of hand** beyond control; definitely and finally. **to hand, at hand, on hand** nearby. **win hands down** win easily.

handbag n woman's small bag for carrying personal articles in.

handbill n small printed notice.

handbook n small reference or instruction book. **handcuff** n one of a linked pair of metal rings designed to be locked round a prisoner's wrists by the police. ▶ v put handcuffs on. **hand-held** adj (of a film camera) held rather than mounted, as in close-up action shots; (of a computer) able to be held in the hand. ▶ n computer that can be held in the

hand. **hand-out** n clothing, food, or money given to a needy person; written information given out at a talk etc. **hands-on** adj involving practical experience of equipment. **handstand** n act of supporting the body on the hands in an upside-down position.

handwriting n (style of) writing by hand.

handful n amount that can be held in the hand; small number; Informal person or animal that is difficult to control.

handicap n physical or mental disability; something that makes progress difficult; contest in which the competitors are given advantages or disadvantages in an attempt to equalize their chances; advantage or disadvantage given. ▶ v make it difficult for (someone) to do something.

handicraft n objects made by hand.

handiwork n result of someone's work or activity.

handkerchief n small square of fabric used to wipe the nose.

handle n part of an object that is held so that it can be used. ▶ v hold, feel, or move with the hands; control or deal with. **handler** n person who controls an animal. **handlebars** pl n curved metal bar used to steer a cycle.

handsome adj (esp. of a man) good-looking; large or generous, e.g. a handsome profit.

handy adj **handier, handiest.** convenient, useful; good at manual work. **handily** adv **handyman** n man who is good at making or repairing things.

hang v hanging, hung. attach or be attached at the top with the lower part free; (past hanged) suspend or be suspended by the neck until dead; fasten to a wall. **get the hang of** Informal begin to understand. **hanger** n curved piece of wood, wire, or plastic, with a hook, for hanging up clothes (also **coat hanger**). **hang back** v hesitate, be reluctant. **hangman** n man who executes people by hanging. **hangover** n headache and nausea as a result of drinking too much alcohol. **hang-up** n Informal emotional or psychological problem.

hangar n large shed for storing aircraft.

hangdog adj guilty, ashamed, e.g. a hangdog look.

hang-glider n glider with a light framework from which the pilot hangs in a harness. **hang-gliding** n

hangi n, pl **-gi, -gis.** NZ Maori oven consisting of a hole in the ground filled with hot stones.

hank n coil, esp. of yarn.

hanker v (foll. by after or for) desire intensely.

hanky, hankie n, pl **hankies.** Informal handkerchief.

hanky-panky n Informal illicit sexual relations.

hansom cab n (formerly) two-wheeled horse-drawn carriage for hire.

haphazard adj not organized or planned. **haphazardly** adv

hapless adj unlucky.

happen v take place, occur; chance (to be or do something). **happening** n event, occurrence.

happy adj **-pier, -piest.** feeling or causing joy; lucky, fortunate. **happily** adv **happiness** n **happy-go-lucky** adj carefree and cheerful.

hara-kiri n (formerly, in Japan) ritual suicide by disembowelling.

harangue v address angrily or forcefully. ▶ n angry or forceful speech.

harass v annoy or trouble constantly. **harassed** adj **harassment** n

harbinger [har-binj-a] n someone or something that announces the approach of something.

harbour n sheltered port. ▶ v maintain secretly in the mind; give shelter or protection to.

hard adj firm, solid, or rigid; difficult; requiring a lot of effort; unkind, unfeeling; causing pain, sorrow, or hardship; (of water) containing calcium salts which stop soap lathering freely; (of a drug) strong and addictive. ▶ adv with great energy or effort; with great intensity. **hard of hearing** unable to hear properly. **hard up** Informal short of money. **harden** v **hardness** n **hardship** n suffering; difficult circumstances. **hard-bitten** adj tough and determined. **hard-boiled** adj (of an egg) boiled until solid; Informal tough, unemotional. **hard copy** computer output printed on paper. **hardfill** n NZ & S Afr stone waste material used for landscaping. **hard-headed** adj shrewd, practical. **hardhearted** adj unsympathetic, uncaring. **hard sell** aggressive sales technique. **hard shoulder** surfaced verge at the edge of a motorway for emergency stops.

hardboard n thin stiff board made of compressed sawdust and wood chips.

hardly adv scarcely or not at all; with difficulty.

hardware n metal tools or implements; machinery used in a computer system; heavy military equipment, such as tanks and missiles.

hardwood n wood of a

broadleaved tree such as oak or ash.

hardy adj **hardier, hardiest.** able to stand difficult conditions. **hardiness** n

hare n animal like a large rabbit, with longer ears and legs. ▶ v (usu. foll. by off) run (away) quickly. **harebell** n blue bell-shaped flower. **harebrained** adj foolish or impractical. **harelip** n slight split in the upper lip.

harem n (apartments of) a Muslim man's wives and concubines.

haricot bean [har-rik-oh] n small pale edible bean, usu. sold dried.

hark v Old-fashioned listen. **hark back** v return to an earlier subject).

harlequin n stock comic character with a diamond-patterned costume and mask. ▶ adj in many colours.

harlot n Lit prostitute.

harm v injure physically, mentally, or morally. ▶ n physical, mental, or moral injury. **harmful** adj **harmless** adj

harmonica n small wind instrument played by sucking and blowing.

harmonium n keyboard instrument like a small organ.

harmony n, pl **-nies.** peaceful agreement and cooperation; pleasant combination of notes sounded at the same time. **harmonious** adj **harmoniously** adv **harmonic** adj of harmony. **harmonics** n science of musical sounds. **harmonize** v blend well together. **harmonization** n

harness n arrangement of straps for attaching a horse to a cart or plough; set of straps fastened round someone's body to attach something, e.g. a safety harness. ▶ v put a harness on; control

(something) in order to make use of it.

harp n large triangular stringed instrument played with the fingers. **harpist** n **harp on about** v talk about continuously.

harpoon n barbed spear attached to a rope used for hunting whales. ▶ v spear with a harpoon.

harpsichord n stringed keyboard instrument.

harpy n, pl **-pies.** nasty or bad-tempered woman.

harridan n nagging or vicious woman.

harrier n cross-country runner.

harrow n implement used to break up lumps of soil. ▶ v draw a harrow over.

harrowing adj very distressing.

harry v **-rying, -ried.** keep asking (someone) to do something, pester.

harsh adj severe and difficult to cope with; unkind, unsympathetic; extremely hard, bright, or rough. **harshly** adv **harshness** n

hart n adult male deer.

harum-scarum adj reckless.

harvest n (season for) the gathering of crops; crops gathered. ▶ v gather (a ripened crop). **harvester** n

has v third person singular of the present tense of HAVE. **has-been** n Informal person who is no longer popular or successful.

hash[1] n dish of diced cooked meat and vegetables reheated. **make a hash of** Informal spoil, do badly.

hash[2] n Informal hashish.

hashish [hash-eesh] n drug made from the cannabis plant, smoked for its intoxicating effects.

hasp n clasp that fits over a staple and is secured by a bolt or padlock, used as a fastening.

hassle Informal ▶ n trouble, bother.

▶ v bother or annoy.

hassock n cushion for kneeling on in church.

haste n (excessive) quickness. **make haste** hurry, rush. **hasten** v (cause to) hurry. **hasty** adj (too) quick. **hastily** adv

hat n covering for the head, often with a brim, usu. worn to give protection from the weather. **keep something under one's hat** keep something secret. **hat trick** any three successive achievements, esp. in sport.

hatch¹ v (cause to) emerge from an egg; devise (a plot).

hatch² n hinged door covering an opening in a floor or wall; opening in the wall between a kitchen and a dining area; door in an aircraft or spacecraft. **hatchback** n car with a lifting door at the back. **hatchway** n opening in the deck of a ship.

hatchet n small axe. **bury the hatchet** become reconciled. **hatchet job** malicious verbal or written attack. **hatchet man** Informal person carrying out unpleasant tasks for an employer.

hate v dislike intensely; be unwilling (to do something). ▶ n intense dislike; person or thing hated. **hateful** adj causing or deserving hate. **hater** n **hatred** n intense dislike.

haughty adj -tier, -tiest. proud, arrogant. **haughtily** adv **haughtiness** n

haul v pull or drag with effort. ▶ n amount gained by effort or theft. **long haul** something that takes a lot of time and effort. **haulage** n (charge for) transporting goods. **haulier** n firm or person that transports goods by road.

haunch n human hip or fleshy hindquarter of an animal.

haunt v visit in the form of a ghost; remain in the memory or thoughts of. ▶ n place visited frequently. **haunted** adj frequented by ghosts; worried. **haunting** adj memorably beautiful or sad.

haute couture [oat koo-**ture**] n French high fashion.

hauteur [oat-**ur**] n haughtiness.

have v has, having, had. possess, hold; receive, take, or obtain; experience or be affected by; (foll. by to) be obliged, must, e.g. I had to go; cause to be done; give birth to; used to form past tenses (with a past participle), e.g. we have looked; she had done enough. **have it out** Informal settle a matter by argument. **have on** v wear; Informal tease or trick. **have up** v bring to trial.

haven n place of safety.

haversack n canvas bag carried on the back or shoulder.

havoc n disorder and confusion.

haw n hawthorn berry.

hawk¹ n bird of prey with a short hooked bill and very good eyesight; Politics supporter or advocate of warlike policies. **hawkish, hawklike** adj **hawk-eyed** adj having very good eyesight.

hawk² v offer (goods) for sale in the street or door-to-door. **hawker** n

hawk³ v cough noisily.

hawser n large rope used on a ship.

hawthorn n thorny shrub or tree.

hay n grass cut and dried as fodder. **hay fever** allergy to pollen, causing sneezing and watery eyes. **haystack** n large pile of stored hay. **haywire** adj **go haywire** Informal not function properly.

hazard n something that could be dangerous. ▶ v put in danger; make (a guess). **hazardous** adj

haze n mist, often caused by heat. **hazy** adj not clear, misty; confused or vague.

hazel n small tree producing edible nuts. ▶ adj (of eyes) greenish-brown. **hazelnut** n

H-bomb n hydrogen bomb.

he pron refers to: male person or animal. ▶ n male person or animal a he-goat.

head n upper or front part of the body, containing the sense organs and the brain; mind and mental abilities; upper or most forward part of anything; person in charge of a group, organization, or school; pus-filled tip of a spot or boil; white froth on beer; (pl **head**) person or animal considered as a unit. ▶ adj chief, principal. ▶ v be at the top or front of; be in charge of; move (in a particular direction); hit (a ball) with the head; provide with a heading. **go to one's head** make one drunk or conceited. **head over heels (in love)** very much in love. **not make head nor tail of** not understand. **off one's head** Slang foolish or insane. **heads** adv Informal with the side of a coin which has a portrait of a head on it uppermost. **header** n striking a ball with the head; headlong fall. **heading** n title written or printed at the top of a page. **heady** adj intoxicating or exciting. **headache** n continuous pain in the head; cause of worry or annoyance. **headboard** n vertical board at the top end of a bed. **headdress** n decorative head covering. **head-hunt** v (of a company) approach and offer a job to (a person working for a

rival company). **head-hunter** n **headland** n area of land jutting out into the sea. **headlight** n powerful light on the front of a vehicle. **headline** n title at the top of a newspaper article, esp. on the front page. ▶ pl main points of a news broadcast. **headlong** adv, adj with the head first; hastily. **headphones** pl n two small loudspeakers held against the ears. **headquarters** pl n centre from which operations are directed. **head start** advantage in a competition. **headstone** n memorial stone on a grave. **headstrong** adj self-willed, obstinate. **headway** n progress. **headwind** n wind blowing against the course of an aircraft or ship.

heal v make or become well. **healer** n

health n normal (good) condition of someone's body. **health food** natural food, organically grown and free from additives. **healthy** adj having good health; of or producing good health; functioning well, sound. **healthily** adv

heap n pile of things one on top of another; (also **heaps**) large number or quantity. ▶ v gather into a pile; (foll. by on) give liberally (to).

hear v hearing, heard. perceive (a sound) by ear; listen to; learn or be informed; Law try (a case). **hear! hear!** exclamation of approval or agreement. **hearer** n **hearing** n ability to hear; trial of a case. **within hearing** close enough to be heard.

hearsay n gossip, rumour.

hearse n funeral car used to carry a coffin.

heart n organ that pumps blood round the body; centre of emotions, esp. love; courage, spirit; central or most important part; figure representing a heart; playing card with red heart heart-shaped symbols. **break someone's heart** cause someone great grief. **by heart** from memory. **set one's heart on something** greatly desire something. **take something to heart** be upset about something. **hearten** v encourage, make cheerful. **heartless** adj cruel, unkind. **hearty** adj substantial, nourishing; friendly, enthusiastic. **heartily** adv **heart attack** sudden severe malfunction of the heart. **heart failure** sudden stopping of the heartbeat. **heart-rending** adj causing great sorrow. **heart-throb** n Slang very attractive man, esp. a film or pop star.

heartache n intense anguish.

heartbeat n one complete pulsation of the heart.

heartbreak n intense grief.

heartburn n burning sensation in the chest caused by indigestion.

heartfelt adj felt sincerely or strongly.

hearth n floor of a fireplace.

heat v make or become hot. ▶ n state of being hot; energy transferred as a result of a difference in temperature; hot weather; intensity of feeling; preliminary eliminating contest in a competition. **on, in heat** (of some female animals) ready for mating. **heated** adj angry and excited. **heatedly** adv **heater** n

heath n Brit area of open uncultivated land.

heathen adj, n (of) a person who does not believe in an established religion.

heather n low-growing plant with small purple, pinkish, or white flowers, growing on heaths and mountains.

heave v lift with effort; throw (something heavy); utter (a sigh); rise and fall; vomit. ▶ n heaving.

heaven n place believed to be the home of God, where good people go when they die; place or state of bliss. **the heavens** sky.

heavenly adj of or like heaven; of or occurring in space; wonderful or beautiful.

heavy adj heavier, heaviest. of great weight; having a high density; great in degree or amount; Informal (of a situation) serious. **heavily** adv **heaviness** n **heavy industry** large-scale production of raw material or machinery. **heavy metal** very loud rock music featuring guitar riffs. **heavyweight** n boxer weighing over 175lb (professional) or 81kg (amateur).

Hebrew n member of an ancient Semitic people; ancient language of the Hebrews; its modern form, used in Israel. ▶ adj of the Hebrews.

heckle v interrupt (a public speaker) with comments, questions, or taunts. **heckler** n

hectare n one hundred ares or 10 000 square metres (2.471 acres).

hectic adj rushed or busy.

hector v bully.

hedge n row of bushes forming a barrier or boundary. ▶ v be evasive or noncommittal; (foll. by against) protect oneself (from). **hedgerow** n bushes forming a hedge.

hedgehog n small mammal with a protective covering of spines.

hedonism n doctrine that pleasure is the most important thing in life. **hedonist** n **hedonistic** adj

heed n careful attention. ▶ v pay careful attention to. **heedless** adj **heedless of** taking no notice of.

heel[1] n back part of the foot; part of a shoe supporting the heel; Old-fashioned contemptible person. ▶ v repair the heel of (a shoe).

heel[2] v (foll. by over) lean to one side.

hefty adj **heftier, heftiest.** large, heavy, or strong.

hegemony [hig-em-on-ee] n political domination.

Hegira n Mohammed's flight from Mecca to Medina in 622 AD.

heifer [hef-fer] n young cow.

height n distance from base to top; distance above sea level; highest degree or topmost point. **heighten** v make or become higher or more intense.

heinous adj evil and shocking.

heir n person entitled to inherit property or rank. **heiress** n fem **heirloom** n object that has belonged to a family for generations.

held v past of HOLD[1].

helical adj spiral.

helicopter n aircraft lifted and propelled by rotating overhead blades. **heliport** n airport for helicopters.

heliotrope n plant with purple flowers. ▶ adj light purple.

helium [heel-ee-um] n Chem very light colourless odourless gas.

helix [heel-iks] n, pl **helices, helixes.** spiral.

hell n place believed to be where wicked people go when they die; place or state of wickedness, suffering, or punishment. **hell for leather** at great speed. **hellish** adj **hellbent** adj (foll. by on) intent.

Hellenic adj of the (ancient) Greeks or their language.

hello interj expression of greeting or surprise.

helm n tiller or wheel for steering a ship.

helmet n hard hat worn for protection.

help v make something easier, better, or quicker for (someone); improve (a situation); refrain from, e.g. I can't help smiling. ▶ n assistance or support. **help oneself** take something, esp. food or drink, without being served; Informal steal something. **helper** n **helpful** adj **helping** n single portion of food. **helpless** adj weak or incapable. **helplessly** adv **helpline** n telephone line set aside for callers to contact an organization for help with a problem. **helpmate** n companion and helper, esp. a husband or wife.

helter-skelter adj haphazard and careless. ▶ adv in a haphazard and careless manner. ▶ n high spiral slide at a fairground.

hem n bottom edge of a garment, folded under and stitched down. ▶ v **hemming, hemmed.** provide with a hem. **hem in** v surround and prevent from moving.

hemline n level to which the hem of a skirt hangs.

hemisphere n half of a sphere, esp. the earth. **hemispherical** adj

hemlock n poison made from a plant with spotted stems and small white flowers.

hemp n (also **cannabis**) Asian plant with tough fibres; its fibre, used to make canvas and rope; narcotic drug obtained from hemp.

hen n female domestic fowl; female of any bird. **hen night, party** party for women only. **henpecked** adj (of a man) dominated by his wife.

hence conj for this reason. ▶ adv from this time. **henceforth** adv from now on.

henchman n person employed by someone powerful to carry out orders.

henna n reddish dye made from a shrub or tree. ▸ v dye (the hair) with henna.

henry n, pl **-ry, -ries, -rys.** unit of electrical inductance.

hepatitis n inflammation of the liver.

heptagon n geometric figure with seven sides.

heptathlon n athletic contest for women, involving seven events.

her pron refers to a female person or animal or anything personified as feminine when the object of a sentence or clause. ▸ adj belonging to her.

herald n person who announces important news; forerunner. ▸ v signal the approach of. **heraldry** n study of coats of arms and family trees. **heraldic** adj

herb n plant used for flavouring in cookery, and in medicine. **herbal** adj **herbalist** n person who grows or specializes in the use of medicinal herbs. **herbaceous** adj (of a plant) soft-stemmed. **herbicide** n chemical used to destroy plants, esp. weeds. **herbivore** n animal that eats only plants. **herbivorous** [her-biv-or-uss] adj

herculean [her-kew-lee-an] adj requiring great strength or effort.

herd n group of animals feeding and living together; large crowd of people. ▸ v collect into a herd. **herdsman** n man who looks after a herd of animals.

here adv in, at, or to this place or point. **hereabouts** adv near here. **hereafter** adv after this point or time. **the hereafter** life after death. **hereby** adv by means of or as a result of this. **herein** adv in this place, matter, or document. **herewith** adv with this.

heredity [hir-red-it-ee] n passing on of characteristics from one generation to another. **hereditary** adj passed on genetically from one generation to another; passed on by inheritance.

heresy [herr-iss-ee] n, pl **-sies.** opinion contrary to accepted opinion or belief. **heretic** [herr-it-ik] n person who holds unorthodox opinions. **heretical** [hir-ret-ik-al] adj

heritage n something inherited; anything from the past, considered as the inheritance of present-day society.

hermaphrodite [her-maf-roe-dite] n animal, plant, or person with both male and female reproductive organs.

hermetic adj sealed so as to be airtight. **hermetically** adv

hermit n person living in solitude, esp. for religious reasons. **hermitage** n home of a hermit.

hernia n protrusion of an organ or part through the lining of the surrounding body cavity.

hero n, pl **heroes.** principal character in a film, book, etc.; man greatly admired for his exceptional qualities or achievements. **heroine** n fem **heroic** adj courageous; of or like a hero. **heroics** pl n extravagant behaviour. **heroically** adv **heroism** [herr-oh-izz-um] n

heroin n highly addictive drug derived from morphine.

heron n long-legged wading bird.

herpes [her-peez] n any of several inflammatory skin diseases, including shingles and cold sores.

Herr [hair] n, pl **Herren.** German term of address equivalent to Mr.

herring n important food fish of northern seas. **herringbone** n pattern of zigzag lines.

hertz n, pl **hertz.** Physics unit of frequency.

hesitate v be slow or uncertain in doing something; be reluctant (to do something). **hesitation** n

hesitant adj undecided or wavering. **hesitantly** adv **hesitancy** n

hessian n coarse jute fabric.

heterodox adj differing from accepted doctrines or beliefs. **heterodoxy** n

heterogeneous [het-er-oh-**jean**-ee-uss] adj composed of diverse elements. **heterogeneity** n

heterosexual n, adj (person) sexually attracted to members of the opposite sex. **heterosexuality** n

heuristic [hew-rist-ik] adj involving learning by investigation.

hew v **hewing, hewed, hewed** or **hewn.** cut with an axe; carve from a substance.

hexagon n geometrical figure with six sides. **hexagonal** adj

hey interj expression of surprise or for catching attention.

heyday n time of greatest success, prime.

hiatus [hie-**ay**-tuss] n, pl **-tuses, -tus.** pause or interruption in continuity.

hibernate v (of an animal) pass the winter as if in a deep sleep. **hibernation** n

Hibernian adj Poetic Irish.

hibiscus n, pl **-cuses.** tropical plant with large brightly coloured flowers.

hiccup, hiccough n spasm of the breathing organs with a sharp coughlike sound; Informal small problem, hitch. ▶ v make a hiccup.

hick n US, Aust & NZ informal unsophisticated country person.

hickory n, pl **-ries.** N American

nut-bearing tree; its wood.

hide¹ v **hiding, hid, hidden.** put (oneself or an object) somewhere difficult to see or find; keep secret. ▶ n place of concealment, esp. for a bird-watcher. **hiding** n state of concealment, e.g. in hiding. **hide-out** n place to hide in.

hide² n skin of an animal. **hiding** n Slang severe beating. **hidebound** adj unwilling to accept new ideas.

hideous [hid-ee-uss] adj ugly, revolting. **hideously** adv

hierarchy [hire-ark-ee] n, pl **-chies.** system of people or things arranged in a graded order. **hierarchical** adj

hieroglyphic [hire-oh-**gliff**-ik] adj of a form of writing using picture symbols, as used in ancient Egypt. ▶ n symbol that is difficult to decipher; (also **hieroglyph**) symbol representing an object, idea, or sound.

hi-fi n set of high-quality sound-reproducing equipment. ▶ adj high-fidelity.

higgledy-piggledy adv, adj in a muddle.

high adj of a great height; far above ground or sea level; being at its peak; greater than usual in intensity or amount; (of a sound) acute in pitch; of great importance, quality, or rank; Informal under the influence of alcohol or drugs. ▶ adv at or to a high level. **highly** adv **highly strung** nervous and easily upset. **Highness** n title used to address or refer to a royal person.

High-Church adj belonging to a section within the Church of England stressing the importance of ceremony and ritual. **higher education** education at colleges and universities. **high-fidelity** adj able to reproduce sound with little or no distortion. **high-flown** adj (of language) extravagant or pretentious. **high-handed** adj excessively forceful. **high-rise** adj (of a building) having many storeys. **high tea** early evening meal consisting of a cooked dish, bread, cakes, and tea. **high time** latest possible time.

highbrow adj, n intellectual and serious (person).

highlands pl n area of high ground.

highlight n outstanding part or feature; light-toned area in a painting or photograph; lightened streak in the hair. ▶ v give emphasis to.

highway n US, Aust & NZ main road. **Highway Code** regulations and recommendations applying to all road users. **highwayman** n (formerly) robber, usu. on horseback, who robbed travellers at gunpoint.

hijack v seize control of (an aircraft or other vehicle) while travelling. **hijacker** n

hike n long walk in the country, esp. for pleasure. ▶ v go for a long walk; (foll. by *up*) pull (up) or raise. **hiker** n

hilarious adj very funny. **hilariously** adv **hilarity** n

hill n raised part of the earth's surface, less high than a mountain. **hilly** adj **hillock** n small hill. **hillbilly** n US unsophisticated country person.

hilt n handle of a sword or knife.

him pron refers to a male person or animal when the object of a sentence or clause.

hind¹ adj hinder, hindmost. situated at the back.

hind² n female deer.

hinder v get in the way of. **hindrance** n

Hindu n person who practises Hinduism. ▶ adj of Hinduism.

Hindi n language of N central India. **Hinduism** n dominant religion of India, which involves the worship of many gods and a belief in reincarnation.

hinge n device for holding together two parts so that one can swing freely. ▶ v (foll. by *on*) depend (on); fit a hinge to.

hint n indirect suggestion; piece of advice; small amount. ▶ v suggest indirectly.

hinterland n land lying behind a coast or near a city, esp. a port.

hip¹ n either side of the body between the pelvis and the thigh.

hip² n rosehip.

hip-hop n pop-culture movement originating in the 1980s, comprising rap music, graffiti, and break dancing.

hippie adj, n same as HIPPY.

hippo n, pl **-pos.** Informal hippopotamus.

hippodrome n music hall, variety theatre, or circus.

hippopotamus n, pl **-muses, -mi.** large African mammal with thick wrinkled skin, living near rivers.

hippy adj, n, pl **-pies.** (esp. in the 1960s) (of) a person whose behaviour and dress imply a rejection of conventional values.

hire v pay to have temporary use of; employ for wages. ▶ n hiring. **for hire** available to be hired. **hireling** n person who works only for wages. **hire-purchase** n system of purchase by which the buyer pays for goods by instalments.

hirsute [her-suit] adj hairy.

his pron, adj (something) belonging to him.

Hispanic adj Spanish or Latin-American.

hiss n sound like that of a long s

(as an expression of contempt).
▶ v utter a hiss; show derision or
anger towards.

histamine [hiss-ta-meen] n
substance released by the body
tissues in allergic reactions.

histogram n statistical graph in
which the frequency of values is
represented by vertical bars of
varying heights and widths.

histology n study of the tissues of
an animal or plant.

history n, pl -ries. (record or
account of) past events and
developments; study of these;
record of someone's past.
historian n writer of history.
historic adj famous or significant
in history. **historical** adj occurring
in the past; based on history.
historically adv

histrionic adj excessively dramatic.
histrionics pl n excessively
dramatic behaviour.

hit v hitting, hit. strike, touch
forcefully; come into violent
contact with; affect badly; reach
(a point or place). ▶ n hitting;
successful record, film, etc.;
Computers single visit to a website.
hit it off Informal get on well
together. **hit the road** Informal
start a journey. **hit-and-miss** adj
sometimes successful and
sometimes not. **hit man** hired
assassin. **hit on** v think of (an
idea).

hitch n minor problem. ▶ v Informal
obtain (a lift) by hitchhiking;
fasten with a knot or tie; (foll. by
up) pull up with a jerk. **hitchhike**
v travel by obtaining free lifts.
hitchhiker n

hi-tech adj using sophisticated
technology.

hither adv Old-fashioned to or
towards this place.

hitherto adv until this time.

HIV human immunodeficiency
virus, the cause of AIDS.

hive n same as BEEHIVE. **hive of
activity** place where people are
very busy. **hive off** v separate
from a larger group.

hives n allergic reaction in which
itchy red or whitish patches
appear on the skin.

HM (in Britain) Her (or His) Majesty.

HMS (in Britain) Her (or His)
Majesty's Ship.

HNC (in Britain) Higher National
Certificate.

HND (in Britain) Higher National
Diploma.

hoard n store hidden away for
future use. ▶ v save or store.
hoarder n

hoarding n large board for
displaying advertisements.

hoarfrost n white ground frost.

hoarse adj (of a voice) rough and
unclear; having a rough and
unclear voice. **hoarsely** adv
hoarseness n

hoary adj hoarier, hoariest. grey
or white-(haired); very old.

hoax n deception or trick. ▶ v
deceive or play a trick upon.
hoaxer n

hob n Brit flat top part of a cooker,
or a separate flat surface,
containing gas or electric rings for
cooking on.

hobble v walk lamely; tie the legs
of (a horse).

hobby n, pl -bies. activity pursued
in one's spare time. **hobbyhorse**
n favourite topic; toy horse.

hobgoblin n mischievous goblin.

hobnail boots pl n heavy boots
with short nails in the soles.

hobnob v -nobbing, -nobbed.
(foll. by with) be on friendly terms
(with).

hobo n, pl -bos. US, Aust & NZ
tramp or vagrant.

hock¹ n joint in the back leg of an animal such as a horse that corresponds to the human ankle.

hock² n white German wine.

hock³ v Informal pawn. **in hock** Informal in debt.

hockey n team game played on a field with a ball and curved sticks; US ice hockey.

hocus-pocus n trickery.

hod n open wooden box attached to a pole, for carrying bricks or mortar.

hoe n long-handled tool used for loosening soil or weeding. ▶ v scrape or weed with a hoe.

hog n castrated male pig; Informal greedy person. ▶ v **hogging, hogged.** Informal take more than one's share of. **hogshead** n large cask. **hogwash** n Informal nonsense.

Hogmanay n (in Scotland) New Year's Eve.

hoick v raise abruptly and sharply.

hoi polloi n the ordinary people.

hoist v raise or lift up. ▶ n device for lifting things.

hoity-toity adj Informal arrogant or haughty.

hokey-pokey n NZ brittle toffee sold in lumps.

hold¹ v **holding, held.** keep or support in or with the hands or arms; arrange for (a meeting, party, etc.) to take place; consider to be as specified, e.g. who are you holding responsible?; maintain in a specified position or state; have the capacity for; Informal wait, esp. on the telephone; restrain or keep back; own, possess. ▶ n act or way of holding; controlling influence. **holder** n

holding n property, such as land or stocks and shares. **holdall** n large strong travelling bag.

hold-up n armed robbery; delay.

hold² n cargo compartment in a ship or aircraft.

hole n area hollowed out in a solid; opening or hollow; animal's burrow; Informal unattractive place; Informal difficult situation. ▶ v make holes in; hit (a golf ball) into the target hole.

holiday n time spent away from home for rest or recreation; day or other period of rest from work or studies.

holiness n state of being holy; (H-) title used to address or refer to the Pope.

holistic adj considering the complete person, physically and mentally, in the treatment of an illness. **holism** n

hollow adj having a hole or space inside; (of a sound) as if echoing in a hollow place; without any real value or worth. ▶ n cavity or space; dip in the land. ▶ v form a hollow in.

holly n evergreen tree with prickly leaves and red berries.

hollyhock n tall garden plant with spikes of colourful flowers.

holocaust n destruction or loss of life on a massive scale.

hologram n three-dimensional photographic image.

holograph n document handwritten by the author.

holster n leather case for a pistol, hung from a belt.

holy adj **-lier, -liest.** of God or a god; devout or virtuous. **holier-than-thou** adj self-righteous. **Holy Communion** Christianity service in which people take bread and wine in remembrance of the death and resurrection of Jesus Christ. **Holy Grail** (in medieval legend) the bowl used by Jesus Christ at the Last Supper. **Holy Spirit, Ghost** Christianity one of the three aspects of God. **Holy Week** *Christianity* week before Easter.

homage n show of respect or honour towards someone or something.

home n place where one lives; institution for the care of the elderly, orphans, etc. ▶ *adj* of one's home, birthplace, or native country; *Sport* played on one's own ground. ▶ *adv* to or at home. ▶ *v* (foll. by *in* or *in on*) direct towards (a point or target). **at home** at ease. **bring home to** make clear to. **home and dry** *Informal* safe or successful.

homeless *adj* having nowhere to live. ▶ *pl n* people who have nowhere to live. **homelessness** n

homely *adj* simple, ordinary, and comfortable; *US* unattractive.

homeward *adj, adv* **homewards** *adv* **home-brew** n beer made at home. **home-made** *adj* made at home or on the premises. **home page** *Computers* introductory information about a website with links to the information or services provided. **home truths** unpleasant facts told to a person about himself or herself.

homeland n country from which a person's ancestors came.

homeopathy [home-ee-**op**-ath-ee] n treatment of disease by small doses of a drug that produces symptoms of the disease in healthy people. **homeopath** n person who practises homeopathy. **homeopathic** *adj*

homesick *adj* sad because missing one's home and family. **homesickness** n

homework n school work done at home.

homicide n killing of a human being; person who kills someone.

homicidal *adj*

homily n, *pl* -**lies**. speech telling people how they should behave.

hominid n man or any extinct forerunner of man.

homo- *combining form* same, like, e.g. *homosexual.*

homogeneous [home-oh-**jean**-ee-uss] *adj* formed of similar parts. **homogeneity** n **homogenize** v break up fat globules in (milk or cream) to distribute them evenly; make homogeneous.

homograph n word spelt the same as another, but with a different meaning.

homologous [hom-**ol**-log-uss] *adj* having a related or similar position or structure.

homonym n word spelt or pronounced the same as another, but with a different meaning.

homophobia n hatred or fear of homosexuals. **homophobic** *adj*

homophone n word pronounced the same as another, but with a different meaning or spelling.

Homo sapiens [hoe-moh sap-ee-enz] n human beings as a species.

homosexual n, *adj* (person) sexually attracted to members of the same sex. **homosexuality** n

hone v sharpen.

honest *adj* truthful and moral; open and sincere. **honestly** *adv* **honesty** n quality of being honest; plant with silvery seed pods.

honey n sweet edible sticky substance made by bees from nectar; term of endearment.

honeycomb n waxy structure of six-sided cells in which honey is stored by bees in a beehive.

honeydew melon melon with a yellow skin and sweet pale flesh.

honeymoon n holiday taken by a

newly married couple.

honeysuckle n climbing shrub with sweet-smelling flowers.

hongi [hong-jee] n NZ Maori greeting in which people touch noses.

honk n sound made by a car horn; sound made by a goose. ▶ v (cause to) make this sound.

honour n sense of honesty and fairness; (award given out of) respect; pleasure or privilege. ▶ pl university degree of a higher standard than an ordinary degree. ▶ v give praise and attention to; give an award to (someone) out of respect; accept or pay (a cheque or bill); keep (a promise). **do the honours** act as host or hostess by pouring drinks or giving out food. **honourable** adj worthy of respect or esteem. **honourably** adv **honorary** adj held or given only as an honour; unpaid. **honorific** adj showing respect.

hood¹ n head covering, often attached to a coat or jacket; folding roof of a convertible car or a pram; US & Aust car bonnet. **hooded** adj (of a garment) having a hood; (of eyes) having heavy eyelids that appear to be half-closed.

hood² n Chiefly US slang hoodlum.

hoodlum n Slang violent criminal, gangster.

hoodoo n, pl **-doos.** (cause of) bad luck.

hoodwink v trick, deceive.

hoof n, pl **hooves, hoofs.** horny covering of the foot of a horse, deer, etc. **hoof it** Slang walk.

hoo-ha n fuss or commotion.

hook n curved piece of metal, plastic, etc., used to hang, hold, or pull something; short swinging punch. ▶ v fasten or catch (as if

with a hook. **hooked** adj bent like a hook; (foll. by on) Slang addicted (to) or obsessed (with).

hooker n Rugby player who uses his feet to get the ball in a scrum.

hook-up n linking of radio or television stations. **hookworm** n blood-sucking worm with hooked mouthparts.

hookah n oriental pipe in which smoke is drawn through water and a long tube.

hooligan n rowdy young person. **hooliganism** n

hoon n Aust & NZ slang loutish youth who drives irresponsibly.

hoop n rigid circular band, used esp. as a child's toy or for animals to jump through in the circus. **jump, be put through the hoops** go through an ordeal or test.

hoopla n fairground game in which hoops are thrown over objects in an attempt to win them.

hooray interj same as HURRAH.

hoot n sound of a car horn; cry of an owl; cry of derision; Informal amusing person or thing. ▶ v sound (a car horn); jeer or yell contemptuously (at someone). **hooter** n device that hoots; Chiefly Brit slang nose.

Hoover n ® vacuum cleaner. ▶ v (h-) clean with a vacuum cleaner.

hooves n a plural of HOOF.

hop¹ v **hopping, hopped.** jump on one foot; move in short jumps; Informal move quickly. ▶ n instance of hopping; Informal dance; short journey, esp. by air. **catch someone on the hop** Informal catch someone unprepared.

hop² n (often pl) climbing plant, the dried flowers of which are used to make beer.

hope v want (something) to happen or be true. ▶ n expectation of something desired;

thing that gives cause for hope or is desired. **hopeful** adj having, expressing, or inspiring hope. ▶ n person considered to be on the brink of success. **hopefully** adv in a hopeful manner; it is hoped. **hopeless** adj

hopper n container for storing substances such as grain or sand.

hopscotch n children's game of hopping in a pattern drawn on the ground.

horde n large crowd.

horizon n apparent line that divides the earth and the sky. ▶ pl limits of scope, interest, or knowledge.

horizontal adj parallel to the horizon, level, flat. **horizontally** adv

hormone n substance secreted by certain glands which stimulates certain organs of the body; synthetic substance with the same effect. **hormonal** adj

horn n one of a pair of bony growths sticking out of the heads of cattle, sheep, etc.; substance of which horns are made; musical instrument with a tube or pipe of brass fitted with a mouthpiece; device on a vehicle sounded as a warning. **horned** adj **horny** adj of or like horn; Slang (easily) sexually aroused. **hornbeam** n tree with smooth grey bark. **hornbill** n bird with a bony growth on its large beak. **hornpipe** n (music for) a solo dance, traditionally performed by sailors.

hornblende n mineral containing aluminium, calcium, sodium, magnesium, and iron.

hornet n large wasp with a severe sting.

horoscope n prediction of a person's future based on the positions of the planets, sun, and moon at his or her birth.

horrendous adj very unpleasant and shocking.

horrible adj disagreeable, unpleasant; causing horror. **horribly** adv

horrid adj disagreeable, unpleasant; Informal nasty.

horrify v -fying, -fied. cause to feel horror or shock. **horrific** adj causing horror.

horror n (thing or person causing) terror or hatred.

hors d'oeuvre [or **durv**] n appetizer served before a main meal.

horse n large animal with hooves, a mane, and a tail, used for riding and pulling carts etc.; piece of gymnastic equipment used for vaulting over. **(straight) from the horse's mouth** from the original source. **horsey, horsy** adj very keen on horses; of or like a horse. **horse around** v Informal play roughly or boisterously. **horse chestnut** tree with broad leaves and inedible large brown shiny nuts in spiky cases. **horsefly** n large bloodsucking fly. **horsehair** n hair from the tail or mane of a horse. **horse laugh** loud coarse laugh. **horseman, horsewoman** n person riding a horse. **horseplay** n rough or rowdy play. **horsepower** n unit of power (equivalent to 745.7 watts), used to measure the power of an engine. **horseradish** n strong-tasting root of a plant, usu. made into a sauce. **horseshoe** n protective U-shaped piece of iron nailed to a horse's hoof, regarded as a symbol of good luck.

horticulture n art or science of cultivating gardens. **horticultural** adj **horticulturalist, horticulturist**

n

hosanna interj exclamation of praise to God.

hose[1] n flexible pipe for conveying liquid. ▶ v water with a hose.

hose[2] n stockings, socks, and tights. **hosiery** n stockings, socks, and tights collectively.

hospice [hoss-piss] n nursing home for the terminally ill.

hospital n place where people who are ill are looked after and treated. **hospitalize** v send or admit to hospital. **hospitalization** n

hospitality n kindness in welcoming strangers or guests. **hospitable** adj welcoming to strangers or guests.

host[1] n (fem **hostess**) person who entertains guests, esp. in his own home; place or country providing the facilities for an event; compere of a show; animal or plant on which a parasite lives. ▶ v be the host of.

host[2] n large number.

Host n Christianity bread used in Holy Communion.

hostage n person who is illegally held prisoner until certain demands are met by other people.

hostel n building providing accommodation at a low cost for a specific group of people such as students, travellers, homeless people, etc.

hostelry n, pl **-ries**. Old-fashioned or facetious inn, pub.

hostile adj unfriendly; (foll. by to) opposed (to); of an enemy. **hostility** n, pl **-ties**. unfriendly and aggressive feelings or behaviour. ▶ pl acts of warfare.

hot adj **hotter, hottest**. having a high temperature; strong, spicy; (of news) very recent; (of a contest) fiercely fought; (of a temper) quick to rouse; liked very much, e.g. a hot favourite; Slang stolen. **in hot water** Informal in trouble. **hotly** adv **hot air** Informal empty talk. **hot-blooded** adj passionate or excitable. **hot dog** long roll split lengthways with a hot frankfurter inside. **hot-headed** adj rash, having a hot temper. **hotline** n direct telephone line for emergency use. **hot pool** NZ geothermally heated pool.

hotbed n any place encouraging a particular activity, e.g. hotbeds of unrest.

hotchpotch n jumbled mixture.

hotel n commercial establishment providing lodging and meals. **hotelier** n owner or manager of a hotel.

hotfoot adv Informal quickly and eagerly. **hotfoot it** Informal go quickly and eagerly.

hothouse n greenhouse.

hotplate n heated metal surface on an electric cooker; portable device for keeping food warm.

hound n hunting dog. ▶ v pursue relentlessly.

hour n twenty-fourth part of a day, sixty minutes; time of day. ▶ pl period regularly appointed for work or business. **hourly** adj, adv (happening) every hour; frequent(ly). **hourglass** n device with two glass compartments, containing a quantity of sand that takes an hour to trickle from the top section to the bottom one.

houri n in Islam any of the nymphs of paradise.

house n building used as a home; building used for some specific purpose, e.g. the opera house; business firm; law-making body or the hall where it meets; family or dynasty; theatre or cinema audience. ▶ v give accommodation to; contain or cover. **get on like a house on fire** *Informal* get on very well together. **on the house** *Informal* provided free by the management. **housing** n (providing of) houses; protective case or covering of a machine. **house arrest** confinement to one's home rather than in prison. **houseboat** n stationary boat used as a home. **housebreaker** n burglar. **housecoat** n woman's long loose coat-shaped garment for wearing at home. **household** n all the people living in a house. **householder** n person who owns or rents a house. **housekeeper** n person employed to run someone else's household. **housekeeping** n (money for) running a household. **housemaid** n female servant employed to do housework. **house-train** v train (a pet) to urinate and defecate outside. **house-warming** n party to celebrate moving into a new home. **housewife** n woman who runs her own household and does not have a job. **housework** n work of running a home, such as cleaning, cooking, and shopping. **House music, House** n electronic funk-based disco music with samples of other recordings edited in.

hovel n small dirty house or hut. **hover** v (of a bird etc.) remain suspended in one place in the air; loiter; be in a state of indecision. **hovercraft** n vehicle which can travel over both land and sea on a cushion of air.

how adv in what way, by what means; to what degree, e.g. *I know how hard it is.* **however** adv nevertheless; by whatever means; no matter how, e.g. *however much*

it hurt, he could do it.

howdah n canopied seat on an elephant's back. **howitzer** n large gun firing shells at a steep angle. **howl** n loud wailing cry; loud burst of laughter. ▶ v utter a howl. **howler** n *Informal* stupid mistake. **hoyden** n *Old-fashioned* wild or boisterous girl.

HP, h.p. hire-purchase; horsepower. **HQ** headquarters. **HRH** Her (or His) Royal Highness. **HRT** hormone replacement therapy. **HTML** hypertext markup language: text description language used on the Internet. **hub** n centre of a wheel, through which the axle passes; central point of activity. **hubbub** n confused noise of many voices. **hubby** n, pl **-bies.** *Informal* husband. **hubris** n [hew-briss] *Formal* pride, arrogance. **huckster** n person using aggressive methods of selling. **huddle** v hunch (oneself) through cold or fear; crowd closely together. ▶ n small group; *Informal* impromptu conference. **hue** n colour, shade. **hue and cry** n public outcry. **huff** n passing mood of anger or resentment. ▶ v blow or puff heavily. **huffy** adj **huffily** adv **hug** v **hugging, hugged.** clasp tightly in the arms, usu. with affection; keep close to (the ground, kerb, etc.). ▶ n tight or fond embrace. **huge** adj very big. **hugely** adv **huh** interj exclamation of derision, bewilderment, or inquiry. **hui** [hoo-ee] n NZ meeting of Maori people; meeting to discuss Maori matters. **hula** n swaying Hawaiian dance.

Hula Hoop ® plastic hoop twirled round the body by gyrating the hips.

hulk n body of an abandoned ship; Offens large heavy person or thing. **hulking** adj bulky, unwieldy.

hull n main body of a boat; leaves round the stem of a strawberry, raspberry, etc. ▶ v remove the hulls from.

hullabaloo n, pl **-loos.** loud confused noise or clamour.

hum v humming, hummed. make a low continuous vibrating sound; sing with the lips closed; Slang (of a place) be very busy. ▶ n humming sound. **hummingbird** n very small American bird whose powerful wings make a humming noise as they vibrate.

human adj of or typical of people. ▶ n human being. **humanly** adv by human powers or means. **human being** man, woman, or child.

humane adj kind or merciful. **humanely** adv

humanism n belief in human effort rather than religion. **humanist** n

humanitarian n, adj (person) having the interests of humankind at heart.

humanity n, pl **-ties.** human race; the quality of being human; kindness or mercy. ▶ pl study of literature, philosophy, and the arts.

humanize v make human or humane.

humankind n human race.

humble adj conscious of one's failings; modest, unpretentious; unimportant. ▶ v cause to feel humble, humiliate. **humbly** adv

humbug n Brit hard striped peppermint sweet; nonsense; dishonest person.

humdinger n Slang excellent person or thing.

humdrum adj ordinary, dull.

humerus [hew-mer-uss] n, pl **-meri** [-mer-rye] bone from the shoulder to the elbow.

humid adj damp and hot.

humidity n **humidify** v **-fying, -fied. humidifier** n device for increasing the amount of water vapour in the air in a room.

humiliate v lower the dignity or hurt the pride of. **humiliating** adj **humiliation** n

humility n quality of being humble.

hummock n very small hill.

humour n ability to say or perceive things that are amusing; amusing quality in a situation, film, etc.; state of mind, mood; Old-fashioned fluid in the body. ▶ v be kind and indulgent to. **humorous** adj **humorously** adv **humorist** n writer or entertainer who uses humour in his or her work.

hump n raised piece of ground; large lump on the back of an animal or person. ▶ v Slang carry or heave. **get, take the hump** Informal be annoyed, sulk. **hump-back, humpbacked bridge** road bridge with a sharp slope on each side.

humus [hew-muss] n decomposing vegetable and animal mould in the soil.

hunch n feeling or suspicion not based on facts. ▶ v draw (one's shoulders) up or together. **hunchback** n an abnormal curvature of the spine.

hundred adj, n ten times ten. ▶ n (often pl) large but unspecified number. **hundredth** adj, n **hundredweight** n Brit unit of weight of 112 pounds (50.8 kilograms).

hung v past of HANG. ▶ adj (of a parliament or jury) with no side having a clear majority. **hung**

over *Informal* suffering the effects of a hangover.

hunger *n* discomfort or weakness from lack of food; desire or craving. ▶ *v* (foll. by *for*) want very much. **hunger strike** refusal of all food, as a means of protest.

hungry *adj* **hungrier, hungriest.** desiring food; (foll. by *for*) having a desire or craving (for). **hungrily** *adv*

hunk *n* large piece; *Slang* sexually attractive man.

hunt *v* seek out and kill (wild animals) for food or sport; (foll. by *for*) search (for). ▶ *n* hunting; (party organized for) hunting wild animals for sport. **huntaway** *n NZ* sheepdog trained to drive sheep by barking. **huntsman** *n* man who hunts wild animals, esp. foxes.

hunter *n* person or animal that hunts wild animals for food or sport.

hurdle *n Sport* light barrier for jumping over in some races; problem or difficulty. ▶ *pl* race involving hurdles. ▶ *v* jump over (something). **hurdler** *n*

hurdy-gurdy *n, pl* **-dies.** mechanical musical instrument, such as a barrel organ.

hurl *v* throw or utter forcefully.

hurling, hurley *n* Irish game like hockey.

hurly-burly *n* loud confusion.

hurrah, hurray *interj* exclamation of joy or applause.

hurricane *n* very strong, often destructive, wind or storm. **hurricane lamp** paraffin lamp with a glass covering.

hurry *v* **-rying, -ried.** (cause to) move or act very quickly. ▶ *n* doing something quickly or the need to do something quickly. **hurriedly** *adv*

hurt *v* **hurting, hurt.** cause physical

or mental pain to; be painful; *Informal* feel pain. ▶ *n* physical or mental pain. **hurtful** *adj* unkind.

hurtle *v* move quickly or violently.

husband *n* woman's partner in marriage. ▶ *v* use economically. **husbandry** *n* farming; management of resources.

hush *v* make or be silent. ▶ *n* stillness or silence. **hush-hush** *adj Informal* secret. **hush up** *v* suppress information about.

husk *n* outer covering of certain seeds and fruits. ▶ *v* remove the husk from.

husky[1] *adj* **huskier, huskiest.** slightly hoarse; *Informal* big and strong. **huskily** *adv*

husky[2] *n, pl* **huskies.** Arctic sledge dog with thick hair and a curled tail.

hussar [hoo-zar] *n Hist* lightly armed cavalry soldier.

hussy *n, pl* **-sies.** immodest or promiscuous woman.

hustings *pl n* political campaigns and speeches before an election.

hustle *v* push about, jostle. ▶ *n* lively activity or bustle.

hut *n* small house, shelter, or shed.

hutch *n* cage for pet rabbits etc.

hyacinth *n* sweet-smelling spring flower that grows from a bulb.

hyaena *n* same as HYENA.

hybrid *n* offspring of two plants or animals of different species; anything of mixed origin. ▶ *adj* of mixed origin.

hydra *n* mythical many-headed water serpent.

hydrangea *n* ornamental shrub with clusters of pink, blue, or white flowers.

hydrant *n* outlet from a water main with a nozzle for a hose.

hydrate *n* chemical compound of water with another substance.

hydraulic *adj* operated by pressure

forced through a pipe by a liquid such as water or oil. **hydraulics** n study of the mechanical properties of fluids as they apply to practical engineering. **hydraulically** adv

hydro[1] n, pl **hydros**. hotel offering facilities for hydropathy.

hydro[2] adj short for HYDROELECTRIC.

hydro- combining form water, e.g. hydroelectric; hydrogen, e.g. hydrochloric acid.

hydrocarbon n compound of hydrogen and carbon.

hydrochloric acid n strong colourless acid used in many industrial and laboratory processes.

hydroelectric adj of the generation of electricity by water pressure.

hydrofoil n fast light boat with its hull raised out of the water on one or more pairs of fins.

hydrogen n Chem light flammable colourless gas that combines with oxygen to form water. **hydrogen bomb** extremely powerful bomb in which energy is released by fusion of hydrogen nuclei to give helium nuclei. **hydrogen peroxide** colourless liquid used as a hair bleach and as an antiseptic.

hydrolysis [hie-drol-iss-iss] n decomposition of a chemical compound reacting with water.

hydrometer [hie-drom-it-er] n instrument for measuring the density of a liquid.

hydropathy n method of treating disease by the use of large quantities of water both internally and externally.

hydrophobia n rabies; fear of water.

hydroplane n light motorboat that skims the water.

hydroponics n method of growing plants in water rather than soil.

hydrotherapy n Med treatment of certain diseases by exercise in water.

hyena n scavenging doglike mammal of Africa and S Asia.

hygiene n principles and practice of health and cleanliness. **hygienic** adj **hygienically** adv

hymen n membrane partly covering the opening of a girl's vagina, which breaks before puberty or at the first occurrence of sexual intercourse.

hymn n Christian song of praise sung to God or a saint. **hymnal** n book of hymns (also **hymn book**).

hype n intensive or exaggerated publicity or sales promotion. ▶ v promote (a product) using intensive or exaggerated publicity.

hyper adj Informal overactive or overexcited.

hyper- prefix over, above, excessively, e.g. hyperactive.

hyperbola [hie-per-bol-a] n Geom curve produced when a cone is cut by a plane at a steeper angle to its base than its side.

hyperbole [hie-per-bol-ee] n deliberate exaggeration for effect. **hyperbolic** adj

hyperlink Computers ▶ n link from a hypertext file that gives users instant access to related material in another file. ▶ v link (files) in this way.

hypermarket n huge self-service store.

hypersensitive adj extremely sensitive to certain drugs, extremes of temperature, etc.; very easily upset.

hypersonic adj having a speed of at least five times the speed of sound.

hypertension n very high blood pressure.

hypertext n computer software and hardware that allows users to

store and view text and move
between related items easily.
hyphen n punctuation mark (-)
indicating that two words or
syllables are connected.
hyphenated adj (of two words or
syllables) having a hyphen
between them. **hyphenation** n
hypnosis n artificially induced state
of relaxation in which the mind is
more than usually receptive to
suggestion. **hypnotic** adj or (as
if) producing hypnosis.
hypnotism n inducing hypnosis in
someone. **hypnotist** n **hypnotize**
v
hypo- prefix beneath, less than, e.g.
hypothermia.
hypoallergenic adj (of cosmetics)
not likely to cause an allergic
reaction.
hypochondria n undue
preoccupation with one's health.
hypochondriac n
hypocrisy [hip-ok-rass-ee] n, pl
-sies. (instance of) pretence of
having standards or beliefs that
are contrary to one's real
character or actual behaviour.
hypocrite [hip-oh-krit] n person
who pretends to be what he or
she is not. **hypocritical** adj
hypocritically adv
hypodermic adj, n (denoting) a
syringe or needle used to inject a
drug beneath the skin.
hypotension n very low blood
pressure.
hypotenuse [hip-pot-a-news] n
side of a right-angled triangle
opposite the right angle.
hypothermia n condition in which
a person's body temperature is
dangerously low as a result of
prolonged exposure to severe cold.
hypothesis [hie-poth-iss-iss] n, pl
-ses [-seez] suggested but
unproved explanation of

something. **hypothetical** adj
based on assumption rather than
fact or reality. **hypothetically**
adv
hyrax n, pl **-raxes** or **-races.** type
of hoofed rodent-like animal of
Africa and Asia.
hysterectomy n, pl **-mies.** surgical
removal of the womb.
hysteria n state of uncontrolled
excitement, anger, or panic.
hysterical adj **hysterically** adv
hysterics pl n attack of hysteria;
Informal uncontrollable laughter.
Hz hertz.

I i

I pron used by a speaker or writer
to refer to himself or herself as the
subject of a verb.
Iberian adj of Iberia, the peninsula
comprising Spain and Portugal.
ibex [ibe-eks] n wild goat of N
with large backward-curving horns.
ibid. (referring to a book, page, or
passage already mentioned) in the
same place.
ibis [ibe-iss] n large wading bird
with long legs.
ice n frozen water; Chiefly Brit
portion of ice cream **the Ice** NZ
informal Antarctica. ▸ v (foll. by up
or over) become covered with ice;
cover with icing. **break the ice**
create a relaxed atmosphere, esp.
between people meeting for the
first time. **iced** adj covered with
icing; (of a drink) containing ice.
icy adj **icier, iciest.** very cold;
covered with ice; aloof and
unfriendly. **icily** adv **iciness** n
Ice Age period when much of the
earth's surface was covered in
glaciers. **iceberg** n large floating
mass of ice. **icebox** n US
refrigerator. **icecap** n mass of ice

permanently covering an area.
ice cream sweet creamy frozen
food. **ice cube** small square block
of ice added to a drink to cool it.
ice floe sheet of ice floating in the
sea. **ice hockey** team game like
hockey played on ice with a puck.
ice lolly flavoured ice on a stick.
ice pick pointed tool for breaking
ice. **ice skate** boot with a steel
blade fixed to the sole, to enable
the wearer to glide over ice.
ice-skate v **ice-skater** n
ichthyology [ik-thi-ol-a-jee] n
scientific study of fish.

icicle n tapering spike of ice
hanging where water has dripped.
icing n mixture of sugar and water
etc., used to cover and decorate
cakes. **icing sugar** finely ground
sugar for making icing.

icon n picture of Christ or another
religious figure, regarded as holy
in the Orthodox Church; picture
on a computer screen
representing a function that can
be activated by moving the cursor
over it.
iconoclast n person who attacks
established ideas or principles.
iconoclastic adj

id n Psychoanalysis the mind's
instinctive unconscious energies.
idea n plan or thought formed in
the mind; thought of something;
belief or opinion.
ideal adj most suitable; perfect. ▶ n
conception of something that is
perfect; perfect person or thing.
ideally adv **idealism** n tendency
to seek perfection in everything.
idealist n **idealistic** adj **idealize**
v regard or portray as perfect or
nearly perfect. **idealization** n
idem pron, adj Latin the same: used
to refer to an article, chapter, or
book already quoted.
identical adj exactly the same.

identically adv
identify v -fying, -fied. prove or
recognize as being a certain
person or thing; (foll. by with)
understand and sympathize with
(a person or group that one
regards as being similar or
similarly situated); treat as being
the same. **identifiable** adj
identification n
Identikit n ® composite picture,
assembled from descriptions
given, of a person wanted by the
police.
identity n, pl -ties. state of being a
specified person or thing;
individuality or personality; state
of being the same.
ideology n, pl -gies. body of ideas
and beliefs of a group, nation, etc.
ideological adj **ideologist** n
idiocy n utter stupidity.
idiom n group of words which
when used together have a
different meaning from the words
individually, e.g. raining cats and
dogs; way of expression natural or
peculiar to a language or group.
idiomatic adj **idiomatically** adv
idiosyncrasy n, pl -sies. personal
peculiarity of mind, habit, or
behaviour.
idiot n foolish or stupid person.
idiotic adj **idiotically** adv
idle adj not doing anything; not
willing to work, lazy; not being
used; useless or meaningless, e.g.
an idle threat. ▶ v (usu. foll. by
away) spend (time) doing very
little; (of an engine) run slowly
with the gears disengaged.
idleness n **idler** n **idly** adv
idol n object of excessive devotion;
image of a god as an object of
worship. **idolatry** n worship of
idols. **idolatrous** adj **idolize** v
love or admire excessively.
idyll [id-ill] n scene or time of

great peace and happiness. **idyllic** adj **idyllically** adv

i.e. that is to say.

if conj on the condition or supposition that; whether; even though. ▶ n uncertainty or doubt, e.g. no ifs, ands, or buts. **iffy** adj Informal doubtful, uncertain.

igloo n, pl **-loos.** dome-shaped Inuit house made of snow and ice.

igneous [ig-nee-uss] adj (of rock) formed as molten rock cools and hardens.

ignite v catch fire or set fire to.

ignition n system that ignites the fuel-and-air mixture to start an engine; igniting.

ignoble adj dishonourable.

ignominy [ig-nom-in-ee] n humiliating disgrace. **ignominious** adj **ignominiously** adv

ignoramus n, pl **-muses.** ignorant person.

ignorant adj lacking knowledge; rude through lack of knowledge of good manners. **ignorance** n

ignore v refuse to notice, disregard deliberately.

iguana n large tropical American lizard.

ileum n lowest part of the small intestine.

ilk n type, e.g. others of his ilk.

ill adj not in good health; harmful or unpleasant, e.g. ill effects. ▶ n evil, harm. ▶ adv badly; hardly, with difficulty, e.g. I can ill afford to lose him. **ill at ease** uncomfortable, unable to relax. **illness** n **ill-advised** adj badly thought out; unwise. **ill-disposed** adj (often foll. by towards) unfriendly, unsympathetic. **ill-fated** adj doomed to end unhappily. **ill-gotten** adj obtained dishonestly. **ill-health** n condition of being unwell. **ill-mannered** adj having bad manners. **ill-treat** v

treat cruelly. **ill will** unkind feeling, hostility.

illegal adj against the law. **illegally** adv **illegality** n, pl **-ties.**

illegible adj unable to be read or deciphered.

illegitimate adj born of parents not married to each other; not lawful. **illegitimacy** n

illicit adj illegal; forbidden or disapproved of by society.

illiterate n, adj (person) unable to read or write. **illiteracy** n

illogical adj unreasonable; not logical. **illogicality** n

illuminate v light up; make clear, explain; decorate with lights; Hist decorate (a manuscript) with designs of gold and bright colours. **illumination** n **illuminating** adj

illusion n deceptive appearance or belief. **illusionist** n conjuror. **illusory** adj seeming to be true, but actually false.

illustrate v explain by use of examples; provide (a book or text) with pictures; be an example of. **illustration** n picture or diagram; example. **illustrative** adj **illustrator** n

illustrious adj famous and distinguished.

image n mental picture of someone or something; impression people have of a person, organization, etc.; representation of a person or thing in a work of art; optical reproduction of someone or something, for example in a mirror; person or thing that looks almost exactly like another; figure of speech, esp. a metaphor or simile. **imagery** n images collectively, esp. in the arts.

imagine v form a mental image of; think, believe, or guess.

imaginable adj **imaginary** adj existing only in the imagination.

imagination n ability to make mental images of things that may not exist in real life; creative mental ability. **imaginative** adj having or showing a lot of creative mental ability. **imaginatively** adv

imago [im-may-go] n, pl **imagoes**, **imagines** [im-maj-in-ees] sexually mature adult insect.

imam n leader of prayers in a mosque; title of some Islamic leaders.

imbalance n lack of balance or proportion.

imbecile [imb-ess-eel] n stupid person. ▶ adj (also **imbecilic**) stupid or senseless. **imbecility** n

imbibe v drink (alcoholic drinks); Lit absorb (ideas etc.).

imbroglio [imb-role-ee-oh] n, pl -ios. confusing and complicated situation.

imbue v -buing, -bued. (usu. foll. by with) fill or inspire with (ideals or principles).

IMF International Monetary Fund.

imitate v take as a model; copy the voice and mannerisms of, esp. for entertainment. **imitation** n copy of an original; imitating. **imitative** adj **imitator** n

immaculate adj completely clean or tidy; completely flawless. **immaculately** adv

immanent adj present within and throughout something. **immanence** n

immaterial adj not important, not relevant.

immature adj not fully developed; lacking wisdom or stability because of youth. **immaturity** n

immediate adj occurring at once; next or nearest in time, space, or relationship. **immediately** adv

immediacy n

immemorial adj since, from time **immemorial** longer than anyone can remember.

immense adj extremely large. **immensely** adv to a very great degree. **immensity** n

immerse v involve deeply, engross; plunge (something or someone) into liquid. **immersion** n

immersion heater electrical device in a domestic hot-water tank for heating water.

immigration n coming to a foreign country in order to settle there. **immigrant** n

imminent adj about to happen. **imminently** adv **imminence** n

immobile adj not moving; unable to move. **immobility** n

immobilize v make unable to move or work.

immoderate adj excessive or unreasonable.

immolate v kill as a sacrifice. **immolation** n

immoral adj morally wrong, corrupt; sexually depraved or promiscuous. **immorality** n

immortal adj living forever; famous for all time. ▶ n person whose fame will last for all time; immortal being. **immortality** n **immortalize** v

immune adj protected against a specific disease; (foll. by to) secure (against); (foll. by from) exempt (from). **immunity** n, pl -ties. ability to resist disease; freedom from prosecution, tax, etc. **immunize** v make immune to a disease. **immunization** n

immunodeficiency n deficiency in or breakdown of a person's ability to fight diseases.

immunology n branch of medicine concerned with the study of immunity. **immunological** adj

immunologist n

immure v Lit imprison.

immutable [im-mute-a-bl] adj unchangeable. **immutability** n

imp n (in folklore) mischievous small creature with magical powers; mischievous child.

impact n strong effect; (force of a) collision. ▶ v press firmly into something.

impair v weaken or damage. **impairment** n

impala [imp-ah-la] n southern African antelope.

impale v pierce with a sharp object.

impalpable adj difficult to define or understand.

impart v communicate (information); give.

impartial adj not favouring one side or the other. **impartially** adv **impartiality** n

impassable adj (of a road etc.) impossible to travel through or over.

impasse [am-pass] n situation in which progress is impossible.

impassioned adj full of emotion.

impassive adj showing no emotion, calm.

impatient adj irritable at any delay or difficulty; restless (to have or do something). **impatiently** adv **impatience** n

impeach v charge with a serious crime against the state. **impeachment** n

impeccable adj without fault, excellent. **impeccably** adv

impecunious adj penniless, poor.

impedance [imp-eed-anss] n Electricity measure of the opposition to the flow of an alternating current.

impede v hinder in action or progress. **impediment** n something that makes action, speech, or progress difficult.

impedimenta pl n objects impeding progress, esp. baggage or equipment.

impel v -pelling, -pelled. push or force (someone) to do something.

impending adj (esp. of something bad) about to happen.

impenetrable adj impossible to get through; impossible to understand.

imperative adj extremely urgent, vital; Grammar denoting a mood of verbs used in commands. ▶ n Grammar imperative mood.

imperceptible adj too slight or gradual to be noticed. **imperceptibly** adv

imperfect adj having faults or mistakes; not complete; Grammar denoting a tense of verbs describing continuous, incomplete, or repeated past actions. ▶ n Grammar imperfect tense. **imperfection** n

imperial adj of or like an empire or emperor; denoting a system of weights and measures formerly used in Britain. **imperialism** n rule by one country over many others. **imperialist** adj, n

imperil v -illing, -illed. put in danger.

imperious adj proud and domineering.

impersonal adj not relating to any particular person, objective; lacking human warmth or sympathy; Grammar (of a verb) without a personal subject, e.g. it is snowing. **impersonality** n

impersonate v pretend to be (another person); copy the voice and mannerisms of, esp. for entertainment. **impersonation** n **impersonator** n

impertinent adj disrespectful or rude. **impertinently** adv **impertinence** n

imperturbable adj calm, not excitable.

impervious adj (foll. by to) not letting (water etc.) through; not influenced by (a feeling, argument, etc.).

impetigo [imp-it-**tie**-go] n contagious skin disease.

impetuous adj done or acting without thought, rash. **impetuously** adv **impetuosity** n

impetus [**imp**-it-uss] n, pl **-tuses.** incentive, impulse; force that starts a body moving.

impinge v (foll. by on) affect or restrict.

impious [**imp**-ee-uss] adj showing a lack of respect or reverence.

impish adj mischievous.

implacable adj not prepared to be appeased, unyielding. **implacably** adv **implacability** n

implant n Med something put into someone's body, usu. by surgical operation. ▶ v put (something) into someone's body, usu. by surgical operation; fix firmly in someone's mind. **implantation** n

implement v carry out (instructions etc.). ▶ n tool, instrument. **implementation** n

implicate v show to be involved, esp. in a crime. **implication** n something implied.

implicit adj expressed indirectly; absolute and unquestioning, e.g. *implicit support.* **implicitly** adv

implore v beg earnestly.

imply v **-plying, -plied.** indicate by hinting, suggest; involve as a necessary consequence.

impolitic adj unwise or inadvisable.

imponderable n, adj (something) impossible to assess.

import v bring in (goods) from another country. ▶ n something imported; importance; meaning. **importation** n **importer** n

important adj of great significance or value; having influence or power. **importance** n

importunate adj persistent or demanding. **importune** v harass with persistent requests. **importunity** n, pl **-ties.**

impose v force the acceptance of; (foll. by on) take unfair advantage (of). **imposing** adj grand, impressive. **imposition** n unreasonable demand.

impossible adj not able to be done or to happen; absurd or unreasonable. **impossibly** adv **impossibility** n, pl **-ties.**

imposter, impostor n person who cheats or swindles by pretending to be someone else.

impotent [**imp**-a-tent] adj powerless; (of a man) incapable of sexual intercourse. **impotence** n **impotently** adv

impound v take legal possession of, confiscate.

impoverish v make poor or weak. **impoverishment** n

impracticable adj incapable of being put into practice.

impractical adj not sensible.

imprecation n curse.

impregnable adj impossible to break into. **impregnability** n

impregnate v saturate, spread all through; make pregnant. **impregnation** n

impresario n, pl **-ios.** person who runs theatre performances, concerts, etc.

impress v affect strongly, usu. favourably; stress, emphasize; imprint, stamp. **impression** n effect, esp. a strong or favourable one; vague idea; impersonation for entertainment; mark made by pressing. **impressionable** adj easily impressed or influenced.

Impressionism n art style that

gives a general effect or mood rather than form or structure. **Impressionist** n **Impressionistic** adj

impressive adj making a strong impression, esp. through size, importance, or quality.

imprimatur [imp-rim-**ah**-ter] n official approval to print a book.

imprint n mark made by printing or stamping; publisher's name and address on a book. ▶ v produce (a mark) by printing or stamping.

imprison v put in prison. **imprisonment** n

improbable adj not likely to be true or to happen. **improbability** n, pl -**ties.**

impromptu adj without planning or preparation.

improper adj indecent; incorrect or irregular. **improper fraction** fraction in which the numerator is larger than the denominator, as in ⅔.

impropriety [imp-roe-**pry**-a-tee] n, pl -**ties.** unsuitable or slightly improper behaviour.

improve v make or become better. **improvement** n

improvident adj not planning for future needs. **improvidence** n

improvise v make use of whatever materials are available; make up (a piece of music, speech, etc.) as one goes along. **improvisation** n

impudent adj cheeky, disrespectful. **impudently** adv **impudence** n

impugn [imp-**yoon**] v challenge the truth or validity of.

impulse n sudden urge to do something; short electrical signal passing along a wire or nerve or through the air. **on impulse** suddenly and without planning. **impulsive** adj acting or done without careful consideration. **impulsively** adv

impunity [imp-**yoon**-it-ee] n **with impunity** without punishment.

impure adj having dirty or unwanted substances mixed in; immoral, obscene. **impurity** n

impute v attribute responsibility to. **imputation** n

in prep indicating position inside, state or situation, etc., e.g. in the net; in tears. ▶ adv indicating position inside, entry into, etc., e.g. she stayed in; come in. ▶ adj fashionable. **inward** adj directed towards the middle; situated within; spiritual or mental. ▶ adv (also **inwards**) towards the inside or middle. **inwardly** adv

inability n lack of means or skill to do something.

inaccurate adj not correct. **inaccuracy** n, pl -**ties.**

inadequate adj not enough; not good enough. **inadequacy** n

inadvertent adj unintentional. **inadvertently** adv

inalienable adj not able to be taken away, e.g. an inalienable right.

inane adj senseless, silly. **inanity** n

inanimate adj not living.

inappropriate adj not suitable.

inarticulate adj unable to express oneself clearly or well.

inasmuch as conj because or in so far as.

inaugurate v open or begin the use of, esp. with ceremony; formally establish (a new leader) in office. **inaugural** adj **inauguration** n

inauspicious adj unlucky, likely to have an unfavourable outcome.

inboard adj (of a boat's engine) inside the hull.

inborn adj existing from birth, natural.

inbred adj produced as a result of inbreeding; inborn or ingrained.

inbreeding n breeding of animals or people that are closely related.

inbuilt adj present from the start.

Inc. US & Aust (of a company) incorporated.

incalculable adj too great to be estimated.

in camera adv see CAMERA.

incandescent adj glowing with heat. **incandescence** n

incantation n ritual chanting of magic words or sounds.

incapable adj (foll. by of) unable (to do something); incompetent.

incapacitate v deprive of strength or ability. **incapacity** n

incarcerate v imprison. **incarceration** n

incarnate adj in human form. **incarnation** n **Incarnation** n Christianity God's coming to earth in human form as Jesus Christ.

incendiary [in-**send**-ya-ree] adj (of a bomb, attack, etc.) designed to cause fires. ▶ n, pl -**aries**. bomb designed to cause fires.

incense[1] v make very angry.

incense[2] n substance that gives off a sweet perfume when burned.

incentive n something that encourages effort or action.

inception n beginning.

incessant adj never stopping. **incessantly** adv

incest n sexual intercourse between two people too closely related to marry. **incestuous** adj

inch n unit of length equal to one twelfth of a foot or 2.54 centimetres. ▶ v move slowly and gradually.

inchoate [in-**koe**-ate] adj just begun and not yet properly developed.

incidence n extent or frequency of occurrence.

incident n something that happens; event involving violence.

incidental adj occurring in connection with or resulting from something more important. **incidentally** adv **incidental music** background music for a film or play.

incinerate v burn to ashes. **incineration** n **incinerator** n furnace for burning rubbish.

incipient adj just starting to appear or happen.

incise v cut into with a sharp tool. **incision** n **incisor** n front tooth, used for biting into food. **incisive** adj direct and forceful.

incite v stir up, provoke. **incitement** n

incivility n, pl -**ties**. rudeness or a rude remark.

inclement adj (of weather) stormy or severe.

incline v lean, slope; (cause to) have a certain disposition or tendency. ▶ n slope. **inclination** n liking, tendency, or preference; slope.

include v have as part of the whole; put in as part of a set or group. **inclusion** n **inclusive** adj including everything (specified). **inclusively** adv

incognito [in-kog-**nee**-toe] adj, adv having adopted a false identity. ▶ n, pl -**tos**. false identity.

incoherent adj unclear and impossible to understand. **incoherence** n **incoherently** adv

income n amount of money earned from work, investments, etc. **income support** (in New Zealand) allowance paid by the government to people with a very low income. **income tax** personal tax levied on annual income.

incoming adj coming in; about to come into office.

incommode v cause inconvenience to.

incommunicado adj, adv deprived of communication with other people.

incomparable adj beyond comparison, unequalled. **incomparably** adv

incompatible adj inconsistent or conflicting. **incompatibility** n

incompetent adj not having the necessary ability or skill to do something. **incompetence** n

inconceivable adj extremely unlikely, unimaginable.

inconclusive adj not giving a final decision or result.

incongruous adj inappropriate or out of place. **incongruously** adv **incongruity** n, pl **-ties.**

inconsequential adj unimportant, insignificant.

inconsiderable adj not inconsiderable fairly large.

inconstant adj liable to change one's loyalties or opinions.

incontinent adj unable to control one's bladder or bowels. **incontinence** n

incontrovertible adj impossible to deny or disprove.

inconvenience n trouble or difficulty. ▶ v cause trouble or difficulty to. **inconvenient** adj

incorporate v include or be included as part of a larger unit. **incorporation** n

incorporeal adj without material form.

incorrigible adj beyond correction or reform.

incorruptible adj too honest to be bribed or corrupted; not subject to decay.

increase v make or become greater in size, number, etc. ▶ n rise in number, size, etc.; amount by which something increases. **increasingly** adv

incredible adj hard to believe or

imagine; Informal marvellous, amazing. **incredibly** adv

incredulous adj not willing to believe something. **incredulity** n

increment n increase in money or value, esp. a regular salary increase. **incremental** adj

incriminate v make (someone) seem guilty of a crime. **incriminating** adj

incubate [in-cube-ate] v (of a bird) hatch (eggs) by sitting on them; grow (bacteria); (of bacteria) remain inactive in an animal or person before causing disease. **incubation** n **incubator** n heated enclosed apparatus for rearing premature babies; apparatus for artificially hatching birds' eggs.

incubus [in-cube-uss] n, pl **-bi, -buses.** (in folklore) demon believed to have sex with sleeping women; nightmarish burden or worry.

inculcate v fix in someone's mind by constant repetition. **inculcation** n

incumbent n person holding a particular office or position. ▶ adj **it is incumbent on it** is the duty of. **incumbency** n, pl **-cies.**

incur v -curring, -curred. cause (something unpleasant) to happen.

incurable adj not able to be cured. **incurably** adv

incurious adj showing no curiosity or interest.

incursion n sudden brief invasion.

indebted adj owing gratitude for help or favours; owing money. **indebtedness** n

indecent adj morally or sexually offensive; unsuitable or unseemly, e.g. indecent haste. **indecently** adv **indecency** n **indecent assault** sexual attack which does not include rape. **indecent exposure** showing of one's genitals in public.

indecipherable adj impossible to read.

indeed adv really, certainly. ▶ interj expression of indignation or surprise.

indefatigable adj never getting tired. **indefatigably** adv

indefensible adj unable to be justified; impossible to defend.

indefinite adj without exact limits, e.g. for an indefinite period; vague, unclear. **indefinite article** Grammar the word a or an. **indefinitely** adv

indelible adj impossible to erase or remove; making indelible marks. **indelibly** adv

indelicate adj offensive or embarrassing.

indemnify v -ifying, -ified. secure against loss, damage, or liability; compensate for loss or damage. **indemnity** n, pl -ties. insurance against loss or damage; compensation for loss or damage.

indent v start (a line of writing) further from the margin than the other lines; order (goods) using a special order form. **indentation** n dent in a surface or edge.

indenture n contract, esp. one binding an apprentice to his or her employer.

independent adj free from the control or influence of others; separate; financially self-reliant; capable of acting for oneself or on one's own. ▶ n politician who does not represent any political party. **independently** adv **independence** n

in-depth adj detailed, thorough.

indescribable adj too intense or extreme for words. **indescribably** adv

indeterminate adj uncertain in extent, amount, or nature.

indeterminacy n

index n, pl **indices** [in-diss-eez] alphabetical list of names or subjects dealt with in a book; file or catalogue used to find things. ▶ v provide (a book) with an index; enter in an index; make index-linked. **index finger** finger next to the thumb. **index-linked** adj (of pensions, wages, etc.) rising or falling in line with the cost of living.

Indian n, adj (person) from India; Native American. **Indian summer** period of warm sunny weather in autumn.

indicate v be a sign or symptom of; point out; state briefly; (of a measuring instrument) show a reading of. **indication** n **indicative** adj (foll. by of) suggesting; Grammar denoting a mood of verbs used to make a statement. ▶ n Grammar indicative mood. **indicator** n something acting as a sign or indication; flashing light on a vehicle showing the driver's intention to turn; dial or gauge.

indict [in-dite] v formally charge with a crime. **indictable** adj **indictment** n

indie adj Informal (of rock music) released by an independent record company.

indifferent adj showing no interest or concern; of poor quality. **indifference** n **indifferently** adv

indigenous [in-dij-in-uss] adj born in or natural to a country.

indigent adj extremely poor. **indigence** n

indigestion n (discomfort or pain caused by) difficulty in digesting food. **indigestible** adj

indignation n anger at something unfair or wrong. **indignant** adj feeling or showing indignation.

indignantly adv

indignity n, pl **-ties.** embarrassing or humiliating treatment.

indigo adj deep violet-blue. ▶ n dye of this colour.

indirect adj done or caused by someone or something else; not by a straight route. **indirect object** Grammar person or thing indirectly affected by the action of a verb, e.g. Amy in I bought Amy a bag. **indirect tax** added to the price of something.

indiscreet adj incautious or tactless in revealing secrets. **indiscreetly** adv **indiscretion** n

indiscriminate adj showing lack of careful thought.

indispensable adj absolutely essential.

indisposed adj unwell, ill. **indisposition** n

indisputable adj beyond doubt. **indisputably** adv

indissoluble adj permanent.

indium n Chem soft silvery-white metallic element.

individual adj characteristic of or meant for a single person or thing; separate, distinct; distinctive, unusual. ▶ n single person or thing. **individually** adv **individuality** n **individualism** n principle of living one's life in one's own way. **individualist** n **individualistic** adj

indoctrinate v teach (someone) to accept a doctrine or belief uncritically. **indoctrination** n

Indo-European adj, n (of) a family of languages spoken in most of Europe and much of Asia, including English, Russian, and Hindi.

indolent adj lazy. **indolence** n

indomitable adj too strong to be defeated or discouraged. **indomitably** adv

indoor adj inside a building. **indoors** adv

indubitable adj beyond doubt, certain. **indubitably** adv

induce v persuade or influence; cause; Med cause (a woman) to go into labour or bring on (labour) by the use of drugs etc. **inducement** n something used to persuade someone to do something.

induct v formally install (someone, esp. a clergyman) in office.

inductance n property of an electric circuit creating voltage by a change of current.

induction n reasoning process by which general conclusions are drawn from particular instances; process by which electrical or magnetic properties are produced by the proximity of an electrified or magnetic object; formal introduction into an office or position. **inductive** adj **induction coil** transformer for producing a high voltage from a low voltage. **induction course** training course to help familiarize someone with a new job.

indulge v allow oneself pleasure; allow (someone) to have or do everything he or she wants. **indulgence** n something allowed because it gives pleasure; act of indulging oneself or someone else; liberal or tolerant treatment. **indulgent** adj **indulgently** adv

industrial adj of, used in, or employed in industry. **industrialize** v develop large-scale industry in (a country or region). **industrialization** n **industrial action** ways in which workers can protest about their conditions, e.g. by striking or working to rule. **industrial estate** area of land set aside for factories and warehouses.

industrial relations relations between management and workers.

industry n, pl **-tries.** manufacture of goods; branch of this, e.g. the music industry; quality of working hard. **industrious** adj hard-working.

inebriate n, adj (person who is) habitually drunk. **inebriated** adj drunk. **inebriation** n

inedible adj not fit to be eaten.

ineffable adj too great for words. **ineffably** adv

ineffectual adj having very little effect.

ineligible adj not qualified for or entitled to something.

ineluctable adj impossible to avoid.

inept adj clumsy, lacking skill. **ineptitude** n

inequitable adj unfair.

ineradicable adj impossible to remove.

inert adj without the power of motion or resistance; chemically unreactive. **inertness** n

inertia n feeling of unwillingness to do anything; Physics tendency of a body to remain still or continue moving unless a force is applied to it.

inescapable adj unavoidable.

inestimable adj too great to be estimated. **inestimably** adv

inevitable adj unavoidable, sure to happen. **the inevitable** something that cannot be prevented. **inevitably** adv **inevitability** n

inexorable adj unable to be prevented from continuing or progressing. **inexorably** adv

inexpert adj lacking skill.

inexplicable adj impossible to explain. **inexplicably** adv

in extremis adv Latin in great difficulty; on the point of death.

inextricable adj impossible to escape from; impossible to disentangle or separate.

infallible adj never wrong. **infallibly** adv **infallibility** n

infamous [in-fam-uss] adj well-known for something bad. **infamously** adv **infamy** n

infant n very young child. **infancy** n early childhood; early stage of development. **infantile** adj childish.

infanticide n murder of an infant; person guilty of this.

infantry n soldiers who fight on foot.

infatuated adj feeling intense unreasoning passion. **infatuation** n intense unreasoning passion.

infect v affect with a disease; affect with a feeling. **infection** n **infectious** adj (of a disease) spreading without actual contact; spreading from person to person, e.g. infectious enthusiasm.

infer v -ferring, -ferred. work out from evidence. **inference** n

inferior adj lower in quality, position, or status. ▶ n person of lower position or status. **inferiority** n

infernal adj of hell; Informal irritating. **infernally** adv

inferno n, pl -nos. intense raging fire.

infertile adj unable to produce offspring; (of soil) barren, not productive. **infertility** n

infest v inhabit or overrun in unpleasantly large numbers. **infestation** n

infidel n person with no religion; person who rejects a particular religion, esp. Christianity or Islam.

infidelity n, pl -ties. (act of) sexual unfaithfulness to one's husband, wife, or lover.

infighting n quarrelling within a group.

infiltrate v enter gradually and secretly. **infiltration** n **infiltrator** n

infinite [in-fin-it] adj without any limit or end. **infinitely** adv

infinitesimal adj extremely small.

infinitive n Grammar form of a verb not showing tense, person, or number, e.g. to sleep.

infinity n endless space, time, or number.

infirm adj physically or mentally weak. **infirmity** n, pl **-ties.**

infirmary n, pl **-ries.** hospital.

inflame v make angry or excited. **inflamed** adj (of part of the body) red, swollen, and painful because of infection. **inflammation** n

inflammable adj easily set on fire.

inflammatory adj likely to provoke anger.

inflate v expand by filling with air or gas; cause economic inflation in. **inflatable** adj able to be inflated. ▶ n plastic or rubber object which can be inflated.

inflation n inflating; increase in prices and fall in the value of money. **inflationary** adj

inflection, inflexion n change in the pitch of the voice; Grammar change in the form of a word to show grammatical use.

inflexible adj unwilling to be persuaded, obstinate; (of a policy etc.) firmly fixed, unalterable. **inflexibly** adv **inflexibility** n

inflict v impose (something unpleasant) on. **infliction** n.

inflorescence n Botany arrangement of flowers on a stem.

influence n effect of one person or thing on another; (person with) the power to have such an effect. ▶ v have an effect on. **influential** adj

influenza n contagious viral disease causing headaches, muscle pains, and fever.

influx n arrival or entry of many people or things.

info n Informal information.

inform v tell; give incriminating information to the police. **informant** n person who gives information. **information** n knowledge or facts. **informative** adj giving useful information. **information superhighway** worldwide network of computers transferring information at high speed. **information technology** use of computers and electronic technology to store and communicate information. **informer** n person who informs to the police.

informal adj relaxed and friendly; appropriate for everyday life or use. **informally** adv **informality** n

infra dig adj Informal beneath one's dignity.

infrared adj of or using rays below the red end of the visible spectrum.

infrastructure n basic facilities, services, and equipment needed for a country or organization to function properly.

infringe v break (a law or agreement). **infringement** n

infuriate v make very angry.

infuse v fill (with an emotion or quality); soak to extract flavour. **infusion** n infusing; liquid obtained by infusing.

ingenious [in-jean-ee-uss] adj showing cleverness and originality. **ingeniously** adv **ingenuity** [in-jen-new-it-ee] n

ingénue [an-jay-new] n naive young woman, esp. as a role played by an actress.

ingenuous [in-jen-new-uss] adj

unsophisticated and trusting.
ingenuously adv

ingest v take (food or liquid) into the body. **ingestion** n

inglorious adj dishonourable, shameful.

ingot n oblong block of cast metal.

ingrained adj firmly fixed.

ingratiate v try to make (oneself) popular with someone. **ingratiating** adj **ingratiatingly** adv

ingredient n component of a mixture or compound.

ingress n act or right of entering.

ingrowing adj (of a toenail) growing abnormally into the flesh.

inhabit v -habiting, -habited. live in. **inhabitable** adj **inhabitant** n

inhale v breathe in (air, smoke, etc.). **inhalation** n **inhalant** n medical preparation inhaled to help breathing problems. **inhaler** n container for an inhalant.

inherent adj existing as an inseparable part. **inherently** adv

inherit v -heriting, -herited. receive (money etc.) from someone who has died; receive (a characteristic) from an earlier generation; receive from a predecessor. **inheritance** n **inheritance tax** tax paid on property left at death. **inheritor** n

inhibit v -hibiting, -hibited. restrain (an impulse or desire); hinder or prevent (action). **inhibited** adj **inhibition** n feeling of fear or embarrassment that stops one from behaving naturally.

inhospitable adj not welcoming, unfriendly; difficult to live in, harsh.

inhuman adj cruel or brutal; not human.

inhumane adj cruel or brutal. **inhumanity** n

inimical adj unfavourable or hostile.

inimitable adj impossible to imitate, unique.

iniquity n, pl **-ties.** injustice or wickedness; wicked act. **iniquitous** adj

initial adj first, at the beginning. ▶ n first letter, esp. of a person's name. ▶ v -tialling, -tialled. sign with one's initials. **initially** adv

initiate v begin or set going; admit (someone) into a closed group; instruct in the basics of something. ▶ n recently initiated person. **initiation** n **initiator** n

initiative n first step, commencing move; ability to act independently.

inject v put (a fluid) into the body with a syringe; introduce (a new element), e.g. try to inject a bit of humour. **injection** n

injudicious adj showing poor judgment, unwise.

injunction n court order not to do something.

injure v hurt physically or mentally. **injury** n, pl **-ries. injury time** Sport playing time added at the end of a match to compensate for time spent treating injured players. **injurious** adj

injustice n unfairness; unfair action.

ink n coloured liquid used for writing or printing. ▶ v (foll. by in) mark in ink (something already marked in pencil). **inky** adj dark or black; covered in ink.

inkling n slight idea or suspicion.

inlaid adj set in another material so that the surface is smooth; made like this, e.g. an inlaid table.

inland adj, adv in or towards the interior of a country, away from the sea. **Inland Revenue** (in Britain) government department that collects taxes.

in-laws pl n one's husband's or wife's family.

inlay n inlaid substance or pattern.

inlet n narrow strip of water extending from the sea into the land; valve etc. through which liquid or gas enters.

in loco parentis *Latin* in place of a parent.

inmate *n* person living in an institution such as a prison.

inmost *adj* innermost.

inn *n* pub or small hotel, esp. in the country. **innkeeper** *n*

innards *pl n Informal* internal organs; working parts of a machine.

innate *adj* being part of someone's nature, inborn.

inner *adj* happening or located inside; relating to private feelings, e.g. *the inner self.* **innermost** *adj* furthest inside. **inner city** parts of a city near the centre, esp. having severe social and economic problems.

innings *n Sport* player's or side's turn of batting; period of opportunity.

innocent *adj* not guilty of a crime; without experience of evil; without malicious intent. ▶ *n* innocent person, esp. a child. **innocently** *adv* **innocence** *n*

innocuous *adj* not harmful. **innocuously** *adv*

innovation *n* new idea or method; introduction of new ideas or methods. **innovate** *v* **innovative** *adj* **innovator** *n*

innuendo *n, pl* **-does.** (remark making) an indirect reference to something rude or unpleasant.

innumerable *adj* too many to be counted.

innumerate *adj* having no understanding of mathematics or science. **innumeracy** *n*

inoculate *v* protect against disease by injecting with a vaccine. **inoculation** *n*

inoperable *adj* (of a tumour or cancer) unable to be surgically removed.

inopportune *adj* badly timed, unsuitable.

inordinate *adj* excessive.

inorganic *adj* not having the characteristics of living organisms; of chemical substances that do not contain carbon.

inpatient *n* patient who stays in a hospital for treatment.

input *n* resources put into a project etc.; data fed into a computer. ▶ *v* **-putting, -put.** enter (data) in a computer.

inquest *n* official inquiry into a sudden death.

inquire *v* seek information or ask (about). **inquirer** *n*

inquiry *n, pl* **-ries.** question; investigation.

inquisition *n* thorough investigation; (**I-**) *Hist* organization within the Catholic Church for suppressing heresy. **inquisitor** *n* **inquisitorial** *adj*

inquisitive *adj* excessively curious about other people's affairs. **inquisitively** *adv*

inquorate *adj* without enough people present to make a quorum.

inroads *pl n* **make inroads into** start affecting or reducing.

insalubrious *adj* unpleasant, unhealthy, or sordid.

insane *adj* mentally ill; stupidly irresponsible. **insanely** *adv* **insanity** *n*

insanitary *adj* dirty or unhealthy.

insatiable [in-saysh-a-bl] *adj* unable to be satisfied.

inscribe *v* write or carve words on. **inscription** *n* words inscribed.

inscrutable *adj* mysterious, enigmatic. **inscrutably** *adv*

insect *n* small animal with six legs and usu. wings, such as an ant or fly. **insecticide** *n* substance for killing insects. **insectivorous** *adj* insect-eating.

insecure *adj* anxious, not confident; not safe or well-protected.

insemination *n* putting semen into a woman's or female animal's body to try to make her pregnant. **inseminate** *v*

insensate *adj* without sensation, unconscious; unfeeling.

insensible *adj* unconscious, without feeling; (foll. by *to* or *of*) not aware (of) or affected (by).

insensitive *adj* unaware of or ignoring other people's feelings. **insensitivity** *n*

inseparable *adj* (of two people) spending most of the time together; (of two things) impossible to separate.

insert *v* put inside or include. ▸ *n* something inserted. **insertion** *n*

inset *n* small picture inserted within a larger one.

inshore *adj* close to the shore. ▸ *adj, adv* towards the shore.

inside *prep* in or to the interior of. ▸ *adj* on or of the inside; by or from someone within an organization, e.g. *inside information*. ▸ *adv* on, in, or to the inside, indoors; *Brit, Aust & NZ slang* in(to) prison. ▸ *n* inner side, surface, or part. ▸ *pl Informal* stomach and bowels. **inside out** with the inside facing outwards. **know inside out** know thoroughly. **insider** *n* member of a group who has privileged knowledge about it.

insidious *adj* subtle or unseen but dangerous. **insidiously** *adv*

insight *n* deep understanding.

insignia *n, pl* **-nias, -nia.** badge or emblem of honour or office.

insignificant *adj* not important. **insignificance** *n*

insincere *adj* showing false feelings, not genuine. **insincerely** *adv* **insincerity** *n, pl* **-ties.**

insinuate *v* suggest indirectly; work (oneself) into a position by gradual manoeuvres. **insinuation** *n*

insipid *adj* lacking interest, spirit, or flavour.

insist *v* demand or state firmly. **insistent** *adj* making persistent demands; demanding attention. **insistently** *adv* **insistence** *n*

in situ *adv, adj Latin* in its original position.

in so far as, insofar as *prep* to the extent that.

insole *n* inner sole of a shoe or boot.

insolent *adj* rude and disrespectful. **insolence** *n* **insolently** *adv*

insoluble *adj* incapable of being solved; incapable of being dissolved.

insolvent *adj* unable to pay one's debts. **insolvency** *n*

insomnia *n* inability to sleep. **insomniac** *n*

insouciant *adj* carefree and unconcerned. **insouciance** *n*

inspect *v* check closely or officially. **inspection** *n* **inspector** *n* person who inspects; high-ranking police officer.

inspire *v* fill with enthusiasm, stimulate; arouse (an emotion). **inspiration** *n* creative influence or stimulus; brilliant idea. **inspirational** *adj*

instability *n* lack of steadiness or reliability.

install *v* put in and prepare (equipment) for use; place (a person) formally in a position or rank. **installation** *n* installing; equipment installed; place containing equipment for a particular purpose, e.g. *oil installations.*

instalment *n* any of the portions

of a thing presented or a debt paid in successive parts.

instance n particular example. ▶ v mention as an example. **for instance** as an example.

instant n very brief time; particular moment. ▶ adj happening at once; (of foods) requiring little preparation. **instantly** adv

instantaneous adj happening at once. **instantaneously** adv

instead adv as a replacement or substitute.

instep n part of the foot forming the arch between the ankle and toes; part of a shoe or boot covering this.

instigate v cause to happen. **instigation** n **instigator** n

instil v **-stilling, -stilled.** introduce (an idea etc.) gradually into someone's mind.

instinct n inborn tendency to behave in a certain way. **instinctive** adj **instinctively** adv

institute n organization set up for a specific purpose, esp. research or teaching. ▶ v start or establish.

institution n large important organization such as a university or bank; hospital etc. for people with special needs; long-established custom. **institutional** adj **institutionalize** v

instruct v order to do something; teach (someone) how to do something. **instruction** n order to do something; teaching. ▶ pl information on how to do or use something. **instructive** adj informative or helpful. **instructor** n

instrument n tool used for particular work; object played to produce a musical sound; measuring device to show height, speed, etc.; Informal someone or something used to achieve an aim. **instrumental** adj (foll. by in) having an important function (in); played by or composed for musical instruments.

instrumentalist n player of a musical instrument.

instrumentation n set of instruments in a car etc.; arrangement of music for instruments.

insubordinate adj not submissive to authority. **insubordination** n

insufferable adj unbearable.

insular adj not open to new ideas, narrow-minded. **insularity** n

insulate v prevent or reduce the transfer of electricity, heat, or sound by surrounding or lining with a nonconducting material; isolate or set apart. **insulation** n **insulator** n

insulin n hormone produced in the pancreas that controls the amount of sugar in the blood.

insult v behave rudely to, offend. ▶ n insulting remark or action. **insulting** adj

insuperable adj impossible to overcome.

insupportable adj impossible to tolerate; impossible to justify.

insurance n agreement by which one makes regular payments to a company who pay an agreed sum if damage, loss, or death occurs; money paid to or by an insurance company; means of protection. **insure** v protect by insurance. **insurance policy** contract of insurance.

insurgent n, adj (person) in revolt against an established authority. **insurrection** n rebellion.

intact adj not changed or damaged in any way.

intaglio [in-tah-lee-oh] n, pl **-lios.** (gem carved with) an engraved design.

intake n amount or number taken in.

integer n positive or negative whole number or zero.

integral adj being an essential part of a whole. ▶ n Maths sum of a large number of very small quantities.

integrate v combine into a whole; amalgamate (a religious or racial group) into a community. **integration** n **integrated circuit** tiny electronic circuit on a chip of semiconducting material.

integrity n quality of having high moral principles; quality of being united.

intellect n power of thinking and reasoning.

intellectual adj of or appealing to the intellect; clever, intelligent. ▶ n intellectual person. **intellectually** adv

intelligent adj able to understand, learn, and think things out quickly; (of a computerized device) able to initiate or modify action in the light of ongoing events. **intelligence** n quality of being intelligent; secret government or military information; people or department collecting such information. **intelligently** adv

intelligentsia n intellectual or cultured people in a society.

intelligible adj able to be understood. **intelligibility** n

intemperate adj unrestrained, uncontrolled; drinking alcohol to excess. **intemperance** n

intend v propose or plan (to do something); have as one's purpose.

intense adj of great strength or degree; deeply emotional. **intensity** n **intensify** v -fying, -fied. make or become more intense. **intensification** n

intensive adj using or needing concentrated effort or resources. **intensively** adv

intent n intention. ▶ adj paying close attention. **intently** adv **intentness** n **intent on doing something** determined to do something.

intention n something intended. **intentional** adj planned in advance, deliberate. **intentionally** adv

inter [in-ter] v -terring, -terred. bury (a corpse). **interment** n

inter- prefix between or among, e.g. international.

interact v act on or in close relation with each other. **interaction** n **interactive** adj

interbreed v breed within a related group.

intercede v try to end a dispute between two people or groups. **intercession** n

intercept v seize or stop in transit. **interception** n

interchange v (cause to) exchange places. ▶ n motorway junction. **interchangeable** adj

Intercity adj ® (in Britain) denoting a fast train (service) travelling between cities.

intercom n internal communication system with loudspeakers.

intercontinental adj travelling between or linking continents.

intercourse n sexual intercourse; communication or dealings between people or groups.

interdiction, interdict n formal order forbidding something.

interdisciplinary adj involving more than one branch of learning.

interest n desire to know or hear more about something; something in which one is interested; (often pl) advantage, benefit; sum paid for the use of borrowed money; (often pl) right or share. ▶ v arouse the interest of. **interested** adj feeling or showing interest; involved in or affected by something. **interesting** adj **interestingly** adv

interface n area where two things interact or link; circuit linking a computer and another device.

interfere v try to influence other people's affairs where one is not involved or wanted; (foll. by with) clash (with); (foll. by with) Brit, Aust & NZ euphemistic abuse (a child) sexually. **interfering** adj **interference** n interfering; Radio interruption of reception by atmospherics or unwanted signals.

interferon n protein that stops the development of an invading virus.

interim adj temporary or provisional.

interior n inside; inland region. ▶ adj inside, inner; mental or spiritual.

interject v make (a remark) suddenly or as an interruption. **interjection** n

interlace v join together as if by weaving.

interlink v connect together.

interlock v join firmly together.

interlocutor [in-ter-lok-yew-ter] n person who takes part in a conversation.

interloper [in-ter-lope-er] n person in a place or situation where he or she has no right to be.

interlude n short rest or break in an activity or event.

intermarry v (of families, races, or religions) become linked by marriage. **intermarriage** n

intermediary n, pl -ries. person trying to create agreement between others.

intermediate adj coming between

two points or extremes.

intermezzo [in-ter-met-so] n, pl -zos. short piece of music, esp. one performed between the acts of an opera.

interminable adj seemingly endless because boring. **interminably** adv

intermingle v mix together.

intermission n interval between parts of a play, film, etc.

intermittent adj occurring at intervals. **intermittently** adv

intern v imprison, esp. during a war. ▶ n trainee doctor in a hospital. **internment** n **internee** n person who is interned.

internal adj of or on the inside; within a country or organization; spiritual or mental. **internally** adv **internal-combustion engine** engine powered by the explosion of a fuel-and-air mixture within the cylinders.

international adj of or involving two or more countries. ▶ n game or match between teams of different countries; player in such a match. **internationally** adv

internecine adj mutually destructive.

Internet, internet n large international computer network.

interplanetary adj of or linking planets.

interplay n action and reaction of two things upon each other.

interpolate [in-ter-pole-ate] v insert (a comment or passage) into (a conversation or text). **interpolation** n

interpose v insert between or among things; say as an interruption.

interpret v explain the meaning of; translate orally from one language into another; convey the meaning of (a poem, song, etc.)

in performance. **interpretation** n
interpreter n person who
translates orally from one
language into another.
interregnum n, pl **-nums, -na.**
interval between reigns.
interrogate v question closely.
interrogation n **interrogative** adj
questioning. ▶ n word used in
asking a question, such as how or
why. **interrogator** n
interrupt v break into (a
conversation etc.); stop (a process
or activity) temporarily.
interruption n
intersect v (of roads) meet and
cross; divide by passing across or
through. **intersection** n
interspersed adj scattered
(among, between, or on).
interstellar adj between or among
stars.
interstice [in-ter-stiss] n small
crack or gap between things.
intertwine v twist together.
interval n time between two
particular moments or events;
break between parts of a play,
concert, etc.; difference in pitch
between musical notes. **at
intervals** repeatedly; with spaces
left between.
intervene v involve oneself in a
situation, esp. to prevent conflict;
happen so as to stop something.
intervention n
interview n formal discussion, esp.
between a job-seeker and an
employer; questioning of a
well-known person about his or
her career, views, etc., by a
reporter. ▶ v conduct an interview
with. **interviewee** n **interviewer**
n
interweave v weave together.
intestate adj not having made a
will. **intestacy** n
intestine n (often pl) lower part of

the alimentary canal between the
stomach and the anus. **intestinal**
adj **intestinally** adv
intimate[1] adj having a close
personal relationship; personal or
private; (of knowledge) extensive
and detailed; (foll. by with)
Euphemistic having a sexual
relationship (with); having a
friendly quiet atmosphere. ▶ n
close friend. **intimately** adv
intimacy n
intimate[2] v hint at or suggest;
announce. **intimation** n
intimidate v subdue or influence
by fear. **intimidating** adj
intimidation n
into prep indicating motion
towards the centre, result of a
change, division, etc., e.g. into the
valley; turned into a madman; cut
into pieces; Informal interested in.
intolerable adj more than can be
endured. **intolerably** adv
intolerant adj refusing to accept
practices and beliefs different from
one's own. **intolerance** n
intonation n sound pattern
produced by variations in the
voice.
intone v speak or recite in an
unvarying tone of voice.
intoxicate v make drunk; excite to
excess. **intoxicant** n intoxicating
drink.
intoxication n state of being
drunk; overexcited state.
intractable adj (of a person)
difficult to control; (of a problem
or issue) difficult to deal with.
intranet n Computers internal
network that makes use of
Internet technology.
intransigent adj refusing to
change one's attitude.
intransigence n
intransitive adj (of a verb) not
taking a direct object.

intrauterine *adj* within the womb.

intravenous [in-tra-vee-nuss] *adj* into a vein. **intravenously** *adv*

intrepid *adj* fearless, bold. **intrepidity** *n*

intricate *adj* involved or complicated; full of fine detail. **intricately** *adv* **intricacy** *n, pl* -cies.

intrigue *v* make interested or curious; plot secretly. ▶ *n* secret plotting; secret love affair. **intriguing** *adj*

intrinsic *adj* essential to the basic nature of something. **intrinsically** *adv*

introduce *v* present (someone) by name (to another person); present (a radio or television programme); bring forward for discussion; bring into use; insert. **introduction** *n* presentation of one person to another; preliminary part or treatment. **introductory** *adj*

introspection *n* examination of one's own thoughts and feelings. **introspective** *adj*

introvert *n* person concerned more with his or her thoughts and feelings than with the outside world. **introverted** *adj* **introversion** *n*

intrude *v* come in or join in without being invited. **intrusion** *n* **intrusive** *adj*

intruder *n* person who enters a place without permission.

intuition *n* instinctive knowledge or insight without conscious reasoning. **intuitive** *adj* **intuitively** *adv*

Inuit *n* indigenous inhabitant of North America or Greenland.

inundate *v* flood; overwhelm. **inundation** *n*

inured *adj* accustomed, esp. to hardship or danger.

invade *v* enter (a country) by military force; enter in large numbers; disturb (someone's privacy). **invader** *n*

invalid[1] *adj, n* disabled or chronically ill (person). ▶ *v* (often foll. by *out*) dismiss from active service because of illness or injury. **invalidity** *n*

invalid[2] *adj* having no legal force; (of an argument etc.) not valid because based on a mistake. **invalidate** *v* make or show to be invalid.

invaluable *adj* of very great value or worth.

invasion *n* invading; intrusion, e.g. *an invasion of privacy.*

invective *n* abusive speech or writing.

inveigh [in-**vay**] *v* (foll. by *against*) criticize strongly.

inveigle *v* coax by cunning or trickery.

invent *v* think up or create (something new); make up (a story, excuse, etc.). **invention** *n* something invented; ability to invent. **inventive** *adj* creative and resourceful. **inventiveness** *n* **inventor** *n*

inventory *n, pl* -tories. detailed list of goods or furnishings.

inverse *adj* reversed in effect, sequence, direction, etc.; *Maths* linking two variables in such a way that one increases as the other decreases. **inversely** *adv*

invert *v* turn upside down or inside out. **inversion** *n* **inverted commas** quotation marks.

invertebrate *n* animal with no backbone.

invest *v* spend (money, time, etc.) on something with the expectation of profit; (foll. by *with*) give (power or rights) to. **investment** *n* money invested; something invested in. **investor** *n*

invest in v buy.

investigate v inquire into, examine. **investigation** n

investigative adj **investigator** n

investiture n formal installation of a person in an office or rank.

inveterate adj firmly established in a habit or condition.

invidious adj likely to cause resentment.

invigilate v supervise people sitting an examination. **invigilator** n

invigorate v give energy to, refresh.

invincible adj impossible to defeat. **invincibility** n

inviolable adj unable to be broken or violated.

inviolate adj unharmed, unaffected.

invisible adj not able to be seen. **invisibly** adv **invisibility** n

invite v request the company of; ask politely for; encourage or provoke, e.g. *the two works inevitably invite comparison.* ▶ n *Informal* invitation. **inviting** adj tempting, attractive. **invitation** n

in-vitro adj happening outside the body in an artificial environment.

invoice v, n (present with) a bill for goods or services supplied.

invoke v put (a law or penalty) into operation; prompt or cause (a certain feeling); call on (a god or spirit) for help, inspiration, etc. **invocation** n

involuntary adj not done consciously, unintentional. **involuntarily** adv

involve v include as a necessary part; affect, concern; implicate (a person). **involved** adj complicated; concerned, taking part. **involvement** n

invulnerable adj not able to be wounded or harmed.

inward adj, adv see IN.

iodine n *Chem* bluish-black element used in medicine and photography. **iodize** v treat with iodine.

ion n electrically charged atom. **ionic** adj **ionize** v change into ions. **ionization** n **ionosphere** n region of ionized air in the upper atmosphere that reflects radio waves.

iota n very small amount.

IOU n signed paper acknowledging debt.

IPA International Phonetic Alphabet.

ipso facto adv *Latin* by that very fact.

IQ intelligence quotient.

IRA Irish Republican Army.

irascible adj easily angered. **irascibility** n

irate adj very angry.

ire n *Lit* anger.

iridescent adj having shimmering changing colours like a rainbow. **iridescence** n

iridium n *Chem* very hard corrosion-resistant metal.

iris n coloured circular membrane of the eye containing the pupil; tall plant with purple, yellow, or white flowers.

Irish adj of Ireland.

irk v irritate, annoy. **irksome** adj irritating, annoying.

iron n strong silvery-white metallic element, widely used for structural and engineering purposes; appliance used, when heated, to press clothes; metal-headed golf club. ▶ pl chains, restraints. ▶ adj made of iron; strong, inflexible, e.g. *iron will.* ▶ v smooth (clothes or fabric) with an iron. **ironing** n clothes to be ironed. **ironing board** long cloth-covered board with folding legs, for ironing clothes. **Iron Age** era when iron tools were used. **iron out** v settle (a problem) through discussion.

ironic, ironical *adj* using irony; odd or amusing because the opposite of what one would expect. **ironically** *adv*

ironmonger *n* shopkeeper or shop dealing in hardware. **ironmongery** *n*

ironstone *n* rock consisting mainly of iron ore.

irony *n, pl* **-nies.** mildly sarcastic use of words to imply the opposite of what is said; aspect of a situation that is odd or amusing because the opposite of what one would expect.

irradiate *v* subject to or treat with radiation. **irradiation** *n*

irrational *adj* not based on or not using logical reasoning.

irredeemable *adj* not able to be reformed or corrected.

irreducible *adj* impossible to put in a simpler form.

irrefutable *adj* impossible to deny or disprove.

irregular *adj* not regular or even; not conforming to accepted practice; (of a word) not following the typical pattern of formation in a language. **irregularly** *adv* **irregularity** *n, pl* **-ties.**

irrelevant *adj* not connected with the matter in hand. **irrelevantly** *adv* **irrelevance** *n*

irreparable *adj* not able to be repaired or put right. **irreparably** *adv*

irreplaceable *adj* impossible to replace.

irreproachable *adj* blameless, faultless.

irresistible *adj* too attractive or strong to resist. **irresistibly** *adv*

irrespective *of prep* without taking account of.

irresponsible *adj* not showing or not done with due care for the consequences of one's actions or attitudes; not capable of accepting responsibility. **irresponsibility** *n*

irreverent *adj* not showing due respect. **irreverence** *n*

irreversible *adj* not able to be reversed or put right again, e.g. *irreversible change.* **irreversibly** *adv*

irrevocable *adj* not possible to change or undo. **irrevocably** *adv*

irrigate *v* supply (land) with water by artificial channels or pipes. **irrigation** *n*

irritate *v* annoy, anger; cause (a body part) to itch or become inflamed. **irritable** *adj* easily annoyed. **irritably** *adv* **irritant** *n, adj* (person or thing) causing irritation. **irritation** *n*

is *v* third person singular present tense of BE.

ISA (in Britain) Individual Savings Account.

isinglass [**ize**-ing-glass] *n* kind of gelatine obtained from some freshwater fish.

Islam *n* Muslim religion teaching that there is one God and that Mohammed is his prophet; Muslim countries and civilization. **Islamic** *adj*

island *n* piece of land surrounded by water. **islander** *n* person who lives on an island; (I-) *NZ* Pacific Islander.

isle *n Poetic* island. **islet** *n* small island.

isobar [**ice**-oh-bar] *n* line on a map connecting places of equal atmospheric pressure.

isolate *v* place apart or alone; *Chem* obtain (a substance) in uncombined form. **isolation** *n* **isolationism** *n* policy of not participating in international affairs. **isolationist** *n, adj*

isomer [**ice**-oh-mer] *n* substance whose molecules contain the same atoms as another but in a different arrangement.

isometric adj relating to muscular contraction without shortening of the muscle. **isometrics** pl n isometric exercises.

isosceles triangle [ice-soss-ill-eez] n triangle with two sides of equal length.

isotherm [ice-oh-therm] n line on a map connecting points of equal temperature.

isotope [ice-oh-tope] n one of two or more atoms with the same number of protons in the nucleus but a different number of neutrons.

ISP Internet service provider.

issue n topic of interest or discussion; reason for quarrelling; particular edition of a magazine or newspaper; outcome or result; Law child or children. ▶ v make (a statement etc.) publicly; supply officially (with); produce and make available. **take issue with** disagree with.

isthmus [iss-muss] n, pl -muses. narrow strip of land connecting two areas of land.

it pron refers to a nonhuman, animal, plant, or inanimate object; refers to a thing mentioned or being discussed; used as the subject of impersonal verbs, e.g. it's windy; Informal crucial or ultimate point. **its** adj, pron belonging to it. **it's** it is; it has. **itself** pron emphatic form of IT.

IT information technology.

italic adj (of printing type) sloping to the right. **italics** pl n this type, used for emphasis. **italicize** v put in italics.

itch n skin irritation causing a desire to scratch; restless desire. ▶ v have an itch. **itchy** adj

item n single thing in a list or

collection; piece of information. **itemize** v make a list of.

iterate v repeat. **iteration** n

itinerant adj travelling from place to place.

itinerary n, pl -aries. detailed plan of a journey.

ITV (in Britain) Independent Television.

IUD intrauterine device: a coil-shaped contraceptive fitted into the womb.

IVF in-vitro fertilization.

ivory n hard white bony substance forming the tusks of elephants. ▶ adj yellowish-white. **ivory tower** remoteness from the realities of everyday life.

ivy n, pl **ivies.** evergreen climbing plant.

iwi [ee-wee] n NZ Maori tribe.

J j

jab v jabbing, jabbed. poke sharply. ▶ n quick punch or poke; Informal injection.

jabber v talk rapidly or incoherently.

jabiru n large white-and-black Australian stork.

jacaranda n tropical tree with sweet-smelling wood.

jack n device for raising a motor vehicle or other heavy object; playing card with a picture of a pageboy; Bowls small white bowl aimed at by the players; socket in electrical equipment into which a plug fits; flag flown at the bow of a ship, showing nationality. **jack-up** n NZ informal something achieved dishonestly. **jack up** v raise with a jack; NZ informal organize by dishonest means.

jackal n doglike wild animal of

Africa and Asia.

jackaroo, jackeroo *n*, *pl* **-roos.**
Aust trainee on a sheep station.

jackass *n* fool; male of the ass.
laughing jackass same as
KOOKABURRA.

jackboot *n* high military boot.

jackdaw *n* black-and-grey Eurasian
bird of the crow family.

jacket *n* short coat; skin of a baked
potato; outer paper cover on a
hardback book.

jackknife *v* (of an articulated truck)
go out of control so that the
trailer swings round at a sharp
angle to the cab. ▶ *n* large clasp
knife.

jackpot *n* largest prize that may be
won in a game. **hit the jackpot**
be very successful through luck.

Jacobean [jak-a-bee-an] *adj* of the
reign of James I of England.

Jacobite *n* supporter of James II of
England and his descendants.

Jacquard [jak-ard] *n* fabric in
which the design is incorporated
into the weave.

Jacuzzi [jak-oo-zee] *n* ® circular
bath with a device that swirls the
water.

jade *n* ornamental semiprecious
stone, usu. dark green. ▶ *adj*
bluish-green.

jaded *adj* tired and unenthusiastic.

jagged [jag-gid] *adj* having an
uneven edge with sharp points.

jaguar *n* large S American spotted
cat.

jail *n* prison. ▶ *v* send to prison.

jailer *n* **jailbird** *n Informal* person
who has often been in prison.

jalopy [jal-lop-ee] *n*, *pl* **-lopies.**
Informal old car.

jam¹ *v* **jamming, jammed.** pack
tightly into a place; crowd or
congest; make or become stuck;
Radio block (another station) with
impulses of equal wavelength. ▶ *n*

hold-up of traffic; *Informal*
awkward situation. **jam on the
brakes** apply brakes fiercely.

jam-packed *adj* filled to capacity.

jam session informal rock or jazz
performance.

jam² *n* food made from fruit boiled
with sugar.

jamb *n* side post of a door or
window frame.

jamboree *n* large gathering or
celebration.

Jan. January.

jandal *n NZ* sandal with a strap
between the toes.

jangle *v* (cause to) make a harsh
ringing noise; (of nerves) be upset
or irritated.

janitor *n* caretaker of a school or
other building.

January *n* first month of the year.

japan *n* very hard varnish, usu.
black. ▶ *v* **-panning, -panned.**
cover with this varnish.

jape *n Old-fashioned* joke or prank.

japonica *n* shrub with red flowers.

jar¹ *n* wide-mouthed container,
usu. round and made of glass.

jar² *v* **jarring, jarred.** have a
disturbing or unpleasant effect;
jolt or bump. ▶ *n* jolt or shock.

jargon *n* specialized technical
language of a particular subject.

jarrah *n* Australian eucalypt
yielding valuable timber.

jasmine *n* shrub with
sweet-smelling yellow or white
flowers.

jasper *n* red, yellow, dark green,
or brown variety of quartz.

jaundice *n* disease marked by
yellowness of the skin. **jaundiced**
adj (of an attitude or opinion)
bitter or cynical; having jaundice.

jaunt *n* short journey for pleasure.

jaunty *adj* **-tier, -tiest.** sprightly
and cheerful; smart. **jauntily** *adv*

javelin *n* light spear thrown in

sports competitions.

jaw *n* one of the bones in which the teeth are set. ▶ *pl* mouth; gripping part of a tool; narrow opening of a gorge or valley. ▶ *v Slang* talk lengthily.

jay *n* bird with a pinkish body and blue-and-black wings.

jaywalker *n* person who crosses the road in a careless or dangerous manner. **jaywalking** *n*

jazz *n* kind of music with an exciting rhythm, usu. involving improvisation. **jazzy** *adj* flashy or showy. **jazz up** *v* make more lively.

JCB *n* ® *Brit* construction machine with a shovel at the front and an excavator at the rear.

jealous *adj* fearful of losing a partner or possession to a rival; envious; suspiciously watchful. **jealously** *adv* **jealousy** *n, pl* **-sies.**

jeans *pl n* casual denim trousers.

Jeep *n* ® four-wheel-drive motor vehicle.

jeer *v* scoff or deride. ▶ *n* cry of derision.

Jehovah *n* God.

jejune *adj* simple or naive; dull or boring.

jell *v* form into a jelly-like substance; take on a definite form.

jelly *n, pl* **-lies.** soft food made of liquid set with gelatine; jam made from fruit juice and sugar. **jellied** *adj* prepared in a jelly.

jellyfish *n* small jelly-like sea animal.

jemmy *n, pl* **-mies.** short steel crowbar used by burglars.

jenny *n, pl* **-nies.** female ass or wren.

jeopardy *n* danger. **jeopardize** *v* place in danger.

jerboa *n* small mouselike rodent with long hind legs.

jerk *v* move or throw abruptly. ▶ *n* sharp or abruptly stopped

movement; *Slang* contemptible person. **jerky** *adj* sudden or abrupt. **jerkily** *adv* **jerkiness** *n*

jerkin *n* sleeveless jacket.

jerry-built *adj* built badly using flimsy materials.

jerry can *n* flat-sided can for carrying petrol etc.

jersey *n* knitted jumper; machine-knitted fabric; **(J-)** breed of cow.

Jerusalem artichoke *n* small yellowish-white root vegetable.

jest *n, v* joke.

jester *n Hist* professional clown at court.

Jesuit [jezz-yoo-it] *n* member of the Society of Jesus, a Roman Catholic order.

jet¹ *n* aircraft driven by jet propulsion; stream of liquid or gas, esp. one forced from a small hole; nozzle from which gas or liquid is forced. ▶ *v* **jetting, jetted.** fly by jet aircraft. **jetboat** *n* motorboat propelled by a jet of water. **jet lag** fatigue caused by crossing time zones in an aircraft. **jet propulsion** propulsion by thrust provided by a jet of gas or liquid. **jet-propelled** *adj* **jet set** rich and fashionable people who travel the world for pleasure.

jet² *n* hard black mineral. **jet-black** *adj* glossy black.

jetsam *n* goods thrown overboard to lighten a ship.

jettison *v* **-soning, -soned.** abandon; throw overboard.

jetty *n, pl* **-ties.** small pier.

Jew *n* person whose religion is Judaism; descendant of the ancient Hebrews. **Jewish** *adj* **Jewry** *n* Jews collectively.

jew's-harp *n* musical instrument held between the teeth and played by plucking a metal strip with one's finger.

jewel n precious stone; special person or thing. **jeweller** n dealer in jewels. **jewellery** n objects decorated with precious stones.

jib¹ n triangular sail set in front of a mast.

jib² v **jibbing, jibbed.** (of a horse, person, etc.) stop and refuse to go on. **jib at** v object to (a proposal etc.).

jib³ n projecting arm of a crane or derrick.

jibe¹ n, v taunt or jeer.

jibe² v same as CYBE.

jiffy n, pl -**fies.** Informal very short period of time.

jig n type of lively dance; music for it; device that holds a component in place for cutting etc. ▶ v **jigging, jigged.** make jerky up-and-down movements.

jiggery-pokery n Informal trickery or mischief.

jiggle v move up and down with short jerky movements.

jigsaw n (also **jigsaw puzzle**) picture cut into interlocking pieces, which the user tries to fit together again; mechanical saw for cutting along curved lines.

jihad n Islamic holy war against unbelievers.

jilt v leave or reject (one's lover).

jingle n catchy verse or song used in a radio or television advert; gentle ringing noise. ▶ v (cause to) make a gentle ringing sound.

jingoism n aggressive nationalism. **jingoistic** adj

jinks pl n **high jinks** boisterous merrymaking.

jinni n, pl **jinn.** spirit in Muslim mythology.

jinx n person or thing bringing bad luck. ▶ v be or put a jinx on.

jitters pl n worried nervousness. **jittery** adj nervous.

jive n lively dance of the 1940s

and '50s. ▶ v dance the jive.

job n occupation or paid employment; task to be done; Informal difficult task; Brit, Aust & NZ informal crime, esp. robbery. **jobbing** adj doing individual jobs for payment. **jobless** adj, pl n unemployed (people). **job lot** assortment sold together. **job sharing** splitting of one post between two people working part-time.

jockey n (professional) rider of racehorses. ▶ v **jockey for position** manoeuvre to obtain an advantage.

jockstrap n belt with a pouch to support the genitals, worn by male athletes.

jocose [joke-kohss] adj playful or humorous.

jocular adj fond of joking; meant as a joke. **jocularity** n **jocularly** adv

jocund [jok-kund] adj Lit merry or cheerful.

jodhpurs pl n riding trousers, loose-fitting above the knee but tight below.

joey n Aust young kangaroo.

jog v **jogging, jogged.** run at a gentle pace, esp. for exercise; nudge slightly. ▶ n slow run. **jogger** n **jogging** n

joggle v shake or move jerkily.

joie de vivre [jwah de veev-ra] n French enjoyment of life.

join v become a member (of); come into someone's company; take part (in); come or bring together. ▶ n place where two things are joined. **join up** v enlist in the armed services.

joiner n maker of finished woodwork. **joinery** n joiner's work.

joint adj shared by two or more. ▶ n place where bones meet but can move; junction of two or more parts or objects; piece of meat for roasting; *Slang* house or place, esp. a disreputable bar or nightclub; *Slang* marijuana cigarette. ▶ v divide meat into joints. **out of joint** disorganized; dislocated. **jointed** adj **jointly** adv

joist n horizontal beam that helps support a floor or ceiling.

jojoba [hoe-**hoe**-ba] n shrub of SW North America whose seeds yield oil used in cosmetics.

joke n thing said or done to cause laughter; amusing or ridiculous person or thing. ▶ v make jokes. **jokey** adj **jokingly** adv **joker** n person who jokes; *Slang* fellow; extra card in a pack, counted as any other in some games.

jolly adj **-lier, -liest.** (of a person) happy and cheerful; (of an occasion) merry and festive. ▶ v **-lying, -lied. jolly along** try to keep (someone) cheerful by flattery or coaxing. **jollity** n **jollification** n merrymaking.

jolt n unpleasant surprise or shock; sudden jerk or bump. ▶ v surprise or shock; move or shake with a jerk.

jonquil n fragrant narcissus.

josh v *Chiefly US slang* tease.

joss stick n stick of incense giving off a sweet smell when burnt.

jostle v knock or push against.

jot v **jotting, jotted.** write briefly. ▶ n very small amount. **jotter** n notebook. **jottings** pl n notes jotted down.

joule [jool] n *Physics* unit of work or energy.

journal n daily newspaper or magazine; daily record of events. **journalese** n superficial style of writing, found in some newspapers. **journalism** n writing in or editing of newspapers and

magazines. **journalist** n **journalistic** adj

journey n act or process of travelling from one place to another. ▶ v travel.

journeyman n qualified craftsman employed by another.

joust *Hist* ▶ n combat with lances between two mounted knights. ▶ v fight on horseback using lances.

jovial adj happy and cheerful. **jovially** adv **joviality** n

jowl[1] n lower jaw. ▶ pl cheeks.

jowl[2] n fatty flesh hanging from the lower jaw.

joy n feeling of great delight or pleasure; cause of this feeling. **joyful** adj **joyless** adj **joyous** adj extremely happy and enthusiastic. **joyriding** n driving for pleasure, esp. in a stolen car. **joyride** n **joyrider** n **joystick** n control device for an aircraft or computer.

JP (in Britain) Justice of the Peace.

JPEG [**jay**-peg] *Computing* standard compressed file format used for pictures; picture held in this file format.

Jr Junior.

JSA jobseeker's allowance: in Britain, a payment made to unemployed people.

jubilant adj feeling or expressing great joy. **jubilantly** adv **jubilation** n

jubilee n special anniversary, esp. 25th (**silver jubilee**) or 50th (**golden jubilee**).

Judaism n religion of the Jews, based on the Old Testament and the Talmud. **Judaic** adj

judder v vibrate violently. ▶ n violent vibration. **judder bar** *NZ* raised strip across a road designed to slow down vehicles.

judge n public official who tries cases and passes sentence in a court of law; person who decides the outcome of a contest. ▶ v act as a judge; appraise critically; consider something to be the case. **judgment, judgement** n opinion reached after careful thought; verdict of a judge; ability to appraise critically. **judgmental, judgemental** adj

judicial adj of or by a court or judge; showing or using judgment. **judicially** adv

judiciary n system of courts and judges.

judicious adj well-judged and sensible. **judiciously** adv

judo n sport in which two opponents try to throw each other to the ground.

jug n container for liquids, with a handle and small spout. **jugged hare** hare stewed in an earthenware pot.

juggernaut n Brit large heavy truck; any irresistible destructive force.

juggle v throw and catch (several objects) so that most are in the air at the same time; manipulate (figures, situations, etc.) to suit one's purposes. **juggler** n

jugular, jugular vein n one of three large veins of the neck that return blood from the head to the heart.

juice n liquid part of vegetables, fruit, or meat; Brit, Aust & NZ informal petrol. ▶ pl fluids secreted by an organ of the body. **juicy** adj full of juice; interesting.

jujitsu n Japanese art of wrestling and self-defence.

juju n W African magic charm or fetish.

jukebox n coin-operated machine on which records, CDs, or videos can be played.

Jul. July.

julep n sweet alcoholic drink.

July n seventh month of the year.

jumble n confused heap or state; articles for a jumble sale. ▶ v mix in a disordered way. **jumble sale** sale of miscellaneous second-hand items.

jumbo adj Informal very large. ▶ n (also **jumbo jet**) large jet airliner.

jumbuck n Aust old-fashioned slang sheep.

jump v leap or spring into the air using the leg muscles; move quickly and suddenly; jerk with surprise; increase suddenly; change the subject abruptly; Informal attack without warning; pass over or miss out (intervening material). ▶ n act of jumping; sudden rise; break in continuity. **jump the gun** act prematurely. **jump the queue** not wait one's turn. **jumpy** adj nervous. **jump at** v accept (a chance etc.) gladly. **jumped-up** adj arrogant because of recent promotion. **jump jet** fixed-wing jet that can take off and land vertically. **jump leads** electric cables to connect a flat car battery to an external battery to aid starting an engine. **jump on** v attack suddenly and forcefully. **jump suit** one-piece garment of trousers and top.

jumper n sweater or pullover.

Jun. June; Junior.

junction n place where routes, railway lines, or roads meet.

juncture n point in time, esp. a critical one.

June n sixth month of the year.

jungle n tropical forest of dense tangled vegetation; confusion or mess; place of intense struggle for survival.

junior adj of lower standing; younger. ▶ n junior person.

juniper n evergreen shrub with purple berries.

junk[1] n discarded or useless objects; *Informal* rubbish; *Slang* narcotic drug, esp. heroin. **junkie, junky** n, pl **junkies**. *Slang* drug addict. **junk food** snack food of low nutritional value. **junk mail** unwanted mail advertising goods or services.

junk[2] n flat-bottomed Chinese sailing boat.

junket n excursion by public officials paid for from public funds; sweetened milk set with rennet.

junta n group of military officers holding power in a country, esp. after a coup.

Jupiter n king of the Roman gods; largest of the planets.

juridical adj of law or the administration of justice.

jurisdiction n right or power to administer justice and apply laws; extent of this right or power.

jurisprudence n science or philosophy of law.

jurist n expert in law.

jury n, pl **-ries**. group of people sworn to deliver a verdict in a court of law. **juror** n member of a jury.

just adv very recently; at this instant; merely; only; exactly; barely; really. ▶ adj fair or impartial in action or judgment; proper or right. **justly** adv **justness** n

justice n quality of being just; judicial proceedings; judge or magistrate. **justice of the peace** (in Britain) person who is authorized to act as a judge in a local court of law.

justify v **-fying, -fied**. prove right or reasonable; explain the reasons for an action; align (text) so the margins are straight. **justifiable** adj **justifiably** adv **justification** n

jut v jutting, jutted. project or

stick out.

jute n plant fibre, used for rope, canvas, etc.

juvenile adj young; of or suitable for young people; immature and rather silly. ▶ n young person or child. **juvenilia** pl n works produced in an author's youth. **juvenile delinquent** young person guilty of a crime.

juxtapose v put side by side. **juxtaposition** n

K k

K *Informal* thousand(s).

kaftan n long loose Eastern garment; woman's dress resembling this.

kaiser [kize-er] n *Hist* German or Austro-Hungarian emperor.

Kalashnikov n Russian-made automatic rifle.

kale n cabbage with crinkled leaves.

kaleidoscope n tube-shaped toy containing loose coloured pieces reflected by mirrors so that intricate patterns form when the tube is twisted. **kaleidoscopic** adj

kamikaze [kam-mee-kah-zee] n (in World War II) Japanese pilot who performed a suicide mission. ▶ adj (of an action) undertaken in the knowledge that it will kill or injure the person performing it.

kangaroo n, pl **-roos**. Australian marsupial which moves by jumping with its powerful hind legs. **kangaroo court** unofficial court set up by a group to discipline its members.

kaolin n fine white clay used to make porcelain and in some medicines.

kapok n fluffy fibre from a tropical tree, used to stuff cushions etc.

kaput [kap-**poot**] *adj Informal* ruined or broken.

karaoke *n* form of entertainment in which people sing over a prerecorded backing tape.

karate *n* Japanese system of unarmed combat using blows with the feet, hands, elbows, and legs.

karma *n Buddhism, Hinduism* person's actions affecting his or her fate in the next reincarnation.

karri *n, pl* **-ris.** Australian eucalypt; its wood, used for building.

katipo *n* small poisonous New Zealand spider.

kayak *n* Inuit canoe made of sealskins stretched over a frame; fibreglass or canvas-covered canoe of this design.

kbyte *Computers* kilobyte.

kebab *n* dish of small pieces of meat grilled on skewers; (also **doner kebab**) grilled minced lamb served in a split slice of unleavened bread.

kedgeree *n* dish of fish with rice and eggs.

keel *n* main lengthways timber or steel support along the base of a ship. **keel over** *v* turn upside down; *Informal* collapse suddenly.

keen[1] *adj* eager or enthusiastic; intense or strong; intellectually acute; (of the senses) capable of recognizing small distinctions; sharp; cold and penetrating; competitive. **keenly** *adv* **keenness** *n*

keen[2] *v* wail over the dead.

keep *v* **keeping, kept.** have or retain possession of; store; stay or cause to stay (in, on, or at a place or position); continue or persist; detain (someone); look after or maintain. ▶ *n* cost of food and everyday expenses. **keeper** *n* person who looks after animals in a zoo; person in charge of a museum or collection; short for GOALKEEPER. **keeping** *n* care or charge. **in, out of keeping with** appropriate or inappropriate for.

keep fit exercises designed to promote physical fitness.

keepsake *n* gift treasured for the sake of the giver. **keep up** *v* maintain at the current level. **keep up with** *v* maintain a pace set by (someone).

keg *n* small metal beer barrel.

kelp *n* large brown seaweed.

kelpie *n* Australian sheepdog with a smooth coat and upright ears.

kelvin *n* SI unit of temperature. **Kelvin scale** temperature scale starting at absolute zero (-273.15° Celsius).

ken *v* **kenning, kenned** *or* **kent.** *Scot* know. **beyond one's ken** beyond one's range of knowledge.

kendo *n* Japanese sport of fencing using wooden staves.

kennel *n* hutlike shelter for a dog. ▶ *pl* place for breeding, boarding, or training dogs.

kept *v* past of KEEP.

keratin *n* fibrous protein found in the hair and nails.

kerb *n* edging to a footpath. **kerb crawling** *Brit* act of driving slowly beside a pavement to pick up a prostitute.

kerchief *n* piece of cloth worn over the head or round the neck.

kerfuffle *n Informal* commotion or disorder.

kernel *n* seed of a nut, cereal, or fruit stone; central and essential part of something.

kerosene *n US, Canadian, Aust & NZ* liquid mixture distilled from petroleum and used as a fuel or solvent.

kestrel *n* type of small falcon.

ketch *n* two-masted sailing ship.

ketchup n thick cold sauce, usu. made of tomatoes.

kettle n container with a spout and handle used for boiling water. **kettledrum** n large bowl-shaped metal drum.

key n device for operating a lock by moving a bolt; device turned to wind a clock, operate a machine, etc.; any of a set of levers or buttons pressed to operate a typewriter, computer, or musical keyboard instrument; *Music* set of related notes; something crucial in providing an explanation or interpretation; means of achieving a desired end; list of explanations of codes, symbols, etc. ▶ adj of great importance. ▶ v (also **key in**) enter (text) using a keyboard. **keyed up** very excited or nervous.

keyboard n set of keys on a piano, computer, etc.; musical instrument played using a keyboard. ▶ v enter (text) using a keyboard.

keyhole n opening for inserting a key into a lock.

keynote n dominant idea of a speech or occasion; basic note of a musical key.

keystone n most important part of a process, organization, etc.; central stone of an arch which locks the others in position.

kg kilogram(s).

KGB n (formerly) Soviet secret police.

khaki adj dull yellowish-brown. ▶ n hard-wearing fabric of this colour used for military uniforms.

kHz kilohertz.

kia ora [kee-a aw-ra] interj NZ Maori greeting.

kibbutz n, pl **kibbutzim.** communal farm or factory in Israel.

kibosh n **put the kibosh on** Slang put a stop to.

kick v drive, push, or strike with the foot; (of a gun) recoil when fired; Informal object or resist; Informal free oneself of (an addiction); Rugby score with a kick. ▶ n thrust or blow with the foot; recoil of a gun; Informal excitement or thrill. **kickback** n money paid illegally for favours done. **kick off** v start a game of soccer; Informal begin. **kick out** v dismiss or expel forcibly. **kick-start** v start (a motorcycle) by kicking a pedal. **kick up** v Informal create (a fuss).

kid¹ n Informal child; young goat; leather made from the skin of a young goat.

kid² v **kidding, kidded.** Informal tease or deceive (someone).

kidnap v **-napping, -napped.** seize and hold (a person) to ransom. **kidnapper** n.

kidney n either of the pair of organs that filter waste products from the blood to produce urine; animal kidney used as food. **kidney bean** reddish-brown kidney-shaped bean, edible when cooked.

kill v cause the death of; Informal cause (someone) pain or discomfort; put an end to; pass (time). ▶ n act of killing; animals or birds killed in a hunt. **killer** n. **killing** Informal ▶ adj very tiring; very funny. ▶ n sudden financial success. **killjoy** n person who spoils others' pleasure.

kiln n oven for baking, drying, or processing pottery, bricks, etc.

kilo n short for KILOGRAM.

kilo- combining form one thousand, e.g. kilometre.

kilobyte n Computers 1024 units of information.

kilogram, kilogramme n one thousand grams.

kilohertz n one thousand hertz.

kilometre n one thousand metres.

kilowatt n Electricity one thousand watts.

kilt n knee-length pleated tartan skirt worn orig. by Scottish Highlanders. **kilted** adj

kimono n, pl **-nos.** loose wide-sleeved Japanese robe, fastened with a sash; European dressing gown resembling this.

kin, kinsfolk n person's relatives collectively. **kinship** n

kind¹ adj considerate, friendly, and helpful. **kindness** n **kindly** adj having a warm-hearted nature; pleasant or agreeable. ▶ adv in a considerate way; please, e.g. will you kindly be quiet! **kindliness** n **kind-hearted** adj

kind² n class or group with common characteristics; essential nature or character. **in kind** (of payment) in goods rather than money; with something similar. **kind of** to a certain extent.

kindergarten n class or school for children under six years old.

kindle v set (a fire) alight; (of a fire) start to burn; arouse or be aroused. **kindling** n dry wood or straw for starting fires.

kindred adj having similar qualities; related by blood or marriage. ▶ n same as KIN.

kindy, kindie n, pl **-dies.** Aust & NZ informal kindergarten.

kinetic [kin-**net**-ik] adj relating to or caused by motion.

king n male ruler of a monarchy; ruler or chief; best or most important of its kind; piece in chess that must be defended; playing card with a picture of a king on it. **kingship** n **kingdom** n state ruled by a king or queen; division of the natural world. **king-size, king-sized** adj larger than standard size.

kingfisher n small bird, often with a bright-coloured plumage, that dives for fish.

kingpin n most important person in an organization.

kink n twist or bend in rope, wire, hair, etc.; Informal quirk in someone's personality. **kinky** adj Slang given to unusual sexual practices; full of kinks.

kiosk n small booth selling drinks, cigarettes, newspapers, etc.; public telephone box.

kip n, v kipping, kipped. Informal sleep.

kipper n cleaned, salted, and smoked herring.

kirk n Scot church.

Kirsch n brandy made from cherries.

kismet n fate or destiny.

kiss v touch with the lips in affection or greeting; join lips with a person in love or desire. ▶ n touch with the lips. **kisser** n Slang mouth or face. **kissagram** n greetings service in which a messenger kisses the person celebrating. **kissing crust** NZ & S Afr soft end of a loaf of bread where two loaves have been separated. **kiss of life** mouth-to-mouth resuscitation.

kist n S Afr large wooden chest.

kit n outfit or equipment for a specific purpose; set of pieces of equipment sold ready to be assembled; NZ flax basket. **kitbag** n bag for a soldier's or traveller's belongings. **kit out** v **kitting, kitted.** provide with clothes or equipment needed for a particular activity. **kitset** n NZ unassembled pieces for constructing a piece of furniture.

kitchen n room used for cooking. **kitchenette** n small kitchen.

kitchen garden garden for growing vegetables, herbs, etc.

kite n light frame covered with a thin material flown on a string in the wind; large hawk with a forked tail. **Kite mark** Brit official mark on articles approved by the British Standards Institution.

kith n **kith and kin** friends and relatives.

kitsch n art or literature with popular sentimental appeal.

kitten n young cat. **kittenish** adj lively and flirtatious.

kittiwake n type of seagull.

kitty n, pl **-ties.** communal fund; total amount wagered in certain gambling games.

kiwi n New Zealand flightless bird with a long beak and no tail; Informal New Zealander. **kiwi fruit** edible fruit with a fuzzy brownish skin and green flesh.

klaxon n loud horn used on emergency vehicles as a warning signal.

kleptomania n compulsive tendency to steal. **kleptomaniac** n

kloof n S Afr mountain pass or gorge.

km kilometre(s).

knack n skilful way of doing something; innate ability.

knacker n Brit buyer of old horses for killing.

knackered adj Slang extremely tired; no longer functioning.

knapsack n soldier's or traveller's bag worn strapped on the back.

knave n jack at cards; Obs dishonest man.

knead v work (dough) into a smooth mixture with the hands; squeeze or press with the hands.

knee n joint between thigh and lower leg; lap; part of a garment covering the knee. ▶ v **kneeing, kneed.** strike or push with the

knee. **kneecap** n bone in front of the knee. ▶ v shoot in the kneecap. **kneejerk** adj (of a reply or reaction) automatic and predictable. **knees-up** n Brit informal party.

kneel v **kneeling, kneeled** or **knelt.** fall or rest on one's knees.

knell n sound of a bell, esp. at a funeral or death; portent of doom.

knew v past tense of KNOW.

knickerbockers pl n loose-fitting short trousers gathered in at the knee.

knickers pl n woman's or girl's undergarment covering the lower trunk and having legs or legholes.

knick-knack n trifle or trinket.

knife n, pl **knives.** cutting tool or weapon consisting of a sharp-edged blade with a handle. ▶ v cut or stab with a knife.

knight n man who has been given a knighthood; Hist man who served his lord as a mounted armoured soldier; chess piece shaped like a horse's head. ▶ v award a knighthood to. **knighthood** n honorary title given to a man by the British sovereign. **knightly** adj

knit v **knitting, knitted** or **knit.** make (a garment) by interlocking a series of loops in wool or other yarn; join closely together; draw (one's eyebrows) together. **knitting** n **knitwear** n knitted clothes, such as sweaters.

knob n rounded projection, such as a switch on a radio; rounded handle on a door or drawer; small amount of butter. **knobbly** adj covered with small bumps.

knobkerrie n S Afr club with a rounded end.

knock v give a blow or push to; rap audibly with the knuckles; make or drive by striking; Informal criticize adversely; (of an engine) make a regular banging noise as a result of a fault. ▸ *n* blow or rap; knocking sound. **knocker** *n* metal fitting for knocking on a door. **knock about, around** *v* wander or spend time aimlessly; hit or kick brutally. **knockabout** *adj* (of comedy) boisterous. **knock back** *v Informal* drink quickly; cost; reject or refuse. **knock down** *v* demolish; reduce the price of. **knockdown** *adj* (of a price) very low. **knock-knees** *pl n* legs that curve in at the knees. **knock off** *v Informal* cease work; *Informal* make or do (something) hurriedly or easily; take (a specified amount) off a price; *Brit, Aust & NZ informal* steal. **knock out** *v* render (someone) unconscious; *Informal* overwhelm or amaze; defeat in a knockout competition. **knockout** *n* blow that renders an opponent unconscious; competition from which competitors are progressively eliminated; *Informal* overwhelmingly attractive person or thing. **knock up** *v Informal* assemble (something) quickly; *Informal* waken. **knock-up** *n* practice session at tennis, squash, or badminton.

knoll *n* small rounded hill.

knot *n* fastening made by looping and pulling tight strands of string, cord, or rope; tangle (of hair); small cluster or huddled group; round lump or spot in timber; feeling of tightness, caused by tension or nervousness; unit of speed used by ships, equal to one nautical mile (1.85 kilometres) per hour. ▸ *v* knotting, knotted. tie with or into a knot. **knotty** *adj* full of knots; puzzling or difficult.

know *v* knowing, knew, known. be or feel certain of the truth of

(information etc.); be acquainted with; have a grasp of or understand (a skill or language); be aware of. **in the know** *Informal* informed or aware. **knowable** *adj* knowing *adj* suggesting secret knowledge. **knowingly** *adv* deliberately; in a way that suggests secret knowledge. **know-all** *n Offens* person who acts as if knowing more than other people. **know-how** *n Informal* ingenuity, aptitude, or skill.

knowledge *n* facts or experiences known by a person; state of knowing; specific information on a subject. **knowledgeable, knowledgable** *adj* intelligent or well-informed.

knuckle *n* bone at the finger joint; knee joint of a calf or pig. **near the knuckle** *Informal* rather rude or offensive. **knuckle-duster** *n* metal appliance worn on the knuckles to add force to a blow. **knuckle under** *v* yield or submit.

KO knockout.

koala *n* tree-dwelling Australian marsupial with dense grey fur.

kohanga reo, kohanga *n NZ* infant class where children are taught in Maori.

kohl *n* cosmetic powder used to darken the edges of the eyelids.

kookaburra *n* large Australian kingfisher with a cackling cry.

koori *n, pl* -ris. Australian Aborigine.

kopje, koppie *n S Afr* small hill.

Koran *n* sacred book of Islam.

kosher [koh-sher] *adj* conforming to Jewish religious law, esp. (of food) to Jewish dietary law; *Informal* legitimate or authentic. ▸ *n* kosher food.

kowhai *n* New Zealand tree with clusters of yellow flowers.

kowtow *v* be servile (towards).

kph kilometres per hour.

kraal n S African village surrounded by a strong fence.

Kremlin n central government of Russia and, formerly, the Soviet Union.

krill n, pl **krill**. small shrimplike sea creature.

krypton n Chem colourless gas present in the atmosphere and used in fluorescent lights.

kudos n fame or credit.

kugel [koog-el] n S Afr rich, fashion-conscious, materialistic young woman.

kumara n NZ tropical root vegetable with yellow flesh.

kumquat [kumm-kwott] n citrus fruit resembling a tiny orange.

kung fu n Chinese martial art combining hand, foot, and weapon techniques.

kura kaupapa Maori n NZ primary school where the teaching is done in Maori.

kurrajong n Australian tree or shrub with tough fibrous bark.

kW kilowatt.

kWh kilowatt-hour.

L l

---

l litre.

L large; learner (driver).

lab n Informal short for LABORATORY.

label n piece of card or other material fixed to an object to show its ownership, destination, etc. ▶ v **-elling, -elled**. give a label to.

labia pl n, sing **labium**. four liplike folds of skin forming part of the female genitals. **labial** [lay-bee-al] adj of the lips.

labor n US & Aust same as LABOUR.

Labor Day (in the US and Canada) public holiday in honour of labour, held on the first Monday in September; (in Australia) public holiday observed on different days in different states.

laboratory n, pl **-ries**. building or room designed for scientific research or for the teaching of practical science.

laborious adj involving great prolonged effort. **laboriously** adv

Labor Party n main left-wing political party in Australia.

labour, (US & Aust) labor n physical work or exertion; workers in industry; final stage of pregnancy, leading to childbirth. ▶ v work hard; stress to excess or too persistently; be at a disadvantage because of a mistake or false belief. **laboured** adj uttered or done with difficulty. **labourer** n person who labours, esp. someone doing manual work for wages. **Labour Day** (in Britain) a public holiday in honour of work, held on May 1; (in New Zealand) a public holiday commemorating the introduction of the eight-hour day, held on the 4th Monday in October. **Labour Party** n main left-wing political party in a number of countries including Britain and New Zealand.

labrador n large retriever dog with a usu. gold or black coat.

laburnum n ornamental tree with yellow hanging flowers.

labyrinth [lab-er-inth] n complicated network of passages; interconnecting cavities in the internal ear. **labyrinthine** adj

lace n delicate decorative fabric made from threads woven into an open weblike pattern; cord drawn through eyelets and tied. ▶ v fasten with laces; thread a cord or string through holes in something;

add a small amount of alcohol, a drug, etc. to (food or drink). **lacy** adj fine, like lace. **lace-ups** pl n shoes which fasten with laces.

lacerate [lass-er-ate] v tear (flesh). **laceration** n

lachrymose adj tearful; sad.

lack n shortage or absence of something needed or wanted. ▶ v need or be short of (something).

lackadaisical adj lazy and careless in a dreamy way.

lackey n servile follower; uniformed male servant.

lacklustre adj lacking brilliance or vitality.

laconic adj using only a few words, terse. **laconically** adv

lacquer n hard varnish for wood or metal; clear sticky substance sprayed onto the hair to hold it in place.

lacrimal adj of tears or the glands which produce them.

lacrosse n sport in which teams catch and throw a ball using long sticks with a pouched net at the end, in an attempt to score goals.

lactation n secretion of milk by female mammals to feed young.

lactic adj of or derived from milk.

lactose n white crystalline sugar found in milk.

lacuna [lak-kew-na] n, pl -nae. gap or missing part, esp. in a document or series.

lad n boy or young man.

ladder n frame of two poles connected by horizontal steps used for climbing; line of stitches that have come undone in tights or stockings. ▶ v have or cause to have such a line of undone stitches.

laden adj loaded; burdened.

la-di-da, lah-di-dah adj Informal affected or pretentious.

ladle n spoon with a long handle

and a large bowl, used for serving soup etc. ▶ v serve out.

lady n, pl -dies. woman regarded as having characteristics of good breeding or high rank; polite term of address for a woman; (L-) title of some female members of the British nobility. **Our Lady** the Virgin Mary. **lady-in-waiting** n, pl **ladies-in-waiting.** female servant of a queen or princess. **ladykiller** n Informal man who is or thinks he is irresistible to women. **ladylike** adj polite and dignified. **ladybird** n small red beetle with black spots.

lag[1] v lagging, lagged. go too slowly, fall behind. ▶ n delay between events. **laggard** n person who lags behind.

lag[2] v lagging, lagged. wrap (a boiler, pipes, etc.) with insulating material. **lagging** n insulating material.

lag[3] n old lag Brit, Aust & NZ slang convict.

lager n light-bodied beer.

lagoon n body of water cut off from the open sea by coral reefs or sand bars.

laid v past of LAY[1]. **laid-back** adj Informal relaxed.

lain v past participle of LIE[2].

lair n resting place of an animal.

laird n Scottish landowner.

laissez-faire [less-ay-fair] n principle of nonintervention, esp. by a government in commercial affairs.

laity [lay-it-ee] n people who are not members of the clergy.

lake[1] n expanse of water entirely surrounded by land. **lakeside** n

lake[2] n red pigment.

lama n Buddhist priest in Tibet or Mongolia.

lamb n young sheep; its meat. ▶ v (of sheep) give birth to a lamb or lambs. **lamb's fry** *Aust & NZ* lamb's liver for cooking. **lambskin** *n* **lambswool** *n*

lambast, lambaste *v* beat or thrash; reprimand severely.

lambent *adj Lit* (of a flame) flickering softly.

lame *adj* having an injured or disabled leg or foot; (of an excuse) unconvincing. ▶ *v* make lame. **lamely** *adv* **lameness** *n* **lame duck** person or thing unable to cope without help.

lamé [lah-may] *n, adj* (fabric) interwoven with gold or silver thread.

lament *v* feel or express sorrow (for). ▶ *n* passionate expression of grief. **lamentable** *adj* very disappointing. **lamentation** *n* **lamented** *adj* grieved for.

laminate *v* make (a sheet of material) by sticking together thin sheets; cover with a thin sheet of material. ▶ *n* laminated sheet. **laminated** *adj*

lamington *n Aust & NZ* sponge cake coated with a sweet coating.

Lammas *n* August 1, formerly a harvest festival.

lamp *n* device which produces light from electricity, oil, or gas. **lamppost** *n* post supporting a lamp in the street. **lampshade** *n*

lampoon *n* humorous satire ridiculing someone. ▶ *v* satirize or ridicule.

lamprey *n* eel-like fish with a round sucking mouth.

lance *n* long spear used by a mounted soldier. ▶ *v* pierce (a boil or abscess) with a lancet. **lancer** *n* formerly, cavalry soldier armed with a lance. **lance corporal** noncommissioned army officer of the lowest rank.

lancet *n* pointed two-edged surgical knife; narrow window in

the shape of a pointed arch.

land *n* solid part of the earth's surface; ground, esp. with reference to its type or use; rural or agricultural area; property consisting of land; country or region. ▶ *v* come or bring to earth after a flight, jump, or fall; go or take from a ship at the end of a voyage; come to or touch shore; come or bring to some point or condition; *Informal* obtain; take (a hooked fish) from the water; *Informal* deliver (a punch). **landed** *adj* possessing or consisting of lands. **landless** *adj* **landward** *adj* nearest to or facing the land. ▶ *adv* (also **landwards**) towards land. **landfall** *n* ship's first landing after a voyage.

landlocked *adj* completely surrounded by land. **land up** *v* arrive at a final point or condition.

landau [lan-daw] *n* four-wheeled carriage with two folding hoods.

landing *n* floor area at the top of a flight of stairs; bringing or coming to land; (also **landing stage**) place where people or goods go onto or come off a boat.

landlord, landlady *n* person who rents out land, houses, etc.; owner or manager of a pub or boarding house.

landlubber *n* person who is not experienced at sea.

landmark *n* prominent object in or feature of a landscape; event, decision, etc. considered as an important development.

landscape *n* extensive piece of inland scenery seen from one place; picture of it. ▶ *v* improve natural features of (a piece of land).

landslide *n* (also **landslip**) falling of soil, rock, etc. down the side of a mountain; overwhelming electoral victory.

lane n narrow road; area of road for one stream of traffic; specified route followed by ships or aircraft; strip of a running track or swimming pool for use by one competitor.

language n system of sounds, symbols, etc. for communicating thought; particular system used by a nation or people; system of words and symbols for computer programming.

languid adj lacking energy or enthusiasm. **languidly** adv

languish v suffer neglect or hardship; lose or diminish in strength or vigour; pine (for).

languor [lang-ger] n state of dreamy relaxation; laziness or weariness. **languorous** adj

lank adj (of hair) straight and limp; thin or gaunt. **lanky** adj ungracefully tall and thin.

lanolin n grease from sheep's wool used in ointments etc.

lantana [lan-tay-na] n shrub with orange or yellow flowers, considered a weed in Australia.

lantern n light in a transparent protective case. **lantern jaw** long thin jaw. **lantern-jawed** adj

lanthanum n Chem silvery-white metallic element. **lanthanide series** class of 15 elements chemically related to lanthanum.

lanyard n cord worn round the neck to hold a knife or whistle; Naut short rope.

lap[1] n part between the waist and knees of a person when sitting. **laptop** adj (of a computer) small enough to fit on a user's lap. ▶ n computer small enough to fit on a user's lap.

lap[2] n single circuit of a racecourse or track; stage of a journey. ▶ v **lapping, lapped.** overtake an

opponent so as to be one or more circuits ahead.

lap[3] v **lapping, lapped.** (of waves) beat softly against (a shore etc.). **lap up** v drink by scooping up with the tongue; accept (information or attention) eagerly.

lapel [lap-pel] n part of the front of a coat or jacket folded back towards the shoulders.

lapidary adj of or relating to stones.

lapis lazuli [lap-iss lazz-yoo-lie] n bright blue gemstone.

lapse n temporary drop in a standard, esp. through forgetfulness or carelessness; instance of bad behaviour by someone usually well-behaved; break in occurrence or usage. ▶ v drop in standard; end or become invalid, esp. through disuse; abandon religious faith; (of time) slip away. **lapsed** adj

lapwing n plover with a tuft of feathers on the head.

larboard adj, n Old-fashioned port (side of a ship).

larceny n, pl **-nies**. Law theft.

larch n deciduous coniferous tree.

lard n soft white fat obtained from a pig. ▶ v insert strips of bacon in (meat) before cooking; decorate (speech or writing) with strange words unnecessarily.

larder n storeroom for food.

large adj great in size, number, or extent. **at large** in general; free, not confined; fully. **largely** adv **largish** adj **large-scale** adj wide-ranging or extensive.

largesse, largess [lar-**jess**] n generous giving, esp. of money.

largo n, pl **-gos**, adv Music (piece to be played) in a slow and dignified manner.

lariat n lasso.

lark[1] n small brown songbird, skylark.

lark² n Informal harmless piece of mischief or fun; unnecessary activity or job. **lark about** v play pranks.

larkspur n plant with spikes of blue, pink, or white flowers with spurs.

larrikin n Aust & NZ old-fashioned slang mischievous or unruly person.

larva n, pl **-vae.** insect in an immature stage, often resembling a worm. **larval** adj

larynx n, pl **larynges.** part of the throat containing the vocal cords. **laryngeal** adj **laryngitis** n inflammation of the larynx.

lasagne, lasagna [laz-**zan**-ya] n pasta in wide flat sheets; dish made from layers of lasagne, meat, and cheese.

lascivious [lass-**iv**-ee-uss] adj showing or producing sexual desire. **lasciviously** adv

laser [**lay**-zer] n device that produces a very narrow intense beam of light, used for cutting very hard materials and in surgery etc.

lash¹ n eyelash; sharp blow with a whip. ▶ v hit with a whip; (of rain or waves) beat forcefully against; attack verbally, scold; flick or wave sharply to and fro. **lash out** v make a sudden physical or verbal attack; Informal spend (money) extravagantly.

lash² v fasten or bind tightly with cord etc.

lashings pl n Old-fashioned large amounts.

lass, lassie n Scot & N English girl.

lassitude n physical or mental weariness.

lasso [lass-**oo**] n, pl **-sos, -soes.** rope with a noose for catching cattle and horses. ▶ v **-soing, -soed.** catch with a lasso.

last¹ adj, adv coming at the end or

after all others; most recent(ly). ▶ adj only remaining. ▶ n last person or thing. **lastly** adv **last-ditch** adj done as a final resort. **last post** army bugle-call played at sunset or funerals. **last straw** small irritation or setback that, coming after others, is too much to bear. **last word** final comment in an argument; most recent or best example of something.

last² v continue; be sufficient for (a specified amount of time); remain fresh, uninjured, or unaltered. **lasting** adj

last³ n model of a foot on which shoes and boots are made or repaired.

latch n fastening for a door with a bar and lever; lock which can only be opened from the outside with a key. ▶ v fasten with a latch. **latch onto** v become attached to (a person or idea).

late adj after the normal or expected time; towards the end of a period; being at an advanced time; recently dead; recent; former. ▶ adv after the normal or expected time; at a relatively advanced age; recently. **lately** adv in recent times. **lateness** n

latent adj hidden and not yet developed. **latency** n

lateral [**lat**-ter-al] adj of or relating to the side or sides. **laterally** adv

latex n milky fluid found in some plants, esp. the rubber tree, used in making rubber.

lath n thin strip of wood used to support plaster, tiles, etc.

lathe n machine for turning wood or metal while it is being shaped.

lather n froth of soap and water; frothy sweat; Informal state of agitation. ▶ v make frothy; rub with soap until lather appears.

Latin n language of the ancient Romans. ▸ adj of or in Latin; of a people whose language derives from Latin. **Latin America** parts of South and Central America whose official language is Spanish or Portuguese. **Latin American** n, adj

latitude n angular distance measured in degrees N or S of the equator; scope for freedom of action or thought. ▸ pl regions considered in relation to their distance from the equator.

latrine n toilet in a barracks or camp.

latter adj second of two; later; recent. **latterly** adv **latter-day** adj modern.

lattice [lat-iss] n framework of intersecting strips of wood, metal, etc.; gate, screen, etc. formed of such a framework. **latticed** adj

laud v praise or glorify. **laudable** adj praiseworthy. **laudably** adv **laudatory** adj praising or glorifying.

laudanum [lawd-a-num] n opium-based sedative.

laugh v make inarticulate sounds with the voice expressing amusement, merriment, or scorn; utter or express with laughter. ▸ n act or instance of laughing; Informal person or thing causing amusement. **laughable** adj ridiculously inadequate. **laughter** n sound or action of laughing. **laughing gas** nitrous oxide as an anaesthetic. **laughing stock** object of general derision. **laugh off** v treat (something serious or difficult) lightly.

launch¹ v put (a ship or boat) into the water, esp. for the first time; begin (a campaign, project, etc.); put a new product on the market; send (a missile or spacecraft) into space or the air. ▸ n launching.

launcher n **launch into** v start doing something enthusiastically. **launch out** v start doing something new.

launch² n open motorboat.

launder v wash and iron (clothes and linen); make (illegally obtained money) seem legal by passing it through foreign banks or legitimate businesses. **laundry** n, pl **-dries.** clothes etc. for washing or which have recently been washed; place for washing clothes and linen. **Launderette** n ® shop with coin-operated washing and drying machines.

laureate [lor-ee-at] adj see POET LAUREATE.

laurel n glossy-leaved shrub, bay tree. ▸ pl wreath of laurel, an emblem of victory or merit.

lava n molten rock thrown out by volcanoes, which hardens as it cools.

lavatory n, pl **-ries.** toilet.

lavender n shrub with fragrant flowers. ▸ adj bluish-purple. **lavender water** light perfume made from lavender.

lavish adj great in quantity or richness; giving or spending generously; extravagant. ▸ v give or spend generously. **lavishly** adv

law n rule binding on a community; system of such rules; Informal police; invariable sequence of events in nature; general principle deduced from facts. **lawful** adj allowed by law. **lawfully** adv **lawless** adj breaking the law, esp. in a violent way. **lawlessness** n **law-abiding** adj obeying the laws. **law-breaker** n **lawsuit** n court case brought by one person or group against another.

lawn¹ n area of tended and mown grass. **lawn mower** machine for cutting grass. **lawn tennis** tennis, esp. when played on a grass court.

lawn² n fine linen or cotton fabric.

lawyer n professionally qualified legal expert.

lax adj not strict. **laxity** n

laxative n, adj (medicine) inducing the emptying of the bowels.

lay¹ v **laying, laid.** cause to lie; devise or prepare; set in a particular place or position; attribute (blame); put forward (a plan, argument, etc.); (of a bird or reptile) produce eggs; arrange (a table) for a meal. **lay waste** devastate. **lay-by** n stopping place for traffic beside a road. **lay off** v dismiss staff during a slack period. **lay-off** n lay off v provide or supply. **lay out** v arrange or spread out; prepare (a corpse) for burial; *Informal* spend money, esp. lavishly; *Informal* knock unconscious. **layout** n arrangement, esp. of matter for printing or of a building.

lay² v past tense of LIE². **layabout** n lazy person.

lay³ adj of or involving people who are not clergymen; nonspecialist. **layman** n person who is not a member of the clergy; person without specialist knowledge.

lay⁴ n short narrative poem designed to be sung.

layer n single thickness of some substance, as a cover or coating on a surface; laying hen; shoot of a plant pegged down and covered with earth to encourage root growth. ▶ v form a layer; propagate plants by layers. **layered** adj

layette n clothes for a newborn baby.

laze v be idle or lazy. ▶ n time spent lazing.

lazy adj **lazier, laziest.** not inclined

to work or exert oneself; done in a relaxed manner without much effort; (of movement) slow and gentle. **lazily** adv **laziness** n

lb pound (weight).

lbw *Cricket* leg before wicket.

lea n *Poetic* meadow.

leach v remove or be removed from a substance by a liquid passing through it.

lead¹ v **leading, led.** guide or conduct; cause to feel, think, or behave in a certain way; be, go, or play first; (of a road, path, etc.) go towards; control or direct; (foll. by *to*) result in; pass or spend (one's life). ▶ n first or most prominent place; amount by which a person or group is ahead of another; clue; length of leather or chain attached to a dog's collar to control it; principal role or actor in a film, play, etc.; cable bringing current to an electrical device. ▶ adj acting as a leader or lead. **leading** adj principal; in the first position. **leading question** question worded to prompt the answer desired. **lead-in** n introduction to a subject.

lead² n soft heavy grey metal; (in a pencil) graphite; lead weight on a line, used for sounding depths of water. **leaded** adj (of windows) made from many small panes of glass held together by lead strips. **leaden** adj heavy or sluggish; dull grey; made from lead.

leader n person who leads; article in a newspaper expressing editorial views. **leadership** n

leaf n, pl **leaves.** flat usu. green blade attached to the stem of a plant; single sheet of paper in a book; very thin sheet of metal; extending flap on a table. **leafy** adj **leafless** adj **leaf mould** rich soil composed of decayed leaves.

leaf through v turn pages without reading them.

leaflet n sheet of printed matter for distribution; small leaf.

league[1] n association promoting the interests of its members; association of sports clubs organizing competitions between its members; *Informal* class or level.

league[2] n *Obs* measure of distance, about three miles.

leak n hole or defect that allows the escape or entrance of liquid, gas, radiation, etc.; liquid etc. that escapes or enters; disclosure of secrets. ▶ v let liquid etc. in or out; (of liquid etc.) find its way through a leak; disclose secret information. **leakage** n act or instance of leaking. **leaky** adj

lean[1] v **leaning, leaned** or **leant.** rest against; bend or slope from an upright position; tend (towards). **leaning** n tendency.

lean on v *Informal* threaten or intimidate; depend on for help or advice. **lean-to** n shed built against an existing wall.

lean[2] adj thin but healthy-looking; (of meat) lacking fat; unproductive. ▶ n lean part of meat. **leanness** n

leap v **leaping, leapt** or **leaped.** make a sudden powerful jump. ▶ n sudden powerful jump; abrupt increase, as in costs or prices. **leapfrog** n game in which a player vaults over another bending down. **leap year** year with February 29th as an extra day.

learn v **learning, learned** or **learnt.** gain skill or knowledge by study, practice, or teaching; memorize (something); find out or discover. **learned** adj erudite, deeply read; showing much learning. **learner** n **learning** n knowledge got by study.

lease n contract by which land or property is rented for a stated time by the owner to a tenant. ▶ v let or rent by lease. **leasehold** n, adj (land or property) held on lease. **leaseholder** n

leash n lead for a dog.

least adj superlative of LITTLE; smallest. ▶ n smallest one. ▶ adv in the smallest degree.

leather n material made from specially treated animal skins. ▶ adj made of leather. ▶ v beat or thrash. **leathery** adj like leather, tough.

leave[1] v **leaving, left.** go away from; allow to remain, accidentally or deliberately; cause to be or remain in a specified state; discontinue membership of; permit; entrust; bequeath. **leave out** v exclude or omit.

leave[2] n permission to be absent from work or duty; period of such absence; permission to do something; formal parting.

leaven [lev-ven] n substance that causes dough to rise; influence that produces a gradual change. ▶ v raise with leaven; spread through and influence (something).

lecher n man who has or shows excessive sexual desire. **lechery** n **lecherous** [letch-er-uss] adj (of a man) having or showing excessive sexual desire.

lectern n sloping reading desk, esp. in a church.

lecture n informative talk to an audience on a subject; lengthy rebuke or scolding. ▶ v give a talk; scold.

lecturer n person who lectures, esp. in a university or college. **lectureship** n appointment as a lecturer.

ledge n narrow shelf sticking out from a wall; shelflike projection

from a cliff etc.
ledger n book of debit and credit accounts of a firm.

lee n sheltered part or side. **leeward** adj, n (on) the lee side. ▶ adv towards this side. **leeway** n room for free movement within limits.

leech n species of bloodsucking worm; person who lives off others.

leek n vegetable of the onion family with a long bulb and thick stem.

leer v look or grin at in a sneering or suggestive manner. ▶ n sneering or suggestive look or grin.

leery adj Informal suspicious or wary (of).

lees pl n sediment of wine.

left[1] adj of the side that faces west when the front faces north. ▶ adv on or towards the left. ▶ n left hand or part; Politics people supporting socialism rather than capitalism. **leftist** n, adj (person) of the political left. **left-handed** adj more adept with the left hand than with the right. **left-wing** adj socialist; belonging to the more radical part of a political party.

left[2] v past of LEAVE[1].

leftover n unused portion of food or material.

leg n one of the limbs on which a person or animal walks, runs, or stands; part of a garment covering the leg; structure that supports, such as one of the legs of a table; stage of a journey; Sport (part of) one game or race in a series. **pull someone's leg** tease someone. **leggy** adj having long legs. **legless** adj without legs; Slang very drunk. **leggings** pl n covering of leather or other material for the legs; close-fitting trousers for women or children.

legacy n, pl -cies. thing left in a

will; thing handed down to a successor.

legal adj established or permitted by law; relating to law or lawyers. **legally** adv **legality** n **legalize** v make legal. **legalization** n

legate n messenger or representative, esp. from the Pope. **legation** n diplomatic minister and his staff; official residence of a diplomatic minister.

legatee n recipient of a legacy.

legato [leg-ah-toe] n, pl -tos, adv Music (piece to be played) smoothly.

legend n traditional story or myth; traditional literature; famous person or event; stories about such a person or event; inscription. **legendary** adj famous; of or in legend.

legerdemain [lej-er-de-main] n sleight of hand; cunning deception.

legible adj easily read. **legibility** n **legibly** adv

legion n large military force; large number; association of veterans; infantry unit in the Roman army. **legionary** adj, n **legionnaire** n member of a legion. **legionnaire's disease** serious bacterial disease similar to pneumonia.

legislate v make laws. **legislative** adj **legislator** n maker of laws. **legislature** n body of people that makes, amends, or repeals laws. **legislation** n legislating; laws made.

legitimate adj authorized by or in accordance with law; fairly deduced; born to parents married to each other. ▶ v make legitimate. **legitimacy** n **legitimately** adv **legitimize** v make legitimate, legalize. **legitimization** n

Lego n ® construction toy of

plastic bricks fitted together by studs.

leguaan [leg-oo-ahn] n large S African lizard.

legume n pod of a plant of the pea or bean family. ▶ *pl* peas or beans. **leguminous** adj (of plants) pod-bearing.

lei n (in Hawaii) garland of flowers.

leisure n time for relaxation or hobbies. **at one's leisure** when one has time. **leisurely** adj deliberate, unhurried. ▶ adv slowly. **leisured** adj with plenty of spare time. **leisure centre** building with facilities such as a swimming pool, gymnasium, and café.

leitmotif [lite-mote-eef] n Music recurring theme associated with a person, situation, or thought.

lekker adj S Afr slang attractive or nice; tasty.

lemming n rodent of arctic regions, reputed to run into the sea and drown during mass migrations.

lemon n yellow oval fruit that grows on trees; Slang useless or defective person or thing. ▶ adj pale-yellow. **lemonade** n lemon-flavoured soft drink, often fizzy. **lemon curd** creamy spread made of lemons, butter, etc. **lemon sole** edible flatfish.

lemur n nocturnal animal like a small monkey, found in Madagascar.

lend v lending, lent. give the temporary use of; provide (money) temporarily, often for interest; add (a quality or effect), e.g. *her presence lent beauty to the scene.* **lend itself to** be suitable for. **lender** n

length n extent or measurement from end to end; period of time for which something happens; quality of being long; piece of something narrow and long. **at length** at last; in full detail.

lengthy adj very long or tiresome. **lengthily** adv **lengthen** v make or become longer. **lengthways, lengthwise** adv

lenient [lee-nee-ent] adj tolerant, not strict or severe. **leniency** n **leniently** adv

lens n, pl **lenses**. piece of glass or similar material with one or both sides curved, used to bring together or spread light rays in cameras, spectacles, telescopes, etc.; transparent structure in the eye that focuses light.

lent v past of LEND.

Lent n period from Ash Wednesday to Easter Saturday. **Lenten** adj of, in, or suitable to Lent.

lentil n edible seed of a leguminous Asian plant.

lento adv, pl **-tos**, adv Music (piece to be played) slowly.

leonine adj like a lion.

leopard n large spotted carnivorous animal of the cat family.

leotard n tight-fitting garment covering the upper body, worn for dancing or exercise.

leper n person suffering from leprosy; ignored or despised person.

lepidoptera pl n order of insects with four wings covered with fine gossamer scales, as moths and butterflies. **lepidopterist** n person who studies or collects butterflies or moths.

leprechaun n mischievous elf of Irish folklore.

leprosy n disease attacking the nerves and skin, resulting in loss of feeling in the affected parts. **leprous** adj

lesbian n homosexual woman. ▶ adj of homosexual women.

lesbianism n

lese-majesty [lezz-**maj**-est-ee] n treason; taking of liberties against people in authority.

lesion n structural change in an organ of the body caused by illness or injury; injury or wound.

less adj smaller in extent, degree, or duration; not so much; comparative of LITTLE. ▶ pron smaller part or quantity. ▶ adv to a smaller extent or degree. ▶ prep after deducting, minus. **lessen** v make or become smaller or not as much. **lesser** adj not as great in quantity, size, or worth.

lessee n person to whom a lease is granted.

lesson n single period of instruction in a subject; content of this; experience that teaches; portion of Scripture read in church.

lest conj so as to prevent any possibility that; for fear that.

let[1] v letting, let. allow, enable, or cause; used as an auxiliary to express a proposal, command, threat, or assumption; grant use of for rent, lease; allow to escape. **let alone** not to mention. **let down** v disappoint; lower; deflate. **letdown** n disappointment. **let off** v excuse from (a duty or punishment); fire or explode (a weapon); emit (gas, steam, etc.). **let on** v Informal reveal (a secret). **let out** v emit; release. **let up** v diminish or stop. **let-up** n lessening.

let[2] n Tennis minor infringement or obstruction of the ball requiring a replay of the point; hindrance.

lethal adj deadly.

lethargy n sluggishness or dullness; abnormal lack of energy. **lethargic** adj **lethargically** adv

letter n written message, usu. sent by post; alphabetical symbol; strict meaning (of a law etc.). ▶ pl literary knowledge or ability. **lettered** adj learned. **lettering** n **letter bomb** explosive device in a parcel or letter that explodes on opening. **letter box** slot in a door through which letters are delivered; box in a street or post office where letters are posted. **letterhead** n printed heading on stationery giving the sender's name and address.

lettuce n plant with large green leaves used in salads.

leucocyte [**loo**-koh-site] n white blood cell.

leukaemia [loo-**kee**-mee-a] n disease caused by uncontrolled overproduction of white blood cells.

levee n US natural or artificial river embankment.

level adj horizontal; having an even surface; at the same height as something else; equal to or even with (someone or something else); not going above the top edge of (a spoon etc.). ▶ v -**elling**, -**elled**. make even or horizontal; make equal in position or status; direct (a gun, accusation, etc.) at; raze to the ground. ▶ n horizontal line or surface; device for showing or testing if something is horizontal; position on a scale; standard or grade; flat area of land. **on the level** Informal honest or trustworthy. **level crossing** point where a railway line and road cross. **level-headed** adj not apt to be carried away by emotion.

lever n handle used to operate machinery; bar used to move a heavy object or to open something; rigid bar pivoted about a fulcrum to transfer a force to a load; means of exerting pressure to achieve an aim. ▶ v

prise or move with a lever.
leverage n action or power of a
lever; influence or strategic
advantage.

leveret [lev-ver-it] n young hare.

leviathan [lev-vie-ath-an] n sea
monster; anything huge or
formidable.

Levis pl n ® denim jeans.

levitation n raising of a solid body
into the air supernaturally.
levitate v rise or cause to rise into
the air.

levity n, pl -ties. inclination to
make a joke of serious matters.

levy [lev-vee] v levying, levied.
impose and collect (a tax); raise
(troops). ▶ n, pl levies. imposition
or collection of taxes; money
levied.

lewd adj lustful or indecent.
lewdly adv **lewdness** n

lexicon n dictionary; vocabulary of
a language. **lexical** adj relating to
the vocabulary of a language.
lexicographer n writer of
dictionaries. **lexicography** n

liable adj legally obliged or
responsible; given to or at risk
from a condition. **liability** n
hindrance or disadvantage; state
of being liable; financial obligation.

liaise v establish and maintain
communication (with). **liaison** n
communication and contact
between groups; secret or
adulterous relationship.

liana n climbing plant in tropical
forests.

liar n person who tells lies.

lib n Informal short for LIBERATION.

libation [lie-bay-shun] n drink
poured as an offering to the gods.

libel n published statement falsely
damaging a person's reputation.
▶ v -belling, -belled. falsely
damage the reputation of
(someone). **libellous** adj

liberal adj having social and
political views that favour progress
and reform; generous in behaviour
or temperament; tolerant;
abundant; (of education) designed
to develop general cultural
interests. ▶ n person who has
liberal ideas or opinions. **liberally**
adv **liberalism** n belief in
democratic reforms and individual
freedom. **liberality** n generosity.
liberalize v make (laws, a country,
etc.) less restrictive. **liberalization**
n **Liberal Democrat, Lib Dem**
member of the Liberal Democrats,
a British political party favouring a
mixed economy and individual
freedom. **Liberal Party** main
right-wing political party in
Australia.

liberate v set free. **liberation** n
liberator n

libertarian n believer in freedom
of thought and action. ▶ adj
having such a belief.

libertine [lib-er-teen] n morally
dissolute person.

liberty n, pl -ties. freedom; act or
comment regarded as forward or
socially unacceptable. **at liberty**
free; having the right. **take
liberties** be presumptuous.

libido [lib-ee-doe] n, pl -dos.
psychic energy; emotional drive,
esp. of sexual origin. **libidinous**
adj lustful.

library n, pl -braries. room or
building where books are kept;
collection of books, records, etc.
for consultation or borrowing.
librarian n keeper of or worker in
a library. **librarianship** n

libretto n, pl -tos, -ti. words of an
opera. **librettist** n

lice n plural of LOUSE.

licence n document giving official
permission to do something;
formal permission; disregard of

conventions for effect, e.g. *poetic licence*; excessive liberty. **license** v grant a licence to. **licensed** *adj* **licensee** *n* holder of a licence, esp. to sell alcohol.

licentiate *n* person licensed as competent to practise a profession.

licentious *adj* sexually unrestrained or promiscuous.

lichen *n* small flowerless plant forming a crust on rocks, trees, etc.

licit *adj* lawful, permitted.

lick *v* pass the tongue over; touch lightly or flicker round; *Slang* defeat. ▶ *n* licking; small amount (of paint etc.); *Informal* fast pace.

licorice *n* same as LIQUORICE.

lid *n* movable cover; short for EYELID.

lido [**lee**-doe] *n*, *pl* **-dos**. open-air centre for swimming and water sports.

lie[1] *v* **lying, lied.** make a deliberately false statement. ▶ *n* deliberate falsehood. **white lie** see WHITE.

lie[2] *v* **lying, lay, lain.** place oneself or be in a horizontal position; be situated; be or remain in a certain state or position; exist or be found. ▶ *n* way something lies. **lie-down** *n* rest. **lie in** *v* remain in bed late into the morning. **lie-in** *n* long stay in bed in the morning.

lied [**leed**] *n*, *pl* **lieder.** *Music* setting for voice and piano of a romantic poem.

liege [**leej**] *adj* bound to give or receive feudal service. ▶ *n* lord.

lien *n Law* right to hold another's property until a debt is paid.

lieu [**lyew**] *n* **in lieu of** instead of.

lieutenant [lef-**ten**-ant] *n* junior officer in the army or navy; main assistant.

life *n*, *pl* **lives.** state of living beings, characterized by growth, reproduction, and response to stimuli; period between birth and death or between birth and the present time; way of living; amount of time something is active or functions; biography; liveliness or high spirits; living beings collectively. **lifeless** *adj* dead; not lively or exciting; unconscious. **lifelike** *adj* **lifelong** *adj* lasting all of a person's life. **life belt, jacket** buoyant device to keep afloat a person in danger of drowning. **lifeboat** *n* boat used for rescuing people at sea. **life cycle** series of changes undergone by each generation of an animal or plant. **lifeline** *n* means of contact or support; rope used in rescuing a person in danger. **life science** any science concerned with living organisms, such as biology, botany, or zoology. **lifestyle** *n* particular attitudes, habits, etc. **life-support** *adj* (of equipment or treatment) necessary to keep a person alive. **lifetime** *n* length of time a person is alive.

lift *v* move upwards in position, status, volume, etc.; revoke or cancel; take (plants) out of the ground for harvesting; (of fog, etc.) disappear; make or become more cheerful. ▶ *n* cage raised and lowered in a vertical shaft to transport people or goods; ride in a car etc. as a passenger; *Informal* feeling of cheerfulness; lifting. **liftoff** *n* moment a rocket leaves the ground.

ligament *n* band of tissue joining bones.

ligature *n* link, bond, or tie.

light[1] *n* electromagnetic radiation by which things are visible; source of this, lamp; anything that lets in light, such as a window; aspect or view; mental vision; means of setting fire to. ▶ *pl* traffic lights.

▶ adj bright; (of a colour) pale. ▶ v **lighting, lighted** or **lit.** ignite; illuminate or cause to illuminate. **lighten** v make less dark. **lighting** n apparatus for and use of artificial light in theatres, films, etc. **light bulb** glass part of an electric lamp. **lighthouse** n tower with a light to guide ships. **light year** Astronomy distance light travels in one year, about six million million miles.

light² adj not heavy, weighing relatively little; relatively low in strength, amount, density, etc.; not clumsy; not serious or profound; easily digested. ▶ adv with little equipment or luggage. ▶ v **lighting, lighted, lit.** (esp. of birds) settle after flight; come (upon) by chance. **lightly** adv **lightness** n **lighten** v make less heavy or burdensome; make more cheerful or lively. **light-fingered** adj skilful at stealing. **light-headed** adj feeling faint, dizzy. **light-hearted** adj carefree. **lightweight** n, adj (person) of little importance. ▶ n boxer weighing up to 135lb (professional) or 60kg (amateur).

lighter¹ n device for lighting cigarettes etc.

lighter² n flat-bottomed boat for unloading ships.

lightning n visible discharge of electricity in the atmosphere. ▶ adj fast and sudden.

lights pl n lungs of animals as animal food.

ligneous adj of or like wood.

lignite [lig-nite] n woody textured rock used as fuel.

like¹ prep, conj, adj, pron indicating similarity, comparison, etc. **liken** v compare. **likeness** n resemblance; portrait. **likewise** adv similarly.

like² v find enjoyable; be fond of; prefer, choose, or wish. **likeable, likable** adj **liking** n fondness; preference.

likely adj tending or inclined; probable; hopeful, promising. ▶ adv probably. **not likely** Informal definitely not. **likelihood** n probability.

lilac n shrub with pale mauve or white flowers. ▶ adj light-purple.

Lilliputian [lil-lip-pew-shun] adj tiny.

Lilo n, pl -**los.** ® inflatable rubber mattress.

lilt n pleasing musical quality in speaking; jaunty rhythm; graceful rhythmic motion. **lilting** adj

lily n, pl **lilies.** plant which grows from a bulb and has large, often white, flowers.

limb n arm, leg, or wing; main branch of a tree.

limber v (foll. by up) loosen stiff muscles by exercising. ▶ adj pliant or supple.

limbo¹ n in limbo not knowing the result or next stage of something and powerless to influence it.

limbo² n, pl -**bos.** West Indian dance in which dancers lean backwards to pass under a bar.

lime¹ n calcium compound used as a fertilizer or in making cement. **limelight** n glare of publicity. **limestone** n sedimentary rock used in building.

lime² n small green citrus fruit. **lime-green** adj greenish-yellow.

lime³ n deciduous tree with heart-shaped leaves and fragrant flowers.

limerick [lim-mer-ik] n humorous verse of five lines.

limey n US slang British person.

limit n ultimate extent, degree, or amount of something; boundary or edge. ▶ *v* **-iting, -ited.** restrict or confine. **limitation** *n* **limitless** *adj* **limited company** company whose shareholders' liability for debts is restricted.

limousine *n* large luxurious car.

limp[1] *v* walk with an uneven step. ▶ *n* limping walk.

limp[2] *adj* without firmness or stiffness. **limply** *adv*

limpet *n* shellfish which sticks tightly to rocks.

limpid *adj* clear or transparent; easy to understand. **limpidity** *n*

linchpin, lynchpin *n* pin to hold a wheel on its axle; essential person or thing.

linctus *n, pl* **-tuses.** syrupy cough medicine.

linden *n* same as LIME[3].

line[1] *n* long narrow mark; indented mark or wrinkle; boundary or limit; edge or contour of a shape; string or wire for a particular use; telephone connection; wire or cable for transmitting electricity; shipping company; railway track; course or direction of movement; prescribed way of thinking; field of interest or activity; row or queue of people; class of goods; row of words. ▶ *pl* words of a theatrical part; school punishment of writing out a sentence a specified number of times. ▶ *v* mark with lines; be or form a border or edge. **in line for** likely to receive. **in line with** in accordance with. **line dancing** form of dancing performed by rows of people to country and western music. **line-up** *n* people or things assembled for a particular purpose.

line[2] *v* give a lining to; cover the inside of.

lineage [lin-ee-ij] *n* descent from an ancestor.

lineament *n* facial feature.

linear [lin-ee-er] *adj* of or in lines.

linen *n* cloth or thread made from flax; sheets, tablecloths, etc.

liner[1] *n* large passenger ship or aircraft.

liner[2] *n* something used as a lining.

linesman *n* (in some sports) an official who helps the referee or umpire; person who maintains railway, electricity, or telephone lines.

ling[1] *n* slender food fish.

ling[2] *n* heather.

linger *v* delay or prolong departure; continue in a weakened state for a long time before dying or disappearing; spend a long time doing something.

lingerie [lan-zher-ee] *n* women's underwear or nightwear.

lingo *n, pl* **-goes.** *Informal* foreign or unfamiliar language or jargon.

lingua franca *n* language used for communication between people of different mother tongues.

lingual *adj* of the tongue.

linguist *n* person skilled in foreign languages; person who studies linguistics. **linguistic** *adj* of languages. **linguistics** *n* scientific study of language.

liniment *n* medicated liquid rubbed on the skin to relieve pain or stiffness.

lining *n* layer of cloth attached to the inside of a garment etc.; inner covering of anything.

link *n* any of the rings forming a chain; person or thing forming a connection; type of communications connection, e.g. *a radio link.* ▶ *v* connect with or as if with links; connect by association. **linkage** *n* **link-up** *n* joining together of two systems or groups.

links *pl n* golf course, esp. one by

the sea.

linnet n songbird of the finch family.

lino n short for LINOLEUM.

linoleum n floor covering of hessian or jute with a smooth decorative coating of powdered cork.

Linotype n ® typesetting machine which casts lines of words in one piece.

linseed n seed of the flax plant.

lint n soft material for dressing a wound.

lintel n horizontal beam at the top of a door or window.

lion n large animal of the cat family, the male of which has a shaggy mane. **lioness** n fem **the lion's share** the biggest part. **lion-hearted** adj brave.

lip n either of the fleshy edges of the mouth; rim of a jug etc.; Slang impudence. **lip-reading** n method of understanding speech by interpreting lip movements. **lip service** insincere tribute or respect. **lipstick** n cosmetic in stick form, for colouring the lips.

liquefy v -fying, -fied. make or become liquid. **liquefaction** n

liqueur [lik-cure] n flavoured and sweetened alcoholic spirit.

liquid n substance in a physical state which can change shape but not size. ▶ adj of or being a liquid; flowing smoothly; (of assets) in the form of money or easily converted into money. **liquidize** v make or become liquid. **liquidizer** n kitchen appliance that liquidizes food. **liquidity** n state of being able to meet financial obligations.

liquidate v pay (a debt); dissolve a company and share its assets among creditors; wipe out or kill. **liquidation** n **liquidator** n official appointed to liquidate a business.

liquor n alcoholic drink, esp. spirits; liquid in which food has been cooked.

liquorice [lik-ker-iss] n black substance used in medicine and as a sweet.

lira n, pl -re, -ras. monetary unit of Turkey and formerly of Italy.

lisle [rhymes with mile] n strong fine cotton thread or fabric.

lisp n speech defect in which s and z are pronounced th. ▶ v speak or utter with a lisp.

lissom, lissome adj supple, agile.

list[1] n item-by-item record of names or things, usu. written one below another. ▶ v make a list of; include in a list.

list[2] v (of a ship) lean to one side. ▶ n leaning to one side.

listen v concentrate on hearing something; heed or pay attention to. **listener** n **listen in** v listen secretly, eavesdrop.

listeriosis n dangerous form of food poisoning.

listless adj lacking interest or energy. **listlessly** adv

lit v past of LIGHT[1] or LIGHT[2].

litany n, pl -nies. prayer with responses from the congregation; any tedious recital.

literacy n ability to read and write.

literal adj according to the explicit meaning of a word or text, not figurative; (of a translation) word for word; actual, true. **literally** adv

literary adj of or knowledgeable about literature; (of a word) formal, not colloquial.

literate adj able to read and write; educated. **literati** pl n literary people.

literature n written works such as novels, plays, and poetry; books and writings of a country, period, or subject.

lithe adj flexible or supple, pliant.

lithium n Chem chemical element, the lightest known metal.

litho n, pl **-thos.** short for LITHOGRAPH. ▶ adj short for LITHOGRAPHIC.

lithography [lith-og-ra-fee] n method of printing from a metal or stone surface in which the printing areas are made receptive to ink. **lithograph** n print made by lithography. ▶ v reproduce by lithography. **lithographic** adj **lithographer** n

litigant n person involved in a lawsuit.

litigation n legal action. **litigate** v bring or contest a law suit; engage in legal action. **litigious** [lit-**ij**-uss] adj frequently going to law.

litmus n blue dye turned red by acids and restored to blue by alkalis. **litmus test** something which is regarded as a simple and accurate test of a particular thing.

litotes [lie-**toe**-teez] n ironical understatement used for effect.

litre n unit of liquid measure equal to 1000 cubic centimetres or 1.76 pints.

litter n untidy rubbish dropped in public places; group of young animals produced at one birth; straw etc. as bedding for an animal; dry material to absorb a cat's excrement; bed or seat on parallel sticks for carrying people. ▶ v strew with litter; scatter or be scattered about untidily; give birth to young.

little adj small or smaller than average; young. ▶ adv not a lot; hardly; not much or often. ▶ n small amount, extent, or duration.

littoral adj of or by the seashore. ▶ n coastal district.

liturgy n, pl **-gies.** prescribed form of public worship. **liturgical** adj

live[1] v be alive; remain in life or existence; exist in a specified way, e.g. we live well; reside; continue or last; subsist; enjoy life to the full. **live down** v wait till people forget a past mistake or misdeed. **live-in** adj resident. **live together** v (of an unmarried couple) share a house and have a sexual relationship. **live up to** v meet (expectations). **live with** v tolerate.

live[2] adj living, alive; (of a broadcast) transmitted during the actual performance; (of a performance) done in front of an audience; (of a wire, circuit, etc.) carrying an electric current; causing interest or controversy; capable of exploding; glowing or burning. ▶ adv in the form of a live performance. **lively** adj full of life or vigour; animated; vivid. **liveliness** n **liven up** v make (more) lively.

livelihood n occupation or employment.

liver n organ secreting bile; animal liver as food. **liverish** adj having a disorder of the liver; touchy or irritable.

livery n, pl **-eries.** distinctive dress, esp. of a servant or servants; distinctive design or colours of a company. **liveried** adj **livery stable** stable where horses are kept at a charge or hired out.

livestock n farm animals.

livid adj Informal angry or furious; bluish-grey.

living adj possessing life, not dead or inanimate; currently in use or existing; of everyday life, e.g. living conditions. ▶ n condition of being alive; manner of life; financial means. **living room** room in a house used for relaxation and entertainment.

lizard n four-footed reptile with a long body and tail.

llama n woolly animal of the camel family used as a beast of burden in S America.

LLB Bachelor of Laws.

loach n carplike freshwater fish.

load n burden or weight; amount carried; source of worry; amount of electrical energy drawn from a source. ▶ pl *Informal* lots. ▶ v put a load on or into; burden or oppress; cause to be biased; put ammunition into (a weapon); put film into (a camera); transfer (a program) into computer memory. **loaded** adj (of a question) containing a hidden trap or implication; (of dice) dishonestly weighted; *Slang* wealthy.

loaf[1] n, pl **loaves.** shaped mass of baked bread; shaped mass of food; *Slang* head, esp. as the source of common sense, e.g. *use your loaf.*

loaf[2] v idle, loiter. **loafer** n

loam n fertile soil.

loan n money lent at interest; lending; thing lent. ▶ v lend. **loan shark** person who lends money at an extremely high interest rate.

loath, loth [rhymes with **both**] adj unwilling or reluctant (to).

loathe v hate, be disgusted by. **loathing** n **loathsome** adj

lob *Sport* ▶ n ball struck or thrown in a high arc. ▶ v **lobbing, lobbed.** strike or throw (a ball) in a high arc.

lobby n, pl **-bies.** corridor into which rooms open; group which tries to influence legislators; hall in a legislative building to which the public has access. ▶ v try to influence (legislators) in the formulation of policy. **lobbyist** n

lobe n rounded projection; soft hanging part of the ear; subdivision of a body organ. **lobed** adj

lobelia n garden plant with blue, red, or white flowers.

lobola [law-**bawl**-a] n *S Afr* (in African custom) price paid by a bridegroom's family to his bride's family.

lobotomy n, pl **-mies.** surgical incision into a lobe of the brain to treat mental disorders.

lobster n shellfish with a long tail and claws, which turns red when boiled.

local adj of or existing in a particular place; confined to a particular place. ▶ n person belonging to a particular district; *Informal* pub close to one's home. **locally** adv **locality** n neighbourhood or area. **localize** v restrict to a particular place. **locale** [loh-**kahl**] n scene of an event. **local anaesthetic** anaesthetic which produces loss of feeling in one part of the body. **local authority** governing body of a county, district, or region. **local government** government of towns, counties, and districts by locally elected political bodies.

locate v discover the whereabouts of; situate or place. **location** n site or position; act of discovering where something is; site of a film production away from the studio; *S Afr* Black African or coloured township.

loch n *Scot* lake; long narrow bay.

lock[1] n appliance for fastening a door, case, etc.; section of a canal shut off by gates between which the water level can be altered to aid boats moving from one level to another; extent to which a vehicle's front wheels will turn; interlocking of parts; mechanism

for firing a gun; wrestling hold.
▶ v fasten or become fastened
securely; become or cause to
become fixed or united; become
or cause to become immovable;
embrace closely. **lockout** n
closing of a workplace by an
employer to force workers to
accept terms. **locksmith** n person
who makes and mends locks.
lockup n prison; garage or storage
place away from the main
premises.

lock² n strand of hair.

locker n small cupboard with a
lock.

locket n small hinged pendant for
a portrait etc.

lockjaw n tetanus.

locomotive n self-propelled engine
for pulling trains. ▶ adj of
locomotion. **locomotion** n action
or power of moving.

locum n temporary stand-in for a
doctor or clergyman.

locus [loh-kuss] n, pl **loci** [loh-sigh]
area or place where something
happens; Maths set of points or
lines satisfying one or more
specified conditions.

locust n destructive African insect
that flies in swarms and eats crops.

lode n vein of ore. **lodestar** n star
used in navigation or astronomy
as a point of reference.

lodestone n magnetic iron ore.

lodge n Chiefly Brit gatekeeper's
house; house or cabin used
occasionally by hunters, skiers,
etc.; porters' room in a university
or college; local branch of some
societies. ▶ v live in another's
house at a fixed charge; stick or
become stuck (in a place); make
(a complaint etc.) formally.
lodger n **lodging** n temporary
residence. ▶ pl rented room or
rooms in another person's house.

loft n space between the top
storey and roof of a building;
gallery in a church etc. ▶ v Sport
strike, throw, or kick (a ball) high
into the air.

lofty adj **loftier, loftiest**. of great
height; exalted or noble; haughty.
loftily adv haughtily.

log¹ n portion of a felled tree
stripped of branches; detailed
record of a journey of a ship,
aircraft, etc. ▶ v **logging, logged**.
saw logs from a tree; record in a
log. **logging** n work of cutting
and transporting logs. **logbook** n
book recording the details about a
car or a ship's journeys. **log in,
out** v gain entrance to or leave a
computer system by keying in a
special command.

log² n short for LOGARITHM.

loganberry n purplish-red fruit,
similar to a raspberry.

logarithm n one of a series of
arithmetical functions used to
make certain calculations easier.

loggerheads pl n **at loggerheads**
quarrelling, disputing.

loggia [loj-ya] n covered gallery at
the side of a building.

logic n philosophy of reasoning;
reasoned thought or argument.
logical adj of logic; capable of or
using clear valid reasoning;
reasonable. **logically** adv **logician**
n

logistics n detailed planning and
organization of a large, esp.
military, operation. **logistical,
logistic** adj

logo [loh-go] n, pl **-os**. emblem
used by a company or other
organization.

loin n part of the body between
the ribs and the hips; cut of meat
from this part of an animal. ▶ pl
hips and inner thighs. **loincloth** n
piece of cloth covering the loins

only.

loiter v stand or wait aimlessly or idly.

loll v lounge lazily; hang loosely.

lollipop n boiled sweet on a small wooden stick. **lollipop man, lady** Brit informal person holding a circular sign on a pole, who controls traffic so that children may cross the road safely.

lolly n, pl **-ies.** Informal lollipop or ice lolly; Aust & NZ informal sweet; Slang money. **lolly scramble** NZ sweets scattered on the ground for children to collect.

lone adj solitary. **lonely** adj sad because alone; resulting from being alone; unfrequented. **loneliness** n **loner** n Informal person who prefers to be alone. **lonesome** adj lonely.

long[1] adj having length, esp. great length, in space or time. ▶ adv for an extensive period.

long-distance adj going between places far apart. **long face** glum expression. **longhand** n ordinary writing, not shorthand or typing. **long johns** Informal long underpants. **long-life** adj (of milk, batteries, etc.) lasting longer than the regular kind. **long-lived** adj living or lasting for a long time. **long-range** adj extending into the future; (of vehicles, weapons, etc.) designed to cover great distances. **long shot** competitor, undertaking, or bet with little chance of success. **long-sighted** adj able to see distant objects in focus but not nearby ones. **long-standing** adj existing for a long time. **long-suffering** adj enduring trouble or unhappiness without complaint. **long-term** adj lasting or effective for a long time. **long wave** radio wave with a wavelength of over 1000 metres.

long-winded adj speaking or writing at tedious length.

long[2] v have a strong desire for. **longing** n yearning. **longingly** adv

longevity [lon-**jev**-it-ee] n long life.

longitude n distance east or west from a standard meridian. **longitudinal** adj of length or longitude; lengthways.

longshoreman n US docker.

loo n Informal toilet.

loofah n sponge made from the dried pod of a gourd.

look v direct the eyes or attention (towards); have the appearance of being; face in a particular direction; search (for); hope (for). ▶ n instance of looking; (often pl) appearance. **look after** v take care of. **lookalike** n person who is the double of another. **look down on** v treat as inferior or unimportant. **look forward to** v anticipate with pleasure. **look on** v be a spectator; consider or regard. **lookout** n guard; place for watching; Informal worry or concern; chances or prospect. **look out** v be careful. **look up** v discover or confirm by checking in a book; improve; visit. **look up to** v respect.

loom[1] n machine for weaving cloth.

loom[2] v appear dimly; seem ominously close.

loony Slang ▶ adj **loonier, looniest.** foolish or insane. ▶ n, pl **loonies.** foolish or insane person.

loop n rounded shape made by a curved line or rope crossing itself. ▶ v form or fasten with a loop. **loop the loop** fly or be flown in a complete vertical circle. **loophole** n means of evading a rule without breaking it.

loose adj not tight, fastened, fixed, or tense; vague; dissolute or promiscuous. ▶ adv in a loose manner. ▶ *v* free; unfasten; slacken; let fly (an arrow, bullet, etc.). **at a loose end** bored, with nothing to do. **loosely** *adv* **looseness** *n* **loosen** *v* make loose. **loosen up** *v* relax, stop worrying. **loose-leaf** *adj* allowing the addition or removal of pages.

loot *n, v* plunder. ▶ *n Informal* money. **looter** *n* **looting** *n*

lop *v* **lopping, lopped.** cut away twigs and branches; chop off.

lope *v* run with long easy strides.

lop-eared *adj* having drooping ears.

lopsided *adj* greater in height, weight, or size on one side.

loquacious *adj* talkative. **loquacity** *n*

lord *n* person with power over others, such as a monarch or master; male member of the British nobility; *Hist* feudal superior; (**L-**) God or Jesus; (**L-**) (in Britain) title given to certain male officials and peers. **House of Lords** unelected upper chamber of the British parliament. **lord it over** act in a superior manner towards. **the Lord's Prayer** prayer taught by Christ to his disciples. **lordly** *adj* imperious, proud. **Lordship** *n* (in Britain) title of some male officials and peers.

lore *n* body of traditions on a subject.

lorgnette [lor-**nyet**] *n* pair of spectacles mounted on a long handle.

lorikeet *n* small brightly coloured Australian parrot.

lorry *n, pl* -**ries.** *Brit & S Afr* large vehicle for transporting loads by road.

lose *v* **losing, lost.** come to be without, esp. by accident or carelessness; fail to keep or maintain; be deprived of; fail to

get or make use of; be defeated in a competition etc.; be or become engrossed, e.g. *lost in thought.*

loser *n* person or thing that loses; *Informal* person who seems destined to fail.

loss *n* losing; that which is lost; damage resulting from losing. **at a loss** confused or bewildered; not earning enough to cover costs. **loss leader** item sold at a loss to attract customers.

lost *v* past of LOSE. ▶ *adj* unable to find one's way; unable to be found.

lot *pron* great number. ▶ *n* collection of people or things; fate or destiny; one of a set of objects drawn at random to make a selection or choice; item at auction. ▶ *pl Informal* great numbers or quantities. **a lot** *Informal* great deal.

loth *adj* same as LOATH.

lotion *n* medical or cosmetic liquid for use on the skin.

lottery *n, pl* -**teries.** method of raising money by selling tickets that win prizes by chance; gamble.

lotto *n* game of chance like bingo; (**L-**) national lottery.

lotus *n* legendary plant whose fruit induces forgetfulness; Egyptian water lily.

loud *adj* relatively great in volume; capable of making much noise; insistent and emphatic; unpleasantly patterned or colourful. **loudly** *adv* **loudness** *n* **loudspeaker** *n* instrument for converting electrical signals into sound.

lough *n Irish* loch.

lounge *n* living room in a private house; more expensive bar in a pub; area for waiting in an airport. ▶ *v* sit, lie, or stand in a relaxed manner. **lounge suit**

man's suit for daytime wear.

lour v same as LOWER[2].

louse n, pl **lice**. wingless parasitic insect; (pl **louses**) unpleasant person. **lousy** adj Slang mean or unpleasant; bad, inferior; unwell.

lout n crude, oafish, or aggressive person. **loutish** adj

louvre [loo-ver] n one of a set of parallel slats slanted to admit air but not rain. **louvred** adj

love v have a great affection for; feel sexual passion for; enjoy (something) very much. ▶ n great affection; sexual passion; wholehearted liking for something; beloved person; Tennis, squash, etc. score of nothing. **fall in love** become in love. **in love (with)** feeling a strong emotional (and sexual) attraction (for). **make love (to)** have sexual intercourse (with). **lovable, loveable** adj **loveless** adj **lovely** adj **-lier, -liest.** very attractive; highly enjoyable. **lover** n person having a sexual relationship outside marriage; person in love; someone who loves a specified person or thing. **loving** adj affectionate, tender. **lovingly** adv **love affair** romantic or sexual relationship between two people who are not married to each other. **lovebird** n small parrot. **love child** Euphemistic child of an unmarried couple. **love life** person's romantic or sexual relationships. **lovelorn** adj miserable because of unhappiness in love. **lovemaking** n

low[1] adj not tall, high, or elevated; of little or less than the usual amount, degree, quality, or cost; coarse or vulgar; dejected; not loud; deep in pitch. ▶ adv in or to a low position, level, or degree. ▶ n low position, level, or degree;

area of low atmospheric pressure, depression. **lowly** adj modest, humble. **lowliness** n **lowbrow** n, adj (person) with nonintellectual tastes and interests. **Low Church** section of the Anglican Church stressing evangelical beliefs and practices. **lowdown** n Informal inside information. **low-down** adj Informal mean, underhand, or dishonest. **low-key** adj subdued, restrained, not intense. **lowland** n low-lying country. ▶ pl (**L-**) less mountainous parts of Scotland. **low profile** position or attitude avoiding prominence or publicity. **low-spirited** adj depressed.

low[2] n cry of cattle, moo. ▶ v moo.

lower[1] adj below one or more other things; smaller or reduced in amount or value. ▶ v cause or allow to move down; lessen. **lower case** small, as distinct from capital, letters.

lower[2], **lour** v (of the sky or weather) look gloomy or threatening. **lowering** adj

loyal adj faithful to one's friends, country, or government. **loyally** adv **loyalty** n **loyalty card** swipe card issued by a supermarket or chain store to a customer, used to record credit points awarded for money spent in the store. **loyalist** n

lozenge n medicated tablet held in the mouth until it dissolves; four-sided diamond-shaped figure.

LP n record playing approximately 20–25 minutes each side.

L-plate n Brit & Aust sign on a car being driven by a learner driver.

LSD lysergic acid diethylamide, a hallucinogenic drug.

Lt Lieutenant.

Ltd Brit Limited (Liability).

lubricate [loo-brik-ate] v oil or grease to lessen friction. **lubricant**

n lubricating substance, such as oil. **lubrication** *n*

lubricious *adj Lit* lewd.

lucerne *n* fodder plant like clover, alfalfa.

lucid *adj* clear and easily understood; able to think clearly; bright and clear. **lucidly** *adv* **lucidity** *n*

Lucifer *n* Satan.

luck *n* fortune, good or bad; good fortune. **lucky** *adj* having or bringing good luck. **lucky dip** game in which prizes are picked from a tub at random. **luckily** *adv* fortunately. **luckless** *adj* having bad luck.

lucrative *adj* very profitable.

lucre [loo-ker] *n* filthy lucre *Facetious* money.

Luddite *n* person opposed to change in industrial methods.

ludicrous *adj* absurd or ridiculous. **ludicrously** *adv*

ludo *n* game played with dice and counters on a board.

lug[1] *v* **lugging, lugged.** carry or drag with great effort.

lug[2] *n* projection serving as a handle; *Brit informal* ear.

luggage *n* traveller's cases, bags, etc.

lugubrious *adj* mournful, gloomy. **lugubriously** *adv*

lugworm *n* large worm used as bait.

lukewarm *adj* moderately warm, tepid; indifferent or half-hearted.

lull *v* soothe (someone) by soft sounds or motions; calm (fears or suspicions) by deception. ▶ *n* brief time of quiet in a storm etc.

lullaby *n, pl* -**bies.** quiet song to send a child to sleep.

lumbago [lum-bay-go] *n* pain in the lower back. **lumbar** *adj* relating to the lower back.

lumber[1] *n Brit* unwanted disused household articles; *Chiefly US* sawn timber. ▶ *v Informal* burden with something unpleasant.

lumberjack *n US* man who fells trees and prepares logs for transport.

lumber[2] *v* move heavily and awkwardly. **lumbering** *adj*

luminous *adj* reflecting or giving off light. **luminosity** *n* **luminary** *n* famous person; *Lit* heavenly body giving off light. **luminescence** *n* emission of light at low temperatures by any process other than burning. **luminescent** *adj*

lump[1] *n* shapeless piece or mass; swelling; *Informal* awkward or stupid person. ▶ *v* consider as a single group. **lump in one's throat** tight dry feeling in one's throat, usu. caused by great emotion. **lumpy** *adj* **lump sum** relatively large sum of money paid at one time.

lump[2] *v* **lump it** *Informal* tolerate or put up with it.

lunar *adj* relating to the moon.

lunatic *adj* foolish and irresponsible. ▶ *n* foolish or annoying person; *Old-fashioned* insane person. **lunacy** *n*

lunch *n* meal taken in the middle of the day. ▶ *v* eat lunch. **luncheon** *n* formal lunch. **luncheon meat** tinned ground mixture of meat and cereal. **luncheon voucher** *Brit* voucher for a certain amount, given to an employee and accepted by some restaurants as payment for a meal.

lung *n* organ that allows an animal or bird to breathe air: humans have two lungs in the chest.

lunge *n* sudden forward motion; thrust with a sword. ▶ *v* move with or make a lunge.

lupin *n* garden plant with tall

spikes of flowers.

lupine adj like a wolf.

lurch¹ v tilt or lean suddenly to one side; stagger. ▶ n lurching movement.

lurch² n **leave someone in the lurch** abandon someone in difficulties.

lurcher n crossbred dog trained to hunt silently.

lure v tempt or attract by the promise of reward. ▶ n person or thing that lures; brightly-coloured artificial angling bait.

lurid adj vivid in shocking detail, sensational; glaring in colour. **luridly** adv

lurk v lie hidden or move stealthily, esp. for sinister purposes; be latent.

luscious [lush-uss] adj extremely pleasurable to taste or smell; very attractive.

lush¹ adj (of grass etc.) growing thickly and healthily; opulent.

lush² n Slang alcoholic.

lust n strong sexual desire; any strong desire. ▶ v have passionate desire (for). **lustful** adj **lusty** adj vigorous, healthy. **lustily** adv

lustre n gloss, sheen; splendour or glory; metallic pottery glaze. **lustrous** adj shining, luminous.

lute n ancient guitar-like musical instrument with a body shaped like a half pear.

Lutheran adj of Martin Luther (1483–1546), German Reformation leader, his doctrines, or a Church following these doctrines.

luxuriant adj rich and abundant; very elaborate. **luxuriance** n **luxuriantly** adv

luxuriate v take self-indulgent pleasure (in); flourish.

luxury n, pl **-ries**. enjoyment of rich, very comfortable living; enjoyable but not essential thing.

▶ adj of or providing luxury.

luxurious adj full of luxury, sumptuous. **luxuriously** adv

lychee [lie-chee] n Chinese fruit with a whitish juicy pulp.

lych gate n roofed gate to a churchyard.

Lycra n ® elastic fabric used for tight-fitting garments, such as swimsuits.

lye n caustic solution made from wood ash.

lying v present participle of LIE¹ or LIE².

lymph n colourless bodily fluid consisting mainly of white blood cells. **lymphatic** adj

lymphocyte n type of white blood cell.

lynch v put to death without a trial.

lynx n animal of the cat family with tufted ears and a short tail.

lyre n ancient musical instrument like a U-shaped harp.

lyric adj (of poetry) expressing personal emotion in songlike style; like a song. ▶ n short poem in a songlike style. ▶ pl words of a popular song. **lyrical** adj lyric; enthusiastic. **lyricist** n person who writes the words of songs or musicals.

— M m —

m metre(s); mile(s); minute(s).

M Motorway; Monsieur.

m. male; married; masculine; meridian; month.

ma n Informal mother.

MA Master of Arts.

ma'am n madam.

mac n Brit informal mackintosh.

macabre [mak-kahb-ra] adj strange and horrible, gruesome.

macadam n road surface of

pressed layers of small broken stones.

macadamia n Australian tree with edible nuts.

macaroni n pasta in short tube shapes.

macaroon n small biscuit or cake made with ground almonds.

macaw n large tropical American parrot.

mace[1] n ceremonial staff of office; medieval weapon with a spiked metal head.

mace[2] n spice made from the dried husk of the nutmeg.

macerate [mass-er-ate] v soften by soaking. **maceration** n

machete [mash-ett-ee] n broad heavy knife used for cutting or as a weapon.

Machiavellian [mak-ee-a-vel-yan] adj unprincipled, crafty, and opportunist.

machinations [mak-in-nay-shunz] pl n cunning plots and ploys.

machine n apparatus, usu. powered by electricity, designed to perform a particular task; vehicle, such as a car or aircraft; controlling system of an organization. ▶ v make or produce by machine. **machinery** n machines or machine parts collectively. **machinist** n person who operates a machine. **machine gun** automatic gun that fires rapidly and continuously. **machine-gun** v fire at with such a gun. **machine-readable** adj (of data) in a form suitable for processing by a computer.

machismo [mak-izz-moh] n exaggerated or strong masculinity.

Mach number [mak] n ratio of the speed of a body in a particular medium to the speed of sound in that medium.

macho [match-oh] adj strongly or

exaggeratedly masculine.

mackerel n edible sea fish.

mackintosh n waterproof raincoat of rubberized cloth.

macramé [mak-rah-mee] n ornamental work of knotted cord.

macrobiotics n dietary system advocating whole grains and vegetables grown without chemical additives. **macrobiotic** adj

macrocosm n the universe; any large complete system.

mad adj **madder, maddest.** mentally deranged, insane; very foolish; Informal angry; frantic; (foll. by about or on) very enthusiastic (about). **like mad** Informal with great energy, enthusiasm, or haste. **madly** adv **madness** n **madden** v infuriate or irritate. **maddening** adj **madman, madwoman** n

madam n polite form of address to a woman; Informal precocious or conceited girl.

madame [mad-dam] n, pl **mesdames** [may-dam] French title equivalent to Mrs.

madcap adj foolish or reckless.

madder n climbing plant; red dye made from its root.

made v past of MAKE.

Madeira [mad-deer-a] n fortified white wine. **Madeira cake** rich sponge cake.

mademoiselle [mad-mwah-zel] n, pl **mesdemoiselles** [maid-mwah-zel] French title equivalent to Miss.

Madonna n the Virgin Mary; picture or statue of her.

madrigal n 16th–17th-century part song for unaccompanied voices.

maelstrom [male-strom] n great whirlpool; turmoil.

maestro [my-stroh] n, pl **-tri, -tros.** outstanding musician or conductor; any master of an art.

Mafia n international secret criminal organization founded in Sicily. **mafioso** n, pl **-sos, -si.** member of the Mafia.

magazine n periodical publication with articles by different writers; television or radio programme made up of short nonfictional items; appliance for automatically supplying cartridges to a gun or slides to a projector; storehouse for explosives or arms.

magenta [maj-**jen**-ta] adj deep purplish-red.

maggot n larva of an insect. **maggoty** adj

Magi [**maje**-eye] pl n wise men from the East who came to worship the infant Jesus.

magic n supposed art of invoking supernatural powers to influence events; mysterious quality or power. ▶ adj (also **magical**) of, using, or like magic; Informal wonderful, marvellous. **magically** adv **magician** n conjuror; person with magic powers.

magistrate n public officer administering the law; Brit justice of the peace; Aust & NZ former name for DISTRICT COURT JUDGE. **magisterial** adj commanding or authoritative; of a magistrate.

magma n molten rock inside the earth's crust.

magnanimous adj noble and generous. **magnanimously** adv **magnanimity** n

magnate n influential or wealthy person, esp. in industry.

magnesia n white tasteless substance used as an antacid and a laxative; magnesium oxide.

magnesium n Chem silvery-white metallic element.

magnet n piece of iron or steel capable of attracting iron and

pointing north when suspended.

magnetic adj having the properties of a magnet; powerfully attractive. **magnetically** adv

magnetism n magnetic property; powerful personal charm; science of magnetic properties.

magnetize v make into a magnet; attract strongly. **magnetic tape** plastic strip coated with a magnetic substance for recording sound or video signals.

magneto [mag-**nee**-toe] n, pl **-tos.** apparatus for ignition in an internal-combustion engine.

magnificent adj splendid or impressive; excellent. **magnificently** adv **magnificence** n

magnify v **-fying, -fied.** increase in apparent size, as with a lens; exaggerate. **magnification** n

magnitude n relative importance or size.

magnolia n shrub or tree with showy white or pink flowers.

magnum n large wine bottle holding about 1.5 litres.

magpie n black-and-white bird.

maharajah n former title of some Indian princes. **maharani** n fem

mah jong, mah-jongg n Chinese table game for four, played with tiles bearing different designs.

mahogany n hard reddish-brown wood of several tropical trees.

mahout [ma-**howt**] n (in India and the East Indies) elephant driver or keeper.

maid n (also **maidservant**) female servant; Lit young unmarried woman.

maiden n Lit young unmarried woman. ▶ adj unmarried; first, e.g. maiden voyage. **maidenly** adj modest. **maidenhair** n fern with delicate fronds. **maidenhead** n virginity. **maiden name** woman's surname before marriage. **maiden**

over *Cricket* over in which no runs are scored.

mail¹ *n* letters and packages transported and delivered by the post office; postal system; single collection or delivery of mail; train, ship, or aircraft carrying mail; same as E-MAIL. ▸ *v* send by mail. **mailbox** *n US, Canadian & Aust* box into which letters and parcels are delivered. **mail order** system of buying goods by post. **mailshot** *n Brit* posting of advertising material to many selected people at once.

mail² *n* flexible armour of interlaced rings or links.

maim *v* cripple or mutilate.

main *adj* chief or principal. ▸ *n* principal pipe or line carrying water, gas, or electricity. ▸ *pl* main distribution network for water, gas, or electricity. **in the main** on the whole. **mainly** *adv* for the most part, chiefly. **mainframe** *n, adj Computers* (denoting) a high-speed general-purpose computer. **mainland** *n* stretch of land which forms the main part of a country. **mainmast** *n* chief mast of a ship. **mainsail** *n* largest sail on a mainmast. **mainspring** *n* chief cause or motive; chief spring of a watch or clock. **mainstay** *n* chief support; rope securing a mainmast. **mainstream** *adj* (of) a prevailing cultural trend.

maintain *v* continue or keep in existence; keep up or preserve; support financially; assert. **maintenance** *n* maintaining; upkeep of a building, car, etc.; provision of money for a separated or divorced spouse.

maisonette *n Brit* flat with more than one floor.

maître d'hôtel [**met**-ra dote-**tell**] *n French* head waiter.

maize *n* type of corn with spikes of yellow grains.

majesty *n, pl* **-ties.** stateliness or grandeur; supreme power. **majestic** *adj* **majestically** *adv*

major *adj* greater in number, quality, or extent; significant or serious. ▸ *n* middle-ranking army officer; scale in music; *US, Canadian, S Afr, Aust & NZ* principal field of study at a university etc. ▸ *v* (foll. by *in*) *US, Canadian, S Afr, Aust & NZ* do one's principal study in (a particular subject). **major-domo** *n, pl* **-domos.** chief steward of a great household.

majority *n, pl* **-ties.** greater number; number by which the votes on one side exceed those on the other; largest party voting together; state of being legally an adult.

make *v* **making, made.** create, construct, or establish; cause to do or be; bring about or produce; perform (an action); serve as or become; amount to; earn. ▸ *n* brand, type, or style. **make do** manage with an inferior alternative. **make it** *Informal* be successful. **on the make** *Informal* out for profit or conquest. **maker** *n* **making** *n* creation or production. ▸ *pl* necessary requirements or qualities. **make-believe** *n* fantasy or pretence. **make for** *v* head towards. **make off with** *v* steal or abduct. **makeshift** *adj* serving as a temporary substitute. **make up** *v* form or constitute; prepare; invent; supply what is lacking, complete; (foll. by *for*) compensate (for); settle a quarrel; apply cosmetics. **make-up** *n* cosmetics; way something is made; mental or physical constitution. **makeweight** n something unimportant added to make up a lack.

mal- combining form bad or badly, e.g. malformation.

malachite [mal-a-kite] n green mineral.

maladjusted adj Psychol unable to meet the demands of society. **maladjustment** n

maladministration n inefficient or dishonest administration.

maladroit adj clumsy or awkward.

malady n, pl **-dies**. disease or illness.

malaise [mal-laze] n vague feeling of unease, illness, or depression.

malapropism n comical misuse of a word by confusion with one which sounds similar, e.g. I am not under the affluence of alcohol.

malaria n infectious disease caused by the bite of some mosquitoes. **malarial** adj

Malay n member of a people of Malaysia or Indonesia; language of this people. **Malayan** adj, n

malcontent n discontented person.

male adj of the sex which can fertilize female reproductive cells. ▶ n male person or animal.

malediction [mal-id-dik-shun] n curse.

malefactor [mal-if-act-or] n criminal or wrongdoer.

malevolent [mal-lev-a-lent] adj wishing evil to others. **malevolently** adv **malevolence** n

malfeasance [mal-fee-zanss] n misconduct, esp. by a public official.

malformed adj misshapen or deformed. **malformation** n

malfunction v function imperfectly or fail to function. ▶ n defective functioning or failure to function.

malice [mal-iss] n desire to cause harm to others. **malicious** adj

maliciously adv

malign [mal-line] v slander or defame. ▶ adj evil in influence or effect. **malignity** n evil disposition.

malignant [mal-lig-nant] adj seeking to harm others; (of a tumour) harmful and uncontrollable. **malignancy** n

malinger v feign illness to avoid work. **malingerer** n

mall [mawl] n street or shopping area closed to vehicles.

mallard n wild duck.

malleable [mal-lee-a-bl] adj capable of being hammered or pressed into shape; easily influenced. **malleability** n

mallee n Aust low-growing eucalypt in dry regions.

mallet n (wooden) hammer; stick with a head like a hammer, used in croquet or polo.

mallow n plant with pink or purple flowers.

malnutrition n inadequate nutrition.

malodorous [mal-lode-or-uss] adj bad-smelling.

malpractice n immoral, illegal, or unethical professional conduct.

malt n grain, such as barley, prepared for use in making beer or whisky.

maltreat v treat badly. **maltreatment** n

mama n Old-fashioned mother.

mamba n deadly S African snake.

mamma n same as MAMA.

mammal n animal of the type that suckles its young. **mammalian** adj

mammary adj of the breasts or milk-producing glands.

mammon n wealth regarded as a source of evil.

mammoth n extinct elephant-like mammal. ▶ adj colossal.

man n, pl **men**. adult male; human being or person; mankind;

manservant; piece used in chess etc. ▶ v **manning, manned.** supply with sufficient people for operation or defence. **manhood** n

mankind n human beings collectively. **manly** adj (possessing qualities) appropriate to a man. **manliness** n **mannish** adj (of a woman) like a man. **man-hour** n work done by one person in one hour. **man-made** adj made artificially.

mana n NZ authority, influence.

manacle [man-a-kl] n, v handcuff or fetter.

manage v succeed in doing; be in charge of, administer; handle or control; cope with (financial) difficulties. **manageable** adj **management** n managers collectively; administration or organization. **manager, manageress** n person in charge of a business, institution, actor, sports team, etc. **managerial** adj

manatee n large tropical plant-eating aquatic mammal.

mandarin n high-ranking government official; kind of small orange.

mandate n official or authoritative command; authorization or instruction from an electorate to its representative or government. ▶ v give authority to. **mandatory** adj compulsory.

mandible n lower jawbone or jawlike part.

mandolin n musical instrument with four pairs of strings.

mandrake n plant with a forked root, formerly used as a narcotic.

mandrel n shaft on which work is held in a lathe.

mandrill n large blue-faced baboon.

mane n long hair on the neck of a horse, lion, etc.

manful adj determined and brave. **manfully** adv

manganese n Chem brittle greyish-white metallic element.

mange n skin disease of domestic animals.

mangelwurzel n variety of beet used as cattle food.

manger n eating trough in a stable or barn.

mangetout [mawnzh-too] n variety of pea with an edible pod.

mangle[1] v destroy by crushing and twisting; spoil.

mangle[2] n machine with rollers for squeezing water from washed clothes. ▶ v put through a mangle.

mango n, pl **-goes, -gos.** tropical fruit with sweet juicy yellow flesh.

mangrove n tropical tree with exposed roots, which grows beside water.

mangy adj **mangier, mangiest.** having mange; scruffy or shabby.

manhandle v treat roughly.

manhole n hole with a cover, through which a person can enter a drain or sewer.

mania n extreme enthusiasm; madness. **maniac** n mad person; Informal person who has an extreme enthusiasm for something. **maniacal** [man-eye-a-kl] adj

manic adj affected by mania.

manicure n cosmetic care of the fingernails and hands. ▶ v care for (the fingernails and hands) in this way. **manicurist** n

manifest adj easily noticed, obvious. ▶ v show plainly; be evidence of. ▶ n list of cargo or passengers for customs. **manifestation** n

manifesto n, pl **-tos, -toes.** declaration of policy as issued by a political party.

manifold adj numerous and varied.

▶ *n* pipe with several outlets, esp. in an internal-combustion engine.

manikin *n* little man or dwarf; model of the human body.

manila, manilla *n* strong brown paper used for envelopes.

manipulate *v* handle skilfully; control cleverly or deviously. **manipulation** *n* **manipulative** *adj* **manipulator** *n*

manna *n Bible* miraculous food which sustained the Israelites in the wilderness; windfall.

mannequin *n* woman who models clothes at a fashion show; life-size dummy of the human body used to fit or display clothes.

manner *n* way a thing happens or is done; person's bearing or behaviour; type or kind; custom or style. ▶ *pl* (polite) social behaviour. **mannered** *adj* affected. **mannerism** *n* person's distinctive habit or trait.

mannikin *n* same as MANIKIN.

manoeuvre [man-noo-ver] *n* skilful movement; contrived, complicated, and possibly deceptive plan or action. ▶ *pl* military or naval exercises. ▶ *v* manipulate or contrive skilfully or cunningly; perform manoeuvres. **manoeuvrable** *adj*

manor *n Brit* large country house and its lands. **manorial** *adj*

manpower *n* available number of workers.

manqué [mong-kay] *adj* would-be, e.g. *an actor manqué.*

mansard roof *n* roof with a break in its slope, the lower part being steeper than the upper.

manse *n* house provided for a minister in some religious denominations.

manservant *n, pl* **menservants.** male servant, esp. a valet.

mansion *n* large house.

manslaughter *n* unlawful but unintentional killing of a person.

mantel *n* structure round a fireplace. **mantelpiece, mantel shelf** *n* shelf above a fireplace.

mantilla *n* (in Spain) a large scarf covering a woman's head and shoulders.

mantis *n, pl* **-tises, -tes.** carnivorous insect like a grasshopper.

mantle *n* loose cloak; covering; responsibilities and duties which go with a particular job or position.

mantra *n Hinduism, Buddhism* any sacred word or syllable used as an object of concentration.

manual *adj* of or done with the hands; by human labour rather than automatic means. ▶ *n* handbook; organ keyboard. **manually** *adv*

manufacture *v* process or make (goods) on a large scale using machinery; invent or concoct (an excuse etc.). ▶ *n* process of manufacturing goods. **manufacturer** *n* company that manufactures goods.

manure *n* animal excrement used as a fertilizer.

manuscript *n* book or document, orig. one written by hand; copy for printing.

Manx *adj* of the Isle of Man or its inhabitants. ▶ *n* almost extinct language of the Isle of Man. **Manx cat** tailless breed of cat.

many *adj* **more, most.** numerous. ▶ *n* large number.

Maoism *n* form of Marxism advanced by Mao Tse-tung in China. **Maoist** *n, adj*

Maori *n, pl* **-ri, -ris.** member of the indigenous race of New Zealand; language of the Maoris. ▶ *adj* of the Maoris or their language.

map 337 **maritime**

map n representation of the earth's surface or some part of it, showing geographical features. ▶ v mapping, mapped. make a map of. **map out** v plan.

maple n tree with broad leaves, a variety of which (**sugar maple**) yields sugar.

mar v marring, marred. spoil or impair.

Mar. March.

marabou n large black-and-white African stork; its soft white down, used to trim hats etc.

maraca [mar-**rak**-a] n shaken percussion instrument made from a gourd containing dried seeds etc.

marae n NZ enclosed space in front of a Maori meeting house; Maori meeting house and its buildings.

maraschino cherry [mar-rass-**kee**-no] n cherry preserved in a cherry liqueur with a taste like bitter almonds.

marathon n long-distance race of 26 miles 385 yards (42.195 kilometres); long or arduous task.

marauding adj wandering or raiding in search of plunder. **marauder** n

marble n kind of limestone with a mottled appearance, which can be highly polished; slab of or sculpture in this; small glass ball used in playing marbles. ▶ pl game of rolling these at one another. **marbled** adj having a mottled appearance like marble.

march¹ v walk with a military step; make (a person or group) proceed; progress steadily. ▶ n action of marching; steady progress; distance covered by marching; piece of music, as for a march. **marcher** n **marching girl** Aust & NZ girl who does team formation marching as a sport.

march² n border or frontier.

March n third month of the year.

marchioness [marsh-on-**ness**] n woman holding the rank of marquis; wife or widow of a marquis.

mare n female horse or zebra. **mare's nest** discovery which proves worthless.

margarine n butter substitute made from animal or vegetable fats.

marge n Informal margarine.

margin n edge or border; blank space round a printed page; additional amount or one greater than necessary; limit. **marginal** adj insignificant, unimportant; near a limit; Politics (of a constituency) won by only a small margin. ▶ n Politics marginal constituency. **marginalize** v make or treat as insignificant. **marginally** adv

marguerite n large daisy.

marigold n plant with yellow or orange flowers.

marijuana [mar-ree-**wah**-na] n dried flowers and leaves of the cannabis plant, used as a drug, esp. in cigarettes.

marina n harbour for yachts and other pleasure boats.

marinade n seasoned liquid in which fish or meat is soaked before cooking. ▶ v same as MARINATE. **marinate** v soak in marinade.

marine adj of the sea or shipping. ▶ n (esp. in Britain and the US) soldier trained for land and sea combat; country's shipping or fleet. **mariner** n sailor.

marionette n puppet worked with strings.

marital adj relating to marriage.

maritime adj relating to shipping; of, near, or living in the sea.

marjoram n aromatic herb used for seasoning food and in salads.

mark¹ n line, dot, scar, etc. visible on a surface; distinguishing sign or symbol; written or printed symbol; letter or number used to grade academic work; indication of position; indication of some quality; target or goal. ▶ v make a mark on; characterize or distinguish; indicate; pay attention to; notice or watch; grade (academic work); stay close to (a sporting opponent) to hamper his or her play. **marked** adj noticeable. **markedly** adv **marker** n

mark² n same as DEUTSCHMARK.

market n assembly or place for buying and selling; demand for goods. ▶ v -keting, -keted. offer or produce for sale. **on the market** for sale. **marketable** adj **marketing** n part of a business that controls the way that goods or services are sold. **market garden** place where fruit and vegetables are grown for sale. **market maker** (in London Stock Exchange) person who uses a firm's money to create a market for a stock. **marketplace** n market; commercial world. **market research** research into consumers' needs and purchases.

marksman n person skilled at shooting. **marksmanship** n

marl n soil formed of clay and lime, used as fertilizer.

marlinespike, marlinspike n pointed hook used to separate strands of rope.

marmalade n jam made from citrus fruits.

marmoreal adj of or like marble.

marmoset n small bushy-tailed monkey.

marmot n burrowing rodent.

maroon¹ adj reddish-purple.

maroon² v abandon ashore, esp. on an island; isolate without resources.

marquee n large tent used for a party or exhibition.

marquess [mar-kwiss] n Brit nobleman of the rank below a duke.

marquetry n ornamental inlaid work of wood.

marquis n (in some European countries) nobleman of the rank above a count.

marram grass n grass that grows on sandy shores.

marrow n fatty substance inside bones; long thick striped green vegetable with whitish flesh.

marry v -rying, -ried. take as a husband or wife; join or give in marriage; unite closely. **marriage** n state of being married; wedding. **marriageable** adj

Mars n Roman god of war; fourth planet from the sun.

Marsala [mar-sah-la] n dark sweet wine.

marsh n low-lying wet land. **marshy** adj

marshal n officer of the highest rank; official who organizes ceremonies or events; US law officer. ▶ v -shalling, -shalled. arrange in order; assemble; conduct with ceremony. **marshalling yard** railway depot for goods trains.

marshmallow n spongy pink or white sweet.

marsupial [mar-soop-ee-al] n animal that carries its young in a pouch, such as a kangaroo.

mart n market.

Martello tower n round tower for coastal defence, formerly used in Europe.

marten n weasel-like animal.

martial adj of war, warlike.
martial art any of various
philosophies and techniques of
self-defence, orig. Eastern, such as
karate. **martial law** law enforced
by military authorities in times of
danger or emergency.
Martian [marsh-an] adj of Mars.
▶ n supposed inhabitant of Mars.
martin n bird with a slightly forked
tail.
martinet n person who maintains
strict discipline.
martini n cocktail of vermouth and
gin.
martyr n person who dies or
suffers for his or her beliefs. ▶ v
make a martyr of. **be a martyr to**
be constantly suffering from.
martyrdom n
marvel v **-velling, -velled.** be filled
with wonder. ▶ n wonderful thing.
marvellous adj amazing;
wonderful.
Marxism n political philosophy of
Karl Marx. **Marxist** n, adj
marzipan n paste of ground
almonds, sugar, and egg whites.
masc. masculine.
mascara n cosmetic for darkening
the eyelashes.
mascot n person, animal, or thing
supposed to bring good luck.
masculine adj relating to males;
manly; Grammar of the gender of
nouns that includes some male
animate things. **masculinity** n
mash n Informal mashed potatoes;
bran or meal mixed with warm
water as food for horses etc. ▶ v
crush into a soft mass.
mask n covering for the face, as a
disguise or protection; behaviour
that hides one's true feelings. ▶ v
cover with a mask; hide or
disguise.
masochism [mass-oh-kiz-zum] n
condition in which (sexual)

pleasure is obtained from feeling
pain or from being humiliated.
masochist n **masochistic** adj
mason n person who works with
stone; **(M-)** Freemason. **Masonic**
adj of Freemasonry. **masonry** n
stonework. **(M-)** Freemasonry.
masque [mask] n Hist
16th–17th-century form of
dramatic entertainment.
masquerade [mask-er-aid] n
deceptive show or pretence; party
at which masks and costumes are
worn. ▶ v pretend to be someone
or something else.
mass n coherent body of matter;
large quantity or number; Physics
amount of matter in a body. ▶ adj
large-scale; involving many
people. ▶ v form into a mass. **the
masses** ordinary people. **massive**
adj large and heavy. **mass-market**
adj for or appealing to a large
number of people. **mass media**
means of communication to many
people, such as television and
newspapers. **mass-produce** v
manufacture (standardized goods)
in large quantities.
Mass n service of the Eucharist,
esp. in the RC Church.
massacre [mass-a-ker] n
indiscriminate killing of large
numbers of people. ▶ v kill in large
numbers.
massage [mass-ahzh] n rubbing
and kneading of parts of the body
to reduce pain or stiffness. ▶ v
give a massage to. **masseur**,
(fem) **masseuse** n person who
gives massages.
massif [mass-seef] n connected
group of mountains.
mast[1] n tall pole for supporting
something, esp. a ship's sails.
mast[2] n fruit of the beech, oak,
etc., used as pig fodder.
mastectomy [mass-tek-tom-ee] n,

pl **-mies.** surgical removal of a breast.

master *n* person in control, such as an employer or an owner of slaves or animals; expert; great artist; original thing from which copies are made; male teacher. ▶ *adj* overall or controlling; main or principal. ▶ *v* acquire knowledge of or skill in; overcome. **masterful** *adj* domineering; showing great skill. **masterly** *adj* showing great skill. **mastery** *n* expertise; control or command. **master key** key that opens all the locks of a set. **mastermind** *v* plan and direct (a complex task). ▶ *n* person who plans and directs a complex task. **masterpiece** *n* outstanding work of art.

mastic *n* gum obtained from certain trees; putty-like substance used as a filler, adhesive, or seal.

masticate *v* chew. **mastication** *n*

mastiff *n* large dog.

mastitis *n* inflammation of a breast or udder.

mastodon *n* extinct elephant-like mammal.

mastoid *n* projection of the bone behind the ear.

masturbate *v* fondle the genitals (of). **masturbation** *n*

mat *n* piece of fabric used as a floor covering or to protect a surface; thick tangled mass. ▶ *v* **matting, matted.** tangle or become tangled into a dense mass.

matador *n* man who kills the bull in bullfights.

match¹ *n* contest in a game or sport; person or thing exactly like, equal to, or in harmony with another; marriage. ▶ *v* be exactly like, equal to, or in harmony with; put in competition (with); find a match for; join (in marriage).

matchless *adj* unequalled.

matchmaker *n* person who schemes to bring about a marriage. **matchmaking** *n, adj*

match² *n* small stick with a tip which ignites when scraped on a rough surface. **matchbox** *n* **matchstick** *n* wooden part of a match. ▶ *adj* (of drawn figures) thin and straight. **matchwood** *n* small splinters.

mate¹ *n* *Informal* friend; associate or colleague, e.g. *team-mate*; sexual partner of an animal; officer in a merchant ship; tradesman's assistant. ▶ *v* pair (animals) or (of animals) be paired for reproduction.

mate² *n, v* *Chess* checkmate.

material *n* substance of which a thing is made; cloth; information on which a piece of work may be based. ▶ *pl* things needed for an activity. ▶ *adj* of matter or substance; not spiritual; affecting physical wellbeing; relevant. **materially** *adv* considerably. **materialism** *n* excessive interest in or desire for money and possessions; belief that only the material world exists. **materialist** *adj, n* **materialistic** *adj* **materialize** *v* actually happen; come into existence or view. **materialization** *n*

maternal *adj* of a mother; related through one's mother. **maternity** *n* motherhood. ▶ *adj* of or for pregnant women.

matey *adj* *Brit informal* friendly or intimate.

mathematics *n* science of number, quantity, shape, and space. **mathematical** *adj* **mathematically** *adv* **mathematician** *n*

maths *n Informal* mathematics.

Matilda *n Aust hist* swagman's bundle of belongings. **waltz**

Matilda *Aust* travel about carrying one's bundle of belongings.

matinée [mat-in-nay] *n* afternoon performance in a theatre or cinema.

matins *pl n* early morning service in various Christian Churches.

matriarch [mate-ree-ark] *n* female head of a tribe or family. **matriarchal** *adj* **matriarchy** *n* society governed by a female, in which descent is traced through the female line.

matricide *n* crime of killing one's mother; person who does this.

matriculate *v* enrol or be enrolled in a college or university. **matriculation** *n*

matrimony *n* marriage. **matrimonial** *adj*

matrix [may-trix] *n, pl* **matrices**. substance or situation in which something originates, takes form, or is enclosed; mould for casting; *Maths* rectangular array of numbers or elements.

matron *n* staid or dignified married woman; woman who supervises the domestic or medical arrangements of an institution; former name for NURSING OFFICER. **matronly** *adj*

matt *adj* dull, not shiny.

matter *n* substance of which something is made; physical substance; event, situation, or subject; written material in general; pus. ▶ *v* be of importance. **what's the matter?** what is wrong?

mattock *n* large pick with one of its blade ends flattened for loosening soil.

mattress *n* large stuffed flat case, often with springs, used on or as a bed.

mature *adj* fully developed or grown-up; ripe. ▶ *v* make or become mature; (of a bill or bond) become due for payment. **maturity** *n* state of being mature. **maturation** *n*

maudlin *adj* foolishly or tearfully sentimental.

maul *v* handle roughly; beat or tear.

maunder *v* talk or act aimlessly or idly.

mausoleum [maw-so-lee-um] *n* stately tomb.

mauve *adj* pale purple.

maverick *n, adj* independent and unorthodox (person).

maw *n* animal's mouth, throat, or stomach.

mawkish *adj* foolishly sentimental.

maxim *n* general truth or principle.

maximum *adj, n, pl* **-mums, -ma**. greatest possible (amount or number). **maximal** *adj* **maximize** *v* increase to a maximum.

may *v, past tense* **might**. used as an auxiliary to express possibility, permission, opportunity, etc.

May *n* fifth month of the year; (**m-**) same as HAWTHORN. **mayfly** *n* short-lived aquatic insect. **maypole** *n* pole set up for dancing round on the first day of May to celebrate spring.

maybe *adv* perhaps, possibly.

Mayday *n* international radio distress signal.

mayhem *n* violent destruction or confusion.

mayonnaise *n* creamy sauce of egg yolks, oil, and vinegar.

mayor *n* head of a municipality. **mayoress** *n* mayor's wife; female mayor. **mayoralty** *n* (term of) office of a mayor.

maze *n* complex network of paths or lines designed to puzzle; any confusing network or system.

mazurka *n* lively Polish dance; music for this.

MB Bachelor of Medicine.

MBE (in Britain) Member of the Order of the British Empire.

MC Master of Ceremonies.

MD Doctor of Medicine.

me *pron* objective form of I.

ME myalgic encephalomyelitis: painful muscles and general weakness sometimes persisting long after a viral illness.

mead *n* alcoholic drink made from honey.

meadow *n* piece of grassland.

meadowsweet *n* plant with dense heads of small fragrant flowers.

meagre *adj* scanty or insufficient.

meal¹ *n* occasion when food is served and eaten; the food itself.

meal² *n* grain ground to powder. **mealy** *adj* **mealy-mouthed** *adj* not outspoken enough.

mealie *n* S Afr maize.

mean¹ *v* **meaning, meant.** intend to convey or express; signify, denote, or portend; intend; have importance as specified. **meaning** *n* sense, significance. **meaningful** *adj* **meaningless** *adj*

mean² *adj* miserly, ungenerous, or petty; despicable or callous; *Chiefly US informal* bad-tempered. **meanly** *adv* **meanness** *n*

mean³ *n* middle point between two extremes; average. ▶ *pl* method by which something is done; money. ▶ *adj* intermediate in size or quantity; average. **by all means** certainly. **by no means** in no way. **means test** inquiry into a person's means to decide on eligibility for financial aid.

meander [mee-**and**-er] *v* follow a winding course; wander aimlessly. ▶ *n* winding course.

meantime *n* intervening period. ▶ *adv* meanwhile.

meanwhile *adv* during the intervening period; at the same time.

measles *n* infectious disease producing red spots. **measly** *adj* *Informal* meagre.

measure *n* size or quantity; graduated scale etc. for measuring size or quantity; unit of size or quantity; extent; action taken; law; poetical rhythm. ▶ *v* determine the size or quantity of; be (a specified amount) in size or quantity. **measurable** *adj* **measured** *adj* slow and steady; carefully considered. **measurement** *n* measuring; size. **measure up to** *v* fulfil (expectations or requirements).

meat *n* animal flesh as food. **meaty** *adj* (tasting) of or like meat; brawny; full of significance or interest.

Mecca *n* holy city of Islam; place that attracts visitors.

mechanic *n* person skilled in repairing or operating machinery. **mechanics** *n* scientific study of motion and force. **mechanical** *adj* of or done by machines; (of an action) without thought or feeling. **mechanically** *adv*

mechanism *n* way a machine works; piece of machinery; process or technique, e.g. *defence mechanism.* **mechanize** *v* equip with machinery; make mechanical or automatic; *Mil* equip (an army) with armoured vehicles. **mechanization** *n*

med. medical; medicine; medieval; medium.

medal *n* piece of metal with an inscription etc., given as a reward or memento. **medallion** *n* disc-shaped ornament worn on a chain round the neck; large medal; circular decorative device in architecture. **medallist** *n* winner of a medal.

meddle *v* interfere annoyingly.

meddler n **meddlesome** adj

media n a plural of MEDIUM; the mass media collectively.

mediaeval adj same as MEDIEVAL.

medial adj of or in the middle.

median adj, n middle (point or line).

mediate v intervene in a dispute to bring about agreement. **mediation** n **mediator** n

medic n Informal doctor or medical student.

medical adj of the science of medicine. ▶ n Informal medical examination. **medically** adv

medicate v treat with a medicinal substance. **medication** n (treatment with) a medicinal substance.

medicine n substance used to treat disease; science of preventing, diagnosing, or curing disease. **medicinal** [med-**diss**-in-al] adj having therapeutic properties. **medicine man** witch doctor.

medieval [med-ee-**eve**-al] adj of the Middle Ages.

mediocre [mee-dee-**oak**-er] adj average in quality; second-rate. **mediocrity** [mee-dee-**ok**-rit-ee] n

meditate v reflect deeply, esp. on spiritual matters; think about or plan. **meditation** n **meditative** adj **meditatively** adv **meditator** n

medium adj midway between extremes, average. ▶ n, pl **-dia**, **-diums**. middle state, degree, or condition; intervening substance producing an effect; means of communicating news or information to the public, such as radio or newspapers; person who can supposedly communicate with the dead; surroundings or environment; category of art according to the material used. **medium wave** radio wave with a wavelength between 100 and 1000 metres.

medlar n apple-like fruit of a small tree, eaten when it begins to decay.

medley n miscellaneous mixture; musical sequence of different tunes.

medulla [mid-**dull**-la] n, pl **-las**, **-lae**. marrow, pith, or inner tissue.

meek adj submissive or humble. **meekly** adv **meekness** n

meerkat n S African mongoose.

meerschaum [**meer**-shum] n white substance like clay; tobacco pipe with a bowl made of this.

meet[1] v **meeting, met.** come together (with); come into contact (with); be at the place of arrival of; make the acquaintance of; satisfy (a need etc.); experience. ▶ n meeting, esp. a sports meeting; assembly of a hunt. **meeting** n coming together; assembly.

meet[2] adj Obs fit or suitable.

mega- combining form denoting one million, e.g. megawatt; very great, e.g. megastar.

megabyte n Computers 2^{20} or 1 048 576 bytes.

megahertz n, pl **-hertz.** one million hertz.

megalith n great stone, esp. as part of a prehistoric monument. **megalithic** adj

megalomania n craving for or mental delusions of power. **megalomaniac** adj, n

megaphone n cone-shaped instrument used to amplify voice.

megaton n explosive power equal to that of one million tons of TNT.

melaleuca [mel-a-**loo**-ka] n Australian shrub or tree with a white trunk and black branches.

melancholy [**mel**-an-kol-lee] n sadness or gloom. ▶ adj sad or gloomy. **melancholia** [mel-an-**kole**-lee-a] n state of depression. **melancholic** adj, n

melange [may-**lahnzh**] n mixture.

melanin n dark pigment found in the hair, skin, and eyes of humans and animals.

mêlée [**mel**-lay] n noisy confused fight or crowd.

mellifluous [mel-**lif**-flew-uss] adj (of sound) smooth and sweet.

mellow adj soft, not harsh; kind-hearted, esp. through maturity; (of fruit) ripe. ▶ v make or become mellow.

melodrama n play full of extravagant action and emotion; overdramatic behaviour or emotion. **melodramatic** adj

melody n, pl -dies. series of musical notes which make a tune; sweet sound. **melodic** [mel-**lod**-ik] adj of melody; melodious. **melodious** [mel-**lode**-ee-uss] adj pleasing to the ear; tuneful.

melon n large round juicy fruit with a hard rind.

melt v (cause to) become liquid by heat; dissolve; disappear; blend (into); soften through emotion. **meltdown** n (in a nuclear reactor) melting of the fuel rods, with the possible release of radiation.

member n individual making up a body or society; limb. **membership** n **Member of Parliament** person elected to parliament.

membrane n thin flexible tissue in a plant or animal body. **membranous** adj

memento n, pl -tos, -toes. thing serving to remind, souvenir.

memo n, pl **memos.** short for MEMORANDUM.

memoir [**mem**-wahr] n biography or historical account based on personal knowledge. ▶ pl collection of these; autobiography.

memorable adj worth remembering, noteworthy. **memorably** adv

memorandum n, pl -dums, -da. written record or communication within a business; note of things to be remembered.

memory n, pl -ries. ability to remember; sum of things remembered; particular recollection; length of time one can remember; commemoration; part of a computer which stores information. **memorize** v commit to memory. **memorial** n something serving to commemorate a person or thing. ▶ adj serving as a memorial.

men n plural of MAN.

menace n threat; Informal nuisance. ▶ v threaten, endanger. **menacing** adj

ménage [may-**nahzh**] n household.

menagerie [min-**naj**-er-ee] n collection of wild animals for exhibition.

mend v repair or patch; recover or heal; make or become better. ▶ n mended area. **on the mend** regaining health.

mendacity n (tendency to) untruthfulness. **mendacious** adj

mendicant adj begging. ▶ n beggar.

menhir [**men**-hear] n single upright prehistoric stone.

menial [**mean**-nee-al] adj involving boring work of low status. ▶ n person with a menial job.

meningitis [men-in-**jite**-iss] n inflammation of the membranes of the brain.

meniscus n curved surface of a liquid; crescent-shaped lens.

menopause n time when a woman's menstrual cycle ceases.

menopausal adj

menstruation n approximately monthly discharge of blood and cellular debris from the womb of a nonpregnant woman. **menstruate** v **menstrual** adj

mensuration n measuring, esp. in geometry.

mental adj of, in, or done by the mind; of or for mental illness; *Informal* insane. **mentally** adv **mentality** n way of thinking.

menthol n organic compound found in peppermint, used medicinally.

mention v refer to briefly; acknowledge. ▶ n brief reference to a person or thing; acknowledgment.

mentor n adviser or guide.

menu n list of dishes to be served, or from which to order; *Computers* list of options displayed on a screen.

MEP Member of the European Parliament.

mercantile adj of trade or traders.

mercenary adj influenced by greed; working merely for reward. ▶ n, pl **-aries.** hired soldier.

merchandise n commodities.

merchant n person engaged in trade, wholesale trader. **merchant bank** bank dealing mainly with businesses and investment.

merchantman n trading ship. **merchant navy** ships or crew engaged in a nation's commercial shipping.

mercury n *Chem* silvery liquid metal; **(M-)** *Roman myth* messenger of the gods; **(M-)** planet nearest the sun. **mercurial** adj lively, changeable.

mercy n, pl **-cies.** compassionate treatment of an offender or enemy who is in one's power; merciful act. **merciful** adj compassionate; giving relief. **merciless** adj

mere[1] adj nothing more than, e.g. *mere chance.* **merely** adv

mere[2] n *Brit obs* lake.

meretricious adj superficially or garishly attractive but of no real value.

merganser [mer-gan-ser] n large crested diving duck.

merge v combine or blend.

merger n combination of business firms into one.

meridian n imaginary circle of the earth passing through both poles.

meringue [mer-rang] n baked mixture of egg whites and sugar; small cake of this.

merino n, pl **-nos.** breed of sheep with fine soft wool; this wool.

merit n excellence or worth. ▶ pl admirable qualities. ▶ v **-iting, -ited.** deserve. **meritorious** adj deserving praise. **meritocracy** [mer-it-**tok**-rass-ee] n rule by people of superior talent or intellect.

merlin n small falcon.

mermaid n imaginary sea creature with the upper part of a woman and the lower part of a fish.

merry adj **-rier, -riest.** cheerful or jolly; *Informal* slightly drunk. **merrily** adv **merriment** n **merry-go-round** n roundabout. **merrymaking** n noisy, cheerful celebrations or fun.

mesdames n plural of MADAME.

mesdemoiselles n plural of MADEMOISELLE.

mesh n network or net; (open space between) strands forming a network. ▶ v (of gear teeth) engage.

mesmerize v hold spellbound; *Obs* hypnotize.

meson [**mee**-zon] n elementary atomic particle.

mess n untidy or dirty confusion; trouble or difficulty; place where servicemen eat; group of servicemen who regularly eat together. ▶ v muddle or dirty; (foll. by about) potter about; (foll. by with) interfere with; Brit, Aust & NZ (of servicemen) eat in a group.

message n communication sent; meaning or moral. **messenger** n bearer of a message.

Messiah n Jews' promised deliverer; Christ. **Messianic** adj

messieurs n plural of MONSIEUR.

Messrs [mess-erz] n plural of MR.

messy adj **messier, messiest**. dirty, confused, or untidy. **messily** adv

met v past of MEET¹.

metabolism [met-tab-oh-liz-zum] n chemical processes of a living body. **metabolic** adj **metabolize** v produce or be produced by metabolism.

metal n chemical element, such as iron or copper, that is malleable and capable of conducting heat and electricity. **metallic** adj **metallurgy** n scientific study of the structure, properties, extraction, and refining of metals. **metallurgical** adj **metallurgist** n **metal road** NZ unsealed road covered in gravel.

metamorphosis [met-a-more-foss-is] n, pl -phoses [-foss-eez] change of form or character. **metamorphic** adj (of rocks) changed in texture or structure by heat and pressure. **metamorphose** v transform.

metaphor n figure of speech in which a term is applied to something it does not literally denote in order to imply a resemblance, e.g. he is a lion in battle. **metaphorical** adj **metaphorically** adv

metaphysics n branch of philosophy concerned with being and knowing. **metaphysical** adj

mete v (usu. with out) deal out as punishment.

meteor n small fast-moving heavenly body, visible as a streak of incandescence if it enters the earth's atmosphere. **meteoric** [meet-ee-or-rik] adj of a meteor; brilliant and very rapid.

meteorite n meteor that has fallen to earth.

meteorology n study of the earth's atmosphere, esp. for weather forecasting. **meteorological** adj **meteorologist** n

meter n instrument for measuring and recording something, such as the consumption of gas or electricity. ▶ v measure by meter.

methane n colourless inflammable gas.

methanol n colourless poisonous liquid used as a solvent and fuel (also **methyl alcohol**).

methinks v, past tense **methought**. Obs it seems to me.

method n way or manner; technique; orderliness. **methodical** adj orderly. **methodically** adv **methodology** n particular method or procedure.

Methodist n member of any of the Protestant churches originated by John Wesley and his followers. ▶ adj of Methodists or their Church. **Methodism** n

meths n Informal methylated spirits.

methyl n (compound containing) a saturated hydrocarbon group of atoms. **methylated spirits** alcohol with methanol added, used as a solvent and for heating.

meticulous adj very careful about details. **meticulously** adv

métier [met-ee-ay] n profession or trade; one's strong point.

metonymy [mit-**on**-im-ee] *n* figure of speech in which one thing is replaced by another associated with it, such as 'the Crown' for 'the queen'.

metre *n* basic unit of length equal to about 1.094 yards (100 centimetres); rhythm of poetry. **metric** *adj* of the decimal system of weights and measures based on the metre. **metrical** *adj* of measurement; of poetic metre. **metrication** *n* conversion to the metric system.

metronome *n* instrument which marks musical time by means of a ticking pendulum.

metropolis [mit-**trop**-oh-liss] *n* chief city of a country or region. **metropolitan** *adj* of a metropolis.

mettle *n* courage or spirit.

mew *n* cry of a cat. ▶ *v* utter this cry.

mews *n* yard or street orig. of stables, now often converted into houses.

mezzanine [mez-zan-een] *n* intermediate storey, esp. between the ground and first floor.

mezzo-soprano [met-so-] *n* voice or singer between a soprano and contralto (also **mezzo**).

mezzotint [met-so-tint] *n* method of engraving by scraping the roughened surface of a metal plate; print so made.

mg milligram(s).

MHz megahertz.

miaow [mee-ow] *n, v* same as MEW.

miasma [mee-**azz**-ma] *n* unwholesome or foreboding atmosphere.

mica [**my**-ka] *n* glasslike mineral used as an electrical insulator.

mice *n* plural of MOUSE.

Michaelmas [**mik**-kl-mass] *n* Sept. 29th, feast of St Michael the archangel. **Michaelmas daisy**

garden plant with small daisy-shaped flowers.

mickey *n* **take the mickey (out of)** *Informal* tease.

micro *n, pl* **-cros**. short for MICROCOMPUTER or MICROPROCESSOR.

microbe *n* minute organism, esp. one causing disease. **microbial** *adj*

microchip *n* small wafer of silicon containing electronic circuits.

microcomputer *n* computer with a central processing unit contained in one or more silicon chips.

microcosm *n* miniature representation of something.

microfiche [**my**-kroh-feesh] *n* microfilm in sheet form.

microfilm *n* miniaturized recording of books or documents on a roll of film.

microlight *n* very small light private aircraft with large wings.

micrometer [my-**krom**-it-er] *n* instrument for measuring very small distances or angles.

micron [**my**-kron] *n* one millionth of a metre.

microorganism *n* organism of microscopic size.

microphone *n* instrument for amplifying or transmitting sounds.

microprocessor *n* integrated circuit acting as the central processing unit in a small computer.

microscope *n* instrument with lens(es) which produces a magnified image of a very small object. **microscopic** *adj* too small to be seen except with a microscope; very small; of a microscope. **microscopically** *adv* **microscopy** *n* use of a microscope.

microsurgery *n* intricate surgery using a special microscope and miniature precision instruments.

microwave *n* electromagnetic

wave with a wavelength of a few centimetres, used in radar and cooking; microwave oven. ▶ v cook in a microwave oven.

microwave oven oven using microwaves to cook food quickly.

mid adj intermediate, middle.

midday n noon.

midden n Brit & Aust dunghill or rubbish heap.

middle adj equidistant from two extremes; medium, intermediate. ▶ n middle point or part. **middle age** period of life between youth and old age. **middle-aged** adj **Middle Ages** period from about 1000 AD to the 15th century. **middle class** social class of business and professional people. **middle-class** adj **Middle East** area around the eastern Mediterranean up to and including Iran. **middleman** n trader who buys from the producer and sells to the consumer. **middle-of-the-road** adj politically moderate; (of music) generally popular. **middleweight** n boxer weighing up to 160lb (professional) or 75kg (amateur).

middling adj mediocre; moderate.

midge n small mosquito-like insect.

midget n very small person or thing.

midland n Brit, Aust & US middle part of a country. ▶ pl (M-) central England.

midnight n twelve o'clock at night.

midriff n middle part of the body.

midshipman n naval officer of the lowest commissioned rank.

midst n in the midst of surrounded by; at a point during.

midsummer n middle of summer; summer solstice. **Midsummer's Day, Midsummer Day** (in Britain and Ireland) June 24th.

midway adj, adv halfway.

midwife n trained person who assists at childbirth. **midwifery** n

midwinter n middle or depth of winter; winter solstice.

mien [meen] n Lit person's bearing, demeanour, or appearance.

miffed adj Informal offended or upset.

might¹ v past tense of MAY.

might² n power or strength. **with might and main** energetically or forcefully. **mighty** adj powerful; important. ▶ adv US & Aust informal very. **mightily** adv

migraine [mee-grain] n severe headache, often with nausea and visual disturbances.

migrate v move from one place to settle in another; (of animals) journey between different habitats at specific seasons. **migration** n **migrant** n person or animal that moves from one place to another. ▶ adj moving from one place to another. **migratory** adj (of an animal) migrating every year.

mike n Informal microphone.

milch adj Chiefly Brit (of a cow) giving milk.

mild not strongly flavoured; gentle; calm or temperate. **mildly** adv **mildness** n

mildew n destructive fungus on plants or things exposed to damp. **mildewed** adj

mile n unit of length equal to 1760 yards or 1.609 kilometres. **mileage** n distance travelled in miles; miles travelled by a motor vehicle per gallon of petrol; Informal usefulness of something. **mileometer** n Brit device that records the number of miles a vehicle has travelled. **milestone** n significant event; stone marker showing the distance to a certain place.

milieu [meal-yer] n, pl milieux,

milieus [meal-**yerz**] environment or surroundings.

militant *adj* aggressive or vigorous in support of a cause. **militancy** *n*

military *adj* of or for soldiers, armies, or war. ▸ *n* armed services. **militarism** *n* belief in the use of military force and methods. **militarist** *n* **militarized** *adj*

militate *v* (usu. with *against* or *for*) have a strong influence or effect.

militia [mill-**ish-a**] *n* military force of trained citizens for use in emergency only.

milk *n* white fluid produced by female mammals to feed their young; milk of cows, goats, etc., used by humans as food; fluid in some plants. ▸ *v* draw milk from; exploit (a person or situation).

milky *adj* **Milky Way** luminous band of stars stretching across the night sky. **milk float** *Brit* small electrically powered vehicle used to deliver milk to houses.

milkmaid *n* (esp. in former times) woman who milks cows. **milkman** *n Brit, Aust & NZ* man who delivers milk to people's houses. **milkshake** *n* frothy flavoured cold milk drink. **milksop** *n* feeble man.

milk teeth first set of teeth in young children.

mill *n* factory; machine for grinding, processing, or rolling. ▸ *v* grind, press, or process in or as if in a mill; cut fine grooves across the edges of (coins); (of a crowd) move in a confused manner.

millennium *n, pl* **-nia, -niums.** period of a thousand years; future period of peace and happiness. **millennium bug** computer problem caused by the date change at the beginning of the 21st century.

miller *n* person who works in a mill.

millet *n* type of cereal grass.

milli- *combining form* denoting a thousandth part, e.g. *millisecond.*

millibar *n* unit of atmospheric pressure.

millimetre *n* thousandth part of a metre.

milliner *n* maker or seller of women's hats. **millinery** *n*

million *n* one thousand thousands. **millionth** *adj, n* **millionaire** *n* person who owns at least a million pounds, dollars, etc.

millipede *n* small animal with a jointed body and many pairs of legs.

millstone *n* flat circular stone for grinding corn.

millwheel *n* waterwheel that drives a mill.

milometer *n Brit* same as MILEOMETER.

milt *n* sperm of fish.

mime *n* acting without the use of words; performer who does this. ▸ *v* act in mime.

mimic *v* **-icking, -icked.** imitate (a person or manner), esp. for satirical effect. ▸ *n* person or animal that is good at mimicking. **mimicry** *n*

min. minimum; minute(s).

minaret *n* tall slender tower of a mosque.

mince *v* cut or grind into very small pieces; walk or speak in an affected manner; soften or moderate (one's words). ▸ *n* minced meat. **mincer** *n* machine for mincing meat. **mincing** *adj* affected in manner. **mincemeat** *n* sweet mixture of dried fruit and spices. **mince pie** pie containing mincemeat.

mind *n* thinking faculties; memory or attention; intention; sanity. ▸ *v* take offence at; pay attention to; take care of; be cautious or careful about (something). **minded** adj having an inclination as specified, e.g. politically minded. **minder** n Informal aide or bodyguard.

mindful adj heedful; keeping aware. **mindless** adj stupid; requiring no thought; careless.

mine[1] pron belonging to me.

mine[2] n deep hole for digging out coal, ores, etc.; bomb placed under the ground or in water; profitable source. ▶ v dig for minerals; dig (minerals) from a mine; place explosive mines in or on. **miner** n person who works in a mine. **minefield** n area of land or water containing mines. **minesweeper** n ship for clearing away mines.

mineral n naturally occurring inorganic substance, such as metal. ▶ adj of, containing, or like minerals. **mineralogy** [min-er-al-a-jee] n study of minerals. **mineral water** water containing dissolved mineral salts or gases.

minestrone [min-ness-**strone**-ee] n soup containing vegetables and pasta.

mingle v mix or blend; come into association (with).

mingy adj **-gier, -giest.** Informal miserly.

mini n, adj (something) small or miniature; short (skirt).

miniature n small portrait, model, or copy. ▶ adj small-scale. **miniaturist** n **miniaturize** v make to a very small scale.

minibar n selection of drinks and confectionery provided in a hotel room.

minibus n small bus.

minicab n Brit ordinary car used as a taxi.

minicomputer n computer smaller than a mainframe but more powerful than a microcomputer.

minidisc n small recordable compact disc.

minim n Music note half the length of a semibreve.

minimum adj, n, pl **-mums, -ma.** least possible (amount or number). **minimal** adj minimum. **minimize** v reduce to a minimum; belittle.

minion n servile assistant.

miniseries n TV programme shown in several parts, often on consecutive days.

minister n head of a government department; diplomatic representative; (in nonconformist churches) member of the clergy. ▶ v (foll. by to) attend to the needs of. **ministerial** adj **ministration** n giving of help. **ministry** n, pl **-tries.** profession or duties of a clergyman; ministers collectively; government department.

mink n stoatlike animal; its highly valued fur.

minnow n small freshwater fish.

minor adj lesser; Music (of a scale) having a semitone between the second and third notes. ▶ n person regarded legally as a child; Music minor scale. **minority** n lesser number; smaller party voting together; group in a minority in any state.

minster n Brit cathedral or large church.

minstrel n medieval singer or musician.

mint[1] n plant with aromatic leaves used for seasoning and flavouring; sweet flavoured with this.

mint[2] n place where money is coined. ▶ v make (coins).

minuet [min-new-**wet**] n stately dance; music for this.

minus prep, adj indicating

subtraction. ▶ *adj* less than zero.
▶ *n* sign (-) denoting subtraction
or a number less than zero.

minuscule [min-niss-skyool] *adj*
very small.

minute[1] [min-it] *n* 60th part of an
hour or degree; moment. ▶ *pl*
record of the proceedings of a
meeting. ▶ *v* record in the minutes.

minute[2] [my-newt] *adj* very small;
precise. **minutely** *adv* **minutiae**
[my-new-shee-eye] *pl n* trifling or
precise details.

minx *n* bold or flirtatious girl.

miracle *n* wonderful supernatural
event; marvel. **miraculous** *adj*
miraculously *adv* **miracle play**
medieval play based on a sacred
subject.

mirage [mir-rahzh] *n* optical
illusion, esp. one caused by hot air.

mire *n* swampy ground; mud.

mirror *n* coated glass surface for
reflecting images. ▶ *v* reflect in or
as if in a mirror.

mirth *n* laughter, merriment, or
gaiety. **mirthful** *adj* **mirthless** *adj*

mis- *prefix* wrong(ly), bad(ly).

misadventure *n* unlucky chance.

misanthrope [miz-zan-thrope] *n*
person who dislikes people in
general. **misanthropic**
[miz-zan-throp-ik] *adj*
misanthropy [miz-zan-throp-ee] *n*

misapprehend *v* misunderstand.
misapprehension *n*

misappropriate *v* take and use
(money) dishonestly.
misappropriation *n*

miscarriage *n* spontaneous
premature expulsion of a fetus
from the womb; failure, e.g. *a
miscarriage of justice.* **miscarry** *v*
have a miscarriage; fail.

miscast *v* **-casting, -cast.** cast (a
role or actor) in (a play or film)
inappropriately.

miscegenation

[miss-ij-in-**nay**-shun] *n*
interbreeding of races.

miscellaneous
[miss-sell-**lane**-ee-uss] *adj* mixed or
assorted. **miscellany**
[miss-**sell**-a-nee] *n* mixed
assortment.

mischance *n* unlucky event.

mischief *n* annoying but not
malicious behaviour; inclination to
tease; harm. **mischievous** *adj* full
of mischief; intended to cause
harm. **mischievously** *adv*

miscible [**miss**-sib-bl] *adj* able to
be mixed.

misconception *n* wrong idea or
belief.

misconduct *n* immoral or
unethical behaviour.

miscreant [**miss**-kree-ant] *n*
wrongdoer.

misdeed *n* wrongful act.

misdemeanour *n* minor
wrongdoing.

miser *n* person who hoards money
and hates spending it. **miserly** *adj*

miserable *adj* very unhappy,
wretched; causing misery; squalid;
mean. **misery** *n*, *pl* **-eries.** great
unhappiness; *Informal* complaining
person.

misfire *v* (of a firearm or engine)
fail to fire correctly; (of a plan) fail
to turn out as intended.

misfit *n* person not suited to his or
her social environment.

misfortune *n* (piece of) bad luck.

misgiving *n* feeling of fear or
doubt.

misguided *adj* mistaken or unwise.

mishandle *v* handle badly or
inefficiently.

mishap *n* minor accident.

misinform *v* give incorrect
information to. **misinformation** *n*

misjudge *v* judge wrongly or
unfairly. **misjudgment,
misjudgement** *n*

mislay v lose (something) temporarily.

mislead v give false or confusing information to. **misleading** adj

mismanage v organize or run (something) badly. **mismanagement** n

misnomer [miss-no-mer] n incorrect or unsuitable name; use of this.

misogyny [miss-oj-in-ee] n hatred of women. **misogynist** n

misplace v mislay; put in the wrong place; give (trust or affection) inappropriately.

misprint n printing error.

misrepresent v represent wrongly or inaccurately.

miss v fail to notice, hear, hit, reach, find, or catch; not be in time for; notice or regret the absence of; avoid; (of an engine) misfire. ▶ n fact or instance of missing. **missing** adj lost or absent.

Miss n title of a girl or unmarried woman.

missal n book containing the prayers and rites of the Mass.

misshapen adj badly shaped, deformed.

missile n object or weapon thrown, shot, or launched at a target.

mission n specific task or duty; group of people sent on a mission; building in which missionaries work; S Afr long and difficult process. **missionary** n, pl -aries. person sent abroad to do religious and social work.

missive n letter.

misspent adj wasted or misused.

mist n thin fog; fine spray of liquid. **misty** adj full of mist; dim or obscure.

mistake n error or blunder. ▶ v -taking, -took, -taken.

misunderstand; confuse (a person or thing) with another.

Mister n polite form of address to a man.

mistletoe n evergreen plant with white berries growing as a parasite on trees.

mistral n strong dry northerly wind of S France.

mistress n woman who has a continuing sexual relationship with a married man; woman in control of people or animals; female teacher.

mistrial n Law trial made void because of some error.

mistrust v have doubts or suspicions about. ▶ n lack of trust. **mistrustful** adj

misunderstand v fail to understand properly. **misunderstanding** n

misuse n incorrect, improper, or careless use. ▶ v use wrongly; treat badly.

mite n very small spider-like animal; very small thing or amount.

mitigate v make less severe. **mitigation** n

mitre [my-ter] n bishop's pointed headdress; joint between two pieces of wood bevelled to meet at right angles. ▶ v join with a mitre joint.

mitt n short for MITTEN; baseball catcher's glove.

mitten n glove with one section for the thumb and one for the four fingers together.

mix v combine or blend into one mass; form (something) by mixing; be sociable. ▶ n mixture. **mixed** adj **mix up** v confuse; make into a mixture. **mixed up** adj **mix-up** n **mixer** n **mixture** n something mixed; combination.

mizzenmast n (on a vessel with

three or more masts) third mast
from the bow.

mm millimetre(s).

mnemonic [nim-on-ik] n, adj
(something, such as a rhyme)
intended to help the memory.

mo n, pl **mos.** Informal short for
MOMENT.

MO Medical Officer.

moa n large extinct flightless New
Zealand bird.

moan n low cry of pain; Informal
grumble. ▶ v make or utter with a
moan; Informal grumble.

moat n deep wide ditch, esp.
round a castle.

mob n disorderly crowd; Slang
gang. ▶ v **mobbing, mobbed.**
surround in a mob to acclaim or
attack.

mobile adj able to move. ▶ n same
as MOBILE PHONE; hanging structure
designed to move in air currents.
mobile phone cordless phone
powered by batteries. **mobility** n

mobilize v (of the armed services)
prepare for active service; organize
for a purpose. **mobilization** n

moccasin n soft leather shoe.

mocha [mock-a] n kind of strong
dark coffee; flavouring made from
coffee and chocolate.

mock v make fun of; mimic. ▶ adj
sham or imitation. **mocks** pl n
Informal (in England and Wales)
practice exams taken before public
exams. **put the mockers on** Brit,
Aust & NZ informal ruin the
chances of success of. **mockery** n
derision; inadequate or worthless
attempt. **mockingbird** n N
American bird which imitates
other birds' songs. **mock orange**
shrub with white fragrant flowers.
mock-up n full-scale model for test
or study.

mod. moderate; modern.

mode n method or manner;

current fashion.

model n (miniature)
representation; pattern; person or
thing worthy of imitation; person
who poses for an artist or
photographer; person who wears
clothes to display them to
prospective buyers. ▶ v **-elling,
-elled.** make a model of; mould;
display (clothing) as a model.

modem [mode-em] n device for
connecting two computers by a
telephone line.

moderate adj not extreme;
self-restrained; average. ▶ n person
of moderate views. ▶ v make or
become less violent or extreme.
moderately adv **moderation** n

moderator n (Presbyterian
Church) minister appointed to
preside over a Church court,
general assembly, etc.; person
who presides over a public or
legislative assembly.

modern adj of present or recent
times; up-to-date. **modernity** n
modernism n (support of) modern
tendencies, thoughts, or styles.
modernist adj, n **modernize** v
bring up to date. **modernization**
n

modest adj not vain or boastful;
not excessive; not showy; shy.
modestly adv **modesty** n

modicum n small quantity.

modify v **-fying, -fied.** change
slightly; tone down; (of a word)
qualify (another word). **modifier**
n word that qualifies the sense of
another. **modification** n

modish [mode-ish] adj in fashion.

modulate v vary in tone; adjust;
change the key of (music).
modulation n **modulator** n

module n self-contained unit,
section, or component with a
specific function.

modus operandi [mode-uss

op-er-an-die] *n Latin* method of operating.

mogul [moh-gl] *n* important or powerful person.

mohair *n* fine hair of the Angora goat; yarn or fabric made from this.

mohican *n* punk hairstyle with shaved sides and a stiff central strip of hair, often brightly coloured.

moiety [moy-it-ee] *n, pl* **-ties.**

moist *adj* slightly wet. **moisten** *v* make or become moist. **moisture** *n* liquid diffused as vapour or condensed in drops. **moisturize** *v* add moisture to (the skin etc.).

molar *n* large back tooth used for grinding.

molasses *n* dark syrup, a by-product of sugar refining.

mole[1] *n* small dark raised spot on the skin.

mole[2] *n* small burrowing mammal; *Informal* spy who has infiltrated and become a trusted member of an organization.

mole[3] *n* unit of amount of substance.

mole[4] *n* breakwater; harbour protected by this.

molecule [mol-lik-kyool] *n* simplest freely existing chemical unit, composed of two or more atoms; very small particle. **molecular** [mol-lek-yew-lar] *adj*

molest *v* interfere with sexually; annoy or injure. **molester** *n* **molestation** *n*

moll *n Slang* gangster's female accomplice.

mollify *v* **-fying, -fied.** pacify or soothe.

mollusc *n* soft-bodied, usu. hard-shelled, animal, such as a snail or oyster.

mollycoddle *v* pamper.

Molotov cocktail *n* petrol bomb.

molten *adj* liquefied or melted.

molybdenum [mol-lib-din-um] *n Chem* hard silvery-white metallic element.

moment *n* short space of time; (present) point in time. **momentary** *adj* lasting only a moment. **momentarily** *adv*

momentous [moh-men-tuss] *adj* of great significance.

momentum *n* impetus of a moving body; product of a body's mass and velocity.

monarch *n* sovereign ruler of a state. **monarchical** *adj* **monarchist** *n* supporter of monarchy. **monarchy** *n* government by or a state ruled by a sovereign.

monastery *n, pl* **-teries.** residence of a community of monks. **monastic** *adj* of monks, nuns, or monasteries; simple and austere. **monasticism** *n*

Monday *n* second day of the week.

monetary *adj* of money or currency. **monetarism** *n* theory that inflation is caused by an increase in the money supply. **monetarist** *n, adj*

money *n* medium of exchange, coins or banknotes. **moneyed, monied** *adj* rich.

mongoose *n, pl* **-gooses.** stoatlike mammal of Asia and Africa that kills snakes.

mongrel *n* animal, esp. a dog, of mixed breed; something arising from a variety of sources. ▶ *adj* of mixed breed or origin.

monitor *n* person or device that checks, controls, warns, or keeps a record of something; *Brit, Aust & NZ* pupil assisting a teacher with duties; television set used in a studio to check what is being transmitted; large lizard of Africa, Asia, and Australia. ▶ *v* watch and check on.

monk n member of an all-male religious community bound by vows. **monkish** adj

monkey n long-tailed primate; mischievous child. ► v (usu. foll. by *about* or *around*) meddle or fool. **monkey nut** Brit peanut. **monkey puzzle** coniferous tree with sharp stiff leaves. **monkey wrench** wrench with adjustable jaws.

mono- combining form single, e.g. monosyllable.

monochrome adj Photog black-and-white; in only one colour.

monocle n eyeglass for one eye only.

monogamy n custom of being married to one person at a time.

monogram n design of combined letters, esp. a person's initials.

monograph n book or paper on a single subject.

monolith n large upright block of stone. **monolithic** adj

monologue n long speech by one person; dramatic piece for one performer.

monomania n obsession with one thing. **monomaniac** n, adj

monoplane n aeroplane with one pair of wings.

monopoly n, pl **-lies.** exclusive possession of or right to do something; **(M-)** ® board game for four to six players who deal in 'property' as they move around the board. **monopolize** v have or take exclusive possession of.

monorail n single-rail railway.

monotheism n belief in only one God. **monotheistic** adj

monotone n unvaried pitch in speech or sound. **monotonous** adj tedious due to lack of variety. **monotonously** adv **monotony** n

Monseigneur [mon-sen-**nyur**] n, pl

Messeigneurs [may-sen-**nyur**] title of French prelates.

monsieur [muss-**syur**] n, pl **messieurs** [may-**syur**] French title of address equivalent to *sir* or *Mr*.

Monsignor n RC Church title attached to certain offices.

monsoon n seasonal wind of SE Asia; rainy season accompanying this.

monster n imaginary, usu. frightening, beast; huge person, animal, or thing; very wicked person. ► adj huge. **monstrosity** n large ugly thing. **monstrous** adj unnatural or ugly; outrageous or shocking; huge. **monstrously** adv

monstrance n RC Church container in which the consecrated Host is exposed for adoration.

montage [mon-**tahzh**] n (making of) a picture composed from pieces of others; method of film editing incorporating several shots to form a single image.

month n one of the twelve divisions of the calendar year; period of four weeks. **monthly** adj happening or payable once a month. ► adv once a month. ► n monthly magazine.

monument n something, esp. a building or statue, that commemorates something. **monumental** adj large, impressive, or lasting; of or being a monument; Informal extreme. **monumentally** adv

moo n long deep cry of a cow. ► v make this noise.

mooch v Slang loiter about aimlessly.

mood[1] n temporary (gloomy) state of mind. **moody** adj sullen or gloomy; changeable in mood. **moodily** adv

mood[2] n Grammar form of a verb indicating whether it expresses a fact, wish, supposition, or command.

moon n natural satellite of the earth; natural satellite of any planet. ▶ v (foll. by *about* or *around*) be idle in a listless or dreamy way. **moonlight** n light from the moon. ▶ v *Informal* work at a secondary job, esp. illegally. **moonshine** n US & Canadian illicitly distilled whisky; nonsense. **moonstone** n translucent semiprecious stone. **moonstruck** adj slightly mad or odd.

moor¹ n *Brit* tract of open uncultivated ground covered with grass and heather. **moorhen** n small black water bird.

moor² v secure (a ship) with ropes etc. **mooring** n place for mooring a ship. ▶ pl ropes etc. used in mooring a ship.

Moor n member of a Muslim people of NW Africa who ruled Spain between the 8th and 15th centuries. **Moorish** adj

moose n large N American deer.

moot adj debatable, e.g. *a moot point.* ▶ v bring up for discussion.

mop n long stick with twists of cotton or a sponge on the end, used for cleaning; thick mass of hair. ▶ v **mopping, mopped.** clean or soak up with or as if with a mop.

mope v be gloomy and apathetic.

moped n light motorized cycle.

moraine n accumulated mass of debris deposited by a glacier.

moral adj concerned with right and wrong conduct; based on a sense of right and wrong; (of support or a victory) psychological rather than practical. ▶ n lesson to be obtained from a story or event. ▶ pl principles of behaviour with respect to right and wrong. **morally** adv **moralist** n person

with a strong sense of right and wrong. **morality** n good moral conduct; moral goodness or badness. **morality play** medieval play with a moral lesson. **moralize** v make moral pronouncements.

morale [mor-**rahl**] n degree of confidence or hope of a person or group.

morass n marsh; mess.

moratorium n, pl **-ria, -riums.** legally authorized ban or delay.

moray n large voracious eel.

morbid adj unduly interested in death or unpleasant events; gruesome.

mordant adj sarcastic or scathing. ▶ n substance used to fix dyes.

more adj greater in amount or degree; comparative of MUCH or MANY; additional or further. ▶ adv to a greater extent; in addition. ▶ pron greater or additional amount or number. **moreover** adv in addition to what has already been said.

mores [**more**-rayz] pl n customs and conventions embodying the fundamental values of a community.

morganatic marriage n marriage of a person of high rank to a lower-ranking person whose status remains unchanged.

morgue n mortuary.

moribund adj without force or vitality.

Mormon n member of a religious sect founded in the USA.

morn n *Poetic* morning.

morning n part of the day before noon. **morning-glory** n plant with trumpet-shaped flowers which close in the late afternoon.

morocco n goatskin leather.

moron n *Informal* foolish or stupid person; (formerly) person with a

low intelligence quotient.
moronic adj
morose [mor-rohss] adj sullen or
moody.
morphine, morphia n drug
extracted from opium, used as an
anaesthetic and sedative.
morphology n science of forms
and structures of organisms or
words. **morphological** adj
morris dance n traditional English
folk dance.
morrow n Poetic next day.
Morse n former system of
signalling in which letters of the
alphabet are represented by
combinations of short and long
signals.
morsel n small piece, esp. of food.
mortal adj subject to death;
causing death. ▸ n human being.
mortally adv **mortality** n state of
being mortal; great loss of life;
death rate. **mortal sin** RC Church
sin meriting damnation.
mortar n small cannon with a
short range; mixture of lime, sand,
and water for holding bricks and
stones together; bowl in which
substances are pounded.
mortarboard n black square
academic cap.
mortgage n conditional pledging
of property, esp. a house, as
security for the repayment of a
loan; the loan itself. ▸ v pledge
(property) as security thus.
mortgagee n creditor in a
mortgage. **mortgagor** n debtor
in a mortgage.
mortice, mortise [more-tiss] n
hole in a piece of wood or stone
shaped to receive a matching
projection on another piece.
mortice lock lock set into a door.
mortify v **-fying, -fied.** humiliate;
subdue by self-denial; (of flesh)
become gangrenous.

mortification n
mortuary n, pl **-aries.** building
where corpses are kept before
burial or cremation.
mosaic [mow-zay-ik] n design or
decoration using small pieces of
coloured stone or glass.
Mosaic adj of Moses.
Moselle n light white German
wine.
Moslem n, adj same as MUSLIM.
mosque n Muslim temple.
mosquito n, pl **-toes, -tos.**
blood-sucking flying insect.
moss n small flowerless plant
growing in masses on moist
surfaces. **mossy** adj
most n greatest number or degree.
▸ adj greatest in number or
degree; superlative of MUCH or
MANY. ▸ adv in the greatest degree.
mostly adv for the most part,
generally.
MOT, MOT test n (in Britain)
compulsory annual test of the
roadworthiness of vehicles over a
certain age.
motel n roadside hotel for
motorists.
motet n short sacred choral song.
moth n nocturnal insect like a
butterfly. **mothball** n small ball of
camphor or naphthalene used to
repel moths from stored clothes.
▸ v store (something operational)
for future use; postpone (a project
etc.). **moth-eaten** adj decayed or
scruffy; eaten or damaged by
moth larvae.
mother n female parent; head of a
female religious community. ▸ adj
native or inborn, e.g. mother wit.
▸ v look after as a mother.
motherhood n **motherly** adj
motherless adj **mother-in-law** n
mother of one's husband or wife.
mother of pearl iridescent lining
of certain shells. **mother tongue**

one's native language.
motif [moh-**teef**] n (recurring) theme or design.
motion n process, action, or way of moving; proposal in a meeting; evacuation of the bowels. ▶ v direct (someone) by gesture. **motionless** adj not moving. **motion picture** cinema film.
motive n reason for a course of action. ▶ adj causing motion. **motivate** v give incentive to. **motivation** n
motley adj miscellaneous; multicoloured.
motocross n motorcycle race over a rough course.
motor n engine, esp. of a vehicle; machine that converts electrical energy into mechanical energy; Chiefly Brit car. ▶ v travel by car. **motorist** n driver of a car. **motorized** adj equipped with a motor or motor transport. **motorbike** n **motorboat** n **motorcar** n **motorcycle** n **motorcyclist** n **motor scooter** light motorcycle with small wheels and an enclosed engine. **motorway** n main road for fast-moving traffic.
mottled adj marked with blotches.
motto n, pl -**toes**, -**tos**. saying expressing an ideal or rule of conduct; verse or maxim in a paper cracker.
mould[1] n hollow container in which metal etc. is cast; shape, form, or pattern; nature or character. ▶ v shape; influence or direct. **moulding** n moulded ornamental edging.
mould[2] n fungal growth caused by dampness. **mouldy** adj stale or musty; dull or boring.
mould[3] n loose soil. **moulder** v decay into dust.
moult v shed feathers, hair, or skin

to make way for new growth. ▶ n process of moulting.
mound n heap, esp. of earth or stones; small hill.
mount v climb or ascend; get up on (a horse etc.); increase or accumulate; fix on a support or backing; organize, e.g. mount a campaign. ▶ n backing or support on which something is fixed; horse for riding; hill.
mountain n hill of great size; large heap. **mountainous** adj full of mountains; huge. **mountaineer** n person who climbs mountains. **mountaineering** n **mountain bike** bicycle with straight handlebars and heavy-duty tyres, for cycling over rough terrain. **mountain oyster** NZ informal sheep's testicle eaten as food.
mountebank n charlatan or fake.
Mountie n Informal member of the Royal Canadian Mounted Police.
mourn v feel or express sorrow for (a dead person or lost thing). **mournful** adj sad or dismal. **mournfully** adv **mourning** n grieving; conventional symbols of grief for death, such as the wearing of black.
mourner n person attending a funeral.
mouse n, pl **mice**. small long-tailed rodent; timid person; Computers hand-held device for moving the cursor without keying. **mouser** n cat used to catch mice. **mousy** adj like a mouse, esp. in hair colour; meek and shy.
mousse n dish of flavoured cream whipped and set.
moustache n hair on the upper lip.
mouth n opening in the head for eating and issuing sounds; entrance; point where a river enters the sea; opening. ▶ v form (words) with the lips without

speaking; speak or utter insincerely, esp. in public.

mouthful n amount of food or drink put into the mouth at any one time when eating or drinking.

mouth organ same as HARMONICA.

mouthpiece n part of a telephone into which a person speaks; part of a wind instrument into which the player blows; spokesperson.

move v change in place or position; change (one's house etc.); take action; stir the emotions of; incite; suggest (a proposal) formally. ▶ n moving; action towards some goal.

movable, moveable adj

movement n action or process of moving; group with a common aim; division of a piece of music; moving parts of a machine.

movie n Informal cinema film.

mow v mowing, mowed, mowed or mown. cut (grass or crops). **mow down** v kill in large numbers.

mower n machine for cutting grass.

mozzarella [mot-sa-rel-la] n moist white cheese originally made in Italy from buffalo milk.

MP Member of Parliament; Military Police(man).

MP3 Computing Motion Picture Expert Group-1, Audio Layer-3: a digital compression format used to compress audio files to a fraction of their original size without loss of sound quality.

MPEG [em-peg] Computing Motion Picture Expert Group: standard compressed file format used for audio and video files; file in this format.

mpg miles per gallon.

mph miles per hour.

Mr Mister.

Mrs n title of a married woman.

Ms [mizz] n title used instead of Miss or Mrs.

MS manuscript; multiple sclerosis.

MSc Master of Science.

MSP (in Britain) Member of the Scottish Parliament.

MSS manuscripts.

Mt Mount.

much adj more, most. large amount or degree of. ▶ n large amount or degree. ▶ adv more, most. to a great degree; nearly.

mucilage [mew-sill-ij] n gum or glue.

muck n dirt, filth; manure. **mucky** adj

mucus [mew-kuss] n slimy secretion of the mucous membranes. **mucous membrane** tissue lining body cavities or passages.

mud n wet soft earth. **muddy** adj **mudguard** n cover over a wheel to prevent mud or water being thrown up by it. **mud pack** cosmetic paste to improve the complexion.

muddle v (often foll. by up) confuse; mix up. ▶ n state of confusion.

muesli [mewz-lee] n mixture of grain, nuts, and dried fruit, eaten with milk.

muezzin [moo-ezz-in] n official who summons Muslims to prayer.

muff¹ n tube-shaped covering to keep the hands warm.

muff² v bungle (an action).

muffin n light round flat yeast cake.

muffle v wrap up for warmth or to deaden sound. **muffler** n Brit scarf; device to reduce the noise of an engine exhaust.

mufti n civilian clothes worn by a person who usually wears a uniform.

mug¹ n large drinking cup.

mug² n Slang face; Slang gullible person. ▶ v mugging, mugged. Informal attack in order to rob.

mugger n

mug³ v **mugging, mugged.** (foll. by up) *Informal* study hard.

muggins n *Informal* stupid or gullible person.

muggy adj **-gier, -giest.** (of weather) damp and stifling.

mulatto [mew-lat-toe] n, pl **-tos, -toes.** child of one Black and one White parent.

mulberry n tree whose leaves are used to feed silkworms; purple fruit of this tree.

mulch n mixture of wet straw, leaves, etc., used to protect the roots of plants. ▶ v cover (land) with mulch.

mule¹ n offspring of a horse and a donkey. **mulish** adj obstinate.

mule² n backless shoe or slipper.

mulga n Australian acacia shrub growing in desert regions; *Aust* the outback.

mull v think (over) or ponder. **mulled** adj (of wine or ale) flavoured with sugar and spices and served hot.

mullah n Muslim scholar, teacher, or religious leader.

mullet¹ n edible sea fish.

mullet² n haircut in which the hair is short at the top and sides and long at the back.

mulligatawny n soup made with curry powder.

mullion n vertical dividing bar in a window. **mullioned** adj

multi- combining form many, e.g. *multicultural; multistorey.*

multifarious [mull-tee-fare-ee-uss] adj having many various parts.

multiple adj having many parts. ▶ n quantity which contains another an exact number of times.

multiplex n purpose-built complex containing several cinemas and usu. restaurants and bars. ▶ adj having many elements, complex.

multiplicity n, pl **-ties.** large number or great variety.

multiply v **-plying, -plied.** (cause to) increase in number, quantity, or degree; add (a number or quantity) to itself a given number of times; increase in number by reproduction. **multiplication** n **multiplicand** n *Maths* number to be multiplied.

multipurpose adj having many uses, e.g. *a multipurpose tool.* **multipurpose vehicle** large vanlike car designed to carry up to eight passengers.

multitude n great number; great crowd. **multitudinous** adj very numerous.

mum¹ n *Informal* mother.

mum² adj **keep mum** remain silent.

mumble v speak indistinctly, mutter.

mumbo jumbo n meaningless language; foolish religious ritual or incantation.

mummer n actor in a traditional English folk play or mime.

mummy¹ n, pl **-mies.** body embalmed and wrapped for burial in ancient Egypt. **mummified** adj (of a body) preserved as a mummy.

mummy² n, pl **-mies.** child's word for MOTHER.

mumps n infectious disease with swelling in the glands of the neck.

munch v chew noisily and steadily.

mundane adj everyday; earthly.

municipal adj relating to a city or town. **municipality** n city or town with local self-government; governing body of this.

munificent [mew-niff-fiss-sent] adj very generous. **munificence** n

muniments pl n title deeds or similar documents.

munitions pl n military stores.

munted adj *NZ slang* destroyed or

ruined; abnormal or peculiar.
mural n painting on a wall.
murder n unlawful intentional killing of a human being. ▷ v kill in this way. **murderer, murderess** n **murderous** adj
murky adj dark or gloomy. **murk** n thick darkness.
murmur v **-muring, -mured.** speak or say in a quiet indistinct way; complain. ▷ n continuous low indistinct sound.
muscle n tissue in the body which produces movement by contracting; strength or power. **muscular** adj with well-developed muscles; of muscles. **muscular dystrophy** disease with wasting of the muscles. **muscle in** v Informal force one's way in.
muse v ponder quietly.
Muse n Greek myth one of nine goddesses, each of whom inspired an art or science; (**m-**) force that inspires a creative artist.
museum n building where natural, artistic, historical, or scientific objects are exhibited and preserved.
mush n soft pulpy mass; Informal cloying sentimentality. **mushy** adj
mushroom n edible fungus with a stem and cap. ▷ v grow rapidly.
music n art form using a melodious and harmonious combination of notes; written or printed form of this. **musical** adj of or like music; talented in or fond of music; pleasant-sounding. ▷ n play or film with songs and dancing. **musically** adv **musician** n **musicology** n scientific study of music. **musicologist** n **music centre** Brit combined record or CD player, radio, and cassette player. **music hall** variety theatre.
musk n scent obtained from a gland of the musk deer or

produced synthetically. **musky** adj
muskrat n N American beaver-like rodent; its fur.
musket n Hist long-barrelled gun. **musketeer** n **musketry** n (use of) muskets.
Muslim n follower of the religion of Islam. ▷ adj of or relating to Islam.
muslin n fine cotton fabric.
mussel n edible shellfish with a dark hinged shell.
must[1] v used as an auxiliary to express obligation, certainty, or resolution. ▷ n essential or necessary thing.
must[2] n newly pressed grape juice.
mustang n wild horse of SW USA.
mustard n paste made from the powdered seeds of a plant, used as a condiment; the plant. **mustard gas** poisonous gas causing blistering burns and blindness.
muster v assemble. ▷ n assembly of military personnel.
musty adj **mustier, mustiest.** smelling mouldy and stale. **mustiness** n
mutable [mew-tab-bl] adj liable to change. **mutability** n
mutation n (genetic) change. **mutate** v (cause to) undergo mutation. **mutant** n mutated animal, plant, etc.
mute adj silent; unable to speak. ▷ n person who is unable to speak; Music device to soften the tone of an instrument. **muted** adj (of sound or colour) softened; (of a reaction) subdued. **mutely** adv
muti [moo-ti] n S Afr informal medicine, esp. herbal medicine.
mutilate [mew-till-ate] v deprive of a limb or other part; damage (a book or text). **mutilation** n
mutiny [mew-tin-ee] n, pl **-nies.** rebellion against authority, esp. by

soldiers or sailors. ▶ v **-nying,
-nied.** commit mutiny. **mutineer**
n **mutinous** adj

mutt n Slang mongrel dog; stupid
person.

mutter v utter or speak indistinctly;
grumble. ▶ n muttered sound or
grumble.

mutton n flesh of sheep, used as
food. **mutton bird** Aust sea bird
with dark plumage; NZ any of a
number of migratory sea birds,
the young of which are a Maori
delicacy.

mutual [mew-chew-al] adj felt or
expressed by each of two people
about the other; common to both
or all. **mutually** adv

Muzak n ® recorded light music
played in shops etc.

muzzle n animal's mouth and
nose; cover for these to prevent
biting; open end of a gun. ▶ v
prevent from being heard or
noticed; put a muzzle on.

muzzy adj **-zier, -ziest.** confused or
muddled; blurred or hazy.

mW milliwatt(s).

MW megawatt(s).

my adj belonging to me.

myall n Australian acacia with hard
scented wood.

mycology n study of fungi.

myna, mynah, mina n Asian bird
which can mimic human speech.

myopia [my-oh-pee-a] n
short-sightedness. **myopic**
[my-op-ik] adj

myriad [mir-ree-ad] adj
innumerable. ▶ n large indefinite
number.

myrrh [mur] n aromatic gum used
in perfume, incense, and medicine.

myrtle [mur-tl] n flowering
evergreen shrub.

myself pron emphatic or reflexive
form of I or ME.

mystery n, pl **-teries.** strange or

inexplicable event or
phenomenon; obscure or secret
thing; story or film that arouses
suspense. **mysterious** adj
mysteriously adv

mystic n person who seeks spiritual
knowledge. ▶ adj mystical.
mystical adj having a spiritual or
religious significance beyond
human understanding. **mysticism**
n

mystify v **-fying, -fied.** bewilder or
puzzle. **mystification** n

mystique [miss-steek] n aura of
mystery or power.

myth n tale with supernatural
characters, usu. of how the world
and mankind began; untrue idea
or explanation; imaginary person
or object. **mythical, mythic** adj
mythology n myths collectively;
study of myths. **mythological** adj

myxomatosis [mix-a-mat-oh-siss] n
contagious fatal viral disease of
rabbits.

— N n —

N Chem nitrogen; Physics
newton(s); North(ern).

n. neuter; noun; number.

Na Chem sodium.

Naafi n Brit canteen or shop for
military personnel.

naan n same as NAN BREAD.

naartjie [nahr-chee] n S Afr
tangerine.

nab v **nabbing, nabbed.** Informal
arrest (someone); catch (someone)
in wrongdoing.

nadir n point in the sky opposite
the zenith; lowest point.

naevus [nee-vuss] n, pl **-vi.**
birthmark or mole.

naff adj Brit slang lacking quality or
taste.

nag¹ v **nagging, nagged.** scold or find fault constantly; be a constant source of discomfort or worry to. ▶ n person who nags. **nagging** adj, n

nag² n Informal old horse.

naiad [nye-ad] n Greek myth nymph living in a lake or river.

nail n pointed piece of metal with a head, hit with a hammer to join two objects together; hard covering of the upper tips of the fingers and toes. ▶ v attach (something) with nails; Informal catch or arrest. **hit the nail on the head** say something exactly correct. **nail file** small metal file used to smooth or shape the finger or toe nails. **nail varnish, polish** cosmetic lacquer applied to the finger or toe nails.

naive [nye-eev] adj innocent and gullible; simple and lacking sophistication. **naively** adv **naivety, naïveté** [nye-eev-tee] n

naked adj without clothes; without any covering. **the naked eye** the eye unassisted by any optical instrument. **nakedness** n

namby-pamby adj Brit, Aust & NZ sentimental or insipid.

name n word by which a person or thing is known; reputation, esp. a good one. ▶ v give a name to; refer to by name; fix or specify. **call someone names, a name** insult someone by using rude words to describe him or her. **nameless** adj without a name; unspecified; too horrible to be mentioned. **namely** adv that is to say. **namesake** n person with the same name as another.

nan bread n slightly leavened Indian bread in a large flat leaf shape.

nanny n, pl **-nies.** woman whose job is looking after young children. **nanny goat** female goat.

nap¹ n short sleep. ▶ v **napping, napped.** have a short sleep.

nap² n raised fibres of velvet or similar cloth.

nap³ n card game similar to whist.

napalm n highly inflammable jellied petrol, used in bombs.

nape n back of the neck.

naphtha n liquid mixture distilled from coal tar or petroleum, used as a solvent and in petrol. **naphthalene** n white crystalline product distilled from coal tar or petroleum, used in disinfectants, mothballs, and explosives.

napkin n piece of cloth or paper for wiping the mouth or protecting the clothes while eating.

nappy n, pl **-pies.** piece of absorbent material fastened round a baby's lower torso to absorb urine and faeces.

narcissism n exceptional interest in or admiration for oneself. **narcissistic** adj

narcissus n, pl **-cissi.** yellow, orange, or white flower related to the daffodil.

narcotic n, adj (of) a drug, such as morphine or opium, which produces numbness and drowsiness, used medicinally but addictive. **narcosis** n effect of a narcotic.

nark Slang ▶ v annoy. ▶ n informer or spy; Brit someone who complains in an irritating manner. **narky** adj Slang irritable or complaining.

narrate v tell (a story); speak the words accompanying and telling what is happening in a film or TV programme. **narration** n **narrator** n

narrative n account, story.

narrow adj small in breadth in comparison to length; limited in range, extent, or outlook; with little margin, e.g. *a narrow escape.* ► *v* make or become narrow; (often foll. by *down*) limit or restrict. **narrows** *pl n* narrow part of a strait, river, or current. **narrowly** *adv* **narrowness** *n* **narrow boat** *Brit* long bargelike canal boat. **narrow-minded** *adj* intolerant or bigoted.

narwhal *n* arctic whale with a long spiral tusk.

NASA *US* National Aeronautics and Space Administration.

nasal *adj* of the nose; (of a sound) pronounced with air passing through the nose. **nasally** *adv*

nascent *adj* starting to grow or develop.

nasturtium *n* plant with yellow, red, or orange trumpet-shaped flowers.

nasty *adj* **-tier, -tiest.** unpleasant; (of an injury) dangerous or painful; spiteful or unkind. **nastily** *adv* **nastiness** *n*

natal *adj* of or relating to birth.

nation *n* people of one or more cultures or races organized as a single state.

national *adj* characteristic of a particular nation. ► *n* citizen of a nation. **nationally** *adv* **National Curriculum** curriculum of subjects taught in state schools in England and Wales since 1989. **National Health Service** (in Britain) system of national medical services financed mainly by taxation. **national insurance** (in Britain) state insurance scheme providing payments to the unemployed, sick, and retired. **national park** area of countryside protected by a government for its natural or environmental importance. **national service** compulsory military service.

nationalism *n* policy of national independence; patriotism, sometimes to an excessive degree. **nationalist** *n, adj*

nationality *n, pl* **-ties.** fact of being a citizen of a particular nation; group of people of the same race.

nationalize *v* put (an industry or a company) under state control. **nationalization** *n*

native *adj* relating to a place where a person was born; born in a specified place; (foll. by *to*) originating (in); inborn. ► *n* person born in a specified place; indigenous animal or plant; member of the original race of a country. **Native American** (person) descended from the original inhabitants of the American continent.

Nativity *n Christianity* birth of Jesus Christ.

NATO North Atlantic Treaty Organization.

natter *Informal* ► *v* talk idly or chatter. ► *n* long idle chat.

natty *adj* **-tier, -tiest.** *Informal* smart and spruce.

natural *adj* normal or to be expected; genuine or spontaneous; of, according to, existing in, or produced by nature; not created by human beings; not synthetic. ► *n* person with an inborn talent or skill. **naturally** *adv* of course; in a natural or normal way; instinctively. **natural gas** gas found below the ground, used mainly as a fuel. **natural history** study of animals and plants in the wild. **natural selection** process by which only creatures and plants well adapted to their environment survive.

naturalism *n* movement in art and

literature advocating detailed realism. **naturalistic** adj

naturalist n student of natural history.

naturalize v give citizenship to (a person born in another country). **naturalization** n

nature n whole system of the existence, forces, and events of the physical world that are not controlled by human beings; fundamental or essential qualities; kind or sort.

naturism n nudism. **naturist** n

naught n Lit nothing.

naughty adj **-tier, -tiest.** disobedient or mischievous; mildly indecent. **naughtily** adv **naughtiness** n

nausea [naw-zee-a] n feeling of being about to vomit. **nauseate** v make (someone) feel sick; disgust. **nauseous** adj as if about to vomit; sickening.

nautical adj of the sea or ships. **nautical mile** 1852 metres (6076.12 feet).

nautilus n, pl **-luses, -li.** shellfish with many tentacles.

naval adj see NAVY.

nave n long central part of a church.

navel n hollow in the middle of the abdomen where the umbilical cord was attached.

navigate v direct or plot the path or position of a ship, aircraft, or car; travel over or through. **navigation** n **navigator** n

navigable adj wide, deep, or safe enough to be sailed through; able to be steered.

navvy n, pl **-vies.** Brit labourer employed on a road or a building site.

navy n, pl **-vies.** branch of a country's armed services comprising warships with their crews and organization; warships of a nation. ▶ adj navy-blue.

naval adj of or relating to a navy or ships. **navy-blue** adj very dark blue.

nay interj Obs no.

Nazi n member of the fascist National Socialist Party, which came to power in Germany in 1933 under Adolf Hitler. ▶ adj of or relating to the Nazis. **Nazism** n

NB note well.

NCO Mil noncommissioned officer.

NE northeast(ern).

Neanderthal [nee-ann-der-tahl] adj of a type of primitive man that lived in Europe before 12 000 BC.

neap tide n tide at the first and last quarters of the moon when there is the smallest rise and fall in tidal level.

near prep, adv, adj indicating a place or time not far away. ▶ adj almost being the thing specified, e.g. a near disaster. ▶ v draw close (to). **nearly** adv almost. **nearness** n **nearby** adj not far away. **nearside** n side of a vehicle that is nearer the kerb.

neat adj tidy and clean; smoothly or competently done; undiluted. **neatly** adv **neatness** n

nebula n, pl **-lae.** Astronomy hazy cloud of particles and gases. **nebulous** adj vague and unclear, e.g. a nebulous concept.

necessary adj needed to obtain the desired result, e.g. the necessary skills; certain or unavoidable, e.g. the necessary consequences. **necessarily** adv **necessitate** v compel or require. **necessity** n circumstances that inevitably require a certain result; something needed.

neck n part of the body joining the head to the shoulders; part of a garment round the neck; long

narrow part of a bottle or violin.
▶ v *Slang* kiss and cuddle. **neck and neck** absolutely level in a race or competition. **neckerchief** n piece of cloth worn tied round the neck. **necklace** n decorative piece of jewellery worn around the neck; *S Afr* burning petrol-filled tyre placed round someone's neck to kill him or her.

necromancy n communication with the dead; sorcery.

necropolis [neck-**rop**-pol-liss] n cemetery.

nectar n sweet liquid collected from flowers by bees; drink of the gods.

nectarine n smooth-skinned peach.

née [nay] *prep* indicating the maiden name of a married woman.

need v require or be in want of; be obliged (to do something). ▶ n condition of lacking something; requirement or necessity; poverty. **needs** adv (preceded or foll. by *must*) necessarily. **needy** adj poor, in need of financial support. **needful** adj necessary or required. **needless** adj unnecessary.

needle n thin pointed piece of metal with an eye through which thread is passed for sewing; long pointed rod used in knitting; pointed part of a hypodermic syringe; small pointed part in a record player that touches the record and picks up the sound signals, stylus; pointer on a measuring instrument or compass; long narrow stiff leaf. ▶ v *Informal* goad or provoke. **needlework** n sewing and embroidery.

ne'er adv *Lit* never. **ne'er-do-well** n useless or lazy person.

nefarious [nif-**fair**-ee-uss] adj wicked.

negate v invalidate; deny the existence of. **negation** n

negative adj expressing a denial or refusal; lacking positive qualities; (of an electrical charge) having the same electrical charge as an electron. ▶ n negative word or statement; *Photog* image with a reversal of tones or colours from which positive prints are made.

neglect v take no care of; fail (to do something) through carelessness; disregard. ▶ n neglecting or being neglected. **neglectful** adj

negligee [neg-lee-zhay] n woman's lightweight usu. lace-trimmed dressing gown.

negligence n neglect or carelessness. **negligent** adj **negligently** adv

negligible adj so small or unimportant as to be not worth considering.

negotiate v discuss in order to reach (an agreement); succeed in passing round or over (a place or problem). **negotiation** n **negotiator** n **negotiable** adj

Negro n, pl **-groes**. *Old-fashioned* member of any of the Black peoples originating in Africa. **Negroid** adj of or relating to the Negro race.

neigh n loud high-pitched sound made by a horse. ▶ v make this sound.

neighbour n person who lives or is situated near another. **neighbouring** adj situated nearby. **neighbourhood** n district; surroundings; people of a district. **neighbourly** adj kind, friendly, and helpful.

neither adj, pron not one nor the other. ▶ conj not.

nemesis [nem-**miss**-iss] n, pl **-ses**. retribution or vengeance.

neo- combining form new, recent, or a modern form of, e.g.

neoclassicism.

Neolithic adj of the later Stone Age.

neologism [nee-ol-a-jiz-zum] n newly-coined word or an established word used in a new sense.

neon n Chem colourless odourless gaseous element used in illuminated signs and lights.

neophyte n beginner or novice; new convert.

nephew n son of one's sister or brother.

nephritis [nif-frite-tiss] n inflammation of a kidney.

nepotism [nep-a-tiz-zum] n favouritism in business shown to relatives and friends.

Neptune n Roman god of the sea; eighth planet from the sun.

nerd n Slang boring person obsessed with a particular subject; stupid and feeble person.

nerve n cordlike bundle of fibres that conducts impulses between the brain and other parts of the body; bravery and determination; impudence. ▶ pl anxiety or tension; ability or inability to remain calm in a difficult situation. **get on someone's nerves** irritate someone. **nerve oneself** prepare oneself (to do something difficult or unpleasant). **nerveless** adj numb, without feeling; fearless. **nervy** adj excitable or nervous. **nerve centre** place from which a system or organization is controlled. **nerve-racking** adj very distressing or harrowing.

nervous adj apprehensive or worried; of or relating to the nerves. **nervously** adv **nervousness** n **nervous breakdown** mental illness in which the sufferer ceases to function properly.

nest n place or structure in which birds or certain animals lay eggs or give birth to young; secluded place; set of things of graduated sizes designed to fit together. ▶ v make or inhabit a nest. **nest egg** fund of money kept in reserve.

nestle v snuggle; be in a sheltered position.

nestling n bird too young to leave the nest.

net[1] n fabric of meshes of string, thread, or wire with many openings; piece of net used to protect or hold things or to trap animals. ▶ v net used to catch (a fish or animal) in a net. **netting** n material made of net.

netball n team game in which a ball has to be thrown through a net hanging from a ring at the top of a pole.

net[2], **nett** adj left after all deductions; (of weight) excluding the wrapping or container. ▶ v **netting, netted.** yield or earn as a clear profit.

nether adj lower.

nettle n plant with stinging hairs on the leaves. **nettled** adj irritated or annoyed.

network n system of intersecting lines, roads, etc.; interconnecting group or system; (in broadcasting) group of stations that all transmit the same programmes simultaneously.

neural adj of a nerve or the nervous system.

neuralgia n severe pain along a nerve.

neuritis [nyoor-rite-tiss] n inflammation of a nerve or nerves.

neurology n scientific study of the nervous system. **neurologist** n

neurosis n, pl **-ses.** mental disorder producing hysteria, anxiety, depression, or obsessive

behaviour. **neurotic** *adj*
emotionally unstable; suffering
from neurosis. ▶ *n* neurotic person.
neuter *adj* belonging to a
particular class of grammatical
inflections in some languages. ▶ *v*
castrate (an animal).
neutral *adj* taking neither side in a
war or dispute; of or belonging to
a neutral party or country; (of a
colour) not definite or striking. ▶ *n*
neutral person or nation; neutral
gear. **neutrality** *n* **neutralize** *v*
make ineffective or neutral.
neutral gear position of the
controls of a gearbox that leaves
the gears unconnected to the
engine.
neutrino [new-tree-no] *n, pl* **-nos**.
elementary particle with no mass
or electrical charge.
neutron *n* electrically neutral
elementary particle of about the
same mass as a proton. **neutron
bomb** nuclear bomb designed to
kill people and animals while
leaving buildings virtually
undamaged.
never *adv* at no time.
nevertheless *adv* in spite of that.
never-never *n Informal*
hire-purchase.
new *adj* not existing before;
recently acquired; having lately
come into some state; additional;
(foll. by *to*) unfamiliar. ▶ *adv*
recently. **newness** *n* **New Age**
philosophy, originating in the late
1980s, characterized by a belief in
alternative medicine and
spirituality. **newborn** *adj* recently
or just born. **newcomer** *n* recent
arrival or participant. **newfangled**
adj objectionably or unnecessarily
modern. **newlyweds** *pl n* recently
married couple. **new moon** moon
when it appears as a narrow
crescent at the beginning of its

cycle.
newel *n* post at the top or bottom
of a flight of stairs that supports
the handrail.
news *n* important or interesting
new happenings; information
about such events reported in the
mass media. **newsy** *adj* full of
news. **newsagent** *n Brit*
shopkeeper who sells newspapers
and magazines. **newsflash** *n* brief
important news item, which
interrupts a radio or television
programme. **newsletter** *n*
bulletin issued periodically to
members of a group. **newspaper**
n weekly or daily publication
containing news. **newsprint** *n*
inexpensive paper used for
newspapers. **newsreader**,
newscaster *n* person who reads
the news on the television or
radio. **newsreel** *n* short film
giving news. **newsroom** *n* room
where news is received and
prepared for publication or
broadcasting. **newsworthy** *adj*
sufficiently interesting to be
reported as news.
newt *n* small amphibious creature
with a long slender body and tail.
newton *n* unit of force.
next *adj, adv* immediately
following; nearest. **next-of-kin** *n*
closest relative.
nexus *n, pl* **nexus**. connection or
link.
NHS (in Britain) National Health
Service.
nib *n* writing point of a pen.
nibble *v* take little bites (of). ▶ *n*
little bite.
nibs *n* **his, her nibs** *Slang* mock
title of respect.
nice *adj* pleasant; kind; good or
satisfactory; subtle, e.g. *a nice
distinction.* **nicely** *adv* **niceness** *n*
nicety *n, pl* **-ties.** subtle point;

refinement or delicacy.

niche [neesh] n hollow area in a wall; suitable position for a particular person.

nick v make a small cut in; *Chiefly Brit slang* steal; *Chiefly Brit slang* arrest. ▶ n small cut; *Slang* prison or police station. **in good nick** *Informal* in good condition. **in the nick of time** just in time.

nickel n *Chem* silvery-white metal often used in alloys; US coin worth five cents.

nickelodeon n *US* early type of jukebox.

nickname n familiar name given to a person or place. ▶ v call by a nickname.

nicotine n poisonous substance found in tobacco.

niece n daughter of one's sister or brother.

nifty adj **-tier, -tiest.** *Informal* neat or smart.

niggardly adj stingy. **niggard** n stingy person.

niggle v worry slightly; continually find fault (with). ▶ n small worry or doubt.

nigh adv, prep *Lit* near.

night n time of darkness between sunset and sunrise. **nightly** adj, adv (happening) each night. **nightcap** n drink taken just before bedtime; soft cap formerly worn in bed. **nightclub** n establishment for dancing, music, etc., open late at night. **nightdress** n woman's loose dress worn in bed. **nightfall** n approach of darkness. **nightie** n *Informal* nightdress. **nightingale** n small bird with a musical song usu. heard at night. **nightjar** n nocturnal bird with a harsh cry. **nightlife** n entertainment and social activities available at night in a town or city. **nightmare** n very bad dream; very unpleasant experience. **night school** place where adults can attend educational courses in the evenings. **nightshade** n plant with bell-shaped flowers which are often poisonous. **nightshirt** n long loose shirt worn in bed. **night-time** n time from sunset to sunrise.

nihilism [nye-ill-liz-zum] n rejection of all established authority and institutions. **nihilist** n **nihilistic** adj

nil n nothing, zero.

nimble adj agile and quick; mentally alert or acute. **nimbly** adv

nimbus n, pl **-bi, -buses.** dark grey rain cloud.

nincompoop n *Informal* stupid person.

nine adj, n one more than eight. **ninth** adj, n (of) number nine in a series. **ninepins** n game of skittles.

nineteen adj, n ten and nine. **nineteenth** adj, n

ninety adj, n ten times nine. **ninetieth** adj, n

niobium n *Chem* white superconductive metallic element.

nip[1] v **nipping, nipped.** *Informal* hurry; pinch or squeeze; bite lightly. ▶ n pinch or light bite; sharp coldness. **nipper** n *Brit, Aust & NZ informal* small child. **nippy** adj frosty or chilly; *Informal* quick or nimble.

nip[2] n small alcoholic drink.

nipple n projection in the centre of a breast.

nirvana [near-vah-na] n *Buddhism, Hinduism* absolute spiritual enlightenment and bliss.

nit n egg or larva of a louse; *Informal* short for NITWIT. **nit-picking** adj *Informal* overconcerned with insignificant detail, esp. to find fault. **nitwit** n *Informal* stupid person.

nitrogen [nite-roj-jen] n Chem colourless odourless gas that forms four fifths of the air. **nitric, nitrous, nitrogenous** adj of or containing nitrogen. **nitrate** n compound of nitric acid, used as a fertilizer. **nitroglycerine, nitroglycerin** n explosive liquid.

nitty-gritty n Informal basic facts.

no interj expresses denial, disagreement, or refusal. ▸ adj not any, not a. ▸ adv not at all. ▸ n, pl **noes, nos.** answer or vote of 'no'; person who answers or votes 'no'. **no-go area** district barricaded off so that the police or army can enter only by force.

no-man's-land n land between boundaries, esp. contested land between two opposing forces. **no-one, no one** pron nobody.

no. number.

nob n Chiefly Brit slang person of wealth or social distinction.

nobble v Brit slang attract the attention of (someone) in order to talk to him or her; bribe or threaten.

nobelium n Chem artificially-produced radioactive element.

Nobel Prize n prize awarded annually for outstanding achievement in various fields.

noble adj showing or having high moral qualities; of the nobility; impressive and magnificent. ▸ n member of the nobility. **nobility** n quality of being noble; class of people holding titles and high social rank. **nobly** adv **nobleman, noblewoman** n

nobody pron no person. ▸ n, pl **-bodies.** person of no importance.

nocturnal adj of the night; active at night.

nocturne n short dreamy piece of music.

nod v nodding, nodded. lower and raise (one's) head briefly in agreement or greeting; let one's head fall forward with sleep. ▸ n act of nodding. **nod off** v Informal fall asleep.

noddle n Chiefly Brit informal the head.

node n point on a plant stem from which leaves grow; point at which a curve crosses itself.

nodule n small knot or lump; rounded mineral growth on the root of a plant.

Noel n Christmas.

noggin n Informal head; small quantity of an alcoholic drink.

noise n sound, usu. a loud or disturbing one. **noisy** adj making a lot of noise; full of noise. **noisily** adv **noiseless** adj

noisome adj (of smells) offensive; harmful or poisonous.

nomad n member of a tribe with no fixed dwelling place, wanderer. **nomadic** adj

nom de plume n, pl **noms de plume.** pen name.

nomenclature n system of names used in a particular subject.

nominal adj in name only; very small in comparison with real worth. **nominally** adv

nominate v suggest as a candidate; appoint to an office or position. **nomination** n **nominee** n candidate. **nominative** n form of a noun indicating the subject of a verb.

non- prefix indicating: negation, e.g. nonexistent; refusal or failure, e.g. noncooperation; exclusion from a specified class, e.g. nonfiction; lack or absence, e.g. nonevent.

nonagenarian n person aged between ninety and ninety-nine.

nonaggression n policy of not attacking other countries.

nonagon n geometric figure with nine sides.

nonalcoholic adj containing no alcohol.

nonaligned adj (of a country) not part of a major alliance or power bloc.

nonce n **for the nonce** for the present.

nonchalant adj casually unconcerned or indifferent. **nonchalantly** adv **nonchalance** n

noncombatant n member of the armed forces whose duties do not include fighting.

noncommissioned officer n (in the armed forces) a subordinate officer, risen from the ranks.

noncommittal adj not committing oneself to any particular opinion.

non compos mentis adj of unsound mind.

nonconductor n substance that is a poor conductor of heat, electricity, or sound.

nonconformist n person who does not conform to generally accepted patterns of behaviour or thought; **(N-)** member of a Protestant group separated from the Church of England. ▸ adj (of behaviour or ideas) not conforming to accepted patterns. **nonconformity** n

noncontributory adj Brit denoting a pension scheme for employees, the premiums of which are paid entirely by the employer.

nondescript adj lacking outstanding features.

none pron not any; no-one. **nonetheless** adv despite that, however.

nonentity [non-enn-tit-tee] n, pl **-ties** insignificant person or thing.

nonevent n disappointing or insignificant occurrence.

nonflammable adj not easily set on fire.

nonintervention n refusal to intervene in the affairs of others.

nonpareil [non-par-rail] n person or thing that is unsurpassed.

nonpayment n failure to pay money owed.

nonplussed adj perplexed.

nonsense n something that has or makes no sense; absurd language; foolish behaviour. **nonsensical** adj

non sequitur [sek-wit-tur] n statement with little or no relation to what preceded it.

nonstandard adj denoting language that is not regarded as correct by educated native speakers.

nonstarter n person or idea that has little chance of success.

nonstick adj coated with a substance that food will not stick to when cooked.

nonstop adj, adv without a stop.

nontoxic adj not poisonous.

noodles pl n long thin strips of pasta.

nook n sheltered place.

noon n twelve o'clock midday. **noonday** adj happening at noon.

noose n loop in the end of a rope, tied with a slipknot.

nor conj and not.

Nordic adj of Scandinavia or its typically tall blond and blue-eyed people.

norm n standard that is regarded as normal.

normal adj usual, regular, or typical; free from mental or physical disorder. **normally** adv **normality** n **normalize** v

Norse n (language) of ancient and medieval Norway.

north n direction towards the North Pole, opposite south; area lying in or towards the north. ▸ adj to or in the north; (of a wind) from the north. ▸ adv in, to, or towards the north. **northerly** *adj* **northern** *adj* **northerner** *n* person from the north of a country or area. **northward** *adj, adv* **northwards** *adv* **North Pole** northernmost point on the earth's axis.

nos. numbers.

nose *n* organ of smell, used also in breathing; front part of a vehicle. ▶ *v* move forward slowly and carefully; pry or snoop. **nose dive** sudden drop. **nosegay** *n* small bunch of flowers. **nosey, nosy** *adj Informal* prying or inquisitive. **nosiness** *n*

nosh *Brit, Aust & NZ slang* ▶ *n* food. ▶ *v* eat.

nostalgia *n* sentimental longing for the past. **nostalgic** *adj*

nostril *n* one of the two openings at the end of the nose.

nostrum *n* quack medicine; favourite remedy.

not *adv* expressing negation, refusal, or denial.

notable *adj* worthy of being noted, remarkable. ▶ *n* person of distinction. **notably** *adv* **notability** *n*

notary *n, pl* **-ries.** person authorized to witness the signing of legal documents.

notation *n* representation of numbers or quantities in a system by a series of symbols; set of such symbols.

notch *n* V-shaped cut; *Informal* step or level. ▶ *v* make a notch in; (foll. by *up*) score or achieve.

note *n* short letter; brief comment or record; banknote; (symbol for) a musical sound; hint or mood. ▶ *v* notice, pay attention to; record in writing; remark upon. **noted** *adj* well-known. **notebook** *n* book for writing in. **noteworthy** *adj* worth noting,

remarkable.

nothing *pron* not anything; matter of no importance; figure 0. ▶ *adv* not at all. **nothingness** *n* nonexistence; insignificance.

notice *n* observation or attention; sign giving warning or an announcement; advance notification of intention to end a contract of employment. ▶ *v* observe, become aware of; point out or remark upon. **noticeable** *adj* easily seen or detected, appreciable.

notify *v* **-fying, -fied.** inform. **notification** *n* **notifiable** *adj* having to be reported to the authorities.

notion *n* idea or opinion; whim. **notional** *adj* speculative, imaginary, or unreal.

notorious *adj* well known for something bad. **notoriously** *adv* **notoriety** *n*

notwithstanding *prep* in spite of.

nougat *n* chewy sweet containing nuts and fruit.

nought *n* figure 0; nothing.

noun *n* word that refers to a person, place, or thing.

nourish *v* feed; encourage or foster (an idea or feeling). **nourishment** *n* **nourishing** *adj* providing the food necessary for life and growth.

nouvelle cuisine [noo-vell kwee-**zeen**] *n* style of preparing and presenting food with light sauces and unusual combinations of flavours.

Nov. November.

nova *n, pl* **-vae, -vas.** star that suddenly becomes brighter and then gradually decreases to its original brightness.

novel[1] *n* long fictitious story in book form. **novelist** *n* writer of novels. **novella** *n, pl* **-las, -lae.** short novel.

novel² adj fresh, new, or original. **novelty** n newness; something new or unusual.

November n eleventh month of the year.

novena [no-vee-na] n, pl -nas. RC Church set of prayers or services on nine consecutive days.

novice n beginner; person who has entered a religious order but has not yet taken vows.

now adv at or for the present time; immediately. ▶ conj seeing that, since. **just now** very recently. **now and again, then** occasionally. **nowadays** adv in these times.

nowhere adv not anywhere.

noxious adj poisonous or harmful; extremely unpleasant.

nozzle n projecting spout through which fluid is discharged.

NSPCC (in Britain) National Society for the Prevention of Cruelty to Children.

NSW New South Wales.

NT (in Britain) National Trust; New Testament; Northern Territory.

nuance [new-ahnss] n subtle difference in colour, meaning, or tone.

nub n point or gist (of a story etc.).

nubile [new-bile] adj (of a young woman) sexually attractive; old enough to get married.

nuclear adj of nuclear weapons or energy; of a nucleus, esp. the nucleus of an atom. **nuclear energy** energy released as a result of nuclear fission or fusion. **nuclear fission** splitting of an atomic nucleus. **nuclear fusion** combination of two nuclei to form a heavier nucleus with the release of energy. **nuclear power** power produced by a nuclear reactor. **nuclear reaction** change in structure and energy content of an atomic nucleus by interaction with another nucleus or particle. **nuclear reactor** device in which a nuclear reaction is maintained and controlled to produce nuclear energy. **nuclear weapon** weapon whose force is due to uncontrolled nuclear fusion or fission. **nuclear winter** theoretical period of low temperatures and little light after a nuclear war.

nucleic acid n complex compound, such as DNA or RNA, found in all living cells.

nucleus n, pl -clei. centre, esp. of an atom or cell; central thing around which others are grouped.

nude adj naked. ▶ n naked figure in painting, sculpture, or photography. **nudity** n **nudism** n practice of not wearing clothes. **nudist** n

nudge v push gently, esp. with the elbow. ▶ n gentle push or touch.

nugatory [new-gat-tree] adj of little value; not valid.

nugget n small lump of gold in its natural state; something small but valuable. ▶ v NZ & S Afr polish footwear.

nuisance n something or someone that causes annoyance or bother.

nuke Slang ▶ v attack with nuclear weapons. ▶ n nuclear weapon.

null adj **null and void** not legally valid. **nullity** n **nullify** v make ineffective; cancel.

nulla-nulla n wooden club used by Australian Aborigines.

numb adj without feeling, as through cold, shock, or fear. ▶ v make numb. **numbly** adv **numbness** n **numbskull** n stupid person.

numbat n small Australian marsupial with a long snout and tongue.

number n sum or quantity; word or symbol used to express a sum

or quantity, numeral; numeral or string of numerals used to identify a person or thing; one of a series, such as a copy of a magazine; song or piece of music; group of people; *Grammar* classification of words depending on how many persons or things are referred to. ▶ *v* count; give a number to; amount to; include in a group.
numberless *adj* too many to be counted. **number crunching** *Computers* large-scale processing of numerical data. **number one** *n Informal* oneself; bestselling pop record in any one week. ▶ *adj* first in importance or quality.
numberplate *n* plate on a car showing the registration number.
numeral *n* word or symbol used to express a sum or quantity.
numerate *adj* able to do basic arithmetic. **numeracy** *n*
numeration *n* act or process of numbering or counting.
numerator *n Maths* number above the line in a fraction.
numerical *adj* measured or expressed in numbers. **numerically** *adv*
numerous *adj* existing or happening in large numbers.
numismatist *n* coin collector.
numskull *n* same as NUMBSKULL.
nun *n* female member of a religious order. **nunnery** *n* convent.
nuncio *n RC Church* pope's ambassador.
nuptial *adj* relating to marriage. **nuptials** *pl n* wedding.
nurse *n* person employed to look after sick people, usu. in a hospital; woman employed to look after children. ▶ *v* look after (a sick person); breast-feed (a baby); try to cure (an ailment); harbour or foster (a feeling). **nursing home**

private hospital or home for old people. **nursing officer** (in Britain) administrative head of the nursing staff of a hospital.
nursery *n, pl* **-ries.** room where children sleep or play; place where children are taken care of while their parents are at work; place where plants are grown for sale.
nurseryman *n* person who raises plants for sale. **nursery school** school for children from 3 to 5 years old. **nursery slopes** gentle ski slopes for beginners.
nurture *n* act or process of promoting the development of a child or young plant. ▶ *v* promote or encourage the development of.
nut *n* fruit consisting of a hard shell and a kernel; small piece of metal that screws onto a bolt; (also **nutcase**) *Slang* insane or eccentric person; *Slang* head.
nutter *n Brit slang* insane person.
nutty *adj* containing or resembling nuts; *Slang* insane or eccentric. **nutcracker** *n* device for cracking the shells of nuts.
nuthatch *n* small songbird.
nutmeg *n* spice made from the seed of a tropical tree.
nutria *n* fur of the coypu.
nutrient *n* substance that provides nourishment.
nutriment *n* food or nourishment required by all living things to grow and stay healthy.
nutrition *n* process of taking in and absorbing nutrients; process of being nourished. **nutritional** *adj* **nutritious, nutritive** *adj* nourishing.
nuzzle *v* push or rub gently with the nose or snout.
NW northwest(ern).
nylon *n* synthetic material used for clothing etc. ▶ *pl* stockings made of nylon.

nymph n mythical spirit of nature, represented as a beautiful young woman; larva of certain insects, resembling the adult form.

nymphet n sexually precocious young girl.

nymphomaniac n woman with an abnormally intense sexual desire.

NZ New Zealand.

NZE New Zealand English.

NZRFU New Zealand Rugby Football Union.

NZSE40 Index New Zealand Share Price 40 Index.

O o

O Chem oxygen.

oaf n stupid or clumsy person. **oafish** adj

oak n deciduous forest tree; its wood, used for furniture. **oaken** adj **oak apple** brownish lump found on oak trees.

oakum n fibre obtained by unravelling old rope.

OAP (in Britain) old-age pensioner.

oar n pole with a broad blade, used for rowing a boat.

oasis n, pl -ses. fertile area in a desert.

oast n Chiefly Brit oven for drying hops.

oat n hard cereal grown as food. ▶ pl grain of this cereal. **sow one's wild oats** have many sexual relationships when young. **oatmeal** adj pale brownish-cream.

oath n solemn promise, esp. to be truthful in court; swearword.

obbligato [ob-lig-gah-toe] n, pl -tos. Music essential part or accompaniment.

obdurate adj hardhearted or stubborn. **obduracy** n

OBE (in Britain) Officer of the Order of the British Empire.

obedient adj obeying or willing to obey. **obedience** n **obediently** adv

obeisance [oh-bay-sanss] n attitude of respect; bow or curtsy.

obelisk [ob-bill-isk] n four-sided stone column tapering to a pyramid at the top.

obese [oh-beess] adj very fat. **obesity** n

obey v carry out instructions or orders.

obfuscate v make (something) confusing.

obituary n, pl -aries. announcement of someone's death, esp. in a newspaper. **obituarist** n

object[1] n physical thing; focus of thoughts or action; aim or purpose; Grammar word that a verb or preposition affects. **no object** not a hindrance.

object[2] v express disapproval. **objection** n **objectionable** adj unpleasant. **objector** n

objective n aim or purpose. ▶ adj not biased; existing in the real world outside the human mind. **objectively** adv **objectivity** n

objet d'art [ob-zhay dahr] n, pl **objets d'art.** small object of artistic value.

oblation n religious offering.

oblige v compel (someone) morally or by law to do something; do a favour for (someone). **obliging** adj ready to help other people. **obligingly** adv **obligated** adj obliged to do something. **obligation** n duty. **obligatory** adj required by a rule or law.

oblique [oh-bleak] adj slanting; indirect. ▶ n the symbol (/). **obliquely** adv **oblique angle** angle that is not a right angle.

obliterate v wipe out, destroy.
obliteration n

oblivious adj unaware. **oblivion** n
state of being forgotten; state of
being unaware or unconscious.

oblong adj having two long sides,
two short sides, and four right
angles. ▶ n oblong figure.

obloquy [ob-**lock**-wee] n, pl **-quies.**
verbal abuse; discredit.

obnoxious adj offensive.

oboe n double-reeded woodwind
instrument. **oboist** n

obscene adj portraying sex
offensively; disgusting. **obscenity**
n

obscure adj not well known; hard
to understand; indistinct. ▶ v make
(something) obscure. **obscurity** n

obsequies [ob-**sick**-weez] pl n
funeral rites.

obsequious [ob-**seek**-wee-uss] adj
overattentive in order to gain
favour. **obsequiousness** n

observe v see or notice; watch
(someone or something) carefully;
remark; act according to (a law or
custom). **observation** n action or
habit of observing; remark.
observable adj **observance** n
observing of a custom. **observant**
adj quick to notice things.
observatory n building equipped
for studying the weather and the
stars.

observer n person who observes,
esp. one who watches someone
or something carefully.

obsess v preoccupy (someone)
compulsively. **obsessed** adj
obsessive adj **obsession** n

obsidian n dark glassy volcanic
rock.

obsolete adj no longer in use.
obsolescent adj becoming
obsolete. **obsolescence** n

obstacle n something that makes
progress difficult.

obstetrics n branch of medicine
concerned with pregnancy and
childbirth. **obstetric** adj
obstetrician n

obstinate adj stubborn; difficult to
remove or change. **obstinately**
adv **obstinacy** n

obstreperous adj unruly, noisy.

obstruct v block with an obstacle.
obstruction n **obstructive** adj

obtain v acquire intentionally; be
customary. **obtainable** adj

obtrude v push oneself or one's
ideas on others. **obtrusive** adj
unpleasantly noticeable.
obtrusively adv

obtuse adj mentally slow; Maths
(of an angle) between 90° and
180°; not pointed. **obtuseness** n

obverse n opposite way of looking
at an idea; main side of a coin or
medal.

obviate v make unnecessary.

obvious adj easy to see or
understand, evident. **obviously**
adv

ocarina n small oval wind
instrument.

occasion n time at which a
particular thing happens; reason,
e.g. no occasion for complaint;
special event. ▶ v cause.
occasional adj happening
sometimes. **occasionally** adv

Occident n Lit the West.
Occidental adj

occiput [ox-**sip**-put] n back of the
head.

occlude v obstruct; close off.
occlusion n **occluded front**
Meteorol front formed when a cold
front overtakes a warm front and
warm air rises.

occult adj relating to the
supernatural. **the occult**
knowledge or study of the
supernatural.

occupant n person occupying a

specified place. **occupancy** n (length of) a person's stay in a specified place.

occupation n profession; activity that occupies one's time; control of a country by a foreign military power; being occupied. **occupational** adj **occupational therapy** purposeful activities, designed to aid recovery from illness etc.

occupy v **-pying, -pied.** live or work in (a building); take up the attention of (someone); take up (space or time); take possession of (a place) by force. **occupier** n

occur v **-curring, -curred.** happen; exist. **occur to** come to the mind of. **occurrence** n something that occurs; fact of occurring.

ocean n vast area of sea between continents. **oceanic** adj **oceanography** n scientific study of the oceans. **ocean-going** adj able to sail on the open sea.

ocelot [oss-ill-lot] n American wild cat with a spotted coat.

oche [ok-kee] n Darts mark on the floor behind which a player must stand.

ochre [oak-er] adj, n brownish-yellow (earth).

o'clock adv used after a number to specify an hour.

Oct. October.

octagon n geometric figure with eight sides. **octagonal** adj

octahedron [ok-ta-heed-ron] n, pl **-drons, -dra.** three-dimensional geometric figure with eight faces.

octane n hydrocarbon found in petrol. **octane rating** measure of petrol quality.

octave n Music (interval between the first and) eighth note of a scale.

octet n group of eight performers; music for such a group.

October n tenth month of the year.

octogenarian n person aged between eighty and eighty-nine.

octopus n, pl **-puses.** sea creature with a soft body and eight tentacles.

ocular adj relating to the eyes or sight.

OD Informal ▶ n overdose. ▶ v **OD'ing, OD'd.** take an overdose.

odd adj unusual; occasional; not divisible by two; not part of a set. **odds** pl n (ratio showing) the probability of something happening. **at odds** in conflict. **odds and ends** small miscellaneous items. **oddity** n odd person or thing. **oddness** n quality of being odd. **oddments** pl n things left over.

ode n lyric poem, usu. addressed to a particular subject.

odium [oh-dee-um] n widespread dislike. **odious** adj offensive.

odour n particular smell. **odorous** adj **odourless** adj

odyssey [odd-iss-ee] n long eventful journey.

OE NZ informal overseas experience, e.g. he's away on his OE.

OECD Organization for Economic Cooperation and Development.

oedema [id-deem-a] n, pl **-mata.** Med abnormal swelling.

oesophagus [ee-soff-a-guss] n pl **-gi.** passage between the mouth and stomach.

oestrogen [ee-stra-jen] n female hormone that controls the reproductive cycle.

of prep belonging to; consisting of; connected with; characteristic of.

off prep away from. ▶ adv away. ▶ adj not operating; cancelled; (of food) gone bad. ▶ n Cricket side of the field to which the batsman's

feet point. **off colour** slightly ill.
off-line adj (of a computer) not directly controlled by a central processor. **off-message** adj (esp. of a politician) not following the official Party line. **off-road** adj (of a motor vehicle) designed for use away from public roads.

offal n edible organs of an animal, such as liver or kidneys. **offal pit, offal hole** NZ place on a farm for the disposal of animal offal.

offcut n piece remaining after the required parts have been cut out.

offend v hurt the feelings of, insult; commit a crime. **offence** n (cause of) hurt feelings or annoyance; illegal act. **offensive** adj disagreeable; insulting; aggressive. ▶ n position or action of attack.

offender n person who commits a crime.

offer v present (something) for acceptance or rejection; provide; be willing (to do something); propose as payment. ▶ n instance of offering something. **offering** n thing offered. **offertory** n Christianity offering of the bread and wine for Communion.

offhand adj casual, curt. ▶ adv without preparation.

office n room or building where people work at desks; department of a commercial organization; formal position of responsibility; place where tickets or information can be obtained.

officer n person in authority in the armed services; member of the police force; person with special responsibility in an organization.

official adj of a position of authority; approved or arranged by someone in authority. ▶ n person who holds a position of authority. **officially** adv

officialdom n officials collectively. **Official Receiver** Brit person who deals with the affairs of a bankrupt company.

officiate v act in an official role.

officious adj interfering unnecessarily.

offing n area of the sea visible from the shore. **in the offing** Brit, Aust & NZ likely to happen soon.

off-licence n Brit shop licensed to sell alcohol for drinking elsewhere.

offset v cancel out, compensate for.

offshoot n something developed from something else.

offside adj, adv Sport (positioned) illegally ahead of the ball.

offspring n, pl **offspring.** child.

often adv frequently, much of the time. **oft** adv Poetic often.

ogle v stare at (someone) lustfully.

ogre n giant that eats human flesh; monstrous or cruel person.

oh interj exclamation of surprise, pain, etc.

ohm n unit of electrical resistance.

OHMS Brit On Her or His Majesty's Service.

oil n viscous liquid, insoluble in water and usu. flammable; same as PETROLEUM; petroleum derivative, used as a fuel or lubricant. ▶ pl oil-based paints used in art. ▶ v lubricate (a machine) with oil. **oily** adj **oilfield** n area containing oil reserves. **oil rig** platform constructed for drilling oil wells. **oilskin** n (garment made from) waterproof material.

ointment n greasy substance used for healing skin or as a cosmetic.

O.K., okay Informal ▶ interj expression of approval. ▶ v approve (something). ▶ n approval.

okapi [ok-**kah**-pee] n African animal related to the giraffe but with a shorter neck.

okra n tropical plant with edible

green pods.

old adj having lived or existed for a long time; of a specified age, e.g. two years old; former. **olden** adj old, e.g. in the olden days. **oldie** n Informal old but popular song or film. **old-fashioned** adj no longer commonly used or valued. **old guard** group of people in an organization who have traditional values. **old hat** boring because so familiar. **old maid** elderly unmarried woman. **old master** European painter or painting from the period 1500–1800. **Old Nick** Brit, Aust & NZ informal the Devil. **old school tie** system of mutual help between former pupils of public schools. **Old Testament** part of the Bible recording Hebrew history. **Old World** world as it was known before the discovery of the Americas.

oleaginous [ol-lee-aj-in-uss] adj oily, producing oil.

oleander [ol-lee-ann-der] n Mediterranean flowering evergreen shrub.

olfactory adj relating to the sense of smell.

oligarchy [ol-lee-gark-ee] n, pl -chies. government by a small group of people; state governed this way. **oligarchic, oligarchical** adj

olive n small green or black fruit used as food or pressed for its oil; tree on which this fruit grows. ▶ adj greyish-green. **olive branch** peace offering.

Olympic Games pl n four-yearly international sports competition.

ombudsman n official who investigates complaints against government organizations.

omelette n dish of eggs beaten and fried.

omen n happening or object thought to foretell success or misfortune. **ominous** adj worrying, seeming to foretell misfortune.

omit v **omitting, omitted.** leave out; neglect (to do something). **omission** n

omnibus n several books or TV or radio programmes made into one; Old-fashioned bus.

omnipotent adj having unlimited power. **omnipotence** n

omnipresent adj present everywhere. **omnipresence** n

omniscient [om-niss-ee-ent] adj knowing everything. **omniscience** n

omnivorous [om-niv-vor-uss] adj eating food obtained from both animals and plants. **omnivore** n omnivorous animal.

on prep indicating position above, attachment, closeness, etc., e.g. lying on the ground; a puppet on a string; on the coast. ▶ adv in operation; continuing; forwards. ▶ adj operating; taking place. In Cricket side of the field on which the batsman stands. **on line, online** adj (of a computer) directly controlled by a central processor; relating to the Internet, e.g. online shopping. **on-message** adj (esp. of a politician) following the official Party line.

once adv on one occasion; formerly. ▶ conj as soon as. **at once** immediately; simultaneously. **once-over** n Informal quick examination.

oncogene [on-koh-jean] n gene that can cause cancer when abnormally activated.

oncoming adj approaching from the front.

one adj single, lone. ▶ n number or figure 1; single unit. ▶ pron any person. **oneness** n unity. **oneself**

pron reflexive form of ONE.
one-armed bandit fruit machine operated by a lever on one side.
one-liner *n* witty remark.
one-night stand sexual encounter lasting one night. **one-sided** *adj* considering only one point of view. **one-way** *adj* allowing movement in one direction only.
onerous [own-er-uss] *adj* (of a task) difficult to carry out.
ongoing *adj* in progress, continuing.
onion *n* strongly flavoured edible bulb.
onlooker *n* person who watches without taking part.
only *adj* alone of its kind. ▶ *adv* exclusively; merely; no more than. ▶ *conj* but.
onomatopoeia [on-a-mat-a-**pee**-a] *n* use of a word which imitates the sound it represents, such as *hiss*. **onomatopoeic** *adj*
onset *n* beginning.
onslaught *n* violent attack.
onto *prep* to a position on; aware of, e.g. *she's onto us.*
ontology *n* branch of philosophy concerned with existence. **ontological** *adj*
onus [**own**-uss] *n*, *pl* onuses. responsibility or burden.
onward *adj* directed or moving forward. ▶ *adv* (also **onwards**) ahead, forward.
onyx *n* type of quartz with coloured layers.
oodles *pl n Informal* great quantities.
ooze[1] *v* flow slowly. ▶ *n* sluggish flow. **oozy** *adj*
ooze[2] *n* soft mud at the bottom of a lake or river.
opal *n* iridescent precious stone. **opalescent** *adj* iridescent like an opal.
opaque *adj* not able to be seen

through, not transparent. **opacity** *n*
op. cit. [op sit] in the work cited.
OPEC Organization of Petroleum-Exporting Countries.
open *adj* not closed; not covered; unfolded; ready for business; free from obstruction, accessible; frank. ▶ *v* (cause to) become open; begin. ▶ *n Sport* competition which all may enter. **in the open** outdoors. **openly** *adv* without concealment. **opening** *n* opportunity; hole. ▶ *adj* first.
opencast mining mining at the surface and not underground.
open day day on which a school or college is open to the public.
open-handed *adj* generous.
open-hearted *adj* generous; frank.
open-heart surgery surgery on the heart during which the blood circulation is maintained by machine. **open house** hospitality to visitors at any time. **open letter** letter to an individual that the writer makes public in a newspaper or magazine.
open-minded *adj* receptive to new ideas. **open-plan** *adj* (of a house or office) having few interior walls. **open prison** prison with minimal security. **open verdict** coroner's verdict not stating the cause of death.
opera[1] *n* drama in which the text is sung to an orchestral accompaniment. **operatic** *adj*
operetta *n* light-hearted comic opera.
opera[2] *n* a plural of OPUS.
operate *v* (cause to) work; direct; perform an operation. **operator** *n*
operation *n* method or procedure of working; medical procedure in which the body is worked on to repair a damaged part.
operational *adj* in working order;

relating to an operation.
operative adj working. ▶ n worker
with a special skill.
ophthalmic adj relating to the eye.
ophthalmology n study of the eye
and its diseases. **ophthalmologist**
n
opiate n narcotic drug containing
opium.
opinion n personal belief or
judgment. **opinionated** adj
having strong opinions. **opine** v
Old-fashioned express an opinion.
opinion poll SEE POLL.
opium n addictive narcotic drug
made from poppy seeds.
opossum n small marsupial of
America or Australasia.
opponent n person one is working
against in a contest, battle, or
argument.
opportunity n, pl -ties. favourable
time or condition; good chance.
opportunity shop Aust & NZ shop
selling second-hand clothes,
sometimes for charity (also
op-shop). **opportune** adj
happening at a suitable time.
opportunist n, adj (person) doing
whatever is advantageous without
regard for principles.
opportunism n
oppose v work against. **be
opposed to** disagree with or
disapprove of. **opposition** n
obstruction or hostility; group
opposing another; political party
not in power.
opposite adj situated on the other
side; facing; completely different.
▶ n person or thing that is
opposite. ▶ prep facing. ▶ adv on
the other side.
oppress v control by cruelty or
force; depress. **oppression** n
oppressor n **oppressive** adj
tyrannical; (of weather) hot and
humid. **oppressively** adv

opprobrium [op-**probe**-ree-um] n
state of being criticized severely
for wrong one has done.
opt v show a preference, choose.
opt out v choose not to be part
(of).
optic adj relating to the eyes or
sight. **optics** n science of sight
and light. **optical** adj **optical
character reader** device that
electronically reads and stores
text. **optical fibre** fine glass-fibre
tube used to transmit information.
optician n (also **ophthalmic
optician**) person qualified to
prescribe glasses; (also **dispensing
optician**) person who supplies and
fits glasses.
optimism n tendency to take the
most hopeful view. **optimist** n
optimistic adj **optimistically** adv
optimum n, pl -ma, -mums. best
possible conditions. ▶ adj most
favourable. **optimal** adj **optimize**
v make the most of.
option n choice; thing chosen;
right to buy or sell something at a
specified price within a given
time. **optional** adj possible but
not compulsory.
optometrist n person qualified to
prescribe glasses. **optometry** n
opulent [op-**yew**-lent] adj having
or indicating wealth. **opulence** n
opus n, pl **opuses, opera**. artistic
creation, esp. a musical work.
or conj used to join alternatives,
e.g. tea or coffee.
oracle n shrine of an ancient god;
prophecy, often obscure, revealed
at a shrine; person believed to
make infallible predictions.
oracular adj
oral adj spoken; (of a drug) to be
taken by mouth. ▶ n spoken
examination. **orally** adv
orange n reddish-yellow citrus
fruit. ▶ adj reddish-yellow.

orangeade n Brit orange-flavoured, usu. fizzy drink.

orangery n greenhouse for growing orange trees.

orang-utan, orang-utang n large reddish-brown ape with long arms.

orator [or-rat-tor] n skilful public speaker. **oration** n formal speech.

oratorio [or-rat-tor-ee-oh] n, pl **-rios.** musical composition for choir and orchestra, usu. with a religious theme.

oratory[1] [or-rat-tree] n art of making speeches. **oratorical** adj

oratory[2] n, pl **-ries.** small private chapel.

orb n ceremonial decorated sphere with a cross on top, carried by a monarch.

orbit n curved path of a planet, satellite, or spacecraft around another body; sphere of influence. ▶ v **orbiting, orbited.** move in an orbit around; put a (satellite or spacecraft) into orbit. **orbital** adj

orchard n area where fruit trees are grown.

orchestra n large group of musicians, esp. playing a variety of instruments; (also **orchestra pit**) area of a theatre in front of the stage, reserved for the musicians. **orchestral** adj **orchestrate** v arrange (music) for orchestra; organize (something) to produce a particular result. **orchestration** n

orchid n plant with flowers that have unusual lip-shaped petals.

ordain v make (someone) a member of the clergy; order or establish with authority.

ordeal n painful or difficult experience.

order n instruction to be carried out; methodical arrangement or sequence; established social system; condition of a law-abiding society; request for goods to be supplied; kind, sort; religious society of monks or nuns. ▶ v give an instruction to; request (something) to be supplied. **in order** so that it is possible.

orderly adj well-organized; well-behaved. ▶ n, pl **-lies.** male hospital attendant. **orderliness** n

ordinal number n number showing a position in a series, e.g. first; second.

ordinance n official rule or order.

ordinary adj usual or normal; dull or commonplace. **ordinarily** adv

ordination n act of making someone a member of the clergy.

ordnance n weapons and military supplies. **Ordnance Survey** official organization making maps of Britain.

ordure n excrement.

ore n (rock containing) a mineral which yields metal.

oregano [or-rig-**gah**-no] n sweet-smelling herb used in cooking.

organ n part of an animal or plant that has a particular function, such as the heart or lungs; musical keyboard instrument in which notes are produced by forcing air through pipes; means of conveying information, esp. a newspaper. **organist** n organ player.

organdie n fine cotton fabric.

organic adj of or produced from animals or plants; grown without artificial fertilizers or pesticides; Chem relating to compounds of carbon; organized systematically. **organically** adv **organism** n any living animal or plant.

organize v make arrangements for; arrange systematically. **organization** n group of people working together; act of organizing. **organizational** adj

organizer n

orgasm n most intense point of sexual pleasure. **orgasmic** adj

orgy n, pl **-gies.** party involving promiscuous sexual activity; unrestrained indulgence, e.g. an orgy of destruction. **orgiastic** adj

oriel window n upper window built out from a wall.

orient, orientate v position (oneself) according to one's surroundings; position (a map) in relation to the points of the compass. **orientation** n

orienteering n sport in which competitors hike over a course using a compass and map.

Orient n the Orient Lit East Asia. **Oriental** adj **Orientalist** n specialist in the languages and history of the Far East.

orifice [**or-rif-fiss**] n opening or hole.

origami [or-rig-gah-mee] n Japanese decorative art of paper folding.

origin n point from which something develops; ancestry. **original** adj first or earliest; new, not copied or based on something else; able to think up new ideas. ▶ n first version, from which others are copied. **original sin** human imperfection and mortality as a result of Adam's disobedience. **originality** n **originally** adv **originate** v come or bring into existence. **origination** n **originator** n

oriole n tropical or American songbird.

ormolu n gold-coloured alloy used for decoration.

ornament n decorative object. ▶ v decorate. **ornamental** adj **ornamentation** n

ornate adj highly decorated, elaborate.

ornithology n study of birds. **ornithological** adj **ornithologist** n

orphan n child whose parents are dead. **orphanage** n children's home for orphans. **orphaned** adj having no living parents.

orrery n, pl **-ries.** mechanical model of the solar system.

orris n kind of iris; (also **orris root**) fragrant root used for perfume.

orthodontics n branch of dentistry concerned with correcting irregular teeth. **orthodontist** n

orthodox adj conforming to established views. **orthodoxy** n **Orthodox Church** dominant Christian Church in Eastern Europe.

orthography n correct spelling.

orthopaedics n branch of medicine concerned with disorders of the bones or joints. **orthopaedic** adj

oryx n large African antelope.

Oscar n award in the form of a statuette given for achievements in films.

oscillate [**oss-ill-late**] v swing back and forth. **oscillation** n **oscillator** n **oscilloscope** [oss-**ill**-oh-scope] n instrument that shows the shape of a wave on a cathode-ray tube.

osier [**oh-zee-er**] n willow tree.

osmium n Chem heaviest known metallic element.

osmosis n movement of a liquid through a membrane from a lower to a higher concentration; process of subtle influence. **osmotic** adj

osprey n large fish-eating bird of prey.

ossify v **-fying, -fied.** (cause to) become bone, harden; become inflexible. **ossification** n

ostensible adj apparent, seeming. **ostensibly** adv

ostentation n pretentious display. **ostentatious** adj **ostentatiously**

adv

osteopathy *n* medical treatment involving manipulation of the joints. **osteopath** *n*

osteoporosis *n* brittleness of the bones, caused by lack of calcium.

ostracize *v* exclude (a person) from a group. **ostracism** *n*

ostrich *n* large African bird that runs fast but cannot fly.

OT Old Testament.

other *adj* remaining in a group of which one or some have been specified; different from the ones specified or understood; additional. ▸ *n* other person or thing. **otherwise** *conj* or else, if not. ▸ *adv* differently, in another way. **otherworldly** *adj* concerned with spiritual rather than practical matters.

otiose [oh-tee-oze] *adj* not useful, e.g. *otiose language*.

otter *n* small brown freshwater mammal that eats fish.

ottoman *n, pl* **-mans**. storage chest with a padded lid for use as a seat. **Ottoman** *n, adj Hist* (member) of the former Turkish empire.

oubliette [oo-blee-ett] *n* dungeon entered only by a trapdoor.

ouch *interj* exclamation of sudden pain.

ought *v* used to express: obligation, e.g. *you ought to pay*; advisability, e.g. *you ought to diet*; probability, e.g. *you ought to know by then*.

Ouija board *n* ® lettered board on which supposed messages from the dead are spelt out.

ounce *n* unit of weight equal to one sixteenth of a pound (28.4 grams).

our *adj* belonging to us. **ours** *pron* thing(s) belonging to us.

ourselves *pron* emphatic and reflexive form of WE or US.

ousel *n* see DIPPER.

oust *v* force (someone) out, expel.

out *adv, adj* denoting movement or distance away from, a state of being used up or extinguished, public availability, etc., e.g. *oil was pouring out; turn the light out; her new book is out*. ▸ *v Informal* name (a public figure) as being homosexual. **out of** at or to a point outside. **out-of-date** *adj* old-fashioned. **outer** *adj* on the outside. **outermost** *adj* furthest out. **outer space** space beyond the earth's atmosphere. **outing** *n* leisure trip. **outward** *adj* apparent. ▸ *adv* (also **outwards**) away from somewhere. **outwardly** *adv*

out- *prefix* surpassing, e.g. *outlive; outdistance*.

outback *n* remote bush country of Australia.

outbid *v* offer a higher price than.

outboard motor *n* engine externally attached to the stern of a boat.

outbreak *n* sudden occurrence (of something unpleasant).

outburst *n* sudden expression of emotion.

outcast *n* person rejected by a particular group.

outclass *v* surpass in quality.

outcome *n* result.

outcrop *n* part of a rock formation that sticks out of the earth.

outcry *n, pl* **-cries**. vehement or widespread protest.

outdo *v* surpass in performance.

outdoors *adv* in(to) the open air. ▸ *n* the open air. **outdoor** *adj*

outface *v* subdue or disconcert (someone) by staring.

outfield *n Cricket* area far from the pitch.

outfit *n* matching set of clothes;

Informal group of people working together. **outfitter** *n* supplier of men's clothes.

outflank *v* get round the side of (an enemy army); outdo (someone).

outgoing *adj* leaving; sociable. **outgoings** *pl n* expenses.

outgrow *v* become too large or too old for. **outgrowth** *n* natural development.

outhouse *n* building near a main building.

outlandish *adj* extremely unconventional.

outlaw *n Hist* criminal deprived of legal protection, bandit. ▶ *v* make illegal; *Hist* make (someone) an outlaw.

outlay *n* expenditure.

outlet *n* means of expressing emotion; market for a product; place where a product is sold; opening or way out.

outline *n* short general explanation; line defining the shape of something. ▶ *v* summarize; show the general shape of.

outlook *n* attitude; probable outcome.

outlying *adj* distant from the main area.

outmanoeuvre *v* get an advantage over.

outmoded *adj* no longer fashionable or accepted.

outnumber *v* exceed in number.

outpatient *n* patient who does not stay in hospital overnight.

outpost *n* outlying settlement.

outpouring *n* passionate outburst.

output *n* amount produced; power, voltage, or current delivered by an electrical circuit; *Computers* data produced. ▶ *v Computers* produce (data) at the end of a process.

outrage *n* great moral indignation; gross violation of morality. ▶ *v* offend morally. **outrageous** *adj* shocking; offensive. **outrageously** *adv*

outré [oo-**tray**] *adj* shockingly eccentric.

outrider *n* motorcyclist acting as an escort.

outrigger *n* stabilizing frame projecting from a boat.

outright *adj, adv* absolute(ly); open(ly) and direct(ly).

outrun *v* run faster than; exceed.

outset *n* beginning.

outshine *v* surpass (someone) in excellence.

outside *prep, adj, adv* indicating movement to or position on the exterior. ▶ *adj* unlikely, e.g. *an outside chance*; coming from outside. ▶ *n* external area or surface. **outsider** *n* person outside a specific group; contestant thought unlikely to win.

outsize, outsized *adj* larger than normal.

outskirts *pl n* outer areas, esp. of a town.

outsmart *v Informal* outwit.

outspan *v S Afr* relax.

outspoken *adj* tending to say what one thinks; said openly.

outstanding *adj* excellent; still to be dealt with or paid.

outstrip *v* surpass; go faster than.

outtake *n* unreleased take from a recording session, film, or TV programme.

outweigh *v* be more important, significant, or influential than.

outwit *v* **-witting, -witted.** get the better of (someone) by cunning.

ouzel [ooze-el] *n* see DIPPER.

ova *n* plural of OVUM.

oval *adj* egg-shaped. ▶ *n* anything that is oval in shape.

ovary *n, pl* **-ries.** female

egg-producing organ. **ovarian** adj

ovation n enthusiastic round of applause.

oven n heated compartment or container for cooking or for drying or firing ceramics.

over prep, adv indicating position on the top of, movement to the other side of, amount greater than, etc., e.g. a room over the garage; climbing over the fence; over fifty pounds. ▶ adj finished. ▶ n Cricket series of six balls bowled from one end. **overly** adv excessively.

over- prefix too much, e.g. overeat; above, e.g. overlord; on top, e.g. overshoe.

overall adj, adv in total. ▶ n coat-shaped protective garment. ▶ pl protective garment consisting of trousers with a jacket or bib and braces attached.

overarm adj, adv (thrown) with the arm above the shoulder.

overawe v affect (someone) with an overpowering sense of awe.

overbalance v lose balance.

overbearing adj unpleasantly forceful.

overblown adj excessive.

overboard adv from a boat into the water. **go overboard** go to extremes, esp. in enthusiasm.

overcast adj (of the sky) covered by clouds.

overcoat n heavy coat.

overcome v gain control over after an effort; (of an emotion) affect strongly.

overcrowded adj containing more people or things than is desirable.

overdo v do to excess; exaggerate (something). **overdo it** do something to a greater degree than is advisable.

overdose n excessive dose of a drug. ▶ v take an overdose.

overdraft n overdrawing; amount overdrawn.

overdraw v withdraw more money than is in (one's bank account).

overdrawn adj having overdrawn one's account; (of an account) in debit.

overdrive n very high gear in a motor vehicle.

overdue adj still due after the time allowed.

overgrown adj thickly covered with plants and weeds.

overhaul v examine and repair. ▶ n examination and repair.

overhead adv, adj above one's head. **overheads** pl n general cost of maintaining a business.

overhear v hear (a speaker or remark) unintentionally or without the speaker's knowledge.

overjoyed adj extremely pleased.

overkill n treatment that is greater than required.

overland adj, adv by land.

overlap v share part of the same space or period of time (as). ▶ n area overlapping.

overleaf adv on the back of the current page.

overlook v fail to notice; ignore; look at from above.

overnight adj, adv (taking place) during one night; (happening) very quickly.

overpower v subdue or overcome (someone).

overreach v **overreach oneself** fail by trying to be too clever.

override v overrule; replace.

overrule v reverse the decision of (a person with less power); reverse (someone else's decision).

overrun v spread over (a place) rapidly; extend beyond a set limit.

overseas adv, adj to, of, or from a distant country.

oversee v watch over from a

position of authority. **overseer** n

overshadow v reduce the significance of (a person or thing) by comparison; sadden the atmosphere of.

oversight n mistake caused by not noticing something.

overspill n Brit rehousing of people from crowded cities in smaller towns.

overstay v **overstay one's welcome** stay longer than one's host or hostess would like. **overstayer** n NZ person who remains in New Zealand after their permit has expired.

overt adj open, not hidden. **overtly** adv

overtake v move past (a vehicle or person) travelling in the same direction.

overthrow v defeat and replace. ▶ n downfall, destruction.

overtime n, adv (paid work done) in addition to one's normal working hours.

overtone n additional meaning.

overture n Music orchestral introduction. ▶ pl opening moves in a new relationship.

overturn v turn upside down; overrule (a legal decision); overthrow (a government).

overweight adj weighing more than is healthy.

overwhelm v overpower, esp. emotionally; defeat by force. **overwhelming** adj **overwhelmingly** adv

overwrought adj nervous and agitated.

ovoid [oh-void] adj egg-shaped.

ovulate [ov-yew-late] v produce or release an egg cell from an ovary. **ovulation** n

ovum [oh-vum] n, pl **ova**. unfertilized egg cell.

owe v be obliged to pay (a sum of money) to (a person). **owing to** as a result of.

owl n night bird of prey. **owlish** adj

own adj used to emphasize possession, e.g. my own idea. ▶ v possess. **owner** n **ownership** n

ox n, pl **oxen**. castrated bull.

Oxfam Oxford Committee for Famine Relief.

oxide n compound of oxygen and one other element. **oxidize** v combine chemically with oxygen, as in burning or rusting.

oxygen n Chem gaseous element essential to life and combustion. **oxygenate** v add oxygen to.

oxymoron [ox-see-more-on] n figure of speech that combines two apparently contradictory ideas, e.g. cruel kindness.

oyez interj Hist shouted three times by a public crier, listen.

oyster n edible shellfish. **oystercatcher** n wading bird with black-and-white feathers.

Oz n Slang Australia.

oz. ounce.

ozone n strong-smelling form of oxygen. **ozone layer** layer of ozone in the upper atmosphere that filters out ultraviolet radiation.

P p

p Brit, Aust & NZ penny; Brit pence.

P parking.

p. pl **pp.** page.

pa n NZ (formerly) a fortified Maori settlement.

PA personal assistant; public-address system.

p.a. each year.

pace n single step in walking; length of a step; rate of progress.

▶ *v* walk up and down, esp. in anxiety; (foll. by *out*) cross or measure with steps. **pacemaker** *n* electronic device surgically implanted in a person with heart disease to regulate the heartbeat; person who, by taking the lead early in a race, sets the pace for the rest of the competitors.

pachyderm [pak-ee-durm] *n* thick-skinned animal such as an elephant.

pacifist *n* person who refuses on principle to take part in war. **pacifism** *n*

pacify *v* **-fying, -fied.** soothe, calm. **pacification** *n*

pack *v* put (clothes etc.) together in a suitcase or bag; put (goods) into containers or parcels; fill with people or things. ▶ *n* bag carried on a person's or animal's back; *Chiefly US* same as PACKET; set of playing cards; group of dogs or wolves that hunt together. **pack ice** mass of floating ice in the sea. **pack in** *v* *Informal* stop doing. **pack off** *v* send away.

package *n* small parcel; (also **package deal**) deal in which separate items are presented together as a unit. ▶ *v* put into a package. **packaging** *n* **package holiday** holiday in which everything is arranged by one company for a fixed price.

packet *n* small container (and contents); small parcel; *Slang* large sum of money.

packhorse *n* horse used for carrying goods.

pact *n* formal agreement.

pad *n* piece of soft material used for protection, support, absorption of liquid, etc.; number of sheets of paper fastened at the edge; fleshy underpart of an animal's paw; place for launching rockets; *Slang*

home. ▶ *v* **padding, padded.** protect or fill with soft material; walk with soft steps. **padding** *n* soft material used to pad something; unnecessary words put into a speech or written work to make it longer.

paddle¹ *n* short oar with a broad blade at one or each end. ▶ *v* move (a canoe etc.) with a paddle. **paddle steamer** ship propelled by paddle wheels. **paddle wheel** wheel with crosswise blades that strike the water successively to propel a ship.

paddle² *v* walk barefoot in shallow water.

paddock *n* small field or enclosure for horses.

paddy *n* *Brit informal* fit of temper. **paddy field** *n* field where rice is grown (also **paddy**).

pademelon, paddymelon [pad-ee-mel-an] *n* small Australian wallaby.

padlock *n* detachable lock with a hinged hoop fastened over a ring on the object to be secured.

padre [pah-dray] *n* chaplain to the armed forces.

paean [pee-an] *n* song of triumph or thanksgiving.

paediatrics *n* branch of medicine concerned with diseases of children. **paediatrician** *n*

paedophilia *n* condition of being sexually attracted to children. **paedophile** *n* person who is sexually attracted to children.

paella [pie-ell-a] *n* Spanish dish of rice, chicken, shellfish, and vegetables.

pagan *n, adj* (person) not belonging to one of the world's main religions.

page¹ *n* (one side of) a sheet of paper forming a book etc.; screenful of information from a website or teletext service.

page n (also **pageboy**) small boy who attends a bride at her wedding; Hist boy in training for knighthood. ▶ v summon (someone) by bleeper or loudspeaker, in order to pass on a message.

pageant n parade or display of people in costume, usu. illustrating a scene from history. **pageantry** n

pagination n numbering of the pages of a book etc.

pagoda n pyramid-shaped Asian temple or tower.

paid v past of PAY. **put paid to** Informal end or destroy.

pail n (contents of) a bucket.

pain n physical or mental suffering. ▶ pl trouble, effort. **on pain of** subject to the penalty of. **painful** adj **painfully** adv **painless** adj **painlessly** adv **painkiller** n drug that relieves pain.

painstaking adj extremely thorough and careful.

paint n coloured substance, spread on a surface with a brush or roller. ▶ v colour or coat with paint; use paint to make a picture of. **painter** n **painting** n

painter n rope at the front of a boat, for tying it up.

pair n set of two things matched for use together. ▶ v group or be grouped in twos.

paisley pattern n pattern of small curving shapes, used in fabric.

Pakeha [pah-kee-ha] n NZ New Zealander who is not of Maori descent.

pal n Informal, old-fashioned in NZ friend.

palace n residence of a king, bishop, etc.; large grand building.

palaeography [pal-ee-og-ra-fee] n study of ancient manuscripts.

Palaeolithic [pal-ee-oh-lith-ik] adj of the Old Stone Age.

palaeontology [pal-ee-on-tol-a-jee] n study of past geological periods and fossils.

Palagi [pa-lang-gee] n, pl -gis. NZ Samoan name for a Pakeha.

palatable adj pleasant to taste.

palate n roof of the mouth; sense of taste.

palatial adj like a palace, magnificent.

palaver [pal-lah-ver] n time-wasting fuss.

pale¹ adj light, whitish; whitish in the face, esp. through illness or shock. ▶ v become pale.

pale² n wooden or metal post used in fences. **beyond the pale** outside the limits of social convention.

palette n artist's flat board for mixing colours on.

palindrome n word or phrase that reads the same backwards as forwards.

paling n wooden or metal post used in fences.

palisade n fence made of wooden posts driven into the ground.

pall¹ n cloth spread over a coffin; dark cloud (of smoke); depressing oppressive atmosphere. **pallbearer** n person who helps to carry the coffin at a funeral.

pall² v become boring.

palladium n Chem silvery-white element of the platinum metal group.

pallet¹ n portable platform for storing and moving goods.

pallet² n straw-filled mattress or bed.

palliate v lessen the severity of (something) without curing it. **palliative** adj giving temporary or partial relief. ▶ n something, for example a drug, that palliates.

pallid adj pale, esp. because ill or weak. **pallor** n

pally adj **-lier, -liest.** Informal on friendly terms.

palm[1] n inner surface of the hand. **palm off** v get rid of (an unwanted thing or person), esp. by deceit.

palm[2] n tropical tree with long pointed leaves growing out of the top of a straight trunk. **Palm Sunday** Sunday before Easter.

palmistry n fortune-telling from lines on the palm of the hand. **palmist** n

palmtop adj (of a computer) small enough to be held in the hand. ▶ n computer small enough to be held in the hand.

palomino n, pl **-nos.** gold-coloured horse with a white mane and tail.

palpable adj obvious, e.g. a palpable hit; so intense as to seem capable of being touched, e.g. the tension is almost palpable. **palpably** adv

palpate v Med examine (an area of the body) by touching.

palpitate v (of the heart) beat rapidly; flutter or tremble. **palpitation** n

palsy [pawl-zee] n paralysis. **palsied** adj affected with palsy.

paltry adj **-trier, -triest.** insignificant.

pampas pl n vast grassy plains in S America. **pampas grass** tall grass with feathery ornamental flower branches.

pamper v treat (someone) with great indulgence, spoil.

pamphlet n thin paper-covered booklet. **pamphleteer** n writer of pamphlets.

pan[1] n wide long-handled metal container used in cooking; bowl of a toilet. ▶ v **panning, panned.** wash gravel from (a river) in a pan to

search for gold; Informal criticize harshly. **pan out** v result.

pan[2] v **panning, panned.** (of a film camera) be moved slowly so as to cover a whole scene or follow a moving object.

pan- combining form all, e.g. pan-American.

panacea [pan-a-**see**-a] n remedy for all diseases or problems.

panache [pan-**ash**] n confident elegant style.

panama hat n straw hat.

panatella n long slender cigar.

pancake n thin flat circle of fried batter.

panchromatic adj Photog sensitive to light of all colours.

pancreas [**pang**-kree-ass] n large gland behind the stomach that produces insulin and helps digestion. **pancreatic** adj

panda n large black-and-white bearlike mammal from China. **panda car** Brit police patrol car.

pandemic adj (of a disease) occurring over a wide area.

pandemonium n wild confusion, uproar.

pander[1] v (foll. by to) indulge (a person his or her desires).

pander[2] n Old-fashioned person who procures a sexual partner for someone.

p & p postage and packing.

pane n sheet of glass in a window or door.

panegyric [pan-ee-**jire**-ik] n formal speech or piece of writing in praise of someone or something.

panel n flat distinct section of a larger surface, for example in a door; group of people as a team in a quiz etc.; list of jurors, doctors, etc.; board or surface containing switches and controls to operate equipment. ▶ v **-elling, -elled.** cover or decorate with

panels. panelling n panels collectively; panels on a wall.

panellist n member of a panel.

panel beater person who repairs damage to car bodies.

pang n sudden sharp feeling of pain or sadness.

pangolin n animal of tropical countries with a scaly body and a long snout for eating ants and termites (also **scaly anteater**).

panic n sudden overwhelming fear, often affecting a whole group of people. ▶ v **-icking, -icked.** feel or cause to feel panic. **panicky** adj **panic-stricken** adj

pannier n bag fixed on the back of a cycle; basket carried by a beast of burden.

panoply n magnificent array.

panorama n wide unbroken view of a scene. **panoramic** adj

pansy n, pl **-sies.** small garden flower with velvety purple, yellow, or white petals.

pant v breathe quickly and noisily during or after exertion.

pantaloons pl n baggy trousers gathered at the ankles.

pantechnicon n large van for furniture removals.

pantheism n belief that God is present in everything. **pantheist** n **pantheistic** adj

pantheon n (in ancient Greece and Rome) temple built to honour all the gods.

panther n leopard, esp. a black one.

panties pl n women's underpants.

pantile n roofing tile with an S-shaped cross section.

pantomime n play based on a fairy tale, performed at Christmas time.

pantry n, pl **-tries.** small room or cupboard for storing food.

pants pl n undergarment for the lower part of the body; US, Canadian, Aust & NZ trousers.

pap n soft food for babies or invalids; worthless entertainment or information.

papacy [pay-pa-see] n, pl **-cies.** position or term of office of a pope. **papal** adj of the pope.

paparazzo [pap-a-rat-so] n, pl **-razzi.** photographer specializing in candid photographs of famous people.

papaya [pa-pie-ya] n large sweet West Indian fruit.

paper n material made in sheets from wood pulp or other fibres; printed sheet of this; newspaper; set of examination questions; article or essay. ▶ v personal documents. ▶ v cover (walls) with wallpaper. **paperback** n book with covers made of flexible card. **paperweight** n heavy decorative object placed on top of loose papers. **paperwork** n clerical work, such as writing reports and letters.

papier-mâché [pap-yay mash-ay] n material made from paper mixed with paste and moulded when moist.

papoose n Native American child.

paprika n mild powdered seasoning made from red peppers.

papyrus [pap-ire-uss] n, pl **-ri, -ruses.** tall water plant; (manuscript written on) a kind of paper made from this plant.

par n usual or average condition, e.g. feeling under par; Golf expected standard score; face value of stocks and shares. **on a par with** equal to.

parable n story that illustrates a religious teaching.

parabola [par-ab-bol-a] n regular curve resembling the course of an object thrown forward and up.

parabolic adj

paracetamol n mild pain-relieving drug.

parachute n large fabric canopy that slows the descent of a person or object from an aircraft. ▶ v land or drop by parachute. **parachutist** n

parade n procession or march; street or promenade. ▶ v display or flaunt; march in procession.

paradigm [par-a-dime] n example or model.

paradise n heaven; place or situation that is near-perfect.

paradox n statement that seems self-contradictory but may be true. **paradoxical** adj **paradoxically** adv

paraffin n Brit & S Afr liquid mixture distilled from petroleum and used as a fuel or solvent.

paragliding n cross-country gliding wearing a parachute shaped like wings.

paragon n model of perfection.

paragraph n section of a piece of writing starting on a new line.

parakeet n small long-tailed parrot.

parallax n apparent change in an object's position due to a change in the observer's position.

parallel adj separated by an equal distance at every point; exactly corresponding. ▶ n line separated from another by an equal distance at every point; thing with similar features to another; line of latitude. ▶ v correspond to.

parallelogram n four-sided geometric figure with opposite sides parallel.

paralysis n inability to move or feel, because of damage to the nervous system. **paralyse** v affect with paralysis; make temporarily unable to move or take action. **paralytic** n, adj (person) affected with paralysis.

paramedic n person working in support of the medical profession. **paramedical** adj

parameter [par-am-it-er] n limiting factor, boundary.

paramilitary adj organized on military lines.

paramount adj of the greatest importance.

paramour n Old-fashioned lover, esp. of a person married to someone else.

paranoia n mental illness causing delusions of grandeur or persecution; Informal intense fear or suspicion. **paranoid, paranoiac** adj, n

paranormal adj beyond scientific explanation.

parapet n low wall or railing along the edge of a balcony or roof.

paraphernalia n personal belongings or bits of equipment.

paraphrase v put (a statement or text) into other words.

paraplegia [para-pleej-ya] n paralysis of the lower half of the body. **paraplegic** adj, n

parapsychology n study of mental phenomena such as telepathy.

Paraquat n ® extremely poisonous weedkiller.

parasite n animal or plant living in or on another; person who lives at the expense of others. **parasitic** adj

parasol n umbrella-like sunshade.

paratrooper n soldier trained to be dropped by parachute into a battle area. **paratroops** pl n

parboil v boil until partly cooked.

parcel n something wrapped up, package. ▶ v **-celling, -celled.** (often foll. by up) wrap up. **parcel out** v divide into parts.

parch v make very hot and dry; make thirsty.

parchment n thick smooth writing

material made from animal skin.
pardon v forgive, excuse. ▶ n
forgiveness; official release from
punishment for a crime.
pardonable adj

pare v cut off the skin or top layer
of; (often foll. by down) reduce in
size or amount. **paring** n piece
pared off.

parent n father or mother.
parental adj **parenthood** n
parentage n ancestry or family.
parenting n activity of bringing
up children.

parenthesis [par-en-thiss-iss] n, pl
-ses. word or sentence inserted
into a passage, marked off by
brackets or dashes. ▶ pl round
brackets, ( ). **parenthetical** adj

pariah [par-rye-a] n social outcast.

parietal [par-rye-it-al] adj of the
walls of a body cavity such as the
skull.

parish n area that has its own
church and a priest or pastor.
parishioner n inhabitant of a
parish.

parity n equality or equivalence.

park n area of open land for
recreational use by the public;
area containing a number of
related enterprises, e.g. a business
park; Brit area of private land
around a large country house. ▶ v
stop and leave (a vehicle)
temporarily.

parka n large waterproof jacket
with a hood.

parky adj **parkier, parkiest.** Brit
informal (of the weather) chilly.

parlance n particular way of
speaking, idiom.

parley n meeting between leaders
or representatives of opposing
forces to discuss terms. ▶ v have a
parley.

parliament n law-making assembly
of a country. **parliamentary** adj

parlour n Old-fashioned living room
for receiving visitors.

parlous adj Old-fashioned dire;
dangerously bad.

Parmesan n hard strong-flavoured
Italian cheese, used grated on
pasta dishes and soups.

parochial adj narrow in outlook; of
a parish. **parochialism** n

parody n, pl **-dies.** exaggerated
and amusing imitation of
someone else's style. ▶ v **-dying,
-died.** make a parody of.

parole n early freeing of a prisoner
on condition that he or she
behaves well. ▶ v put on parole.
on parole (of a prisoner)
released on condition that he or
she behaves well.

paroxysm n uncontrollable
outburst of rage, delight, etc.;
spasm or convulsion of coughing,
pain, etc.

parquet [par-kay] n floor covering
made of wooden blocks arranged
in a geometric pattern.
parquetry n

parricide n crime of killing either
of one's parents; person who does
this.

parrot n tropical bird with a short
hooked beak and an ability to
imitate human speech. ▶ v **-roting,
-roted.** repeat (someone else's
words) without thinking.

parry v **-rying, -ried.** ward off (an
attack); cleverly avoid (an
awkward question).

parse [parz] v analyse (a sentence)
in terms of grammar.

parsimony n extreme caution in
spending money. **parsimonious**
adj

parsley n herb used for seasoning
and decorating food.

parsnip n long tapering
cream-coloured root vegetable.

parson n Anglican parish priest;

any member of the clergy.
parsonage n parson's house.
part n one of the pieces that make
up a whole; one of several equal
divisions; actor's role; (often pl)
region, area; component of a
vehicle or machine. ▶ v divide or
separate; (of people) leave each
other. **take someone's part**
support someone in an argument
etc. **take (something) in good
part** respond to (teasing or
criticism) with good humour.
parting n occasion when one
person leaves another; line of
scalp between sections of hair
combed in opposite directions;
dividing or separating. **partly** adv
not completely.
part of speech
particular grammatical class of
words, such as noun or verb.
part-time adj occupying or
working less than the full working
week. **part with** v give away,
hand over.
partake v **-taking, -took, -taken**.
(foll. by of) take (food or drink);
(foll. by in) take part in.
partial adj not complete;
prejudiced. **partial to** having a
liking for. **partiality** n **partially**
adv
participate v become actively
involved. **participant** n
participation n
participle n form of a verb used in
compound tenses or as an
adjective, e.g. worried; worrying.
particle n extremely small piece or
amount; Physics minute piece of
matter, such as a proton or
electron.
particular adj relating to one
person or thing, not general;
exceptional or special; very exact;
difficult to please, fastidious. ▶ n
item of information, detail.
particularly adv **particularize** v

give details about.
partisan n strong supporter of a
party or group; guerrilla, member
of a resistance movement. ▶ adj
prejudiced or one-sided.
partition n screen or thin wall that
divides a room; division of a
country into independent parts.
▶ v divide with a partition.
partner n either member of a
couple in a relationship or activity;
member of a business partnership.
▶ v be the partner of. **partnership**
n joint business venture between
two or more people.
partridge n game bird of the
grouse family.
parturition n act of giving birth.
party n, pl **-ties**. social gathering
for pleasure; group of people
travelling or working together;
group of people with a common
political aim; person or people
forming one side in a lawsuit or
dispute. **party line** official view of
a political party; telephone line
shared by two or more
subscribers. **party wall** common
wall separating adjoining buildings.
parvenu [par-ven-new] n person
newly risen to a position of power
or wealth.
pascal n unit of pressure.
paspalum [pass-**pale**-um] n Aust &
NZ type of grass with wide leaves.
pass v go by, past, or through; be
successful in (a test or
examination); spend (time) or (of
time) go by; give, hand; be
inherited by; Sport hit, kick, or
throw (the ball) to another player;
(of a law-making body) agree to
(a law); exceed. ▶ n successful
result in a test or examination;
permit or licence. **make a pass
at** Informal make sexual advances
to. **passable** adj (just) acceptable;
(of a road) capable of being

travelled along. **passing** adj brief or transitory; cursory or casual.

pass away v die. **pass out** v Informal faint. **pass up** v Informal fail to take advantage of (something).

passage n channel or opening providing a way through; hall or corridor; section of a book etc.; journey by sea; right or freedom to pass. **passageway** n passage or corridor.

passbook n book issued by a bank or building society for keeping a record of deposits and withdrawals; S Afr formerly, an official identity document.

passé [pas-say] adj out-of-date.

passenger n person travelling in a vehicle driven by someone else; member of a team who does not pull his or her weight.

passer-by n, pl **passers-by.** person who is walking past something or someone.

passim adv Latin everywhere, throughout.

passion n intense sexual love; any strong emotion; great enthusiasm; (P-) Christianity the suffering of Christ. **passionate** adj **passionflower** n tropical American plant. **passion fruit** edible fruit of the passionflower. **Passion play** play about Christ's suffering.

passive adj not playing an active part; submissive and receptive to outside forces; Grammar (of a verb) in a form indicating that the subject receives the action, e.g. was jeered in he was jeered by the crowd. **passivity** n **passive resistance** resistance to a government, law, etc. by nonviolent acts. **passive smoking** inhalation of smoke from others' cigarettes by a nonsmoker.

Passover n Jewish festival

commemorating the sparing of the Jews in Egypt.

passport n official document of nationality granting permission to travel abroad.

password n secret word or phrase that ensures admission.

past adj of the time before the present; ended, gone by; Grammar (of a verb tense) indicating that the action specified took place earlier. ▶ n period of time before the present; person's earlier life, esp. a disreputable period; Grammar past tense. ▶ adv by, along. ▶ prep beyond. **past it** Informal unable to do the things one could do when younger. **past master** person with great talent or experience in a particular subject.

pasta n type of food, such as spaghetti, that is made in different shapes from flour and water.

paste n moist soft mixture, such as toothpaste; adhesive, esp. for paper; Brit pastry dough; shiny glass used to make imitation jewellery. ▶ v fasten with paste. **pasting** n Informal heavy defeat; strong criticism. **pasteboard** n stiff thick paper.

pastel n coloured chalk crayon for drawing; picture drawn in pastels; pale delicate colour. ▶ adj pale and delicate in colour.

pasteurize v sterilize by heating. **pasteurization** n

pastiche [pass-teesh] n work of art that mixes styles or copies the style of another artist.

pastille n small fruit-flavoured and sometimes medicated sweet.

pastime n activity that makes time pass pleasantly.

pastor n member of the clergy in charge of a congregation. **pastoral** adj of or depicting country life; of a clergyman or his duties.

pastrami n highly seasoned smoked beef.

pastry n, pl **-ries.** baking dough made of flour, fat, and water; cake or pie.

pasture n grassy land for farm animals to graze on.

pasty¹ [pay-stee] adj **pastier, pastiest.** (of a complexion) pale and unhealthy.

pasty² [pass-tee] n, pl **pasties.** round of pastry folded over a savoury filling.

pat¹ v **patting, patted.** tap lightly. ▶ n gentle tap or stroke; small shaped mass of butter etc.

pat² adj quick, ready, or glib. **off pat** learned thoroughly.

patch n piece of material sewn on a garment; small contrasting section; plot of ground; protective pad for the eye. ▶ v mend with a patch. **patchy** adj of uneven quality or intensity. **patch up** v repair clumsily; make up (a quarrel). **patchwork** n needlework made of pieces of different materials sewn together.

pate n Old-fashioned head.

pâté [pat-ay] n spread of finely minced liver etc.

patella n, pl **-lae.** kneecap.

patent n document giving the exclusive right to make or sell an invention. ▶ adj open to public inspection, e.g. letters patent; obvious; protected by a patent. ▶ v obtain a patent for. **patently** adv obviously. **patent leather** leather processed to give a hard glossy surface.

paternal adj fatherly; related through one's father. **paternity** n fact or state of being a father. **paternalism** n authority exercised in a way that limits individual

responsibility. **paternalistic** adj

path n surfaced walk or track; course of action.

pathetic adj causing feelings of pity or sadness; distressingly inadequate. **pathetically** adv

pathogen n thing that causes disease. **pathogenic** adj

pathology n scientific study of diseases. **pathological** adj of pathology; Informal compulsively motivated. **pathologist** n

pathos n power of arousing pity or sadness.

patient adj enduring difficulties or delays calmly. ▶ n person receiving medical treatment. **patience** n quality of being patient; card game for one.

patina n fine layer on a surface; sheen of age on woodwork.

patio n, pl **-tios.** paved area adjoining a house.

patois [pat-wah] n, pl **patois** [pat-wahz] regional dialect, esp. of French.

patriarch n male head of a family or tribe; highest-ranking bishop in Orthodox Churches. **patriarchal** adj **patriarchy** n, pl **-chies.** society in which men have most of the power.

patrician n member of the nobility. ▶ adj of noble birth.

patricide n crime of killing one's father; person who does this.

patrimony n, pl **-nies.** property inherited from ancestors.

patriot n person who loves his or her country and supports its interests. **patriotic** adj **patriotism** n

patrol n regular circuit by a guard; person or small group patrolling; unit of Scouts or Guides. ▶ v **-trolling, -trolled.** go round on guard, or reconnoitring.

patron n person who gives

financial support to charities, artists, etc.; regular customer of a shop, pub, etc. **patronage** *n* support given by a patron. **patronize** *v* treat in a condescending way; be a patron of. **patron saint** saint regarded as the guardian of a country or group.

patronymic *n* name derived from one's father or a male ancestor.

patter[1] *v* make repeated soft tapping sounds. ▶ *n* quick succession of taps.

patter[2] *n* glib rapid speech.

pattern *n* arrangement of repeated parts or decorative designs; regular way that something is done; diagram or shape used as a guide to make something. **patterned** *adj* decorated with a pattern.

patty *n, pl* **-ties.** small flattened cake of minced food.

paucity *n* scarcity; smallness of amount or number.

paunch *n* protruding belly.

pauper *n* very poor person.

pause *v* stop for a time. ▶ *n* stop or rest in speech or action.

pave *v* form (a surface) with stone or brick. **pavement** *n* paved path for pedestrians.

pavilion *n* building on a playing field etc.; building for housing an exhibition etc.

paw *n* animal's foot with claws and pads. ▶ *v* scrape with the paw or hoof; *Informal* touch in a rough or overfamiliar way.

pawn[1] *v* deposit (an article) as security for money borrowed. **in pawn** deposited as security with a pawnbroker. **pawnbroker** *n* lender of money on goods deposited.

pawn[2] *n* chessman of the lowest value; person manipulated by someone else.

pay *v* **paid, paid.** give money etc. in return for goods or services; settle a debt or obligation; compensate (for); give; be profitable to. ▶ *n* wages or salary. **payment** *n* act of paying; money paid. **payable** *adj* due to be paid. **payee** *n* person to whom money is paid or due. **paying guest** lodger or boarder. **pay off** *v* pay (debt) in full; turn out successfully. **pay out** *v* spend; release (a rope) bit by bit.

PAYE pay as you earn: system by which income tax is paid by an employer straight to the government.

payload *n* passengers or cargo of an aircraft; explosive power of a missile etc.

payola *n* *Chiefly US informal* bribe to get special treatment, esp. to promote a commercial product.

pc per cent.

PC personal computer; (in Britain) Police Constable; politically correct; (in Britain) Privy Councillor.

PDA personal digital assistant.

PE physical education.

pea *n* climbing plant with seeds growing in pods; its seed, eaten as a vegetable.

peace *n* calm, quietness; absence of anxiety; freedom from war; harmony between people. **peaceable** *adj* inclined towards peace. **peaceably** *adv* **peaceful** *adj* **peacefully** *adv*

peach *n* soft juicy fruit with a stone and a downy skin; *Informal* very pleasing person or thing. ▶ *adj* pinkish-orange.

peacock *n* large male bird with a brilliantly coloured fanlike tail. **peahen** *n fem*

peak *n* pointed top, esp. of a mountain; point of greatest development etc.; projecting piece on the front of a cap. ▶ v form or reach a peak. ▶ adj of or at the point of greatest demand.

peaked adj **peaky** adj pale and sickly.

peal n long loud echoing sound, esp. of bells or thunder. ▶ v sound with a peal or peals.

peanut n pea-shaped nut that ripens underground. ▶ pl Informal trifling amount of money.

pear n sweet juicy fruit with a narrow top and rounded base.

pearl n hard round shiny object found inside some oyster shells and used as a jewel. **pearly** adj

peasant n person working on the land, esp. in poorer countries or in the past. **peasantry** n peasants collectively.

peat n decayed vegetable material found in bogs, used as fertilizer or fuel.

pebble n small roundish stone. **pebbly** adj **pebble dash** coating for exterior walls consisting of small stones set in plaster.

pecan [pee-kan] n edible nut of a N American tree.

peccadillo n, pl **-loes**, **-los**. trivial misdeed.

peck v strike or pick up with the beak; Informal kiss quickly. ▶ n pecking movement. **peckish** adj Informal slightly hungry. **peck at** v nibble, eat reluctantly.

pectin n substance in fruit that makes jam set.

pectoral adj of the chest or thorax. ▶ n pectoral muscle or fin.

peculiar adj strange; distinct, special; belonging exclusively to. **peculiarity** n, pl **-ties**. oddity, eccentricity; distinguishing trait.

pecuniary adj relating to, or consisting of, money.

pedagogue n schoolteacher, esp.

a pedantic one.

pedal n foot-operated lever used to control a vehicle or machine, or to modify the tone of a musical instrument. ▶ v **-alling**, **-alled**. propel (a bicycle) by using its pedals.

pedant n person who is excessively concerned with details and rules, esp. in academic work. **pedantic** adj **pedantry** n

peddle v sell (goods) from door to door.

peddler n person who sells illegal drugs.

pederast n man who has homosexual relations with boys. **pederasty** n

pedestal n base supporting a column, statue, etc.

pedestrian n person who walks. ▶ adj dull, uninspiring. **pedestrian crossing** place marked where pedestrians may cross a road. **pedestrian precinct** Brit (shopping) area for pedestrians only.

pedicure n medical or cosmetic treatment of the feet.

pedigree n register of ancestors, esp. of a purebred animal.

pediment n triangular part over a door etc.

pedlar n person who sells goods from door to door.

pee Informal ▶ v **peeing**, **peed**. urinate. ▶ n act of urinating.

peek v, n peep or glance.

peel v remove the skin or rind of (a vegetable or fruit); (of skin or a surface) come off in flakes. ▶ n rind or skin. **peelings** pl n

peep¹ v look slyly or quickly. ▶ n peeping look. **Peeping Tom** man who furtively watches women undressing.

peep² v make a small shrill noise. ▶ n small shrill noise.

peer[1] *n* (*fem* **peeress**) (in Britain) member of the nobility; person of the same status, age, etc. **peerage** *n Brit* whole body of peers; rank of a peer. **peerless** *adj* unequalled, unsurpassed. **peer group** group of people of similar age, status, etc.

peer[2] *v* look closely and intently.

peeved *adj Informal* annoyed.

peevish *adj* fretful or irritable. **peevishly** *adv*

peewee *n* black-and-white Australian bird.

peewit *n* same as LAPWING.

peg *n* pin or clip for joining, fastening, marking, etc.; hook or knob for hanging things on. ▶ *v* **pegging, pegged.** fasten with pegs; stabilize (prices). **off the peg** (of clothes) ready-to-wear, not tailor-made.

peggy square *n NZ* small hand-knitted square.

peignoir [pay-nwahr] *n* woman's light dressing gown.

pejorative [pij-jor-a-tiv] *adj* (of words etc.) with an insulting or critical meaning.

Pekingese, Pekinese *n, pl* **-ese.** small dog with a short wrinkled muzzle.

pelargonium *n* plant with red, white, purple, or pink flowers.

pelican *n* large water bird with a pouch beneath its bill for storing fish. **pelican crossing** (in Britain) road crossing with pedestrian-operated traffic lights.

pellagra *n* disease caused by lack of vitamin B.

pellet *n* small ball of something.

pell-mell *adv* in utter confusion, headlong.

pellucid *adj* very clear.

pelmet *n* ornamental drapery or board, concealing a curtain rail.

pelt[1] *v* throw missiles at; run fast, rush; rain heavily. **at full pelt** at top speed.

pelt[2] *n* skin of a fur-bearing animal.

pelvis *n* framework of bones at the base of the spine, to which the hips are attached. **pelvic** *adj*

pen[1] *n* instrument for writing in ink. ▶ *v* **penning, penned.** write or compose. **pen friend** friend with whom a person corresponds without meeting. **penknife** *n* small knife with blade(s) that fold into the handle. **pen name** name used by a writer instead of his or her real name.

pen[2] *n* small enclosure for domestic animals. ▶ *v* **penning, penned.** put or keep in a pen.

pen[3] *n* female swan.

penal [pee-nal] *adj* of or used in punishment. **penalize** *v* impose a penalty on; handicap, hinder. **penalty** *n, pl* **-ties.** punishment for a crime or offence; *Sport* handicap or disadvantage imposed for breaking a rule.

penance *n* voluntary self-punishment to make amends for wrongdoing.

pence *n Brit* a plural of PENNY.

penchant [pon-shon] *n* inclination or liking.

pencil *n* thin cylindrical instrument containing graphite, for writing or drawing. ▶ *v* **-cilling, -cilled.** draw, write, or mark with a pencil.

pendant *n* ornament worn on a chain round the neck.

pendent *adj* hanging.

pending *prep* while waiting for. ▶ *adj* not yet decided or settled.

pendulous *adj* hanging, swinging.

pendulum *n* suspended weight swinging to and fro, esp. as a regulator for a clock.

penetrate *v* find or force a way into or through; arrive at the meaning of. **penetrable** *adj*

capable of being penetrated.
penetrating *adj* (of a sound) loud
and unpleasant; quick to
understand. **penetration** *n*

penguin *n* flightless
black-and-white sea bird of the
southern hemisphere.

penicillin *n* antibiotic drug effective
against a wide range of diseases
and infections.

peninsula *n* strip of land nearly
surrounded by water. **peninsular**
adj

penis *n* organ of copulation and
urination in male mammals.

penitent *adj* feeling sorry for
having done wrong. ▶ *n* someone
who is penitent. **penitence** *n*
penitentiary *n, pl* **-ries.** US prison.
▶ *adj* (also **penitential**) relating to
penance.

pennant *n* long narrow flag.

penny *n, pl* **pence, pennies.** British
bronze coin worth one hundredth
of a pound; former British and
Australian coin worth one twelfth
of a shilling. **penniless** *adj* very
poor.

pension[1] *n* regular payment to
people above a certain age,
retired employees, widows, etc.
pensionable *adj* **pensioner** *n*
person receiving a pension.
pension off *v* force (someone) to
retire from a job and pay him or
her a pension.

pension[2] [**pon**-syon] *n* boarding
house in Europe.

pensive *adj* deeply thoughtful,
often with a tinge of sadness.

pentagon *n* geometric figure with
five sides; (**P-**) headquarters of the
US military. **pentagonal** *adj*

pentameter [pen-**tam**-it-er] *n* line
of poetry with five metrical feet.

Pentateuch [**pent**-a-tyuke] *n* first
five books of the Old Testament.

Pentecost *n* Christian festival

celebrating the descent of the
Holy Spirit to the apostles,
Whitsuntide.

penthouse *n* flat built on the roof
or top floor of a building.

pent-up *adj* (of an emotion) not
released, repressed.

penultimate *adj* second last.

penumbra *n, pl* **-brae, -bras.** (in
an eclipse) the partially shadowed
region which surrounds the full
shadow; partial shadow.

penury *n* extreme poverty.
penurious *adj*

peony *n, pl* **-nies.** garden plant
with showy red, pink, or white
flowers.

people *pl n* persons generally; the
community; one's family. ▶ *n* race
or nation. ▶ *v* provide with
inhabitants. **people mover** *Brit,
Aust & NZ* same as MULTIPURPOSE
VEHICLE.

pep *n Informal* high spirits, energy,
or enthusiasm. **pep talk** *Informal*
talk designed to increase
confidence and enthusiasm. **pep
up** *v* **pepping, pepped.** stimulate,
invigorate.

pepper *n* sharp hot condiment
made from the fruit of an East
Indian climbing plant; colourful
tropical fruit used as a vegetable,
capsicum. ▶ *v* season with pepper;
sprinkle, dot; pelt with missiles.
peppery *adj* tasting of pepper;
irritable. **peppercorn** *n* dried
berry of the pepper plant.
peppercorn rent *Chiefly Brit* low
or nominal rent.

peppermint *n* plant that yields an
oil with a strong sharp flavour;
sweet flavoured with this.

peptic *adj* relating to digestion or
the digestive juices.

per *prep* for each. **as per** in
accordance with.

perambulate *v Old-fashioned* walk

through or about (a place).
perambulation n **perambulator** n
pram.
per annum adv Latin in each year.
per capita adj, adv Latin of or for
each person.
perceive v become aware of
(something) through the senses;
understand.
per cent in each hundred.
percentage n proportion or rate
per hundred.
perceptible adj discernible,
recognizable.
perception n act of perceiving;
intuitive judgment. **perceptive** adj
perch¹ n resting place for a bird.
▶ v alight, rest, or place on or as if
on a perch.
perch² n any of various edible
fishes.
perchance adv Old-fashioned
perhaps.
percipient adj quick to notice
things, observant.
percolate v pass or filter through
small holes; spread gradually;
make (coffee) or (of coffee) be
made in a percolator. **percolation**
n **percolator** n coffeepot in
which boiling water is forced
through a tube and filters down
through coffee.
percussion n striking of one thing
against another. **percussion
instrument** musical instrument
played by being struck, such as
drums or cymbals.
perdition n Christianity spiritual
ruin.
peregrination n Obs travels,
roaming.
peregrine falcon n falcon with
dark upper parts and a light
underside.
peremptory adj authoritative,
imperious.
perennial adj lasting through

many years. ▶ n plant lasting more
than two years. **perennially** adv
perfect adj having all the essential
elements; faultless; correct,
precise; utter or absolute;
excellent. ▶ n Grammar perfect
tense. ▶ v improve; make fully
correct. **perfectly** adv **perfection**
n state of being perfect.
perfectionist n person who
demands the highest standards of
excellence. **perfectionism** n
perfidious adj Lit treacherous,
disloyal. **perfidy** n
perforate v make holes in.
perforation n
perforce adv of necessity.
perform v carry out (an action);
act, sing, or present a play before
an audience; fulfil (a request etc.).
performance n **performer** n
perfume n liquid cosmetic worn
for its pleasant smell; fragrance.
▶ v give a pleasant smell to.
perfumery n perfumes in general.
perfunctory adj done only as a
matter of routine, superficial.
perfunctorily adv
pergola n arch or framework of
trellis supporting climbing plants.
perhaps adv possibly, maybe.
pericardium n, pl **-dia.** membrane
enclosing the heart.
perihelion n, pl **-lia.** point in the
orbit of a planet or comet that is
nearest to the sun.
peril n great danger. **perilous** adj
perilously adv
perimeter [per-**rim**-it-er] n (length
of) the outer edge of an area.
perinatal adj of or in the weeks
shortly before or after birth.
period n particular portion of time;
single occurrence of menstruation;
division of time at school etc.
when a particular subject is
taught; US full stop. ▶ adj (of
furniture, dress, a play, etc.)

dating from or in the style of an earlier time. **periodic** adj recurring at intervals. **periodic table** Chem chart of the elements, arranged to show their relationship to each other. **periodical** n magazine issued at regular intervals. ▶ adj periodic.

peripatetic [per-rip-a-**tet**-ik] adj travelling about from place to place.

periphery [per-**if**-er-ee] n, pl **-eries.** boundary or edge; fringes of a field of activity. **peripheral** [per-**if**-er-al] adj unimportant, not central; of or on the periphery.

periscope n instrument used, esp. in submarines, to give a view of objects on a different level.

perish v be destroyed or die; decay, rot. **perishable** adj liable to rot quickly. **perishing** adj Informal very cold.

peritoneum [per-rit-toe-**nee**-um] n, pl **-nea, -neums** membrane lining the internal surface of the abdomen. **peritonitis** [per-rit-tone-**ite**-iss] n inflammation of the peritoneum.

periwinkle[1] n small edible shellfish, the winkle.

periwinkle[2] n plant with trailing stems and blue flowers.

perjury n, pl **-juries.** act or crime of lying while under oath in a court. **perjure oneself** commit perjury.

perk n Informal incidental benefit gained from a job, such as a company car.

perk up v cheer up. **perky** adj lively or cheerful.

perlemoen n S Afr edible sea creature with a shell lined with mother of pearl.

perm n long-lasting curly hairstyle produced by treating the hair with chemicals. ▶ v give (hair) a perm.

permafrost n permanently frozen ground.

permanent adj lasting forever. **permanence** n **permanently** adv

permeate v pervade or pass through the whole of (something). **permeable** adj able to be permeated, esp. by liquid.

permit v **-mitting, -mitted.** give permission, allow. ▶ n document giving permission to do something. **permission** n authorization to do something. **permissible** adj **permissive** adj (excessively) tolerant, esp. in sexual matters.

permutation n any of the ways a number of things can be arranged or combined.

pernicious adj wicked; extremely harmful, deadly.

pernickety adj Informal (excessively) fussy about details.

peroration n concluding part of a speech, usu. summing up the main points.

peroxide n hydrogen peroxide used as a hair bleach; oxide containing a high proportion of oxygen.

perpendicular adj at right angles to a line or surface; upright or vertical. ▶ n line or plane at right angles to another.

perpetrate v commit or be responsible for (a wrongdoing). **perpetration** n **perpetrator** n

perpetual adj lasting forever; continually repeated. **perpetually** adv **perpetuate** v cause to continue or be remembered. **perpetuation** n **in perpetuity** forever.

perplex v puzzle, bewilder. **perplexity** n, pl **-ties.**

perquisite n Formal same as PERK.

perry n, pl **-ries.** alcoholic drink made from fermented pears.

per se [per **say**] *adv Latin* in itself.

persecute *v* treat cruelly because of race, religion, etc.; subject to persistent harassment. **persecution** *n* **persecutor** *n*

persevere *v* keep making an effort despite difficulties. **perseverance** *n*

persimmon *n* sweet red tropical fruit.

persist *v* continue to be or happen; last; continue in spite of obstacles or objections. **persistent** *adj* **persistently** *adv* **persistence** *n*

person *n* human being; body of a human being; *Grammar* form of pronouns and verbs that shows if a person is speaking, spoken to, or spoken of. **in person** actually present.

persona [per-**soh**-na] *n, pl* -**nae** [-nee] someone's personality as presented to others.

personable *adj* pleasant in appearance and personality.

personage *n* important person.

personal *adj* individual or private; of the body, e.g. *personal hygiene*; (of a remark etc.) offensive. **personally** *adv* directly, not by delegation to others; in one's own opinion. **personal computer** small computer used for word processing or computer games. **personal pronoun** pronoun like *I* or *she* that stands for a definite person. **personal stereo** very small portable cassette player with headphones.

personality *n, pl* -**ties**. person's distinctive characteristics; celebrity. ▶ *pl* personal remarks, e.g. *the discussion degenerated into personalities*.

personify *v* -**fying, -fied.** give human characteristics to; be an example of, typify.

personification *n*

personnel *n* people employed in an organization; department in an organization that appoints or keeps records of employees.

perspective *n* view of the relative importance of situations or facts; method of drawing that gives the effect of solidity and relative distances and sizes.

Perspex *n* ® transparent acrylic substitute for glass.

perspicacious *adj* having quick mental insight. **perspicacity** *n*

perspire *v* sweat. **perspiration** *n*

persuade *v* make (someone) do something by argument, charm, etc.; convince. **persuasion** *n* act of persuading; way of thinking or belief. **persuasive** *adj*

pert *adj* saucy and cheeky.

pertain *v* belong or be relevant (to).

pertinacious *adj Formal* very persistent and determined. **pertinacity** *n*

pertinent *adj* relevant. **pertinence** *n*

perturb *v* disturb greatly. **perturbation** *n*

peruse *v* read in a careful or leisurely manner. **perusal** *n*

pervade *v* spread right through (something). **pervasive** *adj*

perverse *adj* deliberately doing something different from what is thought normal or proper. **perversely** *adv* **perversity** *n*

pervert *v* use or alter for a wrong purpose; lead into abnormal (sexual) behaviour. ▶ *n* person who practises sexual perversion. **perversion** *n* sexual act or desire considered abnormal; act of perverting.

pervious *adj* able to be penetrated, permeable.

peseta [pa-**say**-ta] *n* former

monetary unit of Spain.

pessary n, pl **-ries.** appliance worn in the vagina, either to prevent conception or to support the womb; vaginal suppository.

pessimism n tendency to expect the worst in all things. **pessimist** n **pessimistic** adj **pessimistically** adv

pest n annoying person; insect or animal that damages crops.

pesticide n chemical for killing insect pests.

pester v annoy or nag continually.

pestilence n deadly epidemic disease. **pestilent** adj annoying, troublesome; deadly. **pestilential** adj

pestle n club-shaped implement for grinding things to powder in a mortar.

pet n animal kept for pleasure and companionship; person favoured or indulged. ▶ adj particularly cherished. ▶ v **petting, petted.** treat as a pet; pat or stroke affectionately; Old-fashioned kiss and caress erotically.

petal n one of the brightly coloured outer parts of a flower. **petalled** adj

petard n hoist with one's own **petard** being the victim of one's own schemes.

peter out v gradually come to an end.

petite adj (of a woman) small and dainty.

petition n formal request, esp. one signed by many people and presented to parliament. ▶ v present a petition to. **petitioner** n

petrel n sea bird with a hooked bill and tubular nostrils.

petrify v **-fying, -fied.** frighten severely; turn to stone. **petrification** n

petrochemical n substance, such

as acetone, obtained from petroleum.

petrol n flammable liquid obtained from petroleum, used as fuel in internal-combustion engines. **petrol bomb** home-made incendiary device consisting of a bottle filled with petrol.

petroleum n thick dark oil found underground.

petticoat n woman's skirt-shaped undergarment.

pettifogging adj excessively concerned with unimportant detail.

petty adj **-tier, -tiest.** unimportant, trivial; small-minded; on a small scale, e.g. petty crime. **pettiness** n **petty cash** cash kept by a firm to pay minor expenses. **petty officer** noncommissioned officer in the navy.

petulant adj childishly irritable or peevish. **petulance** n **petulantly** adv

petunia n garden plant with funnel-shaped flowers.

pew n fixed benchlike seat in a church; Informal chair, seat.

pewter n greyish metal made of tin and lead.

pH Chem measure of the acidity of a solution.

phalanger n long-tailed Australian tree-dwelling marsupial.

phalanx n, pl **phalanxes.** closely grouped mass of people.

phallus n, pl **-luses, -li.** penis, esp. as a symbol of reproductive power in primitive rites. **phallic** adj

phantasm n unreal vision, illusion. **phantasmal** adj

phantasmagoria n shifting medley of dreamlike figures.

phantom n ghost; unreal vision.

Pharaoh [fare-oh] n title of the ancient Egyptian kings.

pharmaceutical adj of pharmacy.

pharmacology n study of drugs.

pharmacological adj
pharmacologist n
pharmacopoeia
[far-ma-koh-**pee**-a] n book with a list of and directions for the use of drugs.
pharmacy n, pl -**cies.** preparation and dispensing of drugs and medicines; pharmacist's shop.
pharmacist n person qualified to prepare and sell drugs and medicines.
pharynx [**far**-rinks] n, pl **pharynges, pharynxes.** cavity forming the back part of the mouth. **pharyngitis** [far-rin-**jite**-iss] n inflammation of the pharynx.
phase n any distinct or characteristic stage in a development or chain of events.
▶ v arrange or carry out in stages or to coincide with something else. **phase in, out** v introduce or discontinue gradually.
PhD Doctor of Philosophy.
pheasant n game bird with bright plumage.
phenobarbitone n drug inducing sleep or relaxation.
phenol n chemical used in disinfectants and antiseptics.
phenomenon n, pl -**ena.** anything appearing or observed; remarkable person or thing. **phenomenal** adj extraordinary, outstanding. **phenomenally** adv
phial n small bottle for medicine etc.
philadelphus n shrub with sweet-scented flowers.
philanderer n man who flirts or has many casual love affairs. **philandering** adj, n
philanthropy n practice of helping people less well-off than oneself. **philanthropic** adj **philanthropist** n
philately [fill-**lat**-a-lee] n stamp collecting. **philatelist** n
philharmonic adj (in names of orchestras etc.) music-loving.
philistine adj, n boorishly uncultivated (person). **philistinism** n
philology n science of the structure and development of languages. **philological** adj **philologist** n
philosopher n person who studies philosophy.
philosophy n, pl -**phies.** study of the meaning of life, knowledge, thought, etc.; theory or set of ideas held by a particular philosopher; person's outlook on life. **philosophical, philosophic** adj of philosophy; calm in the face of difficulties or disappointments. **philosophically** adv **philosophize** v discuss in a philosophical manner.
philtre n magic drink supposed to arouse love in the person who drinks it.
phlebitis [fleb-**bite**-iss] n inflammation of a vein.
phlegm [flem] n thick yellowish substance formed in the nose and throat during a cold.
phlegmatic [fleg-**mat**-ik] adj not easily excited, unemotional. **phlegmatically** adv
phlox n, pl **phlox, phloxes.** flowering garden plant.
phobia n intense and unreasoning fear or dislike.
phoenix n legendary bird said to set fire to itself and rise anew from its ashes.
phone n, v Informal telephone. **phonecard** n card used to operate certain public telephones. **phone-in** n Brit, Aust & S Afr broadcast in which telephone comments or questions from the public are transmitted live.

phonetic adj of speech sounds; (of spelling) written as it is sounded. **phonetics** n science of speech sounds. **phonetically** adv

phoney, phony Informal ▸ adj **phonier, phoniest.** not genuine; insincere. ▸ n, pl **phoneys, phonies.** phoney person or thing.

phonograph n US old-fashioned record player.

phosphorescence n faint glow in the dark. **phosphorescent** adj

phosphorus n Chem toxic flammable nonmetallic element which appears luminous in the dark. **phosphate** n compound of phosphorus; fertilizer containing phosphorus.

photo n, pl **photos.** short for PHOTOGRAPH. **photo finish** finish of a race in which the contestants are so close that a photograph is needed to decide the result.

photocopy n, pl **-copies.** photographic reproduction. ▸ v **-copying, -copied.** make a photocopy of. **photocopier** n

photoelectric adj using or worked by electricity produced by the action of light.

photogenic adj always looking attractive in photographs.

photograph n picture made by the chemical action of light on sensitive film. ▸ v take a photograph of. **photographic** adj **photography** n art of taking photographs.

photographer n person who takes photographs, esp. professionally.

photostat n copy made by photocopying machine.

photosynthesis n process by which a green plant uses sunlight to build up carbohydrate reserves.

phrase n group of words forming a unit of meaning, esp. within a sentence; short effective expression. ▸ v express in words.

phrasal verb phrase consisting of a verb and an adverb or preposition, with a meaning different from the parts, such as *take in* meaning *deceive.*

phraseology n, pl **-gies.** way in which words are used.

physical adj of the body, as contrasted with the mind or spirit; of material things or nature; of physics. **physically** adv **physical education** training and practice in sports and gymnastics.

physician n doctor of medicine.

physics n science of the properties of matter and energy. **physicist** n person skilled in or studying physics.

physiognomy [fiz-ee-on-om-ee] n face.

physiology n science of the normal function of living things. **physiological** adj **physiologist** n

physiotherapy n treatment of disease or injury by physical means such as massage, rather than by drugs. **physiotherapist** n

physique n person's bodily build and muscular development.

pi n Maths ratio of the circumference of a circle to its diameter.

pianissimo adv Music very quietly.

piano[1] n, pl **pianos.** musical instrument with strings which are struck by hammers worked by a keyboard (also **pianoforte**). **pianist** n **Pianola** n ® mechanically played piano.

piano[2] adv Music quietly.

piazza n square or marketplace, esp. in Italy.

pic n, pl **pics, pix.** Informal photograph or illustration.

picador n mounted bullfighter with a lance.

picaresque adj denoting a type of

fiction in which the hero, a rogue, has a series of adventures.

piccalilli n pickle of vegetables in mustard sauce.

piccolo n, pl **-los.** small flute.

pick[1] v choose; remove (flowers or fruit) from a plant; take hold of and move with the fingers; provoke (a fight etc.) deliberately; open (a lock) by means other than a key. ▶ n choice; best part. **pick-me-up** n Informal stimulating drink, tonic. **pick on** v continually treat unfairly. **pick out** v recognize, distinguish. **pick up** v raise, lift; collect; improve, get better; become acquainted with for a sexual purpose. **pick-up** n small truck; casual acquaintance made for a sexual purpose; device for conversion of vibrations into electrical signals, as in a record player.

pick[2] n tool with a curved iron crossbar and wooden shaft, for breaking up hard ground or rocks.

pickaxe n large pick.

picket n person or group standing outside a workplace to deter would-be workers during a strike; sentry or sentries posted to give warning of an attack; pointed stick used as part of a fence. ▶ v form a picket outside (a workplace). **picket line** line of people acting as pickets.

pickings pl n money easily acquired.

pickle n food preserved in vinegar or salt water; Informal awkward situation. ▶ v preserve in vinegar or salt water. **pickled** adj (of food) preserved; Informal drunk.

pickpocket n thief who steals from someone's pocket.

picnic n informal meal out of doors. ▶ v **-nicking, -nicked.** have a picnic.

Pict n member of an ancient race of N Britain. **Pictish** adj

pictorial adj of or in painting or pictures.

picture n drawing or painting; photograph; mental image; beautiful or picturesque object; image on a TV screen. ▶ pl cinema. ▶ v visualize, imagine; represent in a picture.

picturesque adj (of a place or view) pleasant to look at; (of language) forceful, vivid. **picture window** large window made of a single sheet of glass.

piddle v Informal urinate.

pidgin n language, not a mother tongue, made up of elements of two or more other languages.

pie n dish of meat, fruit, etc. baked in pastry. **pie chart** circular diagram with sectors representing quantities.

piebald n, adj (horse) with irregular black-and-white markings.

piece n separate bit or part; instance, e.g. a piece of luck; example, specimen; literary or musical composition; coin; small object used in draughts, chess, etc. **piece together** v make or assemble bit by bit.

pièce de résistance [pyess de ray-**ziss**-tonss] n French most impressive item.

piecemeal adv bit by bit.

piecework n work paid for according to the quantity produced.

pied adj having markings of two or more colours.

pied-à-terre [pyay da **tair**] n, pl **pieds-à-terre** [pyay da **tair**] small flat or house for occasional use.

pier n platform on stilts sticking out into the sea; pillar, esp. one supporting a bridge.

pierce v make a hole in or through

with a sharp instrument; make a way through. **piercing** adj (of a sound) shrill and high-pitched.

Pierrot [pier-roe] n pantomime clown with a whitened face.

piety n, pl -ties. deep devotion to God and religion.

piffle n Informal nonsense.

pig n animal kept and killed for pork, ham, and bacon; Informal greedy, dirty, or rude person. **piggish, piggy** adj Informal dirty; greedy; stubborn. **piggery** n, pl -geries. place for keeping and breeding pigs. **pig-headed** adj obstinate. **pig iron** crude iron produced in a blast furnace.

pigeon[1] n bird with a heavy body and short legs, sometimes trained to carry messages. **pigeonhole** n compartment for papers in a desk etc. ▶ v classify; put aside and do nothing about. **pigeon-toed** adj with the feet or toes turned inwards.

pigeon[2] n Informal concern or responsibility.

piggyback n ride on someone's shoulders. ▶ adv carried on someone's shoulders.

pigment n colouring matter, paint or dye. **pigmentation** n

Pigmy n, pl -mies. same as PYGMY.

pigtail n plait of hair hanging from the back or either side of the head.

pike[1] n large predatory freshwater fish.

pike[2] n Hist long-handled spear.

pikelet n Aust & NZ small thick pancake.

piker n Aust & NZ slang shirker.

pilaster n square column, usu. set in a wall.

pilau, pilaf, pilaff n Middle Eastern dish of meat, fish, or poultry boiled with rice, spices, etc.

pilchard n small edible sea fish of the herring family.

pile[1] n number of things lying on top of each other; Informal large amount; large building. ▶ v collect into a pile; (foll. by in or out) move in a group. **pile-up** n Informal traffic accident involving several vehicles.

pile[2] n beam driven into the ground, esp. as a foundation for building.

pile[3] n fibres of a carpet or a fabric, esp. velvet, that stand up from the weave.

piles pl n swollen veins in the rectum, haemorrhoids.

pilfer v steal in small quantities.

pilgrim n person who journeys to a holy place. **pilgrimage** n

pill n small ball of medicine swallowed whole. **the pill** pill taken by a woman to prevent pregnancy.

pillage v steal property by violence in war. ▶ n violent seizure of goods, esp. in war.

pillar n upright post, usu. supporting a roof; strong supporter. **pillar box** (in Britain) red pillar-shaped letter box in the street.

pillion n seat for a passenger behind the rider of a motorcycle.

pillory n, pl -ries. Hist frame with holes for the head and hands in which an offender was locked and exposed to public abuse. ▶ v -rying, -ried. ridicule publicly.

pillow n stuffed cloth bag for supporting the head in bed. ▶ v rest as if on a pillow. **pillowcase, pillowslip** n removable cover for a pillow.

pilot n person qualified to fly an aircraft or spacecraft; person employed to steer a ship entering or leaving a harbour. ▶ adj experimental and preliminary. ▶ v act as the pilot of; guide, steer.

pilot light small flame lighting the main one in a gas appliance.

pimento n, pl **-tos.** mild-tasting red pepper.

pimp n man who gets customers for a prostitute in return for a share of his or her earnings. ▶ v act as a pimp.

pimpernel n wild plant with small star-shaped flowers.

pimple n small pus-filled spot on the skin. **pimply** adj

pin n short thin piece of stiff wire with a point and head, for fastening things; wooden or metal peg or stake. ▶ v **pinning, pinned.** fasten with a pin; seize and hold fast. **pin down** v force (someone) to make a decision, take action, etc.; define clearly. **pin money** small amount earned to buy small luxuries. **pin-up** n picture of a sexually attractive person, esp. (partly) naked.

pinafore n apron; dress with a bib top.

pinball n electrically operated table game in which a small ball is shot through various hazards.

pince-nez [panss-nay] n, pl **pince-nez.** glasses kept in place only by a clip on the bridge of the nose.

pincers pl n tool consisting of two hinged arms, for gripping; claws of a lobster etc.

pinch v squeeze between finger and thumb; cause pain by being too tight; Informal steal. ▶ n act of pinching; as much as can be taken up between the finger and thumb. **at a pinch** if absolutely necessary. **feel the pinch** have to economize.

pinchbeck n alloy of zinc and copper, used as imitation gold.

pine[1] n evergreen coniferous tree; its wood. **pine cone** woody seed case of the pine tree. **pine marten** wild mammal of the coniferous forests of Europe and Asia.

pine[2] v (foll. by for) feel great longing (for); become thin and ill through grief etc.

pineal gland n small cone-shaped gland at the base of the brain.

pineapple n large tropical fruit with juicy yellow flesh and a hard skin.

ping v, n (make) a short high-pitched sound.

Ping-Pong n ® table tennis.

pinion[1] n bird's wing. ▶ v immobilize (someone) by tying or holding his or her arms.

pinion[2] n small cogwheel.

pink n pale reddish colour; fragrant garden plant. ▶ adj of the colour pink. ▶ v (of an engine) make a metallic noise because not working properly, knock. **in the pink** in good health.

pinking shears pl n scissors with a serrated edge that give a wavy edge to material to prevent fraying.

pinnacle n highest point of fame or success; mountain peak; small slender spire.

pinotage [pin-no-tajj] n blended red wine of S Africa.

pinpoint v locate or identify exactly.

pinstripe n very narrow stripe in fabric; the fabric itself.

pint n liquid measure, $\frac{1}{8}$ gallon (.568 litre).

pioneer n explorer or early settler of a new country; originator or developer of something new. ▶ v be the pioneer or leader of.

pious adj deeply religious, devout.

pip[1] n small seed in a fruit.

pip[2] n high-pitched sound used as a time signal on radio; Informal star on a junior army officer's shoulder showing rank.

pip³ *n give someone the pip* *Brit, NZ & S Afr slang* annoy.

pipe *n* tube for conveying liquid or gas; tube with a small bowl at the end for smoking tobacco; tubular musical instrument. ▶ *pl* **bagpipes**. ▶ *v* play on a pipe; utter in a shrill tone; convey by pipe; decorate with piping. **piper** *n* player on a pipe or bagpipes. **piping** *n* system of pipes; decoration of icing on a cake etc.; fancy edging on clothes etc. **piped music** recorded music played as background music in public places. **pipe down** *v Informal* stop talking. **pipe dream** fanciful impossible plan. **pipeline** *n* long pipe for transporting oil, water, etc.; means of communication. **in the pipeline** in preparation. **pipe up** *v* speak suddenly or shrilly.

pipette *n* slender glass tube used to transfer or measure fluids.

pipi *n Aust* mollusc often used as bait; *NZ* edible shellfish.

pipit *n* small brownish songbird.

pippin *n* type of eating apple.

piquant [pee-kant] *adj* having a pleasant spicy taste; mentally stimulating. **piquancy** *n*

pique [peek] *n* feeling of hurt pride, baffled curiosity, or resentment. ▶ *v* hurt the pride of; arouse (curiosity).

piqué [pee-kay] *n* stiff ribbed cotton fabric.

piquet [pik-ket] *n* card game for two.

piranha *n* small fierce freshwater fish of tropical America.

pirate *n* sea robber; person who illegally publishes or sells work owned by someone else; person or company that broadcasts illegally. ▶ *v* sell or reproduce

(artistic work etc.) illegally. **piracy** *n* **piratical** *adj*

pirouette *v, n* (make) a spinning turn balanced on the toes of one foot.

pistachio *n, pl* **-chios**. edible nut of a Mediterranean tree.

piste [peest] *n* ski slope.

pistil *n* seed-bearing part of a flower.

pistol *n* short-barrelled handgun.

piston *n* cylindrical part in an engine that slides to and fro in a cylinder.

pit *n* deep hole in the ground; coal mine; dent or depression; servicing and refuelling area on a motor-racing track; same as ORCHESTRA PIT. ▶ *v* **pitting, pitted**. mark with small dents or scars. **pit one's wits against** compete against in a test or contest. **pit bull terrier** strong muscular terrier with a short coat.

pitch¹ *v* throw, hurl; set up (a tent); fall headlong; (of a ship or plane) move with the front and back going up and down alternately; set the level or tone of. ▶ *n* area marked out for playing sport; degree or angle of slope; degree of highness or lowness of a (musical) sound; place where a street or market trader regularly sells; *Informal* persuasive sales talk. **pitch in** *v* join in enthusiastically. **pitch into** *v Informal*

pitch² *n* dark sticky substance obtained from tar. **pitch-black, pitch-dark** *adj* very dark.

pitchblende *n* mineral composed largely of uranium oxide, yielding radium.

pitcher *n* large jug with a narrow neck.

pitchfork *n* large long-handled fork for lifting hay. ▶ *v* thrust abruptly or violently.

pitfall n hidden difficulty or danger.

pith n soft white lining of the rind of oranges etc.; essential part; soft tissue in the stems of certain plants. **pithy** adj short and full of meaning.

piton [**peet**-on] n metal spike used in climbing to secure a rope.

pittance n very small amount of money.

pituitary n, pl **-taries**. gland at the base of the brain, that helps to control growth (also **pituitary gland**).

pity n, pl **pities**. sympathy or sorrow for others' suffering; regrettable fact. ▶ v **pitying, pitied**. feel pity for. **piteous, pitiable** adj arousing pity. **pitiful** adj arousing pity; woeful; contemptible. **pitifully** adv **pitiless** adj feeling no pity or mercy. **pitilessly** adv

pivot n central shaft on which something turns. ▶ v provide with or turn on a pivot. **pivotal** adj of crucial importance.

pix n Informal a plural of PIC.

pixie n (in folklore) fairy.

pizza n flat disc of dough covered with a wide variety of savoury toppings and baked.

pizzazz n Informal attractive combination of energy and style.

pizzicato [pit-see-kah-toe] adj Music played by plucking the string of a violin etc. with the finger.

placard n notice that is carried or displayed in public.

placate v make (someone) stop feeling angry or upset. **placatory** adj

place n particular part of an area or space; particular town, building, etc.; position or point reached; seat or space; duty or right; position of employment; usual position. ▶ v put in a particular place; identify; put in context; make (an order, bet, etc.). **be placed** (of a competitor in a race) be among the first three. **take place** happen, occur.

placebo [plas-**see**-bo] n, pl **-bos, -boes**. sugar pill etc. given to an unsuspecting patient instead of an active drug.

placenta [plass-**ent**-a] n, pl **-tas, -tae**. organ formed in the womb during pregnancy, providing nutrients for the fetus. **placental** adj

placid adj not easily excited or upset, calm. **placidity** n

plagiarize [**play**-jer-ize] v steal ideas, passages, etc. from (someone else's work) and present them as one's own. **plagiarism** n

plague n fast-spreading fatal disease; Hist bubonic plague; widespread infestation. ▶ v **plaguing, plagued**. trouble or annoy continually.

plaice n edible European flatfish.

plaid n long piece of tartan cloth worn as part of Highland dress; tartan cloth or pattern.

plain adj easy to see or understand; expressed honestly and clearly; without decoration or pattern; not beautiful; simple, ordinary. ▶ n large stretch of level country. **plainly** adv **plainness** n **plain clothes** ordinary clothes, as opposed to uniform. **plain sailing** easy progress. **plain speaking** saying exactly what one thinks.

plainsong n unaccompanied singing, esp. in a medieval church.

plaintiff n person who sues in a court of law.

plaintive adj sad, mournful. **plaintively** adv

plait [platt] n intertwined length of

hair. ▶ v intertwine separate strands in a pattern.

plan n way thought out to do or achieve something; diagram showing the layout or design of something. ▶ v **planning, planned.** arrange beforehand; make a diagram of. **planner** n

plane¹ n aeroplane; Maths flat surface; level of attainment etc. ▶ adj perfectly flat or level. ▶ v glide or skim.

plane² n tool for smoothing wood. ▶ v smooth (wood) with a plane.

plane³ n tree with broad leaves.

planet n large body in space that revolves round the sun or another star. **planetary** adj

planetarium n, pl **-iums, -ia.** building where the movements of the stars, planets, etc. are shown by projecting lights on the inside of a dome.

plangent adj (of sounds) mournful and resounding.

plank n long flat piece of sawn timber.

plankton n minute animals and plants floating in the surface water of a sea or lake.

plant n living organism that grows in the ground and has no power to move; equipment or machinery used in industrial processes; factory or other industrial premises. ▶ v put in the ground to grow; place firmly in position; Informal put (a person) secretly in an organization to spy; Informal hide (stolen goods etc.) on a person to make him or her seem guilty. **planter** n owner of a plantation.

plantain¹ n low-growing wild plant with broad leaves.

plantain² n tropical fruit like a green banana.

plantation n estate for the cultivation of tea, tobacco, etc.; wood of cultivated trees.

plaque n inscribed commemorative stone or metal plate; filmy deposit on teeth that causes decay.

plasma n clear liquid part of blood.

plaster n mixture of lime, sand, etc. for coating walls; adhesive strip of material for dressing cuts etc. ▶ v cover with plaster; coat thickly. **plastered** adj Slang drunk. **plaster of Paris** white powder which dries to form a hard solid when mixed with water, used for sculptures and casts for broken limbs.

plastic n synthetic material that can be moulded when soft but sets in a hard long-lasting shape; credit cards etc. as opposed to cash. ▶ adj made of plastic; easily moulded, pliant. **plasticity** n ability to be moulded. **plastic bullet** solid PVC cylinder fired by police in riot control. **plastic surgery** repair or reconstruction of missing or malformed parts of the body.

Plasticine n ® soft coloured modelling material used esp. by children.

plate n shallow dish for holding food; flat thin sheet of metal, glass, etc.; thin coating of metal on another metal; dishes or cutlery made of gold or silver; illustration, usu. on fine quality paper, in a book; Informal set of false teeth. ▶ v cover with a thin coating of gold, silver, or other metal. **plateful** n **plate glass** glass in thin sheets, used for mirrors and windows. **plate tectonics** study of the structure of the earth's crust, esp. the movement of layers of rocks.

plateau n, pl **-teaus, -teaux.** area of level high land; stage when there is no change or development.

platen n roller of a typewriter, against which the paper is held.

platform n raised floor; raised area in a station from which passengers board trains; structure in the sea which holds machinery, stores, etc. for drilling an oil well; programme of a political party.

platinum n Chem valuable silvery-white metal. **platinum blonde** woman with silvery-blonde hair.

platitude n remark that is true but not interesting or original. **platitudinous** adj

platonic adj (of a relationship) friendly or affectionate but not sexual.

platoon n smaller unit within a company of soldiers.

platteland n S Afr rural district.

platter n large dish.

platypus n Australian egg-laying amphibious mammal, with dense fur, webbed feet, and a ducklike bill (also **duck-billed platypus**).

plaudits pl n expressions of approval.

plausible adj apparently true or reasonable; persuasive but insincere. **plausibly** adv **plausibility** n

play v occupy oneself in (a game or recreation); compete against in a game or sport; behave carelessly; act (a part) on the stage; perform on (a musical instrument); cause (a radio, record player, etc.) to give out sound; move lightly or irregularly, flicker. ▶ n story performed on stage or broadcast; activities children take part in for amusement; playing of a game; conduct, e.g. fair play; (scope for) freedom of movement. **playful** adj lively. **play back** v

listen to or watch (something recorded). **playcentre** n NZ & S Afr centre for preschool children run by parents. **play down** v minimize the importance of. **playgroup** n regular meeting of very young children for supervised play. **playhouse** n theatre.

playing card one of a set of 52 cards used in card games.

playing field extensive piece of ground for sport. **play-lunch** n Aust & NZ child's mid-morning snack at school. **play off** v set (two people) against each other for one's own ends. **play on** v exploit or encourage (someone's sympathy or weakness).

playschool n nursery group for young children. **plaything** n toy; person regarded or treated as a toy. **play up** v give prominence to; cause trouble. **playwright** n author of plays.

playboy n rich man who lives only for pleasure.

player n person who plays a game or sport; actor or actress; person who plays a musical instrument.

plaza n open space or square; modern shopping complex.

PLC, plc (in Britain) Public Limited Company.

plea n serious or urgent request, entreaty; statement of a prisoner or defendant; excuse.

plead v ask urgently or with deep feeling; give as an excuse; Law declare oneself to be guilty or innocent of a charge made against one.

pleasant adj pleasing, enjoyable. **pleasantly** adv **pleasantry** n, pl **-tries**. polite or joking remark.

please v give pleasure or satisfaction to. ▶ adv polite word of request. **please oneself** do as one likes. **pleased** adj **pleasing**

adj

pleasure *n* feeling of happiness and satisfaction; something that causes this. **pleasurable** *adj* giving pleasure. **pleasurably** *adv*

pleat *n* fold made by doubling material back on itself. ▶ *v* arrange (material) in pleats.

plebeian [pleb-**ee**-an] *adj* of the lower social classes; vulgar or rough. ▶ *n* (also **pleb**) member of the lower social classes.

plebiscite [pleb-**iss**-ite] *n* decision by direct voting of the people of a country.

plectrum *n, pl* **-trums, -tra.** small implement for plucking the strings of a guitar etc.

pledge *n* solemn promise; something valuable given as a guarantee that a promise will be kept or a debt paid. ▶ *v* promise solemnly; bind by or as if by a pledge.

plenary *adj* (of a meeting) attended by all members.

plenipotentiary *adj* having full powers. ▶ *n, pl* **-aries.** diplomat or representative having full powers.

plenitude *n* completeness, abundance.

plenteous *adj* plentiful.

plenty *n* large amount or number; quite enough. **plentiful** *adj* existing in large amounts or numbers. **plentifully** *adv*

pleonasm *n* use of more words than necessary.

plethora *n* excess.

pleurisy *n* inflammation of the membrane covering the lungs.

pliable *adj* easily bent; easily influenced. **pliability** *n*

pliant *adj* pliable. **pliancy** *n*

pliers *pl n* tool with hinged arms and jaws for gripping.

plight[1] *n* difficult or dangerous situation.

plight[2] *v* **plight one's troth** *Old-fashioned* promise to marry.

Plimsoll line *n* mark on a ship showing the level water should reach when the ship is fully loaded.

plimsolls *pl n Brit* rubber-soled canvas shoes.

plinth *n* slab forming the base of a statue, column, etc.

PLO Palestine Liberation Organization.

plod *v* **plodding, plodded.** walk with slow heavy steps; work slowly but determinedly. **plodder** *n*

plonk[1] *v* put (something) down heavily and carelessly.

plonk[2] *n Informal* cheap inferior wine.

plop *n* sound of an object falling into water without a splash. ▶ *v* **plopping, plopped.** make this sound.

plot[1] *n* secret plan to do something illegal or wrong; story of a film, novel, etc. ▶ *v* **plotting, plotted.** plan secretly, conspire; mark the position or course of (a ship or aircraft) on a map; mark and join up (points on a graph).

plot[2] *n* small piece of land.

plough *n* agricultural tool for turning over soil. ▶ *v* turn over (earth) with a plough; move or work through slowly and laboriously. **ploughman** *n* **ploughshare** *n* blade of a plough.

plover *n* shore bird with a straight bill and long pointed wings.

ploy *n* manoeuvre designed to gain an advantage.

pluck *v* pull or pick off; pull out the feathers of (a bird for cooking); sound the strings of (a guitar etc.) with the fingers or a plectrum. ▶ *n* courage. **plucky** *adj* brave. **pluckily** *adv* **pluck up** *v* summon up (courage).

plug *n* thing fitting into and filling

a hole; device connecting an appliance to an electricity supply; *Informal* favourable mention of a product etc., to encourage people to buy it. ▶ v **plugging, plugged.** block or seal (a hole or gap) with a plug; *Informal* advertise (a product etc.) by constant repetition. **plug away** v *Informal* work steadily. **plug in** v connect (an electrical appliance) to a power source by pushing a plug into a socket.

plum n oval usu. dark red fruit with a stone in the middle. ▶ adj dark purplish-red; very desirable.

plumage n bird's feathers.

plumb v understand (something obscure); test with a plumb line. ▶ adv exactly. **plumb the depths of** experience the worst extremes of (an unpleasant quality or emotion). **plumbing** n pipes and fixtures used in water and drainage systems. **plumb in** v connect (an appliance such as a washing machine) to a water supply. **plumb line** string with a weight at the end, used to test the depth of water or to test whether something is vertical.

plumber n person who fits and repairs pipes and fixtures for water and drainage systems.

plume n feather, esp. one worn as an ornament.

plummet v -**meting, -meted.** plunge downward.

plump[1] adj moderately or attractively fat. **plumpness** n **plump up** v make (a pillow) fuller or rounded.

plump[2] v sit or fall heavily and suddenly. **plump for** v choose, vote for.

plunder v take by force, esp. in time of war. ▶ n things plundered, spoils.

plunge v put or throw forcibly or suddenly (into); descend steeply. ▶ n plunging, dive. **take the plunge** *Informal* embark on a risky enterprise. **plunger** n rubber suction cup used to clear blocked pipes. **plunge into** v become deeply involved in.

plunket baby n *NZ* baby brought up on the diet recommended by the Plunket Society. **plunket nurse** *NZ* nurse working for the Plunket Society.

pluperfect n, adj Grammar (tense) expressing an action completed before a past time, e.g. had gone in his wife had gone already.

plural adj of or consisting of more than one. ▶ n word indicating more than one.

pluralism n existence and toleration of a variety of peoples, opinions, etc. in a society. **pluralist** n **pluralistic** adj

plus prep, adj indicating addition. ▶ adj more than zero; positive; advantageous. ▶ n sign (+) denoting addition; advantage.

plus fours pl n trousers gathered in just below the knee.

plush n fabric with long velvety pile. ▶ adj (also **plushy**) luxurious.

Pluto n Greek god of the underworld; farthest planet from the sun.

plutocrat n person who is powerful because of being very rich. **plutocratic** adj

plutonium n Chem radioactive metallic element used esp. in nuclear reactors and weapons.

ply[1] v plying, plied. work at (a job or trade); use (a tool); (of a ship) travel regularly along or between. **ply with** v supply with or subject to persistently.

ply[2] n thickness of wool, fabric, etc.

plywood n board made of thin

layers of wood glued together.

PM prime minister.

p.m. after noon; postmortem.

PMT premenstrual tension.

pneumatic adj worked by or inflated with wind or air.

pneumonia n inflammation of the lungs.

PO Brit postal order; Post Office.

poach¹ v catch (animals) illegally on someone else's land; encroach on or steal something belonging to someone else.

poach² v simmer (food) gently in liquid.

poacher n person who catches animals illegally on someone else's land.

pocket n small bag sewn into clothing for carrying things; pouchlike container, esp. for catching balls at the edge of a snooker table; isolated or distinct group or area. ▶ v **pocketing, pocketed.** put into one's pocket; take secretly or dishonestly. ▶ adj small. **out of pocket** having made a loss. **pocket money** small regular allowance given to children by parents; money for small personal expenses.

pockmarked adj (of the skin) marked with hollow scars where diseased spots have been.

pod n long narrow seed case of peas, beans, etc.

podgy adj **podgier, podgiest.** short and fat.

podium n, pl **-diums, -dia.** small raised platform for a conductor or speaker.

poem n imaginative piece of writing in rhythmic lines.

poesy n Obs poetry.

poet n writer of poems. **poetry** n poems; art of writing poems; beautiful or pleasing quality.

poetic, poetical adj of or like

poetry. **poetically** adv **poetic justice** suitable reward or punishment for someone's past actions. **poet laureate** poet appointed by the British sovereign to write poems on important occasions.

pogrom n organized persecution and massacre.

poignant adj sharply painful to the feelings. **poignancy** n

poinsettia n Central American shrub widely grown for its clusters of scarlet leaves, which resemble petals.

point n main idea in a discussion, argument, etc.; aim or purpose; detail or item; characteristic; particular position, stage, or time; dot indicating decimals; sharp end; unit for recording a value or score; one of the direction marks of a compass; electrical socket. ▶ v show the direction or position of something or draw attention to it by extending a finger or other pointed object towards it; direct or face towards. **on the point of** very shortly going to. **pointed** adj having a sharp end; (of a remark) obviously directed at a particular person. **pointedly** adv **pointer** n helpful hint; indicator on a measuring instrument; breed of gun dog. **pointless** adj meaningless, irrelevant.

point-blank adj fired at a very close target; (of a remark or question) direct, blunt. ▶ adv directly or bluntly. **point duty** control of traffic by a policeman at a road junction. **point of view** way of considering something.

point-to-point n Brit horse race across open country.

poise n calm dignified manner. **poised** adj absolutely ready; behaving with or showing poise.

poison n substance that kills or injures when swallowed or absorbed. ▸ v give poison to; have a harmful or evil effect on, spoil. **poisoner** n **poisonous** adj **poison-pen letter** malicious anonymous letter.

poke v jab or prod with one's finger, a stick, etc.; thrust forward or out. ▸ n poking. **poky** adj small and cramped.

poker[1] n metal rod for stirring a fire.

poker[2] n card game in which players bet on the hands dealt. **poker-faced** adj expressionless.

polar adj of or near either of the earth's poles. **polar bear** white bear that lives in the regions around the North Pole.

polarize v form or cause to form into groups with directly opposite views; Physics restrict (light waves) to certain directions of vibration. **polarization** n

Polaroid n ® plastic which polarizes light and so reduces glare; camera that develops a print very quickly inside itself.

polder n land reclaimed from the sea, esp. in the Netherlands.

pole[1] n long rounded piece of wood etc.

pole[2] n point furthest north or south on the earth's axis of rotation; either of the opposite ends of a magnet or electric cell. **Pole Star** star nearest to the North Pole in the northern hemisphere.

poleaxe v hit or stun with a heavy blow.

polecat n small animal of the weasel family.

polemic [pol-**em**-ik] n fierce attack on or defence of a particular opinion, belief, etc. **polemical** adj

police n organized force in a state which keeps law and order. ▸ v control or watch over with police or a similar body. **policeman**, **policewoman** n member of a police force.

policy[1] n, pl -**cies**. plan of action adopted by a person, group, or state.

policy[2] n, pl -**cies**. document containing an insurance contract.

polio n disease affecting the spinal cord, which often causes paralysis (also **poliomyelitis**).

polish v make smooth and shiny by rubbing; make more nearly perfect. ▸ n substance used for polishing; pleasing elegant style. **polished** adj accomplished; done or performed well or professionally. **polish off** v finish completely, dispose of.

polite adj showing consideration for others in one's manners, speech, etc.; socially correct or refined. **politely** adv **politeness** n

politic adj wise and likely to prove advantageous.

politics n winning and using of power to govern society; (study of) the art of government; person's beliefs about how a country should be governed. **political** adj of the state, government, or public administration. **politically** adv **politically correct** (of language) intended to avoid any implied prejudice. **political prisoner** person imprisoned because of his or her political beliefs. **politician** n person actively engaged in politics, esp. a member of parliament.

polka n lively 19th-century dance; music for this. **polka dots** pattern of bold spots on fabric.

poll n (also **opinion poll**) questioning of a random sample

of people to find out general opinion; voting; number of votes recorded. ▶ v receive (votes); question in an opinion poll.
pollster n person who conducts opinion polls. **polling station** building where people vote in an election.
pollarded adj (of a tree) growing very bushy because its top branches have been cut short.
pollen n fine dust produced by flowers to fertilize other flowers. **pollinate** v fertilize with pollen. **pollen count** measure of the amount of pollen in the air, esp. as a warning to people with hay fever.
pollute v contaminate with something poisonous or harmful. **pollution** n **pollutant** n something that pollutes.
polo n game like hockey played by teams of players on horseback. **polo neck** sweater with high turned-over collar.
polonaise n old stately dance; music for this.
polonium n Chem radioactive element that occurs in trace amounts in uranium ores.
poltergeist n spirit believed to move furniture and throw objects around.
poltroon n Obs utter coward.
poly- combining form many, much
polyandry n practice of having more than one husband at the same time.
polyanthus n garden primrose.
polychromatic adj many-coloured.
polyester n synthetic material used to make plastics and textile fibres.
polygamy [pol-**ig**-a-mee] n practice of having more than one husband or wife at the same time. **polygamous** adj **polygamist** n

polyglot n, adj (person) able to speak or write several languages.
polygon n geometrical figure with three or more angles and sides. **polygonal** adj
polyhedron n, pl **-drons, -dra.** solid figure with four or more sides.
polymer n chemical compound with large molecules made of simple molecules of the same kind. **polymerize** v form into polymers. **polymerization** n
polyp n small simple sea creature with a hollow cylindrical body; small growth on a mucous membrane.
polyphonic adj Music consisting of several melodies played simultaneously.
polystyrene n synthetic material used esp. as white rigid foam for packing and insulation.
polytechnic n (in New Zealand and formerly in Britain) college offering courses in many subjects at and below degree level.
polytheism n belief in many gods. **polytheistic** adj
polythene n light plastic used for bags etc.
polyunsaturated adj of a group of fats that do not form cholesterol in the blood.
polyurethane n synthetic material used esp. in paints.
pom n Aust & NZ slang person from England (also **pommy**).
pomander n (container for) a mixture of sweet-smelling petals, herbs, etc.
pomegranate n round tropical fruit with a thick rind containing many seeds in a red pulp.
Pomeranian n small dog with long straight hair.
pommel n raised part on the front of a saddle; knob at the top of a

sword hilt.

pomp n stately display or ceremony.

pompom n decorative ball of tufted wool, silk, etc.

pompous adj foolishly serious and grand, self-important. **pompously** adv **pomposity** n

poncho n, pl **-chos.** loose circular cloak with a hole for the head.

pond n small area of still water.

ponder v think thoroughly or deeply (about).

ponderous adj serious and dull; heavy and unwieldy; (of movement) slow and clumsy. **ponderously** adv

pong v, n Informal (give off) a strong unpleasant smell.

pontiff n the Pope. **pontificate** v state one's opinions as if they were the only possible correct ones. ▶ n period of office of a Pope.

pontoon[1] n floating platform supporting a temporary bridge.

pontoon[2] n gambling card game.

pony n, pl **ponies.** small horse. **ponytail** n long hair tied in one bunch at the back of the head.

poodle n dog with curly hair often clipped fancifully.

pool[1] n small body of still water; puddle of spilt liquid; swimming pool.

pool[2] n shared fund or group of workers or resources; game like snooker. ▶ pl Brit short for FOOTBALL POOLS. ▶ v put in a common fund.

poop n raised part at the back of a sailing ship.

poor adj having little money and few possessions; less, smaller, or weaker than is needed or expected; inferior; unlucky, pitiable. **poorly** adv in a poor manner. ▶ adj not in good health.

pop[1] v **popping, popped.** make or cause to make a small explosive sound; Informal go, put, or come unexpectedly or suddenly. ▶ n small explosive sound; Brit nonalcoholic fizzy drink. **popcorn** n grains of maize heated until they puff up and burst.

pop[2] n music of general appeal, esp. to young people.

pop[3] n Informal father.

Pope n head of the Roman Catholic Church.

poplar n tall slender tree.

poplin n ribbed cotton material.

poppadom n thin round crisp Indian bread.

poppy n, pl **-pies.** plant with a large red flower.

populace n the ordinary people.

popular adj widely liked and admired; of or for the public in general. **popularly** adv **popularity** n **popularize** v make popular; make (something technical or specialist) easily understood.

populate v live in, inhabit; fill with inhabitants. **populous** adj densely populated.

population n all the people who live in a particular place; the number of people living in a particular place.

porbeagle n kind of shark.

porcelain n fine china; objects made of it.

porch n covered approach to the entrance of a building.

porcine adj of or like a pig.

porcupine n animal covered with long pointed quills.

pore n tiny opening in the skin or in the surface of a plant.

pork n pig meat. **porker** n pig raised for food.

porn, porno n, adj Informal short for PORNOGRAPHY or PORNOGRAPHIC.

pornography n writing, films, or

pictures designed to be sexually exciting. **pornographer** n producer of pornography. **pornographic** adj

porous adj allowing liquid to pass through gradually. **porosity** n

porphyry [por-fir-ee] n reddish rock with large crystals in it.

porpoise n fishlike sea mammal.

porridge n breakfast food made of oatmeal cooked in water or milk; *Chiefly Brit slang* term in prison.

port[1] n (town with) a harbour.

port[2] n left side of a ship or aircraft when facing the front of it.

port[3] n strong sweet wine, usu. red.

port[4] n opening in the side of a ship; porthole.

portable adj easily carried. **portability** n

portal n large imposing doorway or gate.

portcullis n grating suspended above a castle gateway, that can be lowered to block the entrance.

portend v be a sign of.

portent n sign of a future event. **portentous** adj of great or ominous significance; pompous, self-important.

porter[1] n man who carries luggage; hospital worker who transfers patients between rooms etc.

porter[2] n doorman or gatekeeper of a building.

portfolio n, pl -os. (flat case for carrying) examples of an artist's work; area of responsibility of a government minister; list of investments held by an investor.

porthole n small round window in a ship or aircraft.

portico n, pl -coes, -cos. porch or covered walkway with columns supporting the roof.

portion n part or share; helping of food for one person; destiny or

fate. **portion out** v divide into shares.

portly adj -lier, -liest. rather fat.

portmanteau n, pl -teaus, -teaux. *Old-fashioned* large suitcase that opens into two compartments. ▶ adj combining aspects of different things.

portrait n picture of a person; lifelike description.

portray v describe or represent by artistic means, as in writing or film. **portrayal** n

Portuguese adj of Portugal, its people, or their language. ▶ n person from Portugal; language of Portugal and Brazil. **Portuguese man-of-war** sea creature resembling a jellyfish, with stinging tentacles.

pose v place in or take up a particular position to be photographed or drawn; raise (a problem); ask (a question). ▶ n position while posing; behaviour adopted for effect. **pose as** pretend to be. **poser** n puzzling question; poseur n **poseur** n person who behaves in an affected way to impress others.

posh adj *Informal* smart, luxurious; affectedly upper-class.

posit [pozz-it] v lay down as a basis for argument.

position n place; usual or expected place; way in which something is placed or arranged; attitude, point of view; social standing; job. ▶ v place.

positive adj feeling no doubts, certain; confident; hopeful; helpful, providing encouragement; absolute, downright; *Maths* greater than zero; (of an electrical charge) having a deficiency of electrons. **positively** adv

positive discrimination provision of special opportunities for a disadvantaged group.

positron n Physics particle with same mass as electron but positive charge.

posse [poss-ee] n US group of men organized to maintain law and order; Brit & Aust informal group of friends or associates.

possess v have as one's property; (of a feeling, belief, etc.) have complete control of, dominate. **possessor** n **possession** n state of possessing, ownership. ▶ pl things a person possesses.

possessive adj wanting all the attention or love of another person; (of a word) indicating the person or thing that something belongs to. **possessiveness** n

possible adj able to exist, happen, or be done; worthy of consideration. ▶ n person or thing that might be suitable or chosen. **possibility** n, pl **-ties**. **possibly** adv perhaps, not necessarily.

possum n same as OPOSSUM. **play possum** pretend to be dead or asleep to deceive an opponent.

post¹ n official system of delivering letters and parcels; (single collection or delivery of) letters and parcels sent by this system. ▶ v send by post. **keep someone posted** supply someone regularly with the latest information.

postage n charge for sending a letter or parcel by post. **postal** adj **postal order** Brit written money order sent by post and cashed at a post office by the person who receives it. **postbag** n postman's bag; post received by a magazine, famous person, etc. **postcode** n system of letters and numbers used to aid the sorting of mail. **postie** n Scot, Austral & NZ informal postman. **postman, postwoman** n person who collects

and delivers post. **postmark** n official mark stamped on letters showing place and date of posting. **postmaster, postmistress** n (in some countries) official in charge of a post office. **post office** place where postal business is conducted. **post shop** NZ shop providing postal services.

post² n length of wood, concrete, etc. fixed upright to support or mark something. ▶ v put up (a notice) in a public place.

post³ n job; position to which someone, esp. a soldier, is assigned for duty; military establishment. ▶ v send (a person) to a new place to work; put (a guard etc.) on duty.

post- prefix after, later than, e.g. postwar.

postcard n card for sending a message by post without an envelope.

postdate v write a date on (a cheque) that is later than the actual date.

poster n large picture or notice stuck on a wall.

posterior n buttocks. ▶ adj behind, at the back of.

posterity n future generations, descendants.

postern n small back door or gate.

postgraduate n person with a degree who is studying for a more advanced qualification.

posthaste adv with great speed.

posthumous [poss-tume-uss] adj occurring after one's death. **posthumously** adv

postilion, postillion n Hist person riding one of a pair of horses drawing a carriage.

postmortem n medical examination of a body to establish the cause of death.

postnatal adj occurring after childbirth.

postpone v put off to a later time. **postponement** n

postscript n passage added at the end of a letter.

postulant n candidate for admission to a religious order.

postulate v assume to be true as the basis of an argument or theory.

posture n position or way in which someone stands, walks, etc. ▶ v behave in an exaggerated way to get attention.

posy n, pl -**sies.** small bunch of flowers.

pot¹ n round deep container; teapot. ▶ pl Informal large amount. ▶ v **potting, potted.** plant in a pot; Snooker hit (a ball) into a pocket. **potted** adj grown in a pot; (of meat or fish) cooked or preserved in a pot; Informal abridged. **pot shot** shot taken without aiming carefully. **potting shed** shed where plants are potted.

pot² n Slang cannabis.

potable [**pote**-a-bl] adj drinkable.

potash n white powdery substance obtained from ashes and used as fertilizer.

potassium n Chem silvery metallic element.

potato n, pl -**toes.** roundish starchy vegetable that grows underground.

poteen n (in Ireland) illegally made alcoholic drink.

potent adj having great power or influence; (of a male) capable of having sexual intercourse. **potency** n

potentate n ruler or monarch.

potential adj possible but not yet actual. ▶ n ability or talent not yet fully used; Electricity level of electric pressure. **potentially** adv

potentiality n, pl -**ties.**

pothole n hole in the surface of a road; deep hole in a limestone area. **potholing** n sport of exploring underground caves. **potholer** n

potion n dose of medicine or poison.

potluck n **take potluck** accept whatever happens to be available.

potpourri [po-**poor**-ee] n fragrant mixture of dried flower petals; assortment or medley.

pottage n Old-fashioned thick soup or stew.

potter¹ n person who makes pottery.

potter² v be busy in a pleasant but aimless way.

pottery n, pl -**ries.** articles made from baked clay; place where they are made.

potty¹ adj -**tier, -tiest.** Informal crazy or silly.

potty² n, pl -**ties.** bowl used by a small child as a toilet.

pouch n small bag; baglike pocket of skin on an animal.

pouf, pouffe [poof] n large solid cushion used as a seat.

poulterer n Brit person who sells poultry.

poultice [**pole**-tiss] n moist dressing, often heated, applied to inflamed skin.

poultry n domestic fowls.

pounce v spring upon suddenly to attack or capture. ▶ n pouncing.

pound¹ n monetary unit of Britain and some other countries; unit of weight equal to 0.454 kg.

pound² v hit heavily and repeatedly; crush to pieces or powder; (of the heart) throb heavily; run heavily.

pound³ n enclosure for stray animals or officially removed vehicles.

pour v flow or cause to flow out in a stream; rain heavily; come or go in large numbers.

pout v thrust out one's lips, look sulky. ▶ n pouting look.

poverty n state of being without enough food or money; lack of, scarcity.

POW prisoner of war.

powder n substance in the form of tiny loose particles; medicine or cosmetic in this form. ▶ v apply powder to. **powdered** adj in the form of a powder, e.g. *powdered milk*. **powdery** adj **powder room** ladies' toilet.

power n ability to do or act; strength; position of authority or control; *Maths* product from continuous multiplication of a number by itself; *Physics* rate at which work is done; electricity supply; particular form of energy, e.g. *nuclear power*. **powered** adj having or operated by mechanical or electrical power. **powerful** adj **powerless** adj **power cut** temporary interruption in the supply of electricity. **power point** socket on a wall for plugging in electrical appliances. **power station** installation for generating and distributing electric power.

powwow n *Informal* talk or conference.

pox n disease in which skin pustules form; *Informal* syphilis.

pp (in signing a document) for and on behalf of.

pp. pages.

PPTA (in New Zealand) Post Primary Teachers Association.

PR proportional representation; public relations.

practicable adj capable of being done successfully; usable. **practicability** n

practical adj involving experience or actual use rather than theory; sensible, useful, and effective; good at making or doing things; in effect though not in name. ▶ n examination in which something has to be done or made. **practically** adv **practical joke** trick intended to make someone look foolish.

practice n something done regularly or habitually; repetition of something so as to gain skill; doctor's or lawyer's place of work. **in practice** what actually happens as distinct from what is supposed to happen. **put into practice** carry out, do.

practise v do repeatedly so as to gain skill; take part in, follow (a religion etc.); work at, e.g. *practise medicine*; do habitually.

practitioner n person who practises a profession.

pragmatic adj concerned with practical consequences rather than theory. **pragmatism** n **pragmatist** n

prairie n large treeless area of grassland, esp. in N America and Canada. **prairie dog** rodent that lives in burrows in the N American prairies.

praise v express approval or admiration of (someone or something); express honour and thanks to (one's God). ▶ n something said or written to show approval or admiration. **sing someone's praises** praise someone highly. **praiseworthy** adj

praline [prah-leen] n sweet made of nuts and caramelized sugar.

pram n four-wheeled carriage for a baby, pushed by hand.

prance v walk with exaggerated bouncing steps.

prang v, n *Slang* (have) a crash in a car or aircraft.

prank n mischievous trick.

prat n Brit, Aust & NZ informal stupid person.

prattle v chatter in a childish or foolish way. ▶ n childish or foolish talk.

prawn n edible shellfish like a large shrimp.

praxis n practice as opposed to theory.

pray v say prayers; ask earnestly, entreat.

prayer n thanks or appeal addressed to one's God; set form of words used in praying; earnest request.

pre- prefix before, beforehand, e.g. prenatal; prerecorded; preshrunk.

preach v give a talk on a religious theme as part of a church service; speak in support of (an idea, principle, etc.).

preacher n person who preaches, esp. in church.

preamble n introductory part to something said or written.

prearranged adj arranged beforehand.

prebendary n, pl -daries. clergyman who is a member of the chapter of a cathedral.

precarious adj insecure, unsafe, likely to fall or collapse. **precariously** adv

precaution n action taken in advance to prevent something bad happening. **precautionary** adj

precede v go or be before. **precedence** [press-ee-denss] n formal order of rank or position. **take precedence over** be more important than. **precedent** n previous case or occurrence regarded as an example to be followed.

precentor n person who leads the singing in a church.

precept n rule of behaviour.

preceptive adj

precinct n Brit, Aust & S Afr area in a town closed to traffic; Brit, Aust & S Afr enclosed area round a building; US administrative area of a city. ▶ pl surrounding region.

precious adj of great value and importance; loved and treasured; (of behaviour) affected, unnatural. **precious metal** gold, silver, or platinum. **precious stone** rare mineral, such as a ruby, valued as a gem.

precipice n very steep face of cliff or rockface. **precipitous** adj sheer.

precipitate v cause to happen suddenly; Chem cause to be deposited in solid form from a solution; throw headlong. ▶ adj done rashly or hastily. ▶ n Chem substance precipitated from a solution. **precipitately** adv **precipitation** n precipitating; rain, snow, etc.

précis [pray-see] n, pl précis. short written summary of a longer piece. ▶ v make a précis of.

precise adj exact, accurate in every detail; strict in observing rules or standards. **precisely** adv **precision** n

preclude v make impossible to happen.

precocious adj having developed or matured early or too soon. **precocity** n

precognition n alleged ability to foretell the future.

preconceived adj (of an idea) formed without real experience or reliable information. **preconception** n

precondition n something that must happen or exist before something else can.

precursor n something that precedes and is a signal of something else, forerunner;

predecessor.

predate v occur at an earlier date than; write a date on (a document) that is earlier than the actual date.

predatory [pred-a-tree] adj habitually hunting and killing other animals for food. **predator** n predatory animal.

predecease v die before (someone else).

predecessor n person who precedes another in an office or position; ancestor.

predestination n Theology belief that future events have already been decided by God or fate. **predestined** adj

predetermined adj decided in advance.

predicament n embarrassing or difficult situation.

predicate n Grammar part of a sentence in which something is said about the subject, e.g. went home in I went home. ▶ v declare or assert.

predict v tell about in advance, prophesy. **predictable** adj **prediction** n

predilection n Formal preference or liking.

predispose v influence (someone) in favour of something; make (someone) susceptible to something. **predisposition** n

predominate v be the main or controlling element. **predominance** n **predominant** adj **predominantly** adv

pre-eminent adj excelling all others, outstanding. **pre-eminence** n

pre-empt v prevent an action by doing something which makes it pointless or impossible. **pre-emption** n **pre-emptive** adj

preen v (of a bird) clean or trim (feathers) with the beak. **preen oneself** smarten oneself; show self-satisfaction.

prefab n prefabricated house.

prefabricated adj (of a building) manufactured in shaped sections for rapid assembly on site.

preface [pref-iss] n introduction to a book. ▶ v serve as an introduction to (a book, speech, etc.). **prefatory** adj

prefect n senior pupil in a school, with limited power over others; senior administrative officer in some countries. **prefecture** n office or area of authority of a prefect.

prefer v -ferring, -ferred. like better; Law bring (charges) before a court. **preferable** adj more desirable. **preferably** adv **preference** n **preferential** adj showing preference. **preferment** n promotion or advancement.

prefigure v represent or suggest in advance.

prefix n letter or group of letters put at the beginning of a word to make a new word, such as un- in unhappy. ▶ v put as an introduction or prefix (to).

pregnant adj carrying a fetus in the womb; full of meaning or significance, e.g. a pregnant pause. **pregnancy** n, pl **-cies**.

prehensile adj capable of grasping.

prehistoric adj of the period before written history begins. **prehistory** n

prejudice n unreasonable or unfair dislike or preference. ▶ v cause (someone) to have a prejudice; harm, cause disadvantage to. **prejudicial** adj disadvantageous, harmful.

prelate [prel-it] n bishop or other churchman of high rank.

preliminary adj happening before

and in preparation, introductory.
▶ *n*, *pl* **-naries.** preliminary remark, contest, etc.

prelude *n* introductory movement in music; event preceding and introducing something else.

premarital *adj* occurring before marriage.

premature *adj* happening or done before the normal or expected time; (of a baby) born before the end of the normal period of pregnancy. **prematurely** *adv*

premeditated *adj* planned or in advance. **premeditation** *n*

premenstrual *adj* occurring or experienced before a menstrual period, as in **premenstrual tension.**

premier *n* prime minister. ▶ *adj* chief, leading. **premiership** *n*

première *n* first performance of a play, film, etc.

premise, premiss *n* statement assumed to be true and used as the basis of reasoning.

premises *pl n* house or other building and its land.

premium *n* additional sum of money, as on a wage or charge; (regular) sum paid for insurance. **at a premium** in great demand because scarce. **premium bonds** (in Britain) savings certificates issued by the government, on which no interest is paid but cash prizes can be won.

premonition *n* feeling that something unpleasant is going to happen; foreboding. **premonitory** *adj*

prenatal *adj* before birth, during pregnancy.

preoccupy *v* **-pying, -pied.** fill the thoughts or attention of (someone) to the exclusion of other things. **preoccupation** *n*

preordained *adj* decreed or determined in advance.

prep. preparatory; preposition.

prepacked *adj* sold already wrapped.

prepaid *adj* paid for in advance.

prepare *v* make or get ready. **prepared** *adj* willing; ready.

preparation *n* preparing; something done in readiness for something else; mixture prepared for use as a cosmetic, medicine, etc. **preparatory** [prip-par-a-tree] *adj* preparing for. **preparatory school** *Brit & S Afr* private school for children between 7 and 13.

preponderance *n* greater force, amount, or influence.

preponderant *adj*

preposition *n* word used before a noun or pronoun to show its relationship with other words, such as *by* in *go by bus.* **prepositional** *adj*

prepossessing *adj* making a favourable impression, attractive.

preposterous *adj* utterly absurd.

prep school *n* short for PREPARATORY SCHOOL.

prepuce [**pree**-pyewss] *n* retractable fold of skin covering the tip of the penis, foreskin.

prerecorded *adj* recorded in advance to be played or broadcast later.

prerequisite *n*, *adj* (something) required before something else is possible.

prerogative *n* special power or privilege.

presage [**press**-ij] *v* be a sign or warning of.

Presbyterian *n*, *adj* (member) of a Protestant church governed by lay elders. **Presbyterianism** *n*

presbytery *n*, *pl* **-teries.** *Presbyterian Church* local church court; *RC Church* priest's house.

prescience [**press**-ee-enss] *n* knowledge of events before they happen. **prescient** adj

prescribe v recommend the use of (a medicine); lay down as a rule. **prescription** n written instructions from a doctor for the making up and use of a medicine. **prescriptive** adj laying down rules.

presence n fact of being in a specified place; impressive dignified appearance. **presence of mind** ability to act sensibly in a crisis.

present[1] adj being in a specified place; existing or happening now; Grammar (of a verb tense) indicating that the action specified is taking place now. ▶ n present time or tense. **presently** adv soon; US & Scot now.

present[2] n something given to bring pleasure to another person. ▶ v introduce formally or publicly; introduce and compere (a TV or radio show); cause, e.g. present a difficulty; give, award. **presentation** n **presentable** adj attractive, neat, fit for people to see. **presenter** n person introducing a TV or radio show.

presentiment [priz-**zen**-tim-ent] n sense of something unpleasant about to happen.

preserve v keep from being damaged, changed, or ended; treat (food) to prevent it decaying. ▶ n area of interest restricted to a particular person or group; fruit preserved by cooking in sugar; area where game is kept for private hunting or fishing. **preservation** n **preservative** n chemical that prevents decay.

preshrunk adj (of fabric or a garment) having been shrunk during manufacture so that further shrinkage will not occur when washed.

preside v be in charge, esp. of a

meeting.

president n head of state in many countries; head of a society, institution, etc. **presidential** adj **presidency** n, pl **-cies.**

press[1] v apply force or weight to; squeeze; smooth by applying pressure or heat; urge insistently; crowd, push. ▶ n printing machine. **pressed for** short of. **pressing** adj urgent. **press box** room at a sports ground reserved for reporters. **press conference** interview for reporters given by a celebrity.

press[2] v **press into service** force to be involved or used. **press gang** Hist group of men used to capture men and boys and force them to join the navy.

pressure n force produced by pressing; urgent claims or demands; Physics force applied to a surface per unit of area. **pressure cooker** airtight pot which cooks food quickly by steam under pressure. **pressure group** group that tries to influence policies, public opinion, etc.

prestidigitation n skilful quickness with the hands, conjuring.

prestige n high status or respect resulting from success or achievements. **prestigious** adj

presto adv Music very quickly.

prestressed adj (of concrete) containing stretched steel wires to strengthen it.

presume v suppose to be the case; dare (to). **presumably** adv one supposes (that). **presumption** n bold insolent behaviour; strong probability. **presumptive** adj assumed to be true or valid until the contrary is proved. **presumptuous** adj doing things one has no right to do.

presuppose v need as a previous condition in order to be true. **presupposition** n

pretend v claim or give the appearance of (something untrue) to deceive or in play. **pretender** n person who makes a false or disputed claim to a position of power. **pretence** n behaviour intended to deceive, pretending. **pretentious** adj making (unjustified) claims to special merit or importance. **pretension** n

preternatural adj beyond what is natural, supernatural.

pretext n false reason given to hide the real one.

pretty adj **-tier, -tiest.** pleasing to look at. ▶ adv fairly, moderately, e.g. I'm pretty certain. **prettily** adv **prettiness** n

pretzel n brittle salted biscuit.

prevail v gain mastery; be generally established. **prevailing** adj widespread; predominant. **prevalence** n **prevalent** adj widespread, common.

prevaricate v avoid giving a direct or truthful answer. **prevarication** n

prevent v keep from happening or doing. **preventable** adj **prevention** n **preventive** adj, n

preview n advance showing of a film or exhibition before it is shown to the public.

previous adj coming or happening before. **previously** adv

prey n animal hunted and killed for food by another animal; victim. **bird of prey** bird that kills and eats other birds or animals. **prey on** v hunt and kill for food; worry, obsess.

price n amount of money for which a thing is bought or sold; unpleasant thing that must be endured to get something desirable. ▶ v fix or ask the price

of. **priceless** adj very valuable; Informal very funny. **pricey** adj **pricier, priciest.** Informal expensive.

prick v pierce lightly with a sharp point; cause to feel mental pain; (of an animal) make (the ears) stand erect. ▶ n sudden sharp pain caused by pricking; mark made by pricking; remorse. **prick up one's ears** listen intently.

prickle n thorn or spike on a plant. ▶ v have a tingling or pricking sensation. **prickly** adj **prickly heat** itchy rash occurring in hot moist weather.

pride n feeling of pleasure and satisfaction when one has done well; too high an opinion of oneself; sense of dignity and self-respect; something that causes one to feel pride; group of lions. **pride of place** most important position. **pride oneself on** feel pride about.

priest n (in the Christian church) a person who can administer the sacraments and preach; (in some other religions) an official who performs religious ceremonies. **priestess** n fem **priesthood** n **priestly** adj

prig n self-righteous person who acts as if superior to others. **priggish** adj **priggishness** n

prim adj **primmer, primmest.** formal, proper, and rather prudish. **primly** adv

prima ballerina n leading female ballet dancer.

primacy n, pl **-cies.** state of being first in rank, grade, etc.; office of an archbishop.

prima donna n leading female opera singer; Informal temperamental person.

primaeval adj same as PRIMEVAL.

prima facie [prime-a fay-shee] adv

Latin as it seems at first.

primal *adj* of basic causes or origins.

primary *adj* chief, most important; being the first stage, elementary. **primarily** *adv* **primary colours** (in physics) red, green, and blue or (in art) red, yellow, and blue, from which all other colours can be produced by mixing. **primary school** school for children from five to eleven years or (in New Zealand) between five to thirteen years.

primate[1] *n* member of an order of mammals including monkeys and humans.

primate[2] *n* archbishop.

prime *adj* main, most important; of the highest quality. ▶ *n* time when someone is at his or her best or most vigorous. ▶ *v* give (someone) information in advance to prepare them for something; prepare (a surface) for painting; prepare (a gun, pump, etc.) for use. **primer** *n* special paint applied to bare wood etc. before the main paint. **Prime Minister** leader of a government. **prime number** number that can be divided exactly only by itself and one.

primer *n* beginners' school book or manual.

primeval [prime-ee-val] *adj* of the earliest age of the world.

primitive *adj* of an early simple stage of development; basic, crude.

primogeniture *n* system under which the eldest son inherits all his parents' property.

primordial *adj* existing at or from the beginning.

primrose *n* pale yellow spring flower.

primula *n* type of primrose with brightly coloured flowers.

Primus *n* ® portable cooking stove used esp. by campers.

prince *n* male member of a royal family, the son of the king or queen; male ruler of a small country. **princely** *adj* of or like a prince; generous, lavish, or magnificent. **prince consort** husband of a reigning queen. **Prince of Wales** eldest son of the British sovereign. **princess** *n* female member of a royal family, esp. the daughter of the king or queen. **Princess Royal** title sometimes given to the eldest daughter of the British sovereign.

principal *adj* main, most important. ▶ *n* head of a school or college; person taking a leading part in something; sum of money lent on which interest is paid. **principally** *adv* **principal boy** *Brit* leading male role in pantomime, played by a woman.

principality *n, pl* **-ties.** territory ruled by a prince.

principle *n* moral rule guiding behaviour; general or basic truth; scientific law concerning the working of something. **in principle** in theory but not always in practice. **on principle** because of one's beliefs.

print *v* reproduce (a newspaper, book, etc.) in large quantities by mechanical or electronic means; reproduce (text or pictures) by pressing ink onto paper etc.; write in letters that are not joined up; stamp (fabric) with a design; *Photog* produce (pictures) from negatives. ▶ *n* printed words etc.; printed copy of a painting; printed lettering; photograph; printed fabric; mark left on a surface by something that has pressed against it. **out of print** no longer available from a publisher. **printer** n person or company engaged in printing; machine that prints. **printing** n **printed circuit** electronic circuit with wiring printed on an insulating base. **print-out** n printed information from a computer.

prior[1] adj earlier. **prior to** before.

prior[2] n head monk in a priory. **prioress** n deputy head nun in a convent. **priory** n, pl **-ries**. place where certain orders of monks or nuns live.

priority n, pl **-ties**. most important thing that must be dealt with first; right to be or go before others.

prise v force open by levering.

prism n transparent block usu. with triangular ends and rectangular sides, used to disperse light into a spectrum or refract it in optical instruments. **prismatic** adj of or shaped like a prism; (of colour) as if produced by refraction through a prism, rainbow-like.

prison n building where criminals and accused people are held. **prisoner** n person held captive. **prisoner of war** serviceman captured by an enemy in wartime.

prissy adj **-sier, -siest**. prim, correct, and easily shocked. **prissily** adv

pristine adj clean, new, and unused.

private adj for the use of one person or group only; secret; personal, unconnected with one's work; owned or paid for by individuals rather than by the government; quiet, not likely to be disturbed. ▶ n soldier of the lowest rank. **privately** adv **privacy** n

privateer n Hist privately owned armed vessel authorized by the government to take part in a war; captain of such a ship.

privation n loss or lack of the necessities of life.

privatize v sell (a publicly owned company) to individuals or a private company. **privatization** n

privet n bushy evergreen shrub used for hedges.

privilege n advantage or favour that only some people have. **privileged** adj enjoying a special right or immunity.

privy adj sharing knowledge of something secret. ▶ n, pl **privies**. Obs toilet, esp. an outside one. **Privy Council** private council of the British monarch.

prize[1] n reward given for success in a competition etc. ▶ adj winning or likely to win a prize. **prizefighter** n boxer who fights for money.

prize[2] v value highly.

prize[3] v same as PRISE.

pro[1] adv, prep in favour of. **pros and cons** arguments for and against.

pro[2] n, pl **pros**. Informal professional; prostitute.

pro- prefix in favour of, e.g. pro-Russian; instead of, e.g. pronoun.

probable adj likely to happen or be true. **probability** n, pl **-ties**. **probably** adv in all likelihood.

probate n process of proving the validity of a will; certificate stating that a will is genuine.

probation n system of dealing with law-breakers, esp. juvenile ones, by placing them under supervision; period when someone is assessed for suitability for a job etc. **probationer** n person on probation.

probe v search into or examine closely. ▶ n surgical instrument used to examine a wound, cavity, etc.

probity n honesty, integrity.

problem n something difficult to deal with or solve; question or puzzle set for solution.

problematic, problematical adj

proboscis [pro-boss-iss] n long trunk or snout; elongated mouth of some insects.

procedure n way of doing something, esp. the correct or usual one. **procedural** adj

proceed v start or continue doing; Formal walk, go; start a legal action; arise from. **proceeds** pl n money obtained from an event or activity. **proceedings** pl n organized or related series of events; minutes of a meeting; legal action.

process n series of actions or changes; method of doing or producing something. ▶ v handle or prepare by a special method of manufacture. **processed** adj (of food) treated to prevent it decaying. **processor** n

procession n line of people or vehicles moving forward together in order.

proclaim v declare publicly. **proclamation** n

proclivity n, pl -ties. inclination, tendency.

procrastinate v put off taking action, delay. **procrastination** n

procreate v Formal produce offspring. **procreation** n

procurator fiscal n (in Scotland) law officer who acts as public prosecutor and coroner.

procure v get, provide; obtain (people) to act as prostitutes. **procurement** n **procurer, procuress** n person who obtains people to act as prostitutes.

prod v **prodding, prodded.** poke

with something pointed; goad (someone) to take action. ▶ n prodding.

prodigal adj recklessly extravagant, wasteful. **prodigality** n

prodigy n, pl -gies. person with some marvellous talent; wonderful thing. **prodigious** adj very large, immense; wonderful. **prodigiously** adv

produce v bring into existence; present to view, show; make, manufacture; present on stage, film, or television. ▶ n food grown for sale. **producer** n person with control over the making of a film, record, etc.; person or company that produces something.

product n something produced; number resulting from multiplication. **production** n producing; things produced; presentation of a play, opera, etc. **productive** adj producing large quantities; useful, profitable. **productivity** n

profane adj showing disrespect for religion or holy things; (of language) coarse, blasphemous. ▶ v treat (something sacred) irreverently, desecrate. **profanation** n act of profaning. **profanity** n, pl -ties. profane talk or behaviour, blasphemy.

profess v state or claim (something as true), sometimes falsely; have as one's belief or religion. **professed** adj supposed.

profession n type of work, such as being a doctor, that needs special training; all the people employed in a profession, e.g. the legal profession; declaration of a belief or feeling. **professional** adj working in a profession; taking part in an activity, such as sport or music, for money; very competent. ▶ n person who works in a profession; person paid to take part in sport, music, etc. **professionally** adv **professionalism** n

professor n teacher of the highest rank in a university. **professorial** adj **professorship** n

proffer v offer.

proficient adj skilled, expert. **proficiency** n

profile n outline, esp. of the face, as seen from the side; brief biographical sketch.

profit n money gained; benefit obtained. ▶ v gain or benefit. **profitable** adj making profit. **profitably** adv **profitability** n

profiteer n person who makes excessive profits at the expense of the public. **profiteering** n

profligate adj recklessly extravagant; shamelessly immoral. ▶ n profligate person. **profligacy** n

pro forma adj Latin prescribing a set form.

profound adj showing or needing great knowledge; strongly felt, intense. **profundity** n, pl -ties.

profuse adj plentiful. **profusion** n

progeny [proj-in-ee] n, pl -nies. children. **progenitor** [pro-jen-it-er] n ancestor.

progesterone n hormone which prepares the womb for pregnancy and prevents further ovulation.

prognosis n, pl -noses. doctor's forecast about the progress of an illness; any forecast.

prognostication n forecast or prediction.

program n sequence of coded instructions for a computer. ▶ v -gramming, -grammed. arrange (data) so that it can be processed by a computer; feed a program into (a computer). **programmer** n **programmable** adj

programme n planned series of events; broadcast on radio or television; list of items or performers in an entertainment.

progress n improvement; development; movement forward. ▶ v become more advanced or skilful; move forward. **in progress** taking place. **progression** n

progressive adj favouring political or social reform; happening gradually. **progressively** adv

prohibit v forbid or prevent from happening. **prohibition** n act of forbidding; ban on the sale or drinking of alcohol. **prohibitive** adj (of prices) too high to be affordable. **prohibitively** adv

project n planned scheme to do or examine something over a period. ▶ v make a forecast based on known data; make (a film or slide) appear on a screen; communicate (an impression); stick out beyond a surface or edge. **projector** n apparatus for projecting photographic images, films, or slides on a screen. **projection** n **projectionist** n person who operates a projector.

projectile n object thrown as a weapon or fired from a gun.

prolapse n slipping down of an internal organ of the body from its normal position.

prole adj, n Chiefly Brit slang proletarian.

proletariat [pro-lit-air-ee-at] n working class. **proletarian** adj, n

proliferate v grow or reproduce rapidly. **proliferation** n

prolific adj very productive. **prolifically** adv

prolix adj (of speech or a piece of writing) overlong and boring.

prologue n introduction to a play or book.

prolong v make (something) last longer. **prolongation** n

prom n short for PROMENADE or PROMENADE CONCERT.

promenade n Chiefly Brit paved walkway along the seafront at a holiday resort. ▸ v, n Old-fashioned (take) a leisurely walk.

promenade concert Brit concert at which part of the audience stands rather than sits.

prominent adj very noticeable; famous, widely known. **prominently** adv **prominence** n

promiscuous adj having many casual sexual relationships. **promiscuity** n

promise v say that one will definitely do or not do something; show signs of, seem likely. ▸ n undertaking to do or not to do something; indication of future success. **promising** adj likely to succeed or turn out well.

promo n, pl **-mos.** Informal short film to promote a product.

promontory n, pl **-ries.** point of high land jutting out into the sea.

promote v help to make (something) happen or increase; raise to a higher rank or position; encourage the sale of by advertising. **promoter** n person who organizes or finances an event etc. **promotion** n **promotional** adj

prompt v cause (an action); remind (an actor or speaker) of words that he or she has forgotten. ▸ adj done without delay. ▸ adv exactly, e.g. six o'clock prompt. **promptly** adv immediately, without delay. **promptness** n **prompter, prompt** n person offstage who prompts actors.

promulgate v put (a law etc.) into effect by announcing it officially; make widely known. **promulgation** n

prone adj (foll. by to) likely to do or be affected by (something); lying face downwards.

prong n one spike of a fork or similar instrument. **pronged** adj

pronoun n word, such as she or it, used to replace a noun.

pronounce v form the sounds of (words or letters), esp. clearly or in a particular way; declare formally or officially. **pronounceable** adj **pronounced** adj very noticeable. **pronouncement** n formal announcement. **pronunciation** n way in which a word or language is pronounced.

pronto adv Informal at once.

proof n evidence that shows that something is true or has happened; copy of something printed, such as the pages of a book, for checking before final production. ▸ adj able to withstand, e.g. proof against criticism; denoting the strength of an alcoholic drink, e.g. seventy proof. **proofread** v read and correct (printer's proofs). **proofreader** n

prop¹ v **propping, propped.** support (something) so that it stays upright or in place. ▸ n pole, beam, etc. used as a support.

prop² n movable object used on the set of a film or play.

prop³ n Informal propeller.

propaganda n (organized promotion of) information to assist or damage the cause of a government or movement. **propagandist** n

propagate v spread (information and ideas); reproduce, breed, or grow. **propagation** n

propane n flammable gas found in petroleum and used as a fuel.

propel v **-pelling, -pelled.** cause to

move forward. **propellant** n something that provides or causes propulsion; gas used in an aerosol spray. **propulsion** n method by which something is propelled; act of propelling or state of being propelled.

propeller n revolving shaft with blades for driving a ship or aircraft.

propensity n, pl **-ties.** natural tendency.

proper adj real or genuine; suited to a particular purpose; correct in behaviour; excessively moral; Brit, Aust & NZ informal complete. **properly** adv

property n, pl **-ties.** something owned; possessions collectively; land or buildings owned by somebody; quality or attribute.

prophet n person supposedly chosen by God to spread His word; person who predicts the future. **prophetic** adj **prophetically** adv **prophecy** n, pl **-cies.** prediction; message revealing God's will. **prophesy** v **-sying, -sied.** foretell.

prophylactic n, adj (drug) used to prevent disease.

propitiate v appease, win the favour of. **propitiation** n **propitious** adj favourable or auspicious.

proponent n person who argues in favour of something.

proportion n relative size or extent; correct relation between connected parts; part considered with respect to the whole. ▶ pl dimensions or size. ▶ v adjust in relative amount or size. **in proportion** comparable in size, rate of increase, etc.; without exaggerating. **proportional, proportionate** adj being in proportion. **proportionally, proportionately** adv

propose v put forward for consideration; nominate; intend or plan (to do); make an offer of marriage. **proposal** n **proposition** n offer; statement or assertion; Maths theorem; Informal thing to be dealt with. ▶ v Informal ask (someone) to have sexual intercourse.

propound v put forward for consideration.

proprietor n owner of a business establishment. **proprietress** n fem **proprietary** adj made and distributed under a trade name; denoting or suggesting ownership.

propriety n, pl **-ties.** correct conduct.

propulsion n see PROPEL.

pro rata adv, adj Latin in proportion.

prorogue v suspend (parliament) without dissolving it. **prorogation** n

prosaic [pro-zay-ik] adj lacking imagination, dull. **prosaically** adv

proscenium n, pl **-nia, -niums.** arch in a theatre separating the stage from the auditorium.

proscribe v prohibit, outlaw. **proscription** n **proscriptive** adj

prose n ordinary speech or writing in contrast to poetry.

prosecute v bring a criminal charge against; continue to do. **prosecution** n **prosecutor** n

proselyte [pross-ill-ite] n recent convert.

proselytize [pross-ill-it-ize] v attempt to convert.

prospect n something anticipated; Old-fashioned view from a place. ▶ pl probability of future success. ▶ v explore, esp. for gold. **prospective** adj future; expected. **prospector** n **prospectus** n booklet giving details of a university, company, etc.

prosper v be successful.
  prosperity n success and wealth.
  prosperous adj
prostate n gland in male
  mammals that surrounds the neck
  of the bladder.
prosthesis [pross-**theess**-iss] n, pl
  -ses [-seez] artificial body part,
  such as a limb or breast.
  prosthetic adj
prostitute n person who offers
  sexual intercourse in return for
  payment. ▶ v make a prostitute of;
  offer (oneself or one's talents) for
  unworthy purposes. **prostitution** n
prostrate adj lying face
  downwards; physically or
  emotionally exhausted. ▶ v lie face
  downwards; exhaust physically or
  emotionally. **prostration** n
protagonist n supporter of a
  cause; leading character in a play
  or a story.
protea [**pro**-tee-a] n African shrub
  with showy flowers.
protean [pro-**tee**-an] adj
  constantly changing.
protect v defend from trouble,
  harm, or loss. **protection** n
  protectionism n policy of
  protecting industries by taxing
  competing imports. **protectionist**
  n, adj **protective** adj giving
  protection, e.g. protective clothing;
  tending or wishing to protect
  someone. **protector** n person or
  thing that protects; regent.
  protectorate n territory largely
  controlled by a stronger state;
  (period of) rule of a regent.
protégé, (fem) **protégée**
  [**pro**-ti-zhay] n person who is
  protected and helped by another.
protein n any of a group of
  complex organic compounds that
  are essential for life.
pro tempore adv, adj for the time
  being (also **pro tem**).

protest n declaration or
  demonstration of objection. ▶ v
  object, disagree; assert formally.
  protestation n strong declaration.
Protestant n follower of any of
  the Christian churches that split
  from the Roman Catholic Church
  in the sixteenth century. ▶ adj of
  or relating to such a church.
  Protestantism n
proto- combining form first, e.g.
  protohuman.
protocol n rules of behaviour for
  formal occasions.
proton n positively charged
  particle in the nucleus of an atom.
protoplasm n substance forming
  the living contents of a cell.
prototype n original or model to
  be copied or developed.
protozoan [pro-toe-**zoe**-an] n, pl
  -zoa. microscopic one-celled
  creature.
protracted adj lengthened or
  extended.
protractor n instrument for
  measuring angles.
protrude v stick out, project.
  protrusion n
protuberant adj swelling out,
  bulging. **protuberance** n
proud adj feeling pleasure and
  satisfaction; feeling honoured;
  thinking oneself superior to other
  people; dignified. **proudly** adv
prove v **proving**, **proved**, **proved**
  or **proven**. establish the validity
  of; demonstrate, test; be found to
  be. **proven** adj known from
  experience to work.
provenance [**prov**-in-anss] n place
  of origin.
provender n Old-fashioned fodder.
proverb n short saying that
  expresses a truth or gives a
  warning. **proverbial** adj
provide v make available.
  provider n **provided that**,

providing on condition that.
provide for v take precautions
(against); support financially.
providence n God or nature seen
as a protective force that arranges
people's lives. **provident** adj
thrifty; showing foresight.
providential adj lucky.
province n area governed as a unit
of a country or empire; area of
learning, activity, etc. ▶ pl parts of
a country outside the capital.
provincial adj of a province or the
provinces; unsophisticated and
narrow-minded. ▶ n
unsophisticated person; person
from a province or the provinces.
provincialism n
narrow-mindedness and lack of
sophistication.
provision n act of supplying
something; something supplied;
Law condition incorporated in a
document. ▶ pl food. ▶ v supply
with food. **provisional** adj
temporary or conditional.
provisionally adv
proviso [pro-vize-oh] n, pl **-sos**,
-soes. condition, stipulation.
provoke v deliberately anger;
cause (an adverse reaction).
provocation n **provocative** adj
provost n head of certain
university colleges in Britain; chief
councillor of a Scottish town.
prow n bow of a vessel.
prowess n superior skill or ability;
bravery, fearlessness.
prowl v move stealthily around a
place as if in search of prey or
plunder. ▶ n prowling.
prowler n person who moves
stealthily around a place as if in
search of prey or plunder.
proximity n nearness in space or
time; nearness or closeness in a
series. **proximate** adj
proxy n, pl **proxies**. person

authorized to act on behalf of
someone else; authority to act on
behalf of someone else.
prude n person who is excessively
modest, prim, or proper. **prudish**
adj **prudery** n
prudent adj cautious, discreet, and
sensible. **prudence** n **prudential**
adj Old-fashioned prudent.
prune[1] n dried plum.
prune[2] v cut off dead parts or
excessive branches from (a tree or
plant); shorten, reduce.
prurient adj excessively interested
in sexual matters. **prurience** n
pry v prying, pried. make an
impertinent or uninvited inquiry
into a private matter.
PS postscript.
PSA (in New Zealand) Public
Service Association.
psalm n sacred song. **psalmist** n
writer of psalms.
Psalter n book containing (a
version of) psalms from the Bible.
psaltery n, pl **-ries**. ancient
instrument played by plucking
strings.
PSBR (in Britain) public sector
borrowing requirement.
psephology [sef-fol-a-jee] n
statistical study of elections.
pseud n Informal pretentious
person.
pseudo- combining form false,
pretending, or unauthentic, e.g.
pseudoclassical.
pseudonym n fictitious name
adopted esp. by an author.
pseudonymous adj
psittacosis n disease of parrots
that can be transmitted to humans.
psyche [sye-kee] n human mind or
soul.
psychedelic adj denoting a drug
that causes hallucinations; having
vivid colours and complex
patterns similar to those

experienced during hallucinations.

psychiatry n branch of medicine concerned with mental disorders. **psychiatric** adj **psychiatrist** n

psychic adj (also **psychical**) having mental powers which cannot be explained by natural laws; relating to the mind. ▶ n person with psychic powers.

psycho n, pl **-chos**. Informal psychopath.

psychoanalysis n method of treating mental and emotional disorders by discussion and analysis of one's thoughts and feelings. **psychoanalyse** v **psychoanalyst** n

psychology n, pl **-gies**. study of human and animal behaviour; Informal person's mental make-up. **psychologist** n **psychological** adj of or affecting the mind; of psychology. **psychologically** adv

psychopath n person afflicted with a personality disorder causing him or her to commit antisocial or violent acts. **psychopathic** adj

psychosis n, pl **-ses.** severe mental disorder in which the sufferer's contact with reality becomes distorted. **psychotic** adj

psychosomatic adj (of a physical disorder) thought to have psychological causes.

psychotherapy n treatment of nervous disorders by psychological methods. **psychotherapeutic** adj **psychotherapist** n

psych up v prepare (oneself) mentally for a contest or task.

pt part; point.

PT Old-fashioned physical training.

pt. pint.

PTA Parent-Teacher Association.

ptarmigan [tar-mig-an] n bird of the grouse family which turns white in winter.

pterodactyl [terr-roe-**dak**-til] n

extinct flying reptile with batlike wings.

PTO please turn over.

ptomaine [**toe**-main] n any of a group of poisonous alkaloids found in decaying matter.

Pty Aust, NZ & S Afr Proprietary.

pub n building with a bar licensed to sell alcoholic drinks.

puberty n beginning of sexual maturity. **pubertal** adj

pubic adj of the lower abdomen, e.g. pubic hair.

public adj of or concerning the people as a whole; for use by everyone; well-known; performed or made openly. ▶ n the community, people in general. **publicly** adv **public house** pub. **public relations** promotion of a favourable opinion towards an organization among the public. **public school** private fee-paying school in Britain. **public-spirited** adj having or showing an active interest in the good of the community.

publican n Brit, Aust & NZ person who owns or runs a pub.

publicity n process or information used to arouse public attention; public interest so aroused. **publicist** n person, esp. a press agent or journalist, who publicizes something. **publicize** v bring to public attention.

publish v produce and issue (printed matter) for sale; announce formally or in public. **publication** n **publisher** n

puce adj purplish-brown.

puck n small rubber disc used in ice hockey.

puck n mischievous or evil spirit. **puckish** adj

pucker v gather into wrinkles. ▶ n wrinkle or crease.

pudding n dessert, esp. a cooked

one served hot; savoury dish with pastry or batter, e.g. *steak-and-kidney pudding*; sausage-like mass of meat, e.g. *black pudding*.

puddle *n* small pool of water, esp. of rain.

puerile *adj* silly and childish.

puerperal [pew-**er**-per-al] *adj* concerning the period following childbirth.

puff *n* (sound of) a short blast of breath, wind, etc.; act of inhaling cigarette smoke. ▶ *v* blow or breathe in short quick draughts; take draws at (a cigarette); send out in small clouds; swell. **out of puff** out of breath. **puffy** *adj* **puffball** *n* ball-shaped fungus. **puff pastry** light flaky pastry.

puffin *n* black-and-white sea bird with a brightly-coloured beak.

pug *n* small snub-nosed dog. **pug nose** short stubby upturned nose.

pugilist [**pew**-jil-ist] *n* boxer. **pugilism** *n* **pugilistic** *adj*

pugnacious *adj* ready and eager to fight. **pugnacity** *n*

puissance [**pwee**-sonce] *n* showjumping competition that tests a horse's ability to jump large obstacles.

puke *Slang* ▶ *v* vomit. ▶ *n* act of vomiting; vomited matter.

pulchritude *n Lit* beauty.

pull *v* exert force on (an object) to move it towards the source of the force; strain or stretch; remove or extract; attract. ▶ *n* act of pulling; force used in pulling; act of taking in drink or smoke; *Informal* power, influence. **pull in** *v* (of a vehicle or driver) draw in to the side of the road or stop; reach a destination; attract in large numbers; *Brit, Aust & NZ slang* arrest. **pull off** *v Informal* succeed in performing. **pull out** *v* (of a

vehicle or driver) move away from the side of the road or move out to overtake; (of a train) depart; withdraw; remove by pulling. **pull up** *v* (of a vehicle or driver) stop; remove by the roots; reprimand.

pullet *n* young hen.

pulley *n* wheel with a grooved rim in which a belt, chain, or piece of rope runs in order to lift weights by a downward pull.

Pullman *n, pl* -**mans**. luxurious railway coach.

pullover *n* sweater that is pulled on over the head.

pulmonary *adj* of the lungs.

pulp *n* soft wet substance made from crushed or beaten matter; flesh of a fruit; poor-quality books and magazines. ▶ *v* reduce to pulp.

pulpit *n* raised platform for a preacher.

pulsar *n* small dense star which emits regular bursts of radio waves.

pulse[1] *n* regular beating of blood through the arteries at each heartbeat; any regular beat or vibration. **pulsate** *v* throb, quiver. **pulsation** *n*

pulse[2] *n* edible seed of a pod-bearing plant such as a bean or pea.

pulverize *v* reduce to fine pieces; destroy completely.

puma *n* large American wild cat with a greyish-brown coat.

pumice [**pumm**-iss] *n* light porous stone used for scouring.

pummel *v* -**melling**, -**melled**. strike repeatedly with or as if with the fists.

pump[1] *n* machine used to force a liquid or gas to move in a particular direction. ▶ *v* raise or drive with a pump; supply in large amounts; operate or work in the manner of a pump; extract information from.

pump[2] n light flat-soled shoe.

pumpkin n large round fruit with an orange rind, soft flesh, and many seeds.

pun n use of words to exploit double meanings for humorous effect. ▶ v **punning, punned.** make puns.

punch[1] v strike at with a clenched fist. ▶ n blow with a clenched fist; *Informal* effectiveness or vigour. **punchy** adj forceful. **punch-drunk** adj dazed by or as if by repeated blows to the head.

punch[2] n tool or machine for shaping, piercing, or engraving. ▶ v pierce, cut, stamp, shape, or drive with a punch.

punch[3] n drink made from a mixture of wine, spirits, fruit, sugar, and spices.

punctilious adj paying great attention to correctness in etiquette; careful about small details.

punctual adj arriving or taking place at the correct time. **punctuality** n **punctually** adv

punctuate v put punctuation marks in; interrupt at frequent intervals. **punctuation** n (use of) marks such as commas, colons, etc. in writing, to assist in making the sense clear.

puncture n small hole made by a sharp object, esp. in a tyre. ▶ v pierce a hole in.

pundit n expert who speaks publicly on a subject.

pungent adj having a strong sharp bitter flavour. **pungency** n

punish v cause (someone) to suffer or undergo a penalty for some wrongdoing. **punishing** adj harsh or difficult. **punishment** n

punitive [pew-nit-tiv] adj relating to punishment.

punk n anti-Establishment youth movement and style of rock music of the late 1970s; follower of this music; worthless person.

punnet n small basket for fruit.

punt[1] n open flat-bottomed boat propelled by a pole. ▶ v travel in a punt.

punt[2] *Sport* ▶ n kick of a ball before it touches the ground when dropped from the hands. ▶ v kick (a ball) in this way.

punt[3] n former monetary unit of the Irish Republic.

punter n person who bets; *Brit, Aust & NZ* any member of the public.

puny adj **-nier, -niest.** small and feeble.

pup n young of certain animals, such as dogs and seals.

pupa n, pl **-pae, -pas.** insect at the stage of development between a larva and an adult.

pupil[1] n person who is taught by a teacher.

pupil[2] n round dark opening in the centre of the eye.

puppet n small doll or figure moved by strings or by the operator's hand; person or country controlled by another. **puppeteer** n

puppy n, pl **-pies.** young dog.

purchase v obtain by payment. ▶ n thing that is bought; act of buying; leverage, grip. **purchaser** n

purdah n Muslim and Hindu custom of keeping women in seclusion, with clothing that conceals them completely when they go out.

pure adj unmixed, untainted; innocent; complete, e.g. *pure delight*; concerned with theory only, e.g. *pure mathematics*. **purely** adv **purity** n **purify** v **-fying, -fied.** make or become pure. **purification** n **purist** n person concerned with strict obedience to the traditions of a subject.

purée [pure-ray] n pulp of cooked food. ▶ v **-réeing, -réed.** make into a purée.

purgatory n place or state of temporary suffering; **(P-)** RC Church place where souls of the dead undergo punishment for their sins before being admitted to Heaven. **purgatorial** adj

purge v rid (a thing or place) of (unwanted things or people). ▶ n purging. **purgative** n, adj (medicine) designed to cause defecation.

Puritan n Hist member of the English Protestant group who wanted simpler church ceremonies; **(p-)** person with strict moral and religious principles. **puritanical** adj **puritanism** n

purl n stitch made by knitting a plain stitch backwards. ▶ v knit in purl.

purlieus [per-lyooz] pl n Lit outskirts.

purloin v steal.

purple adj, n (of) a colour between red and blue.

purport v claim (to be or do something). ▶ n apparent meaning, significance.

purpose n reason for which something is done or exists; determination; practical advantage or use, e.g. use the time to good purpose. **purposely** adv intentionally (also **on purpose**).

purr v (of cats) make low vibrant sound, usu. when pleased. ▶ n this sound.

purse n small bag for money; US & NZ handbag; financial resources; prize money. ▶ v draw (one's) lips together into a small round shape.

purser n ship's officer who keeps the accounts.

pursue v chase; follow (a goal); engage in; continue to discuss or ask about (something). **pursuer** n

pursuit n pursuing; occupation or pastime.

purulent [pure-yoo-lent] adj of or containing pus.

purvey v supply (provisions). **purveyor** n

purview n scope or range of activity or outlook.

pus n yellowish matter produced by infected tissue.

push v move or try to move by steady force; drive or spur (oneself or another person) to do something; Informal sell (drugs) illegally. ▶ n act of pushing; special effort. **the push** Slang dismissal from a job or relationship. **pusher** n person who sells illegal drugs. **pushy** adj too assertive or ambitious. **pushchair** n Brit folding chair on wheels for a baby.

pusillanimous adj timid and cowardly. **pusillanimity** n

puss, pussy n, pl **pusses, pussies.** Informal cat.

pussyfoot v Informal behave too cautiously.

pustule n pimple containing pus.

put v **putting, put.** cause to be (in a position, state, or place); express; throw (the shot) in the shot put. ▶ n throw in putting the shot. **put across** v express successfully. **put off** v postpone; disconcert; repel. **put up** v erect; accommodate; nominate.

put-upon adj taken advantage of.

putative adj reputed, supposed.

putrid adj rotten and foul-smelling. **putrefy** v **-fying, -fied.** rot and produce an offensive smell. **putrefaction** n **putrescent** adj rotting.

putsch *n* sudden violent attempt to remove a government from power.

putt *Golf* ▶ *n* stroke on the putting green to roll the ball into or near the hole. ▶ *v* strike (the ball) in this way. **putter** *n* golf club for putting.

putty *n* adhesive used to fix glass into frames and fill cracks in woodwork.

puzzle *v* perplex and confuse or be perplexed or confused. ▶ *n* problem that cannot be easily solved; toy, game, or question that requires skill or ingenuity to solve. **puzzlement** *n* **puzzling** *adj*

PVC polyvinyl chloride: plastic material used in clothes etc.

Pygmy *n, pl* -mies. member of one of the very short peoples of Equatorial Africa. ▶ *adj* (p-) very small.

pyjamas *pl n* loose-fitting trousers and top worn in bed.

pylon *n* steel tower-like structure supporting electrical cables.

pyramid *n* solid figure with a flat base and triangular sides sloping upwards to a point; building of this shape, esp. an ancient Egyptian one. **pyramidal** *adj*

pyre *n* pile of wood for burning a corpse on.

Pyrex *n* ® heat-resistant glassware.

pyromania *n* uncontrollable urge to set things on fire. **pyromaniac** *n*

pyrotechnics *n* art of making fireworks; firework display. **pyrotechnic** *adj*

Pyrrhic victory [pir-ik] *n* victory in which the victor's losses are as great as those of the defeated.

python *n* large nonpoisonous snake that crushes its prey.

Q q

QC Queen's Counsel.

QED which was to be shown or proved.

Qld Queensland.

QM Quartermaster.

qr. quarter; quire.

qt. quart.

qua [kwah] *prep* in the capacity of.

quack[1] *v* (of a duck) utter a harsh guttural sound. ▶ *n* sound made by a duck.

quack[2] *n* unqualified person who claims medical knowledge.

quad *n* see QUADRANGLE; *Informal* quadruplet. ▶ *adj* short for QUADRAPHONIC. **quad bike, quad** vehicle like a small motorcycle with four large wheels, designed for agricultural and sporting uses.

quadrangle *n* (also **quad**) rectangular courtyard with buildings on all four sides; geometric figure consisting of four points connected by four lines. **quadrangular** *adj*

quadrant *n* quarter of a circle; quarter of a circle's circumference; instrument for measuring the altitude of the stars.

quadraphonic *adj* using four independent channels to reproduce or record sound.

quadratic *Maths* ▶ *n* equation in which the variable is raised to the power of two, but nowhere raised to a higher power. ▶ *adj* of the second power.

quadrennial *adj* occurring every four years; lasting four years.

quadri- *combining form* four, e.g. *quadrilateral.*

quadrilateral *adj* having four sides. ▶ *n* polygon with four sides.

quadrille *n* square dance for four

couples.

quadriplegia n paralysis of all four limbs.

quadruped [kwod-roo-ped] n any animal with four legs.

quadruple v multiply by four. ▶ adj four times as much or as many; consisting of four parts.

quadruplet n one of four offspring born at one birth.

quaff [kwoff] v drink heartily or in one draught.

quagmire [kwog-mire] n soft wet area of land.

quail¹ n small game bird of the partridge family.

quail² v shrink back with fear.

quaint adj attractively unusual, esp. in an old-fashioned style. **quaintly** adv

quake v shake or tremble with or as if with fear. ▶ n Informal earthquake.

Quaker n member of a Christian sect, the Society of Friends. **Quakerism** n

qualify v **-fying, -fied.** provide or be provided with the abilities necessary for a task, office, or duty; moderate or restrict (a statement). **qualified** adj **qualification** n official record of achievement in a course or examination; quality or skill needed for a particular activity; condition that modifies or limits; act of qualifying.

quality n, pl **-ties.** degree or standard of excellence; distinguishing characteristic or attribute; basic character or nature of something. ▶ adj excellent or superior. **qualitative** adj of or relating to quality.

qualm [kwahm] n pang of conscience; sudden sensation of misgiving.

quandary n, pl **-ries.** difficult situation or dilemma.

quango n, pl **-gos.** Chiefly Brit quasi-autonomous nongovernmental organization: any partly independent official body set up by a government.

quanta n plural of QUANTUM.

quantify v **-fying, -fied.** discover or express the quantity of. **quantifiable** adj **quantification** n

quantity n, pl **-ties.** specified or definite amount or number; aspect of anything that can be measured, weighed, or counted. **quantitative** adj of or relating to quantity. **quantity surveyor** person who estimates the cost of the materials and labour necessary for a construction job.

quantum n, pl **-ta.** desired or required amount, esp. a very small one. **quantum leap, jump** Informal sudden large change, increase, or advance. **quantum theory** physics theory based on the idea that energy of electrons is discharged in discrete quanta.

quarantine n period of isolation of people or animals to prevent the spread of disease. ▶ v isolate in or as if in quarantine.

quark n Physics subatomic particle thought to be the fundamental unit of matter.

quarrel n angry disagreement; cause of dispute. ▶ v **-relling, -relled.** have a disagreement or dispute. **quarrelsome** adj

quarry¹ n, pl **-ries.** place where stone is dug from the surface of the earth. ▶ v **-rying, -ried.** extract (stone) from a quarry.

quarry² n, pl **-ries.** person or animal that is being hunted.

quart n unit of liquid measure equal to two pints (1.136 litres).

quarter n one of four equal parts of something; fourth part of a year; *Informal* unit of weight equal to 4 ounces; region or district of a town or city; *US* 25-cent piece; mercy or pity, as shown towards a defeated opponent. ▶ *pl* lodgings. ▶ *v* divide into four equal parts; billet or be billeted in lodgings. **quarterly** *adj* occurring, due, or issued at intervals of three months. ▶ *n* magazine issued every three months. ▶ *adv* once every three months. **quarter day** *Brit* any of the four days in the year when certain payments become due. **quarterdeck** *n Naut* rear part of the upper deck of a ship. **quarterfinal** *n* round before the semifinal in a competition. **quartermaster** *n* military officer responsible for accommodation, food, and equipment.

quartet *n* group of four performers; music for such a group.

quarto *n, pl* **-tos**. book size in which the sheets are folded into four leaves.

quartz *n* hard glossy mineral.

quasar [**kway**-zar] *n* extremely distant starlike object that emits powerful radio waves.

quash *v* annul or make void; subdue forcefully and completely.

quasi- [**kway**-zie] *combining form* almost but not really, e.g. *quasi-religious; a quasi-scholar.*

quatrain *n* stanza or poem of four lines.

quaver *v* (of a voice) quiver or tremble. ▶ *n Music* note half the length of a crotchet; tremulous sound or note.

quay [**kee**] *n* wharf built parallel to the shore.

queasy *adj* **-sier, -siest.** having the feeling that one is about to vomit; feeling or causing uneasiness. **queasiness** *n*

queen *n* female sovereign who is the official ruler or head of state; wife of a king; woman, place, or thing considered to be the best of her or its kind; only fertile female in a colony of bees, wasps, or ants; the most powerful piece in chess. **queenly** *adj* **Queen's Counsel** barrister or advocate appointed Counsel to the Crown.

queer *adj* not normal or usual; *Brit* faint, giddy, or queasy. **queer someone's pitch** *Informal* spoil someone's chances of something.

quell *v* suppress; overcome.

quench *v* satisfy (one's thirst); put out or extinguish.

quern *n* stone hand mill for grinding corn.

querulous [**kwer**-yoo-luss] *adj* complaining or whining. **querulously** *adv*

query *n, pl* **-ries.** question, esp. one raising doubt; question mark. ▶ *v* **-rying, -ried.** express uncertainty, doubt, or an objection concerning (something).

quest *n* long and difficult search. ▶ *v* (foll. by *for* or *after*) go in search of.

question *n* form of words addressed to a person in order to obtain an answer; point at issue; difficulty or uncertainty. ▶ *v* put a question or questions to (a person); express uncertainty about. **in question** under discussion. **out of the question** impossible. **questionable** *adj* of disputable value or authority. **questionably** *adv* **questionnaire** *n* set of questions on a form, used to collect information from people. **question mark** punctuation mark (?) written at the end of questions.

queue *n* line of people or vehicles waiting for something. ▶ *v*

queuing or queueing, queued.
(often foll. by up) form or remain
in a line while waiting.

quibble v make trivial objections.
▶ n trivial objection.

quiche [keesh] n savoury flan with
an egg custard filling to which
vegetables etc. are added.

quick adj speedy, fast; lasting or
taking a short time; alert and
responsive; easily excited or
aroused. ▶ n area of sensitive flesh
under a nail. ▶ adv Informal in a
rapid manner. cut someone to
the quick hurt someone's feelings
deeply. quickly adv quicken v
make or become faster; make or
become more lively. quicklime n
white solid used in the
manufacture of glass and steel.
quicksand n deep mass of loose
wet sand that sucks anything on
top of it into it. quicksilver n
mercury. quickstep n fast
modern ballroom dance.

quid n, pl quid. Brit slang pound
(sterling).

quid pro quo n, pl quid pro quos.
one thing, esp. an advantage or
object, given in exchange for
another.

quiescent [kwee-ess-ent] adj quiet,
inactive, or dormant. quiescence
n

quiet adj with little noise; calm or
tranquil; untroubled. ▶ n
quietness. ▶ v make or become
quiet. on the quiet without other
people knowing, secretly. quietly
adv quietness n quieten v (often
foll. by down) make or become
quiet. quietude n quietness,
peace, or tranquillity.

quietism n passivity and calmness
of mind towards external events.

quiff n tuft of hair brushed up
above the forehead.

quill n pen made from the feather

of a bird's wing or tail; stiff hollow
spine of a hedgehog or porcupine.

quilt n padded covering for a bed.
quilted adj consisting of two
layers of fabric with a layer of soft
material between them.

quin n short for QUINTUPLET.

quince n acid-tasting pear-shaped
fruit.

quinine n bitter drug used as a
tonic and formerly to treat malaria.

quinquennial adj occurring every
five years; lasting five years.

quinsy n inflammation of the
throat or tonsils.

quintessence n most perfect
representation of a quality or
state. quintessential adj

quintet n group of five performers;
music for such a group.

quintuplet n one of five offspring
born at one birth.

quip n witty saying. ▶ v quipping,
quipped. make a quip.

quire n set of 24 or 25 sheets of
paper.

quirk n peculiarity of character;
unexpected twist or turn, e.g. a
quirk of fate. quirky adj

quisling n traitor who aids an
occupying enemy force.

quit v quitting, quit. stop (doing
something); give up (a job);
depart from. quitter n person
who lacks perseverance. quits adj
Informal on an equal footing.

quite adv somewhat, e.g. she's
quite pretty; absolutely, e.g. you're
quite right; in actuality, truly.
▶ interj expression of agreement.

quiver¹ v shake with a tremulous
movement. ▶ n shaking or
trembling.

quiver² n case for arrows.

quixotic [kwik-sot-ik] adj romantic
and unrealistic. quixotically adv

quiz n, pl quizzes. entertainment
in which the knowledge of the

players is tested by a series of questions. ▶ v quizzing, quizzed. investigate by close questioning.

quizzical adj questioning and mocking, e.g. *a quizzical look.* **quizzically** adv

quod n Brit slang jail.

quoit n large ring used in the game of quoits. ▶ pl game in which quoits are tossed at a stake in the ground in attempts to encircle it.

quokka n small Australian wallaby.

quorum n minimum number of people required to be present at a meeting before any transactions can take place.

quota n share that is due from, due to, or allocated to a group or person; prescribed number or quantity allowed, required, or admitted.

quote v repeat (words) exactly from (an earlier work, speech, or conversation); state (a price) for goods or a job of work. ▶ n Informal quotation. **quotable** adj **quotation** n written or spoken passage repeated exactly in a later work, speech, or conversation; act of quoting; estimate of costs submitted by a contractor to a prospective client. **quotation marks** raised commas used in writing to mark the beginning and end of a quotation or passage of speech.

quoth v Obs said.

quotidian adj daily; commonplace.

quotient n result of the division of one number or quantity by another.

q.v. which see: used to refer a reader to another item in the same book.

── R r ──

r radius; ratio; right.

R Queen; King; River.

RA (in Britain) Royal Academy; (in Britain) Royal Artillery.

RAAF Royal Australian Air Force.

rabbi [rab-bye] n, pl -bis. Jewish spiritual leader. **rabbinical** adj

rabbit n small burrowing mammal with long ears. **rabbit on** v **rabbiting, rabbited.** Brit informal talk too much.

rabble n disorderly crowd of noisy people.

rabid adj fanatical; having rabies. **rabidly** adv

rabies [ray-beez] n usu. fatal viral disease transmitted by dogs and certain other animals.

RAC (in Britain) Royal Automobile Club.

raccoon n small N American mammal with a long striped tail.

race[1] n contest of speed. ▶ pl meeting for horse racing. ▶ v compete with in a race; run swiftly; (of an engine) run faster than normal. **racer** n **racecourse** n **racehorse** n **racetrack** n

race[2] n group of people of common ancestry with distinguishing physical features, such as skin colour. **racial** adj **racism, racialism** n hostile attitude or behaviour to members of other races, based on a belief in the innate superiority of one's own race. **racist, racialist** adj, n

raceme [rass-eem] n cluster of flowers along a central stem, as in the foxglove.

rack[1] n framework for holding particular articles, such as coats or luggage; Hist instrument of torture that stretched the victim's body.

▶ v cause great suffering to. **rack one's brains** try very hard to remember.

rack² n **go to rack and ruin** be destroyed.

racket¹ n noisy disturbance; occupation by which money is made illegally.

racket², **racquet** n bat with strings stretched in an oval frame, used in tennis etc. **rackets** n ball game played in a four walled court.

racketeer n person making illegal profits.

raconteur [rak-on-**tur**] n skilled storyteller.

racy adj **racier, raciest.** slightly shocking; spirited or lively.

radar n device for tracking distant objects by bouncing high-frequency radio pulses off them.

radial adj spreading out from a common central point; of a radius; (also **radial-ply**) (of a tyre) having flexible sides strengthened with radial cords.

radiant adj looking happy; shining; emitting radiation. **radiance** n

radiate v spread out from a centre; emit or be emitted as radiation. **radiator** n Brit arrangement of pipes containing hot water or steam to heat a room; tubes containing water as cooling apparatus for a car engine; Aust & NZ electric fire.

radiation n transmission of energy from one body to another; particles or waves emitted in nuclear decay; process of radiating.

radical adj fundamental; thorough; advocating fundamental change. ▶ n person advocating fundamental (political) change; number expressed as the root of another. **radically** adv **radicalism** n

radicle n small or developing root.

radii n a plural of RADIUS.

radio n, pl **-dios.** use of electromagnetic waves for broadcasting, communication, etc.; device for receiving and amplifying radio signals; sound broadcasting. ▶ v transmit (a message) by radio.

radio- combining form of radio, radiation, or radioactivity.

radioactive adj emitting radiation as a result of nuclear decay. **radioactivity** n

radiography [ray-dee-**og**-ra-fee] n production of an image on a film or plate by radiation. **radiographer** n

radiology [ray-dee-**ol**-a-jee] n science of using x-rays in medicine. **radiologist** n

radiotherapy n treatment of disease, esp. cancer, by radiation. **radiotherapist** n

radish n small hot-flavoured root vegetable eaten raw in salads.

radium n Chem radioactive metallic element.

radius n, pl **radii, radiuses.** (length of) a straight line from the centre to the circumference of a circle; outer of two bones in the forearm.

radon [ray-don] n Chem radioactive gaseous element.

RAF (in Britain) Royal Air Force.

raffia n prepared palm fibre for weaving mats etc.

raffish adj slightly disreputable.

raffle n lottery with goods as prizes. ▶ v offer as a prize in a raffle.

raft n floating platform of logs, planks, etc.

rafter n one of the main beams of a roof.

rag¹ n fragment of cloth; Brit, Aust & NZ informal newspaper. ▶ pl tattered clothing. **ragged**

[rag-gid] *adj* dressed in shabby or torn clothes; torn; lacking smoothness.

rag² *Brit* ▸ *v* **ragging, ragged.** tease. ▸ *adj, n* (of) events organized by students to raise money for charities.

ragamuffin *n* ragged dirty child.

rage *n* violent anger or passion. ▸ *v* speak or act with fury; proceed violently and without check. **all the rage** very popular.

raglan *adj* (of a sleeve) joined to a garment by diagonal seams from the neck to the underarm.

ragout [rag-**goo**] *n* richly seasoned stew of meat and vegetables.

ragtime *n* style of jazz piano music.

raid *n* sudden surprise attack or search. ▸ *v* make a raid on. **raider** *n*

rail¹ *n* horizontal bar, esp. as part of a fence or track; railway. **railing** *n* fence made of rails supported by posts. **railway** *n* track of iron rails on which trains run; company operating a railway.

rail² *v* (foll. by *at* or *against*) complain bitterly or loudly. **raillery** *n* teasing or joking.

rail³ *n* small marsh bird.

raiment *n Obs* clothing.

rain *n* water falling in drops from the clouds. ▸ *v* fall or pour down as rain; fall rapidly and in large quantities. **rainy** *adj* **rainbow** *n* arch of colours in the sky. **rainbow nation** South African nation. **raincoat** *n* water-resistant overcoat. **rainfall** *n* amount of rain. **rainforest** *n* dense forest in tropical and temperate areas.

raise *v* lift up; set upright; increase in amount or intensity; collect or levy; bring up (a family); put forward for consideration.

raisin *n* dried grape.

raison d'être [ray-zon **det**-ra] *n, pl*

raisons d'être. *French* reason or justification for existence.

Raj *n* the Raj former British rule in India.

raja, rajah *n Hist* Indian prince or ruler.

rake¹ *n* tool with a long handle and a crosspiece with teeth, used for smoothing earth or gathering leaves, hay, etc. ▸ *v* gather or smooth with a rake; search (through); sweep (with gunfire). **rake it in** *Informal* make a large amount of money. **rake-off** *n Slang* share of profits, esp. illegal. **rake up** *v* revive memories of (a forgotten unpleasant event).

rake² *n* dissolute or immoral man. **rakish** *adj*

rakish *adj* dashing or jaunty.

rally *n, pl* **-lies.** large gathering of people for a meeting; marked recovery of strength; *Tennis etc.* lively exchange of strokes; car-driving competition on public roads. ▸ *v* **-lying, -lied.** bring or come together after dispersal or for a common cause; regain health or strength; revive.

ram *n* male sheep; hydraulic machine. ▸ *v* **ramming, rammed.** strike against with force; force or drive; cram or stuff.

RAM *Computers* random access memory.

Ramadan *n* 9th Muslim month; strict fasting from dawn to dusk observed during this time.

ramble *v* walk without a definite route; talk incoherently. ▸ *n* walk, esp. in the country.

rambler *n* person who rambles; climbing rose.

ramekin [**ram**-ik-in] *n* small ovenproof dish for a single serving of food.

ramifications *pl n* consequences resulting from an action.

ramp n slope joining two level surfaces.

rampage v dash about violently. **on the rampage** behaving violently or destructively.

rampant adj growing or spreading uncontrollably; (of a heraldic beast) on its hind legs.

rampart n mound or wall for defence.

ramshackle adj tumbledown, rickety, or makeshift.

ran v past tense of RUN.

ranch n large cattle farm in the American West. **rancher** n

rancid adj (of butter, bacon, etc.) stale and having an offensive smell. **rancidity** n

rancour n deep bitter hate. **rancorous** adj

rand n monetary unit of S Africa.

random adj made or done by chance or without plan. **at random** haphazard(ly).

randy adj **randier, randiest.** Informal sexually aroused.

rang v past tense of RING¹.

range n limits of effectiveness or variation; distance that a missile or plane can travel; distance of a mark shot at; whole set of related things; chain of mountains; place for shooting practice or rocket testing; kitchen stove. ▶ v vary between one point and another; cover or extend over; roam.

ranger n official in charge of a nature reserve etc.; (R-) member of the senior branch of Guides.

rangefinder n instrument for finding how far away an object is.

rangy [**rain**-jee] adj **rangier, rangiest.** having long slender limbs.

rank¹ n relative place or position; status; social class; row or line. ▶ v have a specific rank or position; arrange in rows or lines. **rank**

and file ordinary people or members. **the ranks** common soldiers.

rank² adj complete or absolute, e.g. *rank favouritism*; smelling offensively strong; growing too thickly.

rankle v continue to cause resentment or bitterness.

ransack v search thoroughly; pillage, plunder.

ransom n money demanded in return for the release of someone who has been kidnapped.

rant v talk in a loud and excited way. **ranter** n

rap v **rapping, rapped.** hit with a sharp quick blow; utter (a command) abruptly; perform a rhythmic monologue with musical backing. ▶ n quick sharp blow; rhythmic monologue performed to music. **take the rap** Slang suffer punishment for something whether guilty or not. **rapper** n

rapacious adj greedy or grasping. **rapacity** n

rape¹ v force to submit to sexual intercourse. ▶ n act of raping; any violation or abuse. **rapist** n

rape² n plant with oil-yielding seeds, also used as fodder.

rapid adj quick, swift. **rapids** pl n part of a river with a fast turbulent current. **rapidly** adv **rapidity** n

rapier [**ray**-pyer] n fine-bladed sword.

rapport [rap-**pore**] n harmony or agreement.

rapprochement [rap-**prosh**-mong] n re-establishment of friendly relations, esp. between nations.

rapt adj engrossed or spellbound. **rapture** n ecstasy. **rapturous** adj

rare¹ adj uncommon; infrequent; of uncommonly high quality; (of air at high altitudes) having low

density; thin. **rarely** adv seldom.
rarity n

rare² adj (of meat) lightly cooked.

rarebit n see WELSH RAREBIT.

rarefied [rare-if-ide] adj highly specialized; exalted; (of air) thin.

raring adj **raring to** enthusiastic, willing, or ready to.

rascal n rogue; naughty (young) person. **rascally** adj

rash¹ adj hasty, reckless, or incautious. **rashly** adv

rash² n eruption of spots or patches on the skin; outbreak of (unpleasant) occurrences.

rasher n thin slice of bacon.

rasp n harsh grating noise; coarse file. ▶ v speak in a grating voice; make a scraping noise.

raspberry n red juicy edible berry; Informal spluttering noise made with the tongue and lips, to show contempt.

Rastafarian n, adj (member) of a religion originating in Jamaica and regarding Haile Selassie as God (also **Rasta**).

rat n small rodent; Informal contemptible person, esp. a deserter or informer. ▶ v **ratting, ratted.** Informal inform (on); hunt rats. **ratty** adj Brit & NZ informal bad-tempered, irritable. **rat race** continual hectic competitive activity.

ratafia [rat-a-fee-a] n liqueur made from fruit.

ratatouille [rat-a-twee] n vegetable casserole of tomatoes, aubergines, etc.

ratchet n set of teeth on a bar or wheel allowing motion in one direction only.

rate n degree of speed or progress; proportion between two things; charge. ▶ pl local tax on business. ▶ v consider or value; estimate the value of. **at any rate** in any case.

rateable adj able to be rated; (of property) liable to payment of rates. **ratepayer** n

rather adv to some extent; more truly or appropriately; more willingly.

ratify v **-fying, -fied.** give formal approval to. **ratification** n

rating n valuation or assessment; classification; noncommissioned sailor. ▶ pl size of the audience for a TV programme.

ratio n, pl **-tios.** relationship between two numbers or amounts expressed as a proportion.

ration n fixed allowance of food etc. ▶ v limit to a certain amount per person.

rational adj reasonable, sensible; capable of reasoning. **rationally** adv **rationality** n **rationale** [rash-a-nahl] n reason for an action or decision. **rationalism** n philosophy that regards reason as the only basis for beliefs or actions. **rationalist** n **rationalize** v justify by plausible reasoning; reorganize to improve efficiency or profitability. **rationalization** n

rattan n climbing palm with jointed stems used for canes.

rattle v give out a succession of short sharp sounds; shake briskly causing sharp sounds; Informal confuse or fluster. ▶ n short sharp sound; instrument for making such a sound. **rattlesnake** n poisonous snake with loose horny segments on the tail that make a rattling sound.

raucous adj hoarse or harsh.

raunchy adj **-chier, -chiest.** Slang earthy, sexy.

ravage v cause extensive damage to. **ravages** pl n damaging effects.

rave v talk wildly or with enthusiasm. ▶ n Slang large-scale party with electronic dance music.

raving adj delirious; Informal exceptional, e.g. a raving beauty.

ravel v **-elling, -elled.** tangle or become entangled.

raven n black bird like a large crow. ▶ adj (of hair) shiny black.

ravenous adj very hungry.

ravine [rav-**veen**] n narrow steep-sided valley worn by a stream.

ravioli pl n small squares of pasta with a savoury filling.

ravish v enrapture; Lit rape. **ravishing** adj lovely or entrancing.

raw adj uncooked; not manufactured or refined; inexperienced; chilly. **raw deal** unfair or dishonest treatment. **rawhide** n untanned hide.

ray¹ n single line or narrow beam of light.

ray² n large sea fish with a flat body and a whiplike tail.

rayon n (fabric made of) a synthetic fibre.

raze v destroy (buildings or a town) completely.

razor n sharp instrument for shaving. **razorbill** n sea bird of the North Atlantic with a stout sideways flattened bill.

razzle-dazzle, razzmatazz n Slang showy activity.

RC Roman Catholic; Red Cross.

Rd Road.

re prep with reference to, concerning.

RE (in Britain) religious education.

re- prefix again, e.g. re-enter; retrial.

reach v arrive at; make a movement in order to grasp or touch; succeed in touching; make contact or communication with; extend as far as. ▶ n distance that one can reach; range of influence. ▶ pl stretch of a river. **reachable** adj

react v act in response (to); (foll.

by against) act in an opposing or contrary manner. **reaction** n physical or emotional response to a stimulus; any action resisting another; opposition to change; chemical or nuclear change, combination, or decomposition. **reactionary** n, adj (person) opposed to change, esp. in politics. **reactance** n Electricity resistance to the flow of an alternating current caused by the inductance or capacitance of the circuit. **reactive** adj chemically active. **reactor** n apparatus in which a nuclear reaction is maintained and controlled to produce nuclear energy.

read v **reading, read.** look at and understand or take in (written or printed matter); look at and say aloud; interpret the significance or meaning of; (of an instrument) register; study. ▶ n matter suitable for reading, e.g. a good read. **readable** adj enjoyable to read; legible. **reading** n

reader n person who reads; textbook; Chiefly Brit senior university lecturer. **readership** n readers of a publication collectively.

readjust v adapt to a new situation. **readjustment** n

ready adj **readier, readiest.** prepared for use or action; willing; prompt. **readily** adv **readiness** n **ready-made** adj for immediate use by any customer.

reagent [ree-**age**-ent] n chemical substance that reacts with another, used to detect the presence of the other.

real adj existing in fact; actual; genuine. **really** adv truly. ▶ interj exclamation of dismay, doubt, or surprise. **reality** n state of things as they are. **reality TV** television programmes focusing on members of the public living in conditions created especially by the programme makers. **real ale** *Chiefly Brit* beer allowed to ferment in the barrel. **real estate** property consisting of land and houses.

realistic *adj* seeing and accepting things as they really are, practical. **realistically** *adv* **realism** *n* **realist** *n*

realize *v* become aware or grasp the significance of; achieve (a plan, hopes, etc.); convert into money. **realization** *n*

realm *n* kingdom; sphere of interest.

ream *n* twenty quires of paper, generally 500 sheets. ▶ *pl Informal* large quantity (of written matter).

reap *v* cut and gather (a harvest); receive as the result of a previous activity. **reaper** *n*

reappear *v* appear again. **reappearance** *n*

rear[1] *n* back part; part of an army, procession, etc. behind the others. **bring up the rear** come last. **rearmost** *adj* **rear admiral** high-ranking naval officer. **rearguard** *n* troops protecting the rear of an army.

rear[2] *v* care for and educate (children); breed (animals); (of a horse) rise on its hind feet.

rearrange *v* organize differently, alter. **rearrangement** *n*

reason *n* cause or motive; faculty of rational thought; sanity. ▶ *v* think logically in forming conclusions. **reason with** persuade by logical argument into doing something. **reasonable** *adj* sensible; not excessive; logical. **reasonably** *adv*

reassess *v* reconsider the value or importance of.

reassure *v* restore confidence to.

reassurance *n*

rebate *n* discount or refund.

rebel *v* **-belling, -belled.** revolt against the ruling power; reject accepted conventions. ▶ *n* person who rebels. **rebellion** *n* organized open resistance to authority; rejection of conventions. **rebellious** *adj*

rebore, reboring *v* boring of a cylinder to restore its true shape.

rebound *v* spring back; misfire so as to hurt the perpetrator of a plan or deed. **on the rebound** *Informal* while recovering from rejection.

rebuff *v* reject or snub. ▶ *n* blunt refusal, snub.

rebuke *v* scold sternly. ▶ *n* stern scolding.

rebus *n, pl* **-buses.** puzzle consisting of pictures and symbols representing words or syllables.

rebut *v* **-butting, -butted.** prove that (a claim) is untrue. **rebuttal** *n*

recalcitrant *adj* wilfully disobedient. **recalcitrance** *n*

recall *v* recollect or remember; order to return; annul or cancel. ▶ *n* ability to remember; order to return.

recant *v* withdraw (a statement or belief) publicly. **recantation** *n*

recap *Informal* ▶ *v* **-capping, -capped.** recapitulate. ▶ *n* recapitulation.

recapitulate *v* state again briefly, repeat. **recapitulation** *n*

recapture *v* experience again; capture again.

recce *Chiefly Brit slang* ▶ *v* **-ceing, -ced** *or* **-ceed.** reconnoitre. ▶ *n* reconnaissance.

recede *v* move to a more distant place; (of the hair) stop growing at the front.

receipt *n* written acknowledgment of money or goods received;

receiving or being received.
receive v take, accept, or get; experience; greet (guests).
received adj generally accepted.
receiver n part of telephone that is held to the ear; equipment in a telephone, radio, or television that converts electrical signals into sound; person appointed by a court to manage the property of a bankrupt. **receivership** n state of being administered by a receiver.
recent adj having happened lately; new. **recently** adv
receptacle n object used to contain something.
reception n area for receiving guests, clients, etc.; formal party; manner of receiving; welcome; (in broadcasting) quality of signals received. **receptionist** n person who receives guests, clients, etc.
receptive adj willing to accept new ideas, suggestions, etc. **receptivity** n
recess n niche or alcove; holiday between sessions of work; secret hidden place. **recessed** adj hidden or placed in a recess. **recession** n period of economic difficulty when little is being bought or sold. **recessive** adj receding.
recherché [rish-**air**-shay] adj refined or elegant; known only to experts.
recidivism n habitual relapse into crime. **recidivist** n
recipe n directions for cooking a dish; method for achieving something.
recipient n person who receives something.
reciprocal [ris-**sip**-pro-kl] adj mutual; given or done in return. **reciprocally** adv **reciprocate** v give or feel in return; (of a machine part) move backwards

and forwards. **reciprocation** n **reciprocity** n
recite v repeat (a poem etc.) aloud to an audience. **recital** n musical performance by a soloist or soloists; act of reciting. **recitation** n recital, usu. from memory, of poetry or prose. **recitative** [ress-it-a-**teev**] n speechlike style of singing, used esp. for narrative passages in opera.
reckless adj heedless of danger. **recklessly** adv **recklessness** n
reckon v consider or think; make calculations, count; expect. **reckoning** n
reclaim v regain possession of; make fit for cultivation. **reclamation** n
recline v rest in a leaning position. **reclining** adj
recluse n person who avoids other people. **reclusive** adj
recognize v identify as (a person or thing) already known; accept as true or existing; treat as valid; notice, show appreciation of. **recognition** n **recognizable** adj **recognizance** [rik-**og**-nizz-anss] n undertaking before a court to observe some condition.
recoil v jerk or spring back; draw back in horror; (of an action) go wrong so as to hurt the doer. ▶ n backward jerk; recoiling.
recollect v call back to mind, remember. **recollection** n
recommend v advise or counsel; praise or commend; make acceptable. **recommendation** n
recompense v pay or reward; compensate or make up for. ▶ n compensation; reward or remuneration.
reconcile v harmonize (conflicting beliefs etc.); bring back into friendship; accept or cause to accept (an unpleasant situation).

reconciliation n

recondite adj difficult to understand.

recondition v restore to good condition or working order.

reconnaissance [rik-kon-iss-anss] n survey for military or engineering purposes.

reconnoitre [rek-a-noy-ter] v make a reconnaissance of.

reconsider v think about again, consider changing.

reconstitute v reorganize; restore (dried food) to its former state by adding water. **reconstitution** n

reconstruct v rebuild; use evidence to re-create. **reconstruction** n

record n [rek-ord] document or other thing that preserves information; disc with indentations which a record player transforms into sound; best recorded achievement; known facts about a person's past. ▸ v [rik-kord] put in writing; preserve (sound, TV programmes, etc.) on plastic disc, magnetic tape, etc., for reproduction on a playback device; show or register. **off the record** not for publication.

recorder n person or machine that records, esp. a video, cassette, or tape recorder; type of flute, held vertically; judge in certain courts. **recording** n **record player** instrument for reproducing sound on records.

recount v tell in detail.

re-count v count again. ▸ n second or further count, esp. of votes.

recoup [rik-koop] v regain or make good (a loss); recompense or compensate.

recourse n source of help. **have recourse to** to turn to a source of help or course of action.

recover v become healthy again; regain a former condition; find again; get back (a loss or expense). **recovery** n

recoverable adj

re-create v make happen or exist again.

recreation n agreeable or refreshing occupation, relaxation, or amusement. **recreational** adj

recrimination n mutual blame. **recriminatory** adj

recruit v enlist (new soldiers, members, etc.). ▸ n newly enlisted soldier; new member or supporter. **recruitment** n

rectangle n oblong four-sided figure with four right angles. **rectangular** adj

rectify v **-fying, -fied.** put right, correct; Chem purify by distillation; Electricity convert (alternating current) into direct current. **rectification** n **rectifier** n

rectilinear adj in a straight line; characterized by straight lines.

rectitude n moral correctness.

recto n, pl **-tos.** right-hand page of a book.

rector n clergyman in charge of a parish; head of certain academic institutions. **rectory** n rector's house.

rectum n, pl **-tums, -ta.** final section of the large intestine.

recumbent adj lying down.

recuperate v recover from illness. **recuperation** n **recuperative** adj

recur v **-curring, -curred.** happen again. **recurrence** n repetition. **recurrent** adj

recycle v reprocess (used materials) for further use. **recyclable** adj

red adj redder, reddest. of a colour varying from crimson to orange and seen in blood, fire, etc.; flushed in the face (from anger, shame, etc.) ▸ n a red colour; **(R-)** Informal communist. **in the**

red *Informal* in debt. **see red** *Informal* be angry. **redness** *n*

redden *v* make or become red.

reddish *adj* **red-blooded** *adj Informal* vigorous or virile.

redbrick *adj* (of a university in Britain) founded in the late 19th or early 20th century. **red card** *Soccer* piece of red pasteboard shown by a referee to indicate that a player has been sent off. **red carpet** very special welcome for an important guest. **redcoat** *n Hist* British soldier. **Red Cross** international organization providing help for victims of war or natural disasters. **redcurrant** *n* small round edible red berry.

red-handed *adj Informal* (caught) in the act of doing something wrong or illegal. **red herring** something which diverts attention from the main issue. **red-hot** *adj* glowing red; extremely hot; very keen. **Red Indian** *Offens* A name formerly used for Native American. **red light** traffic signal to stop; danger signal. **red meat** dark meat, esp. beef or lamb. **red tape** excessive adherence to official rules.

redeem *v* make up for; reinstate (oneself) in someone's good opinion; free from sin; buy back; pay off (a loan or debt). **the Redeemer** Jesus Christ. **redeemable** *adj* **redemption** *n* **redemptive** *adj*

redeploy *v* assign to a new position or task. **redeployment** *n*

redevelop *v* rebuild or renovate (an area or building). **redevelopment** *n*

redolent *adj* reminiscent (of); smelling strongly (of).

redouble *v* increase, multiply, or intensify.

redoubt *n* small fort defending a hilltop or pass.

redoubtable *adj* formidable.

redound *v* cause advantage or disadvantage (to).

redox *n* chemical reaction in which one substance is reduced and the other is oxidized.

redress *v* make amends for. ▶ *n* compensation or amends.

reduce *v* bring down, lower; lessen, weaken; bring by force or necessity to some state or action; slim; simplify; make (a sauce) more concentrated. **reducible** *adj* **reduction** *n*

redundant *adj* (of a worker) no longer needed; superfluous. **redundancy** *n*

reed *n* tall grass that grows in swamps and shallow water; tall straight stem of this plant; *Music* vibrating cane or metal strip in certain wind instruments. **reedy** *adj* harsh and thin in tone.

reef¹ *n* ridge of rock or coral near the surface of the sea; vein of ore.

reef² *n* part of a sail which can be rolled up to reduce its area. ▶ *v* take in a reef of. **reefer** *n* short thick jacket worn esp. by sailors; *Old-fashioned slang* hand-rolled cigarette containing cannabis. **reef knot** two simple knots turned opposite ways.

reek *v* smell strongly. ▶ *n* strong unpleasant smell. **reek of** give a strong suggestion of.

reel¹ *n* cylindrical object on which film, tape, thread, or wire is wound; winding apparatus, as of a fishing rod. **reel in** *v* draw in by means of a reel. **reel off** *v* recite or write fluently or quickly.

reel² *v* stagger, sway, or whirl.

reel³ *n* lively Scottish dance.

ref *n Informal* referee in sport.

refectory *n, pl* **-tories**. room for meals in a college etc.

refer v -ferring, -ferred. (foll. by to) allude (to); be relevant (to); send (to) for information; submit (to) for decision. **referral** n

reference n act of referring; citation or direction in a book; written testimonial regarding character or capabilities. **with reference to** concerning.

referee n umpire in sports, esp. soccer or boxing; person willing to testify to someone's character etc.; arbitrator. ▶ v -eeing, -eed. act as referee of.

referendum n, pl -dums, -da. direct vote of the electorate on an important question.

refill v fill again. ▶ n second or subsequent filling; replacement supply of something in a permanent container.

refine v purify; improve. **refined** adj cultured or polite; purified. **refinement** n improvement or elaboration; fineness of taste or manners; subtlety. **refinery** n place where sugar, oil, etc. is refined.

reflation n increase in the supply of money and credit designed to encourage economic activity. **reflate** v **reflationary** adj

reflect v throw back, esp. rays of light, heat, etc.; form an image of; show; consider at length; bring credit or discredit upon. **reflection** n act of reflecting; return of rays of heat, light, etc. from a surface; image of an object given back by a mirror etc.; conscious thought or meditation; attribution of discredit or blame. **reflective** adj quiet, contemplative; capable of reflecting images. **reflector** n polished surface for reflecting light etc.

reflex n involuntary response to a stimulus or situation. ▶ adj (of a muscular action) involuntary; reflected; (of an angle) more than 180°. **reflexive** adj Grammar denoting a verb whose subject is the same as its object, e.g. dress oneself.

reflexology n foot massage as a therapy in alternative medicine.

reform n improvement. ▶ v improve; abandon evil practices. **reformer** n **reformation** n act or instance of something being reformed; (R-) religious movement in 16th-century Europe that resulted in the establishment of the Protestant Churches. **reformatory** n (formerly) institution for reforming young offenders.

refract v change the course of (light etc.) passing from one medium to another. **refraction** n **refractive** adj **refractor** n

refractory adj unmanageable or rebellious; Med resistant to treatment; resistant to heat.

refrain[1] v **refrain from** keep oneself from doing.

refrain[2] n frequently repeated part of a song.

refresh v revive or reinvigorate, as through food, drink, or rest; stimulate (the memory). **refresher** n **refreshing** adj having a reviving effect; pleasantly different or new. **refreshment** n something that refreshes, esp. food or drink.

refrigerate v cool or freeze in order to preserve. **refrigeration** n **refrigerator** n full name for FRIDGE.

refuge n (source of) shelter or protection. **refugee** n person who seeks refuge, esp. in a foreign country.

refulgent adj shining, radiant.

refund v pay back. ▶ n return of

money; amount returned.

refurbish v renovate and brighten up.

refuse¹ v decline, deny, or reject. **refusal** n denial of anything demanded or offered.

refuse² n rubbish or useless matter.

refute v disprove. **refutation** n

regain v get back or recover; reach again.

regal adj of or like a king or queen. **regally** adv **regalia** pl n ceremonial emblems of royalty or high office.

regale v entertain (someone) with stories etc.

regard v consider; look at; heed. ▶ n respect or esteem; attention; look. ▶ pl expression of goodwill. **as regards, regarding** in respect of, concerning. **regardless** adj heedless. ▶ adv in spite of everything.

regatta n meeting for yacht or boat races.

regenerate v (cause to) undergo spiritual, moral, or physical renewal; reproduce or re-create. **regeneration** n **regenerative** adj

regent n ruler of a kingdom during the absence, childhood, or illness of its monarch. ▶ adj ruling as a regent, e.g. *prince regent.* **regency** n status or period of office of a regent.

reggae n style of Jamaican popular music with a strong beat.

regicide n killing of a king; person who kills a king.

regime [ray-**zheem**] n system of government; particular administration.

regimen n prescribed system of diet etc.

regiment n organized body of troops as a unit of the army. **regimental** adj **regimentation** n **regimented** adj very strictly

controlled.

region n administrative division of a country; area considered as a unit but with no definite boundaries; part of the body. **regional** adj

register n (book containing) an official list or record of things; range of a voice or instrument. ▶ v enter in a register or set down in writing; show or be shown on a meter or the face. **registration** n **registration number** numbers and letters displayed on a vehicle to identify it. **registrar** n keeper of official records; senior hospital doctor, junior to a consultant. **register office, registry office** place where births, marriages, and deaths are recorded.

Regius professor [reej-yuss] n (in Britain) professor appointed by the Crown to a university chair founded by a royal patron.

regress v revert to a former worse condition. **regression** n act of regressing; *Psychol* use of an earlier (inappropriate) mode of behaviour. **regressive** adj

regret v **-gretting, -gretted.** feel sorry about; express apology or distress. ▶ n feeling of repentance, guilt, or sorrow. **regretful** adj **regrettable** adj

regular adj normal, customary, or usual; symmetrical or even; done or occurring according to a rule; periodical; employed continuously in the armed forces. ▶ n regular soldier; *Informal* frequent customer. **regularity** n **regularize** v **regularly** adv

regulate v control, esp. by rules; adjust slightly. **regulation** n rule; regulating. **regulator** n device that automatically controls pressure, temperature, etc.

regurgitate v vomit; (of some

birds and animals) bring back (partly digested food) into the mouth; reproduce (ideas, facts, etc.) without understanding them. **regurgitation** n

rehabilitate v help (a person) to readjust to society after illness, imprisonment, etc.; restore to a former position or rank; restore the good reputation of. **rehabilitation** n

rehash v rework or reuse. ▶ n old ideas presented in a new form.

rehearse v practise (a play, concert, etc.); repeat aloud. **rehearsal** n

rehouse v provide with a new (and better) home.

reign n period of a sovereign's rule. ▶ v rule (a country); be supreme.

reimburse v refund, pay back. **reimbursement** n

rein v check or manage with reins; control or limit. **reins** pl n narrow straps attached to a bit to guide a horse; means of control.

reincarnation n rebirth of a soul in successive bodies; one of a series of such transmigrations. **reincarnate** v

reindeer n, pl -deer, -deers. deer of arctic regions with large branched antlers.

reinforce v strengthen with new support, material, or force; strengthen with additional troops, ships, etc. **reinforcement** n **reinforced concrete** concrete strengthened by having steel mesh or bars embedded in it.

reinstate v restore to a former position. **reinstatement** n

reiterate v repeat again and again. **reiteration** n

reject v refuse to accept or believe; rebuff (a person); discard as useless. ▶ n person or thing

rejected as not up to standard. **rejection** n

rejig v -jigging, -jigged. re-equip (a factory or plant); rearrange.

rejoice v feel or express great happiness.

rejoin[1] v join again.

rejoin[2] v reply. **rejoinder** n answer, retort.

rejuvenate v restore youth or vitality to. **rejuvenation** n

relapse v fall back into bad habits, illness, etc. ▶ n return of bad habits, illness, etc.

relate v establish a relation between; have reference or relation to; have an understanding (of people or ideas); tell (a story) or describe (an event). **related** adj

relation n connection between things; relative; connection by blood or marriage; act of relating (a story). ▶ pl social or political dealings; family. **relationship** n dealings and feelings between people or countries; emotional or sexual affair; connection between two things; association by blood or marriage, kinship.

relative adj dependent on relation to something else, not absolute; having reference or relation (to); Grammar referring to a word or clause earlier in the sentence. ▶ n person connected by blood or marriage. **relatively** adv **relativity** n subject of two theories of Albert Einstein, dealing with relationships of space, time, and motion, and acceleration and gravity; state of being relative.

relax v make or become looser, less tense, or less rigid; ease up from effort or attention, rest; be less strict about; become more friendly. **relaxing** adj **relaxation** n

relay n fresh set of people or animals relieving others; Electricity device for making or breaking a local circuit; broadcasting station receiving and retransmitting programmes. ▶ v **-laying, -layed.** pass on (a message). **relay race** *n* race between teams in which each runner races part of the distance.

release *v* set free; let go or fall; issue (a record, film, etc.) for sale or public showing; emit heat, energy, etc. ▶ *n* setting free; statement to the press; act of issuing for sale or publication; newly issued film, record, etc.

relegate *v* put in a less important position; demote (a sports team) to a lower league. **relegation** *n*

relent *v* give up a harsh intention, become less severe. **relentless** *adj* unremitting; merciless.

relevant *adj* to do with the matter in hand. **relevance** *n*

reliable *adj* able to be trusted, dependable. **reliably** *adv* **reliability** *n*

reliance *n* dependence, confidence, or trust. **reliant** *adj*

relic *n* something that has survived from the past; body or possession of a saint, regarded as holy. ▶ *pl* remains or traces. **relict** *n Obs* widow.

relief *n* gladness at the end or removal of pain, distress, etc.; release from monotony or duty; money or food given to victims of disaster, poverty, etc.; freeing of a besieged city etc.; person who replaces another; projection of a carved design from the surface; any vivid effect resulting from contrast, e.g. *comic relief.* **relieve** *v* bring relief to. **relieve oneself** urinate or defecate. **relief map** map showing the shape and height of land by shading.

religion *n* system of belief in and worship of a supernatural power

or god. **religious** *adj* of religion; pious or devout; scrupulous or conscientious. **religiously** *adv*

relinquish *v* give up or abandon.

reliquary *n, pl* **-quaries.** case or shrine for holy relics.

relish *v* enjoy, like very much. ▶ *n* liking or enjoyment; appetizing savoury food, such as pickle; zestful quality or flavour.

relocate *v* move to a new place to live or work. **relocation** *n*

reluctant *adj* unwilling or disinclined. **reluctantly** *adv* **reluctance** *n*

rely *v* **-lying, -lied.** depend (on); trust.

remain *v* continue; stay, be left behind; be left (over); be left to be done, said, etc. **remains** *pl n* relics, esp. of ancient buildings; dead body. **remainder** *n* part which is left; amount left over after subtraction or division. ▶ *v* offer (copies of a poorly selling book) at reduced prices.

remand *v* send back into custody or put on bail before trial. **on remand** in custody or on bail before trial. **remand centre** (in Britain) place where accused people are detained awaiting trial.

remark *v* make a casual comment (on); say; observe or notice. ▶ *n* observation or comment. **remarkable** *adj* worthy of note or attention; striking or unusual. **remarkably** *adv*

remedy *n, pl* **-edies.** means of curing pain or disease; means of solving a problem. ▶ *v* **-edying, -edied.** put right. **remedial** *adj* intended to correct a specific disability, handicap, etc.

remember *v* retain in or recall to one's memory; keep in mind. **remembrance** *n* memory; token or souvenir; honouring of the

memory of a person or event.
remind v cause to remember; put in mind (of). **reminder** n something that recalls the past; note to remind a person of something not done.

reminisce v talk or write of past times, experiences, etc. **reminiscence** n remembering; thing recollected. ▶ pl memoirs. **reminiscent** adj reminding or suggestive of.

remiss adj negligent or careless.

remission n reduction in the length of a prison term; easing of intensity, as of an illness.

remit v [rim-mitt] -mitting, -mitted. send (money) for goods, services, etc., esp. by post; cancel (a punishment or debt); refer (a decision) to a higher authority or later date. ▶ n [ree-mitt] area of competence or authority.

remittance n money sent as payment.

remnant n small piece, esp. of fabric, left over; surviving trace.

remonstrate v argue in protest. **remonstrance** n

remorse n feeling of sorrow and regret for something one did. **remorseful** adj **remorseless** adj pitiless; persistent. **remorselessly** adv

remote adj far away, distant; aloof; slight or faint. **remotely** adv

remote control control of an apparatus from a distance by an electrical device.

remould v Brit renovate (a worn tyre). ▶ n Brit renovated tyre.

remove v take away or off; get rid of; dismiss from office. ▶ n degree of difference. **removable** adj **removal** n removing, esp. changing residence.

remunerate v reward or pay. **remunerative** adj

remuneration n reward or payment.

renaissance n revival or rebirth; (**R-**) revival of learning in the 14th–16th centuries.

renal [ree-nal] adj of the kidneys.

renascent adj becoming active or vigorous again.

rend v **rending, rent.** tear or wrench apart; (of a sound) break (the silence) violently.

render v cause to become; give or provide (aid, a service, etc.); submit or present (a bill); portray or represent; cover with plaster; melt down (fat).

rendezvous [ron-day-voo] n, pl -vous. appointment; meeting place. ▶ v meet as arranged.

rendition n performance; translation.

renegade n person who deserts a cause.

renege [rin-nayg] v go back (on a promise etc.).

renew v begin again; make valid again; grow again; restore to a former state; replace (a worn part); restate or reaffirm. **renewable** adj **renewal** n

rennet n substance for curdling milk to make cheese.

renounce v give up (a belief, habit, etc.) voluntarily; give up (a title or claim) formally. **renunciation** n

renovate v restore to good condition. **renovation** n

renown n widespread good reputation.

renowned adj famous.

rent¹ v give or have use of in return for regular payments. ▶ n regular payment for use of land, a building, machine, etc. **rental** n sum payable as rent.

rent² n tear or fissure. ▶ v past of REND.

renunciation n see RENOUNCE.

reorganize v organize in a new and more efficient way. **reorganization** n

rep¹ n short for REPERTORY COMPANY.

rep² n short for REPRESENTATIVE.

repair¹ v restore to good condition, mend. ▶ n act of repairing; repaired part; state or condition, e.g. *in good repair*. **reparation** n something done or given as compensation.

repair² v go (to).

repartee n interchange of witty retorts; witty retort.

repast n meal.

repatriate v send (someone) back to his or her own country. **repatriation** n

repay v **repaying, repaid.** pay back, refund; do something in return, e.g. *repay hospitality.* **repayable** adj **repayment** n

repeal v cancel (a law) officially. ▶ n act of repealing.

repeat v say or do again; happen again, recur. ▶ n act or instance of repeating; programme broadcast again. **repeatedly** adv **repeater** n firearm that may be discharged many times without reloading.

repel v **-pelling, -pelled.** be disgusting to; drive back, ward off; resist. **repellent** adj distasteful; resisting water etc. ▶ n something that repels, esp. a chemical to repel insects.

repent v feel regret for (a deed or omission). **repentance** n **repentant** adj

repercussions pl n indirect effects, often unpleasant.

repertoire n stock of plays, songs, etc. that a player or company can give.

repertory n, pl **-ries.** repertoire. **repertory company** permanent theatre company producing a succession of plays.

repetition n act of repeating; thing repeated. **repetitive, repetitious** adj full of repetition.

rephrase v express in different words.

repine v fret or complain.

replace v substitute for; put back. **replacement** n

replay n (also **action replay**) immediate reshowing on TV of an incident in sport, esp. in slow motion; second sports match, esp. one following an earlier draw. ▶ v play (a match, recording, etc.) again.

replenish v fill up again, resupply. **replenishment** n

replete adj filled or gorged.

replica n exact copy. **replicate** v make or be a copy of.

reply v **-plying, -plied.** answer or respond. ▶ n, pl **-plies.** answer or response.

report v give an account of; make a report (on); make a formal complaint about; present oneself (to); be responsible (to). ▶ n account or statement; rumour; written statement of a child's progress at school; bang. **reportedly** adv according to rumour. **reporter** n person who gathers news for a newspaper, TV, etc.

repose n peace; composure; sleep. ▶ v lie or lay at rest.

repository n, pl **-ries.** place where valuables are deposited for safekeeping, store.

repossess v (of a lender) take back property from a customer who is behind with payments. **repossession** n

reprehensible adj open to criticism, unworthy.

represent v act as a delegate or substitute for; stand for;

symbolize; make out to be; portray, as in art. **representation** n **representative** n person chosen to stand for a group; (travelling) salesperson. ▶ adj typical.

repress v keep (feelings) in check; restrict the freedom of. **repression** n **repressive** adj

reprieve v postpone the execution of (a condemned person); give temporary relief to. ▶ n (document granting) postponement or cancellation of a punishment; temporary relief.

reprimand v blame (someone) officially for a fault. ▶ n official blame.

reprint v print further copies of (a book). ▶ n reprinted copy.

reprisal n retaliation.

reproach n, v blame, rebuke. **reproachful** adj **reproachfully** adv

reprobate adj, n depraved or disreputable (person).

reproduce v produce a copy of; bring new individuals into existence; re-create. **reproducible** adj **reproduction** n process of reproducing; facsimile, as of a painting etc.; quality of sound from an audio system. **reproductive** adj

reprove v speak severely to (someone) about a fault. **reproof** n severe blaming of someone for a fault.

reptile n cold-blooded egg-laying vertebrate with horny scales or plates, such as a snake or tortoise. **reptilian** adj

republic n form of government in which the people or their elected representatives possess the supreme power; country in which a president is the head of state. **Republican** n, adj (member or supporter) of the Republican

Party, the more conservative of the two main political parties in the US. **Republicanism** n

repudiate [rip-pew-dee-ate] v reject the authority or validity of; disown. **repudiation** n

repugnant adj offensive or distasteful. **repugnance** n

repulse v be disgusting to; drive (an army) back; rebuff or reject. ▶ n driving back; rejection or rebuff. **repulsion** n distaste or aversion; *Physics* force separating two objects. **repulsive** adj loathsome, disgusting.

reputation n estimation in which a person is held. **reputable** adj of good reputation, respectable. **repute** n reputation. **reputed** adj supposed. **reputedly** adv

request v ask. ▶ n asking; thing asked for.

Requiem [rek-wee-em] n Mass for the dead; music for this.

require v want or need; demand. **requirement** n essential condition; specific need or want.

requisite [rek-wizz-it] adj necessary, essential. ▶ n essential thing.

requisition v demand (supplies). ▶ n formal demand, such as for materials or supplies.

requite v return to someone (the same treatment or feeling as received).

reredos [rear-doss] n ornamental screen behind an altar.

rescind v annul or repeal.

rescue v -cuing, -cued. deliver from danger or trouble, save. ▶ n rescuing. **rescuer** n

research n systematic investigation to discover facts or collect information. ▶ v carry out investigations. **researcher** n

resemble v be or look like. **resemblance** n

resent v feel bitter about.
resentful adj **resentment** n

reservation n doubt; exception or limitation; seat, room, etc. that has been reserved; area of land reserved for use by a particular group; (also **central reservation**) Brit strip of ground separating the two carriageways of a dual carriageway or motorway.

reserve v set aside, keep for future use; obtain by arranging beforehand, book; retain. ▶ n something, esp. money or troops, kept for emergencies; area of land reserved for a particular purpose; Sport substitute; concealment of feelings or friendliness. **reserved** adj not showing one's feelings, lacking friendliness; set aside for use by a particular person.
reservist n member of a military reserve.

reservoir n natural or artificial lake storing water for community supplies; store or supply of something.

reshuffle n reorganization. ▶ v reorganize.

reside v dwell permanently.
resident n person who lives in a place. ▶ adj living in a place. **residence** n home or house. **residential** adj (of part of a town) consisting mainly of houses; providing living accommodation.
residue n what is left, remainder. **residual** adj

resign v give up office, a job, etc.; reconcile (oneself) to. **resigned** adj content to endure. **resignation** n resigning; passive endurance of difficulties.

resilient adj (of a person) recovering quickly from a shock etc.; able to return to normal shape after stretching etc. **resilience** n

resin [rezz-in] n sticky substance from plants, esp. pines; similar synthetic substance. **resinous** adj

resist v withstand or oppose; refrain from despite temptation; be proof against. **resistance** n act of resisting; capacity to withstand something; Electricity opposition offered by a circuit to the passage of a current through it. **resistant** adj **resistible** adj **resistor** n component of an electrical circuit producing resistance.

resit v take (an exam) again. ▶ n exam that has to be taken again.

resolute adj firm in purpose. **resolutely** adv

resolution n firmness of conduct or character; thing resolved upon; decision of a court or vote of an assembly; act of resolving.

resolve v decide with an effort of will; form (a resolution) by a vote; separate the component parts of; make clear, settle. **resolved** adj determined.

resonance n echoing, esp. with a deep sound; sound produced in one object by sound waves coming from another object. **resonant** adj **resonate** v

resort v have recourse (to) for help etc. ▶ n place for holidays; recourse.

resound [riz-zownd] v echo or ring with sound. **resounding** adj echoing; clear and emphatic.

resource n thing resorted to for support; ingenuity; means of achieving something. ▶ pl sources of economic wealth; stock that can be drawn on, funds. **resourceful** adj **resourcefulness** n

respect n consideration; deference or esteem; point or aspect; reference or relation, e.g. with respect to. ▶ v treat with esteem; show consideration for. **respecter**

n **respectful** adj **respecting** prep concerning.
respectable adj worthy of respect; fairly good. **respectably** adv **respectability** n
respective adj relating separately to each of those in question. **respectively** adv
respiration [ress-per-**ray**-shun] n breathing. **respirator** n apparatus worn over the mouth and breathed through as protection against dust, poison gas, etc., or to provide artificial respiration. **respiratory** adj **respire** v breathe.
respite n pause, interval of rest; delay.
resplendent adj brilliant or splendid; shining. **resplendence** n
respond v answer; act in answer to any stimulus; react favourably. **respondent** n Law defendant. **response** n answer; reaction to a stimulus. **responsive** adj readily reacting to some influence. **responsiveness** n
responsible adj having control and authority; reporting or accountable (to); sensible and dependable; involving responsibility. **responsibly** adv **responsibility** n, pl **-ties.** state of being responsible; person or thing for which one is responsible.
rest[1] n freedom from exertion etc.; repose; pause, esp. in music; object used for support. ▶ v take a rest; give a rest (to); be supported; place on a support. **restful** adj **restless** adj
rest[2] n what is left; others. ▶ v remain, continue to be.
restaurant n commercial establishment serving meals. **restaurateur** [rest-er-a-**tur**] n person who owns or runs a restaurant.
restitution n giving back;

reparation or compensation.
restive adj restless or impatient.
restore v return (a building, painting, etc.) to its original condition; cause to recover health or spirits; give back, return; re-establish. **restoration** n **restorative** adj restoring. ▶ n food or medicine to strengthen etc. **restorer** n
restrain v hold (someone) back from action; control or restrict. **restrained** adj not displaying emotion. **restraint** n control, esp. self-control; restraining.
restrict v confine to certain limits. **restriction** n **restrictive** adj
restructure v organize in a different way.
result n outcome or consequence; score; number obtained from a calculation; exam mark or grade. ▶ v (foll. by from) be the outcome or consequence (of); (foll. by in) end (in). **resultant** adj
resume v begin again; occupy or take again. **resumption** n
résumé [rezz-yew-may] n summary.
resurgence n rising again to vigour. **resurgent** adj
resurrect v restore to life; use once more (something discarded etc.), revive. **resurrection** n rising again (esp. from the dead); revival.
resuscitate [ris-**suss**-it-tate] v restore to consciousness. **resuscitation** n
retail n selling of goods individually or in small amounts to the public. ▶ adv by retail. ▶ v sell or be sold retail; recount in detail. **retailer** n person or company that sells goods to the public.
retain v keep in one's possession; engage the services of. **retainer** n fee to retain someone's services; old-established servant of a family.
retaliate v repay an injury or

wrong in kind. **retaliation** n
retaliatory adj

retard v delay or slow (progress or development). **retarded** adj underdeveloped, esp. mentally. **retardation** n

retch v try to vomit.

rethink v consider again, esp. with a view to changing one's tactics.

reticent adj uncommunicative, reserved. **reticence** n

retina n, pl -nas. -nae. light-sensitive membrane at the back of the eye.

retinue n band of attendants.

retire v (cause to) give up office or work, esp. through age; go away or withdraw; go to bed. **retired** adj having retired from work etc. **retirement** n **retiring** adj shy.

retort[1] v reply quickly, wittily, or angrily. ▶ n quick, witty, or angry reply.

retort[2] n glass container with a bent neck used for distilling.

retouch v restore or improve by new touches, esp. of paint.

retrace v go back over (a route etc.) again.

retract v withdraw (a statement etc.); draw in or back. **retractable, retractile** adj able to be retracted. **retraction** n

retread v, n same as REMOULD.

retreat v move back from a position, withdraw. ▶ n act of or military signal for retiring or withdrawal; place to which anyone retires, refuge.

retrench v reduce expenditure, cut back. **retrenchment** n

retrial n second trial of a case or defendant in a court of law.

retribution n punishment or vengeance for evil deeds. **retributive** adj

retrieve v fetch back again; restore to a better state; recover

(information) from a computer. **retrievable** adj **retrieval** n

retriever n dog trained to retrieve shot game.

retroactive adj effective from a date in the past.

retrograde adj tending towards an earlier worse condition.

retrogressive adj going back to an earlier worse condition. **retrogression** n

retrorocket n small rocket engine used to slow a spacecraft.

retrospect n in retrospect when looking back on the past.

retrospective adj looking back in time; applying from a date in the past. ▶ n exhibition of an artist's life's work.

retroussé [rit-troo-say] adj (of a nose) turned upwards.

retsina n Greek wine flavoured with resin.

return v go or come back; give, put, or send back; reply; elect. ▶ n returning; (thing) being returned; profit; official report, as of taxable income; return ticket. **returnable** adj **returning officer** person in charge of an election. **return ticket** ticket allowing a passenger to travel to a place and back.

reunion n meeting of people who have been apart. **reunite** v bring or come together again after a separation.

reuse v use again. **reusable** adj

rev Informal ▶ n revolution (of an engine). ▶ v revving, revved. (foll. by up) increase the speed of revolution of (an engine).

Rev., Revd. Reverend.

revalue v adjust the exchange value of (a currency) upwards. **revaluation** n

revamp v renovate or restore.

reveal v make known; expose or show. **revelation** n

reveille [riv-**val**-ee] *n* morning bugle call to waken soldiers.

revel *v* -**elling, -elled.** take pleasure (in); make merry. **revels** *pl n* merrymaking. **reveller** *n* **revelry** *n* festivity.

revenge *n* retaliation for wrong done. ▶ *v* make retaliation for; avenge (oneself or another). **revengeful** *adj*

revenue *n* income, esp. of a state.

reverberate *v* echo or resound. **reverberation** *n*

revere *v* be in awe of and respect greatly. **reverence** *n* awe mingled with respect and esteem. **Reverend** *adj* title of respect for a clergyman. **reverent** *adj* showing reverence. **reverently** *adv* **reverential** *adj* marked by reverence.

reverie *n* absent-minded daydream.

revers [riv-**veer**] *n* turned back part of a garment, such as the lapel.

reverse *v* turn upside down or the other way round; change completely; move (a vehicle) backwards. ▶ *n* opposite; back side; change for the worse; reverse gear. ▶ *adj* opposite or contrary. **reversal** *n* **reversible** *adj* **reverse gear** mechanism enabling a vehicle to move backwards.

revert *v* return to a former state; come back to a subject; (of property) return to its former owner. **reversion** *n*

review *n* critical assessment of a book, concert, etc.; publication with critical articles; general survey; formal inspection. ▶ *v* hold or write a review of; examine, reconsider, or look back on; inspect formally. **reviewer** *n* writer of reviews.

revile *v* be abusively scornful of.

revise *v* change or alter; restudy

(work) in preparation for an examination. **revision** *n*

revive *v* bring or come back to life, vigour, use, etc. **revival** *n* reviving or renewal; movement seeking to restore religious faith. **revivalism** *n* **revivalist** *n*

revoke *v* cancel (a will, agreement, etc.). **revocation** *n*

revolt *n* uprising against authority. ▶ *v* rise in rebellion; cause to feel disgust. **revolting** *adj* disgusting, horrible.

revolution *n* overthrow of a government by the governed; great change; spinning round; complete rotation. **revolutionary** *adj* advocating or engaged in revolution; radically new or different. ▶ *n, pl* -**aries.** person advocating or engaged in revolution. **revolutionize** *v* change considerably.

revolve *v* turn round, rotate. **revolve around** be centred on.

revolver *n* repeating pistol.

revue *n* theatrical entertainment with topical sketches and songs.

revulsion *n* strong disgust.

reward *n* something given in return for a service; sum of money offered for finding a criminal or missing property. ▶ *v* pay or give something to (someone) for a service, information, etc. **rewarding** *adj* giving personal satisfaction, worthwhile.

rewind *v* run (a tape or film) back to an earlier point in order to replay.

rewire *v* provide (a house, engine, etc.) with new wiring.

rewrite *v* write again in a different way. ▶ *n* something rewritten.

rhapsody *n, pl* -**dies.** freely structured emotional piece of music; expression of ecstatic enthusiasm. **rhapsodic** *adj*

rhapsodize v speak or write with extravagant enthusiasm.

rhea [ree-a] n S American three-toed ostrich.

rhenium n Chem silvery-white metallic element with a high melting point.

rheostat n instrument for varying the resistance of an electrical circuit.

rhesus [ree-suss] n small long-tailed monkey of S Asia.

rhesus factor, Rh factor antigen commonly found in human blood.

rhetoric n art of effective speaking or writing; artificial or exaggerated language. **rhetorical** adj (of a question) not requiring an answer. **rhetorically** adv

rheumatism n painful inflammation of joints or muscles. **rheumatic** n, adj (person) affected by rheumatism. **rheumatoid** adj of or like rheumatism.

Rh factor n see RHESUS.

rhinestone n imitation diamond.

rhino n short for RHINOCEROS.

rhinoceros n, pl -oses, -os. large thick-skinned animal with one or two horns on its nose.

rhizome n thick underground stem producing new plants.

rhodium n Chem hard metallic element.

rhododendron n evergreen flowering shrub.

rhombus n, pl -buses, -bi. parallelogram with sides of equal length but no right angles, diamond-shaped figure. **rhomboid** n parallelogram with adjacent sides of unequal length.

rhubarb n garden plant of which the fleshy stalks are cooked as fruit.

rhyme n sameness of the final sounds at the ends of lines of verse, or in words; word identical in sound to another in its final sounds; verse marked by rhyme. ▶ v make a rhyme.

rhythm n any regular movement or beat; arrangement of the durations of and stress on the notes of a piece of music, usu. grouped into a regular pattern; (in poetry) arrangement of words to form a regular pattern of stresses. **rhythmic, rhythmical** adj **rhythmically** adv **rhythm and blues** popular music, orig. Black American, influenced by the blues.

rib¹ n one of the curved bones forming the framework of the upper part of the body; cut of meat including the rib(s); curved supporting part, as in the hull of a boat; raised series of rows in knitting. ▶ v **ribbing, ribbed.** provide or mark with ribs; knit to form a rib pattern. **ribbed** adj **ribbing** n **ribcage** n bony structure of ribs enclosing the lungs.

rib² v **ribbing, ribbed.** Informal tease or ridicule. **ribbing** n

ribald adj humorously or mockingly rude or obscene. **ribaldry** n

ribbon n narrow band of fabric used for trimming, tying, etc.; any long strip, for example of inked tape in a typewriter.

riboflavin [rye-boe-flay-vin] n form of vitamin B.

rice n cereal plant grown on wet ground in warm countries; its seeds as food.

rich adj owning a lot of money or property, wealthy; abounding; fertile; (of food) containing much fat or sugar; mellow; amusing. **riches** pl n wealth. **richly** adv elaborately; fully. **richness** n

rick¹ n stack of hay etc.

rick² v, n sprain or wrench.

rickets n disease of children

marked by softening of the bones, bow legs, etc., caused by vitamin D deficiency.

rickety adj shaky or unstable.

rickshaw n light two-wheeled man-drawn Asian vehicle.

ricochet [rik-osh-ay] v (of a bullet) rebound from a solid surface. ▶ n such a rebound.

rid v **ridding, rid.** clear or relieve (of). **get rid of** free oneself of (something undesirable). **good riddance** relief at getting rid of something or someone.

ridden v past participle of RIDE. ▶ adj afflicted or affected by the thing specified, e.g. *disease-ridden.*

riddle¹ n question made puzzling to test one's ingenuity; puzzling person or thing.

riddle² v pierce with many holes. ▶ n coarse sieve for gravel etc. **riddled with** full of.

ride v **riding, rode, ridden.** sit on and control or propel (a horse, bicycle, etc.); go on horseback or in a vehicle; travel over; be carried on or across; lie at anchor. ▶ n journey on a horse etc., or in a vehicle; type of movement experienced in a vehicle. **ride up** v (of a garment) move up from the proper position.

rider n person who rides; supplementary clause added to a document.

ridge n long narrow hill; long narrow raised part on a surface; line where two sloping surfaces meet; *Meteorol* elongated area of high pressure. **ridged** adj

ridiculous adj deserving to be laughed at, absurd. **ridicule** n treatment of a person or thing as ridiculous. ▶ v laugh at, make fun of.

Riding n former administrative district of Yorkshire.

riesling n type of white wine.

rife adj widespread or common. **rife with** full of.

riff n *Jazz, rock* short repeated melodic figure.

riffle v flick through (pages etc.) quickly.

riffraff n rabble, disreputable people.

rifle¹ n firearm with a long barrel.

rifle² v search and rob; steal.

rift n break in friendly relations; crack, split, or cleft. **rift valley** long narrow valley resulting from subsidence between faults.

rig v **rigging, rigged.** arrange in a dishonest way; equip, esp. a ship. ▶ n apparatus for drilling for oil and gas; way a ship's masts and sails are arranged; *Informal* outfit of clothes. **rigging** n ship's spars and ropes. **rig up** v set up or build temporarily.

right adj just; true or correct; proper; in a satisfactory condition; of the side that faces east when the front is turned to the north; of the outer side of a fabric. ▶ adv properly; straight or directly; on or to the right side. ▶ n claim, title, etc. allowed or due; what is just or due; (**R-**) conservative political party or group. ▶ v bring or come back to a normal or correct state; bring or come back to a vertical position. **in the right** morally or legally correct. **right away** immediately. **rightly** adv **rightful** adj **rightist** n, adj (person) on the political right. **right angle** angle of 90°. **right-handed** adj using or for the right hand. **right-hand man** person's most valuable assistant. **right of way** right of one vehicle to go before another; legal right to pass over someone's land.

righteous [rye-chuss] adj upright,

godly, or virtuous; morally justified. **righteousness** n

rigid adj inflexible or strict; unyielding or stiff. **rigidly** adv **rigidity** n

rigmarole n long complicated procedure.

rigor mortis n stiffening of the body after death.

rigour n harshness, severity, or strictness; hardship. **rigorous** adj harsh, severe, or stern.

rile v anger or annoy.

rill n small stream.

rim n edge or border; outer ring of a wheel. **rimmed** adj

rime n Lit hoarfrost.

rimu n NZ New Zealand tree whose wood is used for building and furniture.

rind n tough outer coating of fruits, cheese, or bacon.

ring[1] v **ringing, rang, rung.** give out a clear resonant sound, as a bell; cause (a bell) to sound; telephone; resound. ▶ n ringing; telephone call. **ring off** v end a telephone call. **ringtone** n tune played by a mobile phone when it receives a call. **ring up** v telephone.

ring[2] n circle of gold etc., esp. for a finger; any circular band, coil, or rim; circle of people; enclosed area, esp. a circle for a circus or a roped-in square for boxing; group operating (illegal) control of a market. ▶ v put a ring round; mark (a bird) with a ring; kill (a tree) by cutting the bark round the trunk. **ringer** n Brit, Aust & NZ slang person or thing apparently identical to another (also **dead ringer**). **ringlet** n curly lock of hair. **ringleader** n instigator of a mutiny, riot, etc. **ring road** Brit, Aust & S Afr main road that bypasses a town (centre).

ringside n row of seats nearest a boxing or circus ring. **ringworm** n fungal skin disease in circular patches.

rink n sheet of ice for skating or curling; floor for roller-skating.

rinse v remove soap from (washed clothes, hair, etc.) by applying clean water; wash lightly. ▶ n rinsing; liquid to tint hair.

riot n disorderly unruly disturbance; Brit, Aust & NZ loud revelry; profusion; Slang very amusing person or thing. ▶ v take part in a riot. **read the riot act** reprimand severely. **run riot** behave without restraint; grow profusely. **riotous** adj unrestrained; unruly or rebellious.

rip v **ripping, ripped.** tear violently; tear away; Informal rush. ▶ n split or tear. **let rip** act or speak without restraint. **ripcord** n cord pulled to open a parachute. **rip off** v Slang cheat by overcharging. **rip-off** n Slang cheat or swindle. **rip-roaring** adj Informal boisterous and exciting.

RIP rest in peace.

riparian [rip-**pair**-ee-an] adj of or on the banks of a river.

ripe adj ready to be reaped, eaten, etc.; matured; ready or suitable. **ripen** v grow ripe; mature.

riposte [rip-**posst**] n verbal retort; counterattack, esp. in fencing. ▶ v make a riposte.

ripple n slight wave or ruffling of a surface; sound like ripples of water. ▶ v flow or form into little waves (on); (of sounds) rise and fall gently.

rise v **rising, rose, risen.** get up from a lying, sitting, or kneeling position; move upwards; (of the sun or moon) appear above the horizon; reach a higher level; (of an amount or price) increase;

rebel; (of a court) adjourn. ▶ *n* rising; upward slope; increase, esp. of wages. **give rise to** cause.
riser *n* person who rises, esp. from bed; vertical part of a step.
rising *n* revolt. ▶ *adj* increasing in rank or maturity.
risible [riz-zib-bl] *adj* causing laughter, ridiculous.
risk *n* chance of disaster or loss; person or thing considered as a potential hazard. ▶ *v* act in spite of the possibility of (injury or loss); expose to danger or loss. **risky** *adj* full of risk, dangerous.
risotto *n*, *pl* **-tos.** dish of rice cooked in stock with vegetables, meat, etc.
risqué [risk-ay] *adj* bordering on indecency.
rissole *n* cake of minced meat, coated with breadcrumbs and fried.
rite *n* formal practice or custom, esp. religious.
ritual *n* prescribed order of rites; regular repeated action or behaviour. ▶ *adj* concerning rites. **ritually** *adv* **ritualistic** *adj* like a ritual.
ritzy *adj* **ritzier, ritziest.** *Slang* luxurious or elegant.
rival *n* person or thing that competes with or equals another for favour, success, etc. ▶ *adj* in the position of a rival. ▶ *v* **-valling, -valled.** (try to) equal. **rivalry** *n* keen competition.
riven *adj* split apart.
river *n* large natural stream of water; plentiful flow.
rivet [riv-vit] *n* bolt for fastening metal plates, the end being put through holes and then beaten flat. ▶ *v* **riveting, riveted.** fasten with rivets; cause to be fixed, as in fascination. **riveting** *adj* very interesting and exciting.

rivulet *n* small stream.
RN (in Britain) Royal Navy.
RNA ribonucleic acid: substance in living cells essential for the synthesis of protein.
RNZ Radio New Zealand.
RNZAF Royal New Zealand Air Force.
RNZN Royal New Zealand Navy.
roach *n* Eurasian freshwater fish.
road *n* way prepared for passengers, vehicles, etc.; route in a town or city with houses along it; way or course, e.g. *the road to fame.* **on the road** travelling.
roadie *n* *Brit, Aust & NZ informal* person who transports and sets up equipment for a band. **roadblock** *n* barricade across a road to stop traffic for inspection etc. **road hog** *Informal* selfish aggressive driver. **roadhouse** *n* *Brit, Aust & S Afr* pub or restaurant on a country road. **roadside** *n, adj* **road test** test of a vehicle etc. in actual use. **roadway** *n* the part of a road used by vehicles. **roadworks** *pl n* repairs to a road, esp. blocking part of the road. **roadworthy** *adj* (of a vehicle) mechanically sound.
roam *v* wander about.
roan *adj* (of a horse) having a brown or black coat sprinkled with white hairs. ▶ *n* roan horse.
roar *v* make or utter a loud deep hoarse sound like that of a lion; shout (something) as in anger; laugh loudly. ▶ *n* such a sound. **a roaring trade** *Informal* brisk and profitable business. **roaring drunk** noisily drunk.
roast *v* cook by dry heat, as in an oven; make or be very hot. ▶ *n* roasted joint of meat. ▶ *adj* roasted. **roasting** *Informal* ▶ *adj* extremely hot. ▶ *n* severe criticism or scolding.
rob *v* **robbing, robbed.** steal from;

deprive. **robber** n **robbery** n

robe n long loose outer garment.
▶ v put a robe on.

robin n small brown bird with a red breast.

robot n automated machine, esp. one performing functions in a human manner; person of machine-like efficiency; *S Afr* set of coloured lights at a junction to control the traffic flow. **robotic** adj **robotics** n science of designing and using robots.

robust adj very strong and healthy. **robustly** adv **robustness** n

roc n monstrous bird of Arabian mythology.

rock[1] n hard mineral substance that makes up part of the earth's crust, stone; large rugged mass of stone; *Brit* hard sweet in sticks. **on the rocks** (of a marriage) about to end; (of an alcoholic drink) served with ice. **rocky** adj having many rocks. **rockery** n mound of stones in a garden for rock plants. **rock bottom** lowest possible level. **rock cake** small fruit cake with a rough surface.

rock[2] v (cause) to sway to and fro; *NZ slang* be very good. ▶ n (also **rock music**) style of pop music with a heavy beat. **rocky** adj shaky or unstable. **rock and roll, rock'n'roll** style of pop music blending rhythm and blues and country music. **rocking chair** chair allowing the sitter to rock backwards and forwards.

rocker n rocking chair; curved piece of wood etc. on which something may rock. **off one's rocker** *Informal* insane.

rocket n self-propelling device powered by the burning of explosive contents (used as a firework, weapon, etc.); vehicle propelled by a rocket engine, as a weapon or carrying a spacecraft.
▶ v **-eting, -eted.** move fast, esp. upwards, like a rocket.

rock melon n *US, Aust & NZ* kind of melon with sweet orange flesh.

rococo [rok-**koe**-koe] adj (of furniture, architecture, etc.) having much elaborate decoration in an early 18th-century style.

rod n slender straight bar, stick; cane.

rode v past tense of RIDE.

rodent n animal with teeth specialized for gnawing, such as a rat, mouse, or squirrel.

rodeo n, pl **-deos.** display of skill by cowboys, such as bareback riding.

roe[1] n mass of eggs in a fish, sometimes eaten as food.

roe[2] n small species of deer.

roentgen [ront-**gan**] n unit measuring a radiation dose.

rogue n dishonest or unprincipled person; mischief-loving person.
▶ adj (of a wild beast) having a savage temper and living apart from the herd. **roguish** adj

roister v make merry noisily or boisterously.

role, rôle n task or function; actor's part.

roll v move by turning over and over; move or sweep along; wind round; undulate; smooth out with a roller; (of a ship or aircraft) turn from side to side about a line from nose to tail. ▶ n act of rolling over or from side to side; piece of paper etc. rolled up; small round individually baked piece of bread; list or register; continuous sound, as of drums, thunder, etc.; swaying unsteady movement or gait. **roll call** calling out of a list of names, as in a school or the army, to check who is present. **rolled gold** metal coated with a thin layer of gold. **rolling pin** cylindrical roller for flattening pastry. **rolling stock** locomotives and coaches of a railway. **rolling stone** restless wandering person.

roll-on/roll-off adj Brit, Aust & NZ denoting a ship allowing vehicles to be driven straight on and off. **roll-top** adj (of a desk) having a flexible lid sliding in grooves. **roll up** v Informal appear or arrive. **roll-up** n Brit informal cigarette made by the smoker from loose tobacco and cigarette paper.

roller n rotating cylinder used for smoothing or supporting a thing to be moved, spreading paint, etc.; long wave of the sea. **Rollerblade** n ® roller skate with the wheels set in one straight line. **roller coaster** (at a funfair) narrow railway with steep slopes. **roller skate** skate with wheels.

rollicking adj boisterously carefree. **roly-poly** adj round or plump. **ROM** Computers read only memory. **Roman** adj of Rome or the Roman Catholic Church. **Roman Catholic** (member) of that section of the Christian Church that acknowledges the supremacy of the Pope. **Roman numerals** the letters I, V, X, L, C, D, M, used to represent numbers. **roman type** plain upright letters in printing.

romance n love affair; mysterious or exciting quality; novel or film dealing with love, esp. sentimentally; story with scenes remote from ordinary life. **Romance** adj (of a language) developed from Latin, such as French or Spanish.

romantic adj of or dealing with love; idealistic but impractical; (of literature, music, etc.) displaying passion and imagination rather than order and form. ▶ n romantic

person or artist. **romantically** adv **romanticism** n **romanticize** v describe or regard in an idealized and unrealistic way.

Romany n, pl **-nies**, adj Gypsy.

romp v play wildly and joyfully. ▶ n boisterous activity. **romp home** win easily. **rompers** pl n child's overalls.

rondo n, pl **-dos**. piece of music with a leading theme continually returned to.

roo n Aust informal kangaroo.

rood n Christianity the Cross; crucifix. **rood screen** (in a church) screen separating the nave from the choir.

roof n, pl **roofs**. outside upper covering of a building, car, etc. ▶ v put a roof on.

rooibos [roy-boss] n S Afr tea prepared from the dried leaves of an African plant.

rook[1] n Eurasian bird of the crow family. **rookery** n, pl **-eries**. colony of rooks, penguins, or seals.

rook[2] n chess piece shaped like a castle.

rookie n Informal new recruit.

room n enclosed area in a building; unoccupied space; scope or opportunity. ▶ pl lodgings. **roomy** adj spacious.

roost n perch for fowls. ▶ v perch.

rooster n domestic fowl.

root[1] n part of a plant that grows down into the earth obtaining nourishment; plant with an edible root, such as a carrot; part of a tooth, hair, etc. below the skin; source or origin; form of a word from which other words and forms are derived; Maths factor of a quantity which, when multiplied by itself the number of times indicated, gives the quantity. ▶ pl person's sense of belonging. ▶ v establish a root and start to grow.

rootless *adj* having no sense of belonging. **root for** *v Informal* cheer on. **root out** *v* get rid of completely.

root² *v* dig or burrow.

rope *n* thick cord. **know the ropes** be thoroughly familiar with an activity. **rope in** *v* persuade to join in.

ropey, ropy *adj* **ropier, ropiest.** *Brit informal* inferior or inadequate; not well.

rorqual *n* toothless whale with a dorsal fin.

rort *Aust informal* ▶ *n* dishonest scheme. ▶ *v* take unfair advantage of something.

rosary *n, pl* -**saries.** series of prayers; string of beads for counting these prayers.

rose¹ *n* shrub or climbing plant with prickly stems and fragrant flowers; flower of this plant; perforated flat nozzle for a hose; pink colour. ▶ *adj* pink. **roseate** [roe-zee-ate] *adj* rose-coloured. **rose window** circular window with spokes branching from the centre. **rosewood** *n* fragrant wood used to make furniture.

rose² *v* past tense of RISE.

rosé [roe-zay] *n* pink wine.

rosehip *n* berry-like fruit of a rose plant.

rosella *n* type of Australian parrot.

rosemary *n* fragrant flowering shrub; its leaves as a herb.

rosette *n* rose-shaped ornament, esp. a circular bunch of ribbons.

rosin [rozz-in] *n* resin used for treating the bows of violins etc.

roster *n* list of people and their turns of duty.

rostrum *n, pl* -**trums, -tra.** platform or stage.

rosy *adj* **rosier, rosiest.** pink-coloured; hopeful or promising.

rot *v* **rotting, rotted.** decompose or decay; slowly deteriorate physically or mentally. ▶ *n* decay; *Informal* nonsense.

rota *n* list of people who take it in turn to do a particular task.

rotary *adj* revolving; operated by rotation.

rotate *v* (cause to) move round a centre or on a pivot; (cause to) follow a set sequence. **rotation** *n*

rote *n* mechanical repetition. **by rote** by memory.

rotisserie *n* rotating spit for cooking meat.

rotor *n* revolving portion of a dynamo, motor, or turbine; rotating device with long blades that provides thrust to lift a helicopter.

rotten *adj* decaying; *Informal* very bad; corrupt.

rotter *n Chiefly Brit slang* despicable person.

Rottweiler [rot-vile-er] *n* large sturdy dog with a smooth black and tan coat and usu. a docked tail.

rotund [roe-tund] *adj* round and plump; sonorous. **rotundity** *n*

rotunda *n* circular building or room, esp. with a dome.

rouble [roo-bl] *n* monetary unit of Russia, Belarus, and Tajikistan.

roué [roo-ay] *n* man given to immoral living.

rouge *n* red cosmetic used to colour the cheeks.

rough *adj* uneven or irregular; not careful or gentle; difficult or unpleasant; approximate; violent, stormy, or boisterous; in preliminary form; lacking refinement. ▶ *v* make rough. ▶ *n* rough state or area. **rough it** live without the usual comforts etc. **roughen** *v* **roughly** *adv* **roughness** *n* **roughage** *n* indigestible constituents of food which aid digestion.

rough-and-ready *adj* hastily prepared but adequate.

rough-and-tumble *n* playful fight.

rough-hewn *adj* roughly shaped.

roughhouse *n Chiefly US slang* fight. **rough out** *v* prepare (a sketch or report) in preliminary form.

roughcast *n* mixture of plaster and small stones for outside walls. ▶ *v* coat with this.

roughshod *adv* **ride roughshod over** act with total disregard for.

roulette *n* gambling game played with a revolving wheel and a ball.

round *adj* spherical, cylindrical, circular, or curved. ▶ *adv, prep* indicating an encircling movement, presence on all sides, etc., e.g. *tied round the waist; books scattered round the room.* ▶ *v* move round. ▶ *n* customary course, as of a milkman; game (of golf); stage in a competition; one of several periods in a boxing match etc.; number of drinks bought at one time; bullet or shell for a gun. **roundly** *adv* thoroughly. **rounders** *n* bat-and-ball team game. **round robin** petition signed with names in a circle to conceal the order; tournament in which each player plays against every other player. **round-the-clock** *adj* throughout the day and night. **round trip** journey out and back again. **round up** *v* gather (people or animals) together. **roundup** *n*

roundabout *n* road junction at which traffic passes round a central island; revolving circular platform on which people ride for amusement. ▶ *adj* not straightforward.

roundel *n* small disc. **roundelay** *n*

simple song with a refrain.

Roundhead *n Hist* supporter of Parliament against Charles I in the English Civil War.

rouse[1] [rhymes with **cows**] *v* wake up; provoke or excite. **rousing** *adj* lively, vigorous.

rouse[2] [rhymes with **mouse**] *v* (foll. by *on*) *Aust* scold or rebuke.

rouseabout *n Aust & NZ* labourer in a shearing shed.

roustabout *n* labourer on an oil rig.

rout *n* overwhelming defeat; disorderly retreat. ▶ *v* defeat and put to flight.

route *n* roads taken to reach a destination; chosen way. **route march** long military training march.

routine *n* usual or regular method of procedure; set sequence. ▶ *adj* ordinary or regular.

roux [roo] *n* fat and flour cooked together as a basis for sauces.

rove *v* wander.

rover *n* wanderer, traveller.

row[1] [rhymes with **go**] *n* straight line of people or things. **in a row** in succession.

row[2] [rhymes with **go**] *v* propel (a boat) by oars. ▶ *n* spell of rowing. **rowing boat** boat propelled by oars.

row[3] [rhymes with **now**] *Informal* ▶ *n* dispute; disturbance; reprimand. ▶ *v* quarrel noisily.

rowan *n* tree producing bright red berries, mountain ash.

rowdy *adj* **-dier, -diest.** disorderly, noisy, and rough. ▶ *n, pl* **-dies.** person like this.

rowel [rhymes with **towel**] *n* small spiked wheel on a spur.

rowlock [rol-luk] *n* device on a boat that holds an oar in place.

royal *adj* of, befitting, or supported by a king or queen; splendid. ▶ *n Informal* member of a royal family.

royally *adv* **royalist** *n* supporter of monarchy. **royalty** *n* royal people; rank or power of a monarch; (*pl* **-ties**) payment to an author, musician, inventor, etc. **royal blue** deep blue.

RPI (in Britain) retail price index: measure of change in the average level of prices.

rpm revolutions per minute.

RSA Republic of South Africa; (in New Zealand) Returned Services Association.

RSI repetitive strain injury.

RSPCA (in Britain) Royal Society for the Prevention of Cruelty to Animals.

RSVP please reply.

rub *v* **rubbing, rubbed.** apply pressure and friction to (something) with a circular or backwards-and-forwards movement; clean, polish, or dry by rubbing; chafe or fray through rubbing. ▶ *n* act of rubbing. **rub it in** emphasize an unpleasant fact. **rub out** *v* remove with a rubber.

rubato *adv, n Music* (with) expressive flexibility of tempo.

rubber[1] *n* strong waterproof elastic material, orig. made from the dried sap of a tropical tree, now usu. synthetic; piece of rubber used for erasing writing. ▶ *adj* made of or producing rubber. **rubbery** *adj* **rubberneck** *v* stare with unthinking curiosity. **rubber stamp** device for imprinting the date, a name, etc.; automatic authorization.

rubber[2] *n* match consisting of three games of bridge, whist, etc.; series of matches.

rubbish *n* waste matter; anything worthless; nonsense. **rubbishy** *adj*

rubble *n* fragments of broken stone, brick, etc.

rubella *n* same as GERMAN MEASLES.

rubicund *adj* ruddy.

rubidium *n Chem* soft highly reactive radioactive element.

rubric *n* heading or explanation inserted in a text.

ruby *n, pl* **-bies.** red precious gemstone. ▶ *adj* deep red.

ruck[1] *n* rough crowd of common people; *Rugby* loose scrummage.

ruck[2] *n, v* wrinkle or crease.

rucksack *n Brit, Aust & S Afr* large pack carried on the back.

ructions *pl n Informal* noisy uproar.

rudder *n* vertical hinged piece at the stern of a boat or at the rear of an aircraft, for steering.

ruddy *adj* **-dier, -diest.** of a fresh healthy red colour.

rude *adj* impolite or insulting; coarse, vulgar, or obscene; unexpected and unpleasant; roughly made; robust. **rudely** *adv* **rudeness** *n*

rudiments *pl n* simplest and most basic stages of a subject. **rudimentary** *adj* basic, elementary.

rue[1] *v* **ruing, rued.** feel regret for. **rueful** *adj* regretful or sorry. **ruefully** *adv*

rue[2] *n* plant with evergreen bitter leaves.

ruff *n* starched and frilled collar; natural collar of feathers, fur, etc. on certain birds and animals.

ruffian *n* violent lawless person.

ruffle *v* disturb the calm of; annoy, irritate. ▶ *n* frill or pleat.

rug *n* small carpet; thick woollen blanket.

rugby *n* form of football played with an oval ball which may be handled by the players.

rugged [**rug**-gid] *adj* rocky or steep; uneven and jagged; strong-featured; tough and sturdy.

rugger *n Chiefly Brit informal* rugby.

ruin *v* destroy or spoil completely;

impoverish. ▶ *n* destruction or decay; loss of wealth, position, etc.; broken-down unused building. **ruination** *n* act of ruining; state of being ruined; cause of ruin. **ruinous** *adj* causing ruin; more expensive than can be afforded. **ruinously** *adv*

rule *n* statement of what is allowed, for example in a game or procedure; what is usual; government, authority, or control; measuring device with a straight edge. ▶ *v* govern; be pre-eminent; give a formal decision; mark with straight line(s); restrain. **as a rule** usually. **ruler** *n* person who governs; measuring device with a straight edge. **ruling** *n* formal decision. **rule of thumb** practical but imprecise approach. **rule out** *v* exclude.

rum *n* alcoholic drink distilled from sugar cane.

rumba *n* lively ballroom dance of Cuban origin.

rumble *v* make a low continuous noise; *Brit informal* discover the (disreputable) truth about. ▶ *n* deep resonant sound.

rumbustious *adj* boisterous or unruly.

ruminate *v* chew the cud; ponder or meditate. **ruminant** *adj, n* cud-chewing (animal, such as a cow, sheep, or deer). **rumination** *n* quiet meditation and reflection. **ruminative** *adj*

rummage *v* search untidily and at length. ▶ *n* untidy search through a collection of things.

rummy *n* card game in which players try to collect sets or sequences.

rumour *n* unproved statement; gossip or common talk. **rumoured** *adj* suggested by rumour.

rump *n* buttocks; rear of an animal.

rumple *v* make untidy, crumpled, or dishevelled.

rumpus *n, pl* **-puses.** noisy commotion.

run *v* **running, ran, run.** move with a more rapid gait than walking; compete in a race, election, etc.; travel according to schedule; function; manage; continue in a particular direction or for a specified period; expose oneself to (a risk); flow; spread; (of stitches) unravel. ▶ *n* act or spell of running; ride in a car; continuous period; series of unravelled stitches, ladder. **run away** *v* make one's escape, flee. **run down** *v* be rude about; reduce in number or size; stop working. **rundown** *n* **run-down** *adj* exhausted. **run into** *v* meet. **run-of-the-mill** *adj* ordinary. **run out** *v* be completely used up. **run over** *v* knock down (a person) with a moving vehicle. **run up** *v* incur (a debt).

rune *n* any character of the earliest Germanic alphabet. **runic** *adj*

rung[1] *n* crossbar on a ladder.

rung[2] *v* past participle of RING[1].

runnel *n* small brook.

runner *n* competitor in a race; messenger; part underneath an ice skate etc., on which it slides; slender horizontal stem of a plant, such as a strawberry, running along the ground and forming new roots at intervals; long strip of carpet or decorative cloth. **runner-up** *n* person who comes second in a competition.

running *adj* continuous; consecutive; (of water) flowing. ▶ *n* act of moving or flowing quickly; management of a business etc. **in, out of the running** having or not having a good chance in a competition.

runny adj **-nier, -niest.** tending to flow; exuding moisture.

runt n smallest animal in a litter; undersized person.

runway n hard level roadway where aircraft take off and land.

rupee n monetary unit of India and Pakistan.

rupture n breaking, breach; hernia. ▶ v break, burst, or sever.

rural adj in or of the countryside.

ruse [rooz] n stratagem or trick.

rush[1] v move or do very quickly; force (someone) to act hastily; make a sudden attack upon (a person or place). ▶ n sudden quick or violent movement. ▶ pl first unedited prints of a scene for a film. ▶ adj done with speed, hasty.

rush hour period at the beginning and end of the working day, when many people are travelling to or from work.

rush[2] n marsh plant with a slender pithy stem. **rushy** adj full of rushes.

rusk n hard brown crisp biscuit, used esp. for feeding babies.

russet adj reddish-brown. ▶ n apple with rough reddish-brown skin.

rust n reddish-brown coating formed on iron etc. that has been exposed to moisture; disease of plants which produces rust-coloured spots. ▶ adj reddish-brown. ▶ v become coated with rust. **rusty** adj coated with rust; of a rust colour; out of practice.

rustic adj of or resembling country people; rural; crude, awkward, or uncouth; (of furniture) made of untrimmed branches. ▶ n person from the country.

rustle[1] v, n (make) a low whispering sound.

rustle[2] v US steal (cattle). **rustler** n

US cattle thief. **rustle up** v prepare at short notice.

rut[1] n furrow made by wheels; dull settled habits or way of living.

rut[2] n recurrent period of sexual excitability in male deer. ▶ v rutting, rutted. be in a period of sexual excitability.

ruthenium n Chem rare hard brittle white element.

ruthless adj pitiless, merciless. **ruthlessly** adv **ruthlessness** n

rye n kind of grain used for fodder and bread; US whiskey made from rye.

rye-grass n any of several grasses cultivated for fodder.

S s

s second(s).

S South(ern).

SA Salvation Army; South Africa; South Australia.

SAA South African Airways.

Sabbath n day of worship and rest: Saturday for Jews, Sunday for Christians. **sabbatical** adj, n (denoting) leave for study.

SABC South African Broadcasting Corporation.

sable n dark fur from a small weasel-like Arctic animal. ▶ adj black.

sabot [sab-oh] n wooden shoe traditionally worn by peasants in France.

sabotage n intentional damage done to machinery, systems, etc. ▶ v damage intentionally. **saboteur** n person who commits sabotage.

sabre n curved cavalry sword.

sac n pouchlike structure in an animal or plant.

saccharin n artificial sweetener.

saccharine adj excessively sweet.

sacerdotal adj of priests.

sachet n small envelope or bag containing a single portion.

sack¹ n large bag made of coarse material; *Informal* dismissal; *Slang* bed. ▶ v *Informal* dismiss.
sackcloth n coarse fabric used for sacks, formerly worn as a penance.

sack² n plundering of a captured town. ▶ v plunder (a captured town).

sacrament n ceremony of the Christian Church, esp. Communion. **sacramental** adj

sacred adj holy; connected with religion; set apart, reserved.

sacrifice n giving something up; thing given up; making of an offering to a god; thing offered. ▶ v offer as a sacrifice; give (something) up. **sacrificial** adj

sacrilege n misuse or desecration of something sacred. **sacrilegious** adj

sacristan n person in charge of the contents of a church. **sacristy** n, pl -ties. room in a church where sacred objects are kept.

sacrosanct adj regarded as sacred, inviolable.

sacrum [say-krum] n, pl -cra. wedge-shaped bone at the base of the spine.

sad adj **sadder, saddest.** sorrowful, unhappy; deplorably bad. **sadden** v make sad. **sadly** adv **sadness** n

saddle n rider's seat on a horse or bicycle; joint of meat. ▶ v put a saddle on (a horse); burden (with a responsibility). **saddler** n maker or seller of saddles.

sadism [say-dizz-um] n gaining of (sexual) pleasure from inflicting pain. **sadist** n **sadistic** adj **sadistically** adv

sadomasochism n combination of sadism and masochism.

sadomasochist n

s.a.e. *Brit, Aust & NZ* stamped addressed envelope.

safari n, pl -ris. expedition to hunt or observe wild animals, esp. in Africa. **safari park** park where lions, elephants, etc. are kept uncaged so that people can see them from cars.

safe adj secure, protected; uninjured, out of danger; not involving risk. ▶ n strong lockable container. **safely** adv

safe-conduct n permit allowing travel through a dangerous area.

safekeeping n protection.

safeguard v protect. ▶ n protection.

safety n, pl -ties. state of being safe. **safety net** net to catch performers on a trapeze or high wire if they fall. **safety pin** pin with a spring fastening and a guard over the point when closed.
safety valve valve that allows steam etc. to escape if pressure becomes excessive.

saffron n orange-coloured flavouring obtained from a crocus. ▶ adj orange.

sag v **sagging, sagged.** sink in the middle; tire; (of clothes) hang loosely. ▶ n droop.

saga [sah-ga] n legend of Norse heroes; any long story or series of events.

sagacious adj wise. **sagacity** n

sage¹ n very wise man. ▶ adj *Lit* wise. **sagely** adv

sage² n aromatic herb with grey-green leaves.

sago n starchy cereal from the powdered pith of the sago palm tree.

said v past of SAY.

sail n sheet of fabric stretched to catch the wind for propelling a sailing boat; arm of a windmill. ▶ v travel by water; begin a voyage;

move smoothly. **sailor** n member of a ship's crew. **sailboard** n board with a mast and single sail, used for windsurfing.

saint n Christianity person venerated after death as specially holy; exceptionally good person. **saintly** adj **saintliness** n

sake¹ n benefit; purpose. **for the sake of** for the purpose of; to please or benefit (someone).

sake², **saki** [sah-kee] n Japanese alcoholic drink made from fermented rice.

salaam [sal-ahm] n low bow of greeting among Muslims.

salacious adj excessively concerned with sex.

salad n dish of raw vegetables, eaten as a meal or part of a meal.

salamander n amphibian which looks like a lizard.

salami n highly spiced sausage.

salary n, pl **-ries.** fixed regular payment, usu. monthly, to an employee. **salaried** adj

sale n exchange of goods for money; selling of goods at unusually low prices; auction. **saleable** adj fit or likely to be sold.

salesman, **saleswoman**, **salesperson** n person who sells goods. **salesmanship** n skill in selling.

salient [say-lee-ent] adj prominent, noticeable. ▶ n Mil projecting part of a front line.

saline [say-line] adj containing salt. **salinity** n

saliva n liquid that forms in the mouth, spittle. **salivary** adj **salivate** v produce saliva.

sallow adj of an unhealthy pale or yellowish colour.

sally n, pl **-lies.** witty remark; sudden brief attack by troops. ▶ v **-lying, -lied.** (foll. by forth) rush out; go out.

salmon n large fish with orange-pink flesh valued as food. ▶ adj orange-pink.

salmonella n, pl **-lae.** bacterium causing food poisoning.

salon n commercial premises of a hairdresser, beautician, etc.; elegant reception room for guests.

saloon n two-door or four-door car with body closed off from rear luggage area; large public room, as on a ship; US bar serving alcoholic drinks. **saloon bar** more expensive bar in a pub.

salt n white crystalline substance used to season food; chemical compound of acid and metal. ▶ v season or preserve with salt. **old salt** experienced sailor. **with a pinch of salt** allowing for exaggeration. **worth one's salt** efficient. **salty** adj **salt cellar** small container for salt at table.

saltire n Heraldry diagonal cross on a shield.

saltpetre n compound used in gunpowder and as a preservative.

salubrious adj favourable to health.

Saluki n tall hound with a silky coat.

salutary adj producing a beneficial result.

salute n motion of the arm as a formal military sign of respect; firing of guns as a military greeting of honour. ▶ v greet with a salute; make a salute; acknowledge with praise. **salutation** n greeting by words or actions.

salvage n saving of a ship or other property from destruction; property so saved. ▶ v save from destruction or waste.

salvation n fact or state of being saved from harm or the consequences of sin.

salve n healing or soothing

ointment. ▶ v soothe or appease.

salver n (silver) tray on which something is presented.

salvia n plant with blue or red flowers.

salvo n, pl **-vos, -voes.** simultaneous discharge of guns etc.; burst of applause or questions.

sal volatile [sal vol-**at**-ill-ee] n preparation of ammonia, used to revive a person who feels faint.

SAM surface-to-air missile.

Samaritan n person who helps people in distress.

samba n lively Brazilian dance.

same adj identical, not different, unchanged; just mentioned. **sameness** n

samovar n Russian tea urn.

Samoyed n dog with a thick white coat and tightly curled tail.

sampan n small boat with oars used in China.

samphire n plant found on rocks by the seashore.

sample n part taken as representative of a whole; Music short extract from an existing recording mixed into a backing track to produce a new recording. ▶ v take and test a sample of; Music take a short extract from (one recording) and mix it into a backing track; record (a sound) and feed it into a computerized synthesizer so that it can be reproduced at any pitch. **sampler** n piece of embroidery showing the embroiderer's skill; Music piece of electronic equipment used for sampling. **sampling** n

samurai n, pl **-rai.** member of an ancient Japanese warrior caste.

sanatorium n, pl **-riums, -ria.** institution for invalids or convalescents; room for sick pupils at a boarding school.

sanctify v **-fying, -fied.** make holy.

sanctimonious adj pretending to be religious and virtuous.

sanction n permission, authorization; coercive measure or penalty. ▶ v allow, authorize.

sanctity n sacredness, inviolability.

sanctuary n, pl **-aries.** holy place; part of a church nearest the altar; place of safety for a fugitive; place where animals or birds can live undisturbed.

sanctum n, pl **-tums, -ta.** sacred place; person's private room.

sand n substance consisting of small grains of rock, esp. on a beach or in a desert. ▶ pl stretches of sand forming a beach or desert. ▶ v smooth with sandpaper.

sandy adj covered with sand; (of hair) reddish-fair. **sandbag** n bag filled with sand, used as protection against gunfire or flood water. **sandblast** v, n (clean with) a jet of sand blown from a nozzle under pressure. **sandpaper** n paper coated with sand for smoothing a surface. **sandpiper** n shore bird with a long bill and slender legs. **sandstone** n rock composed of sand. **sandstorm** n desert wind that whips up clouds of sand.

sandal n light shoe consisting of a sole attached by straps.

sandalwood n sweet-scented wood.

sander n power tool for smoothing surfaces.

sandwich n two slices of bread with a layer of food between. ▶ v insert between two other things. **sandwich board** pair of boards hung over a person's shoulders to display advertisements in front and behind.

sane adj of sound mind; sensible, rational. **sanity** n

sang v past tense of SING.

sang-froid [sahng-**frwah**] n composure and calmness in a difficult situation.

sangoma n S Afr witch doctor or herbalist.

sanguinary adj accompanied by bloodshed; bloodthirsty.

sanguine adj cheerful, optimistic.

sanitary adj promoting health by getting rid of dirt and germs. **sanitation** n sanitary measures, esp. drainage or sewerage.

sank v past tense of SINK.

Sanskrit n ancient language of India.

sap¹ n moisture that circulates in plants; Informal gullible person.

sap² v sapping, sapped. undermine; weaken. **sapper** n soldier in an engineering unit.

sapient [**say**-pee-ent] adj Lit wise, shrewd.

sapling n young tree.

sapphire n blue precious stone. ▶ adj deep blue.

sarabande, saraband n slow stately Spanish dance.

Saracen n Hist Arab or Muslim who opposed the Crusades.

sarcasm n (use of) bitter or wounding ironic language. **sarcastic** adj **sarcastically** adv

sarcophagus n, pl **-gi, -guses**. stone coffin.

sardine n small fish of the herring family, usu. preserved tightly packed in tins.

sardonic adj mocking or scornful. **sardonically** adv

sargassum, sargasso n type of floating seaweed.

sari, saree n long piece of cloth draped around the body and over one shoulder, worn by Hindu women.

sarmie n S Afr slang sandwich.

sarong n long piece of cloth

tucked around the waist or under the armpits, worn esp. in Malaysia.

sarsaparilla n soft drink, orig. made from the root of a tropical American plant.

sartorial adj of men's clothes or tailoring.

SAS (in Britain) Special Air Service.

sash¹ n decorative strip of cloth worn round the waist or over one shoulder.

sash² n wooden frame containing the panes of a window. **sash window** window consisting of two sashes that can be opened by sliding one over the other.

sassafras n American tree with aromatic bark used medicinally.

Sassenach n Scot English person.

sat v past of SIT.

Satan n the Devil. **satanic** adj of Satan; supremely evil. **Satanism** n worship of Satan.

satay, saté [sat-ay] n Indonesian and Malaysian dish consisting of pieces of chicken, pork, etc., grilled on skewers and served with peanut sauce.

satchel n bag, usu. with a shoulder strap, for carrying books.

sate v satisfy (a desire or appetite) fully.

satellite n man-made device orbiting in space; heavenly body that orbits another; country that is dependent on a more powerful one. ▶ adj of or used in the transmission of television signals from a satellite to the home.

satiate [**say**-she-ate] v provide with more than enough, so as to disgust. **satiety** [sat-**tie**-a-tee] n feeling of having had too much.

satin n silky fabric with a glossy surface on one side. **satiny** adj or like satin. **satinwood** n tropical tree yielding hard wood.

satire n use of ridicule to expose

vice or folly; poem or other work that does this. **satirical** adj

satirist n **satirize** v ridicule by means of satire.

satisfy v **-fying, -fied.** please, content; provide amply for (a need or desire); convince, persuade. **satisfaction** n **satisfactory** adj

satnav n Motoring, informal satellite navigation.

satsuma n kind of small orange.

saturate v soak thoroughly; cause to absorb the maximum amount of something. **saturation** n

Saturday n seventh day of the week.

Saturn n Roman god of agriculture; sixth planet from the sun. **saturnine** adj gloomy in temperament or appearance. **saturnalia** n wild party or orgy.

satyr n woodland god, part man, part goat; lustful man.

sauce n liquid added to food to enhance flavour; Chiefly Brit informal impudence. **saucy** adj impudent; pert, jaunty. **saucily** adv **saucepan** n cooking pot with a long handle.

saucer n small round dish put under a cup.

sauerkraut n shredded cabbage fermented in brine.

sauna n Finnish-style steam bath.

saunter v walk in a leisurely manner, stroll. ▶ n leisurely walk.

sausage n minced meat in an edible tube-shaped skin. **sausage roll** skinless sausage covered in pastry.

sauté [so-tay] v **-téing** or **-teeing, -téed.** fry quickly in a little fat.

savage adj wild, untamed; cruel and violent; uncivilized, primitive. ▶ n uncivilized person. ▶ v attack ferociously. **savagely** adv **savagery** n

savannah, savanna n extensive open grassy plain in Africa.

savant n learned person.

save v rescue or preserve from harm, protect; keep for the future; set aside (money); Sport prevent the scoring of (a goal). ▶ n Sport act of preventing a goal. **saver** n **saving** n economy. ▶ pl money put by for future use.

saveloy n Brit, Aust & NZ spicy smoked sausage.

saviour n person who rescues another; (**S-**) Christ.

savoir-faire [sav-wahr-**fair**] n French ability to do and say the right thing in any situation.

savory n aromatic herb used in cooking.

savour v enjoy, relish; (foll. by of) have a flavour or suggestion of. ▶ n characteristic taste or odour; slight but distinctive quality. **savoury** adj salty or spicy. ▶ n, pl **-vouries.** savoury dish served before or after a meal.

savoy n variety of cabbage.

savvy Slang ▶ v **-vying, -vied.** understand. ▶ n understanding, intelligence.

saw[1] n cutting tool with a toothed metal blade. ▶ v **sawing, sawed, sawed** or **sawn.** cut with a saw; move (something) back and forth. **sawyer** n person who saws timber for a living. **sawdust** n fine wood fragments made in sawing. **sawfish** n fish with a long toothed snout. **sawmill** n mill where timber is sawn into planks.

saw[2] v past tense of SEE[1].

saw[3] n wise saying, proverb.

sax n Informal short for SAXOPHONE.

saxifrage n alpine rock plant with small flowers.

Saxon n member of the W Germanic people who settled widely in Europe in the early

Middle Ages. ▶ *adj* of the Saxons.

saxophone *n* brass wind instrument with keys and a curved body. **saxophonist** *n*

say *v* **saying, said.** speak or utter; express (an idea) in words; give as one's opinion; suppose as an example or possibility. ▶ *n* right or chance to speak; share in a decision. **saying** *n* maxim, proverb.

scab *n* crust formed over a wound; *Offens* blackleg. **scabby** *adj* covered with scabs; *Informal* despicable.

scabbard *n* sheath for a sword or dagger.

scabies [**skay-beez**] *n* itchy skin disease.

scabrous [**skay-bruss**] *adj* rough and scaly; indecent.

scaffold *n* temporary platform for workmen; gallows. **scaffolding** *n* (materials for building) scaffolds.

scalar *n, adj* (variable quantity) having magnitude but no direction.

scald *v* burn with hot liquid or steam; sterilize with boiling water; heat (liquid) almost to boiling point. ▶ *n* injury by scalding.

scale¹ *n* one of the thin overlapping plates covering fishes and reptiles; thin flake; coating which forms in kettles etc. due to hard water; tartar formed on the teeth. ▶ *v* remove scales from; come off in scales. **scaly** *adj*

scale² *n* (often pl) weighing instrument.

scale³ *n* graduated table or sequence of marks at regular intervals, used as a reference in making measurements; ratio of size between a thing and a representation of it; relative degree or extent; fixed series of notes in music. ▶ *v* climb. **scale**

up, down *v* increase or decrease proportionately in size.

scalene *adj* (of a triangle) with three unequal sides.

scallop *n* edible shellfish with two fan-shaped shells; one of a series of small curves along an edge. **scalloped** *adj* decorated with small curves along the edge.

scallywag *n Informal* scamp, rascal.

scalp *n* skin and hair on top of the head. ▶ *v* cut off the scalp of.

scalpel *n* small surgical knife.

scam *n Informal* dishonest scheme.

scamp *n* mischievous child.

scamper *v* run about hurriedly or in play. ▶ *n* scampering.

scampi *pl n* large prawns.

scan *v* **scanning, scanned.** scrutinize carefully; glance over quickly; examine or search (an area) by passing a radar or sonar beam over it; (of verse) conform to metrical rules. ▶ *n* scanning. **scanner** *n* electronic device used for scanning. **scansion** *n* metrical scanning of verse.

scandal *n* disgraceful action or event; malicious gossip. **scandalize** *v* shock by scandal. **scandalous** *adj*

scandium *n Chem* rare silvery-white metallic element.

scant *adj* barely sufficient, meagre.

scanty *adj* **scantier, scantiest.** barely sufficient or not sufficient. **scantily** *adv*

scapegoat *n* person made to bear the blame for others.

scapula *n, pl* **-lae, -las.** shoulder blade. **scapular** *adj*

scar *n* mark left by a healed wound; permanent emotional damage left by an unpleasant experience. ▶ *v* **scarring, scarred.** mark or become marked with a scar.

scarab *n* sacred beetle of ancient

Egypt.

scarce *adj* insufficient to meet demand; not common, rarely found. **make oneself scarce** *Informal* go away. **scarcely** *adv* hardly at all; definitely or probably not. **scarcity** *n*

scare *v* frighten or be frightened. ▶ *n* fright, sudden panic. **scary** *adj Informal* frightening.

scarecrow *n* figure dressed in old clothes, set up to scare birds away from crops; raggedly dressed person. **scaremonger** *n* person who spreads alarming rumours.

scarf[1] *n, pl* **scarves, scarfs.** piece of material worn round the neck, head, or shoulders.

scarf[2] *n* joint between two pieces of timber made by notching the ends and fastening them together. ▶ *v* join in this way.

scarify *v* **-fying, -fied.** scratch or cut slightly all over; break up and loosen (topsoil); criticize mercilessly. **scarification** *n*

scarlatina *n* scarlet fever.

scarlet *adj, n* brilliant red. **scarlet fever** infectious fever with a scarlet rash.

scarp *n* steep slope.

scarper *v Brit slang* run away.

scat[1] *v* **scatting, scatted.** *Informal* go away.

scat[2] *n* jazz singing using improvised vocal sounds instead of words.

scathing *adj* harshly critical.

scatological *adj* preoccupied with obscenity, esp. with references to excrement. **scatology** *n*

scatter *v* throw about in various directions; disperse. **scatterbrain** *n* empty-headed person.

scatty *adj* **-tier, -tiest.** *Informal* empty-headed.

scavenge *v* search for (anything usable) among discarded material.

scavenger *n* person who scavenges; animal that feeds on decaying matter.

scenario *n, pl* **-rios.** summary of the plot of a play or film; imagined sequence of future events.

scene *n* place of action of a real or imaginary event; subdivision of a play or film in which the action is continuous; view of a place; display of emotion; *Informal* specific activity or interest, e.g. *the fashion scene.* **behind the scenes** backstage; in secret. **scenery** *n* natural features of a landscape; painted backcloths or screens used on stage to represent the scene of action. **scenic** *adj* picturesque.

scent *n* pleasant smell; smell left in passing, by which an animal can be traced; series of clues; perfume. ▶ *v* detect by smell; suspect; fill with fragrance.

sceptic [skep-tik] *n* person who habitually doubts generally accepted beliefs. **sceptical** *adj* **sceptically** *adv* **scepticism** *n*

sceptre *n* ornamental rod symbolizing royal power.

schedule *n* plan of procedure for a project; list; timetable. ▶ *v* plan to occur at a certain time.

schema *n, pl* **-mata.** overall plan or diagram. **schematic** *adj* presented as a plan or diagram.

scheme *n* systematic plan; secret plot. ▶ *v* plan in an underhand manner. **scheming** *adj, n*

scherzo [skairt-so] *n, pl* **-zos, -zi.** brisk lively piece of music.

schism [skizz-um] *n* (group resulting from) division in an organization. **schismatic** *adj, n*

schist [skist] *n* crystalline rock which splits into layers.

schizoid *adj* abnormally introverted; *Informal* contradictory.

▶ n schizoid person.

schizophrenia n mental disorder involving deterioration of or confusion with the personality; *Informal* contradictory behaviour or attitudes. **schizophrenic** adj, n

schmaltz n excessive sentimentality. **schmaltzy** adj

schnapps n strong alcoholic spirit.

schnitzel n thin slice of meat, esp. veal.

scholar n learned person; student receiving a scholarship; pupil. **scholarly** adj learned. **scholarship** n learning; financial aid given to a student because of academic merit. **scholastic** adj of schools or scholars.

school[1] n place where children are taught or instruction is given in a subject; group of artists, thinkers, etc. with shared principles or methods. ▶ v educate or train.

school[2] n shoal of fish, whales, etc.

schooner n sailing ship rigged fore-and-aft; large glass.

sciatica n severe pain in the large nerve in the back of the leg. **sciatic** adj of the hip; or of afflicted with sciatica.

science n systematic study and knowledge of natural or physical phenomena. **scientific** adj of science; systematic. **scientifically** adv **scientist** n person who studies or practises a science. **science fiction** stories making imaginative use of scientific knowledge. **science park** area where scientific research and commercial development are carried on in cooperation.

sci-fi n short for SCIENCE FICTION.

scimitar n curved oriental sword.

scintillate v give off sparks. **scintillating** adj very lively and amusing.

scion [sy-on] n descendant or heir; shoot of a plant for grafting.

scissors pl n cutting instrument with two crossed pivoted blades.

sclerosis n, pl **-ses**. abnormal hardening of body tissues.

scoff[1] v express derision.

scoff[2] v *Informal* eat rapidly.

scold v find fault with, reprimand. ▶ n person who scolds. **scolding** n

sconce n bracket on a wall for holding candles or lights.

scone n small plain cake baked in an oven or on a griddle.

scoop n shovel-like tool for ladling or hollowing out; news story reported in one newspaper before all its rivals. ▶ v take up or hollow out with or as if with a scoop; beat (rival newspapers) in reporting a news item.

scoot v *Slang* leave or move quickly.

scooter n child's vehicle propelled by pushing on the ground with one foot; light motorcycle.

scope n opportunity for using abilities; range of activity.

scorch v burn on the surface; parch or shrivel from heat. ▶ n slight burn. **scorcher** n *Informal* very hot day.

score n points gained in a game or competition; twenty; written version of a piece of music showing parts for each musician; mark or cut; grievance, e.g. *settle old scores*. ▶ pl lots. ▶ v gain (points) in a game; keep a record of points; mark or cut; (foll. by *out*) cross out; arrange music (for); achieve a success.

scorn n open contempt. ▶ v despise; reject with contempt. **scornful** adj **scornfully** adv

scorpion n small lobster-shaped animal with a sting at the end of a jointed tail.

Scot n person from Scotland.

Scottish adj of Scotland, its people, or their languages. **Scotch** n whisky distilled in Scotland. **Scots** adj Scottish. **Scotsman, Scotswoman** n

scotch v put an end to.

scot-free adj without harm or punishment.

scoundrel n Old-fashioned cheat or deceiver.

scour¹ v clean or polish by rubbing with something rough; clear or flush out. **scourer** n small rough nylon pad used for cleaning pots and pans.

scour² v search thoroughly and energetically.

scourge n person or thing causing severe suffering; whip. ▶ v cause severe suffering; whip.

scout n person sent out to reconnoitre; **(S-)** member of the Scout Association, an organization for young people which aims to develop character and promotes outdoor activities. ▶ v act as a scout; reconnoitre.

scowl v, n (have) an angry or sullen expression.

scrabble v scrape at with the hands, feet, or claws.

scrag n thin end of a neck of mutton. **scraggy** adj thin, bony.

scram v scramming, scrammed. Informal go away quickly.

scramble v climb or crawl hastily or awkwardly; struggle with others (for); mix up; cook (eggs beaten up with milk); (of an aircraft or aircrew) take off hurriedly in an emergency; make (transmitted speech) unintelligible by the use of an electronic device. ▶ n scrambling; rough climb; disorderly struggle; motorcycle race over rough ground. **scrambler** n electronic device that makes transmitted speech

unintelligible.

scrap¹ n small piece; waste metal collected for reprocessing. ▶ pl leftover food. ▶ v scrapping, scrapped. discard as useless. **scrappy** adj fragmentary, disjointed. **scrapbook** n book with blank pages in which newspaper cuttings or pictures are stuck.

scrap² n, v scrapping, scrapped. Informal fight or quarrel.

scrape v rub with something rough or sharp; clean or smooth thus; rub with a harsh noise; economize. ▶ n act or sound of scraping; mark or wound caused by scraping; Informal awkward situation. **scraper** n scrape through v succeed in scrape or obtain with difficulty.

scratch v mark or cut with claws, nails, or anything rough or sharp; scrape (skin) with nails or claws to relieve itching; withdraw from a race or competition. ▶ n wound, mark, or sound made by scratching. ▶ adj put together at short notice. **from scratch** from the very beginning. **up to scratch** up to standard. **scratchy** adj **scratchcard** n ticket that reveals whether or not the holder has won a prize when the surface is removed by scratching.

scrawl v write carelessly or hastily. ▶ n scribbled writing.

scrawny adj scrawnier, scrawniest. thin and bony.

scream v utter a piercing cry, esp. of fear or pain; utter with a scream. ▶ n shrill piercing cry; Informal very funny person or thing.

scree n slope of loose shifting stones.

screech v, n (utter) a shrill cry.

screed n long tedious piece of

writing.

screen *n* surface of a television set, VDU, etc., on which an image is formed; white surface on which films or slides are projected; movable structure used to shelter, divide, or conceal something. ▸ *v* shelter or conceal with or as if with a screen; examine (a person or group) to determine suitability for a task or to detect the presence of disease or weapons; show (a film). **the screen** cinema generally. **screen saver** *Computers* software that produces changing images on a monitor when the computer is operative but idle.

screw *n* metal pin with a spiral ridge along its length, twisted into materials to fasten them together; *Slang* prison guard. ▸ *v* turn (a screw); twist; fasten with screw(s); *Informal* extort. **screwy** *adj Informal* crazy or eccentric. **screwdriver** *n* tool for turning screws. **screw up** *v Informal* bungle; distort.

scribble *v* write hastily or illegibly; make meaningless or illegible marks. ▸ *n* something scribbled.

scribe *n* person who copied manuscripts before the invention of printing; *Bible* scholar of the Jewish Law.

scrimmage *n* rough or disorderly struggle.

scrimp *v* be very economical.

scrip *n* certificate representing a claim to stocks or shares.

script *n* text of a film, play, or TV programme; particular system of writing, e.g. *Arabic script*; handwriting.

scripture *n* sacred writings of a religion. **scriptural** *adj*

scrofula *n* tuberculosis of the lymphatic glands. **scrofulous** *adj*

scroggin *n NZ* mixture of nuts and dried fruits.

scroll *n* roll of parchment or paper; ornamental carving shaped like a scroll. ▸ *v* move (text) up or down on a VDU screen.

scrotum *n, pl* **-ta, -tums.** pouch of skin containing the testicles.

scrounge *v Informal* get by cadging or begging. **scrounger** *n*

scrub¹ *v* **scrubbing, scrubbed.** clean by rubbing, often with a hard brush and water; *Informal* delete or cancel. ▸ *n* scrubbing.

scrub² *n* stunted trees; area of land covered with scrub. **scrubby** *adj* covered with scrub; stunted; *Informal* shabby.

scruff¹ *n* nape (of the neck).

scruff² *n Informal* untidy person. **scruffy** *adj* unkempt or shabby.

scrum, scrummage *n Rugby* restarting of play in which opposing packs of forwards push against each other to gain possession of the ball; disorderly struggle.

scrumptious *adj Informal* delicious.

scrunch *v* crumple or crunch or be crumpled or crunched. ▸ *n* act or sound of scrunching.

scruple *n* doubt produced by one's conscience or morals. ▸ *v* have doubts on moral grounds. **scrupulous** *adj* very conscientious; very careful or precise. **scrupulously** *adv*

scrutiny *n, pl* **-nies.** close examination. **scrutinize** *v* examine closely.

scuba diving *n* sport of swimming under water using cylinders containing compressed air attached to breathing apparatus.

scud *v* **scudding, scudded.** move along swiftly.

scuff *v* drag (the feet) while walking; scrape (one's shoes) by doing so. ▸ *n* mark caused by scuffing.

scuffle v fight in a disorderly manner. ▸ n disorderly struggle; scuffling sound.

scull n small oar. ▸ v row (a boat) using sculls.

scullery n, pl **-leries.** small room where washing-up and other kitchen work is done.

sculpture n art of making figures or designs in wood, stone, etc.; product of this art. ▸ v (also **sculpt**) represent in sculpture. **sculptor, sculptress** n **sculptural** adj

scum n impure or waste matter on the surface of a liquid; worthless people. **scummy** adj

scungy adj **-ier, -iest.** Aust & NZ informal sordid or dirty.

scupper v Informal defeat or ruin.

scurf n flaky skin on the scalp.

scurrilous adj untrue and defamatory.

scurry v **-rying, -ried.** move hastily. ▸ n act or sound of scurrying.

scurvy n disease caused by lack of vitamin C.

scut n short tail of the hare, rabbit, or deer.

scuttle[1] n fireside container for coal.

scuttle[2] v run with short quick steps. ▸ n hurried run.

scuttle[3] v make a hole in (a ship) to sink it.

scythe n long-handled tool with a curved blade for cutting grass. ▸ v cut with a scythe.

SE southeast(ern).

sea n mass of salt water covering three quarters of the earth's surface; particular area of this; vast expanse. **at sea** in a ship on the ocean; confused or bewildered. **sea anemone** sea animal with suckers like petals. **seaboard** n coast. **sea dog** experienced sailor. **seafaring** adj working or

travelling by sea. **seafood** n edible saltwater fish or shellfish. **seagull** n gull. **sea horse** small sea fish with a plated body and horselike head. **sea level** average level of the sea's surface in relation to the land. **sea lion** kind of large seal. **seaman** n sailor. **seaplane** n aircraft designed to take off from and land on water. **seasick** adj suffering from nausea caused by the motion of a ship. **seasickness** n **seaside** n area, esp. a holiday resort, on the coast. **sea urchin** sea animal with a round spiky shell. **seaweed** n plant growing in the sea. **seaworthy** adj (of a ship) in fit condition for a sea voyage.

seal[1] n piece of wax, lead, etc. with a special design impressed upon it, attached to a letter or document as a mark of authentication; device or material used to close an opening tightly. ▸ v close with or as if with a seal; make airtight or watertight; affix a seal to or stamp with a seal; decide (one's fate) irrevocably. **sealant** n any substance used for sealing. **seal off** enclose or isolate (a place) completely.

seal[2] n amphibious mammal with flippers as limbs. **sealskin** n

seam n line where two edges are joined, as by stitching; thin layer of coal or ore. ▸ v mark with furrows or wrinkles. **seamless** adj **seamy** adj sordid.

seamstress n woman who sews, esp. professionally.

seance [say-anss] n meeting at which spiritualists attempt to communicate with the dead.

sear v scorch, burn the surface of. **searing** adj (of pain) very sharp; highly critical.

search v examine closely in order

to find something. ▸ *n* searching.
searching *adj* keen or thorough.
search engine *Computers* Internet
service enabling users to search
for items of interest. **searchlight**
n powerful light with a beam that
can be shone in any direction.
season *n* one of four divisions of
the year, each of which has
characteristic weather conditions;
period during which a thing
happens or is plentiful; fitting or
proper time. ▸ *v* flavour with salt,
herbs, etc.; dry (timber) till ready
for use. **seasonable** *adj*
appropriate for the season; timely
or opportune. **seasonal** *adj*
depending on or varying with the
seasons. **seasoned** *adj*
experienced. **seasoning** *n* salt,
herbs, etc. added to food to
enhance flavour. **season ticket**
ticket for a series of journeys or
events within a specified period.
seat *n* thing designed or used for
sitting on; place to sit in a theatre,
esp. one that requires a ticket;
buttocks; *Brit* country house;
membership of a legislative or
administrative body. ▸ *v* cause to
sit; provide seating for. **seat belt**
belt worn in a car or aircraft to
prevent a person being thrown
forward in a crash.
sebaceous *adj* of, like, or secreting
fat or oil.
secateurs *pl n* small pruning shears.
secede *v* withdraw formally from a
political alliance or federation.
secession *n*
seclude *v* keep (a person) from
contact with others. **secluded** *adj*
private, sheltered. **seclusion** *n*
second[1] *adj* coming directly after
the first; alternate, additional;
inferior. ▸ *n* person or thing
coming second; attendant in a
duel or boxing match. ▸ *pl* inferior

goods. ▸ *v* express formal support
for (a motion proposed in a
meeting). **secondly** *adv*
second-class *adj* inferior; cheaper,
slower, or less comfortable than
first-class. **second-hand** *adj*
bought after use by another.
second nature something so
habitual that it seems part of
one's character. **second sight**
supposed ability to predict events.
second thoughts revised opinion
on a matter already considered.
second wind renewed ability to
continue effort.
second[2] *n* sixtieth part of a minute
of an angle or time; moment.
second[3] [si-**kond**] *v* transfer (a
person) temporarily to another
job. **secondment** *n*
secondary *adj* of less importance;
coming after or derived from what
is primary or first; relating to the
education of people between the
ages of 11 and 18 or, in New
Zealand, between 13 and 18.
secret *adj* kept from the
knowledge of others. ▸ *n*
something kept secret; mystery;
underlying explanation, e.g. *the
secret of my success.* **in secret**
without other people knowing.
secretly *adv* **secrecy** *n* **secretive**
adj inclined to keep things secret.
secretiveness *n*
secretariat *n* administrative office
or staff of a legislative body.
secretary *n, pl* **-ries.** person who
deals with correspondence and
general clerical work; (**S-**) head of
a state department, e.g. *Home
Secretary.* **secretarial** *adj*
Secretary of State head of a
major governmental department.
secrete[1] *v* (of an organ, gland,
etc.) produce and release (a
substance). **secretion** *n*
secretory [sek-**reet**-or-ee] *adj*

secrete[2] v hide or conceal.

sect n subdivision of a religious or political group, esp. one with extreme beliefs. **sectarian** adj of a sect; narrow-minded.

section n part cut off; part or subdivision of something; distinct part of a country or community; cutting; drawing of something as if cut through. ▶ v cut or divide into sections. **sectional** adj

sector n part or subdivision; part of a circle enclosed by two radii and the arc which they cut off.

secular adj worldly, as opposed to sacred; not connected with religion or the church.

secure adj free from danger; free from anxiety; firmly fixed; reliable. ▶ v obtain; make safe; make firm; guarantee payment of (a loan) by giving something as security. **securely** adv **security** n, pl **-ties**. precautions against theft, espionage, or other danger; state of being secure; certificate of ownership of a share, stock, or bond; something given or pledged to guarantee payment of a loan.

sedan n US, Aust & NZ two-door or four-door car with the body closed off from the rear luggage area. **sedan chair** Hist enclosed chair for one person, carried on poles by two bearers.

sedate[1] adj calm and dignified; slow or unhurried. **sedately** adv

sedate[2] v give a sedative drug to. **sedation** n **sedative** adj having a soothing or calming effect. ▶ n sedative drug.

sedentary adj done sitting down, involving little exercise.

sedge n coarse grasslike plant growing on wet ground.

sediment n matter which settles to the bottom of a liquid; material deposited by water, ice, or wind. **sedimentary** adj

sedition n speech or action encouraging rebellion against the government. **seditious** adj

seduce v persuade into sexual intercourse; tempt into wrongdoing. **seducer, seductress** n **seduction** n **seductive** adj

sedulous adj diligent or persevering. **sedulously** adv

see[1] v **seeing, saw, seen.** perceive with the eyes or mind; understand; watch; find out; make sure (of something); consider or decide; have experience of; meet or visit; accompany. **seeing** conj in view of the fact that.

see[2] n diocese of a bishop.

seed n mature fertilized grain of a plant; such grains used for sowing; origin; Obs offspring; Sport player ranked according to his or her ability. ▶ v sow with seed; remove seeds from; arrange (the draw of a sports tournament) so that the outstanding competitors will not meet in the early rounds. **go, run to seed** (of plants) produce or shed seeds after flowering; lose vigour or usefulness. **seedling** n young plant raised from a seed. **seedy** adj shabby.

seek v **seeking, sought.** try to find or obtain; try (to do something).

seem v appear to be. **seeming** adj apparent but not real. **seemingly** adv

seemly adj proper or fitting.

seen v past participle of SEE[1].

seep v trickle through slowly, ooze. **seepage** n

seer n prophet.

seersucker n light cotton fabric with a slightly crinkled surface.

seesaw n plank balanced in the middle so that two people seated on either end ride up and down alternately. ▶ v move up and down.

seethe v **seething, seethed.** be very agitated; (of a liquid) boil or foam.

segment n one of several sections into which something may be divided. ▶ v divide into segments. **segmentation** n

segregate v set apart. **segregation** n

seine [sane] n large fishing net that hangs vertically from floats.

seismic adj relating to earthquakes. **seismology** n study of earthquakes. **seismological** adj **seismologist** n **seismograph**, **seismometer** n instrument that records the strength of earthquakes.

seize v take hold of forcibly or quickly; take immediate advantage of; (usu. foll. by up) (of mechanical parts) stick tightly through overheating. **seizure** n sudden violent attack of an illness; seizing or being seized.

seldom adv not often, rarely.

select v pick out or choose. ▶ adj chosen in preference to others; restricted to a particular group, exclusive. **selection** n selecting; things that have been selected; range from which something may be selected. **selective** adj chosen or choosing carefully. **selectively** adv **selectivity** n **selector** n

selenium n Chem nonmetallic element with photoelectric properties.

self n, pl **selves.** distinct individuality or identity of a person or thing; one's basic nature; one's own welfare or interests. **selfish** adj caring too much about oneself and not enough about others. **selfishly** adv **selfishness** n **selfless** adj unselfish.

self- prefix used with many main words to mean: of oneself or itself; by, to, in, due to, for, or from the self; automatic(ally).

self-assured adj confident.

self-catering adj (of accommodation) for people who provide their own food.

self-coloured adj having only a single colour. **self-conscious** adj embarrassed at being the object of others' attention.

self-contained adj containing everything needed, complete; (of a flat) having its own facilities.

self-determination n the right of a nation to decide its own form of government. **self-evident** adj obvious without proof. **self-help** n use of one's own abilities to solve problems; practice of solving one's problems within a group of people with similar problems.

self-interest n one's own advantage. **self-made** adj having achieved wealth or status by one's own efforts. **self-possessed** adj having control of one's emotions, calm. **self-raising** adj (of flour) containing a raising agent.

self-righteous adj thinking oneself more virtuous than others.

selfsame adj the very same.

self-seeking adj, n seeking to promote only one's own interests.

self-service adj denoting a shop, café, or garage where customers serve themselves and then pay a cashier. **self-styled** adj using a title or name that one has taken without right. **self-sufficient** adj able to provide for oneself without help. **self-willed** adj stubbornly determined to get one's own way.

sell v **selling, sold.** exchange (something) for money; stock, deal in; (of goods) be sold; (foll.

by for) have a specified price; *Informal* persuade (someone) to accept (something). ▶ *n* manner of selling. **seller** *n* **sell-by date** *Brit* date on packaged food after which it should not be sold. **sell out** *v* dispose of (something) completely by selling; *Informal* betray. **sellout** *n* performance of a show etc. for which all the tickets are sold; *Informal* betrayal.

Sellotape *n* ® type of adhesive tape. ▶ *v* stick with Sellotape.

selvage, selvedge *n* edge of cloth, woven so as to prevent unravelling.

selves *n* plural of SELF.

semantic *adj* relating to the meaning of words. **semantics** *n* study of linguistic meaning.

semaphore *n* system of signalling by holding two flags in different positions to represent letters of the alphabet.

semblance *n* outward or superficial appearance.

semen *n* sperm-carrying fluid produced by male animals.

semester *n* either of two divisions of the academic year.

semi *n Brit & S Afr informal* semidetached house.

semi- *prefix* used with many main words to mean: half, e.g. *semicircle*; partly or almost, e.g. *semiprofessional*.

semibreve *n* musical note four beats long.

semicolon *n* the punctuation mark (;).

semiconductor *n* substance with an electrical conductivity that increases with temperature.

semidetached *adj* (of a house) joined to another on one side.

semifinal *n* match or round before the final. **semifinalist** *n*

seminal *adj* original and influential;

capable of developing; of semen or seed.

seminar *n* meeting of a group of students for discussion.

seminary *n, pl* **-ries.** college for priests.

semiprecious *adj* (of gemstones) having less value than precious stones.

semiquaver *n* musical note half the length of a quaver.

Semite *n* member of the group of peoples including Jews and Arabs.

Semitic *adj* of the group of peoples including Jews and Arabs.

semitone *n* smallest interval between two notes in Western music.

semitrailer *n Aust* large truck in two separate sections joined by a pivoted bar (also **semi**).

semolina *n* hard grains of wheat left after the milling of flour, used to make puddings and pasta.

Senate *n* upper house of some parliaments; governing body of some universities. **senator** *n* member of a Senate. **senatorial** *adj*

send *v* **sending, sent.** cause (a person or thing) to go to or be taken or transmitted to a place; bring into a specified state or condition. **sendoff** *n* demonstration of good wishes at a person's departure. **send up** *v Informal* make fun of by imitating. **send-up** *n Informal* imitation.

senile *adj* mentally or physically weak because of old age. **senility** *n*

senior *adj* superior in rank or standing; older; of or for older pupils. ▶ *n* senior person. **seniority** *n*

senna *n* tropical plant; its dried leaves or pods used as a laxative.

señor [sen-**nyor**] *n, pl* **-ores.**

Spanish term of address equivalent to *sir* or *Mr.* **señora** [sen-**nyor**-a] *n* Spanish term of address equivalent to *madam* or *Mrs.* **señorita** [sen-nyor-**ee**-ta] *n* Spanish term of address equivalent to *madam* or *Miss.*

sensation *n* ability to feel things physically; physical feeling; general feeling or awareness; state of excitement; exciting person or thing. **sensational** *adj* causing intense shock, anger, or excitement; *Informal* very good. **sensationalism** *n* deliberate use of sensational language or subject matter. **sensationalist** *adj, n*

sense *n* any of the faculties of perception or feeling (sight, hearing, touch, taste, or smell); ability to perceive; feeling perceived through one of the senses; awareness; (sometimes *pl*) sound practical judgment or intelligence; specific meaning. ▶ *v* perceive. **senseless** *adj*

sensible *adj* having or showing good sense; practical, e.g. *sensible shoes*; (foll. by *of*) aware. **sensibly** *adv* **sensibility** *n* ability to experience deep feelings.

sensitive *adj* easily hurt or offended; responsive to external stimuli; (of a subject) liable to arouse controversy or strong feelings; (of an instrument) responsive to slight changes. **sensitively** *adv* **sensitivity** *n* **sensitize** *v* make sensitive.

sensor *n* device that detects or measures the presence of something, such as radiation.

sensory *adj* of the senses or sensation.

sensual *adj* giving pleasure to the body and senses rather than the mind; having a strong liking for physical pleasures. **sensually** *adv*

sensuality *n* **sensualist** *n*

sensuous *adj* pleasing to the senses. **sensuously** *adv*

sent *v* past of SEND.

sentence *n* sequence of words capable of standing alone as a statement, question, or command; punishment passed on a criminal. ▶ *v* pass sentence on (a convicted person).

sententious *adj* trying to sound wise; pompously moralizing.

sentient [sen-**tee**-ent] *adj* capable of feeling. **sentience** *n*

sentiment *n* thought, opinion, or attitude; feeling expressed in words; exaggerated or mawkish emotion. **sentimental** *adj* excessively romantic or nostalgic. **sentimentalism** *n* **sentimentality** *n* **sentimentalize** *v* make sentimental.

sentinel *n* sentry.

sentry *n, pl* **-tries.** soldier on watch.

sepal *n* leaflike division of the calyx of a flower.

separate *v* act as a barrier between; distinguish between; divide up into parts; (of a couple) stop living together. ▶ *adj* not the same, different; set apart; not shared, individual. **separately** *adv* **separation** *n* separating or being separated; *Law* living apart of a married couple without divorce. **separable** *adj* **separatist** *n* person who advocates the separation of a group from an organization or country. **separatism** *n*

sepia *adj, n* reddish-brown (pigment).

sepsis *n* poisoning caused by pus-forming bacteria.

Sept. September.

September *n* ninth month of the year.

septet *n* group of seven

performers; music for such a
group.

septic *adj* (of a wound) infected;
of or caused by harmful bacteria.
septic tank tank in which sewage
is decomposed by the action of
bacteria.

septicaemia [sep-tis-**see**-mee-a] *n*
infection of the blood.

septuagenarian *n* person aged
between seventy and seventy-nine.

sepulchre [**sep**-pull-ker] *n* tomb or
burial vault. **sepulchral**
[sip-**pulk**-ral] *adj* gloomy.

sequel *n* novel, play, or film that
continues the story of an earlier
one; consequence.

sequence *n* arrangement of two or
more things in successive order;
the successive order of two or
more things; section of a film
showing a single uninterrupted
episode. **sequential** *adj*

sequester *v* seclude; sequestrate.

sequestrate *v* confiscate
(property) until its owner's debts
are paid or a court order is
complied with. **sequestration** *n*

sequin *n* small ornamental metal
disc on a garment. **sequined** *adj*

sequoia *n* giant Californian
coniferous tree.

seraglio [sir-**ah**-lee-oh] *n, pl*
-raglios. harem of a Muslim
palace; Turkish sultan's palace.

seraph *n, pl* **-aphs, -aphim.**
member of the highest order of
angels. **seraphic** *adj*

Serbian, Serb *adj* of Serbia. ▶ *n*
person from Serbia. **Serbo-Croat,
Serbo-Croatian** *adj, n* (of) the
chief official language of Serbia
and Croatia.

serenade *n* music played or sung
to a woman by a lover. ▶ *v* sing or
play a serenade to (someone).

serendipity *n* gift of making
fortunate discoveries by accident.

serene *adj* calm, peaceful.
serenely *adv* **serenity** *n*

serf *n* medieval farm labourer who
could not leave the land he
worked on. **serfdom** *n*

serge *n* strong woollen fabric.

sergeant *n* noncommissioned
officer in the army; police officer
ranking between constable and
inspector. **sergeant at arms**
parliamentary or court officer with
ceremonial duties. **sergeant
major** highest rank of
noncommissioned officer in the
army.

serial *n* story or play produced in
successive instalments. ▶ *adj* of or
forming a series; published or
presented as a serial. **serialize** *v*
publish or present as a serial.
serial killer person who commits
a series of murders.

series *n, pl* **-ries.** group or
succession of related things, usu.
arranged in order; set of radio or
TV programmes about the same
subject or characters.

serious *adj* giving cause for
concern; concerned with
important matters; not cheerful,
grave; sincere; not joking.
seriously *adv* **seriousness** *n*

sermon *n* speech on a religious or
moral subject by a clergyman in a
church service; long moralizing
speech. **sermonize** *v* make a long
moralizing speech.

serpent *n Lit* snake. **serpentine**
adj twisting like a snake.

serrated *adj* having a notched or
sawlike edge.

serried *adj* in close formation.

serum [**seer**-um] *n* watery fluid left
after blood has clotted; this fluid
from the blood of immunized
animals used for inoculation or
vaccination.

servant *n* person employed to do

household work for another.

serve v work for (a person, community, or cause); perform official duties; attend to (customers); provide (someone) with (food or drink); provide with a service; be a member of the armed forces; spend (time) in prison; be useful or suitable; *Tennis etc.* put (the ball) into play. ▶ n *Tennis etc.* act of serving the ball.

server n player who serves in racket games; *Computers* computer or program that supplies data to other machines on a network.

service n system that provides something needed by the public; department of public employment and its employees; availability for use; overhaul of a machine or vehicle; formal religious ceremony; *Tennis etc.* act, manner, or right of serving the ball. ▶ pl armed forces. ▶ v overhaul (a machine or vehicle). **serviceable** adj useful or helpful; able or ready to be used. **service area** area beside a motorway with garage, restaurant, and toilet facilities. **serviceman, servicewoman** n member of the armed forces. **service road** narrow road giving access to houses and shops. **service station** garage selling fuel for motor vehicles.

serviette n table napkin.

servile adj too eager to obey people, fawning; suitable for a slave. **servility** n

servitude n bondage or slavery.

sesame [sess-am-ee] n plant cultivated for its seeds and oil, which are used in cooking.

session n period spent in an activity; meeting of a court, parliament, or council; series or period of such meetings; academic term or year.

set¹ v **setting, set.** put in a specified position or state; make ready; make or become firm or rigid; establish, arrange; prescribe, assign; (of the sun) go down. ▶ n scenery used in a play or film. ▶ adj fixed or established beforehand; rigid or inflexible; determined (to do something). **setback** n anything that delays progress. **set square** flat right-angled triangular instrument used for drawing angles. **set up** v arrange or establish. **setup** n way in which anything is organized or arranged.

set² n number of things or people grouped or belonging together; *Maths* group of numbers or objects that satisfy a given condition or share a property; television or radio receiver; *Sport* group of games in a match.

sett, set n badger's burrow.

settee n couch.

setter n long-haired gun dog.

setting n background or surroundings; time and place where a film, book, etc. is supposed to have taken place; music written for the words of a text; decorative metalwork in which a gem is set; plates and cutlery for a single place at table; position or level to which the controls of a machine can be adjusted.

settle¹ v arrange or put in order; come to rest; establish or become established as a resident; make quiet, calm, or stable; pay (a bill); bestow (property) legally. **settlement** n act of settling; place newly colonized; subsidence (of a building); property bestowed legally. **settler** n colonist.

settle² n long wooden bench with high back and arms.

seven adj, n one more than six. **seventh** adj, n (of) number seven in a series. **seventeen** adj, n ten and seven. **seventeenth** adj, n **seventy** adj, n ten times seven. **seventieth** adj, n

sever v cut through or off; break off (a relationship). **severance** n **severance pay** compensation paid by a firm to an employee who leaves because the job he or she was appointed to do no longer exists.

several adj some, a few; various, separate. **severally** adv separately.

severe adj strict or harsh; very intense or unpleasant; strictly restrained in appearance. **severely** adv **severity** n

sew v sewing, sewed, sewn or sewed. join with thread repeatedly passed through with a needle; make or fasten by sewing.

sewage n waste matter or excrement carried away in sewers.

sewer n drain to remove waste water and sewage. **sewerage** n system of sewers.

sewn v a past participle of sew.

sex n state of being male or female; male or female category; sexual intercourse; sexual feelings or behaviour. ▶ v find out the sex of. **sexy** adj sexually exciting or attractive; Informal exciting or trendy. **sexism** n discrimination on the basis of a person's sex. **sexist** adj, n **sexual** adj **sexually** adv **sexuality** n **sexual intercourse** sexual act in which the male's penis is inserted into the female's vagina.

sexagenarian n person aged between sixty and sixty-nine.

sextant n navigator's instrument for measuring angles, as between the sun and horizon, to calculate one's position.

sextet n group of six performers; music for such a group.

sexton n official in charge of a church and churchyard.

SF science fiction.

shabby adj -bier, -biest. worn or dilapidated in appearance; mean or unworthy, e.g. shabby treatment. **shabbily** adv **shabbiness** n

shack n rough hut. **shack up with** v Slang live with (one's lover).

shackle n one of a pair of metal rings joined by a chain, for securing a person's wrists or ankles. ▶ v fasten with shackles.

shad n herring-like fish.

shade n relative darkness; place sheltered from sun; screen or cover used to protect from a direct source of light; depth of colour; slight amount; Lit ghost. ▶ pl Slang sunglasses. ▶ v screen from light; darken; represent (darker areas) in drawing; change slightly or by degrees. **shady** adj situated in or giving shade; of doubtful honesty or legality.

shadow n dark shape cast on a surface when something stands between a light and the surface; patch of shade; slight trace; threatening influence; inseparable companion. ▶ v cast a shadow over; follow secretly. **shadowy** adj **shadow-boxing** n boxing against an imaginary opponent for practice. **Shadow Cabinet** members of the main opposition party in Parliament who would be ministers if their party were in power.

shaft n long narrow straight handle of a tool or weapon; ray of light; revolving rod that transmits power in a machine; vertical passageway, as for a lift or a mine; one of the bars between which an animal is harnessed to a vehicle.

shag[1] n coarse shredded tobacco.
▶ adj (of a carpet) having a long pile. **shaggy** adj covered with rough hair or wool; tousled, unkempt. **shaggy-dog story** long anecdote with a humorous twist at the end.

shag[2] n kind of cormorant.

shagreen n sharkskin; rough grainy untanned leather.

shah n formerly, ruler of Iran.

shake v **shaking, shook, shaken.** move quickly up and down or back and forth; make unsteady; tremble; grasp (someone's hand) in greeting or agreement; shock or upset. ▶ n shaking; vibration; *Informal* short period of time. **shaky** adj unsteady; uncertain or questionable. **shakily** adv

shale n flaky sedimentary rock.

shall v, past tense **should.** used as an auxiliary to make the future tense or to indicate intention, obligation, or inevitability.

shallot n kind of small onion.

shallow adj not deep; lacking depth of character or intellect. **shallows** pl n area of shallow water. **shallowness** n

sham n thing or person that is not genuine. ▶ adj not genuine. ▶ v **shamming, shammed.** fake, feign.

shamble v walk in a shuffling awkward way.

shambles n disorderly event or place.

shame n painful emotion caused by awareness of having done something dishonourable or foolish; capacity to feel shame; cause of shame; cause for regret. ▶ v cause to feel shame; disgrace; compel by shame. ▶ interj S Afr *informal* exclamation of sympathy or endearment. **shameful** adj

causing or deserving shame. **shamefully** adv **shameless** adj with no sense of shame. **shamefaced** adj looking ashamed.

shammy n, pl **-mies.** *Informal* piece of chamois leather.

shampoo n liquid soap for washing hair, carpets, or upholstery; process of shampooing. ▶ v wash with shampoo.

shamrock n clover leaf, esp. as the Irish emblem.

shandy n, pl **-dies.** drink made of beer and lemonade.

shanghai v **-haiing, -haied.** force or trick (someone) into doing something. ▶ n *Aust & NZ* catapult.

shank n lower leg; shaft or stem.

shan't shall not.

shantung n soft Chinese silk with a knobbly surface.

shanty[1] n, pl **-ties.** shack or crude dwelling. **shantytown** n slum consisting of shanties.

shanty[2] n, pl **-ties.** sailor's traditional song.

shape n outward form of an object; way in which something is organized; pattern or mould; condition or state. ▶ v form or mould; devise or develop. **shapeless** adj **shapely** adj having an attractive shape.

shard n broken piece of pottery or glass.

share[1] n part of something that belongs to or is contributed by a person; one of the equal parts into which the capital stock of a public company is divided. ▶ v give or take a share of (something); join with others in doing or using (something). **shareholder** n **sharemilker** NZ person who works on a dairy farm belonging to someone else.

share[2] n blade of a plough.

shark n large usu. predatory sea fish; person who cheats others.

sharkskin n stiff glossy fabric.

sharp adj having a keen cutting edge or fine point; not gradual; clearly defined; mentally acute; shrill; bitter or sour in taste; Music above the true pitch. ▸ adv promptly; Music too high in pitch. ▸ n Music symbol raising a note one semitone above natural pitch. **sharply** adv **sharpness** n **sharpen** v make or become sharp or sharper. **sharpener** n **sharpshooter** n marksman.

shatter v break into pieces; destroy completely. **shattered** adj Informal completely exhausted; badly upset.

shave v **shaving, shaved, shaved** or **shaven.** remove (hair) from (the face, head, or body) with a razor or shaver; pare away; touch lightly in passing. ▸ n shaving. **close shave** Informal narrow escape. **shaver** n electric razor. **shavings** pl n parings.

shawl n piece of cloth worn over a woman's head or shoulders or wrapped around a baby.

she pron refers to: female person or animal previously mentioned; something regarded as female, such as a car, ship, or nation.

sheaf n, pl **sheaves.** bundle of papers; tied bundle of reaped corn.

shear v **shearing, sheared, sheared** or **shorn.** clip hair or wool from; cut through. **shears** pl n large scissors or a cutting tool shaped like these. **shearer** n **shearing shed** Aust & NZ farm building with equipment for shearing sheep.

shearwater n medium-sized sea bird.

sheath n close-fitting cover, esp. for a knife or sword; Brit, Aust &

NZ condom. **sheathe** v put into a sheath.

shebeen n Scot, Irish & S Afr place where alcohol is sold illegally.

shed[1] n building used for storage or shelter or as a workshop.

shed[2] v **shedding, shed.** pour forth (tears); cast off (skin, hair, or leaves).

sheen n glistening brightness on the surface of something.

sheep n, pl **sheep.** ruminant animal bred for wool and meat. **sheep-dip** n liquid disinfectant in which sheep are immersed. **sheepdog** n dog used for herding sheep. **sheepskin** n skin of a sheep with the fleece still on, used for clothing or rugs.

sheepish adj embarrassed because of feeling foolish. **sheepishly** adv

sheer[1] adj absolute, complete, e.g. sheer folly; perpendicular, steep; (of material) so fine as to be transparent.

sheer[2] v change course suddenly.

sheet[1] n large piece of cloth used as an inner bed cover; broad thin piece of any material; large expanse.

sheet[2] n rope for controlling the position of a sail. **sheet anchor** strong anchor for use in an emergency; person or thing relied on.

sheikh, sheik [shake] n Arab chief. **sheikhdom, sheikdom** n

sheila n Aust & NZ slang girl or woman.

shekel n monetary unit of Israel. ▸ pl Informal money.

shelf n, pl **shelves.** board fixed horizontally for holding things; ledge. **shelf life** time a packaged product will remain fresh.

shell n hard outer covering of an egg, nut, or certain animals; external frame of something;

explosive projectile fired from a large gun. ▷ v take the shell from; fire at with artillery shells.
shellfish n sea-living animal, esp. one that can be eaten, with a shell. **shell out** v Informal pay out or hand over (money). **shell shock** nervous disorder caused by exposure to battle conditions. **shell suit** Brit lightweight tracksuit made of a waterproof nylon layer over a cotton layer.
shellac n resin used in varnishes. ▷ v -lacking, -lacked. coat with shellac.
shelter n structure providing protection from danger or the weather; protection. ▷ v give shelter to; take shelter.
shelve[1] v put aside or postpone; provide with shelves. **shelving** n (material for) shelves.
shelve[2] v slope.
shenanigans pl n Informal mischief or nonsense; trickery.
shepherd n person who tends sheep. ▷ v guide or watch over (people). **shepherdess** n fem **shepherd's pie** baked dish of mince covered with mashed potato.
sherbet n Brit, Aust & NZ fruit-flavoured fizzy powder; US, Canadian & S Afr flavoured water ice.
sheriff n (in the US) chief law enforcement officer of a county; (in England and Wales) chief executive officer of the Crown in a county; (in Scotland) chief judge of a district; (in Australia) officer of the Supreme Court.
Sherpa n member of a people of Tibet and Nepal.
sherry n, pl -ries. pale or dark brown fortified wine.
shibboleth n slogan or principle, usu. considered outworn,

characteristic of a particular group.
shield n piece of armour carried on the arm to protect the body from blows or missiles; anything that protects; sports trophy in the shape of a shield. ▷ v protect.
shift v move; transfer (blame or responsibility); remove or be removed. ▷ n shifting; group of workers who work during a specified period; period of time during which they work; loose-fitting straight underskirt or dress. **shiftless** adj lacking in ambition or initiative. **shifty** adj evasive or untrustworthy. **shiftiness** n
shillelagh [shil-lay-lee] n (in Ireland) a cudgel.
shilling n former British coin, replaced by the 5p piece; former Australian coin, worth one twentieth of a pound.
shillyshally v -lying, -lied. Informal be indecisive.
shimmer v, n (shine with) a faint unsteady light.
shin n front of the lower leg. ▷ v shinning, shinned. climb by using the hands or arms and legs. **shinbone** n tibia.
shindig n Informal noisy party; brawl.
shine v shining, shone. give out or reflect light; aim a (light); polish; excel. ▷ n brightness or lustre. **shiny** adj **take a shine to** Informal take a liking to (someone). **shiner** n Informal black eye.
shingle[1] n wooden roof tile. ▷ v cover (a roof) with shingles.
shingle[2] n coarse gravel found on beaches. **shingle slide** NZ loose stones on a steep slope.
shingles n disease causing a rash of small blisters along a nerve.
Shinto n Japanese religion in which ancestors and nature spirits are

worshipped. **Shintoism** n

shinty n game like hockey.

ship n large seagoing vessel. ▶ v **shipping, shipped.** send or transport by carrier, esp. a ship; bring or go aboard a ship.

shipment n act of shipping cargo; consignment of goods shipped.

shipping n freight transport business; ships collectively.

shipshape adj orderly or neat.

shipwreck n destruction of a ship through storm or collision. ▶ v cause to undergo shipwreck.

shipyard n place where ships are built.

shire n Brit county; Aust rural area with an elected council.

shire horse n large powerful breed of horse.

shirk v avoid (duty or work). **shirker** n

shirt n garment for the upper part of the body.

shirty adj **-tier, -tiest.** Chiefly Brit slang bad-tempered or annoyed.

shish kebab n meat and vegetable dish cooked on a skewer.

shiver[1] v tremble, as from cold or fear. ▶ n shivering.

shiver[2] v splinter into pieces.

shoal[1] n large number of fish swimming together.

shoal[2] n stretch of shallow water; sandbank.

shock[1] v horrify, disgust, or astonish. ▶ n sudden violent emotional disturbance; sudden violent blow or impact; something causing this; state of bodily collapse caused by physical or mental shock; pain and muscular spasm caused by an electric current passing through the body. **shocker** n **shocking** adj causing horror, disgust, or astonishment; Informal very bad.

shock[2] n bushy mass (of hair).

shod v past of SHOE.

shoddy adj **-dier, -diest.** made or done badly.

shoe n outer covering for the foot, ending below the ankle; horseshoe. ▶ v shoeing, shod. fit with a shoe or shoes. **shoehorn** n smooth curved implement inserted at the heel of a shoe to ease the foot into it. **shoestring** n **on a shoestring** using a very small amount of money.

shone v past of SHINE.

shonky adj **-kier, -kiest.** Aust & NZ informal unreliable or unsound.

shoo interj go away! ▶ v drive away as by saying 'shoo'.

shook v past tense of SHAKE.

shoot v shooting, shot. hit, wound, or kill with a missile fired from a weapon; fire (a missile from) a weapon; hunt; send out or move rapidly; (of a plant) sprout; photograph or film; Sport take a shot at goal. ▶ n new branch or sprout of a plant; hunting expedition. **shooting star** meteor. **shooting stick** stick with a spike at one end and a folding seat at the other.

shop n place for sale of goods and services; workshop. ▶ v shopping, shopped. visit a shop or shops to buy goods; Brit, Aust & NZ slang inform against (someone). **talk shop** discuss one's work, esp. on a social occasion. **shop around** v visit various shops to compare goods and prices. **shop floor** production area of a factory; workers in a factory. **shoplifter** n person who steals from a shop. **shop-soiled** adj soiled or faded from being displayed in a shop. **shop steward** (in some countries) trade-union official elected to represent his or her fellow workers.

shore[1] n edge of a sea or lake.

shore² v (foll. by *up*) prop or support.

shorn v a past participle of SHEAR.

short adj not long; not tall; not lasting long, brief; deficient, e.g. *short of cash*; abrupt, rude; (of a drink) consisting chiefly of a spirit; (of pastry) crumbly. ▶ adv abruptly. ▶ n drink of spirits; short film; *Informal* short circuit. ▶ pl short trousers. **shortage** n deficiency. **shorten** v make or become shorter. **shortly** adv soon; rudely. **shortbread**, **shortcake** n crumbly biscuit made with butter. **short-change** v give (someone) less than the correct amount of change; *Slang* swindle. **short circuit** faulty or accidental connection in a circuit, which deflects current through a path of low resistance. **shortcoming** n failing or defect. **short cut** quicker route or method. **shortfall** n deficit. **shorthand** n system of rapid writing using symbols to represent words. **short-handed** adj not having enough workers. **short list** selected list of candidates for a job or prize, from which the final choice will be made. **short-list** v put on a short list. **short shrift** brief and unsympathetic treatment. **short-sighted** adj unable to see distant things clearly; lacking in foresight. **short wave** radio wave with a wavelength of less than 60 metres.

shot¹ n shooting; small lead pellets used in a shotgun; person with specified skill in shooting; *Slang* attempt; *Sport* act or instance of hitting, kicking, or throwing the ball; photograph; uninterrupted film sequence; *Informal* injection. **shotgun** n gun for firing a charge of shot at short range.

shot² v past of SHOOT. ▶ adj woven to show changing colours.

shot put n athletic event in which contestants hurl a heavy metal ball as far as possible. **shot-putter** n

should v past tense of SHALL used as an auxiliary to make the subjunctive mood or to indicate obligation or possibility.

shoulder n part of the body to which an arm, foreleg, or wing is attached; cut of meat including the upper foreleg; side of a road. ▶ v bear (a burden or responsibility); push with one's shoulder; put on one's shoulder. **shoulder blade** large flat triangular bone at the shoulder.

shouldn't should not.

shout n loud cry; *Informal* person's turn to buy a round of drinks. ▶ v cry out loudly; *Aust & NZ informal* treat (someone) to (something, such as a drink). **shout down** v silence (someone) by shouting.

shove v push roughly; *Informal* put. ▶ n rough push. **shove off** v *Informal* go away.

shovel n tool for lifting or moving loose material. ▶ v -elling, -elled. lift or move as with a shovel.

show v showing, showed, shown or showed. make, be, or become noticeable or visible; exhibit or display; indicate; instruct by demonstration; prove; guide; reveal or display (an emotion). ▶ n public exhibition; theatrical or other entertainment; mere display or pretence. **showy** adj gaudy; ostentatious. **showily** adv **show business** the entertainment industry. **showcase** n situation in which something is displayed to best advantage; glass case used to display objects. **showdown** n confrontation that settles a dispute. **showjumping** n competitive sport of riding horses to demonstrate skill in jumping.

showman n man skilled at presenting anything spectacularly. **showmanship** n **show off** v exhibit to invite admiration; Informal behave flamboyantly in order to attract attention.

show-off n Informal person who shows off. **showpiece** n excellent specimen shown for display or as an example. **showroom** n room in which goods for sale are on display. **show up** v reveal or be revealed clearly; expose the faults or defects of; Informal embarrass; Informal arrive.

shower n kind of bath in which a person stands while being sprayed with water; wash in this; short period of rain, hail, or snow; sudden abundant fall of objects. ▶ v wash in a shower; bestow (things) or present (someone) with things liberally. **showery** adj

shown v a past participle of SHOW.

shrank v a past tense of SHRINK.

shrapnel n artillery shell filled with pellets which scatter on explosion; fragments from this.

shred n long narrow strip torn from something; small amount. ▶ v shredding, shredded or shred. tear to shreds.

shrew n small mouselike animal; bad-tempered nagging woman. **shrewish** adj

shrewd adj clever and perceptive. **shrewdly** adv **shrewdness** n

shriek n shrill cry. ▶ v utter (with) a shriek.

shrike n songbird with a heavy hooked bill.

shrill adj (of a sound) sharp and high-pitched. **shrillness** n **shrilly** adv

shrimp n small edible shellfish;

Informal small person. **shrimping** n fishing for shrimps.

shrine n place of worship associated with a sacred person or object.

shrink v shrinking, shrank or shrunk, shrunk or shrunken. become or make smaller; recoil or withdraw. ▶ n Slang psychiatrist.

shrinkage n decrease in size, value, or weight.

shrivel v -elling, -elled. shrink and wither.

shroud n piece of cloth used to wrap a dead body; anything which conceals. ▶ v conceal.

Shrove Tuesday n day before Ash Wednesday.

shrub n woody plant smaller than a tree. **shrubbery** n, pl -beries. area planted with shrubs.

shrug v shrugging, shrugged. raise and then drop (the shoulders) as a sign of indifference, ignorance, or doubt. ▶ n shrugging. **shrug off** v dismiss as unimportant.

shrunk v a past of SHRINK.

shrunken v a past participle of SHRINK.

shudder v shake or tremble violently, esp. with horror. ▶ n shaking or trembling.

shuffle v walk without lifting the feet; jumble together; rearrange. ▶ n shuffling; rearrangement.

shun v shunning, shunned. avoid.

shunt v move (objects or people) to a different position; move (a train) from one track to another.

shush interj be quiet!

shut v shutting, shut. bring together or fold, close; prevent access to; (of a shop etc.) stop operating for the day. **shutter** n hinged doorlike cover for closing off a window; device in a camera letting in the light required to expose a film. **shut down** v close or stop (a factory, machine, or business). **shutdown** n

shuttle n vehicle going to and fro over a short distance; instrument which passes the weft thread between the warp threads in weaving. ▸ v travel by or as if by shuttle.

shuttlecock n small light cone with feathers stuck in one end, struck to and fro in badminton.

shy¹ adj not at ease in company; timid; (foll. by of) cautious or wary. ▸ v shying, shied. start back in fear; (foll. by away from) avoid (doing something) through fear or lack of confidence. **shyly** adv **shyness** n

shy² v shying, shied. throw. ▸ n, pl **shies.** throw.

SI French Système International (d'Unités), international metric system of units of measurement.

Siamese adj of Siam, former name of Thailand. **Siamese cat** breed of cat with cream fur, dark ears and face, and blue eyes. **Siamese twins** twins born joined to each other at some part of the body.

sibilant adj hissing. ▸ n consonant pronounced with a hissing sound.

sibling n brother or sister.

sibyl n (in ancient Greece and Rome) prophetess.

sic Latin thus: used to indicate that an odd spelling or reading is in fact accurate.

sick adj vomiting or likely to vomit; physically or mentally unwell; Informal amused by or fascinated by something sadistic or morbid; (foll. by of) Informal disgusted (by) or weary (of). **sickness** n **sicken** v make nauseated or disgusted; become ill. **sickly** adj unhealthy, weak; causing revulsion or nausea. **sick bay** place for sick people,

such as that on a ship.

sickle n tool with a curved blade for cutting grass or grain.

side n line or surface that borders anything; either of two halves into which something can be divided; either surface of a flat object; area immediately next to a person or thing; aspect or part; one of two opposing groups or teams. ▸ adj at or on the side; subordinate. **on the side** as an extra; unofficially. **siding** n short stretch of railway track on which trains or wagons are shunted from the main line. **sideboard** n piece of furniture for holding plates, cutlery, etc. in a dining room. **sideburns, sideboards** pl n man's side whiskers. **side effect** additional undesirable effect. **sidekick** n Informal close friend or associate. **sidelight** n either of two small lights on the front of a vehicle. **sideline** n subsidiary interest or source of income; Sport line marking the boundary of a playing area. **sidelong** adj sideways. ▸ adv obliquely. **side-saddle** n saddle designed to allow a woman rider to sit with both legs on the same side of the horse. **sidestep** v dodge (an issue); avoid by stepping sideways. **sidetrack** v divert from the main topic. **sidewalk** n US paved path for pedestrians, at the side of a road. **sideways** adv to or from the side; obliquely. **side with** v support (one side in a dispute).

sidereal [side-eer-ee-al] adj of or determined with reference to the stars.

sidle v walk in a furtive manner.

SIDS sudden infant death syndrome, cot death.

siege n surrounding and blockading of a place.

sienna n reddish- or yellowish-brown pigment made from natural earth.

sierra n range of mountains in Spain or America with jagged peaks.

siesta n afternoon nap, taken in hot countries.

sieve [siv] n utensil with mesh through which a substance is sifted or strained. ▶ v sift or strain through a sieve.

sift v remove the coarser particles from a substance with a sieve; examine (information or evidence) to select what is important.

sigh n long audible breath expressing sadness, tiredness, relief, or longing. ▶ v utter a sigh.

sight n ability to see; instance of seeing; range of vision; device for guiding the eye while using a gun or optical instrument; thing worth seeing; Informal a lot. ▶ v catch sight of. **sightless** adj blind. **sight-read** v play or sing printed music without previous preparation. **sightseeing** n visiting places of interest. **sightseer** n

sign n indication of something not immediately or outwardly observable; gesture, mark, or symbol conveying a meaning; notice displayed to advertise, inform, or warn; omen. ▶ v write (one's name) on (a document or letter) to show its authenticity or one's agreement; communicate using sign language; make a sign or gesture. **sign language** system of communication by gestures, as used by deaf people (also **signing**). **sign on** v register as unemployed; sign a document committing oneself to a job, course, etc. **signpost** n post bearing a sign that shows the way.

signal n sign or gesture to convey information; sequence of electrical impulses or radio waves transmitted or received. ▶ adj Formal very important. ▶ v -nalling, -nalled. convey (information) by signal. **signally** adv **signal box** building from which railway signals are operated. **signalman** n railwayman in charge of signals and points.

signatory n, pl -ries. one of the parties who sign a document.

signature n person's name written by himself or herself in signing something; sign at the start of a piece of music to show the key or tempo. **signature tune** tune used to introduce a particular television or radio programme.

signet n small seal used to authenticate documents. **signet ring** finger ring bearing a signet.

significant adj important; having or expressing a meaning. **significantly** adv **significance** n

signify v -fying, -fied. indicate or suggest; be a symbol or sign for; be important. **signification** n

signor [see-nyor] n Italian term of address equivalent to sir or Mr. **signora** [see-nyor-a] n Italian term of address equivalent to madam or Mrs. **signorina** [see-nyor-ee-na] n Italian term of address equivalent to madam or Miss.

Sikh [seek] n member of an Indian religion having only one God.

silage [sile-ij] n fodder crop harvested while green and partially fermented in a silo or plastic bags.

silence n absence of noise or speech. ▶ v make silent; put a stop to. **silent** adj **silently** adv **silencer** n device to reduce the noise of an engine exhaust or gun.

silhouette n outline of a dark

shape seen against a light background. ▸ v show in silhouette.

silica n hard glossy mineral found as quartz and in sandstone. **silicosis** n lung disease caused by inhaling silica dust.

silicon n Chem brittle nonmetallic element widely used in chemistry and industry. **silicone** n tough synthetic substance made from silicon and used in lubricants, paints, and resins. **silicon chip** tiny wafer of silicon processed to form an integrated circuit.

silk n fibre made by the larva (**silkworm**) of a certain moth; thread or fabric made from this. **silky, silken** adj of or like silk.

sill n ledge at the bottom of a window or door.

silly adj -lier, -liest. foolish. **silliness** n

silo n, pl -los. pit or airtight tower for storing silage or grains; underground structure in which nuclear missiles are kept ready for launching.

silt n mud deposited by moving water. ▸ v (foll. by up) fill or be choked with silt.

silvan adj same as SYLVAN.

silver n white precious metal; coins or articles made of silver. ▸ adj made of or of the colour of silver. **silverbeet** n Aust & NZ leafy green vegetable with white stalks. **silver birch** tree with silvery-white bark. **silver fern** NZ sporting symbol of New Zealand. **silverfish** n small wingless silver-coloured insect. **silverside** n cut of beef from below the rump and above the leg. **silver wedding** twenty-fifth wedding anniversary.

simian adj, n (of or like) a monkey or ape.

similar adj alike but not identical. **similarity** n **similarly** adv

simile [sim-ill-ee] n figure of speech comparing one thing to another, using 'as' or 'like', e.g. as blind as a bat.

similitude n similarity, likeness.

simmer v cook gently at just below boiling point; be in a state of suppressed rage. **simmer down** v Informal calm down.

simnel cake n Brit fruit cake covered with marzipan.

simper v smile in a silly or affected way; utter (something) with a simper. ▸ n simpering smile.

simple adj easy to understand or do; plain or unpretentious; not combined or complex; sincere or frank; feeble-minded. **simply** adv **simplicity** n **simplify** v make less complicated. **simplification** n **simplistic** adj too simple or naive. **simpleton** n foolish or half-witted person.

simulate v make a pretence of; imitate the conditions of (a particular situation); have the appearance of. **simulation** n **simulator** n

simultaneous adj occurring at the same time. **simultaneously** adv

sin[1] n breaking of a religious or moral law; offence against a principle or standard. ▸ v **sinning, sinned.** commit a sin. **sinful** adj guilty of sin; being a sin. **sinfully** adv **sinner** n

sin[2] Maths sine.

since prep during the period of time after. ▸ conj from the time when; for the reason that. ▸ adv from that time.

sincere adj without pretence or deceit. **sincerely** adv **sincerity** n

sine n (in trigonometry) ratio of the length of the opposite side to that of the hypotenuse in a right-angled triangle.

sinecure [sin-ee-cure] n paid job with minimal duties.

sine die [sin-ay **dee**-ay] adv Latin with no date fixed for future action.

sine qua non [sin-ay kwah **non**] n Latin essential requirement.

sinew n tough fibrous tissue joining muscle to bone; muscles or strength. **sinewy** adj

sing v singing, sang, sung. make musical sounds with the voice; perform (a song); make a humming or whistling sound.
singing telegram service in which a messenger presents greetings to a person by singing. **singsong** n informal singing session. ▶ adj (of the voice) repeatedly rising and falling in pitch.

singe v singeing, singed. burn the surface of. ▶ n superficial burn.

singer n person who sings, esp. professionally.

single adj one only; distinct from others of the same kind; unmarried; designed for one user; formed of only one part; (of a ticket) valid for an outward journey only. ▶ n single thing; thing intended for one person; record with one short song or tune on each side; single ticket. ▶ pl game between two players. ▶ v (foll. by out) pick out from others. **singly** adv **single file** (of people or things) arranged in one line. **single-handed** adj without assistance. **single-minded** adj having one aim only.

singlet n sleeveless vest.

singular adj (of a word or form) denoting one person or thing; remarkable, unusual. ▶ n singular form of a word. **singularity** n **singularly** adv

sinister adj threatening or suggesting evil or harm.

sink v sinking, sank, sunk or sunken. submerge (in liquid); descend or cause to descend; decline in value or amount; become weaker in health; dig or drill (a hole or shaft); invest (money); Golf, snooker hit (a ball) into a hole or pocket. ▶ n fixed basin with a water supply and drainage pipe. **sinker** n weight for a fishing line. **sink in** v penetrate the mind. **sinking fund** money set aside regularly to repay a long-term debt.

Sino- combining form Chinese.

sinuous adj curving; lithe. **sinuously** adv

sinus [sine-uss] n hollow space in a bone, esp. an air passage opening into the nose.

sip v sipping, sipped. drink in small mouthfuls. ▶ n amount sipped.

siphon n bent tube which uses air pressure to draw liquid from a container. ▶ v draw off thus; redirect (resources).

sir n polite term of address for a man; (S-) title of a knight or baronet.

sire n male parent of a horse or other domestic animal; respectful term of address to a king. ▶ v father.

siren n device making a loud wailing noise as a warning; dangerously alluring woman.

sirloin n prime cut of loin of beef.

sirocco n, pl -cos. hot wind blowing from N Africa into S Europe.

sis interj S Afr informal exclamation of disgust.

sisal [size-al] n (fibre of) plant used in making ropes.

siskin n yellow-and-black finch.

sissy adj, n, pl -sies. weak or cowardly (person).

sister n girl or woman with the same parents as another person; female fellow-member of a group; senior nurse; nun. ▸ adj closely related, similar. **sisterhood** n state of being a sister; group of women united by common aims or beliefs. **sisterly** adj
sister-in-law n, pl **sisters-in-law.** sister of one's husband or wife; one's brother's wife.
sit v **sitting, sat.** rest one's body upright on the buttocks; cause to sit; perch; occupy an official position; (of an official body) hold a session; take (an examination). **sitting room** room in a house where people sit and relax. **sit-in** n protest in which demonstrators occupy a place and refuse to move.
sitar n Indian stringed musical instrument.
sitcom n Informal situation comedy.
site n place where something is, was, or is intended to be located; same as WEBSITE. ▸ v provide with a site.
situate v place.
situation n state of affairs; location and surroundings; position of employment. **situation comedy** radio or television series involving the same characters in various situations.
six adj, n one more than five.
sixth adj, n (of) number six in a series. **sixteen** adj, n six and ten. **sixteenth** adj, n **sixty** adj, n six times ten. **sixtieth** adj, n
size[1] n dimensions, bigness; one of a series of standard measurements of goods. ▸ v arrange according to size. **sizeable, sizable** adj quite large. **size up** v Informal assess.
size[2] n gluey substance used as a protective coating.
sizzle v make a hissing sound like

frying fat.
skate[1] n boot with a steel blade or sets of wheels attached to the sole for gliding over ice or a hard surface. ▸ v glide on or as if on skates. **skateboard** n board mounted on small wheels for riding on while standing up. **skateboarding** n **skate over, round** v avoid discussing or dealing with (a matter) fully.
skate[2] n large marine flatfish.
skedaddle v Informal run off.
skein n yarn wound in a loose coil; flock of geese in flight.
skeleton n framework of bones inside a person's or animal's body; essential framework of a structure. ▸ adj reduced to a minimum. **skeletal** adj **skeleton key** key which can open many different locks.
sketch n rough drawing; brief description; short humorous play. ▸ v make a sketch (of). **sketchy** adj incomplete or inadequate.
skew v make slanting or crooked. ▸ adj slanting or crooked. **skew-whiff** adj Brit informal slanting or crooked.
skewer n pin to hold meat together during cooking. ▸ v fasten with a skewer.
ski n one of a pair of long runners fastened to boots for gliding over snow or water. ▸ v **skiing, skied** or **ski'd.** travel on skis. **skier** n
skid v **skidding, skidded.** (of a moving vehicle) slide sideways uncontrollably. ▸ n skidding.
skiff n small boat.
skill n special ability or expertise; something requiring special training or expertise. **skilful** adj having or showing skill. **skilfully** adv **skilled** adj
skillet n small frying pan or shallow cooking pot.

skim v skimming, skimmed.
remove floating matter from the
surface of (a liquid); glide
smoothly over; read quickly.
skimmed, skim milk milk from
which the cream has been
removed.

skimp v not invest enough time,
money, material, etc. **skimpy** adj
scanty or insufficient.

skin n outer covering of the body;
complexion; outer layer or
covering; film on a liquid; animal
skin used as a material or
container. ▶ v **skinning, skinned.**
remove the skin of. **skinless** adj
skinny adj thin. **skin-deep** adj
superficial. **skin diving**
underwater swimming using
flippers and light breathing
apparatus. **skin-diver** n **skinflint**
n miser. **skinhead** n youth with
very short hair.

skint adj Brit slang having no
money.

skip¹ v **skipping, skipped.** leap
lightly from one foot to the other;
jump over a rope as it is swung
under one; Informal pass over,
omit. ▶ n skipping.

skip² n large open container for
builders' rubbish.

skipper n, v captain.

skirl n sound of bagpipes.

skirmish n brief or minor fight or
argument. ▶ v take part in a
skirmish.

skirt n woman's garment hanging
from the waist; part of a dress or
coat below the waist; cut of beef
from the flank. ▶ v border; go
round; avoid dealing with (an
issue). **skirting board** narrow
board round the bottom of an
interior wall.

skit n brief satirical sketch.

skite v, n Aust & NZ boast.

skittish adj playful or lively.

skittle n bottle-shaped object used
as a target in some games. ▶ pl
game in which players try to
knock over skittles by rolling a ball
at them.

skive v Brit informal evade work or
responsibility.

skivvy n, pl -vies. Brit female
servant who does menial work.

skua n large predatory gull.

skulduggery n Informal trickery.

skulk v move stealthily; lurk.

skull n bony framework of the
head. **skullcap** n close-fitting
brimless cap.

skunk n small black-and-white N
American mammal which emits a
foul-smelling fluid when attacked;
Slang despicable person.

sky n, pl skies. upper atmosphere
as seen from the earth. **skydiving**
n sport of jumping from an
aircraft and performing
manoeuvres before opening one's
parachute. **skylark** n lark that
sings while soaring at a great
height. **skylight** n window in a
roof or ceiling. **skyscraper** n very
tall building.

slab n broad flat piece.

slack adj not tight; negligent; not
busy. ▶ n slack part. ▶ pl informal
trousers. ▶ v neglect one's work or
duty. **slackness** n **slacken** v
make or become slack. **slacker** n

slag n waste left after metal is
smelted. ▶ v slagging, slagged.
(foll. by off) Brit, Aust & NZ slang
criticize.

slain v past participle of SLAY.

slake v satisfy (thirst or desire);
combine (quicklime) with water.

slalom n skiing or canoeing race
over a winding course.

slam v slamming, slammed. shut,
put down, or hit violently and
noisily; Informal criticize harshly.
▶ n act or sound of slamming.

grand slam see GRAND.

slander n false and malicious statement about a person; crime of making such a statement. ▶ v utter slander about. **slanderous** adj

slang n very informal language. **slangy** adj **slanging match** abusive argument.

slant v lean at an angle, slope; present (information) in a biased way. ▶ n slope; point of view, esp. a biased one. **slanting** adj

slap n blow with the open hand or a flat object. ▶ v **slapping, slapped.** strike with the open hand or a flat object; Informal place forcefully or carelessly. **slapdash** adj careless and hasty. **slap-happy** adj Informal cheerfully careless. **slapstick** n boisterous knockabout comedy. **slap-up** adj (of a meal) large and luxurious.

slash v cut with a sweeping stroke; gash; reduce drastically. ▶ n sweeping stroke; gash.

slat n narrow strip of wood or metal.

slate[1] n rock which splits easily into thin layers; piece of this for covering a roof or, formerly, for writing on.

slate[2] v Informal criticize harshly.

slattern n Old-fashioned slovenly woman. **slatternly** adj

slaughter v kill (animals) for food; kill (people) savagely or indiscriminately. ▶ n slaughtering. **slaughterhouse** n place where animals are killed for food.

Slav n member of any of the peoples of E Europe or the former Soviet Union who speak a Slavonic language. **Slavonic** n language group including Russian, Polish, and Czech. ▶ adj of this language group.

slave n person owned by another

for whom he or she has to work; person dominated by another or by a habit; drudge. ▶ v work like a slave. **slaver** n person or ship engaged in the slave trade. **slavery** n state or condition of being a slave; practice of owning slaves. **slavish** adj of or like a slave; imitative. **slave-driver** n person who makes others work very hard.

slaver [slav-ver] v dribble saliva from the mouth.

slay v **slaying, slew, slain.** kill.

sleazy adj **-zier, -ziest.** run-down or sordid. **sleaze** n

sledge[1], **sled** n carriage on runners for sliding on snow; light wooden frame for sliding over snow. ▶ v travel by sledge.

sledge[2], **sledgehammer** n heavy hammer with a long handle.

sleek adj glossy, smooth, and shiny.

sleep n state of rest characterized by unconsciousness; period of this. ▶ v **sleeping, slept.** be in or as if in a state of sleep; have sleeping accommodation for (a specified number). **sleeper** n railway car fitted for sleeping in; beam supporting the rails of a railway; ring worn in a pierced ear to stop the hole from closing up; person who sleeps. **sleepy** adj **sleepily** adv **sleepiness** n **sleepless** adj **sleeping bag** padded bag for sleeping in. **sleeping sickness** African disease spread by the tsetse fly. **sleepout** n NZ small building for sleeping in. **sleep with, together** v have sexual intercourse (with).

sleet n rain and snow or hail falling together.

sleeve n part of a garment which covers the arm; tubelike cover; gramophone record cover. **up one's sleeve** secretly ready.

sleeveless *adj*

sleigh *n, v* sledge.

sleight of hand [slite] *n* skilful use of the hands when performing conjuring tricks.

slender *adj* slim; small in amount.

slept *v* past of SLEEP.

sleuth [slooth] *n* detective.

slew¹ *v* past tense of SLAY.

slew² *v* twist or swing round.

slice *n* thin flat piece cut from something; share; kitchen tool with a broad flat blade; *Sport* hitting of a ball so that it travels obliquely. ▶ *v* cut into slices; *Sport* hit (a ball) with a slice.

slick *adj* persuasive and glib; skilfully devised or carried out; well-made and attractive, but superficial. ▶ *n* patch of oil on water. ▶ *v* make smooth or sleek.

slide *v* **sliding, slid.** slip smoothly along (a surface); pass unobtrusively. ▶ *n* sliding; piece of glass holding an object to be viewed under a microscope; photographic transparency; surface or structure for sliding on or down; ornamental hair clip.

slide rule mathematical instrument formerly used for rapid calculations. **sliding scale** variable scale according to which things such as wages alter in response to changes in other factors.

slight *adj* small in quantity or extent; not important; slim and delicate. ▶ *v, n* snub. **slightly** *adv*

slim *adj* **slimmer, slimmest.** not heavy or stout; thin; slight. ▶ *v* **slimming, slimmed.** make or become slim by diet and exercise.

slimmer *n*

slime *n* unpleasant thick slippery substance. **slimy** *adj* of, like, or covered with slime; ingratiating.

sling¹ *n* bandage hung from the neck to support an injured hand or arm; rope or strap for lifting something; strap with a string at each end for throwing a stone. ▶ *v* **slinging, slung.** throw; carry, hang, or throw with or as if with a sling.

sling² *n* sweetened drink with a spirit base, e.g. *gin sling.*

slink *v* **slinking, slunk.** move furtively or guiltily. **slinky** *adj* (of clothes) figure-hugging.

slip¹ *v* **slipping, slipped.** lose balance by sliding; move smoothly, easily, or quietly; (foll. by *on* or *off*) put on or take off easily or quickly; pass out of (the mind). ▶ *n* slipping; mistake; petticoat. **give someone the slip** escape from someone. **slippy** *adj Informal* slippery. **slipknot** *n* knot tied so that it will slip along the rope round which it is made.

slipped disc painful condition in which one of the discs connecting the bones of the spine becomes displaced. **slip road** narrow road giving access to a motorway. **slipshod** *adj* (of an action) careless. **slipstream** *n* stream of air forced backwards by a fast-moving object. **slip up** *v* make a mistake. **slipway** *n* launching slope on which ships are built or repaired.

slip² *n* small piece (of paper).

slip³ *n* clay mixed with water used for decorating pottery.

slipper *n* light shoe for indoor wear.

slippery *adj* so smooth or wet as to cause slipping or be difficult to hold; (of a person) untrustworthy.

slit *n* long narrow cut or opening. ▶ *v* **slitting, slit.** make a long straight cut in.

slither *v* slide unsteadily.

sliver [sliv-ver] *n* small thin piece.

slob *n Informal* lazy and untidy

person. **slobbish** adj

slobber v dribble or drool.
slobbery adj

sloe n sour blue-black fruit.

slog v **slogging, slogged.** work
hard and steadily; make one's way
with difficulty; hit hard. ▶ n long
and exhausting work or walk.

slogan n catchword or phrase used
in politics or advertising.

sloop n small single-masted ship.

slop v **slopping, slopped.** splash or
spill. ▶ n spilt liquid; liquid food.
▶ pl liquid refuse and waste food
used to feed animals. **sloppy** adj
careless or untidy; gushingly
sentimental.

slope v slant. ▶ n sloping surface;
degree of inclination. ▶ pl hills.
slope off v Informal go furtively.

slosh v splash carelessly; Slang hit
hard. ▶ n splashing sound.
sloshed adj Slang drunk.

slot n narrow opening for inserting
something; Informal place in a
series or scheme. ▶ v **slotting,
slotted.** make a slot or slots in; fit
into a slot. **slot machine**
automatic machine worked by
placing a coin in it.

sloth [rhymes with **both**] n
slow-moving animal of tropical
America; laziness. **slothful** adj lazy
or idle.

slouch v sit, stand, or move with a
drooping posture. ▶ n drooping
posture. **be no slouch** Informal be
very good or talented.

slough[1] [rhymes with **now**] n bog.

slough[2] [sluff] v (of a snake) shed
(its skin) or (of a skin) be shed.
slough off v get rid of (something
unwanted or unnecessary).

sloven n habitually dirty or untidy
person. **slovenly** adj dirty or
untidy; careless.

slow adj taking a longer time than
is usual or expected; not fast; (of

a clock or watch) showing a time
earlier than the correct one;
stupid. ▶ v reduce the speed (of).
slowly adv **slowness** n

slowcoach n Informal person who
moves or works slowly.

slowworm n small legless lizard.

sludge n thick mud; sewage.

slug[1] n land snail with no shell.
sluggish adj slow-moving, lacking
energy. **sluggishly** adv
sluggishness n **sluggard** n lazy
person.

slug[2] n bullet; Informal mouthful of
an alcoholic drink.

slug[3] v **slugging, slugged.** hit
hard. ▶ n heavy blow.

sluice n channel carrying off water;
sliding gate used to control the
flow of water in this; water
controlled by a sluice. ▶ v pour a
stream of water over or through.

slum n squalid overcrowded house
or area. ▶ v **slumming, slummed.**
temporarily and deliberately
experience poorer places or
conditions than usual.

slumber v, n Lit sleep.

slump v (of prices or demand)
decline suddenly; sink or fall
heavily. ▶ n sudden decline in
prices or demand; time of
substantial unemployment.

slung v past of SLING[1].

slunk v past of SLINK.

slur v **slurring, slurred.** pronounce
or utter (words) indistinctly; Music
sing or play (notes) smoothly
without a break. ▶ n slurring of
words; remark intended to
discredit someone; Music slurring
of notes; curved line indicating
notes to be slurred.

slurp Informal ▶ v eat or drink
noisily. ▶ n slurping sound.

slurry n, pl **-ries.** muddy liquid
mixture.

slush n watery muddy substance;

sloppy sentimental talk or writing.

slushy adj **slush fund** fund for financing bribery or corruption.

sly adj **slyer, slyest** or **slier, sliest.** crafty; secretive and cunning; roguish. **on the sly** secretly.

slyly adv **slyness** n

smack [1] v slap sharply; open and close (the lips) loudly in enjoyment or anticipation. ▶ n sharp slap; loud kiss; slapping sound. ▶ adv Informal squarely or directly, e.g. smack in the middle.

smacker n Slang loud kiss.

smack [2] n slight flavour or trace; Slang heroin. ▶ v have a slight flavour or trace (of).

smack [3] n small single-masted fishing boat.

small adj not large in size, number, or amount; unimportant; mean or petty. ▶ n narrow part of the lower back. ▶ pl Informal underwear. **smallness** n

smallholding n small area of farming land. **small hours** hours just after midnight. **small-minded** adj intolerant, petty. **smallpox** n contagious disease with blisters that leave scars. **small talk** light social conversation. **small-time** adj insignificant or minor.

smarmy adj **smarmier, smarmiest.** Informal unpleasantly suave or flattering.

smart adj well-kept and neat; astute; witty; fashionable; brisk. ▶ v feel or cause stinging pain. ▶ n stinging pain. **smartly** adv **smartness** n **smart aleck** Informal irritatingly clever person. **smart card** plastic card used for storing and processing computer data. **smarten** v make or become smart.

smash v break violently and noisily; throw (against) violently; collide forcefully; destroy. ▶ n act or sound of smashing; violent

collision of vehicles; Informal popular success; Sport powerful overhead shot. **smasher** n Informal attractive person or thing. **smashing** adj Informal excellent.

smattering n slight knowledge.

smear v spread with a greasy or sticky substance; rub so as to produce a dirty mark or smudge; slander. ▶ n dirty mark or smudge; slander; Med sample of a secretion smeared on to a slide for examination under a microscope.

smell v smelling, smelt or smelled. perceive (a scent or odour) by means of the nose; have or give off a smell; have an unpleasant smell; detect by instinct. ▶ n ability to perceive odours by the nose; odour or scent; smelling. **smelly** adj having a nasty smell. **smelling salts** preparation of ammonia used to revive a person who feels faint.

smelt [1] v extract (a metal) from (an ore) by heating.

smelt [2] n small fish of the salmon family.

smelt [3] v a past of SMELL.

smelter n industrial plant where smelting is carried out.

smile n turning up of the corners of the mouth to show pleasure, amusement, or friendliness. ▶ v give a smile. **smiley** n symbol depicting a smile or other facial expression, used in e-mail. **smile on, upon** v regard favourably.

smirch v, n stain.

smirk n smug smile. ▶ v give a smirk.

smite v smiting, smote, smitten. Old-fashioned strike hard; affect severely.

smith n worker in metal. **smithy** n blacksmith's workshop.

smithereens pl n shattered fragments.

smitten v past participle of SMITE.

smock n loose overall; woman's loose blouselike garment. ▶ v gather (material) by sewing in a honeycomb pattern. **smocking** n

smog n mixture of smoke and fog.

smoke n cloudy mass that rises from something burning; act of smoking tobacco. ▶ v give off smoke; inhale and expel smoke of (a cigar, cigarette, or pipe); do this habitually; cure (meat, fish, or cheese) by treating with smoke. **smokeless** adj **smoker** n **smoky** adj **smoke screen** something said or done to hide the truth.

smooch Informal ▶ v kiss and cuddle. ▶ n smooching.

smooth adj even in surface, texture, or consistency; without obstructions or difficulties; charming and polite but possibly insincere; free from jolts; not harsh in taste. ▶ v make smooth; calm. **smoothie** n Informal charming but possibly insincere man; thick drink made from puréed fresh fruit. **smoothly** adv

smorgasbord n buffet meal of assorted dishes.

smote v past tense of SMITE.

smother v suffocate or stifle; suppress; cover thickly.

smoulder v burn slowly with smoke but no flame; (of feelings) exist in a suppressed state.

SMS short message system: used for sending data to mobile phones.

smudge v make or become smeared or soiled. ▶ n dirty mark; blurred form. **smudgy** adj

smug adj **smugger, smuggest.** self-satisfied. **smugly** adv **smugness** n

smuggle v import or export (goods) secretly and illegally; take somewhere secretly. **smuggler** n

smut n obscene jokes, pictures, etc.; speck of soot or dark mark left by soot. **smutty** adj

snack n light quick meal. **snack bar** place where snacks are sold.

snaffle n jointed bit for a horse. ▶ v Brit, Aust & NZ slang steal.

snag n difficulty or disadvantage; sharp projecting point; hole in fabric caused by a sharp object. ▶ v snagging, snagged. catch or tear on a point.

snail n slow-moving mollusc with a spiral shell. **snail mail** Informal conventional post, as opposed to e-mail. **snail's pace** very slow speed.

snake n long thin scaly limbless reptile. ▶ v move in a winding course like a snake. **snake in the grass** treacherous person. **snaky** adj twisted or winding.

snap v snapping, snapped. break suddenly; (cause to) make a sharp cracking sound; move suddenly; bite (at) suddenly; speak sharply and angrily; take a snapshot of. ▶ n act or sound of snapping; Informal snapshot; sudden brief spell of cold weather; card game in which the word 'snap' is called when two similar cards are put down. ▶ adj made on the spur of the moment. **snappy** adj (also **snappish**) irritable; Slang quick; Slang smart and fashionable.

snapdragon n plant with flowers that can open and shut like a mouth. **snapshot** n informal photograph. **snap up** v take eagerly and quickly.

snare n trap with a noose. ▶ v catch in or as if in a snare.

snarl[1] v (of an animal) growl with bared teeth; speak or utter fiercely. ▶ n act or sound of snarling.

snarl[2] n tangled mess. ▶ v make tangled. **snarl-up** n Informal confused situation such as a traffic jam.

snatch v seize or try to seize suddenly; take (food, rest, etc.) hurriedly. ▶ n snatching; fragment.

snazzy adj **-zier, -ziest.** Informal stylish and flashy.

sneak v move furtively; bring, take, or put furtively; Informal tell tales. ▶ n cowardly or underhand person. **sneaking** adj slight but persistent; secret. **sneaky** adj

sneakers pl n canvas shoes with rubber soles.

sneer n contemptuous expression or remark. ▶ v show contempt by a sneer.

sneeze v expel air from the nose suddenly, involuntarily, and noisily. ▶ n act or sound of sneezing.

snicker n, v same as SNIGGER.

snide adj critical in an unfair and nasty way.

sniff v inhale through the nose in short audible breaths; smell by sniffing. ▶ n act or sound of sniffing. **sniffle** v sniff repeatedly, as when suffering from a cold. ▶ n slight cold. **sniff at** v express contempt for. **sniffer dog** police dog trained to detect drugs or explosives by smell.

snifter n Informal small quantity of alcoholic drink.

snigger n sly disrespectful laugh, esp. one partly stifled. ▶ v utter a snigger.

snip v **snipping, snipped.** cut in small quick strokes with scissors or shears. ▶ n Informal bargain; act or sound of snipping. **snippet** n small piece.

snipe n wading bird with a long straight bill. ▶ v (foll. by at) shoot at (a person) from cover; make critical remarks about.

sniper n person who shoots at

someone from cover.

snitch Informal ▶ v act as an informer; steal. ▶ n informer.

snivel v **-elling, -elled.** cry in a whining way.

snob n person who judges others by social rank; person who feels smugly superior in his or her tastes or interests. **snobbery** n **snobbish** adj

snoek n S Afr edible marine fish.

snood n pouch, often of net, loosely holding a woman's hair at the back.

snook n **cock a snook at** show contempt for.

snooker n game played on a billiard table. ▶ v leave (a snooker opponent) in a position such that another ball blocks the target ball; Informal put (someone) in a position where he or she can do nothing.

snoop Informal ▶ v pry. ▶ n snooping. **snooper** n

snooty adj **snootier, snootiest.** Informal haughty.

snooze Informal ▶ v take a brief light sleep. ▶ n brief light sleep.

snore v make snorting sounds while sleeping. ▶ n sound of snoring.

snorkel n tube allowing a swimmer to breathe while face down on the surface of the water. ▶ v **-kelling, -kelled.** swim using a snorkel.

snort v exhale noisily through the nostrils; express contempt or anger by snorting. ▶ n act or sound of snorting.

snot n Slang mucus from the nose.

snout n animal's projecting nose and jaws.

snow n frozen vapour falling from the sky in flakes; Slang cocaine. ▶ v fall as or like snow. **be snowed under** be overwhelmed, esp. with

paperwork. **snowy** adj **snowball**
n snow pressed into a ball for
throwing. ► v increase rapidly.
snowboard n board on which a
person stands to slide across the
snow. **snowboarding** n
snowdrift n bank of deep snow.
snowdrop n small white
bell-shaped spring flower.
snowflake n single crystal of
snow. **snow line** (on a mountain)
height above which there is
permanent snow. **snowman** n
figure shaped out of snow.
snowplough n vehicle for clearing
away snow. **snowshoes** pl n
racket-shaped shoes for travelling
on snow.
snub v **snubbing, snubbed.** insult
deliberately. ► n deliberate insult.
► adj (of a nose) short and blunt.
snub-nosed adj
snuff¹ n powdered tobacco for
sniffing up the nostrils.
snuff² v extinguish (a candle).
snuff it Informal die.
snuffle v breathe noisily or with
difficulty.
snug adj **snugger, snuggest.** warm
and comfortable; comfortably
close-fitting. ► n (in Britain and
Ireland) small room in a pub.
snugly adv
snuggle v nestle into a person or
thing for warmth or from affection.
so adv to such an extent; in such a
manner; very; also; thereupon.
► conj in order that; with the result
that; therefore. ► interj exclamation
of surprise, triumph, or realization.
so-and-so n Informal person whose
name is not specified; unpleasant
person or thing. **so-called** adj
called (in the speaker's opinion,
wrongly) by that name. **so long**
goodbye. **so that** in order that.
soak v make wet; put or lie in
liquid so as to become thoroughly

wet; (of liquid) penetrate. ► n
soaking; Slang drunkard. **soaking**
n, adj **soak up** v absorb.
soap n compound of alkali and fat,
used with water as a cleaning
agent; Informal soap opera. ► v
apply soap to. **soapy** adj **soap
opera** radio or television serial
dealing with domestic themes.
soar v rise or fly upwards; increase
suddenly.
sob v **sobbing, sobbed.** weep with
convulsive gasps; utter with sobs.
► n act or sound of sobbing. **sob
story** tale of personal distress told
to arouse sympathy.
sober adj not drunk; serious; (of
colours) plain and dull. ► v make
or become sober. **soberly** adv
sobriety n state of being sober.
sobriquet [so-brik-ay] n nickname.
soccer n football played by two
teams of eleven kicking a spherical
ball.
sociable adj friendly or
companionable; (of an occasion)
providing companionship.
sociability n **sociably** adv
social adj living in a community; of
society or its organization;
sociable. ► n informal gathering.
socially adv **socialite** n member
of fashionable society. **socialize** v
meet others socially. **social
security** state provision for the
unemployed, elderly, or sick.
social services welfare services
provided by local authorities or
the state. **social work** work
which involves helping or advising
people with serious financial or
family problems.
socialism n political system which
advocates public ownership of
industries, resources, and
transport. **socialist** n, adj
society n, pl **-ties.** human beings
considered as a group; organized

community; structure and institutions of such a community; organized group with common aims and interests; upper-class or fashionable people collectively; companionship.

sociology n study of human societies. **sociological** adj **sociologist** n

sock[1] n knitted covering for the foot.

sock[2] Slang ▶ v hit hard. ▶ n hard blow.

socket n hole or recess into which something fits.

sod n (piece of) turf.

soda n compound of sodium; soda water. **soda water** fizzy drink made from water charged with carbon dioxide.

sodden adj soaked.

sodium n Chem silvery-white metallic element. **sodium bicarbonate** white soluble compound used in baking powder.

sodomy n anal intercourse. **sodomite** n person who practises sodomy.

sofa n couch.

soft adj easy to shape or cut; not hard, rough, or harsh; (of a breeze or climate) mild; (too) lenient; easily influenced or imposed upon; (of drugs) not liable to cause addiction. **softly** adv **soften** v make or become soft or softer. **soft drink** nonalcoholic drink. **soft furnishings** curtains, rugs, lampshades, and furniture covers. **soft option** easiest alternative. **soft-pedal** v deliberately avoid emphasizing something. **soft-soap** v Informal flatter. **software** n computer programs. **softwood** n wood of a coniferous tree.

soggy adj **-gier, -giest.** soaked; moist and heavy. **sogginess** n

soigné, (fem) **soignée** [swah-nyay] adj well-groomed, elegant.

soil[1] n top layer of earth; country or territory.

soil[2] v make or become dirty; disgrace.

soiree [swah-ray] n evening party or gathering.

sojourn [soj-urn] n temporary stay. ▶ v stay temporarily.

solace [sol-iss] n, v comfort in distress.

solar adj of the sun; using the energy of the sun. **solar plexus** network of nerves at the pit of the stomach; that part of the stomach. **solar system** the sun and the heavenly bodies that go round it.

solarium n, pl **-lariums, -laria.** place with beds and ultraviolet lights used for acquiring an artificial suntan.

sold v past of SELL.

solder n soft alloy used to join two metal surfaces. ▶ v join with solder. **soldering iron** tool for melting and applying solder.

soldier n member of an army. ▶ v serve in an army. **soldierly** adj **soldier on** v persist doggedly.

sole[1] adj one and only; not shared, exclusive. **solely** adv only, completely; singly. **sole charge school** NZ country school with only one teacher.

sole[2] n underside of the foot; underside of a shoe. ▶ v provide (a shoe) with a sole.

sole[3] n small edible flatfish.

solecism [sol-iss-izz-um] n minor grammatical mistake; breach of etiquette.

solemn adj serious, deeply sincere; formal. **solemnly** adv **solemnity** n

solenoid [sole-in-oid] n coil of wire magnetized by passing a current through it.

sol-fa n system of syllables used as

names for the notes of a scale.

solicit *v* **-iting, -ited.** request; (of a prostitute) offer (a person) sex for money. **solicitation** *n*

solicitor *n* Brit, Aust & NZ lawyer who advises clients and prepares documents and cases.

solicitous *adj* anxious about someone's welfare. **solicitude** *n*

solid *adj* (of a substance) keeping its shape; not liquid or gas; not hollow; of the same substance throughout; strong or substantial; sound or reliable; having three dimensions. ▶ *n* three-dimensional shape; solid substance. **solidly** *adv* **solidify** *v* make or become solid or firm. **solidity** *n*

solidarity *n* agreement in aims or interests, total unity.

soliloquy *n, pl* **-quies.** speech made by a person while alone, esp. in a play.

solipsism *n* doctrine that the self is the only thing known to exist. **solipsist** *n*

solitaire *n* game for one person played with pegs set in a board; gem set by itself.

solitary *adj* alone, single; (of a place) lonely. **solitude** *n* state of being alone.

solo *n, pl* **-los.** music for one performer; any act done without assistance. ▶ *adj* done alone. ▶ *adv* by oneself, alone. **soloist** *n* **solo parent** NZ parent bringing up a child or children alone.

solstice *n* either the shortest (in winter) or longest (in summer) day of the year.

soluble *adj* able to be dissolved; able to be solved. **solubility** *n*

solution *n* answer to a problem; act of solving a problem; liquid with something dissolved in it; process of dissolving.

solve *v* find the answer to (a problem). **solvable** *adj*

solvent *adj* having enough money to pay one's debts. ▶ *n* liquid capable of dissolving other substances. **solvency** *n* **solvent abuse** deliberate inhaling of intoxicating fumes from certain solvents.

sombre *adj* dark, gloomy.

sombrero *n, pl* **-ros.** wide-brimmed Mexican hat.

some *adj* unknown or unspecified; unknown or unspecified quantity or number of; considerable number or amount of; *Informal* remarkable. ▶ *pron* certain unknown or unspecified people or things; unknown or unspecified number or quantity. **somebody** *pron* some person. ▶ *n* important person. **somehow** *adv* in some unspecified way. **someone** *pron* somebody. **something** *pron* unknown or unspecified thing or amount; impressive or important thing. **sometime** *adv* at some unspecified time. ▶ *adj* former. **sometimes** *adv* from time to time, now and then. **somewhat** *adv* to some extent, rather. **somewhere** *adv* in, to, or at some unspecified or unknown place.

somersault *n* leap or roll in which the trunk and legs are turned over the head. ▶ *v* perform a somersault.

somnambulism *n* person who walks in his or her sleep. **somnambulism** *n*

somnolent *adj* drowsy.

son *n* male offspring. **son-in-law** *n, pl* **sons-in-law.** daughter's husband.

sonar *n* device for detecting underwater objects by the reflection of sound waves.

sonata *n* piece of music in several movements for one instrument with or without piano.

son et lumière [sawn eh

loo-mee-er] n French night-time entertainment with lighting and sound effects, telling the story of the place where it is staged.

song n music for the voice; tuneful sound made by certain birds; singing. **for a song** very cheaply.

songster, songstress n singer.

songbird n any bird with a musical call.

sonic adj of or producing sound. **sonic boom** loud bang caused by an aircraft flying faster than sound.

sonnet n fourteen-line poem with a fixed rhyme scheme.

sonorous adj (of sound) deep or resonant. **sonorously** adv **sonority** n

soon adv in a short time.

sooner adv rather, e.g. I'd sooner go alone. **sooner or later** eventually.

soot n black powder formed by the incomplete burning of an organic substance. **sooty** adj

soothe v make calm; relieve (pain etc.).

soothsayer n seer or prophet.

sop n concession to pacify someone. ▶ v **sopping, sopped.** mop up or absorb (liquid). **sopping** adj completely soaked.

soppy adj Informal oversentimental.

sophist n person who uses clever but invalid arguments.

sophisticate v make less natural or innocent; make more complex or refined. ▶ n sophisticated person.

sophisticated adj having or appealing to refined or cultured tastes and habits; complex and refined.

sophistry, sophism n clever but invalid argument.

sophomore n US student in second year at college.

soporific adj causing sleep. ▶ n drug that causes sleep.

soprano n, pl **-pranos.** (singer with) the highest female or boy's voice; highest pitched of a family of instruments.

sorbet n flavoured water ice.

sorcerer n magician. **sorceress** fem **sorcery** n witchcraft or magic.

sordid adj dirty, squalid; base, vile; selfish and grasping. **sordidly** adv **sordidness** n

sore adj painful; causing annoyance; resentful; (of need) urgent. ▶ n painful area on the body. ▶ adv Obs greatly. **sorely** adv greatly. **soreness** n

sorghum n kind of grass cultivated for grain.

sorrel n bitter-tasting plant.

sorrow n grief or sadness; cause of sorrow. ▶ v grieve. **sorrowful** adj **sorrowfully** adv

sorry adj **-rier, -riest.** feeling pity or regret; pitiful or wretched.

sort n group all sharing certain qualities or characteristics; Informal type of character. ▶ v arrange according to kind; mend or fix. **out of sorts** slightly unwell or bad-tempered.

sortie n relatively short return trip; operational flight made by military aircraft.

SOS n international code signal of distress; call for help.

so-so adj Informal mediocre.

sot n habitual drunkard.

sotto voce [sot-toe voe-chay] adv in an undertone.

soubriquet [so-brik-ay] n same as SOBRIQUET.

soufflé [soo-flay] n light fluffy dish made with beaten egg whites and other ingredients.

sough [rhymes with now] v (of the wind) make a sighing sound.

sought [sawt] v past of SEEK.

souk [sook] n marketplace in Muslim countries, often open-air.

soul n spiritual and immortal part of a human being; essential part or fundamental nature; deep and sincere feelings; person regarded as typifying some quality; person; type of Black music combining blues, pop, and gospel. **soulful** adj full of emotion. **soulless** adj lacking human qualities, mechanical; (of a person) lacking sensitivity.

sound¹ n something heard, noise. ▶ v make or cause to make a sound; seem to be as specified; pronounce. **sound barrier** Informal sudden increase in air resistance against an object as it approaches the speed of sound. **sound bite** short pithy sentence or phrase extracted from a longer speech, esp. by a politician, for use on television or radio. **soundproof** adj not penetrable by sound. ▶ v make soundproof. **soundtrack** n recorded sound accompaniment to a film.

sound² adj in good condition; firm, substantial; financially reliable; showing good judgment; ethically correct; (of sleep) deep; thorough. **soundly** adv

sound³ v find the depth of (water etc.); examine (the body) by tapping or with a stethoscope; ascertain the views of. **soundings** pl n measurements of depth taken by sounding. **sounding board** person or group used to test a new idea.

sound⁴ n channel or strait.

soup n liquid food made from meat, vegetables, etc. **soupy** adj **soup kitchen** place where food and drink is served to needy people. **souped-up** adj (of an engine) adjusted so as to be more powerful than normal.

soupçon [soop-sonn] n small amount.

sour adj sharp-tasting; (of milk) gone bad; (of a person's temperament) sullen. ▶ v make or become sour. **sourly** adv **sourness** n

source n origin or starting point; person, book, etc. providing information; spring where a river or stream begins.

souse v plunge (something) into liquid; drench; pickle.

soutane [soo-tan] n Roman Catholic priest's cassock.

south n direction towards the South Pole, opposite north; area lying in or towards the south. ▶ adj to or in the south; (of a wind) from the south. ▶ adv in, to, or towards the south. **southerly** adj **southern** adj **southerner** n person from the south of a country or area. **southward** adj, adv **southwards** adv **southpaw** n Informal left-handed person, esp. a boxer. **South Pole** southernmost point on the earth's axis.

souvenir n keepsake, memento.

sou'wester n seaman's waterproof hat covering the head and back of the neck.

sovereign n king or queen; former British gold coin worth one pound. ▶ adj (of a state) independent; supreme in rank or authority; excellent. **sovereignty** n

soviet n formerly, elected council at various levels of government in the USSR. ▶ adj (S-) of the former USSR.

sow¹ [rhymes with **know**] v **sowing, sowed, sown** or **sowed.** scatter or plant (seed) in or on (the ground); implant or introduce.

sow² [rhymes with **cow**] n female adult pig.

soya n plant whose edible bean (**soya bean**) is used for food and as a source of oil. **soy sauce** sauce made from fermented soya beans, used in Chinese and Japanese cookery.

sozzled *adj Brit, Aust & NZ slang* drunk.

spa *n* resort with a mineral-water spring.

space *n* unlimited expanse in which all objects exist and move; interval; blank portion; unoccupied area; the universe beyond the earth's atmosphere. ▶ *v* place at intervals. **spacious** *adj* having a large capacity or area. **spacecraft, spaceship** *n* vehicle for travel beyond the earth's atmosphere. **space shuttle** manned reusable vehicle for repeated space flights. **spacesuit** *n* sealed pressurized suit worn by an astronaut.

spade[1] *n* tool for digging. **spadework** *n* hard preparatory work.

spade[2] *n* playing card of the suit marked with black leaf-shaped symbols.

spaghetti *n* pasta in the form of long strings.

span *n* space between two points; complete extent; distance from thumb to little finger of the expanded hand. ▶ *v* **spanning, spanned.** stretch or extend across.

spangle *n* small shiny metallic ornament. ▶ *v* decorate with spangles.

spaniel *n* dog with long ears and silky hair.

spank *v* slap with the open hand, on the buttocks or legs. ▶ *n* such a slap. **spanking** *n*

spanking *adj Informal* outstandingly fine or smart; quick. **spanner** *n* tool for gripping and turning a nut or bolt.

spar[1] *n* pole used as a ship's mast, boom, or yard.

spar[2] *v* **sparring, sparred.** box or fight using light blows for practice; argue (with someone).

spare *adj* extra; in reserve; (of a person) thin. ▶ *n* duplicate kept in case of damage or loss. ▶ *v* refrain from punishing or harming; protect (someone) from (something unpleasant); afford to give. **to spare** in addition to what is needed. **sparing** *adj* economical. **spare ribs** pork ribs with most of the meat trimmed off.

spark *n* fiery particle thrown out from a fire or caused by friction; flash of light produced by an electrical discharge; trace or hint (of a particular quality). ▶ *v* give off sparks; initiate. **sparkie** *n NZ informal* electrician. **spark plug** device in an engine that ignites the fuel by producing an electric spark.

sparkle *v* glitter with many points of light; be vivacious or witty. ▶ *n* sparkling points of light; vivacity or wit. **sparkler** *n* hand-held firework that emits sparks. **sparkling** *adj* (of wine or mineral water) slightly fizzy.

sparrow *n* small brownish bird. **sparrowhawk** *n* small hawk.

sparse *adj* thinly scattered. **sparsely** *adv* **sparseness** *n*

spartan *adj* strict and austere.

spasm *n* involuntary muscular contraction; sudden burst of activity or feeling. **spasmodic** *adj* occurring in spasms. **spasmodically** *adv*

spastic *n* person with cerebral palsy. ▶ *adj* suffering from cerebral palsy; affected by spasms.

spat[1] *n* slight quarrel.

spat[2] *v* past of SPIT[1].

spate *n* large number of things

happening within a period of time; sudden outpouring or flood.

spatial adj of or in space.

spats pl n coverings formerly worn over the ankle and instep.

spatter v scatter or be scattered in drops over (something). ▶ n spattering sound; something spattered.

spatula n utensil with a broad flat blade for spreading or stirring.

spawn n jelly-like mass of eggs of fish, frogs, or molluscs. ▶ v (of fish, frogs, or molluscs) lay eggs; generate.

spay v remove the ovaries from (a female animal).

speak v **speaking, spoke, spoken.** say words, talk; communicate or express in words; give a speech or lecture; know how to talk in (a specified language). **speaker** n person who speaks, esp. at a formal occasion; loudspeaker; **(S-)** official chairman of a body.

spear[1] n weapon consisting of a long shaft with a sharp point. ▶ v pierce with or as if with a spear. **spearhead** v lead (an attack or campaign). ▶ n leading force in an attack or campaign.

spear[2] n slender shoot.

spearmint n type of mint.

spec n **on spec** Informal as a risk or gamble.

special adj distinguished from others of its kind; for a specific purpose; exceptional; particular. **specially** adv **specialist** n expert in a particular activity or subject. **speciality** n special interest or skill; product specialized in. **specialize** v be a specialist. **specialization** n

specie n coins as distinct from paper money.

species n, pl -cies. group of plants or animals that are related closely enough to interbreed naturally.

specific adj particular, definite. ▶ n drug used to treat a particular disease. ▶ pl particular details. **specifically** adv **specification** n detailed description of something to be made or done. **specify** v refer to or state specifically.

specific gravity ratio of the density of a substance to that of water.

specimen n individual or part typifying a whole; sample of blood etc. taken for analysis.

specious [spee-shuss] adj apparently true, but actually false.

speck n small spot or particle.

speckle n small spot. ▶ v mark with speckles.

specs pl n Informal short for SPECTACLES.

spectacle n strange, interesting, or ridiculous sight; impressive public show. ▶ pl pair of glasses for correcting faulty vision. **spectacular** adj impressive. ▶ n spectacular public show. **spectacularly** adv

spectator n person viewing anything, onlooker. **spectate** v watch.

spectre n ghost; menacing mental image. **spectral** adj

spectrum n pl -tra. range of different colours, radio waves, etc. in order of their wavelengths; entire range of anything. **spectroscope** n instrument for producing or examining spectra.

speculate v guess, conjecture; buy property, shares, etc. in the hope of selling them at a profit. **speculation** n **speculative** adj **speculator** n

sped v a past of SPEED.

speech n act, power, or manner of speaking; talk given to an audience; language or dialect. **speechless** adj unable to speak because of great emotion.

speed n swiftness; rate at which something moves or acts; *Slang* amphetamine. ▶ v **speeding, sped** or **speeded.** go quickly; drive faster than the legal limit. **speedy** adj prompt; rapid. **speedily** adv

speedboat n light fast motorboat.

speed camera *Brit, Aust & NZ* camera for photographing vehicles breaking the speed limit.

speedometer n instrument to show the speed of a vehicle.

speed up v accelerate. **speedway** n track for motorcycle racing; *US, Canadian & NZ* track for motor racing. **speedwell** n plant with small blue flowers.

speleology n study and exploration of caves.

spell[1] v **spelling, spelt** or **spelled.** give in correct order the letters that form (a word); (of letters) make up (a word); indicate.

spelling n way a word is spelt; person's ability to spell.

spellchecker n *Computing* program that highlights wrongly spelled words in a word-processed document. **spell out** v make explicit.

spell[2] n formula of words supposed to have magic power; effect of a spell; fascination. **spellbound** adj entranced.

spell[3] n period of time of weather or activity; *Scot, Aust & NZ* period of rest.

spelt v a past of SPELL[1].

spend v **spending, spent.** pay out (money); use or pass (time); use up completely. **spendthrift** n person who spends money wastefully.

sperm n, pl **sperms** or **sperm.** male reproductive cell; semen. **spermicide** n substance that kills sperm. **sperm whale** large toothed whale.

spermaceti [sper-ma-set-ee] n waxy solid obtained from the sperm whale.

spermatozoon [sper-ma-toe-zoe-on] n, pl -**zoa.** sperm.

spew v vomit; send out in a stream.

sphagnum n moss found in bogs.

sphere n perfectly round solid object; field of activity. **spherical** adj

sphincter n ring of muscle which controls the opening and closing of a hollow organ.

Sphinx n statue in Egypt with a lion's body and human head; (**s-**) enigmatic person.

spice n aromatic substance used as flavouring; something that adds zest or interest. ▶ v flavour with spices. **spicy** adj flavoured with spices; *Informal* slightly scandalous.

spick-and-span adj neat and clean.

spider n small eight-legged creature which spins a web to catch insects for food. **spidery** adj

spiel n speech made to persuade someone to do something.

spigot n stopper for, or tap fitted to, a cask.

spike n sharp point; sharp pointed metal object. ▶ pl sports shoes with spikes for greater grip. ▶ v put spikes on; pierce or fasten with a spike; add alcohol to (a drink). **spike someone's guns** thwart someone. **spiky** adj

spill[1] v **spilling, spilt** or **spilled.** pour from or as if from a container. ▶ n fall; amount spilt. **spill the beans** *Informal* give away a secret. **spillage** n

spill[2] n thin strip of wood or paper for lighting pipes or fires.

spin v **spinning, spun.** revolve or cause to revolve rapidly; draw out and twist (fibres) into thread;

Informal present information in a way that creates a favourable impression. ▸ *n* revolving motion; continuous spiral descent of an aircraft; *Informal* short drive for pleasure; *Informal* presenting of information in a way that creates a favourable impression. **spin a yarn** tell an improbable story. **spinner** *n* **spin doctor** *Informal* person who provides a favourable slant to a news item or policy on behalf of a politician or a political party. **spin-dry** *v* dry (clothes) in a spin-dryer. **spin-dryer** *n* machine in which washed clothes are spun in a perforated drum to remove excess water. **spin-off** *n* incidental benefit. **spin out** *v* prolong.

spina bifida *n* condition in which part of the spinal cord protrudes through a gap in the backbone, often causing paralysis.

spinach *n* dark green leafy vegetable.

spindle *n* rotating rod that acts as an axle; weighted rod rotated for spinning thread by hand. **spindly** *adj* long, slender, and frail.

spindrift *n* spray blown up from the sea.

spine *n* backbone; edge of a book on which the title is printed; sharp point on an animal or plant. **spinal** *adj* of the spine. **spineless** *adj* lacking courage. **spiny** *adj* covered with spines.

spinet *n* small harpsichord.

spinifex *n* coarse spiny Australian grass.

spinnaker *n* large sail on a racing yacht.

spinney *n Chiefly Brit* small wood.

spinster *n* unmarried woman.

spiral *n* continuous curve formed by a point winding about a central axis at an ever-increasing distance from it; steadily accelerating increase or decrease. ▸ *v* **-ralling, -ralled.** move in a spiral; increase or decrease with steady acceleration. ▸ *adj* having the form of a spiral.

spire *n* pointed part of a steeple.

spirit[1] *n* nonphysical aspect of a person concerned with profound thoughts; nonphysical part of a person believed to live on after death; courage and liveliness; essential meaning as opposed to literal interpretation; ghost. ▸ *pl* emotional state. ▸ *v* **-iting, -ited.** carry away mysteriously. **spirited** *adj* lively.

spirit[2] *n* liquid obtained by distillation. **spirit level** glass tube containing a bubble in liquid, used to check whether a surface is level.

spiritual *adj* relating to the spirit; relating to sacred things. ▸ *n* type of religious folk song originating among Black slaves in America. **spiritually** *adv* **spirituality** *n*

spiritualism *n* belief that the spirits of the dead can communicate with the living. **spiritualist** *n*

spit[1] *v* **spitting, spat.** eject (saliva or food) from the mouth; throw out particles explosively; rain slightly; utter (words) in a violent manner. ▸ *n* saliva. **spitting image** *Informal* person who looks very like another. **spittle** *n* fluid produced in the mouth, saliva. **spittoon** *n* bowl to spit into.

spit[2] *n* sharp rod on which meat is skewered for roasting; long narrow strip of land jutting out into the sea.

spite *n* deliberate nastiness. ▸ *v* annoy or hurt from spite. **in spite of** in defiance of. **spiteful** *adj* **spitefully** *adv*

spitfire *n* person with a fiery

spiv n Brit, Aust & NZ slang smartly dressed man who makes a living by shady dealings.

splash v scatter liquid on (something); scatter (liquid) or (of liquid) be scattered in drops; print (a story or photograph) prominently in a newspaper. ▶ n splashing sound; patch (of colour or light); extravagant display; small amount of liquid added to a drink. **splash out** v Informal spend extravagantly.

splatter v, n splash.

splay v spread out, with ends spreading in different directions.

spleen n abdominal organ which filters bacteria from the blood; bad temper. **splenetic** adj spiteful or irritable.

splendid adj excellent; brilliant in appearance. **splendidly** adv **splendour** n

splice v join by interweaving or overlapping ends. **get spliced** Slang get married.

splint n rigid support for a broken bone.

splinter n thin sharp piece broken off, esp. from wood. ▶ v break into fragments. **splinter group** group that has broken away from an organization.

split v **splitting, split.** break into separate pieces; separate; share. ▶ n crack or division caused by splitting. ▶ pl an act of sitting with the legs outstretched in opposite directions. **split second** very short period of time.

splotch, splodge n, v splash, daub.

splurge v spend money extravagantly. ▶ n bout of extravagance.

splutter v utter with spitting or choking sounds; make hissing spitting sounds. ▶ n spluttering.

spoil v **spoiling, spoilt** or **spoiled.** damage; harm the character of (a child) by giving it all it wants; rot, go bad. **spoils** pl n booty. **spoiling for** eager for. **spoilsport** n person who spoils the enjoyment of others.

spoke[1] v past tense of SPEAK.

spoke[2] n bar joining the hub of a wheel to the rim.

spoken v past participle of SPEAK.

spokesman, spokeswoman, spokesperson n person chosen to speak on behalf of a group.

spoliation n plundering.

sponge n sea animal with a porous absorbent skeleton; skeleton of a sponge, or a substance like it, used for cleaning; type of light cake. ▶ v wipe with a sponge; live at the expense of others. **sponger** n Slang person who sponges on others. **spongy** adj

sponsor n person who promotes something; person who agrees to give money to a charity on completion of a specified activity by another; godparent. ▶ v act as a sponsor for. **sponsorship** n

spontaneous adj not planned or arranged; occurring through natural processes without outside influence. **spontaneously** adv **spontaneity** n

spoof n mildly satirical parody.

spook n Informal ghost. **spooky** adj

spool n cylinder round which something can be wound.

spoon n shallow bowl attached to a handle for eating, stirring, or serving food. ▶ v lift with a spoon. **spoonful** n **spoon-feed** v feed with a spoon; give (someone) too much help.

spoonerism n accidental changing over of the initial sounds of a pair of words, such as half-warmed fish for *half-formed wish*.

spoor *n* trail of an animal.

sporadic *adj* intermittent, scattered. **sporadically** *adv*

spore *n* minute reproductive body of some plants.

sporran *n* pouch worn in front of a kilt.

sport *n* activity for pleasure, competition, or exercise; such activities collectively; enjoyment; playful joking; person who reacts cheerfully. ▶ *v* wear proudly. **sporting** *adj* of sport; behaving in a fair and decent way. **sporting chance** reasonable chance of success. **sporty** *adj* **sportive** *adj* playful. **sports car** fast low-built car, usu. open-topped. **sports jacket** man's casual jacket. **sportsman, sportswoman** *n* person who plays sports; person who plays fair and is good-humoured when losing. **sportsmanlike** *adj* **sportsmanship** *n*

spot *n* small mark on a surface; pimple; location; *Informal* small quantity; *Informal* awkward situation. ▶ *v* **spotting, spotted.** notice; mark with spots; watch for and take note of. **on the spot** at the place in question; immediately; in an awkward predicament. **spotless** *adj* absolutely clean. **spotlessly** *adv* **spotty** *adj* with spots. **spot check** random examination. **spotlight** *n* powerful light illuminating a small area; centre of attention. **spot-on** *adj Informal* absolutely accurate.

spouse *n* husband or wife.

spout *v* pour out in a stream or jet; *Slang* utter (a stream of words) lengthily. ▶ *n* projecting tube or lip for pouring liquids; stream or jet of liquid.

sprain *v* injure (a joint) by a

sudden twist. ▶ *n* such an injury.

sprang *v* a past tense of SPRING.

sprat *n* small sea fish.

sprawl *v* lie or sit with the limbs spread out; spread out in a straggling manner. ▶ *n* part of a city that has spread untidily over a large area.

spray¹ *n* (device for producing) fine drops of liquid. ▶ *v* scatter in fine drops; cover with a spray. **spray gun** device for spraying paint etc.

spray² *n* branch with buds, leaves, flowers, or berries; ornament like this.

spread *v* **spreading, spread.** open out or be displayed to the fullest extent; extend over a larger expanse; apply as a coating; send or be sent in all directions. ▶ *n* spreading; extent; *Informal* large meal; soft food which can be spread. **spread-eagled** *adj* with arms and legs outstretched. **spreadsheet** *n* computer program for manipulating figures.

spree *n* session of overindulgence, usu. in drinking or spending money.

sprig *n* twig or shoot; *NZ* stud on the sole of a soccer or rugby boot.

sprightly *adj* **-lier, -liest.** lively and brisk. **sprightliness** *n*

spring *v* **springing, sprang** or **sprung, sprung.** move suddenly upwards or forwards in a single motion, jump; develop unexpectedly; originate (from); *Informal* arrange the escape of (someone) from prison. ▶ *n* season between winter and summer; jump; coil which can be compressed, stretched, or bent and returns to its original shape when released; natural pool forming the source of a stream; elasticity. **springy** *adj* elastic.

springboard n flexible board used to gain height or momentum in diving or gymnastics.

spring-clean v clean (a house) thoroughly. **spring tide** high tide at new or full moon.

springbok n S African antelope.

springer n small spaniel.

sprinkle v scatter (liquid or powder) in tiny drops or particles over (something). **sprinkler** n **sprinkling** n small quantity or number.

sprint n short race run at top speed; fast run. ▶ v run a short distance at top speed. **sprinter** n

sprite n elf.

sprocket n wheel with teeth on the rim, that drives or is driven by a chain.

sprout v put forth shoots; begin to grow or develop. ▶ n shoot; short for BRUSSELS SPROUT.

spruce[1] n kind of fir.

spruce[2] adj neat and smart. **spruce up** v make neat and smart.

sprung v a past of SPRING.

spry adj spryer, spryest or sprier, spriest. active or nimble.

spud n Informal potato.

spume n, v froth.

spun v past of SPIN.

spunk n Informal courage, spirit. **spunky** adj

spur n stimulus or incentive; spiked wheel on the heel of a rider's boot used to urge on a horse; projection. ▶ v spurring, spurred. urge on, incite (someone). **on the spur of the moment** on impulse.

spurge n plant with milky sap.

spurious adj not genuine.

spurn v reject with scorn.

spurt v gush or cause to gush out in a jet. ▶ n short sudden burst of activity or speed; sudden gush.

sputnik n early Soviet artificial satellite.

sputter v, n splutter.

sputum n, pl **-ta**. spittle, usu. mixed with mucus.

spy n, pl **spies**. person employed to obtain secret information; person who secretly watches others. ▶ v spying, spied. act as a spy; catch sight of.

Sq. Square.

squabble v, n (engage in) a petty or noisy quarrel.

squad n small group of people working or training together.

squadron n division of an air force, fleet, or cavalry regiment.

squalid adj dirty and unpleasant; morally sordid. **squalor** n disgusting dirt and filth.

squall[1] n sudden strong wind.

squall[2] v cry noisily, yell. ▶ n harsh cry.

squander v waste (money or resources).

square n geometric figure with four equal sides and four right angles; open area in a town in this shape; product of a number multiplied by itself. ▶ adj square in shape; denoting a measure of area; straight or level; fair and honest; with all accounts or debts settled. ▶ v multiply (a number) by itself; make square; be or cause to be consistent. ▶ adv squarely, directly. **squarely** adv in a direct way; in an honest and frank manner. **square dance** formation dance in which the couples form squares. **square meal** substantial meal. **square root** number of which a given number is the square. **square up to** v prepare to confront (a person or problem).

squash[1] v crush flat; suppress; push into a confined space; humiliate with a crushing retort. ▶ n sweet fruit drink diluted with water;

crowd of people in a confined space; game played in an enclosed court with a rubber ball and long-handled rackets. **squashy** adj

squash[2] n marrow-like vegetable.

squat v **squatting, squatted.** crouch with the knees bent and the weight on the feet; occupy unused premises to which one has no legal right. ► n place where squatters live. ► adj short and broad.

squatter n illegal occupier of unused premises.

squawk n loud harsh cry. ► v utter a squawk.

squeak n short shrill cry or sound. ► v make or utter a squeak. **squeaky** adj

squeal n long shrill cry or sound. ► v make or utter a squeal; Slang inform on someone to the police.

squeamish adj easily sickened or shocked.

squeegee n tool with a rubber blade for clearing water from a surface.

squeeze v grip or press firmly; crush or press to extract liquid; push into a confined space; hug; obtain (something) by force or great effort. ► n squeezing; amount extracted by squeezing; hug; crush of people in a confined space; restriction on borrowing.

squelch v make a wet sucking sound, as by walking through mud. ► n squelching sound.

squib n small firework that hisses before exploding.

squid n sea creature with a long soft body and ten tentacles.

squiggle n wavy line. **squiggly** adj

squint v have eyes which face in different directions; glance sideways. ► n squinting condition of the eye; Informal glance. ► adj

crooked.

squire n country gentleman, usu. the main landowner in a community; Hist knight's apprentice.

squirm v wriggle, writhe; feel embarrassed. ► n wriggling movement.

squirrel n small bushy-tailed tree-living animal.

squirt v force (a liquid) or (of a liquid) be forced out of a narrow opening; squirt liquid at. ► n jet of liquid; Informal small or insignificant person.

squish v, n (make) a soft squelching sound. **squishy** adj

Sr Senior; Señor.

SS Schutzstaffel: Nazi paramilitary security force; steamship.

St Saint; Street.

st. stone (weight).

stab v **stabbing, stabbed.** pierce with something pointed; jab (at). ► n stabbing; sudden unpleasant sensation; Informal attempt.

stabilize v make or become stable. **stabilization** n **stabilizer** n device for stabilizing a child's bicycle, an aircraft, or a ship.

stable[1] n building in which horses are kept; establishment that breeds and trains racehorses; establishment that manages or trains several entertainers or athletes. ► v put or keep (a horse) in a stable.

stable[2] adj firmly fixed or established; firm in character; Science not subject to decay or decomposition. **stability** n

staccato [stak-ah-toe] adj, adv Music with the notes sharply separated. ► adj consisting of short abrupt sounds.

stack n ordered pile; large amount; chimney. ► v pile in a stack; control (aircraft waiting to land).

so that they fly at different altitudes.

stadium n, pl **-diums, -dia.** sports arena with tiered seats for spectators.

staff¹ n people employed in an organization; stick used as a weapon, support, etc. ▶ v supply with personnel.

staff² n, pl **staves.** set of five horizontal lines on which music is written.

stag n adult male deer. **stag beetle** beetle with large branched jaws. **stag night, party** party for men only.

stage n step or period of development; platform in a theatre where actors perform; portion of a journey. ▶ v put (a play) on stage; organize and carry out (an event). **the stage** theatre as a profession. **stagey** adj overtheatrical. **stagecoach** n large horse-drawn vehicle formerly used to carry passengers and mail. **stage fright** nervousness felt by a person about to face an audience. **stage whisper** loud whisper intended to be heard by an audience.

stagger v walk unsteadily; astound; set apart to avoid congestion. ▶ n staggering.

stagnant adj (of water or air) stale from not moving; not growing or developing. **stagnate** v be stagnant. **stagnation** n

staid adj sedate, serious, and rather dull.

stain v discolour, mark; colour with a penetrating pigment. ▶ n discoloration or mark; moral blemish or slur; penetrating liquid used to colour things. **stainless** adj **stainless steel** steel alloy that does not rust.

stairs pl n flight of steps between

floors, usu. indoors. **staircase, stairway** n flight of stairs with a handrail or banisters.

stake¹ n pointed stick or post driven into the ground as a support or marker. ▶ v support or mark out with stakes. **stake a claim to** claim a right to. **stake out** v Slang (of police) keep (a place) under surveillance.

stake² n money wagered; interest, usu. financial, held in something. ▶ v wager, risk; support financially. **at stake** being risked.

stalactite n lime deposit hanging from the roof of a cave.

stalagmite n lime deposit sticking up from the floor of a cave.

stale adj not fresh; lacking energy or ideas through overwork or monotony; uninteresting from overuse. **staleness** n

stalemate n Chess position in which any of a player's moves would put his king in check, resulting in a draw; deadlock, impasse.

stalk¹ n plant's stem.

stalk² v follow or approach stealthily; pursue persistently and, sometimes, attack (a person with whom one is obsessed); walk in a stiff or haughty manner. **stalker** n person who follows or stealthily approaches a person or an animal; person who persistently pursues and, sometimes, attacks someone with whom he or she is obsessed. **stalking-horse** n pretext.

stall¹ n small stand for the display and sale of goods; compartment in a stable; small room or compartment. ▶ pl ground-floor seats in a theatre or cinema; row of seats in a church for the choir or clergy. ▶ v stop (a motor vehicle or engine) or (of a motor vehicle or engine) stop accidentally.

stall² v employ delaying tactics.

stallion n uncastrated male horse.

stalwart [stawl-wart] adj strong and sturdy; dependable. ▶ n stalwart person.

stamen n pollen-producing part of a flower.

stamina n enduring energy and strength.

stammer v speak or say with involuntary pauses or repetition of syllables. ▶ n tendency to stammer.

stamp n (also **postage stamp**) piece of gummed paper stuck to an envelope or parcel to show that the postage has been paid; act of stamping; instrument for stamping a pattern or mark; pattern or mark stamped; characteristic feature. ▶ v bring (one's foot) down forcefully; walk with heavy footsteps; characterize; impress (a pattern or mark) on; stick a postage stamp on. **stamping ground** favourite meeting place. **stamp out** v suppress by force.

stampede n sudden rush of frightened animals or of a crowd. ▶ v (cause to) take part in a stampede.

stance n attitude; manner of standing.

stanch [stahnch] v same as STAUNCH².

stanchion n upright bar used as a support.

stand v **standing, stood.** be in, rise to, or place in an upright position; be situated; be in a specified state or position; remain unchanged or valid; tolerate; offer oneself as a candidate; Informal treat to. ▶ n stall for the sale of goods; structure for spectators at a sports ground; firmly held opinion; US & Aust witness box;

rack or piece of furniture on which things may be placed. **standing** adj permanent, lasting. ▶ n reputation or status; duration. **stand for** v represent or mean; Informal tolerate. **stand in** v act as a substitute. **stand-in** n substitute. **standoffish** adj reserved or haughty. **stand up for** v support or defend.

standard n level of quality; example against which others are judged or measured; moral principle; distinctive flag; upright pole. ▶ adj usual, regular, or average; of recognized authority; accepted as correct. **standardize** v cause to conform to a standard. **standardization** n **standard lamp** lamp attached to an upright pole on a base.

standpipe n tap attached to a water main to provide a public water supply.

standpoint n point of view.

standstill n complete halt.

stank v a past tense of STINK.

stanza n verse of a poem.

staple¹ n U-shaped piece of metal used to fasten papers or secure things. ▶ v fasten with staples. **stapler** n small device for fastening papers together.

staple² adj of prime importance, principal. ▶ n main constituent of anything.

star n hot gaseous mass in space, visible in the night sky as a point of light; star-shaped mark used to indicate excellence; asterisk; celebrity in the entertainment or sports world. ▶ pl astrological forecast, horoscope. ▶ v **starring, starred.** feature or be featured as a star; mark with a star or stars. ▶ adj leading, famous. **stardom** n status of a star in the entertainment or sports world.

starry adj full of or like stars.
starry-eyed adj full of naive
optimism. **starfish** n star-shaped
sea creature.

starboard n right-hand side of a
ship, when facing forward. ▶ adj
of or on this side.

starch n carbohydrate forming the
main food element in bread,
potatoes, etc., and used mixed
with water for stiffening fabric. ▶ v
stiffen (fabric) with starch.
starchy adj containing starch; stiff
and formal.

stare v look or gaze fixedly (at).
▶ n fixed gaze.

stark adj harsh, unpleasant, and
plain; desolate, bare; absolute.
▶ adv completely.

starling n songbird with glossy
black speckled feathers.

start v take the first step, begin;
set or be set in motion; make a
sudden involuntary movement
from fright; establish or set up. ▶ n
first part of something; place or
time of starting; advantage or lead
in a competitive activity; sudden
movement made from fright.
starter n first course of a meal;
device for starting a car's engine;
person who signals the start of a
race. **start-up** n recently launched
project or business enterprise.
▶ adj recently launched, e.g.
start-up grants.

startle v slightly surprise or
frighten.

starve v die or suffer or cause to
die or suffer from hunger; deprive
of something needed. **starvation**
n

stash Informal ▶ v store in a secret
place. ▶ n secret store.

state n condition of a person or
thing; sovereign political power or
its territory; (**S-**) the government;
Informal excited or agitated

condition; pomp. ▶ adj of or
concerning the State; involving
ceremony. ▶ v express in words.
stately adj dignified or grand.
statehouse n NZ publicly-owned
house rented to a low-income
tenant. **statement** n something
stated; printed financial account.
stateroom n private cabin on a
ship; large room in a palace, used
for ceremonial occasions.
statesman, stateswoman n
experienced and respected
political leader. **statesmanship** n

static adj stationary or inactive; (of
a force) acting but producing no
movement. ▶ n crackling sound or
speckled picture caused by
interference in radio or television
reception; (also **static electricity**)
electric sparks produced by friction.

station n place where trains stop
for passengers; headquarters or
local offices of the police or a fire
brigade; building with special
equipment for a particular
purpose, e.g. power station;
television or radio channel;
position in society; large Australian
sheep or cattle property. ▶ v
assign (someone) to a particular
place. **station wagon** US & Aust
car with a rear door and luggage
space behind the rear seats.

stationary adj not moving.

stationery n writing materials such
as paper and pens. **stationer** n
dealer in stationery.

statistic n numerical fact collected
and classified systematically.
statistics n science of classifying
and interpreting numerical
information. **statistical** adj
statistically adv **statistician** n
person who compiles and studies
statistics.

statue n large sculpture of a
human or animal figure. **statuary**

n statues collectively. **statuesque** *adj* (of a woman) tall and well-proportioned. **statuette** *n* small statue.

stature *n* person's height; reputation of a person or their achievements.

status *n* social position; prestige; person's legal standing. **status quo** existing state of affairs.

statute *n* written law. **statutory** *adj* required or authorized by law.

staunch[1] *adj* loyal, firm.

staunch[2], **stanch** *v* stop (a flow of blood).

stave *n* one of the strips of wood forming a barrel; *Music* same as STAFF[2]. **stave in** *v* **staving, stove.** burst a hole in. **stave off** *v* **staving, staved.** ward off.

stay[1] *v* remain in a place or condition; reside temporarily; endure; *Scot & S Afr* live permanently, e.g. *where do you stay?* ▶ *n* period of staying in a place; postponement. **staying power** stamina.

stay[2] *n* prop or buttress. ▶ *pl* corset.

stay[3] *n* rope or wire supporting a ship's mast.

STD sexually transmitted disease; *Brit, Aust & S Afr* subscriber trunk dialling; *NZ* subscriber toll dialling.

stead *n* **in someone's stead** in someone's place. **stand someone in good stead** be useful to someone.

steadfast *adj* firm, determined. **steadfastly** *adv*

steady *adj* **steadier, steadiest.** not shaky or wavering; regular or continuous; sensible and dependable. ▶ *v* **steadying, steadied.** make steady. ▶ *adv* in a steady manner. **steadily** *adv* **steadiness** *n*

steak *n* thick slice of meat, esp. beef; slice of fish.

steal *v* **stealing, stole, stolen.** take unlawfully or without permission; move stealthily.

stealth *n* secret or underhand behaviour. **stealthy** *adj* **stealthily** *adv*

steam *n* vapour into which water changes when boiled; power, energy, or speed. ▶ *v* give off steam; (of a vehicle) move by steam power; cook or treat with steam. **steamer** *n* steam-propelled ship; container used to cook food in steam. **steam engine** engine worked by steam. **steamroller** *n* steam-powered vehicle with heavy rollers, used to level road surfaces. ▶ *v* use overpowering force to make (someone) do what one wants.

steed *n Lit* horse.

steel *n* hard malleable alloy of iron and carbon; steel rod used for sharpening knives; hardness of character or attitude. ▶ *v* prepare (oneself) for something unpleasant. **steely** *adj*

steep[1] *adj* sloping sharply; *Informal* (of a price) unreasonably high. **steeply** *adv* **steepness** *n*

steep[2] *v* soak or be soaked in liquid. **steeped in** filled with.

steeple *n* church tower with a spire. **steeplejack** *n* person who repairs steeples and chimneys.

steeplechase *n* horse race with obstacles to jump; track race with hurdles and a water jump.

steer[1] *v* direct the course of (a vehicle or ship); direct (one's course). **steerage** *n* cheapest accommodation on a passenger ship. **steering wheel** wheel turned by the driver of a vehicle in order to steer it.

steer[2] *n* castrated male ox.

stein [stine] *n* earthenware beer

mug.

stellar adj of stars.

stem[1] n long thin central part of a plant; long slender part, as of a wineglass; part of a word to which inflections are added. ▶ v **stemming, stemmed. stem from** originate from.

stem[2] v **stemming, stemmed.** stop (the flow of something).

stench n foul smell.

stencil n thin sheet with cut-out pattern through which ink or paint passes to form the pattern on the surface below; pattern made thus. ▶ v **-cilling, -cilled.** make (a pattern) with a stencil.

stenographer n shorthand typist.

stent n surgical implant used to keep an artery open.

stentorian adj (of a voice) very loud.

step v **stepping, stepped.** move and set down the foot, as when walking; walk a short distance. ▶ n stepping; distance covered by a step; sound made by stepping; foot movement in a dance; one of a sequence of actions taken in order to achieve a goal; degree in a series or scale; flat surface for placing the foot on when going up or down. ▶ pl **stepladder. step in** v intervene. **stepladder** n folding portable ladder with supporting frame. **stepping stone** one of a series of stones for stepping on in crossing a stream; means of progress towards a goal. **step up** v increase (something) by stages.

step- prefix denoting a relationship created by the remarriage of a parent, e.g. stepmother.

steppes pl n wide grassy treeless plains in Russia and Ukraine.

stereo adj short for STEREOPHONIC. ▶ n stereophonic record player;

stereophonic sound.

stereophonic adj using two separate loudspeakers to give the effect of naturally distributed sound.

stereotype n standardized idea of a type of person or thing. ▶ v form a stereotype of.

sterile adj free from germs; unable to produce offspring or seeds; lacking inspiration or vitality. **sterility** n **sterilize** v make sterile. **sterilization** n

sterling n British money system. ▶ adj genuine and reliable.

stern[1] adj severe, strict. **sternly** adv **sternness** n

stern[2] n rear part of a ship.

sternum n, pl **-na, -nums.** same as BREASTBONE.

steroid n organic compound containing a carbon ring system, such as many hormones.

stethoscope n medical instrument for listening to sounds made inside the body.

Stetson n ® tall broad-brimmed hat, worn mainly by cowboys.

stevedore n person who loads and unloads ships.

stew n food cooked slowly in a closed pot; Informal troubled or worried state. ▶ v cook slowly in a closed pot.

steward n person who looks after passengers on a ship or aircraft; official who helps at a public event such as a race; person who administers another's property. **stewardess** n fem

stick[1] n long thin piece of wood; such a piece of wood shaped for a special purpose, e.g. hockey stick; something like a stick, e.g. stick of celery; Slang verbal abuse, criticism.

stick[2] v **sticking, stuck.** push (a pointed object) into (something); fasten or be fastened by or as if by pins or glue; (foll. by *out*) extend beyond something else, protrude; *Informal* put; remain for a long time. **sticker** *n* adhesive label or sign. **sticky** *adj* covered with an adhesive substance; *Informal* difficult, unpleasant; (of weather) warm and humid.

stick-in-the-mud *n* person who does not like anything new.

stick-up *n Slang* robbery at gunpoint. **stick up for** *v Informal* support or defend.

stickleback *n* small fish with sharp spines on its back.

stickler *n* person who insists on something, e.g. *stickler for detail*.

stiff *adj* not easily bent or moved; severe, e.g. *stiff punishment*; unrelaxed or awkward; firm in consistency; strong, e.g. *a stiff drink*. ▶ *n Slang* corpse. **stiffly** *adv* **stiffness** *n* **stiffen** *v* make or become stiff. **stiff-necked** *adj* haughtily stubborn.

stifle *v* suppress; suffocate.

stigma *n*, *pl* **-mas**, **-mata**. mark of social disgrace; part of a plant that receives pollen. **stigmata** *pl n* marks resembling the wounds of the crucified Christ. **stigmatize** *v* mark as being shameful.

stile *n* set of steps allowing people to climb a fence.

stiletto *n*, *pl* **-tos**. high narrow heel on a woman's shoe; small slender dagger.

still[1] *adv* now or in the future as before; up to this or that time; even or yet, e.g. *still more insults*; quietly or without movement. ▶ *adj* motionless; silent and calm, undisturbed; (of a drink) not fizzy. ▶ *n* photograph from a film scene. ▶ *v* make still. **stillness** *n* **stillborn** *adj* born dead. **still life** painting of inanimate objects.

still[2] *n* apparatus for distilling

alcoholic drinks.

stilted *adj* stiff and formal in manner.

stilts *pl n* pair of poles with footrests for walking raised from the ground; long posts supporting a building above ground level.

stimulus *n*, *pl* **-li.** something that rouses a person or thing to activity. **stimulant** *n* something, such as a drug, that acts as a stimulus. **stimulate** *v* act as a stimulus (on). **stimulation** *n*

sting *v* **stinging, stung.** (of certain animals or plants) wound by injecting with poison; feel or cause to feel sharp physical or mental pain; *Slang* cheat (someone) by overcharging. ▶ *n* wound or pain caused by or as if by stinging; mental pain; sharp pointed organ of certain animals or plants by which poison can be injected.

stingy *adj* **-gier, -giest.** mean or miserly. **stinginess** *n*

stink *n* strong unpleasant smell; *Slang* unpleasant fuss. ▶ *v* **stinking, stank** or **stunk, stunk.** give off a strong unpleasant smell; *Slang* be very unpleasant.

stint *v* (foll. by *on*) be miserly with (something). ▶ *n* allotted amount of work.

stipend [sty-pend] *n* regular allowance or salary, esp. that paid to a clergyman. **stipendiary** *adj* receiving a stipend.

stipple *v* paint, draw, or engrave using dots.

stipulate *v* specify as a condition of an agreement. **stipulation** *n*

stir *v* **stirring, stirred.** mix up (a liquid) by moving a spoon etc. around in it; move; excite or stimulate (a person) emotionally. ▶ *n* a stirring; strong reaction, usu. of excitement. **stir-fry** *v* **-fries,**

-frying, -fried. cook (food) quickly by stirring it in a pan over a high heat. ▶ *n, pl* **-fries.** dish cooked in this way.

stirrup *n* metal loop attached to a saddle for supporting a rider's foot.

stitch *n* link made by drawing thread through material with a needle; loop of yarn formed round a needle or hook in knitting or crochet; sharp pain in the side. ▶ *v* sew. **in stitches** *Informal* laughing uncontrollably. **not a stitch** *Informal* no clothes at all.

stoat *n* small mammal of the weasel family, with brown fur that turns white in winter.

stock *n* total amount of goods available for sale in a shop; supply stored for future use; financial shares in, or capital of, a company; liquid produced by boiling meat, fish, bones, or vegetables. ▶ *pl Hist* instrument of punishment consisting of a wooden frame with holes into which the hands and feet of the victim were locked. ▶ *adj* kept in stock, standard; hackneyed. ▶ *v* keep for sale or future use; supply (a farm) with livestock or (a lake etc.) with fish. **stockist** *n* dealer who stocks a particular product.

stocky *adj* (of a person) broad and sturdy. **stockbroker** *n* person who buys and sells stocks and shares for customers. **stock car** car modified for a form of racing in which the cars often collide. **stock exchange, market** institution for the buying and selling of shares. **stockpile** *v* store a large quantity of (something) for future use. ▶ *n* accumulated store. **stock-still** *adj* motionless. **stocktaking** *n* counting and valuing of the goods in a shop. **stockade** *n* enclosure or barrier

made of stakes.

stocking *n* close-fitting covering for the foot and leg.

stodgy *adj* **stodgier, stodgiest.** (of food) heavy and starchy; (of a person) serious and boring. **stodge** *n Brit, Aust & NZ* heavy starchy food.

stoep [stoop] *n S Afr* verandah.

stoic [stow-ik] *n* person who suffers hardship without showing his or her feelings. ▶ *adj* (also **stoical**) suffering hardship without showing one's feelings. **stoically** *adv* **stoicism** [stow-iss-izz-um] *n*

stoke *v* feed and tend (a fire or furnace). **stoker** *n*

stole[1] *v* past tense of STEAL.

stole[2] *n* long scarf or shawl.

stolen *v* past participle of STEAL.

stolid *adj* showing little emotion or interest. **stolidly** *adv*

stomach *n* organ in the body which digests food; front of the body around the waist; desire or inclination. ▶ *v* put up with.

stomp *v Informal* tread heavily.

stone *n* material of which rocks are made; piece of this; gem; hard central part of a fruit; unit of weight equal to 14 pounds or 6.350 kilograms; hard deposit formed in the kidney or bladder. ▶ *v* throw stones at; remove stones from (a fruit). **stoned** *adj Slang* under the influence of alcohol or drugs. **stony** *adj* of or like stone; unfeeling or hard. **stony-broke** *adj Slang* completely penniless. **stonily** *adv* **Stone Age** prehistoric period when tools were made of stone. **stone-cold** *adj* completely cold. **stone-deaf** *adj* completely deaf. **stonewall** *v* obstruct or hinder discussion. **stoneware** *n* hard kind of pottery fired at a very high temperature.

stood *v* past of STAND.

stooge n actor who feeds lines to a comedian or acts as the butt of his jokes; *Slang* person taken advantage of by a superior.

stool n chair without arms or back; piece of excrement.

stool pigeon n informer for the police.

stoop v bend (the body) forward and downward; carry oneself habitually in this way; degrade oneself. ▶ n stooping posture.

stop v **stopping, stopped.** cease or cause to cease from doing (something); bring to or come to a halt; prevent or restrain; withhold; block or plug; stay or rest. ▶ n stopping or being stopped; place where something stops; full stop; knob on an organ that is pulled out to allow a set of pipes to sound. **stoppage** n **stoppage time** same as INJURY TIME. **stopper** n plug for a bottle etc. **stopcock** n valve to control or stop the flow of fluid in a pipe. **stopgap** n temporary substitute. **stopover** n short break in a journey. **stop press** news item put into a newspaper after printing has been started. **stopwatch** n watch which can be stopped instantly for exact timing of a sporting event.

store v collect and keep (things) for future use; put (furniture etc.) in a warehouse for safekeeping; stock (goods); *Computers* enter or retain (data). ▶ n shop; supply kept for future use; storage place, such as a warehouse. ▶ pl stock of provisions. **in store** about to happen. **set great store by** value greatly. **storage** n storing; space for storing. **storage heater** electric device that can accumulate and radiate heat generated by off-peak electricity.

storey n floor or level of a building.

stork n large wading bird.

storm n violent weather with wind, rain, or snow; strongly expressed reaction. ▶ v attack or capture (a place) suddenly; shout angrily; rush violently or angrily. **stormy** adj characterized by storms; involving violent emotions.

story n, pl **-ries.** description of a series of events told or written for entertainment; plot of a book or film; news report; *Informal* lie.

stoup [stoop] n small basin for holy water.

stout adj fat; thick and strong; brave and resolute. ▶ n strong dark beer. **stoutly** adv

stove[1] n apparatus for cooking or heating.

stove[2] v a past of STAVE.

stow v pack or store. **stowaway** n person who hides on a ship or aircraft in order to travel free. **stow away** v hide as a stowaway.

straddle v have one leg or part on each side of (something).

strafe v attack (an enemy) with machine guns from the air.

straggle v go or spread in a rambling or irregular way. **straggler** n **straggly** adj

straight adj not curved or crooked; level or upright; honest or frank; (of spirits) undiluted; *Slang* heterosexual. ▶ adv in a straight line; immediately; in a level or upright position. ▶ n straight part, esp. of a racetrack; *Slang* heterosexual person. **go straight** *Informal* reform after being a criminal. **straighten** v **straightaway** adv immediately. **straight face** serious facial expression concealing a desire to laugh. **straightforward** adj honest, frank; (of a task) easy.

strain[1] v cause (something) to be

used or tested beyond its limits; make an intense effort; injure by overexertion; sieve. ▶ *n* tension or tiredness; force exerted by straining; injury from overexertion; great demand on strength or resources; melody or theme. **strained** *adj* not natural, forced; not relaxed, tense. **strainer** *n* sieve.

strain² *n* breed or race; trace or streak.

strait *n* narrow channel connecting two areas of sea. ▶ *pl* position of acute difficulty. **straitjacket** *n* strong jacket with long sleeves used to bind the arms of a violent person. **strait-laced, straight-laced** *adj* prudish or puritanical.

straitened *adj* in **straitened circumstances** not having much money.

strand¹ *v* run aground; leave in difficulties. ▶ *n Poetic* shore.

strand² *n* single thread of string, wire, etc.

strange *adj* odd or unusual; not familiar; inexperienced (in) or unaccustomed (to). **strangely** *adv* **strangeness** *n*

stranger *n* person who is not known or is new to a place or experience.

strangle *v* kill by squeezing the throat; prevent the development of. **strangler** *n* **strangulation** *n* strangling. **stranglehold** *n* strangling grip in wrestling; powerful control.

strap *n* strip of flexible material for lifting, fastening, or holding in place. ▶ *v* **strapping, strapped.** fasten with a strap or straps. **strapping** *adj* tall and sturdy.

strata *n* plural of STRATUM.

stratagem *n* clever plan, trick.

strategy *n, pl* **-gies.** overall plan;

art of planning in war. **strategic** [strat-**ee**-jik] *adj* advantageous; (of weapons) aimed at an enemy's homeland. **strategically** *adv* **strategist** *n*

strathspey *n* Scottish dance with gliding steps.

stratosphere *n* atmospheric layer between about 15 and 50 kilometres above the earth.

stratum [**strah**-tum] *n, pl* **strata.** layer, esp. of rock; social class. **stratified** *adj* divided into strata. **stratification** *n*

straw *n* dried stalks of grain; single stalk of straw; long thin tube used to suck up liquid into the mouth. **straw poll** unofficial poll taken to determine general opinion.

strawberry *n* sweet fleshy red fruit with small seeds on the outside. **strawberry mark** red birthmark.

stray *v* wander; digress; deviate from certain moral standards. ▶ *adj* having strayed; scattered, random. ▶ *n* stray animal.

streak *n* long band of contrasting colour or substance; quality or characteristic; short stretch (of good or bad luck). ▶ *v* mark with streaks; move rapidly; *Informal* run naked in public. **streaker** *n* **streaky** *adj*

stream *n* small river; steady flow, as of liquid, speech, or people; schoolchildren grouped together because of similar ability. ▶ *v* flow steadily; move in unbroken succession; float in the air; group (pupils) in streams. **streamer** *n* strip of coloured paper that unrolls when tossed; long narrow flag.

streamline *v* make more efficient by simplifying; give (a car, plane, etc.) a smooth even shape to offer least resistance to the flow of air or water.

street n public road, usu. lined with buildings. **streetcar** n US tram. **streetwise** adj knowing how to survive in big cities.

strength n quality of being strong; quality or ability considered an advantage; degree of intensity; total number of people in a group. **on the strength of** on the basis of. **strengthen** v

strenuous adj requiring great energy or effort. **strenuously** adv

streptococcus [strep-toe-**kok**-uss] n, pl **-cocci**. bacterium occurring in chains, many species of which cause disease.

stress n tension or strain; emphasis; stronger sound in saying a word or syllable; Physics force producing strain. ▶ v emphasize; put stress on (a word or syllable). **stressed-out** adj Informal suffering from tension.

stretch v extend or be extended; be able to be stretched; extend the limbs or body; strain (resources or abilities) to the utmost. ▶ n stretching; continuous expanse; period; Informal term of imprisonment. **stretchy** adj

stretcher n frame covered with canvas, on which an injured person is carried.

strew v **strewing, strewed, strewed** or **strewn**. scatter (things) over a surface.

striated adj having a pattern of scratches or grooves.

stricken adj seriously affected by disease, grief, pain, etc.

strict adj stern or severe; adhering closely to specified rules; complete, absolute. **strictly** adv **strictness** n

stricture n severe criticism.

stride v **striding, strode, stridden**. walk with long steps. ▶ n long step; regular pace. ▶ pl progress.

strident adj loud and harsh. **stridently** adv **stridency** n

strife n conflict, quarrelling.

strike v **striking, struck**. cease work as a protest; hit; attack suddenly; ignite (a match) by friction; (of a clock) indicate (a time) by sounding a bell; enter the mind of; afflict; discover (gold, oil, etc.); agree (a bargain). ▶ n stoppage of work as a protest. **striking** adj impressive; noteworthy. **strike camp** dismantle and pack up tents. **strike home** have the desired effect. **strike off, out** v cross out. **strike up** v begin (a conversation or friendship); begin to play music.

striker n striking worker; attacking player at soccer.

string n thin cord used for tying; set of objects threaded on a string; series of things or events; stretched wire or cord on a musical instrument that produces sound when vibrated. ▶ pl restrictions or conditions; section of an orchestra consisting of stringed instruments. ▶ v **stringing, strung**. provide with a string or strings; thread on a string. **stringed** adj (of a musical instrument) having strings that are plucked or played with a bow. **stringy** adj like string; (of meat) fibrous. **pull strings** use one's influence. **string along** v deceive over a period of time. **string up** v Informal kill by hanging.

stringent [strin-jent] adj strictly controlled or enforced. **stringently** adv **stringency** n

strip[1] v **stripping, stripped**. take (the covering or clothes) off; take a title or possession away from (someone); dismantle (an engine). **stripper** n person who performs a striptease. **striptease** n entertainment in which a performer undresses to music.

strip² n long narrow piece; *Brit, Aust & NZ* clothes a sports team plays in. **strip cartoon** sequence of drawings telling a story.

stripe n long narrow band of contrasting colour or substance; chevron or band worn on a uniform to indicate rank. **striped, stripy, stripey** adj

stripling n youth.

strive v **striving, strove, striven.** make a great effort.

strobe n short for STROBOSCOPE.

stroboscope n instrument producing a very bright flashing light.

strode v past tense of STRIDE.

stroke v touch or caress lightly with the hand. ▶ n light touch or caress with the hand; rupture of a blood vessel in the brain; blow; action or occurrence of the kind specified, e.g. *a stroke of luck*; chime of a clock; mark made by a pen or paintbrush; style or method of swimming.

stroll v walk in a leisurely manner. ▶ n leisurely walk.

strong adj having physical power; not easily broken; great in degree or intensity; having moral force; having a specified number, e.g. *twenty strong*. **strongly** adv **stronghold** n area of predominance of a particular belief; fortress. **strongroom** n room designed for the safekeeping of valuables.

strontium n *Chem* silvery-white metallic element.

strop n leather strap for sharpening razors.

stroppy adj **-pier, -piest.** *Slang* angry or awkward.

strove v past tense of STRIVE.

struck v past of STRIKE.

structure n complex construction; manner or basis of construction or organization. ▶ v give a structure to. **structural** adj **structuralism** n approach to literature, social sciences, etc., which sees changes in the subject as caused and organized by a hidden set of universal rules. **structuralist** n, adj

strudel n thin sheet of filled dough rolled up and baked, usu. with an apple filling.

struggle v work, strive, or make one's way with difficulty; move about violently in an attempt to get free; fight (with someone). ▶ n striving; fight.

strum v **strumming, strummed.** play (a guitar or banjo) by sweeping the thumb or a plectrum across the strings.

strumpet n *Old-fashioned* prostitute.

strung v past of STRING.

strut v **strutting, strutted.** walk pompously, swagger. ▶ n bar supporting a structure.

strychnine [strik-neen] n very poisonous drug used in small quantities as a stimulant.

stub n short piece left after use; counterfoil of a cheque or ticket. ▶ v **stubbing, stubbed.** strike (the toe) painfully against an object; put out (a cigarette) by pressing the end against a surface. **stubby** adj short and broad.

stubble n short stalks of grain left in a field after reaping; short growth of hair on the chin of a man who has not shaved recently. **stubbly** adj

stubborn adj refusing to agree or give in; difficult to deal with. **stubbornly** adv **stubbornness** n

stucco n plaster used for coating or decorating walls.

stuck v past of STICK². **stuck-up** adj *Informal* conceited or snobbish.

stud[1] n small piece of metal attached to a surface for decoration; disc-like removable fastener for clothes; one of several small round objects fixed to the sole of a football boot to give better grip. ▶ v **studding, studded.** set with studs.

stud[2] n male animal, esp. a stallion, kept for breeding; (also **stud farm**) place where horses are bred; Slang virile or sexually active man.

student n person who studies a subject, esp. at university.

studio n, pl **-dios.** workroom of an artist or photographer; room or building in which television or radio programmes, records, or films are made. **studio flat** Brit one-room flat with a small kitchen and bathroom.

study v **studying, studied.** be engaged in learning (a subject); investigate by observation and research; scrutinize. ▶ n, pl **studies.** act or process of studying; room for studying in; book or paper produced as a result of study; sketch done as practice or preparation; musical composition designed to improve playing technique. **studied** adj carefully practised or planned. **studious** adj fond of study; careful and deliberate. **studiously** adv

stuff n substance or material; collection of unnamed things. ▶ v pack, cram, or fill completely; fill (food) with a seasoned mixture; fill (an animal's skin) with material to restore the shape of the live animal. **stuffing** n seasoned mixture with which food is stuffed; padding.

stuffy adj **stuffier, stuffiest.** lacking fresh air; Informal dull or conventional.

stultifying adj very boring and repetitive.

stumble v trip and nearly fall; walk in an unsure way; make frequent mistakes in speech. ▶ n stumbling. **stumble across** v discover accidentally. **stumbling block** obstacle or difficulty.

stump n base of a tree left when the main trunk has been cut away; part of a thing left after a larger part has been removed; Cricket one of the three upright sticks forming the wicket. ▶ v baffle; Cricket dismiss (a batsman) by breaking his wicket with the ball; walk with heavy steps. **stumpy** adj short and thick. **stump up** v Informal give (the money required).

stun v **stunning, stunned.** shock or overwhelm; knock senseless. **stunning** adj very attractive or impressive.

stung v past of STING.

stunk v a past of STINK.

stunt[1] v prevent or impede the growth of. **stunted** adj

stunt[2] n acrobatic or dangerous action; anything spectacular done to gain publicity.

stupefy v **-fying, -fied.** make insensitive or lethargic; astound. **stupefaction** n

stupendous adj very large or impressive. **stupendously** adv

stupid adj lacking intelligence; silly; in a stupor. **stupidity** n **stupidly** adv

stupor n dazed or unconscious state.

sturdy adj **-dier, -diest.** healthy and robust; strongly built. **sturdily** adv

sturgeon n fish from which caviar is obtained.

stutter v speak with repetition of initial consonants. ▶ n tendency to stutter.

sty n, pl **sties.** pen for pigs.

stye, sty n, pl **styes, sties.** inflammation at the base of an eyelash.

style n shape or design; manner of writing, speaking, or doing something; elegance, refinement; prevailing fashion. ► v shape or design; name or call. **stylish** adj smart, elegant, and fashionable. **stylishly** adv **stylist** n hairdresser; person who writes or performs with great attention to style. **stylistic** adj of literary or artistic style. **stylize** v cause to conform to an established stylistic form.

stylus n needle-like device on a record player that rests in the groove of the record and picks up the sound signals.

stymie v **-mieing, -mied.** hinder or thwart.

styptic n, adj (drug) used to stop bleeding.

suave [swahv] adj smooth and sophisticated in manner. **suavely** adv

sub n subeditor; submarine; subscription; substitute; Brit informal advance payment of wages or salary. ► v **subbing, subbed.** act as a substitute; grant advance payment to.

sub- prefix used with many main words to mean: under or beneath, e.g. submarine; subordinate, e.g. sublieutenant; falling short of, e.g. subnormal; forming a subdivision, e.g. subheading.

subaltern n British army officer below the rank of captain.

subatomic adj of or being one of the particles which make up an atom.

subcommittee n small committee formed from some members of a larger committee.

subconscious adj happening or existing without one's awareness. ► n Psychoanalysis that part of the mind of which one is not aware but which can influence one's behaviour. **subconsciously** adv

subcontinent n large land mass that is a distinct part of a continent.

subcontract n secondary contract by which the main contractor for a job puts work out to others. ► v put out (work) on a subcontract. **subcontractor** n

subcutaneous [sub-cute-**ayn**-ee-uss] adj under the skin.

subdivide v divide (a part of something) into smaller parts. **subdivision** n

subdue v **-duing, -dued.** overcome; make less intense.

subeditor n person who checks and edits text for a newspaper or magazine.

subject n person or thing being dealt with or studied; Grammar word or phrase that represents the person or thing performing the action of the verb in a sentence; person under the rule of a monarch or government. ► adj being under the rule of a monarch or government. ► v (foll. by to) cause to undergo. **subject to** liable to; conditional upon. **subjection** n **subjective** adj based on personal feelings or prejudices. **subjectively** adv

sub judice [sub joo-**diss**-ee] adj Latin before a court of law and therefore prohibited from public discussion.

subjugate v bring (a group of people) under one's control. **subjugation** n

subjunctive Grammar ► n mood of verbs used when the content of the clause is doubted, supposed, or wished. ▸ *adj* in or of that mood.

sublet *v* **-letting, -let.** rent out (property rented from someone else).

sublimate *v Psychol* direct the energy of (a strong desire, esp. a sexual one) into socially acceptable activities. **sublimation** *n*

sublime *adj* of high moral, intellectual, or spiritual value; unparalleled, supreme. ▸ *v Chem* change from a solid to a vapour without first melting. **sublimely** *adv*

subliminal *adj* relating to mental processes of which the individual is not aware.

sub-machine-gun *n* portable machine gun with a short barrel.

submarine *n* vessel which can operate below the surface of the sea. ▸ *adj* below the surface of the sea.

submerge *v* put or go below the surface of water or other liquid. **submersion** *n*

submit *v* **-mitting, -mitted.** surrender; put forward for consideration; be (voluntarily) subjected to a process or treatment. **submission** *n* submitting; something submitted for consideration; state of being submissive. **submissive** *adj* meek and obedient.

subordinate *adj* of lesser rank or importance. ▸ *n* subordinate person or thing. ▸ *v* make or treat as subordinate. **subordination** *n*

suborn *v Formal* bribe or incite (a person) to commit a wrongful act.

subpoena [sub-pee-na] *n* writ requiring a person to appear before a lawcourt. ▸ *v* summon (someone) with a subpoena.

subscribe *v* pay (a subscription); give support or approval (to). **subscriber** *n* **subscription** *n* payment for issues of a publication over a period; money contributed to a charity etc.; membership fees paid to a society.

subsection *n* division of a section.

subsequent *adj* occurring after, succeeding. **subsequently** *adv*

subservient *adj* submissive, servile. **subservience** *n*

subside *v* become less intense; sink to a lower level. **subsidence** *n* act or process of subsiding.

subsidiary *adj* of lesser importance. ▸ *n, pl* **-aries.** subsidiary person or thing.

subsidize *v* help financially. **subsidy** *n, pl* **-dies.** financial aid.

subsist *v* manage to live. **subsistence** *n*

subsonic *adj* moving at a speed less than that of sound.

substance *n* physical composition of something; solid, powder, liquid, or paste; essential meaning of something; solid or meaningful quality; wealth. **substantial** *adj* of considerable size or value; (of food or a meal) sufficient and nourishing; solid or strong; real. **substantially** *adv* **substantiate** *v* support (a story) with evidence. **substantiation** *n* **substantive** *n* noun. ▸ *adj* of or being the essential element of a thing.

substitute *v* take the place of or put in place of another. ▸ *n* person or thing taking the place of (another). **substitution** *n*

subsume *v* include (an idea, case, etc.) under a larger classification or group.

subterfuge *n* trick used to achieve an objective.

subterranean *adj* underground.

subtitle *n* secondary title of a

book. ▶ *pl* printed translation at the bottom of the picture in a film with foreign dialogue. ▶ *v* provide with a subtitle or subtitles.

subtle *adj* not immediately obvious; having or requiring ingenuity. **subtly** *adv* **subtlety** *n*

subtract *v* take (one number or quantity) from another. **subtraction** *n*

subtropical *adj* of the regions bordering on the tropics.

suburb *n* residential area on the outskirts of a city. **suburban** *adj* of or inhabiting a suburb; narrow or unadventurous in outlook. **suburbia** *n* suburbs and their inhabitants.

subvention *n Formal* subsidy.

subvert *v* overthrow the authority of. **subversion** *n* **subversive** *adj*, *n*

subway *n* passage under a road or railway; underground railway.

succeed *v* accomplish an aim; turn out satisfactorily; come next in order after (something); take over a position from (someone). **success** *n* achievement of something attempted; attainment of wealth, fame, or position; successful person or thing. **successful** *adj* having success. **successfully** *adv* **succession** *n* series of people or things following one another in order; act or right by which one person succeeds another in a position. **successive** *adj* consecutive. **successively** *adv* **successor** *n* person who succeeds someone in a position.

succinct *adj* brief and clear. **succinctly** *adv*

succour *v, n* help in distress.

succulent *adj* juicy and delicious; (of a plant) having thick fleshy leaves. ▶ *n* succulent plant.

succulence *n*

succumb *v* (foll. by *to*) give way (to something overpowering); die (of an illness).

such *adj* of the kind specified; so great, so much. ▶ *pron* such things. **such-and-such** *adj* specific, but not known or named. **suchlike** *pron* such or similar things.

suck *v* draw (liquid or air) into the mouth; take (something) into the mouth and moisten, dissolve, or roll it around with the tongue; (foll. by *in*) draw in by irresistible force. ▶ *n* sucking. **sucker** *n Slang* person who is easily deceived or swindled; organ or device which adheres by suction; shoot coming from a plant's root or the base of its main stem. **suck up to** *v Informal* flatter (someone) for one's own profit.

suckle *v* feed at the breast. **suckling** *n* unweaned baby or young animal.

sucrose [soo-kroze] *n* chemical name for sugar.

suction *n* sucking; force produced by drawing air out of a space to make a vacuum that will suck in a substance from another space.

sudden *adj* done or occurring quickly and unexpectedly. **all of a sudden** quickly and unexpectedly. **suddenly** *adv* **suddenness** *n* **sudden death** *Sport* period of extra time in which the first competitor to score wins.

sudorific [syoo-dor-**if**-ik] *n, adj* (drug) causing sweating.

suds *pl n* froth of soap and water, lather.

sue *v* suing, sued. start legal proceedings against.

suede *n* leather with a velvety finish on one side.

suet *n* hard fat obtained from

sheep and cattle, used in cooking.

suffer v undergo or be subjected to; tolerate. **sufferer** n **suffering** n **sufferance** n **on sufferance** tolerated with reluctance.

suffice [suf-**fice**] v be enough for a purpose. **sufficient** adj enough, adequate. **sufficiency** n adequate amount. **sufficiently** adv

suffix n letter or letters added to the end of a word to form another word, such as -s and -ness in dogs and softness.

suffocate v kill or be killed by deprivation of oxygen; feel uncomfortable from heat and lack of air. **suffocation** n

suffragan n bishop appointed to assist an archbishop.

suffrage n right to vote in public elections. **suffragette** n (in Britain in the early 20th century) a woman who campaigned militantly for the right to vote.

suffuse v spread through or over (something). **suffusion** n

sugar n sweet crystalline carbohydrate found in many plants and used to sweeten food and drinks. ▶ v sweeten or cover with sugar. **sugary** adj **sugar beet** beet grown for the sugar obtained from its roots. **sugar cane** tropical grass grown for the sugar obtained from its canes. **sugar daddy** Slang elderly man who gives a young woman money and gifts in return for sexual favours.

suggest v put forward (an idea) for consideration; bring to mind by the association of ideas; give a hint of. **suggestible** adj easily influenced. **suggestion** n thing suggested; hint or indication. **suggestive** adj suggesting something indecent; conveying a

hint (of). **suggestively** adv

suicide n killing oneself intentionally; person who kills himself intentionally; self-inflicted ruin of one's own prospects or interests. **suicidal** adj liable to commit suicide. **suicidally** adv

suit n set of clothes designed to be worn together; outfit worn for a specific purpose; one of the four sets into which a pack of cards is divided; lawsuit. ▶ v be appropriate for; be acceptable to. **suitable** adj appropriate or proper. **suitably** adv **suitability** n

suitcase n portable travelling case for clothing.

suite n set of connected rooms in a hotel; matching set of furniture; set of musical pieces in the same key.

suitor n Old-fashioned man who is courting a woman.

sulk v be silent and sullen because of resentment or bad temper. ▶ n resentful or sullen mood. **sulky** adj **sulkily** adv

sullen adj unwilling to talk or be sociable. **sullenly** adv **sullenness** n

sully v -lying, -lied. ruin (someone's reputation); make dirty.

sulphate n salt or ester of sulphuric acid.

sulphide n compound of sulphur with another element.

sulphite n salt or ester of sulphurous acid.

sulphonamide [sulf-**on**-a-mide] n any of a class of drugs that prevent the growth of bacteria.

sulphur n Chem pale yellow nonmetallic element. **sulphuric, sulphurous** adj of or containing sulphur.

sultan n sovereign of a Muslim country. **sultana** n kind of raisin; sultan's wife, mother, or daughter.

sultanate n territory of a sultan.

sultry adj **-trier, -triest.** (of weather or climate) hot and humid; passionate, sensual.

sum n result of addition, total; problem in arithmetic; quantity of money. **sum total** complete or final total. **sum up** v **summing, summed.** summarize; form a quick opinion of.

summary n, pl **-ries.** brief account giving the main points of something. ▶ adj done quickly, without formalities. **summarily** adv **summarize** v make or be a summary of (something). **summation** n summary; adding up.

summer n warmest season of the year, between spring and autumn. **summery** adj **summerhouse** n small building in a garden. **summertime** n period or season of summer.

summit n top of a mountain or hill; highest point; conference between heads of state or other high officials.

summon v order (someone) to come; call upon (someone) to do something; gather (one's courage, strength, etc.). **summons** n command summoning someone; order requiring someone to appear in court. ▶ v order (someone) to appear in court.

sumo n Japanese style of wrestling.

sump n container in an internal-combustion engine into which oil can drain; hollow into which liquid drains.

sumptuous adj lavish, magnificent. **sumptuously** adv

sun n star around which the earth and other planets revolve; any star around which planets revolve; heat and light from the sun. ▶ v **sunning, sunned.** expose (oneself) to the sun's rays. **sunless** adj

sunny adj full of or exposed to sunlight; cheerful. **sunbathe** v lie in the sunshine in order to get a suntan. **sunbeam** n ray of sun. **sunburn** n painful reddening of the skin caused by overexposure to the sun. **sunburnt, sunburned** adj **sundial** n device showing the time by means of a pointer that casts a shadow on a marked dial. **sundown** n sunset. **sunflower** n tall plant with large golden flowers. **sunrise** n daily appearance of the sun above the horizon; time of this. **sunset** n daily disappearance of the sun below the horizon; time of this. **sunshine** n light and warmth from the sun. **sunspot** n dark patch appearing temporarily on the sun's surface; Aust small area of skin damage caused by exposure to the sun. **sunstroke** n illness caused by prolonged exposure to intensely hot sunlight. **suntan** n browning of the skin caused by exposure to the sun.

sundae n ice cream topped with fruit etc.

Sunday n first day of the week and the Christian day of worship. **Sunday school** school for teaching children about Christianity.

sundry adj several, various. **sundries** pl n several things of various sorts. **all and sundry** everybody.

sung v past participle of SING.

sunk v a past participle of SINK.

sunken v a past participle of SINK.

sup v **supping, supped.** take (liquid) by sips. ▶ n sip.

super adj Informal excellent.

super- prefix used with many main words to mean: above or over, e.g. superimpose; outstanding, e.g. superstar; of greater size or extent, e.g. supermarket.

superannuation n regular payment by an employee into a pension fund; pension paid from this. **superannuated** adj discharged with a pension, owing to old age or illness.

superb adj excellent, impressive, or splendid. **superbly** adv

superbug n Informal bacterium resistant to antibiotics.

supercharged adj (of an engine) having a supercharger. **supercharger** n device that increases the power of an internal-combustion engine by forcing extra air into it.

supercilious adj showing arrogant pride or scorn.

superconductor n substance which has almost no electrical resistance at very low temperatures. **superconductivity** n

superficial adj not careful or thorough; (of a person) without depth of character, shallow; or of on the surface. **superficially** adv **superficiality** n

superfluous [soo-per-flew-uss] adj more than is needed. **superfluity** n

superhuman adj beyond normal human ability or experience.

superimpose v place (something) on or over something else.

superintendent n senior police officer; supervisor. **superintend** v supervise (a person or activity).

superior adj greater in quality, quantity, or merit; higher in position or rank; believing oneself to be better than others. ▶ n person of greater rank or status. **superiority** n

superlative [soo-per-lat-iv] adj of outstanding quality; Grammar denoting the form of an adjective or adverb indicating most. ▶ n Grammar superlative form of a word.

superman n man with great physical or mental powers.

supermarket n large self-service store selling food and household goods.

supermodel n famous and highly-paid fashion model.

supernatural adj of or relating to things beyond the laws of nature. **the supernatural** supernatural forces, occurrences, and beings collectively.

supernova n, pl -vae, -vas. star that explodes and briefly becomes exceptionally bright.

supernumerary adj exceeding the required or regular number. ▶ n, pl -ries. supernumerary person or thing.

superpower n extremely powerful nation.

superscript n, adj (character) printed above the line.

supersede v replace, supplant.

supersonic adj of or travelling at a speed greater than the speed of sound.

superstition n belief in omens, ghosts, etc.; idea or practice based on this. **superstitious** adj

superstore n large supermarket.

superstructure n structure erected on something else; part of a ship above the main deck.

supervene v occur as an unexpected development.

supervise v watch over to direct or check. **supervision** n **supervisor** n **supervisory** adj

supine adj lying flat on one's back.

supper n light evening meal.

supplant v take the place of, oust.

supple adj (of a person) moving and bending easily and gracefully; bending easily without damage. **suppleness** n

supplement n thing added to

complete something or make up for a lack; magazine inserted into a newspaper; section added to a publication to supply further information. ▸ v provide or be a supplement to (something). **supplementary** adj

supplication n humble request.

supplicant n person who makes a humble request.

supply v **-plying, -plied.** provide with something required. ▸ n, pl **-plies.** supplying; amount available; Economics willingness and ability to provide goods and services. ▸ pl food or equipment. **supplier** n

support v bear the weight of; provide the necessities of life for; give practical or emotional help to; take an active interest in (a sports team, political principle, etc.); help to prove (a theory etc.); speak in favour of. ▸ n supporting; means of support. **supporter** n person who supports a team, principle, etc. **supportive** adj

suppose v presume to be true; consider as a proposal for the sake of discussion. **supposed** adj presumed to be true without proof, doubtful. **supposed to** expected or required to, e.g. you were supposed to phone me; permitted to, e.g. we're not supposed to swim here. **supposedly** adv **supposition** n supposing; something supposed.

suppository n, pl **-ries.** solid medication inserted into the rectum or vagina and left to melt.

suppress v put an end to; prevent publication of (information); restrain (an emotion or response). **suppression** n

suppurate v (of a wound etc.) produce pus.

supreme adj highest in authority, rank, or degree. **supremely** adv extremely. **supremacy** n supreme power; state of being supreme. **supremo** n Informal person in overall authority.

surcharge n additional charge.

surd n Maths number that cannot be expressed in whole numbers.

sure adj free from uncertainty or doubt; reliable; inevitable. ▸ adv, interj Informal certainly. **surely** adv it must be true that. **sure-footed** adj unlikely to slip or stumble.

surety n, pl **-ties.** person who takes responsibility, or thing given as a guarantee, for the fulfilment of another's obligation.

surf n foam caused by waves breaking on the shore. ▸ v take part in surfing; move quickly through a medium such as the Internet. **surfing** n sport of riding towards the shore on a surfboard on the crest of a wave. **surfer** n **surfboard** n long smooth board used in surfing.

surface n outside or top of an object; material covering the surface of an object; superficial appearance. ▸ v rise to the surface; put a surface on.

surfeit n excessive amount.

surge n sudden powerful increase; strong rolling movement, esp. of the sea. ▸ v increase suddenly; move forward strongly.

surgeon n doctor who specializes in surgery. **surgery** n treatment in which the patient's body is cut open in order to treat the affected part; (pl **-geries**) place where, or time when, a doctor, dentist, etc. can be consulted; Brit occasion when an elected politician can be consulted. **surgical** adj **surgically** adv

surly adj **-lier, -liest.** ill-tempered

and rude. **surliness** n

surmise v, n guess, conjecture.

surmount v overcome (a problem); be on top of (something). **surmountable** adj

surname n family name.

surpass v be greater than or superior to.

surplice n loose white robe worn by clergymen and choristers.

surplus n amount left over in excess of what is required.

surprise n unexpected event; amazement and wonder. ▶ v cause to feel amazement or wonder; come upon, attack, or catch suddenly and unexpectedly.

surrealism n movement in art and literature involving the combination of incongruous images, as in a dream. **surreal** adj bizarre. **surrealist** n, adj **surrealistic** adj

surrender v give oneself up; give (something) up to another; yield (to a temptation or influence). ▶ n surrendering.

surreptitious adj done secretly or stealthily. **surreptitiously** adv

surrogate n substitute. **surrogate mother** woman who gives birth to a child on behalf of a couple who cannot have children.

surround v be, come, or place all around (a person or thing). ▶ n border or edging. **surroundings** pl n area or environment around a person, place, or thing.

surveillance n close observation.

survey v view or consider in a general way; make a map of (an area); inspect (a building) to assess its condition and value; find out the incomes, opinions, etc. of (a group of people). ▶ n surveying; report produced by a survey. **surveyor** n

survive v continue to live or exist

after (a difficult experience); live after the death of (another). **survival** n condition of having survived. **survivor** n

susceptible adj liable to be influenced or affected by. **susceptibility** n

sushi [soo-shee] n Japanese dish of small cakes of cold rice with a topping of raw fish.

suspect v believe (someone) to be guilty without having any proof; think (something) to be false or questionable; believe (something) to be the case. ▶ adj not to be trusted. ▶ n person who is suspected.

suspend v hang from a high place; cause to remain floating or hanging; cause to cease temporarily; remove (someone) temporarily from a job or team. **suspenders** pl n straps for holding up stockings; US braces.

suspense n state of uncertainty while awaiting news, an event, etc.

suspension n suspending or being suspended; system of springs and shock absorbers supporting the body of a vehicle; mixture of fine particles of a solid in a fluid. **suspension bridge** bridge hanging from cables attached to towers at each end.

suspicion n feeling of not trusting a person or thing; belief that something is true without definite proof; slight trace. **suspicious** adj feeling or causing suspicion. **suspiciously** adv

suss out v Slang work out using one's intuition.

sustain v maintain or prolong; keep up the vitality or strength of; suffer (an injury or loss); support. **sustenance** n food.

suture [soo-cher] n stitch joining the edges of a wound.

suzerain n state or sovereign with limited authority over another self-governing state. **suzerainty** n

svelte adj attractively or gracefully slim.

SW southwest(ern).

swab n small piece of cotton wool used to apply medication, clean a wound, etc. ▶ v **swabbing, swabbed.** clean (a wound) with a swab; clean (the deck of a ship) with a mop.

swaddle v wrap (a baby) in swaddling clothes. **swaddling clothes** long strips of cloth formerly wrapped round a newborn baby.

swag n Slang stolen property. **swagman** n Aust hist tramp who carries his belongings in a bundle on his back.

swagger v walk or behave arrogantly. ▶ n arrogant walk or manner.

swain n Poetic suitor; country youth.

swallow[1] v cause to pass down one's throat; make a gulping movement in the throat, as when nervous; Informal believe (something) gullibly; refrain from showing (a feeling); engulf or absorb. ▶ n swallowing; amount swallowed.

swallow[2] n small migratory bird with long pointed wings and a forked tail.

swam v past tense of SWIM.

swamp n watery area of land, bog. ▶ v cause (a boat) to fill with water and sink; overwhelm. **swampy** adj

swan n large usu. white water bird with a long graceful neck. ▶ v **swanning, swanned.** Informal wander about idly. **swan song** person's last performance before retirement or death.

swank Slang ▶ v show off or boast.

▶ n showing off or boasting. **swanky** adj Slang expensive and showy, stylish.

swanndri [swan-dry] n ® NZ weatherproof woollen shirt or jacket (also **swannie**).

swap v **swapping, swapped.** exchange (something) for something else. ▶ n exchange.

sward n stretch of short grass.

swarm[1] n large group of bees or other insects; large crowd. ▶ v move in a swarm; (of a place) be crowded or overrun.

swarm[2] v (foll. by up) climb (a ladder or rope) by gripping with the hands and feet.

swarthy adj **-thier, -thiest.** dark-complexioned.

swashbuckling adj having the exciting behaviour of pirates, esp. those depicted in films. **swashbuckler** n

swastika n symbol in the shape of a cross with the arms bent at right angles, used as the emblem of Nazi Germany.

swat v **swatting, swatted.** hit sharply. ▶ n sharp blow.

swatch n sample of cloth.

swath [swawth] n see SWATHE.

swathe v wrap in bandages or layers of cloth. ▶ n long strip of cloth wrapped around something; (also **swath**) the width of one sweep of a scythe or mower.

sway v swing to and fro or from side to side; waver or cause to waver in opinion. ▶ n power or influence; swaying motion.

swear v **swearing, swore, sworn.** use obscene or blasphemous language; state or promise on oath; state earnestly. **swear by** v have complete confidence in. **swear in** v cause to take an oath. **swearword** n word considered obscene or blasphemous.

sweat n salty liquid given off through the pores of the skin; Slang drudgery or hard labour. ▶ v have sweat coming through the pores; be anxious. **sweaty** adj **sweatband** n strip of cloth tied around the forehead or wrist to absorb sweat. **sweatshirt** n long-sleeved cotton jersey. **sweatshop** n place where employees work long hours in poor conditions for low pay.

sweater n (woollen) garment for the upper part of the body.

swede n kind of turnip.

sweep v **sweeping, swept.** remove dirt from (a floor) with a broom; move smoothly and quickly; spread rapidly; move majestically; carry away suddenly or forcefully; stretch in a long wide curve. ▶ n sweeping; sweeping motion; wide expanse; sweepstake; chimney sweep. **sweeping** adj wide-ranging; indiscriminate. **sweepstake** n lottery in which the stakes of the participants make up the prize.

sweet adj tasting of or like sugar; kind and charming; agreeable to the senses or mind; (of wine) with a high sugar content. ▶ n shaped piece of food consisting mainly of sugar; dessert. **sweetly** adv **sweetness** n **sweeten** v **sweetener** n sweetening agent that does not contain sugar; Brit, Aust & NZ slang bribe. **sweetbread** n animal's pancreas used as food. **sweet corn** type of maize with sweet yellow kernels, eaten as a vegetable. **sweetheart** n lover. **sweetmeat** n Old-fashioned sweet delicacy such as a small cake. **sweet pea** climbing plant with bright fragrant flowers. **sweet potato** tropical root vegetable with yellow flesh. **sweet-talk** v Informal coax or flatter. **sweet tooth** strong liking for sweet foods.

swell v **swelling, swelled, swollen** or **swelled.** expand or increase; (of a sound) become gradually louder. ▶ n swelling or being swollen; movement of waves in the sea; Old-fashioned slang fashionable person. ▶ adj US slang excellent or fine. **swelling** n enlargement of part of the body, caused by injury or infection.

swelter v feel uncomfortably hot.

sweltering adj uncomfortably hot.

swept v past of SWEEP.

swerve v turn aside from a course sharply or suddenly. ▶ n swerving.

swift adj moving or able to move quickly. ▶ n fast-flying bird with pointed wings. **swiftly** adv **swiftness** n

swig n large mouthful of drink. ▶ v **swigging, swigged.** drink in large mouthfuls.

swill v drink greedily; rinse (something) in large amounts of water. ▶ n sloppy mixture containing waste food, fed to pigs; deep drink.

swim v **swimming, swam, swum.** move along in water by movements of the limbs; be covered or flooded with liquid; reel, e.g. her head was swimming. ▶ n act or period of swimming. **swimmer** n **swimmingly** adv successfully and effortlessly. **swimming pool** (building containing) an artificial pond for swimming in.

swindle v cheat (someone) out of money. ▶ n instance of swindling. **swindler** n

swine n contemptible person; pig.

swing v **swinging, swung.** move to and fro, sway; move in a curve; (of an opinion or mood) change sharply; hit out with a sweeping motion; *Slang* be hanged. ▶ *n* swinging; suspended seat on which a child can swing to and fro; sudden or extreme change.

swingeing [**swin**-jing] *adj* punishing, severe.

swipe *v* strike (at) with a sweeping blow; *Slang* steal; pass (a credit card or debit card) through a machine that electronically reads information stored in the card. ▶ *n* hard blow. **swipe card** credit card or debit card that is passed through a machine that electronically reads information stored in the card.

swirl *v* turn with a whirling motion. ▶ *n* whirling motion; twisting shape.

swish *v* move with a whistling or hissing sound. ▶ *n* whistling or hissing sound. ▶ *adj Informal* fashionable, smart.

Swiss *adj* of Switzerland or its people. ▶ *n, pl* **Swiss.** person from Switzerland. **swiss roll** sponge cake spread with jam or cream and rolled up.

switch *n* device for opening and closing an electric circuit; abrupt change; exchange or swap; flexible rod or twig. ▶ *v* change abruptly; exchange or swap. **switchback** *n* road or railway with many sharp hills or bends. **switchboard** *n* installation in a telephone exchange or office where telephone calls are connected. **switch on, off** *v* turn (a device) on or off by means of a switch.

swivel *v* **-elling, -elled.** turn on a central point. ▶ *n* coupling device that allows an attached object to turn freely.

swizzle stick *n* small stick used to stir cocktails.

swollen *v* a past participle of SWELL.

swoon *v, n* faint.

swoop *v* sweep down or pounce on suddenly. ▶ *n* swooping.

swop *v* **swopping, swopped,** *n* same as SWAP.

sword *n* weapon with a long sharp blade. **swordfish** *n* large fish with a very long upper jaw. **swordsman** *n* person skilled in the use of a sword.

swore *v* past tense of SWEAR.

sworn *v* past participle of SWEAR. ▶ *adj* bound by or as if by an oath, e.g. *sworn enemies.*

swot *Informal* ▶ *v* **swotting, swotted.** study hard. ▶ *n* person who studies hard.

swum *v* past participle of SWIM.

swung *v* past of SWING.

sybarite [**sib**-bar-ite] *n* lover of luxury. **sybaritic** *adj*

sycamore *n* tree with five-pointed leaves and two-winged fruits.

sycophant *n* person who uses flattery to win favour from people with power or influence. **sycophantic** *adj* **sycophancy** *n*

syllable *n* part of a word pronounced as a unit. **syllabic** *adj*

syllabub *n* dessert of beaten cream, sugar, and wine.

syllabus *n, pl* **-buses, -bi.** list of subjects for a course of study.

syllogism *n* form of logical reasoning consisting of two premises and a conclusion.

sylph *n* slender graceful girl or woman; imaginary being supposed to inhabit the air. **sylphlike** *adj*

sylvan *adj Lit* relating to woods and trees.

symbiosis *n* close association of two species living together to their mutual benefit. **symbiotic** *adj*

symbol *n* sign or thing that stands for something else. **symbolic** *adj*

symbolically adv **symbolism** n representation of something by symbols; movement in art and literature using symbols to express abstract and mystical ideas. **symbolist** n, adj **symbolize** v be a symbol of; represent with a symbol.

symmetry n state of having two halves that are mirror images of each other. **symmetrical** adj **symmetrically** adv

sympathy n, pl **-thies.** compassion for someone's pain or distress; agreement with someone's feelings or interests. **sympathetic** adj feeling or showing sympathy; likeable or appealing. **sympathetically** adv **sympathize** v feel or express sympathy. **sympathizer** n

symphony n, pl **-nies.** composition for orchestra, with several movements. **symphonic** adj

symposium n, pl **-siums, -sia.** conference for discussion of a particular topic.

symptom n sign indicating the presence of an illness; sign that something is wrong. **symptomatic** adj

synagogue n Jewish place of worship and religious instruction.

sync, synch Informal ▶ v synchronization. ▶ v synchronize.

synchromesh adj (of a gearbox) having a device that synchronizes the speeds of gears before they engage.

synchronize v (of two or more people) perform (an action) at the same time; set (watches) to show the same time; match (the soundtrack and action of a film) precisely. **synchronization** n **synchronous** adj happening or existing at the same time.

syncopate v Music stress the weak beats in (a rhythm) instead of the strong ones. **syncopation** n

syncope [sing-kop-ee] n Med a faint.

syndicate n group of people or firms undertaking a joint business project; agency that sells material to several newspapers; association of individuals who control organized crime. ▶ v publish (material) in several newspapers; form a syndicate. **syndication** n

syndrome n combination of symptoms indicating a particular disease; set of characteristics indicating a particular problem.

synergy n potential ability for people or groups to be more successful working together than on their own.

synod n church council.

synonym n word with the same meaning as another. **synonymous** adj

synopsis n, pl **-ses.** summary or outline.

syntax n Grammar way in which words are arranged to form phrases and sentences. **syntactic** adj

synthesis n, pl **-ses.** combination of objects or ideas into a whole; artificial production of a substance. **synthesize** v produce by synthesis. **synthesizer** n electronic musical instrument producing a range of sounds. **synthetic** adj (of a substance) made artificially; not genuine, insincere. **synthetically** adv

syphilis n serious sexually transmitted disease. **syphilitic** adj

syphon n, v same as SIPHON.

syringe n device for withdrawing or injecting fluids, consisting of a hollow cylinder, a piston, and a hollow needle. ▶ v wash out or inject with a syringe.

syrup n solution of sugar in water; thick sweet liquid. **syrupy** adj

system n method or set of methods; scheme of classification or arrangement; network or assembly of parts that form a whole. **systematic** adj **systematically** adv **systematize** v organize using a system. **systematization** n **systemic** adj affecting the entire animal or body.

systole [**siss-tol-ee**] n regular contraction of the heart as it pumps blood. **systolic** adj

T t

t tonne.

T n **to a T** in every detail; perfectly.

t. ton.

ta interj Informal thank you.

TA (in Britain) Territorial Army.

tab n small flap or projecting label. **keep tabs on** Informal watch closely.

TAB (in New Zealand) Totalisator Agency Board.

tabard n short sleeveless tunic decorated with a coat of arms, worn in medieval times.

Tabasco n ® very hot red pepper sauce.

tabby n, pl -**bies**, adj (cat) with dark stripes on a lighter background.

tabernacle n portable shrine of the Israelites; Christian place of worship not called a church; RC Church receptacle for the consecrated Host.

tabla n, pl -**bla**, -**bias**. one of a pair of Indian drums played with the hands.

table n piece of furniture with a flat top supported by legs; arrangement of information in columns. ▸ v submit (a motion) for discussion by a meeting; US suspend discussion of (a proposal).

tableland n high plateau.

tablespoon n large spoon for serving food. **table tennis** game like tennis played on a table with small bats and a light ball.

tableau [**tab-loh**] n, pl -**leaux**. silent motionless group arranged to represent some scene.

table d'hôte [**tah-bla dote**] n, pl **tables d'hôte**, adj (meal) having a set number of dishes at a fixed price.

tablet n pill of compressed medicinal substance; inscribed slab of stone etc.

tabloid n small-sized newspaper with many photographs and a concise, usu. sensational style.

taboo n, pl -**boos**. prohibition resulting from religious or social conventions. ▸ adj forbidden by a taboo.

tabular adj arranged in a table. **tabulate** v arrange (information) in a table. **tabulation** n

tachograph n device for recording the speed and distance travelled by a motor vehicle.

tachometer n device for measuring speed, esp. that of a revolving shaft.

tacit [**tass-it**] adj implied but not spoken. **tacitly** adv

taciturn [**tass-it-turn**] adj habitually uncommunicative. **taciturnity** n

tack[1] n short nail with a large head; long loose stitch. ▸ v fasten with tacks; stitch with tacks. **tack on** v append.

tack[2] n course of a ship sailing obliquely into the wind; course of action. ▸ v sail into the wind on a zigzag course.

tack[3] n riding harness for horses.

tackies, takkies pl n, sing **tacky**. S

African *informal* tennis shoes or plimsolls.

tackle *v* deal with (a task); confront (an opponent); *Sport* attempt to get the ball from (an opposing player). ▶ *n Sport* act of tackling an opposing player; equipment for a particular activity; set of ropes and pulleys for lifting heavy weights.

tacky[1] *adj* **tackier, tackiest.** slightly sticky.

tacky[2] *adj* **tackier, tackiest.** *Informal* vulgar and tasteless; shabby.

taco [tah-koh] *n, pl* **tacos.** Mexican cookery tortilla fried until crisp, served with a filling.

tact *n* skill in avoiding giving offence. **tactful** *adj* **tactfully** *adv* **tactless** *adj* **tactlessly** *adv*

tactics *n* art of directing military forces in battle. **tactic** *n* method or plan to achieve an end. **tactical** *adj* **tactician** *n*

tactile *adj* of or having the sense of touch.

tadpole *n* limbless tailed larva of a frog or toad.

TAFE *Aust* Technical and Further Education.

taffeta *n* shiny silk or rayon fabric.

tag[1] *n* label bearing information; pointed end of a cord or lace; trite quotation. ▶ *v* **tagging, tagged.** attach a tag to. **tag along** *v* accompany someone, esp. if uninvited.

tag[2] *n* children's game where the person being chased becomes the chaser upon being touched. ▶ *v* **tagging, tagged.** touch and catch in this game.

tagliatelle *n* pasta in long narrow strips.

tail *n* rear part of an animal's body, usu. forming a flexible appendage; rear or last part or parts of

something; *Informal* person employed to follow and spy on another. ▶ *pl Informal* tail coat. ▶ *adj* at the rear. ▶ *v Informal* follow (someone) secretly. **turn tail** run away. **tailless** *adj* **tails** *adv* with the side of a coin uppermost that does not have a portrait of a head on it. **tailback** *n Brit* queue of traffic stretching back from an obstruction. **tailboard** *n* removable or hinged rear board on a truck etc. **tail coat** man's coat with a long back split into two below the waist. **tail off, away** *v* diminish gradually. **tailplane** *n* small stabilizing wing at the rear of an aircraft. **tailspin** *n* uncontrolled spinning dive of an aircraft. **tailwind** *n* wind coming from the rear.

tailor *n* person who makes men's clothes. ▶ *v* adapt to suit a purpose. **tailor-made** *adj* made by a tailor; perfect for a purpose.

taint *v* spoil with a small amount of decay, contamination, or other bad quality. ▶ *n* something that taints.

taipan *n* large poisonous Australian snake.

take *v* **taking, took, taken.** remove from a place; carry or accompany; use; get possession of, esp. dishonestly; capture; require (time, resources, or ability); assume; accept. ▶ *n* one of a series of recordings from which the best will be used. **take place** happen. **taking** *adj* charming. **takings** *pl n* money received by a shop. **take after** *v* look or behave like (a parent etc.). **take away** *v* remove or subtract. **takeaway** *n* shop or restaurant selling meals for eating elsewhere; meal bought at a takeaway. **take in** *v* understand; deceive or swindle; make (clothing) smaller. **take off** v (of an aircraft) leave the ground; *Informal* depart; *Informal* parody. **takeoff** n **takeover** n act of taking control of a company by buying a large number of its shares. **take up** v occupy or fill (space or time); adopt the study or activity of; shorten (a garment); accept (an offer).

talc n talcum powder; soft mineral of magnesium silicate. **talcum powder** powder, usu. scented, used to dry or perfume the body.

tale n story; malicious piece of gossip.

talent n natural ability; ancient unit of weight or money. **talented** adj

talisman n, pl **-mans**. object believed to have magic power. **talismanic** adj

talk v express ideas or feelings by means of speech; utter; discuss, e.g. *let's talk business*; reveal information; (be able to) speak in a specified language. ▶ n speech or lecture. **talker** n **talkative** adj fond of talking. **talk back** v answer impudently. **talkback** n NZ broadcast in which telephone comments or questions from the public are transmitted live.

talking-to n *Informal* telling-off.

tall adj higher than average; of a specified height. **tall order** difficult task. **tall story** unlikely and probably untrue tale.

tallboy n high chest of drawers.

tallow n hard animal fat used to make candles.

tally v **-lying, -lied.** (of two things) correspond. ▶ n, pl **-lies.** record of a debt or score.

tally-ho interj huntsman's cry when the quarry is sighted.

Talmud n body of Jewish law. **Talmudic** adj

talon n bird's hooked claw.

tamarind n tropical tree; its acid fruit.

tamarisk n evergreen shrub with slender branches and feathery flower clusters.

tambourine n percussion instrument like a small drum with jingling metal discs attached.

tame adj (of animals) brought under human control; (of animals) not afraid of people; meek or submissive; uninteresting. ▶ v make tame. **tamely** adv

tamer n person who tames wild animals.

Tamil n member of a people of Sri Lanka and S India; their language.

tam-o'-shanter n brimless wool cap with a bobble in the centre.

tamp v pack down by repeated taps.

tamper v (foll. by *with*) interfere.

tampon n absorbent plug of cotton wool inserted into the vagina during menstruation.

tan n brown coloration of the skin from exposure to sunlight. ▶ v **tanning, tanned.** (of skin) go brown from exposure to sunlight; convert (a hide) into leather. ▶ adj yellowish-brown. **tannery** n place where hides are tanned.

tandem n bicycle for two riders, one behind the other. **in tandem** together.

tandoori adj (of food) cooked in an Indian clay oven.

tang n strong taste or smell; trace or hint. **tangy** adj

tangata whenua [tang-ah-tah fen-noo-ah] pl n NZ original Polynesian settlers in New Zealand.

tangent n line that touches a curve without intersecting it; (in trigonometry) ratio of the length of the opposite side to that of the adjacent side of a right-angled triangle. **go off at a tangent** suddenly take a completely different line of thought or action. **tangential** *adj* of superficial relevance only; of a tangent. **tangentially** *adv*

tangerine *n* small orange-like fruit of an Asian citrus tree.

tangible *adj* able to be touched; clear and definite. **tangibly** *adv*

tangle *n* confused mass or situation. ▶ *v* twist together in a tangle; (often foll. by *with*) come into conflict.

tango *n, pl* **-gos.** S American dance. ▶ *v* dance a tango.

taniwha [**tun-ee-fah**] *n NZ* mythical Maori monster that lives in water.

tank *n* container for liquids or gases; armoured fighting vehicle moving on tracks. **tanker** *n* ship or truck for carrying liquid in bulk.

tankard *n* large beer-mug, often with a hinged lid.

tannin, tannic acid *n* vegetable substance used in tanning.

Tannoy *n* ® *Brit* type of public-address system.

tansy *n, pl* **-sies.** yellow-flowered plant.

tantalize *v* torment by showing but withholding something desired. **tantalizing** *adj* **tantalizingly** *adv*

tantalum *n Chem* hard greyish-white metallic element.

tantamount *adj* **tantamount to** equivalent in effect to.

tantrum *n* childish outburst of temper.

tap¹ *v* **tapping, tapped.** knock lightly and usu. repeatedly. ▶ *n* light knock. **tap dancing** style of dancing in which the feet beat out an elaborate rhythm.

tap² *n* valve to control the flow of liquid from a pipe or cask. ▶ *v* **tapping, tapped.** listen in on (a telephone call) secretly by making an illegal connection; draw off with or as if with a tap. **on tap** *Informal* readily available; (of beer etc.) drawn from a cask.

tape *n* narrow long strip of material; (recording made on) a cassette containing magnetic tape; string stretched across a race track to mark the finish. ▶ *v* record on magnetic tape; bind or fasten with tape. **tape measure** tape marked off in centimetres or inches for measuring. **tape recorder** device for recording and reproducing sound on magnetic tape.

tapeworm *n* long flat parasitic worm living in the intestines of vertebrates.

taper *v* become narrower towards one end. ▶ *n* long thin candle. **taper off** *v* become gradually less.

tapestry *n, pl* **-tries.** fabric decorated with coloured woven designs.

tapioca *n* beadlike starch made from cassava root, used in puddings.

tapir [**tape-er**] *n* piglike mammal of tropical America and SE Asia, with a long snout.

tappet *n* short steel rod in an engine, transferring motion from one part to another.

taproot *n* main root of a plant, growing straight down.

tar *n* thick black liquid distilled from coal etc. ▶ *v* **tarring, tarred.** coat with tar. **tar-seal** *n NZ* tarred road surface.

taramasalata *n* creamy pink pâté made from fish roe.

tarantella *n* lively Italian dance; music for this.

tarantula *n* large hairy spider with a poisonous bite.

tardy *adj* **tardier, tardiest.** slow or late. **tardily** *adv* **tardiness** *n*

tare n type of vetch plant; Bible weed.

target n object or person a missile is aimed at; goal or objective; object of criticism. ▶ v **-geting, -geted.** aim or direct.

tariff n tax levied on imports; list of fixed prices.

Tarmac n ® mixture of tar, bitumen, and crushed stones used for roads etc.; (**t-**) airport runway.

tarn n small mountain lake.

tarnish v make or become stained or less bright; damage or taint. ▶ n discoloration or blemish.

tarot [**tarr**-oh] n special pack of cards used mainly in fortune-telling. **tarot card** card in a tarot pack.

tarpaulin n (sheet of) heavy waterproof fabric.

tarragon n aromatic herb.

tarry v **-rying, -ried.** Old-fashioned linger or delay; stay briefly.

tarsus n, pl **-si.** bones of the heel and ankle collectively.

tart[1] n pie or flan with a sweet filling.

tart[2] adj sharp or bitter. **tartly** adv **tartness** n

tart[3] n Informal sexually provocative or promiscuous woman. **tart up** Informal dress or decorate in a smart or flashy way.

tartan n design of straight lines crossing at right angles, esp. one associated with a Scottish clan; cloth with such a design.

tartar[1] n hard deposit on the teeth; deposit formed during the fermentation of wine.

tartar[2] n fearsome or formidable person.

tartare sauce n mayonnaise sauce mixed with chopped herbs and capers, served with seafood.

tartrazine [**tar**-traz-zeen] n artificial yellow dye used in food etc.

TAS Tasmania.

task n (difficult or unpleasant) piece of work to be done. **take to task** criticize or scold. **task force** (military) group formed to carry out a specific task. **taskmaster** n person who enforces hard work.

Tasmanian n, adj (person) from Tasmania. **Tasmanian devil** small carnivorous Tasmanian marsupial. **Tasmanian tiger** extinct doglike Tasmanian marsupial.

tassel n decorative fringed knot of threads.

taste n sense by which the flavour of a substance is distinguished in the mouth; distinctive flavour; small amount tasted; brief experience of something; liking; ability to appreciate what is beautiful or excellent. ▶ v distinguish the taste of (a substance); take a small amount of (something) into the mouth; have a specific taste; experience briefly. **tasteful** adj having or showing good taste. **tastefully** adv **tasteless** adj bland or insipid; showing bad taste. **tastelessly** adv **tasty** adj pleasantly flavoured. **taste bud** small organ on the tongue which perceives flavours.

tat n Brit tatty or tasteless article(s).

tattered adj ragged or torn. **in tatters** in ragged pieces.

tattle v, n Brit, Aust & NZ gossip or chatter.

tattoo[1] n pattern made on the body by pricking the skin and staining it with indelible dye. ▶ v **-tooing, -tooed.** make such a pattern on the skin. **tattooist** n

tattoo[2] n military display or pageant; drumming or tapping.

tatty adj **-tier, -tiest.** shabby or worn out.

taught v past of TEACH.

taunt v tease with jeers. ▶ n jeering remark.

taupe adj brownish-grey.

taut adj drawn tight; showing nervous strain. **tauten** v make or become taut.

tautology n, pl -gies. use of words which merely repeat something already stated. **tautological** adj

tavern n Old-fashioned pub.

tawdry adj -drier, -driest. cheap, showy, and of poor quality.

tawny adj -nier, -niest. yellowish-brown.

tax n compulsory payment levied by a government on income, property, etc. to raise revenue. ▶ v levy a tax on; make heavy demands on. **taxable** adj **taxation** n levying of taxes. **tax-free** adj (of goods, services and income) not taxed. **taxpayer** n **tax relief** reduction in the amount of tax a person or company has to pay. **tax return** statement of personal income for tax purposes.

taxi n (also **taxicab**) car with a driver that may be hired to take people to any specified destination. ▶ v **taxiing, taxied.** (of an aircraft) run along the ground before taking off or after landing. **taxi meter** meter in a taxi that registers the fare. **taxi rank** place where taxis wait to be hired.

taxidermy n art of stuffing and mounting animal skins to give them a lifelike appearance. **taxidermist** n

taxonomy n classification of plants and animals into groups. **taxonomic** adj **taxonomist** n

TB tuberculosis.

tbs., tbsp. tablespoon(ful).

tea n drink made from infusing the dried leaves of an Asian bush in boiling water; leaves used to make this drink; Brit, Aust & NZ main evening meal; Chiefly Brit light afternoon meal of tea, cakes, etc.; drink like tea, made from other plants. **tea bag** small porous bag of tea leaves. **tea cosy** covering for a teapot to keep the tea warm. **teapot** n container with a lid, spout, and handle for making and serving tea. **teaspoon** n small spoon for stirring tea. **tea towel, tea cloth** towel for drying dishes.

teach v **teaching, taught.** tell or show (someone) how to do something; give lessons in (a subject); cause to learn or understand. **teaching** n

teacher n person who teaches, esp. in a school.

teak n very hard wood of an E Indian tree.

teal n kind of small duck.

team n group of people forming one side in a game; group of people or animals working together. **teamster** n US commercial vehicle driver. **team up** v make or join a team. **teamwork** n cooperative work by a team.

tear¹, teardrop n drop of fluid appearing in and falling from the eye. **in tears** weeping. **tearful** adj weeping or about to weep. **tear gas** gas that stings the eyes and causes temporary blindness. **tear-jerker** n Informal excessively sentimental film or book.

tear² v **tearing, tore, torn.** rip a hole in; rip apart; rush. ▶ n hole or split. **tearaway** n wild or unruly person.

tease v make fun of (someone) in a provoking or playful way. ▶ n person who teases. **teasing** adj, n

tease out v remove tangles from (hair etc.) by combing.

teasel, teazel, teazle n plant with prickly leaves and flowers.

teat n nipple of a breast or udder; rubber nipple of a feeding bottle.

tech n Informal technical college.

technetium [tek-**neesh**-ee-um] n Chem artificially produced silvery-grey metallic element.

technical adj of or specializing in industrial, practical, or mechanical arts and applied sciences; skilled in technical subjects; relating to a particular subject; according to the letter of the law; showing technique, e.g. technical brilliance. **technically** adv **technicality** n petty point based on a strict application of rules. **technician** n person skilled in a particular technical field. **technical college** higher educational institution with courses in art and technical subjects.

Technicolor n ® system of colour photography used for the cinema.

technique n method or skill used for a particular task; technical proficiency.

techno n type of electronic dance music with a very fast beat.

technocracy n, pl **-cies.** government by technical experts. **technocrat** n

technology n application of practical or mechanical sciences to industry or commerce; scientific methods used in a particular field. **technological** adj **technologist** n

tectonics n study of the earth's crust and the forces affecting it.

teddy n, pl **-dies.** teddy bear; combined camisole and knickers. **teddy bear** soft toy bear.

tedious adj causing fatigue or boredom. **tediously** adv **tedium** n monotony.

tee n small peg from which a golf ball can be played at the start of each hole; area of a golf course from which the first stroke of a hole is made. **tee off** v make the first stroke of a hole in golf.

teem[1] v be full of.

teem[2] v rain heavily.

teenager n person aged between 13 and 19. **teenage** adj

teens pl n period of being a teenager.

teepee n same as TEPEE.

tee-shirt n same as T-SHIRT.

teeter v wobble or move unsteadily.

teeth n plural of TOOTH.

teethe v (of a baby) grow his or her first teeth. **teething troubles** problems during the early stages of something.

teetotal adj drinking no alcohol. **teetotaller** n

TEFL Teaching of English as a Foreign Language.

Teflon n ® substance used for nonstick coatings on saucepans etc.

tele- combining form distance, e.g. telecommunications; telephone or television, e.g. teleconference.

telecommunications n communications using telephone, radio, television, etc.

telegram n formerly, a message sent by telegraph.

telegraph n formerly, a system for sending messages over a distance along a cable. ▶ v communicate by telegraph. **telegraphic** adj **telegraphist** n **telegraphy** n science or use of a telegraph.

telekinesis n movement of objects by thought or willpower.

telemetry n use of electronic devices to record or measure a distant event and transmit the data to a receiver.

teleology *n* belief that all things have a predetermined purpose. **teleological** *adj*

telepathy *n* direct communication between minds. **telepathic** *adj* **telepathically** *adv*

telephone *n* device for transmitting sound over a distance along wires. ▸ *v* call or talk to (a person) by telephone. **telephony** *n* **telephonic** *adj* **telephonist** *n* person operating a telephone switchboard.

telephoto lens *n* camera lens producing a magnified image of a distant object.

teleprinter *n* Brit apparatus like a typewriter for sending and receiving typed messages by wire.

telesales *n* selling of a product or service by telephone.

telescope *n* optical instrument for magnifying distant objects. ▸ *v* shorten. **telescopic** *adj*

Teletext *n* ® system which shows information and news on television screens.

television *n* system of producing a moving image and accompanying sound on a distant screen; device for receiving broadcast signals and converting them into sound and pictures; content of television programmes. **televise** *v* broadcast on television. **televisual** *adj*

telex *n* international communication service using teleprinters; message sent by telex. ▸ *v* transmit by telex.

tell *v* **telling, told.** make known in words; order or instruct; give an account of; discern or distinguish; have an effect; Informal reveal secrets. **teller** *n* narrator; bank cashier; person who counts votes. **telling** *adj* having a marked effect. **tell off** *v* reprimand. **telling-off** *n*

telltale *n* person who reveals secrets. ▸ *adj* revealing.

tellurium *n* Chem brittle silvery-white nonmetallic element.

telly *n, pl* **-lies.** Informal television.

temerity [tim-merr-it-tee] *n* boldness or audacity.

temp Brit informal ▸ *n* temporary employee, esp. a secretary. ▸ *v* work as a temp.

temp. temperature; temporary.

temper *n* outburst of anger; tendency to become angry; calm mental condition, e.g. *I lost my temper;* frame of mind. ▸ *v* make less extreme; strengthen or toughen (metal).

tempera *n* painting medium for powdered pigments.

temperament *n* person's character or disposition. **temperamental** *adj* having changeable moods; Informal erratic and unreliable. **temperamentally** *adv*

temperate *adj* (of climate) not extreme; self-restrained or moderate. **temperance** *n* moderation; abstinence from alcohol.

temperature *n* degree of heat or cold; Informal abnormally high body temperature.

tempest *n* violent storm. **tempestuous** *adj* violent or stormy.

template *n* pattern used to cut out shapes accurately.

temple[1] *n* building for worship.

temple[2] *n* region on either side of the forehead. **temporal** *adj*

tempo *n, pl* **-pi, -pos.** rate or pace; speed of a piece of music.

temporal *adj* of time; worldly rather than spiritual.

temporary *adj* lasting only for a short time. **temporarily** *adv*

temporize *v* gain time by negotiation or evasiveness; adapt to circumstances.

tempt v entice (a person) to do something wrong. **tempt fate** take foolish or unnecessary risks. **tempter, temptress** n **temptation** n tempting; tempting thing. **tempting** adj attractive or inviting.

ten adj, n one more than nine. **tenth** adj, n (of) number ten in a series.

tenable adj able to be upheld or maintained.

tenacious adj holding fast; stubborn. **tenaciously** adv **tenacity** n

tenant n person who rents land or a building. **tenancy** n

tench n, pl **tench.** freshwater game fish of the carp family.

tend¹ v be inclined; go in the direction of. **tendency** n inclination to act in a certain way. **tendentious** adj biased, not impartial.

tend² v take care of.

tender¹ adj not tough; gentle and affectionate; vulnerable or sensitive. **tenderly** adv **tenderness** n **tenderize** v soften (meat) by pounding or treatment with a special substance.

tender² v offer; make a formal offer to supply goods or services at a stated cost. ▶ n such an offer. **legal tender** currency that must, by law, be accepted as payment.

tender³ n small boat that brings supplies to a larger ship in a port; carriage for fuel and water attached to a steam locomotive.

tendon n strong tissue attaching a muscle to a bone.

tendril n slender stem by which a climbing plant clings.

tenement n (esp. in Scotland or the US) building divided into several flats.

tenet [ten-nit] n doctrine or belief.

tenner n Brit informal ten-pound note.

tennis n game in which players use rackets to hit a ball back and forth over a net.

tenon n projecting end on a piece of wood fitting into a slot in another.

tenor n (singer with) the second highest male voice; general meaning. ▶ adj (of a voice or instrument) between alto and baritone.

tenpin bowling n game in which players try to knock over ten skittles by rolling a ball at them.

tense¹ adj emotionally strained; stretched tight. ▶ v make or become tight.

tense² n Grammar form of a verb showing the time of action.

tensile adj of tension.

tension n hostility or suspense; emotional strain; degree of stretching.

tent n portable canvas shelter.

tentacle n flexible organ of many invertebrates, used for grasping, feeding, etc.

tentative adj provisional or experimental; cautious or hesitant. **tentatively** adv

tenterhooks pl n **on tenterhooks** in anxious suspense.

tenuous adj slight or flimsy. **tenuously** adv

tenure n (period of) the holding of an office or position.

tepee [tee-pee] n cone-shaped tent, formerly used by Native Americans.

tepid adj slightly warm; half-hearted.

tequila n Mexican alcoholic drink.

tercentenary adj, n, pl **-naries.** (of) a three hundredth anniversary.

term n word or expression; fixed period; period of the year when a school etc. is open or a lawcourt holds sessions. ▶ *pl* conditions; mutual relationship. ▶ *v* name or designate.

terminal *adj* (of an illness) ending in death; at or being an end. ▶ *n* place where people or vehicles begin or end a journey; point where current enters or leaves an electrical device; keyboard and VDU having input and output links with a computer. **terminally** *adv*

terminate *v* bring or come to an end. **termination** *n*

terminology *n* technical terms relating to a subject.

terminus *n*, *pl* **-ni**, **-nuses**. railway or bus station at the end of a line.

termite *n* white antlike insect that destroys timber.

tern *n* gull-like sea bird with a forked tail and pointed wings.

ternary *adj* consisting of three parts.

Terpsichorean *adj* of dancing.

terrace *n* row of houses built as one block; paved area next to a building; level tier cut out of a hill. ▶ *pl* (also **terracing**) tiered area in a stadium where spectators stand. ▶ *v* form into or provide with a terrace.

terracotta *adj*, *n* (made of) brownish-red unglazed pottery. ▶ *adj* brownish-red.

terra firma *n Latin* dry land or solid ground.

terrain *n* area of ground, esp. with reference to its physical character.

terrapin *n* small turtle-like reptile.

terrarium *n*, *pl* **-raria**, **-rariums.** enclosed container for small plants or animals.

terrazzo *n*, *pl* **-zos.** floor of marble chips set in mortar and polished.

terrestrial *adj* of the earth; of or living on land.

terrible *adj* very serious; *Informal* very bad; causing fear. **terribly** *adv*

terrier *n* any of various breeds of small active dog.

terrific *adj* great or intense; *Informal* excellent.

terrify *v* **-fying, -fied.** fill with fear. **terrified** *adj* **terrifying** *adj*

terrine [terr-**reen**] *n* earthenware dish with a lid; pâté or similar food.

territory *n*, *pl* **-ries.** district; area under the control of a particular government; area inhabited and defended by an animal; area of knowledge. **territorial** *adj* **Territorial Army** (in Britain) reserve army.

terror *n* great fear; terrifying person or thing; *Brit, Aust & NZ informal* troublesome person or thing. **terrorism** *n* use of violence and intimidation to achieve political ends. **terrorist** *n*, *adj* **terrorize** *v* force or oppress by fear or violence.

terry *n* fabric with small loops covering both sides, used esp. for making towels.

terse *adj* neat and concise; curt. **tersely** *adv*

tertiary [**tur**-shar-ee] *adj* third in degree, order, etc.

Terylene *n* ® synthetic polyester yarn or fabric.

tessellated *adj* paved or inlaid with a mosaic of small tiles.

test *v* try out to ascertain the worth, capability, or endurance of; carry out an examination on. ▶ *n* critical examination; Test match. **testing** *adj* **test case** lawsuit that establishes a precedent. **Test match** one of a series of international cricket or rugby matches. **test tube** narrow round-bottomed glass tube used

in scientific experiments.
test-tube baby baby conceived outside the mother's body.

testament n proof or tribute; *Law* will; **(T-)** one of the two main divisions of the Bible.

testator [test-**tay**-tor], *(fem)* **testatrix** [test-**tay**-triks] n maker of a will.

testicle n either of the two male reproductive glands.

testify v -**fying, -fied.** give evidence under oath. **testify to** be evidence of.

testimony n, pl -**nies.** declaration of truth or fact; evidence given under oath. **testimonial** n recommendation of the worth of a person or thing; tribute for services or achievement.

testis n, pl -**tes.** testicle.

testosterone n male sex hormone secreted by the testes.

testy adj -**tier, -tiest.** irritable or touchy. **testily** adv **testiness** n

tetanus n acute infectious disease producing muscular spasms and convulsions.

tête-à-tête n, pl -**têtes, -tête.** private conversation.

tether n rope or chain for tying an animal to a spot. ▶ v tie up with rope. **at the end of one's tether** at the limit of one's endurance.

tetrahedron [tet-ra-**heed**-ron] n, pl -**drons, -dra.** solid figure with four faces.

tetralogy n, pl -**gies.** series of four related works.

Teutonic [tew-**tonn**-ik] adj of or like the (ancient) Germans.

text n main body of a book as distinct from illustrations etc.; passage of the Bible as the subject of a sermon; novel or play studied for a course; text message. ▶ v send a text message to (someone). **textual** adj **textbook**

n standard book on a particular subject. ▶ adj perfect, e.g. a textbook landing. **text message** message sent in text form, esp. by means of a mobile phone.

textile n fabric or cloth, esp. woven.

texture n structure, feel, or consistency. **textured** adj **textural** adj

thalidomide [thal-**lid**-oh-mide] n drug formerly used as a sedative, but found to cause abnormalities in developing fetuses.

thallium n *Chem* highly toxic metallic element.

than conj, prep used to introduce the second element of a comparison.

thane n *Hist* Anglo-Saxon or medieval Scottish nobleman.

thank v express gratitude to; hold responsible. **thanks** pl n words of gratitude. ▶ interj (also **thank you**) polite expression of gratitude. **thanks to** because of. **thankful** adj grateful. **thankless** adj unrewarding or unappreciated. **Thanksgiving Day** autumn public holiday in Canada and the US.

that adj, pron used to refer to something already mentioned or familiar, or further away. ▶ conj used to introduce a clause. ▶ pron used to introduce a relative clause.

thatch n roofing material of reeds or straw. ▶ v roof (a house) with reeds or straw.

thaw v make or become unfrozen; become more relaxed or friendly. ▶ n thawing; weather causing snow or ice to melt.

the adj the definite article, used before a noun.

theatre n place where plays etc. are performed; hospital operating room; drama and acting in general. **theatrical** adj of the

theatre; exaggerated or affected.
theatricals pl n (amateur) dramatic performances.
theatrically adv **theatricality** n
thee pron Obs objective form of THOU.

theft n act or an instance of stealing.

their adj of or associated with them. **theirs** pron (thing or person) belonging to them.

theism [thee-iz-zum] n belief in a God or gods. **theist** n, adj **theistic** adj

them pron refers to people or things other than the speaker or those addressed. **themselves** pron emphatic and reflexive form of THEY or THEM.

theme n main idea or subject being discussed; recurring melodic figure in music. **thematic** adj **theme park** leisure area in which all the activities and displays are based on a single theme.

then adv at that time; after that; that being so.

thence adv from that place or time; therefore.

theocracy n, pl -**cies**. government by a god or priests. **theocratic** adj

theodolite [thee-odd-oh-lite] n surveying instrument for measuring angles.

theology n, pl -**gies**. study of religions and religious beliefs. **theologian** n **theological** adj **theologically** adv

theorem n proposition that can be proved by reasoning.

theory n, pl -**ries**. set of ideas to explain something; abstract knowledge or reasoning; idea or opinion. **in theory** in an ideal or hypothetical situation. **theoretical** adj based on theory rather than practice or fact. **theoretically** adv **theorist** n **theorize** v form

theories, speculate.

theosophy n religious or philosophical system claiming to be based on intuitive insight into the divine nature. **theosophical** adj

therapy n, pl -**pies**. curing treatment. **therapist** n **therapeutic** [ther-rap-**pew**-tik] adj curing. **therapeutics** n art of curing.

there adv in or to that place; in that respect. **thereby** adv by that means. **therefore** adv consequently, that being so. **thereupon** adv immediately after that.

therm n unit of measurement of heat.

thermal adj of heat; hot or warm; (of clothing) retaining heat. ► n rising current of warm air.

thermodynamics n scientific study of the relationship between heat and other forms of energy.

thermometer n instrument for measuring temperature.

thermonuclear adj involving nuclear fusion.

thermoplastic adj (of a plastic) softening when heated and resetting on cooling.

Thermos n ® vacuum flask.

thermosetting adj (of a plastic) remaining hard when heated.

thermostat n device for automatically regulating temperature. **thermostatic** adj **thermostatically** adv

thesaurus [thiss-**sore**-uss] n, pl -**ruses**. book containing lists of synonyms and related words.

these adj, pron plural of THIS.

thesis n, pl **theses**. written work submitted for a degree; opinion supported by reasoned argument.

Thespian n actor or actress. ► adj of the theatre.

they *pron* refers to: people or things other than the speaker or people addressed; people in general; *Informal* he or she.

thiamine *n* vitamin found in the outer coat of rice and other grains.

thick *adj* of great or specified extent from one side to the other; having a dense consistency; *Informal* stupid or insensitive; *Brit, Aust & NZ informal* friendly. **a bit thick** *Informal* unfair or unreasonable. **the thick** busiest or most intense part. **thick with** full of. **thicken** *v* make or become thick or thicker. **thickly** *adv* **thickness** *n* state of being thick; dimension through an object; layer. **thickset** *adj* stocky in build.

thicket *n* dense growth of small trees.

thief *n, pl* **thieves**. person who steals. **thieve** *v* steal. **thieving** *adj*

thigh *n* upper part of the human leg.

thimble *n* cap protecting the end of the finger when sewing.

thin *adj* **thinner, thinnest**. not thick; slim or lean; sparse or meagre; of low density; poor or unconvincing. ▶ *v* **thinning, thinned**. make or become thin. **thinly** *adv* **thinness** *n*

thine *pron, adj Obs* (something) of or associated with you (thou).

thing *n* material object; object, fact, or idea considered as a separate entity; *Informal* obsession. ▶ *pl* possessions, clothes, etc.

think *v* thinking, **thought**. consider, judge, or believe; make use of the mind; be considerate enough or remember to do something. **thinker** *n* **thinking** *adj, n* **think-tank** *n* group of experts studying specific problems. **think up** *v* invent or devise.

third *adj* of number three in a series; rated or graded below the second level. ▶ *n* one of three equal parts. **third degree** violent interrogation. **third party** (applying to) a person involved by chance or only incidentally in legal proceedings, an accident, etc. **Third World** developing countries of Africa, Asia, and Latin America.

thirst *n* desire to drink; craving or yearning. ▶ *v* feel thirst. **thirsty** *adj* **thirstily** *adv*

thirteen *adj, n* three plus ten. **thirteenth** *adj, n*

thirty *adj, n* three times ten. **thirtieth** *adj, n*

this *adj, pron* used to refer to a thing or person nearby, just mentioned, or about to be mentioned. ▶ *adj* used to refer to the present time, e.g. *this morning.*

thistle *n* prickly plant with dense flower heads.

thither *adv Obs* to or towards that place.

thong *n* thin strip of leather etc.; skimpy article of underwear or beachwear that covers the genitals while leaving the buttocks bare.

thorax *n, pl* **thoraxes, thoraces**. part of the body between the neck and the abdomen. **thoracic** *adj*

thorn *n* prickle on a plant; bush with thorns. **thorn in one's side, flesh** source of irritation. **thorny** *adj*

thorough *adj* complete; careful or methodical. **thoroughly** *adv* **thoroughness** *n* **thoroughbred** *n, adj* (animal) of pure breed. **thoroughfare** *n* way through from one place to another.

those *adj, pron* plural of THAT.

thou *pron Obs* singular form of YOU.

though *conj* despite the fact that. ▶ *adv* nevertheless.

thought v past of THINK. ▶ n thinking; concept or idea; ideas typical of a time or place; consideration; intention or expectation. **thoughtful** adj considerate; showing careful thought; pensive or reflective. **thoughtless** adj inconsiderate.

thousand adj, n ten hundred; large but unspecified number. **thousandth** adj, n (of) number one thousand in a series.

thrall n state of being in the power of another person.

thrash v beat, esp. with a stick or whip; defeat soundly; move about wildly; thresh. **thrashing** n severe beating. **thrash out** v solve by thorough argument.

thread n fine strand or yarn; unifying theme; spiral ridge on a screw, nut, or bolt. ▶ v pass thread through; pick (one's way etc.). **threadbare** adj (of fabric) with the nap worn off; hackneyed; shabby.

threat n declaration of intent to harm; dangerous person or thing. **threaten** v make or be a threat to; be a menacing indication of.

three adj, n one more than two. **threesome** n group of three. **three-dimensional, 3-D** adj having three dimensions.

threnody n, pl **-dies.** lament for the dead.

thresh v beat (wheat etc.) to separate the grain from the husks and straw. **thresh about** move about wildly.

threshold n bar forming the bottom of a doorway; entrance; starting point; point at which something begins to take effect.

threw v past tense of THROW.

thrice adv Lit three times.

thrift n wisdom and caution with money; low-growing plant with pink flowers. **thrifty** adj

thrill n sudden feeling of excitement. ▶ v (cause to) feel a thrill. **thrilling** adj

thriller n book, film, etc. with an atmosphere of mystery or suspense.

thrive v thriving, thrived or throve, thrived or thriven. flourish or prosper; grow well.

throat n passage from the mouth and nose to the stomach and lungs; front of the neck. **throaty** adj (of the voice) hoarse.

throb v throbbing, throbbed. pulsate repeatedly; vibrate rhythmically. ▶ n throbbing.

throes pl n violent pangs or pains. **in the throes of** struggling to cope with.

thrombosis n, pl **-ses.** forming of a clot in a blood vessel or the heart.

throne n ceremonial seat of a monarch or bishop; sovereign power.

throng n, v crowd.

throstle n song thrush.

throttle n device controlling the amount of fuel entering an engine. ▶ v strangle.

through prep from end to end or side to side of; because of; during. ▶ adj finished; (of transport) going directly to a place. **through and through** completely. **throughout** prep, adv in every part (of). **throughput** n amount of material processed.

throve v a past tense of THRIVE.

throw v throwing, threw, thrown. hurl through the air; move or put suddenly or carelessly; bring into a specified state, esp. suddenly; give (a party); Informal baffle or disconcert. ▶ n throwing; distance thrown. **throwaway** adj done or said casually; designed to be discarded after use. **throwback** n person or thing that reverts to an earlier type. **throw up** v vomit.

thrush[1] n brown songbird.

thrush[2] n fungal disease of the mouth or vagina.

thrust v **thrusting, thrust.** push forcefully. ▶ n forceful stab; force or power; intellectual or emotional drive.

thud n dull heavy sound. ▶ v **thudding, thudded.** make such a sound.

thug n violent man, esp. a criminal. **thuggery** n **thuggish** adj

thumb n short thick finger set apart from the others. ▶ v touch or handle with the thumb; signal with the thumb for a lift in a vehicle. **thumb through** flick through (a book or magazine).

thump n (sound of) a dull heavy blow. ▶ v strike heavily.

thunder n loud noise accompanying lightning. ▶ v rumble with thunder; shout; move fast, heavily, and noisily. **thunderous** adj **thundery** adj **thunderbolt** n lightning flash; something sudden and unexpected. **thunderclap** n peal of thunder. **thunderstruck** adj amazed.

Thursday n fifth day of the week.

thus adv therefore; in this way.

thwack v, n whack.

thwart v foil or frustrate. ▶ n seat across a boat.

thy adj Obs of or associated with you (thou). **thyself** pron Obs emphatic form of THOU.

thyme [time] n aromatic herb.

thymus n, pl **-muses, -mi.** small gland at the base of the neck.

thyroid adj, n (of) a gland in the neck controlling body growth.

tiara n semicircular jewelled headdress.

tibia n, pl **tibiae, tibias.** inner bone of the lower leg. **tibial** adj

tic n spasmodic muscular twitch.

tick[1] n mark (✓) used to check off or indicate the correctness of something; recurrent tapping sound, as of a clock; Informal moment. ▶ v mark with a tick; make a ticking sound. **tick off** v mark with a tick; reprimand. **tick over** v (of an engine) idle; function smoothly. **ticktack** n Brit bookmakers' sign language.

tick[2] n tiny bloodsucking parasitic animal.

tick[3] n Informal credit or account.

ticket n card or paper entitling the holder to admission, travel, etc.; label, esp. showing price; official notification of a parking or traffic offence; Chiefly US & NZ declared policy of a political party. ▶ v **-eting, -eted.** attach or issue a ticket to.

ticking n strong material for mattress covers.

tickle v touch or stroke (a person) to produce laughter; itch or tingle; please or amuse. ▶ n tickling. **ticklish** adj sensitive to tickling; requiring care or tact.

tiddler n Informal very small fish.

tiddly[1] adj **-dlier, -dliest.** tiny.

tiddly[2] adj **-dlier, -dliest.** Informal slightly drunk.

tiddlywinks n game in which players try to flip small plastic discs into a cup.

tide n rise and fall of the sea caused by the gravitational pull of the sun and moon; current caused by this; widespread feeling or tendency. **tidal** adj **tidal wave** large destructive wave. **tide over** v help (someone) temporarily.

tidings pl n news.

tidy adj **-dier, -diest.** neat and orderly; Brit, Aust & NZ informal considerable. ▶ v **-dying, -died.**

put in order. **tidily** adv **tidiness** n

tie v **tying, tied.** fasten or be fastened with string, rope, etc.; make (a knot or bow) in (something); restrict or limit; score the same as another competitor. ▶ n long narrow piece of material worn knotted round the neck; bond or fastening; drawn game or contest. **tied** adj Brit (of a cottage etc.) rented to the tenant only as long as he or she is employed by the owner.

tier n one of a set of rows placed one above and behind the other.

tiff n petty quarrel.

tiger n large yellow-and-black striped Asian cat. **tigress** n female tiger; Informal fierce woman.

tight adj stretched or drawn taut; closely fitting; secure or firm; cramped; Brit, Aust & NZ informal not generous; (of a match or game) very close; Informal drunk. **tights** pl n one-piece clinging garment covering the body from the waist to the feet. **tightly** adv **tighten** v make or become tight or tighter. **tightrope** n rope stretched taut on which acrobats perform.

tiki n NZ small carving of a grotesque person worn as a pendant.

tikka adj Indian cookery marinated in spices and dry-roasted.

tilde n mark (˜) used in Spanish to indicate that the letter 'n' is to be pronounced in a particular way.

tile n flat piece of ceramic, plastic, etc. used to cover a roof, floor, or wall. ▶ v cover with tiles. **tiled** adj **tiling** n tiles collectively.

till[1] conj, prep until.

till[2] v cultivate (land). **tillage** n

till[3] n drawer for money, usu. in a cash register.

tiller n lever to move a rudder of a boat.

tilt v slant at an angle; Hist compete against in a jousting contest. ▶ n slope; Hist jousting contest; attempt. **at full tilt** at full speed or force.

timber n wood as a building material; trees collectively; wooden beam in the frame of a house, boat, etc. **timbered** adj **timber line** limit beyond which trees will not grow.

timbre [tam-bra] n distinctive quality of sound of a voice or instrument.

time n past, present, and future as a continuous whole; specific point in time; unspecified interval; instance or occasion; period with specific features; musical tempo; Brit, Aust & NZ slang imprisonment. ▶ v note the time taken by; choose a time for. **timeless** adj unaffected by time; eternal. **timely** adj at the appropriate time. **time-honoured** adj sanctioned by custom. **time-lag** n period between cause and effect. **timepiece** n watch or clock. **timeserver** n person who changes his or her views to gain support or favour. **time sharing** n system of part ownership of a holiday property for a specified period each year. **timetable** n plan showing the times when something takes place, the departure and arrival times of trains or buses, etc.

timid adj easily frightened; shy, not bold. **timidly** adv **timidity** n **timorous** adj timid.

timpani [tim-pan-ee] pl n set of kettledrums. **timpanist** n

tin n soft metallic element; (airtight) metal container. **tinned** adj (of food) preserved by being sealed in a tin. **tinny** adj (of sound) thin and metallic. **tinpot** adj Informal worthless or unimportant.

tincture n medicinal extract in a solution of alcohol.

tinder n dry easily-burning material used to start a fire. **tinderbox** n

tine n prong of a fork or antler.

ting n high metallic sound, as of a small bell.

tinge n slight tint; trace. ▶ v **tingeing, tinged.** give a slight tint or trace to.

tingle v, n (feel) a prickling or stinging sensation.

tinker n travelling mender of pots and pans; Scot & Irish Gypsy. ▶ v fiddle with (an engine etc.) in an attempt to repair it.

tinkle v ring with a high tinny sound like a small bell. ▶ n this sound or action.

tinsel n decorative metallic strips or threads.

tint n (pale) shade of a colour; dye for the hair. ▶ v give a tint to.

tiny adj **tinier, tiniest.** very small.

tip¹ n narrow or pointed end of anything; small piece forming an end. ▶ v **tipping, tipped.** put a tip on.

tip² n money given in return for service; helpful hint or warning; piece of inside information. ▶ v **tipping, tipped.** give a tip to.

tipster n person who sells tips about races.

tip³ v **tipping, tipped.** tilt or overturn; dump (rubbish). ▶ n rubbish dump.

tipple v drink alcohol habitually, esp. in small quantities. ▶ n alcoholic drink. **tippler** n

tipsy adj **-sier, -siest.** slightly drunk.

tiptoe v **-toeing, -toed.** walk quietly with the heels off the ground.

tiptop adj of the highest quality or condition.

tirade n long angry speech.

tire v reduce the energy of, as by exertion; weary or bore. **tired** adj exhausted; hackneyed or stale. **tiring** adj **tireless** adj energetic and determined. **tiresome** adj boring and irritating.

tissue n substance of an animal body or plant; piece of thin soft paper used as a handkerchief etc.; interwoven series.

tit n any of various small songbirds.

titanic adj huge or very important.

titanium n Chem strong light metallic element used to make alloys.

titbit n tasty piece of food; pleasing scrap of scandal.

tit-for-tat adj done in retaliation.

tithe n esp. formerly, one tenth of one's income or produce paid to the church as a tax.

Titian [tish-an] adj (of hair) reddish-gold.

titillate v excite or stimulate pleasurably. **titillating** adj **titillation** n

titivate v smarten up.

title n name of a book, film, etc.; name signifying rank or position; formal designation, such as Mrs; Sport championship; Law legal right of possession. **titled** adj aristocratic. **title deed** legal document of ownership.

titter v laugh in a suppressed way. ▶ n suppressed laugh.

tittle-tattle n, v gossip.

titular adj in name only; of a title.

tizzy n, pl **-zies.** Informal confused or agitated state.

TNT n trinitrotoluene, a powerful explosive.

to prep indicating movement towards, equality or comparison, etc., e.g. walking to school; forty *miles to the gallon;* used to mark the indirect object or infinitive of a verb. ▸ *adv* to a closed position, e.g. *pull the door to.* **to and fro** back and forth.

toad *n* animal like a large frog.

toad-in-the-hole *n Brit* sausages baked in batter.

toadstool *n* poisonous fungus like a mushroom.

toady *n, pl* **toadies**. ingratiating person. ▸ *v* **toadying, toadied.** be ingratiating.

toast[1] *n* sliced bread browned by heat. ▸ *v* brown (bread) by heat; warm or be warmed. **toaster** *n* electrical device for toasting bread.

toast[2] *n* tribute or proposal of health or success marked by people raising glasses and drinking together; person or thing so honoured. ▸ *v* drink a toast to.

tobacco *n, pl* **-cos, -coes.** plant with large leaves dried for smoking. **tobacconist** *n* person or shop selling tobacco, cigarettes, etc.

toboggan *n* narrow sledge for sliding over snow. ▸ *v* **-ganing, -ganed.** ride a toboggan.

toby jug *n Chiefly Brit* mug in the form of a stout seated man.

toccata [tok-kah-ta] *n* rapid piece of music for a keyboard instrument.

today *n* this day; the present age. ▸ *adv* on this day; nowadays.

toddler *n* child beginning to walk.

toddle *v* walk with short unsteady steps.

toddy *n, pl* **-dies.** sweetened drink of spirits and hot water.

to-do *n, pl* **-dos.** *Brit, Aust & NZ* fuss or commotion.

toe *n* digit of the foot; part of a shoe or sock covering the toes. ▸ *v* **toeing, toed.** touch or kick with the toe. **toe the line** conform.

toff *n Brit slang* well-dressed or upper-class person.

toffee *n* chewy sweet made of boiled sugar.

tofu *n* soft food made from soya-bean curd.

tog *n* unit for measuring the insulating power of duvets.

toga [toe-ga] *n* garment worn by citizens of ancient Rome.

together *adv* in company; simultaneously. ▸ *adj Informal* organized.

toggle *n* small bar-shaped button inserted through a loop for fastening; switch used to turn a machine or computer function on or off.

toil *n* hard work. ▸ *v* work hard; progress with difficulty.

toilet *n* (room with) a bowl connected to a drain for receiving and disposing of urine and faeces; washing and dressing. **toiletry** *n, pl* **-ries.** object or cosmetic used to clean or groom oneself. **toilet water** light perfume.

token *n* sign or symbol; voucher exchangeable for goods of a specified value; disc used as money in a slot machine. ▸ *adj* nominal or slight. **tokenism** *n* policy of making only a token effort, esp. to comply with a law.

told *v* past of TELL.

tolerate *v* allow to exist or happen; endure patiently. **tolerable** *adj* bearable; *Informal* quite good. **tolerably** *adv* **tolerance** *n* acceptance of other people's rights to their own opinions or actions; ability to endure something. **tolerant** *adj* **tolerantly** *adv* **toleration** *n*

toll[1] *v* ring (a bell) slowly and regularly, esp. to announce a death. ▸ *n* tolling.

toll[2] *n* charge for the use of a

bridge or road; total loss or damage from a disaster.

tom n male cat.

tomahawk n fighting axe of the Native Americans.

tomato n, pl **-toes**. red fruit used in salads and as a vegetable.

tomb n grave; monument over a grave. **tombstone** n gravestone.

tombola n lottery with tickets drawn from a revolving drum.

tomboy n girl who acts or dresses like a boy.

tome n large heavy book.

tomfoolery n foolish behaviour.

Tommy gun n light sub-machine-gun.

tomorrow adv, n (on) the day after today; (in) the future.

tom-tom n drum beaten with the hands.

ton n unit of weight equal to 2240 pounds or 1016 kilograms (**long ton**) or, in the US, 2000 pounds or 907 kilograms (**short ton**). **tonnage** n weight capacity of a ship.

tone n sound with reference to its pitch, volume, etc.; US musical note; Music (also **whole tone**) interval of two semitones; quality of a sound or colour; general character; healthy bodily condition. ▶ v harmonize (with); give tone to. **tonal** adj Music written in a key. **tonality** n **toneless** adj **tone-deaf** adj unable to perceive subtle differences in pitch. **tone down** v make or become more moderate.

tongs pl n large pincers for grasping and lifting.

tongue n muscular organ in the mouth, used in speaking and tasting; language; animal tongue as food; thin projecting strip; flap of leather on a shoe.

tonic n medicine to improve body tone. ▶ adj invigorating. **tonic water** mineral water containing quinine.

tonight adv, n (in or during) the night or evening of this day.

tonne [tunn] n unit of weight equal to 1000 kilograms.

tonsil n small gland in the throat. **tonsillectomy** n surgical removal of the tonsils. **tonsillitis** n inflammation of the tonsils.

tonsure n shaving of all or the top of the head as a religious or monastic practice; shaved part of the head. **tonsured** adj

too adv also, as well; to excess; extremely.

took v past tense of TAKE.

tool n implement used by hand; person used by another to perform unpleasant or dishonourable tasks.

toot n short hooting sound. ▶ v (cause to) make such a sound.

tooth n, pl **teeth**. bonelike projection in the jaws of most vertebrates for biting and chewing; toothlike prong or point. **sweet tooth** strong liking for sweet food. **toothless** adj **toothpaste** n paste used to clean the teeth. **toothpick** n small stick for removing scraps of food from between the teeth.

top[1] n highest point or part; lid or cap; highest rank; garment for the upper part of the body. ▶ adj at or of the top. ▶ v **topping, topped**. form a top on; be at the top of; exceed or surpass. **topping** n sauce or garnish for food. **topless** adj (of a costume or woman) with no covering for the breasts. **topmost** adj highest or best. **top brass** most important officers or leaders. **top hat** man's tall cylindrical hat. **top-heavy** adj unstable through being

overloaded at the top. **top-notch**
adj excellent, first-class. **topsoil** n
surface layer of soil.

top² n toy which spins on a
pointed base.

topaz [toe-pazz] n semiprecious
stone in various colours.

topee, topi [toe-pee] n
lightweight hat worn in tropical
countries.

topiary [tope-yar-ee] n art of
trimming trees and bushes into
decorative shapes.

topic n subject of a conversation,
book, etc. **topical** adj relating to
current events. **topicality** n

topography n, pl **-phies.** (science
of describing) the surface features
of a place. **topographer** n
topographical adj

topology n geometry of the
properties of a shape which are
unaffected by continuous
distortion. **topological** adj

topple v (cause) to fall over;
overthrow (a government etc.).

topsy-turvy adj upside down; in
confusion.

toque [toke] n small round hat.

tor n high rocky hill.

Torah n body of traditional Jewish
teaching.

torch n small portable
battery-powered lamp; wooden
shaft dipped in wax and set
alight. ▶ v Informal deliberately set
(a building) on fire.

tore n past tense of TEAR².

toreador [torr-ee-a-dor] n
bullfighter.

torment v cause (someone) great
suffering; tease cruelly. ▶ n great
suffering; source of suffering.
tormentor n

torn v past participle of TEAR².

tornado n, pl **-dos, -does.** violent
whirlwind.

torpedo n, pl **-does.** self-propelled

underwater missile. ▶ v **-doing,**
-doed. attack or destroy with or
as if with torpedoes.

torpid adj sluggish and inactive.
torpor n torpid state.

torque [tork] n force causing
rotation; Celtic necklace or
armband of twisted metal.

torrent n rushing stream; rapid
flow of questions, abuse, etc.
torrential adj (of rain) very heavy.

torrid adj very hot and dry; highly
emotional.

torsion n twisting of a part by
equal forces being applied at both
ends but in opposite directions.

torso n, pl **-sos.** trunk of the
human body; statue of a nude
human trunk.

tort n Law civil wrong or injury for
which damages may be claimed.

tortilla n thin Mexican pancake.

tortoise n slow-moving land
reptile with a dome-shaped shell.
tortoiseshell n mottled brown
shell of a turtle, used for making
ornaments. ▶ adj having brown,
orange, and black markings.

tortuous adj winding or twisting;
not straightforward.

torture v cause (someone) severe
pain or mental anguish. ▶ n severe
physical or mental pain; torturing.
torturer n

Tory n, pl **Tories.** member of the
Conservative Party in Great Britain
or Canada. ▶ adj of Tories.
Toryism n

toss v throw lightly; fling or be
flung about; coat (food) by gentle
stirring or mixing; (of a horse)
throw (its rider); throw up (a coin)
to decide between alternatives by
guessing which side will land
uppermost. ▶ n tossing. **toss up** v
toss a coin. **toss-up** n even
chance or risk.

tot¹ n small child; small drink of

spirits.

tot² v **totting, totted. tot up** add (numbers) together.

total n whole, esp. a sum of parts. ▶ adj complete; of or being a total. ▶ v **-talling, -talled.** amount to; add up. **totally** adv **totality** n

totalitarian adj of a dictatorial one-party government. **totalitarianism** n

tote¹ v carry (a gun etc.).

tote² n short for TOTALIZATOR.

totem n tribal badge or emblem. **totem pole** post carved or painted with totems by Native Americans.

totter v move unsteadily; be about to fall.

toucan n tropical American bird with a large bill.

touch v come into contact with; tap, feel, or stroke; affect; move emotionally; eat or drink; equal or match; Brit, Aust & NZ slang ask for money. ▶ n sense by which an object's qualities are perceived when they come into contact with part of the body; gentle tap, push, or caress; small amount; characteristic style; detail. ▶ adj of a non-contact version of particular sport, e.g. touch rugby. **touch and go** risky or critical. **touched** adj emotionally moved; slightly mad. **touching** adj emotionally moving. **touchy** adj easily offended. **touch down** v (of an aircraft) land. **touchline** n side line of the pitch in some games. **touch-on** v refer to in passing. **touch-type** v type without looking at the keyboard.

touché [too-shay] interj acknowledgment of the striking home of a remark or witty reply.

touchstone n standard by which a judgment is made.

tough adj strong or resilient; difficult to chew or cut; firm and determined; rough and violent; difficult; Informal unlucky or unfair. ▶ n Informal rough violent person. **toughness** n **toughen** v make or become tough or toughened.

toupee [too-pay] n small wig.

tour n journey visiting places of interest along the way; trip to perform or play in different places. ▶ v make a tour (of). **tourism** n tourist travel as an industry. **tourist** n person travelling for pleasure. **touristy** adj Informal full of tourists or tourist attractions.

tour de force n, pl **tours de force.** French brilliant stroke or achievement.

tournament n sporting competition with several stages to decide the overall winner; Hist contest between knights on horseback.

tourniquet [tour-nick-kay] n something twisted round a limb to stop bleeding.

tousled adj ruffled and untidy.

tout [rhymes with **shout**] v seek business in a persistent manner; recommend (a person or thing). ▶ n person who sells tickets for a popular event at inflated prices.

tow¹ v drag, esp. by means of a rope. ▶ n towing. **in tow** following closely behind. **on tow** being towed. **towbar** n metal bar on a car for towing vehicles. **towpath** n path beside a canal or river, originally for horses towing boats.

tow² n fibre of hemp or flax.

towards, toward prep in the direction of; with regard to; as a contribution to.

towel n cloth for drying things. **towelling** n material used for making towels.

tower n tall structure, often forming part of a larger building.

tower of strength person who supports or comforts. **tower over** v be much taller than.

town n group of buildings larger than a village; central part of this; people of a town. **township** n small town; (in S Africa) urban settlement of Black or Coloured people. **town hall** large building used for council meetings, concerts, etc.

toxaemia [tox-seem-ya] n blood poisoning; high blood pressure in pregnancy.

toxic adj poisonous; caused by poison. **toxicity** n **toxicology** n study of poisons. **toxin** n poison of bacterial origin.

toy n something designed to be played with. ▶ adj (of a dog) of a variety much smaller than is normal for that breed. **toy with** v play or fiddle with.

toy-toy S Afr ▶ n dance of political protest. ▶ v perform this dance.

trace v track down and find; follow the course of; copy exactly by drawing on a thin sheet of transparent paper set on top of the original. ▶ n track left by something; minute quantity; indication. **traceable** adj **tracer** n projectile which leaves a visible trail. **tracery** n pattern of interlacing lines. **tracing** n traced copy. **trace element** chemical element occurring in very small amounts in soil etc.

traces pl n strap by which a horse pulls a vehicle. **kick over the traces** escape or defy control.

trachea [track-kee-a] n, pl **tracheae**. windpipe. **tracheotomy** [track-ee-ot-a-mee] n surgical incision into the trachea.

track n rough road or path; mark or trail left by the passage of anything; railway line; course for racing; separate section on a record, tape, or CD; course of action or thought; endless band round the wheels of a tank, bulldozer, etc. ▶ v follow the trail or path of. **track down** v hunt for and find. **track event** athletic sport held on a running track.

track record past accomplishments of a person or organization. **tracksuit** n warm loose-fitting suit worn by athletes etc., esp. during training.

tract[1] n wide area; Anat system of organs with a particular function.

tract[2] n pamphlet, esp. a religious one.

tractable adj easy to manage or control.

traction n pulling, esp. by engine power; Med application of a steady pull on an injured limb by weights and pulleys; grip of the wheels of a vehicle on the ground. **traction engine** old-fashioned steam-powered vehicle for pulling heavy loads.

tractor n motor vehicle with large rear wheels for pulling farm machinery.

trade n buying, selling, or exchange of goods; person's job or craft; (people engaged in) a particular industry or business. ▶ v buy and sell; exchange; engage in trade. **trader** n **trading** n **trade-in** n used article given in part payment for a new one. **trademark** n (legally registered) name or symbol used by a firm to distinguish its goods. **trade-off** n exchange made as a compromise. **tradesman** n skilled worker; shopkeeper. **trade union** society of workers formed to protect their interests. **trade wind** wind blowing steadily towards the equator.

tradition n body of beliefs, customs, etc. handed down from generation to generation; custom or practice of long standing. **traditional** adj **traditionally** adv

traduce v slander.

traffic n vehicles coming and going on a road; (illicit) trade. ▶ v **-ficking, -ficked.** trade, usu. illicitly. **trafficker** n **traffic lights** set of coloured lights at a junction to control the traffic flow. **traffic warden** Brit person employed to control the movement and parking of traffic.

tragedy n, pl **-dies.** shocking or sad event; serious play, film, etc. in which the hero is destroyed by a personal failing in adverse circumstances. **tragedian** [traj-**jee**-dee-an], **tragedienne** [traj-jee-dee-**enn**] n person who acts in or writes tragedies. **tragic** adj of or like a tragedy. **tragically** adv **tragicomedy** n play with both tragic and comic elements.

trail n path, track, or road; tracks left by a person, animal, or object. ▶ v drag along the ground; lag behind; follow the tracks of.

trailer n vehicle designed to be towed by another vehicle; extract from a film or programme used to advertise it.

train v instruct in a skill; learn the skills needed to do a particular job or activity; prepare for a sports event etc.; aim (a gun etc.); cause (an animal) to perform or (a plant) to grow in a particular way. ▶ n line of railway coaches or wagons drawn by an engine; sequence or series; long trailing back section of a dress. **trainer** n person who trains an athlete or sportsman; sports shoe. **trainee** n person being trained.

traipse v Informal walk wearily.

trait n characteristic feature.

traitor n person guilty of treason or treachery. **traitorous** adj

trajectory n, pl **-ries.** line of flight, esp. of a projectile.

tram n public transport vehicle powered by an overhead wire and running on rails laid in the road. **tramlines** pl n track for trams.

tramp v travel on foot, hike; walk heavily. ▶ n homeless person who travels on foot; hike; sound of tramping; cargo ship available for hire; US, Aust & NZ slang promiscuous woman.

trample v tread on and crush.

trampoline n tough canvas sheet attached to a frame by springs, used by acrobats etc. ▶ v bounce on a trampoline.

trance n unconscious or dazed state.

tranche n portion of something large, esp. a sum of money.

tranquil adj calm and quiet. **tranquilly** adv **tranquillity** n

tranquillize v make calm. **tranquillizer** n drug which reduces anxiety or tension.

trans- prefix across, through, or beyond.

transact v conduct or negotiate (a business deal).

transaction n business deal transacted.

transatlantic adj on, from, or to the other side of the Atlantic.

transceiver n transmitter and receiver of radio or electronic signals.

transcend v rise above; be superior to. **transcendence** n **transcendent** adj **transcendental** adj based on intuition rather than experience; supernatural or mystical. **transcendentalism** n

transcribe v write down (something said); record for a

later broadcast; arrange (music) for a different instrument.
transcript n copy.
transducer n device that converts one form of energy to another.
transept n either of the two shorter wings of a cross-shaped church.
transfer v -ferring, -ferred. move or send from one person or place to another. ▶ n transferring; design which can be transferred from one surface to another. **transferable** adj **transference** n transferring.
transfer station NZ depot where rubbish is sorted for recycling.
transfigure v change in appearance. **transfiguration** n
transfix v astound or stun; pierce through.
transform v change the shape or character of. **transformation** n
transformer n device for changing the voltage of an alternating current.
transfusion n injection of blood into the blood vessels of a patient. **transfuse** v give a transfusion to; permeate or infuse.
transgress v break (a moral law). **transgression** n **transgressor** n
transient adj lasting only for a short time. **transience** n
transistor n semiconducting device used to amplify electric currents; portable radio using transistors.
transit n movement from one place to another. **transition** n change from one state to another. **transitional** adj **transitive** adj Grammar (of a verb) requiring a direct object. **transitory** adj not lasting long.
translate v turn from one language into another. **translation** n **translator** n
transliterate v convert to the

letters of a different alphabet. **transliteration** n
translucent adj letting light pass through, but not transparent. **translucency, translucence** n
transmigrate v (of a soul) pass into another body. **transmigration** n
transmit v -mitting, -mitted. pass (something) from one person or place to another; send out (signals) by radio waves; broadcast (a radio or television programme). **transmission** n transmitting; shafts and gears through which power passes from a vehicle's engine to its wheels. **transmittable** adj **transmitter** n
transmogrify v -fying, -fied. Informal change completely.
transmute v change the form or nature of. **transmutation** n
transom n horizontal bar across a window; bar separating a door from the window over it.
transparent adj able to be seen through, clear; easily understood or recognized. **transparently** adv **transparency** n transparent quality; colour photograph on transparent film that can be viewed by means of a projector.
transpire v become known; Informal happen; give off water vapour through pores. **transpiration** n
transplant v transfer (an organ or tissue) surgically from one part or body to another; remove and replace (a plant) to another place. ▶ n surgical transplanting; thing transplanted. **transplantation** n
transport v convey from one place to another; Hist exile (a criminal) to a penal colony; enrapture. ▶ n business or system of transporting; vehicle used in transport; ecstasy or rapture. **transportation** n

transporter n large goods vehicle.

transpose v interchange two things; put (music) into a different key. **transposition** n

transsexual, transexual n person of one sex who believes his or her true identity is of the opposite sex.

transubstantiation n Christianity doctrine that the bread and wine consecrated in Communion changes into the substance of Christ's body and blood.

transuranic [tranz-yoor-**ran**-ik] adj (of an element) having an atomic number greater than that of uranium.

transverse adj crossing from side to side.

transvestite n person who seeks sexual pleasure by wearing the clothes of the opposite sex. **transvestism** n

trap n device for catching animals; plan for tricking or catching a person; bend in a pipe containing liquid to prevent the escape of gas; stall in which greyhounds are enclosed before a race; two-wheeled carriage; Brit, Aust & NZ slang mouth. ▶ v **trapping, trapped.** catch; trick. **trapper** n person who traps animals for their fur. **trapdoor** n door in floor or roof.

trapeze n horizontal bar suspended from two ropes, used by circus acrobats.

trapezium n, pl **-ziums, -zia.** quadrilateral with two parallel sides of unequal length. **trapezoid** [trap-**piz**-zoid] n quadrilateral with no sides parallel; Chiefly US trapezium.

trappings pl n accessories that symbolize an office or position.

Trappist n member of an order of Christian monks who observe strict silence.

trash n anything worthless; US & Afr rubbish. **trashy** adj

trauma [**traw**-ma] n emotional shock; injury or wound. **traumatic** adj **traumatize** v

travail n Lit labour or toil.

travel v **-elling, -elled.** go from one place to another, through an area, or for a specified distance. ▶ n travelling, esp. as a tourist. ▶ pl (account of) travelling. **traveller** n **travelogue** n film or talk about someone's travels.

traverse v move over or back and forth over.

travesty n, pl **-ties.** grotesque imitation or mockery.

trawl n net dragged at deep levels behind a fishing boat. ▶ v fish with such a net.

trawler n trawling boat.

tray n flat board, usu. with a rim, for carrying things; open receptacle for office correspondence.

treachery n, pl **-eries.** wilful betrayal. **treacherous** adj disloyal; unreliable or dangerous. **treacherously** adv

treacle n thick dark syrup produced when sugar is refined. **treacly** adj

tread v **treading, trod, trodden** or **trod.** set one's foot on; crush by walking on. ▶ n way of walking or dancing; upper surface of a step; part of a tyre or shoe that touches the ground. **treadmill** n Hist cylinder turned by treading on steps projecting from it; dreary routine.

treadle [**tred**-dl] n lever worked by the foot to turn a wheel.

treason n betrayal of one's sovereign or country; treachery or disloyalty. **treasonable** adj

treasure n collection of wealth, esp. gold or jewels; valued person or thing. ▶ v prize or cherish.

treasury n storage place for treasure; (**T-**) government department in charge of finance.

treasure-trove n treasure found with no evidence of ownership.

treasurer n official in charge of funds.

treat v deal with or regard in a certain manner; give medical treatment to; subject to a chemical or industrial process; provide (someone) with (something) as a treat. ▶ n pleasure, entertainment, etc. given or paid for by someone else.

treatment n medical care; way of treating a person or thing.

treatise [treat-izz] n formal piece of writing on a particular subject.

treaty n, pl **-ties.** signed contract between states.

treble adj triple; Music high-pitched. ▶ n (singer with or part for) a soprano voice. ▶ v increase three times. **trebly** adv

tree n large perennial plant with a woody trunk. **treeless** adj **tree surgery** repair of damaged trees. **tree surgeon**

trefoil [tref-foil] n plant, such as clover, with a three-lobed leaf; carved ornament like this.

trek n long difficult journey, esp. on foot; S Afr migration by ox wagon. ▶ v **trekking, trekked.** make such a journey.

trellis n framework of horizontal and vertical strips of wood.

tremble v shake or quiver; feel fear or anxiety. ▶ n trembling. **trembling** adj

tremendous adj huge; Informal great in quality or amount. **tremendously** adv

tremolo n, pl **-los.** Music quivering effect in singing or playing.

tremor n involuntary shaking;

minor earthquake.

tremulous adj trembling, as from fear or excitement.

trench n long narrow ditch, esp. one used as a shelter in war. **trench coat** double-breasted waterproof coat.

trenchant adj incisive; effective.

trencher n Hist wooden plate for serving food. **trencherman** n hearty eater.

trend n general tendency or direction; fashion. **trendy** adj, n Informal consciously fashionable (person). **trendiness** n

trepidation n fear or anxiety.

trespass v go onto another's property without permission. ▶ n trespassing; Old-fashioned sin or wrongdoing. **trespasser** n **trespass on** v take unfair advantage of (someone's friendship, patience, etc.).

tresses pl n long flowing hair.

trestle n board fixed on pairs of spreading legs, used as a support.

trevally n, pl **-lies.** Aust & NZ any of various food and game fishes.

trews pl n close-fitting tartan trousers.

tri- combining form three.

triad n group of three; (**T-**) Chinese criminal secret society.

trial n Law investigation of a case before a judge; trying or testing; thing or person straining endurance or patience. ▶ pl sporting competition for individuals.

triangle n geometric figure with three sides; triangular percussion instrument; situation involving three people. **triangular** adj

tribe n group of clans or families believed to have a common ancestor. **tribal** adj **tribalism** n loyalty to a tribe.

tribulation n great distress.

tribunal n board appointed to inquire into a specific matter; lawcourt.

tribune n people's representative, esp. in ancient Rome.

tributary n, pl **-taries**. stream or river flowing into a larger one. ▸ adj (of a stream or river) flowing into a larger one.

tribute n sign of respect or admiration; tax paid by one state to another.

trice n **in a trice** instantly.

triceps n muscle at the back of the upper arm.

trichology [trick-ol-a-jee] n study and treatment of hair and its diseases. **trichologist** n

trick n deceitful or cunning action or plan; joke or prank; feat of skill or cunning; mannerism; cards played in one round. ▸ v cheat or deceive. **trickery** n **trickster** n

tricky adj difficult, needing careful handling; crafty.

trickle v (cause to) flow in a thin stream or drops; move gradually. ▸ n gradual flow.

tricolour [trick-kol-lor] n three-coloured striped flag.

tricycle n three-wheeled cycle.

trident n three-pronged spear.

triennial adj happening every three years.

trifle n insignificant thing or amount; dessert of sponge cake, fruit, custard, and cream. **trifling** adj insignificant. **trifle with** v toy with.

trigger n small lever releasing a catch on a gun or machine; action that sets off a course of events. ▸ v (usu. foll. by off) set (an action or process) in motion.

trigger-happy adj too quick to use guns.

trigonometry n branch of mathematics dealing with relations of the sides and angles of triangles.

trike n Informal tricycle.

trilateral adj having three sides.

trilby n, pl **-bies**. man's soft felt hat.

trill n Music rapid alternation between two notes; shrill warbling sound made by some birds. ▸ v play or sing a trill.

trillion n one million million, 10^{12}; (formerly) one million million, 10^{18}.

trilobite [trile-oh-bite] n small prehistoric animal.

trilogy n, pl **-gies**. series of three related books, plays, etc.

trim adj trimmer, trimmest. neat and smart; slender. ▸ v trimming, trimmed. cut or prune into good shape; decorate with lace, ribbons, etc.; adjust the balance of (a ship or aircraft) by shifting the cargo etc. ▸ n decoration; upholstery and decorative facings in a car; trim state; haircut that neatens the existing style.

trimming n decoration. ▸ pl usual accompaniments.

trimaran [trime-a-ran] n three-hulled boat.

trinitrotoluene n full name for TNT.

trinity n, pl **-ties**. group of three; (**T-**) Christianity union of three persons, Father, Son, and Holy Spirit, in one God.

trinket n small or worthless ornament or piece of jewellery.

trio n, pl **trios**. group of three; piece of music for three performers.

trip n journey to a place and back, esp. for pleasure; stumble; Informal hallucinogenic drug experience; switch on a mechanism. ▸ v tripping, tripped. (cause to) stumble; (often foll. by up) catch (someone) in a mistake; move or tread lightly; Informal experience the hallucinogenic effects of a drug. **tripper** n tourist.

tripe n stomach of a cow used as food; Brit, Aust & NZ informal nonsense.

triple adj having three parts; three times as great or as many. ▶ v increase three times. **triplet** n one of three babies born at one birth. **triple jump** athletic event in which competitors make a hop, a step, and a jump as a continuous movement.

triplicate [tripe-pod] triple. **in triplicate** in three copies.

tripod [tripe-pod] n three-legged stand, stool, etc.

tripos [tripe-poss] n final examinations for an honours degree at Cambridge University.

triptych [trip-tick] n painting or carving on three hinged panels, often forming an altarpiece.

trite adj (of a remark or idea) commonplace and unoriginal.

tritium n radioactive isotope of hydrogen.

triumph n (happiness caused by) victory or success. ▶ v be victorious or successful; rejoice over a victory. **triumphal** adj celebrating a triumph. **triumphant** adj feeling or showing triumph.

triumvirate [try-umm-vir-rit] n group of three people in joint control.

trivet [triv-vit] n metal stand for a pot or kettle.

trivial adj of little importance. **trivially** adv **trivia** pl n trivial things or details. **triviality** n **trivialize** v make (something) seem less important or complex than it is.

trod v past tense and a past participle of TREAD.

trodden v a past participle of TREAD.

troglodyte n cave dweller.

troika n Russian vehicle drawn by three horses abreast; group of three people in authority.

troll n giant or dwarf in Scandinavian folklore.

trolley n small wheeled table for food and drink; wheeled cart for moving goods. **trolley bus** bus powered by electricity from an overhead wire but not running on rails.

trollop n Old-fashioned promiscuous or slovenly woman.

trombone n brass musical instrument with a sliding tube. **trombonist** n

troop n large group; artillery or cavalry unit; Scout company. ▶ pl soldiers. ▶ v move in a crowd. **trooper** n cavalry soldier.

trope n figure of speech.

trophy n, pl **-phies**. cup, shield, etc. given as a prize; memento of success.

tropic n either of two lines of latitude at 23½°N (**tropic of Cancer**) or 23½°S (**tropic of Capricorn**). ▶ pl part of the earth's surface between these lines. **tropical** adj of or in the tropics; (of climate) very hot.

trot v **trotting, trotted.** (of a horse) move at a medium pace, lifting the feet in diagonal pairs; (of a person) move at a steady brisk pace. ▶ n trotting. **trotter** n pig's foot. **trot out** v repeat (old ideas etc.) without fresh thought.

troth [rhymes with **growth**] n Obs pledge of devotion, esp. a betrothal.

troubadour [troo-bad-oor] n medieval travelling poet and singer.

trouble n (cause of) distress or anxiety; disease or malfunctioning; state of disorder or unrest; care or effort. ▶ v (cause to) worry; exert oneself; cause inconvenience to. **troubled** adj **troublesome** adj

troubleshooter n person employed to locate and deal with faults or problems.

trough [troff] n long open container, esp. for animals' food or water; narrow channel between two waves or ridges; Meteorol area of low pressure.

trounce v defeat utterly.

troupe [troop] n company of performers. **trouper** n

trousers pl n two-legged outer garment with legs reaching usu. to the ankles. **trouser** adj of trousers.

trousseau [troo-so] n, pl **-seaux, -seaus.** bride's collection of clothing etc. for her marriage.

trout n game fish related to the salmon.

trowel n hand tool with a wide blade for spreading mortar, lifting plants, etc.

troy weight, troy n system of weights used for gold, silver, and jewels.

truant n pupil who stays away from school without permission. **play truant** stay away from school without permission. **truancy** n

truce n temporary agreement to stop fighting.

truck¹ n railway goods wagon; large vehicle for transporting loads by road. **trucker** n truck driver.

truck² n **have no truck with** refuse to be involved with.

truculent [truck-yew-lent] adj aggressively defiant. **truculence** n

trudge v walk heavily or wearily. ▶ n long tiring walk.

true adj **truer, truest.** in accordance with facts; genuine; faithful; exact. **truly** adv **truism** n self-evident truth. **truth** n state of

being true; something true. **truthful** adj honest; exact. **truthfully** adv

truffle n edible underground fungus; sweet flavoured with chocolate.

trug n Brit long shallow basket used by gardeners.

trump¹ n, adj (card) of the suit outranking the others. ▶ v play a trump card on (another card). ▶ pl n suit outranking the others. **turn up trumps** achieve an unexpected success. **trumped up** invented or concocted.

trump² n Lit (sound of) a trumpet.

trumpet n valved brass instrument with a flared tube. ▶ v **-peting, -peted.** proclaim loudly; (of an elephant) cry loudly. **trumpeter** n

truncate v cut short.

truncheon n club carried by a policeman.

trundle v move heavily on wheels.

trunk n main stem of a tree; large case or box for clothes etc.; person's body excluding the head and limbs; elephant's long nose; US car boot. ▶ pl man's swimming shorts. **trunk call** Chiefly Brit long-distance telephone call. **trunk road** main road.

truss v tie or bind up. ▶ n device for holding a hernia in place; framework supporting a roof, bridge, etc.

trust v believe in and rely on; consign to someone's care; expect or hope. ▶ n confidence in the truth, reliability, etc. of a person or thing; obligation arising from responsibility; arrangement in which one person administers property, money, etc. on another's behalf; property held for another; Brit self-governing hospital or group of hospitals within the National Health Service;

group of companies joined to control a market. **trustee** n person holding property on another's behalf. **trustful, trusting** adj inclined to trust others. **trustworthy** adj reliable or honest. **trusty** adj faithful or reliable.

truth n see TRUE.

try v **trying, tried.** make an effort or attempt; test or sample; put strain on, e.g. *he tries my patience*; investigate (a case); examine (a person) in a lawcourt. ▶ n, pl **tries.** attempt or effort; *Rugby* score gained by touching the ball down over the opponent's goal line. **try it on** *Informal* try to deceive or fool someone. **trying** adj *Informal* difficult or annoying.

tryst n arrangement to meet.

tsar, czar [zahr] n *Hist* Russian emperor.

tsetse fly [tset-see] n bloodsucking African fly whose bite transmits disease, esp. sleeping sickness.

T-shirt n short-sleeved casual shirt or top.

tsp. teaspoon.

T-square n T-shaped ruler.

tsunami n, pl **-mis, -mi.** tidal wave, usu. caused by an earthquake under the sea.

TT teetotal.

tuatara n large lizard-like New Zealand reptile.

tub n open, usu. round container; bath. **tubby** adj (of a person) short and fat.

tuba [tube-a] n valved low-pitched brass instrument.

tube n hollow cylinder; flexible cylinder with a cap to hold pastes. **the tube** underground railway, esp. the one in London. **tubing** n length of tube; system of tubes. **tubular [tube-yew-lar]** adj of or

shaped like a tube.

tuber [tube-er] n fleshy underground root of a plant such as a potato. **tuberous** adj

tubercle [tube-er-kl] n small rounded swelling.

tuberculosis [tube-berk-yew-lohss-iss] n infectious disease causing tubercles, esp. in the lungs. **tubercular** adj **tuberculin** n extract from a bacillus used to test for tuberculosis.

TUC (in Britain and S Africa) Trades Union Congress.

tuck v push or fold into a small space; stitch in folds. ▶ n stitched fold; *Brit informal* food. **tuck away** v eat (a large amount of food).

tucker n *Aust & NZ informal* food.

Tudor adj of the English royal house ruling from 1485–1603.

Tuesday n third day of the week.

tufa [tew-fa] n porous rock formed as a deposit from springs.

tuffet n small mound or seat.

tuft n bunch of feathers, grass, hair, etc. held or growing together at the base.

tug v **tugging, tugged.** pull hard. ▶ n hard pull; (also **tugboat**) small ship used to tow other vessels. **tug of war** contest in which two teams pull against one another on a rope.

tuition n instruction, esp. received individually or in a small group.

tulip n plant with bright cup-shaped flowers.

tulle [tewl] n fine net fabric of silk etc.

tumble v (cause to) fall, esp. awkwardly or violently; roll or twist, esp. in play; rumple. ▶ n fall; somersault. **tumbler** n stemless drinking glass; acrobat; spring catch in a lock. **tumbledown** adj dilapidated. **tumble dryer, drier**

machine that dries laundry by rotating it in warm air. **tumble to** v Informal realize, understand.

tumbril, tumbrel n farm cart used during the French Revolution to take prisoners to the guillotine.

tumescent [tew-**mess**-ent] adj swollen or becoming swollen.

tummy n, pl **-mies.** Informal stomach.

tumour [**tew**-mer] n abnormal growth in or on the body.

tumult n uproar or commotion. **tumultuous** [tew-mull-tew-uss] adj

tumulus n, pl **-li.** burial mound.

tun n large beer cask.

tuna n large marine food fish.

tundra n vast treeless Arctic region with permanently frozen subsoil.

tune n (pleasing) sequence of musical notes; correct musical pitch, e.g. she sang out of tune. ▶ v adjust (a musical instrument) so that it is in tune; adjust (a machine) to obtain the desired performance. **tuneful** adj **tunefully** adv **tuneless** adj **tuner** n **tune in** v adjust (a radio or television) to receive (a station or programme).

tungsten n Chem greyish-white metal.

tunic n close-fitting jacket forming part of some uniforms; loose knee-length garment.

tunnel n underground passage. ▶ v **-nelling, -nelled.** make a tunnel (through).

tunny n, pl **-nies, -ny.** same as TUNA.

tup n male sheep.

turban n Muslim, Hindu, or Sikh man's head covering, made by winding cloth round the head.

turbid adj muddy, not clear.

turbine n machine or generator driven by gas, water, etc. turning blades.

turbot n large European edible

flatfish.

turbulence n confusion, movement, or agitation; atmospheric instability causing gusty air currents. **turbulent** adj

tureen n serving dish for soup.

turf n, pl **turfs, turves.** short thick even grass; square of this with roots and soil attached. ▶ v cover with turf. **the turf** racecourse; horse racing. **turf accountant** bookmaker. **turf out** v Informal throw out.

turgid [**tur**-jid] adj (of language) pompous; swollen and thick.

turkey n large bird bred for food.

Turkish adj of Turkey, its people, or their language. ▶ n Turkish language. **Turkish bath** steam bath. **Turkish delight** jelly-like sweet coated with icing sugar.

turmeric n yellow spice obtained from the root of an Asian plant.

turmoil n agitation or confusion.

turn v change the position or direction (of); move around an axis, rotate; (usu. foll. by into) change in nature or character; reach or pass in age, time, etc., e.g. she has just turned twenty; shape on a lathe; become sour. ▶ n turning; opportunity to do something as part of an agreed succession; direction or drift; period or spell; short theatrical performance. **good, bad turn** helpful or unhelpful act. **turner** n **turning** n road or path leading off a main route. **turncoat** n person who deserts one party or cause to join another. **turn down** v reduce the volume or brightness (of); refuse or reject. **turn in** v go to bed; hand in. **turning point** moment when a decisive change occurs. **turn off** v stop (something) working by using a knob etc. **turn on** v start (something) working by using a knob etc.; become aggressive towards; *Informal* excite, esp. sexually. **turnout** *n* number of people appearing at a gathering. **turnover** *n* total sales made by a business over a certain period; small pastry; rate at which staff leave and are replaced. **turnpike** *n Brit* road where a toll is collected at barriers. **turnstile** *n* revolving gate for admitting one person at a time. **turntable** *n* revolving platform. **turn up** *v* arrive or appear; find or be found; increase the volume or brightness (of). **turn-up** *n* turned-up fold at the bottom of a trouser leg; *Informal* unexpected event.

turnip *n* root vegetable with orange or white flesh.

turpentine *n* (oil made from) the resin of certain trees. **turps** *n* turpentine oil.

turpitude *n* wickedness.

turquoise *adj* blue-green. ▶ *n* blue-green precious stone.

turret *n* small tower; revolving gun tower on a warship or tank.

turtle *n* sea tortoise. **turn turtle** capsize. **turtledove** *n* small wild dove. **turtleneck** *n* (sweater with) a round high close-fitting neck.

tusk *n* long pointed tooth of an elephant, walrus, etc.

tussle *n, v* fight or scuffle.

tussock *n* tuft of grass.

tutelage [tew-till-lij] *n* instruction or guidance, esp. by a tutor; state of being instructed by a guardian or tutor. **tutelary** [tew-till-lar-ee] *adj*

tutor *n* person teaching individuals or small groups. ▶ *v* act as a tutor to. **tutorial** *n* period of instruction with a tutor.

tutu *n* short stiff skirt worn by ballerinas.

tuxedo *n, pl* -**dos.** *US & Aust* dinner jacket.

TV television.

twaddle *n* silly or pretentious talk or writing.

twain *n Obs* two.

twang *n* sharp ringing sound; nasal speech. ▶ *v* (cause to) make a twang.

tweak *v* pinch or twist sharply. ▶ *n* tweaking.

twee *adj Informal* too sentimental, sweet, or pretty.

tweed *n* thick woollen cloth. ▶ *pl* suit of tweed. **tweedy** *adj*

tweet *n, v* chirp.

tweeter *n* loudspeaker reproducing high-frequency sounds.

tweezers *pl n* small pincer-like tool.

twelve *adj, n* two more than ten. **twelfth** *adj, n* (of) number twelve in a series.

twenty *adj, n* two times ten. **twentieth** *adj, n*

twenty-four-seven, 24/7 *adv Informal* all the time.

twerp *n Informal* silly person.

twice *adv* two times.

twiddle *v* fiddle or twirl in an idle way. **twiddle one's thumbs** be bored, have nothing to do.

twig[1] *n* small branch or shoot.

twig[2] *v* **twigging, twigged.** *Informal* realize or understand.

twilight *n* soft dim light just after sunset.

twill *n* fabric woven to produce parallel ridges.

twin *n* one of a pair, esp. of two children born at one birth. ▶ *v* **twinning, twinned.** pair or be paired.

twine *n* string or cord. ▶ *v* twist or coil round.

twinge *n* sudden sharp pain or emotional pang.

twinkle *v* shine brightly but

intermittently. ▸ n flickering brightness.

twirl v turn or spin around quickly; twist or wind, esp. idly.

twist v turn out of the natural position; distort or pervert; wind or twine. ▸ n twisting; twisted thing; unexpected development in the plot of a film, book, etc.; bend or curve; distortion. **twisted** adj (of a person) cruel or perverted. **twister** n Brit informal swindler.

twit[1] v **twitting, twitted.** poke fun at (someone).

twit[2] n Informal foolish person.

twitch v move spasmodically; pull sharply. ▸ n nervous muscular spasm; sharp pull.

twitter v (of birds) utter chirping sounds. ▸ n act or sound of twittering.

two adj, n one more than one. **two-edged** adj (of a remark) having both a favourable and an unfavourable interpretation. **two-faced** adj deceitful, hypocritical. **two-time** v Informal deceive (a lover) by having an affair with someone else.

tycoon n powerful wealthy businessman.

tyke n Brit, Aust & NZ informal small cheeky child.

type n class or category; Informal person, esp. of a specified kind; block with a raised character used for printing; printed text. ▸ v print with a typewriter or word processor; typify; classify. **typist** n person who types with a typewriter or word processor. **typecast** v continually cast (an actor or actress) in similar roles. **typewriter** n machine which prints a character when the appropriate key is pressed.

typhoid fever n acute infectious feverish disease.

typhoon n violent tropical storm.

typhus n infectious feverish disease.

typical adj true to type, characteristic. **typically** adv

typify v **-fying, -fied.** be typical of.

typography n art or style of printing. **typographical** adj **typographer** n

tyrannosaurus [tirr-ran-oh-**sore**-uss] n large two-footed flesh-eating dinosaur.

tyrant n oppressive or cruel ruler; person who exercises authority oppressively. **tyrannical** adj like a tyrant, oppressive. **tyrannize** v exert power (over) oppressively or cruelly. **tyrannous** adj **tyranny** n tyrannical rule.

tyre n rubber ring, usu. inflated, over the rim of a vehicle's wheel to grip the road.

tyro n, pl **-ros.** novice or beginner.

U u

ubiquitous [yew-**bik**-wit-uss] adj being or seeming to be everywhere at once. **ubiquity** n

udder n large baglike milk-producing gland of cows, sheep, or goats.

UFO unidentified flying object.

ugly adj **uglier, ugliest.** of unpleasant appearance; ominous or menacing. **ugliness** n

UHF ultrahigh frequency.

UHT (of milk or cream) ultra-heat-treated.

UK United Kingdom.

ukulele, ukelele [yew-kal-**lay**-lee] n small guitar with four strings.

ulcer n open sore on the surface of the skin or mucous membrane. **ulcerated** adj made or becoming ulcerous. **ulceration** n **ulcerous**

adj of, like, or characterized by ulcers.

ulna *n, pl* **-nae, -nas.** inner and longer of the two bones of the human forearm.

ulterior *adj* (of an aim, reason, etc.) concealed or hidden.

ultimate *adj* final in a series or process; highest or supreme. **ultimately** *adv*

ultimatum [ult-im-**may**-tuhm] *n* final warning stating that action will be taken unless certain conditions are met.

ultra- *prefix* beyond a specified extent, range, or limit, e.g. *ultrasonic*; extremely, e.g. *ultramodern.*

ultrahigh frequency *n* radio frequency between 3000 and 300 megahertz.

ultramarine *adj* vivid blue.

ultrasonic *adj* of or producing sound waves with a higher frequency than the human ear can hear.

ultraviolet *adj, n* (of) light beyond the limit of visibility at the violet end of the spectrum.

ululate [**yewl**-yew-late] *v* howl or wail. **ululation** *n*

umber *adj* dark brown to reddish-brown.

umbilical *adj* of the navel.

umbilical cord long flexible tube of blood vessels that connects a fetus with the placenta.

umbrage *n* **take umbrage** feel offended or upset.

umbrella *n* portable device used for protection against rain, consisting of a folding frame covered in material attached to a central rod; single organization, idea, etc. that contains or covers many different organizations, ideas, etc.

umpire *n* official who rules on the playing of a game. ▸ *v* act as umpire in (a game).

umpteen *adj Informal* very many. **umpteenth** *n, adj*

UN United Nations.

un- *prefix* not, e.g. *unidentified*; denoting reversal of an action, e.g. *untie*; denoting removal from, e.g. *unthrone.*

unable *adj* **unable to** lacking the necessary power, ability, or authority to (do something).

unaccountable *adj* unable to be explained; (foll. by *to*) not answerable to. **unaccountably** *adv*

unadulterated *adj* with nothing added, pure.

unanimous [yew-**nan**-im-uss] *adj* in complete agreement; agreed by all. **unanimity** *n*

unarmed *adj* without weapons.

unassuming *adj* modest or unpretentious.

unaware *adj* not aware or conscious. **unawares** *adv* by surprise, e.g. *caught unawares*; without knowing.

unbalanced *adj* biased or one-sided; mentally deranged.

unbearable *adj* not able to be endured. **unbearably** *adv*

unbeknown *adv* **unbeknown to** without the knowledge of (a person).

unbend *v Informal* become more strict or more informal in one's attitudes or behaviour. **unbending** *adj*

unbidden *adj* not ordered or asked.

unborn *adj* not yet born.

unbosom *v* relieve (oneself) of (secrets or feelings) by telling someone.

unbridled *adj* (of feelings or behaviour) not controlled in any way.

unburden *v* relieve (one's mind or oneself) of a worry by confiding in someone.

uncalled-for adj not fair or justified.

uncanny adj weird or mysterious. **uncannily** adv

unceremonious adj relaxed and informal; abrupt or rude. **unceremoniously** adv

uncertain adj not able to be accurately known or predicted; not able to be depended upon; changeable. **uncertainty** n

un-Christian adj not in accordance with Christian principles.

uncle n brother of one's father or mother; husband of one's aunt.

unclean adj lacking moral, spiritual, or physical cleanliness.

uncomfortable adj not physically relaxed; anxious or uneasy.

uncommon adj not happening or encountered often; in excess of what is normal. **uncommonly** adv

uncompromising adj not prepared to compromise.

unconcerned adj lacking in concern or involvement. **unconcernedly** adv

unconditional adj without conditions or limitations.

unconscionable adj having no principles, unscrupulous; excessive in amount or degree.

unconscious adj lacking normal awareness through the senses; not aware of one's actions or behaviour. ▶ n part of the mind containing instincts and ideas that exist without one's awareness. **unconsciously** adv **unconsciousness** n

uncooperative adj not willing to help other people with what they are doing.

uncouth adj lacking in good manners, refinement, or grace.

uncover v reveal or disclose; remove the cover, top, etc., from.

unction n act of anointing with oil in sacramental ceremonies.

unctuous adj pretending to be kind and concerned.

undecided adj not having made up one's mind; (of an issue or problem) not agreed or decided upon.

undeniable adj unquestionably true. **undeniably** adv

under prep, adj indicating movement to or position beneath the underside or base. ▶ prep less than; subject to.

under- prefix below, e.g. underground; insufficient or insufficiently, e.g. underrate.

underage adj below the required or standard age.

underarm adj Sport denoting a style of throwing, bowling, or serving in which the hand is swung below shoulder level. ▶ adv Sport in an underarm style.

undercarriage n landing gear of an aircraft; framework supporting the body of a vehicle.

underclass n class consisting of the most disadvantaged people, such as the long-term unemployed.

undercoat n coat of paint applied before the final coat.

undercover adj done or acting in secret.

undercurrent n current that is not apparent at the surface; underlying opinion or emotion.

undercut v charge less than (a competitor) to obtain trade.

underdog n person or team in a weak or underprivileged position.

underdone adj not cooked enough.

underestimate v make too low an estimate; not realize the full potential of.

underfoot adv under the feet.

undergarment n any piece of underwear.

undergo v experience, endure, or

sustain.

undergraduate n person studying in a university for a first degree.

underground adj occurring, situated, used, or going below ground level; secret. ▶ n electric passenger railway operated in underground tunnels; movement dedicated to overthrowing a government or occupation forces.

undergrowth n small trees and bushes growing beneath taller trees in a wood or forest.

underhand adj sly, deceitful, and secretive.

underlie v lie or be placed under; be the foundation, cause, or basis of. **underlying** adj fundamental or basic.

underline v draw a line under; state forcibly, emphasize.

underling n subordinate.

undermine v weaken gradually.

underneath prep, adv under or beneath. ▶ adj, n lower (part or surface).

underpants pl n man's undergarment for the lower part of the body.

underpass n section of a road that passes under another road or a railway line.

underpin v give strength or support to.

underprivileged adj lacking the rights and advantages of other members of society.

underrate v not realize the full potential of. **underrated** adj

underseal n Chiefly Brit coating of tar etc. applied to the underside of a motor vehicle to prevent corrosion.

underside n bottom or lower surface.

understand v know and comprehend the nature or meaning of; realize or grasp

(something); assume, infer, or believe. **understandable** adj **understandably** adv

understanding n ability to learn, judge, or make decisions; personal interpretation of a subject; mutual agreement, usu. an informal or private one. ▶ adj kind and sympathetic.

understate v describe or represent (something) in restrained terms; state that (something, such as a number) is less than it is. **understatement** n

understudy n actor who studies a part in order to be able to replace the usual actor if necessary. ▶ v act as an understudy for.

undertake v agree or commit oneself to (something) or to do (something); promise. **undertaking** n task or enterprise; agreement to do something.

undertaker n person whose job is to prepare corpses for burial or cremation and organize funerals.

undertone n quiet tone of voice; underlying quality or feeling.

undertow n strong undercurrent flowing in a different direction from the surface current.

underwear n clothing worn under the outer garments and next to the skin.

underworld n criminals and their associates; Greek & Roman myth regions below the earth's surface regarded as the abode of the dead.

underwrite v accept responsibility for (a commercial project); sign and issue (an insurance policy), thus accepting liability. **underwriter** n person who underwrites (esp. an insurance policy).

undesirable adj not desirable or pleasant, objectionable. ▶ n objectionable person.

undo v open, unwrap; reverse the effects of; cause the downfall of. **undone** adj **undoing** n cause of someone's downfall.

undoubted adj certain or indisputable. **undoubtedly** adv

undue adj greater than is reasonable, excessive. **unduly** adv

undulate v move in waves. **undulation** n

undying adj never ending, eternal.

unearth v reveal or discover by searching; dig up out of the earth.

unearthly adj ghostly or eerie; ridiculous or unreasonable.

uneasy adj (of a person) anxious or apprehensive; (of a condition) precarious or uncomfortable. **uneasily** adv **uneasiness** n **unease** n feeling of anxiety; state of dissatisfaction.

unemployed adj out of work. **unemployment** n

unequivocal adj completely clear in meaning. **unequivocally** adv

unerring adj never mistaken, consistently accurate.

unexceptionable adj beyond criticism or objection.

unfailing adj continuous or reliable. **unfailingly** adv

unfair adj not right, fair, or just. **unfairly** adv **unfairness** n

unfaithful adj having sex with someone other than one's regular partner; not true to a promise or vow. **unfaithfulness** n

unfeeling adj without sympathy.

unfit adj unqualified or unsuitable; in poor physical condition.

unflappable adj Informal not easily upset. **unflappability** n

unfold v open or spread out from a folded state; reveal or be revealed.

unforgettable adj impossible to forget, memorable.

unfortunate adj unlucky, unsuccessful, or unhappy; regrettable or unsuitable. **unfortunately** adv

unfrock v deprive (a priest in holy orders) of his or her priesthood.

ungainly adj **-lier, -liest.** lacking grace when moving.

ungodly adj Informal unreasonable or outrageous, e.g. an ungodly hour; wicked or sinful.

ungrateful adj not grateful or thankful.

unguarded adj not protected; incautious or careless.

unguent [ung-gwent] n Lit ointment.

unhand v Old-fashioned or lit release from one's grasp.

unhappy adj sad or depressed; unfortunate or wretched. **unhappily** adv **unhappiness** n

unhealthy adj likely to cause poor health; not fit or well; morbid, unnatural.

unhinge v derange or unbalance (a person or his or her mind).

uni n Informal short for UNIVERSITY.

uni- combining form of, consisting of, or having only one, e.g. unicellular.

unicorn n imaginary horselike creature with one horn growing from its forehead.

uniform n special identifying set of clothes for the members of an organization, such as soldiers. ▶ adj regular and even throughout, unvarying; alike or like. **uniformly** adv **uniformity** n

unify v **-fying, -fied.** make or become one. **unification** n

unilateral adj made or done by only one person or group. **unilaterally** adv

unimpeachable adj completely honest and reliable.

uninterested adj having or

showing no interest in someone or something.

union *n* uniting or being united; short for TRADE UNION; association or confederation of individuals or groups for a common purpose. **unionist** *n* member or supporter of a trade union. **unionize** *v* organize (workers) into a trade union. **unionization** *n* **Union Jack, Flag** national flag of the United Kingdom.

unique [yoo-**neek**] *adj* being the only one of a particular type; without equal or like. **uniquely** *adv*

unisex *adj* designed for use by both sexes.

unison *n* complete agreement; *Music* singing or playing of the same notes together at the same time.

unit *n* single undivided entity or whole; group or individual regarded as a basic element of a larger whole; fixed quantity etc., used as a standard of measurement; piece of furniture designed to be fitted with other similar pieces. **unit trust** investment trust that issues units for public sale and invests the money in many different businesses.

Unitarian *n* person who believes that God is one being and rejects the Trinity. **Unitarianism** *n*

unitary *adj* consisting of a single undivided whole; of a unit or units.

unite *v* make or become an integrated whole; (cause to) enter into an association or alliance.

unity *n* state of being one; mutual agreement.

universe *n* whole of all existing matter, energy, and space; the world. **universal** *adj* of or typical of the whole of mankind or of

nature; existing everywhere. **universally** *adv* **universality** *n*

university *n, pl* **-ties.** institution of higher education with the authority to award degrees.

unkempt *adj* (of the hair) not combed; slovenly or untidy.

unknown *adj* not known; not famous. ▶ *n* unknown person, quantity, or thing.

unleaded *adj* (of petrol) containing less tetraethyl lead, in order to reduce environmental pollution.

unless *conj* except under the circumstances that.

unlike *adj* dissimilar or different. ▶ *prep* not like or typical of.

unlikely *adj* improbable.

unload *v* remove (cargo) from (a ship, truck, or plane); remove the ammunition from (a firearm).

unmask *v* remove the mask or disguise from; (cause to) appear in true character.

unmentionable *adj* unsuitable as a topic of conversation.

unmistakable, unmistakeable *adj* not ambiguous, clear. **unmistakably, unmistakeably** *adv*

unmitigated *adj* not reduced or lessened in severity etc.; total and complete.

unmoved *adj* not affected by emotion, indifferent.

unnatural *adj* strange and frightening because not usual; not in accordance with accepted standards of behaviour.

unnerve *v* cause to lose courage, confidence, or self-control.

unnumbered *adj* countless; not counted or given a number.

unorthodox *adj* (of ideas, methods, etc.) unconventional and not generally accepted; (of a person) having unusual opinions or methods.

unpack *v* remove the contents of

(a suitcase, trunk, etc.); take (something) out of a packed container.

unparalleled adj not equalled, supreme.

unpick v undo (the stitches) of (a piece of sewing).

unpleasant adj not pleasant or agreeable. **unpleasantly** adv **unpleasantness** n

unprintable adj unsuitable for printing for reasons of obscenity or libel.

unprofessional adj contrary to the accepted code of a profession. **unprofessionally** adv

unqualified adj lacking the necessary qualifications; total or complete.

unravel v -elling, -elled. reduce (something knitted or woven) to separate strands; become unravelled; explain or solve.

unremitting adj never slackening or stopping.

unrequited adj not returned, e.g. unrequited love.

unrest n rebellious state of discontent.

unrivalled adj having no equal.

unroll v open out or unwind (something rolled or coiled) or (of something rolled or coiled) become opened out or unwound.

unruly adj -lier, -liest. difficult to control or organize.

unsavoury adj distasteful or objectionable.

unscathed adj not harmed or injured.

unscrupulous adj prepared to act dishonestly, unprincipled.

unseat v throw or displace from a seat or saddle; depose from an office or position.

unsettled adj lacking order or stability; disturbed and restless; constantly changing or moving

from place to place.

unsightly adj unpleasant to look at.

unsocial adj (also **unsociable**) avoiding the company of other people; falling outside the normal working day, e.g. unsocial hours.

unsound adj unhealthy or unstable; not based on truth or fact.

unstable adj lacking stability or firmness; having abrupt changes of mood or behaviour.

unsuitable adj not right or appropriate for a particular purpose. **unsuitably** adv

unsuited adj not appropriate for a particular task or situation.

unswerving adj firm, constant, not changing.

unthinkable adj out of the question, inconceivable.

untidy adj messy and disordered. **untidily** adv **untidiness** n

untie v open or free (something that is tied); free from constraint.

until conj up to the time that. ▶ prep in or throughout the period before. **not until** not before (a time or event).

untimely adj occurring before the expected or normal time; inappropriate to the occasion or time.

unto prep Old-fashioned to.

untold adj incapable of description; incalculably great in number or quantity.

untouchable adj above reproach or suspicion; unable to be touched. ▶ n member of the lowest Hindu caste in India.

untoward adj causing misfortune or annoyance.

untrue adj incorrect or false; disloyal or unfaithful. **untruth** n statement that is not true, lie.

unusual adj uncommon or extraordinary. **unusually** adv

unutterable adj incapable of being expressed in words. **unutterably** adv

unvarnished adj not elaborated upon, e.g. the unvarnished truth.

unwieldy adj too heavy, large, or awkward to be easily handled.

unwind v relax after a busy or tense time; slacken, undo, or unravel.

unwitting adj not intentional; not knowing or conscious. **unwittingly** adv

unwonted adj out of the ordinary.

unworthy adj not deserving or worthy; lacking merit or value. **unworthy of** beneath the level considered befitting (to).

unwrap v remove the wrapping from (something).

unwritten adj not printed or in writing; operating only through custom.

up prep, adv indicating movement to or position at a higher place. ▶ adv indicating readiness, intensity or completeness, etc., e.g. warm up; drink up. ▶ adj of a high or higher position; out of bed. ▶ v upping, upped. increase or raise. **up against** having to cope with. **up and** Informal do something suddenly, e.g. he upped and left. **ups and downs** alternating periods of good and bad luck. **what's up?** Informal what is wrong? **upward** adj directed or moving towards a higher place or level. ▶ adv (also **upwards**) from a lower to a higher place, level, or condition.

upbeat adj Informal cheerful and optimistic. ▶ n Music unaccented beat.

upbraid v scold or reproach.

upbringing n education of a person during the formative years.

update v bring up to date.

upend v turn or set (something) on its end.

upfront adj open and frank. ▶ adv, adj (of money) paid out at the beginning of a business arrangement.

upgrade v promote (a person or job) to a higher rank.

upheaval n strong, sudden, or violent disturbance.

uphill adj sloping or leading upwards; requiring a great deal of effort. ▶ adv up a slope. ▶ n S Afr difficulty.

uphold v maintain or defend against opposition; give moral support to. **upholder** n

upholster v fit (a chair or sofa) with padding, springs, and covering. **upholsterer** n

upholstery n soft covering on a chair or sofa.

upkeep n act, process, or cost of keeping something in good repair.

upland adj of or in an area of high or relatively high ground.

uplands pl n area of high or relatively high ground.

uplift v raise or lift up; raise morally or spiritually. ▶ n act or process of improving moral, social, or cultural conditions. **uplifting** adj

upon prep on; up and on.

upper adj higher or highest in physical position, wealth, rank, or status. ▶ n part of a shoe above the sole. **uppermost** adj highest in position, power, or importance. ▶ adv in or into the highest place or position. **upper class** highest social class. **upper-class** adj **upper crust** Brit, Aust & NZ informal upper class. **upper hand** position of control.

uppish, uppity adj Brit informal snobbish, arrogant, or presumptuous.

upright adj vertical or erect; honest or just. ▶ adv vertically or in an erect position. ▶ n vertical support, such as a post.
uprightness n

uprising n rebellion or revolt.

uproar n disturbance characterized by loud noise and confusion.
uproarious adj very funny; (of laughter) loud and boisterous.
uproariously adv

uproot v pull up by or as if by the roots; displace (a person or people) from their native or usual surroundings.

upset adj emotionally or physically disturbed or distressed. ▶ v tip over; disturb the normal state or stability of; disturb mentally or emotionally; make physically ill. ▶ n unexpected defeat or reversal; disturbance or disorder of the emotions, mind, or body.
upsetting adj

upshot n final result or conclusion.

upside down adj turned over completely; Informal confused or jumbled. ▶ adv in an inverted fashion; in a chaotic manner.

upstage adj at the back half of the stage. ▶ v Informal draw attention to oneself from (someone else).

upstairs adv to or on an upper floor of a building. ▶ n upper floor. ▶ adj situated on an upper floor.

upstanding adj of good character.

upstart n person who has risen suddenly to a position of power and behaves arrogantly.

upstream adv, adj in or towards the higher part of a stream.

upsurge n rapid rise or swell.

uptake n Quick, slow on the uptake Informal quick or slow to understand or learn.

uptight adj Informal nervously tense, irritable, or angry.

up-to-date adj modern or fashionable.

upturn n upward trend or improvement. **upturned** adj facing upwards.

uranium n Chem radioactive silvery-white metallic element, used chiefly as a source of nuclear energy.

Uranus n Greek myth god of the sky; seventh planet from the sun.

urban adj of or living in a city or town; denoting modern pop music of African-American origin, such as hip-hop. **urbanize** v make (a rural area) more industrialized and urban. **urbanization** n

urbane adj characterized by courtesy, elegance, and sophistication. **urbanity** n

urchin n mischievous child.

urethra [yew-reeth-ra] n canal that carries urine from the bladder out of the body.

urge n strong impulse, inner drive, or yearning. ▶ v plead with or press (a person to do something); advocate earnestly; force or drive onwards.

urgent adj requiring speedy action or attention. **urgency** n **urgently** adv

urine n pale yellow fluid excreted by the kidneys to the bladder and passed as waste from the body. **urinary** adj **urinate** v discharge urine. **urination** n **urinal** n sanitary fitting used by men for urination.

URL uniform resource locator: a standardized address of a location on the Internet.

urn n vase used as a container for the ashes of the dead; large metal container with a tap, used for making and holding tea or coffee.

ursine adj of or like a bear.

us pron objective case of WE.

US, USA United States (of America).

use v put into service or action; take advantage of, exploit; consume or expend. ▶ n using or being used; ability or permission to use; usefulness or advantage; purpose for which something is used. **user** n **user-friendly** adj easy to familiarize oneself with, understand, and use. **usable** adj able to be used. **usage** n regular or constant use; way in which a word is used in a language. **use-by date** Aust, NZ & S Afr date on packaged food after which it should not be sold. **used** adj second-hand. **used** adj accustomed to. ▶ v used as an auxiliary to express past habitual or accustomed actions, e.g. *I used to live there*. **useful** adj **usefully** adv **usefulness** n **useless** adj **uselessly** adv **uselessness** n

usher n official who shows people to their seats, as in a church. ▶ v conduct or escort. **usherette** n female assistant in a cinema who shows people to their seats.

USSR (formerly) Union of Soviet Socialist Republics.

usual adj of the most normal, frequent, or regular type. **usually** adv most often, in most cases.

usurp [yewz-**zurp**] v seize (a position or power) without authority. **usurpation** n **usurper** n

usury n practice of lending money at an extremely high rate of interest. **usurer** [**yewz**-yoor-er] n

ute [yoot] n Aust & NZ informal utility truck.

utensil n tool or container for practical use, e.g. *cooking utensils*.

uterus [**yew**-ter-russ] n womb. **uterine** adj

utilitarian adj useful rather than beautiful; of utilitarianism.

utilitarianism n Ethics doctrine that the right action is the one that brings about the greatest good for the greatest number of people.

utility n usefulness; (pl **-ties**) public service, such as electricity. ▶ adj designed for use rather than beauty. **utility room** room used for large domestic appliances and equipment. **utility truck** Aust & NZ small truck with an open body and low sides.

utilize v make practical use of. **utilization** n

utmost adj, n (of) the greatest possible degree or amount, e.g. *the utmost point; I was doing my utmost to comply*.

Utopia [yew-**tope**-ee-a] n any real or imaginary society, place, or state considered to be perfect or ideal. **Utopian** adj

utter[1] v express (something) in sounds or words. **utterance** n something uttered; act or power of uttering.

utter[2] adj total or absolute. **utterly** adv

uttermost adj, n same as UTMOST.

U-turn n turn, made by a vehicle, in the shape of a U, resulting in a reversal of direction; complete change in policy, e.g. *a humiliating U-turn by the Prime Minister*.

UV ultraviolet.

uvula [**yew**-view-la] n small fleshy part of the soft palate that hangs in the back of the throat. **uvular** adj

uxorious [ux-**or**-ee-uss] adj excessively fond of or dependent on one's wife.

— V v —

V volt.

v. versus; very.

vacant adj (of a toilet, room, etc.) unoccupied; without interest or understanding. **vacantly** adv

vacancy n, pl **-cies.** unfilled job; unoccupied room in a guesthouse; state of being unoccupied.

vacate v cause (something) to be empty by leaving; give up (a job or position). **vacation** n time when universities and law courts are closed; *Chiefly US* holiday.

vaccinate v inject with a vaccine. **vaccination** n **vaccine** n substance designed to cause a mild form of a disease to make a person immune to the disease itself.

vacillate [**vass**-ill-late] v keep changing one's mind or opinions. **vacillation** n

vacuous adj not expressing intelligent thought. **vacuity** n

vacuum n, pl **vacuums, vacua.** empty space from which all or most air or gas has been removed. ▶ v clean with a vacuum cleaner. **vacuum cleaner** electrical appliance which sucks up dust and dirt from carpets and upholstery. **vacuum flask** double-walled flask with a vacuum between the walls that keeps drinks hot or cold.

vacuum-packed adj contained in packaging from which the air has been removed.

vagabond n person with no fixed home, esp. a beggar.

vagary [**vaig**-a-ree] n, pl **-garies.** unpredictable change.

vagina [vaj-**jine**-a] n (in female mammals) passage from the womb to the external genitals. **vaginal** adj

vagrant [**vaig**-rant] n person with no settled home. ▶ adj wandering. **vagrancy** n

vague adj not clearly explained; unable to be seen or heard clearly; absent-minded. **vaguely** adv

vain adj excessively proud, esp. of one's appearance; bound to fail, futile. **in vain** unsuccessfully.

vainglorious adj *Lit* boastful.

valance [**val**-lenss] n piece of drapery round the edge of a bed.

vale n *Lit* valley.

valedictory [val-lid-**dik**-tree] adj (of a speech, performance, etc.) intended as a farewell. **valediction** n farewell speech.

valence [**vale**-ence] n molecular bonding between atoms.

valency n, pl **-cies.** power of an atom to make molecular bonds.

valentine n (person to whom one sends) a romantic card on Saint Valentine's Day, 14th February.

valerian n herb used as a sedative.

valet n man's personal male servant.

valetudinarian [val-lit-yew-din-**air**-ee-an] n person with a long-term illness; person overconcerned about his or her health.

valiant adj brave or courageous.

valid adj soundly reasoned; having legal force. **validate** v make valid. **validation** n **validity** n

valise [val-**leez**] n *Old-fashioned* small suitcase.

Valium n ® drug used as a tranquillizer.

valley n low area between hills, often with a river running through it.

valour n *Lit* bravery.

value n importance, usefulness;

monetary worth. ▶ *pl* moral principles. ▶ *v* **valuing, valued.** assess the worth or desirability of; have a high regard for. **valuable** *adj* having great worth. **valuables** *pl n* valuable personal property. **valuation** *n* assessment of worth. **valueless** *adj* **valuer** *n* **value-added tax** *Brit & S Afr* VAT. **value judgment** opinion based on personal belief.

valve *n* device to control the movement of fluid through a pipe; *Anat* flap in a part of the body allowing blood to flow in one direction only; *Physics* tube containing a vacuum, allowing current to flow from a cathode to an anode. **valvular** *adj*

vamp[1] *n Informal* sexually attractive woman who seduces men.

vamp[2] *v* **vamp up** make (a story, piece of music, etc.) seem new by inventing additional parts.

vampire *n* (in folklore) corpse that rises at night to drink the blood of the living. **vampire bat** tropical bat that feeds on blood.

van[1] *n* motor vehicle for transporting goods; railway carriage for goods, luggage, or mail.

van[2] *n* short for VANGUARD.

vanadium *n Chem* metallic element, used in steel.

vandal *n* person who deliberately damages property. **vandalism** *n* **vandalize** *v*

vane *n* flat blade on a rotary device such as a weathercock or propeller.

vanguard *n* unit of soldiers leading an army; most advanced group or position in a movement or activity.

vanilla *n* seed pod of a tropical climbing orchid, used for flavouring.

vanish *v* disappear suddenly or mysteriously; cease to exist.

vanity *n, pl* **-ties.** (display of) excessive pride.

vanquish *v Lit* defeat (someone) utterly.

vantage *n* **vantage point** position that gives an overall view.

vapid *adj* lacking character, dull.

vapour *n* moisture suspended in air as steam or mist; gaseous form of something that is liquid or solid at room temperature. **vaporize** *v* **vaporizer** *n* **vaporous** *adj*

variable *adj* not always the same, changeable. ▶ *n Maths* expression with a range of values. **variability** *n*

variant *adj* differing from a standard or type. ▶ *n* something that differs from a standard or type. **at variance** in disagreement.

variation *n* something presented in a slightly different form; difference in level, amount, or quantity; *Music* repetition in different forms of a basic theme.

varicose veins *pl n* knotted and swollen veins, esp. in the legs.

variegated *adj* having patches or streaks of different colours. **variegation** *n*

variety *n, pl* **-ties.** state of being diverse or various; different things of the same kind; particular sort or kind; light entertainment composed of unrelated acts.

various *adj* of several kinds. **variously** *adv*

varnish *n* solution of oil and resin, put on a surface to make it hard and glossy. ▶ *v* apply varnish to.

vary *v* **varying, varied.** change; cause differences in. **varied** *adj*

vascular *adj Biol* relating to vessels.

vas deferens *n, pl* **vasa deferentia.** *Anat* sperm-carrying duct in each testicle.

vase *n* ornamental jar, esp. for

flowers.

vasectomy n, pl **-mies.** surgical removal of part of the vas deferens, as a contraceptive method.

Vaseline n ® thick oily cream made from petroleum, used in skin care.

vassal n Hist man given land by a lord in return for military service; subordinate person or nation. **vassalage** n

vast adj extremely large. **vastly** adv **vastness** n

vat n large container for liquids.

VAT Brit & S Afr value-added tax: tax on the difference between the cost of materials and the selling price.

Vatican n the Pope's palace.

vaudeville n variety entertainment of songs and comic turns.

vault¹ n secure room for storing valuables; underground burial chamber. **vaulted** adj having an arched roof.

vault² v jump over (something) by resting one's hand(s) on it. ▶ n such a jump.

vaunt v describe or display (success or possessions) boastfully. **vaunted** adj

VC Vice Chancellor; Victoria Cross.

VCR video cassette recorder.

VD venereal disease.

VDU visual display unit.

veal n calf meat.

vector n Maths quantity that has size and direction, such as force; animal, usu. an insect, that carries disease.

veer v change direction suddenly.

vegan [vee-gan] n person who eats no meat, fish, eggs, or dairy products. ▶ adj suitable for a vegan. **veganism** n

vegetable n edible plant; Informal severely brain-damaged person.

▶ adj of or like plants or vegetables.

vegetarian n person who eats no meat or fish. ▶ adj suitable for a vegetarian. **vegetarianism** n

vegetate v live a dull boring life with no mental stimulation.

vegetation n plant life of a given place.

vehement adj expressing strong feelings. **vehemence** n **vehemently** adv

vehicle n machine, esp. with an engine and wheels, for carrying people or objects; something used to achieve a particular purpose or as a means of expression. **vehicular** adj

veil n piece of thin cloth covering the head or face; something that masks the truth, e.g. a veil of secrecy. ▶ v cover with or as if with a veil. **take the veil** become a nun. **veiled** adj disguised.

vein n tube that takes blood to the heart; line in a leaf or an insect's wing; layer of ore or mineral in rock; streak in marble, wood, or cheese; feature of someone's writing or speech, e.g. a vein of humour; mood or style, e.g. in a lighter vein. **veined** adj

Velcro n ® fastening consisting of one piece of fabric with tiny hooked threads and another with a coarse surface that sticks to it.

veld, veldt n high grassland in southern Africa. **veldskoen, velskoen** n S Afr leather ankle boot.

vellum n fine calfskin parchment; type of strong good-quality paper.

velocity n, pl **-ties.** speed of movement in a given direction.

velour, velours [vel-loor] n fabric similar to velvet.

velvet n fabric with a thick soft pile. **velvety** adj soft and smooth. **velveteen** n cotton velvet.

venal adj easily bribed; characterized by bribery.

vend v sell. **vendor** n **vending machine** machine that dispenses goods when coins are inserted.

vendetta n prolonged quarrel between families, esp. one involving revenge killings.

veneer n thin layer of wood etc. covering a cheaper material; superficial appearance, e.g. a veneer of sophistication.

venerable adj worthy of deep respect. **venerate** v hold (a person) in deep respect. **veneration** n

venereal disease [ven-eer-ee-al] n disease transmitted sexually.

Venetian adj of Venice, port in NE Italy. **Venetian blind** window blind made of thin horizontal slats that turn to let in more or less light.

vengeance n revenge. **vengeful** adj wanting revenge.

venial [veen-ee-al] adj (of a sin or fault) easily forgiven.

venison n deer meat.

venom n malice or spite; poison produced by snakes etc. **venomous** adj

venous adj Anat of veins.

vent[1] n outlet releasing fumes or fluid. ▶ v express (an emotion) freely. **give vent to** release (an emotion) in an outburst.

vent[2] n vertical slit in a jacket.

ventilate v let fresh air into; discuss (ideas or feelings) openly. **ventilation** n **ventilator** n

ventral adj relating to the front of the body.

ventricle n Anat one of the four cavities of the heart or brain.

ventriloquist n entertainer who can speak without moving his or her lips, so that a voice seems to come from elsewhere.

ventriloquism n

venture n risky undertaking, esp. in business. ▶ v do something risky; dare to express (an opinion); go to an unknown place. **venturesome** adj daring.

venue n place where an organized gathering is held.

Venus n planet second nearest to the sun; Roman goddess of love. **Venus flytrap** plant that traps and digests insects between hinged leaves.

veracity n habitual truthfulness. **veracious** adj

verandah, veranda n open porch attached to a house.

verb n word that expresses the idea of action, happening, or being. **verbal** adj spoken; of a verb. **verbally** adv **verbalize** v express (something) in words.

verbatim [verb-bait-im] adv, adj word for word.

verbena n plant with sweet-smelling flowers.

verbiage n excessive use of words.

verbose [verb-bohss] adj speaking at tedious length. **verbosity** n

verdant adj Lit covered in green vegetation.

verdict n decision of a jury; opinion formed after examining the facts.

verdigris [ver-dig-riss] n green film on copper, brass, or bronze.

verdure n Lit flourishing green vegetation.

verge n grass border along a road. **on the verge of** having almost reached (a point or condition). **verge on** v be near to (a condition).

verger n C of E church caretaker.

verify v -ifying, -ified. check the truth or accuracy of. **verifiable** adj **verification** n

verily adv Obs in truth.

verisimilitude n appearance of being real or true.

veritable adj rightly called, without exaggeration, e.g. *a veritable feast.* **veritably** adv

verity n, pl **-ties.** true statement or principle.

vermicelli [ver-me-**chell**-ee] n fine strands of pasta.

vermiform adj shaped like a worm. **vermiform appendix** Anat same as APPENDIX.

vermilion adj orange-red.

vermin pl n animals, esp. insects and rodents, that spread disease or cause damage. **verminous** adj

vermouth [ver-muth] n wine flavoured with herbs.

vernacular [ver-**nak**-yew-lar] n most widely spoken language of a particular people or place.

vernal adj occurring in spring.

vernier [ver-nee-er] n movable scale on a graduated measuring instrument for taking readings in fractions.

veronica n plant with small blue, pink, or white flowers.

verruca [ver-**roo**-ka] n wart, usu. on the foot.

versatile adj having many skills or uses. **versatility** n

verse n group of lines forming part of a song or poem; poetry as distinct from prose; subdivision of a chapter of the Bible. **versed in** knowledgeable about.

versification n writing in verse.

version n form of something, such as a piece of writing, with some differences from other forms; account of an incident from a particular point of view.

verso n, pl **-sos.** left-hand page of a book.

versus prep in opposition to or in contrast with; *Sport, Law* against.

vertebra n, pl **vertebrae.** one of

the bones that form the spine. **vertebral** adj **vertebrate** n, adj (animal) having a spine.

vertex n, pl **-texes, -tices.** Maths point on a geometric figure where the sides form an angle; highest point of a triangle.

vertical adj straight up and down. ▶ n vertical direction.

vertigo n dizziness, usu. when looking down from a high place. **vertiginous** adj

vervain n plant with spikes of blue, purple, or white flowers.

verve n enthusiasm or liveliness.

very adv more than usually, extremely. ▶ adj absolute, exact, e.g. *the very top; the very man.*

vesicle n Biol sac or small cavity, esp. one containing fluid.

vespers pl n RC Church (service of) evening prayer.

vessel n ship; Lit container, esp. for liquids; Biol tubular structure in animals and plants that carries body fluids, such as blood or sap.

vest n undergarment worn on the top half of the body; US & Aust waistcoat. ▶ v (foll. by in or with) give (authority) to (someone).

vested interest n someone has in a matter because he or she might benefit from it.

vestibule n small entrance hall.

vestige [vest-ij] n small amount or trace. **vestigial** adj

vestments pl n priest's robes.

vestry n, pl **-tries.** room in a church used as an office by the priest or minister.

vet[1] n short for VETERINARY SURGEON. ▶ v **vetting, vetted.** check the suitability of.

vet[2] n US, Aust & NZ military veteran.

vetch n climbing plant with a beanlike fruit used as fodder.

veteran n person with long

experience in a particular activity, esp. military service. ▶ *adj* long-serving.

veterinary *adj* concerning animal health. **veterinary surgeon** medical specialist who treats sick animals.

veto *n, pl* **-toes.** official power to cancel a proposal. ▶ *v* **-toing, -toed.** enforce a veto against.

vex *v* frustrate, annoy. **vexation** *n* something annoying; being annoyed. **vexatious** *adj* **vexed question** much debated subject.

VHF very high frequency: radio frequency band between 30 and 300 MHz.

VHS ® Video Home System: format for recording on video.

via *prep* by way of.

viable *adj* able to be put into practice; *Biol* able to live and grow independently. **viability** *n*

viaduct *n* bridge over a valley.

Viagra [vie-**ag**-ra] *n* ® drug used to treat impotence in men.

vial *n* same as PHIAL.

viands *pl n Obs* food.

vibes *pl n Informal* emotional reactions between people; atmosphere of a place; short for VIBRAPHONE.

vibrant [**vibe**-rant] *adj* vigorous in appearance, energetic; (of a voice) resonant; (of a colour) strong and bright.

vibraphone *n* musical instrument with metal bars that resonate electronically when hit.

vibrate *v* move back and forth rapidly; (cause to) resonate. **vibration** *n* **vibrator** *n* device that produces vibratory motion, used for massage or as a sex aid. **vibratory** *adj*

vibrato *n, pl* **-tos.** *Music* rapid fluctuation in the pitch of a note.

Vic Victoria.

vicar *n C of E* member of the clergy in charge of a parish. **vicarage** *n* vicar's house.

vicarious [vick-**air**-ee-uss] *adj* felt indirectly by imagining what another person experiences; delegated. **vicariously** *adv*

vice¹ *n* immoral or evil habit or action; habit regarded as a weakness in someone's character; criminal immorality, esp. involving sex.

vice² *n* tool with a pair of jaws for holding an object while working on it.

vice³ *adj* serving in place of.

vice chancellor *n* chief executive of a university.

viceroy *n* governor of a colony who represents the monarch. **viceregal** *adj*

vice versa [vie-see **ver**-sa] *adv Latin* conversely, the other way round.

vicinity [viss-**in**-it-ee] *n* surrounding area.

vicious *adj* cruel and violent. **viciously** *adv* **vicious circle, cycle** situation in which an attempt to resolve one problem creates new problems that recreate the original one.

vicissitudes [viss-**iss**-it-yewds] *pl n* changes in fortune.

victim *n* person or thing harmed or killed. **victimize** *v* punish unfairly; discriminate against. **victimization** *n*

victor *n* person who has defeated an opponent, esp. in war or in sport.

Victoria Cross *n Brit* highest award for bravery in battle.

Victorian *adj* of or in the reign of Queen Victoria (1837–1901); characterized by prudery or hypocrisy; of or relating to the Australian state of Victoria.

victory n winning of a battle or contest. **victorious** adj

victuals [vit-tals] pl n Old-fashioned food and drink.

vicuña [vik-koo-nya] n S American animal like the llama; fine cloth made from its wool.

video n, pl -os. short for VIDEO CASSETTE (RECORDER). ▶ v **videoing, videoed.** record (a TV programme or event) on video. ▶ adj relating to or used in producing television images. **video nasty** horrific or pornographic film, usu. made for video. **videotext** n means of representing on a TV screen information that is held in a computer.

video cassette n cassette containing video tape. **video cassette recorder** tape recorder for recording and playing back TV programmes and films.

video tape n magnetic tape used to record video-frequency signals in TV production; magnetic tape used to record programmes when they are broadcast. **videotape** v record (a TV programme) on video tape. **video tape recorder** tape recorder for vision signals, used in TV production.

vie v **vying, vied.** compete (with someone).

view n opinion or belief; everything that can be seen from a given place; picture of this. ▶ v think of (something) in a particular way. **in view of** taking into consideration. **on view** exhibited to the public. **viewer** n person who watches television; hand-held device for looking at photographic slides. **viewfinder** n window on a camera showing what will appear in a photograph.

Viewdata n ® videotext service linking users to a computer by telephone.

vigil [vij-ill] n night-time period of staying awake to look after a sick person, pray, etc. **vigilant** adj watchful in case of danger. **vigilance** n

vigilante [vij-ill-ant-ee] n person, esp. as one of a group, who takes it upon himself or herself to enforce the law.

vignette [vin-yet] n concise description of the typical features of something; small decorative illustration in a book.

vigour n physical or mental energy. **vigorous** adj **vigorously** adv

Viking n Hist seafaring raider and settler from Scandinavia.

vile adj very wicked; disgusting. **vilely** adv **vileness** n

vilify v **-ifying, -ified.** attack the character of. **vilification** n

villa n large house with gardens; holiday home, usu. in the Mediterranean.

village n small group of houses in a country area; rural community. **villager** n

villain n wicked person; main wicked character in a play. **villainous** adj **villainy** n

villein [vill-an] n Hist peasant bound in service to his lord.

vinaigrette n salad dressing of oil and vinegar.

vindicate v clear (someone) of guilt; provide justification for. **vindication** n

vindictive adj maliciously seeking revenge. **vindictiveness** n **vindictively** adv

vine n climbing plant, esp. one producing grapes. **vineyard** [vinn-yard] n plantation of grape vines, esp. for making wine.

vinegar n acid liquid made from wine, beer, or cider. **vinegary** adj

vino [vee-noh] n Informal wine.

vintage n wine from a particular harvest of grapes. ▶ adj best and most typical. **vintage car** car built between 1919 and 1930.

vintner n dealer in wine.

vinyl [vine-ill] n type of plastic, used in mock leather and records.

viol [vie-oll] n early stringed instrument preceding the violin.

viola¹ [vee-oh-la] n stringed instrument higher in pitch than a violin.

viola² [vie-ol-la] n variety of pansy.

violate v break (a law or agreement); disturb (someone's privacy); treat (a sacred place) disrespectfully; rape. **violation** n **violator** n

violence n use of physical force, usu. intended to cause injury or destruction; great force or strength in action, feeling, or expression. **violent** adj **violently** adv

violet n plant with bluish-purple flowers. ▶ adj bluish-purple.

violin n small four-stringed musical instrument played with a bow. **violinist** n

VIP very important person.

viper n poisonous snake.

virago [vir-**rah**-go] n, pl **-goes, -gos.** aggressive woman.

viral adj of or caused by a virus.

virgin n person, esp. a woman, who has not had sexual intercourse. ▶ adj not having had sexual intercourse; not yet exploited or exploited. **virginal** adj like a virgin. ▶ n early keyboard instrument like a small harpsichord. **virginity** n

virile adj having the traditional male characteristics of physical strength and a high sex drive. **virility** n

virology n study of viruses.

virtual adj having the effect but not the form of; of or relating to virtual reality. **virtual reality** computer-generated environment that seems real to the user. **virtually** adv practically, almost.

virtue n moral goodness; positive moral quality; merit. **by virtue of** by reason of. **virtuous** adj morally good. **virtuously** adv

virtuoso n, pl **-sos, -si.** person with impressive esp. musical skill. **virtuosity** n

virulent [vir-yew-lent] adj very infectious; violently harmful.

virus n microorganism that causes disease in humans, animals, and plants; Computers program that propagates itself, via disks and electronic networks, to cause disruption.

visa n permission to enter a country, granted by its government and shown by a stamp on one's passport.

visage [viz-zij] n Lit face.

vis-à-vis [veez-ah-**vee**] prep in relation to, regarding.

viscera [viss-er-a] pl n large abdominal organs.

visceral [viss-er-al] adj instinctive; of or relating to the viscera.

viscid [viss-id] adj sticky.

viscose n synthetic fabric made from cellulose.

viscount [vie-count] n British nobleman ranking between an earl and a baron.

viscountess [vie-count-iss] n woman holding the rank of viscount in her own right; wife or widow of a viscount.

viscous adj thick and sticky. **viscosity** n

visible adj able to be seen; able to be perceived by the mind. **visibly** adv **visibility** n range or clarity of vision.

vision n ability to see; mental image of something; foresight; hallucination. **visionary** adj showing foresight; idealistic but impractical. ▶ n visionary person.

visit v **-iting, -ited.** go or come to see; stay temporarily with; (foll. by **upon**) Lit afflict. ▶ n instance of visiting; official call. **visitor** n

visitation n formal visit or inspection; catastrophe seen as divine punishment.

visor [**vize**-or] n transparent part of a helmet that pulls down over the face; eyeshade, esp. in a car; peak on a cap.

vista n (beautiful) extensive view.

visual adj done by or used in seeing; designed to be looked at. **visualize** v form a mental image of. **visualization** n **visual display unit** device with a screen for displaying data held in a computer.

vital adj essential or highly important; lively; necessary to maintain life. **vitals** pl n bodily organs necessary to maintain life. **vitally** adv **vitality** n physical or mental energy. **vital statistics** statistics of births, deaths, and marriages; Informal woman's bust, waist, and hip measurements.

vitamin n one of a group of substances that are essential in the diet for specific body processes.

vitiate [**vish**-ee-ate] v spoil the effectiveness of.

viticulture n cultivation of grapevines.

vitreous adj like or made from glass.

vitriol n language expressing bitterness and hatred; sulphuric acid. **vitriolic** adj

vituperative [vite-**tyew**-pra-tiv] adj bitterly abusive. **vituperation** n

viva¹ interj long live (a person or thing).

viva² n Brit examination in the form of an interview.

vivace [viv-**vah**-chee] adv Music in a lively manner.

vivacious adj full of energy and enthusiasm. **vivacity** n

viva voce [vive-a-**voh**-chee] adv by word of mouth. ▶ n same as VIVA².

vivid adj very bright; conveying images that are true to life. **vividly** adv **vividness** n

vivisection n performing surgical experiments on living animals. **vivisectionist** n

vixen n female fox; Brit, Aust & NZ informal spiteful woman.

viz. (introducing specified items) namely.

vizier [viz-**zeer**] n high official in certain Muslim countries.

vizor n same as VISOR.

vocabulary n, pl **-aries.** all the words that a person knows; all the words in a language; specialist terms used in a given subject; list of words in another language with their translation.

vocal adj relating to the voice; outspoken. **vocals** pl n singing part of a piece of pop music. **vocally** adv **vocalist** n singer. **vocalize** v express with or use the voice. **vocalization** n **vocal cords** membranes in the larynx that vibrate to produce sound.

vocation n profession or trade; occupation that someone feels called to. **vocational** adj directed towards a particular profession or trade.

vociferous adj shouting, noisy.

vodka n (Russian) spirit distilled from potatoes or grain.

vogue n popular style; period of popularity.

voice n (quality of) sound made when speaking or singing;

expression of opinion by a person or group; property of verbs that makes them active or passive. ▶ *v* express verbally. **voiceless** *adj*
voice mail electronic system for the transfer and storage of telephone messages, which can be dealt with by the user at a later time. **voice-over** *n* film commentary spoken by someone off-camera.

void *adj* not legally binding; empty. ▶ *n* empty space. ▶ *v* make invalid; empty.

voile [voyl] *n* light semitransparent fabric.

vol. volume.

volatile *adj* liable to sudden change, esp. in behaviour; evaporating quickly. **volatility** *n*

vol-au-vent [voll-oh-von] *n* small puff-pastry case with a savoury filling.

volcano *n, pl* **-noes, -nos.** mountain with a vent through which lava is ejected. **volcanic** *adj*

vole *n* small rodent.

volition *n* ability to decide things for oneself. **of one's own volition** through one's own choice.

volley *n* simultaneous discharge of ammunition; burst of questions or critical comments; *Sport* stroke or kick at a moving ball before it hits the ground. ▶ *v* discharge (ammunition) in a volley; hit or kick (a ball) in a volley. **volleyball** *n* team game where a ball is hit with the hands over a high net.

volt *n* unit of electric potential. **voltage** *n* electric potential difference expressed in volts. **voltmeter** *n* instrument for measuring voltage.

volte-face [volt-**fass**] *n* reversal of opinion.

voluble *adj* talking easily and at length. **volubility** *n* **volubly** *adv*

volume *n* size of the space occupied by something; amount; loudness of sound; book, esp. one of a series. **voluminous** *adj* (of clothes) large and roomy; (of writings) extensive. **volumetric** *adj* relating to measurement by volume.

voluntary *adj* done by choice; done or maintained without payment; (of muscles) controlled by the will. ▶ *n, pl* **-taries.** organ solo in a church service. **voluntarily** *adv*

volunteer *n* person who offers voluntarily to do something; person who voluntarily undertakes military service. ▶ *v* offer one's services; give (information) willingly; offer the services of (another person).

voluptuous *adj* (of a woman) sexually alluring through fullness of figure; sensually pleasurable. **voluptuary** *n* person devoted to sensual pleasures.

volute *n* spiral or twisting turn, form, or object.

vomit *v* **-iting, -ited.** eject (the contents of the stomach) through the mouth. ▶ *n* matter vomited.

voodoo *n* religion involving ancestor worship and witchcraft, practised by Black people in the West Indies, esp. in Haiti.

voracious *adj* craving great quantities of food; insatiably eager. **voraciously** *adv* **voracity** *n*

vortex *n, pl* **-texes, -tices.** whirlpool.

vote *n* choice made by a participant in a shared decision, esp. in electing a person; right to this choice; total number of votes cast; collective voting power of a given group, e.g. the Black vote. ▶ *v* make a choice by a vote; authorize (something) by vote.

voter n

votive adj done or given to fulfil a vow.

vouch v **vouch for** give one's personal assurance about; provide evidence for.

voucher n ticket used instead of money to buy specified goods; record of a financial transaction, receipt.

vouchsafe v Old-fashioned give, entrust.

vow n solemn and binding promise. ► pl formal promises made when marrying or entering a religious order. ► v promise solemnly.

vowel n speech sound made without obstructing the flow of breath; letter representing this.

vox pop n Brit interviews with members of the public on TV or radio.

vox populi n public opinion.

voyage n long journey by sea or in space. ► v make a voyage. **voyager** n

voyeur n person who obtains pleasure from watching people undressing or having sex. **voyeurism** n

vs versus.

V-sign n offensive gesture made by sticking up the index and middle fingers with the palm inwards; similar gesture, with the palm outwards, meaning victory or peace.

VSO (in Britain) Voluntary Service Overseas.

VSOP (of brandy or port) very superior old pale.

VTOL vertical takeoff and landing.

VTR video tape recorder.

vulcanize v strengthen (rubber) by treating it with sulphur.

vulgar adj showing lack of good taste, decency, or refinement.

vulgarly adv **vulgarity** n

vulgarian n vulgar (rich) person.

vulgar fraction simple fraction.

Vulgate n fourth-century Latin version of the Bible.

vulnerable adj liable to be physically or emotionally hurt; exposed to attack. **vulnerability** n

vulpine adj of or like a fox.

vulture n large bird that feeds on the flesh of dead animals.

vulva n woman's external genitals.

vying n present participle of VIE.

—— W w ——

W watt; West(ern).

WA Western Australia.

wacky adj **wackier, wackiest.** Informal eccentric or funny. **wackiness** n

wad n small mass of soft material; roll or bundle, esp. of banknotes. **wadding** n soft material used for padding or stuffing.

waddle v walk with short swaying steps. ► n swaying walk.

waddy n, pl **-dies.** heavy wooden club used by Australian Aborigines.

wade v walk with difficulty through water or mud; proceed with difficulty. **wader** n long-legged water bird. ► pl angler's long waterproof boots.

wadi [wod-dee] n, pl **-dies.** (in N Africa and Arabia) river which is dry except in the wet season.

wafer n thin crisp biscuit; thin disc of unleavened bread used at Communion; thin slice.

waffle¹ Informal ► v speak or write in a vague wordy way. ► n vague wordy talk or writing.

waffle² n square crisp pancake with a gridlike pattern.

waft v drift or carry gently through

the air. ▶ *n* something wafted.

wag *v* **wagging, wagged.** move rapidly from side to side. ▶ *n* wagging movement; *Old-fashioned* humorous witty person. **wagtail** *n* small long-tailed bird.

wage *n* (often *pl*) payment for work done, esp. when paid weekly. ▶ *v* engage in (an activity).

wager *n, v* bet on the outcome of something.

waggle *v* move with a rapid shaking or wobbling motion.

wagon, waggon *n* four-wheeled vehicle for heavy loads; railway freight truck.

waif *n* young person who is, or seems, homeless or neglected.

wail *v* cry out in pain or misery. ▶ *n* mournful cry.

wain *n* *Poetic* farm wagon.

wainscot, wainscoting *n* wooden lining of the lower part of the walls of a room.

waist *n* part of the body between the ribs and hips; narrow middle part. **waistband** *n* band of material sewn on to the waist of a garment to strengthen it. **waistcoat** *n* sleeveless garment which buttons up the front, usu. worn over a shirt and under a jacket. **waistline** *n* (size of) the waist of a person or garment.

wait *v* remain inactive in expectation (of something); be ready (for something); delay or be delayed; serve in a restaurant etc. ▶ *n* act or period of waiting. **waiter** *n* man who serves in a restaurant etc. **waitress** *n fem*

Waitangi Day *n* February 6th, the national day of New Zealand commemorating the Treaty Of Waitangi in 1840.

waive *v* refrain from enforcing (a law, right, etc.).

waiver *n* act or instance of

voluntarily giving up a claim, right, etc.

waka *n* NZ Maori canoe.

wake¹ *v* **waking, woke, woken.** rouse from sleep or inactivity. ▶ *n* vigil beside a corpse the night before the funeral. **waken** *v* wake. **wakeful** *adj*

wake² *n* track left by a moving ship. **in the wake of** following, often as a result.

walk *v* move on foot with at least one foot always on the ground; pass through or over on foot; escort or accompany on foot. ▶ *n* act or instance of walking; distance walked; manner of walking; place or route for walking. **walk of life** social position or profession. **walker** *n* **walkabout** *n* informal walk among the public by royalty etc. **walkie-talkie** *n* portable radio transmitter and receiver. **walking stick** stick used as a support when walking. **walk into** *v* meet with unwittingly. **Walkman** *n* ® small portable cassette player with headphones. **walkout** *n* strike; act of leaving as a protest. **walkover** *n* easy victory.

wall *n* structure of brick, stone, etc. used to enclose, divide, or support; something having the function or effect of a wall. ▶ *v* enclose or seal with a wall or walls. **wallflower** *n* fragrant garden plant; (at a dance) woman who remains seated because she has no partner. **wallpaper** *n* decorative paper to cover interior walls.

wallaby *n, pl* **-bies.** marsupial like a small kangaroo.

wallet *n* small folding case for paper money, documents, etc.

wallop *Informal* ▶ *v* **-loping, -loped.** hit hard. ▶ *n* hard blow.

walloping *Informal* ▶ *n* thrashing. ▶ *adj* large or great.

wallow *v* revel in an emotion; roll in liquid or mud. ▶ *n* act or instance of wallowing.

wally *n, pl* **-lies.** *Brit slang* stupid person.

walnut *n* edible nut with a wrinkled shell; tree it grows on; its wood, used for making furniture.

walrus *n, pl* **-ruses, -rus.** large sea mammal with long tusks.

waltz *n* ballroom dance; music for this. ▶ *v* dance a waltz; *Informal* move in a relaxed confident way.

wampum [**wom**-pum] *n* shells woven together, formerly used by Native Americans for money and ornament.

wan [rhymes with **swan**] *adj* **wanner, wannest.** pale and sickly looking.

wand *n* thin rod, esp. one used in performing magic tricks.

wander *v* move about without a definite destination or aim; go astray, deviate. ▶ *n* act or instance of wandering. **wanderer** *n* **wanderlust** *n* great desire to travel.

wane *v* decrease gradually in size or strength; (of the moon) decrease in size. **on the wane** decreasing in size, strength, or power.

wangle *v* *Informal* get by devious methods.

want *v* need or long for; desire or wish. ▶ *n* act or instance of wanting; thing wanted; lack or absence; state of being in need, poverty. **wanted** *adj* sought by the police. **wanting** *adj* lacking; not good enough.

wanton *adj* without motive, provocation, or justification; *Old-fashioned* (of a woman) sexually unrestrained or immodest.

WAP Wireless Application Protocol:

a system that allows mobile phone users to access the Internet and other information services.

war *n* fighting between nations; conflict or contest. ▶ *adj* of, like, or caused by war. ▶ *v* **warring, warred.** conduct a war. **warring** *adj* **warlike** *adj* of or relating to war; hostile and eager to have a war. **war crime** crime, such as killing, committed during a war in violation of accepted conventions. **war criminal** person who has committed war crimes. **warfare** *n* fighting or hostilities. **warhead** *n* explosive front part of a missile. **warmonger** *n* person who encourages war. **warship** *n* ship designed and equipped for naval combat.

waratah *n* Australian shrub with crimson flowers.

warble *v* sing in a trilling voice. **warbler** *n* any of various small songbirds.

ward *n* room in a hospital for patients needing a similar kind of care; electoral division of a town; child under the care of a guardian or court. **warder** *n* prison officer. **wardress** *n fem* **ward off** *v* avert or repel. **wardroom** *n* officers' quarters on a warship.

warden *n* person in charge of a building and its occupants; official responsible for the enforcement of regulations.

wardrobe *n* cupboard for hanging clothes in; person's collection of clothes; costumes of a theatrical company.

ware *n* articles of a specified type or material, e.g. *silverware*. ▶ *pl* goods for sale. **warehouse** *n* building for storing goods prior to sale or distribution.

warlock *n* man who practises black magic.

warm *adj* moderately hot; providing warmth; (of a colour) predominantly yellow or red; affectionate; enthusiastic. ▶ *v* make or become warm. **warmly** *adv* **warmth** *n* mild heat; cordiality; intensity of emotion. **warm up** *v* make or become warmer; do preliminary exercises before a race or more strenuous exercise; make or become more lively. **warm-up** *n*

warn *v* make aware of possible danger or harm; caution or scold; inform (someone) in advance. **warning** *n* something that warns; scolding or caution. **warn off** *v* advise (someone) not to become involved with.

warp *v* twist out of shape; pervert. ▶ *n* state of being warped; lengthwise threads on a loom.

warrant *n* (document giving) official authorization. ▶ *v* make necessary; guarantee. **warranty** *n*, *pl* **-ties.** (document giving) a guarantee. **warrant officer** officer in certain armed services with a rank between a commissioned and noncommissioned officer.

warren *n* series of burrows in which rabbits live; overcrowded building or part of a town.

warrigal *Aust n* ▶ *n* dingo. ▶ *adj* wild.

warrior *n* person who fights in a war.

wart *n* small hard growth on the skin. **wart hog** kind of African wild pig.

wary [ware-ree] *adj* **warier, wariest.** watchful or cautious. **warily** *adv* **wariness** *n*

was *v* first and third person singular past tense of BE.

wash *v* clean (oneself, clothes, etc.) with water and usu. soap; be washable; flow or sweep over or against; *Informal* be believable or acceptable, e.g. *that excuse won't*

wash. ▶ *n* act or process of washing; clothes washed at one time; thin coat of paint; disturbance in the water after a ship has passed by. **washable** *adj* **washer** *n* ring put under a nut or bolt or in a tap as a seal.

washing *n* clothes to be washed. **washing-up** *n* (washing of) dishes and cutlery needing to be cleaned after a meal. **wash away** *v* carry or be carried off by moving water. **washout** *n* *Informal* complete failure. **wash up** *v* wash dishes and cutlery after a meal.

wasp *n* stinging insect with a slender black-and-yellow striped body. **waspish** *adj* bad-tempered.

waste *v* use pointlessly or thoughtlessly; fail to take advantage of. ▶ *n* act of wasting or state of being wasted; anything wasted; rubbish. ▶ *pl* desert. ▶ *adj* rejected as worthless or surplus to requirements; not cultivated or inhabited. **waste away** (cause to) decline in health or strength. **wastage** *n* loss by wear or waste; reduction in size of a workforce by not filling vacancies. **wasteful** *adj* extravagant. **wastefully** *adv* **waster, wastrel** *n* layabout. **wastepaper basket** container for discarded paper.

watch *v* look at closely; guard or supervise. ▶ *n* portable timepiece for the wrist or pocket; (period of) watching; sailor's spell of duty. **watchable** *adj* **watcher** *n* **watchful** *adj* vigilant or alert. **watchfully** *adv* **watchdog** *n* dog kept to guard property; person or group guarding against inefficiency or illegality. **watch for** *v* be keenly alert to or cautious about. **watchman** *n* man employed to guard a building or property. **watchword** *n* word or phrase that sums up the attitude of a particular group.

water n clear colourless tasteless liquid that falls as rain and forms rivers etc.; body of water, such as a sea or lake; level of the tide; urine. ▶ v put water on or into; (of the eyes) fill with tears; (of the mouth) salivate. **watery** adj **water buffalo** oxlike Asian animal. **water closet** Old-fashioned (room containing) a toilet flushed by water. **watercolour** n paint thinned with water; painting done in this. **watercourse** n bed of a stream or river. **watercress** n edible plant growing in clear ponds and streams. **water down** v dilute, make less strong. **waterfall** n place where the waters of a river drop vertically. **waterfront** n part of a town alongside a body of water. **water lily** water plant with large floating leaves. **watermark** n faint translucent design in a sheet of paper. **watermelon** n melon with green skin and red flesh. **water polo** team game played by swimmers with a ball. **waterproof** adj not letting water through. ▶ n waterproof garment. ▶ v make waterproof. **watershed** n important period or factor serving as a dividing line; line separating two river systems. **watersider** n NZ person employed to load and unload ships. **water-skiing** n sport of riding over water on skis towed by a speedboat. **watertight** adj not letting water through; with no loopholes or weak points. **water wheel** large wheel which is turned by flowing water to drive machinery.

watt [wott] n unit of power. **wattage** n electrical power

expressed in watts.

wattle [wott-tl] n branches woven over sticks to make a fence.

wave v move the hand to and fro as a greeting or signal; move or flap to and fro. ▶ n moving ridge on water; curve(s) in the hair; prolonged spell of something; gesture of waving; vibration carrying energy through a medium. **wavy** adj **wavelength** n distance between the same points of two successive waves. **waver** v hesitate or be irresolute; be or become unsteady. **waverer** n

wax[1] n solid shiny fatty or oily substance used for sealing, making candles, etc.; similar substance made by bees; waxy secretion of the ear. ▶ v coat or polish with wax. **waxen** adj made of or like wax. **waxy** adj **waxwork** n lifelike wax model of a (famous) person. ▶ pl place exhibiting these.

wax[2] v increase in size or strength; (of the moon) get gradually larger.

way n manner or method; characteristic manner; route or direction; track or path; distance; room for movement or activity, e.g. you're in the way; passage or journey. **wayfarer** n Lit traveller. **waylay** v lie in wait for and accost or attack. **wayside** adj, n (situated by the) side of a road.

wayward adj erratic, selfish, or stubborn. **waywardness** n

WC water closet.

we pron (used as the subject of a verb) the speaker or writer and one or more others; people in general; formal word for 'I' used by editors and monarchs.

weak adj lacking strength; liable to give way; unconvincing; lacking flavour. **weaken** v make or become weak. **weakling** n feeble person or animal. **weakly** adv feebly. **weakness** n being weak; failing; self-indulgent liking.

weal n raised mark left on the skin by a blow.

wealth n state of being rich; large amount of money and valuables; great amount or number. **wealthy** adj

wean v accustom (a baby or young mammal) to food other than mother's milk; coax (someone) away from former habits.

weapon n object used in fighting; anything used to get the better of an opponent. **weaponry** n weapons collectively.

wear v **wearing, wore, worn.** have on the body as clothing or ornament; show as one's expression; (cause to) deteriorate by constant time or action; endure constant use. ▶ n clothes suitable for a particular time or purpose, e.g. beach wear; damage caused by use; ability to endure constant use. **wearer** n **wear off** v gradually decrease in intensity. **wear on** v (of time) pass slowly.

weary adj **-rier, -riest.** tired or exhausted; tiring. ▶ v **-rying, -ried.** make or become weary. **wearily** adv **weariness** n **wearisome** adj tedious.

weasel n small carnivorous mammal with a long body and short legs.

weather n day-to-day atmospheric conditions of a place. ▶ v (cause to) be affected by the weather; come safely through. **under the weather** Informal slightly ill. **weather-beaten** adj worn, damaged, or (of skin) tanned by exposure to the weather. **weathercock, weathervane** n device that revolves to show the

direction of the wind.

weave v **weaving, wove** or **weaved, woven** or **weaved.** make (fabric) by interlacing (yarn) on a loom; compose (a story); move from side to side while going forwards. **weaver** n

web n net spun by a spider; anything intricate or complex, e.g. web of deceit; skin between the toes of a duck, frog, etc. **the Web** short for WORLD WIDE WEB. **webbed** adj **webbing** n strong fabric woven in strips. **webcam** n camera that transmits images over the Internet. **webcast** n broadcast of an event over the Internet. **website** n group of connected pages on the World Wide Web.

wed v **wedding, wedded** or **wed.** marry; unite closely. **wedding** n act or ceremony of marriage. **wedlock** n marriage.

wedge n piece of material thick at one end and thin at the other. ▶ v fasten or split with a wedge; squeeze into a narrow space.

Wednesday n fourth day of the week.

wee adj Brit, Austral & NZ informal small or short.

weed n plant growing where undesired; Informal thin ineffectual person. ▶ v clear of weeds. **weedy** adj Informal (of a person) thin and weak. **weed out** v remove or eliminate (what is unwanted).

weeds pl n Obs widow's mourning clothes.

week n period of seven days, esp. one beginning on a Sunday; hours or days of work in a week. **weekly** adj, adv happening, done, etc. once a week. ▶ n, pl **-lies.** newspaper or magazine published once a week. **weekday** n any day of the week except Saturday or Sunday. **weekend** n Saturday and Sunday.

weep v weeping, wept. shed tears; ooze liquid. **weepy** adj liable to cry. **weeping willow** willow with drooping branches.

weevil n small beetle which eats grain etc.

weft n cross threads in weaving.

weigh v have a specified weight; measure the weight of; consider carefully; be influential; be burdensome. **weigh anchor** raise a ship's anchor or (of a ship) have its anchor raised. **weighbridge** n machine for weighing vehicles by means of a metal plate set into the road.

weight n heaviness of an object; unit of measurement of weight; object of known mass used for weighing; heavy object; importance or influence. ▶ v add weight to; slant (a system) so that it favours one side rather than another. **weightless** adj **weightlessness** n

weighting n Brit extra allowance paid in special circumstances.

weighty adj weightier, weightiest. important or serious; very heavy. **weightily** adv

weir n river dam.

weird adj strange or bizarre; unearthly or eerie.

weirdo n, pl -dos. Informal peculiar person.

welch v same as WELSH.

welcome v -coming, -comed. greet with pleasure; receive gladly. ▶ n kindly greeting. ▶ adj received gladly; freely permitted.

weld v join (pieces of metal or plastic) by softening with heat; unite closely. ▶ n welded joint. **welder** n

welfare n wellbeing; help given to people in need. **welfare state** system in which the government takes responsibility for the wellbeing of its citizens.

well¹ adv better, best. satisfactorily; skilfully; completely; intimately; considerably; very likely. ▶ adj in good health. ▶ interj exclamation of surprise, interrogation, etc.

well² n hole sunk into the earth to reach water, oil, or gas; deep open shaft. ▶ v flow upwards or outwards.

wellbeing n state of being well, happy, or prosperous.

well-disposed adj inclined to be friendly or sympathetic.

wellies pl n Brit & Aust informal wellingtons.

wellingtons pl n Brit & Aust high waterproof rubber boots.

well-meaning adj having good intentions.

well-spoken adj speaking in a polite or articulate way.

well-worn adj (of a word or phrase) stale from overuse; so much used as to be affected by wear.

welsh v fail to pay a debt or fulfil an obligation.

Welsh adj of Wales. ▶ n language or people of Wales. **Welsh rarebit, rabbit** dish of melted cheese on toast.

welt n raised mark on the skin produced by a blow; raised or strengthened seam.

welter n jumbled mass.

welterweight n boxer weighing up to 147lb (professional) or 67kg (amateur).

wen n cyst on the scalp.

wench n Facetious young woman.

wend v go or travel.

went v past tense of GO.

wept v past of WEEP.

were v form of the past tense of **be** used after *we, you, they,* or a plural noun; subjunctive of BE.

we're we are.

weren't were not.

werewolf n (in folklore) person who can turn into a wolf.

west n (direction towards) the part of the horizon where the sun sets; region lying in this direction; (**W-**) western Europe and the US. ▶ adj to or in the west; (of a wind) from the west. ▶ adv in, to, or towards the west. **westerly** adj **western** adj of or in the west. ▶ n film or story about cowboys in the western US. **westernize** v adapt to the customs and culture of the West. **westward** adj, adv **westwards** adv

wet adj **wetter, wettest.** covered or soaked with water or another liquid; not yet dry; rainy; *Brit informal* (of a person) feeble or foolish. ▶ n moisture or rain; *Brit informal* feeble or foolish person. ▶ v **wetting, wet** or **wetted.** make wet. **wet blanket** *Informal* person who has a depressing effect on others. **wetland** n area of marshy land. **wet nurse** woman employed to breast-feed another's child. **wet suit** close-fitting rubber suit worn by divers etc.

whack v strike with a resounding blow. ▶ n such a blow; *Informal* share; *Informal* attempt. **whacked** adj exhausted. **whacking** adj *Informal* huge.

whale n large fish-shaped sea mammal. **have a whale of a time** *Informal* enjoy oneself very much. **whaler** n ship or person involved in whaling. **whaling** n hunting of whales for food and oil.

wharf n, pl **wharves, wharfs.** platform at a harbour for loading and unloading ships. **wharfie** n

Aust person employed to load and unload ships.

what pron which thing; that which; request for a statement to be repeated. ▶ interj exclamation of anger, surprise, etc. ▶ adv in which way, how much, e.g. *what do you care?* **what for?** why? **whatever** pron everything or anything that; no matter what. **whatnot** n *Informal* similar unspecified things. **whatsoever** adj at all.

wheat n grain used in making flour, bread, and pasta; plant producing this. **wheaten** adj **wheatear** n small songbird.

wheedle v coax or cajole.

wheel n disc that revolves on an axle; pivoting movement. ▶ v push or pull (something with wheels); turn as if on an axis; turn round suddenly. **wheeling and dealing** use of shrewd and sometimes unscrupulous methods to achieve success. **wheeler-dealer** n **wheelbarrow** n shallow box for carrying loads, with a wheel at the front and two handles. **wheelbase** n distance between a vehicle's front and back axles. **wheelchair** n chair mounted on wheels for use by people who cannot walk. **wheel clamp** immobilizing device fixed to one wheel of an illegally parked car.

wheeze v breathe with a hoarse whistling noise. ▶ n wheezing sound; *Informal* trick or plan. **wheezy** adj

whelk n edible snail-like shellfish.

whelp n pup or cub. ▶ v (of an animal) give birth.

when adv at what time? ▶ conj at the time that; although; considering the fact that. ▶ pron at which time. **whenever** adv, conj at whatever time.

whence adv, conj *Obs* from what

place or source.

where adv in, at, or to what place?
▶ pron in, at, or to which place.
▶ conj in the place at which.
whereabouts n present position.
▶ adv at what place. **whereas**
conj but on the other hand. **whereby**
pron by which. **wherefore** Obs
▶ adv why. ▶ conj consequently.
whereupon conj at which point.
wherever conj, adv at whatever
place. **wherewithal** n necessary
funds, resources, etc.

whet v **whetting, whetted.**
sharpen (a tool). **whet
someone's appetite** increase
someone's desire. **whetstone** n
stone for sharpening tools.

whether conj used to introduce an
indirect question or a clause
expressing doubt or choice.

whey [way] n watery liquid that
separates from the curd when
milk is clotted.

which adj, pron used to request or
refer to a choice from different
possibilities. ▶ pron used to refer to
a thing already mentioned.
whichever adj, pron any out of
several; no matter which.

whiff n puff of air or odour; trace
or hint.

Whig n member of a British
political party of the 18th–19th
centuries that sought limited
reform.

while conj at the same time that;
whereas. ▶ n period of time.
whilst conj while. **while away** v
pass (time) idly but pleasantly.

whim n sudden fancy. **whimsy** n
caprious idea; light or fanciful
humour. **whimsical** adj unusual,
playful, and fanciful.

whimper v cry in a soft whining
way. ▶ n soft plaintive whine.

whin n Brit gorse.

whine n high-pitched plaintive cry;

peevish complaint. ▶ v make such
a sound. **whining** n, adj

whinge Brit, Aust & NZ informal ▶ v
complain. ▶ n complaint.

whinny v **-nying, -nied.** neigh
softly. ▶ n, pl **-nies.** soft neigh.

whip n cord attached to a handle,
used for beating animals or
people; politician responsible for
organizing and disciplining fellow
party or caucus members; call
made on members of Parliament
to attend for important votes;
dessert made from beaten cream
or egg whites. ▶ v **whipping,
whipped.** strike with a whip,
strap, or cane; Informal pull,
remove, or move quickly; beat
(esp. eggs or cream) to a froth;
rouse into a particular condition;
Informal steal. **whiplash injury**
neck injury caused by a sudden
jerk to the head, as in a car crash.
whip-round n Informal collection
of money.

whippet n racing dog like a small
greyhound.

whirl v spin or revolve; be dizzy or
confused. ▶ n whirling movement;
bustling activity; confusion or
giddiness. **whirlpool** n strong
circular current of water.
whirlwind n column of air
whirling violently upwards in a
spiral. ▶ adj much quicker than
normal.

whirr, whir n prolonged soft buzz.
▶ v **whirring, whirred. (**cause to)
make a whirr.

whisk v move or remove quickly;
beat (esp. eggs or cream) to a
froth. ▶ n egg-beating utensil.

whisker n any of the long stiff
hairs on the face of a cat or other
mammal. ▶ pl hair growing on a
man's face. **by a whisker** Informal
only just.

whisky n, pl **-kies.** spirit distilled

from fermented cereals. **whiskey** *n*, *pl* **-keys.** Irish or American whisky.

whisper *v* speak softly, without vibration of the vocal cords; rustle. ▶ *n* soft voice; *Informal* rumour; rustling sound.

whist *n* card game in which one pair of players tries to win more tricks than another pair.

whistle *v* produce a shrill sound, esp. by forcing the breath through pursed lips; signal by a whistle. ▶ *n* whistling sound; instrument blown to make a whistling sound. **blow the whistle on** *Informal* inform on or put a stop to. **whistling** *n*, *adj*

whit *n* not a whit not the slightest amount.

white *adj* of the colour of snow; pale; light in colour; (of coffee) served with milk. ▶ *n* colour of snow; clear fluid round the yolk of an egg; white part, esp. of the eyeball; (**W-**) member of the race of people with light-coloured skin. **whiten** *v* make or become white or whiter. **whiteness** *n* **whitish** *adj* **white-collar** *adj* denoting professional and clerical workers. **white elephant** useless or unwanted possession. **white flag** signal of surrender or truce. **white goods** large household appliances such as cookers and fridges. **white-hot** *adj* very hot. **white lie** minor unimportant lie. **white paper** report by the government, outlining its policy on a matter.

whitebait *n* small edible fish.

whitewash *n* substance for whitening walls. ▶ *v* cover with whitewash; conceal or gloss over unpleasant facts.

whither *adv Obs* to what place.

whiting *n* edible sea fish.

Whitsun *n* Christian festival celebrating the descent of the Holy Spirit to the apostles.

whittle *v* cut or carve (wood) with a knife. **whittle down, away** *v* reduce or wear away gradually.

whizz, whiz *v* **whizzing, whizzed.** make a loud buzzing sound; *Informal* move quickly. ▶ *n*, *pl* **whizzes.** loud buzzing sound; *Informal* person skilful at something. **whizz kid, whiz kid** *Informal* person who is outstandingly able for his or her age.

who *pron* which person; used to refer to a person or people already mentioned. **whoever** *pron* any person who; no matter who.

whodunnit, whodunit [hoo-**dun**-nit] *n Informal* detective story, play, or film.

whole *adj* containing all the elements or parts; uninjured or undamaged. ▶ *n* complete thing or system. **on the whole** taking everything into consideration. **wholly** *adv* **wholefood** *n* food that has been processed as little as possible. **wholehearted** *adj* sincere or enthusiastic. **wholemeal** *adj* (of flour) made from the whole wheat grain; made from wholemeal flour. **whole number** number that does not contain a fraction. **wholesale** *adj*, *adv* dealing by selling goods in large quantities to retailers; on a large scale. **wholesaler** *n*

wholesome *adj* physically or morally beneficial.

whom *pron* objective form of WHO.

whoop *v*, *n* shout or cry to express excitement.

whoopee *interj Informal* cry of joy.

whooping cough *n* infectious disease marked by convulsive coughing and noisy breathing.

whopper n Informal anything unusually large; huge lie.

whopping adj

whorl n ring of leaves or petals; one turn of a spiral.

whose pron of whom or of which.

why adv for what reason. ▶ pron because of which.

wick n cord through a lamp or candle which carries fuel to the flame.

wicked adj morally bad; mischievous. **wickedly** adv **wickedness** n

wicker adj made of woven cane. **wickerwork** n

wicket n set of three cricket stumps and two bails; ground between the two wickets on a cricket pitch.

wide adj large from side to side; having a specified width; spacious or extensive; far from the target; opened fully. ▶ adv to the full extent; over an extensive area; far from the target. **widely** adv

widen v make or become wider.

widespread adj affecting a wide area or a large number of people.

widgeon n same as WIGEON.

widow n woman whose husband is dead and who has not remarried. **widowed** adj **widowhood** n **widower** n man whose wife is dead and who has not remarried.

width n distance from side to side; quality of being wide.

wield v hold and use (a weapon); have and use (power).

wife n, pl **wives**. woman to whom a man is married.

wig n artificial head of hair.

wigeon n duck found in marshland.

wiggle v move jerkily from side to side. ▶ n wiggling movement.

wigwam n Native American's tent.

wild adj (of animals) not tamed or domesticated; (of plants) not cultivated; lacking restraint or control; violent or stormy; Informal excited; Informal furious; random. **wilds** pl n desolate or uninhabited place. **wildly** adv **wildness** n **wild-goose chase** search that has little chance of success.

wildcat n European wild animal like a large domestic cat. **wildcat strike** sudden unofficial strike.

wildebeest n gnu.

wilderness n uninhabited uncultivated region.

wildfire n **spread like wildfire** spread quickly and uncontrollably.

wildlife n wild animals and plants collectively.

wiles pl n tricks or ploys. **wily** adj crafty or sly.

wilful adj headstrong or obstinate; intentional. **wilfully** adv

will[1] v, past **would**. used as an auxiliary to form the future tense or to indicate intention, ability, or expectation.

will[2] n strong determination; desire or wish; directions written for disposal of one's property after death. ▶ v use one's will in an attempt to do (something); wish or desire; leave (property) by a will. **willing** adj ready or inclined (to do something); keen and obliging. **willingly** adv **willingness** n **willpower** n ability to control oneself and one's actions.

will-o'-the-wisp n elusive person or thing; pale light sometimes seen over marshes at night.

willow n tree with thin flexible branches; its wood, used for making cricket bats. **willowy** adj slender and graceful.

willy-nilly adv whether desired or not.

willy wagtail n Aust black-and-white flycatcher.

willy-willy n Aust small tropical dust storm.

wilt v (cause to) become limp or lose strength.

wimp n Informal feeble ineffectual person.

wimple n garment framing the face, worn by medieval women and now by nuns.

win v **winning, won.** come first in (a competition, fight, etc.); gain (a prize) in a competition; get by effort. ▶ n victory, esp. in a game. **winner** n **winning** adj gaining victory; charming. **winnings** pl n sum won, esp. in gambling. **win over** v gain the support or consent of (someone).

wince v draw back, as if in pain. ▶ n wincing.

winch n machine for lifting or hauling using a cable or chain wound round a drum. ▶ v lift or haul using a winch.

wind¹ n current of air; hint or suggestion; breath; flatulence; idle talk. ▶ v render short of breath. **windy** adj **windward** adj, n (of or in) the direction from which the wind is blowing. **windfall** n unexpected good luck; fallen fruit. **wind instrument** musical instrument played by blowing. **windmill** n machine for grinding or pumping driven by sails turned by the wind. **windpipe** n tube linking the throat and the lungs. **windscreen** n front window of a motor vehicle. **windscreen wiper** device that wipes rain etc. from a windscreen. **windsock** n cloth cone on a mast at an airfield to indicate wind direction. **windsurfing** n sport of riding on water using a surfboard propelled and steered by a sail.

wind² v **winding, wound.** coil or wrap around; tighten the spring of (a clock or watch); move in a twisting course. **wind up** v bring to or reach an end; tighten the spring of (a clock or watch); Informal make tense or agitated; Slang tease.

windlass n winch worked by a crank.

window n opening in a wall to let in light or air; glass pane or panes fitted in such an opening; display area behind the window of a shop; area on a computer screen that can be manipulated separately from the rest of the display area; period of unbooked time in a diary or schedule. **window-dressing** n arrangement of goods in a shop window; attempt to make something more attractive than it really is. **window-shopping** n looking at goods in shop windows without intending to buy.

wine n alcoholic drink made from fermented grapes; similar drink made from other fruits. **wine and dine** entertain or be entertained with fine food and drink.

wing n one of the limbs or organs of a bird, insect, or bat that are used for flying; one of the winglike supporting parts of an aircraft; projecting side part of a building; faction of a political party; part of a car body surrounding the wheels; Sport (player on) either side of the pitch. ▶ pl sides of a stage. ▶ v fly; wound slightly in the wing or arm. **winged** adj **winger** n Sport player positioned on a wing.

wink v close and open (an eye) quickly as a signal; twinkle. ▶ n winking; smallest amount of sleep.

winkle n shellfish with a spiral

shell. **winkle up** v *Informal* extract or prise out.

winnow v separate (chaff) from (grain); examine to select desirable elements.

winsome adj charming or winning.

winter n coldest season. ▶ v spend the winter. **wintry** adj of or like winter; cold or unfriendly. **winter sports** open-air sports held on snow or ice.

wipe v clean or dry by rubbing; erase (a tape). ▶ n wiping. **wipe out** v destroy completely.

wire n thin flexible strand of metal; length of this used to carry electric current; *Obs* telegram. ▶ v equip with wires. **wiring** n system of wires. **wiry** adj lean and tough; like wire. **wire-haired** adj (of a dog) having a stiff wiry coat.

wireless n *Old-fashioned* same as RADIO.

wireless adj (of a computer network) connected by radio rather than by cables or fibre optics. ▶ n *Old-fashioned* same as RADIO.

wisdom n good sense and judgment; accumulated knowledge. **wisdom tooth** any of the four large molar teeth that come through usu. after the age of twenty.

wise[1] adj having wisdom. **wisely** adv **wiseacre** n person who wishes to seem wise.

wise[2] n *Obs* manner.

wisecrack *Informal* ▶ n clever, sometimes unkind, remark. ▶ v make a wisecrack.

wish v want or desire; feel or express a hope about someone's wellbeing, success, etc. ▶ n expression of a desire; thing desired. **wishful** adj too optimistic. **wishbone** n V-shaped bone above the breastbone of a fowl.

wishy-washy adj *Informal* insipid or bland.

wisp n light delicate streak; twisted bundle or tuft. **wispy** adj

wisteria n climbing shrub with blue or purple flowers.

wistful adj sadly longing. **wistfully** adv

wit n ability to use words or ideas in a clever and amusing way; person with this ability; (sometimes pl) practical intelligence. **witless** adj foolish.

witch n person, usu. female, who practises (black) magic; ugly or wicked woman. **witchcraft** n use of magic. **witch doctor** (in certain societies) a man appearing to cure or cause injury or disease by magic. **witch-hunt** n campaign against people with unpopular views.

witchetty grub n wood-boring edible Australian caterpillar.

with prep indicating presence alongside, possession, means of performance, characteristic manner, etc., e.g. *walking with his dog; a man with two cars; hit with a hammer; playing with skill.*

within prep, adv in or inside.

without prep not accompanied by, using, or having.

withdraw v -drawing, -drew, -drawn. take or move out or away. **withdrawal** n **withdrawn** adj unsociable.

wither v wilt or dry up. **withering** adj (of a look or remark) scornful.

withers pl n ridge between a horse's shoulder blades.

withhold v -holding, -held. refrain from giving.

withstand v -standing, -stood. oppose or resist successfully.

witness n person who has seen something happen; person giving evidence in court; evidence or testimony. ▶ v see at first hand; sign (a document) to certify that it is genuine.

witter v Chiefly Brit chatter pointlessly or at unnecessary length.

wittingly adv intentionally.

witty adj **wittier, wittiest.** clever and amusing. **wittily** adv **witticism** n witty remark.

wives n plural of WIFE.

wizard n magician; person with outstanding skill in a particular field. **wizardry** n

wizened [wiz-zend] adj shrivelled or wrinkled.

woad n blue dye obtained from a plant, used by the ancient Britons as a body dye.

wobbegong n Australian shark with brown-and-white skin.

wobble v move unsteadily; shake. ▶ n wobbling movement or sound. **wobbly** adj

wodge n Informal thick lump or chunk.

woe n grief. **woeful** adj extremely sad; pitiful. **woefully** adv **woebegone** adj looking miserable.

wok n bowl-shaped Chinese cooking pan, used for stir-frying.

woke v past tense of WAKE[1].

woken v past participle of WAKE[1].

wold n high open country.

wolf n, pl **wolves.** wild predatory canine mammal. ▶ v eat ravenously. **cry wolf** raise a false alarm. **wolf whistle** whistle by a man indicating that he thinks a woman is attractive.

wolverine n carnivorous mammal of Arctic regions.

woman n, pl **women.** adult human female; women collectively. **womanhood** n **womanish** adj effeminate. **womanly** adj having qualities traditionally associated with a woman. **womanizing** n practice of indulging in casual affairs with women. **womanizer** n

Women's Liberation movement for the removal of inequalities between women and men (also **women's lib**).

womb n hollow organ in female mammals where babies are conceived and develop.

wombat n small heavily-built burrowing Australian marsupial.

won v past of WIN.

wonder v be curious about; be amazed. ▶ n wonderful thing; emotion caused by an amazing or unusual thing, e.g. a wonder drug. **wonderful** adj spectacularly successful, e.g. a wonder drug. **wonderful** adj very fine; remarkable. **wonderfully** adv **wonderment** n **wondrous** adj Old-fashioned wonderful.

wonky adj **-kier, -kiest.** Brit, Aust & NZ informal shaky or unsteady.

wont [rhymes with **don't**] adj accustomed. ▶ n custom.

won't will not.

woo v try to persuade; Old-fashioned try to gain the love of.

wood n substance trees are made of, used in carpentry and as fuel; area where trees grow; long-shafted golf club, usu. with wooden head. **wooded** adj covered with trees. **wooden** adj made of wood; without expression. **woody** adj **woodbine** n honeysuckle. **woodcock** n game bird. **woodcut** n (print made from) an engraved block of wood. **woodland** n forest. **woodlouse** n small insect-like creature with many legs. **woodpecker** n bird which searches tree trunks for insects. **woodwind** adj, n (of) a type of wind instrument made of wood.

woodworm n insect larva that bores into wood.

woof¹ n cross threads in weaving.

woof² n barking noise made by a dog. **woofer** n loudspeaker reproducing low-frequency sounds.

wool n soft hair of sheep, goats, etc.; yarn spun from this. **woollen** adj **woolly** adj of or like wool; vague or muddled. ▸ n knitted woollen garment.

woomera n notched stick used by Australian Aborigines to aid the propulsion of a spear.

woozy adj **woozier, wooziest.** Informal weak, dizzy, and confused.

wop-wops pl n NZ informal remote rural areas.

word n smallest single meaningful unit of speech or writing; chat or discussion; brief remark; message; promise; command. ▸ v express in words. **wordy** adj using too many words. **wording** n choice and arrangement of words. **word processor** keyboard, microprocessor, and VDU for electronic organization and storage of text. **word processing** n

wore v past tense of WEAR.

work n physical or mental effort directed to making or doing something; paid employment; duty or task; something made or done. ▸ pl factory; total of a writer's or artist's achievements; Informal full treatment; mechanism of a machine. ▸ adj of or for work. ▸ v (cause) to do work; be employed; (cause) to operate; (of a plan etc.) to be successful; cultivate (land); manipulate, shape, or process; (cause) to reach a specified condition. **work-to-rule** n protest in which workers keep strictly to all regulations to reduce the rate of work. **workable** adj WEAR. **worker** n **workaholic** n person

obsessed with work. **workhorse** n person or thing that does a lot of dull or routine work. **workhouse** n (in England, formerly) institution where the poor were given food and lodgings in return for work. **working class** social class consisting of wage earners, esp. manual workers. **working-class** adj **working party** committee investigating a specific problem. **workman** n manual worker. **workmanship** n skill with which an object is made. **workshop** n room or building for a manufacturing process. **worktop** n surface in a kitchen, used for food preparation.

world n the planet earth; mankind; society of a particular area or period; sphere of existence. ▸ adj of the whole world. **worldly** adj not spiritual; concerned with material things; wise in the ways of the world. **world-weary** adj no longer finding pleasure in life. **World Wide Web** global network of linked computer files.

worm n small limbless invertebrate animal; Informal wretched or spineless person; shaft with a spiral thread forming part of a gear system; Computers type of virus. ▸ pl illness caused by parasitic worms in the intestines. ▸ v rid of worms. **worm one's way** crawl; insinuate (oneself). **wormy** adj **worm-eaten** adj eaten into by worms. **worm out** v extract (information) craftily. **wormwood** n bitter plant.

worn v past participle of WEAR.

worry v **-rying, -ried.** (cause to) be anxious or uneasy; annoy or bother; (of a dog) chase and try to bite (sheep etc.). ▸ n, pl **-ries.** (cause of) anxiety or concern. **worried** adj **worrying** adj, n

worse adj, adv comparative of BAD or BADLY. **worst** adj, adv superlative of BAD or BADLY. ▶ n worst thing. **worsen** v make or grow worse.

worship v **-shipping, -shipped.** show religious devotion to; love and admire. ▶ n act or instance of worshipping; **(W-)** title for a mayor or magistrate. **worshipper** n **worshipful** adj worshipping.

worsted [wooss-tid] n type of woollen yarn or fabric.

worth prep having a value of; meriting or justifying. ▶ n value or price; excellence; amount to be had for a given sum. **worthless** adj **worthy** adj deserving admiration or respect. ▶ n Informal notable person. **worthily** adv **worthiness** n **worthwhile** adj worth the time or effort involved.

would v used as an auxiliary to express a request, describe a habitual past action, or form the past tense or subjunctive mood of WILL[1]. **would-be** adj wishing or pretending to be.

wouldn't would not.

wound[1] n injury caused by violence; injury to the feelings. ▶ v inflict a wound on.

wound[2] v past of WIND[2].

wove v a past tense of WEAVE.

woven v a past participle of WEAVE.

wow interj exclamation of astonishment. ▶ n Informal astonishing person or thing.

wowser n Aust & NZ slang puritanical person; teetotaller.

wpm words per minute.

wrack n seaweed.

wraith n ghost.

wrangle v argue noisily. ▶ n noisy argument.

wrap v **wrapping, wrapped.** fold (something) round (a person or thing) so as to cover. ▶ n garment

wrapped round the shoulders; sandwich made by wrapping a filling in a tortilla. **wrapper** n cover for a product. **wrapping** n material used to wrap. **wrap up** v fold paper round; put warm clothes on; Informal finish or settle (a matter).

wrasse n colourful sea fish.

wrath [roth] n intense anger. **wrathful** adj

wreak v **wreak havoc** cause chaos. **wreak vengeance on** take revenge on.

wreath n twisted ring or band of flowers or leaves used as a memorial or tribute. **wreathed** adj surrounded or encircled.

wreck v destroy. ▶ n remains of something that has been destroyed or badly damaged, esp. a ship; person in very poor condition. **wrecker** n **wreckage** n wrecked remains.

wren n small brown songbird.

Wren n Informal (in Britain) member of the former Women's Royal Naval Service.

wrench v twist or pull violently; sprain (a joint). ▶ n violent twist or pull; sprain; difficult or painful parting; adjustable spanner.

wrest v twist violently; take by force.

wrestle v fight, esp. as a sport, by grappling with and trying to throw down an opponent; struggle hard with. **wrestler** n **wrestling** n

wretch n despicable person; pitiful person.

wretched [retch-id] adj miserable or unhappy; worthless. **wretchedly** adv **wretchedness** n

wrier adj a comparative of WRY.

wriest adj a superlative of WRY.

wriggle v move with a twisting action; manoeuvre oneself by devious means. ▶ *n* wriggling movement.

wright *n* maker, e.g. *wheelwright*.

wring *v* **wringing, wrung.** twist, esp. to squeeze liquid out of; clasp and twist (the hands); obtain by forceful means.

wrinkle *n* slight crease, esp. one in the skin due to age. ▶ *v* make or become slightly creased. **wrinkly** *adj*

wrist *n* joint between the hand and the arm. **wristwatch** *n* watch worn on the wrist.

writ *n* written legal command.

write *v* **writing, wrote, written.** mark paper etc. with symbols or words; set down in words; communicate by letter; be the author or composer of. **writing** *n* **writer** *n* author; person who has written something specified. **write-off** *n Informal* something damaged beyond repair. **write-up** *n* published account of something.

writhe *v* twist or squirm in or as if in pain.

wrong *adj* incorrect or mistaken; immoral or bad; not intended or suitable; not working properly. ▶ *adv* in a wrong manner. ▶ *n* something immoral or unjust. ▶ *v* treat unjustly; malign. **wrongly** *adv* **wrongful** *adj* **wrongfully** *adv* **wrongdoing** *n* immoral or illegal behaviour. **wrongdoer** *n*

wrote *v* past tense of WRITE.

wrought [rawt] *v Lit* past of WORK. ▶ *adj* (of metals) shaped by hammering or beating. **wrought iron** pure form of iron used for decorative work.

wrung *v* past of WRING.

wry *adj* **wrier, wriest** or **wryer, wryest.** drily humorous; (of a facial expression) contorted. **wryly** *adv*

wt. weight.

WWW World Wide Web.

wych-elm *n* elm with large rough leaves.

X x

X indicating an error, a choice, or a kiss; indicating an unknown, unspecified, or variable factor, number, person, or thing.

xenon *n Chem* colourless odourless gas found in very small quantities in the air.

xenophobia [zen-oh-**fobe**-ee-a] *n* fear or hatred of people from other countries.

Xerox [**zeer**-ox] *n* ® machine for copying printed material; ® copy made by a Xerox machine. ▶ *v* copy (a document) using such a machine.

Xmas [**eks**-mass] *n Informal* Christmas.

X-ray, x-ray *n* stream of radiation that can pass through some solid materials; picture made by sending X-rays through someone's body to examine internal organs. ▶ *v* photograph, treat, or examine using X-rays.

xylem [**zy**-lem] *n* plant tissue that conducts water and minerals from the roots to all other parts.

xylophone [**zile**-oh-fone] *n* musical instrument made of a row of wooden bars played with hammers.

Y y

Y2K *n Informal* name for the year 2000 AD (esp. referring to the millennium bug).

ya *interj S Afr* yes.

yabby n, pl **-bies**. Aust small freshwater crayfish; marine prawn used as bait.

yacht [yott] n large boat with sails or an engine, used for racing or pleasure cruising. **yachting** n **yachtsman, yachtswoman** n

yak¹ n Tibetan ox with long shaggy hair.

yak² v **yakking, yakked**. Slang talk continuously about unimportant matters.

yakka n Aust & NZ informal work.

yam n tropical root vegetable.

yank v pull or jerk suddenly. ▶ n sudden pull or jerk.

Yankee, Yank n Slang person from the United States.

yap v **yapping, yapped**. bark with a high-pitched sound; Informal talk continuously. ▶ n high-pitched bark.

yard¹ n unit of length equal to 36 inches or about 91.4 centimetres. **yardstick** n standard against which to judge other people or things.

yard² n enclosed area, usu. next to a building and often used for a particular purpose, e.g. builder's yard.

yarmulke [yar-mull-ka] n skullcap worn by Jewish men.

yarn n thread used for knitting or making cloth; Informal long involved story.

yashmak n veil worn by a Muslim woman to cover her face in public.

yaw v (of an aircraft or ship) turn to one side or from side to side while moving.

yawl n two-masted sailing boat.

yawn v open the mouth wide and take in air deeply, often when sleepy or bored; (of an opening) be large and wide. ▶ n act of yawning. **yawning** adj

yd yard.

ye [yee] pron Obs you.

year n time taken for the earth to make one revolution around the sun, about 365 days; twelve months from January 1 to December 31. **yearly** adj, adv (happening) every year or once a year. **yearling** n animal between one and two years old.

yearn v want (something) very much. **yearning** n, adj

yeast n fungus used to make bread rise and to ferment alcoholic drinks. **yeasty** adj

yebo interj S Afr informal yes.

yell v shout or scream in a loud or piercing way. ▶ n loud cry of pain, anger, or fear.

yellow n the colour of gold, a lemon, etc. ▶ adj of this colour; Informal cowardly. ▶ v make or become yellow. **yellow fever** serious infectious tropical disease. **yellowhammer** n European songbird with a yellow head and body. **Yellow Pages** ® telephone directory which lists businesses under the headings of the type of service they provide.

yelp v, n (give) a short sudden cry.

yen¹ n, pl **yen**. monetary unit of Japan.

yen² n Informal longing or desire.

yeoman [yo-man] n, pl **-men**. Hist farmer owning and farming his own land. **yeoman of the guard** member of the ceremonial bodyguard of the British monarchy.

yes interj expresses consent, agreement, or approval; used to answer when one is addressed. **yes man** person who always agrees with their superior.

yesterday adv, n (on) the day before today; (in) the recent past.

yet conj nevertheless, still. ▶ adv until then or now; still; now.

yeti n same as ABOMINABLE SNOWMAN.

yew n evergreen tree with needle-like leaves and red berries.

Yiddish adj, n (of or in) a language of German origin spoken by many Jews in Europe and elsewhere.

yield v produce or bear; give up control of, surrender; give in. ▶ n amount produced. **yielding** adj submissive; soft or flexible.

YMCA Young Men's Christian Association.

yob, yobbo n Slang bad-mannered aggressive youth.

yodel v **-delling, -delled.** sing with abrupt changes between a normal and a falsetto voice.

yoga n Hindu method of exercise and discipline aiming at spiritual, mental, and physical wellbeing. **yogi** n person who practises yoga.

yogurt, yoghurt n slightly sour custard-like food made from milk that has had bacteria added to it, often sweetened and flavoured with fruit.

yoke n wooden bar put across the necks of two animals to hold them together; frame fitting over a person's shoulders for carrying buckets; Lit oppressive force, e.g. the yoke of the tyrant; fitted part of a garment to which a fuller part is attached. ▶ v put a yoke on; unite or link.

yokel n Old-fashioned slang person who lives in the country and is usu. simple and old-fashioned.

yolk n yellow part of an egg that provides food for the developing embryo.

Yom Kippur n annual Jewish religious holiday.

yonder adj, adv (situated) over there.

yonks pl n Informal very long time.

yore n Lit **of yore** a long time ago.

Yorkshire pudding n baked batter made from flour, milk, and eggs.

you pron refers to: the person or people addressed; unspecified person or people in general.

young adj in an early stage of life or growth. ▶ pl n young people in general; offspring, esp. young animals. **youngster** n young person.

your adj of, belonging to, or associated with you; of, belonging to, or associated with an unspecified person or people in general. **yours** pron something belonging to you. **yourself** pron

youth n time of being young; boy or young man; young people as a group. **youthful** adj **youthfulness** n **youth club** club that provides leisure activities for young people. **youth hostel** inexpensive lodging place for young people travelling cheaply.

yowl v, n (produce) a loud mournful cry.

yo-yo n, pl **-yos.** toy consisting of a spool attached to a string, by which it is repeatedly spun out and reeled in.

yttrium [it-tree-um] n Chem silvery metallic element used in various alloys.

yucca n tropical plant with spikes of white leaves.

yucky adj **yuckier, yuckiest.** Slang disgusting, nasty.

Yule n Lit Christmas (season).

yuppie n young highly-paid professional person, esp. one who has a materialistic way of life. ▶ adj typical of or reflecting the values of yuppies.

YWCA Young Women's Christian Association.

Z z

zany [zane-ee] *adj* **zanier, zaniest.** comical in an endearing way.

zap *v* **zapping, zapped.** *Slang* kill (by shooting); change TV channels rapidly by remote control.

zeal *n* great enthusiasm or eagerness. **zealot** [zel-lot] *n* fanatic or extreme enthusiast. **zealous** [zel-luss] *adj* extremely eager or enthusiastic. **zealously** *adv*

zebra *n* black-and-white striped African animal of the horse family. **zebra crossing** pedestrian crossing marked by black and white stripes on the road.

zebu [zee-boo] *n* Asian ox with a humped back and long horns.

Zen *n* Japanese form of Buddhism that concentrates on learning through meditation and intuition.

zenith *n* highest point of success or power; point in the sky directly above an observer.

zephyr [zef-fer] *n* soft gentle breeze.

zeppelin *n Hist* large cylindrical airship.

zero *n, pl* **-ros, -roes.** (symbol representing) the number 0; point on a scale of measurement from which the graduations commence; lowest point; nothing, nil. ▶ *adj* having no measurable quantity or size. **zero in on** *v* aim at; *Informal* concentrate on.

zest *n* enjoyment or excitement; interest, flavour, or charm; peel of an orange or lemon.

zigzag *n* line or course having sharp turns in alternating directions. ▶ *v* **-zagging, -zagged.** move in a zigzag. ▶ *adj* formed in or proceeding in a zigzag.

zinc *n Chem* bluish-white metallic element used in alloys and to coat metal.

zing *n Informal* quality in something that makes it lively or interesting.

Zionism *n* movement to found and support a Jewish homeland in Israel. **Zionist** *n, adj*

zip *n* fastener with two rows of teeth that are closed or opened by a small clip pulled between them; *Informal* energy, vigour; short whizzing sound. ▶ *v* **zipping, zipped.** fasten with a zip; move with a sharp whizzing sound.

zircon *n* mineral used as a gemstone and in industry.

zirconium *n Chem* greyish-white metallic element that is resistant to corrosion.

zither *n* musical instrument consisting of strings stretched over a flat box and plucked to produce musical notes.

zodiac *n* imaginary belt in the sky within which the sun, moon, and planets appear to move, divided into twelve equal areas, called signs of the zodiac, each named after a constellation.

zombie, zombi *n* person who appears to be lifeless, apathetic, or totally lacking in independent judgment; corpse brought back to life by witchcraft.

zone *n* area with particular features or properties; one of the divisions of the earth's surface according to temperature. ▶ *v* divide into zones. **zonal** *adj*

zoo *n, pl* **zoos.** place where live animals are kept for show.

zoology *n* study of animals. **zoologist** *n* **zoological** *adj* **zoological garden** zoo.

zoom *v* move or rise very rapidly; make or move with a buzzing or humming sound. **zoom lens** lens that can make the details of a picture larger or smaller while keeping the picture in focus.

zucchini [zoo-**keen**-ee] *n, pl* -**ni,** -**nis.** *US & Aust* courgette.

Zulu *n* member of a tall Black people of southern Africa; language of this people.

zygote *n* fertilized egg cell.

WORD POWER
AND
FACT FINDER

CONTENTS

CONTENTS

CONTENTS

PARTS OF SPEECH

Every word in the dictionary belongs to one or more of the classes of words called the parts of speech. Knowing the part of speech of a particular word helps us understand what sort of idea the word represents, and how it can be combined with other words.

►ADJECTIVE

An adjective is a word that tells you something about a noun or pronoun. Adjectives are sometimes called "describing words":

> e.g. *three* boats ◦ *silly* me ◦ an *enormous* cloud ◦ Her dress is *green*. ◦ They are probably *Danish*. ◦ one *long* and two *short* sticks ◦ a *southern* accent

Most short adjectives have three different forms. These forms are called the **positive**, the **comparative** and the **superlative**.

1 The **positive** form is used when no comparison is being made:

> e.g. She lived in a *big* house.

2 The **comparative** form is made by adding *-er* to the positive form. It is used to show that the thing being described has more of a quality than the thing it is being compared with:

> e.g. Our garden is *bigger* than yours.

3 The **superlative** form is made by adding *-est* to the positive form. It is used to show that the thing being described has more of a quality than all the others it is

PARTS OF SPEECH

being compared with:

e.g. He ordered the **biggest** pizza on the menu.

4 Another way of making a comparative or superlative is to use the word *more* or *most* before the positive form. For many longer adjectives this is the only way to express a comparative or superlative:

e.g. *more beautiful* [= comparative] ● *most beautiful* [= superlative]

►ADVERB

An adverb is a word that gives more information about a verb, an adjective, or another adverb. Many adverbs end in *-ly*:

e.g. Mark laughed **loudly**. ● She fell **awkwardly**. ● a **horribly** violent film ● It should arrive **fairly** soon.

However, some have the same form as the adjective:

e.g. The river runs **south**. ● Children travel **free**. ● It should arrive **soon**.

Sometimes an adverb can refer to a whole sentence:

e.g. **Unfortunately**, she can't come to the party.

►ARTICLES

1 The word *a* (or *an*) is known as the **indefinite article**. The indefinite article is used before a singular noun to refer to any example of that noun, or to avoid being specific about which example you mean. The form *a* is used before nouns that begin with, or sound as if they

begin with, a consonant. *An* is used before nouns that
begin with, or sound as if they begin with, a vowel:

> e.g. *a man* ● *a country* ● *a union* ● *an elephant*
> ● *an honour*

2 The word *the* is known as the **definite article**.
The definite article is used before a singular or a plural
noun to refer to a specific example or examples of that
noun:

> e.g. *the man standing by the door* ● *the countries of
> Europe*

►CONJUNCTION

A conjunction is a word that joins two words or two
parts of a sentence together. Conjunctions are
sometimes called "joining words":

> e.g. *salt **and** pepper* ● *tea **or** coffee* ● *strange **but** true* ●
> *It's faded **because** it's been washed so often.*

Sometimes conjunctions are used in pairs:

> e.g. *She speaks **both** French **and** Spanish* ● *Use **either**
> butter **or** margarine.* ● *That's **neither** here **nor** there.*

►INTERJECTION

An interjection is a word or short phrase that expresses
a feeling or emotion:

> e.g. *Ouch!* ● *Good gracious!* ● *Whew!* ● *Mmm!* ● *Hooray!*
> ● *Tut, tut!* ● *Hi.* ● *Congratulations!* ● *Thanks.*

Interjections often stand alone, but if an interjection is

PARTS OF SPEECH

used within a sentence, it is usually separated by commas or dashes:

> e.g. *I turned the key and,* **hey presto**, *the engine started.*

►NOUN

A noun is a word that refers to a person, thing or idea. Nouns are sometimes called "naming words".
Common nouns, which start with small letters, are the words used for every example of a certain type of thing:

> e.g. *wizard* ● *country* ● *book*

1 Some common nouns are concrete nouns; these name things you can touch:

> e.g. *chair* ● *water* ● *hand*

2 Other common nouns are abstract nouns; these name things you cannot touch:

> e.g. *hatred* ● *beauty* ● *ambition* ● *popularity*

3 Some common nouns are collective nouns; these are words used to indicate groups or collections of things:

> e.g. *flock* ● *team* ● *furniture*

Proper nouns, which start with capital letters, give the name of a particular person, place or object:

> e.g. *Harry Potter* ● *New Zealand* ● *Great Expectations*

►PREPOSITION

A preposition is a word that is used before a noun or

PARTS OF SPEECH

pronoun to relate it to other words. Prepositions may tell you the place of something in relation to another thing, or indicate movement or time:

> e.g. *an owl **in** the tree* ◦ *The marble rolled **under** the bed.* ◦ *Put the cart **before** the horse.* ◦ *He burst **through** the doors.* ◦ *They're only here **for** the day.* ◦ *We'll arrive **on** Monday.*

▶PRONOUN

A pronoun is a word that is used in place of a noun, or instead of naming a person or thing:

> e.g. *The cat likes fish. **It** likes cream too.* ◦ *Molly rang yesterday. **She** rings every week.*

1 The **personal pronouns** are the words *I, me, we, us, you, he, him, she, her, they, them* and *it*. Personal pronouns replace the subject or object of a sentence:

> e.g. ***He** phoned **me**.*

2 The **reflexive pronouns** replace the object of a sentence when the object is the same person or thing as the subject:

> e.g. *Kathy burnt **herself**.*

3 The **possessive pronouns** are the words *mine, ours, yours, his, hers* and *theirs*:

> e.g. ***Mine** is better than **yours**.* ◦ *I didn't know he was a friend of **theirs**.* ◦ ***Ours** is on the left.*

4 Indefinite pronouns replace a subject or object and are used to refer to a broad or vague range of people

PARTS OF SPEECH

or things:

e.g. **Somebody** must know the answer. ☀ Can you see **anything**?

5 The **demonstrative pronouns** are the words *this*, *that*, *these* and *those*. Demonstrative pronouns replace the subject or object of a sentence:

e.g. **That** is a novel. ☀ **Those** are dictionaries. ☀ Have you seen **this**?

6 The **interrogative pronouns** - used to ask questions - are the words *what, which, who, whose* and *whom*:

e.g. **What** are you doing? ☀ **Who** are you going to see? ☀ **Which** is best?

7 The **relative pronouns** are the words *which, who, whom, whose*, and *that*. Relative pronouns are used to link two different parts of a sentence and always refer back to a word in the earlier part of the sentence:

e.g. We ate at the local café, **which** serves very good snacks. ☀ They have friends **who** live in the country. ☀ He is a man in **whom** you can put your trust. ☀ a boy **whose** name I didn't know ☀ Paris is a city **that** I visit regularly.

▶VERB

A verb is a word that describes an action or state of being. Verbs are sometimes called "doing words".

1 An **auxiliary verb** is a verb used in combination with other verbs to form tenses. The basic auxiliary verbs are *be, have,* and *do*:

PARTS OF SPEECH

e.g. *He is living abroad right now.* • *They **were** laughing.* • *She **has** decided to stay.* • *We **had** already gone home.* • *I **didn't** want to disturb you.* • ***Do** you know where I can find him?*

2 Modal verbs – *can, could, may, might, must, should, would* and *ought* – are usually used as auxiliary verbs to change the tone of the meaning of other verbs. They can express requests, intentions, politeness, likelihood, or obligation:

e.g. ***Can** we go now?* • ***Could** you pass me the salt?* • *I **might** go shopping tomorrow.* • *It **may** be possible to go another day.* • *I **would** be grateful if you **could** return it straight away.* • *She **must** finish her essay by Monday.* • *I thought we **ought** to get out and help.*

3 A phrasal verb consists of a verb followed by either a preposition or an adverb. The two words taken together have a special meaning which is different from their literal meanings:

e.g. *come up with* [= find] • *pass away* [= die] • *nod off* [= go to sleep]

10

PHRASES, CLAUSES AND SENTENCES

►PHRASES

A phrase is a group of words that forms a unit of meaning, but requires additional words to form a meaningful sentence.

Phrases often form part of a sentence and may act as nouns, verbs, adjectives or adverbs:

e.g. **The tall thin man** is my uncle. ❋ He **used to play rugby.** ❋ That's **a bit odd.** ❋ It disappeared **in the blink of an eye.**

►CLAUSES

A clause is a group of words that forms part of a sentence and expresses an idea or describes a situation.

1 A **main clause** is the core of a sentence, and every sentence contains a main clause. Main clauses make sense on their own.

e.g. *John caught a fish* that was bigger than anything he had caught before.

2 A **subordinate clause** is a less important part of a sentence, which gives information about the main clause. Subordinate clauses would not make sense on their own:

e.g. He put the fish back **because it was too small.**

3 A **relative clause** gives more information about the person or thing mentioned in the main clause:

e.g. This is my sister, **who you've met once before.**

PHRASES, CLAUSES AND SENTENCES

►SENTENCES

A sentence is a group of words that expresses an idea or describes a situation. Sentences begin with a capital letter and should end with either a full stop, question mark or exclamation mark.

Sentences have a subject indicating a person or thing that the sentence is about. The subject is usually the first word or group of words in the sentence:

e.g. ***Anna*** *laughed.* ● ***A pale moon*** *rose above the darkened hills.*

Most sentences have a verb. The verb says what the subject of the sentence is doing or what is happening to the subject. The verb usually follows immediately after the subject:

e.g. *Anna **laughed**.* ● *A pale moon **rose** above the darkened hills.*

1 A **simple sentence** has only one main clause and no subordinate clause:

e.g. *John went to bed.*

2 A **compound sentence** is made up of two or more main clauses joined to each other by a conjunction:

e.g. *John went to bed but Paul stayed up to watch TV.*

3 A **complex sentence** is made up of a main clause with one or more subordinate clauses joined to it:

e.g. *After John went to bed, Paul stayed up late watching TV, which is why he was late for work the next morning.*

12

PUNCTUATION

Punctuation marks are essential parts of written language. They help the reader understand what the writer wants to convey, and how something should be read.

▶APOSTROPHE

1 The apostrophe (') is used to show that something belongs to someone. It is usually added to the end of a word and followed by an *s*:

e.g. *a baby's pushchair* ✳ *children's games* ✳ *Hannah's book* ✳ *James's pen*

If the word ends in an *s* and is a plural, an apostrophe is added after the *s* that is already there:

e.g. *Your grandparents are your parents' parents.*

2 An apostrophe is used in shortened forms of words to show that one or more letters have been missed out:

e.g. *it's* [= it is] ✳ *he'll* [= he will] ✳ *she'd* [= she had or she would] ✳ *don't* [= do not] ✳ *rock'n'rock* [= rock and roll]

⚠ An apostrophe is <u>not</u> used to form possessive pronouns:

e.g. *Is the responsibility yours or theirs?* [<u>not</u> *your's* or *their's*] ✳ *Its cover is torn.* [<u>not</u> *It's cover is torn.*]

⚠ An apostrophe is <u>not</u> used to form the plurals of words:

e.g. *2 kilos of potatoes* [<u>not</u> *potato's*] ✳ *The girls laughed.* (<u>not</u> *The girl's laughed.*)

13

PUNCTUATION

►BRACKET

1 Brackets ( ) are used to enclose a word or words which can be left out and still leave a meaningful sentence:

e.g. *The area planted with conifers (see map below) is approximately 4000 hectares.*

2 Brackets are also used to show alternatives or options:

e.g. *Any student(s) interested in taking part should speak to their tutor about it.*

►COLON

The colon (:) is used to introduce a list, a quotation, or an explanation:

e.g. *I used three colours: green, blue and pink.* ⊛ *He received a telegram which read: "Return home immediately."* ⊛ *They didn't like the room: it was small and dingy.*

►COMMA

The comma (,) marks a short pause between different elements in a sentence.

1 A comma is used between two main clauses joined by a conjunction:

e.g. *He was talking quite loudly, but I couldn't hear him.*

2 A comma is often used to separate an introductory

WORD POWER

PUNCTUATION

word or phrase from the main clause in a sentence, or to separate a subordinate clause or short phrase that comes after the main clause:

e.g. *If we get another goal before full-time, we'll have won the league.* ❋ *He'll be there, come what may.*

3 When words like *however, therefore,* and *moreover* are put into a sentence to show how a train of thought is progressing, these words should be marked off by commas:

e.g. *The forecasters got it wrong. There was no warning, therefore, of the heavy rain and flooding that hit the south.*

4 Commas are also used to separate off a subordinate clause inserted into a main clause:

e.g. *A new model, which will be made in Spain, is to be introduced in the Spring.*

5 Commas are used to separate the name of a person or people being addressed from the rest of the sentence:

e.g. *And now, ladies and gentlemen, please raise your glasses in a toast.*

6 Commas are also used to separate items in a list or series:

e.g. *bread, butter and jam* ❋ *Winners of a Highly-Commended Prize: Alice Howard, Ayesha Singh, Thomas McAdam.*

7 A comma is used to separate words in quotation marks from the rest of the sentence, if there is no question mark or exclamation mark at the end of the quotation:

e.g. *"I don't understand this question," said Peter.*

►DASH

1 The dash (–) marks an abrupt change in the flow of a sentence, showing a sudden change of subject:

e.g. *Now children – Kenneth, stop that immediately! – open your books at page 20.*

2 The dash also marks off extra information:

e.g. *Boots and shoes – all shapes, sizes and colours – tumbled out of the cupboard.*

3 The dash is also used to indicate a range:

e.g. *pages 26–42.*

►EXCLAMATION MARK

The exclamation mark (!) is used after exclamations and emphatic expressions:

e.g. *I can't believe it! • Oh, no! Look at this mess!*

⚠ The exclamation mark can lose its effect if it is overused. It is better to use a full stop after a sentence expressing only mild excitement or humour:

e.g. *It was such a beautiful day.*

►FULL STOP

1 A full stop (.) is used to mark the end of a sentence

PUNCTUATION

that is not a question or an exclamation:

e.g. *Harry loves football.*

2 Full stops are also used after abbreviations or initials:

e.g. *etc. * Rev. Adams * George W. Bush*

3 A full stop is used after an indirect question or a polite request:

e.g. *He asked if the London train had arrived. * May I see the menu.*

►HYPHEN

The hyphen (-) separates words or parts of words.

1 A hyphen is used to join two or more words which together form an adjective, where this adjective is used <u>before</u> the noun it describes in a sentence or phrase:

e.g. *a twentieth-century painter * an up-to-date account of the issues * a last-minute dash to the airport * a step-by-step guide to giving up smoking*

The hyphen is left out when the adjective formed comes <u>after</u> the noun it describes:

e.g. *the account is up to date * a painter from the twentieth century*

2 Some common multi-word phrases are usually written with hyphens:

e.g. *mother-in-law*

3 Hyphens can be used to split words formed by adding a prefix to another word, especially to avoid an

PUNCTUATION

awkward or misleading situation:

e.g. *re-elect* ● *re-covering furniture*

4 Numbers from 21 to 99 are usually written with hyphens:

e.g. *sixty-two* ● *fifty-five*

5 Hyphens are used at the ends of lines where a word has been split, to warn the reader that the word continues on the next line:

e.g. *He was just leaving the house when he remembered he'd left his lunch on the kitchen table.*

►QUESTION MARK

The question mark (?) marks the end of a question:

e.g. *When will we be arriving? Do you like hockey and netball?* ● *"What? No ice cream?" said William in astonishment.* ● *Not your best effort, eh?*

A full stop, rather than a question mark, is used after an indirect question or a polite request:

e.g. *George asked when we would be arriving.* ● *Will you please return the completed forms to me.*

►SEMICOLON

The semicolon (;) marks a stronger break than a comma, but a weaker one than a full stop.

1 It is used to mark a break between two main clauses when there is a balance or contrast between the clauses:

PUNCTUATION

e.g. *I'm not that interested in jazz; I prefer classical music.*

2 The semicolon is used to separate clauses or items in a long list:

e.g. *The holiday was a disaster: the flight was four hours late; the hotel was overbooked; and it rained for the whole fortnight.*

▶SLASH

The slash (/) separates letters, words, or numbers. It is used to indicate alternatives, ratios and ranges, and in web site addresses:

e.g. *he/she/it* ● *200 km/hr* ● *the 2001/2 accounting year*
● *http://www.collinsdictionaries.com*

▶SPEECH MARKS, INVERTED COMMAS or QUOTATION MARKS

1 Speech marks, inverted commas or quotation marks (" " or ' ') mark the beginning and end of **direct speech** (a speaker's words written down exactly as they were said):

e.g. *"I didn't understand the question," said Peter.* ● *Mr Evans declared abruptly, "We're leaving."*

2 Speech marks are used to indicate the title of a book, poem, piece of music, film or work of art:

e.g. *Have you read "The Lord of the Rings"?* ● *music from "Swan Lake" by Tchaikovsky*

PUNCTUATION

3 Speech marks are also used to show that a word is being used in an unusual way, or that the word itself is being discussed:

> e.g. *Braille allows a blind person to "see" with the fingers.* • *What is the French for "egg"?*

⚠ Speech marks are **not** used for **indirect** or **reported speech** (what someone has said, but not in their exact words):

> e.g. *Peter said that he didn't understand the question.* • *Mr Evans declared abruptly that they were leaving.*

SPELLING RULES

1 ie or ei The rule is: *i* before *e*, except after *c*:

ach**ie**ve	br**ie**f	ch**ie**f
f**ie**rce	gr**ie**ve	n**ie**ce
rel**ie**f	s**ie**ge	th**ie**f
c**ei**ling	conc**ei**t	dec**ei**t
dec**ei**ve	rec**ei**pt	rec**ei**ve

2 -ize or -ise In this dictionary, only the *-ize* (and *-ization*) endings are shown for verbs (and their nouns) such as *emphasize, organize (organization)* and *patronize*. Many of these words can also be spelled with the endings *-ise* (and *-isation*), and this is quite acceptable in British English. Care should be taken, however, because some words can only be spelled with *-ize* and others only with *-ise*.

Verbs (and nouns) only spelled with *-ize*:

> caps**ize**
> pr**ize** [= *value highly*]

Verbs (and nouns) only spelled with *-ise*:

advert**ise**	adv**ise**	chast**ise**
compr**ise**	comprom**ise**	desp**ise**
dev**ise**	disgu**ise**	exc**ise**
exerc**ise**	franch**ise**	improv**ise**
pr**ise** [= *force open*]	rev**ise**	superv**ise**
surpr**ise**	telev**ise**	

3 a. A final silent *e* is dropped when an ending that begins with a vowel is added:

servile + ity	=	servil**ity**
response + ible	=	respons**ible**
tolerate + ing	=	tolerat**ing**

21

SPELLING RULES

value + able	=	valu**able**
excuse + ed	=	excus**ed**

3 b. But the *e* is kept if an ending beginning with a vowel is added to a word that ends in *-ce* or *-ge*:

change + able	=	chang**eable**
notice + able	=	notic**eable**
outrage + ous	=	outrag**eous**
peace + able	=	peac**eable**

4 When an ending beginning with a vowel is added to a word that ends in a single vowel + a consonant, the consonant is doubled if the stress is on the end of the word:

admit + ance	=	admi**tt**ance
begin + ing	=	begi**nn**ing
occur +ence	=	occu**rr**ence
equip + ed	=	equi**pp**ed

5 When an ending beginning with a vowel is added to a word that ends in a vowel + *l* or *p*, the *l* or *p* is usually doubled:

cancel + ation	=	cance**ll**ation
dial + ing	=	dia**ll**ing
fulfil + ed	=	fulfi**ll**ed
kidnap + er	=	kidna**pp**er
slip + ing	=	sli**pp**ing

6 When the adverb suffix *-ly* is added to an adjective that ends in a consonant followed by *-le*, the *-le* in the adjective is usually dropped:

gentle + ly	=	gent**ly**
idle + ly	=	id**ly**

SPELLING RULES

subtle + ly = subt**ly**

7 When the adjective suffix *-ous* or *-ary* is added to a word that ends in *-our*, the *u* of the *-our* is dropped:

glamour + ous = glam**o**rous
honour + ary = hon**o**rary
humour + ous = hum**o**rous

8 When an ending beginning with *e, i* or *y* is added to a word that ends in *c*, a *k* is added to the *c* to keep its hard sound:

mimic + ed = mimi**ck**ed
picnic + ing = picni**ck**ing

9 a. When an ending is added to a word that ends in a consonant + *y*, the *y* changes to *i*:

beauty + ful = beaut**i**ful
crazy + ly = craz**i**ly
woolly + er = wooll**i**er

9 b. But, with certain short adjectives that end in a consonant + *y*, the *-ly* ending to make an adverb is added after the *y*:

shy + ly = shy**ly**
wry + ly = wry**ly**

10 The plural of a word that ends in a consonant + *y* is made by changing the *y* to *i* and adding *-es*:

story + es = stor**ies**
quality + es = qualit**ies**
spy + es = sp**ies**

11 The plural of a word that ends in a vowel plus *y* is made by adding *-s*:

SPELLING RULES

donkey + s	=	donkey**s**
holiday + s	=	holiday**s**
boy + s	=	boy**s**
buoy + s	=	buoy**s**

12 The plural of a word that ends in *s, x, z, sh* or *ch* is made by adding *-es*:

bus + es	=	bus**es**
mass + es	=	mass**es**
fox + es	=	fox**es**
buzz + es	=	buzz**es**
rash + es	=	rash**es**
match + es	=	match**es**

13 The plural of a word that ends in *-eau* is made by adding *-x*:

gateau + x	=	gateau**x**
bureau + x	=	bureau**x**

(bureaus is also allowable)

14 The suffix *-ful* is always spelt with one *l*:

grateful   faithful   cupful

But *-fully* is always spelt with two:

gratefully   faithfully   beautifully

WORDS AND SPELLINGS THAT CAN BE CONFUSED

accept – VERB   *Please accept my apologies.*
except – PREP   *He works every day except Tuesday.*

---

affect – VERB   *Tiredness affects concentration.*
effect – NOUN   *the beneficial effects of the medicine*

---

allude – VERB   *She alluded to the recent reports in the newspapers.*

elude – VERB   *I recognized his face, but his name eluded me.*

---

altar – NOUN   *The couple stood before the altar to take their marriage vows.*

alter – VERB   *His tone altered suddenly.*

---

ascent – NOUN   *the ascent of Everest by Edmund Hilary and Sherpa Tensing*

assent – NOUN   *The king gave his assent to the government's revised bill.*

---

aural – ADJ   *high- and low-pitched sounds which test aural function*

oral – ADJ   *He stumbled over his words in the oral examination.*

---

breath – NOUN   *There wasn't a breath of wind.*
breathe – VERB   *Breathe deeply a couple of times.*

---

broach – VERB   *She didn't dare broach the subject of a pay rise.*

brooch – NOUN   *a gold brooch set with emeralds and diamonds*

---

canvas – NOUN   *a hammock made from heavy canvas*
canvass – VERB   *TV reporters canvassing opinion*

25

WORDS AND SPELLINGS THAT CAN BE CONFUSED

coarse – ADJ	*a coarse cloth which scratched the skin*	
course – NOUN	*The river widens along its course.*	
complement – NOUN	*Rice is a good complement to curry.*	
compliment – NOUN	*My compliments to the chef.*	
council – NOUN	*the local council • a council of war*	
counsel – VERB & NOUN	*He counsels victims of crime. • give good counsel*	
cue – NOUN	*That's the leading lady's cue.*	
queue – NOUN	*a long queue at the post office*	
curb – VERB	*trying hard to curb her appetite for chocolate*	
kerb – NOUN	*The taxi drew up at the kerb.*	
currant – NOUN	*raisins, sultanas and currants*	
current – NOUN & ADJ	*ocean currents • current affairs.*	
dependant – NOUN	*Do you have children or other dependants?*	
dependent – ADJ	*The flood victims are dependent on international aid.*	
desert – NOUN & VERB	*the Gobi Desert • The sentry deserted his post.*	
dessert – NOUN	*Would you like ice-cream or fresh fruit for dessert?*	
draft – NOUN & VERB	*a first draft of the report • He's drafting a letter to his MP.*	
draught – NOUN	*There's a draught coming under that door.*	

WORDS AND SPELLINGS THAT CAN BE CONFUSED

dual – ADJ	*Their children have dual citizenship of Britain and France.*
duel – NOUN	*The two men fought a duel with pistols at dawn.*
dyeing – VERB	*Have you been dyeing your hair again?*
dying – VERB	*The weakest are dying first, of hunger and cold.*
envelop – VERB	*A greenish haze seemed to envelop the landscape.*
envelope – NOUN	*Send a stamped addressed envelope.*
flair – NOUN	*a flair for design*
flare – NOUN & VERB	*The fishermen lit a flare to attract attention.* ✷ *The horse's nostrils flared.*
forth – ADV	*They rode forth from the black gates in a great mass.*
fourth – ADJ	*the fourth of July*
gamble – VERB	*gambling on the lottery*
gambol – VERB	*puppies gambolling in the sunshine*
gilt – NOUN	*a clock decorated with silver gilt*
guilt – NOUN	*The evidence proves his guilt.*
hoard – NOUN & VERB	*a hoard of treasure* ✷ *Many people hoard cooking ingredients years past their sell-by date.*
horde – NOUN	*hordes of noisy football fans*

WORDS AND SPELLINGS THAT CAN BE CONFUSED

its – ADJ & PRON	The dog broke free of its lead and ran off.
it's – SHORT FORM	It's rude to stare.
lead – VERB & NOUN	You lead the way. ＊ pipes made of lead
led – VERB	He was led astray by the other children.
leant – VERB	He leant against the tree.
lent – VERB	She lent me her bike.
licence – NOUN	a driver's licence
license – VERB	licensed to drive heavy goods vehicles
loath – ADJ	I'm loath to ask him for money.
loathe – VERB	We loathe each other.
loose – ADJ	His front tooth is loose.
lose – VERB	Be careful not to lose your pocket money.
miner – NOUN	a coal miner
minor – ADJ & NOUN	a minor inconvenience ＊ a 14-year-old minor
practice – NOUN	a common practice ＊ a dental practice
practise – VERB	He has a law degree but has never practised.
precede – VERB	Summer precedes autumn.
proceed – VERB	Let's proceed with the meeting.

28

WORDS AND SPELLINGS THAT CAN BE CONFUSED

principal – ADJ & NOUN   *the principal reason* ∗ *the school principal*

principle – NOUN   *Telling fibs is against my principles.*

---

stationary – ADJ   *The bus skidded and hit a stationary vehicle.*

stationery – NOUN   *paper, envelopes and other office stationery*

---

their – ADJ   *It's not their fault.*

they're – SHORT FORM   *They're not to blame.*

there – ADV   *There is no reason to punish them.*

---

vain – ADJ   *He's vain and self-opinionated.* ∗ *She searched in vain for her keys.*

vein – NOUN   *Veins carry blood back to the heart.*

THE EARTH

COUNTRIES, CAPITALS AND CURRENCIES

Country	Capital	Currency
Afghanistan	Kabul	Afghani
Albania	Tirana	Lek
Algeria	Algiers	Dinar
Andorra	Andorra la Vella	euro
Angola	Luanda	Kwanza
Antigua and Barbuda	St John's	East Caribbean Dollar
Argentina	Buenos Aires	Peso
Armenia	Erevan	Dram
Australia	Canberra	Australian Dollar
Austria	Vienna	euro
Azerbaijan	Baku	Manat
Bahamas	Nassau	Bahamian Dollar
Bahrain	Manama	Dinar
Bangladesh	Dhaka	Taka
Barbados	Bridgetown	Barbados Dollar
Belarus	Minsk	Rouble
Belgium	Brussels	euro
Belize	Belmopan	Belize Dollar
Benin	Porto Novo	CFA Franc
Bhutan	Thimphu	Ngultrum
Bolivia	Sucre/La Paz	Boliviano
Bosnia and Herzegovina	Sarajevo	Convertible Marka
Botswana	Gaborone	Pula
Brazil	Brasília	Real
Brunei	Bandar Seri Begawan	Brunei Dollar
Bulgaria	Sofia	Lev
Burkina-Faso	Ouagadougou	CFA Franc
Burundi	Bujumbura	Burundi Franc
Cambodia	Phnom Penh	Riel
Cameroon	Yaoundé	CFA Franc
Canada	Ottawa	Canadian Dollar
Cape Verde	Praia	Escudo
Central African Republic	Bangui	CFA Franc

THE EARTH

COUNTRIES, CAPITALS AND CURRENCIES

Country	Capital	Currency
Chad	Ndjaména	CFA Franc
Chile	Santiago	Peso
China	Beijing	Yuan
Colombia	Bogotá	Peso
Comoros	Moroni	Comorian Franc
Congo (Republic of)	Brazzaville	CFA Franc
Congo (Democratic Republic of)	Kinshasa	Congolese Franc
Costa Rica	San José	Colón
Côte d'Ivoire	Yamoussoukro	CFA Franc
Croatia	Zagreb	Kuna
Cuba	Havana	Peso
Cyprus	Nicosia	Pound
Czech Republic	Prague	Koruna
Denmark	Copenhagen	Krone
Djibouti	Djibouti	Djibouti Franc
Dominica	Roseau	East Caribbean Dollar
Dominican Republic	Santo Domingo	Pesó
East Timor	Dili	US Dollar
Ecuador	Quito	US Dollar
Egypt	Cairo	Pound
El Salvador	San Salvador	Cólon
Equatorial Guinea	Malabo	CFA Franc
Eritrea	Asmara	Nakfa
Estonia	Tallinn	Kroon
Ethiopia	Addis Ababa	Birr
Fiji	Suva	Fiji Dollar
Finland	Helsinki	euro
France	Paris	euro
Gabon	Libreville	CFA Franc
Gambia	Banjul	Dalasi
Georgia	Tbilisi	Lari
Germany	Berlin	euro
Ghana	Accra	Cedi
Greece	Athens	euro
Grenada	St George's	East Caribbean Dollar

THE EARTH

COUNTRIES, CAPITALS AND CURRENCIES

Country	Capital	Currency
Guatemala	Guatemala City	Quetzal
Guinea	Conakry	Guinea Franc
Guinea-Bissau	Bissau	CFA Franc
Guyana	Georgetown	Guyana Dollar
Haiti	Port-au-Prince	Gourde
Honduras	Tegucigalpa	Lempira
Hungary	Budapest	Forint
Iceland	Reykjavik	Króna
India	Delhi	Rupee
Indonesia	Jakarta	Rupiah
Iran	Tehran	Rial
Iraq	Baghdad	Dinar
Ireland	Dublin	euro
Israel	Tel Aviv/Jerusalem	Shekel
Italy	Rome	euro
Jamaica	Kingston	Jamaican Dollar
Japan	Tokyo	Yen
Jordan	Amman	Dinar
Kazakhstan	Astana	Tenge
Kenya	Nairobi	Shilling
Kiribati	Tarawa	Australian Dollar
Kosovo (Federal Republic of Yugoslavia)	Pristina	Dinar & euro
Kuwait	Kuwait	Dinar
Kyrgyzstan	Bishkek	Som
Laos	Vientiane	Kip
Latvia	Riga	Lat
Lebanon	Beirut	Pound
Lesotho	Maseru	Loti
Liberia	Monrovia	Liberian Dollar
Libya	Tripoli	Dinar
Liechtenstein	Vaduz	Swiss Franc
Lithuania	Vilnius	Litas
Luxembourg	Luxembourg	euro
Macedonia	Skopje	Denar
Madagascar	Antananarivo	Malagasy Franc

THE EARTH

COUNTRIES, CAPITALS AND CURRENCIES

Country	Capital	Currency
Malawi	Lilongwe	Kwacha
Malaysia	Kuala Lumpur	Ringgit
Maldives	Malé	Rufiyaa
Mali	Bamako	CFA franc
Malta	Valletta	Lira
Marshall Islands	Majuro	US Dollar
Mauritania	Nouakchott	Ouguiya
Mauritius	Port Louis	Rupee
Mexico	Mexico City	Peso
Micronesia	Palikir	US Dollar
Moldova	Kishinev	Leu
Monaco	Monaco-Ville	euro
Mongolia	Ulan Bator	Tugrik
Morocco	Rabat	Dirham
Mozambique	Maputo	Metical
Myanmar (Burma)	Yangon (Rangoon)	Kyat
Namibia	Windhoek	Namibian Dollar
Nauru	Yaren	Australian Dollar
Nepal	Kathmandu	Rupee
Netherlands	Amsterdam/ The Hague	euro
New Zealand	Wellington	New Zealand Dollar
Nicaragua	Managua	Córdoba
Niger	Niamey	CFA Franc
Nigeria	Abuja	Naira
North Korea	Pyongyang	Won
Norway	Oslo	Krone
Oman	Muscat	Rial
Pakistan	Islamabad	Rupee
Palau	Koror	US Dollar
Panama	Panama City	Balboa
Papua New Guinea	Port Moresby	Kina
Paraguay	Asunción	Guaraní
Peru	Lima	New Sol
Philippines	Manila	Peso
Poland	Warsaw	Zloty

THE EARTH

COUNTRIES, CAPITALS AND CURRENCIES

Country	Capital	Currency
Portugal	Lisbon	euro
Qatar	Doha	Riyal
Romania	Bucharest	Leu
Russia	Moscow	Rouble
Rwanda	Kigali	Rwanda Franc
St Kitts and Nevis	Basseterre	East Caribbean Dollar
St Lucia	Castries	East Caribbean Dollar
St Vincent and Grenadines	Kingstown	East Caribbean Dollar
Samoa	Apia	Tala
San Marino	San Marino	euro
São Tomé and Príncipe	São Tomé	Dobra
Saudi Arabia	Riyadh	Riyal
Senegal	Dakar	CFA Franc
Seychelles	Victoria	Rupee
Sierra Leone	Freetown	Leone
Singapore	Singapore	Singapore Dollar
Slovakia	Bratislava	Koruna
Slovenia	Ljubljana	Tolar
Solomon Islands	Honiara	Solomon Islands Dollar
Somalia	Mogadishu	Shilling
South Africa	Pretoria/ Cape Town	Rand
South Korea	Seoul	Won
Spain	Madrid	euro
Sri Lanka	Colombo	Rupee
Sudan	Khartoum	Dinar
Suriname	Paramaribo	Guilder
Swaziland	Mbabane	Lilangeni
Sweden	Stockholm	Krona
Switzerland	Berne	Swiss Franc
Syria	Damascus	Pound
Taiwan	Taipei	Taiwan Dollar
Tajikistan	Dushanbe	Somoni
Tanzania	Dodoma	Shilling

THE EARTH

COUNTRIES, CAPITALS AND CURRENCIES

Country	Capital	Currency
Thailand	Bangkok	Baht
Togo	Lomé	CFA Franc
Tonga	Nuku'alofa	Pa'anga
Trinidad and Tobago	Port of Spain	Trinidad and Tobago Dollar
Tunisia	Tunis	Dinar
Turkey	Ankara	Lira
Turkmenistan	Ashkhabad	Manat
Tuvalu	Funafuti	Australian Dollar
Uganda	Kampala	Shilling
Ukraine	Kiev	Hryvna
United Arab Emirates	Abu Dhabi	Dirham
United Kingdom	London	Pound Sterling
United States of America	Washington	US Dollar
Uruguay	Montevideo	Peso
Uzbekistan	Tashkent	Sum
Vanuatu	Port Vila	Vatu
Vatican City	Vatican City	euro
Venezuela	Caracas	Bolívar
Vietnam	Hanoi	Dong
Yemen	Sana`a	Riyal
Yugoslavia (Serbia and Montenegro)	Belgrade (Federal Republic of Yugoslavia and Serbia) and Podgorica (Montenegro)	Dinar (euros in Montenegro)
Zambia	Lusaka	Kwacha
Zimbabwe	Harare	Zimbabwe Dollar

THE EARTH

STATES OF THE USA

State	Capital	Abbreviation
Alabama	Montgomery	AL
Alaska	Juneau	AK
Arizona	Phoenix	AZ
Arkansas	Little Rock	AR
California	Sacramento	CA
Colorado	Denver	CO
Connecticut	Hartford	CT
Delaware	Dover	DE
Florida	Tallahassee	FL
Georgia	Atlanta	GA
Hawaii	Honolulu	HI
Idaho	Boise	ID
Illinois	Springfield	IL
Indiana	Indianapolis	IN
Iowa	Des Moines	IA
Kansas	Topeka	KS
Kentucky	Frankfort	KY
Louisiana	Baton Rouge	LA
Maine	Augusta	ME
Maryland	Annapolis	MD
Massachusetts	Boston	MA
Michigan	Lansing	MI
Minnesota	St Paul	MN
Mississippi	Jackson	MS
Missouri	Jefferson City	MO

THE EARTH

STATES OF THE USA

State	Capital	Abbreviation
Montana	Helena	MT
Nebraska	Lincoln	NE
Nevada	Carson City	NV
New Hampshire	Concord	NH
New Jersey	Trenton	NJ
New Mexico	Santa Fe	NM
New York	Albany	NY
North Carolina	Raleigh	NC
North Dakota	Bismarck	ND
Ohio	Columbus	OH
Oklahoma	Oklahoma City	OK
Oregon	Salem	OR
Pennsylvania	Harrisburg	PA
Rhode Island	Providence	RI
South Carolina	Columbia	SC
South Dakota	Pierre	SD
Tennessee	Nashville	TN
Texas	Austin	TX
Utah	Salt Lake City	UT
Vermont	Montpelier	VT
Virginia	Richmond	VA
Washington	Olympia	WA
West Virginia	Charleston	WV
Wisconsin	Madison	WI
Wyoming	Cheyenne	WY

FACT FINDER

THE EARTH

PROVINCES AND TERRITORIES OF CANADA

Province/Territory	Capital	Abbreviation
Alberta	Edmonton	AB
British Columbia	Victoria	BC
Manitoba	Winnipeg	MB
New Brunswick	Fredericton	NB
Newfoundland	St John's	NF
Northwest Territories	Yellowknife	NWT
Nova Scotia	Halifax	NS
Nunavut	Iqaluit	NT
Ontario	Toronto	ON
Prince Edward Island	Charlottetown	PE
Quebec	Quebec	QC
Saskatchewan	Regina	SK
Yukon	Whitehorse	YT

AUSTRALIAN STATES

State	Capital
Northern Territory	Darwin
Western Australia	Perth
Queensland	Brisbane
New South Wales	Sydney
Victoria	Melbourne
South Australia	Adelaide
Tasmania	Hobart

THE EARTH

CONTINENTS OF THE WORLD

Name	Area (sq km)
Africa	29,800,000
America*	41,918,000
Antarctica	13,980,000
Asia	43,998,000
Europe (including European Russia)	9,699,000
Oceania (Australia, New Zealand and non-Asian Pacific islands)	7,618,490

* Usually divided politically into North/Central America and South America; North/Central America is approx. 24,255,000 sq km.

LARGEST ISLANDS

Name	Ocean	Area (sq km)
Greenland	Arctic	2,175,600
New Guinea	Pacific	821,030
Borneo	Pacific	744,366
Madagascar	Indian	587,040
Baffin	Arctic	476,068

LARGEST OCEANS

Name	Area (sq km)	Greatest Depth (m)
Pacific	165,241,000	11,020
Atlantic	86,550,000	9,460
Indian	73,427,000	7,542
Arctic	13,230,000	5,400

THE EARTH

LARGEST SEAS

Name	Area (sq km)	Greatest Depth (m)
South China	2,974,600	7,260
Caribbean	2,753,000	8,600
Mediterranean	2,503,000	5,100
Bering	2,226,100	3,930
Gulf of Mexico	1,542,985	3,505

LARGEST DESERTS

Name	Continent	Area (sq km)
Sahara	Africa	8,400,000
Australian	Oceania	1,550,000
Arabian	Asia	1,300,000
Gobi	Asia	1,040,000
Kalahari	Africa	520,000

HIGHEST MOUNTAINS

Name	Height (m)
All in the Himalayas.	
Everest	8,863
K2	8,607
Kangchenjunga	8,597
Lhotse	8,511
Makalu I	8,481

THE EARTH

HIGHEST MOUNTAINS BY CONTINENT

Continent	Name	Height (m)
Africa	Mt Kilimanjaro	5,895
North/Central America	Mt McKinley	6,194
South America	Aconcagua	6,960
Antarctica	Vinson Massif	5,140
Asia	Mt Everest	8,850
Europe	Mont Blanc	4,807
Oceania	Mt Kosciusko	2,228

LARGEST VOLCANOES (ACTIVE)

Name	Country	Height (m)
Guallatiri	Chile	6,060
Cotopaxi	Ecuador	5,897
Tupungatito	Chile	5,640
Lascar	Chile	5,590
Nevado del Ruiz	Colombia	5,400

LARGEST LAKES

Name	Continent	Area (sq km)
Caspian Sea	Asia	380,000
Superior	(N) America	82,100
Victoria	Africa	69,485
Aral Sea*	Asia	64,000
Huron	(N) America	59,600

The Aral Sea is a saltwater lake.

THE EARTH

LONGEST RIVERS

Name	Continent	Length (km)
Nile	Africa	6,670
Amazon	(S) America	6,448
Yangtze-Kiang	Asia	6,300
Mississippi-Missouri	(N) America	6,020
Yenisey-Angara	Asia	5,540

HIGHEST WATERFALLS

Name	Country	Height (m)
Angel	Venezuela	979
Tugela	South Africa	947
Utigard	Norway	800
Mongefossen	Norway	774
Yosemite	USA	739

FACT FINDER

THE EARTH

RICHTER AND MERCALLI SCALES (earthquakes)

The Richter Scale is used to measure an earthquake's magnitude and the Mercalli Scale is used to measure its intensity.

Mercalli	Richter	Characteristics
1	less than 3.5	only detected by seismograph
2	3.5	only noticed by people at rest
3	4.2	similar to vibrations from HGV
4	4.5	felt indoors; rocks parked cars
5	4.8	generally felt; awakens sleepers
6	5.4	trees sway; causes some damage
7	6.1	causes general alarm; building walls crack
8	6.5	walls collapse
9	6.9	some houses collapse; cracks appear in ground
10	7.3	buildings destroyed; rails buckle
11	8.1	most buildings destroyed; landslides
12	greater than 8.1	total destruction of area

FACT FINDER

THE EARTH

BEAUFORT SCALE (wind speed)

Scale No.	Description	Speed (kph)	Characteristics
0	Calm	Less than 1	smoke goes straight up
1	Light air	1–5	smoke blows in wind
2	Light breeze	6–12	wind felt on face; leaves rustle
3	Gentle breeze	13–20	light flag flutters; leaves in constant motion
4	Moderate breeze	21–29	dust and loose paper blown; small branches move
5	Fresh breeze	30–39	small trees sway
6	Strong breeze	40–50	hard to use umbrellas
7	Moderate gale	51–61	hard to walk into; whole trees in motion
8	Fresh gale	62–74	twigs break off trees
9	Strong gale	75–87	chimney pots and slates lost
10	Whole gale	88–102	trees uprooted; considerable structural damage
11	Storm	103–120	widespread damage
12–17	Hurricane	over 120	violent, massive damage

THE EARTH

THE EARTH'S STRUCTURE

The Earth is composed of the following layers:

Crust – the solid outer shell of the Earth, with an average thickness of 30–35 km in continental regions and 5km beneath the oceans. It represents only 0.1% of the Earth's total volume. Continental crust is composed of granite, while the oceanic crust is made of basalt.

Mantle – the largest layer, accounting for more than 82% of the Earth's volume. The mantle is 2809 km deep and thought to be largely composed of the rock *peridotite*.

Core – the innermost layer, consisting mainly of iron and nickel. The **outer core** is 2000km deep and the **inner core** is 1482km deep.

THE EARTH'S ATMOSPHERE

The atmosphere is the mixture of gases surrounding the earth. It is composed of oxygen (21%), nitrogen (78%) carbon dioxide, argon, helium and other gases in tiny quantities. The atmosphere can be divided into the following atmospheric layers:

Exosphere:	Up to 8000 km
Thermosphere:	Up to 350 km
Mesosphere:	Up to 80 km
Stratosphere:	Up to 50 km
Troposphere:	Up to 6 km at the Poles and 18 km at the equator.

THE EARTH

WEATHER

Weather is the swirling movement of the atmosphere's lowest layer (the **troposphere**). Air is heated at the equator and rises to the top of the troposphere and then moves towards the poles. Cold air at the poles sinks and moves down towards the equator. Rising and sinking air forms weather zones or "cells" either side of the equator (the **tropical climate zone**), between the equator and the poles (the **temperate climate zones**), and at the poles (the **polar climate zones**). In temperate latitudes where there are sharp temperature differences, fast moving currents of air (**jet streams**) are formed at high altitudes and drag disturbed zones of weather around the globe. Areas of high pressure (**anticyclones**) give dry settled weather. Areas of low pressure (**depressions**) create unsettled stormy weather. An area of low pressure between two highs is a **trough**, and an area of high pressure between two lows is a **ridge**.

THE EARTH

THUNDER STORMS

Electricity builds up in storm clouds, and is then suddenly discharged into the air as **lightning.** The air disturbed by the bolt of lightning presses against the air around it creating **thunder.** Lightning is seen before thunder is heard because light travels much faster than sound.

TROPICAL STORMS

Cyclones, hurricanes and typhoons rotate in an anticlockwise direction in the northern hemisphere, and clockwise in the southern hemisphere. The centre of a hurricane or typhoon is called the eye, and it is produced by a strong downdraught of air.

Type of storm	Areas affected	Time of year
Hurricane	USA, Caribbean	July to October
Typhoon	China, Japan	July to October
Cyclone	Indian subcontinent	April to June, September to December
Tropical cyclone	Philippines, etc	December to March
Willy-willy	Australia	December to March

THE SOLAR SYSTEM

Planet	Equatorial diameter (km)	Mean distance from sun (millions of km)
Mercury	4,878	58
Venus	12,104	108
Earth	12,756	150
Mars	6,795	227
Jupiter	142,800	778
Saturn	120,000	1,427
Uranus	50,800	2,869
Neptune	48,500	4,497
Pluto	3,000	5,888

THE SOLAR SYSTEM

Period of from Rotation (length of 'day')	Period of revolution or Sidereal period (length of 'year')	Number of known moons
58.6 days	87.97 days	0
243 days	224.70 days	0
23.9 hours	365.26 days	1
24.6 hours	686.98 days	2
9.8 hours	11.86 years	16
10.2 hours	29.46 years	22
16.2 hours	84.01 years	15
16 hours	164.79 years	8
6.3 days	247.70 years	1

FACT FINDER

WEIGHTS AND MEASURES

THE METRIC SYSTEM

Linear Measure

1 millimetre	= 0.039 37 inch	
10 millimetres	= 1 centimetre	= 0.3937 inch
10 decimetres	= 1 metre	= 39.37 inches or 3.2808 feet
1 kilometre	= 0.621 mile or 3280.8 feet	

Square Measure

1 square millimetre	= 0.001 55 square inch
100 square millimetres	= 1 square centimetre
	= 0.154 99 square inch
100 square decimetres	= 1 square metre
	= 1549. 9 square inches or
	1.196 square yards
100 square hectometres	= 1 square kilometre
	= 0.386 square mile or 247.1 acres

Land Measure

100 centiares	= 1 are	= 119.6 square yards	
100 ares	= 1 hectare	= 2.471 acres	
100 hectares	= 1 square kilometre		
	= 0.386 square mile or 247.1 acres		

Volume Measure

1000 cubic millimetres	= 1 cubic centimetre
	= 0.061 02 cubic inch
1000 cubic centimetres	= 1 cubic decimetre (1 litre)
	= 61.023 cubic inches or
	0.0353 cubic foot
1000 cubic decimetres	= 1 cubic metre
	= 35.314 cubic feet or 1.308 cubic yards

Weights

10 decigrammes	= 1 gram	
	= 15.432 grains or 0.035 274 ounce (avdp.)	
10 hectogrammes	= 1 kilogram	= 2.2046 pounds
10 quintals	= 1 metric ton	= 2204.6 pounds

50

WEIGHTS AND MEASURES

THE IMPERIAL SYSTEM

Linear Measure

1 mil	= 0.001 inch	= 0.0254 millimetre		
1 inch	= 1000 mils	= 2.54 centimetres		
12 inches	= 1 foot	= 0.3048 metre		
3 feet	= 1 yard	= 0.9144 metre		
5½ yards or 16½ feet	= 1 rod (or pole or perch)	= 5.029 metres		
40 rods	= 1 furlong	= 201.168 metres		
8 furlongs or 1760 yards or 5280 feet	= 1 (statute) mile	= 1.6093 kilometres		

Square Measure

1 square inch	= 6.452 square centimetres	
144 square inches	= 1 square foot	= 929.03 square centimetres
9 square feet	= 1 square yard	= 0.8361 square metre
30¼ square yards	= 1 square rod (or square pole or square perch) = 25.292 square metres	
160 square rods or 4840 square yards or 43 560 square feet	= 1 acre	= 0.4047 hectare
640 acres	= 1 square mile	= 259.00 hectares or 2.590 square kilometres

Cubic Measure

1 cubic inch	= 16.387 cubic centimetres
1728 cubic inches	= 1 cubic foot = 0.0283 cubic metre
27 cubic feet	= 1 cubic yard = 0.7646 cubic metre

Nautical Measure

6 feet	= 1 fathom	= 1.829 metres
100 fathoms	= 1 cable's length	

(in the Royal Navy, 608 feet, or 185.319 metres = 1 cable's length)

10 cables' length	= 1 international nautical mile	
	= 1.852 kilometres (exactly)	
1 international nautical mile	= 1.150 779 statute miles	

(the length of a minute of latitude at the equator)

60 nautical miles	= 1 degree of a great circle of the earth
	= 69.047 statute miles

FACT FINDER

WEIGHTS AND MEASURES

Liquid and Dry Measure

1 gill	= 5 fluid ounces	= 9.0235 cubic inches	= 0.1480 litre
4 gills	= 1 pint	= 34.68 cubic inches	= 0.568 litre
2 pints	= 1 quart	= 69.36 cubic inches	= 1.136 litres
4 quarts	= 1 gallon	= 277.4 cubic inches	= 4.546 litres
2 gallons	= 1 peck	= 554.8 cubic inches	= 9.092 litres
4 pecks	= 1 bushel	= 2219.2 cubic inches	= 36.37 litres

The U.S. Gallon (4 U.S. Quarts) = 231 cubic inches = 3.7854 litres.

Apothecaries' Fluid Measure

1 minim = 0.0038 cubic inch = 0.616 millilitre
60 minims = 1 fluid dram = 0.2256 cubic inch = 3.6966 millilitres
8 fluid drams = 1 fluid ounce = 1.8047 cubic inches = 0.0296 litre
20 fluid ounces = 1 pint = 34.68 cubic inches = 0.568 litre
The U.S. pint = 16 fluid ounces

Avoirdupois Weight

(The grain, equal to 0.0648 gram, is the same in all three tables of weight)

1 dram or 27.34 grains	= 1.722 grams
16 drams or 437.5 grains	= 1 ounce = 28.3495 grams
16 ounces or 7000 grains	= 1 pound = 453.59 grams
14 pounds	= 1 stone = 6.35 kilograms
112 pounds	= 1 hundredweight = 50.80 kilograms
2240 pounds	= 1 (long) ton = 1016.05 kilograms
2000 pounds	= 1 (short) ton = 907.18 kilograms

Troy Weight

(The grain, equal to 0.0648 gram, is the same in all three tables of weight)

3.086 grains = 1 carat = 200.00 milligrams
24 grains = 1 pennyweight = 1.5552 grams
20 pennyweights or 480 grains = 1 ounce = 31.1035 grams
12 ounces or 5760 grains = 1 pound = 373.24 grams

Apothecaries' Weight

(The grain, equal to 0.0648 gram, is the same in all three tables of weight)

20 grains	=	1 scruple	= 1.296 grams
3 scruples	=	1 dram	= 3.888 grams
8 drams or 480 grains		= 1 ounce	= 31.1035 grams

WEIGHTS AND MEASURES

SI UNITS

Prefixes used with SI Units

Factor	Name of prefix	Symbol
10^{-1}	deci-	d
10^{-2}	centi-	c
10^{-3}	milli-	m
10^{-6}	micro-	μ
10^{-9}	nano-	n
10^{-12}	pico-	p
10^{-15}	femto-	f
10^{-18}	atto-	a
10	deca-	da
10^{2}	hecto-	h
10^{3}	kilo-	k
10^{6}	mega-	M
10^{9}	giga-	G
10^{12}	tera-	T
10^{15}	peta-	P
10^{18}	exa-	E

Base SI Units

Physical quantity	Name	Symbol
length	metre	m
mass	kilogram	kg
time	second	s
electric current	ampere	A
thermodynamic temperature	kelvin	K
amount of substance	mole	mol
luminous intensity	candela	cd

Supplementary SI Units

Physical quantity	Name	Symbol
plane angle	radian	rad
solid angle	steradian	sr

WEIGHTS AND MEASURES

Derived SI Units with Special Names

Physical quantity	Name	Symbol
frequency	hertz	Hz
energy	joule	J
force	newton	N
power	watt	W
pressure	pascal	Pa
electric charge	coulomb	C
electric potential difference	volt	V
electric resistance	ohm	Ω
electric conductance	siemens	S
electric capacitance	farad	F
magnetic flux	weber	Wb
inductance	henry	H
magnetic flux density	tesla	T

FACT FINDER

GEOMETRY

POLYGONS

Name of polygon		Number of sides	Each internal angle	Sum of internal angles
Triangle	△	3	60°	180°
Square	□	4	90°	360°
Pentagon	⬠	5	108°	540°
Hexagon	⬡	6	120°	720°
Heptagon	⬠	7	128.6°	900°
Octagon	◯	8	135°	1080°
Nonagon	◯	9	140°	1260°
Decagon	◯	10	144°	1440°
Undecagon	◯	11	147.3°	1620°
Dodecagon	◯	12	150°	1800°

GEOMETRY

QUADRILATERALS

A quadrilateral is a four-sided polygon.

1 Square   Sides are equal length; angles are right angles.

2 Rectangle   Opposite sides are equal; angles are right angles.

3 Rhombus   Sides are equal; none of the angles are right angles.

4 Parallelogram   Opposite sides are parallel and of equal length.

5 Trapezium   One pair of opposite sides is parallel.

6 Kite   Adjacent sides are equal; diagonals intersect at right angles

GEOMETRY

TRIANGLES

A triangle is a three-sided polygon that can be classified by angle.

1 Equilateral   Sides are equal; all the angles are equal.

2 Isosceles   Two sides are equal; two angles are equal.

3 Scalene   Sides are different lengths and all angles are different sizes.

4 Right angle   Has one right angle.

5 Obtuse angle   Has one obtuse angle (between 90° and 180°).

6 Acute angle   Has three acute angles (less than 90°).

CHEMICAL ELEMENTS

1	hydrogen	H	28	nickel	Ni
2	helium	He	29	copper	Cu
3	lithium	Li	30	zinc	Zn
4	beryllium	Be	31	gallium	Ga
5	boron	B	32	germanium	Ge
6	carbon	C	33	arsenic	As
7	nitrogen	N	34	selenium	Se
8	oxygen	O	35	bromine	Br
9	fluorine	F	36	krypton	Kr
10	neon	Ne	37	rubidium	Rb
11	sodium	Na	38	strontium	Sr
12	magnesium	Mg	39	yttrium	Y
13	aluminium	Al	40	zirconium	Zr
14	silicon	Si	41	niobium	Nb
15	phosphorus	P	42	molybdenum	Mo
16	sulphur	S	43	technetium	Tc
17	chlorine	Cl	44	ruthenium	Ru
18	argon	Ar	45	rhodium	Rh
19	potassium	K	46	palladium	Pd
20	calcium	Ca	47	silver	Ag
21	scandium	Sc	48	cadmium	Cd
22	titanium	Ti	49	indium	In
23	vanadium	V	50	tin	Sn
24	chromium	Cr	51	antimony	Sb
25	manganese	Mn	52	tellurium	Te
26	iron	Fe	53	iodine	I
27	cobalt	Co	54	xenon	Xe

CHEMICAL ELEMENTS

55	caesium	Cs
56	barium	Ba
57	lanthanum	La
58	cerium	Ce
59	praseodymium	Pr
60	neodymium	Nd
61	promethium	Pm
62	samarium	Sm
63	europium	Eu
64	gadolinium	Gd
65	terbium	Tb
66	dysprosium	Dy
67	holmium	Ho
68	erbium	Er
69	thulium	Tm
70	ytterbium	Yb
71	lutetium	Lu
72	hafnium	Hf
73	tantalum	Ta
74	tungsten	W
75	rhenium	Re
76	osmium	Os
77	iridium	Ir
78	platinum	Pt
79	gold	Au
80	mercury	Hg
81	thallium	Tl
82	lead	Pb

83	bismuth	Bi
84	polonium	Po
85	astatine	At
86	radon	Rn
87	francium	Fr
88	radium	Ra
89	actinium	Ac
90	thorium	Th
91	protactinium	Pa
92	uranium	U
93	neptunium	Np
94	plutonium	Pu
95	americium	Am
96	curium	Cm
97	berkelium	Bk
98	californium	Cf
99	einsteinium	Es
100	fermium	Fm
101	mendelevium	Md
102	nobelium	No
103	lawrencium	Lr
104	rutherfordium	Rf
105	dubnium	Db
106	seaborgium	Sg
107	bohrium	Bh
108	hassium	Hs
109	meitnerium	Mt

FACT FINDER

TIME

UNITS OF TIME

millennium	1000 years
century	100 years
decade	10 years
leap year	366 days
year	12 months
year	52 weeks
year	365 days
month	28–31 days
week	7 days
day	24 hours
hour	60 minutes
minute	60 seconds
millisecond	10^{-3} s 0.001 seconds
microsecond	10^{-6} s 0.000001 seconds
nanosecond	10^{-9} s 0.000000001 seconds

TIME

SOLSTICES AND EQUINOXES

The summer solstice is the longest day of the year and the winter solstice is the shortest. Equinoxes are when the day and night are of equal length.

Date	Northern hemisphere	Southern hemisphere
21 June	summer solstice	winter solstice
23 September	autumn equinox	spring equinox
22 December	winter solstice	summer solstice
21 March	spring equinox	autumn equinox

FACT FINDER

POLITICAL LEADERS

US PRESIDENTS

Name	Party	Term of office
1. George Washington	Federalist	1789–97
2. John Adams	Federalist	1797–1801
3. Thomas Jefferson	Democratic Republican	1801–1809
4. James Madison	Democratic Republican	1809–1817
5. James Monroe	Democratic Republican	1817–25
6. John Quincy Adams	Democratic Republican	1825–29
7. Andrew Jackson	Democrat	1829–37
8. Martin Van Buren	Democrat	1837–41
9. William Henry Harrison	Whig	1841
10. John Tyler	Whig	1841–45
11. James K. Polk	Democrat	1845–49
12. Zachary Taylor	Whig	1849–50
13. Millard Fillmore	Whig	1850–53
14. Franklin Pierce	Democrat	1853–57
15. James Buchanan	Democrat	1857–61
16. Abraham Lincoln	Republican	1861–65
17. Andrew Johnson	Republican	1865–69
18. Ulysses S. Grant	Republican	1869–77
19. Rutherford B. Hayes	Republican	1877–81
20. James A. Garfield	Republican	1881
21. Chester A. Arthur	Republican	1881–85
22. Grover Cleveland	Democrat	1885–89

POLITICAL LEADERS

US PRESIDENTS

Name	Party	Term of office
23. Benjamin Harrison	Republican	1889–93
24. Grover Cleveland	Democrat	1893–97
25. William McKinley	Republican	1897–1901
26. Theodore Roosevelt	Republican	1901–1909
27. William Howard Taft	Republican	1909–13
28. Woodrow Wilson	Democrat	1913–21
29. Warren G. Harding	Republican	1921–23
30. Calvin Coolidge	Republican	1923–29
31. Herbert C. Hoover	Republican	1929–33
32. Franklin D. Roosevelt	Democrat	1933–45
33. Harry S. Truman	Democrat	1945–53
34. Dwight D. Eisenhower	Republican	1953–61
35. John F. Kennedy	Democrat	1961–63
36. Lyndon B. Johnson	Democrat	1963–69
37. Richard M. Nixon	Republican	1969–74
38. Gerald R. Ford	Republican	1974–77
39. James E. Carter, Jr	Democrat	1977–81
40. Ronald W. Reagan	Republican	1981–89
41. George H. W. Bush	Republican	1989–93
42. William J. Clinton	Democrat	1993–2001
43. George W. Bush	Republican	2001–

POLITICAL LEADERS

BRITISH PRIME MINISTERS

Name	Party	Term of office
Robert Walpole	Whig	1721–42
Earl of Wilmington	Whig	1742–43
Henry Pelham	Whig	1743–54
Duke of Newcastle	Whig	1754–56
Duke of Devonshire	Whig	1756–57
Duke of Newcastle	Whig	1757–62
Earl of Bute	Tory	1762–63
George Grenville	Whig	1763–65
Marquess of Rockingham	Whig	1765–66
Duke of Grafton	Whig	1766–70
Lord North	Tory	1770–82
Marquess of Rockingham	Whig	1782
Earl of Shelburne	Whig	1782–83
Duke of Portland	Coalition	1783
William Pitt	Tory	1783–1801
Henry Addington	Tory	1801–04
William Pitt	Tory	1804–06
Lord Grenville	Whig	1806–07
Duke of Portland	Tory	1807–09
Spencer Perceval	Tory	1809–12
Earl of Liverpool	Tory	1812–27
George Canning	Tory	1827
Viscount Goderich	Tory	1827–28
Duke of Wellington	Tory	1828–30
Earl Grey	Whig	1830–34
Viscount Melbourne	Whig	1834
Robert Peel	Conservative	1834–35
Viscount Melbourne	Whig	1835–41
Robert Peel	Conservative	1841–46
Lord John Russell	Liberal	1846–52
Earl of Derby	Conservative	1852
Lord Aberdeen	Peelite	1852–55
Viscount Palmerston	Liberal	1855–58
Earl of Derby	Conservative	1858–59
Viscount Palmerston	Liberal	1859–65
Lord John Russell	Liberal	1865–66
Earl of Derby	Conservative	1866–68

POLITICAL LEADERS

BRITISH PRIME MINISTERS

Name	Party	Term of office
Benjamin Disraeli	Conservative	1868
William Gladstone	Liberal	1868–74
Benjamin Disraeli	Conservative	1874–80
William Gladstone	Liberal	1880–85
Marquess of Salisbury	Conservative	1885–86
William Gladstone	Liberal	1886
Marquess of Salisbury	Conservative	1886–92
William Gladstone	Liberal	1892–94
Earl of Rosebery	Liberal	1894–95
Marquess of Salisbury	Conservative	1895–1902
Arthur James Balfour	Conservative	1902–05
Henry Campbell-Bannerman	Liberal	1905–08
Herbert Henry Asquith	Liberal	1908–15
Herbert Henry Asquith	Coalition	1915–16
David Lloyd George	Coalition	1916–22
Andrew Bonar Law	Conservative	1922–23
Stanley Baldwin	Conservative	1923–24
James Ramsay MacDonald	Labour	1924
Stanley Baldwin	Conservative	1924–29
James Ramsay MacDonald	Labour	1929–31
James Ramsay MacDonald	Nationalist	1931–35
Stanley Baldwin	Nationalist	1935–37
Arthur Neville Chamberlain	Nationalist	1937–40
Winston Churchill	Coalition	1940–45
Clement Attlee	Labour	1945–51
Winston Churchill	Conservative	1951–55
Anthony Eden	Conservative	1955–57
Harold Macmillan	Conservative	1957–63
Alec Douglas-Home	Conservative	1963–64
Harold Wilson	Labour	1964–70
Edward Heath	Conservative	1970–74
Harold Wilson	Labour	1974–76
James Callaghan	Labour	1976–79
Margaret Thatcher	Conservative	1979–90
John Major	Conservative	1990–97
Tony Blair	Labour	1997–

POLITICAL LEADERS

CANADIAN PRIME MINISTERS

Name	Party	Term of office
John A. MacDonald	Conservative	1867–73
Alexander Mackenzie	Liberal	1873–78
John A. MacDonald	Conservative	1878–91
John J.C. Abbot	Conservative	1891–92
John S.D. Thompson	Conservative	1892–94
Mackenzie Bowell	Conservative	1894–96
Charles Tupper	Conservative	1896
Wilfrid Laurier	Liberal	1896–1911
Robert Borden	Conservative	1911–20
Arthur Meighen	Conservative	1920–21
William Lyon MacKenzie King	Liberal	1921–26
Arthur Meighen	Conservative	1926
William Lyon MacKenzie King	Liberal	1926–30
Richard Bedford Bennet	Conservative	1930–35
William Lyon MacKenzie King	Liberal	1935–48
Louis St. Laurent	Liberal	1948–57
John George Diefenbaker	Conservative	1957–63
Lester Bowles Pearson	Liberal	1963–68
Pierre Elliott Trudeau	Liberal	1968–79
Joseph Clark	Conservative	1979–80
Pierre Elliott Trudeau	Liberal	1980–84
John Turner	Liberal	1984
Brian Mulroney	Conservative	1984–93
Kim Campbell	Conservative	1993
Joseph Jacques Jean Chrétien	Liberal	1993–

POLITICAL LEADERS

AUSTRALIAN PRIME MINISTERS

Name	Party	Term of office
Edmund Barton	Protectionist	1901–03
Alfred Deakin	Protectionist	1903–04
John Christian Watson	Labor	1904
George Houston Reid	Free Trade	1904–05
Alfred Deakin	Protectionist	1905–08
Andrew Fisher	Labor	1908–09
Alfred Deakin	Fusion	1909–10
Andrew Fisher	Labor	1910–13
Joseph Cook	Liberal	1913–14
Andrew Fisher	Labor	1914–15
William Morris Hughes	National Labor	1915–17
William Morris Hughes	Nationalist	1917–23
Stanley Melbourne Bruce	Nationalist	1923–29
James Henry Scullin	Labor	1929–31
Joseph Aloysius Lyons	United	1931–39
Earle Christmas Page	Country	1939
Robert Gordon Menzies	United	1939–41
Arthur William Fadden	Country	1941
John Joseph Curtin	Labor	1941–45
Joseph Benedict Chifley	Labor	1945–49
Robert Gordon Menzies	Liberal	1949–66
Harold Edward Holt	Liberal	1966–67
John McEwen	Country	1967–68
John Grey Gorton	Liberal	1968–71
William McMahon	Liberal	1971–72
Edward Gough Whitlam	Labor	1972–75
John Malcolm Fraser	Liberal	1975–83
Robert James Lee Hawke	Labor	1983–91
Paul Keating	Labor	1991–96
John Howard	Liberal	1996–

POLITICAL LEADERS

NEW ZEALAND PRIME MINISTERS

Name	Party	Term of office
Henry Sewell	—	1856
William Fox	—	1856
Edward William Stafford	—	1856–61
William Fox	—	1861–62
Alfred Domett	—	1862–63
Frederick Whitaker	—	1863–64
Frederick Aloysius Weld	—	1864–65
Edward William Stafford	—	1865–69
William Fox	—	1869–72
Edward William Stafford	—	1872
William Fox	—	1873
Julius Vogel	—	1873–75
Daniel Pollen	—	1875–76
Julius Vogel	—	1876
Harry Albert Atkinson	—	1876–77
George Grey	—	1877–79
John Hall	—	1879–82
Frederick Whitaker	—	1882–83
Harry Albert Atkinson	—	1883–84
Robert Stout	—	1884
Harry Albert Atkinson	—	1884
Robert Stout	—	1884–87
Harry Albert Atkinson	—	1887–91
John Ballance	—	1891–93
Richard John Seddon	Liberal	1893–1906

POLITICAL LEADERS

NEW ZEALAND PRIME MINISTERS

Name	Party	Term of office
William Hall-Jones	Liberal	1906
Joseph George Ward	Liberal/National	1906–12
Thomas Mackenzie	National	1912
William Ferguson Massey	Reform	1912–25
Francis Henry Dillon Bell	Reform	1925
Joseph Gordon Coates	Reform	1925–28
Joseph George Ward	Liberal/National	1928–30
George William Forbes	United	1930–35
Michael Joseph Savage	Labour	1935–40
Peter Fraser	Labour	1940–49
Sidney George Holland	National	1949–57
Keith Jacka Holyoake	National	1957
Walter Nash	Labour	1957–60
Keith Jacka Holyoake	National	1960–72
John Ross Marshall	National	1972
Norman Eric Kirk	Labour	1972–74
Wallace Edward Rowling	Labour	1974–75
Robert David Muldoon	National	1975–84
David Russell Lange	Labour	1984–89
Geoffrey Palmer	Labour	1989–90
Mike Moore	Labour	1990
Jim Bolger	National	1990–97
Jenny Shipley	National	1997–99
Helen Clark	Labour	1999–

POLITICAL LEADERS

SOUTH AFRICAN LEADERS
Governor General

Name	Term of office
Herbert, Viscount Gladstone	1910–14
Sydney, Earl Buxton	1914–20
Arthur, Duke of Connaught	1920–24
Alexander, Earl of Athlone	1924–31
George Herbert Hyde Villiers	1931–37
Patrick Duncan	1937–43
Nicolaas Jacobus de Wet	1943–45
Gideon Brand Van Zyl	1945–51
Ernest George Jansen	1951–59
Lucas Cornelius Steyn	1959
Charles Robberts Swart	1959–61

REPUBLIC
President

Name	Term of office
Charles Robberts Swart	1961–67
Theophilus Ebenhaezer Dönges	1967
Jozua François Nandé	1967–68
Jacobus Johannes Fouché	1968–75
Nicolaas Diederichs	1975–78
Balthazar Johannes Vorster	1978–79
Marais Viljoen	1979–84
Pieter Willem Botha	1984–89
Frederick Willem de Klerk	1989–94
Nelson Rolihlahla Mandela	1994–99
Thabo Mbeki	1999–